Studies in Fiction

Studies in Fiction

ENLARGED THIRD EDITION

Blaze O. Bonazza

CALIFORNIA STATE UNIVERSITY, LONG BEACH

Emil Roy

UNIVERSITY OF SOUTH CAROLINA

Sandra Roy

UNIVERSITY OF SOUTH CAROLINA

HARPER & ROW, PUBLISHERS, New York
Cambridge, Philadelphia, San Francisco,
London, Mexico City, São Paulo, Sydney

1817

Sponsoring Editor: Phillip Leininger
Project Editor: Linda Buchanan
Designer: Robert Sugar
Production Manager: Marion Palen
Compositor: University Graphics, Inc.
Printer and Binder: Halliday Lithograph Corporation
Cover: Robert Sugar/Mies Hora
Cover sculpture: Marisol, *The Family* (1962). Painted wood and other materials in three sections, 6′10 5/8″ x 65 1/2″ (209.8 x 166.3 cm). Collection, The Museum of Modern Art, New York. Advisory Committee Fund.

Studies in Fiction, Enlarged Third Edition

Library of Congress Cataloging in Publication Data
Main entry under title:

Studies in fiction.

Bibliography: p.
1. Short stories. I. Bonazza, Blaze Odell. II. Roy, Emil. III. Roy, Sandra.
PN6120.2.S88 1982 808.83′1 81-7016
ISBN 0-06-040832-4 AACR2

To Rosalind, Marita, and Lisa

Contents

Contents by Chronology

Contents by Theme

Part I
The Forming Self and Others

GROUP ONE / THE INDIVIDUAL AND THE FAMILY

GROUP TWO / MAN AND WOMAN

GROUP THREE / MAN VERSUS WOMAN

Part II
The Inner World: Self and Symbols

GROUP FOUR / SELF-KNOWLEDGE AND SELF-DECEPTION

GROUP FIVE / EVIL WITHIN AND WITHOUT

Part III
Dream and Reality

GROUP SIX / LIFE AS NIGHTMARE

GROUP SEVEN / LIFE AS COMIC FANTASY

Preface

This enlarged, third edition of *Studies in Fiction* contains more stories than did its two predecessors and offers a chronological table of contents in addition to a thematic table of contents. The added selections bring the total to 101, and give the collection not only a greater number of authors but also a greater variety in the types of stories represented. Although they were selected primarily for their intrinsic literary merit and anticipated reader appeal, the new stories were also chosen with an eye toward their usefulness in advancing the purpose of the collection, which is to develop in the reader an understanding of the short story as a highly artistic literary form deserving of a careful, disciplined approach.

The collection is international in scope and spans nearly two centuries, beginning with early masters, such as Dickens, Dostoevsky, and Poe, and progressing toward contemporary experimental writers, such as Donald Barthelme and Robert Coover. The stories themselves are widely diversified as to type and style, ranging from detective fiction to black humor and antifiction, and offer attractions to a multiplicity of tastes and interests. They also provide the opportunity for selective approaches organized around related themes.

Women writers are well represented, as the inclusion of 27 stories by writers such as Willa Cather, Doris Lessing, Ursula Le Guin, Dorothy Parker, Ann Petry, Katherine Anne Porter, Dorothy L. Sayers, Eudora Welty, Edith Wharton, and others will attest. All of the stories, by women and by men, were selected for their literary merit. The fact that women are so well represented is gratifying to us as editors and critics, but the provenance of the stories in relation to gender was not the basis for the decision to include any particular story. Each story stood on its own as one worthy of an initial reading, a subsequent closer examination, and finally, rereading at a later date.

In addition, black writers are represented by James Baldwin, Ralph Ellison, Ernest J. Gaines, Langston Hughes, and Ann Petry. Here again, the decision to include was always based on the criterion of literary quality, and the works selected differ widely among themselves as to the fictional experiences dealt with and the attitudes conveyed.

We have included three stories each by Sherwood Anderson, James Baldwin, Donald Barthelme, Anton Chekhov, Ursula Le Guin, James Joyce, Luigi Pirandello, Katherine Anne Porter, and Eudora Welty to invite comparisons and contrasts among stories by the same author, taking into account the possible use of variations on recurring themes or the use of similar or dissimilar techniques in different works.

We have included in this anthology, as we did in the earlier editions, an introduction, "The Short Story: A Structural Approach," dealing with the art of reading short fiction. This section, in revised and updated form, applies a number of critical concepts and techniques to various aspects of the short story as a preliminary guide to close reading. In this edition the questions for discussion ("For Discussion") following each story are preceded by a brief analytical and critical comment ("For Thought") that is intended to assist the student in coming to grips with the issues raised by the questions. While these questions are designed to be suggestive and illuminating rather than necessarily definitive in scope, they will serve to concentrate the student's attention on the quintessential elements of the story. They will also provide a practical basis for class discussions that are pertinent and purposeful rather than merely desultory and often overly subjective on the part of the students. They may also be used to elicit written responses from the students, whether as theme topics or as essay questions on examination. In appreciative response to suggestions from teachers and students who have used the earlier versions of this text, we have altered some types of questions and have added new ones to sharpen the focus by avoiding some ambiguities and overlapping. All of the questions have been formulated so as to be answerable on the basis of the story alone, but only after the student has given it close, thoughtful attention. At the end of the book, there is a Glossary that reflects terms introduced and defined in "The Short Story: A Structural Approach."

Suggestions from fellow teachers who have used this book in its earlier forms have been very helpful in every phase of this revision. We are thankful to those who have so graciously proffered their comments to assist us in the preparation of this new edition. We hope that those who use this product of our present endeavors will find it useful in the attempt to teach the short story in a way that makes it a pleasant and rewarding experience for the teacher and student alike.

Acknowledgments

When a book is finally in its desired form and is ready to be published, the question arises as to how to thank the many people who helped make the venture possible. Knowing full well that this attempt at expressing gratitude is doomed to inadequacy, we will make the effort nonetheless because of the magnitude of our debt.

We would like to thank Phil Leininger, sponsoring editor, Linda Buchanan, project editor, and the staff at Harper & Row for their work on the project. We would also like to thank the many colleagues and other users of the previous editions of this book for the helpful recommendations they offered as we were in the process of preparing this, the third edition. Among those we wish to single out for personal encomia are Gene Dinielli, Elliot Fried, Gerald Locklin, Charles Stetler, Luster Williams, and Ora Williams of California State University, Long Beach. Each of them contributed significantly by urging the inclusion of certain stories and by generously agreeing to read and comment upon our treatment of a number of selections.

William Bonnycastle and John Dowden of Cerritos Community College in Norwalk, California, also merit praise and thanks for providing the kind of expert advice gained from long experience in teaching literature to college students.

We owe a special debt of gratitude to Kathy Billing, thesis reviewer at California State University, Long Beach, for her superhuman patience in editing and typing the final manuscript for the Instructor's Manual that accompanies the text. Hers was a formidable task that would have daunted the faint of heart, considering the "foul papers" turned over to her to be transmogrified into neat and accurate copy ready for the printer. Without her unflagging perseverance and helpful attitude the task would have been tedious at best. With her dedicated but relaxed approach, what would have been travail became a gratifyingly productive joint effort. Her assistant for proofreading the typed copy, Linda Fogerlund, performed admirably in ferreting out elusive typographical errors that might have otherwise escaped detection and correction. For this fine close reading, we give her our thanks.

Blaze O. Bonazza
Emil Roy
Sandra Roy

To the Student

By generally accepted convention, a short story is characterized by its economical literary technique. It demands a high degree of selectivity in the choice of details for the creation of character and situation and whatever plot development and theme the writer chooses to employ to tie all the elements together. The relatively compressed nature of the form usually requires that you, the reader, pay close attention to details in order to appreciate the full significance of the story and enjoy the maximum emotional impact. As worthy examples of the form, the stories that have been selected for this collection cannot be dismissed with a cursory reading without your losing a great deal. Quite frequently you will find your perceptiveness and comprehension challenged and perhaps even temporarily frustrated by some of the more obscure ones, employing as they often do subtle ironies, elusive symbols, or sometimes a strong element of unreality achieved through the use of bizarre imaginative details.

Because of the difficulties characteristic of much literary analysis, we have tried to approach the problem of developing understanding and appreciation of the short story by providing a guide to systematic critical reading. The method employed here is as old as the socratic dialogue. It uses a series of suggestive, and often leading, questions at the end of each story. Some of the questions may elicit a brief and fairly obvious answer; others may seem baffling at first but ultimately answerable after careful thought. Most of them are designed to bring to your attention or to remind you of something you may have passed over in the first reading. The remaining questions usually direct your attention to some technical aspect of the work to point out the choices made by the author in producing the effect desired. The questions are also generally intended to sharpen your powers of perception by combining seemingly unrelated points which, on closer examination, emerge as parts of an integrated and sometimes complex pattern.

We suggest that you read a story through once without considering the discussion questions in order to familiarize yourself with the basic elements of situation and character and to obtain an initial overall impression of the work. This process might be likened to one in an art gallery, where you would first stand back to look at a painting, then examine it in detail at closer range, and finally stand back again to view it with an awareness of both the grand design and the minutiae that contribute to it. A careful second reading, with the questions in mind, should make you aware of the minute details in the story and the contributions they make to the total impression, so that you emerge from the process with an understanding and insight you may not have had after a first reading.

Judging from the reported experience of students and teachers who have used earlier editions of this text, we would expect that a conscientious application of this method will provide you with a satisfying approach to your reading of prose fiction. The method should also stimulate your interest in literature generally, develop confidence in your powers of perception, and enhance your enjoyment from reading, for perhaps a lifetime.

Blaze O. Bonazza
Emil Roy
Sandra Roy

Studies in Fiction

The Short Story
A Structural Approach

The term *structure* as applied to a short story, or to any form of literary art, is a metaphorical expression referring to the architecturallike pattern of the work. Much like a building, a short story is an orderly arrangement of individual parts put together to form a cohesive whole. In a building, the constituent elements are physical and exist in space; in a short story, the elements are intangibles, but they too are arranged in accordance with a carefully conceived plan. Instead of existing in space, these elements exist as ideas in the mind of the writer that are transferred to the mind of the reader through the medium of the printed page. The structure is then re-created in the reader's mind as the story is read. Behind this concept of structure lies the assumption that the author has an awareness and understanding of the need for structure in the work and that, in writing the story, has made deliberate choices in the selection of details and has carefully arranged these details into a meaningful, aesthetic pattern. A further assumption is that full appreciation of a story by the reader demands some awareness and understanding of its structure.

In its broadest sense, structure includes all the elements in a story: plot, character and characterization, point of view, language, which can be realistic, symbolic or allegorical, and theme. In studying literature from a structural point of view, one may deal with these elements separately, at first; however, the ultimate objective is to see the work as a whole and to become aware of how the parts are integrated to produce a composite effect.

Although many stories have similar basic narrative patterns and deal with the same or similar subjects, the final effect of such stories may differ markedly. For example, both "Araby" and "The Killers" focus on the subject of a disillusioning revelation about life that is experienced by a boy approaching early adulthood; yet, the language, point of view, and theme of the two stories are vastly different.

Similarly, "The Druggist's Wife" and "The Catbird Seat" center on comic relationships between the sexes, but with an entirely different polarity. The men are attracted to the woman in the Chekhov story, but repelled by the one in the Thurber story. By contrast, "During the Retreat" combines both attraction and rejection. "Has Anybody Seen Miss Dora Dean?," "The Fall of the House of Usher," and "In the Penal Colony" all employ the fairly common motif of an outsider trying to solve an enigma, but the separate treatments of this motif vary radically among these three examples. One story is rationally objective, one is melodramatically gothic, and one is highly allegorical. Furthermore, even though some short stories may incorporate similar themes, the author's tone or attitude may completely alter the final impact of the individual stories. For example, stories such as "Miss Brill," "The Sojourner," and "Cruel and Barbarous Treatment," concentrate on the conflict between illusion and reality and the way people try to shelter themselves in a carapace of illusion to ward off an unpleasant reality. In the first story, the author's attitude toward the protagonist, or central character, is sympathetic; in the second, the author's tone is relatively objective, but not void of sympathy; and in the last of the trio, the author's attitude is hostile. Stories such as "Death of a Traveling Salesman" and "In the Penal Colony" combine the motif of the mysterious journey with a milieu that seems like a surrealistic nightmare. Both authors use fantasy to disguise universal truth yet ultimately reveal this truth, but in a complex and cryptic fashion. Whereas Welty uses American folklore in her adaptation of the motif, Kafka brings into play the entire religious and ethical code of the Judaeo-Christian tradition to support the motif. On the other hand, "The Bride Comes to Yellow Sky" joins a comic variation of the perilous journey motif with the one of the outsider trying to solve an enigma. Here the two motifs are brought together and unified by the author's pervasive use of an irony that is genial rather than satiric in nature. In the story by Italo Svevo, "The Mother," we have a comic fable that parodies the motif of the dangerous quest by making the seeker-protagonist a young rooster instead of a human being.

Although there are many more narrative patterns than those mentioned above, the supply is not inexhaustible. There are only so many patterns available in our culture, and even when an apparently unorthodox writer appears to be ignoring conventional motifs, he or she may still be using them in disguised form, as Barthelme does in "A Shower of Gold," where the pattern of the rogue-adventurer in conflict with society is camouflaged under seemingly nonsensical and unconnected events. In "Don't Call Me by My Right Name," Purdy takes advantage of the comic possibilities arising out of a conversation at cross-purposes with shifting word meanings, a laugh provoking situation traceable to ancient Greek and Roman comedy.

Elements of Plot

Simply stated, *plot* is the arrangement of the events in a story into a causal sequence. Although the short story is one of the most flexible vehicles for the diverse elements of plot, as is demonstrated by the Barthelme, Brautigan, Coover, and Purdy selections, this flexibility and variety does not reduce the value of a systematic and even orthodox approach to plot construction. Among the formal elements of plot are: *exposition*, background; *conflict*, the opposition of forces, internal or external; *complication*, the development of predictable or unforeseen contingencies in the action; *foreshadowing*, a hint of what is to come; *reversal*, a change in fortune experienced by the protagonist; *denouement*, the final outcome of the sequence of events; and *insight*, recognition by the protagonist of his or her nature or fate.

Although these and numerous other technical terms referring to elements of the short story frequently appear in the discussion questions following the stories in this collection, they are important not in themselves, but as devices to encourage closer scrutiny and develop better understanding of the story being read. The questions should not make the reading of literature a didactic chore, but should provide an adventure of the mind that will produce both pleasure and insight.

Even if possessed to a high degree, technical competence on the part of an author in manipulating plot does not make a literary work great, or even worth a second reading. What does make a work great and worthy of repeated reading is its power to engage the reader's intellect and emotions. This power is achieved by the author's creative imagination working through the skillful manipulation of all the elements that go into the making of a story.

Character and Characterization

Character and *characterization* are closely related but essentially different concepts. Character refers to one of the persons in the story—the end result of the author's effort to create a fictional personality. Characterization, on the other hand, refers to the means by which the writer creates the sum of traits, thoughts, and actions which, taken together, constitute a character.

At the simplest level, literary characters may belong to a number of stock types: a euphoric, newly wed husband, as in Wharton's "The Other Two"; a romantically frustrated young married woman, as in Chekhov's "The Druggist's Wife"; a frivolous and shallow sophisticate, as in McCarthy's "Cruel and Barbarous Treatment"; a mild-mannered, self-effacing office worker, as in Thurber's "The Catbird Seat"; a diffident, but resourceful and brave frontier sheriff, as in Crane's "The Bride Comes to Yellow Sky"; or an impractically gallant adolescent boy, as in Updike's "A & P." With uninspired treatment, such figures might never rise above the level of stock types. With creative imagination, however, a writer may start out with commonplace characters and develop them into universal figures, far beyond the original cardboard dimensions of the stereotypes to which they are related. Don Quixote, Hamlet, or Huck Finn, to name a few, escape the confines of their types—the impractical do-gooder, the slow-to-act intellectual, and the boy who rebels against the mores of his society—and transcend their literary confines to become symbols of human aspiration.

Another concept relating to character is that of flatness, or its opposite, roundedness. If the story is a short one, the author may create only *flat characters*, that is, characters whose essence may be summed up in a phrase, as Irwin Shaw does in "The Girls in Their Summer Dresses." If the story requires it, as is usually the case, a writer may create a *rounded character,* that is, a character who is so complex as to require extended analysis. Both types of characters may appear in the same story, depending on their importance to the action and the length of the story. In Tolstoy's "After the Ball," for example, the host's wife is a flat character whose function in the story can be encapsuled in the phrase, "a gracious, if somewhat officious giver of elaborate parties." Conversely, however, any attempt to summarize the character of Ivan, the narrator-protagonist, would require more thought and effort in order to recognize and reconcile the conflicting elements in his more detailed characterization. In the same way, in "The Bride Comes to Yellow Sky," Scratchy Wilson may be identified simply as a "hell-raising cowhand," whereas Sheriff Potter is a far more complex blend of contradictory traits and attitudes. As a caveat, it should be mentioned that one should not expect all the characters in a story to be rounded. For the good of the story, since it is a short story and not a novel, the author may create only a few rounded characters and, sometimes, only one, as Mansfield and Borges do in "Miss Brill" and in "The Secret Miracle," respectively.

Literary characters have also been described as being *static* or *developing,* depending upon whether they remain the same from the beginning to the end of the story or whether they undergo some significant, internal change in the course of events. The concept of developing suggests that the character achieves a different view of life as a result of some insight gained from conflict and is no longer quite the same person as before. The concept of static suggests the opposite.

While the author's choice of individuals and types to write about makes up the gallery of characters, the point of view and tone determine, to a very large extent, the method of characterization. A writer may choose to analyze and pass judgment on a character through the use of an omniscient, editorializing narrator. With this approach, the narrator's tone would help to achieve the desired characterization. This is the method Fitzgerald uses, in part, with his protagonist, Anson Hunter, in "The Rich Boy." Characterization can also be effected by using highly selective language or by using sequential ironies of situation as in "Cruel and Barbarous Treatment" and "The Other Two." At the other extreme, the author may present only the speech and actions of the characters, along with a motivating setting, and let the reader arrive at an inductive conclusion, as Hemingway does in "The Killers." Or a writer may have one character directly characterize another, as the character Buddy does in Capote's "A Christmas Memory." Sometimes, the comments of a character, and also those of the narrator, may be ironic or disingenuous, as in "Cruel and Barbarous Treatment" or "The Druggist's Wife." The author may have one character describe, judge, and react to another character at various points in the action, thereby telling the reader something about both of them. Lessing uses this method both in "The Nuisance" and in "Our Friend Judith," in a way that achieves both effective characterization and dramatic intensity. In some stories, a character may say one thing and do precisely the opposite, thus increasing the complexity and requiring the reader to modify an interpretation or to suspend judgment until the end. Regardless of the method of characterization that the author selects, whether direct or indirect, explicit or ironic, the task is to create believable characters who could conceivably do the things they do in the story, whether the background is mundanely realistic, as in most stories, or highly fantastic, as in some; "The Killers" is an example of the former and "A Pedestrian Accident" is an example of the latter variety.

Point of View

The concept of *point of view* introduced in the discussion on character and characterization requires a more detailed explanation because of its importance to the structure of a story. There are several questions about the way a story can be told that will help lead us to an understanding of exactly what point of view is, what varieties there are, and how different purposes are served by these different varieties. Chief among these questions are the following: through whose eyes and ears do we know what is going on? How much does this observer-spokesperson, or *narrator*, know about the people and events in the story? Does he or she know all there is to know about everyone and everything or is the knowledge possessed less than total? Does the spokesperson see into the minds of all the major characters or into the mind of just one? For ease of naming and for subsequent identification, we may ask: in what person is the story being told—first or third? We also need to consider the degree of participation that the author's spokesperson-observer has in the action of the story. For example, is this spokesperson an agent in the events, merely an observer at the periphery of the action, or an outsider reporting secondhand information? Finally, we might inquire: how does the point of view chosen serve the author's purpose and how is it better suited to the needs of the story than other options might have been when one considers the overall effect the author is attempting to produce? In asking all of these questions, and particularly the last one, one should keep in mind that the point of view selected by the author should unify and give a sense of direction to the story. At the same time, it should also blend smoothly with all the other elements of the story.

For the purpose of convenient reference, several different points of view have been traditionally distinguished and named. One of the earliest employed and most familiar is the *first-person* point of view, in which the narrator may be a major character, a minor character, or a bystander. The narrator may give a firsthand account, or one mixed with conjecture and hearsay. The narrator may be at the edge of the action and basically objective in attitude, as is the case in "The Fall of the House of Usher." Or the narrator may be at the center of the action and highly involved emotionally, as is the young man in "I'm a Fool." On the other hand, the author may elect to use the *third-person* point of view, in which the reader sees and interprets everything through the mind of a single character, who may be at the center of the story, as with Miss Brill in the Mansfield selection; or at the periphery, as with the townsman-narrator in "A Rose for Emily" (who actually operates from the third-person point of view, even though he employs the pronoun "we"); or outside the action entirely, as in "The Minister's Black Veil." When a single character at the center of the action is used as the focus of impressions, the term *central intelligence* is often applied. In the central intelligence point of view, the character is aware of all that occurs in the story and every significant thought he or she has is made known to the reader. Although a central intelligence character is involved in or witnesses all that is happening, the character may be temporarily confused, self-deluded, or naive enough to be unaware of its full meaning. However, even in such instances, the reader may expect to be provided with the necessary information to allow a correct interpretation of the significance of what is going on. Sometimes this point of view is referred to as *limited omniscience*, since the author provides access to the mind of only one character in the story.

Another possibility is the one in which the writer may choose not to invade the inner sanctum of the mind of any of the characters. Instead, the author may decide to function as the "camera-eye" and "tape-recorder" and abstain from any judgmental comment, relying only on the careful selection of significant details, as Hemingway does in "The Killers." This ostensibly *objective* point of view is variously referred to as "the stage-setting" or "scenic" technique of telling a story because of its emphasis on straightforward representation and deliberate avoidance of explicit interpretation of motives and actions.

Opposed to these points of view with varying degrees of limited knowledge is the *omniscient* point of view, one in which the author provides access to the thoughts of any and all the characters, in any place at any time he or she chooses. Usually, the author speaks in the third person, but the method may, once in a while, be used with a first-person narrator. Although writers of the eighteenth and nineteenth centuries who employed this point of view often indulged in comments made directly to the reader, modern writers using this method usually refrain from such statements. Instead, they maintain an aesthetic distance through irony, scrupulous attempts at impartiality, or some other tonal device, as is the case with Fitzgerald and Maugham in this collection.

Occasionally, a story may combine different points of view. For example, "After the Ball" joins the first-person peripheral point of view in the frame story with the first-person central-character variety in the main story. In the frame story (or subplot), the narrator speaks from the first-person point of view, but is, in fact, telling someone else's story rather than his own. "The Outstation" employs the third-person limited omniscience point of view for the greater part of the story, but toward the end of the story the point of view becomes omniscient by the delving into the mind of Cooper, Warburton's assistant. "The Rich Boy" starts out as a first-person peripheral observer story, becomes virtually omniscient in the large middle section, and reverts to the first-person peripheral observer at the end. The reader might be tempted to decry these shifts in point of view, but they are successful because the tone and attitude of the work are consistent and not misleading to the reader.

Although distinctions among different points of view are helpful for discussion purposes, the reader should not assume that any one point of view is inherently better than any other merely because it works well in a particular story. One point of view is not "more true to life," "more objective," "more modern," than any other. A writer who refrains from explicit comment on the characters and action in a story may be trying to influence the reader's judgment just as much as the writer of the nineteenth century who uses the editorial-omniscient point of view.

The influencing is done through the careful selection of details that can weight the case as heavily as the author's conscience permits or as the tolerance of the author's readers will allow. The real value in being aware of point of view is that one's sensitivity to subtleties of tone and attitude will be sharpened and the reader will become aware of nuances that might otherwise escape observation. In this regard, the Keith Fort story, "The Coal Shoveller," offers deliberate examples of how important point of view, along with style, is in determining the direction a story will take and the ultimate effect it will have upon the reader.

Language

Linked as it is to the pattern of action, character and characterization, and point of view, *language*, besides being the medium, is also another important element in the structure of a story. As the term is used here, *language* refers to the way in which words are put together for the creation of special effects. Among these special effects are: attitude, tone, atmosphere and mood, setting, pace and rhythm, and dialogue.

The *attitude* of a work is the relation the author assumes toward the subject, characters, and action in the story. Usually it can be described on a continuum from sympathetic, through neutral, to antipathetic. *Tone* is the verbal stance the author assumes toward the reader. It may be anything from sober earnestness to tongue-in-cheek levity. The author's tone may be straightforward and explicit or devious and ironic. In "The Bride Comes to Yellow Sky," the tone is clearly that of parodying irony, suggesting, from the beginning, that the threatened danger is not to be taken seriously. Through the special effect of tone, Crane is putting his reader into a mood that anticipates amusement, not one of fearful apprehension, as the bare facts of the long-standing feud between Scratchy and Potter might warrant the reader to experience. Poe, on the other hand, with his ominous tone of revelatory seriousness, is preparing the reader to expect something startling and frightening to happen in the decaying mansion of the wild-eyed, last scion of a doomed family.

The *atmosphere* is a feeling of "something in the air" that an author develops, through either description or dialogue, to serve as a conditioning or motivating force in the action. The febrile oppressiveness in "Death of a Traveling Salesman" is as crucial to the events and theme of the story as is the heavy miasmic mist settled about the crumbling family mansion in Poe's gothic horror story. The odor of decomposition pervading "A Rose for Emily" is another instance of the skillful use of atmosphere to arouse curiosity, to create suspense, and to prepare the reader for the outcome of the action. Pirandello accomplishes the same thing with the depressing aura of funereal darkness and torpid air that he creates as the ambience for the opening scene in "The Soft Touch of Grass."

The term *mood* is applied to the emotional content of a scene or entire story and it is created by the combined effect of atmosphere and setting, exposition and foreshadowing, dialogue and action. It can range from happiness to sadness, from complacency to fear, from contentment to deep frustration, and so forth.

Along with atmosphere and mood, the author may employ a spatial and temporal *setting,* which helps determine the outcome of the conflict and the protagonist's fate. The events in "The Killers," for example, happens in a time of rampant lawlessness and wanton murder, such as during the era of Prohibition in the 1920s. In the same way, the events in the Chekhov story, "The Druggist's Wife," seem credible, almost inevitable, because of the dullness and boredom emanating from the dusty streets and drab houses of the provincial, nineteenth-century Russian village the author chose as the locale for his story.

Language also helps to establish any underlying *motif.* A motif, as used in this connection, is any recurring idea, phrase, image, or action that unifies a story by repeatedly recalling its earlier occurrences. In "Death of a Traveling Salesman," for example, Welty uses the name "Beulah," with its strong religious implications, to reinforce the theme of love and acceptance, redemption and salvation. D. H. Lawrence does much the same thing in "The Rocking Horse Winner," by using the reiterated whispered importunities about the incessant need for more money that urge the boy frenetically onward to the chilling climax.

Language also helps to establish the *pace* and *rhythm* of a story. Pace and rhythm may be achieved through variations in the length of words and word groups, through contrasting or matching syntactical constructions, through the sense of pauses or the rapid flow of speech, through the deliberate selection of words for ease or difficulty of pronunciation, and through the verbatim repetition of words or phrases. Hemingway uses short, simple sentences and words that have a flat, reportorial quality about them, which suggests an objective recording of bare facts and lends an air of tense realism and swift-moving action to the scene. Fitzgerald, on the contrary, uses balanced, antithetical sentences that deliberately slow the rhythm down and invite deep reflection rather than quick response or hasty judgment.

Another function of language is the expression of character through speech, that is, *dialogue.* In "The Valiant Woman," while Mrs. Stoner's profanity, hackneyed allusions to popular literature, and use of faulty grammar indicate her shallow, untrained mind, so do the author's descriptive terms of speech—"cut" and "spit"—classify her as an overbearing person who is devoid of all Christian charity, despite her protestations of piety and noble motives.

Although the language in a well-written story may seem effortless and natural, it is only so because a great deal of care and artistry has gone into controlling it properly in order to create the various special effects that embellish the narrative understructure. It may not be an easy task for the reader to analyze the language of a story in complete detail. Nevertheless, in order to understand clearly what one reads, close attention must be paid to the individual words and word patterns in the story to see how and what they contribute to the other elements.

Symbolism and Allegory

In a story employing *symbolism,* the literal element remains basic and is not merely a vehicle for ideas. In such a story, the emphasis is on the characters who exhibit varying degrees of roundedness, and on the pattern of action, which is usually realistically oriented. Symbols are employed to amplify meaning and to extend the scope of meaning through *metaphor,* or figurative language. Symbols express the relationship of the literal figure to its real world by establishing a parallel relationship on the nonliteral level. For example, in "Araby," the bazaar is literally a large hall consisting of separate booths set up to provide entertainment and to sell curios to people drawn to it. On the symbolic level, however, for the protagonist, the bazaar stands for a number of things—"beauty," "romance," "the mysterious Orient," or anything aesthetically and emotionally inviting, but normally out of reach. For the boy in the story, the bazaar is a thing of compelling beauty and veiled allure that outrivals the mundane and ugly of ordinary existence. But this is only in anticipation, for when he finally gets to the bazaar and sees it as it really is, in all its tawdriness and banality, the magic vanishes. The shattering revelation tarnishes the boy's world of illusion and romantic imagination, which has enraptured his heart and mind for days. Thus, by the use of this symbol, Joyce expands and enriches the meaning of his story beyond that of the disillusionment of a young boy enthralled by romantic fancies. The use of symbolism enables Joyce to deal with universal human hopes and their frustration by reality. However, unlike a story utilizing allegory, the story using symbolism does not exist primarily to convey a moral message. A story like "Araby" can exist apart from its symbols, but its meaning and effect are immeasurably enhanced by the writer's symbolic use of language.

In a story organized as fully developed *allegory*, which is like symbolism in that it, too, is a nonliteral mode of expression, every character, object, and place stands more for the abstract idea than for the literal figure in the narrative. It is the idea represented that is important, not the semirealistic character, object, or place. Since characters in allegory personify abstract concepts such as "Love," "Mercy," "Forgiveness," "Sin," and "Death," the characters are of necessity flat and undeveloped, having little real personality of their own apart from what they represent. In a story using complex allegory, such as Kafka's "In the Penal Colony," the figures of the officer, explorer, the old and new commandants, and the soldier and condemned man are allegorical on several different levels—theological, political, psychological, philosophical, and mythological—yet they still emerge as relatively flat characters. The explanation for this flatness lies in the intent of allegory: to convey through narrative form a message, usually moralistic or philosophical, to a reader who is aware of and accepts the worth of the idea represented. The story line, with its personified abstractions and specially contrived situations, is merely a vehicle for the message. In the hands of a consummate artist such as Kafka, the traditional one-to-one, figure-to-concept structure of allegory is considerably amplified. In spite of its elaboration and subtlety, however, "In the Penal Colony" is as much an allegory as a medieval morality play or Dante's *Divine Comedy*. Allegory, when it is artistically executed, can be as entertaining and absorbing as it is edifying; however, when it is mechanically done, it can be soporifically boring and stultifying. As literary fashions have changed over the centuries, the allegorical form has attracted fewer writers than has fiction grounded in reality. It would appear that modern fiction has substituted stories of bizarre fantasy for the abstractions of allegory to convey important ideas under the surface of reality, as the selections in this collection by Coover, Barthelme, and Hughes would suggest. Another distinction between symbolism and allegory is that while symbolism is usually associated with considerable realistic detail, allegory frequently pays little attention to realistic detail and the demands of credibility. In a nonallegorical story employing symbolism, such as "The Fall of the House of Usher," Poe carefully describes the size, appearance, and depth of the tarn near the doomed mansion. Besides being a symbol of the oblivion that will engulf the last of the Ushers, the tarn and its miasma are used to create a sense of foreboding on the literal and narrative level. "In the Penal Colony" provides little realistic detail to orient the reader in a specific time or place, although it does give a detailed description of the fanciful apparatus central to the bizarre action. The description is so fanciful, however, as to suggest it is not intended to be taken as representative of a real object.

A further difference between symbolism and allegory is that a story employing symbolism may be probable, logical, and understandable whether or not the reader recognizes the symbolic meaning inherent in certain elements in the story. A symbolic story, such as "Araby," would be intellectually rewarding and entertaining even if the reader failed to recognize the bazaar as the unifying symbol. A story employing an allegorical pattern, however, is apt to be improbable, absurd, and incomprehensible if read on the literal level alone. An allegory usually stands or falls on the reader's awareness of the ideas that are being personified in the characters and represented by the action and setting.

It should also be noted that while allegory develops its meaning by the forward movement of the plot in a series of conflicts between interrelated abstractions, symbolism is amplified chiefly by repetition in varying contexts and by increasing the associations grouped around the symbols, a device sometimes referred to as "incremental repetition." In "Miss Brill," for example, the fox fur is much more suggestive and important symbolically for being ridiculed and then hastily packed away to the accompaniment of sobs than had it been simply petted and worn with pride. In essence, both symbolism and allegory depend upon the texture of the whole work for whatever value they possess. To be warranted artistically, they must clarify and extend the scope of the story, not limit or warp its total effect to the point that it becomes a catalogue of ideas or a dull moral tract rather than an engrossing work of the imagination.

Theme

The *theme* of a story is the generalization about human life that can be drawn from the outcome of the conflict and from the support provided by tone, attitude, atmosphere, setting, and symbolism or allegory. In attempting to come to grips with the meaning of a story, the reader should not be misled into accepting the statement of any of the characters as a necessarily accurate or complete expression of the theme. A character in "After the Ball" may say, "It's all a question of chance," but the story itself may be saying much more. A themelike statement by one of the characters may simply reflect that particular character's limited or biased perception of the truth. In some cases, the statement may be absolutely wrong. Or it may be an ironic statement, as is the case with the young protagonist in "I'm a Fool," who sees less of the truth than the reader does.

In regard to *irony*, or reversal of meaning, the reader should always be on the alert for its presence. Reversal of meaning, or *verbal irony*, may be present when the author, through whatever point of view, means precisely the opposite of what he or she seems to be saying. For example, in "The Bride Comes to Yellow Sky," the narrator may profess apprehension of imminent danger, all the while knowing full well that in fact there is nothing of which to be afraid. Or, on the other hand, the narrator may speak blandly and unconcernedly about horrifying possibilities, as in the Kafka story. Verbal irony may be inherent in the language of the various characters. The insights and resolves they make known to the reader may be completely spurious or insincere, as is the case with She in "Cruel and Barbarous Treatment."

Verbal irony may be genial, philosophically detached, or satirical in intent. The satirical variety occurs when the author's tone clearly implies censure, even though the words used may appear to be sympathetic, appreciative, or even flattering in meaning. Examples of *satirical irony* can be seen in "A Shower of Gold," "One off the Short List," "Lawley Road," and "The Lottery Ticket." In all of these stories, someone or something is ostensibly being praised or treated tolerantly, when actually the real intent of the author is to ridicule the type of human folly exhibited.

Irony may also exist in actions and situations, where the reversal is not one of meaning but of expectation. This *situational irony* can give a direct clue to the meaning of the story. For instance, in "Araby," it is ironic that the place that holds the greatest promise of fulfillment for the boy should drive him away and deprive him of his illusions of romance. *Irony of fate* is a variant of situational irony and is a frequently used device. It occurs when circumstances come about that are the opposite of the outcome anticipated by the protagonist, but not necessarily by the reader. In Chekhov's "The Druggist's Wife," the twist of fate occurs when the husband, instead of the pretty young wife, answers the bell on the lieutenant's return, thus stifling the possibility of a romantic liaison that would dispel her boredom and frustration.

In the effort to become aware of irony, either verbal or situational, one might well start with the title, which is frequently ironic or symbolic, as well as being descriptive, and continue being on the alert, to the very last word in the story. If one remains insensitive to irony, attempts to arrive at a proper understanding of a story may end in an unperceptive distortion of the author's intent.

With some stories, it may be difficult to arrive at a simple formulation of the theme. A subtle writer may even include several plausible thematic statements in the text to increase the irony and complexity of the story. At the end of "The Real Thing," for example, the author presents two possible concepts as the theme. "Art for art's sake," as proposed by Hawley, is contrasted to the artist's humanitarian reflection that he is somehow better for having known the Monarchs. Although neither view is patently wrong, both are only partially supportable—as are most of the views we have of life, the author seems to be suggesting. Neither the aesthetic rationalism of the painter's friend nor the sentimental concern of the painter himself sums up the whole truth or theme of the story. We would be misreading if we argued for either view to the exclusion of the other or to the exclusion of some synthesis of the two views.

In most great literature, the theme is implied rather than explicitly stated. For Welty to say, "Money can't buy love," or Malamud, "Misery can be comic," or Kafka, "The choices in life are clear but equally unsatisfying," would rob the stories of their challenging complexity and rich ambiguity, or multiple layers of meaning. It may be good practice for the reader to try to state the theme explicitly, because by so doing, it forces one to read the story carefully and to think about it on more than a superficial level. However, if the author too explicitly states the theme, it may be considered gratuitous and inartistic. If the story is structured properly, the author should not have to belabor the reader with a bald statement of meaning.

It should be understood, however, that even when the reader has arrived at a satisfactory statement of the theme, he or she should not assume that the theme itself is the story. The story always remains greater than any of its parts because it is a work of art, not a column of figures to be added up with the end result being all that really matters.

Finally, the value of thematic ideas in a story can be considered only in their relation to the entire work. Regardless of how true, universal, or appealing an idea may seem or not seem, the primary concern of a perceptive reader should be with how well the idea is exemplified and brought to life in the story. What matters is how artistically, how concretely, and how compellingly the author gives shape and substance to a guiding principle, apart from the reader's appraisal of the validity, intellectual worth, or originality of the idea embodied.

Evaluation of Literature

Upon reading a work of literature, we inevitably arrive at some evaluation of the artistic merit it possesses. We can best arrive at a fair and reasonable judgment by asking ourselves some pertinent questions relating to the elements of structure previously discussed. First of all, we might ask: does the action add up? Given the situation at the beginning of the story, do the subsequent events follow some kind of meaningful pattern, no matter how odd that pattern may seem in terms of ordinary logic? For instance, even the apparently illogical behavior of the characters in the stories by Purdy, Friedman, and Coover exhibits a narrative consistency, no matter how incredible it may have seemed initially. Even though as a reader one may be willing to suspend disbelief at the beginning of a story, one expects subsequent action to be meaningful and to follow a logic of sorts. Furthermore, the outcome of the events should be reasonably predictable from the initial situation. Suspense and surprise may enhance the effect of the story, but the reader has a right to expect that whenever events take a surprising turn, such surprises should be inherent in the characters and plot, and not belatedly contrived to rescue the author from an impasse he or she has been too inept to surmount. Hence, if the author has conscientiously and artfully structured the elements into a meaningful, aesthetic structure, the pattern of events will seem plausible and acceptable to the reader.

We may proceed along this line of inquiry by asking additional questions concerning the writer's handling of the other elements of structure. Does the author reveal the past, when necessary, in such a way that action and characterization are not impeded? Does the author handle this exposition without confusing the tone or detracting from the contributing effect of atmosphere and mood? Has the author created believable characters or are they stereotypes from beginning to end, manipulated externally rather than being credibly motivated? How does the author handle the patterns of conflict and tension in the story? Is there a rhythm of increasing intensity, followed by a release that is emotionally and intellectually satisfying, as in "Who Am I This Time?" or "The Conversion of the Jews"? Or do action and interest bog down in unintentional anticlimax or become trapped in a repetition of incidents devoid of tension?

The question of how well an author uses language and its special effects is also important when evaluating literature. Does the author use language skillfully to creative a pervasive mood, a motivating atmosphere, and an appropriate setting; or are these elements inert or, worse, in conflict with one another? Has the author selected a suitable point of view, and is it employed consistently throughout the story, without annoying shifts that disrupt the tone and destroy the aesthetic distance necessary to sustain reader interest?

After examining the individual parts of a story, we may also examine its cohesiveness: is the story tied together and balanced with the proper stress on the important elements? Are the symbols and images an integral part of the story, as they are in Oates's "Four Summers," or are they merely tacked on to lend an air of artistry and profundity to an otherwise facile and shallow effort? Finally, we might ask whether the theme is an artificial appendage grafted onto the work; or does the theme develop out of the structure of the story, out of the characters given, and out of the situation in which the characters find themselves, their conflicts, and the resolution or failure to resolve these conflicts?

Theoretically, a great story should sustain superbly all of the elements of structure—plot, characterization, point of view, language, tone, atmosphere, mood, setting, imagery, symbolism, and theme. Even with the best of stories, however, we may feel that one or another element falls below the high standard set by the others. For example, an author may shift the point of view upon reaching an impasse in characterization, or may impede the story's progress with dilatory exposition or excessively involuted language. Yet, if the heart of the story—characterization, conflict, and resolution—is sound, one may be willing to overlook an awkward development of some element, considering the overall strength of the story.

Many of the stories in this collection may seem to be close to perfection; others may appear slightly flawed in one important aspect or another, but may still possess strong appeal because of their overall conception or skillful execution of a dominant element. Regardless of the degree of excellence, however, most of the stories should prove both entertaining and rewarding, hopefully even more so for having been approached structurally, as we recommend in this introduction.

Conrad Aiken
Silent Snow, Secret Snow

I

Just why it should have happened, or why it should have happened just when it did, he could not, of course, possibly have said; nor perhaps would it even have occurred to him to ask. The thing was above all a secret, something to be preciously concealed from Mother and Father; and to that very fact it owed an enormous part of its deliciousness. It was like a peculiarly beautiful trinket to be carried unmentioned in one's trouser pocket—a rare stamp, an old coin, a few tiny gold links found trodden out of shape on the path in the park, a pebble of carnelian, a seashell distinguishable from all others by an unusual spot or stripe—and, as if it were any one of these, he carried around with him everywhere a warm and persistent and increasingly beautiful sense of possession. Nor was it only a sense of possession—it was also a sense of protection. It was as if, in some delightful way, his secret gave him a fortress, a wall behind which he could retreat into heavenly seclusion. This was almost the first thing he had noticed about it—apart from the oddness of the thing itself—and it was this that now again, for the fiftieth time, occurred to him, as he sat in the little schoolroom. It was the half-hour for geography. Miss Buell was revolving with one finger, slowly, a huge terrestrial globe which had been placed on her desk. The green and yellow continents passed and repassed, questions were asked and answered, and now the little girl in front of him, Deirdre, who had a funny little constellation of freckles on the back of her neck, exactly like the Big Dipper, was standing up and telling Miss Buell that the equator was the line that ran round the middle.

Miss Buell's face, which was old and grayish and kindly, with gray stiff curls beside the cheeks, and eyes that swam very brightly, like little minnows, behind thick glasses, wrinkled itself into a complication of amusements.

"Ah! I see. The earth is wearing a belt, or a sash. Or someone drew a line round it!"

"Oh no—not that—I mean—"

In the general laughter, he did not share, or only a very little. He was thinking about the Arctic and Antarctic regions, which of course, on the globe, were white. Miss Buell was now telling them about the tropics, the jungles, the steamy heat of equatorial swamps, where the birds and butterflies, and even the snakes, were like living jewels. As he listened to these things, he was already, with a pleasant sense of half-effort, putting his secret between himself and the words. Was it really an effort at all? For effort implied something voluntary, and perhaps even something one did not especially want; whereas this was distinctly pleasant, and came almost of its own accord. All he needed to do was to think of that morning, the first one, and then of all the others—

But it was all so absurdly simple! It had amounted to so little. It was nothing, just an idea—and just why it should have become so wonderful, so permanent, was a mystery—a very pleasant one, to be sure, but also, in an amusing way, foolish. However, without ceasing to listen to Miss Buell, who had now moved up to the north temperate zones, he deliberately invited his memory of the first morning. It was only a moment or two after he had waked up—or perhaps the moment itself. But was there, to be exact, an exact moment? Was one awake all at once? or was it gradual? Anyway, it was after he had stretched a lazy hand up toward the headrail, and yawned, and then relaxed again among his warm covers, all the more grateful on a December morning, that the thing had happened. Suddenly, for no reason, he had thought of the postman, he remembered the postman. Perhaps there was nothing so odd in that. After all, he heard the postman almost every morning in his life—his heavy boots could be heard clumping round the corner at the top of the little cobbled hill-street, and then, progressively nearer, progressively louder, the double knock at each door, the crossings and re-crossings of the street, till finally the clumsy steps came stumbling across to the very door, and the tremendous knock came which shook the house itself.

(Miss Buell was saying, "Vast wheat-growing areas in North America and Siberia."

Deirdre had for the moment placed her left hand across the back of her neck.)

But on this particular morning, the first morning, as he lay there with his eyes closed, he had for some reason *waited* for the postman. He wanted to hear him come round the corner. And that was precisely the joke—he never did. He never came. He never had come—*round the corner*—again. For when at last the steps *were* heard, they had already, he was quite sure, come a little down the hill, to the first house; and even so, the steps were curiously different—they were softer, they had a new secrecy about them, they were muffled and indistinct; and while the rhythm of them was the same, it now said a new thing—it said peace, it said remoteness, it said cold, it said sleep. And he had understood the situation at once—nothing could have seemed simpler—there had been snow in the night, such as all winter he had been longing for; and it was this which had rendered the postman's first footsteps inaudible, and the later ones faint. Of course! How lovely! And even now it must be snowing—it was going to be a snowy day—the long white ragged lines were drifting and sifting across the street, across the faces of the old houses, whispering and hushing, making little triangles of white in the corners between cobblestones, seething a little when the wind blew them over the ground to a drifted corner; and so it would be all day, getting deeper and deeper and silenter and silenter.

(Miss Buell was saying, "Land of perpetual snow.")

All this time, of course (while he lay in bed), he had kept his eyes closed, listening to the nearer progress of the postman, the muffled footsteps thumping and slipping on the snow-sheathed cobbles; and all the other sounds—the double knocks, a frosty far-off voice or two, a bell ringing thinly and softly as if under a sheet of ice—had the same slightly abstracted quality, as if removed by one degree from actuality—as if everything in the world had been insulated by snow. But when at last, pleased, he opened his eyes, and turned them toward the window, to see for himself this long-desired and now so clearly imagined miracle—what he saw instead was brilliant sunlight on a roof; and when, astonished, he jumped out of bed and stared down into the street, expecting to see the cobbles obliterated by the snow, he saw nothing but the bare bright cobbles themselves.

Queer, the effect this extraordinary surprise had had upon him—all the following morning he had kept with him a sense as of snow falling about him, a secret screen of new snow between himself and the world. If he had not dreamed such a thing—and how could he have dreamed it while awake?—how else could one explain it? In any case, the delusion had been so vivid as to affect his entire behavior. He could not now remember whether it was on the first or the second morning—or was it even the third?—that his mother had drawn attention to some oddness in his manner.

"But my darling"—she had said at the breakfast table—"what has come over you? You don't seem to be listening. . . ."

And how often that very thing had happened since!

(Miss Buell was now asking if anyone knew the difference between the North Pole and the Magnetic Pole. Deirdre was holding up her flickering brown hand, and he could see the four white dimples that marked the knuckles.)

Perhaps it hadn't been either the second or third morning—or even the fourth or fifth. How could he be sure? How could he be sure just when the delicious *progress* had become clear? Just when it had really *begun?* The intervals weren't very precise. . . . All he now knew was, that at some point or other—perhaps the second day, perhaps the sixth—he had noticed that the presence of the snow was a little more insistent, the sound of it clearer; and, conversely, the sound of the postman's footsteps more indistinct. Not only could he not hear the steps come round the corner, he could not even hear them at the first house. It was below the first house that he heard them; and then, a few days later, it was below the second house that he heard them; and a few days later again, below the third. Gradually, gradually, the snow was becoming heavier, the sound of its seething louder, the cobblestones more and more muffled. When he found, each morning, on going to the window, after the ritual of listening, that the roofs and cobbles were as bare as ever, it made no difference. This was, after all, only what he had expected. It was even what pleased him, what rewarded him: the thing was his own, belonged to no one else. No one else knew about it, not even his mother and father. There, outside, were the bare cobbles; and here, inside, was the snow. Snow growing heavier each day, muffling the world, hiding the ugly, and deadening increasingly—above all—the steps of the postman.

"But, my darling"—she had said at the luncheon table—"what has come over you? You don't seem to listen when people speak to you. That's the third time I've asked you to pass your plate. . . ."

How was one to explain this to Mother? or to Father? There was, of course, nothing to be done about it: nothing. All one could do was to laugh embarrassedly, pretend to be a little ashamed, apologize, and take a sudden and somewhat disingenuous interest in what was being done or said. The cat had stayed out all night. He had a curious swelling on his left cheek—perhaps somebody had kicked him, or a stone had struck him. Mrs. Kempton was or was not coming to tea. The house was going to be housecleaned, or "turned out," on Wednesday instead of Friday. A new lamp was provided for his evening work—perhaps it was eyestrain which accounted for this new and so peculiar vagueness of his—Mother was looking at him with amusement as she said this, but with something else as well. A new lamp? A new lamp. Yes, Mother, No, Mother, Yes, Mother. School is going very well. The geometry is very easy. The history is very dull. The geography is very interesting—particularly when it takes one to the North Pole. Why the North Pole? Oh, well, it would be fun to be an explorer. Another Peary or Scott or Shackleton. And then abruptly he found his interest in the talk at an end, stared at the pudding on his plate, listened, waited, and began once more—ah, how heavenly, too, the first beginnings—to hear or feel—for could he actually hear it?—the silent snow, the secret snow.

(Miss Buell was telling them about the search for the Northwest Passage, about Hendrik Hudson, the *Half Moon*.)

This had been, indeed, the only distressing feature of the new experience; the fact that it so increasingly had brought him into a kind of mute misunderstanding, or even conflict, with his father and mother. It was as if he were trying to lead a double life. On the one hand, he had to be Paul Hasleman, and keep up the appearance of being that person—dress, wash, and answer intelligently when spoken to—; on the other, he had to explore this new world which had been opened to him. Nor could there be the slightest doubt—not the slightest—that the new world was the profounder and more wonderful of the two. It was irresistible. It was miraculous. Its beauty was simply beyond anything—beyond speech as beyond thought—utterly incommunicable. But how then, between the two worlds, of which he was thus constantly aware, was he to keep a balance? One must get up, one must go to breakfast, one must talk with Mother, go to school, do one's lessons—and, in all this, try not to appear too much of a fool. But if all the while one was also trying to extract the full deliciousness of another and quite separate existence, one which could not easily (if at all) be spoken of—how was one to manage? How was one to explain? Would it be safe to explain? Would it be absurd? Would it merely mean that he would get into some obscure kind of trouble?

These thoughts came and went, came and went, as softly and secretly as the snow; they were not precisely a disturbance, perhaps they were even a pleasure; he liked to have them; their presence was something almost palpable, something he could stroke with his hand, without closing his eyes, and without ceasing to see Miss Buell and the schoolroom and the globe and the freckles on Deirdre's neck; nevertheless he did in a sense cease to see, or to see the obvious external world, and substituted for this vision the vision of snow, the sound of snow, and the slow, almost soundless, approach of the postman. Yesterday, it had been only at the sixth house that the postman had become audible; the snow was much deeper now, it was falling more swiftly and heavily, the sound of its seething was more distinct, more soothing, more persistent. And this morning, it had been—as nearly as he could figure—just above the seventh house—perhaps only a step or two above; at most, he had heard two or three footsteps before the knock had sounded. . . . And with each such narrowing of the sphere, each nearer approach of the limit at which the postman was first audible, it was odd how sharply was increased the amount of illusion which had to be carried into the ordinary business of daily life. Each day, it was harder to get out of bed, to go to the window, to look out at the—as always—perfectly empty and snowless street. Each day it was more difficult to go through the perfunctory motions of greeting Mother and Father at breakfast, to reply to their questions, to put his books together and go to school. And at school, how extraordinarily hard to conduct with success simultaneously the public life and the life that was secret! There were times when he longed—positively ached—to tell everyone about it—to burst out with it—only to be checked almost at once by a far-off feeling as of some faint absurdity which was inherent in it—but *was* it absurd?—and more importantly by a sense of mysterious power in his very secrecy. Yes; it must be kept secret. That, more and more, became clear. At whatever cost to himself, whatever pain to others—

(Miss Buell looked straight at him, smiling, and said, "Perhaps we'll ask Paul. I'm sure Paul will come out of his daydream long enough to be able to tell us. Won't you, Paul?" He rose slowly from his chair, resting one hand on the brightly varnished desk, and deliberately stared through the snow toward the blackboard. It was an effort, but it was amusing to make it. "Yes," he said slowly, "it was what we now call the Hudson River. This he thought to be the Northwest Passage. He was disappointed." He sat down again, and as he did so Deirdre half turned in her chair and gave him a shy smile, of approval and admiration.)

At whatever pain to others.

This part of it was very puzzling, very puzzling. Mother was very nice, and so was Father. Yes, that was all true enough. He wanted to be nice to them, to tell them everything—and yet, was it really wrong of him to want to have a secret place of his own?

At bed-time, the night before, Mother had said, "If this goes on, my lad, we'll have to see a doctor, we will! We can't have our boy—" But what was it she had said? "Live in another world"? "Live so far away"? The word "far" had been in it, he was sure, and then Mother had taken up a magazine again and laughed a little, but with an expression which wasn't mirthful. He had felt sorry for her. . . .

The bell rang for dismissal. The sound came to him through long curved parallels of falling snow. He saw Deirdre rise, and had himself risen almost as soon—but not quite as soon—as she.

II

On the walk homeward, which was timeless, it pleased him to see through the accompaniment, or counterpoint, of snow, the items of mere externality on his way. There were many kinds of brick in the sidewalks, and laid in many kinds of pattern. The garden walls, too, were various, some of wooden palings, some of plaster, some of stone. Twigs of bushes leaned over the walls: the little hard green winter-buds of lilac, on gray stems, sheathed and fat; other branches very thin and fine and black and desiccated. Dirty sparrows huddled in the bushes, as dull in color as dead fruit left in leafless trees. A single starling creaked on a weather vane. In the gutter, beside a drain, was a scrap of torn and dirty newspaper, caught in a little delta of filth; the word ECZEMA appeared in large capitals, and below it was a letter from Mrs. Amelia D. Cravath, 2100 Pine Street, Fort Worth, Texas, to the effect that after being a sufferer for years she had been cured by Caley's Ointment. In the little delta, beside the fan-shaped and deeply runneled continent of brown mud, were lost twigs, descended from their parent trees, dead matches, a rusty horse-chestnut burr, a small concentration of eggshell, a streak of yellow sawdust which had been wet and now was dry and congealed, a brown pebble, and a broken feather. Farther on was a cement sidewalk, ruled into geometrical parallelograms, with a brass inlay at one end commemorating the contractors who had laid it, and, halfway across, an irregular and random series of dog-tracks, immortalized in synthetic stone. He knew these well, and always stepped on them; to cover the little hollows with his own foot had always been a queer pleasure; today he did it once more, but perfunctorily and detachedly, all the while thinking of something else. That was a dog, a long time ago, who had made a mistake and walked on the cement while it was still wet. He had probably wagged his tail, but that hadn't been recorded. Now, Paul Hasleman, aged twelve, on his way home from school, crossed the same river, which in the meantime had frozen into rock. Homeward through the snow, the snow falling in bright sunshine. Homeward?

Then came the gateway with the two

posts surmounted by egg-shaped stones which had been cunningly balanced on their ends, as if by Columbus, and mortared in the very act of balance; a source of perpetual wonder. On the brick wall just beyond, the letter H had been stenciled, presumably for some purpose.

H? H.

The green hydrant, with a little green-painted chain attached to the brass screw-cap.

The elm tree, with the great gray wound in the bark, kidney-shaped, into which he always put his hand—to feel the cold but living wood. The injury, he had been sure, was due to the gnawings of a tethered horse. But now it deserved only a passing palm, a merely tolerant eye. There were more important things. Miracles. Beyond the thoughts of trees, mere elms. Beyond the thoughts of sidewalks, mere stone, mere brick, mere cement. Beyond the thoughts even of his own shoes, which trod these sidewalks obediently, bearing a burden—far above—of elaborate mystery. He watched them. They were not very well polished; he had neglected them, for a very good reason: they were one of the many parts of the increasing difficulty of the daily return to daily life, the morning struggle. To get up, having at last opened one's eyes, to go to the window, and discover no snow, to wash, to dress, to descend the curving stairs to breakfast—

At whatever pain to others, nevertheless, one must persevere in severance, since the incommunicability of the experience demanded it. It was desirable, of course, to be kind to Mother and Father, especially as they seemed to be worried, but it was also desirable to be resolute. If they should decide—as appeared likely—to consult the doctor, Doctor Howells, and have Paul inspected, his heart listened to through a kind of dictaphone, his lungs, his stomach—well, that was all right. He would go through with it. He would give them answer for question, too—perhaps such answers as they hadn't expected? No. That would never do. For the secret world must, at all costs, be preserved.

The bird-house in the apple tree was empty—it was the wrong time of year for wrens. The little round black door had lost its pleasure. The wrens were enjoying other houses, other nests, remoter trees. But this too was a notion which he only vaguely and grazingly entertained—as if, for the moment, he merely touched an edge of it; there was something further on, which was already assuming a sharper importance; something which already teased at the corners of his eyes, teasing also at the corner of his mind. It was funny to think that he so wanted this, so awaited it—and yet found himself enjoying this momentary dalliance with the bird-house, as if for a quite deliberate postponement and enhancement of the approaching pleasure. He was aware of his delay, of his smiling and detached and now almost uncomprehending gaze at the little bird-house; he knew what he was going to look at next: it was his own little cobbled hill-street, his own house, the little river at the bottom of the hill, the grocer's shop with the cardboard man in the window—and now, thinking of all this, he turned his head, still smiling, and looking quickly right and left through the snow-laden sunlight.

And the mist of snow, as he had foreseen, was still on it—a ghost of snow falling in the bright sunlight, softly and steadily floating and turning and pausing, soundlessly meeting the snow that covered, as with a transparent mirage, the bare bright cobbles. He loved it—he stood still and loved it. Its beauty was paralyzing—beyond all words, all experience, all dream. No fairy story he had ever read could be compared with it—none had ever given him this extraordinary combination of ethereal loveliness with a something else, unnameable, which was just faintly and deliciously terrifying. What was this thing? As he thought of it, he looked upward toward his own bedroom window, which was open—and it was as if he looked straight into the room and saw himself lying half awake in his bed. There he was—at this very instant he was still perhaps actually there—more truly there than standing here at the edge of the cobbled hill-street, with one hand lifted to shade his eyes against the snow-sun. Had he indeed ever left his room in all this time? since that very first morning? Was the whole progress still being enacted there, was it still the same morning, and himself not yet wholly awake? And even now, had the postman not yet come round the corner? . . .

This idea amused him, and automatically, as he thought of it, he turned his head and looked toward the top of the hill. There was, of course, nothing there—nothing and no one. The street was empty and quiet. And all the more because of its emptiness it occurred to him to count the houses—a thing which, oddly enough, he hadn't before thought of doing. Of course, he had known there weren't many—many, that is, on his own side of the street, which were the ones that figured in the postman's progress—but nevertheless it came as something of a shock to find that there were precisely *six*, above his own house—his own house was the seventh.

Six!

Astonished, he looked at his own house—looked at the door, on which was the number thirteen—and then realized that the whole thing was exactly and logically and absurdly what he ought to have known. Just the same, the realization gave him abruptly, and even a little frighteningly, a sense of hurry. He was being hurried—he was being rushed. For—he knit his brow—he couldn't be mistaken—it was just above the *seventh* house, his *own* house, that the postman had first been audible this very morning. But in that case—in that case—did it mean that tomorrow he would hear nothing? The knock he had heard must have been the knock of their own door. Did it mean—and this was an idea which gave him a really extraordinary feeling of surprise—that he would never hear the postman again?—that tomorrow morning the postman would already have passed the house, in a snow so deep as to render his footsteps completely inaudible? That he would have made his approach down the snow-filled street so soundlessly, so secretly, that he, Paul Hasleman, there lying in bed, would not have waked in time, or waking, would have heard nothing?

But how could that be? Unless even the knocker should be muffled in the snow—frozen tight, perhaps? . . . But in that case—

A vague feeling of disappointment came over him; a vague sadness as if he felt himself deprived of something which he had long looked forward to, something much prized. After all this, all this beautiful progress, the slow delicious advance of the postman through the silent and secret snow, the knock creeping closer each day, and the footsteps nearer, the audible compass of the world thus daily narrowed, narrowed, narrowed, as the snow soothingly and beautifully encroached and deepened, after all this, was he to be defrauded of the one thing he had so wanted—to be able to count, as it were, the last two or three solemn footsteps, as they finally approached his own door? Was it all going to happen, at the end, so suddenly? or indeed, had it already happened? with no slow and subtle gradations of menace, in which he could luxuriate?

He gazed upward again, toward his own window which flashed in the sun; and this time almost with a feeling that it would be better if he *were* still in bed, in that room; for in that case this must still be the first morning, and there would be six more mornings to come—or, for that matter, seven or eight or nine—how could he be sure?—or even more.

III

After supper, the inquisition began. He stood before the doctor, under the lamp, and submitted silently to the usual thumpings and tappings.

"Now will you please say 'Ah!'?"

"Ah!"

"Now again, please, if you don't mind."

"Ah."

"Say it slowly, and hold it if you can—"

"Ah-h-h-h-h-h—"

"Good."

How silly all this was. As if it had anything to do with his throat! Or his heart, or lungs!

Relaxing his mouth, of which the corners, after all this absurd stretching, felt uncomfortable, he avoided the doctor's eyes, and stared toward the fireplace, past his mother's feet (in gray slippers) which projected from the green chair, and his father's feet (in brown slippers) which stood neatly side by side on the hearth rug.

"Hm. There is certainly nothing wrong there . . . ?"

He felt the doctor's eyes fixed upon him, and, as if merely to be polite, returned the look, but with a feeling of justifiable evasiveness.

"Now, young man, tell me—do you feel all right?"

"Yes, sir, quite all right."

"No headaches? no dizziness?"

"No, I don't think so."

"Let me see. Let's get a book, if you don't mind—yes, thank you, that will do splendidly—and now, Paul, if you'll just read it, holding it as you would normally hold it—"

He took the book and read:

"And another praise have I to tell for this the city our mother, the gift of a great god, a glory of the land most high; the might of horses, the might of young horses, the might of the sea . . . For thou, son of Cronus, our lord Poseidon, hath throned herein this pride, since in these roads first thou didst show forth the curb that cures the rage of steeds. And the shapely oar, apt to men's hands, hath a wondrous speed on the brine, following the hundred-footed Nereids. . . . O land that art praised above all lands, now is it for thee to make those bright praises seen in deeds."

He stopped, tentatively, and lowered the heavy book.

"No—as I thought—there is certainly no superficial sign of eyestrain."

Silence thronged the room, and he was aware of the focused scrutiny of the three people who confronted him. . . .

"We could have his eyes examined—but I believe it is something else."

"What could it be?" That was his father's voice.

"It's only this curious absent-mindedness—" This was his mother's voice.

In the presence of the doctor, they both seemed irritatingly apologetic.

"I believe it is something else. Now Paul—I would like very much to ask you a question or two. You will answer them, won't you—you know I'm an old, old friend of yours, eh? That's right! . . ."

His back was thumped twice by the doctor's fat fist—then the doctor was grinning at him with false amiability, while with one fingernail he was scratching the top button of his waistcoat. Beyond the doctor's shoulder was the fire, the fingers of flame making light prestidigitation against the sooty fireback, the soft sound of their random flutter the only sound.

"I would like to know—is there anything that worries you?"

The doctor was again smiling, his eyelids low against the little black pupils, in each of which was a tiny white bead of light. Why answer him? why answer him at all? "At whatever pain to others"—but it was all a nuisance, this necessity for resistance, this necessity for attention; it was as if one had been stood up on a brilliantly lighted stage, under a great round blaze of spotlight; as if one were merely a trained seal, or a performing dog, or a fish, dipped out of an aquarium and held up by the tail. It would serve them right if he were merely to bark or growl. And meanwhile, to miss these last few precious hours, these hours of which each minute was more beautiful than the last, more menacing—! He still looked, as if from a great distance, at the beads of light in the doctor's eyes, at the fixed false smile, and then, beyond, once more at his mother's slippers, his father's slippers, the soft flutter of the fire. Even here, even amongst these hostile presences, and in this arranged light, he could see the snow, he could hear it—it was in the corners of the room, where the shadow was deepest, under the sofa, behind the half-opened door which led to the dining room. It was gentler here, softer, its seethe the quietest of whispers, as if, in deference to a drawing room, it had quite deliberately put on its "manners"; it kept itself out of sight, obliterated itself, but distinctly with an air of saying, "Ah, but just wait! Wait till we are alone together! Then I will begin to tell you something new! Something white! something cold! something sleepy! something of cease, and peace, and the long bright curve of space! Tell them to go away. Banish them. Refuse to speak. Leave them, go upstairs to your room, turn out the light and get into bed—I will go with you, I will be waiting for you, I will tell you a better story than Little Kay of the Skates, or The Snow Ghost—I will surround your bed, I will close the windows, pile a deep drift against the door, so that none will ever again be able to enter. Speak to them! . . ." It seemed as if the little hissing voice came from a slow white spiral of falling flakes in the corner by the front window—but he could not be sure. He felt himself smiling, then, and said to the doctor, but without looking at him, looking beyond him still—

"Oh no, I think not—"

"But are you sure, my boy?"

His father's voice came softly and coldly then—the familiar voice of silken warning.

"You needn't answer at once, Paul—remember we're trying to help you—think it over and be quite sure, won't you?"

He felt himself smiling again, at the notion of being quite sure. What a joke! As if he weren't so sure that reassurance was no longer necessary, and all this cross-examination a ridiculous farce, a grotesque parody! What could they know about it? these gross intelligences, these humdrum minds so bound to the usual, the ordinary? Impossible to tell them about it! Why, even now, even now, with the proof so abundant, so formidable, so imminent, so appallingly present here in this very room, could they believe it?—could even his mother believe it? No—it was only too plain that if anything were said about it, the merest hint given, they would be incredulous—they would laugh—they would say "Absurd!"—think things about him which weren't true. . . .

"Why no, I'm not worried—why should I be?"

He looked then straight at the doctor's low-lidded eyes, looked from one of them to the other, from one bead of light to the other, and gave a little laugh.

The doctor seemed to be disconcerted by this. He drew back in his chair, resting a fat white hand on either knee. The smile faded slowly from his face.

"Well, Paul!" he said, and paused gravely, "I'm afraid you don't take this quite seriously enough. I think you perhaps don't quite realize—don't quite realize—" He took a deep quick breath and turned, as if helplessly, at a loss for words, to the others. But Mother and Father were both silent—no help was forthcoming.

"You must surely know, be aware, that you have not been quite yourself, of late? Don't you know that? . . ."

It was amusing to watch the doctor's renewed attempt at a smile, a queer disorganized look, as of confidential embarrassment.

"I feel all right, sir," he said, and again gave the little laugh.

"And we're trying to help you." The doctor's tone sharpened.

"Yes, sir, I know. But why? I'm all right. I'm just *thinking*, that's all."

His mother made a quick movement forward, resting a hand on the back of the doctor's chair.

"Thinking?" she said. "But my dear, about what?"

This was a direct challenge—and would have to be directly met. But before he met it, he looked again into the corner by the door, as if for reassurance. He smiled again at what he saw, at what he heard. The little spiral was still there, still softly whirling, like the ghost of a white kitten chasing the ghost of a white tail, and making as it did so the faintest of whispers. It was all right! If only he could remain firm, everything was going to be all right.

"Oh, about anything, about nothing—*you* know the way you do!"

"You mean—daydreaming?"

"Oh, no—thinking!"

"But thinking about *what?*"

"Anything."

He laughed a third time—but this time, happening to glance upward toward his mother's face, he was appalled at the effect his laughter seemed to have upon her. Her mouth had opened in an expression of horror.... This was too bad! Unfortunate! He had known it would cause pain, of course—but he hadn't expected it to be quite so bad as this. Perhaps—perhaps if he just gave them a tiny gleaming hint—?

"About the snow," he said.

"What on earth?" This was his father's voice. The brown slippers came a step nearer on the hearth-rug.

"But my dear, what do you mean?" This was his mother's voice.

The doctor merely stared.

"Just *snow*, that's all. I like to think about it."

"Tell us about it, my boy."

"But that's all it is. There's nothing to tell. *You* know what snow is?"

This he said almost angrily, for he felt that they were trying to corner him. He turned sideways so as no longer to face the doctor, and the better to see the inch of blackness between the window-sill and the lowered curtain—the cold inch of beckoning and delicious night. At once he felt better, more assured.

"Mother—can I go to bed, now, please? I've got a headache."

"But I thought you said—"

"It's just come. It's all these questions—! Can I, mother?"

"You can go as soon as the doctor has finished."

"Don't you think this thing ought to be gone into thoroughly, and *now?*" This was Father's voice. The brown slippers again came a step nearer, the voice was the well-known "punishment" voice, resonant and cruel.

"Oh, what's the use, Norman—"

Quite suddenly, everyone was silent. And without precisely facing them, nevertheless he was aware that all three of them were watching him with an extraordinary intensity—staring hard at him—as if he had done something monstrous, or was himself some kind of monster. He could hear the soft irregular flutter of the flames; the cluck-click-cluck-click of the clock; far and faint, two sudden spurts of laughter from the kitchen, as quickly cut off as begun; a murmur of water in the pipes; and then, the silence seemed to deepen, to spread out, to become world-long and world-wide, to become timeless and shapeless, and to center inevitably and rightly, with a slow and sleepy but enormous concentration of all power, on the beginning of a new sound. What this new sound was going to be, he knew perfectly well. It might begin with a hiss, but it would end with a roar—there was no time to lose—he must escape. It mustn't happen here—

Without another word, he turned and ran up the stairs.

IV

Not a moment too soon. The darkness was coming in long white waves. A prolonged sibilance filled the night—a great seamless seethe of wild influence went abruptly across it—a cold low humming shook the windows. He shut the door and flung off his clothes in the dark. The bare black floor was like a little raft tossed in waves of snow, almost overwhelmed, washed under whitely, up again, smothered in curled billows of feather. The snow was laughing; it spoke from all sides at once; it pressed closer to him as he ran and jumped exulting into his bed.

"Listen to us!" it said. "Listen! We have come to tell you the story we told you about. You remember? Lie down. Shut your eyes, now—you will no longer see much—in this white darkness who could see, or want to see? We will take the place of everything. . . . Listen—"

A beautiful varying dance of snow began at the front of the room, came forward and then retreated, flattened out toward the floor, then rose fountain-like to the ceiling, swayed, recruited itself from a new stream of flakes which poured laughing in through the humming window, advanced again, lifted long white arms. It said peace, it said remoteness, it said cold—it said—

But then a gash of horrible light fell brutally across the room from the opening door—the snow drew back hissing—something alien had come into the room—something hostile. This thing rushed at him, clutched at him, shook him—and he was not merely horrified, he was filled with such a loathing as he had never known. What was this? this cruel disturbance? this act of anger and hate? It was as if he had to reach up a hand toward another world for any understanding of it—an effort of which he was only barely capable. But of that other world he still remembered just enough to know the exorcising words. They tore themselves from his other life suddenly—

"Mother! Mother! Go away! I hate you!"

And with that effort, everything was solved, everything became all right: the seamless hiss advanced once more, the long white wavering lines rose and fell like enormous whispering sea-waves, the whisper becoming louder, the laughter more numerous.

"Listen!" it said. "We'll tell you the last, the most beautiful and secret story—shut your eyes—it is a very small story—a story that gets smaller and smaller—it comes inward instead of opening like a flower—it is a flower becoming a seed—a little cold seed—do you hear? we are leaning closer to you—"

The hiss was now becoming a roar—the whole world was a vast moving screen of snow—but even now it said peace, it said remoteness, it said cold, it said sleep.

[1932]

For Thought

"Silent Snow, Secret Snow" describes a boy's descent into mental illness. While Paul appears intelligent and aware of the external world, he chooses to withdraw from the reality that is complex and threatening to him. In two contrasting settings (the external world that includes Paul's home and his school, and the interior world of Paul's mind, which is filled with a dream of snow), the story explores ideas about thought, and about the human experience of dream and reality.

For Discussion

1. How is the postman significant in Paul's withdrawal from reality?
2. How are the class's studies of geography related symbolically to Paul's deepening mental illness? What parts do Deirdre and Miss Buell play in this process?
3. The author chose to relate the story from Paul's point of view. How and why is this the most effective method of telling the story?

4. What human characteristics does the snow take on in Paul's mind? What other characteristics does it take on?
5. Why are Paul's parents and the family doctor incapable of understanding Paul's difficulties and dealing with them?
6. What are the themes of each of the story's four parts? How do the four parts reflect distinct stages in the development of Paul's illness?

Sherwood Anderson
The Egg

My father was, I am sure, intended by nature to be a cheerful, kindly man. Until he was thirty-four years old he worked as a farmhand for a man named Thomas Butterworth whose place lay near the town of Bidwell, Ohio. He had then a horse of his own, and on Saturday evenings drove into town to spend a few hours in social intercourse with other farmhands. In town he drank several glasses of beer and stood about in Ben Head's saloon—crowded on Saturday evenings with visiting farmhands. Songs were sung and glasses thumped on the bar. At ten o'clock father drove home along a lonely country road, made his horse comfortable for the night, and himself went to bed, quite happy in his position in life. He had at that time no notion of trying to rise in the world.

It was in the spring of his thirty-fifth year that father married my mother, then a country schoolteacher, and in the following spring I came wriggling and crying into the world. Something happened to the two people. They became ambitious. The American passion for getting up in the world took possession of them.

It may have been that mother was responsible. Being a schoolteacher she had no doubt read books and magazines. She had, I presume, read of how Garfield, Lincoln, and other Americans rose from poverty to fame and greatness, and as I lay beside her—in the days of her lying-in—she may have dreamed that I would some day rule men and cities. At any rate she induced father to give up his place as a farmhand, sell his horse, and embark on an independent enterprise of his own. She was a tall silent woman with a long nose and troubled gray eyes. For herself she wanted nothing. For father and myself she was incurably ambitious.

The first venture into which the two people went turned out badly. They rented ten acres of poor stony land on Grigg's Road, eight miles from Bidwell, and launched into chicken-raising. I grew into boyhood on the place and got my first impression of life there. From the beginning they were impressions of disaster, and if, in my turn, I am a gloomy man inclined to see the darker side of life, I attribute it to the fact that what should have been for me the happy joyous days of childhood were spent on a chicken farm.

One unversed in such matters can have no notion of the many and tragic things that can happen to a chicken. It is born out of an egg, lives for a few weeks as a tiny fluffy thing such as you will see pictured on Easter cards, then becomes hideously naked, eats quantities of corn and meal bought by the sweat of your father's brow, gets diseases called pip, cholera, and other names, stands looking with stupid eyes at the sun, becomes sick and dies. A few hens and now and then a rooster, intended to serve God's mysterious ends, struggle through to maturity. The hens lay eggs out of which come other chickens and the dreadful cycle is thus made complete. It is all unbelievably complex. Most philosophers must have been raised on chicken farms. One hopes for so much from a chicken and is so dreadfully disillusioned. Small chickens just setting out on the journey of life, look so bright and alert and they are in fact so dreadfully stupid. They are so much like people they mix one up in one's judgments of life. If disease does not kill them, they wait until your expectations are thoroughly aroused and then walk under the wheels of a wagon—to go squashed and dead back to their maker. Vermin infest their youth, and fortunes must be spent for curative powders. In later life I have seen how a literature has been built up on the subject of fortunes to be made out of the raising of chickens. It is intended to be read by the gods who have just eaten of the tree of the knowledge of good and evil. It is a hopeful literature and declares that much may be done by simple ambitious people who own a few hens. Do not be led astray by it. It was not written for you. Go hunt for gold on the frozen hills of Alaska, put your faith in the honesty of a politician, believe if you will that the world is daily growing better and that good will triumph over evil, but do not read and believe the literature that is written concerning the hen. It was not written for you.

I, however, digress. My tale does not primarily concern itself with the hens. If correctly told it will center on the egg. For ten years my father and mother struggled to make our chicken farm pay and then they gave up that struggle and began another. They moved into the town of Bidwell, Ohio, and embarked in the restaurant business. After ten years of worry with incubators that did not hatch, and with tiny—and in their own way lovely—balls of fluff that passed on into seminaked pullethood and from that into dead henhood, we threw all aside and, packing our belongings on a wagon, drove down Grigg's Road toward Bidwell, a tiny caravan of hope looking for a new place from which to start on our upward journey through life.

We must have been a sad-looking lot, not, I fancy, unlike refugees fleeing from a battlefield. Mother and I walked in the road. The wagon that contained our goods had been borrowed for the day from Mr. Albert Griggs, a neighbor. Out of its sides stuck the legs of cheap chairs, and at the back of the pile of beds, tables, and boxes filled with kitchen utensils was a crate of live chickens, and on top of that the baby carriage in which I had been wheeled about in my infancy. Why we stuck to the baby carriage I don't know. It was unlikely other children would be born and the wheels were broken. People who have few possessions cling tightly to those they have. That is one of the facts that make life so discouraging.

Father rode on top of the wagon. He was then a bald-headed man of forty-five, a little fat, and from long association with mother and the chickens he had become habitually silent and discouraged. All during our ten years on the chicken farm he had worked as a laborer on neighboring farms and most of the money he had earned had been spent for remedies to cure chicken diseases, on Wilmer's White Wonder Cholera Cure or Professor Bidlow's Egg Producer or some other preparations that mother found advertised in the poultry papers. There were two little patches of hair on father's head just above his ear. I remember that as a child I used to sit looking at him when he had gone to sleep in a chair before the stove on Sunday afternoons in the winter. I had at that time already begun to read books and have notions of my own, and the bald path that led over the top of his head was, I fancied, something like a broad road, such a road as Caesar might have made on which to lead his legions out of Rome and into the wonders of an unknown world. The tufts of hair that grew above father's ears were, I thought, like forests. I fell into a half-sleeping, half-waking state and dreamed I was a tiny thing going along the road into a far beautiful place where there were no chicken farms and where life was a happy eggless affair.

One might write a book concerning our flight from the chicken farm into town. Mother and I walked the entire eight miles—she to be sure that nothing fell from the wagon and I to see the wonders of the world. On the seat of the wagon beside father was his greatest treasure. I will tell you of that.

On a chicken farm, where hundreds and even thousands of chickens come out of eggs, surprising things sometimes happen. Grotesques are born out of eggs as out of people. The accident does not often occur—perhaps once in a thousand births. A chicken is, you see, born that has four legs, two pairs of wings, two heads, or what not. The things do not live. They go quickly back to the hand of their maker that has for a moment trembled. The fact that the poor little things could not live was one of the tragedies of life to father. He had some sort of notion that if he could but bring into henhood or roosterhood a five-legged hen or a two-headed rooster his fortune would be made. He dreamed of taking the wonder about the county fairs and of growing rich by exhibiting it to other farmhands.

At any rate, he saved all the little monstrous things that had been born on our chicken farm. They were preserved in alcohol and put each in its own glass bottle. These he had carefully put into a box, and on our journey into town it was carried on the wagon seat beside him. He drove the horses with one hand and with the other clung to the box. When we got to our destination, the box was taken down at once and the bottles removed. All during our days as keepers of a restaurant in the town of Bidwell, Ohio, the grotesques in their little glass bottles sat on a shelf back of the counter. Mother sometimes protested, but father was a rock on the subject of his treasure. The grotesques were, he declared, valuable. People, he said, liked to look at strange and wonderful things.

Did I say that we embarked in the restaurant business in the town of Bidwell, Ohio? I exaggerated a little. The town itself lay at the foot of a low hill and on the shore of a small river. The railroad did not run through the town and the station was a mile away to the north at a place called Pickleville. There had been a cider mill and pickle factory at the station, but before the time of our coming they had both gone out of business. In the morning and in the evening buses came down to the station along a road called Turner's Pike from the hotel on the main street of Bidwell. Our going to the out-of-the-way place to embark in the restaurant business was mother's idea. She talked of it for a year and then one day went off and rented an empty store building opposite the railroad station. It was her idea that the restaurant would be profitable. Traveling men, she said, would be always waiting around to take trains out of town and town people would come to the station to await incoming trains. They would come to the restaurant to buy pieces of pie and drink coffee. Now that I am older I know that she had another motive in going. She was ambitious for me. She wanted me to rise in the world, to get into a town school and become a man of the towns.

At Pickleville father and mother worked hard, as they always had done. At first there was the necessity of putting our place into shape to be a restaurant. That took a month. Father built a shelf on which he put tins of vegetables. He painted a sign on which he put his name in large red letters. Below his name was the sharp command—"EAT HERE"—that was so seldom obeyed. A showcase was bought and filled with cigars and tobacco. Mother scrubbed the floor and the walls of the room. I went to school in the town and was glad to be away from the farm, from the presence of the discouraged, sad-looking chickens. Still I was not very joyous. In the evening I walked home from school along Turner's Pike and remembered the children I had seen playing in the town schoolyard. A troop of little girls had gone hopping about and singing. I tried that. Down along the frozen road I went hopping solemnly on one leg. "Hippity Hop to the Barber Shop," I sang shrilly. Then I stopped and looked doubtfully about. I was afraid of being seen in my gay mood. It must have seemed to me that I was doing a thing that should not be done by one who, like myself, had been raised on a chicken farm where death was a daily visitor.

Mother decided that our restaurant should remain open at night. At ten in the evening a passenger train went north past our door followed by a local freight. The freight crew had switching to do in Pickleville, and when the work was done they came to our restaurant for hot coffee and food. Sometimes one of them ordered a fried egg. In the morning at four they returned north-bound and again visited us. A little trade began to grow up. Mother slept at night and during the day tended the restaurant and fed our boarders while father slept. He slept in the same bed mother had occupied during the night and I went off to the town of Bidwell and to school. During the long nights, while mother and I slept, father cooked meats that were to go into sandwiches for the lunch baskets of our boarders. Then an idea in regard to getting up in the world came into his head. The American spirit took hold of him. He also became ambitious.

In the long nights when there was little to do, father had time to think. That was his undoing. He decided that he had in the past been an unsuccessful man because he had not been cheerful enough and that in the future he would adopt a cheerful outlook on life. In the early morning he came upstairs and got into bed with mother. She woke and the two talked. From my bed in the corner I listened.

It was father's idea that both he and mother should try to entertain the people who came to eat at our restaurant. I cannot now remember his words but he gave the impression of one about to become in some obscure way a kind of public entertainer. When people, particularly young people from the town of Bidwell, came into our place, as on very rare occasions they did, bright entertaining conversation was to be made. From father's words I gathered that something of the jolly innkeeper effect was to be sought. Mother must have been doubtful from the first, but she said nothing discouraging. It was father's notion that a passion for the company of himself and mother would spring up in the breasts of the younger people of the town of Bidwell. In the evening bright happy groups would come singing down Turner's Pike. They would troop shouting with joy and laughter into our place. There would be song and festivity. I do not mean to give the impression that father spoke so elaborately of the matter. He was, as I have said, an uncommunicative man. "They want some place to go. I tell you they want some place to go," he said over and over. That was as far as he got. My own imagination has filled in the blanks.

For two or three weeks this notion of father's invaded our house. We did not talk much, but in our daily lives tried earnestly to make smiles take the place of glum looks. Mother smiled at the boarders and I, catching the infection, smiled at our cat. Father became a little feverish in his anxiety to please. There was, no doubt, lurking somewhere in him, a touch of the spirit of the showman. He did not waste much of his ammunition on the railroad men he served at night, but seemed to be waiting for a young man or woman from Bidwell to come in to show what he could do. On the counter in the restaurant there was a wire basket kept always filled with eggs, and it must have been before his eyes when the idea of being entertaining was born in his brain. There was something pre-natal about the way eggs kept themselves connected with the development of his idea. At any rate, an egg ruined his new impulse in life. Late one night I was awakened by a roar of anger coming from father's throat. Both mother and I sat upright in our beds. With trembling hands she lighted a lamp that stood on a table by her head. Downstairs the front door of our restaurant went shut with a bang and in a few minutes father tramped up the stairs. He held an egg in his hand and his hand trembled as though he were having a chill. There was a half-insane light in his eyes. As he stood glaring at us I was sure he intended throwing the egg at either mother or me. Then he laid it gently on the table beside the lamp and dropped on his knees beside mother's bed. He began to cry like a boy, and I, carried away by his grief, cried with him. The two of us filled the little upstairs room with our wailing voices. It is ridiculous, but of the picture we made I can remember only the fact that mother's hand continually stroked the bald path that ran across the top of his head. I have forgotten what mother said to him and how she induced him to tell her of what had happened downstairs. His explanation also has gone out of my mind. I remember only my own grief and fright and the shiny path over father's head glowing in the lamplight as he knelt by the bed.

As to what happened downstairs. For some unexplainable reason I know the story as well as though I had been a witness to my father's discomfiture. One in time gets to know many unexplainable things. On that evening young Joe Kane, son of a merchant of Bidwell, came to Pickleville to meet his father, who was expected on the ten-o-clock evening train from the South. The train was three hours late and Joe came into our place to loaf about and to wait for its arrival. The local freight train came in and the freight crew were fed. Joe was left alone in the restaurant with father.

From the moment he came into our place the Bidwell young man must have been puzzled by my father's actions. It was his notion that father was angry at him for hanging around. He noticed that the restaurant-keeper was apparently disturbed by his presence and he thought of going out. However, it began to rain and he did not fancy the long walk to town and back. He bought a five-cent cigar and ordered a cup of coffee. He had a newspaper in his pocket and took it out and began to read. "I'm waiting for the evening train. It's late," he said apologetically.

For a long time father, whom Joe Kane had never seen before, remained silently gazing at his visitor. He was no doubt suffering from an attack of stage fright. As so often happens in life he had thought so much and so often of the situation that now confronted him that he was somewhat nervous in its presence.

For one thing, he did not know what to do with his hands. He thrust one of them nervously over the counter and shook hands with Joe Kane. "How-de-do," he said. Joe Kane put his newspaper down and stared at him. Father's eyes lighted on the basket of eggs that sat on the counter and he began to talk. "Well," he began hesitatingly, "well, you have heard of Christopher Columbus, eh?" He seemed to be angry. "That Christopher Columbus was a cheat," he declared emphatically. "He talked of making an egg stand on its end. He talked, he did, and then he went and broke the end of the egg."

My father seemed to his visitor to be beside himself at the duplicity of Christopher Columbus. He muttered and swore. He declared it was wrong to teach children that Christopher Columbus was a great man when, after all, he cheated at the critical moment. He had declared he would make an egg stand on end and then, when his bluff had been called, he had done a trick. Still grumbling at Columbus, father took an egg from the basket on the counter and began to walk up and down. He rolled the egg between the palms of his hands. He smiled genially. He began to mumble words regarding the effect to be produced on an egg by the electricity that comes out of the human body. He declared that, without breaking its shell and by virtue of rolling it back and forth in his hands, he could stand the egg on its end. He explained that the warmth of his hands and the gentle rolling movement he gave the egg created a new center of gravity, and Joe Kane was mildly interested. "I have handled thousands of eggs," father said. "No one knows more about eggs than I do."

He stood the egg on the counter and it fell on its side. He tried the trick again and again, each time rolling the egg between the palms of his hands and saying the words regarding the wonders of electricity and the laws of gravity. When after a half-hour's effort he did succeed in making the egg stand for a moment, he looked up to find that his visitor was no longer watching. By the time he had succeeded in calling Joe Kane's attention to the success of his effort, the egg had rolled over and lay on its side.

Afire with the showman's passion and at the same time a good deal disconcerted by the failure of his first effort, father now took the bottles containing the poultry monstrosities down from their place on the shelf and began to show them to his visitor. "How would you like to have seven legs and two heads like this fellow?" he asked, exhibiting the most remarkable of his treasures. A cheerful smile played over his face. He reached over the counter and tried to slap Joe Kane on the shoulder as he had seen men do in Ben Head's saloon when he was a young farmhand and drove to town on Saturday evenings. His visitor was made a little ill by the sight of the body of the terribly deformed bird floating in the alcohol in the bottle and got up to go. Coming from behind the counter, father took hold of the young man's arm and led him back to his seat. He grew a little angry and for a moment had to turn his face away and force himself to smile. Then he put the bottles back on the shelf. In an outburst of generosity he fairly compelled Joe Kane to have a fresh cup of coffee and another cigar at his expense. Then he took a pan and filling it with vinegar, taken from a jug that sat beneath the counter, he declared himself about to do a new trick. "I will heat this egg in this pan of vinegar," he said. "Then I will put it through the neck of a bottle without breaking the shell. When the egg is inside the bottle it will resume its normal shape and the shell will become hard again. Then I will give the bottle with the egg in it to you. You can take it about with you wherever you go. People will want to know how you got the egg in the bottle. Don't tell them. Keep them guessing. That is the way to have fun with this trick."

Father grinned and winked at his visitor. Joe Kane decided that the man who confronted him was mildly insane but harmless. He drank the cup of coffee that had been given him and began to read his paper again. When the egg had been heated in vinegar, father carried it on a spoon to the counter and going into a back room got an empty bottle. He was angry because his visitor did not watch him as he began to do his trick, but neverthless went cheerfully to work. For a long time he struggled, trying to get the egg to go through the neck of the bottle. He put the pan of vinegar back on the stove, intending to reheat the egg, then picked it up and burned his fingers. After a second bath in the hot vinegar, the shell of the egg had been softened a little, but not enough for his purpose. He worked and worked and a spirit of desperate determination took possession of him. When he thought that at last the trick was about to be consummated, the delayed train came in at the station and Joe Kane started to go nonchalantly out at the door. Father made a last desperate effort to conquer the egg and make it do the thing that would establish his reputation as one who knew how to entertain guests who came into his restaurant. He worried the egg. He attempted to be somewhat rough with it. He swore and the sweat stood out on his forehead. The egg broke under his hand. When the contents spurted over his clothes, Joe Kane, who had stopped at the door, turned and laughed.

A roar of anger rose from my father's throat. He danced and shouted a string of inarticulate words. Grabbing another egg from the basket on the counter, he threw it, just missing the head of the young man as he dodged through the door and escaped.

Father came upstairs to mother and me with an egg in his hand. I do not know what he intended to do. I imagine he had some idea of destroying it, of destroying all eggs, and that he intended to let mother and me see him begin. When, however, he got into the presence of mother, something happened to him. He laid the egg gently on the table and dropped on his knees by the bed as I have already explained. He later decided to close the restaurant for the night and to come upstairs and get into bed. When he did so, he blew out the light and after much muttered conversation both he and mother went to sleep. I suppose I went to sleep also, but my sleep was troubled. I awoke at dawn and for a long time looked at the egg that lay on the table. I wondered why eggs had to be and why from the egg came the hen who again laid the egg. The question got into my blood. It has stayed there, I imagine, because I am the son of my father. At any rate, the problem remains unsolved in my mind. And that, I conclude, is but another evidence of the complete and final triumph of the egg—at least as far as my family is concerned.

[1920]

For Thought

Anderson has written what appears to be a biographical story. Although the author, like the narrator, was born and raised in Ohio, the story is not a factual one. However, Anderson is known for his gloomy outlook. And it is gloom that permeates the story. The narrator relates a tale of financial failure and frustration brought on by ambition and ineptitude as well as by fate, in the form of an egg. Throughout this tale, the narrator's attitude is one of humor and sympathy for the father; however, it is Anderson's pessimistic tone that pervades and affects the atmosphere of the story.

For Discussion

1. What point of view does the author use? If Anderson had used the father as narrator or had chosen an omniscient point of view, allowing the reader to see into the minds of all the characters, how would the story have been different?
2. Although, basically, "The Egg" is about the serious subject of a man's failure in business, there are some humorous elements in the story. How many of the humorous incidents are ironic? Why does Anderson use humorous elements in the story?
3. What is the narrator's character like? Does he resemble either parent in any way? Does the influence of his parents have an impact on his outlook on life? If so, how?

4. What does the narrator mean by his comment, "Most philosophers must have been raised on chicken farms"?
5. The narrator compares his family's caravan to Bidwell to that of the refugees fleeing from a battlefield. How is this comparison symbolic?
6. How does the action in the first part of the story prepare the reader for what happens in the second part as well as for the conclusion of the story?
7. In what way is the egg an ironic symbol? How does it sum up the theme of the story?
8. In what ways is the mother's ambition the motivating force behind all the action in the story? Why is the father's ambitious plan unsuccessful?
9. Why does the father break the egg at the end of the story?
10. Except for the name of the man the father worked for as a farmhand, why is Joe Kane the only character named in the story?

Sherwood Anderson
Death in the Woods

I

She was an old woman and lived on a farm near the town in which I lived. All country and small-town people have seen such old women, but no one knows much about them. Such an old woman comes into town driving an old worn-out horse or she comes afoot carrying a basket. She may own a few hens and have eggs to sell. She brings them in a basket and takes them to a grocer. There she trades them in. She gets some salt pork and some beans. Then she gets a pound or two of sugar and some flour.

Afterwards she goes to the butcher's and asks for some dog-meat. She may spend ten or fifteen cents, but when she does she asks for something. Formerly the butchers gave liver to anyone who wanted to carry it away. In our family we were always having it. Once one of my brothers got a whole cow's liver at the slaughterhouse near the fair grounds in our town. We had it until we were sick of it. It never cost a cent. I have hated the thought of it ever since.

The old farm woman got some liver and a soup-bone. She never visited with anyone, and as soon as she got what she wanted she lit out for home. It made quite a load for such an old body. No one gave her a lift. People drive right down a road and never notice an old woman like that.

There was such an old woman who used to come into town past our house one summer and fall when I was a young boy and was sick with what was called inflammatory rheumatism. She went home later carrying a heavy pack on her back. Two or three large gaunt-looking dogs followed at her heels.

The old woman was nothing special. She was one of the nameless ones that hardly anyone knows, but she got into my thoughts. I have just suddenly now, after all these years, remembered her and what happened. It is a story. Her name was Grimes, and she lived with her husband and son in a small unpainted house on the bank of a small creek four miles from town.

The husband and son were a tough lot. Although the son was but twenty-one, he had already served a term in jail. It was whispered about that the woman's husband stole horses and ran them off to some other county. Now and then, when a horse turned up missing, the man had also disappeared. No one ever caught him. Once, when I was loafing at Tom Whitehead's livery-barn, the man came there and sat on the bench in front. Two or three other men were there, but no one spoke to him. He sat for a few minutes and then got up and went away. When he was leaving he turned around and stared at the men. There was a look of defiance in his eyes. "Well, I have tried to be friendly. You don't want to talk to me. It has been so wherever I have gone in this town. If, some day, one of your fine horses turns up missing, well, then what?" He did not say anything actually. "I'd like to bust one of you on the jaw," was about what his eyes said. I remember how the look in his eyes made me shiver.

The old man belonged to a family that had had money once. His name was Jake Grimes. It all comes back clearly now. His father, John Grimes, had owned a sawmill when the country was new, and had made money. Then he got to drinking and running after women. When he died there wasn't much left.

Jake blew in the rest. Pretty soon there wasn't any more lumber to cut and his land was nearly all gone.

He got his wife off a German farmer, for whom he went to work one June day in the wheat harvest. She was a young thing then and scared to death. You see, the farmer was up to something with the girl—she was, I think, a bound girl and his wife had her suspicions. She took it out on the girl when the man wasn't around. Then, when the wife had to go off to town for supplies, the farmer got after her. She told young Jake that nothing really ever happened, but he didn't know whether to believe it or not.

He got her pretty easy himself, the first time he was out with her. He wouldn't have married her if the German farmer hadn't tried to tell him where to get off. He got her to go riding with him in his buggy one night when he was threshing on the place, and then he came for her the next Sunday night.

She managed to get out of the house without her employer's seeing, but when she was getting into the buggy he showed up. It was almost dark, and he just popped up suddenly at the horse's head. He grabbed the horse by the bridle and Jake got out his buggy-whip.

They had it out all right! The German was a tough one. Maybe he didn't care whether his wife knew or not. Jake hit him over the face and shoulders with the buggy-whip, but the horse got to acting up and he had to get out.

Then the two men went for it. The girl didn't see it. The horse started to run away and went nearly a mile down the road before the girl got him stopped. Then she managed to tie him to a tree beside the road. (I wonder how I know all this. It must have stuck in my mind from small-town tales when I was a boy.) Jake found her there after he got through with the German. She was huddled up in the buggy seat, crying, scared to death. She told Jake a lot of stuff, how the German had tried to get her, how he chased her once into the barn, how another time, when they happened to be alone in the house together, he tore her dress open clear down the front. The German, she said, might have got her that time if he hadn't heard his old woman drive in at the gate. She had been off to town for supplies. Well, she would be putting the horse in the barn. The German managed to sneak off to the fields without his wife seeing. He told the girl he would kill her if she told. What could she do? She told a lie about ripping her dress in the barn when she was feeding the stock. I remember now that she was a bound girl and did not know where her father and mother were. Maybe she did not have any father. You know what I mean.

Such bound children were often enough

cruelly treated. They were children who had no parents, slaves really. There were very few orphan homes then. They were legally bound into some home. It was a matter of pure luck how it came out.

II

She married Jake and had a son and daughter, but the daughter died.

Then she settled down to feed stock. That was her job. At the German's place she had cooked the food for the German and his wife. The wife was a strong woman with big hips and worked most of the time in the fields with her husband. She fed them and fed the cows in the barn, fed the pigs, the horses and the chickens. Every moment of every day, as a young girl, was spent feeding something.

Then she married Jake Grimes and he had to be fed. She was a slight thing, and when she had been married for three or four years, and after the two children were born, her slender shoulders became stooped.

Jake always had a lot of big dogs around the house, that stood near the unused sawmill near the creek. He was always trading horses when he wasn't stealing something and had a lot of poor bony ones about. Also he kept three or four pigs and a cow. They were all pastured in the few acres left of the Grimes place and Jake did little enough work.

He went into debt for a threshing outfit and ran it for several years, but it did not pay. People did not trust him. They were afraid he would steal the grain at night. He had to go a long way off to get work and it cost too much to get there. In the winter he hunted and cut a little firewood, to be sold in some nearby town. When the son grew up he was just like the father. They got drunk together. If there wasn't anything to eat in the house when they came home the old man gave his old woman a cut over the head. She had a few chickens of her own and had to kill one of them in a hurry. When they were all killed she wouldn't have any eggs to sell when she went to town, and then what would she do?

She had to scheme all her life about getting things fed, getting the pigs fed so they would grow fat and could be butchered in the fall. When they were butchered her husband took most of the meat off to town and sold it. If he did not do it first the boy did. They fought sometimes and when they fought the old woman stood aside trembling.

She had got the habit of silence anyway—that was fixed. Sometimes, when she began to look old—she wasn't forty yet—and when the husband and son were both off, trading horses or drinking or hunting or stealing, she went around the house and the barnyard muttering to herself.

How was she going to get everything fed?—that was her problem. The dogs had to be fed. There wasn't enough hay in the barn for the horses and the cow. If she didn't feed the chickens how could they lay eggs? Without eggs to sell how could she get things in town, things she had to have to keep the life of the farm going? Thank heaven, she did not have to feed her husband—in a certain way. That hadn't lasted long after their marriage and after the babies came. Where he went on his long trips she did not know. Sometimes he was gone from home for weeks, and after the boy grew up they went off together.

They left everything at home for her to manage and she had no money. She knew no one. No one ever talked to her in town. When it was winter she had to gather sticks of wood for her fire, had to try to keep the stock fed with very little grain.

The stock in the barn cried to her hungrily, the dogs followed her about. In the winter the hens laid few enough eggs. They huddled in the corners of the barn and she kept watching them. If a hen lays an egg in the barn in the winter and you do not find it, it freezes and breaks.

One day in winter the old woman went off to town with a few eggs and the dogs followed her. She did not get started until nearly three o'clock and the snow was heavy. She hadn't been feeling very well for several days and so she went muttering along, scantily clad, her shoulders stooped. She had an old grain bag in which she carried her eggs, tucked away down in the bottom. There weren't many of them, but in winter the price of eggs is up. She would get a little meat in exchange for the eggs, some salt pork, a little sugar, and some coffee perhaps. It might be the butcher would give her a piece of liver.

When she had got to town and was trading in her eggs the dogs lay by the door outside. She did pretty well, got the things she needed, more than she had hoped. Then she went to the butcher and he gave her some liver and some dog-meat.

It was the first time anyone had spoken to her in a friendly way for a long time. The butcher was alone in his shop when she came in and was annoyed by the thought of such a sick-looking old woman out on such a day. It was bitter cold and the snow, that had let up during the afternoon, was falling again. The butcher said something about her husband and her son, swore at them, and the old woman stared at him, a look of mild surprise in her eyes as he talked. He said that if either the husband or the son were going to get any of the liver or the heavy bones with scraps of meat hanging to them that he had put into the grain bag, he'd see him starve first.

Starve, eh? Well, things had to be fed. Men had to be fed, and the horses that weren't any good but maybe could be traded off, and the poor thin cow that hadn't given any milk for three months.

Horses, cows, pigs, dogs, men.

III

The old woman had to get back before darkness came if she could. The dogs followed at her heels, sniffing at the heavy grain bag she had fastened on her back. When she got to the edge of town she stopped by a fence and tied the bag on her back with a piece of rope she had carried in her dress-pocket for just that purpose. That was an easier way to carry it. Her arms ached. It was hard when she had to crawl over fences and once she fell over and landed in the snow. The dogs went frisking about. She had to struggle to get to her feet again, but she made it. The point of climbing over the fences was that there was a short cut over a hill and through a woods. She might have gone around by the road, but it was a mile farther that way. She was afraid she couldn't make it. And then, besides, the stock had to be fed. There was a little hay left and a little corn. Perhaps her husband and son would bring some home when they came. They had driven off in the only buggy the Grimes family had, a rickety thing, a rickety horse hitched to the buggy, two other rickety horses led by halters. They were going to trade horses, get a little money if they could. They might come home drunk. It would be well to have something in the house when they came back.

The son had an affair on with a woman at the county seat, fifteen miles away. She was a rough enough woman, a tough one. Once, in the summer, the son had brought her to the house. Both she and the son had been drinking. Jake Grimes was away and the son and his woman ordered the old woman about like a servant. She didn't mind much; she was used to it. Whatever happened she never said anything. That was her way of getting along. She had managed that way when she was a young girl at the German's and ever since she had married Jake. That time her son brought his woman to the house they stayed all night, sleeping together just as though they were married. It hadn't shocked the old woman, not much. She had got past being shocked early in life.

With the pack on her back she went painfully along across an open field, wading in the deep snow, and got into the woods.

There was a path, but it was hard to follow. Just beyond the top of the hill, where the woods was thickest, there was a small clearing. Had someone once thought of building a house there? The clearing was as large as a building lot in town, large enough for a house and a garden. The path ran along the side of the clearing, and when she got there the old woman sat down to rest at the foot of a tree.

It was a foolish thing to do. When she got herself placed, the pack against the tree's trunk, it was nice, but what about getting up again? She worried about that for a moment and then quietly closed her eyes.

She must have slept for a time. When you are about so cold you can't get any colder. The afternoon grew a little warmer and the snow came thicker than ever. Then after a time the weather cleared. The moon even came out.

There were four Grimes dogs that had followed Mrs. Grimes into town, all tall gaunt fellows. Such men as Jake Grimes and his son always keep just such dogs. They kick and abuse them, but they stay. The Grimes dogs, in order to keep from starving, had to do a lot of foraging for themselves, and they had been at it while the old woman slept with her back to the tree at the side of the clearing. They had been chasing rabbits in the woods and in adjoining fields and in their ranging had picked up three other farm dogs.

After a time all the dogs came back to the clearing. They were excited about something. Such nights, cold and clear and with a moon, do things to dogs. It may be that some old instinct, come down from the time when they were wolves and ranged the woods in packs on winter nights, comes back into them.

The dogs in the clearing, before the old woman, had caught two or three rabbits and their immediate hunger had been satisfied. They began to play, running in circles in the clearing. Round and round they ran, each dog's nose at the tail of the next dog. In the clearing, under the snow-laden trees and under the wintry moon they made a strange picture, running thus silently, in a circle their running had beaten in the soft snow. The dogs made no sound. They ran around and around in the circle.

It may have been that the old woman saw them doing that before she died. She may have awakened once or twice and looked at the strange sight with dim old eyes.

She wouldn't be very cold now, just drowsy. Life hangs on a long time. Perhaps the old woman was out of her head. She may have dreamed of her girlhood, at the German's, and before that, when she was a child and before her mother lit out and left her.

Her dreams couldn't have been very pleasant. Not many pleasant things had happened to her. Now and then one of the Grimes dogs left the running circle and came to stand before her. The dog thrust his face close to her face. His red tongue was hanging out.

The running of the dogs may have been a kind of death ceremony. It may have been that the primitive instinct of the wolf, having been aroused in the dogs by the night and the running, made them somehow afraid.

"Now we are no longer wolves. We are dogs, the servants of men. Keep alive, man! When man dies we become wolves again."

When one of the dogs came to where the old woman sat with her back against the tree and thrust his nose close to her face he seemed satisfied and went back to run with the pack. All the Grimes dogs did it at some time during the evening, before she died. I knew all about it afterward, when I grew to be a man, because once in a woods in Illinois, on another winter night, I saw a pack of dogs act just like that. The dogs were waiting for me to die as they had waited for the old woman that night when I was a child, but when it happened to me I was a young man and had no intention whatever of dying.

The old woman died softly and quietly. When she was dead and when one of the

Grimes dogs had come to her and had found her dead all the dogs stopped running.

They gathered about her.

Well, she was dead now. She had fed the Grimes dogs when she was alive, what about now?

There was the pack on her back, the grain bag containing the piece of salt pork, the liver the butcher had given her, the dog-meat, the soup bones. The butcher in town, having been suddenly overcome with a feeling of pity, had loaded her grain bag heavily. It had been a big haul for the old woman.

It was a big haul for the dogs now.

IV

One of the Grimes dogs sprang suddenly out from among the others and began worrying the pack on the old woman's back. Had the dogs really been wolves that one would have been the leader of the pack. What he did, all the others did.

All of them sank their teeth into the grain bag the old woman had fastened with ropes to her back.

They dragged the old woman's body out into the open clearing. The worn-out dress was quickly torn from her shoulders. When she was found, a day or two later, the dress had been torn from her body clear to the hips, but the dogs had not touched her body. They had got the meat out of the grain bag, that was all. Her body was frozen stiff when it was found, and the shoulders were so narrow and the body so slight that in death it looked like the body of some charming young girl.

Such things happened in towns of the Middle West, on farms near town, when I was a boy. A hunter out after rabbits found the old woman's body and did not touch it. Something, the beaten round path in the little snow-covered clearing, the silence of the place, the place where the dogs had worried the body trying to pull the grain bag away or tear it open—something startled the man and he hurried off to town.

I was in Main Street with one of my brothers who was town newsboy and who was taking the afternoon papers to the stores. It was almost night.

The hunter came into a grocery and told his story. Then he went to a hardware shop and into a drugstore. Men began to gather on the sidewalks. Then they started out along the road to the place in the woods.

My brother should have gone on about his business of distributing papers but he didn't. Everyone was going to the woods. The undertaker went and the town marshal. Several men got on a dray and rode out to where the path left the road and went into the woods, but the horses weren't very sharply shod and slid about on the slippery roads. They made no better time than those of us who walked.

The town marshal was a large man whose leg had been injured in the Civil War. He carried a heavy cane and limped rapidly along the road. My brother and I followed at his heels, and as we went other men and boys joined the crowd.

It had grown dark by the time we got to where the old woman had left the road but the moon had come out. The marshal was thinking there might have been a murder. He kept asking the hunter questions. The hunter went along with his gun across his shoulders, a dog following at his heels. It isn't often a rabbit hunter has a chance to be so conspicuous. He was taking full advantage of it, leading the procession with the town marshal. "I didn't see any wounds. She was a beautiful young girl. Her face was buried in the snow. No, I didn't know her." As a matter of fact, the hunter had not looked closely at the body. He had been frightened. She might have been murdered and someone might spring out from behind a tree and murder him. In a woods, in the late afternoon, when the trees are all bare and there is white snow on the ground, when all is silent, something creepy steals over the mind and body. If something strange or uncanny has happened in the neighborhood all you think about is getting away from there as fast as you can.

The crowd of men and boys had got to where the old woman had crossed the field and went, following the marshal and the hunter, up the slight incline and into the woods.

My brother and I were silent. He had his bundle of papers in a bag slung across his shoulder. When he got back to town he would have to go on distributing his papers before he went home to supper. If I went along, as he had no doubt already determined I should, we would both be late. Either mother or our older sister would have to warm our supper.

Well, we would have something to tell. A boy did not get such a chance very often. It was lucky we just happened to go into the grocery when the hunter came in. The hunter was a country fellow. Neither of us had ever seen him before.

Now the crowd of men and boys had got to the clearing. Darkness comes quickly on such winter nights, but the full moon made everything clear. My brother and I stood near the tree, beneath which the old woman had died.

She did not look old, lying there in that light, frozen and still. One of the men turned her over in the snow and I saw everything. My body trembled with some strange mystical feeling and so did my brother's. It might have been the cold.

Neither of us had ever seen a woman's body before. It may have been the snow, clinging to the frozen flesh, that made it look so white and lovely, so like marble. No woman had come with the party from town; but one of the men, he was the town blacksmith, took off his overcoat and spread it over her. Then he gathered her into his arms and started off to town, all the others following silently. At that time no one knew who she was.

V

I had seen everything, had seen the oval in the snow, like a miniature race track, where the dogs had run, had seen how the men were mystified, had seen the white bare young-looking shoulders, had heard the whispered comments of the men.

The men were simply mystified. They took the body to the undertaker's, and when the blacksmith, the hunter, the marshal and several others had got inside they closed the door. If father had been there perhaps he could have got in, but we boys couldn't.

I went with my brother to distribute the rest of his papers and when we got home it was my brother who told the story.

I kept silent and went to bed early. It may have been I was not satisfied with the way he told it.

Later, in the town, I must have heard other fragments of the old woman's story. She was recognized the next day and there was an investigation.

The husband and son were found somewhere and brought to town and there was an attempt to connect them with the woman's death, but it did not work. They had perfect enough alibis.

However, the town was against them. They had to get out. Where they went I never heard.

I remember only the picture there in the forest, the men standing about, the naked girlish-looking figure, face down in the snow, the tracks made by the running dogs and the clear cold winter sky above. White fragments of clouds were drifting across the sky. They went racing across the little open space among the trees.

The scene in the forest had become for me, without my knowing it, the foundation for the real story I am now trying to tell. The fragments, you see, had to be picked up slowly, long afterwards.

Things happened. When I was a young man I worked on the farm of a German. The hired-girl was afraid of her employer. The farmer's wife hated her.

I saw things at that place. Once later, I had a half-uncanny, mystical adventure with dogs in an Illinois forest on a clear, moonlit winter night. When I was a schoolboy, and on a summer day, I went with a boy friend out along a creek some miles from town and came to the house where the old woman had lived. No one had lived in the house since her death. The doors were broken from the hinges; the window lights were all broken. As the boy and I stood in the road outside, two dogs, just roving farm dogs no doubt, came running around the corner of the house. The dogs were tall, gaunt fellows and came down to the fence and glared through at us, standing in the road.

The whole thing, the story of the old woman's death, was to me as I grew older like music heard from far off. The notes had to be picked up slowly one at a time. Something had to be understood.

The woman who died was one destined to feed animal life. Anyway, that is all she ever did. She was feeding animal life before she was born, as a child, as a young woman working on the farm of the German, after she married, when she grew old and when she died. She fed animal life in cows, in chickens, in pigs, in horses, in dogs, in men. Her daughter had died in childhood and with her one son she had no articulate relations. On the night when she died she was hurrying homeward, bearing on her body food for animal life.

She died in the clearing in the woods and even after her death continued feeding animal life.

You see it is likely that, when my brother told the story, that night when we got home and my mother and sister sat listening, I did not think he got the point. He was too young and so was I. A thing so complete has its own beauty.

I shall not try to emphasize the point. I am only explaining why I was dissatisfied then and have been ever since. I speak of that only that you may understand why I have been impelled to try to tell the simple story over again.

[1922]

For Thought

"Death in the Woods" packs the history of a nameless old woman into a series of telling incidents. By adopting the point of view of an impressionable young boy, Anderson endows his narrative with suspense and innocence. The author employs the motif of the necessity to feed life to help create the characterization of the old woman. The death of the old woman becomes a symbol of both waste and mercy.

For Discussion

1. The author states, "All country and small-town people have seen such old women. . . ." By making this statement, the author has stereotyped the old woman's character. Is this an accurate description of the old woman? Explain.
2. How does the author establish the narrator's character and background?
3. The story is divided into five sections. What happens in each section? Why does Anderson choose this particular way of organizing his story?
4. What evidence is there that the old man was "a tough lot"?
5. How does the girl of the story manage physically and emotionally? How does she manage as an old woman?
6. What are the conflicts in the story and how are they resolved?
7. What did the old woman's body, which looked "lovely . . . like marble," symbolize?
8. What elements of the uncanny are there in the story?

9. Why was the narrator dissatisfied with his brother's story, so dissatisfied that he felt compelled to retell it?
10. From what point of view is the story written? How does the narrator know what happened in the woods?
11. The old woman's dress was ripped to the waist twice. Of what is this act symbolic? How does it reflect the theme of the story?

Sherwood Anderson
I'm a Fool

It was a hard jolt for me, one of the most bitterest I ever had to face. And it all came about through my own foolishness, too. Even yet sometimes, when I think of it I want to cry or swear or kick myself. Perhaps, even now, after all this time, there will be a kind of satisfaction in making myself look cheap by telling of it.

It began at three o'clock one October afternoon as I sat in the grandstand at the fall trotting and pacing meet at Sandusky, Ohio.

To tell the truth, I felt a little foolish that I should be sitting in the grandstand at all. During the summer before, I had left my home town with Harry Whitehead and, with a nigger named Burt, had taken a job as swipe with one of the two horses Harry was campaigning through the fall race meets that year. Mother cried and my sister Mildred, who wanted to get a job as a schoolteacher in our town that fall, stormed and scolded about the house all during the week before I left. They both thought it something disgraceful that one of our family should take a place as a swipe with race horses. I've an idea Mildred thought my taking the place would stand in the way of her getting the job she'd been working so long for.

But after all, I had to work, and there was no other work to be got. A big lumbering fellow of nineteen couldn't just hang around the house and I had got too big to mow people's lawns and sell newspapers. Little chaps who could get next to people's sympathies by their sizes were always getting jobs away from me. There was one fellow who kept saying to everyone who wanted a lawn mowed or a cistern cleaned that he was saving money to work his way through college, and I used to lay awake nights thinking up ways to injure him without being found out. I kept thinking of wagons running over him and bricks falling on his head as he walked along the street. But never mind him.

I got the place with Harry and I liked

Burt fine. We got along splendid together. He was a big nigger with a lazy sprawling body and soft, kind eyes, and when it came to a fight he could hit like Jack Johnson. He had Bucephalus, a big black pacing stallion that could do 2:09 or 2:10, if he had to, and I had a little gelding named Doctor Fritz that never lost a race all fall when Harry wanted him to win.

We set out from home late in July in a boxcar with the two horses and after that, until late November, we kept moving along to the race meets and the fairs. It was a peachy time for me, I'll say that. Sometimes now I think that boys who are raised regular in houses, and never have a fine nigger like Burt for best friend, and go to high schools and college, and never steal anything, or get drunk a little, or learn to swear from fellows who know how, or come walking up in front of a grandstand in their shirt sleeves and with dirty horsey pants on when the races are going on and the grandstand is full of people all dressed up—What's the use of talking about it? Such fellows don't know nothing at all. They've never had no opportunity.

But I did. Burt taught me how to rub down a horse and put the bandages on after a race and steam a horse out and a lot of valuable things for any man to know. He could wrap a bandage on a horse's leg so smooth that if it had been the same color you would think it was his skin, and I guess he'd have been a big driver, too, and got to the top like Murphy and Walter Cox and the others if he hadn't been black.

Gee whizz, it was fun. You got to a county seat town, maybe say on a Saturday or Sunday, and the fair began the next Tuesday and lasted until Friday afternoon. Doctor Fritz would be, say in the 2:25 trot on Tuesday afternoon and on Thursday afternoon Bucephalus would knock 'em cold in the "free-for-all" pace. It left you a lot of time to hang around and listen to horse talk, and see Burt knock some yap cold that got too gay, and you'd find out about horses and men and pick up a lot of stuff you could use all the rest of your life, if you had some sense and salted down what you heard and felt and saw.

And then at the end of the week when the race meet was over, and Harry had run home to tend up to his livery stable business, you and Burt hitched the two horses to carts and drove slow and steady across country, to the place for the next meeting, so as to not overheat the horses, etc., etc., you know.

Gee whizz, Gosh amighty, the nice hickory nut and beechnut and oaks and other kinds of trees along the roads, all brown and red, and the good smells, and Burt singing a song that was called "Deep River," and the country girls at the windows of houses and everything. You can stick your colleges up your nose for all me. I guess I know where I got my education.

Why, one of those little burgs of towns you come to on the way, say now on a Saturday afternoon, and Burt says, "Let's lay up here." And you did.

And you took the horses to a livery stable and fed them, and you got your good clothes out of a box and put them on.

And the town was full of farmers gaping, because they could see you were race horse people, and the kids maybe never see a nigger before and was afraid and run away when the two of us walked down their main street.

And that was before prohibition and all that foolishness, and so you went into a saloon, the two of you, and all the yaps come and stood around, and there was always someone pretended he was horsey and knew things and spoke up and began asking questions, and all you did was to lie and lie all you could about what horses you had, and I said I owned them, and then some fellow said "Will you have a drink of whisky?" and Burt knocked his eye out the way he could say, off-hand like, "Oh, well, all right, I'm agreeable to a little nip. I'll split a quart with you." Gee whizz.

But that isn't what I want to tell my story about. We got home late in November and I promised Mother I'd quit the race horses for good. There's a lot of things you've got to promise a mother because she don't know any better.

And so, there not being any work in our town any more than when I left there to go to the races, I went off to Sandusky and got a pretty good place taking care of horses for a man who owned a teaming and delivery and storage and coal and real estate business there. It was a pretty good place with good eats, and a day off each week, and sleeping on a cot in a big barn, and mostly just shoveling in hay and oats to a lot of big good-enough skates of horses, that couldn't have trotted a race with a toad. I wasn't dissatisfied and I could send money home.

And then, as I started to tell you, the fall races come to Sandusky and I got the day off and I went. I left the job at noon and had on my good clothes and my new brown derby hat I'd just bought the Saturday before, and a stand-up collar.

First of all I went downtown and walked about with the dudes. I've always thought to myself, "put up a good front" and so I did it. I had forty dollars in my pocket and so I went into the West House, a big hotel, and walked up to the cigar stand. "Give me three twenty-five-cent cigars," I said. There was a lot of horsemen and strangers and dressed-up people from other towns standing around in the lobby and in the bar, and I mingled amongst them. In the bar there was a fellow with a cane and a Windsor tie on, that it made me sick to look at him. I like a man to be a man and dress up, but not to go put on that kind of airs. So I pushed him aside, kind of rough, and had me a drink of whisky. And then he looked at me as though he thought maybe he'd get gay, but he changed his mind and didn't say anything. And then I had another drink of whisky, just to show him something, and went out and had a hack out to the races, all to myself, and when I got there I bought myself the best seat I could get up in the grandstand, but didn't go in for any of these boxes. That's putting on too many airs.

And so there I was, sitting up in the grandstand as gay as you please and looking down on the swipes coming out with their horses, and with their dirty horsey pants on and the horse blankets swung over their shoulders, same as I had been doing all the year before. I liked one thing about the same as the other, sitting up there and feeling grand and being down there and looking up at the yaps and feeling grander and more important, too. One thing's about as good as another, if you take it just right. I've often said that.

Well, right in front of me, in the grandstand that day, there was a fellow with a couple of girls and they was about my age. The young fellow was a nice guy all right. He was the kind maybe that goes to college and then comes to be a lawyer or maybe a newspaper editor or something like that, but he wasn't stuck on himself. There are some of that kind are all right and he was one of the ones.

He had his sister with him and another girl, and the sister looked around over his shoulder, accidental at first, not intending to start anything—she wasn't that kind—and her eyes and mine happened to meet.

You know how it is. Gee, she was a peach! She had on a soft dress, kind of a blue stuff and it looked carelessly made, but was well sewed and made and everything. I knew that much. I blushed when she looked right at me and so did she. She was the nicest girl I've ever seen in my life. She wasn't stuck on herself and she could talk proper grammar without being like a schoolteacher or something like that. What I mean is, she was O.K. I think maybe her father was well-to-do, but not rich to make her chesty because she was his daughter, as some are. Maybe he owned a drugstore or a drygoods store in their home town, or something like that. She never told me and I never asked.

My own people are all O.K. too, when

you come to that. My grandfather was Welsh and over in the old country, in Wales he was—But never mind that.

The first heat of the first race came off and the young fellow setting there with the two girls left them and went down to make a bet. I knew what he was up to, but he didn't talk big and noisy and let everyone around know he was a sport, as some do. He wasn't that kind. Well, he come back and I heard him tell the two girls what horse he'd bet on, and when the heat was trotted they all half got to their feet and acted in the excited, sweaty way people do when they've got money down on a race, and the horse they bet on is up there pretty close at the end, and they think maybe he'll come on with a rush, but he never does because he hasn't got the old juice in him, come right down to it.

And then, pretty soon, the horses came out for the 2:18 pace and there was a horse in it I knew. He was a horse Bob French had in his string but Bob didn't own him. He was a horse owned by a Mr. Mathers down at Marietta, Ohio.

This Mr. Mathers had a lot of money and owned some coal mines or something, and he had a swell place out in the country, and he was stuck on race horses, but was a Presbyterian or something, and I think more than likely his wife was one, too, maybe a stiffer one than himself. So he never raced his horses hisself, and the story round the Ohio race tracks was that when one of his horses got ready to go to the races he turned him over to Bob French and pretended to his wife he was sold.

So Bob had the horses and he did pretty much as he pleased, and you can't blame Bob, at least I never did. Sometimes he was out to win and sometimes he wasn't. I never cared much about that when I was swiping a horse. What I did want to know was that my horse had the speed and could go out in front, if you wanted him to.

And, as I'm telling you, there was Bob in this race with one of Mr. Mathers' horses, was named "About Ben Ahem" or something like that, and was fast as a streak. He was a gelding and had a mark of 2:21, but could step in :08 or :09.

Because when Burt and I were out, as I've told you, the year before, there was a nigger Burt knew, worked for Mr. Mathers, and we went out there one day when we didn't have no race on at the Marietta Fair and our boss Harry was gone home.

And so everyone was gone to the fair but just this one nigger and he took us all through Mr. Mathers' swell house and he and Burt tapped a bottle of wine Mr. Mathers had hid in his bedroom, back in a closet, without his wife knowing, and he showed us this Ahem horse. Burt was always stuck on being a driver but didn't have much chance to get to the top, being a nigger, and he and the other nigger gulped that whole bottle of wine and Burt got a little lit up.

So the nigger let Burt take this About Ben Ahem and step him a mile in a track Mr. Mathers had all to himself, right there on the farm. And Mr. Mathers had one child, a daughter, kinda sick and not very good-looking, and she came home and we had to hustle and get About Ben Ahem stuck back in the barn.

I'm only telling you to get everything straight. At Sandusky, that afternoon I was at the fair, this young fellow with the two girls was fussed, being with the girls and losing his bet. You know how a fellow is that way. One of them was his girl and the other his sister. I had figured that out.

"Gee whizz," I says to myself, "I'm going to give him the dope."

He was mighty nice when I touched him on the shoulder. He and the girls were nice to me right from the start and clear to the end. I'm not blaming them.

And so he leaned back and I give him the dope on About Ben Ahem. "Don't bet a cent on this first heat because he'll go like an oxen hitched to a plow, but when the first heat is over go right down and lay on your pile." That's what I told him.

Well, I never saw a fellow treat anyone sweller. There was a fat man sitting beside the little girl, that had looked at me twice by this time, and I at her, and both blushing, and what did he do but have the nerve to turn and ask the fat man to get up and change places with me so I could set with his crowd.

Gee whizz, craps amighty. There I was. What a chump I was to go and get gay up there in the West House bar, and just because that dude was standing there with a cane and that kind of a necktie on, to go and get all balled up and drink that whisky, just to show off.

Of course she would know, me setting right beside her and letting her smell of my breath. I could have kicked myself right down out of that grandstand and all around that race track and made a faster record than most of the skates of horses they had there that year.

Because that girl wasn't any mutt of a girl. What wouldn't I have give right then for a stick of chewing gum to chew, or a lozenger, or some liquorice, or most anything. I was glad I had those twenty-five-cent cigars in my pocket and right away I give that fellow one and lit one myself. Then that fat man got up and we changed places and there I was, plunked right down beside her.

They introduced themselves and the fellow's best girl, he had with him, was named Miss Elinor Woodbury, and her father was a manufacturer of barrels from a place called Tiffin, Ohio. And the fellow himself was named Wilbur Wessen and his sister was Miss Lucy Wessen.

I suppose it was their having such swell names got me off my trolley. A fellow, just because he has been a swipe with a race horse, and works taking care of horses for a man in the teaming, delivery, and storage business, isn't any better or worse than anyone else. I've often thought that, and said it too.

But you know how a fellow is. There's something in that kind of nice clothes, and the kind of nice eyes she had, and the way she had looked at me, awhile before, over her brother's shoulder, and me looking back at her, and both of us blushing.

I couldn't show her up for a boob, could I?

I made a fool of myself, that's what I did. I said my name was Walter Mathers from Marietta, Ohio, and then I told all three of them the smashingest lie you ever heard. What I said was that my father owned the horse About Ben Ahem and that he had let him out to this Bob French for racing purposes, because our family was proud and had never gone into racing that way, in our own name, I mean. Then I had got started and they were all leaning over and listening, and Miss Lucy Wessen's eyes were shining, and I went the whole hog.

I told about our place down at Marietta, and about the big stables and the grand brick house we had on a hill, up above the Ohio River, but I knew enough not to do it in no bragging way. What I did was to start things and then let them drag the rest out of me. I acted just as reluctant to tell as I could. Our family hasn't got any barrel factory, and, since I've known us, we've always been pretty poor, but not asking anything of anyone at that, and my grandfather, over in Wales—but never mind that.

We sat there talking like we had known each other for years and years, and I went and told them that my father had been expecting maybe this Bob French wasn't on the square, and had sent me up to Sandusky on the sly to find out what I could.

And I bluffed it through I had found out all about the 2:18 pace, in which About Ben Ahem was to start.

I said he would lose the first heat by pacing like a lame cow and then he would come back and skin 'em alive after that. And to back up what I said I took thirty dollars out of my pocket and handed it to Mr. Wilbur Wessen and asked him, would he mind, after the first heat, to go down and place it on About Ben Ahem for whatever odds he could get. What I said was that I didn't want Bob French to see me and none of the swipes.

Sure enough the first heat come off and About Ben Ahem went off his stride, up the back stretch, and looked like a wooden horse or a sick one, and come in to be last. Then this Wilbur Wessen went down to the betting place under the grandstand and there I was with the two girls, and when that Miss Woodbury was looking the other way once, Lucy Wessen kinda, with her shoulder you know, kinda touched me. Not just tucking down, I don't mean. You know how a woman can do. They get close, but not getting gay either. You know what they do. Gee whizz.

And then they give me a jolt. What they had done, when I didn't know, was to get together, and they had decided Wilbur Wessen would bet fifty dollars, and the two girls had gone and put in ten dollars each, of their own money, too. I was sick then, but I was sicker later.

About the gelding, About Ben Ahem, and their winning their money, I wasn't worried a lot about that. It come out O.K. Ahem stepped the next three heats like a bushel of spoiled eggs going to market before they could be found out, and Wilbur Wessen had got nine to two for the money. There was something else eating at me.

Because Wilbur come back, after he had bet the money, and after that he spent most of his time talking to that Miss Woodbury, and Lucy Wessen and I was left alone together like on a desert island. Gee, if I'd only been on the square or if there had been any way of getting myself on the square. There ain't any Walter Mathers, like I said to her and them, and there hasn't ever been one, but if there was, I bet I'd go to Marietta, Ohio, and shoot him tomorrow.

There I was, big boob that I am. Pretty soon the race was over, and Wilbur had gone down and collected our money, and we had a hack downtown, and he stood us a swell supper at the West House, and a bottle of champagne beside.

And I was with that girl and she wasn't saying much, and I wasn't saying much either. One thing I know. She wasn't stuck on me because of the lie about my father being rich and all that. There's a way you know.... Craps amighty. There's a kind of girl, you see just once in your life, and if you don't get busy and make hay, then you're gone for good and all, and might as well go jump off a bridge. They give you a look from inside of them somewhere, and it ain't no vamping, and what it means is—you want that girl to be your wife, and you want nice things around her like flowers and swell clothes, and you want her to have the kids you're going to have, and you want good music played and no ragtime. Gee whizz.

There's a place over near Sandusky, across a kind of bay, and it's called Cedar Point. And after we had supper we went over to it in a launch, all by ourselves. Wilbur and Miss Lucy and that Miss Woodbury had to catch a ten-o'clock train back to Tiffin, Ohio, because, when you're out with girls like that, you can't get careless and miss any trains and stay out all night, like you can with some kinds of Janes.

And Wilbur blowed himself to the launch and it cost him fifteen cold plunks, but I wouldn't never have knew if I hadn't listened. He wasn't no tinhorn kind of a sport.

Over at the Cedar Point place, we didn't stay around where there was a gang of common kind of cattle at all.

There was big dance halls and dining places for yaps, and there was a beach you could walk along and get where it was dark, and we went there.

She didn't talk hardly at all and neither did I, and I was thinking how glad I was my mother was all right, and always made us kids learn to eat with a fork at table, and not swill soup, and not be noisy and rough like a gang you see around a race track that way.

Then Wilbur and his girl went away up the beach and Lucy and I sat down in a dark place, where there was some roots of old trees, the water had washed up, and after that the time, till we had to go back in the launch and they had to catch their trains, wasn't nothing at all. It went like winking your eye.

Here's how it was. The place we were setting in was dark, like I said, and there was the roots from that cold stump sticking up like arms, and there was a watery smell, and the night was like—as if you could put your hand out and feel it—so warm and soft and dark and sweet like an orange.

I most cried and I most swore and I most jumped up and danced, I was so mad and happy and sad.

When Wilbur come back from being alone with his girl, and she saw him coming, Lucy she says, "We got to go to the train now," and she was most crying too, but she never knew nothing I knew, and she couldn't be so all busted up. And then, before Wilbur and Miss Woodbury got up to where we was, she put her face up and kissed me quick and put her head up against me and she was all quivering and—Gee whizz.

Sometimes I hope I have cancer and die. I guess you know what I mean. We went in the launch across the bay to the train like that, and it was dark, too. She whispered and said it was like she and I could get out of the boat and walk on the water, and it sounded foolish, but I knew what she meant.

And then quick we were right at the depot, and there was a big gang of yaps, the kind that goes to the fairs, and crowded and milling around like cattle, and how could I tell her? "It won't be long because you'll write and I'll write to you." That's all she said.

I got a chance like a hay barn afire. A swell chance I got.

And maybe she would write me, down at Marietta that way, and the letter would come back, and stamped on the front of it by the U.S.A. "there ain't any such guy," or something like that, whatever they stamp on a letter that way.

And me trying to pass myself off for a bigbug and a swell—to her, as decent a little body as God ever made. Craps amighty—a swell chance I got!

And then the train come in, and she got on it, and Wilbur Wessen he come and shook hands with me, and that Miss Woodbury was nice too and bowed to me, and I at her, and the train went and I busted out and cried like a kid.

Gee, I could have run after that train and made Dan Patch look like a freight train after a wreck but, socks amighty, what was the use? Did you ever see such a fool?

I'll bet you what—if I had an arm broke right now or a train had run over my foot—I wouldn't go to no doctor at all. I'd go set down and let her hurt and hurt—that's what I'd do.

I'll bet you what—if I hadn't a drunk that booze I'd a never been such a boob as to go tell such a lie—that couldn't never be made straight to a lady like her.

I wish I had that fellow right here that had on a Windsor tie and carried a cane. I'd smash him for fair. Gosh darn his eyes. He's a big fool—that's what he is.

And if I'm not another you just go find me one and I'll quit working and be a bum and give him my job. I don't care nothing for working, and earning money, and saving it for no such boob as myself.

[1926]

For Thought

Anderson selected the limited-omniscience point of view for the story "I'm a Fool." Consequently, though the narrator considers himself to be knowing and mature, the reader is able to view him as young and inexperienced. Because he is overanxious, he creates a false identity for himself in order to impress new friends at a race track. He discovers too late that he and a new girl will never see their newfound passion ripen. Sometimes, Anderson's theme suggests, a promising new direction in one's life is choked off forever by a trivial mistake. Anderson also uses language to establish the race-track setting as well as the characterization of the narrator.

For Discussion

1. What traits about the narrator does Anderson reveal that the boy himself is unaware of?
2. How does Anderson build suspense in the story?
3. How are the horses of the story linked to its ironic treatment of appearance and reality?
4. What recognitions are achieved by the boy?
5. What truths unknown to the boy are seen by the reader?
6. How does the author's use of language help establish the setting for the story?

Isaac Babel
The Sin of Jesus

Arina was a servant at the hotel. She lived next to the main staircase, while Serega, the janitor's helper, he lived over the backstairs. Between them there was shame. On Palm Sunday Arina gave Serega a present—twins. Water flows, stars shine, a man lusts, and soon Arina was big again, her sixth month was rolling by—they're slippery, a woman's months. And now Serega must go into the army. There's a mess for you!

So Arina goes and says: "No sense, Sergunia, there's no sense in my waiting for you. For four years we'll be parted, and in four years, whatever way you look at it, I'll be sure to bring two or three more into this world. It's like walking around with your skirt turned up, working at the hotel. Whoever stops here, he's your master, let him be a Jew, let him be anybody at all. By the time you come home, my insides will be no good anymore, I'll be a used-up woman, no match for you."

"That's so," Serega nodded.

"There's many that want me. Trofimych the contractor—but he's no gentleman. And Isai Abramych, the warden of Nikolo-Sviatski church, a feeble old man, but anyway I'm sick to the stomach of your murderous strength. I tell you this now, and I say it like I would at confession, I've got the wind plain knocked out of me. . . . I'll spill my load in three months, then I'll take the baby to the orphanage and marry the old man."

When Serega heard this, he took off his belt and beat her like a hero, right on the belly.

"Look out there," Arina says to him, "go soft on the belly, it's your stuffing, no one else's. . . ."

There was no end to the beating, no end to the man's tears and the woman's blood, but that is neither here nor there.

Then the woman came to Jesus Christ.

"So and so," she says, "Lord Jesus. I am the woman Arina from the Hotel Madrid and Louvre, the one on Tverskaya Street. Working at the hotel, it's like going around with your skirt up. Just let a man stop there, and he's your lord and master, let him be a Jew, let him be anybody at all. There is another slave of yours walking the earth, the janitor's helper, Serega. Last year on Palm Sunday I bore him twins. . . ."

And so she described it all to the Lord.

"And what if Serega were not to go into the army at all?" the Saviour suggested.

"Try and get away with it—not with the policeman around. He'll drag him off as sure as daylight. . . ."

"Oh yes, the policeman," the Lord bowed his head, "I never thought of him. . . . Then perhaps you ought to live in purity for a while?. . ."

"For four years?" the woman cried. "To hear you talk, all people should deny their animal nature. That's just your old ways all over again. And where will the increase come from? No, you'd better give me some sensible advice. . . ."

The Lord's cheeks turned scarlet, the woman's words had touched a tender spot. But he said nothing. You cannot kiss your own ear—even God knows that.

"I'll tell you what, God's servant, glorious sinner, maiden Arina," the Lord proclaimed in all his glory, "I have a little angel here in heaven, hanging around uselessly. His name is Alfred. Lately he's gotten out of hand altogether, keeps crying and nagging all the time: 'What have you done to me, Lord, why did you turn me into an angel in my twentieth year, and me a hale young fellow?' So I'll give you Alfred the angel as a husband for four years. He'll be your prayer, he'll be your protection, and he'll be your solace. And as for offspring, you've nothing to worry about—you can't bear a duckling from him, let alone a baby, for there's a lot of fun in him, but no seriousness. . . ."

"That's just what I need," the maid Arina wept gratefully. "Their seriousness takes me to the doorstep of the grave three times every two years. . . ."

"You'll have a sweet respite, God's child Arina, may your prayer be light as a song. Amen."

And so it was decided. Alfred was brought in—a frail young fellow, delicate, two wings fluttering behind his pale-blue shoulders, rippling with rosy lights like two doves playing in heaven. Arina threw her hefty arms about him, weeping out of tenderness, out of her woman's soft heart.

"Alfred, my soul, my consolation, my bridegroom. . . ."

In parting, the Lord gave her strict instructions to take off the angel's wings every night before he went to bed. His wings were attached to hinges, like a door, and every night she was to take them off and wrap them in a clean sheet, because they were brittle, his wings, and could snap as he tossed in bed—for what were they made of but the sighs of babes, no more than that.

For the last time the Lord blessed the union, while the choir of bishops, called in for the occasion, rendered thunderous praises. No food was served, not a crumb—that wasn't the style in heaven—and then Arina and Alfred, their arms about each other, ran down a silken ladder, straight back to earth. They came to Petrovka, where nothing but the best is sold—the woman would do right by her Alfred!—(and he, if one might say so, not only lacking socks, but altogether natural just as his mother bore him)—and she bought him patent leather half-boots, checked jersey trousers, a fine hunting jacket, and an electric blue vest.

"The rest," she says, "we'll find at home. . . ."

That day Arina begged off from work. Serega came, raised a fuss, but she did not even come out to him, only said from behind her locked door:

"Sergei Nifantich, I am at present laving my feet and beg you to retire without more noise. . . ."

He went away without a word—the angel's power was already beginning to manifest itself!

In the evening Arina set out a supper fit for a merchant—the woman had devilish vanity! A half-pint of vodka, wine on the side, a Danube herring with potatoes, a samovar of tea. When Alfred had partaken of all these earthly blessings, he keeled over in a dead sleep. Quick as a wink, Arina lifted off his wings from the hinges, packed them away, and carried him to bed in her arms.

There it lies, the snowy wonder on the eiderdown pillows of her tattered, sinful bed, sending forth a heavenly radiance; moon-silver shafts of light pass and repass, alternate with red ones, float across the room, sway over his shiny feet. Arina weeps and rejoices, sings and prays. Arina, thou hast been granted a happiness unheard of on this battered earth, blessed art thou among women!

They had drunk the vodka to the last drop, and now it took effect. As soon as they fell asleep, she went and rolled over on top of Alfred with her hot, six-months'-big belly. Not enough for her to sleep with an angel, not enough that nobody beside her spat at the wall, snored and snorted—that wasn't enough for the clumsy, ravening slut. No, she had to warm her belly too, her burning belly big with Serega's lust. And so she smothered him in her fuddled sleep, smothered him in the midst of her rejoicing like a week-old babe, crushed him under her bloated weight, and he gave up the ghost, and his wings, wrapped in her sheet, wept pale tears.

Dawn came—and all the trees bowed low to the ground. In distant northern forests each fir tree turned into a priest, each fir tree bent its knees in silent worship.

Once more the woman stands before the Lord's throne—broad in the shoulders, mighty, the young corpse drooping in her huge red arms.

"Behold, Lord. . . ."

But here the gentle heart of Jesus could endure no longer, and he cursed the woman in his anger:

"As it is on earth, so shall it be with you, Arina, from this day on. . . ."

"How is it then, Lord," the woman replied in a scarce audible voice, "was it I who made my body heavy, was it I that brewed vodka on earth, was it I that created a woman's soul, stupid and lonely?. . ."

"I don't wish to be bothered with you," exclaimed the Lord Jesus, "you've smothered my angel, you filthy scum. . . ."

And Arina was thrown back to earth on a putrid wind, straight down to Tverskaya Street, to the Hotel Madrid and Louvre, where she was doomed to spend her days. And once there—the sky's the limit. Serega was carousing, drinking away his last days, seeing as he was a recruit. The contractor Trofimych, just come from Koloma, took one look at Arina, hefty and red-cheeked: "Oh, you cute little belly," he says, and so forth.

Isai Abramych, the old codger, heard about this cute little belly and he is right there too, wheezing toothlessly:

"I cannot wed you lawfully," he says, "after all that happened. However, I can lie with you the same as anyone. . . ."

The old man ought to be lying in cold mother earth instead of thinking such things, but no, he too must take his turn at spitting into her soul. It was like everybody breaking off a chain—kitchen boys, merchants, foreigners. A trading man—he likes to have his fun.

And that is the end of my tale.

Before she was laid up, because three months had rolled by in the meantime, Arina went out into the backyard, behind the janitor's rooms, raised her monstrous huge belly to the silken sky and said stupidly:

"See, Lord, what a belly. They hammer at it like peas out of a bursting pod. And what's the sense in it—I cannot see. And furthermore, I have no wish to see. . . ."

With his tears Jesus washed Arina when he heard these words, on his knees the Saviour dropped before her.

"Forgive me, Arinushka, forgive your sinful God. What have I done to you?. . ."

But Arina shook her head and would not listen.

"There's no forgiveness for you, Jesus Christ," she said, "no forgiveness at all, none."

[1955]

For Thought

Babel has written a modern parable complete with earthy sinners, sincere heavenly beings and pithy folk wisdom. Arina is a tainted heroine who is stressed to the limit yet manages to view her woes with realism and even humor. Her bargaining dialogues with Jesus treat prayer and the heavenly realm quite literally, slyly calling into question some basic religious tenets. Babel uses satire of religious abstractions to probe deeply into the everyday lives of the Russian poor.

For Discussion

1. What problems is Arina forced to deal with? Why has she such difficulty taking control of her life?
2. Why are Jesus's initial suggestions to Arina—that Serega not go into the army or that Arina remain "pure"—so impractical? How do they satirize the assumptions of well-meaning advice givers?
3. Why is it so ironic that Jesus should be placed in the position of bargaining face-to-face with Arina, that he should be forced to deal with the complaints of an unhappy angel, and that he should decide to unite Arina with a fragile angel?
4. How is Arina's and Alfred's wedding night comic and ironic instead of shocking and pathetic?
5. Why does Jesus come to believe he needs forgiveness? Why does Arina refuse to forgive him?
6. What theme emerges from the story?

James Baldwin
Going to Meet the Man

"What's the matter?" she asked.

"I don't know," he said, trying to laugh, "I guess I'm tired."

"You've been working too hard," she said. "I keep telling you."

"Well, goddammit, woman," he said, "it's not my fault!" He tried again; he wretchedly failed again. Then he just lay there, silent, angry, and helpless. Excitement filled him like a toothache, but it refused to enter his flesh. He stroked her breast. This was his wife. He could not ask her to do just a little thing for him, just to help him out, just for a little while, the way he could ask a nigger girl to do it. He lay there, and he sighed. The image of a black girl caused a distant excitement in him, like a far-away light; but, again, the excitement was more like pain; instead of forcing him to act, it made action impossible.

"Go to sleep," she said, gently, "you got a hard day tomorrow."

"Yeah," he said, and rolled over on his side, facing her, one hand still on one breast. "Goddamn the niggers. The black stinking coons. You'd think they'd learn. Wouldn't you think they'd learn? I mean, *wouldn't* you?"

"They going to be out there tomorrow," she said, and took his hand away, "get some sleep."

He lay there, one hand between his legs, staring at the frail sanctuary of his wife. A faint light came from the shutters; the moon was full. Two dogs, far away, were barking at each other, back and forth, insistently, as though they were agreeing to make an appointment. He heard a car coming north on the road and he half sat up, his hand reaching for his holster, which was on a chair near the bed, on top of his pants. The lights hit the shutters and seemed to travel across the room and then went out. The sound of the car slipped away, he heard it hit gravel, then heard it no more. Some liver-lipped students, probably, heading back to that college—but coming from where? His watch said it was two in the morning. They could be coming from anywhere, from out of state most likely, and they would be at the court house tomorrow. The niggers were getting ready. Well, they would be ready, too.

He moaned. He wanted to let whatever was in him out; but it wouldn't come out. Goddamn! he said aloud, and turned again, on his side, away from Grace, staring at the shutters. He was a big, healthy man and he had never had any trouble sleeping. And he wasn't old enough yet to have any trouble getting it up—he was only forty-two. And he was a good man, a God-fearing man, he had tried to do his duty all his life, and he had been a deputy sheriff for several years. Nothing had ever bothered him before, certainly not getting it up. Sometimes, sure, like any other man, he knew that he wanted a little more spice than Grace could give him and he would drive over yonder and pick up a black piece or arrest her, it came to the same thing, but he couldn't do that now, no more. There was no telling what might happen once your ass was in the air. And they were low enough to kill a man then, too, everyone of them, or the girl herself might do it, right while she was making believe you made her feel so good. The niggers. What had the good Lord Almighty had in mind when he made the niggers? Well. They were pretty good at that, all right. Damn. Damn. Goddamn.

This wasn't helping him to sleep. He turned again, toward Grace again, and moved close to her warm body. He felt something he had never felt before. He felt that he would like to hold her, hold her, hold her, and be buried in her like a child and never have to get up in the morning again and go downtown to face those faces, good Christ, they were ugly! and never have to enter that jail house again and smell that smell and hear that singing; never again feel that filthy, kinky, greasy hair under his hand, never again watch those black breasts leap against the leaping cattle prod, never hear those moans again or watch that blood run down or the fat lips split or the sealed eyes struggle open. They were animals, they were no better than animals, what could be done with people like that? Here they had been in a civilized country for years and they still lived like animals. Their houses were dark, with oil cloth or cardboard in the windows, the smell was enough to make you puke your guts out, and there they sat, a whole tribe, pumping out kids, it looked like, every damn five minutes, and laughing and talking and playing music like they didn't have a care in the world, and he reckoned they didn't, neither, and coming to the door, into the sunlight, just standing there, just looking foolish, not thinking of anything but just getting back to what they were doing, saying, Yes suh, Mr. Jesse. I surely will, Mr. Jesse. Fine weather, Mr. Jesse. Why, I thank you, Mr. Jesse. He had worked for a mail-order house for a while and it had been his job to collect the payments for the stuff they bought. They were too dumb to know that they were being cheated blind, but that was no skin off his ass—he was just supposed to do his job. They would be late—they didn't have the sense to put money aside; but it was easy to scare them, and he never really had any trouble. Hell, they all liked him, the kids used to smile when he came to the door. He gave them candy, sometimes, or chewing gum, and rubbed their rough bullet heads—maybe the candy should have been poisoned. Those kids were grown now. He had had trouble with one of them today.

"There was this nigger today," he said; and stopped; his voice sounded peculiar. He touched Grace. "You awake?" he asked. She mumbled something, impatiently, she was probably telling him to go to sleep. It was all right. He knew that he was not alone.

"What a funny time," he said, "to be thinking about a thing like that—you listening?" She mumbled something again. He rolled over on his back. "This nigger's one of the ringleaders. We had trouble with him before. We must have had him out there at the work farm three or four times. Well, Big Jim C. and some of the boys really had to whip that nigger's ass today." He looked over at Grace; he could not tell whether she was listening or not; and he was afraid to ask again. "They had this line you know, to register"—he laughed, but she did not—"and they wouldn't stay where Big Jim C. wanted them, no, they had to start blocking traffic all around the court house so couldn't nothing or nobody get through, and Big Jim C. told them to disperse and they wouldn't move, they just kept up that singing, and Big Jim C. figured that the others would move if this nigger would move, him being the ring-leader, but he wouldn't move and he wouldn't let the others move, so they had to beat him and a couple of the others and they threw them in the wagon—but *I* didn't see this nigger till I got to the jail. They were still singing and I was supposed to make them stop. Well, I couldn't make them stop for me but I knew he could make them stop. He was lying on the ground jerking and moaning, they had threw him in a cell by himself, and blood was coming out his ears from where Big Jim C. and his boys had whipped him. Wouldn't you think they'd learn? I put the prod to him and he jerked some more and he kind of screamed—but he didn't have much voice left. "You make them stop that singing," I said to him, "you hear me? You make them stop that singing." He acted like he didn't hear me and I put it to him again, under his arms, and he just rolled around on the floor and blood started coming from his mouth. He'd pissed his pants already." He paused. His mouth felt dry and his throat was as rough as sandpaper; as he talked, he began to hurt all over with that peculiar excitement which refused to be released. "You all are going to stop your singing, I said to him, and you are going to stop coming down to the court house and disrupting traffic and molesting the people and keeping us from our duties and keeping doctors from getting to sick white women and getting all them Northerners in this town to give our town a bad name—!" As he said this, he kept prodding the boy, sweat pouring from beneath the helmet he had not yet taken off. The boy rolled around in his own dirt and water and blood and tried to scream again as the prod hit his testicles, but the scream did not come out, only a kind of rattle and a moan. He stopped. He was not supposed to kill the nigger. The cell was filled with a terrible odor. The boy was still. "You hear me?" he called. "You had enough?" The singing went on. "You had enough?" His foot leapt out, he had not known it was going to, and caught the boy flush on the jaw. *Jesus*, he thought, *this ain't no nigger, this is a goddamn bull,* and he screamed again, "You had enough? You going to make them stop that singing now?"

But the boy was out. And now he was shaking worse than the boy had been shaking. He was glad no one could see him. At the same time, he felt very close to a very peculiar, particular joy; something deep in him and deep in his memory was stirred, but whatever was in his memory eluded him. He took off his helmet. He walked to the cell door.

"White man," said the boy, from the floor, behind him.

He stopped. For some reason, he grabbed his privates.

"You remember Old Julia?"

The boy said, from the floor, with his mouth full of blood, and one eye, barely open, glaring like the eye of a cat in the dark, "My grandmother's name was Mrs. Julia Blossom. *Mrs.* Julia Blossom. You going to call our women by their right names yet.—And those kids ain't going to stop singing. We going to keep on singing until every one of you miserable white mothers go stark raving out of your minds." Then he closed the one eye; he spat blood; his head fell back against the floor.

He looked down at the boy, whom he had been seeing, off and on, for more than a year, and suddenly remembered him: Old Julia had been one of his mail-order customers, a nice old woman. He had not seen her for years, he supposed that she must be dead.

He had walked into the yard, the boy had been sitting in a swing. He had smiled at the boy, and asked, "Old Julia home?"

The boy looked at him for a long time before he answered. "Don't no Old Julia live here."

"This is her house. I know her. She's lived here for years."

The boy shook his head. "You might know a Old Julia someplace else, white man. But don't nobody by that name live here."

He watched the boy; the boy watched him. The boy certainly wasn't more than ten. *White man.* He didn't have time to be fooling around with some crazy kid. He yelled, "Hey! Old Julia!"

But only silence answered him. The expression on the boy's face did not change. The sun beat down on them both, still and silent; he had the feeling that he had been caught up in a nightmare, a nightmare dreamed by a child; perhaps one of the nightmares he himself had dreamed as a child. It had that feeling—everything familiar, without undergoing any other change, had been subtly and hideously displaced: the trees, the sun, the patches of grass in the yard, the leaning porch and the weary porch steps and the card-board in the windows and the black hole of the door which looked like the entrance to a cave, and the eyes of the pickaninny, all, all, were charged with malevolence. *White man.* He looked at the boy. "She's gone out?"

The boy said nothing.

"Well," he said, "tell her I passed by and I'll pass by next week." He started to go; he stopped. "You want some chewing gum?"

The boy got down from the swing and started for the house. He said, "I don't want nothing you got, white man." He walked into the house and closed the door behind him.

Now the boy looked as though he were dead. Jesse wanted to go over to him and pick him up and pistol whip him until the boy's head burst open like a melon. He began to tremble with what he believed was rage, sweat, both cold and hot, raced down his body, the singing filled him as though it were a weird, uncontrollable, monstrous howling rumbling up from the depths of his own belly, he felt an icy fear rise in him and raise him up, and he shouted, he howled, "You lucky we *pump* some white blood into you every once in a while—your women! Here's what I got for all the black bitches in the world—!" Then he was, abruptly, almost too weak to stand; to his bewilderment, his horror, beneath his own fingers, he felt himself violently stiffen—with no warning at all; he dropped his hands and he stared at the boy and he left the cell.

"All that singing they do," he said. "All that singing." He could not remember the first time he had heard it; he had been hearing it all his life. It was the sound with which he was most familiar—though it was also the sound of which he had been least conscious—and it had always contained an obscure comfort. They were singing to God. They were singing for mercy and they hoped to go to heaven, and he had even sometimes felt, when looking into the eyes of some of the old women, a few of the very old men, that they were singing for mercy for his soul, too. Of course he had never thought of their heaven or of what God was, or could be, for them; God was the same for everyone, he supposed, and heaven was where good people went—he supposed. He had never thought much about what it meant to be a good person. He tried to be a good person and treat everybody right; it wasn't his fault if the niggers had taken it into their heads to fight against God and go against the rules laid down in the Bible for everyone to read! Any preacher would tell you that. He was only doing his duty: protecting white people from the niggers and the niggers from themselves. And there were still lots of good niggers around—he had to remember that; they weren't all like that boy this afternoon; and the good niggers must be mighty sad to see what was happening to their people. They would thank him when this was over. In that way they had, the best of them, not quite looking him in the eye, in a low voice, with a little smile: We surely thanks you, Mr. Jesse. From the bottom of our hearts, we thanks you. He smiled. They hadn't all gone crazy. This trouble would pass.—He knew that the young people had changed some of the words to the songs. He had scarcely listened to the words before and he did not listen to them now; but he knew that the words were different; he could hear that much. He did not know if the faces were different, he had never, before this trouble began, watched them as they sang, but he certainly did not like what he saw now. They hated him, and this hatred was blacker than their hearts, blacker than their skins, redder than their blood, and harder, by far, than his club. Each day, each night, he felt worn out, aching, with their smell in his nostrils and filling his lungs, as though he were drowning—drowning in niggers; and it was all to be done again when he awoke. It would never end. It would never end. Perhaps this was what the singing had meant all along. They had not been singing black folks into heaven, they had been singing white folks into hell.

Everyone felt this black suspicion in many ways, but no one knew how to express it. Men much older than he, who had been responsible for law and order much longer than he, were now much quieter than they had been, and the tone of their jokes, in a way that he could not quite put his finger on, had changed. These men were his models, they had been friends to his father, and they had taught him what it meant to be a man. He looked to them for courage now. It wasn't that he didn't know that what he was doing was right—he knew that, nobody had to tell him that; it was only that he missed the ease of former years. But they didn't have much time to hang out with each other these days. They tended to stay close to their families every free minute because nobody knew what might happen next. Explosions rocked the night of their tranquil town. Each time each man wondered silently if perhaps this time the dynamite had not fallen into the wrong hands. They thought that they knew where all the guns were; but they could not possibly know every move that was made in that secret place where the darkies lived. From time to time it was suggested that they form a posse and search the home of every nigger, but they hadn't done it yet. For one thing, this might have brought the bastards from the North down on their backs; for another, although the niggers were scattered throughout the town—down in the hollow near the railroad tracks, way west near the mills, up on the hill, the well-off ones, and some out near the college—nothing seemed to happen in one part of town without the niggers immediately knowing it in the other. This meant that they could not take them by surprise. They rarely mentioned it, but they *knew* that some of the niggers had guns. It stood to reason, as they said, since, after all, some of them had been in the Army. There were niggers in the Army right now and God knows they wouldn't have had any trouble stealing this half-assed government blind—the whole world was doing it, look at the European countries and all those countries in Africa. They made jokes about it—bitter jokes; and they cursed the government in Washington, which had betrayed them; but they had not yet formed a posse. Now, if their town had been laid out like some towns in the North, where all the niggers lived together in one locality, they could have gone down and set fire to the houses and brought about peace that way. If the niggers had all lived in one place, they could have kept the fire in one place. But the way this town was laid out, the fire could hardly be controlled. It would spread all over town—and the niggers would probably be helping it to spread. Still, from time to time, they spoke of doing it, anyway; so that now there was a real fear among them that somebody might go crazy and light the match.

They rarely mentioned anything not directly related to the war that they were fighting, but this had failed to establish between them the unspoken communication of soldiers during a war. Each man, in the thrilling silence which sped outward from their exchanges, their laughter, and their anecdotes, seemed wrestling, in various degrees of darkness, with a secret which he could not articulate to himself, and which, however directly it related to the war, related yet more surely to his privacy and his past. They could no longer be sure, after all, that they had all done the same things. They had never dreamed that their privacy could contain any element of terror, could threaten, that is, to reveal itself, to the scrutiny of a judgment day, while remaining unreadable and inaccessible to themselves; nor had they dreamed that the past, while certainly refusing to be forgotten, could yet so stubbornly refuse to be remembered. They felt themselves mysteriously set at naught, as no longer entering into the real concerns of other people—while here they were, out-numbered, fighting to save the civilized world. They had thought that people would care—people didn't care; not enough, anyway, to help them. It would have been a help, really, or at least a relief, even to have been forced to surrender. Thus they had lost, probably forever, their old and easy connection with each other. They were forced to depend on each other more and, at the same time, to trust each other less. Who could tell when one of them might not betray them all, for money, or for the ease of confession? But no one dared imagine what there might be to confess. They were soldiers fighting a war, but their relationship to each other was that of accomplices in a crime. They all had to keep their mouths shut.

I stepped in the river at Jordan.

Out of the darkness of the room, out of nowhere, the line came flying up at him, with the melody and the beat. He turned wordlessly toward his sleeping wife. *I stepped in the river at Jordan*. Where had he heard that song?

"Grace," he whispered. "You awake?"

She did not answer. If she was awake, she wanted him to sleep. Her breathing was slow and easy, her body slowly rose and fell.

I stepped in the river at Jordan.
The water came to my knees.

He began to sweat. He felt an overwhelming fear, which yet contained a curious and dreadful pleasure.

I stepped in the river at Jordan.
The water came to my waist.

It had been night, as it was now, he was in the car between his mother and his father, sleepy, his head in his mother's lap, sleepy, and yet full of excitement. The singing came from far away, across the dark fields. There were no lights anywhere. They had said good-bye to all the others and turned off on this dark dirt road. They were almost home.

I stepped in the river at Jordan,
The water came over my head,
I looked way over to the other side,
He was making up my dying bed!

"I guess they singing for him," his father said, seeming very weary and subdued now. "Even when they're sad, they sound like they just about to go and tear off a piece." He yawned and leaned across the boy and slapped his wife lightly on the shoulder, allowing his hand to rest there for a moment. "Don't they?"

"Don't talk that way," she said.

"Well, that's what we going to do," he

said, "you can make up your mind to that." He started whistling. "You see? When I begin to feel it, I gets kind of musical, too."

> Oh, Lord! Come on and ease my troubling mind!

He had a black friend, his age, eight, who lived nearby. His name was Otis. They wrestled together in the dirt. Now the thought of Otis made him sick. He began to shiver. His mother put her arm around him.

"He's tired," she said.

"We'll be home soon," said his father. He began to whistle again.

"We didn't see Otis this morning," Jesse said. He did not know why he said this. His voice, in the darkness of the car, sounded small and accusing.

"You haven't seen Otis for a couple of mornings," his mother said.

That was true. But he was only concerned about *this* morning.

"No," said his father, "I reckon Otis's folks was afraid to let him show himself this morning."

"But Otis didn't do nothing!" Now his voice sounded questioning.

"Otis *can't* do nothing," said his father, "he's too little." The car lights picked up their wooden house, which now solemnly approached them, the lights falling around it like yellow dust. Their dog, chained to a tree, began to bark.

"We just want to make sure Otis *don't* do nothing," said his father, and stopped the car. He looked down at Jesse. "And you tell him what your Daddy said, you hear?"

"Yes sir," he said.

His father switched off the lights. The dog moaned and pranced, but they ignored him and went inside. He could not sleep. He lay awake, hearing the night sounds, the dog yawning and moaning outside, the sawing of the crickets, the cry of the owl, dogs barking far away, then no sounds at all, just the heavy, endless buzzing of the night. The darkness pressed on his eyelids like a scratchy blanket. He turned, he turned again. He wanted to call his mother, but he knew his father would not like this. He was terribly afraid. Then he heard his father's voice in the other room, low, with a joke in it; but this did not help him, it frightened him more, he knew what was going to happen. He put his head under the blanket, then pushed his head out again, for fear, staring at the dark window. He heard his mother's moan, his father's sigh; he gritted his teeth. Then their bed began to rock. His father's breathing seemed to fill the world.

That morning, before the sun had gathered all its strength, men and women, some flushed and some pale with excitement, came with news. Jesse's father seemed to know what the news was before the first jalopy stopped in the yard, and he ran out, crying, "They got him, then? They got him?"

The first jalopy held eight people, three men and two women and three children. The children were sitting on the laps of the grown-ups. Jesse knew two of them, the two boys; they shyly and uncomfortably greeted each other. He did not know the girl.

"Yes, they got him," said one of the women, the older one, who wore a wide hat and a fancy, faded blue dress. "They found him early this morning."

"How far had he got?" Jesse's father asked.

"He hadn't got no further than Harkness," one of the men said. "Look like he got lost up there in all them trees—or maybe he just got so scared he couldn't move." They all laughed.

"Yes, and you know it's near a graveyard, too," said the younger woman, and they laughed again.

"Is that where they got him now?" asked Jesse's father.

By this time there were three cars piled behind the first one, with everyone looking excited and shining, and Jesse noticed that they were carrying food. It was like a Fourth of July picnic.

"Yeah, that's where he is," said one of

the men, "declare, Jesse, you going to keep us here all day long, answering your damn fool questions. Come on, we ain't got no time to waste."

"Don't bother putting up no food," cried a woman from one of the other cars, "we got enough. Just come on."

"Why, thank you," said Jesse's father, "we be right along, then."

"I better get a sweater for the boy," said his mother, "in case it turns cold."

Jesse watched his mother's thin legs cross the yard. He knew that she also wanted to comb her hair a little and maybe put on a better dress, the dress she wore to church. His father guessed this, too, for he yelled behind her, "Now don't you go trying to turn yourself into no movie star. You just come on." But he laughed as he said this, and winked at the men; his wife was younger and prettier than most of the other women. He clapped Jesse on the head and started pulling him toward the car. "You all go on," he said. "I'll be right behind you. Jesse, you go tie up that there dog while I get this car started."

The cars sputtered and coughed and shook; the caravan began to move; bright dust filled the air. As soon as he was tied up, the dog began to bark. Jesse's mother came out of the house, carrying a jacket for his father and a sweater for Jesse. She had put a ribbon in her hair and had an old shawl around her shoulders.

"Put these in the car, son," she said, and handed everything to him. She bent down and stroked the dog, looked to see if there was water in his bowl, then went back up the three porch steps and closed the door.

"Come on," said his father, "ain't nothing in there for nobody to steal." He was sitting in the car, which trembled and belched. The last car of the caravan had disappeared but the sound of singing floated behind them.

Jesse got into the car, sitting close to his father, loving the smell of the car, and the trembling, and the bright day, and the sense of going on a great and unexpected journey. His mother got in and closed the door and the car began to move. Not until then did he ask, "Where are we going? Are we going on a picnic?"

He had a feeling that he knew where they were going, but he was not sure.

"That's right," his father said, "we're going on a picnic. You won't ever forget *this* picnic—!"

"Are we," he asked, after a moment, "going to see the bad nigger—the one that knocked down old Miss Standish?"

"Well, I reckon," said his mother, "that we *might* see him."

He started to ask, *Will a lot of niggers be there? Will Otis be there?*—but he did not ask his question, to which, in a strange and uncomfortable way, he already knew the answer. Their friends, in the other cars, stretched up the road as far as he could see; other cars had joined them; there were cars behind them. They were singing. The sun seemed suddenly very hot, and he was, at once very happy and a little afraid. He did not quite understand what was happening, and he did not know what to ask—he had no one to ask. He had grown accustomed, for the solution of such mysteries, to go to Otis. He felt that Otis knew everything. But he could not ask Otis about this. Anyway, he had not seen Otis for two days; he had not seen a black face anywhere for more than two days; and he now realized, as they began chugging up the long hill which eventually led to Harkness, that there were no black faces on the road this morning, no black people anywhere. From the houses in which they lived, all along the road, no smoke curled, no life stirred—maybe one or two chickens were to be seen, that was all. There was no one at the windows, no one in the yard, no one sitting on the porches, and the doors were closed. He had come this road many a time and seen women washing in the yard (there were no clothes on the clotheslines), men working in the fields, children playing in the dust; black men passed them on the road other mornings, other days, on foot, or in wagons, sometimes in cars, tipping their hats, smiling, joking, their teeth a solid white against their skin, their eyes as warm as the sun, the blackness of their skin like dull fire against the white of the blue or the grey of their torn clothes. They passed the nigger church—dead-white, desolate, locked up; and the graveyard, where no one knelt or walked, and he saw no flowers. He wanted to ask, *Where are they? Where are they all?* But he did not dare. As the hill grew steeper, the sun grew colder. He looked at his mother and his father. They looked straight ahead, seeming to be listening to the singing which echoed and echoed in this graveyard silence. They were strangers to him now. They were looking at something he could not see. His father's lips had a strange, cruel curve, he wet his lips from time to time, and swallowed. He was terribly aware of his father's tongue, it was as though he had never seen it before. And his father's body suddenly seemed immense, bigger than a mountain. His eyes, which were grey-green, looked yellow in the sunlight; or at least there was a light in them which he had never seen before. His mother patted her hair and adjusted the ribbon, leaning forward to look into the car mirror. "You look all right," said his father, and laughed. "When that nigger looks at you, he's going to swear he throwed his life away for nothing. Wouldn't be surprised if he don't come back to haunt you." And he laughed again.

The singing now slowly began to cease; and he realized that they were nearing their destination. They had reached a straight, narrow, pebbly road, with trees on either side. The sunlight filtered down on them from a great height, as though they were under-water; and the branches of the trees scraped against the cars with a tearing sound. To the right of them, and beneath them, invisible now, lay the town; and to the left, miles of trees which led to the high mountain range which his ancestors had crossed in order to settle in this valley. Now, all was silent, except for the bumping of the tires against the rocky road, the sputtering of motors, and the sound of a crying child. And they seemed to move more slowly. They were beginning to climb again. He watched the cars ahead as they toiled patiently upward, disappearing into the sunlight of the clearing. Presently, he felt their vehicle also rise, heard his father's changed breathing, the sunlight hit his face, the trees moved away from them, and they were there. As their car crossed the clearing, he looked around. There seemed to be millions, there were certainly hundreds of people in the clearing, staring toward something he could not see. There was a fire. He could not see the flames, but he smelled the smoke. Then they were on the other side of the clearing, among the trees again. His father drove off the road and parked the car behind a great many other cars. He looked down at Jesse.

"You all right?" he asked.

"Yes sir," he said.

"Well, come on, then," his father said. He reached over and opened the door on his mother's side. His mother stepped out first. They followed her into the clearing. At first he was aware only of confusion, of his mother and father greeting and being greeted, himself being handled, hugged, and patted, and told how much he had grown. The wind blew the smoke from the fire across the clearing into his eyes and nose. He could not see over the backs of the people in front of him. The sounds of laughing and cursing and wrath—and something else—rolled in waves from the front of the mob to the back. Those in front expressed their delight at what they saw, and this delight rolled backward, wave upon wave, across the clearing, more acrid than the smoke. His father reached down suddenly and sat Jesse on his shoulders.

Now he saw the fire—of twigs and boxes, piled high; flames made pale orange and yellow and thin as a veil under the steadier light of the sun; grey-blue smoke rolled upward and poured over their heads. Beyond the shifting curtain of fire and smoke, he made out first only a length of gleaming chain, attached to a great limb of the tree; then he saw that this chain bound two black hands together at the wrist, dirty yellow palm facing dirty yellow palm. The smoke poured up; the hands dropped out of sight; a cry went up from the crowd. Then the hands slowly came into view again, pulled upward by the chain. This time he saw the kinky, sweating, bloody head—he had never before seen a head with so much hair on it, hair so black and so tangled that it seemed like another jungle. The head was hanging. He saw the forehead, flat and high, with a kind of arrow of hair in the center, like he had, like his father had; they called it a widow's peak; and the mangled eye brows, the wide nose, the closed eyes, and the glinting eye lashes and the hanging lips, all streaming with blood and sweat. His hands were straight above his head. All his weight pulled downward from his hands; and he was a big man, a bigger man than his father, and black as an African jungle Cat, and naked. Jesse pulled upward; his father's hands held him firmly by the ankles. He wanted to say something, he did not know what, but nothing he said could have been heard, for now the crowd roared again as a man stepped forward and put more wood on the fire. The flames leapt up. He thought he heard the hanging man scream, but he was not sure. Sweat was pouring from the hair in his armpits, poured down his sides, over his chest, into his navel and his groin. He was lowered again; he was raised again. Now Jesse knew that he heard him scream. The head went back, the mouth wide open, blood bubbling from the mouth; the veins of the neck jumped out; Jesse clung to his father's neck in terror as the cry rolled over the crowd. The cry of all the people rose to answer the dying man's cry. He wanted death to come quickly. They wanted to make death wait; and it was they who held death, now, on a leash which they lengthened little by little. *What did he do?* Jesse wondered. *What did the man do? What did he do?*—but he could not ask his father. He was seated on his father's shoulders, but his father was far away. There were two older men, friends of his father's, raising and lowering the chain; everyone, indiscriminately, seemed to be responsible for the fire. There was no hair left on the nigger's privates, and the eyes, now, were wide open, as white as the eyes of a clown or a doll. The smoke now carried a terrible odor across the clearing, the odor of something burning which was both sweet and rotten.

He turned his head a little and saw the field of faces. He watched his mother's face. Her eyes were very bright, her mouth was open: she was more beautiful than he had ever seen her, and more strange. He began to feel a joy he had never felt before. He watched the hanging, gleaming body, the most beautiful and terrible object he had ever seen till then. One of his father's friends reached up and in his hands he held a knife: and Jesse wished that he had been that man. It was a long, bright knife and the sun seemed to catch it, to play with it, to caress it—it was brighter than the fire. And a wave of laughter swept the crowd. Jesse felt his father's hands on his ankles slip and tighten. The man with the knife walked toward the crowd, smiling slightly; as though this were a signal, silence fell; he heard his mother cough. Then the man with the knife walked up to the hanging body. He turned and smiled again. Now there was a silence all over the field. The hanging head looked up. It seemed fully conscious now, as though the fire had burned out terror and pain. The man with the knife took the nigger's privates in his hand, one hand, still smiling, as though he were weighing them. In the cradle of the one white hand, the nigger's privates seemed as remote as meat being weighed in the scales; but seemed heavier, too, much heavier, and Jesse felt his scrotum tighten; and huge, huge, much bigger than his father's, flaccid, hairless, the largest thing he had ever seen till then, and the blackest. The white hand stretched them, cradled them, caressed them. Then the dying man's eyes looked straight into Jesse's eyes—it could not have been as long as a second, but it seemed longer than a year. Then Jesse screamed, and the crowd screamed as the knife flashed, first up, then down, cutting the dreadful thing away, and the blood came roaring down. Then the crowd rushed forward, tearing at the body with their hands, with knives, with rocks, with stones, howling and cursing. Jesse's head, of its own weight, fell downward toward his father's head. Someone stepped forward and drenched the body with kerosene. Where the man had been, a great sheet of flame appeared. Jesse's father lowered him to the ground.

"Well, I told you," said his father, "you wasn't never going to forget *this* picnic." His father's face was full of sweat, his eyes were very peaceful. At that moment Jesse loved his father more than he had ever loved him. He felt that his father had carried him through a mighty test, had revealed to him a great secret which would be the key to his life forever.

"I reckon," he said. "I reckon."

Jesse's father took him by the hand and, with his mother a little behind them, talking and laughing with the other women, they walked through the crowd, across the clearing. The black body was on the ground, the chain which had held it was being rolled up by one of his father's friends. Whatever the fire had left undone, the hands and the knives and the stones of the people had accomplished. The head was caved in, one eye was torn out, one ear was hanging. But one had to look carefully to realize this, for it was, now, merely, a black charred object on the black, charred ground. He lay spread-eagled with what had been a wound between what had been his legs.

"They going to leave him here, then?" Jesse whispered.

"Yeah," said his father, "they'll come and get him by and by. I reckon we better get over there and get some of that food before it's all gone."

"I reckon," he muttered now to himself, "I reckon." Grace stirred and touched him on the thigh: the moonlight covered her like glory. Something bubbled up in him, his nature again returned to him. He thought of the boy in the cell; he thought of the man in the fire; he thought of the knife and grabbed himself and stroked himself and a terrible sound, something between a high laugh and a howl, came out of him and dragged his sleeping wife up on one elbow. She stared at him in a moonlight which had now grown cold as ice. He thought of the morning and grabbed her, laughing and crying, crying and laughing, and he whispered, as he stroked her, as he took her, "Come on, sugar, I'm going to do you like a nigger, just like a nigger, come on, sugar, and love me just like you'd love a nigger." He thought of the morning as he labored and she moaned, thought of morning as he labored harder than he ever had before, and before his labors had ended, he heard the first cock crow and the dogs begin to bark, and the sound of tires on the gravel road.

[1948]

For Thought

"Going to Meet the Man" illustrates an awakening of consciousness among whites and blacks in the American South. The plot of the story enables Baldwin to treat the failing confidence of a Southern deputy sheriff with insight and to chronicle the deputy sheriff's participation in two incidents of racial violence a generation apart. Beneath the blind mob violence lies the powerful motif of sexuality, which brutalizes both the oppressor and the oppressed. By choosing a general locale for the setting and by using flat characters, or characters with little individualization, Baldwin universalizes a pivotal era in American history.

For Discussion

1. What has Baldwin gained by telling his story from the point of view of a white deputy sheriff? What had he supposedly learned from his job collecting payments for a mail order house? How does he rationalize his brutality toward blacks?
2. How is the deputy sheriff affected by the beatings of blacks attempting to register? How is his experience a common one among the other whites in the town?
3. How is it ironic that the whites make a picnic out of their lynching party? How does the lynching itself resemble and differ from the white reaction to the black registration drive? Why does Baldwin end the story with an incident that had supposedly occurred a generation before the registration drive?

James Baldwin
Previous Condition

I woke up shaking, alone in my room. I was clammy cold with sweat; under me the sheet and the mattress were soaked. The sheet was gray and twisted like a rope. I breathed like I had been running.

I couldn't move for the longest while. I just lay on my back, spread-eagled, looking up at the ceiling, listening to the sounds of people getting up in other parts of the house, alarm clocks ringing and water splashing and doors opening and shutting and feet on the stairs. I could tell when people left for work: the hall doorway downstairs whined and shuffled as it opened and gave a funny kind of double slam as it closed. One thud and then a louder thud and then a little final click. While the door was open I could hear the street sounds too, horses' hoofs and delivery wagons and people in the streets and big trucks and motor cars screaming on the asphalt.

I had been dreaming. At night I dreamt and woke up in the morning trembling, but not remembering the dream, except that in the dream I had been running. I could not remember when the dream—or dreams—had started; it had been long ago. For long periods maybe, I would have no dreams at all. And then they would come back, every night, I would try not to go to bed, I would go to sleep frightened and wake up frightened and have another day to get through with the nightmare at my shoulder. Now I was back from Chicago, busted, living off my friends in a dirty furnished room downtown. The show I had been with had folded in Chicago. It hadn't been much of a part—or much of a show either, to tell the truth. I played a kind of intellectual Uncle Tom, a young college student working for his race. The playwright had wanted to prove he was a liberal, I guess. But, as I say, the show had folded and here I was, back in New York and hating it. I knew that I should be getting another job, making the rounds, pounding the pavement. But I didn't. I couldn't face it. It was summer. I seemed to be fagged out. And every day I hated myself more. Acting's a rough life, even if you're white. I'm not tall and I'm not good looking and I can't sing or dance and I'm not white; so even at the best of times I wasn't in much demand.

The room I lived in was heavy ceilinged, perfectly square, with walls the color of chipped dry blood. Jules Weissman, a Jewboy, had got the room for me. It's a room to sleep in, he said, or maybe to die in but God knows it wasn't meant to live in. Perhaps because the room was so hideous it had a fantastic array of light fixtures: one on the ceiling, one on the left wall, two on the right wall, and a lamp on the table beside my bed. My bed was in front of the window through which nothing ever blew but dust. It was a furnished room and they'd thrown enough stuff in it to furnish three rooms its size. Two easy chairs and a desk, the bed, the table, a straight-backed chair, a bookcase, a cardboard wardrobe; and my books and my suitcase, both unpacked; and my dirty clothes flung in a corner. It was the kind of room that defeated you. It had a fireplace, too, and a heavy marble mantelpiece and a great gray mirror above the mantelpiece. It was hard to see anything in the mirror very clearly—which was perhaps just as well—and it would have been worth your life to have started a fire in the fireplace.

"Well, you won't have to stay here long," Jules told me the night I came. Jules smuggled me in, sort of, after dark, when everyone had gone to bed.

"Christ, I hope not."

"I'll be moving to a big place soon," Jules said. "You can move in with me." He turned all the lights on. "Think it'll be all right for a while?" He sounded apologetic, as though he had designed the room himself.

"Oh, sure. D'you think I'll have any trouble?"

"I don't think so. The rent's paid. She can't put you out."

I didn't say anything to that.

"Sort of stay undercover," Jules said. "You know."

"Roger," I said.

I had been living there for three days, timing it so I left after everyone else had gone, coming back late at night when everyone else was asleep. But I knew it wouldn't work. A couple of the tenants had seen me on the stairs, a woman had surprised me coming out of the john. Every morning I waited for the landlady to come banging on the door. I didn't know what would happen. It might be all right. It might not be. But the waiting was getting me.

The sweat on my body was turning cold. Downstairs a radio was tuned in to the Breakfast Symphony. They were playing Beethoven. I sat up and lit a cigarette. "Peter," I said, "don't let them scare you to death. You're a man, too." I listened to Ludwig and I watched the smoke rise to the dirty ceiling. Under Ludwig's drums and horns I listened to hear footsteps on the stairs.

I'd done a lot of traveling in my time. I'd knocked about through St. Louis, Frisco, Seattle, Detroit, New Orleans, worked at just about everything. I'd run away from my old lady when I was about sixteen. She'd never been able to handle me. You'll never be nothin' *but* a bum, she'd say. We lived in an old shack in a town in New Jersey in the nigger part of town, the kind of houses colored people live in all over the U.S. I hated my mother for living there. I hated all the people in my neighborhood. They went to church and they got drunk. They were nice to the white people. When the landlord came around they paid him and took his crap.

The first time I was ever called nigger I was seven years old. It was a little white girl with long black curls. I used to leave the front of my house and go wandering by myself through town. This little girl was playing ball alone and as I passed her the ball rolled out of her hands into the gutter.

I threw it back to her.

"Let's play catch," I said.

But she held the ball and made a face at me.

"My mother don't let me play with niggers," she told me.

I did not know what the word meant. But my skin grew warm. I stuck my tongue out at her.

"I don't care. Keep your old ball." I started down the street.

She screamed after me: "Nigger, nigger, nigger!"

I screamed back: "Your mother was a nigger!"

I asked my mother what a nigger was.

"Who called you that?"

"I heard somebody say it."

"Who?"

"Just somebody."

"Go wash your face," she said. "You dirty as sin. Your supper's on the table."

I went to the bathroom and splashed water on my face and wiped my face and hands on the towel.

"You call that clean?" my mother cried. "Come here, boy!"

She dragged me back to the bathroom and began to soap my face and neck.

"You run around dirty like you do all the time, everybody'll call you a little nigger, you hear?" She rinsed my face and looked at my hands and dried me. "Now, go on and eat your supper."

I didn't say anything. I went to the kitchen and sat down at the table. I remember I wanted to cry. My mother sat down across from me.

"Mama," I said. She looked at me. I started to cry.

She came around to my side of the table and took me in her arms.

"Baby, don't fret. Next time somebody calls you nigger you tell them you'd rather be your color than be lowdown and nasty like some white folks is."

We formed gangs when I was older, my friends and I. We met white boys and their friends on the opposite sides of fences and we threw rocks and tin cans at each other. I'd come home bleeding. My mother would slap me and scold me and cry.

"Boy, you wanna get killed? You wanna end up like your father?"

My father was a bum and I had never seen him. I was named for him: Peter.

I was always in trouble: truant officers, welfare workers, everybody else in town.

"You ain't never gonna be nothin' *but* a bum," my mother said.

By and by older kids I knew finished school and got jobs and got married and settled down. They were going to settle down and bring more black babies into the world and pay the same rents for the same old shacks and it would go on and on—

When I was sixteen I ran away. I left a note and told Mama not to worry, I'd come back one day and I'd be all right. But when I was twenty-two she died. I came back and put my mother in the ground. Everything was like it had been. Our house had not been painted and the porch floor sagged and there was somebody's raincoat stuffed in the broken window. Another family was moving in.

Their furniture was stacked along the walls and their children were running through the house and laughing and somebody was frying pork chops in the kitchen. The oldest boy was tacking up a mirror.

Last year Ida took me driving in her big car and we passed through a couple of towns upstate. We passed some crumbling houses on the left. The clothes on the line were flying in the wind.

"Are people living there?" asked Ida.

"Just darkies," I said.

Ida passed the car ahead, banging angrily on the horn. "D'you know you're becoming paranoiac, Peter?"

"All right. All right. I know a lot of white people are starving too."

"You're damn right they are. I know a little about poverty myself."

Ida had come from the kind of family called shanty Irish. She was raised in Boston. She's a very beautiful woman who married young and married for money—so now I can afford to support attractive young men, she'd giggle. Her husband was a ballet dancer who was forever on the road. Ida suspected that he went with boys. Not that I give a damn, she said, as long as he leaves me alone. When we met last year she was thirty and I was twenty-five. We had a pretty stormy relationship but we stuck. Whenever I got to town I called her; whenever I was stranded out of town I'd let her know. We never let it get too serious. She went her way and I went mine.

In all this running around I'd learned a few things. Like a prizefighter learns to take a blow or a dancer learns to fall, I'd learned how to get by. I'd learned never to be belligerent with policemen, for instance. No matter who was right, I was certain to be wrong. What might be accepted as just good old American independence in someone else would be insufferable arrogance in me. After the first few times I realized that I had to play smart, to act out the role I was expected to play. I only had one head and it was too easy to get it broken. When I faced a policeman I acted like I didn't know a thing. I let my jaw drop and I let my eyes get big. I didn't give him any smart answers, none of the crap about my rights. I figured out what answers he wanted and I gave them to him. I never let him think he wasn't king. If it was more than routine, if I was picked up on suspicion of robbery or murder in the neighborhood, I looked as humble as I could and kept my mouth shut and prayed. I took a couple of beatings but I stayed out of prison and I stayed off chain gangs. That was also due to luck, Ida pointed out once. "Maybe it would've been better for you if you'd been a little less lucky. Worse things have happened than chain gangs. Some of them have happened to you."

There was something in her voice. "What are you talking about?" I asked.

"Don't lose your temper. I said maybe."

"You mean you think I'm a coward?"

"I didn't say that, Peter."

"But you meant that. Didn't you?"

"No. I didn't mean that. I didn't mean anything. Let's not fight."

There are times and places when a Negro can use his color like a shield. He can trade on the subterranean Anglo-Saxon guilt and get what he wants that way; or some of what he wants. He can trade on his nuisance value, his value as forbidden fruit; he can use it like a knife, he can twist it and get his vengeance that way. I knew these things long before I realized that I knew them and in the beginning I used them, not knowing what I was doing. Then when I began to see it, I felt betrayed. I felt beaten as a person. I had no honest place to stand.

This was the year before I met Ida. I'd been acting in stock companies and little theaters; sometimes fairly good parts. People were nice to me. They told me I had talent. They said it sadly, as though they were thinking, What a pity, he'll never get anywhere. I had got to the point where I resented praise and I resented pity and I wondered what people were thinking when they shook my hand. In New York I met some pretty fine people; easygoing, hard-drinking, flotsam and jetsam; and they liked me; and I wondered if I trusted them; if I was able any longer to trust anybody. Not on top, where all the world could see, but underneath where everybody lives.

Soon I would have to get up. I listened to Ludwig. He shook the little room like the footsteps of a giant marching miles away. On summer evenings (and maybe we would go this summer) Jules and Ida and I would go up to the Stadium and sit beneath the pillars on the cold stone steps. There it seemed to me the sky was far away; and I was not myself, I was high and lifted up. We never talked, the three of us. We sat and watched the blue smoke curl in the air and watched the orange tips of cigarettes. Every once in a while the boys who sold popcorn and soda pop and ice cream climbed the steep steps chattering; and Ida shifted slightly and touched her blue-black hair; and Jules scowled. I sat with my knee up, watching the lighted half-moon below, the blackcoated, straining conductor, the faceless men beneath him moving together in a rhythm like the sea. There were pauses in the music for the rushing, calling, halting piano. Everything would stop except the climbing soloist; he would reach a height and everything would join him, the violins first and then the horns; and then the deep blue bass and the flute and the bitter trampling drums; beating, beating and mounting together and stopping with a crash like daybreak. When I first heard the *Messiah* I was alone; my blood bubbled like fire and wine; I cried; like an infant crying for its mother's milk; or a sinner running to meet Jesus.

Now below the music I heard footsteps on the stairs. I put out my cigarette. My heart was beating so hard I thought it would tear my chest apart. Someone knocked on the door.

I thought: Don't answer. Maybe she'll go away.

But the knocking came again, harder this time.

Just a minute, I said. I sat on the edge of the bed and put on my bathrobe. I was trembling like a fool. For Christ's sake, Peter, you've been through this before. What's the worst thing that can happen? You won't have a room. The world's full of rooms.

When I opened the door the landlady stood there, red-and-whitefaced and hysterical.

"Who are you? I didn't rent this room to you."

My mouth was dry. I started to say something.

"I can't have no colored people here," she said. "All my tenants are complainin'. Women afraid to come home nights."

"They ain't gotta be afraid of me," I said. I couldn't get my voice up; it rasped and rattled in my throat; and I began to be angry. I wanted to kill her. "My friend rented this room for me," I said.

"Well, I'm sorry, he didn't have no right to do that, I don't have nothin' against you, but you gotta get out."

Her glasses blinked, opaque in the light on the landing. She was frightened to death. She was afraid of me but she was more afraid of losing her tenants. Her face was mottled with rage and fear, her breath came rushed and little bits of spittle gathered at the edges of her mouth; her breath smelled bad, like rotting hamburger on a July day.

"You can't put me out," I said. "This room was rented in my name." I started to close the door, as though the matter was finished: "I live here, see, this is my room, you can't put me out."

"You get outa my house!" she screamed. "I got the right to know who's in my house! This is a white neighborhood. I don't rent to colored people. Why don't you go on uptown, like you belong?"

"I can't stand niggers," I told her. I started to close the door again but she moved and stuck her foot in the way. I wanted to kill her, I watched her stupid, wrinkled frightened white face and I wanted to take a club, a hatchet, and bring it down with all my weight, splitting her skull down the middle where she parted her iron-grey hair.

"Get out of the door," I said. "I want to get dressed."

But I knew that she had won, that I was already on my way. We stared at each other. Neither of us moved. From her came an emanation of fear and fury and something else. You maggot-eaten bitch, I thought. I said evilly, "You wanna come in and watch me?" Her face didn't change, she didn't take her foot away. My skin prickled, tiny hot needles punctured my flesh. I was aware of my body under the bathrobe; and it was as though I had done something wrong, something monstrous, years ago, which no one had forgotten and for which I would be killed.

"If you don't get out," she said, "I'll get a policeman to put you out."

I grabbed the door to keep from touching her. "All right. All right. You can have the goddamn room. Now get out and let me dress."

She turned away. I slammed the door. I heard her going down the stairs. I threw stuff into my suitcase. I tried to take as long as possible but I cut myself while shaving because I was afraid she would come back upstairs with a policeman.

Jules was making coffee when I walked in.

"Good morning, good morning! What happened to you?"

"No room at the inn," I said. "Pour a cup of coffee for the notorious son of man." I sat down and dropped my suitcase on the floor.

Jules looked at me. "Oh. Well. Coffee coming up."

He got out the coffee cups. I lit a cigarette and sat there. I couldn't think of anything to say. I knew that Jules felt bad and I wanted to tell him that it wasn't his fault.

He pushed coffee in front of me and sugar and cream.

"Cheer up, baby. The world's wide and life—life, she is very long."

"Shut up. I don't want to hear any of your bad philosophy."

"Sorry."

"I mean, let's not talk about the good, the true, and the beautiful."

"All right. But don't sit there holding onto your table manners. Scream if you want to."

"Screaming won't do any good. Besides I'm a big boy now."

I stirred my coffee. "Did you give her a fight?" Jules asked.

I shook my head. "No."

"Why the hell not?"

I shrugged, a little ashamed now. I couldn't have won it. What the hell.

"You might have won it. You might have given her a couple of bad moments."

"Goddamit to hell, I'm sick of it. Can't I get a place to sleep without dragging it through the courts? I'm goddamn tired of battling every Tom, Dick, and Harry for what everybody else takes for granted. I'm tired, man, tired! Have you ever been sick to death of something? Well, I'm sick to death. And I'm scared. I've been fighting so goddamn long I'm not a person any more. I'm not Booker T. Washington. I've got no vision of emancipating anybody. I want to emancipate myself. If this goes on much longer, they'll send me to Bellevue, I'll blow my top, I'll break somebody's head. I'm not worried about that miserable little room. I'm worried about what's happening to me, *to me*, inside. I don't walk the streets, I crawl. I've never been like this before. Now when I go to a strange place I wonder what will happen, will I be accepted, if I'm accepted, can I accept?—"

"Take it easy," Jules said.

"Jules, I'm beaten."

"I don't think you are. Drink your coffee."

"Oh," I cried, "I know you think I'm making it dramatic, that I'm paranoiac and just inventing trouble! Maybe I think so sometimes, how can I tell? You get so used to being hit you find you're always waiting for it. Oh, I know, you're Jewish, you get kicked around, too, but you can walk into a bar and nobody *knows* you're Jewish and if you go looking for a job you'll get a better job than mine! How can I say what it feels like? I don't know. I know everybody's in trouble and nothing is easy, but how can I explain to you what it feels like to be black when I don't understand it and don't want to and spend all my time trying to forget it? I don't want to hate anybody—but now maybe, I can't love anybody either—are we friends? Can we be really friends?"

"We're friends," Jules said, "don't

worry about it." He scowled. "If I wasn't Jewish I'd ask you why you don't live in Harlem." I looked at him. He raised his hand and smiled—"But I'm Jewish, so I didn't ask you. Ah Peter," he said, "I can't help you—take a walk, get drunk, we're all in this together."

I stood up. "I'll be around later. I'm sorry."

"Don't be sorry. I'll leave my door open. Bunk here for awhile."

"Thanks," I said.

I felt that I was drowning; that hatred had corrupted me like cancer in the bone.

I saw Ida for dinner. We met in a restaurant in the Village, an Italian place in a gloomy cellar with candles on the tables.

It was not a busy night, for which I was grateful. When I came in there were only two other couples on the other side of the room. No one looked at me. I sat down in a corner booth and ordered a Scotch old-fashioned. Ida was late and I had three of them before she came.

She was very fine in black, a high-necked dress with a pearl choker; and her hair was combed page-boy style, falling just below her ears.

"You look real sweet, baby."

"Thank you. It took fifteen extra minutes but I hoped it would be worth it."

"It was worth it. What're you drinking?"

"Oh—what're you drinking?"

"Old-fashioneds."

She sniffed and looked at me. "How many?"

I laughed. "Three."

"Well," she said, "I suppose you had to do something." The waiter came over. We decided on one Manhattan and one lasagna and one spaghetti with clam sauce and another old-fashioned for me.

"Did you have a constructive day, sweetheart? Find a job?"

"Not today," I said. I lit her cigarette. "Metro offered me a fortune to come to the coast and do the lead in *Native Son* but I turned it down. Type casting, you know. It's so difficult to find a decent part."

"Well, if they don't come up with a decent offer soon tell them you'll go back to Selznick. *He'll* find you a part with guts—the very *idea* of offering you *Native Son!* I wouldn't stand for it."

"You ain't gotta tell me. I told them if they didn't find me a decent script in two weeks I was through, that's all."

"Now that's talking, Peter my lad."

The drinks came and we sat in silence for a minute or two. I finished half of my drink at a swallow and played with the toothpicks on the table. I felt Ida watching me.

"Peter, you're going to be awfully drunk."

"Honeychile, the first thing a southern gentleman learns is how to hold his liquor."

"That myth is older than the rock of ages. And anyway you come from Jersey."

I finished my drink and snarled at her: "That's just as good as the South."

Across the table from me I could see that she was readying herself for trouble: her mouth tightened slightly, setting her chin so that the faint cleft showed: "What happened to you today?"

I resented her concern; I resented my need. "Nothing worth talking about," I muttered, "just a mood."

And I tried to smile at her, to wipe away the bitterness.

"Now I know something's the matter. Please tell me."

It sounded trivial as hell: "You know the room Jules found for me? Well, the landlady kicked me out of it today."

"God save the American republic," Ida said. "D'you want to waste some of my husband's money? We can sue her."

"Forget it. I'll end up with lawsuits in every state in the union."

"Still, as a gesture—"

"The devil with the gesture. I'll get by."

The food came. I didn't want to eat. The first mouthful hit my belly like a gong. Ida began cutting up lasagna.

"Peter," she said, "try not to feel so badly. We're all in this together, the whole world. Don't let it throw you. What can't be helped you have to learn to live with."

"That's easy for you to say," I told her.

She looked at me quickly and looked away. "I'm not pretending that it's easy to do," she said.

I didn't believe that she could really understand it; and there was nothing I could say. I sat like a child being scolded, looking down at my plate, not eating, not saying anything. I wanted her to stop talking, to stop being intelligent about it, to stop being calm and grown-up about it; good Lord, none of us has ever grown up, we never will.

"It's no better anywhere else," she was saying. "In all of Europe there's famine and disease, in France and England they hate the Jews—nothing's going to change, baby, people are too empty-headed, too empty-hearted—it's always been like that, people always try to destroy what they don't understand—and they hate almost everything because they understand so little—"

I began to sweat in my side of the booth. I wanted to stop her voice. I wanted her to eat and be quiet and leave me alone. I looked around for the waiter so I could order another drink. But he was on the far side of the restaurant, waiting on some people who had just come in; a lot of people had come in since we had been sitting there.

"Peter," Ida said, "Peter please don't look like that."

I grinned: the painted grin of the professional clown. "Don't worry, baby, I'm all right. I know what I'm going to do. I'm gonna go back to my people where I belong and find me a nice, black nigger wench and raise me a flock of babies."

Ida had an old maternal trick; the grin tricked her into using it now. She raised her fork and rapped me with it across the knuckles. "Now, stop that. You're too old for that."

I screamed and stood up screaming and knocked the candle over: "Don't *do* that, you bitch, don't *ever* do that!"

She grabbed the candle and set it up and glared at me. Her face had turned perfectly white: "Sit down! Sit *down!*"

I fell back into my seat. My stomach felt like water. Everyone was looking at us. I turned cold, seeing what they were seeing: a black boy and a white woman, alone together. I knew it would take nothing to have them at my throat.

"I'm sorry," I muttered, "I'm sorry, I'm sorry."

The waiter was at my elbow. "Is everything all right, miss?"

"Yes, quite, thank you." She sounded like a princess dismissing a slave. I didn't look up. The shadow of the waiter moved away from me.

"Baby," Ida said, "forgive me, please forgive me."

I stared at the tablecloth. She put her hand on mine, brightness and blackness.

"Let's go," I said, "I'm terribly sorry."

She motioned for the check. When it came she handed the waiter a ten dollar bill without looking. She picked up her bag.

"Shall we go to a nightclub or a movie or something?"

"No, honey, not tonight." I looked at her. "I'm tired, I think I'll go on over to Jules's place. I'm gonna sleep on his floor for a while. Don't worry about me. I'm all right."

She looked at me steadily. She said: "I'll come see you tomorrow?"

"Yes, baby, please."

The waiter brought the change and she tipped him. We stood up; as we passed the tables (not looking at the people) the ground under me seemed falling, the doorway seemed impossibly far away. All my muscles tensed; I seemed ready to spring; I was waiting for the blow.

I put my hands in my pockets and we walked to the end of the block. The lights were green and red, the lights from the theater across the street exploded blue and yellow, off and on.

"Peter?"

"Yes?"

"I'll see you tomorrow?"

"Yeah. Come by Jules's. I'll wait for you."

"Goodnight, darling."

"Goodnight."

I started to walk away. I felt her eyes on my back. I kicked a bottle-top on the sidewalk.

God save the American republic.

I dropped into the subway and got on an uptown train, not knowing where it was going and not caring. Anonymous, islanded people surrounded me, behind newspapers, behind make-up, fat, fleshy masks and flat eyes. I watched the empty faces. (No one looked at me.) I looked at the ads, unreal women and pink-cheeked men selling cigarettes, candy, shaving cream, nightgowns, chewing gum, movies, sex; sex without organs, drier than sand and more secret than death. The train stopped. A white boy and a white girl got on. She was nice, short, svelte. Nice legs. She was hanging on his arm. He was the football type, blond, ruddy. They were dressed in summer clothes. The wind from the doors blew her print dress. She squealed, holding the dress at the knees and giggled and looked at him. He said something I didn't catch and she looked at me and the smile died. She stood so that she faced him and had her back to me. I looked back at the ads. Then I hated them. I wanted to do something to make them hurt, something that would crack the pink-cheeked mask. The white boy and I did not look at each other again. They got off at the next stop.

I wanted to keep on drinking. I got off in Harlem and went to a rundown bar on Seventh Avenue. My people, my people. Sharpies stood on the corner, waiting. Women in summer dresses pranced by on wavering heels. Click clack. Click clack. There were white mounted policemen in the streets. On every block there was another policeman on foot. I saw a black cop.

God save the American republic.

The juke box was letting loose with "Hamps' Boogie." The place was jumping, I walked over to the man.

"Rye," I said.

I was standing next to somebody's grandmother. "Hello, papa. What you puttin' down?"

"Baby, you can't pick it up," I told her. My rye came and I drank.

"Nigger," she said, "you must think you's somebody."

I didn't answer. She turned away, back to her beer, keeping time to the juke box, her face sullen and heavy and aggrieved. I watched her out of the side of my eye. She had been good looking once, pretty even, before she hit the bottle and started crawling into too many beds. She was flabby now, flesh heaved all over in her thin dress. I wondered what she'd be like in bed; then I realized that I was a little excited by her; I laughed and set my glass down.

"The same," I said. "And a beer chaser."

The juke box was playing something else now, something brassy and commercial which I didn't like. I kept on drinking, listening to the voices of my people, watching the faces of my people. (God pity us, the terrified republic.) Now I was sorry to have angered the woman who still sat next to me, now deep in conversation with another, younger woman. I longed for some opening, some sign, something to make me part of the life around me. But there was nothing except my color. A white outsider coming in would have seen a young Negro drinking in a Negro bar, perfectly in his element, in his place, as the saying goes. But the people here knew differently, as I did. I didn't seem to have a place.

So I kept on drinking by myself, saying to myself after each drink, Now I'll go. But I was afraid; I didn't want to sleep on Jules's floor; I didn't want to go to sleep. I kept on drinking and listening to the juke box. They were playing Ella Fitzgerald, "Cow-Cow Boogie."

"Let me buy you a drink," I said to the woman.

She looked at me, startled, suspicious, ready to blow her top.

"On the level," I said. I tried to smile. "Both of you."

"I'll take a beer," the young one said.

I was shaking like a baby. I finished my drink.

"Fine," I said. I turned to the bar.

"Baby," said the old one, "what's your story?"

The man put three beers on the counter.

"I got no story, Ma," I said.

[1948]

For Thought

In "Previous Condition," Baldwin utilizes the first-person point of view to explore the mind of a black man who is caught between a past that fills him with rage and a future that drives him to despair. In this story, the motif of "acting" has symbolical and ironical connotations. Peter had learned to act in his youth in order to protect himself from brutality and punishment. Though he has been acting all his life and has, thus, chosen acting as a career, Peter, because of his race, is considered not to have enough talent to gain lasting success as an actor. He is only allowed typecasting parts. In the end, he returns to a black ghetto, a "previous condition."

For Discussion

1. What sources of anxiety torment Peter at the beginning of the story? Who has chosen to befriend him, and why?
2. How is Peter's confrontation with the landlady like his first encounter with the white person who called him "nigger"? How is it different? Why doesn't he fight eviction?
3. What influence has the narrator's mother had on his life?
4. Why does the narrator first repel and then welcome friendliness in the Harlem bar? Has he resolved any of his problems?

James Baldwin
This Morning, This Evening, So Soon

"You are full of nightmares," Harriet tells me. She is in her dressing gown and has cream all over her face. She and my older sister, Louisa, are going out to be girls together. I suppose they have many things to talk about—they have *me* to talk about, certainly—and they do not want my presence. I have been given a bachelor's evening. The director of the film which has brought us such incredible and troubling riches will be along later to take me out to dinner.

I watch her face. I know that it is quite impossible for her to be as untroubled as she seems. Her self-control is mainly for my benefit—my benefit, and Paul's. Harriet comes from orderly and progressive Sweden and has reacted against all the advanced doctrines to which she has been exposed by becoming steadily and beautifully old-fashioned. We never fought in front of Paul, not even when he was a baby. Harriet does not so much believe in protecting children as she does in helping them to build a foundation on which they can build and build again, each time life's high-flying steel ball knocks down everything they have built.

Whenever I become upset, Harriet becomes very cheerful and composed. I think she began to learn how to do this over eight years ago, when I returned from my only visit to America. Now, perhaps, it has become something she could not control if she wished to. This morning, at breakfast, when I yelled at Paul, she averted Paul's tears and my own guilt by looking up and saying, "My God, your father is cranky this morning, isn't he?"

Paul's attention was immediately distracted from his wounds, and the unjust inflicter of those wounds, to his mother's laughter. He watched her.

"It is because he is afraid they will not like his songs in New York. Your father is an *artiste, mon chou,* and they are very mysterious people, *les artistes.* Millions of people are waiting for him in New York,

SOURCE: "This Morning, This Evening, So Soon" by James Baldwin. Copyright © 1960 by James Baldwin. Originally published in *Atlantic Monthly.* Reprinted from *Going to Meet the Man* by James Baldwin with permission of The Dial Press.

they are begging him to come, and they will give him a *lot* of money, but he is afraid they will not like him. Tell him he is wrong."

She succeeded in rekindling Paul's excitement about places he has never seen. I was also, at once, reinvested with all my glamour. I think it is sometimes extremely difficult for Paul to realize that the face he sees on record sleeves and in the newspapers and on the screen is nothing more or less than the face of his father—who sometimes yells at him. Of course, since he is only seven—going on eight, he will be eight years old this winter—he cannot know that I am baffled, too.

"Of course, you are wrong, you are silly," he said with passion—and caused me to smile. His English is strongly accented and is not, in fact, as good as his French, for he speaks French all day at school. French is really his first language, the first he ever heard. "You are the greatest singer in France"—sounding exactly as he must sound when he makes this pronouncement to his schoolmates—"the greatest *American* singer"—this concession was so gracefully made that it was not a concession at all, it added inches to my stature, America being only a glamorous word for Paul. It is the place from which his father came, and to which he now is going, a place which very few people have ever seen. But his aunt is one of them and he looked over at her. "Mme. Dumont says so, and she says he is a *great actor, too.*" Louisa nodded, smiling. "And she has seen *Les Fauves Nous Attendent*—five times." This clinched it, of course. Mme. Dumont is our concierge and she has known Paul all his life. I suppose he will not begin to doubt anything she says until he begins to doubt everything.

He looked over at me again. "So you are wrong to be afraid."

"I was wrong to yell at you, too. I won't yell at you any more today."

"All right." He was very grave.

Louisa poured more coffee. "He's going to knock them dead in New York. You'll see."

"*Mais bien sur,*" said Paul, doubtfully. He does not quite know what "knock them dead" means, though he was sure, from her tone, that she must have been agreeing with him. He does not quite understand this aunt, whom he met for the first time two months ago, when she arrived to spend the summer with us. Her accent is entirely different from anything he has ever heard. He does not really understand why, since she is my sister and his aunt, she should be unable to speak French.

Harriet, Louisa, and I looked at each other and smiled. "Knock them dead," said Harriet, "means *d'avoir un succès fou.* But you will soon pick up all the American expressions." She looked at me and laughed. "So will I."

"That's what he's afraid of." Louisa grinned. "We have *got* some expressions, believe me. Don't let anybody ever tell you America hasn't got a culture. Our culture is as thick as clabber milk."

"Ah," Harriet answered, "I know. I know."

"I'm going to be practicing later," I told Paul.

His face lit up. "*Bon.*" This meant that, later, he would come into my study and lie on the floor with his papers and crayons while I worked out with the piano and the tape recorder. He knew that I was offering this as an olive branch. All things considered, we get on pretty well, my son and I.

He looked over at Louisa again. She held a coffee cup in one hand and a cigarette in the other; and something about her baffled him. It was early, so she had not yet put on her face. Her short, thick, graying hair was rougher than usual, almost as rough as my own—later, she would be going to the hairdresser's; she is fairer than I, and better-looking; Louisa, in fact, caught all the looks in the family. Paul knows that she is my older sister and that she helped to raise me, though he does not, of course, know what this means. He knows that she is a schoolteacher in the *American* South, which is not, for some reason, the same place as South America. I could see him trying to fit all these exotic details together into a pattern which would explain her strangeness—strangeness of accent, strangeness of manner. In comparison with the people he has always known, Louisa must seem, for all her generosity and laughter and affection, peculiarly uncertain of herself, peculiarly hostile and embattled.

I wondered what he would think of his Uncle Norman, older and much blacker than I, who lives near the Alabama town in which we were born. Norman will meet us at the boat.

Now Harriet repeats, "Nightmares, nightmares. Nothing ever turns out as badly as you think it will—in fact," she adds laughing, "I am happy to say that that would scarcely be possible."

Her eyes seek mine in the mirror—dark-blue eyes, pale skin, black hair. I had always thought of Sweden as being populated entirely by blondes, and I thought that Harriet was abnormally dark for a Swedish girl. But when we visited Sweden, I found out differently. "It is all a great racial salad, Europe, that is why I am sure that I will never understand your country," Harriet said. That was in the days when we never imagined that we would be going to it.

I wonder what she is really thinking. Still, she is right, in two days we will be on a boat, and there is simply no point in carrying around my load of apprehension. I sit down on the bed, watching her fix her face. I realize that I am going to miss this old-fashioned bedroom. For years, we've talked about throwing out the old junk which came with the apartment and replacing it with less massive, modern furniture. But we never have.

"Oh, everything will probably work out," I say. "I've been in a bad mood all day long. I just can't sing any more." We both laugh. She reaches for a wad of tissues and begins wiping off the cream. "I wonder how Paul will like it, if he'll make friends—that's all."

"Paul will like any place where you are, where we are. Don't you worry about Paul."

Paul has never been called any names, so far. Only, once he asked us what the word *métis* meant and Harriet explained to him that it meant mixed blood, adding that the blood of just about everybody in the world was mixed by now. Mme. Dumont contributed bawdy and detailed corroboration from her own family tree, the roots of which were somewhere in Corsica; the moral of the story, as she told it, was that women were weak, men incorrigible, and *le bon Dieu* appallingly clever. Mme. Dumont's version is the version I prefer, but it may not be, for Paul, the most utilitarian.

Harriet rises from the dressing table and comes over to sit in my lap. I fall back with her on the bed, and she smiles down into my face.

"Now, don't worry," she tells me, "please try not to worry. Whatever is coming, we will manage it all very well, you will see. We have each other and we have our son and we know what we want. So, we are luckier than most people."

I kiss her on the chin. "I'm luckier than most men."

"I'm a very lucky woman, too."

And for a moment we are silent, alone in our room, which we have shared so long. The slight rise and fall of Harriet's breathing creates an intermittent pressure against my chest, and I think how, if I had never left America, I would never have met her and would never have established a life of my own, would never have entered my own life. For everyone's life begins on a level where races, armies, and churches stop. And yet everyone's life is always shaped by races, churches, and armies; races, churches, armies menace, and have taken, many lives. If Harriet had been born in America, it would have taken her a long time, perhaps forever, to look on me as a man like other men; if I had met her in

America, I would never have been able to look on her as a woman like all other women. The habits of public rage and power would also have been our private compulsions, and would have blinded our eyes. We would never have been able to love each other. And Paul would never have been born.

Perhaps, if I had stayed in America, I would have found another woman and had another son. But that other woman, that other son are in the limbo of vanished possibilities. I might also have become something else, instead of an actor-singer, perhaps a lawyer, like my brother, or a teacher, like my sister. But no, I am what I have become and this woman beside me is my wife, and I love her. All the sons I might have had mean nothing, since I *have* a son, I named him, Paul, for my father, and I love him.

I think of all the things I have seen destroyed in America, all the things that I have lost there, all the threats it holds for me and mine.

I grin up at Harriet. "Do you love me?"

"Of course not. I simply have been madly plotting to get to America all these years."

"What a patient wench you are."

"The Swedes are very patient."

She kisses me again and stands up. Louisa comes in, also in a dressing gown.

"I hope you two aren't sitting in her yakking about the *subject*." She looks at me. "My, you are the sorriest-looking celebrity I've ever seen. I've always wondered why people like you hired press agents. Now I know." She goes to Harriet's dressing table. "Honey, do you mind if I borrow some of the *mad* nail polish?"

Harriet goes over to the dressing table. "I'm not sure I know *which* mad nail polish you mean."

Harriet and Louisa, somewhat to my surprise, get on very well. Each seems to find the other full of the weirdest and most delightful surprises. Harriet has been teaching Louisa French and Swedish expressions, and Louisa has been teaching Harriet some of the saltier expressions of the black South. Whenever one of them is not playing straight man to the other's accent, they become involved in long speculations as to how a language reveals the history and the attitudes of a people. They discovered that all the European languages contain a phrase equivalent to "to work like a nigger." ("Of course," says Louisa, "they've had black men working for them for a long time.") "Language is experience and language is power," says Louisa, after regretting that she does not know any of the African dialects. "That's what I keep trying to tell those dirty bastards down South. They get their own experience into the language, we'll have a great language. But, no, they all want to talk like white folks." Then she leans forward, grasping Harriet by the knee. "I tell them, honey, white folks ain't saying *nothing*. Not a thing are they saying—and *some* of them know it, they *need* what you got, the whole world needs it." Then she leans back, in disgust. "You think they listen to me? Indeed they do not. They just go right on, trying to talk like white folks." She leans forward again, in tremendous indignation. "You know some of them folks are *ashamed* of Mahalia Jackson? *Ashamed* of her, one of the greatest singers alive! They think she's common." Then she looks about the room as though she held a bottle in her hand and were looking for a skull to crack.

I think it is because Louisa has never been able to talk like this to any white person before. All the white people she has ever met needed, in one way or another, to be reassured, consoled, to have their consciences pricked but not blasted; could not, could not afford to hear a truth which would shatter, irrevocably, their image of themselves. It is astonishing the lengths to which a person, or a people, will go in order to avoid a truthful mirror. But Harriet's necessity is precisely the opposite: it is of the utmost importance that she learn everything that Louisa can tell her, and then learn more, much more. Harriet is really trying to learn from Louisa how best to protect her husband and her son. This is why they are going out alone tonight. They will have, tonight, as it were, a final council of war. I may be moody, but they, thank God, are practical.

Now Louisa turns to me while Harriet rummages about on the dressing table. "What time is Vidal coming for you?"

"Oh, around seven-thirty, eight o'clock. He says he's reserved tables for us in some very chic place, but he won't say where." Louisa wriggles her shoulders, raises her eyebrows, and does a tiny bump and grind. I laugh. "That's right. And then I guess we'll go out and get drunk."

"I hope to God you do. You've been about as cheerful as a cemetery these last few days. And, that way, your hangover will keep you from bugging us tomorrow."

"What about *your* hangovers? I know the way you girls drink."

"Well, we'll be paying for our own drinks," says Harriet, "so I don't think we'll have that problem. But *you're* going to be feted, like an international movie star."

"You sure you don't want to change your mind and come out with Vidal and me?"

"We're sure," Louisa says. She looks down at me and gives a small, amused grunt. "An international movie star. And I used to change your diapers. I'll be damned." She is grave for a moment. "Mama'd be proud of you, you know that?" We look at each other and the air between us is charged with secrets which not even Harriet will ever know. "Now, get the hell out of here, so we can get dressed."

"I'll take Paul on down to Mme. Dumont's."

Paul is to have supper with her children and spend the night there.

"For the last time," says Mme. Dumont and she rubs her hand over Paul's violently curly black hair. "*Tu vas nous manquer, tu sais?*" Then she looks up at me and laughs. "He doesn't care. He is only interested in seeing the big ship and all the wonders of New York. Children are never sad to make journeys."

"I would be very sad to go," says Paul, "but my father must go to New York to work and he wants me to come with him."

Over his head, Mme. Dumont and I smile at each other. "*Il est malin, ton gosse!*" She looks down at him again. "And do you think, my little diplomat, that you will like New York?"

"We aren't only going to New York," Paul answers, "we are going to California, too."

"Well, do you think you will like California?"

Paul looks at me. "I don't know. If we don't like it, we'll come back."

"So simple. Just like that," says Mme. Dumont. She looks at me. "It is the best way to look at life. Do come back. You know, we feel that you belong to us, too, here in France."

"I hope you do," I say. "I hope you do. I have always felt—always felt at home here." I bend down and Paul and I kiss each other on the cheek. We have always done so—but will we be able to do so in America? American fathers never kiss American sons. I straighten, my hand on Paul's shoulder. "You be good. I'll pick you up for breakfast, or, if you get up first you come and pick me up and we can hang out together tomorrow, while your *Maman* and your Aunt Louisa finish packing. They won't want two men hanging around the house."

"*D'accord.* Where shall we hang out?" On the last two words he stumbles a little and imitates me.

"Maybe we can go to the zoo, I don't know. And I'll take you to lunch at the Eiffel Tower, would you like that?"

"Oh, yes," he says, "I'd love that." When he is pleased, he seems to glow. All the energy of his small, tough, concentrated being charges an unseen battery and adds an incredible luster to his eyes, which are large and dark brown—like mine—and to his skin, which always reminds me of the colors of honey and the fires of the sun.

"Ok, then." I shake hands with Mme. Dumont. "*Bonsoir, Madame.*" I ring for the elevator, staring at Paul. "*Ciao, Pauli.*"

"*Bonsoir, Papa.*"

And Mme. Dumont takes him inside.

Upstairs, Harriet and Louisa are finally powdered, perfumed, and jeweled, and ready to go: dry martinis at the Ritz, supper, "in some *very* expensive little place," says Harriet, and perhaps the Folies Bergère afterwards. "A real cornball, tourist evening," says Louisa. "I'm working on the theory that if I can get Harriet to act like an American now, she won't have so much trouble later."

"I very much doubt," Harriet says, "that I will be able to endure the Folies Bergère for three solid hours."

"Oh, then we'll duck across town to Harry's New York bar and drink mint juleps," says Louisa.

I realize that, quite apart from everything else, Louisa is having as much fun as she has ever had in her life. Perhaps she, too, will be sad to leave Paris, even though she has only known it for such a short time.

"Do people drink those in New York?" Harriet asks. I think she is making a list of the things people do or do not do in New York.

"*Some* people do." Louisa winks at me. "Do you realize that this Swedish chick's picked up an Alabama drawl?"

We laugh together. The elevator chugs to a landing.

"We'll stop and say goodnight to Paul," Harriet says. She kisses me. "Give our best to Vidal."

"Right. Have a good time. Don't let any Frenchmen run off with Louisa."

"I did not come to Paris to be protected, and if I had, this wild chick *you* married couldn't do it. I just *might* upset everybody and come home with a French count." She presses the elevator button and the cage goes down.

I walk back into our dismantled apartment. It stinks of departure. There are bags and crates in the hall which will be taken away tomorrow, there are no books in the bookcases, the kitchen looks as though we never cooked a meal there, never dawdled there, in the early morning or late at night, over coffee. Presently, I must shower and shave but now I pour myself a drink and light a cigarette and step out on our balcony. It is dusk, the brilliant light of Paris is beginning to fade, and the green of the trees is darkening.

I have lived in this city for twelve years. This apartment is on the top floor of a corner building. We look out over the trees and the roof tops of the Champ de Mars, where the Eiffel Tower stands. Beyond this field is the river, which I have crossed so often, in so many states of mind. I have crossed every bridge in Paris, I have walked along every *quai*. I know the river as one finally knows a friend, know it when it is black, guarding all the lights of Paris in its depths, and seeming, in its vast silence, to be communing with the dead who lie beneath it; when it is yellow, evil, and roaring, giving a rough time to tugboats and barges, and causing people to remember that it has been known to rise, it has been known to kill; when it is peaceful, a slick dark, dirty green, playing host to rowboats and *les bateaux mouches* and throwing up from time to time an extremely unhealthy fish. The men who stand along the *quais* all summer with their fishing lines gratefully accept the slimy object and throw it in a rusty can. I have always wondered who eats those fish.

And I walk up and down, up and down, glad to be alone.

It is August, the month when all Parisians desert Paris and one has to walk miles to find a barbershop or a laundry open in some tree-shadowed, silent side street. There is a single person on the avenue, a paratrooper walking toward École Militaire. He is also walking, almost certainly, and rather sooner than later, toward Algeria. I have a friend, a good-natured boy who was always hanging around the clubs in which I worked in the old days, who has just returned from Algeria, with a recurring, debilitating fever, and minus one eye. The government has set his pension at the sum, arbitrary if not occult, of fifty-three thousand francs every three months. Of course, it is quite impossible to live on this amount of money without working—but who will hire a half-blind invalid? This boy has been spoiled forever, long before his thirtieth birthday, and there are thousands like him all over France.

And there are fewer Algerians to be found on the streets of Paris now. The rug sellers, the peanut vendors, the postcard peddlers and money-changers have vanished. The boys I used to know during my first years in Paris are scattered—or corralled—the Lord knows where.

Most of them had no money. They lived three and four together in rooms with a single skylight, a single hard cot, or in buildings that seemed abandoned, with cardboard in the windows, with erratic plumbing in a wet, cobblestoned yard, in dark, dead-end alleys, or on the outer, chilling heights of Paris.

The Arab cafés are closed—those dark, acrid cafés in which I used to meet with them to drink tea, to get high on hashish, to listen to the obsessive, stringed music which has no relation to any beat, any time, that I have ever known. I once thought of the North Africans as my brothers and that is why I went to their cafés. They were very friendly to me, perhaps one or two of them remained really fond of me even after I could no longer afford to smoke Lucky Strikes and after my collection of American sport shirts had vanished—mostly into their wardrobes. They seemed to feel that they had every right to them, since I could only have wrested these things from the world by cunning—it meant nothing to say that I had had no choice in the matter; perhaps I had wrested these things from the world by treason, by refusing to be identified with the misery of my people. Perhaps, indeed, I identified myself with those who were responsible for this misery.

And this was true. Their rage, the only note in all their music which I could not fail to recognize, to which I responded, yet had the effect of setting us more than ever at a division. They were perfectly prepared to drive all Frenchmen into the sea, and to level the city of Paris. But I could not hate the French, because they left me alone. And I love Paris, I will always love it, it is the city which saved my life. It saved my life by allowing me to find out who I am.

It was on a bridge, one tremendous, April morning, that I knew I had fallen in love. Harriet and I were walking hand in hand. The bridge was the Pont Royal, just before us was the great *horloge*, high and lifted up, saying ten to ten; beyond this, the golden statue of Joan of Arc, with her sword uplifted. Harriet and I were silent, for we had been quarreling about something. Now, when I look back, I think we had reached that state when an affair must either end or become something more than an affair.

I looked sideways at Harriet's face, which was still. Her dark-blue eyes were narrowed against the sun, and her full, pink lips were still slightly sulky, like a child's. In those days, she hardly ever wore make-up. I was in my shirt sleeves. Her face made me want to laugh and run my hand over her short dark hair. I wanted to pull her to me and say, *Baby, don't be mad at me,* and at that moment something tugged at my heart and made me catch my breath. There were millions of people all around us, but I was alone with Harriet. She was alone with me. Never, in all my life, until that moment, had I been alone with anyone. The world had always been with us, between us, defeating the quarrel we could not achieve, and making love impossible. During all the years of my life, until that moment, I had carried the menacing, the hostile, killing world with me everywhere. No matter what I was doing or saying or feeling, one eye had always been on the world—that world which I had learned to distrust almost as soon as I learned my name, that world on which I knew one could never turn one's back, the white man's world. And for the first time in my life I was free of it; it had not existed for me; I had been quarreling with my girl. It was our quarrel, it was entirely between us, it had nothing to do with anyone else in the world. For the first time in my life I had not been afraid of the patriotism of the mindless, in uniform or out, who would beat me up and treat the woman who was with me as though she were the lowest of untouchables. For the first time in my life I felt that no force jeopardized my right, my power, to possess and to protect a woman; for the first time, the first time, felt that the woman was not, in her own eyes or in the eyes of the world, degraded by my presence.

The sun fell over everything, like a blessing, people were moving all about us, I will never forget the feeling of Harriet's small hand in mine, dry and trusting, and I turned to her, slowing our pace. She looked up at me with her enormous, blue eyes, and she seemed to wait. I said, "*Harriet. Harriet. Tu sais, il y a quelque chose de très grave qui m'est arrivé. Je t'aime. Je t'aime. Tu me comprends*, or shall I say it in English?"

This was eight years ago, shortly before my first and only visit home.

That was when my mother died. I stayed in America for three months. When I came back, Harriet thought that the change in me was due to my grief—I was very silent, very thin. But it had not been my mother's death which accounted for the change. I had known that my mother was going to die. I had not known what America would be like for me after nearly four years away.

I remember standing at the rail and watching the distance between myself and Le Havre increase. Hands fell, ceasing to wave, handkerchiefs ceased to flutter, people turned away, they mounted their bicycles or got into their cars and rode off. Soon, Le Havre was nothing but a blur. I thought of Harriet, already miles from me in Paris, and I pressed my lips tightly together in order not to cry.

Then, as Europe dropped below the water, as the days passed and passed, as we left behind us the skies of Europe and the eyes of everyone on the ship began, so to speak, to refocus, waiting for the first glimpse of America, my apprehension began to give way to a secret joy, a checked anticipation. I thought of such details as showers, which are rare in Paris, and I thought of such things as rich, cold, American milk and heavy, chocolate cake. I wondered about my friends, wondered if I had any left, and wondered if they would be glad to see me.

The Americans on the boat did not seem to be so bad, but I was fascinated, after such a long absence from it, by the nature of their friendliness. It was a friendliness which did not suggest, and was not intended to suggest, any possibility of friendship. Unlike Europeans, they dropped titles and used first names almost at once, leaving themselves, unlike the Europeans, with nowhere thereafter to go. Once one had become "Pete" or "Jane" or "Bill" all that could decently be known was known and any suggestion that there might be further depths, a person, so to speak, behind the name, was taken as a violation of that privacy which did not, paradoxically, since they trusted it so little, seem to exist among Americans. They apparently equated privacy with the unspeakable things they did in the bathroom or the bedroom, which they related only to the analyst, and then read about in the pages of best sellers. There was an eerie and unnerving irreality about everything they said and did, as though they were all members of the same team and were acting on orders from some invincibly cheerful and tirelessly inventive coach. I was fascinated by it. I found it oddly moving, but I cannot say that I was displeased. It had not occurred to me before that Americans, who had never treated me with any respect, had no respect for each other.

On the last night but one, there was a gala in the big ballroom and I sang. It had been a long time since I had sung before so many Americans. My audience had mainly been penniless French students, in the weird, Left Bank bistros I worked in those days. Still, I was a great hit with them and by this time I had become enough of a drawing card, in the Latin quarter and in St. Germain des Prés, to have attracted a couple of critics, to have had my picture in *France-soir*, and to have acquired a legal work permit which allowed me to make a little more money. Just the same, no matter how industrious and brilliant some of the musicians had been, or how devoted my audience, they did not know, they could not know, what my songs came out of. They did not know what was funny about it. It was impossible to translate: It damn well better be funny, or Laughing to keep from crying, or What did *I* do to be so black and blue?

The moment I stepped out on the floor, they began to smile, something opened in them, they were ready to be pleased. I found in their faces, as they watched me, smiling, waiting, an artless relief, a profound reassurance. Nothing was more familiar to them than the sight of a dark boy, singing, and there were few things on earth more necessary. It was under cover of darkness, my own darkness, that I could sing for them of the joys, passions, and terrors they smuggled about with them like steadily depreciating contraband. Under cover of the midnight fiction that I was unlike them because I was black, they could stealthily gaze at those treasures which they had been mysteriously forbidden to possess and were never permitted to declare.

I sang *I'm Coming, Virginia*, and *Take This Hammer*, and *Precious Lord*. They wouldn't let me go and I came back and sang a couple of the oldest blues I knew. Then someone asked me to sing *Swanee River*, and I did, astonished that I could, astonished that this song, which I had put down long ago, should have the power to move me. Then, if only, perhaps, to make the record complete, I wanted to sing *Strange Fruit*, but, on this number, no one can surpass the great, tormented Billie Holiday. So I finished with *Great Getting-Up Morning* and I guess I can say that if I didn't stop the show I certainly ended it. I got a big hand and I drank at a few tables and I danced with a few girls.

After one more day and one more night, the boat landed in New York. I woke up, I was bright awake at once, and I thought, *We're here.* I turned on all the lights in my small cabin and I stared into the mirror as though I were committing my face to memory. I took a shower and I took a long time shaving and I dressed myself very carefully. I walked the long ship corridors to the dining room, looking at the luggage piled high before the elevators and beside the steps. The dining room was nearly half empty and full of a quick and joyous excitement which depressed me even more. People ate quickly, chattering to each other, anxious to get upstairs and go on deck. Was it my imagination or was it true that they seemed to avoid my eyes? A few people waved and smiled, but let me pass; perhaps it would have made them uncomfortable, this morning, to try to share their excitement with me; perhaps they did not want to know whether or not it was possible for me to share it. I walked to my table and sat down. I munched toast as dry as paper and drank a pot of coffee. Then I tipped my waiter, who bowed and smiled and called me "sir" and said that he hoped to see me on the boat again. "I hope so, too," I said.

And was it true, or was it my imagination, that a flash of wondering comprehension, a flicker of wry sympathy, then appeared in the waiter's eyes? I walked upstairs to the deck.

There was a breeze from the water but the sun was hot and made me remember how ugly New York summers could be. All of the deck chairs had been taken away and people milled about in the space where the deck chairs had been, moved from one side of the ship to the other, clambered up and down the steps, crowded the rails, and they were busy taking photographs—of the harbor, of each other, of the sea, of the gulls. I walked slowly along the deck, and an impulse stronger than myself drove me to the rail. There it was, the great, unfinished city, with all its towers blazing in the sun. It came toward us slowly and patiently, like some enormous, cunning, and murderous beast, ready to devour, impossible to escape. I watched it come closer and I listened to the people around me, to their excitement and their pleasure. There was no doubt that it was real. I watched their shining faces and wondered if I were mad. For a moment I longed, with all my heart, to be able to feel whatever they were feeling, if only to know what such a feeling was like. As the boat moved slowly into the harbor, they were being moved into safety. It was only I who was being floated into danger. I turned my head, looking for Europe, but all that stretched behind me was the sky, thick with gulls. I moved away from the rail. A big, sandy-haired man held his daughter on his shoulders, showing her the Statue of Liberty. I would never know what this statue meant to others, she had always been an ugly joke for me. And the American flag was flying from the top of the ship, above my head. I had seen the French flag drive the French into the most unspeakable frenzies, I had seen the flag which was nominally mine used to dignify the vilest purposes: now I would never, as long as I lived, know what others saw when they saw a flag. "There's no place like home," said a voice close by, and I thought, *There damn sure isn't*. I decided to go back to my cabin and have a drink.

There was a cablegram from Harriet in my cabin. It said: Be good. Be quick. I'm waiting. I folded it carefully and put it in my breast pocket. Then I wondered if I would ever get back to her. How long would it take me to earn the money to get out of this land? Sweat broke out on my forehead and I poured myself some whiskey from my nearly empty bottle. I paced the tiny cabin. It was silent. There was no one down in the cabins now.

I was not sober when I faced the uniforms in the first-class lounge. There were two of them; they were not unfriendly. They looked at my passport, they looked at me. "You've been away a long time," said one of them.

"Yes," I said, "it's been a while."

"What did you do over there all that time?"—with a grin meant to hide more than it revealed, which hideously revealed more than it could hide.

I said, "I'm a singer," and the room seemed to rock around me. I held on to what I hoped was a calm, open smile. I had not had to deal with these faces in so long that I had forgotten how to do it. I had once known how to pitch my voice precisely between curtness and servility, and known what razor's edge of a pickaninny's smile would turn away wrath. But I had forgotten all the tricks on which my life had once depended. Once I had been an expert at baffling these people, at setting their teeth on edge, and dancing just outside the trap laid for me. But I was not an expert now. These faces were no longer merely the faces of two white men, who were my enemies. They were the faces of two white people whom I did not understand, and I could no longer plan my moves in accordance with what I knew of their cowardice and their needs and their strategy. That moment on the bridge had undone me forever.

"That's right," said one of them, "that's what it says, right here on the passport. Never heard of you, though." They looked up at me. "Did you do a lot of singing over there?"

"Some."

"What kind—concerts?"

"No." I wondered what I looked like, sounded like. I could tell nothing from their eyes. "I worked a few nightclubs."

"Nightclubs, eh? I guess they liked you over there."

"Yes," I said, "they seemed to like me all right."

"Well"—and my passport was stamped and handed back to me—"let's hope they like you over here."

"Thanks." They laughed—was it at me, or was it my imagination? and I picked up the one bag I was carrying and threw my trench coat over one shoulder and walked out of the first-class lounge. I stood in the slow-moving, murmuring line which led to the gangplank. I looked straight ahead and watched heads, smiling faces, step up to the shadow of the gangplank awning and then swiftly descend out of sight. I put my passport back in my breast pocket—*Be quick. I'm waiting*— and I held my landing card in my hand. Then, suddenly, there I was, standing on the edge of the boat, staring down the long ramp to the ground. At the end of the plank, on the ground, stood a heavy man in a uniform. His cap was pushed back from his gray hair and his face was red and wet. He looked up at me. This was the face I remembered, the face of my nightmares; perhaps hatred had caused me to know this face better than I would ever know the face of any lover. "Come on, boy," he cried, "come on, come on!"

And I almost smiled. I was home. I touched my breast pocket. I thought of a song I sometimes sang, *When will I ever get to be a man?* I came down the gangplank, stumbling a little, and gave the man my landing card.

Much later in the day, a customs inspector checked my baggage and waved me away. I picked up my bags and started walking down the long stretch which led to the gate, to the city.

And I heard someone call my name.

I looked up and saw Louisa running toward me. I dropped my bags and grabbed her in my arms and tears came to my eyes and rolled down my face. I did not know whether the tears were for joy at seeing her, or from rage, or both.

"How are you? How are you? You look wonderful, but, oh, haven't you lost weight? It's wonderful to see you again."

I wiped my eyes. "It's wonderful to see you, too, I bet you thought I was never coming back."

Louisa laughed. "I wouldn't have blamed you if you hadn't. These people are just as corny as ever, I swear I don't believe there's any hope for them. How's your French? Lord, when I think that it was I who studied French and now I can't speak a word. And you never went near it and you probably speak it like a native."

I grinned. "*Pas mal. Te me défends pas mal.*" We started down the wide steps into the street. "My God," I said. "New York." I was not aware of its towers now. We were in the shadow of the elevated highway but the thing which most struck me was neither light nor shade, but noise. It came from a million things at once, from trucks and tires and clutches and brakes and doors; from machines shuttling and stamping and rolling and cutting and pressing; from the building of tunnels, the checking of gas mains, the laying of wires, the digging of foundations; from the chattering of rivets, the scream of the pile driver, the clanging of great shovels; from the battering down and the raising up of walls; from millions of radios and television sets and juke boxes. The human voices distinguished themselves from the roar only by their note of strain and hostility. Another fleshy man, uniformed and red faced, hailed a cab for us and touched his cap politely but could only manage a peremptory growl: "Right this way, miss. Step up, sir." He slammed the cab door behind us. Louisa directed the driver to the New Yorker Hotel.

"Do they take us there?"

She looked at me. "They got laws in New York, honey, it'd be the easiest thing in the world to spend all your time in court. But over at the New Yorker, I believe they've already got the message." She took my arm. "You see? In spite of all this chopping and booming, this place hasn't really changed very much. You still can't hear yourself talk."

And I thought to myself, Maybe that's the point.

Early the next morning we checked out of the hotel and took the plane for Alabama.

I am just stepping out of the shower when I hear the bell ring. I dry myself hurriedly and put on a bathrobe. It is Vidal, of course, and very elegant he is, too, with his bushy gray hair quite lustrous, his swarthy, cynical, gypsylike face shaved and lotioned. Usually he looks just any old way. But tonight his brief bulk is contained in a dark-blue suit and he has an ironical pearl stickpin in his blue tie.

"Come in, make yourself a drink. I'll be with you in a second."

"I am, *hélas!*, on time. I trust you will forgive me for my thoughtlessness."

But I am already back in the bathroom. Vidal puts on a record: Mahalia Jackson, singing *I'm Going to Live the Life I Sing About in My Song.*

When I am dressed, I find him sitting in a chair before the open window. The daylight is gone, but it is not exactly dark. The trees are black now against the darkening sky. The lights in windows and the lights of motorcars are yellow and ringed. The street lights have not yet been turned on. It is as though, out of deference to the departed day, Paris waited a decent interval before assigning her role to a more theatrical but inferior performer.

Vidal is drinking a whiskey and soda. I pour myself a drink. He watches me.

"Well. How are you, my friend? You are nearly gone. Are you happy to be leaving us?"

"No." I say this with more force than I had intended. Vidal raises his eyebrows, looking amused and distant. "I never really intended to go back there. I certainly never intended to raise my kid there—"

"*Mais, mon cher,*" Vidal says, calmly, "you are an intelligent man, you must have known that you would probably be returning one day." He pauses. "And, as for Pauli—did it never occur to you that he might wish one day to see the country in which his father and his father's fathers were born?"

"To do that, really, he'd have to go to Africa."

"America will always mean more to him than Africa, you know that."

"I don't know." I throw my drink down and pour myself another. "Why should he want to cross all that water just to be called a nigger? America never gave him anything."

"It gave him his father."

I look at him. "You mean, his father escaped."

Vidal throws back his head and laughs. If Vidal likes you, he is certain to laugh at you and his laughter can be very unnerving. But the look, the silence which follows this laughter can be very unnerving, too. And, now, in the silence, he asks me, "Do you really think that you have escaped anything? Come. I know you for a better man than that." He walks to the table which holds the liquor. "In that movie of ours which has made you so famous, and, as I now see, so troubled, what are you playing, after all? What is the tragedy of this half-breed troubadour if not, precisely, that he has taken all the possible roads to escape and that all these roads have failed him?" He pauses, with the bottle in one hand, and looks at me. "Do you remember the trouble I had to get a performance out of you? How you hated me, you sometimes looked as though you wanted to shoot me! And do you remember when the role of Chico began to come alive?" He pours his drink. "Think back, remember. I am a very great director, *mais pardon!* I could not have got such a performance out of anyone but you.

And what were you thinking of, what was in your mind, what nightmare were you living with when you began, at last, to play the role—truthfully?" He walks back to his seat.

Chico, in the film, is the son of a Martinique woman and a French *colon* who hates both his mother and his father. He flees from the island to the capital, carrying his hatred with him. This hatred has now grown, naturally, to include all dark women and all white men, in a word, everyone. He descends into the underworld of Paris, where he dies. *Les fauves*—the wild beasts—refers to the life he has fled and to the life which engulfs him. When I agreed to do the role, I felt that I could probably achieve it by bearing in mind the North Africans I had watched in Paris for so long. But this did not please Vidal. The blowup came while we were rehearsing a fairly simple, straightforward scene. Chico goes into a sleazy Pigalle dance hall to beg the French owner for a particularly humiliating job. And this Frenchman reminds him of his father.

"You are playing this boy as though you thought of him as the noble savage," Vidal said, icily. "*Ça vient d'où*—all these ghastly mannerisms you are using all the time?"

Everyone fell silent, for Vidal rarely spoke this way. This silence told me that everyone, the actor with whom I was playing the scene and all the people in the "dance hall," shared Vidal's opinion of my performance and were relieved that he was going to do something about it. I was humiliated and too angry to speak; but perhaps I also felt, at the very bottom of my heart, a certain relief, an unwilling respect.

"You are doing it all wrong," he said, more gently. Then, "Come, let us have a drink together."

We walked into his office. He took a bottle and two glasses out of his desk. "Forgive me, but you put me in mind of some of those English *lady* actresses who love to play *putain* as long as it is always absolutely clear to the audience that they are really ladies. So perhaps they read a book, not usually, *hélas!, Fanny Hill,* and they have their chauffeurs drive them through Soho once or twice—and they come to the stage with a performance so absolutely loaded with detail, every bit of it meaningless, that there can be no doubt that they are acting. It is what the British call a triumph." He poured two cognacs. "That is what you are doing. Why? Who do you think this boy is, what do you think he is feeling, when he asks for this job?" He watched me carefully and I bitterly resented his look. "You come from America. The situation is not so pretty there for boys like you. I know you may not have been as poor as—as some—but is it really impossible for you to understand what a boy like Chico feels? Have you never, yourself, been in a similar position?"

I hated him for asking the question because I knew he knew the answer to it. "I would have had to be a very lucky black man not to have been in such a position."

"You would have had to be a very lucky *man*."

"Oh, God," I said, "please don't give me any of this equality-in-anguish business."

"It is perfectly possible," he said, sharply, "that there is not another kind."

Then he was silent. He sat down behind his desk. He cut a cigar and lit it, puffing up clouds of smoke, as though to prevent us from seeing each other too clearly. "Consider this," he said. "I am a French director who has never seen your country. I have never done you any harm, except, perhaps, historically—I mean, because I am white—but I cannot be blamed for that—"

"But *I* can be," I said, "and I am! I've never understood why, if *I* have to pay for the history written in the color of my skin, *you* should get off scot-free!" But I was surprised at my vehemence, I had not known I was going to say these things, and by the fact that I was trembling and from the way he looked at me I knew that, from a professional point of view anyway, I was playing into his hands.

"What makes you think I *do?*" His face looked weary and stern. "I am a Frenchman. Look at France. You think that I—we—are not paying for our history?" He walked to the window, staring out at the rather grim little town in which the studio was located. "If it is revenge that you want, well, then, let me tell you, you will have it. You will probably have it, whether you want it or not, our stupidity will make it inevitable." He turned back into the room. "But I beg you not to confuse me with the happy people of your country, who scarcely know that there is such a thing as history and so, naturally, imagine that they can escape, as you put it, scot-free. That is what you are doing, that is what I was about to say. I was about to say that I am a French director and I have never been in your country and I have never done you any harm—but you are not talking to that man, in this room, now. You are not talking to Jean Luc Vidal, but to some other white man, whom you remember, who has nothing to do with me." He paused and went back to his desk. "Oh, most of the time you are not like this, I know. But it is there all the time, it must be, because when you are upset, this is what comes out. So you are not playing Chico truthfully, you are lying about him, and I will not let you do it. When you go back, now, and play this scene again, I want you to remember what has just happened in this room. You brought your past into this room. That is what Chico does when he walks into the dance hall. The Frenchman whom he begs for a job is not merely a Frenchman—he is the father who disowned and betrayed him and all the Frenchmen whom he hates." He smiled and poured me another cognac. "Ah! If it were not for *my* history, I would not have so much trouble to get the truth out of you." He looked into my face, half smiling. "And you, you are angry—are you not?—that I *ask* you for the truth. You think I have no right to ask." Then he said something which he knew would enrage me. "Who are you then, and what good has it done you to come to France, and how will you raise your son? Will you teach him never to tell the truth to anyone?" And he moved behind his desk and looked at me, as though from behind a barricade.

"You have no right to talk to me this way."

"Oh, yes, I do," he said. "I have a film to make and a reputation to maintain and I am going to get a performance out of you." He looked at his watch. "Let us go back to work."

I watch him now, sitting quietly in my living room, tough, cynical, crafty old Frenchman, and I wonder if he knows that the nightmare at the bottom of my mind, as I played the role of Chico, was all the possible fates of Paul. This is but another way of saying that I relived the disasters which had nearly undone me; but, because I was thinking of Paul, I discovered that I did not want my son ever to feel toward me as I had felt toward my own father. He had died when I was eleven, but I had watched the humiliations he had to bear, and I had pitied him. But was there not, in that pity, however painfully and unwillingly, also some contempt? For how could I *know* what he had borne? I knew only that I was his son. However he had loved me, whatever he had borne, I, his son, was despised. Even had he lived, he could have done nothing to prevent it, nothing to protect me. The best that he could hope to do was to prepare me for it; and even at that he had failed. How can one be prepared for the spittle in the face, all the tireless ingenuity which goes into the spite and fear of small, unutterably miserable people, whose greatest terror is the singular identity, whose joy, whose safety, is entirely dependent on the humiliation and anguish of others?

But for Paul, I swore it, such a day would never come. I would throw my life and my work between Paul and the nightmare of the world. I would make it impossible for the world to treat Paul as it had treated my father and me.

Mahalia's record ends. Vidal rises to turn it over. "Well?" He looks at me very affectionately. "Your nightmares, please!"

"Oh, I was thinking of that summer I spent in Alabama, when my mother died." I stop. "You know, but when we finally filmed that bar scene, I was thinking of New York. I was scared in Alabama, but I almost went crazy in New York. I was sure I'd never make it back here—back here to Harriet. And I knew if I didn't, it was going to be the end of me." Now Mahalia is singing *When the Saints Go Marching In*. "I got a job in the town as an elevator boy, in the town's big department store. It was a special favor, one of my father's white friends got it for me. For a long time, in the South, we all—depended—on the —*kindness*—of white friends." I take out a handkerchief and wipe my face. "But this man didn't like me. I guess I didn't seem grateful enough, wasn't enough like my father, what he thought my father was. And I couldn't get used to the town again, I'd been away too long, I hated it. It's a terrible town, anyway, the whole thing looks as though it's been built around a jailhouse. There's a room in the courthouse, a room where they beat you up. Maybe you're walking along the street one night, it's usually at night, but it happens in the daytime, too. And the police car comes up behind you and the cop says, 'Hey, boy. Come on over here.' So you go on over. He says, 'Boy, I believe you're drunk.' And, you see, if you say, 'No, no sir,' he'll beat you because you're calling him a liar. And if you say anything else, unless it's something to make him laugh, he'll take you in and beat you, just for fun. The trick is to think of some way for them to have their fun without beating you up."

The street lights of Paris click on and turn all the green leaves silver. "Or to go along with the ways *they* dream up. And they'll do anything, anything at all, to prove that you're no better than a dog and to make you feel like one. And they hated me because I'd been North and I'd been to Europe. People kept saying, I hope you didn't bring no foreign notions back here with you, boy. And I'd say, 'No sir,' or 'No ma'am,' but I never said it right. And there was a time, all of them remembered it, when I *had* said it right. But now they could tell that I despised them—I guess, no matter what, I wanted them to know that I despised them. But I didn't despise them any more than everyone else did, only the others never let it show. They knew how to keep the white folks happy, and it was easy—you just had to keep them feeling like they were God's favor to the universe. They'd walk around with great, big, foolish grins on their faces and the colored folks loved to see this, because they hated them so much. 'Just look at So-and-So,' somebody'd say. 'His white is *on* him today.' And when we didn't hate them, we pitied them. In America, that's usually what it means to have a white friend. You pity the poor bastard because he was born believing the world's a great place to be, and you know it's not, and you can see that he's going to have a terrible time getting used to this idea, if he ever gets used to it."

Then I think of Paul again, those eyes which still imagine that I can do anything, that skin, the color of honey and fire, his jet-black, curly hair. I look out at Paris again, and I listen to Mahalia. "Maybe it's better to have the terrible times first. I don't know. Maybe, then, you can have, *if* you live, a better life, a real life, because you had to fight so hard to get it away—you know?—from the mad dog who held it in his teeth. But then your life has all those tooth marks, too, all those tatters, and all that blood." I walk to the bottle and raise it. "One for the road?"

"Thank you," says Vidal.

I pour us a drink, and he watches me. I have never talked so much before, not about those things anyway. I know that Vidal has nightmares, because he knows so much about them, but he has never told me what his are. I think that he probably does not talk about his nightmares any more. I know that the war cost him his wife and his son, and that he was in prison in Germany. He very rarely refers to it. He has a married daughter who lives in England, and he rarely speaks of her. He is like a man who has learned to live on what is left of an enormous fortune.

We are silent for a moment.

"Please go on," he says, with a smile. "I am curious about the reality behind the reality of your performance."

"My sister, Louisa, never married," I say, abruptly, "because, once, years ago, she and the boy she was going with and two friends of theirs were out driving in a car and the police stopped them. The girl who was with them was very fair and the police pretended not to believe her when she said she was colored. They made her get out and stand in front of the headlights of the car and pull down her pants and raise her dress—they said that was the only way they could be sure. And you can imagine what they said, and what they did—and they were lucky, at that, that it didn't go any further. But none of the men could do anything about it. Louisa couldn't face the boy again, and I guess he couldn't face her." Now it is really growing dark in the room and I cross to the light switch. "You know, I know what that boy felt, I've felt it. They want you to feel that you're not a man, maybe that's the only way they can feel like men, I don't know. I walked around New York with Harriet's cablegram in my pocket as though it were some atomic secret, in *code*, and they'd kill me if they ever found out what it meant. You know, there's something wrong with people like that. And thank God Harriet was here, she *proved* that the world was bigger than the world they wanted me to live in, I *had* to get back here, get to a place where people were too busy with their own lives, *their private lives*, to make fantasies about mine, to set up walls around mine." I look at him. The light in the room has made the night outside blue-black and golden and the great searchlight of the Eiffel Tower is turning in the sky. "That's what it's like in America, for me, anyway. I always feel that I don't exist there, except in someone else's—usually dirty—mind. I don't know if you know what that means, but I do, and I don't want to put Harriet through that and I don't want to raise Paul there."

"Well," he says at last, "you are not required to remain in America forever, are you? You will sing in that elegant club which apparently feels that it cannot, much longer, so much as open its doors without you, and you will probably accept the movie offer, you would be very foolish not to. You will make a lot of money. Then, one day, you will remember that airlines and steamship companies are still in business and that France still exists. *That* will certainly be cause for astonishment."

Vidal was a Gaullist before de Gaulle came to power. But he regrets the manner of de Gaulle's rise and he is worried about de Gaulle's regime. "It is not the fault of *mon général*," he sometimes says, sadly. "Perhaps it is history's fault. I *suppose* it must be history which always arranges to bill a civilization at the very instant it is least prepared to pay."

Now he rises and walks out on the balcony, as though to reassure himself of the reality of Paris. Mahalia is singing *Didn't It Rain?* I walk out and stand beside him.

"You are a good boy—Chico," he says. I laugh. "You believe in love. You do not know all the things love cannot do, but"—he smiles—"love will teach you that."

We go, after dinner, to a Left Bank discothèque which can charge outrageous prices because Marlon Brando wandered in there one night. By accident, according to Vidal. "Do you know how many people in Paris are becoming rich—to say nothing of those, *hélas!*, who are going broke—on the off chance that Marlon Brando will lose his way again?"

He has not, presumably, lost his way tonight, but the discothèque is crowded with those strangely faceless people who are part of the night life of all great cities, and who always arrive, moments, hours, or decades late, on the spot made notorious by an event or a movement or a handful of personalities. So here are American boys, anything but beardless, scratching around for Hemingway; American girls, titillating themselves with Frenchmen and existentialism, while waiting for the American boys to shave off their beards; French painters, busily pursuing the revolution which ended thirty years ago; and the young, bored, perverted, American *arrivistes* who are buying their way into the art world via flattery and liquor, and the production of canvases as arid as their greedy little faces. Here are boys, of all nations, one step above the pimp, who are occasionally walked across a stage or trotted before a camera. And the girls, their enemies, whose faces are sometimes seen in ads, one of whom will surely have a tantrum before the evening is out.

In a corner, as usual, surrounded, as usual, by smiling young men, sits the drunken blonde woman who was once the mistress of a famous, dead painter. She is a figure of some importance in the art world, and so rarely has to pay for either her drinks or her lovers. An older Frenchman, who was once a famous director, is playing *quatre cent vingt-et-un* with the woman behind the cash register. He nods pleasantly to Vidal and me as we enter, but makes no move to join us, and I respect him for this. Vidal and I are obviously cast tonight in the role vacated by Brando: our entrance justifies the prices and sends a kind of shiver through the room. It is marvelous to watch the face of the waiter as he approaches, all smiles and deference and grace, not so much honored by our presence as achieving his reality from it; excellence, he seems to be saying, gravitates naturally toward excellence. We order two whiskey and sodas. I know why Vidal sometimes comes here. He is lonely. I do not think that he expects ever to love one woman again, and so he distracts himself with many.

Since this is a discothèque, jazz is blaring from the walls and record sleeves are scattered about with a devastating carelessness. Two of them are mine and no doubt, presently, someone will play the recording of the songs I sang in the film.

"I thought," says Vidal, with a malicious little smile, "that your farewell to Paris would not be complete without a brief exposure to the perils of fame. Perhaps it will help prepare you for America, where, I am told, the populace is yet more carnivorous than it is here."

I can see that one of the vacant models is preparing herself to come to our table and ask for an autograph, hoping, since she is pretty—she has, that is, the usual female equipment, dramatized in the usual, modern way—to be invited for a drink. Should the maneuver succeed, one of her boy friends or girl friends will contrive to come by the table, asking for a light or a pencil or a lipstick, and it will be extremely difficult not to invite this person to join us, too. Before the evening ends, we will be surrounded. I don't, now, know what I expected of fame, but I suppose it never occurred to me that the light could be just as dangerous, just as killing, as the dark.

"Well, let's make it brief," I tell him. "Sometimes I wish that you weren't quite so fond of me."

He laughs. "There are some very interesting people here tonight. Look."

Across the room from us, and now staring at our table, are a group of American Negro students, who are probably visiting Paris for the first time. There are four of them, two boys and two girls, and I suppose that they must be in their late teens or early twenties. One of the boys, a gleaming, curly-haired, golden-brown type—the color of his mother's fried chicken—is carrying a guitar. When they realize we have noticed them, they smile and wave—wave as though I were one of their possessions, as, indeed, I am. Golden-brown is a mime. He raises his guitar, drops his shoulders, and his face falls into the lugubrious lines of Chico's face as he approaches death. He strums a little of the film's theme music, and I laugh and the table laughs. It is as though we were all back home and had met for a moment, on a Sunday morning, say, before a church or a poolroom or a barbershop.

And they have created a sensation in the discothèque, naturally, having managed, with no effort whatever, to outwit all the gleaming boys and girls. Their table, which had been of no interest only a moment before, has now become the focus of a rather pathetic attention; their smiles have made it possible for the others to smile, and to nod in our direction.

"Oh," says Vidal, "he does that far better than you ever did, perhaps I will make him a star."

"Feel free, *m'sieu, le bon Dieu,* I got mine." But I can see that his attention has really been caught by one of the girls, slim, tense, and dark, who seems, though it is hard to know how one senses such things, to be treated by the others with a special respect. And, in fact, the table now seems to be having a council of war, to be demanding her opinion or her cooperation. She listens, frowning, laughing; the quality, the force of her intelligence causes her face to keep changing all the time, as though a light played on it. And, presently, with a gesture she might once have used to scatter feed to chickens, she scoops up from the floor one of those dangling rag bags women love to carry. She holds it loosely by the drawstrings, so that it is banging somewhere around her ankle, and walks over to our table. She has an honest, forthright walk, entirely unlike the calculated, pelvic workout by means of which most women get about. She is small, but sturdily, economically, put together.

As she reaches our table, Vidal and I rise, and this throws her for a second. (It has been a long time since I have seen such an attractive girl.)

Also, everyone, of course, is watching us. It is really a quite curious moment. They have put on the record of Chico singing a sad, angry Martinique ballad; my own voice is coming at us from the walls as the girl looks from Vidal to me, and smiles.

"I guess you know," she says, "we weren't *about* to let you get out of here without bugging you just a little bit. We've only been in Paris just a couple of days and we thought for sure that we wouldn't have a chance of running into you anywhere, because it's in all the papers that you're coming home."

"Yes," I say, "yes. I'm leaving the day after tomorrow."

"Oh!" She grins. "Then we really *are* lucky." I find that I have almost forgotten the urchin-like grin of a colored girl. "I guess, before I keep babbling on, I'd better introduce myself. My name is Ada Holmes."

We shake hands. "This is Monsieur Vidal, the director of the film."

"I'm very honored to meet you, sir."

"Will you join us for a moment? Won't you sit down?" And Vidal pulls a chair out for her.

But she frowns contritely. "I really ought to get back to my friends." She looks at me. "I really just came over to say, for myself and all the kids, that we've got your records and we've seen your movie, and it means so much to us"—and she laughs, breathlessly, nervously, it is somehow more moving than tears—"more than I can say. Much more. And we wanted to know if you and your friend"—she looks at Vidal—"your *director,* Monsieur Vidal, would allow us to buy you a drink? We'd be very honored if you would."

"It is we who are honored," says Vidal, promptly, "*and* grateful. We were getting terribly bored with one another, thank God you came along."

The three of us laugh, and we cross the room.

The three at the table rise, and Ada makes the introductions. The other girl, taller and paler than Ada, is named Ruth. One of the boys is named Talley—"short for Talliafero"—and Golden-brown's name is Pete. "Man," he tells me, "I dig you the most. You tore me up, baby, tore me *up*."

"You tore up a lot of people," Talley says, cryptically, and he and Ruth laugh. Vidal does not know, but I do, that Talley is probably referring to white people.

They are from New Orleans and Tallahassee and North Carolina; are college students, and met on the boat. They have been in Europe all summer, in Italy and Spain, but are only just getting to Paris.

"We meant to come sooner," says Ada, "but we could never make up our minds to leave a place. I thought we'd never pry Ruth loose from Venice."

"I resigned myself," says Pete, "and just sat in the Piazza San Marco, drinking gin fizz and being photographed with the pigeons, while Ruth had herself driven *all* up and down the Grand Canal." He looks at Ruth. "Finally, thank heaven, it rained."

"She was working off her hostilities," says Ada, with a grin. "We thought we might as well let her do it in Venice, the opportunities in North Carolina are really terribly limited."

"There are some very upset people walking around down there," Ruth says, "and a couple of tours around the Grand Canal might do them a world of good."

Pete laughs. "Can't you just see Ruth escorting them to the edge of the water?"

"I haven't lifted my hand in anger yet," Ruth says, "but, oh Lord," and she laughs, clenching and unclenching her fists.

"You haven't been back for a long time, have you?" Talley asks me.

"Eight years. I haven't really lived there for twelve years."

Pete whistles. "I fear you are in for some surprises, my friend. There have been some changes made." Then, "Are you afraid?"

"A little."

"We all are," says Ada, "that's why I was so glad to get away for a little while."

"Then you haven't been back since Black Monday," Talley says. He laughs. "That's how it's gone down in Confederate history." He turns to Vidal. "What do people think about it here?"

Vidal smiles, delighted. "It seems extraordinarily infantile behavior, even for Americans, from whom, I must say, I have never expected very much in the way of maturity." Everyone at the table laughs. Vidal goes on. "But I cannot really talk about it, I do not understand it. I have never really understood Americans; I am an old man now, and I suppose I never will. There is something very nice about them, something very winning, but they seem so ignorant—so ignorant of life. Perhaps it is strange, but the only people from your country with whom I have ever made contact are black people—like my good friend, my discovery, here," and he slaps me on the shoulder. "Perhaps it is because we, in Europe, whatever else we do not know, or have forgotten, know about suffering. We have suffered here. You have suffered, too. But most Americans do not yet know what anguish is. It is too bad, because the life of the West is in their hands." He turns to Ada. "I cannot help saying that I think it is a scandal—and we may all pay very dearly for it—that a civilized nation should elect to represent it a man who is so simple that he thinks the world is simple." And silence falls at the table and the four young faces stare at him.

"Well," says Pete, at last, turning to me, "you won't be bored, man, when you get back there."

"It's much too nice a night," I say, "to stay cooped up in this place, where all I can hear is my own records." We laugh. "Why don't we get out of here and find a sidewalk café?" I tap Pete's guitar. "Maybe we can find out if you've got any talent."

"Oh, talent I've got," says Pete, "but character, man, I'm lacking."

So, after some confusion about the bill, for which Vidal has already made himself responsible, we walk out into the Paris night. It is very strange to feel that, very soon now, these boulevards will not exist for me. People will be walking up and down, as they are tonight, and lovers will be murmuring in the black shadows of the plane trees, and there will be these same still figures on the benches or in the parks—but they will not exist for me, I will not be here. For a long while Paris will no longer exist for me, except in my mind; and only in the minds of some people will I exist any longer for Paris. After departure, only invisible things are left, perhaps the life of the world is held together by invisible chains of memory and loss and love. So many things, so many people, depart! And we can only repossess them in our minds. Perhaps this is what the old folks meant, what my mother and my father meant, when they counseled us to keep the faith.

We have taken a table at the Deux Magots and Pete strums on his guitar and begins to play this song:

Preach the word, preach the word, preach the word!
If I never, never see you any more.
Preach the word, preach the word.
And I'll meet you on Canaan's shore.

He has a strong, clear, boyish voice, like a young preacher's, and he is smiling as he sings his song. Ada and I look at each other and grin, and Vidal is smiling. The waiter looks a little worried, for we are already beginning to attract a crowd, but it is a summer night, the gendarmes on the corner do not seem to mind, and there will be time, anyway, to stop us.

Pete was not there, none of us were, the first time this song was needed; and no one now alive can imagine what that time was like. But the song has come down the bloodstained ages. I suppose this to mean that the song is still needed, still has its work to do.

The others are all, visibly, very proud of Pete; and we all join him, and people stop to listen:

Testify! Testify!
If I never, never see you any more!
Testify! Testify!
I'll meet you on Canaan's shore!

In the crowd that has gathered to listen to us, I see a face I know, the face of a North African prize fighter, who is no longer in the ring. I used to know him well in the old days, but have not seen him for a long time. He looks quite well, his face is shining, he is quite decently dressed. And something about the way he holds himself, not quite looking at our table, tells me that he has seen me, but does not want to risk a rebuff. So I call him. "Boona!"

And he turns, smiling, and comes loping over to our table, his hands in his pockets. Pete is still singing and Ada and Vidal have taken off on a conversation of their own. Ruth and Talley look curiously, expectantly, at Boona. Now that I have called him over, I feel somewhat uneasy. I realize that I do not know what he is doing now, or how he will get along with any of these people, and I can see in his eyes that he is delighted to be in the presence of two young girls. There are virtually no North African women in Paris, and not even the dirty, rat-faced girls who live, apparently, in cafés are willing to go with an Arab. So Boona is always looking for a girl, and because he is so deprived and because he is not Western, his techniques can be very unsettling. I know he is relieved that the girls are not French and not white. He looks briefly at Vidal and Ada. Vidal, also, though for different reasons, is always looking for a girl.

But Boona has always been very nice to me. Perhaps I am sorry that I called him over, but I did not want to snub him.

He claps one hand to the side of my head, as is his habit. "*Comment vas-tu, mon frère?* I have not see you, oh, for long time." And he asks me, as in the old days, "You all right? Nobody bother you?" And he laughs. "*Ah! Tu as fait le chemin, toi!* Now you are *vedette*, big star—wonderful!" He looks around the table, made a little uncomfortable by the silence that has fallen, now that Pete has stopped singing. "I have seen you in the movies—you know?—and I tell everybody, I know *him!*" He points to me, and laughs, and Ruth and Talley laugh with him. "That's right, man, you make me real proud, you make me cry!"

"Boona, I want you to meet some friends of mine." And I go round the table: "Ruth, Talley, Ada, Pete"—and he bows and shakes hands, his dark eyes gleaming with pleasure—"*et Monsieur Vidal, le metteur en scène du film qui t'a arrache des larmes.*"

"*Enchanté.*" But his attitude toward Vidal is colder, more distrustful. "Of course I have heard of Monsieur Vidal. He is the director of many films, many of them made me cry." This last statement is utterly, even insolently, insincere.

But Vidal, I think, is relieved that I will now be forced to speak to Boona and will leave him alone with Ada.

"Sit down," I say, "have a drink with us, let me have your news. What's been happening with you, what are you doing with yourself these days?"

"Ah," he sits down, "nothing very brilliant, my brother." He looks at me quickly, with a little smile. "You know, we have been having hard times here."

"Where are you from?" Ada asks him.

His brilliant eyes take her in entirely, but she does not flinch. "I am from Tunis." He says it proudly, with a little smile.

"From Tunis. I have never been to Africa, I would love to go one day."

He laughs. "Africa is a big place. Very big. There are many countries in Africa, many"—he looks briefly at Vidal—"different kinds of people, many colonies."

"But Tunis," she continues, in her innocence, "is free? Freedom is happening all over Africa. That's why I would like to go there."

"I have not been back for a long time," says Boona, "but all the news I get from Tunis, from my people, is not good."

"Wouldn't you like to go back?" Ruth asks.

Again he looks at Vidal. "That is not so easy."

Vidal smiles. "You know what I would like to do? There's a wonderful Spanish place not far from here, where we can listen to live music and dance a little." He turns to Ada. "Would you like that?"

He is leaving it up to me to get rid of Boona, and it is, of course, precisely for this reason that I cannot do it. Besides, it is no longer so simple.

"Oh, I'd love that," says Ada, and she turns to Boona. "Won't you come, too?"

"Thank you, mam'selle," he says, softly, and his tongue flicks briefly over his lower lip, and he smiles. He is very moved, people are not often nice to him.

In the Spanish place there are indeed a couple of Spanish guitars, drums, castanets, and a piano, but the uses to which these are being put carry one back, as Pete puts it, to the levee. "These are the wailingest Spanish cats I ever heard," says Ruth. "They didn't learn how to do this in Spain, no, they didn't, they been rambling. You ever hear anything like this going on in Spain?" Talley takes her out on the dance floor, which is already crowded. A very handsome Frenchwoman is dancing with an enormous, handsome black man, who seems to be her lover, who seems to have taught her how to dance. Apparently, they are known to the musicians, who egg them on with small cries of "*Olé!*" It is a very good-natured crowd, mostly foreigners, Spaniards, Swedes, Greeks. Boona takes Ada out on the dance floor while Vidal is answering some questions put to him by Pete on the entertainment situation in France. Vidal looks a little put out, and I am amused.

We are there for perhaps an hour, dancing, talking, and I am, at last, a little drunk. In spite of Boona, who is a very good and tireless dancer, Vidal continues his pursuit of Ada, and I begin to wonder if he will make it and I begin to wonder if I want him to.

I am still puzzling out my reaction when Pete, who has disappeared, comes in through the front door, catches my eye, and signals to me. I leave the table and follow him into the streets.

He looks very upset. "I don't want to bug you, man," he says, "but I fear your boy has goofed."

I know he is not joking. I think he is probably angry at Vidal because of Ada, and I wonder what I can do about it and why he should be telling me.

I stare at him, gravely, and he says, "It looks like he stole some money."

"Stole *money?* Who, Vidal?"

And then, of course, I get it, in the split second before he says, impatiently, "No, are you kidding? Your friend, the Tunisian."

I do not know what to say or what to do, and so I temporize with questions. All the time I am wondering if this can be true and what I can do about it if it is. The trouble is, I know that Boona steals, he would probably not be alive if he didn't, but I cannot say so to these children, who probably still imagine that everyone who steals is a thief. But he has never, to my knowledge, stolen from a friend. It seems unlike him. I have always thought of him as being better than that, and smarter than that. And so I cannot believe it, but neither can I doubt it. I do not know anything about Boona's life, these days. This causes me to realize that I do not really know much about Boona.

"Who did he steal it from?"

"From Ada. Out of her bag."

"How much?"

"Ten dollars. It's not an awful lot of money, but"—he grimaces—"none of us *have* an awful lot of money."

"I know." The dark side street on which we stand is nearly empty. The only sound on the street is the muffled music of the Spanish club. "How do you know it was Boona?"

He anticipates my own unspoken rejoinder. "Who else could it be? Besides—somebody *saw* him do it."

"Somebody saw him?"

"Yes."

I do not ask him who this person is, for fear that he will say it is Vidal.

"Well," I say, "I'll try to get it back." I think that I will take Boona aside and then replace the money myself. "Was it in dollars or in francs?"

"In francs."

I have no dollars and this makes it easier. I do not know how I can possibly face Boona and accuse him of stealing money from my friends. I would rather give him the benefit of even the faintest doubt. But, "Who saw him?" I ask.

"Talley. But we didn't want to make a thing about it—"

"Does Ada know it's gone?"

"Yes." He looks at me helplessly. "I know this makes you feel pretty bad, but we thought we'd better tell you, rather than"—lamely—"anybody else."

Now, Ada comes out of the club, carrying her ridiculous handbag, and with her face all knotted and sad. "Oh," she says, "I hate to cause all this trouble, it's not worth it, not for ten lousy dollars." I am astonished to see that she has been weeping, and tears come to her eyes now.

I put my arm around her shoulder. "Come on, now. You're not causing anybody any trouble and, anyway, it's nothing to cry about."

"It isn't your fault, Ada," Pete says, miserably.

"Oh, I ought to get a sensible handbag," she says, "like you're always telling me to do," and she laughs a little, then looks at me. "Please don't try to do anything about it. Let's just forget it."

"What's happening inside?" I ask her.

"Nothing. They're just talking. I think Mr. Vidal is dancing with Ruth. He's a great dancer, that little Frenchman."

"He's a great talker, too," Pete says.

"Oh, he doesn't mean anything," says Ada, "he's just having fun. He probably doesn't get a chance to talk to many American girls."

"He certainly made up for lost time tonight."

"Look," I say, "if Talley and Boona are alone, maybe you better go back in. We'll be in in a minute. Let's try to keep this as quiet as we can."

"Yeah," he says, "okay. We're going soon anyway, okay?"

"Yes," she tells him, "right away."

But as he turns away, Boona and Talley step out into the street, and it is clear that Talley feels that he has Boona under arrest.

I almost laugh, the whole thing is beginning to resemble one of those mad French farces with people flying in and out of doors; but Boona comes straight to me.

"They say I stole money, my friend. You know me, you are the only one here who knows me, you know I would not do such a thing."

I look at him and I do not know what to say. Ada looks at him with her eyes full of tears and looks away. I take Boona's arm.

"We'll be back in a minute," I say. We walk a few paces up the dark, silent street.

"She say I take her money," he says. He, too, looks as though he is about to weep—but I do not know for which reason. "You know me, you know me almost twelve years, you think I do such a thing?"

Talley saw you, I want to say, but I cannot say it. Perhaps Talley only thought he saw him. Perhaps it is easy to see a boy who looks like Boona with his hand in an American girl's purse.

"If you not believe me," he says, "search me. Search me!" And he opens his arms wide, theatrically, and now there are tears standing in his eyes.

I do not know what his tears mean, but I certainly cannot search him. I want to say, I know you steal, I know you have to steal. Perhaps you took the money out of this girl's purse in order to eat tomorrow, in order not to be thrown into the streets tonight, in order to stay out of jail. This girl means nothing to you, after all, she is only an American, an American like me. Perhaps, I suddenly think, no girl means anything to you, or ever will again, they have beaten you too hard and kept you out in the gutter too long. And I also think, if you would steal from her, then of course you would lie to me, neither of us means anything to you; perhaps, in your eyes, we are simply luckier gangsters in a world which is run by gangsters. But I cannot say any of these things to Boona. I cannot say, Tell me the truth, nobody cares about the money any more.

So I say, "Of course I will not search you." And I realize that he knew I would not.

"I think it is that Frenchman who say I am a thief. They think we all are thieves." His eyes are bright and bitter. He looks over my shoulder. "They have all come out of the club now."

I look around and they are all there, in a little dark knot on the sidewalk.

"Don't worry," I say. "It doesn't matter."

"You believe me? My brother?" And his eyes look into mine with a terrible intensity.

"Yes," I force myself to say, "yes, of course, I believe you. Someone made a mistake, that's all."

"You know, the way American girls run around, they have their sack open all the time, she could have lost the money anywhere. Why she blame me? Because I come from Africa?" Tears are glittering on his face. "Here she come now."

And Ada comes up the street with her straight, determined walk. She walks straight to Boona and takes his hand. "I am sorry," she says, "for everything that happened. Please believe me. It isn't worth all this fuss. I'm sure you're a very nice person, and"—she falters—"I must have lost the money, I'm sure I lost it." She looks at him. "It isn't worth hurting your feelings, and I'm terribly sorry about it."

"I no take your money," he says. "Really, truly, I no take it. Ask him"—pointing to me, grabbing me by the arm, shaking me—"he know me for years, he will tell you that I never, never steal!"

"I'm sure," she says. "I'm sure."

I take Boona by the arm again. "Let's forget it. Let's forget it all. We're all going home now, and one of these days we'll have a drink again and we'll forget all about it, all right?"

"Yes," says Ada, "let us forget it." And she holds out her hand.

Boona takes it, wonderingly. His eyes take her in again. "You are a very nice girl. Really. A very nice girl."

"I'm sure you're a nice person, too." She pauses. "Goodnight."

"Goodnight," he says, after a long silence.

Then he kisses me on both cheeks. "*Au revoir, mon frère.*"

"*Au revoir, Boona.*"

After a moment we turn and walk away, leaving him standing there.

"Did he take it?" asks Vidal.

"I tell you, I *saw* him," says Talley.

"Well," I say, "it doesn't matter now." I look back and see Boona's stocky figure disappearing down the street.

"No," says Ada, "it doesn't matter." She looks up. "It's almost morning."

"I would gladly," says Vidal, stammering, "gladly—"

But she is herself again. "I wouldn't think of it. We had a wonderful time tonight, a wonderful time, and I wouldn't think of it." She turns to me with that urchin-like grin. "It was wonderful meeting you. I hope you won't have too much trouble getting used to the States again."

"Oh, I don't think I will," I say. And then, "I hope you won't."

"No," she says, "I don't think anything they can do will surprise me any more."

"Which way are we all going?" asks Vidal. "I hope someone will share my taxi with me."

But he lives in the sixteenth arrondissement, which is not in anyone's direction. We walk him to the line of cabs standing under the clock at Odéon.

And we look each other in the face, in the growing morning light. His face looks weary and lined and lonely. He puts both hands on my shoulders and then puts one hand on the nape of my neck. "Do not forget me, Chico," he says. "You must come back and see us, one of these days. Many of us depend on you for many things."

"I'll be back," I say. "I'll never forget you."

He raises his eyebrows and smiles. "*Alors, Adieu.*"

"*Adieu, Vidal.*"

"I was happy to meet all of you," he says. He looks at Ada. "Perhaps we will meet again before you leave."

"Perhaps," she says. "Goodby, Monsieur Vidal."

"Goodby."

Vidal's cab drives away. "I also leave you now," I say. "I must go home and wake up my son and prepare for our journey."

I leave them standing on the corner, under the clock, which points to six. They look very strange and lost and determined, the four of them. Just before my cab turns off the boulevard, I wave to them and they wave back.

Mme. Dumont is in the hall, mopping the floor.

"Did all my family get home?" I ask. I feel very cheerful, I do not know why.

"Yes," she says, "they are all here. Paul is still sleeping."

"May I go in and get him?"

She looks at me in surprise. "Of course."

So I walk into her apartment and walk into the room where Paul lies sleeping. I stand over his bed for a long time.

Perhaps my thoughts traveled—travel through to him. He opens his eyes and smiles up at me. He puts a fist to his eye and raises his arms. "*Bonjour, Papa.*"

I lift him up. "*Bonjour.* How do you feel today?"

"Oh, I don't know yet," he says.

I laugh. I put him on my shoulder and walk out into the hall. Mme. Dumont looks up at him with her radiant, aging face.

"Ah," she says, "you are going on a journey! How does it feel?"

"He doesn't know yet," I tell her. I walk to the elevator door and open it, dropping Paul down to the crook of my arm.

She laughs again. "He will know later. What a journey! *Jusqu'au nouveau monde!*"

I open the cage and we step inside. "Yes," I say, "all the way to the new world." I press the button and the cage, holding my son and me, goes up.

[1960]

For Thought

Baldwin has adapted several ancient story telling motifs to a modern situation. The narrator is attempting to return home, to rediscover his roots and his identity after having become a successful actor and singer in France. The author brings him randomly into contact with his director, touring young countrymen, a Tunisian fighter down on his luck and others as tests of his sensibility and maturity. In the end, he discovers that the more things change, the more they remain the same.

For Discussion

1. What factors seem to bother the narrator as he prepares to leave Paris? To what extent does he feel a sense of loss? How would his Swedish wife, his son, and his artistic successes have been impossible elsewhere?
2. What does the narrator learn about himself and about the history of others while in contact with his director?
3. What conflicts are forced upon the narrator by his chance meeting with Boona and the American couples? Why does he feel relieved and upbeat after parting from them? What new insight does he come upon through the episode?

Donald Barthelme
I Bought a Little City

So I bought a little city (it was Galveston, Texas) and told everybody that nobody had to move, we were going to do it just gradually, very relaxed, no big changes overnight. They were pleased and suspicious. I walked down to the harbor where there were cotton warehouses and fish markets and all sorts of installations having to do with the spread of petroleum throughout the Free World, and I thought, A few apple trees here might be nice. Then I walked out this broad boulevard which has all these tall thick palm trees maybe forty feet high in the center and oleanders on both sides, it runs for blocks and blocks and ends up opening up to the broad Gulf of Mexico—stately homes on both sides and a big Catholic church that looks more like a mosque and the Bishop's Palace and a handsome red brick affair where the Shriners meet. I thought, What a nice little city, it suits me fine.

It suited me fine so I started to change it. But softly, softly. I asked some folks to move out of a whole city block on I Street, and then I tore down their houses. I put the people into the Galvez Hotel, which is the nicest hotel in town, right on the seawall, and I made sure that every room had a beautiful view. Those people had wanted to stay at the Galvez Hotel all their lives and never had a chance before because they didn't have the money. They were delighted. I tore down their houses and made that empty block a park. We planted it all to hell and put some nice green iron benches in it and a little fountain—all standard stuff, we didn't try to be imaginative.

I was pleased. All the people who lived in the four blocks surrounding the empty block had something they hadn't had before, a park. They could sit in it, and like that. I went and watched them sitting in it. There was already a black man there playing bongo drums. I hate bongo drums. I started to tell him to stop playing those goddamn bongo drums but then I said to myself, No, that's not right. You got to let him play his goddamn bongo drums if he feels like it, it's part of the misery of democracy, to which I subscribe. Then I started thinking about new housing for the people I had displaced, they couldn't stay in that fancy hotel forever.

But I didn't have any ideas about new housing, except that it shouldn't be too imaginative. So I got to talking to one of these people, one of the ones we had moved out, guy by the name of Bill Caulfield who worked in a wholesale-tobacco place down on Mechanic Street.

"So what kind of a place would you like to live in?" I asked him.

"Well," he said, "not too big."

"Uh-huh."

"Maybe with a veranda around three sides," he said, "so we could sit on it and look out. A screened porch, maybe."

"Whatcha going to look out at?"

"Maybe some trees and, you know, the lawn."

"So you want some ground around the house."

"That would be nice, yeah."

"'Bout how much ground are you thinking of?"

"Well, not too much."

"You see, the problem is, there's only *x* amount of ground and everybody's going to want to have it to look at and at the same time they don't want to be staring at the neighbors. Private looking, that's the thing."

"Well, yes," he said. "I'd like it to be kind of private."

"Well," I said, "get a pencil and let's see what we can work out."

We started with what there was going to be to look at, which was damned difficult. Because when you look you don't want to be able to look at just one thing, you want to be able to shift your gaze. You need to be able to look at at least three things, maybe four. Bill Caulfield solved the problem. He showed me a box. I opened it up and inside was a jigsaw puzzle with a picture of the Mona Lisa on it.

"Lookee here," he said. "If each piece of ground was like a piece of this-here puzzle, and the tree line on each piece of property followed the outline of a piece of the puzzle—well, there you have it, Q.E.D. and that's all she wrote."

"Fine," I said. "Where are the folk going to park their cars?"

"In the vast underground parking facility," he said.

"O.K., but how does each householder gain access to his household?"

"The tree lines are double and shade beautifully paved walkways possibly bordered with begonias," he said.

"A lurkway for potential muggists and rapers," I pointed out.

"There won't be any such," Caulfield said, "because you've bought our whole city and won't allow that class of person to hang out here no more."

That was right. I had bought the whole city and could probably do that. I had forgotten.

"Well," I said finally, "let's give 'er a try. The only thing I don't like about it is that it seems a little imaginative."

We did and it didn't work out badly. There was only one complaint. A man named A. G. Bartie came to see me.

"Listen," he said, his eyes either gleaming or burning, I couldn't tell which, it was a cloudy day, "I feel like I'm living in this gigantic jiveass jigsaw puzzle."

He was right. Seen from the air, he was living in the middle of a titanic reproduction of the Mona Lisa, too, but I thought it best not to mention that. We allowed him to square off his property into a standard 60 x 100 foot lot and later some other people did that too—some people just like rectangles, I guess. I must say it improved the concept. You run across an occasional rectangle in Shady Oaks (we didn't want to call the development anything too imaginative) and it surprises you. That's nice.

I said to myself:

Got a little city
Ain't it pretty

By now I had exercised my proprietorship so lightly and if I do say so myself tactfully that I wondered if I was enjoying myself enough (and I had paid a heavy penny too—near to half my fortune). So I went out on the streets then and shot six thousand dogs. This gave me great satisfaction and you have no idea how wonderfully it improved the city for the better. This left us with a dog population of 165,000, as opposed to a human population of something like 89,000. Then I went down to the Galveston *News*, the morning paper, and wrote an editorial denouncing myself as the vilest creature the good God had ever placed upon the earth, and were we, the citizens of this fine community, who were after all free Americans of whatever race or creed, going to sit still while one man, *one man*, if indeed so vile a critter could be so called, etc. etc.? I gave it to the city desk and told them I wanted it on the front page in fourteen-point type, boxed. I did this just in case they might have hesitated to do it themselves, and because I'd seen that Orson Welles picture where the guy writes a nasty notice about his own wife's terrible singing, which I always thought was pretty decent of him, from some points of view.

A man whose dog I'd shot came to see me.

"You shot Butch," he said.

"Butch? Which one was Butch?"

"One brown ear and one white ear," he said. "Very friendly."

"Mister," I said, "I've just shot six thousand dogs, and you expect me to remember Butch?"

"Butch was all Nancy and me had," he said. "We never had no children."

"Well, I'm sorry about that," I said, "but I own this city."

"I know that," he said.

"I am the sole owner and I make all the rules."

"They told me," he said.

"I'm sorry about Butch but he got in the way of the big campaign. You ought to have had him on a leash."

"I don't deny it," he said.

"You ought to have had him inside the house."

"He was just a poor animal that had to go out sometimes."

"And mess up the streets something awful?"

"Well," he said, "it's a problem. I just wanted to tell you how I feel."

"You didn't tell me," I said. "How do you feel?"

"I feel like bustin' your head," he said, and showed me a short length of pipe he had brought along for the purpose.

"But of course if you do that you're going to get your ass in a lot of trouble," I said.

"I realize that."

"It would make you feel better, but then I own the jail and the judge and the po-lice and the local chapter of the American Civil Liberties Union. All mine. I could hit you with a writ of mandamus."

"You wouldn't do that."

"I've been known to do worse."

"You're a black-hearted man," he said. "I guess that's it. You'll roast in Hell in the eternal flames and there will be no mercy or cooling drafts from any quarter."

He went away happy with this explanation. I was happy to be a black-hearted man in his mind if that would satisfy the issue between us because that was a bad-looking piece of pipe he had there and I was still six thousand dogs ahead of the game, in a sense. So I owned this little city which was very, very pretty and I couldn't think of any more new innovations just then or none that wouldn't get me punctuated like the late Huey P. Long, former governor of Louisiana. The thing is, I had fallen in love with Sam Hong's wife. I had wandered into this store on Tremont Street where they sold Oriental novelties, paper lanterns, and cheap china and bamboo birdcages and wicker footstools and all that kind of thing. She was smaller than I was and I thought I had never seen that much goodness in a woman's face before. It was hard to credit. It was the best face I'd ever seen.

"I can't do that," she said, "because I am married to Sam."

"Sam?"

She pointed over to the cash register where there was a Chinese man, young and intelligent-looking and pouring that intelligent look at me with considered unfriendliness.

"Well, that's dismal news," I said. "Tell me, do you love me?"

"A little bit," she said, "but Sam is wise and kind and we have one and one-third lovely children."

She didn't look pregnant but I congratulated her anyhow, and then went out on the street and found a cop and sent him down to H Street to get me a bucket of Colonel Sanders' Kentucky Fried Chicken, extra crispy. I did that just out of meanness. He was humiliated but he had no choice. I thought:

> I own a little city
> Awful pretty
> Can't help people
> Can hurt them though
> Shoot their dogs
> Mess 'em up
> Be imaginative
> Plant trees
> Best to leave 'em alone?
> Who decides?
> Sam's wife is Sam's wife and coveting
> Is not nice.

So I ate the Colonel Sanders' Kentucky Fried Chicken, extra crispy, and sold Galveston, Texas, back to the interests. I took a bath on that deal, there's no denying it, but I learned something—don't play God. A lot of other people already knew that, but I have never doubted for a minute that a lot of other people are smarter than me, and figure things out quicker, and have grace and statistical norms on their side. Probably I went wrong by being too imaginative, although really I was guarding against that. I did very little, I was fairly restrained. God does a lot worse things, every day, in one little family, any family, than I did in that whole little city. But He's got a better imagination than I do. For instance, I still covet Sam Hong's wife. That's torment. Still covet Sam Hong's wife, and probably always will. It's like having a tooth pulled. For a year. The same tooth. That's a sample of His imagination. It's powerful.

So what happened? What happened was that I took the other half of my fortune and went to Galena Park, Texas, and lived inconspicuously there, and when they asked me to run for the school board I said No, I don't have any children.

[1970]

For Thought

Barthelme achieves his bizarre comic effect by positing an incredible situation and then, in a matter-of-fact tone, dealing with the humdrum details of working out the narrator's grandiose pipe dream as though it were practicable. Underneath the amusing nonsense in the story lurks a very shrewd observation on human nature generally and on modern American life in particular.

For Discussion

1. What are we supposed to deduce about the narrator-protagonist in the story?
2. How does Barthelme use the belief in American ingenuity and know-how in a comic fashion?
3. How does the author satirize the naiveté of some American social customs and traditions?
4. What does the narrator-protagonist represent or symbolize?
5. What is the central meaning of the story? How do the poems contribute to the meaning?

Donald Barthelme

A Shower of Gold

Because he needed the money Peterson answered an ad that said "*We'll pay you* to be on TV if your opinions are strong enough or your personal experiences have a flavor of the unusual." He called the number and was told to come to Room 1551 in the Graybar Building on Lexington. This he did and after spending twenty minutes with a Miss Arbor who asked him if he had ever been in analysis was okayed for a program called *Who Am I?* "What do you have strong opinions about?" Miss Arbor asked. "Art," Peterson said, "life, money." "For instance?" "I believe," Peterson said, "that the learning ability of mice can be lowered or increased by regulating the amount of serotonin in the brain. I believe that schizophrenics have a high incidence of unusual fingerprints, including lines that make almost complete circles. I believe that the dreamer watches his dream in sleep, by moving his eyes." "*That's very interesting!*" Miss Arbor cried. "It's all in the *World Almanac,*" Peterson replied.

"I see you're a sculptor," Miss Arbor said, "that's wonderful." "What is the nature of the program?" Peterson asked. "I've never seen it." "Let me answer your question with another question," Miss Arbor said. "Mr. Peterson, are you absurd?" Her enormous lips were smeared with a glowing white cream. "I beg your pardon?" "I mean," Miss Arbor said earnestly, "do you encounter your own existence as gratuitous? Do you feel *de trop?* Is there nausea?" "I have an enlarged liver," Peterson offered. "That's *excellent!*" Miss Arbor exclaimed. "That's a *very* good beginning! *Who Am I?* tries, Mr. Peterson, to discover what people *really are*. People today, we feel, are hidden away inside themselves, alienated, desperate, living in anguish, despair and bad faith. Why have we been thrown here, and abandoned? That's the question we try to answer, Mr. Peterson. Man stands alone in a featureless, anonymous landscape, in fear and trembling and sickness unto death. God is dead. Nothingness everywhere. Dread. Estrangement. Finitude. *Who Am I?* approaches these problems in a root radical way." "On television?" "We're interested in basics, Mr. Peterson. We don't play around." "I see," Peterson said, wondering about the amount of the fee. "What I want to know now, Mr. Peterson, is this: are you *interested* in absurdity?" "Miss Arbor," he said, "to tell you the truth, I don't know. I'm not sure I believe in it." "Oh, Mr. Peterson!" Miss Arbor said, shocked. "Don't *say* that! You'll be . . ." "Punished?" Peterson suggested. "*You* may not be interested in absurdity," she said firmly, "but absurdity is interested in *you*." "I have a lot of problems, if that helps," Peterson said. "Existence is problematic for you," Miss Arbor said, relieved. "The fee is two hundred dollars."

"I'm going to be on television," Peterson said to his dealer. "A terrible shame," Jean-Claude responded. "Is it unavoidable?" "It's unavoidable," Peterson said, "if I want to eat." "How much?" Jean-Claude asked and Peterson said: "Two hundred." He looked around the gallery to see if any of his works were on display. "A ridiculous compensation considering the infamy. Are you using your own name?" "You haven't by any chance . . ." "No one is buying," Jean-Claude said. "Undoubtedly it is the weather. People are thinking in terms of—what do you call those things?—Chris-Crafts. To boat with. You would not consider again what I spoke to you about before?" "No," Peterson said, "I wouldn't consider it." "Two little ones would move much, much faster than a single huge big one," Jean-Claude said, looking away. "To saw it across the middle would be a very simple matter." "It's supposed to be a work of art," Peterson said, as calmly as possible. "You don't go around sawing works of art across the middle, remember?" "That place where it saws," Jean-Claude said, "is not very difficult. I can put my two hands around it." He made a circle with his two hands to demonstrate. "Invariably when I look at that piece I see two pieces. Are you absolutely sure you didn't conceive it wrongly in the first instance?" "Absolutely," Peterson said. Not a single piece of his was on view, and his liver expanded in rage and hatred. "You have a very romantic impulse," Jean-Claude said. "I admire, dimly, the posture. You read too much in the history of art. It estranges you from those possibilities for authentic selfhood that inhere in the present century." "I know," Peterson said, "could you let me have twenty until the first?"

Peterson sat in his loft on lower Broadway drinking Rheingold and thinking about the President. He had always felt close to the President but felt now that he had, in agreeing to appear on the television program, done something slightly disgraceful, of which the President would not approve. But I needed the money, he told himself, the telephone is turned off and the kitten is crying for milk. And I'm running out of beer. The President feels that the arts should be encouraged, Peterson reflected, surely he doesn't want me to go without beer? He wondered if what he was feeling was simple guilt at having sold himself to television or something more elegant: nausea? His liver groaned within him and he considered a situation in which his new relationship with the President was announced. He was working in the loft. The piece in hand was to be called *Season's Greetings* and combined three auto radiators, one from a Chevrolet Tudor, one from a Ford pickup, one from a 1932 Essex, with part of a former telephone switchboard and other items. The arrangement seemed right and he began welding. After a time the mass was freestanding. A couple of hours had passed. He put down the torch, lifted off the mask. He walked over to the refrigerator and found a sandwich left by a friendly junk dealer. It was a sandwich made hastily and without inspiration: a thin slice of ham between two pieces of bread. He ate it gratefully nevertheless. He stood looking at the work, moving from time to time so as to view it from a new angle.

Then the door to the loft burst open and the President ran in, trailing a sixteen-pound sledge. His first blow cracked the principal weld in *Season's Greetings,* the two halves parting like lovers, clinging for a moment and then rushing off in opposite directions. Twelve Secret Service men held Peterson in a paralyzing combination of secret grips. He's looking good, Peterson thought, very good, healthy, mature, fit, trustworthy. I like his suit. The President's second and third blows smashed the Essex radiator and the Chevrolet radiator. Then he attacked the welding torch, the plaster sketches on the workbench, the Rodin cast and the Giacometti stickman Peterson had bought in Paris. *"But Mr. President!"* Peterson shouted. *"I thought we were friends!"* A Secret Service man bit him in the back of the neck. Then the President lifted the sledge high in the air, turned toward Peterson, and said: "Your liver is diseased? That's a good sign. You're making progress. You're thinking."

"I happen to think that guy in the White House is doing a pretty darn good job." Peterson's barber, a man named Kitchen who was also a lay analyst and the author of four books titled *The Decision To Be,* was the only person in the world to whom he had confided his former sense of community with the President. "As far as his relationship with you personally goes," the barber continued, "it's essentially a kind of I-Thou relationship, if you know what I mean. You got to handle it with full awareness of the implications. In the end one experiences only oneself, Nietzsche said. When you're angry with the President, what you experience is self-as-angry-with-the-President. When things are okay between you and him, what you experience is self-as-swinging-with-the-President. Well and good. *But,*" Kitchen said, lathering up, "you want the relationship to be such that what you experience is the-President-as-swinging-with-you. You want *his* reality, get it? So that you can break out of the hell of solipsism. How about a little more off the sides?" "Everybody knows the language but me," Peterson said irritably. "Look," Kitchen said, "when you talk about me to somebody else, you say 'my barber,' don't you? Sure you do. In the same way, I look at you as being 'my' customer and I don't regard myself as 'your' barber. Oh, it's hell all right." The razor moved like a switchblade across the back of Peterson's neck. "Like Pascal said: 'The natural misfortune of our mortal and feeble condition is so wretched that when we consider it closely, nothing can console us.'" The razor rocketed around an ear. "Listen," Peterson said, "what do you think of this television program called *Who Am I?* Ever seen it?" "Frankly," the barber said, "it smells of the library. But they do a job on those people, I'll tell you that." "What do you mean?" Peterson said excitedly. "What kind of a job?" The cloth was whisked away and shaken with a sharp popping sound. "It's too horrible even to talk about," Kitchen said. "But it's what they deserve, those crumbs." "Which crumbs?" Peterson asked.

That night a tall foreign-looking man with a switchblade big as a butcherknife open in his hand walked into the loft without knocking and said "Good evening, Mr. Peterson, I am the cat-piano player, is there anything you'd particularly like to hear?" "Cat-piano?" Peterson said, gasping, shrinking from the knife. "What are you talking about? What do you want?" A biography of Nolde slid from his lap to the floor. "The cat-piano," said the visitor, "is an instrument of the devil, a diabolical instrument. You needn't sweat quite so much," he added, sounding aggrieved. Peterson tried to be brave. "I don't understand," he said. "Let me explain," the tall foreign-looking man said graciously. "The keyboard consists of eight cats—the octave—encased in the body of the instrument in such a way that only their heads and forepaws protrude. The player presses upon the appropriate paws, and the appropriate cats respond—with a kind of shriek. There is also provision made for pulling their tails. A tail-puller, or perhaps I should say tail *player*" (he smiled a disingenuous smile) "is stationed at the rear of the instrument, where the tails are. At the correct moment the tail-puller pulls the correct tail. The tail-note is of course quite different from the paw-note and produces sounds in the upper registers. Have you ever seen such an instrument, Mr. Peterson?" "No, and I don't believe it exists," Peterson said heroically. "There is an excellent early seventeenth-century engraving by Franz van der Wyngaert, Mr. Peterson, in which a cat-piano appears. Played, as it happens, by a man with a wooden leg. You will observe my own leg." The cat-piano player hoisted his trousers and a leglike contraption of wood, metal and plastic appeared. "And now, would you like to make a request? 'The Martyrdom of St. Sebastian'? The 'Romeo and Juliet' overture? 'Holiday for Strings?'" "But why—" Peterson began. "The kitten is crying for milk, Mr. Peterson. And whenever a kitten cries, the cat-piano plays." "But it's not my kitten," Peterson said reasonably. "It's just a kitten that wished itself on me. I've been trying to give it away. I'm not sure it's still around. I haven't seen it since the day before yesterday." The kitten appeared, looked at Peterson reproachfully, and then rubbed itself against the cat-piano player's mechanical leg. "Wait a minute!" Peterson exclaimed. "This thing is rigged! That cat hasn't been here in two days. What do you want from me? What am I supposed to do?" "Choices, Mr. Peterson, choices. You *chose* that kitten as a way of encountering that which you are not, that is to say, kitten. An effort on the part of the *pour-soi* to—" "But it chose me!" Peterson cried, "the door was open and the first thing I knew it was lying in my bed, under the Army blanket. I didn't have anything to do with it!" The cat-piano player repeated his disingenuous smile. "Yes, Mr. Peterson, I know, I know. Things are done to you, it is all a gigantic conspiracy. I've heard the story a hundred times. But the kitten is here, is it not? The kitten is weeping, is it not?" Peterson looked at the kitten, which was crying huge tigerish tears into its empty dish. "*Listen* Mr. Peterson," the cat-piano player said, "*listen!*" The blade of his immense knife jumped back into the handle with a thwack! and the hideous music began.

The day after the hideous music began the three girls from California arrived. Peterson opened his door, hesitantly, in response to an insistent ringing, and found himself being stared at by three girls in blue jeans and heavy sweaters, carrying suitcases. "I'm Sherry," the first girl said, "and this is Ann and this is Louise. We're from California and we need a place to stay." They were homely and extremely purposeful. "I'm sorry," Peterson said, "I can't—" "We sleep anywhere," Sherry said, looking past him into the vastness of his loft, "on the floor if we have to. We've done it before." Ann and Louise stood on their toes to get a good look. "What's that funny music?" Sherry asked, "it sounds pretty far-out. We really won't be any trouble at all and it'll just be a little while until we make a connection." "Yes," Peterson said, "but why me?" "You're an artist," Sherry said sternly, "we saw the A.I.R. sign downstairs." Peterson cursed the fire laws which made posting of the signs obligatory. "Listen," he said, "I can't even feed the cat. I can't even keep myself in beer. This is not the place. You won't be happy here. My work isn't authentic. I'm a minor artist." "The natural misfortune of our mortal and feeble condition is so wretched that when we consider it closely, nothing can console us," Sherry said. "That's Pascal." "I know," Peterson said, weakly. "Where is the john?" Louise asked. Ann marched into the kitchen and began to prepare, from supplies removed from her rucksack, something called *veal engagé*. "Kiss me," Sherry said, "I need love." Peterson flew to his friendly neighborhood bar, ordered a double brandy, and wedged himself into a telephone booth. "Miss Arbor? This is Hank Peterson. Listen, Miss Arbor, I can't do it. No, I mean really. I'm being punished horribly for even thinking about it. No, I mean it. You can't imagine what's going on around here. Please, get somebody else? I'd regard it as a great personal favor. Miss Arbor? Please?"

The other contestants were a young man in white pajamas named Arthur Pick, a karate expert, and an airline pilot in full uniform, Wallace E. Rice. "Just be natural," Miss Arbor said, "and of course be frank. We score on the basis of the validity of your answers, and of course that's measured by the polygraph." "What's this about a polygraph?" the airline pilot said. "The polygraph measures the validity of your answers," Miss Arbor said, her lips glowing whitely. "How else are we going to know if you're . . ." "Lying?" Wallace E. Rice supplied. The contestants were connected to the machine and the machine to a large illuminated tote board hanging over their heads. The master of ceremonies, Peterson noted without pleasure, resembled the President and did not look at all friendly.

The program began with Arthur Pick. Arthur Pick got up in his white pajamas and gave a karate demonstration in which he broke three half-inch pine boards with a single kick of his naked left foot. Then he told how he had disarmed a bandit, late at night at the A&P where he was an assistant manager, with a maneuver called a "rip-choong" which he demonstrated on the announcer. "How about that?" the announcer caroled. "Isn't that something? Audience?" The audience responded enthusiastically and Arthur Pick stood modestly with his hands behind his back. "Now," the announcer said, "let's play *Who Am I?* And here's you host, *Bell Lemmon!*" No, he doesn't look like the President, Peterson decided. "Arthur," Bill Lemmon said, "for twenty dollars—do you love your mother?" "Yes," Arthur Pick said. "Yes, of course." A bell rang, the tote board flashed, and the audience screamed. "He's lying!" the announcer shouted, "lying! lying! lying!" "Arthur," Bill Lemmon said, looking at his index cards, "the polygraph shows that the validity of your answer is . . . questionable. Would you like to try it again? Take another crack at it?" "You're crazy," Arthur Pick said. "Of course I love my mother." He was fishing around inside his pajamas for a handkerchief. "Is your mother watching the show tonight, Arthur?" "Yes, Bill, she is." "How long have you been studying karate?" "Two years, Bill." "And who paid for the lessons?" Arthur Pick hesitated. Then he said: "My mother, Bill." "They were pretty expensive, weren't they, Arthur?" "Yes, Bill, they were." "How expensive?" "Five dollars an hour." "Your mother doesn't make very much money, does she, Arthur?" "No, Bill, she doesn't." "Arthur, what does your mother do for a living?" "She's a garment worker, Bill. In the garment district." "And how long has she worked down there?" "All her life, I guess. Since my old man died." "And she doesn't make very much money, you said." "No. But she *wanted* to pay for the lessons. She *insisted* on it." Bill Lemmon said: "She wanted a son who could break boards with his feet?" Peterson's liver leaped and the tote board spelled out, in huge, glowing white letters, the words BAD FAITH. The airline pilot, Wallace E. Rice, was led to reveal that he had been caught, on a flight from Omaha to Miami, with a stewardess sitting on his lap and wearing his captain's cap, that the flight engineer had taken a Polaroid picture, and that he had been given involuntary retirement after nineteen years of faithful service. "It was perfectly safe," Wallace E. Rice said, "you don't understand, the automatic pilot can fly that plane better than I can." He further confessed to a lifelong and intolerable itch after stewardesses which had much to do, he said, with the way their jackets fell just on top of their hips, and his own jacket with the three gold stripes on the sleeve darkened with sweat until it was black.

I was wrong, Peterson thought, the world is absurd. The absurdity is punishing me for not believing in it. I affirm the absurdity. On the other hand, absurdity is itself absurd. Before the emcee could ask the first question, Peterson began to talk. "Yesterday," Peterson said to the television audience, "in the typewriter in front of the Olivetti showroom on Fifth Avenue, I found a recipe for Ten Ingredient Soup that included a stone from a toad's head. And while I stood there marveling a nice old lady pasted on the elbow of my best Haspel suit a little blue sticker reading THIS INDIVIDUAL IS A PART OF THE COMMUNIST CONSPIRACY FOR GLOBAL DOMINATION OF THE ENTIRE GLOBE. Coming home I passed a sign that said in ten-foot letters COWARD SHOES and heard a man singing "Golden Earrings" in a horrible voice, and last night I dreamed there was a shoot-out at our house on Meat Street and my mother shoved me in a closet to get me out of the line of fire." The emcee waved at the floor manager to turn Peterson off, but Peterson kept talking. "In this kind of a world," Peterson said, "absurd if you will, possibilities nevertheless proliferate and escalate all around us and there are opportunities for beginning again. I am a minor artist and my dealer won't even display my work if he can help it but minor is as minor does and lightning may strike even yet. Don't be reconciled. Turn off your television sets," Peterson said, "cash in your life insurance, indulge in a mindless optimism. Visit girls at dusk. Play the guitar. How can you be alienated without first having been connected? Think back and remember how it was." A man on the floor in front of Peterson was waving a piece of cardboard on which something threatening was written but Peterson ignored him and concentrated on the camera with the little red light. The little red light jumped from camera to camera in an attempt to throw him off balance but Peterson was too smart for it and followed wherever it went. "My mother was a royal virgin," Peterson said, "and my father a shower of gold. My childhood was pastoral and energetic and rich in experiences which developed my character. As a young man I was noble in reason, infinite in faculty, in form express and admirable, and in apprehension . . ." Peterson went on and on and although he was, in a sense, lying, in a sense he was not.

[1962]

For Thought

In the loose format of a rogue-adventurer tale, Barthelme uses deliberately flat characters that are outrageous caricatures of the types they represent. Through the misadventures of his artist-protagonist, he holds up to ridicule the fatuous notions and values we are led to accept uncritically as a result of mass conditioning brought about by constant exposure.

For Discussion

1. What does Miss Arbor represent in the way of a value system? How is her name ironic in this context?
2. What is the cat-piano a parody of in modern life?
3. What is Barthelme holding up to satirical laughter in the barber-shop scene?
4. What elements of the ridiculous are there in the TV-program scene? How close to reality is the exaggerated satire?
5. What are the comic and the serious aspects of Peterson's soliloquy at the end of the story?

Donald Barthelme
The King of Jazz

Well I'm the king of jazz now, thought Hokie Mokie to himself as he oiled the slide on his trombone. Hasn't been a 'bone man been king of jazz for many years. But now that Spicy MacLammermoor, the old king, is dead, I guess I'm it. Maybe I better play a few notes out of this window here, to reassure myself.

"Wow!" said somebody standing on the sidewalk. "Did you hear that?"

"I did," said his companion.

"Can you distinguish our great homemade American jazz performers, each from the other?"

"Used to could."

"Then who was that playing?"

"Sounds like Hokie Mokie to me. Those few but perfectly selected notes have the real epiphanic glow."

"The what?"

"The real epiphanic glow, such as is obtained only by artists of the caliber of Hokie Mokie, who's from Pass Christian, Mississippi. He's the king of jazz, now that Spicy MacLammermoor is gone."

Hokie Mokie put his trombone in its trombone case and went to a gig. At the gig everyone fell back before him, bowing.

"Hi Bucky! Hi Boot! Hi Freddie! Hi George! Hi Thad! Hi Roy! Hi Dexter! Hi Jo! Hi Willie! Hi Greens!"

"What we gonna play, Hokie? You the king of jazz now, you gotta decide."

"How 'bout 'Smoke'?"

"Wow!" everybody said. "Did you hear that? Hokie Mokie can just knock a fella out, just the way he pronounces a word. What a intonation on that boy! God Almight!"

"I don't want to play 'Smoke,'" somebody said.

"Would you repeat that, stranger?"

"I don't want to play 'Smoke.' 'Smoke' is dull. I don't like the changes. I refuse to play 'Smoke.'"

"He refuses to play 'Smoke'! But Hokie Mokie is the king of jazz and he says 'Smoke'!"

"Man, you from outa town or something? What do you mean you refuse to play 'Smoke'? How'd you get on this gig anyhow? Who hired you?"

"I am Hideo Yamaguchi, from Tokyo, Japan."

"Oh you're one of those Japanese cats, eh?"

"Yes I'm the top trombone man in all of Japan."

"Well you're welcome here until we hear you play. Tell me, is the Tennessee Tea Room still the top jazz place in Tokyo?"

"No, the top jazz place in Tokyo is the Square Box now."

"That's nice. O.K., now we gonna play 'Smoke' just like Hokie said. You ready, Hokie? O.K., give you four for nothin'. One! Two! Three! Four!"

The two men who had been standing under Hokie's window had followed him to the club. Now they said:

"Good God!"

"Yes, that's Hokie's famous 'English sunrise' way of playing. Playing with lots of rays coming out of it, some red rays, some blue rays, some green rays, some green stemming from a violet center, some olive stemming from a tan center—"

"That young Japanese fellow is pretty good, too."

"Yes, he is pretty good. And he holds his horn in a peculiar way. That's frequently the mark of a superior player."

"Bent over like that with his head between his knees—good God, he's sensational!"

He's sensational, Hokie thought. Maybe I ought to kill him.

But at that moment somebody came in the door pushing in front of him a four-and-one-half-octave marimba. Yes, it was Fat Man Jones, and he began to play even before he was fully in the door.

"What're we playing?"

"'Billie's Bounce.'"

"That's what I thought it was. What're we in?"

"F."

"That's what I thought we were in. Didn't you use to play with Maynard?"

"Yeah I was on that band for a while until I was in the hospital."

"What for?"

"I was tired."

"What can we add to Hokie's fantastic playing?"

"How 'bout some rain or stars?"

"Maybe that's presumptuous?"

"Ask him if he'd mind."

"You ask him, I'm scared. You don't fool around with the king of jazz. That young Japanese guy's pretty good, too."

"He's sensational."

"You think he's playing in Japanese?"

"Well I don't think it's English."

This trombone's been makin' my neck green for thirty-five years, Hokie thought. How come I got to stand up to yet another challenge, this late in life?

"Well, Hideo—"

"Yes, Mr. Mokie?"

"You did well on both 'Smoke' and 'Billie's Bounce.' You're just about as good as me, I regret to say. In fact, I've decided you're *better* than me. It's a hideous thing to contemplate, but there it is. I have only been the king of jazz for twenty-four hours, but the unforgiving logic of this art demands we bow to Truth, when we hear it."

"Maybe you're mistaken?"

"No, I got ears. I'm not mistaken. Hideo Yamaguchi is the new king of jazz."

"You want to be king emeritus?"

"No, I'm just going to fold up my horn and steal away. This gig is yours, Hideo. You can pick the next tune."

"How 'bout 'Cream'?"

"O.K., you heard what Hideo said, it's 'Cream.' You ready, Hideo?"

"Hokie, you don't have to leave. You can play too. Just move a little over to the side there—"

"Thank you, Hideo, that's very gracious of you. I guess I will play a little, since I'm still here. Sotto voce, of course."

"Hideo is wonderful on 'Cream'!"

"Yes, I imagine it's his best tune."

"What's that sound coming in from the side there?"

"Which side?"

"The left."

"You mean that sound that sounds like the cutting edge of life? That sounds like polar bears crossing Arctic ice pans? That sounds like a herd of musk ox in full flight? That sounds like male walruses diving to the bottom of the sea? That sounds like fumaroles smoking on the slopes of Mt. Katmai? That sounds like the wild turkey walking through the deep, soft forest? That sounds like beavers chewing trees in an Appalachian marsh? That sounds like an oyster fungus growing on an aspen trunk? That sounds like a mule deer wandering a montane of the Sierra Nevada? That sounds like prairie dogs kissing? That sounds like witchgrass tumbling or a river meandering? That sounds like manatees munching seaweed at Cape Sable? That sounds like coatimundis moving in packs across the face of Arkansas? That sounds like—"

"Good God, it's Hokie! Even with a cup mute on, he's blowing Hideo right off the stand!"

"Hideo's playing on his knees now! Good God, he's reaching into his belt for a large steel sword—Stop him!"

"Wow! That was the most exciting 'Cream' ever played! Is Hideo all right?"

"Yes, somebody is getting him a glass of water."

"You're my man, Hokie! That was the dadblangedest thing I ever saw!"

"You're the king of jazz once again!"

"Hokie Mokie is the most happening thing there is!"

"Yes, Mr. Hokie sir, I have to admit it, you blew me right off the stand. I see I have many years of work and study before me still."

"That's O.K., son. Don't think a thing about it. It happens to the best of us. Or it almost happens to the best of us. Now I want everybody to have a good time because we're gonna play 'Flats.' 'Flats' is next."

"With your permission, sir, I will return to my hotel and pack. I am most grateful for everything I have learned here."

"That's O.K., Hideo. Have a nice day. He-he. Now, 'Flats.'"

[1970]

For Thought

In this battle of comic giants, Barthelme fashions a parodying variation of the cowboy movie in which two formidable rivals engage one another in a jazz blow-out instead of in a deadly shoot-out. He makes artful use of the third-person peripheral observer point of view and employs disarmingly simple language, marked by comic understatement, to set a swift pace and establish an upbeat rhythm for this amusing comment on an important element in our culture.

For Discussion

1. What is the conflict? How is it rendered comic?
2. How are the two rivals characterized in view of the variation on the cowboy and gunfight elements employed by Barthelme?
3. Discuss the use of rhetorical devices for comic effect.
4. What role do the listeners play in the action? How is this role made comic?
5. What comic comment is Barthelme making on life?

Saul Bellow
Looking for Mr. Green

Whatsoever thy hand findeth to do, do it with thy might. . . .

Ecclesiastes 9:10

Hard work? No, it wasn't really so hard. He wasn't used to walking and stair-climbing, but the physical difficulty of his new job was not what George Grebe felt most. He was delivering relief checks in the Negro district, and although he was a native Chicagoan this was not a part of the city he knew much about—it needed a depression to introduce him to it. No, it wasn't literally hard work, not as reckoned in foot-pounds, but yet he was beginning to feel the strain of it, to grow aware of its peculiar difficulty. He could find the streets and numbers, but the clients were not where they were supposed to be, and he felt like a hunter inexperienced in the camouflage of his game. It was an unfavorable day, too—fall, and cold, dark weather, windy. But, anyway, instead of shells in his deep trenchcoat pocket he had the cardboard of checks, punctured for the spindles of the file, the holes reminding him of the holes in player-piano paper. And he didn't look much like a hunter, either; his was a city figure entirely, belted up in this Irish conspirator's coat. He was slender without being tall, stiff in the back, his legs looking shabby in a pair of old tweed pants gone through and fringy at the cuffs. With this stiffness, he kept his head forward, so that his face was red from the sharpness of the weather, and it was an indoors sort of face with gray eyes that persisted in some kind of thought and yet seemed to avoid definiteness of conclusion. He wore sideburns that surprised you somewhat by the tough curl of the blond hair and the effect of assertion in their length. He was not so mild as he looked, nor so youthful; and nevertheless there was no effort on his part to seem what he was not. He was an educated man: he was a bachelor; he was in some ways simple; without lushing, he liked a drink: his luck had not been good. Nothing was deliberately hidden.

He felt that his luck was better than usual today. When he had reported for work that morning he had expected to be shut up in the relief office at a clerk's job, for he had been hired downtown as a clerk, and he was glad to have, instead, the freedom of the streets and welcomed, at least at first, the vigor of the cold and even the blowing of the hard wind. But on the other hand he was not getting on with the distribution of the checks. It was true that it was a city job; nobody expected you to push too hard at a city job. His supervisor, that young Mr. Raynor, had practically told him that. Still, he wanted to do well at it. For one thing, when he knew how quickly he could deliver a batch of checks, he would know also how much time he could expect to clip for himself. And then, too, the clients would be waiting for their money. That was not the most important consideration, though it certainly mattered to him. No, but he wanted to do well, simply for doing-well's sake, to acquit himself decently of a job because he so rarely had a job to do that required just this sort of energy. Of this peculiar energy he now had a superabundance; once it had started to flow, it flowed all too heavily. And, for the time being anyway, he was balked. He could not find Mr. Green.

So he stood in his big-skirted trenchcoat with a large envelope in his hand and papers showing from his pocket, wondering why people should be so hard to locate who were too feeble or sick to come to the station to collect their own checks. But Raynor had told him that tracking them down was not easy at first and had offered him some advice on how to proceed. "If you can see the postman, he's your first man to ask, and your best bet. If you can't connect with him, try the stores and tradespeople around. Then the janitor and the neighbors. But you'll find the closer you come to your man the less people will tell you. They don't want to tell you anything."

"Because I'm a stranger."

"Because you're white. We ought to have a Negro doing this, but we don't at the moment, and of course you've got to eat, too, and this is public employment. Jobs have to be made. Oh, that holds for me too. Mind you, I'm not letting myself out. I've got three years of seniority on you, that's all. And a law degree. Otherwise, you might be back of the desk and I might be going out into the field this cold day. The same dough pays us both and for the same, exact, identical reason. What's my law degree got to do with it? But you have to pass out these checks, Mr. Grebe, and it'll help if you're stubborn, so I hope you are."

"Yes, I'm fairly stubborn."

Raynor sketched hard with an eraser in the old dirt of his desk, left-handed, and said, "Sure, what else can you answer to such a question. Anyhow, the trouble you're going to have is that they don't like to give information about anybody. They think you're a plain-clothes dick or an installment collector, or summons-server or something like that. Till you've been seen around the neighborhood for a few months and people know you're only from the relief."

It was dark, ground-freezing, pre-Thanksgiving weather; the wind played hob with the smoke, rushing it down, and Grebe missed his gloves, which he had left in Raynor's office. And no one would admit knowing Green. It was past three o'clock and the postman had made his last delivery. The nearest grocer, himself a Negro, had never heard the name Tulliver Green, or said he hadn't. Grebe was inclined to think that it was true, that he had in the end convinced the man that he wanted only to deliver a check. But he wasn't sure. He needed experience in interpreting looks and signs and, even more, the will not to be put off or denied and even the force to bully if need be. If the grocer did know, he had got rid of him easily. But since most of his trade was with reliefers, why should he prevent the delivery of a check? Maybe Green, or Mrs. Green, if there was a Mrs. Green, patronized another grocer. And was there a Mrs. Green? It was one of Grebe's great handicaps that he hadn't looked at any of the case records. Raynor should have let him read files for a few hours. But he apparently saw no need for that, probably considering the job unimportant. Why prepare systematically to deliver a few checks?

But now it was time to look for the janitor. Grebe took in the building in the wind and gloom of the late November day—trampled, frost-hardened lots on one side; on the other, an automobile junk yard and then the infinite work of Elevated frames, weak-looking, gaping with rubbish fires; two sets of leaning brick porches three stories high and a flight of cement stairs to the cellar. Descending, he entered the underground passage, where he tried the doors until one opened and he found himself in the furnace room. There someone rose toward him and approached, scraping on the coal grit and bending under the canvas-jacketed pipes.

"Are you the janitor?"

"What do you want?"

"I'm looking for a man who's supposed to be living here. Green"

"What Green?"

"Oh, you maybe have more than one Green?" said Grebe with new, pleasant hope. "This is Tulliver Green."

"I don't think I c'n help you, mister, I don't know any."

"A crippled man."

The janitor stood bent before him. Could it be that he was crippled? Oh, God! what if he was. Grebe's gray eyes sought with excited difficulty to see. But no, he was only very short and stooped. A head awakened from meditation, a strong-haired beard, low, wide shoulders. A staleness of sweat and coal rose from his black shirt and the burlap sack he wore as an apron.

"Crippled how?"

Grebe thought and then answered with the light voice of unmixed candor. "I don't know. I've never seen him." This was damaging, but his only other choice was to make a lying guess, and he was not up to it. "I'm delivering checks for the relief to shut-in cases. If he weren't crippled he'd come to collect himself. That's why I said crippled. Bedridden, chair-ridden—is there anybody like that?"

This sort of frankness was one of Grebe's oldest talents, going back to childhood. But it gained him nothing here.

"No suh. I've got four buildin's same as this that I take care of. I don't know all the tenants, leave alone the tenants' tenants. The rooms turn over so fast, people movin' in and out every day. I can't tell you."

The janitor opened his grimy lips but Grebe did not hear him in the piping of the valves and the consuming pull of air to flame in the body of the furnace. He knew, however, what he had said.

"Well, all the same, thanks. Sorry I bothered you. I'll prowl around upstairs again and see if I can turn up someone who knows him."

Once more in the cold air and early darkness he made the short circle from the cellarway to the entrance crowded between the brickwork pillars and began to climb to the third floor. Pieces of plaster ground under his feet; strips of brass tape from which the carpeting had been torn away marked old boundaries at the sides. In the passage, the cold reached him worse than in the street; it touched him to the bone. The hall toilets ran like springs. He thought grimly as he heard the wind burning around the building with a sound like that of the furnace, that this was a great piece of constructed shelter. Then he struck a match in the gloom and searched for names and numbers among the writings and scribbles on the walls. He saw WHOODY-DOODY GO TO JESUS, and zigzags, caricatures, sexual scrawls, and curses. So the sealed rooms of pyramids were also decorated, and the caves of human dawn.

The information on his card was, TULLIVER GREEN—APT 3D. There were no names, however, and no numbers. His shoulders drawn up, tears of cold in his eyes, breathing vapor, he went the length of the corridor and told himself that if he had been lucky enough to have the temperament for it he would bang on one of the doors and bawl out "Tulliver Green!" until he got results. But it wasn't in him to make an uproar and he continued to burn matches, passing the light over the walls. At the rear, in a corner off the hall, he discovered a door he had not seen before and he thought it best to investigate. It sounded empty when he knocked, but a young Negress answered, hardly more than a girl. She opened only a bit, to guard the warmth of the room.

"Yes suh?"

"I'm from the district relief station on Prairie Avenue. I'm looking for a man named Tulliver Green to give him his check. Do you know him?"

No, she didn't; but he thought she had not understood anything of what he had said. She had a dream-bound, dream-blind face, very soft and black, shut off. She wore a man's jacket and pulled the ends together at her throat. Her hair was parted in three directions, at the sides and transversely, standing up at the front in a dull puff.

"Is there somebody around here who might know?"

"I jus' taken this room las' week."

He observed that she shivered, but even her shiver was somnambulistic and there was no sharp consciousness of cold in the big smooth eyes of her handsome face.

"All right, miss, thank you. Thanks," he said, and went to try another place.

Here he was admitted. He was grateful, for the room was warm. It was full of people, and they were silent as he entered—ten people, or a dozen, perhaps more, sitting on benches like a parliament. There was no light, properly speaking, but a tempered darkness that the window gave, and everyone seemed to him enormous, the men padded out in heavy work clothes and winter coats, and the women huge, too, in their sweaters, hats, and old furs. And, besides, bed and bedding, a black cooking range, a piano piled towering to the ceiling with papers, a dining-room table of the old style of prosperous Chicago. Among these people Grebe, with his cold-heightened fresh color and his smaller stature, entered like a schoolboy. Even though he was met with smiles and good will, he knew, before a single word was spoken, that all the currents ran against him and that he would make no headway. Nevertheless he began. "Does anybody here know how I can deliver a check to Mr. Tulliver Green?"

"Green?" It was the man that had let him in who answered. He was in short sleeves, in a checkered shirt, and had a queer, high head, profusely overgrown and long as a shako; the veins entered it strongly from his forehead. "I never heard mention of him. Is this where he live?"

"This is the address they gave me at the station. He's a sick man, and he'll need his check. Can't anybody tell me where to find him?"

He stood his ground and waited for a reply, his crimson wool scarf wound about his neck and drooping outside his trenchcoat, pockets weighted with the block of checks and official forms. They must have realized that he was not a college boy employed afternoons by a bill collector trying foxily to pass for a relief clerk, recognized that he was an older man who knew himself what need was, who had had more than an average seasoning in hardship. It was evident enough if you looked at the marks under his eyes and at the sides of his mouth.

"Anybody know this sick man?"

"No suh." On all sides he saw heads shaken and smiles of denial. No one knew. And maybe it was true, he considered, standing silent in the earthen, musky human gloom of the place as the rumble continued. But he could never really be sure.

"What's the matter with this man?" said shako-head.

"I've never seen him. All I can tell you is that he can't come in person for his money. It's my first day in this district."

"Maybe they given you the wrong number?"

"I don't believe so. But where else can I ask about him?" He felt that this persistence amused them deeply, and in a way he shared their amusement that he should stand up so tenaciously to them. Though smaller, though slight, he was his own man, he retracted nothing about himself, and he looked back at them, gray-eyed, with amusement and also with a sort of courage. On the bench some man spoke in his throat, the words impossible to catch, and a woman answered with a wild, shrieking laugh, which was quickly cut off.

"Well, so nobody will tell me?"

"Ain't nobody who knows."

"At least, if he lives here, he pays rent to someone. Who manages the building?"

"Greatham Company. That's on Thirty-ninth Street."

Grebe wrote it in his pad. But, in the street again, a sheet of wind-driven paper clinging to his leg while he deliberated what direction to take next, it seemed a feeble lead to follow. Probably this Green didn't rent a flat, but a room. Sometimes there were as many as twenty people in an apartment; the real-estate agent would know only the lessee. And not even the agent could tell you who the renters were. In some places the beds were even used in shifts, watchmen or jitney drivers or short-order cooks in night joints turning out after a day's sleep and surrendering their beds to a sister, a nephew, or perhaps a stranger, just off the bus. There were large numbers of newcomers in this terrific, blight-bitten portion of the city between Cottage Grove and Ashland, wandering from house to house and room to room. When you saw them, how could you know them? They didn't carry bundles on their backs or look picturesque. You only saw a man, a Negro, walking in the street or riding in the car, like everyone else, with his thumb closed on a transfer. And therefore how were you supposed to tell? Grebe thought the Greatham agent would only laugh at his question.

But how much it would have simplified the job to be able to say that Green was old, or blind, or consumptive. An hour in the files, taking a few notes, and he needn't have been at such a disadvantage. When Raynor gave him the block of checks he asked, "How much should I know about these people?" Then Raynor had looked as though he were preparing to accuse him of trying to make the job more important than it was. He smiled, because by then they were on fine terms, but nevertheless he had been getting ready to say something like that when the confusion began in the station over Staika and her children.

Grebe had waited a long time for this job. It came to him through the pull of an old schoolmate in the Corporation Counsel's office, never a close friend, but suddenly sympathetic and interested—pleased to show, moreover, how well he had done, how strongly he was coming on even in these miserable times. Well, he was coming through strongly, along with the Democratic administration itself. Grebe had gone to see him in City Hall, and they had had a counter lunch or beers at least once a month for a year, and finally it had been possible to swing the job. He didn't mind being assigned the lowest clerical grade, nor even being a messenger, though Raynor thought he did.

This Raynor was an original sort of guy and Grebe had taken to him immediately. As was proper on the first day, Grebe had come early, but he waited long, for Raynor was late. At last he darted into his cubicle of an office as though he had just jumped from one of those hurtling huge red Indian Avenue cars. His thin, rough face was wind-stung and he was grinning and saying something breathlessly to himself. In his hat, a small fedora, and his coat, the velvet collar a neat fit about his neck, and his silk muffler that set off the nervous twist of his chin, he swayed and turned himself in his swivel chair, feet leaving the ground; so that he pranced a little as he sat. Meanwhile he took Grebe's measure out of his eyes, eyes of an unusual vertical length and slightly sardonic. So the two men sat for a while, saying nothing, while the supervisor raised his hat from his miscombed hair and put it in his lap. His cold-darkened hands were not clean. A steel beam passed through the little makeshift room, from which machine belts once had hung. The building was an old factory.

"I'm younger than you; I hope you won't find it hard taking orders from me," said Raynor. "But I don't make them up, either. You're how old, about?"

"Thirty-five."

"And you thought you'd be inside doing paper work. But it so happens I have to send you out."

"I don't mind."

"And it's mostly a Negro load we have in this district."

"So I thought it would be."

"Fine. You'll get along. *C'est un bon boulot*. Do you know French?"

"Some."

"I thought you'd be a university man."

"Have you been in France?" said Grebe.

"No, that's the French of the Berlitz School. I've been at it for more than a year, just as I'm sure people have been, all over the world, office boys in China and braves in Tanganyika. In fact, I damn well know it. Such is the attractive power of civilization. It's overrated, but what do you want? *Que voulez-vous?* I get *Le Rire* and all the spicy papers, just like in Tanganyika. It must be mystifying, out there. But my reason is that I'm aiming at the diplomatic service. I have a cousin who's a courier, and the way he describes it is awfully attractive. He rides in the *wagon-lits* and reads books. While we—What did you do before?"

"I sold."

"Where?"

"Canned meat at Stop and Shop. In the basement."

"And before that?"

"Window shades, at Goldblatt's."

"Steady work?"

"No, Thursdays and Saturdays. I also sold shoes."

"You've been a shoe-dog too. Well. And prior to that? Here it is in your folder." He opened the record. "Saint Olaf's College, instructor in classical languages. Fellow, University of Chicago, 1926–27. I've had Latin, too. Let's trade quotations—'*Dum spiro spero*.'"

"'Da dextram misero.'"

"'Alea jacta est.'"

"'Excelsior.'"

Raynor shouted with laughter, and other workers came to look at him over the partition. Grebe also laughed, feeling pleased and easy. The luxury of fun on a nervous morning.

When they were done and no one was watching or listening, Raynor said rather seriously, "What made you study Latin in the first place? Was it for the priesthood?"

"No."

"Just for the hell of it? For the culture? Oh, the things people think they can pull!" He made his cry hilarious and tragic. "I ran my pants off so I could study for the bar, and I've passed the bar, so I get twelve dollars a week more than you as a bonus for having seen life straight and whole. I'll tell you, as a man of culture, that even though nothing looks to be real, and everything stands for something else, and that thing for another thing, and that thing for a still further one—there ain't any comparison between twenty-five and thirty-seven dollars a week, regardless of the last reality. Don't you think that was clear to your Greeks? They were a thoughtful people, but they didn't part with their slaves."

This was a great deal more than Grebe had looked for in his first interview with his supervisor. He was too shy to show all the astonishment he felt. He laughed a little, aroused, and brushed at the sunbeam that covered his head with its dust. "Do you think my mistake was so terrible?"

"Damn right it was terrible, and you know it now that you've had the whip of hard times laid on your back. You should have been preparing yourself for trouble. Your people must have been well off to send you to the university. Stop me, if I'm stepping on your toes. Did your mother pamper you? Did your father give in to you? Were you brought up tenderly, with permission to go and find out what were the last things that everything else stands for while everybody else labored in the fallen world of appearances?"

"Well, no it wasn't exactly like that." Grebe smiled. *The fallen world of appearances!* no less. But now it was his turn to deliver a surprise. "We weren't rich. My father was the last genuine English butler in Chicago—"

"Are you kidding?"

"Why should I be?"

"In a livery?"

"In a livery. Up on the Gold Coast."

"And he wanted you to be educated like a gentleman?"

"He did not. He sent me to the Armour Institute to study chemical engineering. But when he died I changed schools."

He stopped himself, and considered how quickly Raynor had reached him. In no time he had your valise on the table and all your stuff unpacked. And afterward, in the streets, he was still reviewing how far he might have gone, and how much he might have been led to tell if they had not been interrupted by Mrs. Staika's great noise.

But just then a young woman, one of Raynor's workers, ran into the cubicle exclaiming. "Haven't you heard all the fuss?"

"We haven't heard anything."

"It's Staika, giving out with all her might. The reporters are coming. She said she phoned the papers, and you know she did."

"But what is she up to?" said Raynor.

"She brought her wash and she's ironing it here, with our current, because the relief won't pay her electric bill. She has her ironing board set up by the admitting desk, and her kids are with her, all six. They never are in school more than once a week. She's always dragging them around with her because of her reputation."

"I don't want to miss any of this," said Raynor, jumping up. Grebe, as he followed with the secretary, said, "Who is this Staika?"

"They call her the 'Blood Mother of Federal Street.' She's a professional donor at the hospitals. I think they pay ten dollars a pint. Of course it's no joke, but she makes a very big thing out of it and she and the kids are in the papers all the time."

A small crowd, staff and clients divided by a plywood barrier, stood in the narrow space of the entrance, and Staika was shouting in a gruff, mannish voice, plunging the iron on the board and slamming it on the metal rest.

"My father and mother came in a steerage, and I was born in our house, Robey by Huron. I'm no dirty immigrant. I'm a U.S. citizen. My husband is a gassed veteran from France with lungs weaker'n paper, that hardly can he go to the toilet by himself. These six children of mine, I have to buy the shoes for their feet with my own blood. Even a lousy little white Communion necktie, that's a couple of drops of blood; a little piece of mosquito veil for my Vadja so she won't be ashamed in church for the other girls, they take my blood for it by Goldblatt. That's how I keep goin.' A fine thing if I had to depend on the relief. And there's plenty of people on the rolls—fakes! There's nothin' *they* can't get, that can go and wrap bacon at Swift and Armour any time. They're lookin' for them by the Yards. They never have to be out of work. Only they rather lay in their lousy beds and eat the public's money." She was not afraid, in a predominantly Negro station, to shout this way about Negroes.

Grebe and Raynor worked themselves forward to get a closer view of the woman. She was flaming with anger and with pleasure at herself, broad and huge, a golden-headed woman who wore a cotton cap laced with pink ribbon. She was barelegged and had on black gym shoes, her Hoover apron was open and her great breasts, not much restrained by a man's undershirt, hampered her arms as she worked at the kid's dress on the ironing board. And the children, silent and white, with a kind of locked obstinacy, in sheepskins and lumberjackets, stood behind her. She had captured the station, and the pleasure this gave her was enormous. Yet her grievances were true grievances. She was telling the truth. But she behaved like a liar. The look of her small eyes were hidden, and while she raged she also seemed to be spinning and planning.

"They send me out college case workers in silk pants to talk me out of what I got comin'. Are they better'n me? Who told them? Fire them. Let 'em go and get married, and then you won't have to cut electric from people's budget."

The chief supervisor, Mr. Ewing, couldn't silence her and he stood with folded arms at the head of his staff, bald, bald-headed, saying to his subordinates like the ex-school principal he was, "Pretty soon she'll be tired and go."

"No she won't," said Raynor to Grebe. "She'll get what she wants. She knows more about the relief even then Ewing. She's been on the rolls for years, and she always gets what she wants because she puts on a noisy show. Ewing knows it. He'll give in soon. He's only saving face. If he gets bad publicity, the Commissioner'll have him on the carpet, downtown. She's got him submerged; she'll submerge everybody in time, and that includes nations and governments."

Grebe replied with his characteristic smile, disagreeing completely. Who would take Staika's orders, and what changes could her yelling ever bring about?

No, what Grebe saw in her, the power that made people listen, was that her cry expressed the war of flesh and blood, perhaps turned a little crazy and certainly ugly, on this place and this condition. And at first, when he went out, the spirit of Staika somehow presided over the whole district for him, and it took color from her; he saw her color, in the spotty curb fires, and the fires under the El, the straight alley of flamy gloom. Later, too, when he went into a tavern for a shot of rye, the sweat of beer, association with West Side Polish streets, made him think of her again.

He wiped the corners of his mouth with his muffler, his handkerchief being inconvenient to reach for, and went out again to get on with the delivery of his checks. The air bit cold and hard and a few flakes of snow formed near him. A train struck by and left a quiver in the frames and a bristling icy hiss over the rails.

Crossing the street, he descended a flight of board steps into a basement grocery, setting off a little bell. It was a dark long store and it caught you with its stinks of smoked meat, soap, dried peaches, and fish. There was a fire wrinkling and flapping in the little stove, and the proprietor was waiting, an Italian with a long, hollow face and stubborn bristles. He kept his hands warm under his apron.

No, he didn't know Green. You knew people but not names. The same man might not have the same name twice. The police didn't know, either, and mostly didn't care. When somebody was shot or knifed they took the body away and didn't look for the murderer. In the first place, nobody would tell them anything. So they made up a name for the coroner and called it quits. And in the second place, they didn't give a goddamn anyhow. But they couldn't get to the bottom of a thing even if they wanted to. Nobody would get to know even a tenth of what went on among these people. They stabbed and stole, they did every crime and abomination you ever heard of, men and men, women and women, parents and children, worse than the animals. They carried on their own way, and the horrors passed off like a smoke. There was never anything like it in the history of the whole world.

It was a long speech, deepening with every word in its fantasy and passion and becoming increasingly senseless and terrible: a swarm amassed by suggestion and invention, a huge, hugging, despairing knot, a human wheel of heads, legs, bellies, arms, rolling through his shop.

Grebe felt that he must interrupt him. He said sharply, "What are you talking about! All I asked was whether you knew this man."

"That isn't even the half of it. I been here six years. You probably don't want to believe this. But suppose it's true?"

"All the same," said Grebe, "there must be a way to find a person."

The Italian's close-spaced eyes had been queerly concentrated, as were his muscles, while he leaned across the counter trying to convince Grebe. Now he gave up the effort and sat down on his stool. "Oh—I suppose. Once in a while. But I been telling you, even the cops don't get anywhere."

"They're always after somebody. It's not the same thing."

"Well, keep trying if you want. I can't help you."

But he didn't keep trying. He had no more time to spend on Green. He slipped Green's check to the back of the block. The next name on the list was FIELD, WINSTON.

He found the back-yard bungalow without the least trouble; it shared a lot with another house, a few feet of yard between. Grebe knew these two-shack arrangements. They had been built in vast numbers in the days before the swamps were filled and the streets raised, and they were all the same—a boardwalk along the fence, well under street level, three or four ball-headed posts for clotheslines, greening wood, dead shingles, and a long, long flight of stairs to the rear door.

A twelve-year-old boy let him into the kitchen, and there the old man was, sitting by the table in a wheel chair.

"Oh, it's d'Government man," he said to the boy when Grebe drew out his checks. "Go bring me my box of papers." He cleared a space on the table.

"Oh, you don't have to go to all that trouble," said Grebe. But Field laid out his papers. Social Security card, relief certification, letters from the state hospital in Manteno, and a naval discharge dated San Diego, 1920.

"That's plenty," Grebe said. "Just sign."

"You got to know who I am," the old man said. "You're from the Government. It's not your check, it's a Government check and you got no business to hand it over till everything is proved."

He loved the ceremony of it, and Grebe made no more objections. Field emptied his box and finished out the circle of cards and letters.

"There's everything I done and been. Just the death certificate and they can close book on me." He said this with a certain happy pride and magnificence. Still he did not sign; he merely held the little pen upright on the golden-green corduroy of his thigh. Grebe did not hurry him. He felt the old man's hunger for conversation.

"I got to get better coal," he said. "I send my little gran'son to the yard with my order and they fill his wagon with screening. The stove ain't made for it. It fall through the grate. The order says Franklin County egg-size coal."

"I'll report it and see what can be done."

"Nothing can be done, I expect. You know and I know. There ain't no little ways to make things better, and the only big thing is money. That's the only sunbeams, money. Nothing is black where it shines, and the only place you see black is where it ain't shining. What we colored have to have is our own rich. There ain't no other way."

Grebe sat, his reddened forehead bridged levelly by his close-cut hair and his cheeks lowered in the wings of his collar—the caked fire shone hard within the isinglass-and-iron frames but the room was not comfortable—sat and listened while the old man unfolded his scheme. This was to create one Negro millionaire a month by subscription. One clever, good-hearted young fellow elected every month would sign a contract to use the money to start a business employing Negroes. This would be advertised by chain letters and word of mouth, and every Negro wage earner would contribute a dollar a month. Within five years there would be sixty millionaires.

"That'll fetch respect," he said with a throat-stopped sound that came out like a foreign syllable. "You got to take and organize all the money that gets thrown away on the policy wheel and horse race. As long as they can take it away from you, they got no respect for you. Money, that's d' sun of human kind!" Field was a Negro of mixed blood, perhaps Cherokee, or Natchez; his skin was reddish. And he sounded, speaking about a golden sun in this dark room, and looked, shaggy and slab-headed, with the mingled blood of his face and broad lips, the little pen still upright in his hand, like one of the underground kings of mythology, old judge Minos himself.

And now he accepted the check and signed. Not to soil the slip, he held it down with his knuckles. The table budged and creaked, the center of the gloomy, heathen midden of the kitchen covered with bread, meat, and cans, and the scramble of papers.

"Don't you think my scheme'd work?"

"It's worth thinking about. Something ought to be done, I agree."

"It'll work if people will do it. That's all. That's the only thing, any time. When they understand it in the same way, all of them."

"That's true," said Grebe, rising. His glance met the old man's.

"I know you got to go," he said. "Well, God bless you, boy, you ain't been sly with me. I can tell it in a minute."

He went back through the buried yard. Someone nursed a candle in a shed, where a man unloaded kindling wood from a sprawl-wheeled baby buggy and two voices carried on a high conversation. As he came up the sheltered passage he heard the hard boost of the wind in the branches and against the house fronts, and then, reaching the sidewalk, he saw the needle-eye red of cable towers in the open icy height hundreds of feet above the river and the factories—those keen points. From here, his view was obstructed all the way to the South Branch and its timber banks, and the cranes beside the water. Rebuilt after the Great Fire, this part of the city was, not fifty years later, in ruins again, factories boarded up, buildings deserted or fallen, gaps of prairie between. But it wasn't desolation that this made you feel, but rather a faltering of organization that set free a huge energy, an escaped, unattached unregulated power from the giant raw place. Not only must people feel it but, it seemed to Grebe, they were compelled to match it. In their very bodies. He no less than others, he realized. Say that his parents had been servants in their time, whereas he was not supposed to be one. He thought that they had never done any service like this, which no one visible asked for, and probably flesh and blood could not even perform. Nor could anyone show why it should be performed; or see where the performance would lead. That did not mean that he wanted to be released from it, he realized with a grimly pensive face. On the contrary. He had something to do. To be compelled to feel this energy and yet have no task to do—that was horrible; that was suffering; he knew what that was. It was now quitting time. Six o'clock. He could go home if he liked, to his room, that is, to wash in hot water, to pour a drink, lie down on his quilt, read the paper, eat some liver paste on crackers before going out to dinner. But to think of this actually made him feel a little sick, as though he had swallowed hard air. He had six checks left and he was determined to deliver at least one of these: Mr. Green's check.

So he started again. He had four or five dark blocks to go, past open lots, condemned houses, old foundations, closed schools, black churches, mounds, and he reflected that there must be many people alive who had once seen the neighborhood rebuilt and new. Now there was a second layer of ruins; centuries of history accomplished through human massing. Numbers had given the place forced growth; enormous numbers had also broken it down. Objects once so new, so concrete that it could have occurred to anyone they stood for other things, had crumbled. Therefore, reflected Grebe, the secret of them was out. It was that they stood for themselves by agreement, and were natural and not unnatural by agreement, and when the things themselves collapsed the agreement became visible. What was it, otherwise, that kept cities from looking peculiar? Rome, that was almost permanent, did not give rise to thoughts like these. And was it abidingly real? But in Chicago, where the cycles were so fast and the familiar died out, and again rose changed, and died again in thirty years, you saw the common agreement or covenant, and you were forced to think about appearances and realities. (He remembered Raynor and he smiled. Raynor was a clever boy.) Once you had grasped this, a great many things became intelligible. For instance, why Mr. Field should conceive such a scheme. Of course, if people were to agree to create a millionaire, a real millionaire would come into existence. And if you wanted to know how Mr. Field was inspired to think of this, why, he had within sight of his kitchen window the chart, the very bones of a successful scheme—the El with its blue and green confetti of signals. People consented to pay dimes and ride the crash-box cars, and so it was a success. Yet how absurd it looked; how little reality there was to start with. And yet Yerkes, the great financier who built it, had known that he could get people to agree to do it. Viewed as itself, what a scheme of a scheme it seemed, how close to an appearance. Then why wonder at Mr. Field's idea? He had grasped a principle. And then Grebe remembered, too, that Mr. Yerkes had established the Yerkes Observatory and endowed it with millions. Now how did the notion come to him in his New York museum of a palace or his Aegean-bound yacht to give money to astronomers? Was he awed by the success of his bizarre enterprise and therefore ready to spend money to find out where in the universe being and seeming were identical? Yes, he wanted to know what abides; and whether flesh is Bible grass; and he offered money to be burned in the fire of suns. Okay, then, Grebe thought further, these things exist because people consent to exist with them—we have got so far—and also there is reality which doesn't depend on consent but within which consent is a game. But what about need, the need that keeps so many vast thousands in position? You tell me that, you *private* little gentleman and *decent* soul—he used these words against himself scornfully. Why is the consent given to misery? And why so painfully ugly? Because there is *something* that is dismal and permanently ugly? Here he sighed and gave it up, and thought it was enough for the present moment that he had a real check in his pocket for a Mr. Green who must be real beyond question. If only his neighbors didn't think they had to conceal him.

This time he stopped at the second floor. He struck a match and found a door. Presently a man answered his knock and Grebe had the check ready and showed it even before he began. "Does Tulliver Green live here? I'm from the relief."

The man narrowed the opening and spoke to someone at his back.

"Does he live here?"

"Uh-uh. No."

"Or anywhere in this building? He's a sick man and he can't come for his dough." He exhibited the check in the light, which was smoky—the air smelled of charred lard—and the man held off the brim of his cap to study it.

"Uh-uh. Never seen the name."

"There's nobody around here that uses crutches?"

He seemed to think, but it was Grebe's impression that he was simply waiting for a decent interval to pass.

"No, suh. Nobody I ever see."

"I've been looking for this man all afternoon"—Grebe spoke out with sudden force—"and I'm going to have to carry this check back to the station. It seems strange not to be able to find a person to *give* him something when you're looking for him for a good reason. I suppose if I had bad news for him I'd find him quick enough."

There was a responsive motion in the other man's face. "That's right, I reckon."

"It almost doesn't do any good to have a name if you can't be found by it. It doesn't stand for anything. He might as well not have any," he went on, smiling. It was as much of a concession as he could make to his desire to laugh.

"Well, now, there's a little old knot-back man I see once in a while. He might be the one you lookin' for. Downstairs."

"Where? Right side or left? Which door?"

"I don't know which. Thin-face little knot-back with a stick."

But no one answered at any of the doors on the first floor. He went to the end of the corridor, searching by matchlight, and found only a stairless exit to the yard, a drop of about six feet. But there was a bungalow near the alley, an old house like Mr. Field's. To jump was unsafe. He ran from the front door, through the underground passage and into the yard. The place was occupied. There was a light through the curtains, upstairs. The name on the ticket under the broken, scoop-shaped mailbox was Green! He exultantly rang the bell and pressed against the locked door. Then the lock clicked faintly and a long staircase opened before him. Someone was slowly coming down—a woman. He had the impression in the weak light that she was shaping her hair as she came, making herself presentable, for he saw her arms raised. But it was for support that they were raised; she was feeling her way downward, down the wall, stumbling. Next he wondered about the pressure of her feet on the treads; she did not seem to be wearing shoes. And it was a freezing stairway. His ring had got her out of bed, perhaps, and she had forgotten to put them on. And then he saw that she was not only shoeless but naked; she was entirely naked, climbing down while she talked to herself, a heavy woman, naked and drunk. She blundered into him. The contact of her breasts, though they touched only his coat, made him go back against the door with a blind shock. See what he had tracked down, in his hunting game!

The woman was saying to herself, furious with insult, "So I cain't—k, huh? I'll show that son-of-a-bitch kin I, cain't I."

What should he do now? Grebe asked himself. Why, he should go. He should turn away and go. He couldn't talk to this woman. He couldn't keep her standing naked in the cold. But when he tried he found himself unable to turn away.

He said, "Is this where Mr. Green lives?"

But she was still talking to herself and did not hear him.

"Is this Mr. Green's house?"

At last she turned her furious drunken glance on him. "What do you want?"

Again her eyes wandered from him; there was a dot of blood in their enraged brilliance. He wondered why she didn't feel the cold.

"I'm from the relief."

"Awright, what?"

"I've got a check for Tulliver Green."

This time she heard him and put out her hand.

"No, no, for *Mr.* Green. He's got to sign," he said. How was he going to get Green's signature tonight!

"I'll take it. He cain't."

He desperately shook his head, thinking of Mr. Field's precautions about identification. "I can't let you have it. It's for him. Are you Mrs. Green?"

"Maybe I is, and maybe I ain't. Who want to know?"

"Is he upstairs?"

"Awright. Take it up yourself, you goddamn fool."

Sure, he was a goddamn fool. Of course he could not go up because Green would probably be drunk and naked, too. And perhaps he would appear on the landing soon. He looked eagerly upward. Under the light was a high narrow brown wall. Empty! It remained empty!

"Hell with you, then!" he heard her cry. To deliver a check for coal and clothes, he was keeping her in the cold. She did not feel it, but his face was burning with frost and self-ridicule. He backed away from her.

"I'll come tomorrow, tell him."

"Ah, hell with you. Don' never come. What you doin' here in the nighttime? Don' come back." She yelled so that he saw the breadth of her tongue. She stood astride in the long cold box of the hall and held on to the banister and the wall. The bungalow itself was shaped something like a box, a clumsy, high box pointing into the freezing air with its sharp, wintry lights.

"If you are Mrs. Green, I'll give you the check." he said, changing his mind.

"Give here, then." She took it, took the pen offered with it in her left hand, and tried to sign the receipt on the wall. He looked around, almost as though to see whether his madness was being observed, and came near believing that someone was standing on a mountain of used tires in the auto-junking shop next door.

"But are you Mrs. Green?" he now thought to ask. But she was already climbing the stairs with the check, and it was too late, if he had made an error, if he was now in trouble, to undo the thing. But he wasn't going to worry about it. Though she might not be Mrs. Green, he was convinced that Mr. Green was upstairs. Whoever she was, the woman stood for Green, whom he was not to see this time. Well, you silly bastard, he said to himself, so you think you found him. So what? Maybe you really did find him—what of it? But it was important that there was a real Mr. Green whom they could not keep him from reaching because he seemed to come as an emissary from hostile appearances. And though the self-ridicule was slow to diminish, and his face still blazed with it, he had, nevertheless, a feeling of elation, too." "For after all," he said, "he *could* be found!"

[1951]

For Thought

Bellow has adapted the old motif of a quest through a labyrinth to the setting of Chicago's street slums. "Looking for Mr. Green" is filled with realistic characters who each reflect a different aspect of poverty. George Grebe meets these characters at the welfare center while trying to find a welfare check recipient; however, George Grebe is also in quest of himself. His failure to find Mr. Green points up the difficulty of defining or fixing anyone's identity beyond a name on a piece of paper.

For Discussion

1. How is George Grebe characterized? How does Bellow compare him with and contrast him to Raynor? How is it unusual that both of them are working in a city welfare office?
2. How do each of the characters reflect a particular outlook on life?
3. Explain why Grebe seeks Tulliver Green so stubbornly.
4. Why is the setting of the story appropriate for Bellow to compare it implicitly with the Labyrinth of "old judge Minor" of Crete?
5. What is the significance of the author's initial use of a quote from Ecclesiastes 9:10?

Ambrose Bierce
Chickamauga

One sunny autumn afternoon a child strayed away from its rude home in a small field and entered a forest unobserved. It was happy in a new sense of freedom from control, happy in the opportunity of exploration and adventure; for this child's spirit, in bodies of its ancestors, had for thousands of years been trained to memorable feats of discovery and conquest—victories in battles whose critical moments were centuries, whose victors' camps were cities of hewn stone. From the cradle of its race it had conquered its way through two continents and passing a great sea had penetrated a third, there to be born to war and dominion as a heritage.

The child was a boy aged about six years, the son of a poor planter. In his younger manhood the father had been a soldier, had fought against naked savages and followed the flag of his country into the capital of a civilized race to the far South. In the peaceful life of a planter the warrior-fire survived; once kindled, it is never extinguished. The man loved military books and pictures and the boy had understood enough to make himself a wooden sword, though even the eye of his father would hardly have known it for what it was. This weapon he now bore bravely, as became the son of an heroic race, and pausing now and again in the sunny space of the forest assumed, with some exaggeration, the postures of aggression and defense that he had been taught by the engraver's art. Made reckless by the ease with which he overcame invisible foes attempting to stay his advance, he committed the common enough military error of pushing the pursuit to a dangerous extreme, until he found himself upon the margin of a wide but shallow brook, whose rapid waters barred his direct advance against the flying foe that had crossed with illogical ease. But the intrepid victor was not to be baffled; the spirit of the race which had passed the great sea burned unconquerable in that small breast and would not be denied. Finding a place where some boulders in the bed of the stream lay but a step or a leap apart, he

SOURCE "Chickamauga" by Ambrose Bierce. Reprinted from *Tales of Soldiers and Civilians*, 1891.

made his way across and fell again upon the rearguard of his imaginary foe, putting all to the sword.

Now that the battle had been won, prudence required that he withdraw to his base of operations. Alas; like many a mightier conqueror, and like one, the mightiest, he could not

> curb the lust for war,
> Nor learn that tempted Fate will leave
> the loftiest star.

Advancing from the bank of the creek he suddenly found himself confronted with a new and more formidable enemy: in the path that he was following, sat, bolt upright, with ears erect and paws suspended before it, a rabbit! With a startled cry the child turned and fled, he knew not in what direction, calling with inarticulate cries for his mother, weeping, stumbling, his tender skin cruelly torn by brambles, his little heart beating hard with terror—breathless, blind with tears—lost in the forest! Then, for more than an hour, he wandered with erring feet through the tangled undergrowth, till at last, overcome by fatigue, he lay down in a narrow space between two rocks, within a few yards of the stream and still grasping his toy sword, no longer a weapon but a companion, sobbed himself to sleep. The wood birds sang merrily above his head; the squirrels whisking their bravery of tail, ran barking from tree to tree, unconscious of the pity of it, and somewhere far away was a strange, muffled thunder, as if the partridges were drumming in celebration of nature's victory over the son of her immemorial enslavers. And back at the little plantation, where white men and black were hastily searching the fields and hedges in alarm, a mother's heart was breaking for her missing child.

Hours passed, and then the little sleeper rose to his feet. The chill of the evening was in his limbs, the fear of the gloom in his heart. But he had rested, and he no longer wept. With some blind instinct which impelled him to action he struggled through the undergrowth about him and came to a more open ground—on his right the brook, to the left a gentle acclivity studded with infrequent trees; over all, the gathering gloom of twilight. A thin, ghostly mist rose along the water. It frightened and repelled him; instead of recrossing, in the direction whence he had come, he turned his back upon it, and went forward toward the dark inclosing wood. Suddenly he saw before him a strange moving object which he took to be some large animal—a dog, a pig—he could not name it; perhaps it was a bear. He had seen pictures of bears, but knew of nothing to their discredit and had vaguely wished to meet one. But something in form or movement of this object—something in the awkwardness of its approach—told him that it was not a bear, and curiosity was stayed by fear. He stood still and as it came slowly on gained courage every moment, for he saw that at least it had not the long, menacing ears of the rabbit. Possibly his impressionable mind was half conscious of something familiar in its shambling, awkward gait. Before it had approached near enough to resolve his doubts he saw that it was followed by another and another. To right and to left were many more; the whole open space about him was alive with them—all moving toward the brook.

They were men. They crept upon their hands and knees. They used their hands only, dragging their legs. They used their knees only, their arms hanging idle at their sides. They strove to rise to their feet, but fell prone in the attempt. They did nothing naturally, and nothing alike, save only to advance foot by foot in the same direction. Singly, in pairs and in little groups, they came on through the gloom, some halting now and again while others crept slowly past them, then resuming their movement. They came by dozens and by hundreds; as far on either hand as one could see in the deepening gloom they extended and the black wood behind them appeared to be inexhaustible. The very ground seemed in motion toward the creek. Occasionally one who had paused did not again go on, but lay motionless. He was dead. Some, pausing, made strange gestures with their hands, erected their arms and lowered them again, clasped their heads; spread their palms upward, as men are sometimes seen to do in public prayer.

Not all of this did the child note; it is what would have been noted by an elder observer; he saw little but that these were men, yet crept like babes. Being men, they were not terrible, though unfamiliarity clad. He moved among them freely, going from one to another and peering into their faces with childish curiosity. All their faces were singularly white and many were streaked and gouted with red. Something in this—something too, perhaps, in their grotesque attitudes and movements—reminded him of the painted clown whom he had seen last summer in the circus, and he laughed as he watched them. But on and ever on they crept, these maimed and bleeding men, as heedless as he of the dramatic contrast between his laughter and their own ghastly gravity. To him it was a merry spectacle. He had seen his father's negroes creep upon their hands and knees for his amusement—had ridden them so, "making believe" they were his horses. He now approached one of these crawling figures from behind and with an agile movement mounted it astride. The man sank upon his breast, recovered, flung the small boy fiercely to the ground as an unbroken colt might have done, then turned upon him a face that lacked a lower jaw—from the upper teeth to the throat was a great red gap fringed with hanging shreds of flesh and splinters of bone. The unnatural prominence of nose, the absence of chin, the fierce eyes, gave this man the appearance of a great bird of prey crimsoned in throat and breast by the blood of its quarry. The man rose to his knees, the child to his feet. The man shook his fist at the child; the child, terrified at last, ran to a tree near by, got upon the farther side of it and took a more serious view of the situation. And so the clumsy multitude dragged itself slowly and painfully along in hideous pantomime—moved forward down the slope like a swarm of great black beetles, with never a sound of going—in silence profound, absolute.

Instead of darkening, the haunted landscape began to brighten. Through the belt of trees beyond the brook shone a strange red light, the trunks and branches of the trees making a black lacework against it. It struck the creeping figures and gave them monstrous shadows, which caricatured their movements on the lit grass. It fell upon their faces, touching their whiteness with a ruddy tinge, accentuating the stains with which so many of them were freaked and maculated. It sparkled on buttons and bits of metal in their clothing. Instinctively the child turned toward the growing splendor and moved down the slope with his horrible companions; in a few moments had passed the foremost of the throng—not much of a feat, considering his advantages. He placed himself in the lead, his wooden sword still in hand, and solemnly directed the march, conforming his pace to theirs and occasionally turning as if to see that his forces did not straggle. Surely such a leader never before had such a following.

Scattered about upon the ground now slowly narrowing by the encroachment of this awful march to water, were certain articles to which, in the leader's mind, were coupled no significant associations: an occasional blanket, tightly rolled lengthwise, doubled and the ends bound together with a string; a heavy knapsack here, and there a broken rifle—such things, in short, as are found in the rear of retreating troops, the "spoor" of men flying from their hunters. Everywhere near the creek, which here had a margin of lowland, the earth was trodden into mud by the feet of men and horses. An observer of better experience in the use of his eyes would have noticed that these footprints pointed in both directions; the ground had been twice passed over—in advance and in retreat. A few hours before, these desperate, stricken men, with their more fortunate and now distant comrades, had penetrated the forest in thousands. Their successive battalions, breaking into swarms and re-forming in lines, had passed the child on every side—had almost trodden on him as he slept. The rustle and murmur of their march had not awakened him. Almost within a stone's throw of where he lay they had fought a battle; but all unheard by him were the roar of the musketry, the shock of the cannon, "the thunder of the captains and the shouting." He had slept through it all, grasping his little wooden sword with perhaps a tighter clutch in unconscious sympathy with his martial environment, but as heedless of the grandeur of the struggle as the dead who had died to make the glory.

The fire beyond the belt of woods on the farther side of the creek, reflected to earth from the canopy of its own smoke, was now suffusing the whole landscape. It transformed the sinuous line of mist to the vapour of gold. The water gleamed with dashes of red, and red, too, were many of the stones protruding above the surface. But that was blood; the less desperately wounded had stained them in crossing. On them, too, the child now crossed with eager steps; he was going to the fire. As he stood upon the farther bank he turned about to look at the companions of his march. The advance was arriving at the creek. The stronger had already drawn themselves to the brink and plunged their faces into the flood. Three or four who lay without motion appeared to have no heads. At this the child's eyes expanded with wonder; even his hospitable understanding could not accept a phenomenon implying such vitality as that. After slaking their thirst these men had not had the strength to back away from the water, nor to keep their heads above it. They were drowned. In rear of these, the open spaces of the forest showed the leader as many formless figures of his grim command as at first; but not nearly so many were in motion. He waved his cap for their encouragement and smilingly pointed with his weapon in the direction of the guiding light—a pillar of fire to this strange exodus.

Confident of the fidelity of his forces, he now entered the belt of woods, passed through it easily in the red illumination, climbed a fence, ran across a field, turning now and again to coquet with his responsive shadow, and so approached the blazing ruin of a dwelling. Desolation everywhere! In all the wide glare not a living thing was visible. He cared nothing for that; the spectacle pleased, and he danced with glee in imitation of the wavering flames. He ran about, collecting fuel, but every object that he found was too heavy for him to cast in from the distance to which the heat limited his approach. In despair he flung in his sword—a surrender to the superior forces of nature. His military career was at an end.

Shifting his position, his eyes fell upon some outbuildings which had an oddly familiar appearance, as if he had dreamed of them. He stood considering them with wonder, when suddenly the entire plantation, with its inclosing forest, seemed to turn as if upon a pivot. His little world swung half around; the points of the compass were reversed. He recognized the blazing building as his own home!

For a moment he stood stupefied by the power of the revelation, then ran with stumbling feet, making a half-circuit of the ruin. There, conspicuous in the light of the conflagration, lay the dead body of a woman—the white face turned upward, the hands thrown out and clutched full of grass, the clothing deranged, the long dark hair in tangles and full of clotted blood. The greater part of the forehead was torn away, and from the jagged hole the brain protruded, overflowing the temple, a frothy mass of gray, crowned with clusters of crimson bubbles—the work of a shell.

The child moved his little hands, making wild, uncertain gestures. He uttered a series of inarticulate and indescribable cries—something between the chattering of an ape and the gobbling of a turkey—a startling, soulless, unholy sound, the language of a devil. The child was a deaf mute.

Then he stood motionless, with quivering lips, looking down upon the wreck.

[1891]

For Thought

Bierce has chosen to portray the aftermath of a bloody battle during the American Civil War from the "camera eye" point of view of a deaf-mute child. The story's violent carnage climaxes with the burning of the family farm and the boy's discovery of his dead mother. Although war may seem to be child's play to adults deaf to its horrors, it is not. The wanton destruction of war mocks the ideals which drive people to enter it.

For Discussion

1. In the story, the boy pretends to lead a conquering army, gets lost and goes to sleep, treats a retreat of wounded soldiers as if it were a game, and then discovers a scene of violence. How have the opposing armies experienced a similar chain of actions and feelings?
2. Critics have complained that Bierce does not play fair with the reader. He conceals the child's handicaps for the sake of a shocking climax. How and where does the author hint at the boy's handicaps? How do the boy's actions reflect his inability to speak or hear?
3. The wounded soldiers are not identified as individuals or even as members of a particular army. How does Bierce use animal imagery? Explain the impact of this imagery on the boy and upon the reader.
4. Aside from the title, the story could deal with any battle fought in the last century or so. What themes emerge from the child's view and the apparently senseless nature of the conflict?

Jorge Luis Borges
The Secret Miracle

And God had him die for a hundred years and then revived him and said: "How long have you been here?" "A day or a part of a day," he answered.

Koran, II, 261

The night of March 14, 1943, in an apartment in the Zeltnergasse of Prague, Jaromir Hladik, the author of the unfinished drama entitled *The Enemies*, of *Vindication of Eternity* and of a study of the indirect Jewish sources of Jakob Böhme, had a dream of a long game of chess. The players were not two persons, but two illustrious families; the game had been going on for centuries. Nobody could remember what the stakes were, but it was rumored that they were enormous, perhaps infinite; the chessmen and the board were in a secret tower. Jaromir (in his dream) was the first-born of one of the contending families. The clock struck the hour for the game, which could not be postponed. The dreamer raced over the sands of a rainy desert, and was unable to recall either the pieces or the rules of chess. At that moment he awoke. The clangor of the rain and of the terrible clocks ceased. A rhythmic, unanimous noise, punctuated by shouts of command, arose from the Zeltnergasse. It was dawn, and the armored vanguard of the Third Reich was entering Prague.

On the nineteenth the authorities received a denunciation; that same nineteenth, toward evening, Jaromir Hladik was arrested. He was taken to an aseptic, white barracks on the opposite bank of the Moldau. He was unable to refute a single one of the Gestapo's charges; his mother's family name was Jaroslavski, he was of Jewish blood, his study on Böhme had a marked Jewish emphasis, his signature had been one more on the protest against the *Anschluss*. In 1928 he had translated the *Sepher Yezirah* for the publishing house of Hermann Barsdorf. The fulsome catalogue of the firm had exaggerated, for publicity purposes, the translator's reputation, and the catalogue had been examined by Julius Rothe, one of the officials who held Hladik's fate in his hands. There is not a person who, except in the field of his own specialization, is not credulous; two or three adjectives in Gothic type were enough to persuade Julius Rothe of Hladik's importance, and he ordered him sentenced to death *pour encourager les autres*. The execution was set for March 29th, at 9:00 A.M. This delay (whose importance the reader will grasp later) was owing to the desire on the authorities' part to proceed impersonally and slowly, after the manner of vegetables and plants.

Hladik's first reaction was mere terror. He felt he would not have shrunk from the gallows, the block, or the knife, but that death by a firing squad was unbearable. In vain he tried to convince himself that the plain, unvarnished fact of dying was the fearsome thing, not the attendant circumstances. He never wearied of conjuring up these circumstances, senselessly trying to exhaust all their possible variations. He infinitely anticipated the process of his dying, from the sleepless dawn to the mysterious volley. Before the day set by Julius Rothe he died hundreds of deaths in courtyards whose forms and angles strained geometrical probabilities, machine-gunned by variable soldiers in changing numbers, who at times killed him from a distance, at others from close by. He faced these imaginary executions with real terror (perhaps with real bravery); each simulacrum lasted a few seconds. When the circle was closed, Jaromir returned once more and interminably to the tremulous vespers of his death. Then he reflected that reality does not usually coincide with our anticipation of it; with a logic of his own he inferred that to foresee a circumstantial detail is to prevent its happening. Trusting in this weak magic, he invented, *so that they would not happen,* the most gruesome details. Finally, as was natural, he came to fear that they were prophetic. Miserable in the night, he endeavored to find some way to hold fast to the fleeting substance of time. He knew that it was rushing headlong toward the dawn of the twenty-ninth. He reasoned aloud: "I am now in the night of the twenty-second; while this night lasts (and for six nights more), I am invulnerable, immortal." The nights of sleep seemed to him deep, dark pools in which he could submerge himself. There were moments when he longed impatiently for the final burst of fire that would free him, for better or for worse, from the vain compulsion of his imaginings. On the twenty-eight, as the last sunset was reverberating from the high barred windows, the thought of his drama, *The Enemies,* deflected him from these abject considerations.

Hladik had rounded forty. Aside from a few friendships and many habits, the problematic exercise of literature constituted his life. Like all writers, he measured the achievements of others by what they had accomplished, asking of them that they measure him by what he envisaged or planned. All the books he had published had left him with a complex feeling of repetance. His studies of the work of Böhme, of Ibn Ezra, and of Fludd had been characterized essentially by mere application; his translation of the *Sepher Yezirah,* by carelessness, fatigue, and conjecture. *Vindication of Eternity* perhaps had fewer shortcomings. The first volume gave a history of man's various concepts of eternity, from the immutable Being of Parmenides to the modifiable Past of Hinton. The second denied (with Francis Bradley) that all the events of the universe make up a temporal series, arguing that the number of man's possible experiences is not infinite, and that a single "repetition" suffices to prove that time is a fallacy . . . Unfortunately, the arguments that demonstrate this fallacy are equally fallacious. Hladik was in the habit of going over them with a kind of contemptuous perplexity. He had also composed a series of Expressionist poems; to the poet's chagrin they had been included in an anthology published in 1924, and no subsequent anthology but inherited them. From all this equivocal, uninspired past Hladik had hoped to redeem himself with his drama in verse, *The Enemies*. (Hladik felt the verse form to be essential because it makes it impossible for the spectators to lose sight of irreality, one of art's requisites.)

The drama observed the unities of time, place, and action. The scene was laid in

Hradčany, in the library of Baron von Roemerstadt, on one of the last afternoons of the nineteenth century. In the first scene of the first act a strange man visits Roemerstadt. (A clock was striking seven, the vehemence of the setting sun's rays glorified the windows, a passionate, familiar Hungarian music floated in the air.) This visit is followed by others; Roemerstadt does not know the people who are importuning him, but he has the uncomfortable feeling that he has seen them somewhere, perhaps in a dream. They all fawn upon him, but it is apparent—first to the audience and then to the Baron—that they are secret enemies, in league to ruin him. Roemerstadt succeeds in checking or evading their involved schemings. In the dialogue mention is made of his sweetheart, Julia von Weidenau, and a certain Jaroslav Kubin, who at one time pressed his attentions on her. Kubin has now lost his mind, and believes himself to be Roemerstadt. The dangers increase; Roemerstadt, at the end of the second act, is forced to kill one of the conspirators. The third and final act opens. The incoherencies gradually increase; actors who had seemed out of the play reappear; the man Roemerstadt killed returns for a moment. Someone points out that evening has not fallen; the clock strikes seven, the high windows reverberate in the western sun, the air carries an impassioned Hungarian melody. The first actor comes on and repeats the lines he had spoken in the first scene of the first act. Roemerstadt speaks to him without surprise; the audience understands that Roemerstadt is the miserable Jaroslav Kubin. The drama has never taken place; it is the circular delirium that Kubin lives and relives endlessly.

Hladik had never asked himself whether this tragicomedy of errors was preposterous or admirable, well thought out or slipshod. He felt that the plot I have just sketched was best contrived to cover up his defects and point up his abilities and held the possibility of allowing him to redeem (symbolically) the meaning of his life. He had finished the first act and one or two scenes of the third; the metrical nature of the work made it possible for him to keep working it over, changing the hexameters, without the manuscript in front of him. He thought how he still had two acts to do, and that he was going to die very soon. He spoke with God in the darkness: "If in some fashion I exist, if I am not one of Your repetitions and mistakes, I exist as the author of *The Enemies*. To finish this drama, which can justify You, I need another year. Grant me these days, You to whom the centuries and time belong." This was the last night, the most dreadful of all, but ten minutes later sleep flooded over him like a dark water.

Toward dawn he dreamed that he had concealed himself in one of the naves of the Clementine Library. A librarian wearing dark glasses asked him: "What are you looking for?" Hladik answered: "I am looking for God." The librarian said to him: "God is in one of the letters on one of the pages of one of the four hundred thousand volumes of the Clementine. My fathers and the fathers of my fathers have searched for this letter; I have grown blind seeking it." He removed his glasses, and Hladik saw his eyes, which were dead. A reader came in to return an atlas. "This atlas is worthless," he said, and handed it to Hladik, who opened it at random. He saw a map of India as in a daze. Suddenly sure of himself, he touched one of the tiniest letters. A ubiquitous voice said to him: "The time of your labor has been granted." At this point Hladik awoke.

He remembered that men's dreams belong to God, and that Maimonides had written that the words heard in a dream are divine when they are distinct and clear and the person uttering them cannot be seen. He dressed: two soldiers came into the cell and ordered him to follow them.

From behind the door, Hladik had envisaged a labyrinth of passageways, stairs, and separate buildings. The reality was less spectacular: they descended to an inner court by a narrow iron stairway. Several soldiers—some with uniform unbuttoned—were examining a motorcycle and discussing it. The sergeant looked at the clock; it was 8:44. They had to wait until it struck nine. Hladik, more insignificant than pitiable, sat down on a pile of wood. He noticed that the soldiers' eyes avoided his. To ease his wait, the sergeant handed him a cigarette. Hladik did not smoke; he accepted it out of politeness or humility. As he lighted it, he noticed that his hands were shaking. The day was clouding over; the soldiers spoke in a low voice as though he were already dead. Vainly he tried to recall the woman of whom Julia von Weidenau was the symbol.

The squad formed and stood at attention. Hladik, standing against the barracks wall, waited for the volley. Someone pointed out that the wall was going to be stained with blood; the victim was ordered to step forward a few paces. Incongruously, this reminded Hladik of the fumbling preparations of photographers. A big drop of rain struck one of Hladik's temples and rolled slowly down his cheek, the sergeant shouted the final order.

The physical universe came to a halt.

The guns converged on Hladik, but the men who were to kill him stood motionless. The sergeant's arm eternized an unfinished gesture. On a paving stone of the courtyard a bee cast an unchanging shadow. The wind had ceased, as in a picture. Hladik attempted a cry, a word, a movement of the hand. He realized that he was paralyzed. Not a sound reached him from the halted world. He thought: "I am in hell, I am dead." He thought: "I am mad." He thought: "Time has stopped." Then he reflected that if that was the case, his mind would have stopped too. He wanted to test this; he repeated (without moving his lips) Vergil's mysterious fourth Eclogue. He imagined that the now remote soldiers must be sharing his anxiety; he longed to be able to communicate with them. It astonished him not to feel the least fatigue, not even the numbness of his protracted immobility. After an indeterminate time he fell asleep. When he awoke the world continued motionless and mute. The drop of water still clung to his cheek, the shadow of the bee to the stone. The smoke from the cigarette he had thrown away had not dispersed. Another "day" went by before Hladik understood.

He had asked God for a whole year to finish his work; His omnipotence had granted it. God had worked a secret miracle for him; German lead would kill him at the set hour, but in his mind a year would go by between the order and its execution. From perplexity he passed to stupor, from stupor to resignation, from resignation to sudden gratitude.

He had no document but his memory; the training he had acquired with each added hexameter gave him a discipline unsuspected by those who set down and forget temporary, incomplete paragraphs. He was not working for posterity or even for God, whose literary tastes were unknown to him. Meticulously, motionlessly, secretly, he wrought in time his lofty, invisible labyrinth. He worked the third act over twice. He eliminated certain symbols as over-obvious, such as the repeated striking of the clock, the music. Nothing hurried him. He omitted, he condensed, he amplified. In certain instances he came back to the original version. He came to feel an affection for the courtyard, the barracks; one of the faces before him modified his conception of Roemerstadt's character. He discovered that the wearying cacophonies that bothered Flaubert so much are mere visual superstitions, weakness and limitation of the written word, not the spoken . . . He concluded his drama. He had only the problem of a single phrase. He found it. The drop of water slid down his cheek. He opened his mouth in a maddened cry, moved his face, dropped under the quadruple blast.

Jaromir Hladik died on March 29, at 9:02 A.M.

[1956]

For Thought

In the "Secret Miracle" Borges tells a number of stories within a story. The crux of the tale is one of choice: What would one do if one had only a year to live? His central character is blessed with time to create the best play of which he is capable. But the blessing is coupled with a curse. The play, once finished, will have no audience but that of its own maker. Borges suggests that the ideal reader must recreate the work of literature in his or her own mind; all creative work is a deeply private experience.

For Discussion

1. What point of view does Borges choose? Why is it so effective?
2. How is the ending of the story foreshadowed? How does Borges manage to build suspense?
3. How does the game of chess symbolically resemble the creative process? In what way does it sum up the meaning of Hladik's life up until the point of his condemnation to death?
4. How is Hladik's condemnation to death ironic?
5. What truth regarding the creative process emerges from the granting of Haldik's prayer—a year in which to complete his play? How is it ironic that he has prayed to a God in which he has no belief?

Kay Boyle
Rest Cure

He sat in the sun with the blanket about him, considering, with his hands lying out like emaciated strangers before him, that today the sun would endure a little longer. Certainly it would survive until the trees below the terrace effaced it, towards four o'clock, like opened parasols. A crime it had been, the invalid thought, turning his head this way and that, to have ever built up one house before another in such a way that one man's habitation cast a shadow upon another's. The whole sloping coast should have been left a wilderness with no order to it, stalked and leafed with the great strong trunks and foliage of these parts. Cactus plants with petals a yard wide and yucca tongues as thick as elephant trunks were sullenly and viciously flourishing all about the house. Upon the terrace had a further attempt at nicety and precision been made: there his wife had seen to it that geraniums were potted into the wooden boxes that stood along the wall.

From his lounging chair he could reach out and, with no effort beyond that of raising the skeleton of his hand, finger the parched stems of the geraniums. The south, and the Mediterranean wind, had blistered them past all belief. They bore their rosy top-knots or their soiled white flowers balanced upon their thick Italian heads. There they were, within his reach, a row of weary washerwomen leaning back from the villainous descent of the coast. What parched scions had thrust forth from their stems now served to obliterate in part the vision of the sun. With arms akimbo they surrounded him: thin burned Italian women with their meager bundles of dirty linen on their heads. One after another, with a flicker of irritation for his wife lighting his eye, he fingered them at the waist a moment, and then snapped off each stem. One after another he broke their stalks in two and dropped them away onto the pavings beneath his lounging chair. When he had finished off what plants grew within his reach, he lay back exhausted, sank, thin as an archer's bow, into the depths of his cushions.

'They kept the sun off me,' he was thinking in absolution.

In spite of the garden and its vegetation, he would have the last drops of sun. He had closed his eyes, and there he lay looking straight ahead of him into the fathomless black pits of his lids. Even here, in the south, in the sun even, the coal-mines remained. His nostrils were sick with the smell of them and on his cheeks he felt lingering the slipping mantle of the English fog. He had not seen the mines since he was a young man, but nothing he had ever done between would alter them. There he sat in the sun with his eyes closed, looking into their depths.

Because his father had been a miner, he was thinking, the black of the pits had put some kind of blasphemy on his own blood. He sat with his eyes closed looking directly into the blank awful mines. Against their obscurity he set the icicles of one winter when the war was on, when he had spent his twilights seeking for pinecones under the tall trees in the woods behind the house. In Cornwall. What a vision! How beautiful that year, and many other years, might have been had it not been for the sour thought of war. Every time his heart had lifted for a hillside or a wave, or for the wind blowing, the thought of the turmoil going on had beset and stricken him. It had lain like a burden on his conscience every morning when he was coming awake. The first light moments of day coming had warned him that despite the blood rising in his body, it was no time to rejoice. The war. Ah, yes, the war. After the mines, it had been the war. Whenever he had believed for half a minute in man, then he had remembered that the war was going on.

For a little while one February, it had seemed that the colors set out in Monte Carlo, facing the Casino, would obliterate forever the angry memories his heart had stored away. The great mauve, white, and deep royal purple bouquets had thrived a week or more, as if rooted in his eyes. Such banks and beds of richly petaled flowers set thick as thieves or thicker on the cultivated lawns conveyed the wish. Their artificial physiognomics masked the earth as well as he would have wished his own features to stand guard before his spirit. The invalid lifted his hand and touched his beard. His mouth and chin, he thought with cunning satisfaction, were marvelously concealed.

The sound of his wife's voice speaking in the room that opened behind him onto the terrace roused him a little as he sat pondering in the sun. She seemed to be moving from one long window to another, arranging flowers in the vases, for her voice would come across the pavings, now strong and close, now distant as if turned away, and she was talking to their guest about some sort of shrub or fern. A special kind, the like of which she could find nowhere on the Riviera. It thrived in the cool brisk fogs of their own land, she was saying. Her voice had turned towards him again and was ringing clearly across the terrace.

'Those are beautiful ones you have there now,' said the voice of the gentleman.

'Ah, take care!' cried out his wife's voice, somewhat dimmed as though she had again turned towards the room. 'I was afraid you had pierced your hand,' she said in a moment.

When the invalid opened his eyes, he saw that the sun was even now beginning to glimmer through the upper branches of the trees, was lolling along the prosperous dark upper boughs as if in preparation for descent. Not yet, he thought, not yet. He raised himself on his elbows and scanned the sky. Scarcely three-thirty, surely, he was thinking. The sun can't be going down at once.

'The sun can't be down yet awhile, can it?' he called out to the house.

He heard the gravel of the pathway sparkling and spitting out from under the soles of their feet as they crossed it, and then his wife's heels and the boots of the guest struck and advanced across the paving stones.

'Oh, oh, the geraniums—' said his wife suddenly by his side. The guest had raised his head and stood squinting up at the sun.

'I should say it were going down,' he said after a moment.

He had deliberately stepped before the rays of it and stood leaning back against the terrace-wall. His solid gray head had served to cork the sunlight. Like a wooden stopper, thought the invalid, painted to resemble a man. With the nose of a wooden stopper. And the sightless eyes. And the creases when he speaks or smiles.

'But think what it must be like in Paris now,' said the gentleman. 'I don't know how you feel, but I can't find words to say how grateful I am for being here.' The guest, thought the invalid as he surveyed him, was very conscious of being a guest—of accepting meals, bed, tea, society—and his smile was permanently set beneath his nose.

'Of course you don't know how I feel,' said the invalid. He lay looking sourly up at his guest. 'Would you mind moving out of the sun?' As the visiting gentleman skipped out of the way, the invalid cleared his throat, dissolved the little pellet of phlegm which had leapt to being on his tongue so as not to spit before them, and sank back into his chair.

'The advantage—or rather *one* of the advantages of being a writer,' said the visiting gentleman with a smile, 'is that he can settle down wherever the fancy takes him. Now a publisher—'

'Why be a publisher?' said the invalid in irritation. He was staring again into the black blank mines.

His wife was squatting and stooping about his chair, gathering up in her dress the butchered geraniums. She said not a word, but crouched there picking them carefully up, one by one. By her side had appeared a little covered basket, and within it rattled a pair of castanets.

'I am sure I can very easily turn these into slips,' she said gently, as if speaking to herself. 'A little snip in the right place and they'll be as good as new.'

'You can make soup out of them,' said the invalid bitterly. 'What's in the basket,' he said, 'making a noise?'

'Oh, a *langouste!*' cried out his wife. She had just remembered. 'We bought you a *langouste,* alive, at the Beausoleil market. It's as lively as a rig!'

The visiting gentleman burst into laughter. The invalid could hear him gasping with enjoyment by his side.

'I can't bear them alive,' said the invalid testily. He lay listening curiously to the animal rattling his jaws and clawing under the basket's lid.

'Oh, but with mayonnaise!' cried his wife. 'Tomorrow!'

'Why doesn't Mr. What-do-you-call him answer the question I put him?' asked the invalid sourly. His mind was possessed with the thought of the visiting man. 'I asked him why he was a publisher,' said the invalid. What a viper, what a felon, he was thinking, to come and live on me and not give me the satisfaction of a quarrel! He was not a young man, thought the invalid, with his little remains of graying hair, but he had all the endurance and patience of a younger man in the presence of a master. All the smiling and bowing, thought the invalid with contempt, and all the obsequious ways. The man was standing so near to his chair that he could hear his breath whistling through his nostrils. Maybe his eyes were on him, the invalid was thinking. It gave him a turn to think that he was lying there exposed in the sun where the visitor could examine him pore by pore. Hair by hair could the visitor take him in and record him.

'Oh, I beg you pardon,' said the gentleman. 'I'm afraid I owe you an apology. You see, I'm not accustomed to it.'

'To what?' said the invalid sharply. He had flashed his eyes open and looked suspiciously into the publisher's face.

'To seeing you flat on your back,' said the gentleman promptly.

'You covered that over very nicely,' said the invalid. He clasped his hands across his sunken bosom. 'You meant to say something else. You meant to say DEATH,' said the invalid calmly. 'I heard the first letter of it on your tongue.'

He lay back in his chair again with his lids fallen. He could distinctly smell the foul fumes of the pits.

'Elsa,' he said, as he lay twitching in the light, 'I would like some champagne. JUST BECAUSE,' he said sitting up abruptly, 'I've written a few books doesn't mean that you have to keep the truth about me to yourself.'

His wife went off across the terrace, leaving the two men together.

'Don't make a mistake,' said the invalid smiling grimly. 'Don't make any mistake. I'm not quite finished. Not QUITE. I still have a little more to write about,' he said. 'Don't you fool yourself, my dear.'

'Oh, I flatter myself that I don't,' said the gentleman agreeably. 'I'm convinced there's an unlimited amount still to come. And I hope to have the honor of publishing some of it. I'm counting on that, you know.' He ended on a playful note and looked coyly at the invalid. But every spark of life had suddenly expired in the ill man's face.

'I didn't know the sun would be off the terrace so soon,' he said blankly. His wife had returned and was opening the bottle, carefully and without error, with the end of her pliant thumb. The invalid turned on his side and regarded her: a great strong woman whom he would never forget, never, nor the surprisingly slim crescent of her flexible thumb. All of her fingers, he lay thinking as he watched her, were soft as skeins of silk, and tied in at the joints and knuckles by invisible satin bands of faintest rose. And there was the visiting gentleman hovering about her, with his oh-let-me-please-mrs-oh-do-let-me-now. But her grip on the neck of the bottle was as tenacious as a snake's. She lifted her head, smiled, and shook it at their guest.

'Oh, no,' she said, 'I'm doing beautifully.'

Just as she spoke the cork flew out and hit the gentleman square in the forehead. After it streamed a geyser of purest gold.

'Oh, oh, oh,' cried the invalid. He held out his hands to the golden spray. 'Oh, pour it here!' he cried. 'Oh, buckets of it going! Oh, pour it over me, Elsa!'

The color had flown into Elsa's face and she was laughing. Softly and breathlessly she ran from glass to glass. There in the stems played the clear living liquid, like a fountain springing upward. Ah, that, ah, that, in the inwards of a man, thought the invalid joyfully! Ah, that, springing again and again in the belly and heart! There in the glass it ran, cascaded in needlepoints the length of his throat, went whistling to his pulses.

The invalid set down his empty glass.

'Elsa,' he said gently, 'could I have a little more champagne?'

His wife had risen with the bottle in her hand, but she looked doubtfully at him.

'Do you really think you should?' she asked.

'Yes,' said the invalid. He watched the unbelievable pure stuff flowing out all over his glass. 'Yes,' he said. 'Of course. Of course, I should.'

A sweet shy look of love had begun to arch in his eyes.

'I'd love to see the *langouste*,' he said gently. 'Do you think you could let him out and let me see him run around?'

Elsa set down her glass and stooped to lift the cover of the basket. There was the green armored beast lifting its eyes, as if on hinges, to examine the light. Such an expression he had seen before, thought the invalid immediately. There was a startling likeness in those small audacious eyes. Such a look had there been in his father's eyes: that look and the long smooth mustaches drooping across the wee clefted chin, gave the *langouste* such a look of his father that he exclaimed aloud.

'Be careful,' said Elsa. 'His claws are tied, but still—'

'I must have him out,' said the invalid. He gripped the *langouste* firmly about the hips. He looks like my father, he was thinking. I must have him out where I can see.

In spite of its shackles, the animal contrived to wave his wide pinions in the air as the invalid lifted him up and set him on the rug across his knees. There was the same line of sparkling dewlike substance pearling the *langouste's* lip, the same weak disappointed lip, like the eagle's lip, and the bold suspicious eye. Across the sloping shoulders of the beast lay a sprinkling of brilliant dust, as black as coal dust and quite as luminous. Just as his father had looked coming home at night, with the coal dust showered across his shoulders like a deadly mantle. Just such a deadly cloak of quartz and mica and the rotted roots of fern. Even the queer blue toothless look of his father about the jaws. The invalid took another deep swallow of champagne and let it seep quietly through his flesh and blood. Then he lifted his hand and stroked the *langouste* gently. You've never counted, he was thinking mildly. I've led my life very well without you in it. You better go back to the mines where you belong.

When he lifted up the *langouste* to peer into his face, the arms of the beast fell ludicrously open as if he were seeking to embrace the ailing man. He could see his father very well in him, coming home with the coal dirt all over him in the evening, standing by the door that opened in by halves, opening first the upper half and then the lower, swaying a little as he felt for the latch of the lower half of the door. With the beer he had been drinking, or the dew of the Welsh mist shining on his long mustaches. The invalid gave him a gentle shake and set him down again.

I got on very well without you, he was thinking. He sipped at his champagne and regarded the animal upon his knees. As far as I was concerned. As far as I was concerned you need never have been my father at all. Slowly and warily the wondrous eyes and feelers of the beast moved in distrust across the invalid's lap and bosom. A lot of good you ever did me, he was thinking. As he watched the *langouste* groping about as if in darkness, he began to think of the glowing miner's lamp his father had worn strapped upon his brow. Feeling about in the dark and choking to death underground, he was thinking impatiently. I might have been anybody's son. The strong shelly odor of the *langouste* was seasoning the air.

'I've got on very well without you,' he was thinking bitterly. From his wife's face he gathered that he had spoken aloud. The visiting gentleman looked into the depths of his glass of champagne.

'Don't misunderstand me,' said the guest with a forbearing smile. 'I'm quite aware of the fact that, long before you met me, you had one of the greatest publics and following of any living writer—'

The invalid looked in bewilderment at his wife's face and at the face of the visiting man. If they scold me, he thought, I am going to cry. He felt his underlip quivering. Scold me! he thought suddenly in indignation. A man with a beard! His hand fled to his chin for confirmation. A man with a beard, he thought with a cunning evil gleam narrowing his eye.

'You haven't answered my question,' he said aggressively to the visitor. 'You haven't answered it yet, have you?'

His hand had fallen against the hard brittle armor of the the *langouste's* hide. There were the eyes raised to his and the canny feelers lifted. His fingers closed for comfort about the *langouste's* unwieldy paw. Father, he said in his heart, father, help me. Father, father, he said, I don't want to die.

[1933]

For Thought

In "Rest Cure," Kay Boyle imagines the last days of the dying D. H. Lawrence, who had tuberculosis. The story is set in Vence, near Nice, in southern France. With the use of the images such as the lobster and the geraniums, Boyle is able to stress Lawrence's alternating periods of irascibility and dreaminess. While his illness appears to heighten his pettiness and spikiness, he remains true to his creative vision. Lawrence finally emerges as a flawed human being but a passionately committed artist.

For Discussion

1. Lawrence deliberately attempts to anger his wife and would-be publisher. Why does he try so hard to provoke them into quarreling with him?
2. How do Lawrence's wife and would-be publisher treat him, and why?
3. How is it ironic that the writer of the story thinks mostly of earlier days in England while dying in France?
4. How is the title of the story ironic?
5. What similarities are suggested between the lobster *(langouste)* and Lawrence's father?
6. What combination of disagreeable and admirable qualities does Lawrence reveal?

Ray Bradbury
And the Rock Cried Out

The raw carcasses, hung in the sunlight, rushed at them, vibrated with heat and red color in the green jungle air, and were gone. The stench of rotting flesh gushed through the car windows, and Leonora Webb quickly pressed the button that whispered her door window up.

"Good Lord," she said, "those open-air butcher shops."

The smell was still in the car, a smell of war and horror.

"Did you see the flies?" she asked.

"When you buy any kind of meat in those markets," John Webb said, "you slap the beef with your hand. The flies lift from the meat so you can get a look at it."

He turned the car around a lush bend in the green rain-jungle road.

"Do you think they'll let us into Juatala when we get there?"

"I don't know."

"Watch out!"

He saw the bright things in the road too late, tried to swerve, but hit them. There was a terrible sighing from the right front tire, the car heaved about and sank to a stop. He opened his side of the car and stepped out. The jungle was hot and silent and the highway empty, very empty and quiet at noon.

He walked to the front of the car and bent, all the while checking his revolver in its underarm holster.

Leonora's window gleamed down. "Is the tire hurt much?"

"Ruined, utterly ruined!" He picked up the bright thing that had stabbed and slashed the tire.

"Pieces of a broken machete," he said, "placed in adobe holders pointing toward our car wheels. We're lucky it didn't get all our tires."

"But *why*?"

"You know as well as I." He nodded to the newspaper beside her, at the date, the headlines:

OCTOBER 4TH, 1983: UNITED STATES,
EUROPE SILENT!
The radios of the U.S.A. and Europe are dead. There is a great silence.
The War has spent itself.

It is believed that most of the population of the United States is dead. It is believed that most of Europe, Russia, and Siberia is equally decimated. The day of the white people of the earth is over and finished.

"It all came so fast," said Webb. "One week we're on another tour, a grand vacation from home. The next week—this."

They both looked away from the black headlines to the jungle.

The jungle looked back at them with a vastness, a breathing moss-and-leaf silence, with a billion diamond and emerald insect eyes.

"Be careful, Jack."

He pressed two buttons. An automatic lift under the front wheels hissed and hung the car in the air. He jammed a key nervously into the right wheel plate. The tire, frame and all, with a sucking pop, bounced from the wheel. It was a matter of seconds to lock the spare in place and roll the shattered tire back to the luggage compartment. He had his gun out while he did all this.

"Don't stand in the open, please, Jack."

"So it's starting already." He felt his hair burning hot on his skull. "News travels fast."

"For God's sake," said Leonora. "They can *hear* you!"

He stared at the jungle.

"I know you're in there!"

"Jack!"

He aimed at the silent jungle. "I see you!" He fired four, five times, quickly, wildly.

The jungle ate the bullets with hardly a quiver, a brief slit sound like torn silk where the bullets bored and vanished into a million acres of green leaves, trees, silence, and moist earth. The brief echo of the shots died. Only the car muttered its exhaust behind Webb. He walked around the car, got in, and shut the door and locked it.

He reloaded the gun, sitting in the front seat. Then they drove away from the place.

They drove steadily.

"Did you see anyone?"

"No. You?"

She shook her head.

"You're going too fast."

He slowed only in time. As they rounded a curve another clump of the bright flashing objects filled the right side of the road. He swerved to the left and passed.

"Sons-of-bitches!"

"They're not sons-of-bitches, they're just people who never had a car like this or anything at all."

Something ticked across the window pane.

There was a streak of colorless liquid on the glass.

Leonora glanced up. "Is it going to rain?"

"No, an insect hit the pane."

Another tick.

"Are you sure that was an insect?"

Tick, tick, tick.

"Shut the window!" he said, speeding up.

Something fell in her lap.

She looked down at it. He reached over to touch the thing. "Quick!"

She pressed the button. The window snapped up.

Then she examined her lap again.

The tiny blowgun dart glistened there.

"Don't get any of the liquid on you," he said."Wrap it in your handkerchief—we'll throw it away later."

He had the car up to sixty miles an hour.

"If we hit another road block, we're done."

"This is a local thing," he said. "We'll drive out of it."

The panes were ticking all the time. A shower of things blew at the window and fell away in their speed.

"Why," said Leonora Webb, "they don't even *know* us!"

"I only wish they did." He gripped the wheel. "It's hard to kill people you know. But not hard to kill strangers."

"I don't want to die," she said simply, sitting there.

He put his hand inside his coat. "If anything happens to me, my gun is here. Use it, for God's sake, and don't waste time."

She moved over close to him and they drove seventy-five miles an hour down a straight stretch in the jungle road, saying nothing.

With the windows up, the heat was oven-thick in the car.

"It's so silly," she said, at last. "Putting the knives in the road. Trying to hit us with the blowguns. How could they know that the next car along would be driven by white people?"

"Don't ask them to be that logical," he said. "A car is a car. It's big, it's rich. The money in one car would last them a lifetime. And anyway, if you road-block a car, chances are you'll get either an American tourist or a rich Spaniard, comparatively speaking, whose ancestors should have behaved better. And if you happen to road-block another Indian, hell, all you do is go out and help him change tires."

"What time is it?" she asked.

For the thousandth time he glanced at his empty wrist. Without expression or surprise, he fished in his coat pocket for the glistening gold watch with the silent sweep hand. A year ago he had seen a native stare at this watch and stare at it and stare at it with almost a hunger. Then the native had examined him, not scowling, not hating, not sad or happy; nothing except puzzled.

He had taken the watch off that day and never worn it since.

"Noon," he said.

Noon.

The border lay ahead. They saw it and both cried out at once. They pulled up, smiling, not knowing they smiled. . . .

John Webb leaned out the window, started gesturing to the guard at the border station, caught himself, and got out of his car. He walked ahead to the station where three young men, very short, in lumpy uniforms, stood talking. They did not look up at Webb, who stopped before them. They continued conversing in Spanish, ignoring him.

"I beg your pardon," said John Webb at last. "Can we pass over the border into Juatala?"

One of the men turned for a moment. "Sorry, *señor*."

The three men talked again.

"You don't understand," said Webb, touching the first man's elbow. "We've *got* to get through."

The man shook his head. "Passports are no longer good. Why should you want to leave our country, anyway?"

"It was announced on the radio. All Americans to leave the country, immediately."

"Ah, *si, si*." All three soldiers nodded and leered at each other with shining eyes.

"Or be fined or imprisoned, or both," said Webb.

"We could let you over the border, but Juatala would give you twenty-four hours to leave, also. If you don't believe me, listen!" The guard turned and called across the border, "Aye, there! Aye!"

In the hot sun, forty yards distant, a pacing man turned, his rifle in his arms.

"Aye there, Paco, you want these two people?"

"No, *gracias—gracias*, no," replied the man, smiling.

"You see?" said the guard, turning to John Webb.

All of the soldiers laughed together.

"I have money," said Webb.

The men stopped laughing. The first guard stepped up to John Webb and his face was now not relaxed or easy; it was like brown stone.

"Yes," he said. "They always have money. I know. They come here and they think money will do everything. But what is money? It is only a promise, *señor*. This I know from books. And when somebody no longer likes your promise, what then?"

"I will give you anything you ask."

"Will you?" The guard turned to his friends. "He will give me *anything* I ask."

To Webb: "It was a joke. *We* were always a joke to you, weren't we?"

"No."

"*Mañana*, you laughed at us; *mañana*, you laughed at our siestas and our *mañanas*, didn't you?"

"Not me. Someone else."

"Yes, you."

"I've never been to this particular station before."

"I know you, anyway. Run here, do this, do that. Oh, here's a peso, buy yourself a house. Run over there, do this, do that."

"It wasn't me."

"He looked like you, anyway."

They stood in the sun with their shadows dark under them, and the perspiration coloring their armpits. The soldier moved closer to John Webb. "I don't have to do anything for you any more."

"You never had to before. I never asked it."

"You're trembling, *señor*."

"I'm all right. It's the sun."

"How much money have you got?" asked the guard.

"A thousand pesos to let us through, and a thousand for the other man over there."

The guard turned again. "Will a thousand pesos be enough?"

"No," said the other guard. "Tell him to report us!"

"Yes," said the guard, back to Webb again. "Report me. Get me fired. I was fired once, years ago, by you."

"It was someone else."

"Take my name. It is Carlos Rodriguez Ysotl. Go on now."

"I see."

"No, you don't see," said Carlos Rodriguez Ysotl. "Now give me two thousand pesos."

John Webb took out his wallet and handed over the money. Carlos Rodriguez Ysotl licked his thumb and counted the money slowly under the blue glazed sky of his country as noon deepened and sweat arose from hidden sources and people breathed and panted above their shadows.

"Two thousand pesos." He folded it and put it in his pocket quietly. "Now turn your car around and head for another border."

"Hold on now, damn it!"

The guard looked at him. "Turn your car."

They stood a long time that way, with the sun blazing on the rifle in the guard's hands, not speaking. And then John Webb turned and walked slowly, one hand to his face, back to the car and slid into the front seat.

"What're we going to do?" said Leonora.

"Rot. Or try to reach Porto Bello."

"But we need gas and our spare fixed. And going back over those highways . . . This time they might drop logs, and—"

"I know, I know." He rubbed his eyes and sat for a moment with his head in his hands. "We're alone, my God, we're alone. Remember how safe we used to feel? How safe? We registered in all the big towns with the American Consuls. Remember how the joke went? 'Everywhere you go you can hear the rustle of the eagle's wings!' Or was it the sound of paper money? I forget. Jesus, Jesus, the world got empty awfully quick. Who do I call on now?"

She waited a moment and then said, "I guess just me. That's not much."

He put his arm around her. "You've been swell. No hysterics, nothing."

"Tonight maybe I'll be screaming, when we're in bed, if we ever find a bed again. It's been a million miles since breakfast."

He kissed her, twice, on her dry mouth. Then he sat slowly back. "First thing is to try to find gas. If we get that, we're ready to head for Porto Bello."

The three soldiers were talking and joking as they drove away.

After they had been driving a minute, he began to laugh quietly.

"What were you thinking?" asked his wife.

"I remember an old spiritual. It goes like this:

"'"I went to the Rock to hide my face
And the Rock cried out, "No Hiding Place,
There's no Hiding Place down here."'"

"I remember that," she said.

"It's an appropriate song right now," he said. "I'd sing the whole thing for you if I could rememmber it all. And if I felt like singing."

He put his foot harder to the accelerator.

They stopped at a gas station and after a minute, when the attendant did not appear, John Webb honked the horn. Then, appalled, he snapped his hand away from the horn-ring, looking at it as if it were the hand of a leper.

"I shouldn't have done that."

The attendant appeared in the shadowy doorway of the gas station. Two other men appeared behind him.

The three men came out and walked around the car, looking at it, touching it, feeling it.

Their faces were like burnt copper in the daylight. They touched the resilient tires, they sniffed the rich new smell of the metal and upholstery.

"*Señor,*" said the gas attendant at last.

"We'd like to buy some gas, please."

"We are all out of gas, *señor*."

"But your tank reads full. I see the gas in the glass container up there."

"We are all out of gas," said the man.

"I'll give you ten pesos a gallon!"

"*Gracias*, no."

"We haven't enough gas to get anywhere from here." Webb checked the gauge. "Not even a quarter gallon left. We'd better leave the car here and go into town and see what we can do there."

"I'll watch the car for you, *señor,*" said the station attendant. "If you leave the keys."

"We can't do that!" said Leonora. "Can we?"

"I don't see what choice we have. We can stall it on the road and leave it to anyone who comes along, or leave it with this man."

"That's better," said the man.

They climbed out of the car and stood looking at it.

"It was a beautiful car," said John Webb.

"Very beautiful," said the man, his hand out for the keys. "I will take good care of it, *señor.*"

"But, Jack—"

She opened the back door and started to take out the luggage. Over her shoulder, he saw the bright travel stickers, the storm of color that had descended upon and covered the worn leather now after years of travel, after years of the best hotels in two dozen countries.

She tugged at the valises, perspiring, and he stopped her hands and they stood gasping there for a moment, in the open door of the car, looking at these fine rich suitcases, inside which were the beautiful tweeds and woolens and silks of their lives and living, the forty-dollar-an-ounce perfumes and the cool dark furs and the silvery golf shafts. Twenty years were packed into each of the cases; twenty years and four dozen parts they had played in Rio, in Paris, in Rome and Shanghai, but the part they played most frequently and best of all was the rich and buoyant, amazingly happy Webbs, the smiling people, the ones who could make that rarely balanced martini known as the Sahara.

"We can't carry it all into town," he said. "We'll come back for it later. Later."

"But . . ."

He silenced her by turning her away and starting her off down the road.

"But we can't leave it there, we can't leave all our luggage and we can't leave our car! O look here now, I'll roll up the windows and lock myself in the car, while you go for the gas, why not?" she said.

He stopped and glanced back at the three men standing by the car, which blazed in the yellow sun. Their eyes were shining and looking at the woman.

"There's your answer," he said. "Come on."

"But you just *don't* walk off and leave a four-thousand-dollar automobile!" she cried.

He moved her along, holding her elbow firmly and with quiet decision. "A car is to travel in. When it's not traveling, it's useless. Right now, we've got to travel; that's everything. The car isn't worth a dime without gas in it. A pair of good strong legs is worth a hundred cars, if you use the legs. We've just begun to toss things overboard. We'll keep dropping ballast until there's nothing left to heave but our hides."

He let her go. She was walking steadily now, and she fell into step with him. "It's so strange. So strange. I haven't walked like this in years." She watched the motion of her feet beneath her, she watched the road pass by, she watched the jungle moving to either side, she watched her husband striding quickly along, until she seemed hypnotized by the steady rhythm. "But I guess you can learn anything over again," she said, at last.

The sun moved in the sky and they moved for a long while on the hot road. When he was quite ready, the husband began to think aloud. "You know, in a way, I think it's good to be down to essentials. Now instead of worrying over a dozen damned things, it's just two items—you and me."

"Watch it, here comes a car—we'd better . . ."

They half turned, yelled, and jumped. They fell away from the highway and lay watching the automobile hurtle past at seventy miles an hour. Voices sang, men laughed, men shouted, waving. The car sped away into the dust and vanished around a curve, blaring its double horns again and again.

He helped her up and they stood in the quiet road.

"Did you see it?"

They watched the dust settle slowly.

"I hope they remember to change the oil and check the battery, at least. I hope they think to put water in the radiator," she said, and paused. "They were singing, weren't they?"

He nodded. They stood blinking at the great dust cloud filtering down like yellow pollen upon their heads and arms. He saw a few bright splashes flick from her eyelids when she blinked.

"Don't," he said. "After all, it was only a machine."

"I loved it."

"We're always loving everything too much."

Walking, they passed a shattered wine bottle which steamed freshly as they stepped over it.

They were not far from the town, walking single file, the wife ahead, the husband following, looking at their feet as they walked, when a sound of tin and steam and bubbling water made them turn and look at the road behind them. An old man in a 1929 Ford drove along the road at a moderate speed. The car's fenders were gone, and the sun had flaked and burnt the paint badly, but he rode in the seat with a great deal of quiet dignity, his face a thoughtful darkness under a dirty Panama hat, and when he saw the two people he drew the car up, steaming, the engine joggling under the hood, and opened the squealing door as he said, "This is no day for walking."

"Thank you," they said.

"It is nothing." The old man wore an ancient yellowed white summer suit, with a rather greasy tie knotted loosely at his wrinkled throat. He helped the lady into the rear seat with a gracious bow of his head. "Let us men sit up front," he suggested, and the husband sat up front and the car moved off in trembling vapors.

"Well. My name is Garcia."

There were introductions and noddings.

"Your car broke down? You are on your way for help?" said *Señor* Garcia.

"Yes."

"Then let me drive you and a mechanic back out," offered the old man.

They thanked him and kindly turned

the offer aside and he made it once again, but upon finding that his interest and concern caused them embarrassment, he very politely turned to another subject.

He touched a small stack of folded newspapers on his lap.

"Do you read the papers? Of course, you do. But do you read them as I read them? I rather doubt that you have come upon my system. No, it was not exactly myself that came upon it; the system was forced upon me. But now I know what a clever thing it has turned out to be. I always get the newspapers a week late. All of us, those who are interested, get the papers a week late, from the Capital. And this circumstance makes for a man being a clear-thinking man. You are very careful with your thinking when you pick up a week-old paper."

The husband and wife asked him to continue.

"Well," said the old man, "I remember once, when I lived in the Capital for a month and bought the paper fresh each day, I went wild with love, anger, irritation, frustration; all of passions boiled in me. I was young. I exploded at everything I saw. But then I saw what I was doing: I was believing what I read. Have you noticed? You believe a paper printed on the very day you buy it? This has happened but only an hour ago, you think! It must be true." He shook his head. "So I learned to stand back away and let the paper age and mellow. Back here, in Colonia, I saw the headlines diminish to nothing. The week-old paper—why, you can spit on it if you wish. It is like a woman you once loved, but you now see, a few days later, she is not quite what you thought. She has rather a plain face. She is no deeper than a cup of water."

He steered the car gently, his hands upon the wheel as upon the heads of his good children, with care and affection. "So here I am, returning to my home to read my weekly papers, to peek sideways at them, to toy with them." He spread one on his knee, glancing down to it on occasion as he drove. "How white this paper is, like the mind of a child that is an idiot, poor thing, all blank. You can put anything into an empty place like that. Here, do you see? This paper speaks and says that the light-skinned people of the world are dead. Now that is a very silly thing to say. At this very moment, there are probably millions upon millions of white men and women eating their noon meals or their suppers. The earth trembles, a town collapses, people run from the town, screaming, *All is lost!* In the next village, the population wonders what all of the shouting is about, since *they* have had a most splendid night's repose. Ah, ah, what a sly world it is. People do not see how sly it is. It is either night or day to them. Rumor flies. This very afternoon all of the little villages upon this highway, behind us and ahead of us, are in carnival. The white man is dead, the rumors say, and yet here I come into the town with two very lively ones. I hope you don't mind my speaking in this way? If I do not talk to you I would then be talking to this engine up in the front, which makes a great noise speaking back."

They were at the edge of town.

"Please," said John Webb, "it wouldn't be wise for you to be seen with us today. We'll get out here."

The old man stopped his car reluctantly and said, "You are most kind and thoughtful of me." He turned to look at the lovely wife.

"When I was a young man I was very full of wildness and ideas. I read all of the books from France by a man named Jules Verne. I see you know his name. But at night I many times thought I must be an inventor. That is all gone by; I never did what I thought I might do. But I remember clearly that one of the machines I wished to put together was a machine that would help every man, for an hour, to be like any other man. The machine was full of colors and smells and it had film in it, like a theater, and the machine was like a coffin. You lay in it. And you touched a button. And for an hour you could be one of those Eskimos in the cold wind up there, or you could be an Arab gentlemen on a horse. Everything a New York man felt, you could feel. Everything a man from Sweden smelled, you could smell. Everything a man from China tasted, your tongue knew. The machine was like another man—do you see what I was after? And by touching many of the buttons, each time you got into my machine, you could be a white man or a yellow man or a Negrito. You could be a child or a woman, even, if you wished to be very funny."

The husband and wife climbed from the car.

"Did you ever try to invent that machine?"

"It was so very long ago. I had forgotten until today. And today I was thinking, we could make use of it, we are in need of it. What a shame I never tried to put it all together. Someday some other man will do it."

"Someday," said John Webb.

"It has been a pleasure talking with you," said the old man. "God go with you."

"*Adiós, Señor* Garcia," they said.

The car drove slowly away, steaming. They stood watching it go, for a full minute. Then, without speaking, the husband reached over and took his wife's hand.

They entered the small town of Colonia on foot. They walked past the little shops—the butcher shop, the photographer's. People stopped and looked at them as they went by and did not stop looking at them as long as they were in sight. Every few seconds, as he walked, Webb put up his hand to touch the holster hidden under his coat, secretly, tentatively, like someone feeling for a tiny boil that is growing and growing every hour and every hour . . .

The patio of the Hotel Esposa was cool as a grotto under a blue waterfall. In it caged birds sang, and footsteps echoed like small rifle shots, clear and smooth.

"Remember? We stopped her years ago," said Webb, helping his wife up the steps. They stood in the cool grotto, glad of the blue shade.

"*Señor* Esposa," said John Webb, when a fat man came forward from the desk, squinting at them. "Do you remember me—John Webb? Five years ago—we played cards one night."

"Of course, of course." *Señor* Esposa bowed to the wife and shook hands briefly. There was an uncomfortable silence.

Webb cleared his throat. "We've had a bit of trouble, *señor*. Could we have a room for tonight only?"

"Your money is always good here."

"You mean you'll actually give us a room? We'll be glad to pay in advance. Lord, we need the rest. But, more than that, we need gas."

Leonora picked at her husband's arm. "Remember? We haven't a car anymore."

"Oh. Yes." He fell silent for a moment and then sighed. "Well. Never mind the gas. Is there a bus out of here for the Capital soon?"

"All will be attended to, in time," said the manager nervously. "This way."

As they were climbing the stairs they heard a noise. Looking out they saw their car riding around and around the plaza, eight times, loaded with men who were shouting and singing and hanging on to the front fenders, laughing. Children and dogs ran after the car.

"I would like to own a car like that," said *Señor* Esposa.

He poured a little cool wine for the three of them, standing in the room on the third floor of the Esposa Hotel.

"To 'change,'" said *Señor* Esposa.

"I'll drink to that."

They drank. *Señor* Esposa licked his lips and wiped them on his coat sleeve. "We are always surprised and saddened to see the world change. It is insane, they have run out on us, you say. It is unbelievable. And now, well—you are safe for the night. Shower and have a good supper. I won't be able to keep you more than one night, to repay you for your kindness to me five years ago."

"And tomorrow?"

"Tomorrow? Do not take any bus to Capital, please. There are riots in the streets there. A few people from the North have been killed. It is nothing. It will pass in a few days. But you must be careful until those few days pass and the blood cools. There are many wicked people taking advantage of this day, *señor*. For forty-eight hours anyway, under the guise of a great resurgence of nationalism, these people will try to gain power. Selfishness and patriotism, *señor;* today I cannot tell one from the other. So—you must hide. That is a problem. The town will know you are here in another few hours. This might be dangerous to my hotel. I cannot say."

"We understand. It's good of you to help *this* much."

"If you need anything, call me." *Señor* Esposa drank the rest of the wine in his glass. "Finish the bottle," he said.

The fireworks began at nine that evening. First one skyrocket then another soared into the dark sky and burst out upon the winds, building architectures of flame. Each skyrocket, at the top of its ride, cracked open and let out a formation of streamers in red and white flame that made something like the dome of a beautiful cathedral.

Leonora and John Webb stood by the open window in their unlit room, watching and listening. As the hour latened, more people streamed into town from every road and path and began to roam, arm, in arm, around the plaza, singing, barking like dogs, crowing like roosters, and then falling down on the tile sidewalks, sitting there, laughing, their heads thrown back, while the skyrockets burst explosive colors on the tilted faces. A brass band began to thump and wheeze.

"So here we are," said John Webb, "after a few hundred years of living high. So this is what's left of our white supremacy—you and I in a dark room in a hotel three hundred miles inside a celebrating country."

"You've got to see their side of it."

"Oh, I've seen it ever since I was that high. In a way, I'm glad they're happy. God knows they've waited long enough to be. But I wonder how long that happiness will last. Now that the scapegoat is gone, who will they blame for oppression, who will be as handy and as obvious and as guilty as you and I and the man who lived in this room before us?"

"I don't know."

"We were so convenient. The man who rented this room last month, he was convenient, he stood out. He made loud jokes about the natives' siestas. He refused to learn even a smattering of Spanish. Let them learn English, by God, and speak like men, he said. And he drank too much and whored too much with this country's women." He broke off and moved back from the window. He stared at the room.

The furniture, he thought. Where *he* put his dirty shoes upon the sofa, where *he* burnt holes in the carpet with cigarettes; the wet spot on the wall near the bed, God knows what or how he did *that*. The chairs scarred and kicked. It wasn't his hotel or his room; it was borrowed, it meant nothing. So this son-of-a-bitch went around the country for the past one hundred years, a traveling commercial, a Chamber of Commerce, and now here *we* are, enough like him to be his brother and sister, and there *they* are down there on the night of the Butlers' Ball. They don't know, or if they know they won't think of it, that tomorrow they'll be just as poor, just as oppressed as ever, that the whole machine will only have shifted into another gear.

Now the band had stopped playing below; a man had leaped up, shouting, on the bandstand. There was a flash of machetes in the air and the brown gleam of half-naked bodies.

The man on the bandstand faced the hotel and looked up at the dark room where John and Leonora Webb now stood back out of the intermittent flares.

The man shouted.

"What does he say?" asked Leonora.

John Webb translated: "It is now a free world, he says."

The man yelled.

John Webb translated again. "He says, 'We are *free*!'"

The man lifted himself on his toes and made a motion of breaking manacles. "He says, 'No one owns us, no one in all the world.'"

The crowd roared and the band began to play, and while it was playing, the man on the grandstand stood glaring up at the room window, with all of the hatred of the universe in his eyes.

During the night there were fights and pummelings and voices lifted, arguments and shots fired. John Webb lay awake and heard the voice of *Señor* Esposa below, reasoning, talking quietly, firmly. And then the fading away of the tumult, the last rockets in the sky, the last breakings of bottles on the cobbles.

At five in the morning the air was warming into a new day. There was the softest of taps on the bedroom door.

"It is me, it is Esposa," said a voice.

John Webb hesitated, half-dressed, numbed on his feet from lack of sleep, then opened the door.

"What a night, what a night!" said *Señor* Esposa, coming in, shaking his head, laughing gently. "Did you hear that noise? Yes? They tried to come up here to your room. I prevented this."

"Thank you," said Leonora, still in bed, turned to the wall.

"They were all old friends. I made an agreement with them, anyway. They were drunk enough and happy enough so they agreed to wait. I am to make a proposition to you two." Suddenly he seemed embarrassed. He moved to the window. "Everyone is sleeping late. A few are up. A few men. See them there on the far side of the plaza?"

John Webb looked out at the plaza. He saw the brown men talking quietly there about the weather, the world, the sun, this town, and perhaps the wine.

"*Señor*, have you every been hungry in your life?"

"For a day, once."

"Only for a day. Have you always had a house to live in and a car to drive?"

"Until yesterday."

"Were you every without a job?"

"Never."

"Did all of your brothers and sisters live to be twenty-one years old?"

"All of them."

"Even I," said *Señor* Esposa, "even *I* hate you a little bit now. For *I* have been hungry. *I* have three brothers and one sister buried in that graveyard on the hill beyond the town, all dead of tuberculosis before they were nine years old."

Señor Esposa glanced at the men in the plaza. "Now, I am no longer hungry or poor, I have a car, I am alive. But I am one in a thousand. What can *you* say to them out there today?"

"I'll try to think of something."

"Long ago I stopped trying. *Señor*, we have *always* been a minority, we white people. I am Spanish, but I was born here. They tolerate me."

"We have never let ourselves think about our being a minority," said Webb, "and now it's hard to get used to the fact."

"You have behaved beautifully."

"Is that a virtue?"

"In the bull ring, yes; in war, yes; in anything like this, most assuredly yes. You do not complain, you do not make excuses. You do not run and make a spectacle of yourself. I think you are both very brave."

The hotel manager sat down, slowly, helplessly.

"I've come to offer you the chance to settle down," he said.

"We wanted to move on, if possible."

The manager shrugged. "Your car is stolen, I can do nothing to get it back. You cannot leave town. Remain then and accept my offer of a position in my hotel."

"You don't think there is any way for us to travel?"

"It might be twenty days, *señor*, or twenty years. You cannot exist without money, food, lodging. Consider my hotel and the work I can give you."

The manager arose and walked unhappily to the door and stood by the chair, touching Webb's coat, which was draped over it.

"What's the job?" asked Webb.

"In the kitchen," said the manager, and looked away.

John Webb sat on the bed and said nothing. His wife did not move. *Señor* Esposa said, "It is the best I can do. What more can you ask of me? Last night, those others down in the plaza wanted both of you. Did you see the machetes? I bargained with them. You were lucky. I told them you would be employed in my hotel for the next twenty years, that you were my employees and deserve my protection!"

"You said *that*!"

"*Señor, señor*, be thankful! Consider! Where will you go? The jungle? You will be dead in two hours from the snakes. Then can you walk five hundred miles to a capital which will not welcome you? No—you must face the reality." *Señor* Esposa opened the door. "I offer you an honest job and you will be paid the standard wages of two pesos a day, plus meals. Would you rather be with me, or out in the plaza at noon with our friends? Consider."

The door was shut. *Señor* Esposa was gone.

Webb stood looking at the door for a long while.

Then he walked to the chair and fumbled with the holster under the draped white shirt. The holster was empty. He held it in his hands and blinked at its emptiness and looked again at the door through which *Señor* Esposa had just passed. He went over and sat down on the bed beside his wife. He stretched out beside her and took her in his arms and kissed her, and they lay there, watching the room get brighter with the new day.

At eleven o'clock in the morning, with the great doors on the windows of their room flung back, they began to dress. There were soap, towels, shaving equipment, even perfume in the bathroom, provided by Mr. Esposa.

John Webb shaved and dressed carefully.

At eleven-thirty he turned on the small radio near their bed. You could usually get New York or Cleveland or Houston on such a radio. But the air was silent. John Webb turned the radio off.

"There's nothing to go back to—nothing to go back for—nothing."

His wife sat on a chair near the door, looking at the wall.

"We could stay here and work," he said.

She stirred at last. "No. We couldn't do that, not really. Could we?"

"No, I guess not."

"There's no way we could do that. We're being consistent, anyway; spoiled, but consistent."

He thought a moment. "We could make for the jungle."

"I don't think we can move from the hotel without being seen. We don't want to try to escape and be caught. It would be far worse that way."

He nodded.

They both sat a moment.

"It might not be too bad, working here," he said.

"What would we be living for? Everyone's dead—your father, mine, your mother, mine, your brothers, mine, all our friends, everything gone, everything we understood."

He nodded.

"Or if we took the job, one day soon one

of the men would touch me and you'd go after him, you know you would. Or someone would do something to you, and *I'd* do something."

He nodded again.

They sat for fifteen minutes, talking quietly. Then, at last, he picked up the telephone and ticked the cradle with his finger.

"*Bueno,*" said a voice on the other end.

"*Señor* Esposa?"

"*Si.*"

"*Señor* Esposa," he paused and licked his lips, "tell your friends we will be leaving the hotel at noon."

The phone did not immediately reply. Then with a sigh *Señor* Esposa said, "As you wish. You are sure—?"

The phone was silent for a full minute. Then it was picked up again and the manager said quietly, "My friends say they will be waiting for you on the far side of the plaza."

"We will meet them there," said John Webb.

"And *señor*—"

"Yes."

"Do not hate me, do not hate us."

"I don't hate anybody."

"It is a bad world, *señor*. None of us know how we got here or what we are doing. These men don't know what they are mad at, except they are mad. Forgive them and do not hate them."

"I don't hate them or you."

"Thank you, thank you." Perhaps the man on the far end of the telephone wire was crying. There was no way to tell. There were great lapses in his talking, in his breathing. After a while he said, "We don't know why we do anything. Men hit each other for no reason except they are unhappy. Remember that. I am your friend. I would help you if I could. But I cannot. It would be me against the town. Good-by, *señor.*" He hung up.

John Webb sat in the chair with his hand on the silent phone. It was a moment before he glanced up. It was a moment before his eyes focused on an object immediately before him. When he saw it clearly, he still did not move, but sat regarding it, until a look of immensely tired irony appeared on his mouth. "Look here," he said at last.

Leonora followed his motion, his pointing.

They both sat looking at his cigarette which, neglected on the rim of the table while he telephoned, had burnt down so that now it had charred a black hole in the clean surface of the wood.

It was noon, with the sun directly over them, pinning their shadows under them as they started down the steps of the Hotel Esposa. Behind them, the birds fluted in their bamboo cages, and water ran in a little fountain bath. They were as neat as they could get, their faces and hands washed, their nails clean, their shoes polished.

Across the plaza two hundred yards away stood a small group of men, in the shade of a store-front overhang. Some of the men were natives from the jungle area, with machetes gleaming at their sides. They were all facing the plaza.

John Webb looked at them for a long while. That isn't everyone, he thought, that isn't the whole country. That's only the surface. That's only the thin skin over the flesh. It's not the body at all. Just the shell of an egg? Remember the crowds back home, the mobs, the riots? Always the same, there or here. A few mad faces up front, and the quiet ones far back, not taking part, letting things go, not wanting to be in it. The majority not moving. And so the few, the handful, take over and move for them.

His eyes did not blink. If we could break through that shell—God knows it's thin! he thought. If we could talk our way through that mob and get to the quiet people beyond . . . Can I do it? Can I say the right things? Can I keep my voice down?

He fumbled in his pockets and brought out a rumpled cigarette package and some matches.

I can try, he thought. How would the old man in the Ford have done it? I'll try to do it his way. When we get across the plaza, I'll start talking, I'll whisper if necessary. And if we move slowly through the mob, we might just possibly find our way to the other people and we'll be on high ground and we'll be safe.

Leonora moved beside him. She was so fresh, so well groomed in spite of everything, so new in all this oldness, so startling, that his mind flinched and jerked. He found himself staring at her as if she'd betrayed him by her salt-whiteness, her wonderfully brushed hair and her cleanly manicured nails and her bright-red mouth.

Standing on the bottom step, Webb lit a cigarette, took two or three long drags on it, tossed it down, stepped on it, kicked the flattened butt into the street, and said, "Here we go."

They stepped down and started around the far side of the plaza, past the few shops that were still open. They walked quietly.

"Perhaps they'll be decent to us."

"We can hope so."

They passed a photographic shop.

"It's another day. Anything can happen. I believe that. No—I don't really believe it. I'm only talking. I've got to talk or I wouldn't be able to walk," she said.

They passed a candy shop.

"Keep talking, then."

"I'm afraid," she said. "This can't be happening to us! Are we the last ones in the world?"

"Maybe next to the last."

They approached an open air *carneceria*.

God! he thought. How the horizons narrowed, how they came in. A year ago there weren't four directions, there were a million for us. Yesterday they got down to four; we could go to Juatala, Porto Bello, San Juan Clementas, or Brioconbria. We were satisfied to have our car. Then when we couldn't get gas, we were satisfied to have our clothes, then when they took our clothes, we were satisfied to have a place to sleep. Each pleasure they took away left us with one other creature comfort to hold on to. Did you see how we let go of one thing and clutched another so quickly? I guess that's human. So they took away everything. There's nothing left. Except us. It all boils down to just you and me walking along here, and thinking too goddamn much for my own good. And what counts in the end is whether they can take you away from me or me away from you, Lee, and I don't think they can do that. They've got everything else and I don't blame them. But they can't really do anything else to us now. When you strip all the clothes away and the doodads, you have two human beings who were either happy or unhappy together, and we have no complaints.

"Walk slowly," said John Webb.

"I am."

"Not too slowly, to look reluctant. Not too fast, to look as if you want to get it over with. Don't give them the satisfaction, Lee, don't give them a damn bit."

"I won't."

They walked. "Don't even touch me," he said, quietly. "Don't even hold my hand."

"Oh, please!"

"No, not even that."

He moved away a few inches and kept walking steadily. His eyes were straight ahead and their pace was regular.

"I'm beginning to cry, Jack."

"Goddamn it!" he said, measuredly, between his teeth, not looking aside. "Stop it! Do you want me to run? Is that what you want—do you want me to take you and run into the jungle, and let them hunt us, is that what you want, goddamn it, do you want me to fall down in the street here and grovel and scream, shut up, let's do this right, don't give them *anything*!"

"All right," she said, hands tight, her head coming up. "I'm not crying now. I won't cry."

"Good, damn it, that's good."

And still, strangely, they were not past the *carneceria*. The vision of red horror was on their left as they paced steadily forward on the hot tile sidewalk. The things that hung from hooks looked like brutalities and sins, like bad consciences, evil dreams, like gored flags and slaughtered promises. The redness, oh, the hanging, evil-smelling wetness and redness, the hooked and hung-high carcasses, unfamiliar, unfamiliar.

As he passed the shop, something made John Webb strike out a hand. He slapped it smartly against a strung-up side of beef. A mantle of blue buzzing flies lifted angrily and swirled in a bright cone over the meat.

Leonora said, looking ahead, walking, "They're all strangers! I don't know any of them. I wish I knew even *one* of them. I wish even *one* of them knew me!"

They walked on past the *carneceria.* The side of beef, red and irritable-looking, swung in the hot sunlight after they passed.

The flies came down in a feeding cloak to cover the meat, once it had stopped swinging.

[1953]

For Thought

"And the Rock Cried Out" is science fiction to the extent that it is placed in the future thirty years after it was written: in 1983. Bradbury uses the hostile setting of a jungle town to reflect the belligerent atmosphere and tone of the story. After a catastrophic war, in which devastation is world-wide, Bradbury's central characters struggle to save the few possessions which make them feel human. In the end, however, they decide that the virtue of grace under fire is more important than material objects or mere survival.

For Discussion

1. How does the country in which the story is set combine the familiar and the unfamiliar?
2. How does Bradbury portray John and Leonora Webb? How do they resemble the average American tourist? How are they different?
3. How does Bradbury foreshadow the ending of the story?
4. What is the symbolism of the hanging meat carcasses?
5. How is it significant that the old man in the Ford befriends the Webbs? How do his ideas contribute to the story's theme?
6. What factors motivate the proprietor of the Hotel Esposa, Señor Garcia, to help the Webbs? What prevents him from doing so?
7. Why don't the Webbs accept Garcia's offer of a job in the kitchen?
8. Why do the Webbs prefer death at the hands of the waiting mob to either running away or taking Garcia's offer of a job?

Richard Brautigan
Greyhound Tragedy

She wanted her life to be a movie magazine tragedy like the death of a young star with long lines of people weeping and a corpse more beautiful than a great painting, but she was never able to leave the small Oregon town that she was born and raised in and go to Hollywood and die.

Though it was the Depression, her life was comfortable and untouched because her father was the manager of the local Penney's and financially compassionate to his family.

Movies were the religion of her life and she attended every service with a bag of popcorn. Movie magazines were her Bible that she studied with the zealousness of a doctor of divinity. She probably knew more about movies than the Pope.

The years passed like the subscriptions to her magazines: 1931, 1932, 1933, 1934, 1935, 1936, 1937, until September 2, 1938.

Finally it was time to make her move if she were ever going to go to Hollywood. There was a young man who wanted to marry her. Her parents were very enthusiastic about his prospects. They approved of him because he was a Ford salesman. "It's a company with fine tradition," her father said. Things did not look good for her.

She spent months building up the courage to go down to the bus station to find out how much the fare to Hollywood cost. Sometimes she spent whole days thinking about the bus station. A few times she even got dizzy and had to sit down. It never dawned on her that she could have called on the telephone.

She made it a point during those nervous months never to go by the bus station. Thinking about it all the time was one thing but actually seeing it was another.

Once she was driving downtown with her mother and her mother turned onto the street where the bus station was located and she asked her mother to *please* turn down another street because she wanted to buy something at a store on that street.

Some shoes.

Her mother thought nothing of it and

made the turn. She didn't think to ask her daughter why her face was red but that was not unusual because she seldom thought to ask her anything.

One morning she was going to talk to her about all the movie magazines that came in the mail. Some days they would jam up the mailbox, so that she would have to use a screwdriver to get the mail out. But her mother had forgotten about it by noon. Her mother's memory had never been able to last until twelve. It usually pooped out around 11:30, but she was a good cook if the recipes were simple.

Time was running out like the popcorn at a Clark Gable picture. Her father had been dropping a lot of "hints" lately about her being out of high school for three years and perhaps it was time for her to think about doing something with her life.

He was not the local manager of Penney's for nothing. Recently, actually about a year ago, he had become tired of watching his daughter sit around the house all the time reading movie magazines with her eyes wide as saucers. He had begun to think of her as a bump on a log.

Her father's hints happened to coincide with the young Ford salesman's fourth proposal of marriage. She had turned down the other three saying that she needed time to think it over which really meant that she was trying to build up enough courage to go down to the bus station and find out what the fare to Hollywood cost.

At last the pressure of her own longings and her father's "hints" made her leave the house early one warm twilight, after getting out of doing the dinner dishes, and walk slowly down to the bus station. From March 10, 1938 until the evening of September 2, 1938, she had been wondering what a bus ticket to Hollywood cost.

The bus station was stark, unromantic and very distant from the silver screen. Two old people were sitting there on a bench waiting for a bus. The old people were tired. They wanted to be now at wherever they were going. Their suitcase was like a burned-out light bulb.

The man who sold the tickets looked as if he could have sold anything. He could just as well be selling washing machines or lawn furniture as tickets to other places.

She was red-faced and nervous. Her heart felt out of place in the bus station. She tried to act as if she were waiting for somebody to come in on the next bus, an aunt, as she worked desperately to build up enough courage to go ask how much it cost to go to Hollywood but it didn't make any difference to anybody else what games she pretended.

Nobody looked at her, though she could have rented herself out as an earthquake beet. They simply didn't care. It was a stupid night in September and she just didn't have enough nerve to find out how much the fare to Hollywood cost.

She cried all the way home through the warm gentle Oregon night, wanting to die every time her feet touched the ground. There was no wind and all the shadows were comforting. They were like cousins to her, so she married the young Ford salesman and drove a new car every year except for the Second World War.

She had two children that she named Jean and Rudolph and tried to let her beautiful movie star death go at that, but now, thirty-one years later, she still blushes when she passes the bus station.

[1963]

For Thought

Brautigan deals here with the comically pathetic illusions engendered by Hollywood movies at a time when they were a major source of entertainment and cultural values for millions of Americans. Possessing an allure that was virtually hypnotic, the movies were powerfully attractive, especially to the young and impressionable, and fostered visions and desires that were impossible to fulfill anyplace but on the silver screen.

For Discussion

1. What is the chief advantage of the point of view Brautigan adopts?
2. Examine the figures of speech used and discuss their contribution to the tone of the story.
3. What is Brautigan's attitude toward his protagonist? How is it revealed?
4. How is the title comically ironic?
5. What serious comment on life arises out of the comic catastrophe?

Erskine Caldwell
Masses of Men

Hugh Miller worked for the street railway company. Hugh had a silver button, a gold button, a bronze watch-fob made like a trolley-car, and a small tin disk with the numeral 7 almost worn off. He had worked for the company twenty-six years repairing tracks, and the company had once told him that some day he would be retired with a comfortable pension.

After all those years, Hugh was still trying to get along in the world. He still hoped to be made superintendent of construction. For some reason, though, he had never got far. He was still repairing tracks. Even though there were other men who were stepped ahead when the time came to fill up the ranks, Hugh kept his job as a laborer, repairing the tracks year after year, and hoped he would be made superintendent before he got too old to work any longer.

"I'll get it yet," he told himself. "I'll get it as sure as shooting. They've got to promote me some day, and I've been working long enough now to get it. I'll get it as sure as shooting."

Hugh had put off marrying Cora until he was promoted. Cora told him that she did not mind waiting a little longer, because she was working then in a store in town and earning as much as Hugh himself was. But after the twelfth year, Hugh decided that if he ever was going to get married, he ought to do it without further delay. He was growing old, and, although Cora was still as youthful in appearance as she was when they became engaged, she was beginning to complain of the long hours she was compelled to stand on her feet behind the counter in the notion store.

"We'll get married right now," Hugh told her one Sunday night while they were riding home on his company pass. "There's no sense in waiting any longer. If you are ready, we'll be married next week. I've been thinking about it a long time, and there's no sense in waiting till I get promoted."

"I'd love to, Hugh," she said, clutching his arm in the crowded car. "I think it's silly to put it off any longer. I've been hoping for it to happen for I don't know how long. We don't have to wait until you get promoted."

They got off the car at the boulevard stop and walked slowly home. They lived next door to each other, in boarding houses, and there was no hurry since it was Saturday night.

That was the beginning. They walked slowly down the dark street talking about next week, and Hugh kept saying to himself under his breath that he would surely be promoted the next time the company filled up the ranks. He was certain of it. He told Cora he was. She believed him.

After they were married, Hugh rented a five-room house not far from the carbarn. It was just a step down the alley from the tree-lined street where the trollies passed all day long. It was a good house, for the money, and it was comfortable. Having their door-step in an alley did not really matter so much after all. They did not mind that. The house was almost on the corner, and the upstairs windows looked out over the tree-lined street. They could step out the front door, walk a few steps, and be in the street. It was not a bad place to live, and Cora liked it.

First there was a girl; they named her Pearl. Later there was a boy, John; after another year there was another girl, and they named her Ruby.

Hugh still looked forward to the time when he would be made superintendent of construction for the street railway company, but after Ruby was born, he did not think about it any more. Cora had stopped working in the notion store; she stayed at home and attended to the house and cared for the children. She was beginning to wonder what she could do to her skin to keep it from turning so dark; in the meantime, she hid her face when people for some reason or another came to the door. She knew there was nothing wrong with her skin; it was merely becoming darker and darker every day. But she wished she knew what to do about it. Her hair already had a streak of gray in it.

She would have mentioned it to Hugh, but Hugh never talked any more. When he came home from work, he ate his supper and went to bed. She did not have a chance to tell Hugh anything like that. He was too tired to listen to her.

When Pearl, the oldest child, was nine, Hugh was knocked down by an automobile one day while he was jacking up a rail to replace a rotted cross-tie, and run over and killed. The company sent his body home that evening, when the rest of the workers got off at five o'clock, and Cora did not know what to do. After she had put the children to bed, she went out and walked down the street until she saw a policeman. She told him what had happened to Hugh, and he said he would have the body taken away the next morning. She went back home and looked at Hugh, but she could not notice any difference in him; at home, he was always asleep.

Cora knew there would be a little money coming in from the company. She was certain there would be something, but she was afraid it would not be enough to pay for Hugh's funeral and burial, and leave enough for them to live on until she could find work of some kind.

The policeman had the body taken away the next morning, and it was buried somewhere. Cora did not know where, but she did know it was the only thing she could do about it. The children had to have food, and they had to have a little heat in the house.

She waited a month for the money to come from the street railway company, and still it did not come. After that she went to the office and asked for it. There was no one there who seemed to know anything about the matter. Nobody in the big brick building had ever heard of Hugh Miller, and when they looked up the name, no one was certain which Hugh Miller she had inquired about. Cora stayed there all day, but when the people in the building went home at dark, she did not know what else to do except to go home, too.

After that she did not bother the people at the street railway company any more. She did not have time to go there, for one thing; and she had a lot to do at home. The three children had to be taken care of, and she had to go out every day and find enough food to keep them from being hungry. Sometimes it took her all day long to get enough just for one small meal; other times she could find nothing at all for them to eat, but she kept on walking because the children had to be fed.

Pearl was going on ten. She was the oldest, and Ruby was still just a baby. But Pearl was growing up. She had long yellow hair and a blue gingham dress, and she tried to help her mother all she could. She cared for the other children while Cora was out trying to get some food, and at night she helped her mother put them to bed. After they were asleep, Cora would tell her about her father, Hugh.

"Your father worked for the street railway company," she told Pearl. "The company would help us out, but they are so busy up there they can't seem to find time to do anything about it. They would help us if they could get all the Hugh Millers who have worked for them straight in their minds. Your father was just one of them."

"I can work," Pearl told her mother. "I'm old enough now. I'll see if I can find something to do. You take me with you, Mama, and I'll ask about it. John and Ruby can take care of each other if we lock them in a room before we go out."

"You're not very big for your age," Cora said. "People wouldn't believe you when you told them you are going on ten."

"But I can work. I'll show them how much I can do."

"Hugh worked for the street railway company, Pearl. He was your father. Some day the company will help us. They're busy right now. I don't like to bother them so much."

Pearl went to bed telling her mother that she was old enough to work. Cora did not say anything else to her, but she could not think of any kind of work that Pearl was capable of doing.

The next morning John and Ruby went out early to bring back some wood for the stove. They had no shoes to wear, and their coats were not warm enough. It was midwinter, but the ground was bare of snow. When they came back that afternoon, their feet were bleeding around the toes and their heels had cracked open in several places.

"Where's the fire-wood, John?" Cora asked him.

"We couldn't find any."

Cora put her cloak around her head and shoulders and went out into the alley. There was no wood of any kind there, but up at the other end there was a coal bin that sometimes overflowed into the narrow way. She filled her apron with coal and ran back to the house. The children huddled around the stove, shivering and whimpering, while she kindled the fire.

"I'm hungry, Mama," Ruby said.

"I'll get you something to eat," Cora promised her.

"When are we going to have something to eat again?" John asked her.

"I'll bring you something when I come back."

Pearl piled the quilts on the floor beside the stove and held John and Ruby close beside her in the warmth. Her gingham dress was torn, but her long yellow hair was thick and warm over her shoulders. She held the children close to her and rubbed their toes and heels.

Cora put on her cloak and went out into the alley. She ran to the street and stood there indecisively for a moment until she could make up her mind which direction she would take. She turned down the street this time, instead of going up it.

After she had run and walked for five or six blocks, she came to a cluster of one-story suburban stores. There were several men standing at the curb in front of the buildings. They were waiting for a street car to take them into town. The men turned and looked at Cora when they saw that she was running towards them.

"Mister, give me half a dollar for my children," she pleaded.

The men turned all the way around and looked her up and down. One of them laughed at her.

"Sister," one of them said, "I wouldn't give a dime for you and a dozen more like you."

The others laughed at what he had said. The trolley was coming down the street; it was two or three blocks away, and its bell was clanging. The men stepped out into the street and stood beside the tracks waiting for it to stop. Cora followed them into the street.

"Mister," she said to the man who had spoken to her, "Mister, what would you—"

"Don't call me 'Mister,'" he said angrily. "My name's Johnson."

The others laughed at her again. Johnson stepped forward and looked down at her while his friends continued laughing at her.

"Mr. Johnson," Cora said, "what would you give me a half a dollar for?"

"What would I give you half a dollar for?" he asked.

"Yes, Mr. Johnson. What would you give it to me for?"

He turned around and winked at the other men before answering her. They urged him on.

"Have you got a girl at home?" he asked her.

"Yes, sir. I've got Pearl, and Ruby, too."

"Well, I couldn't give you half a dollar, but I might be able to give you a quarter."

The street car stopped and the door sprang open. The other two men hopped on, calling to Johnson to hurry. He looked at Cora for a moment longer, but when she continued to stand there with her mouth open, unable to say anything, he ran and jumped aboard.

Cora was left standing beside the tracks. When the car started, she stood on her toes and tried to see the man inside. She called to him frantically, trying to make him understand her; and she waved her arms excitedly, attempting to attract his attention. All three of them ran to the rear end of the car and pressed their faces against the glass to see her better. Cora ran down the middle of the street, calling to them and waving her arms to stop them, but the car was soon out of sight and she was left alone on the car tracks. She went to the sidewalk and walked back up the street until she reached the corner in front of the stores where the men had been standing when she first saw them. When she got to the corner, she sat down on the curb to wait.

Cora did not know how long she had waited, but she had promised the children she would bring back some food when she returned, and she had to wait no matter how long the time was. But Johnson finally came back. He got off the street car and walked towards her at the curb. He was surprised to see her there, and he stopped before her and looked at her in amazement. Cora was glad the other men had not come back with him.

She led him up the street, running ahead and urging him to hurry. Even though he followed her without protest, he did not walk fast enough to please Cora, and she was continually asking him to hurry. He stopped once and struck a match for his cigarette against an iron street-light pole, and Cora ran back and pulled at his coat, begging him to follow her as fast as he could walk.

When he got inside the house, Cora awakened Pearl. The man stood close to the door, debating within himself whether to remain or to leave. Cora got behind him and held the door shut so he could not leave.

"How old is she?" he asked Cora.

"She's almost ten now."

"It's cold as hell in this house. Why don't you have some heat in here? You've got a stove there."

"Give me the quarter, and I'll try to get a little coal somewhere."

"Tell her to stand up."

"Stand up, Pearl," Cora told her.

Pearl shrank against the foot of the bed; she was bewildered and frightened. She wished to run to her mother, but the strange man was between them. She was afraid he could catch her before she could reach the door where Cora stood.

"You're lying to me," Johnson said. "She's nowhere near ten."

"I swear to God, Mr. Johnson, she's almost ten. Please, Mr. Johnson, don't go off now."

Johnson looked around the room and saw John and Ruby asleep under the quilts on the bed.

"How old is the other girl?"

"She's eight."

"I don't believe you. You're lying to me. Neither of them is over eight."

"Pearl's almost ten, Mr. Johnson. I swear before God, she is. Please give me the quarter."

He walked across the room towards Pearl. She tried to run away, but Cora caught her and made her stand beside the foot of the bed. Cora waited behind Johnson.

"Tell her to turn around," he said.

"Turn around, Pearl," Cora told her.

"It's too damn cold in here," he said, his hands trembling. "My feet are frozen. Why don't you make a fire in that stove?"

"If you'll give me the quarter, I'll try to get a little coal somewhere."

"How do I know you're on the level?" he asked her. "I'm afraid of you. You don't look right to me. How do I know you won't go yelling for a cop the first thing?"

"I wouldn't do that. Give me the quarter."

"I'd be in a pretty fix, caught like that. They'd give me twenty years at hard labor. I'd never come out alive."

"I won't tell anybody, Mr. Johnson. I swear to God, I won't. Just give me the quarter."

Johnson pushed his hands into his pockets and looked at Pearl again. His hands were cold, and his feet were, too. His breath looked like smoke in the cold house.

"Tell her to let me see her," he said.

"Let him see you, Pearl," Cora said.

Johnson waited, looking at her and at Cora. He could not stand still while he watched her against the foot of the bed.

"Hurry up, Pearl, and let him see you," Cora urged.

Pearl began to cry.

"They'd give me life for that," Johnson said, backing towards the door. "You'd get a cop after me before I could get out of the house. I don't like the way you look. Why don't you have some heat in here? You've got a stove."

"Honest to God, Mr. Johnson, I wouldn't tell on you. Give me the quarter, and you can trust me."

"Get some heat in here first," he said. "My feet are freezing."

"I can't get any coal till you give me the quarter."

"You can go steal some, can't you?"

"Give me the quarter first, Mr. Johnson."

"How do I know you're on the level? I don't like the way you look."

"I swear to God, I won't tell on you, Mr. Johnson."

Johnson lit a cigarette and inhaled the smoke in the manner of a man grasping for breath. With his lungs and mouth and nostrils dense with smoke, he dropped the stub into the stove and thrust his hands back into his pockets.

"Tell her to come over here," he said.

"Go over there, Pearl."

Johnson bent down and looked at Pearl in the dim light. He straightened up once for a moment, and bent down again and looked at her more closely.

"They'd hang me before tomorrow night if they caught me," he said jerkily.

"Give me the quarter, Mr. Johnson, and I swear to God I won't tell anybody."

"Tell her to stand still."

"Stand still, Pearl."

"For God's sake get some heat in here."

"Give me the quarter first, Mr. Johnson," Cora begged.

"And then go out and tell a cop," he said shrilly.

"Just give me the quarter first."

"You're crazy," he shouted at her. "I don't like the looks of you. How do I know what you'll do? You might run out of here the first thing yelling for a cop."

"Give me the quarter, and I'll get a little coal."

"And tell a cop."

"I swear I won't do that, Mr. Johnson. Give me the quarter, and I'll get some coal."

Johnson turned his back on Cora and went closer to Pearl. He took his hands out of his pockets and blew into them.

"Tell her to stop that crying."

"Stop crying, Pearl."

Johnson reached down and put his hands under Pearl's thick yellow hair, but the moment he touched her, she whirled around and ran to Cora.

"They'd screw my head off of my neck so quick I wouldn't have a chance to think about it."

"Give me the quarter, Mr. Johnson, and I swear to God I won't tell on you."

He hesitated a moment; looking at Pearl, he shoved his hands into his pants pocket and brought out a twenty-five cent piece. Cora grabbed it from his hand and bolted for the door.

"Wait a minute!" he shouted, running and catching her. "Come back here and tell her to keep still before you go."

"Keep still, Pearl," her mother told her.

"Hurry up and get some coal before I freeze to death. And if you tell a policeman, I'll kill the last one of you before they take me. I ought to have better sense than to let you go. I don't like the way you look."

Cora ran out the door and into the alley before he could say anything more to her. She slammed the door and ran with all her might to the end of the alley. Without losing a moment, she raced down the street towards the one-story stores. After she had gone a block, she stopped and carefully laid the quarter on her tongue and closed her lips tightly so she would be sure not to drop it or lose it on the dark street.

One of the grocery stores was still open. She took the coin out of her mouth, pointing at bread and pressed meat, and placed it in the clerk's hand. He dropped the wet silver piece as though it were white-hot steel and wiped his hands on his apron.

When Cora got back, the children were asleep. John and Ruby were rolled tightly in the quilts, and Pearl was lying on the bed with the coat over her. She had been crying, and the tears had not fully dried on her cheeks; her eyes were inflamed, and her face was swollen across the bridge of her nose. Cora went to the side of the bed and threw the coat from her and looked down at her. Pearl had doubled herself into a knot, with her arms locked around her knees, and her head was thrust forward over her chest. Cora looked at her for a while, and then she carefully replaced the coat over her.

After unwrapping the bread and pressed meat, she stuffed the paper into the stove and struck a match to it. She drew her chair closer and bent forward so she could stretch her arms around the sides of the stove and feel the heat as much as possible before it burned out.

When the stove became cold again, Cora laid the bread and pressed meat on a chair beside her and rolled up in her quilt to wait for day. When the children woke up, the food would be there for them.

[1933]

For Thought

Caldwell's story, "Masses of Men," focuses on the grim struggle of a desperate woman who tries to keep her starving children alive, anyway she can. The period is the Great Depression. While the characters are flat and are not remarkable in any way, Cora Miller's intense loyalty to her children dominates the story. Caldwell brings irony into play when temporary relief from hunger and cold must be bought at the cost of the destruction of her daughter's innocence.

For Discussion

1. How does Caldwell characterize Hugh and Cora Miller?
2. Why does the author leave the era and identity of the large city in which the Millers live so vague?
3. Why is there no compensation paid to Cora for Hugh's accidental death? Should the blame for this wrong be shared by both the company and Cora?
4. How is Cora's desperate plight the result of both her situation and her own shortcomings?
5. Cora's long bargaining session with Johnson is sordid and degrading to both of them. What conflicts within and between both characters give the scene its emotional power?
6. What accounts for the sense of calm that accompanies the conclusion of the story?

Truman Capote
A Christmas Memory

Imagine a morning in late November. A coming of winter morning more than twenty years ago. Consider the kitchen of a spreading old house in a country town. A great black stove is its main feature; but there is also a big round table and a fireplace with two rocking chairs placed in front of it. Just today the fireplace commenced its seasonal roar.

A woman with shorn white hair is standing at the kitchen window. She is wearing tennis shoes and a shapeless gray sweater over a summery calico dress. She is small and sprightly, like a bantam hen; but, due to a long youthful illness, her shoulders are pitifully hunched. Her face is remarkable—not unlike Lincoln's, craggy like that, and tinted by sun and wind; but it is delicate too, finely boned, and her eyes are sherry-colored and timid. "Oh my," she exclaims, her breath smoking the windowpane, "it's fruitcake weather!"

The person to whom she is speaking is myself. I am seven; she is sixty-something. We are cousins, very distant ones, and we have lived together—well, as long as I can remember. Other people inhabit the house, relatives; and though they have power over us, and frequently make us cry, we are not, on the whole, too much aware of them. We are each other's best friend. She calls me Buddy, in memory of a boy who was formerly her best friend. The other Buddy died in the 1880's, when she was still a child. She is still a child.

"I knew it before I got out of bed," she says turning away from the window with a purposeful excitement in her eyes. "The courthouse bell sounded so cold and clear. And there were no birds singing; they've gone to warmer country, yes indeed. Oh, Buddy, stop stuffing biscuit and fetch our buggy. Help me find my hat. We've thirty cakes to bake."

It's always the same: a morning arrives in November, and my friend, as though officially inaugurating the Christmas time of year that exhilarates her imagination and fuels the blaze of her heart, announces: "It's fruitcake weather! Fetch our buggy. Help me find my hat."

The hat is found, a straw cartwheel corsaged with velvet roses out-of-doors has faded: it once belonged to a more fashionable relative. Together, we guide our buggy, a dilapidated baby carriage, out to the garden and into a grove of pecan trees. The buggy is mine; that is, it was bought for me when I was born. It is made of wicker, rather unraveled, and the wheels wobble like a drunkard's legs. But it is a faithful object; springtimes, we take it to the woods and fill it with flowers, herbs, wild fern for our porch pots; in the summer, we pile it with picnic paraphernalia and sugar-cane fishing poles and roll it down to the edge of a creek; it has its winter uses, too: as a truck for hauling firewood from the yard to the kitchen, as a warm bed for Queenie, our tough little orange and white rat terrier who has survived distemper and two rattlesnake bites. Queenie is trotting beside it now.

Three hours later we are back in the kitchen hulling a heaping buggyload of windfall pecans. Our backs hurt from gathering them: how hard they were to find (the main crop having been shaken off the trees and sold by the orchard's owners, who are not us) among the concealing leaves, the frosted, deceiving grass. Caarackle! A cheery crunch, scraps of miniature thunder sound as the shells collapse and the golden mound of sweet oily ivory meat mounts in the milk-glass bowl. Queenie begs to taste, and now and again my friend sneaks her a mite, though insisting we deprive ourselves. "We mustn't, Buddy. If we start, we won't stop. And there's scarcely enough as there is. For thirty cakes." The kitchen is growing dark. Dusk turns the window into a mirror: our reflections mingle with the rising moon as we work by the fireside in the firelight. At last, when the moon is quite high, we toss the final hull into the fire and, with joined sighs, watch it catch flame. The buggy is empty, the bowl is brimful.

We eat our supper (cold biscuits, bacon, blackberry jam) and discuss tomorrow. Tomorrow the kind of work I like best begins: buying. Cherries and citron, ginger and vanilla and canned Hawaiian pineapple, rinds and raisins and walnuts and whiskey and oh, so much flour, butter, so many eggs, spices, flavorings: why, we'll need a pony to pull the buggy home.

But before these purchases can be made, there is the question of money. Neither of us has any. Except for skinflint sums persons in the house occasionally provide (a dime is considered very big money); or what we earn ourselves from various activities: holding rummage sales, selling buckets of hand-picked blackberries, jars of homemade jam and apple jelly and peach preserves, rounding up flowers for funerals and weddings. Once we won seventy-ninth prize, five dollars, in a national football contest. Not that we know a fool thing about football. It's just that we enter any contest we hear about: at the moment our hopes are centered on the fifty-thousand-dollar Grand Prize being offered to name a new brand of coffee (we suggested "A.M."; and, after some hesitation, for my friend thought it perhaps sacrilegious, the slogan "A.M.! Amen!"). To tell the truth, our only *really* profitable enterprise was the Fun and Freak Museum we conducted in a back-yard woodshed two summers ago. The Fun was a stereopticon with slide views of Washington and New York lent us by a relative who had been to those places (she was furious when she discovered why we'd borrowed it); the Freak was a three-legged biddy chicken hatched by one of our own hens. Everybody hereabouts wanted to see that biddy: we charged grownups a nickel, kids two cents. And took in a good twenty dollars before the museum shut down due to the decease of the main attraction.

But one way and another we do each year accumulate Christmas savings, a Fruitcake Fund. These moneys we keep hidden in an ancient bead purse under a loose board under the floor under a chamber pot under my friend's bed. The purse is seldom removed from this safe location except to make a deposit, or, as happens every Saturday, a withdrawal; for on Saturdays I am allowed ten cents to go to the picture show. My friend has never been to a picture show, nor does she intend to: "I'd rather hear you tell the story, Buddy. That way I can imagine it more. Besides, a person my age shouldn't squander their eyes. When the Lord comes, let me see him clear." In addition to never having seen a movie, she has never: eaten in a restaurant, traveled more than five miles from home, received or sent a telegram, read anything except funny papers and the Bible, worn cosmetics, cursed, wished someone harm, told a lie on purpose, let a hungry dog go hungry. Here are a few things she has done, does do: killed with a hoe the biggest rattlesnake ever seen in this county (sixteen rattles), dip snuff (secretly), tame hummingbirds (just try it) till they balance on her finger, tell ghost stories (we both believe in ghosts) so tingling they chill you in July, talk to herself, take walks in the rain, grow the prettiest japonicas in town, know the recipe for every sort of old-time Indian cure, including a magical wart-remover.

Now, with supper finished, we retire to the room in a faraway part of the house where my friend sleeps in a scrap-quilt-covered iron bed painted rose pink, her favorite color. Silently, wallowing in the pleasures of conspiracy, we take the bead purse from its secret place and spill its contents on the scrap quilt. Dollar bills, tightly rolled and green as May buds. Somber fifty-cent pieces, heavy enough to weight a dead man's eyes. Lovely dimes, the liveliest coin, the one that really jingles. Nickels and quarters, worn smooth as creek pebbles. But mostly a hateful heap of bitter-odored pennies. Last summer others in the house contracted to pay us a penny for every twenty-five flies we killed. Oh, the carnage of August: the flies that flew to heaven! Yet it was not work in which we took pride. And, as we sit counting pennies, it is as though we were back tabulating dead flies. Neither of us has a head for figures; we count slowly, lose track, start again. According to her calculations, we have $12.73. According to mine, exactly $13. "I do hope you're wrong, Buddy. We can't mess around with thirteen. The cakes will fall. Or put somebody in the cemetery. Why, I wouldn't dream of getting out of bed on the thirteenth." This is true: she always spends thirteenths in bed. So, to be on the safe side, we subtract a penny and toss it out the window.

Of the ingredients that go into our fruitcakes, whiskey is the most expensive, as well as the hardest to obtain: State law forbid its sale. But everybody knows you can buy a bottle from Mr. Haha Jones. And the next day, having completed our more prosaic shopping, we set out for Mr. Haha's business address, a "sinful" (to quote public opinion) fish-fry and dancing café down by the river. We've been there before, and on the same errand; but in previous years our dealings have been with Haha's wife, an iodine-dark Indian woman with brazzy peroxided hair and a dead-tired disposition. Actually, we've never laid eyes on her husband, though we've heard that he's an Indian too. A giant with razor scars across his cheeks. They call him Haha because he's so gloomy, a man who never laughs. As we approach his café (a large log cabin festooned inside and out with chains of garish-gay naked lightbulbs and standing by the river's muddy edge under the shade of river trees where moss drifts through the branches like gray mist) our steps slow down. Even Queenie stops prancing and sticks close by. People have been murdered in Haha's café. Cut to pieces. Hit on the head. There's a case coming up in court next month. Naturally these goings-on happen at night when the colored lights cast crazy patterns and the victrola wails. In the daytime Haha's is shabby and deserted. I knock at the door, Queenie barks, my friend calls: "Mrs. Haha, ma'am? Anyone to home?"

Footsteps. The door opens. Our hearts overturn. It's Mr. Haha Jones himself! And he *is* a giant; he *does* have scars; he *doesn't* smile. No, he glowers at us through Satan-tilted eyes and demands to know: "What you want with Haha?"

For a moment we are too paralyzed to tell. Presently my friend half-finds her voice, a whispery voice at best: "If you please, Mr. Haha, we'd like a quart of your finest whiskey."

His eyes tilt more. Would you believe it? Haha is smiling! Laughing, too. "Which one of you is a drinkin man?"

"It's for making fruitcakes, Mr. Haha. Cooking."

This sobers him. He frowns. "That's no way to waste good whiskey." Nevertheless, he retreats into the shadowed café and seconds later appears carrying a bottle of daisy yellow unlabeled liquor. He demonstrates its sparkle in the sunlight and says: "Two dollars."

We pay him with nickels and dimes and pennies. Suddenly, jangling the coins in his hand like a fistful of dice, his face softens. "Tell you what," he proposes, pouring the money back into our bead purse, "just send me one of them fruitcakes instead."

"Well," my friend remarks on our way home, "there's a lovely man. We'll put an extra cup of raisins in *his* cake."

The black stove, stoked with coal and firewood, glows like a lighted pumpkin. Eggbeaters whirl, spoons spin round in bowls of butter and sugar, vanilla sweetens the air, ginger spices it; melting, nose-tingling odors saturate the kitchen, suffuse the house, drift out to the world on puffs of chimney smoke. In four days our work is done. Thirty-one cakes, dampened with whiskey, bask on window sills and shelves.

Who are they for?

Friends. Not necessarily neighbor friends: indeed, the larger share are intended for persons we've met maybe once, perhaps not at all. People who've struck our fancy. Like President Roosevelt. Like the Reverend and Mrs. J. C. Lucey, Baptist missionaries to Borneo who lectured here last winter. Or the little knife grinder who comes through town twice a year. Or Abner Packer, the driver of the six o'clock bus from Mobile, who exchanges waves with us every day as he passes in a dust-cloud whoosh. Or the young Wistons, a California couple whose car one afternoon broke down outside the house and who spent a pleasant hour chatting with us on the porch (young Mr. Wiston snapped our picture, the only one we've ever had taken). Is it because my friend is shy with everyone *except* strangers that these strangers, and merest acquaintances, seem to us our truest friends? I think yes. Also, the scrapbooks we keep of thank-you's on White House stationery, time-to-time communications from California and Borneo, the knife grinder's penny post cards, make us feel connected to eventful worlds beyond the kitchen with its view of a sky that stops.

Now a nude December fig branch grates against the window. The kitchen is empty, the cakes are gone; yesterday we carted the last of them to the post office, where the cost of stamps turned our purse inside out. We're broke. That rather depresses me, but my friend insists on celebrating—with two inches of whiskey left in Haha's bottle. Queenie has a spoonful in a bowl of coffee (she likes her coffee chicory-flavored and strong). The rest we divide between a pair of jelly glasses. We're both quite awed at the prospect of drinking straight whiskey; the taste of it brings screwed-up expressions and sour shudders. But by and by we begin to sing, the two of us singing different songs simultaneously. I don't know the words to mine, just: *Come on along, come on along, to the dark-town strutters' ball.* But I can dance: that's what I mean to be, a tap dancer in the movies. My dancing shadow rollicks on the walls; our voices rock the chinaware; we giggle: as if unseen hands were tickling us. Queenie rolls on her back, her paws plow the air, something like a grin stretches her black lips. Inside myself, I feel warm and sparky as those crumbling logs, carefree as the wind in the chimney. My friend waltzes round the stove, the hem of her poor calico skirt pinched between her fingers as though it were a party dress: *Show me the way to go home* she sings, her tennis shoes squeaking on the floor. *Show me the way to go home.*

Enter: two relatives. Very angry. Potent with eyes that scold, tongues that scald. Listen to what they have to say, the words tumbling together into a wrathful tune: "A child of seven whiskey on his breath! are you out of your mind? feeding a child of seven! must be loony! road to ruination! remember Cousin Kate? Uncle Charlie? Uncle Charlie's brother-in-law? shame! scandal! humiliation! kneel, pray, beg the Lord!"

Queenie sneaks under the stove. My friend gazes at her shoes, her chin quivers, she lifts her skirt and blows her nose and runs to her room. Long after the town has gone to sleep and the house is silent except for the chimings of clocks and the sputter of fading fires, she is weeping into a pillow already as wet as a widow's handkerchief.

"Don't cry," I say, sitting at the bottom of her bed and shivering despite my flannel nightgown that smells of last winter's cough syrup, "don't cry," I beg, teasing her toes, tickling her feet, "you're too old for that."

"It's because," she hiccups, "I *am* too old. Old and funny."

"Not funny. Fun. More fun than anybody. Listen. If you don't stop crying you'll be so tired tomorrow we can't go cut a tree."

She straightens up. Queenie jumps on the bed (where Queenie is not allowed) to lick her cheeks. "I know where we'll find pretty trees, Buddy. And holly, too. With berries big as your eyes. It's way off in the woods. Farther than we've ever been. Papa used to bring us Christmas trees from there: carry them on his shoulder. That's fifty years ago. Well, now: I can't wait for morning."

Morning. Frozen rime lusters the grass; the sun, round as an orange and orange as hot-weather moons, balances on the horizon, burnishes the silvered winter woods. A wild turkey calls. A renegade hog grunts in the undergrowth. Soon, by the edge of knee-deep, rapid-running water, we have to abandon the buggy. Queenie wades the stream first, paddles across barking complaints at the swiftness of the current, the pneumonia-making coldness of it. We follow, holding our shoes and equipment (a hatchet, a burlap sack) above our heads. A mile more: of chastising thorns, burs and briers that catch at our clothes; of rusty pine needles brilliant with gaudy fungus and molted feathers. Here, there, a flash, a flutter, an ecstasy of shrillings remind us that not all the birds have flown south. Always, the path unwinds through lemony sun pools and pitch vine tunnels. Another creek to cross: a disturbed armada of speckled trout froths the water round us, and frogs the size of plates practice belly flops; beaver workmen are building a dam. On the farther shore, Queenie shakes herself and trembles. My friend shivers, too: not with cold but enthusiasm. One of her hat's ragged roses sheds a petal as she lifts her head and inhales the pine-heavy air. "We're almost there; can you smell it, Buddy?" she says, as though we were approaching an ocean.

And, indeed, it is a kind of ocean. Scented acres of holiday trees, prickly-leafed holly. Red berries shiny as Chinese bells: black crows swoop upon them screaming. Having stuffed our burlap sacks with enough greenery and crimson to garland a dozen windows, we set about choosing a tree. "It should be," muses my friend, "twice as tall as a boy. So a boy can't steal the star." The one we pick is twice as tall as me. A brave handsome brute that survives thirty hatchet strokes before it keels with a creaking rending cry. Lugging it like a kill, we commence the long trek out. Every few yards we abandon the struggle, sit down and pant. But we have the strength of triumphant huntsmen; that and the tree's virile, icy perfume revive us, goad us on. Many compliments accompany our sunset return along the red clay road to town; but my friend is sly and noncommittal when passers-by praise the treasure perched on our buggy: what a fine tree and where did it come from? "Yonderways," she murmurs vaguely. Once a car stops and the rich mill owner's lazy wife leans out and whines: "Giveya two-bits cash for that ol tree." Ordinarily my friend is afraid of saying no; but on this occasion she promptly shakes her head: "We wouldn't take a dollar." The mill owner's wife persists. "A dollar, my foot! Fifty cents. That's my last offer. Goodness, woman, you can get another one." In answer, my friend gently reflects: "I doubt it. There's never two of anything."

Home: Queenie slumps by the fire and sleeps till tomorrow, snoring loud as a human.

A trunk in the attic contains: a shoebox of ermine tails (off the opera cape of a curious lady who once rented a room in the house), coils of frazzled tinsel gone gold with age, one silver star, a brief rope of dilapidated, undoubtedly dangerous candy-like light bulbs. Excellent decorations, as far as they go, which isn't far enough: my friend wants our tree to blaze "like a Baptist window," droop with weighty snows of ornament. But we can't afford the made-in-Japan splendors at the five-and-dime. So we do what we've always done: sit for days at the kitchen table with scissors and crayons and stacks of colored paper. I make sketches and my friend cuts them out: lots of cats, fish too (because they're easy to draw), some apples, some watermelons, a few winged angels devised from saved-up sheets of Hershey-bar tin foil. We use safety pins to attach these creations to the tree; as a final touch, we sprinkle the branches with shredded cotton (picked in August for this purpose). My friend, surveying the effect, clasps her hands together. "Now honest, Buddy. Doesn't it look good enough to eat?" Queenie tries to eat an angel.

After weaving and ribboning holly wreaths for all the front windows, our next project is the fashioning of family gifts. Tie-dye scarves for the ladies, for the men a home-brewed lemon and licorice and aspirin syrup to be taken "at the first Symptoms of a Cold and after Hunting." But when it comes time for making each other's gift, my friend and I separate to work secretly. I would like to buy her a pearl-handled knife, a radio, a whole pound of chocolate-covered cherries (we tasted some once, and she always swears: "I could live on them, Buddy, Lord yes I could—and that's not taking His name in vain"). Instead, I am building her a kite. She would like to give me a bicycle (she's said so on several million occasions: "If only I could, Buddy. It's bad enough in life to do without something *you* want; but confound it, what gets my goat is not being able to give somebody something you want *them* to have. Only one of these days I will, Buddy. Locate you a bike. Don't ask how. Steal it, maybe"). Instead, I'm fairly certain that she is building me a kite—the same as last year, and the year before: the year before that we exchanged slingshots. All of which is fine by me. For we are champion kite-fliers who study the wind like sailors; my friend, more accomplished than I, can get a kite aloft when there isn't enough breeze to carry clouds.

Christmas Eve afternoon we scrape together a nickel and go to the butcher's to buy Queenie's traditional gift, a good gnawable beef bone. The bone, wrapped in funny paper, is placed high in the tree near the silver star. Queenie knows it's there. She squats at the foot of the tree staring up in a trance of greed: when bedtime arrives she refuses to budge. Her excitement is equaled by my own. I kick the covers and turn my pillow as though it were a scorching summer's night. Somewhere a rooster crows: falsely, for the sun is still on the other side of the world.

"Buddy, are you awake?" It is my friend, calling from her room, which is next to mine; and an instant later she is sitting on my bed holding a candle. "Well, I can't sleep a hoot," she declares. "My mind's jumping like a jack rabbit. Buddy, do you think Mrs. Roosevelt will serve our cake at dinner?" We huddle in the bed, and she squeezes my hand I-love-you. "Seems like your hand used to be so much smaller. I guess I hate to see you grow up. When you're grown up, will we still be friends?" I say always. "But I feel so bad, Buddy. I wanted so bad to give you a bike. I tried to sell my cameo Papa gave me. Buddy"—she hesitates, as though embarrassed—"I made you another kite." Then I confess that I made her one, too; and we laugh. The candle burns too short to hold. Out it goes, exposing the starlight, the stars spinning at the window like a visible caroling that slowly, slowly daybreak silences. Possibly we doze; but the beginnings of dawn splash us like cold water: we're up, wide-eyed and wandering while we wait for others to waken. Quite deliberately my friend drops a kettle on the kitchen floor. I tap-dance in front of closed doors. One by one the household emerges, looking as though they'd like to kill us both; but it's Christmas, so they can't. First, a gorgeous breakfast: just everything you can imagine—from flapjacks and fried squirrel to hominy grits and honey-on-the-comb. Which puts everyone in a good humor except my friend and I. Frankly, we're so impatient to get at the presents we can't eat a mouthful.

Well, I'm disappointed. Who wouldn't be? With socks, a Sunday school shirt, some handkerchiefs, a hand-me-down sweater and a year's subscription to a religious magazine for children. *The Little Shepherd*. It makes me boil. It really does.

My friend has a better haul. A sack of Satsumas, that's her best present. She is proudest, however, of a white wool shawl knitted by her married sister. But she *says* her favorite gift is the kite I built her. And it *is* very beautiful though not as beautiful as the one she made me, which is blue and scattered with gold and green Good Conduct stars; moreover, my name is painted on it, "Buddy."

"Buddy, the wind is blowing."

The wind is blowing, and nothing will do till we've run to a pasture below the house where Queenie has scooted to bury her bone (and where, a winter hence, Queenie will be buried, too). There, plunging through the healthy waist-high grass, we unreel our kites, feel them twitching at the string like sky fish as they swim into the wind. Satisfied, sun-warmed, we sprawl in the grass and peel Satsumas and watch our kites cavort. Soon I forget the socks and hand-me-down sweater. I'm as happy as if we'd already won the fifty-thousand-dollar Grand Prize in that coffee-naming contest.

"My, how foolish I am!" my friend cries, suddenly alert, like a woman remembering too late she has biscuits in the oven. "You know what I've always thought?" she asks in a tone of discovery, and not smiling at me but a point beyond. "I've always thought a body would have to be sick and dying before they saw the Lord. And I imagined that when He came it would be like looking at the Baptist window: pretty as colored glass with the sun pouring through, such a shine you don't know it's getting dark. And it's been a comfort: to think of that shine taking away all the spooky feeling. But I'll wager it never happens. I'll wager at the very end a body realizes the Lord has already shown Himself. That things as they are"—her hand circles in a gesture that gathers clouds and kites and grass and Queenie pawing earth over her bone—"just what they've always seen, was seeing Him. As for me, I could leave the world with today in my eyes."

This is our last Christmas together.

Life separates us. Those who Know Best decide that I belong in a military school. And so follows a miserable succession of bugle-blowing prisons, grim reveille-ridden summer camps. I have a new home too. But it doesn't count. Home is where my friend is, and there I never go.

And there she remains, puttering around the kitchen. Alone with Queenie.

Then alone. ("Buddy dear," she writes in her wild hard-to-read script, "yesterday Jim Macy's horse kicked Queenie bad. Be thankful she didn't feel much. I wrapped her in a Fine Linen sheet and rode her in the buggy down to Simpson's pasture where she can be with all her Bones . . ."). For a few Novembers she continues to bake her fruitcakes single-handed; not as many, but some: and, of course, she always sends me "the best of the batch." Also, in every letter she encloses a dime wadded in toilet paper: "See a picture show and write me the story." But gradually in her letters she tends to confuse me with her other friend, the Buddy who died in the 1880's; more and more thirteenths are not the only days she stays in bed: a morning arrives in November, a leafless birdless coming of winter morning, when she cannot rouse herself to exclaim: "Oh my, it's fruitcake weather!"

And when that happens, I know it. A message saying so merely confirms a piece of news some secret vein had already received, severing from me an irreplaceable part of myself, letting it loose like a kite on a broken string. That is why, walking across a school campus on this particular December morning, I keep searching the sky. As if I expected to see, rather like hearts, a lost pair of kites hurrying toward heaven.

[1956]

For Thought

With a masterful use of vivid sensory detail and gently ironic dialogue, Capote creates, against a setting and atmosphere of rural, pioneerlike austerity, a pervasive mood of great happiness and joy arising out of the simple activities of an unlikely pair of friends in the midst of a family situation where they appear to be virtual outcasts. Through the first-person central-participant point of view, the author relates how a seven-year-old boy and his "sixty-something"-year-old lady friend rise above neglect and material shortcomings to achieve a spiritual union that defies separation. Capote attains characterization in depth by having Buddy characterize the friend while indirectly characterizing himself at the same time.

For Discussion

1. How is the friend characterized by the things she has never done and by the things she has done and now does?
2. How do the Christmas fruitcakes serve as a central symbol in the story?
3. What elements of humor are there in the story (that is, in the couple's situation, in their character, and in the language employed by the author)?
4. Compare and contrast the encounter with Haha and that with the rich mill owner's wife.
5. Compare and contrast the gifts the boy and the old woman would like to give to one another and those they actually give and receive. How does this activity relate to the theme of the story?

Willa Cather
Paul's Case

It was Paul's afternoon to appear before the faculty of the Pittsburgh High School to account for his various misdemeanors. He had been suspended a week ago, and his father had called at the Principal's office and confessed his perplexity about his son. Paul entered the faculty room suave and smiling. His clothes were a trifle outgrown, and the tan velvet on the collar of his open overcoat was frayed and worn; but for all that there was something of the dandy about him, and he wore an opal pin in his neatly knotted black four-in-hand, and a red carnation in his buttonhole. This latter adornment the faculty somehow felt was not properly significant of the contrite spirit befitting a boy under the ban of suspension.

Paul was tall for his age and very thin, with high, cramped shoulders and a narrow chest. His eyes were remarkable for a certain hysterical brilliancy, and he continually used them in a conscious, theatrical sort of way, peculiarly offensive in a boy. The pupils were abnormally large, as though he were addicted to belladonna, but there was a glassy glitter about them which that drug does not produce.

When questioned by the Principal as to why he was there, Paul stated, politely enough, that he wanted to come back to school. This was a lie, but Paul was quite accustomed to lying; found it, indeed, indispensable for overcoming friction. His teachers were asked to state their respective charges against him, which they did with such a rancour and aggrievedness as evinced that this was not a usual case. Disorder and impertinence were among the offences named, yet each of his instructors felt that it was scarcely possible to put into words the real cause of the trouble, which lay in a sort of hysterically defiant manner of the boy's; in the contempt which they all knew he felt for them, and which he seemingly made not the least effort to conceal. Once, when he had been making a synopsis of a paragraph at the blackboard, his English teacher had stepped to his side and attempted to guide his hand. Paul had started back with a shudder and thrust his hands violently behind him. The astonished woman could scarcely have been more hurt and embarrassed had he struck at her. The insult was so involuntary and definitely personal as to be unforgettable. In one way and another, he had made all his teachers, men and women alike, conscious of the same feeling of physical aversion. In one class he habitually sat with his hand shading his eyes; in another he always looked out of the window during the recitation; in another he made a running commentary on the lecture, with humorous intent.

His teachers felt this afternoon that his whole attitude was symbolized by his shrug and his flippantly red carnation flower, and they fell upon him without mercy, his English teacher leading the pack. He stood through it smiling, his pale lips parted over his white teeth. (His lips were continually twitching, and he had a habit of raising his eyebrows that was contemptuous and irritating to the last degree.) Older boys than Paul had broken down and shed tears under that ordeal, but his set smile did not once desert him, and his only sign of discomfort was the nervous trembling of the fingers that toyed with the buttons of his overcoat, and an occasional jerking of the other hand which held his hat. Paul was always smiling, always glancing about him, seeming to feel that people might be watching him and trying to detect something. This conscious expression, since it was as far as possible from boyish mirthfulness, was usually attributed to insolence or "smartness."

As the inquisition proceeded, one of his instructors repeated an impertinent remark of the boy's, and the Principal asked him whether he thought that a courteous speech to make to a woman. Paul shrugged his shoulders slightly and his eyebrows twitched.

"I don't know," he replied. "I didn't mean to be polite or impolite, either. I guess it's a sort of way I have, of saying things regardless."

The Principal asked him whether he didn't think that a way it would be well to get rid of. Paul grinned and said he guessed so. When he was told that he could go, he bowed gracefully and went out. His bow was like a repetition of the scandalous red carnation.

His teachers were in despair, and his drawing-master voiced the feeling of them all when he declared there was something about the boy which none of them understood. He added: "I don't really believe that smile of his comes altogether from insolence; there's something sort of haunted about it. The boy is not strong, for one thing. There is something wrong about the fellow."

The drawing-master had come to realize that, in looking at Paul, one saw only his white teeth and the forced animation of his eyes. One warm afternoon the boy had gone to sleep at his drawing-board, and his master had noted with amazement what a white, blue-veined face it was; drawn and wrinkled like an old man's about the eyes, the lips twitching even in his sleep.

His teachers left the building dissatisfied and unhappy; humiliated to have felt so vindictive toward a mere boy, to have uttered this feeling in cutting terms, and to have set each other on, as it were, in the gruesome game of intemperate reproach. One of them remembered having seen a miserable street cat set at bay by a ring of tormentors.

As for Paul, he ran down the hill whistling the Soldiers' Chorus from "Faust," looking behind him now and then to see whether some of his teachers were not there to witness his light-heartedness. As it was now late in the afternoon and Paul was on duty that evening as usher at Carnegie Hall, he decided that he would not go home to supper.

When he reached the concert hall, the doors were not yet open. It was chilly outside, and he decided to go up into the picture gallery—always deserted at this hour—where there were some of Raffelli's gay studies of Paris streets and an airy blue

Venetian scene or two that always exhilarated him. He was delighted to find no one in the gallery but the old guard, who sat in the corner, a newspaper on his knee, a black patch over one eye and the other closed. Paul possessed himself of the place and walked confidently up and down, whistling under his breath. After a while he sat down before a blue Rico and lost himself. When he bethought him to look at his watch, it was after seven o'clock, and he rose with a start and ran downstairs, making a face at Augustus Caesar, peering out from the cast-room, and an evil gesture at the Venus of Milo as he passed her on the stairway.

When Paul reached the ushers' dressing-room, half a dozen boys were there already, and he began excitedly to tumble into his uniform. It was one of the few that at all approached fitting, and Paul thought it very becoming—though he knew the tight, straight coat accentuated his narrow chest, about which he was exceedingly sensitive. He was always excited while he dressed, twanging all over the tuning of the strings and the preliminary flourishes of the horns in the music-room; but tonight he seemed quite beside himself, and he teased and plagued the boys until, telling him that he was crazy, they put him down on the floor and sat on him.

Somewhat calmed by his suppression, Paul dashed out to the front of the house to seat the early comers. He was a model usher. Gracious and smiling he ran up and down the aisles. Nothing was too much trouble for him; he carried messages and brought programmes as though it were his greatest pleasure in life, and all the people in his section thought him a charming boy, feeling that he remembered and admired them. As the house filled, he grew more and more vivacious and animated, and the colour came to his cheeks and lips. It was very much as though this were a great reception and Paul were the host. Just as the musicians came out to take their places, his English teacher arrived with cheques for the seats which a prominent manufacturer had taken for the season. She betrayed some embarrassment when she handed Paul the tickets, and a hauteur which subsequently made her feel very foolish. Paul was startled for a moment, and had the feeling of wanting to put her out; what business had she here among all these fine people and gay colours? He looked her over and decided that she was not appropriately dressed and must be a fool to sit downstairs in such togs. The tickets had probably been sent her out of kindness, he reflected, as he put down a seat for her, and she had about as much right to sit there as he had.

When the symphony began, Paul sank into one of the rear seats with a long sigh of relief, and lost himself as he had done before the Rico. It was not that symphonies, as such, meant anything in particular to Paul, but the first sigh of the instruments seemed to free some hilarious spirit within him; something that struggled there like the Genius in the bottle found by the Arab fisherman. He felt a sudden zest of life; the lights danced before his eyes and the concert hall blazed into unimaginable splendour. When the soprano soloist came on, Paul forgot even the nastiness of his teacher's being there, and gave himself up to the peculiar intoxication such personages always had for him. The soloist chanced to be a German woman, by no means in her first youth, and the mother of many children; but she wore a satin gown and a tiara, and she had that indefinable air of achievement, that world-shine upon her, which always blinded Paul to any possible defects.

After a concert was over, Paul was often irritable and wretched until he got to sleep—and to-night he was even more than usually restless. He had the feeling of not being able to let down; of its being impossible to give up this delicious excitement which was the only thing that could be called living at all. During the last number he withdrew and, after hastily changing his clothes in the dressing-room, slipped out to the side door where the singer's carriage stood. Here he began pacing rapidly up and down the walk, waiting to see her come out.

Over yonder the Schenley, in its vacant stretch, loomed big and square through the fine rain, the windows of its twelve stories glowing like those of a lighted cardboard house under a Christmas tree. All the actors and singers of any importance stayed there when they were in Pittsburgh, and a number of the big manufacturers of the place lived there in the winter. Paul had often hung about the hotel, watching the people go in and out, longing to enter and leave schoolmasters and dull care behind him forever.

At last the singer came out, accompanied by the conductor, who helped her into her carriage and closed the door with a cordial *auf wiedersehen*—which set Paul to wondering whether she were not an old sweetheart of his. Paul followed the carriage over to the hotel, walking so rapidly as not to be far from the entrance when the singer alighted and disappeared behind the swinging glass doors which were opened by a Negro in a tall hat and a long coat. In the moment that the door was ajar, it seemed to Paul that he, too, entered. He seemed to feel himself go after her up the steps, into the warm, lighted building, into an exotic, a tropical world of shiny, glistening surfaces and basking ease. He reflected upon the mysterious dishes that were brought into the dining-room, the green bottles in buckets of ice, as he had seen them in the supper-party pictures of the Sunday supplement. A quick gust of wind brought the rain down with sudden vehemence, and Paul was startled to find that he was still outside in the slush of the gravel driveway; that his boots were letting in the water and his scanty overcoat was clinging wet about him; that the lights in front of the concert hall were out, and that the rain was driving in sheets between him and the orange glow of the windows above him. There it was, what he wanted—tangibly before him, like the fairy world of a Christmas pantomime; as the rain beat in his face, Paul wondered whether he were destined always to shiver in the black night outside, looking up at it.

He turned and walked reluctantly toward the car tracks. The end had to come sometime; his father in his night-clothes at the top of the stairs, explanations that did not explain, hastily improvised fictions that were forever tripping him up, his upstairs room and its horrible yellow wallpaper, the creaking bureau with the greasy plush collar-box, and over his painted wooden bed the pictures of George Washington and John Calvin, and the framed motto, 'Feed my Lambs,' which had been worked in red worsted by his mother, whom Paul could not remember.

Half an hour later, Paul alighted from the Negley Avenue car and went slowly down one of the side streets off the main thoroughfare. It was a highly respectable street, where all the houses were exactly alike, and where business men of moderate means begot and reared large families of children, all of whom went to Sabbath School and learned the shorter catechism, and were interested in arithmetic; all of whom were as exactly alike as their homes, and of a piece with the monotony in which they lived. Paul never went up Cordelia Street without a shudder of loathing. His home was next to the house of the Cumberland minister. He approached it tonight with the nerveless sense of defeat, the hopeless feeling of sinking back forever into ugliness and commonness that he had always had when he came home. The moment he turned into Cordelia Street he felt the waters close above his head. After each of these orgies of living, he experienced all the physical depression which follows a debauch; the loathing of respectable beds, of common food, of a house permeated by kitchen odours; a shuddering repulsion for the flavourless, colourless mass of every-day existence; a morbid desire for cool things and soft lights and fresh flowers.

The nearer he approached the house, the more absolutely unequal Paul felt to the sight of it all: his ugly sleeping chamber; the cold bathroom with the grimy zinc tub, the cracked mirror, the dripping spigots; his father, at the top of the stairs, his hairy legs sticking out from his nightshirt, his feet thrust into carpet slippers. He was so much later than usual that there would certainly be enquiries and reproaches. Paul stopped short before the door. He felt that he could not be accosted by his father to-night; that he could not toss again on that miserable bed. He would not go in. He would tell his father that he had no car-fare, and it was raining so hard he had gone home with one of the boys and stayed all night.

Meanwhile, he was wet and cold. He went around to the back of the house and tried one of the basement windows, found it open, raised it cautiously, and scrambled down the cellar wall to the floor. There he stood, holding his breath, terrified by the noise he had made; but the floor above him was silent, and there was no creak on the stairs. He found a soap-box, and carried it over to the soft ring of light that streamed from the furnace door, and sat down. He was horribly afraid of rats, so he did not try to sleep, but sat looking distrustfully at the dark, still terrified lest he might have awakened his father.

In such reactions, after one of the experiences which made days and nights out of the dreary blanks of the calendar, when his senses were deadened, Paul's head was always singularly clear. Suppose his father had heard him getting in at the window and had come down and shot him for a burglar? Then, again, suppose his father had come down, pistol in hand, and he had cried out in time to save himself, and his father had been horrified to think how nearly he had killed him? Then, again, suppose a day should come when his father would remember that night, and wish there had been no warning cry to stay his hand? With this last supposition Paul entertained himself until daybreak.

The following Sunday was fine; the sodden November chill was broken by the last flash of autumnal summer. In the morning Paul had to go to church and Sabbath School, as always. On seasonable Sunday afternoons the burghers of Cordelia Street usually sat out on their front "stoops," and talked to their neighbours on the next stoop, or called to those across the street in neighbourly fashion. The men sat placidly on gay cushions placed upon the steps that led down to the sidewalk, while the women, in the Sunday "waists," sat in rockers on the cramped porches, pretending to be greatly at their ease. The children played in the streets; there were so many of them that the place resembled the recreation grounds of a kindergarten. The men on the steps, all in their shirt-sleeves, their vests unbuttoned, sat with their legs well apart, their stomachs comfortably protruding, and talked of the prices of things, or told anecdotes of the sagacity of their various chiefs and overlords. They occasionally looked over the multitude of squabbling children, listened affectionately to their high-pitched, nasal voices, smiling to see their own proclivities reproduced in their offspring, and interspersed their legends of the iron kings with remarks about their sons' progress at school, their grades in arithmetic, and the amounts they had saved in their toy banks.

On this last Sunday of November, Paul sat all the afternoon on the lowest step of his "stoop," staring into the street, while his sisters, in their rockers, were talking to the minister's daughters next door about how many shirtwaists they had made in the last week, and how many waffles someone had eaten at the last church supper. When the weather was warm, and his father was in a particularly jovial frame of mind, the girls made lemonade, which was always brought out in a red-glass pitcher, ornamented with forget-me-nots in blue enamel. This the girls thought very fine, and the neighbours joked about the suspicious colour of the pitcher.

To-day Paul's father, on the top step, was talking to a young man who shifted a restless baby from knee to knee. He happened to be the young man who was daily held up to Paul as a model, and after whom it was his father's dearest hope that he would pattern. This young man was of a ruddy complexion, with a compressed, red mouth, and faded, nearsighted eyes, over which he wore thick spectacles, with gold bows that curved about his ears. He was clerk to one of the magnates of a great steel corporation, and was looked upon in Cordelia Street as a young man with a future. There was a story that, some five years ago—he was now barely twenty-six—he had been a trifle "dissipated," but in order to curb his appetites and save the loss of time and strength that a sowing of wild oats might have entailed, he had taken his chief's advice, oft reiterated to his employees, and at twenty-one had married the first woman he could persuade to share his fortunes. She happened to be an angular schoolmistress, much older than he, who also wore thick glasses, and who had now borne him four children, all nearsighted like herself.

The young man was relating how his chief, now cruising in the Mediterranean, kept in touch with all the details of the business, arranging his office hours on his yacht just as though he were at home, and "knocking off work enough to keep two stenographers busy." His father told, in turn, the plan his corporation was considering, of putting in an electric railway plant at Cairo. Paul snapped his teeth; he had an awful apprehension that they might spoil it all before he got there. Yet he rather liked to hear these legends of the iron kings, that were told and retold on Sundays and holidays; these stories of palaces in Venice, yachts on the Mediterranean, and high play at Monte Carlo appealed to his fancy, and he was interested in the triumphs of cash-boys who had become famous, though he had no mind for the cash-boy stage.

After supper was over, and he had helped to dry the dishes, Paul nervously asked his father whether he could go to George's to get some help in his geometry, and still more nervously asked for car-fare. This latter request he had to repeat, as his father, on principle, did not like to hear requests for money, whether much or little. He asked Paul whether he could not go to some boy who lived nearer, and told him that he ought not to leave his school work until Sunday; but he gave him the dime. He was not a poor man, but he had a worthy ambition to come up in the world. His only reason for allowing Paul to usher was that he thought a boy ought to be earning a little.

Paul bounded upstairs, scrubbed the greasy odour of the dishwater from his hands with the ill-smelling soap he hated, and then shook over his fingers a few drops of violet water from the bottle he kept hidden in his drawer. He left the house with his geometry conspicuously under his arm, and the moment he got out of Cordelia Street and boarded a downtown car, he shook off the lethargy of two deadening days, and began to live again.

The leading juvenile of the permanent stock company which played at one of the downtown theatres was an acquaintance of Paul's, and the boy had been invited to drop in at the Sunday-night rehearsals whenever he could. For more than a year Paul had spent every available moment loitering about Charley Edwards's dressing-room. He had won a place among Edwards's following not only because the young actor, who could not afford to employ a dresser, often found him useful, but because he recognized in Paul something akin to what churchmen term "vocation."

It was at the theatre and at Carnegie Hall that Paul really lived; the rest was but a sleep and a forgetting. This was Paul's fairy tale, and it had for him all the allurement of a secret love. The moment he inhaled the gassy, painty, dusty odour behind the scenes, he breathed like a prisoner set free, and felt within him the possibility of doing or saying splendid, brilliant things. The moment the cracked orchestra beat out the overture from "Martha," or jerked at the serenade from "Rigoletto," all stupid and ugly things slid from him, and his senses were deliciously, yet delicately fired.

Perhaps it was because, in Paul's world, the natural nearly always wore the guise of ugliness, that a certain element of artificiality seemed to him necessary in beauty. Perhaps it was because his experience of life elsewhere was so full of Sabbath-School picnics, petty economies, wholesome advice as to how to succeed in life, and the unescapable odours of cooking, that he found this existence so alluring, these smartly clad men and women so attractive, that he was so moved by these starry apple orchards that bloomed perennially under the limelight. It would be difficult to put it strongly enough how convincingly the stage entrance of that theatre was for Paul the actual portal of Romance. Certainly none of the company ever suspected it, least of all Charley Edwards. It was very like the old stories that used to float about London of fabulously rich Jews, who had subterranean halls, with palms, and fountains, and soft lamps and richly apparelled women who never saw the disenchanting light of London day. So, in the midst of that smoke-palled city, enamoured of figures and grimy toil, Paul had his secret temple, his wishing-carpet, his bit of blue-and-white Mediterranean shore bathed in perpetual sunshine.

Several of Paul's teachers had a theory that his imagination had been perverted by garish fiction; but the truth was he scarcely ever read at all. The books at home were not such as would either tempt or corrupt a youthful mind, and as for reading the novels that some of his friends urged upon him—well, he got what he wanted much more quickly from music; any sort of music, from an orchestra to a barrel-organ. He needed only the spark, the indescribable thrill that made his imagination master of his senses, and he could make plots and pictures enough of his own. It was equally true that he was not stage-struck—not, at any rate, in the usual acceptation of that expression. He had no desire to become an actor, any more than he had to become a musician. He felt no necessity to do any of these things; what he wanted was to see, to be in the atmosphere, float on the wave of it, to be carried out, blue league after league, away from everything.

After a night behind the scenes, Paul found the schoolroom more than ever repulsive; the bare floors and naked walls; the prosy men who never wore frock coats, or violets in their buttonholes; the women with their dull gowns, shrill voices, and pitiful seriousness about prepositions that govern the dative. He could not bear to have the other pupils think, for a moment, that he took these people seriously; he must convey to them that he considered it all trivial, and was there only by way of a joke, anyway. He had autographed pictures of all the members of the stock company which he showed his classmates, telling them the most incredible stories of his familiarity with these people, of his acquaintance with the soloists who came to Carnegie Hall, his suppers with them and the flowers he sent them. When these stories lost their effect, and his audience grew listless, he would bid all the boys goodbye, announcing that he was going to travel for a while; going to Naples, to California, to Egypt. Then, next Monday, he would slip back, conscious and nervously smiling; his sister was ill, and he would have to defer his voyage until spring.

Matters went steadily worse with Paul at school. In the itch to let his instructors know how heartily he despised them, and how thoroughly he was appreciated elsewhere, he mentioned once or twice that he had no time to fool with theorems; adding—with a twitch of the eyebrows and a touch of that nervous bravado which so perplexed them—that he was helping the people down at the stock company, they were old friends of his.

The upshot of the matter was that the Principal went to Paul's father, and Paul was taken out of school and put to work.

The manager at Carnegie Hall was told to get another usher in his stead; the doorkeeper at the theatre was warned not to admit him to the house; and Charley Edwards remorsefully promised the boy's father not to see him again.

The members of the stock company were vastly amused when some of Paul's stories reached them—especially the women. They were hard-working women, most of them supporting indolent husbands or brothers, and they laughed rather bitterly at having stirred the boy to such fervid and florid inventions. They agreed with the faculty and with his father, that Paul's was a bad case.

The east-bound train was ploughing through a January snowstorm; the dull dawn was beginning to show grey when the engine whistled a mile out of Newark. Paul started up from the seat where he had lain curled in uneasy slumber, rubbed the breath-misted window-glass with his hand, and peered out. The snow was whirling in curling eddies above the white bottom lands, and the drifts lay already deep in the fields and along the fences, while here and there the tall dead grass and dried weed stalks protruded black above it. Lights shone from the scattered houses, and a gang of labourers who stood beside the track waved their lanterns.

Paul had slept very little, and he felt grimy and uncomfortable. He had made the all-night journey in a day coach because he was afraid if he took a Pullman he might be seen by some Pittsburgh business man who had noticed him in Denny and Carson's office. When the whistle woke him, he clutched quickly at his breast pocket, glancing about him with an uncertain smile. But the little, clay-bespattered Italians were still sleeping, the slatternly women across the aisle were in open-mouthed oblivion, and even the crumby, crying babies were for the time stilled. Paul settled back to struggle with his impatience as best he could.

When he arrived at the Jersey City station, he hurried through his breakfast, manifestly ill at ease and keeping a sharp eye about him. After he reached the Twenty-Third Street station, he consulted a cabman, and had himself driven to a men's furnishing establishment which was just opening for the day. He spent upward of two hours there, buying with endless reconsidering and great care. His new street suit he put on in the fitting-room; the frock coat and dress clothes he had bundled into the cab with his new shirts. Then he drove to a hatter's and a shoe house. His next errand was at Tiffany's, where he selected silver-mounted brushes and a scarf-pin. He would not wait to have his silver marked, he said. Lastly, he stopped at a trunk shop on Broadway, and had his purchases packed into various travelling-bags.

It was a little after one o'clock when he drove up to the Waldorf, and, after settling with the cabman, went into the office. He registered from Washington; said his mother and father had been abroad, and that he had come down to await the arrival of their steamer. He told his story plausibly and had no trouble, since he offered to pay for them in advance, in engaging his rooms; a sleeping-room, sitting-room, and bath.

Not once, but a hundred times Paul had planned this entry into New York. He had gone over every detail of it with Charley Edwards, and in his scrapbook at home there were pages of description about New York hotels, cut from the Sunday papers.

When he was shown to his sitting-room on the eighth floor, he saw at a glance that everything was as it should be; there was but one detail in his mental picture that the place did not realize, so he rang for the bell-boy and sent him down for flowers. He moved about nervously until the boy returned, putting away his new linen and fingering it delightedly as he did so. When the flowers came, he put them hastily into water, and then tumbled into a hot bath. Presently he came out of his white bathroom, resplendent in his new silk underwear, and playing with the tassels of his red robe. The snow was whirling so fiercely outside his windows that he could scarcely see across the street; but within, the air was deliciously soft and fragrant. He put the violets and jonquils on the tabouret beside the couch, and threw himself down with a long sigh, covering himself with a Roman blanket. He was thoroughly tired; he had been in such haste, he had stood up to such a strain, covered so much ground in the last twenty-four hours, that he wanted to think how it had all come about. Lulled by the sound of the wind, the warm air, and the cool fragrance of the flowers, he sank into deep, drowsy retrospection.

It had been wonderfully simple; when they had shut him out of the theatre and concert hall, when they had taken away his bone, the whole thing was virtually determined. The rest was a mere matter of opportunity. The only thing that at all surprised him was his own courage—for he realized well enough that he had always been tormented by fear, a sort of apprehensive dread which, of late years, as the meshes of the lies he had told closed about him, had been pulling the muscles of his body tighter and tighter. Until now, he could not remember a time when he had not been dreading something. Even when he was a little boy, it was always there—behind him, or before, or on either side. There had always been the shadowed corner, the dark place into which he dared not look, but from which something seemed always to be watching him—and Paul had done things that were not pretty to watch, he knew.

But now he had a curious sense of relief, as though he had at last thrown down the gauntlet to the thing in the corner.

Yet it was but a day since he had been sulking in the traces; but yesterday afternoon that he had been sent to the bank with Denny and Carson's deposit, as usual—but this time he was instructed to leave the book to be balanced. There was above two thousand dollars in cheques, and nearly a thousand in the banknotes which he had taken from the book and quietly transferred to his pocket. At the bank he had made out a new deposit slip. His nerves had been steady enough to permit of his returning to the office, where he had finished his work and asked for a full day's holiday tomorrow, Saturday, giving a perfectly reasonable pretext. The bank book, he knew, would not be returned before Monday or Tuesday, and his father would be out of town for the next week. From the time he slipped the banknotes into his pocket until he boarded the night train for New York, he had not known a moment's hesitation.

How astonishingly easy it had all been; here he was, the thing done; and this time there would be no awakening, no figure at the top of the stairs. He watched the snowflakes whirling by his window until he fell asleep.

When he awoke, it was four o'clock in the afternoon. He bounded up with a start; one of his precious days gone already! He spent nearly an hour in dressing, watching every stage of his toilet carefully in the mirror. Everything was quite perfect; he was exactly the kind of boy he had always wanted to be.

When he went downstairs, Paul took a carriage and drove up Fifth Avenue toward the Park. The snow had somewhat abated; carriages and tradesmen's wagons were hurrying soundlessly to and fro in the winter twilight; boys in woollen mufflers were shovelling off the doorsteps; the Avenue stages made fine spots of colour against the white street. Here and there on the corners whole flower gardens blooming behind glass windows, against which the snowflakes stuck and melted; violets, roses, carnations, lilies-of-the-valley—somehow vastly more lovely and alluring that they blossomed thus unnaturally in the snow. The Park itself was a wonderful stage winter-piece.

When he returned, the pause of the twilight had ceased, and the tune of the streets had changed. The snow was falling faster, lights streamed from the hotels that reared their many stories fearlessly up into the storm, defying the raging Atlantic winds. A long, black stream of carriages poured down the Avenue, intersected here and there by other streams, tending horizontally. There were a score of cabs about the entrance of his hotel, and his driver had to wait. Boys in livery were running in and out of the awning stretched across the sidewalk, up and down the red velvet carpet laid from the door to the street. Above, about, within it all, was the rumble and roar, the hurry and toss of thousands of human beings as hot for pleasure as himself, and on every side of him towered the glaring affirmation of the omnipotence of wealth.

The boy set his teeth and drew his shoulders together in a spasm of realization; the plot of all dramas, the text of all romances, the nerve-stuff of all sensations was whirling about him like the snowflakes. He burnt like a fagot in a tempest.

When Paul came down to dinner, the music of the orchestra floated up the elevator shaft to greet him. As he stepped into the thronged corridor, he sank back into one of the chairs against the wall to get his breath. The lights, the chatter, the perfumes, the bewildering medley of colour—he had, for a moment, the feeling of not being able to stand it. But only for a moment; these were his own people, he told himself. He went slowly about the corridors, through the writing-rooms, smoking-rooms, reception-rooms, as though he were exploring the chambers of an enchanted palace, built and peopled for him alone.

When he reached the dining-room he sat down at a table near a window. The flowers, the white linen, the many-coloured wine-glasses, the gay toilettes of the women, the low popping of corks, the undulating repetitions of the "Blue Danube" from the orchestra, all flooded Paul's dream with bewildering radiance. When the roseate tinge of his champagne was added—that cold, precious, bubbling stuff that creamed and foamed in his glass—Paul wondered that there were honest men in the world at all. This was what all the world was fighting for, he reflected; this was what all the struggle was about. He doubted the reality of his past. Had he ever known a place called Cordelia Street, a place where fagged-looking business men boarded the early car? Mere rivets in a machine they seemed to Paul—sickening men, with combings of children's hair always hanging to their coats, and the smell of cooking in their clothes. Cordelia Street—Ah, that belonged to another time and country! Had he not always been thus, had he not sat here night after night, from as far back as he could remember, looking pensively over just such shimmering textures, and slowly twirling the stem of a glass like this one between his thumb and middle finger? He rather thought he had.

He was not in the least abashed or lonely. He had no especial desire to meet or to know any of these people; all he demanded was the right to look on and conjecture, to watch the pageant. The mere stage properties were all he contended for. Nor was he lonely later in the evening, in his loge at the Opera. He was entirely rid of his nervous misgivings, of his forced aggressiveness, of the imperative desire to show himself different from his surroundings. He felt now that his surroundings explained him. Nobody questioned the purple; he had only to wear it passively. He had only to glance down at his dress coat to reassure himself that here it would be impossible for anyone to humiliate him.

He found it hard to leave his beautiful sitting-room to go to bed that night, and sat long watching the raging storm from his turrent window. When he went to sleep, it was with the lights turned on in his bedroom; partly because of his old timidity, and partly so that, if he should wake in the night, there would be no wretched moment of doubt, no horrible suspicion of yellow wallpaper, or of Washington and Calvin above his bed.

On Sunday morning the city was practically snowbound. Paul breakfasted late, and in the afternoon he fell in with a wild San Francisco boy, a freshman at Yale, who said he had run down for a "little flyer" over Sunday. The young man offered to show Paul the night side of the town, and the two boys went off together after dinner, not returning to the hotel until seven o'clock the next morning. They had started out in the confiding warmth of a champagne friendship, but their parting in the elevator was singularly cool. The freshman pulled himself together to make his train, and Paul went to bed. He awoke at two o'clock in the afternoon, very thirsty and dizzy, and rang for ice-water, coffee, and the Pittsburgh papers.

On the part of the hotel management, Paul excited no suspicion. There was this to be said for him, that he wore his spoils with dignity and in no way made himself conspicuous. His chief greediness lay in his ears and eyes, and his excesses were not offensive ones. His dearest pleasures were the grey winter twilights in his sitting-room; his quiet enjoyment of his flowers, his clothes, his wide divan, his cigarette, and his sense of power. He could not remember a time when he had felt so at peace with himself. The mere release from the necessity of petty lying, lying every day and every day, restored his self-respect. He had never lied for pleasure, even at school; but to make himself noticed and admired, to assert his difference from other Cordelia Street boys; and he felt a good deal more manly, more honest, even, now that he had no need for boastful pretensions, now that he could, as his actor friends used to say, "dress the part." It was characteristic that remorse did not occur to him. His golden days went by without a shadow, and he made each as perfect as he could.

On the eighth day after his arrival in New York, he found the whole affair exploited in the Pittsburgh papers, exploited with a wealth of detail which indicated that local news of a sensational nature was at a low ebb. The firm of Denny and Carson announced that the boy's father had refunded the full amount of his theft, and that they had no intention of prosecuting. The Cumberland minister had been interviewed, and expressed his hope of yet reclaiming the motherless lad, and Paul's Sabbath-School teacher declared that she would spare no effort to that end. The rumour had reached Pittsburgh that the boy had been seen in a New York hotel, and his father had gone East to find him and bring him home.

Paul had just come in to dress for dinner; he sank into a chair, weak in the knees, and clasped his head in his hands. It was to be worse than jail, even; the tepid waters of Cordelia Street were to close over him finally and forever. The grey monotony stretched before him in hopeless, unrelieved years;—Sabbath-School, Young People's Meeting, the yellow-papered room, the damp dish-towels; it all rushed back upon him with sickening vividness. He had the old feeling that the orchestra had suddenly stopped, the sinking sensation that the play was over. The sweat broke out on his face, and he sprang to his feet, looked about him with his white, conscious smile, and winked at himself in the mirror. With something of the childish belief in miracles with which he had so often gone to class, all his lessons unlearned, Paul dressed and dashed whistling down the corridor to the elevator.

He had no sooner entered the dining-room and caught the measure of the music than his remembrance was lightened by his old elastic power of claiming the moment, mounting with it, and finding it all-sufficient. The glare and glitter about him, the mere scenic accessories had again, and for the last time, their old potency. He would show himself that he was game, he would finish the thing splendidly. He doubted, more than ever, the existence of Cordelia Street, and for the first time he drank his wine recklessly. Was he not, after all, one of these fortunate beings? Was he not still himself, and in his own place? He drummed a nervous accompaniment to the music and looked about him telling himself over and over that it had paid.

He reflected drowsily, to the swell of the violin and the chill sweetness of his wine, that he might have done it more wisely. He might have caught an outbound steamer and been well out of their clutches before now. But the other side of the world had seemed too far away and too uncertain then; he could not have waited for it; his need had been too sharp. If he had to choose over again, he would do the same thing to-morrow. He looked affectionately about the dining-room, now gilded with a soft mist. Ah, it had paid indeed!

Paul was awakened next morning by a painful throbbing in his head and feet. He had thrown himself across the bed without undressing, and had slept with his shoes on. His limbs and hands were lead-heavy, and his tongue and throat were parched. There came upon him one of those fateful attacks of clear-headedness that never occurred except when he was physically exhausted and his nerves hung loose. He lay still and closed his eyes and let the tide of realities wash over him.

His father was in New York; "stopping at some joint or other," he told himself. The memory of successive summers on the front stoop fell upon him like a weight of black water. He had not a hundred dollars left; and he knew now, more than ever, that money was everything, the wall that stood between all he loathed and all he wanted. The thing was winding itself up; he had thought of that on his first glorious day in New York, and had even provided a way to snap the thread. It lay on his dressing-table now; he had got it out last night when he came blindly up from dinner—but the shiny metal hurt his eyes, and he disliked the look of it, anyway.

He rose and moved about with a painful effort, succumbing now and again to attacks of nausea. It was the old depression exaggerated; all the world had become Cordelia Street. Yet somehow he was not afraid of anything, was absolutely calm; perhaps because he had looked into the dark corner at last, and knew. It was bad enough, what he saw there; but somehow not so bad as his long fear of it had been. He saw everything clearly now. He had a feeling that he had made the best of it, that he had lived the sort of life he was meant to live, and for half an hour he sat staring at the revolver. But he told himself that was not the way, so he went downstairs and took a cab to the ferry.

When Paul arrived at Newark, he got off the train and took another cab, directing the driver to follow the Pennsylvania tracks out of the town. The snow lay heavy on the roadways and had drifted deep in the open fields. Only here and there the dead grass or dried weed stalks projected, singularly black, above it.

Once well into the country, Paul dismissed the carriage and walked, floundering along the tracks, his mind a medley of irrelevant things. He seemed to hold in his brain an actual picture of everything he had seen that morning. He remembered every feature of both his drivers, the toothless old woman from whom he had bought the red flowers in his coat, the agent from whom he had got his ticket, and all of his fellow-passengers on the ferry. His mind, unable to cope with vital matters near at hand, worked feverishly and deftly at sorting and grouping these images. They made for him a part of the ugliness of the world, of the ache in his head, and the bitter burning on his tongue. He stooped and put a handful of snow into his mouth as he walked, but that, too, seemed hot. When he reached a little hillside, where the tracks ran through a cut some twenty feet below him, he stopped and sat down.

The carnations in his coat were drooping with the cold, he noticed; their red glory over. It occurred to him that all the flowers he had seen in the show windows that first night must have gone the same way, long before this. It was only one splendid breath they had, in spite of their brave mockery at the winter outside the glass. It was a losing game in the end, it seemed, this revolt against the homilies by which the world is run. Paul took one of the blossoms carefully from his coat and scooped a little hole in the snow, where he covered it up. Then he dozed awhile, from his weak condition, seeming insensible to the cold.

The sound of an approaching train woke him and he started to his feet, remembering only his resolution, and afraid lest he should be too late. He stood watching the approaching locomotive, his teeth chattering, his lips drawn away from them in a frightened smile; once or twice he glanced nervously sidewise, as though he were being watched. When the right moment came, he jumped. As he fell, the folly of his haste occurred to him with merciless clearness, the vastness of what he had left undone. There flashed through his brain, clearer than every before, the blue of Adriatic water, the yellow of Algerian sands.

He felt something strike his chest—his body was being thrown swiftly through the air, on and on, immeasurably far and fast, while his limbs gently relaxed. Then, because the picture-making mechanism was crushed, the disturbing visions flashed into black, and Paul dropped back into the immense design of things.

[1904]

For Thought

Throughout the story, without moralizing censure or extenuating sentimentality and by the carefully organized use of sensory details and perceptions garnered from Paul's consciousness, Cather establishes the fragile, mothlike quality of the boy's tortured, short-lived existence. By her use of a modified form of the omniscient point of view, she creates in the reader a compassionate awareness of the constraints on human life that make a tragic ending seem inevitable in the life of someone doomed by an irreconcilable conflict between temperament and circumstance.

For Discussion

1. What is the advantage of using the omniscient point of view, with its primary focus on Paul, rather than using the first-person technique, with Paul telling his own story?
2. What preparation is there for Paul's critical decision to steal the money and go to New York to stay at an elegant hotel?
3. What makes Paul's fate tragic and meaningful rather than merely pathetic and regrettable?
4. What is the flaw in Paul's nature that leads to his downfall?
5. How are the stage scenery at the theater and the flowers in the store window in New York used as ironic symbols?
6. How do the setting and atmosphere serve as motivating forces in the action?
7. What is the conflict, the turning point or crisis, and the resolution of the action?
8. Do the events in the story proceed in a logical order and with a sense of inevitability, or do they arise from chance and whim?

John Cheever
The Country Husband

To begin at the beginning, the airplane from Minneapolis in which Francis Weed was travelling East ran into heavy weather. The sky had been a hazy blue, with the clouds below the plane lying so close together that nothing could be seen of the earth. Then mist began to form outside the windows, and they flew into a white cloud of such density that it reflected the exhaust fires. The color of the cloud darkened to gray, and the plane began to rock. Francis had been in heavy weather before, but he had never been shaken up so much. The man in the seat beside him pulled a flask out of his pocket and took a drink. Francis smiled at his neighbor, but the man looked away; he wasn't sharing his painkiller with anyone. The plane had begun to drop and flounder wildly. A child was crying. The air in the cabin was overheated and stale, and Francis' left foot went to sleep. He read a little from a paper book that he had bought at the airport, but the violence of the storm divided his attention. The exhaust fires blazed and shed sparks in the dark, and, inside, the shaded lights, the stuffiness, and the window curtains gave the cabin an atmosphere of intense and misplaced domesticity. Then the lights flickered and went out. "You know what I've always wanted to do?" the man beside Francis said suddenly. "I've always wanted to buy a farm in New Hampshire and raise beef cattle." The stewardess announced that they were going to make an emergency landing. All but the child saw in their minds the spreading wings of the Angel of Death. The pilot could be heard singing faintly, "I've got sixpence, jolly, jolly sixpence. I've got sixpence to last me all my life . . ." There was no other sound.

The loud groaning of the hydraulic valves swallowed up the pilot's song, and there was a shrieking high in the air, like automobile brakes, and the plane hit flat on its belly in a cornfield and shook them so violently that an old man up forward howled, "Me kidneys! Me kidneys!" The stewardess flung open the door, and someone opened an emergency door at the back, letting in the sweet noise of their continuing mortality—the idle splash and smell of a heavy rain. Anxious for their lives, they filed out of the doors and scattered over the cornfield in all directions, praying that the thread would hold. It did. Nothing happened. When it was clear that the plane would not burn or explode, the crew and the stewardess gathered the passengers together and led them to the shelter of a barn. They were not far from Philadelphia, and in a little while a string of taxis took them into the city. "It's just like the Marne," someone said, but there was surprisingly little relaxation of that suspiciousness with which many Americans regard their fellow-travellers.

In Philadelphia, Francis Weed got a train to New York. At the end of that journey, he crossed the city and caught, just as it was about to pull out, the commuting train that he took five nights a week to his home in Shady Hill.

He sat with Trace Bearden. "You know, I was in the plane that just crashed outside Philadelphia," he said. "We came down in a field . . ." He had traveled faster than the newspapers or the rain, and the weather in New York was sunny and mild. It was a day in late September, as fragrant and shapely as an apple. Trace listened to the story, but how could he get excited? Francis has no powers that would let him recreate a brush with death—particularly in the atmosphere of a commuting train, journeying through a sunny countryside where already, in the slum gardens, there were signs of harvest. Trace picked up his newspaper, and Francis was left alone with his thoughts. He said good night to Trace on the platform at Shady Hill and drove in his second-hand Volkswagen up to the Blenhollow neighborhood, where he lived.

The Weeds' Dutch Colonial house was larger than it appeared to be from the driveway. The living room was spacious and divided like Gaul into three parts. Around an ell to the left as one entered from the vestibule was the long table, laid for six, with candles and a bowl of fruit in the center. The sounds and smells that came from the open kitchen door were appetizing, for Julia Weed was a good cook. The largest part of the living room centered around a fireplace. On the right were some bookshelves and a piano. The room was polished and tranquil, and from the windows that opened to the west there was some late-summer sunlight, brilliant and as clear as water. Nothing here was neglected; nothing had not been burnished. It was not the kind of household where, after prying open a stuck cigarette box, you would find an old shirt button and a tarnished nickel. The hearth was swept, the roses on the piano were reflected in the polish of the broad top, and there was an album of Schubert waltzes on the rack. Louisa Weed, a pretty girl of nine, was looking out the western windows. Her younger brother Henry was standing beside her. Her still younger brother, Toby, was studying the figures of some tonsured monks drinking beer on the polished brass of the wood box. Francis, taking off his hat and putting down his paper, was not consciously pleased with the scene; he was not that reflective. It was his element, his creation, and he returned to it with that sense of lightness and strength with which any creature returns to its home. "Hi, everybody," he said. "The plane from Minneapolis . . ."

Nine times out of ten, Francis would be greeted with affection, but tonight the children are absorbed in their own antagonisms. Francis had not finished his sentence about the plane crash before Henry plants a kick in Louisa's behind. Louisa swings around, saying "Damn you!" Francis makes the mistake of scolding Louisa for bad language before he punishes Henry. Now Louisa turns on her father and accuses him of favoritism. Henry is always right; she is persecuted and lonely; her lot is hopeless. Francis turns to his son, but the boy has justification for the kick—she hit him first; she hit him on the ear, which is dangerous. Louisa agrees with this passionately. She hit him on the ear, and she meant to hit him on the ear, because he messed up her china collection. Henry says that this is a lie. Little Toby turns away from the wood box to throw in some evidence for Louisa. Henry claps his hand over little Toby's mouth. Francis separates the two boys but accidentally pushes Toby into the wood box. Toby begins to cry. Louisa is already crying. Just then, Julia Weed comes into that part of the room where the table is laid. She is a pretty, intelligent woman, and the white in her hair is premature. She does not seem to notice the fracas. "Hello, darling," she says serenely to Francis. "Wash your hands, everyone. Dinner is ready." She strikes a match and lights the six candles in this vale of tears.

This simple announcement, like the war cries of the Scottish chieftains, only refreshes the ferocity of the combatants. Louisa gives Henry a blow on the shoulder. Henry, although he seldom cries, has pitched nine innings and is tired. He bursts into tears. Little Toby discovers a splinter in his hand and begins to howl. Francis says loudly that he has been in a plane crash and that he is tired. Julia appears again, from the kitchen, and still ignoring the chaos, asks Francis to go upstairs and tell Helen that everything is ready. Francis is happy to go; it is like getting back to headquarters company. He is planning to tell his oldest daughter about the airplane crash, but Helen is lying on her bed reading a *True Romance* magazine, and the first thing Francis does is to take the magazine from her hand and remind Helen that he has forbidden her to buy it. She did not buy it, Helen replies. It was given to her by her best friend, Bessie Black. Everybody reads *True Romance*. Bessie Black's father reads *True Romance*. There isn't a girl in Helen's class who doesn't read *True Romance*. Francis expresses his detestation of the magazine and then tells her that dinner is ready—although from the sounds downstairs it doesn't seem so. Helen follows him down the stairs. Julia has seated herself in the candle-light and spread a napkin over her lap. Neither Louisa nor Henry has come to the table. Little Toby is still howling, lying face down on the floor. Francis speaks to him gently: "Daddy was in a plane crash this afternoon, Toby. Don't you want to hear about it?" Toby goes on crying. "If you don't come to the table now, Toby," Francis says, "I'll have to send you to bed without any supper." The little boy rises, gives him a cunning look, flies up the stairs to his bedroom, and slams the door. "Oh, dear," Julia says, and starts to go after him. Francis says that she will spoil him. Julia says that Toby is ten pounds underweight and has to be encouraged to eat. Winter is coming, and he will spend the cold months in bed unless he has his dinner. Julia goes upstairs. Francis sits down at the table with Helen. Helen is suffering from the dismal feeling of having read too intently on a fine day, and she gives her father and the room a jaded look. She doesn't understand about the plane crash, because there wasn't a drop of rain in Shady Hill.

Julia returns with Toby, and they all sit down and are served. "Do I have to look at that big, fat slob?" Henry says, of Louisa. Everybody but Toby enters into this skirmish, and it rages up and down the table for five minutes. Toward the end, Henry puts his napkin over his head and, trying to eat that way, spills spinach all over his shirt. Francis asks Julia if the children couldn't have their dinner earlier. Julia's guns are loaded for this. She can't cook two dinners and lay two tables. She paints with lightning strokes that panorama of drudgery in which her youth, her beauty, and her wit have been lost. Francis says that he must be understood; he was nearly killed in an airplane crash, and he doesn't like to come home every night to a battlefield. Now Julia is deeply committed. Her voice trembles. He doesn't come home every night to a battlefield. The accusation is stupid and mean. Everything was tranquil until he arrived. She stops speaking, puts down her knife and fork, and looks into her plate as if it is a gulf. She begins to cry. "Poor

Mummy," Toby says, and when Julia gets up from the table, drying her tears with a napkin, Toby goes to her side. "Poor Mummy!" he says. "Poor Mummy!" And they climb the stairs together. The other children drift away from the battlefield and Francis goes into the back garden for a cigarette and some air.

It was a pleasant garden, with walks and flower beds and places to sit. The sunset had nearly burned out, but there was still plenty of light. Put into a thoughtful mood by the crash and the battle, Francis listened to the evening sounds of Shady Hill. "Varmits! Rascals!" old Mr. Nixon shouted to the squirrels in his bird-feeding station. "Avaunt and quit my sight!" A door slammed. Someone was playing tennis on the Babcocks' court; someone was cutting grass. Then Donald Goslin, who lived at the corner, began to play the "Moonlight Sonata." He did this nearly every night. He threw the tempo out the window and played it rubato from beginning to end, like an outpouring of tearful petulance, lonesomeness, and self-pity—of everything it was Beethoven's greatness not to know. The music rang up and down the street beneath the trees like an appeal for love, for tenderness, aimed at some lonely housemaid—some fresh-faced, homesick girl from Galway, looking at old snapshots in her third-floor room. "Here, Jupiter, here, Jupiter," Francis called to the Mercers' retriever. Jupiter crashed through the tomato vines with the remains of a felt hat in his mouth.

Jupiter was an anomaly. His retrieving instincts and his high spirits were out of place in Shady Hill. He was as black as coal, with a long alert, intelligent, rakehell face. His eyes gleamed with mischief, and he held his head high. It was the fierce, heavily collared dog's head that appears in heraldry, in tapestry, and that used to appear on umbrella handles and walking sticks. Jupiter went where he pleased, ransacking wastebaskets, clotheslines, garbage pails, and shoe bags. He broke up garden parties and tennis matches, and got mixed up in the processional at Christ's Church on Sunday, barking at the men in red dresses. He crashed through old Mr. Nixon's rose garden two or three times a day, cutting a wide swath through the Condesa de Sastagos, and as soon as Donald Goslin lighted his barbecue fire on Thursday nights, Jupiter would get the scent. Nothing the Goslins did could drive him away. Sticks and stones and rude commands only moved him to the edge of the terrace, where he remained, with his gallant and heraldic muzzle, waiting for Donald Goslin to turn his back and reach for the salt. Then he would spring onto the terrace, lift the steak lightly off the fire, and run away with the Goslins' dinner. Jupiter's days were numbered. The Wrightsons' German gardener or the Farquarsons' cook would soon poison him. Even old Mr. Nixon might put some arsenic in the garbage that Jupiter loved. "Here, Jupiter, Jupiter!" Francis called, but the dog pranced off, shaking the hat in his white teeth. Looking in at the windows of his house, Francis saw that Julia had come down and was blowing out the candles.

Julia and Francis Weed went out a great deal. Julia was well liked and gregarious, and her love of parties sprang from a most natural dread of chaos and loneliness. She went through her morning mail with real anxiety, looking for invitations, and she usually found some, but she was insatiable, and if she had gone out seven nights a week, it would not have cured her of a reflective look—the look of someone who hears distant music—for she would always suppose that there was a more brilliant party somewhere else. Francis limited her to two week-night parties, putting a flexible interpretation on Friday, and rode through the weekend like a dory in a gale. The day after the airplane crash, the Weeds were to have dinner with the Farquarsons.

Francis got home late from town, and Julia got the sitter while he dressed, and then hurried him out of the house. The party was small and pleasant, and Francis settled down to enjoy himself. A new maid passed the drinks. Her hair was dark, and her face was round and pale and seemed familiar to Francis. He had not developed his memory as a sentimental faculty. Wood smoke, lilac, and other such perfumes did not stir him, and his memory was something like his appendix—a vestigial repository. It was not his limitation at all to be unable to escape the past; it was perhaps his limitation that he had escaped it so successfully. He might have seen the maid at other parties, he might have seen her taking a walk on Sunday afternoons, but in either case he would not be searching his memory now. Her face was, in a wonderful way, a moon face—Norman or Irish—but it was not beautiful enough to account for his feeling that he had seen her before, in circumstances that he ought to be able to remember. He asked Nellie Farquarson who she was. Nellie said that the maid had come through an agency, and that her home was Trénon, in Normandy—a small place with a church and a restaurant that Nellie had once visited. While Nellie talked on about her travels abroad, Francis realized where he had seen the woman before. It had been at the end of the war. He had left a replacement depot with some men and taken a three-day pass in Trénon. On their second day, they had walked out to a crossroads to see the public chastisement of a young woman who had lived with the German commandant during the Occupation.

It was a cool morning in the fall. The sky was overcast, and poured down onto the dirt crossroads a very discouraging light. They were on high land and could see how like one another the shapes of the clouds and the hills were as they stretched off towards the sea. The prisoner arrived sitting on a three-legged stool in a farm cart. She stood by the cart while the mayor read the accusation and the sentence. Her head was bent and her face was set in that empty half smile behind which the whipped soul is suspended. When the mayor was finished, she undid her hair and let it fall across her back. A little man with a gray mustache cut off her hair with shears and dropped it on the ground. Then, with a bowl of soapy water and a straight razor, he shaved her skull clean. A woman approached and began to undo the fastenings of her clothes, but the prisoner pushed her aside and undressed herself. When she pulled her chemise over her head and threw it on the ground, she was naked. The women jeered; the men were still. There was no change in the falseness or the plaintiveness of the prisoner's smile. The cold wind made her white skin rough and hardened the nipples of her breasts. The jeering ended gradually, put down by the recognition of their common humanity. One woman spat on her, but some inviolable grandeur in her nakedness lasted through the ordeal. When the crowd was quiet, she turned—she had begun to cry—and, with nothing on but a pair of worn black shoes and stockings, walked down the dirt road alone away from the village. The round white face had aged a little, but there was no question but that the maid who passed his cocktails and later served Francis his dinner was the woman who had been punished at the crossroads.

The war seemed now so distant and that world where the cost of partisanship had been death or torture so long ago. Francis had lost track of the men who had been with him in Vésey. He could not count on Julia's discretion. He could not tell anyone. And if he had told the story now, at the dinner table, it would have been a social as well as a human error. The people in the Farquarsons' living room seemed united in their tacit claim that there had been no past, no war—that there was no danger or trouble in the world. In the recorded history of human arrangements, this extraordinary meeting would have fallen into place, but the atmosphere of Shady Hill made the memory unseemly and impolite. The prisoner withdrew after passing the coffee, but the encounter left Francis feeling languid; it had opened his memory and his senses, and left them dilated. He and Julia drove home when the party ended, and Julia went into the house. Francis stayed in the car to take the sitter home.

Expecting to see Mrs. Henlein, the old lady who usually stayed with the children, he was surprised when a young girl opened the door and came out onto the lighted stoop. She stayed in the light to count her textbooks. She was frowning and beautiful. Now, the world is full of beautiful young girls, but Francis saw here the difference between beauty and perfection. All those endearing flaws, moles, birthmarks, and healed wounds were missing, and he experienced in his consciousness that moment when music breaks glass, and felt a pang of recognition as strange, deep, and wonderful as anything in his life. It hung from her frown, from an impalpable darkness in her face—a look that impressed him as a direct appeal for love. When she had counted her books, she came down the steps and opened the car door. In the light, he saw that her cheeks were wet. She got in and shut the door.

"You're new," Francis said.

"Yes, Mrs. Henlein is sick. I'm Anne Murchison."

"Did the children give you any trouble?"

"Oh, no, no." She turned and smiled at him unhappily in the dim dashboard light. Her light hair caught on the collar of her jacket, and she shook her head to set it loose.

"You've been crying."

"Yes."

"I hope it was nothing that happened in our house."

"No, no, it was nothing that happened in your house." Her voice was bleak. "It's no secret. Everybody in the village knows. Daddy's an alcoholic, and he just called me from some saloon and gave me a piece of his mind. He thinks I'm immoral. He called just before Mrs. Weed came back."

"I'm sorry."

"Oh, Lord!" She gasped and began to cry. She turned toward Francis, and he took her in his arms and let her cry on his shoulder. She shook in his embrace, and this movement accentuated his sense of the fineness of her flesh and bone. The layers of their clothing felt thin, and when her shuddering began to diminish, it was so much like a paroxysm of love that Francis lost his head and pulled her roughly against him. She drew away. "I live on Belleview Avenue," she said. "You go down Lansing Street to the railroad bridge."

"All right." He started the car.

"You turn left at the traffic light. . . . Now you turn right here and go straight on toward the tracks."

The road Francis took brought him out of his own neighborhood, across the tracks, and toward the river, to a street where the near-poor lived, in houses whose peaked gables and trimmings of wooden lace conveyed the purest feelings of pride and romance, although the houses themselves could not have offered much privacy or comfort, they were all so small. The street was dark, and stirred by the grace and beauty of the troubled girl, he seemed, in turning in to it, to have come into the deepest part of some submerged memory. In the distance, he saw a porch light burning. It was the only one, and she said that the house with the light was where she lived. When he stopped the car, he could see beyond the porch light into a dimly lighted hallway with an old-fashioned clothes tree. "Well, here we are," he said, conscious that a young man would have said something different.

She did not move her hands from the books, where they were folded, and she turned and faced him. There were tears of lust in his eyes. Determinedly—not sadly—he opened the door on his side and walked around to open hers. He took her free hand, letting his fingers in between hers, climbed at her side the two concrete steps, and went up a narrow walk through a front garden where dahlias, marigolds, and roses—things that had withstood the light frosts—still bloomed, and made a bittersweet smell in the night air. At the steps, she freed her hand and then turned and kissed him swiftly. Then she crossed the porch and shut the door. The porch light went out, then the light in the hall. A second later, a light went on upstairs at the side of the house, shining into a tree that was still covered with leaves. It took her only a few minutes to undress and get into bed, and then the house was dark.

Julia was asleep when Francis got home. He opened a second window and got into bed to shut his eyes on that night, but as soon as they were shut—as soon as he had dropped off to sleep—the girl entered his mind, moving with perfect freedom through its shut doors and filling chamber after chamber with her light, her perfume, and the music of her voice. He was crossing the Atlantic with her on the old Mauretania and, later, living with her in Paris. When he woke from this dream, he got up and smoked a cigarette at the open window. Getting back into bed, he cast around in his mind for something he desired to do that would injure no one, and he thought of skiing. Up through the dimness in his mind rose the image of a mountain deep in snow. It was late in the day. Wherever his eyes looked, he saw broad and heartening things. Over his shoulder, there was a snow-filled valley, rising into wooded hills where the trees dimmed the whiteness like a sparse coat of hair. The cold deadened all sound but the loud, iron clanking of the lift machinery. The light on the trails was blue, and it was harder than it had been a minute or two earlier to pick the turns, harder to judge—now that the snow was all deep blue—the crust, the ice, the bare spots, and the deep piles of dry powder. Down the mountain he swung, matching his speed against the contours of a slope that had been formed in the first ice age, seeking with ardor some simplicity of feeling and circumstances. Night fell then, and he drank a Martini with some old friend in a dirty country bar.

In the morning, Francis' snow-covered mountain was gone, and he was left with his vivid memories of Paris and the Mauretania. He had been bitten gravely. He washed his body, shaved his jaws, drank his coffee, and missed the seven-thirty-one. The train pulled out just as he brought his car to the station, and the longing he felt for the coaches as they drew stubbornly away from him reminded him of the humors of love. He waited for the eight-two, on what was now an empty platform. It was a clear morning; the morning seemed thrown like a gleaming bridge of light over his mixed affairs. His spirits were feverish and high. The image of the girl seemed to put him into a relationship to the world that was mysterious and enthralling. Cars were beginning to fill up the parking lot, and he noticed that those that had driven down from the high land above Shady Hill were white with hoarfrost. This first clear sign of autumn thrilled him. An express train—a night from Buffalo or Albany—came down the tracks between the platforms, and he saw that the roofs of the foremost cars were covered with a skin of ice. Struck by the miraculous physicalness of everything, he smiled at the passengers in the dining car, who could be seen eating eggs and wiping their mouths with napkins as they travelled. The sleeping-car compartments, with their soiled bed linen, trailed through the fresh morning like a string of rooming-house windows. Then he saw an extraordinary thing; at one of the bedroom windows sat an unclothed woman of exceptional beauty, combing her golden hair. She passed like an apparition through Shady Hill, combing and combing her hair, and Francis followed her with his eyes until she was out of sight. Then old Mrs. Wrightson joined him on the platform and began to talk.

"Well, I guess you must be surprised to see me here the third morning in a row," she said, "but because of my window curtains I'm becoming a regular commuter. The curtains I bought on Monday I returned on Tuesday, and the curtains I bought on Tuesday, I'm returning today.

On Monday, I got exactly what I wanted—it's a wool tapestry with roses and birds—but when I got them home, I found they were the wrong length. Well, I exchanged them yesterday, and when I got them home, I found they were still the wrong length. Now I'm praying to high Heaven that the decorator will have them in the right length, because you know my house, you know my living-room windows, and you can imagine what a problem they present. I don't know what to do with them."

"I know what to do with them," Francis said.

"What?"

"Paint them black on the inside, and shut up."

There was a gasp from Mrs. Wrightson, and Francis looked down at her to be sure that she knew he meant to be rude. She turned and walked away from him, so damaged in spirit that she limped. A wonderful feeling enveloped him, as if light were being shaken about him, and he thought again of Venus combing and combing her hair as she drifted through the Bronx. The realization of how many years had passed since he had enjoyed being deliberately impolite sobered him. Among his friends and neighbors, there were brilliant and gifted people—he saw that—but many of them, also, were bores and fools, and he had made the mistake of listening to them all with equal attention. He had confused a lack of discrimination with Christian love, and the confusion seemed general and destructive. He was grateful to the girl for this bracing sensation of independence. Birds were singing—cardinals and the last of robins. The sky shone like enamel. Even the smell of ink from his morning paper honed his appetite for life, and the world that was spread out around him was plainly a paradise.

If Francis had believed in some hierarchy of love—in spirits armed with hunting bows, in the capriciousness of Venus and Eros—or even in magical potions, philtres, and stems, in scapulae and quarters of the moon, it might have explained his susceptibility and his feverish high spirits. The autumnal loves of middle age are well publicized, and he guessed that he was face to face with one of these, but there was not a trace of autumn in what he felt. He wanted to sport in the green woods, scratch where he itched, and drink from the same cup.

His secretary, Miss Rainey, was late that morning—she went to a psychiatrist three mornings a week—and when she came in, Francis wondered what advice a psychiatrist would have for him. But the girl promised to bring back into his life something like the sound of music. The realization that this music might lead him straight to a trial for statutory rape at the county courthouse collapsed his happiness. The photograph of his four children laughing into the camera on the beach at Gay Head reproached him. On the letterhead of his firm there was a drawing of the Laocoön, and the figure of the priest and his sons in the coils of the snake appeared to him to have the deepest meaning.

He had lunch with Pinky Trabert, who told him a couple of dirty stories. At a conversational level, the mores of his friends were robust and elastic, but he knew that the moral card house would come down on them all—on Julia and the children as well—if he got caught taking advantage of a baby-sitter. Looking back over the recent history of Shady Hill for some precedent, he found there was none. There was no turpitude; there had not been a divorce since he lived there; there had not even been a breath of scandal. Things seemed arranged with more propriety even than in the Kingdom of Heaven. After leaving Pinky, Francis went to a jeweller's and bought the girl a bracelet. How happy this clandestine purchase made him, how stuffy and comical the jeweller's clerks seemed, how sweet the women who passed at his back smelled! On Fifth Avenue, passing Atlas with his shoulders bent under the weight of the world, Francis thought of the strenuousness of containing his physicalness within the patterns he had chosen.

He did not know when he would see the girl next. He had the bracelet in his inside pocket when he got home. Opening the door of his house, he found her in the hall. Her back was to him, and she turned when she heard the door close. Her smile was open and loving. Her perfection stunned him like a fine day—a day after a thunderstorm. He seized her and covered her lips with his, and she struggled but she did not have to struggle for long, because just then little Gertrude Flannery appeared from somewhere and said, "Oh, Mr. Weed . . ."

Gertrude was a stray. She had been born with a taste for exploration, and she did not have it in her to center her life with her affectionate parents. People who did not know the Flannerys concluded from Gertrude's behavior that she was the child of a bitterly divided family, where drunken quarrels were the rule. This was not true. The fact that little Gertrude's clothing was ragged and thin was her own triumph over her mother's struggle to dress her warmly and neatly. Garrulous, skinny, and unwashed, she drifted from house to house around the Blenhollow neighborhood, forming and breaking alliances based on an attachment to babies, animals, children her own age, adolescents, and sometimes adults. Opening your front door in the morning, you would find Gertrude sitting on your stoop. Going into the bathroom to shave, you would find Gertrude using the toilet. Looking into your son's crib, you find it empty, and, looking further, you would find that Gertrude had pushed him in his baby carriage into the next village. She was helpful, pervasive, honest, hungry, and loyal. She never went home of her own choice. When the time to go arrived, she was indifferent to all its signs. "Go home, Gertrude," people could be heard saying in one house or an other, night after night. "Go home, Gertrude." "It's time for you to go home now, Gertrude." "You had better go home and get your supper, Gertrude." "I told you to go home twenty minutes ago, Gertrude." "Your mother will be worrying about you, Gertrude." "Go home, Gertrude, go home."

There are times when the lines around the human eye seem like shelves of eroded stone and when the staring eye itself strikes us with such a wilderness of animal feeling that we are at a loss. The look Francis gave the little girl was ugly and queer, and it frightened her. He reached into his pocket—his hands were shaking—and took out a quarter. "Go home, Gertrude, go home, and don't tell anyone, Gertrude. Don't—" He choked and ran into the living room as Julia called to him from upstairs to hurry and dress.

The thought that he would drive Anne Murchison home later that night ran like a golden thread through the events of the party that Francis and Julia went to, and he laughed uproariously at dull jokes, dried a tear when Mabel Mercer told him about the death of her kitten, and stretched, yawned, sighed, and grunted like any other man with a rendezvous at the back of his mind. The bracelet was in his pocket. As he sat talking, the smell of grass was in his nose, and he was wondering where he would park the car. Nobody lived in the old Parker mansion, and the driveway was used as a lovers' lane. Townsend Street was a dead end, and he could park there, beyond the last house. The old lane that used to connect Elm Street to the riverbanks was overgrown, but he had walked there with his children, and he could drive his car deep enough into the brushwoods to be concealed.

The Weeds were the last to leave the party, and their host and hostess spoke of their own marriage happiness while they all four stood in the hallway saying good night. "She's my girl," their host said, squeezing his wife. "She's my blue sky. After sixteen years, I still bite her shoulders. She makes me feel like Hannibal crossing the Alps."

The Weeds drove home in silence.

Francis brought the car up the driveway and sat still, with the motor running. "You can put the car in the garage," Julia said as she got out. "I told the Murchison girl she could leave at eleven. Someone drove her home." She shut the door, and Francis sat in the dark. He would be spared nothing then, it seemed, that a fool was not spared: ravening lewdness, jealousy, this hurt to his feelings that put tears in his eyes, even scorn—for he could see clearly the image he now presented, his arms spread over the steering wheel and his head buried in them for love.

Francis had been a dedicated Boy Scout when he was young, and, remembering the precepts of his youth, he left his office early the next afternoon and played some round-robin squash, but, with his body toned up by exercise and a shower, he realized that he might better have stayed at his desk. It was a frosty night when he got home. The air smelled sharply of change. When he stepped into the house, he sensed an unusual stir. The children were in their best clothes, and when Julia came down, she was wearing a lavender dress and her diamond sunburst. She explained the stir. Mr. Hubber was coming at seven to take their photograph for the Christmas card. She had put out Francis' blue suit and a tie with some color in it because the picture was going to be in color this year. Julia was lighthearted at the thought of being photographed for Christmas. It was the kind of ceremony she enjoyed.

Francis went upstairs to change his clothes. He was tired from the day's work and tired with longing, and sitting on the edge of the bed had the effect of deepening his weariness. He thought of Anne Murchison, and the physical need to express himself, instead of being restrained by the pink lamps on Julia's dressing table, engulfed him. He went to Julia's desk, took a piece of writing paper, and began to write on it. "Dear Anne, I love you, I love you, I love you . . ." No one would see the letter, and he used no restraint. He used phrases like "heavenly bliss," and "love nest." He salivated, sighed, and trembled. When Julia called to come down, the abyss between his fantasy and the practical world opened so wide that he felt the muscles of his heart.

Julia and the children were on the stoop, and the photographer and his assistant had set up a double battery of floodlights to show the family and the architectural beauty of the entrance to their house. People who had come home on a late train slowed their cars to see the Weeds being photographed for their Christmas card. A few waved and called to the family. It took half an hour of smiling and wetting their lips before Mr. Hubber was satisfied. The heat of the lights made an unfresh smell in the frosty air, and when they were turned off, they lingered on the retina of Francis' eyes.

Later that night, while Francis and Julia were drinking their coffee in the living room, the doorbell rang. Julia answered the door and let in Clayton Thomas. He had come to pay her for some theatre tickets that she had given his mother some time ago, and that Helen Thomas had scrupulously insisted on paying for, though Julia had asked her not to. Julia invited him in to have a cup of coffee. "I won't have any coffee," Clayton said, "but I will come in for a minute." He followed her into the living room, said good evening to Francis, and sat awkwardly in a chair.

Clayton's father had been killed in the war, and the young man's fatherlessness surrounded him like an element. This may have been conspicuous in Shady Hill because the Thomases were the only family that lacked a piece; all the other marriages were intact and productive. Clayton was in his second or third year of college, and he and his mother lived alone in a large house, which she hoped to sell. Clayton had once made some trouble. Years ago, he had stolen some money and run away; he had got to California before they caught up with him. He was tall and homely, wore horn-rimmed glasses, and spoke in a deep voice.

"When do you go back to college, Clayton?" Francis asked.

"I'm not going back," Clayton said. "Mother doesn't have the money, and there's no sense in all this pretense. I'm going to get a job, and if we sell the house, we'll take an apartment in New York."

"Won't you miss Shady Hill?" Julia asked.

"No," Clayton said. "I don't like it."

"Why not?" Francis asked.

"Well, there's a lot here I don't approve of," Clayton said gravely. "Things like the club dances. Last Saturday night, I looked in toward the end and saw Mr. Granner trying to put Mrs. Minot into the trophy case. They were both drunk. I disapprove of so much drinking."

"It was Saturday night," Francis said.

"And all the dovecotes are phoney," Clayton said. "And the way people clutter up their lives. I've thought about it a lot, and what seems to me to be really wrong with Shady Hill is that it doesn't have any future. So much energy is spent in perpetuating the place—in keeping out undesirables, and so forth—that the only idea of the future anyone has is just more and more commuting trains and more parties. I don't think that's healthy. I think people ought to be able to dream big dreams about the future. I think people ought to be able to dream great dreams."

"It's too bad you couldn't continue with college," Julia said.

"I wanted to go to divinity school," Clayton said.

"What's your church?" Francis asked.

"Unitarian, Theosophist, Transcendentalist, Humanist," Clayton said.

"Wasn't Emerson a transcendentalist?" Julia asked.

"I mean the English transcendentalists," Clayton said. "All the American transcendentalists were goops."

"What kind of a job do you expect to get?" Francis asked.

"Well, I'd like to work for a publisher," Clayton said, "but everyone tells me there's nothing doing. But it's the kind of thing I'm interested in. I'm writing a long verse play about good and evil. Uncle Charlie might get me into a bank, and that would be good for me. I need the discipline. I have a long way to go in forming my character. I have some terrible habits. I talk too much. I think I ought to take vows of silence. I ought to try not to speak for a week, and discipline myself. I've thought of making a retreat at one of the Episcopalian monasteries, but I don't like Trinitarianism."

"Do you have any girl friends?" Francis asked.

"I'm engaged to be married," Clayton said. "Of course, I'm not old enough or rich enough to have my engagement observed or respected or anything, but I bought a simulated emerald for Anne Murchison with the money I made cutting lawns this summer. We're going to be married as soon as she finishes school."

Francis recoiled at the mention of the girl's name. Then a dingy light seemed to emanate from his spirit, showing everything—Julia, the boy, the chairs—in their true colorlessness. It was like a bitter turn of the weather.

"We're going to have a large family," Clayton said. "Her father's a terrible rummy, and I've had my hard times, and we want to have lots of children. Oh, she's wonderful, Mr. and Mrs. Weed, and we have so much in common. We like all the same things. We sent out the same Christmas card last year without planning it, and we both have an allergy to tomatoes, and our eyebrows grow together in the middle. Well, good night."

Julia went to the door with him. When she returned, Francis said that Clayton was lazy, irresponsible, affected, and smelly. Julia said that Francis seemed to be getting intolerant; the Thomas boy was young and should be given a chance. Julia had noticed other cases where Francis had been short-tempered. "Mrs. Wrightson has asked everyone in Shady Hill to her anniversary party but us," she said.

"I'm sorry, Julia."

"Do you know why they didn't ask us?"

"Why?"

"Because you insulted Mrs. Wrightson."

"Then you know about it?"

"June Masterson told me. She was standing behind you." Julia walked in front of the sofa with a small step that expressed, Francis knew, a feeling of anger.

"I did insult Mrs. Wrightson, Julia, and I meant to. I've never liked her parties, and I'm glad she's dropped us."

"What about Helen?"

"How does Helen come into this?"

"Mrs. Wrightson's the one who decides who goes to the assemblies."

"You mean she can keep Helen from going to the dances?"

"Yes."

"I hadn't thought of that."

"Oh, I knew you hadn't thought of it," Julia cried, thrusting hilt-deep into this chink of his armor. "And it makes me furious to see this kind of stupid thoughtlessness wreck everyone's happiness."

"I don't think I've wrecked anyone's happiness."

"Mrs. Wrightson runs Shady Hill and has run it for the last forty years. I don't know what makes you think that in a community like this you can indulge every impulse you have to be insulting, vulgar, and offensive."

"I have very good manners," Francis said, trying to give the evening a turn toward the light.

"Damn you, Francis Weed!" Julia cried, and the spit of her words struck him in the face. "I've worked hard for the social position we enjoy in this place, and I won't stand by and see you wreck it. You must have understood when you settled here that you couldn't expect to live like a bear in a cave."

"I've got to express my likes and dislikes."

"You can conceal your dislikes. You don't have to meet everything head-on, like a child. Unless you're anxious to be a social leper. It's no accident that we get asked out a great deal. It's no accident that Helen has so many friends. How would you like to spend your Saturday nights at the movies? How would you like to spend your Sundays raking up leaves? How would you like it if your daughter spent the assembly nights sitting at her window, listening to the music from the club? How would you like it—" He did something then that was, after all, not so unaccountable, since her words seemed to raise up between them a wall so deadening that he gagged: He struck her full in the face. She went up the stairs to their room. She didn't slam the door. When Francis followed, a few minutes later, he found her packing a suitcase.

"Julia, I'm very sorry."

"It doesn't matter," she said. She was crying.

"Where do you think you're going?"

"I don't know. I just looked at a timetable. There's an eleven-sixteen into New York. I'll take that."

"You can't go, Julia."

"I can't stay. I know that."

"I'm sorry about Mrs. Wrightson, Julia, and I'm—"

"It doesn't matter about Mrs. Wrightson. That isn't the trouble."

"What is the trouble?"

"You don't love me."

"I do love you, Julia."

"No, you don't."

"Julia, I do love you, and I would like to be as we were—sweet and bawdy and dark—but now there are so many people."

"You hate me."

"I don't hate you, Julia."

"You have no idea of how much you hate me. I think it's subconscious. You don't realize the cruel things you've done."

"What cruel things, Julia?"

"The cruel acts your subconscious drives you to in order to express your hatred of me."

"What, Julia?"

"I've never complained."

"Tell me."

"You don't know what you're doing."

"Tell me."

"Your clothes."

"What do you mean?"

"I mean the way you leave your dirty clothes around in order to express your subconscious hatred for me."

"I don't understand."

"I mean your dirty socks and your dirty pajamas and your dirty underwear and your dirty shirts!" She rose from kneeling by the suitcase and faced him, her eyes blazing and her voice ringing with emotion. "I'm talking about the fact that you've never learned to hang up anything. You just leave your clothes all over the floor where they drop, in order to humiliate me. You do it on purpose!" She fell on the bed, sobbing.

"Julia, darling!" he said, but when she felt his hand on her shoulder she got up.

"Leave me alone," she said. "I have to go." She brushed past him to the closet and came back with a dress. "I'm not taking any of the things you've given me," she said. "I'm leaving my pearls and the fur jacket."

"Oh, Julia!" Her figure, so helpless in its self-deceptions, bent over the suitcase made him nearly sick with pity. She did not understand how desolate her life would be without him. She didn't understand the hours that working women have to keep. She didn't understand that most of her friendships existed within the framework of their marriage, and that without this she would find herself alone. She didn't understand about travel, about hotels, about money. "Julia, I can't let you go! What you don't understand, Julia, is that you've come to be dependent on me."

She tossed her head back and covered her face with her hands. "Did you say that I was dependent on you?" she asked. "Is that what you said? And who is it that tells you what time to get up in the morning and when to go to bed at night? Who is it that prepares your meals and picks up your dirty clothes and invites your friends to dinner? If it weren't for me, your neckties would be greasy and your clothing would be full of moth holes. You were alone when I met you, Francis Weed, and you'll be alone when I leave. When Mother asked you for a list to send out invitations to our wedding, how many names did you have to give her? Fourteen!"

"Cleveland wasn't my home, Julia."

"And how many of your friends came to the church? Two!"

"Cleveland wasn't my home, Julia."

"Since I'm not taking the fur jacket," she said quietly, "you'd better put it back into storage. There's an insurance policy on the pearls that comes due in January. The name of the laundry and the maid's telephone number—all those things are in my desk. I hope you won't drink too much, Francis. I hope that nothing bad will happen to you. If you do get into serious trouble, you can call me."

"Oh my darling, I can't let you go!" Francis said. "I can't let you go, Julia!" He took her in his arms.

"I guess I'd better stay and take care of you for a little while longer," she said.

Riding to work in the morning, Francis saw the girl walk down the aisle of the coach. He was surprised; he hadn't realized that the school she went to was in the city, but she was carrying books, she seemed to be going to school. His surprise delayed his reaction, but then he got up clumsily and stepped into the aisle. Several people had come between them, but he could see her ahead of him, waiting for someone to open the car door, and then, as the train swerved, putting out her hand to support herself as she crossed the platform into the next car. He followed her through that car and halfway through another before calling her name—"Anne! Anne!"—but she didn't turn. He followed her into still another car, and she sat down in an aisle seat. Coming up to her, all his feelings warm and bent in her direction, he put his hand on the back of her seat—even this touch warmed him—and, leaning down to speak to her, he saw it was not Anne. It was an older woman wearing glasses. He went on deliberately into another car, his face red with embarrassment and the much deeper feeling of having his good sense challenged; for if he couldn't tell one person from another, what evidence was there that his life with Julia and the children had as much reality as his dreams of iniquity in Paris or the litter, the grass smell, and the cave-shaped trees in Lovers' Lane.

Late that afternoon, Julia called to remind Francis that they were going out for dinner. A few minutes later, Trace Beardon called. "Look, feller," Trace said. "I'm calling for Mrs. Thomas. You know? Clayton, that boy of hers, doesn't seem able to get a job, and I wondered if you could help. If you'd call Charlie Bell—I know he's indebted to you—and say a good word for the kid, I think Charlie would—"

"Trace, I hate to say this," Francis said, "but I don't feel that I can do anything for that boy. The kid's worthless. I know it's a harsh thing to say, but it's a fact. Any kindness done for him would backfire in everybody's face. He's just a worthless kid, Trace, and there's nothing to be done about it. Even if we got him a job, he wouldn't be able to keep it for a week. I know that to be a fact. It's an awful thing, Trace, and I know it is, but instead of recommending that kid, I'd feel obliged to warn people against him—people who knew his father and would naturally want to step in and do something. I'd feel obliged to warn them. He's a thief . . ."

The moment this conversation was finished, Miss Rainey came in and stood by his desk. "I'm not going to be able to work for you any more, Mr. Weed," she said. "I can stay until the seventeenth if you need me, but I've been offered a whirlwind of a job, and I'd like to leave as soon as possible."

She went out, leaving him to face alone the wickedness of what he had done to the Thomas boy. His children in their photograph laughed and laughed, glazed with all the bright colors of summer, and he remembered that they had met a bagpiper on the beach that day and he had paid the piper a dollar to play them a battle song of the Black Watch. The girl would be at the house when he got home. He would spend another evening among his kind neighbors, picking and choosing dead-end streets, cart tracks, and the driveways of abandoned houses. There was nothing to mitigate his feeling—nothing that laughter or a game of softball with the children would change—and, thinking back over the plane crash, the Farquarsons' new maid, and Anne Murchison's difficulties with her drunken father, he wondered how he could have avoided arriving at just where he was. He was in trouble. He had been lost once in his life, coming back from a trout stream in the north woods, and he had now the same bleak realization that no amount of cheerfulness or hopefulness or valor or perseverance could help him find, in the gathering dark, the path that he'd lost. He smelled the forest. The feeling of bleakness was intolerable, and he saw clearly that he had reached the point where he would have to make a choice.

He could go to a psychiatrist, like Miss Rainey; he could go to church and confess his lusts; he could go to a Danish massage parlor in the West Seventies that had been recommended by a salesman; he could rape the girl or trust that he would somehow be prevented from doing this; or he could get drunk. It was his life, his boat, and, like every other man, he was made to be the father of thousands, and what harm could there be in a tryst that would make them both feel more kindly toward the world? This was the wrong train of thought, and he came back to the first, the psychiatrist. He had the telephone number of Miss Rainey's doctor, and he called and asked for an immediate appointment. He was insistent with the doctor's secretary—it was his manner in business—and when she said that the doctor's schedule was full for the next few weeks, Francis demanded an appointment that day and was told to come at five.

The psychiatrist's office was in a build ing that was used mostly by doctors and dentists, and the hallways were filled with the candy smell of mouth-wash and memories of pain. Francis' character had been formed upon a series of private resolves—resolves about cleanliness, about going off the high diving board or repeating any other feat that challenged his courage, about punctuality, honesty, and virtue. To abdicate the perfect loneliness in which he had made his most vital decisions shattered his concept of character and left him now in a condition that felt like shock. He was stupefied. The scene for his *miserere mei Deus* was, like the waiting room of so many doctors' offices, a crude token gesture toward the sweets of domestic bliss: a place arranged with antiques, coffee tables, potted plants, and etchings of snow-covered bridges and geese in flight, although there were no children, no marriage bed, no stove, even, in this travesty of a house, where no one had ever spent the night and where the curtained windows looked straight onto a dark air shaft. Francis gave his name and address to a secretary and then saw, at the side of the room, a policeman moving toward him. "Hold it, hold it," the policeman said. "Don't move. Keep your hands where they are."

"I think it's all right, Officer," the secretary began. "I think it will be—"

"Let's make sure," the policeman said, and he began to slap Francis' clothes, looking for what—pistols, knives, an icepick? Finding nothing, he went off, and the secretary began a nervous apology: "When you called on the telephone, Mr. Weed, you seemed very excited, and one of the doctor's patients has been threatening his life, and we have to be careful. If you want to go in now?" Francis pushed open a door connected to an electrical chime, and in the doctor's lair sat down heavily, blew his nose into a handkerchief, searched in his pockets for cigarettes, for matches, for something, and said hoarsely, with tears in his eyes, "I'm in love, Dr. Herzog."

It is a week or ten days later in Shady Hill. The seven-fourteen has come and gone, and here and there dinner is finished and the dishes are in the dish-washing machine. The village hangs, morally and economically, from a thread; but it hangs by its thread in the evening light. Donald Goslin has begun to worry the "Moonlight Sonata" again. *Marcato ma sempre pianissimo!* He seems to be wringing out a wet bath towel, but the housemaid does not heed him. She is writing a letter to Arthur Godfrey. In the cellar of his house, Francis Weed is building a coffee table. Dr. Herzog recommended woodwork as a therapy, and Francis finds some true consolation in the simple arithmetic involved and in the holy smell of new wood. Francis is happy. Upstairs, little Toby is crying, because he is tired. He puts off his cowboy hat, gloves, and fringed jacket, unbuckles the belt studded with gold and rubies, the silver bullets and holsters, slips off his suspenders, his checked shirt, and Levis, and sits on the edge of his bed to pull off his high boots. Leaving this equipment in a heap, he goes to the closet and takes his space suit off a nail. It is a struggle for him to get into the long tights, but he succeeds. He loops the magic cape over his shoulders and, climbing onto the footboard of his bed, he spreads his arms and flies the short distance to the floor, landing with a thump that is audible to everyone in the house but himself.

"Go home, Gertrude, go home," Mrs. Matterson says. "I told you to go home an hour ago, Gertrude. It's way past your suppertime, and your mother will be worried. Go home!" A door on the Babcocks' terrace flies open, and out comes Mrs. Babcock without any clothes on, pursued by her naked husband. (Their children are away at boarding school, and their terrace is screened by a hedge.) Over the terrace they go in at the kitchen door, as passionate and handsome a nymph and satyr as you will find on any wall in Venice. Cutting the last of the roses in her garden, Julia hears old Mr. Nixon shouting at the squirrels in his bird-feeding station. "Rapscallions! Varmints! Avaunt and quit my sight!" A miserable cat wanders into the garden, sunk in spiritual and physical discomfort. Tied to its head is a small straw hat—a doll's hat—and it is securely buttoned into a doll's dress, from the skirts of which protrudes its long, hairy tail. As it walks, it shakes its feet, as if it had fallen into water.

"Here, pussy, pussy, pussy," Julia calls. "Here, pussy, here, poor pussy!" But the cat gives her a skeptical look and stumbles away in its skirts. The last to come is Jupiter. He prances through the tomato vines, holding in his generous mouth the remains of an evening slipper. Then it is dark; it is a night where kings in golden suits ride elephants over the mountains.

[1954]

For Thought

Cheever's story examines the boredom and frustration experienced by an apparently successful middle-aged American husband and father. Ironically, the author heightens Weed's sense of desperation by allowing him to experience a series of sensational adventures. He experiences a near plane crash, a reminder of a wartime disgrace, an unsettling flirtation, a violent domestic quarrel, and terror in a psychiatrist's office. When emotions are bottled up for the sake of appearances, Cheever suggests, life becomes meaningless.

For Discussion

1. What opportunities for escape from boredom arise for Francis Weed? Why can he not act upon them?
2. To what extent is Weed both a type and an individual?
3. What point of view does Cheever adopt in the story?
4. Compare and contrast Julia Weed with the French maid, and Anne Murchison with Mrs. Wrightson.
5. What symbolism is involved in Cheever's references to classical mythology, the "Moonlight Sonata," the wandering Gertrude Flannery, the unclothed woman in the sleeping car, and the retriever Jupiter?
6. The Weed family has evidently achieved financial security and material comfort. What price have they paid in terms of tranquillity and self-esteem?

Anton Chekhov
The Darling

Olenka Plemyannikova, the daughter of a retired collegiate assessor, was sitting on her porch, which gave on the courtyard, deep in thought. It was hot, the flies were persistent and annoying, and it was pleasant to think that it would soon be evening. Dark rainclouds were gathering in the east and there was a breath of moisture in the wind that occasionally blew from that direction.

Kukin, a theater manager who ran a summer garden known as The Tivoli and lodged in the wing of the house, was standing in the middle of the courtyard, staring at the sky.

"Again!" he was saying in despair. "It's going to rain again! Rain every day, every day, as if to spite me! It will be the death of me! It's ruin! Such a frightful loss every day!"

He struck his hands together and continued, turning to Olenka:

"There, Olga Semyonovna, that's our life. It's enough to make you weep! You work, you try your utmost, you wear yourself out, you lie awake nights, you rack your brains trying to make a better thing of it, and what's the upshot? In the first place, the public is ignorant, barbarous. I give them the very best operetta, an elaborate spectacle, first-rate vaudeville artists. But do you think they want that? It's all above their heads. All they want is slapstick! Give them trash! And then look at the weather! Rain almost every evening. It started raining on the tenth of May, and it has kept it up all May and June. It's simply terrible! The public doesn't come, but don't I have to pay the rent? Don't I have to pay the artists?"

The next day toward evening the sky would again be overcast and Kukin would say, laughing hysterically:

"Well, go on, rain! Flood the garden, drown me! Bad luck to me in this world and the next! Let the artists sue me! Let them send me to prison—to Siberia—to the scaffold! Ha, ha, ha!"

The next day it was the same thing all over again.

Olenka listened to Kukin silently, gravely, and sometimes tears would come to her eyes. In the end his misfortunes moved her and she fell in love with him. He was a short, thin man with a sallow face, and wore his hair combed down over his temples. He had a thin tenor voice and when he spoke, his mouth twisted, and his face perpetually wore an expression of despair. Nevertheless he aroused a genuine, deep feeling in her. She was always enamored of someone and could not live otherwise. At first it had been her papa, who was now ill and sat in an armchair in a darkened room, breathing with difficulty. Then she had devoted her affections to her aunt, who used to come from Bryansk every other year. Still earlier, when she went to school, she had been in love with her French teacher. She was a quiet, kind, softhearted girl, with meek, gentle eyes, and she enjoyed very good health. At the sight of her full pink cheeks, her soft white neck with a dark birthmark on it, and the kind artless smile that came into her face when she listened to anything pleasant, men said to themselves, "Yes, not half bad," and smiled too, while the ladies present could not refrain from suddenly seizing her hand in the middle of the conversation and exclaiming delightedly, "You darling!"

The house in which she lived all her life and which was to be hers by her father's will, was situated on the outskirts of the city on what was known as Gypsy Road, not far from The Tivoli. In the evening and at night she could hear the band play and the skyrockets go off, and it seemed to her that it was Kukin fighting his fate and assaulting his chief enemy, the apathetic public. Her heart contracted sweetly, she had no desire to sleep, and when he returned home at dawn, she would tap softly at her bedroom window and, showing him only her face and one shoulder through the curtain, give him a friendly smile.

He proposed to her, and they were married. And when he had a good look at her neck and her plump firm shoulders, he struck his hands together, and exclaimed, "Darling!"

He was happy, but as it rained on their wedding day and the night that followed, the expression of despair did not leave his face.

As a married couple, they got on well together. She presided over the box office, looked after things in the summer garden, kept accounts and paid salaries; and her rosy cheeks, the radiance of her sweet artless smile showed now in the box office window, now in the wings of the theater, now at the buffet. And she was already telling her friends that the theater was the most remarkable, the most important, and the most essential thing in the world, and that it was only the theater that could give true pleasure and make you a cultivated and humane person.

"But do you suppose the public understands that?" she would ask. "What it wants is slapstick! Yesterday we gave 'Faust Inside Out,' and almost all the boxes were empty, and if Vanichka and I had put on something vulgar, I assure you the theater would have been packed. Tomorrow Vanichka and I are giving 'Orpheus in Hell.' Do come."

And what Kukin said about artists and the theater she would repeat. Like him she despised the public for its ignorance and indifference to art; she took a hand in the rehearsals, correcting the actors, kept an eye on the musicians, and when there was an unfavorable notice in the local paper, she wept and went to see the editor about it.

The actors were fond of her and called her "the darling," and "Vanichka-and-I." She was sorry for them and would lend them small sums, and if they cheated her, she cried in private but did not complain to her husband.

The pair got on just as well together when winter came. They leased the municipal theater for the season and sublet it for short periods to a Ukrainian troupe, a magician, or a local dramatic club. Olenka was gaining weight and beamed with happiness, but Kukin was getting thinner and more sallow and complained of terrible losses, although business was fairly good during the winter. He coughed at night, and she would make him drink an infusion of raspberries and linden blossoms, rub him with eau de Cologne and wrap him in her soft shawls.

"What a sweet thing you are!" she would say quite sincerely, smoothing his hair. "My handsome sweet!"

At Lent he left for Moscow to engage a company of actors for the summer season, and she could not sleep with him away. She sat at the window and watched the stars. It occurred to her that she had something in common with the hens: they too stayed awake all night and were disturbed when the cock was absent from the henhouse. Kukin was detained in Moscow, and wrote that he would return by Easter, and in his letters he sent instructions about The Tivoli. But on the Monday of Passion Week, late in the evening, there was a sudden ominous knock at the gate; someone was banging at the wicket as though it were a barrel—boom, boom, boom! The sleepy cook, her bare feet splashing through the puddles, ran to open the gate.

"Open, please!" someone on the other side of the gate was saying in a deep voice. "There's a telegram for you."

Olenka had received telegrams from her husband before, but this time for some reason she was numb with fright. With trembling hands she opened the telegram and read the following:

"Ivan Petrovich died suddenly today awaiting prot instructions tuneral Tuesday."

That is exactly how the telegram had it: "tuneral," and there was also the incomprehensible word "prot"; the signature was that of the director of the comic opera company.

"My precious!" Olenka sobbed. "Vanichka, my precious, my sweet! Why did we ever meet! Why did I get to know you and to love you! To whom can your poor unhappy Olenka turn?"

Kukin was buried on Tuesday in the Vagankovo Cemetery in Moscow. Olenka returned home on Wednesday, and no sooner did she enter her room than she sank onto the bed and sobbed so loudly that she could be heard in the street and in the neighboring courtyards.

"The darling!" said the neighbors, crossing themselves. "Darling Olga Semyonovna! How the poor soul takes on!"

Three months later Olenka was returning from Mass one day in deep mourning and very sad. It happened that one of her neighbors, Vasily Andreich Pustovalov, the manager of Babakayev's lumberyard, who was also returning from church, was walking beside her. He was wearing a straw hat and a white waistcoat, with a gold watch-chain, and he looked more like a landowner than a businessman.

"There is order in all things, Olga Semyonovna," he was saying sedately, with a note of sympathy in his voice; "and if one of our dear ones passes on, then it means that this was the will of God, and in that case we must keep ourselves in hand and bear it submissively."

Having seen Olenka to her gate, he took leave of her and went further. All the rest of the day she heard his sedate voice, and as soon as she closed her eyes she had a vision of his dark beard. She liked him very much. And apparently she too had made an impression on him because a little later a certain elderly lady, whom she scarcely knew, called to have coffee with her, and no sooner was she seated at table than the visitor began to talk about Pustovalov, saying that he was a fine, substantial man, and that any marriageable woman would be glad to go to the altar with him. Three days later Pustovalov himself paid her a visit. He did not stay more than ten minutes and he said little, but Olenka fell in love with him, so deeply that she stayed awake all night burning as with fever, and in the morning she sent for the elderly lady. The match was soon arranged and then came the wedding.

As a married couple Pustovalov and Olenka got on very well together. As a rule he was in the lumberyard till dinnertime, then he went out on business and was replaced by Olenka, who stayed in the office till evening, making out bills and seeing that orders were shipped.

"We pay twenty per cent more for lumber every year," she would say to customers and acquaintances. "Why, we used to deal in local timber, and now Vasichka has to travel to the province of Mogilev for timber regularly. And the freight rates!" she would exclaim, putting her hands to her cheeks in horror. "The freight rates!"

It seemed to her that she had been in the lumber business for ages, that lumber was the most important, the most essential thing in the world, and she found something intimate and touching in the very sound of such words as beam, log, batten, plank, box board, lath, scantling, slab . . .

At night she would dream of whole mountains of boards and planks, of endless caravans of carts hauling lumber out of town to distant points. She would dream that a regiment of beams, 28 feet by 8 inches, standing on end, was marching in the lumberyard, that beams, logs, and slabs were crashing against each other with the hollow sound of dry wood, that they kept tumbling down and rising again, piling themselves on each other. Olenka would scream in her sleep and Pustovalov would say to her tenderly: "Olenka, what's the matter, darling? Cross yourself!"

Whatever ideas her husband had, she adopted as her own. If he thought that the room was hot or that business was slow, she thought so too. Her husband did not care for entertainments and on holidays stayed home—so did she.

"You are always at home or in the office," her friends would say. "You ought to go to the theater, darling, or to the circus."

"Vasichka and I have no time for the theater," she would answer sedately, "We are working people, we're not interested in such foolishness. What good are these theaters?"

On Saturdays the two of them would go to evening service, on holidays they attended early Mass, and returning from the church they walked side by side, their faces wearing a softened expression. There was an agreeable aroma about them, and her silk dress rustled pleasantly. At home they had tea with shortbread, and various kinds of jam, and afterwards they ate pie. Every day at noon, in the yard and on the street just outside the gate, there was a delicious smell of *borshch* and roast lamb or duck, and on fast days there was the odor of fish, and one could not pass the Pustovalov gate without one's mouth watering.

In the office the samovar was always boiling and the customers were treated to tea with doughnuts. Once a week the pair went to the baths and returned side by side, both with red faces.

"Yes, everything goes well with us, thank God," Olenka would say to her friends. "I wish everyone were as happy as Vasichka and I."

When Pustovalov went off to the provinces of Mogilev for timber, she missed him badly and lay awake nights, crying. Sometimes, in the evening, a young army veterinary, by the name of Smirnin, who rented the wing of their house, would call on her. He chatted or played cards with her and that diverted her. What interested her most was what he told her about his domestic life. He had been married and had a son, but was separated from his wife because she had been unfaithful to him, and now he hated her; he sent her forty rubles a month for the maintenance of the child. And listening to him, Olenka would sigh and shake her head: she was sorry for him.

"Well, God keep you," she would say to him as she took leave of him, going to the stairs with him, candle in hand. "Thank you for relieving my boredom, and may the Queen of Heaven give you health!"

She always expressed herself in this sedate and reasonable manner, in imitation of her husband. Just as the veterinary would be closing the door behind him, she would recall him and say:

"You know, Vladimir Platonych, you had better make up with your wife. You ought to forgive her, at least for your son's sake! I am sure the little boy understands everything."

And when Pustovalov came back, she would tell him in low tones about the veterinary and his unhappy domestic life, and both of them would sigh and shake their heads and speak of the boy, who was probably missing his father. Then by a strange association of ideas they would both turn to the icons, bow down to the ground before them and pray that the Lord would grant them children.

Thus the Pustovalovs lived in peace and quiet, in love and harmony for six years. But one winter day, right after having hot tea at the office, Vasily Andreich went out without his cap to see about shipping some lumber, caught a chill and was taken sick. He was treated by the best doctors, but the illness had its own way with him, and he died after four months. Olenka was a widow again.

"To whom can I turn now, my darling?" she sobbed when she had buried her husband. "How can I live without you, wretched and unhappy as I am? Pity me, good people, left all alone in the world—"

She wore a black dress with white cuffs and gave up wearing hat and gloves for good. She hardly ever left the house except to go to church or to visit her husband's grave, and at home she lived like a nun. Only at the end of six months did she take off her widow's weeds and open the shutters. Sometimes in the morning she was seen with her cook going to market for provisions, but how she lived now and what went on in her house could only be guessed. People based their guesses on such facts as that they saw her having tea with the veterinary in her little garden, he reading the newspaper aloud to her, and that, meeting an acquaintance at the post office, she would say:

"There is no proper veterinary inspection in our town, and that's why there is so much illness around. So often you hear of people getting ill from the milk or catching infections from horses and cows. When you come down to it, the health of domestic animals must be as well cared for as the health of human beings."

She now repeated the veterinary's words and held the same opinions about everything that he did. It was plain that she could not live even for one year without an attachment and that she had found new happiness in the wing of her house. Another woman would have been condemned for this, but of Olenka no one could think ill: everything about her was so unequivocal. Neither she nor the veterinary mentioned to anyone the change that had occurred in their relations; indeed, they tried to conceal it, but they didn't succeed, because Olenka could not keep a secret. When he had visitors, his regimental colleagues, she, pouring the tea or serving the supper, would begin to talk of the cattle plague, of the pearl disease, of the municipal slaughterhouses. He would be terribly embarrassed and when the guests had gone, he would grasp her by the arms and hiss angrily:

"I've asked you before not to talk about things that you don't understand! When veterinaries speak among themselves, please don't butt in! It's really annoying!"

She would look at him amazed and alarmed and ask, "But Volodichka, what shall I talk about?"

And with tears in her eyes she would hug him and beg him not to be angry, and both of them were happy.

Yet this happiness did not last long. The veterinary left, left forever, with his regiment, which was moved to some remote place, it may have been Siberia. And Olenka remained alone.

Now she was quite alone. Her father had died long ago, and his armchair stood in the attic, covered with dust and minus one leg. She got thinner and lost her looks, and passers-by in the street did not glance at her and smile as they used to. Obviously, her best years were over, were behind her, and now a new kind of life was beginning for her, an unfamiliar kind that did not bear thinking of. In the evening Olenka sat on her porch, and heard the band play at The Tivoli and the rockets go off, but this no longer suggested anything to her mind. She looked apathetically at the empty courtyard, thought of nothing, and later, when night came, she would go to bed and dream of the empty courtyard. She ate and drank as though involuntarily.

Above all, and worst of all, she no longer had any opinions whatever. She saw objects about her and understood what was going on, but she could not form an opinion about anything and did not know what to talk about. And how terrible it is not to have any opinions! You see, for instance, a bottle, or the rain, or a peasant driving in a cart, but what is the bottle for, or the rain, or the peasant, what is the meaning of them, you can't tell, and you couldn't, even if they paid you a thousand rubles. When Kukin was about, or Pustovalov or, later, the veterinary, Olenka could explain it all and give her opinions about anything you like, but now there was the same emptiness in her head and in her heart as in her courtyard. It was weird, and she felt as bitter as if she had been eating wormwood.

Little by little the town was extending in all directions. Gypsy Road was now a regular street, and where The Tivoli had been and the lumberyards, houses had sprung up and lanes had multiplied. How swiftly time passes! Olenka's house had taken on a shabby look, the roof was rusty, the shed sloped, and the whole yard was invaded by burdock and stinging nettles. Olenka herself had aged and grown homely. In the summer she sat on the porch, feeling empty and dreary and bitter, as before; in the winter she sat by the window and stared at the snow. Sometimes at the first breath of spring or when the wind brought her the chime of church bells, memories of the past would overwhelm her, her heart would contract sweetly and her eyes would brim over with tears. But this only lasted a moment, and then there was again emptiness and once more she was possessed by a sense of the futility of life; Trot, the black kitten, rubbed against her and purred softly, but Olenka was not affected by these feline caresses. Is that what she needed? She needed an affection that would take possession of her whole being, her soul, her mind, that would give her ideas, a purpose in life, that would warm her aging blood. And she would shake the kitten off her lap, and say irritably: "Scat! Scat! Don't stick to me!"

And so it went, day after day, year after year, and no joy, no opinion! Whatever Mavra the cook would say, was well enough.

One hot July day, toward evening, when the cattle were being driven home and the yard was filled with clouds of dust, suddenly someone knocked at the gate. Olenka herself went to open it and was dumfounded at what she saw: at the gate stood Smirnin, the veterinary, already gray, and wearing civilian clothes. She suddenly recalled everything and, unable to control herself, burst into tears, silently letting her head drop on his breast. She was so agitated that she scarcely noticed how the two of them entered the house and sat down to tea.

"My dear," she murmured, trembling with joy, "Vladimir Platonych, however did you get here?"

"I have come here for good," he explained. "I have retired from the army and want to see what it's like to be on my own and live a settled life. And besides, my son is ready for high school. I have made up with my wife, you know."

"Where is she?"

"She's at the hotel with the boy, and I'm out looking for lodgings."

"Goodness, Vladimir Platonych, take my house! You don't need to look further! Good Lord, and you can have it free," exclaimed Olenka, all in a flutter and beginning to cry again. "You live here in the house, and the wing will do for me. Heavens, I'm so glad!"

The next day they began painting the roof and whitewashing the walls, and Olenka, her arms akimbo, walked about the yard, giving orders. The old smile had come back to her face, and she was lively and spry, as though she had waked from a long sleep. Presently the veterinary's wife arrived, a thin, homely lady with bobbed hair who looked as if she were given to caprices. With her was the little boy, Sasha, small for his age (he was going on ten), chubby, with clear blue eyes and dimples in his cheeks.

No sooner did he walk into the yard than he began chasing the cat, and immediately his eager, joyous laughter rang out.

"Auntie, is that your cat?" he asked Olenka. "When she has little ones, please give us a kitten. Mama is terribly afraid of mice."

Olenka chatted with him, then gave him tea, and her heart suddenly grew warm and contracted sweetly, as if this little boy were her own son. And in the evening, as he sat in the dining-room doing his homework, she looked at him with pity and tenderness and whispered:

"My darling, my pretty one, my little one! How blond you are, and so clever!"

"An island," he was reciting from the book, "is a body of land entirely surrounded by water."

"An island is a body of land . . ." she repeated and this was the first opinion she expressed with conviction after so many years of silence and mental vacuity.

She now had opinions of her own, and at supper she had a conversation with Sasha's parents, saying that studying in high school was hard on the children, but that nevertheless the classical course was better than the scientific one because a classical education opened all careers to you: you could be either a doctor or an engineer.

Sasha started going to high school. His mother went off to Kharkov to visit her sister and did not come back; every day his father left town to inspect herds and sometimes he stayed away for three days together, and it seemed to Olenka that Sasha was wholly abandoned, that he was unwanted, that he was being starved, and she moved him into the wing with her and settled him in a little room there.

For six months now Sasha has been living in her wing. Every morning Olenka comes into his room; he is fast asleep, his hand under his cheek, breathing quietly. She is sorry to wake him.

"Sashenka," she says sadly, "get up, my sweet! It's time to go to school."

He gets up, dresses, says his prayers, and sits down to his breakfast: he drinks three glasses of tea and eats two large doughnuts, and half a buttered French roll. He is hardly awake and consequently cross.

"You haven't learned the fable, Sashenka," says Olenka, looking at him as though she were seeing him off on a long journey. "You worry me. You must do your best, darling, study. And pay attention to your teachers."

"Please leave me alone!" says Sasha.

Then he walks down the street to school, a small boy in a big cap, with his books in a rucksack. Olenka follows him noiselessly.

"Sashenka!" she calles after him. He turns around and she thrusts a date or a caramel into his hand. When they turn into the school lane, he feels ashamed at being followed by a tall stout woman; he looks round and says: "You'd better go home, auntie; I can go alone now."

She stands still and stares after him until he disappears at the school entrance. How she loves him! Not one of her former attachments was so deep; never had her soul surrendered itself so unreservedly, so disinterestedly and with such joy as now when her maternal instinct was increasingly asserting itself. For this little boy who was not her own, for the dimples in his cheeks, for his very cap, she would have laid down her life, would have laid it down with joy, with tears of tenderness. Why? But who knows why?

Having seen Sasha off to school, she goes quietly home, contented, tranquil, brimming over with love; her face, grown younger in the last six months, beams with happiness; people meeting her look at her with pleasure and say:

"Good morning, Olga Semyonovna, darling! How are you, darling?"

"They make the children work so hard at high school nowadays," she says, as she does her marketing. "Think of it: yesterday in the first form they had a fable to learn by heart, a Latin translation and a problem for homework. That's entirely too much for a little fellow."

And she talks about the teachers, the lessons, the textbooks—saying just what Sasha says about them.

At three o'clock they have dinner together, in the evening they do the homework together, and cry. When she puts him to bed, she takes a long time making the sign of the cross over him and whispering prayers. Then she goes to bed and thinks of the future, distant and misty, when Sasha, having finished his studies, will become a doctor or an engineer, will have a large house of his own, horses, a carriage, will marry and become a father. She falls asleep and her dreams are of the same thing, and tears flow down her cheeks from her closed eyes. The black kitten lies beside her purring: Purr-purrr-purrr.

Suddenly there is a loud knock at the gate. Olenka wakes up, breathless with fear, her heart palpitating. Half a minute passes, and there is another knock.

"That's a telegram from Kharkov," she thinks, beginning to tremble from head to foot. "Sasha's mother is sending for him from Kharkov—O Lord!"

She is in despair. Her head, her hands, her feet grow chill and it seems to her that she is the most unhappy woman in the whole world. But another minute passes, voices are heard: it's the veterinary returning from the club.

"Well, thank God!" she thinks.

Little by little the load rolls off her heart and she is again at ease; she goes back to bed and thinks of Sasha who is fast asleep in the next room and sometimes shouts in his sleep:

"I'll give it to you! Scram! No fighting!"

[1899]

For Thought

In Olenka, the twice bereaved widow and foster mother, Chekhov creates a female character of almost mythic proportions. His characterization of her, achieved mainly through the use of irony as he follows her through life, emphasizes her extraordinary chameleon-like nature in the comic facility she possesses of being able to alter her personality to match the interests and tastes of the person she loves, whether it be father, husband, or adopted child. With a balanced view of the tragic and the comic, Chekhov treats his main character as the object of both genial laughter and sympathetic tears, all the while marveling at the wonder of her loving nature.

For Discussion

1. How does the characterization of each husband contribute to the comic effect of Olenka's relationship to them?
2. How is Olenka's relationship with Smirnin comical?
3. What are the methods Chekhov employs to keep the characterization of Olenka from being simply inane and ridiculous?
4. How does Chekhov convert the sequential emotional disasters into comedy rather than tragedy?
5. What is the central irony in the story? In what way is Olenka symbolic?

Anton Chekhov
The Druggist's Wife

Village B, consisting of some two or three twisting streets, was fast asleep. Silence hung on the listless air. The only sound was that of a dog barking in a hoarse tenor somewhere far off, probably outside of town. It was almost dawn.

Everything had been asleep for a long time. The only person still awake was the young wife of the pharmacist, who ran the town drugstore. She had lain down three times already, but sleep stubbornly evaded her, and she didn't know why. She was sitting in her chemise by an open window, looking out on the street. She felt uncomfortably hot, bored, and annoyed . . . so annoyed that she even felt like crying, but why . . . again she didn't know. There was some sort of lump in her chest that kept working its way up into her throat . . . A few feet behind her, curled up against the wall, lay her husband, snoring peacefully. A hungry flea bit him in the bridge of the nose, but he didn't feel it. Instead, he smiled as if he were dreaming that everyone in town had a cough and had to keep buying cough drops from him. Pinpricks, gunfire, or caresses could not have awakened him.

The drugstore was located almost at the edge of town so that the druggist's wife could see far across the fields. She could see the eastern rim of the sky lighting up little by little, then turning purple as if from a large fire. Unexpectedly from behind the distant bushes a large broadfaced moon appeared. It was crimson (usually when it comes out from behind bushes, the moon seems to be frightfully embarrassed).

Suddenly in the midst of the nocturnal silence she could hear someone's footsteps and jingling spurs. Next, she heard voices.

"It's probably officers going back to camp from the police inspector's," she thought.

A moment later two figures in white officers' summer tunics appeared; one was tall and heavy-set, the other, somewhat shorter and thinner. . . . They were sauntering along beside the fence, dragging one foot after the other, and talking loudly about something. As they came near the drugstore, they began to walk still more slowly and looked at the windows.

"It smells like a drugstore . . ." said the thinner one. "And sure enough, it is a drugstore. Ah, I remember . . . I was here last week and bought some castor oil. The druggist is a sourpuss with a jaw like a jackass. Boy, what a jaw! Just like the one Samson slew the Philistines with."

"Mm . . . yes . . ." said the heavy-set one in a deep voice. "He's asleep. And so is his wife. She's a real pretty one, Obtyosoff."

"Yes, I've seen her. She really appeals to

SOURCE: "The Druggist's Wife" by Anton Chekhov. Translation by Blaze Bonazza and Emil Roy.

me . . . Say, Doctor, she can't possibly be in love with that jawbone of an ass, can she?"

"No, very likely she doesn't love him," sighed the doctor with an expression of pity for the druggist. "That cute little wife of his is sleeping behind that window right now . . . stretched out from the heat, with her sweet little mouth half open . . . and her tiny little foot dangling over the edge of the bed. I'll bet that jackass of a druggist doesn't realize how lucky he is."

"You know what, Doctor?" said the other, coming to a halt. "We should go in and buy something. Maybe we'll get to see the druggist's wife."

"Are you out of your mind—it's the middle of the night!"

"So what? They carry on business at night. Let's go in, chum."

"All right."

The druggist's wife, hiding behind the curtain, heard the muffled tingling of the bell. Glancing at her husband, who was snoring peacefully as before and smiling, she threw on her dress, slipped her bare feet into a pair of bedroom slippers, and hurried into the shop.

On the other side of the glass door two shadows were visible. Turning up the lamp, she hurried to unlock the door. She was no longer bored or annoyed, and she didn't feel like crying. It was just that her heart was pounding strongly. The heavy-set doctor and his slender fellow officer entered the shop. Now she could get a good look at them. The heavy-set one was dark, bearded, and slow-moving. With the least movement his tunic crackled and the sweat stood out on his face. The other officer, a lieutenant, was pink-cheeked, clean-shaven, effeminate, and supple-looking.

"What can I do for you?" asked the druggist's wife, clutching her dress at the neckline.

"Give me . . . a . . . a . . . fifteen kopeck's worth of peppermint drops!"

Without hurrying, she got a jar down from the shelf and began to weigh out the candy. The customers stared at her back without blinking—the doctor with half-closed eyes, like a well-fed cat; the lieutenant with an expression of solemnity.

"It's the first time I've ever seen a woman working in a drugstore," remarked the doctor.

"It's not a bit unusual . . ." answered the druggist's wife, looking out of the corner of her eye at the pink-cheeked lieutenant. "My husband doesn't have an assistant so I have to help him."

"Ah . . . but what a nice little store you have here! You have such a variety of . . . jars! Aren't you afraid to move about among all these poisons! Brrr!"

The druggist's wife sealed the small package and handed it to the doctor. The lieutenant gave her the fifteen kopecks. A half-minute went by in silence. The men looked at one another, took a step toward the door, and once again looked at one another.

"Let's have ten kopeck's worth of soda water," said the doctor. The druggist's wife, moving languidly and dispiritedly, once again stretched her hand out to the shelf.

"Don't you have something in the store . . ." mumbled the lieutenant, gesturing with his fingers, "something more refreshing . . . you know . . . Seltzer water, perhaps. Do you have any Seltzer water?"

"Yes," she answered.

"Bravo! You're a goddess, not a woman. Let's have three bottles."

She quickly sealed up the bottle of soda water and disappeared through the door into the darkness behind.

"What a peach!" said the doctor, winking. "You couldn't find a more luscious peach on the island of Madeira itself, Obtyosoff. What do you say? But listen to that snoring. Our friend the druggist is obliging enough to be sound asleep."

A minute later the druggist's wife returned and set five bottles on the counter. She had just come from the cellar and was rosy-cheeked and a bit flustered.

'Shh . . . quiet!" said the lieutenant, when she dropped the cork-screw as she was opening the bottles. "Don't make such a racket or you'll wake up your husband."

"Well . . . what if I do wake him up?"

"It's just that he's sleeping so sweetly . . . and is probably seeing you in his dreams . . . Here's to you!"

"Besides," grumbled the doctor in his deep voice, as he belched from the Seltzer water, "husbands are such dull characters, it would be better if they slept all the time. Oh, for some red wine to add to this fine water!"

"What'll you think of next!" laughed the druggist's wife.

"How wonderful it would be! Too bad they don't sell alcoholic beverages in a drugstore! But wait a minute . . . you certainly must sell wine as a medicine. Don't you have any *vinum gallicum rubrum?*"

"Yes."

"Hell, let's have some then. Get some for us."

"How much do you want?"

"*Quantum satis.* Start out by giving us an ounce each and we'll take it from there . . . What do you say, Obtyosoff? First we'll try it with water and then by itself."

The doctor and the lieutenant then sat down on the counter, took off their caps, and began drinking the red wine.

"This wine is horrible stuff, you'll have to admit! *Vinum plochissimum!* But then, in the presence of . . . er . . . it tastes like ambrosia. You are positively ravishing, madam. I mentally kiss your dainty fingertips."

"I would give anything to really do it," said the lieutenant. "Cross my heart, I would give my life."

"You'd better stop all this," said the druggist's wife, blushing and putting on a serious expression.

"What a flirt you are, though!" the doctor laughed softly, looking roguishly at her from under his brows. "How those sweet little eyes of yours fire away. Bang! Bang! I congratulate you. You have conquered us. We are vanquished."

The druggist's wife looked at their flushed faces, listened to their banter, and soon became quite excited herself. Oh, now she felt so happy. She entered into conversation with them, laughed, flirted, and even, after repeated invitations, drank a couple of ounces of red wine.

"You officers should come to town more often. It's so dreary around here. I'm simply dying of boredom."

"I can well imagine," sighed the doctor. "Such a peach . . . such a miracle of nature . . . and wasted on this wilderness!"

"Well, I'm afraid it's time for us to leave. It was very nice meeting you . . . very nice! How much do we owe you?"

"Twelve roubles, forty-eight kopecks," she said.

The lieutenant took a thick wallet out of his pocket, fumbled through a roll of bills, and then paid her.

"Your husband is sleeping soundly . . . he must be dreaming," he mumbled, as he squeezed her hand at parting.

"I don't like to listen to nonsense."

"What nonsense? On the contrary, it's not nonsense at all. Even Shakespeare says, 'Blessed is he who when he was young took advantage of his youth.'"

"Let go of my hand."

Finally, after some further conversation, the customers kissed her hand and hesitantly left the store as if wondering whether they had perhaps forgotten something.

The druggist's wife ran quickly into the bedroom and sat down beside the window again. She saw the doctor and the lieutenant leave the shop and walk slowly away for twenty paces or so. Then they stopped and began to whisper about something. About what? Her heart beat excitedly and her temples pounded fiercely, but why she didn't know. Her heart was beating as violently as if the two men whispering outside were settling her fate.

Five minutes later, the doctor left his friend and went off, but the lieutenant started to come back. He walked past the shop once, then again. . . . He stopped near the door and then took a few more steps. Finally, he timidly rang the bell.

"What is it? Who's there?" suddenly she

heard her husband's voice. " . . . They're ringing and you don't even hear it!" growled the druggist. "Some system we have around here!"

He got up, put on his bathrobe, and stumbled, half-asleep, into the shop.

"What do you want?" he asked the lieutenant.

"Give me . . . give me fifteen kopecks' worth of peppermint drops."

With endless wheezing, yawning, and dozing off as he stumbled about and bumped his knees against the counter, the druggist reached up and took the jar of candy from the shelf.

Two minutes later, the druggist's wife saw the lieutenant leave the drugstore, take a few steps, and then toss the peppermint drops on the dusty road. From around the corner came the doctor toward his friend. . . . They walked toward one another, waved their arms about, and disappeared into the morning mist.

"How unhappy I am," said the druggist's wife, casting a bitter glance at her husband, who was undressing rapidly in order to get back into bed. "Oh, how unhappy I am!" she repeated, suddenly shedding large, bitter tears. "And no one knows, no one knows. . . ."

"I left fifteen kopecks on the counter," muttered the druggist, pulling the blankets up over him. "Put it away in the cash drawer, would you?"

And all at once he fell back to sleep.

[1886]

For Thought

All the ingredients for a successful seduction seem to be present in this amusing tale of a bored young housewife who longs to have some excitement and romance enter her dreary existence. However, Chekhov, with his ruefully comic view of life, uses the irony of fate to frustrate his character's desire. The trigger for action in the story is made believable by the character contrast he establishes between the druggist and his wife and by the aggressive, opportunistic personalities of the two young officers. Along with this skillful characterization, Chekhov makes use of the dull, boring provincial setting of the story to help create a motivating atmosphere and mood conducive to the seduction motif. The attempt at seduction is foiled, not by the purposeful action of one of the characters, but by sheer chance.

For Discussion

1. How do the details of the setting help to establish the mood and the atmosphere of the story?
2. What character contrast is there between the druggist and his wife?
3. What conflict is established?
4. What tone does the moon imagery create?
5. How does the officers' conversation about the druggist serve to characterize them?
6. What is ironic about the conversation between the officers regarding the druggist's wife and for what does it prepare?
7. How does the phrase "clutching her dress at the neckline" characterize the wife and further the action?
8. How do the peppermint drops function as a central symbol?
9. What diversity within the repetition is there between the first purchase of peppermint drops and the second?
10. How do the physical and temperamental differences between the doctor and Obtyosoff help to maintain the comic tone of the story?
11. What part does chance play in the outcome of the story?

Anton Chekhov
The Lottery Ticket

Ivan Dmitritch, a middle-class man who lived with his family on an income of twelve hundred a year and was very well satisfied with his lot, sat down on the sofa after supper and began reading the newspaper.

"I forgot to look at the newspaper today," his wife said to him as she cleared the table. "Look and see whether the list of drawings is there."

"Yes, it is," said Ivan Dmitritch: "but hasn't your ticket lapsed?"

"No; I took the interest on Tuesday."

"What is the number?"

"Series 9,499, number 26."

"All right . . . we will look . . . 9,499 and 26."

Ivan Dmitritch had no faith in lottery luck, and would not, as a rule, have consented to look at the lists of winning numbers, but now, as he had nothing else to do and as the newspaper was before his eyes, he passed his finger downwards along the column of numbers. And immediately, as though in mockery of his scepticism, no further than the second line from the top, his eye was caught by the figure 9,499! Unable to believe his eyes, he hurriedly dropped the paper on his knees without looking to see the number of the ticket, and, just as though some one had given him a douche of cold water, he felt an agreeable chill in the pit of the stomach; tingling and terrible and sweet!

"Masha, 9,499 is there!" he said in a hollow voice.

His wife looked at his astonished and panic-stricken face, and realized that he was not joking.

"9,499?" she asked, turning pale and dropping the folded tablecloth on the table.

"Yes, yes . . . it really is there!"

"And the number of the ticket?"

"Oh, yes! There's the number of the ticket too. But stay . . . wait! No, I say! Anyway, the number of our series is there! Anyway, you understand. . . ."

Looking at his wife, Ivan Dmitritch gave a broad, senseless smile, like a baby when a bright object is shown it. His wife smiled too; it was as pleasant to her as to him that he only mentioned the series, and did not try to find out the number of the winning ticket. To torment and tantalize oneself with hopes of possible fortune is so sweet, so thrilling!

"It is our series," said Ivan Dmitritch, after a long silence. "So there is a probability that we have won. It's only a probability, but there it is!"

"Well, now look!"

"Wait a little. We have plenty of time to be disappointed. It's on the second line from the top, so the prize is seventy-five thousand. That's not money, but power, capital! And in a minute I shall look at the list, and there—26! Eh? I say, what if we really have won?"

The husband and wife began laughing and staring at one another in silence. The possibility of winning bewildered them; they could not have said, could not have dreamed, what they both needed that seventy-five thousand for, what they would buy, where they would go. They thought only of the figures 9,499 and 75,000 and pictured them in their imagination, while somehow they could not think of the happiness itself which was so possible.

Ivan Dmitritch, holding the paper in his hand, walked several times from corner to corner, and only when he had recovered from the first impression began dreaming a little.

"And if we have won," he said—"why, it will be a new life, it will be a transformation! The ticket is yours, but if it were mine I should, first of all, of course, spend twenty-five thousand on real property in the shape of an estate; ten thousand on immediate expenses, new furnishing . . . travelling . . . paying debts, and so on. . . . The other forty thousand I would put in the bank and get interest on it."

"Yes, an estate, that would be nice," said his wife, sitting down and dropping her hands in her lap.

"Somewhere in the Tula or Oryol provinces. . . . In the first place we shouldn't need a summer villa, and besides, it would always bring in an income."

And pictures came crowding on his imagination, each more gracious and poetical than the last. And in all these pictures he saw himself well fed, serene, healthy, felt warm, even hot! Here, after eating a summer soup, cold as ice, he lay on his back on the burning sand close to a stream or in the garden under a lime-tree. . . . It is hot. . . . His little boy and girl are crawling about near him, digging in the sand or catching ladybirds in the grass. He dozes sweetly, thinking of nothing, and feeling all over that he need not go to the office today, tomorrow, or the day after. Or, tired of lying still, he goes to the hayfield, or to the forest for mushrooms, or watches the peasants catching fish with a net. When the sun sets he takes a towel and soap and saunters to the bathingshed, where he undresses at his leisure, slowly rubs his bare chest with his hands, and goes into the water. And in the water, near the opaque soapy circles, little fish flit to and fro and green waterweeds nod their heads. After bathing there is tea with cream and milk rolls. . . . In the evening a walk or *vint* with the neighbors.

"Yes, it would be nice to buy an estate," said his wife, also dreaming, and from her face it was evident that she was enchanted by her thoughts.

Ivan Dmitritch pictured to himself autumn with its rains, its cold evenings, and its St. Martin's summer. At that season he would have to take longer walks about the garden and beside the river, so as to get thoroughly chilled, and then drink a big glass of vodka and eat a salted mushroom or a soused cucumber, and then—drink another. . . . The children would come running from the kitchen-garden, bringing a carrot and a radish smelling of fresh earth. . . . And then, he would lie stretched full length on the sofa, and in leisurely fashion turn over the pages of some illustrated magazine, or, covering his face with it and unbuttoning his waistcoat, give himself up to slumber.

The St. Martin's summer is followed by cloudy, gloomy weather. It rains day and night, the bare trees weep, the wind is damp and cold. The dogs, the horses, the fowls—all are wet, depressed, downcast. There is nowhere to walk; one can't go out for days together; one has to pace up and down the room, looking despondently at the grey window. It is dreary!

Ivan Dmitritch stopped and looked at his wife.

"I should go abroad, you know, Masha," he said.

And he began thinking how nice it would be in late autumn to go abroad somewhere to the South of France . . . to Italy . . . to India!

"I should certainly go abroad too," his wife said. "But look at the number of the ticket!"

"Wait, wait! . . ."

He walked about the room and went on thinking. It occurred to him: what if his wife really did go abroad? It is pleasant to travel alone, or in the society of light, careless women who live in the present, and not such as think and talk all the journey about nothing but their children, sigh, and tremble with dismay over every farthing. Ivan Dmitritch imagined his wife in the train with a multitude of parcels, baskets, and bags; she would be sighing over something, complaining that the train made her head ache, that she had spent so much money. . . . At the stations he would continually be having to run for boiling water, bread and butter. . . . She wouldn't have dinner because of its being too dear. . . .

"She would begrudge me every farthing," he thought, with a glance at his wife. "The lottery ticket is hers, not mine! Besides, what is the use of her going abroad? What does she want there? She would shut herself up in the hotel, and not let me out of her sight. . . . I know!"

And for the first time in his life his mind dwelt on the fact that his wife had grown elderly and plain, and that she was saturated through and through with the smell of cooking, while he was still young, fresh, and healthy, and might well have got married again.

"Of course, all that is silly nonsense," he thought: "but . . . why should she go abroad? What would she make of it? And yet she would go, of course. . . . I can fancy. . . . In reality it is all one to her, whether it is Naples or Klin. She would only be in my way. I should be dependent upon her. I can fancy how, like a regular woman, she will lock the money up as soon as she gets it. . . . She will look after her relations and grudge me every farthing."

Ivan Dmitritch thought of her relations. All those wretched brothers and sisters and aunts and uncles would come crawling about as soon as they heard of the winning ticket, would begin whining like beggars, and fawning upon them with oily, hypocritical smiles. Wretched, detestable people! If they were given anything, they would ask for more; while if they were refused, they would swear at them, slander them, and wish them every kind of misfortune.

Ivan Dmitritch remembered his own relations, and their faces, at which he had looked impartially in the past, struck him now as repulsive and hateful.

"They are such reptiles!" he thought.

And his wife's face, too, struck him as repulsive and hateful. Anger surged up in his heart against her, and he thought malignantly:

"She knows nothing about money, and so she is stingy. If she won it she would give me a hundred roubles, and put the rest away under lock and key."

And he looked at his wife, not with a smile now, but with hatred. She glanced at him too, and also with hatred and anger. She had her own daydreams, her own plans, her own reflections; she understood perfectly well what her husband's dreams were. She knew who would be the first to try to grab her winnings.

"It's very nice making daydreams at other people's expense!" is what her eyes expressed. "No, don't you dare!"

Her husband understood her look;

hatred began stirring again in his breast, and in order to annoy his wife he glanced quickly, to spite her, at the fourth page on the newspaper and read out triumphantly:

"Series 9,499, number 46! Not 26!"

Hatred and hope both disappeared at once, and it began immediately to seem to Ivan Dmitritch and his wife that their rooms were dark and small and low-pitched, that the supper they had been eating was not doing them good, but lying heavy on their stomachs, that the evenings were long and wearisome. . . .

"What the devil's the meaning of it?" said Ivan Dmitritch, beginning to be ill-humored. "Wherever one steps there are bits of paper under one's feet, crumbs, husks. The rooms are never swept! One is simply forced to go out. Damnation take my soul entirely! I shall go and hang myself on the first aspen-tree!"

[1887]

For Thought

In this vignette focusing on a comic reversal of intention, Chekhov illuminates the monotonous existence of a middle-class couple by adopting a mildly satiric and ironic tone in a situation that takes only seconds to develop and unravel. He creates two different moods in the mind of his protagonist to generate the conflict, the complication, the reversal, the denouement, and the insight that arise out of the inciting action of merely checking something in the evening newspaper.

For Discussion

1. What is the mood at the beginning of the story? At the end? What details establish the mood?
2. What is the inciting factor; the complication; the crisis; the climax; the resolution of the story?
3. Given the situation as it is, how is the point of view Chekhov uses appropriate and well chosen?
4. How is Ivan Dmitritch characterized by the fantasies he entertains?
5. What comment is Chekhov making on human nature and the institution of marriage?

Walter Van Tilburg Clark
The Portable Phonograph

The red sunset, with narrow black cloud strips like threats across it, lay on the curved horizon of the prairie. The air was still and cold, and in it settled the mute darkness and greater cold of night. High in the air there was wind, for through the veil of the dusk the clouds could be seen gliding rapidly south and changing shapes. A queer sensation of torment, of two-sided, unpredictable nature, arose from the stillness of the earth air beneath the violence of the upper air. Out of the sunset, through the dead, matted grass and isolated weed stalks of the prairie, crept the narrow and deeply rutted remains of a road. In the road, in places, there were crusts of shallow, brittle ice. There were little islands of an old oiled pavement in the road too, but most of it was mud, now frozen rigid. The frozen mud still bore the toothed impress of great tanks, and a wanderer on the neighboring undulations might have stumbled, in this light, into large, partially filled-in and weed-grown cavities, their banks channeled and beginning to spread into badlands. These pits were such as might have been made by falling meteors, but they were not. They were the scars of gigantic bombs, their rawness already made a little natural by rain, seed, and time. Along the road there were rakish remnants of fence. There was also, just visible, one portion of tangled and multiple barbed wire still erect, behind which was a shelving ditch with small caves, now very quiet and empty, at intervals in its back wall. Otherwise there was no structure or remnant of a structure visible over the dome of the darkling earth, but only, in sheltered hollows, the darker shadows of young trees trying again.

Under the wuthering arch of the high wind a V of wild geese fled south. The rush of their pinions sounded briefly, and the faint, plaintive notes of their expeditionary talk. Then they left a still greater vacancy. There was the smell and expectation of snow, as there is likely to be when the wild geese fly south. From the remote distance, towards the red sky, came faintly the protracted howl and quick yap-yap of a prairie wolf.

North of the road, perhaps a hundred yards, lay the parallel and deeply intrenched course of a small creek, lined with leafless alders and willows. The creek was already silent under ice. Into the bank above it was dug a sort of cell, with a single opening, like the mouth of a mine tunnel. Within the cell there was a little red of fire, which showed dully through the opening, like a reflection or a deception of the imagination. The light came from the chary burning of four blocks of poorly aged peat, which gave off a petty warmth and much acrid smoke. But the precious remnants of wood, old fenceposts and timbers from the long-deserted dugouts, had to be saved for the real cold, for the time when a man's breath blew white, the moisture in his nostrils stiffened at once when he stepped out, and the expansive blizzards paraded for days over the vast open, swirling and settling and thickening, till the dawn of the cleared day when the sky was thin blue-green and the terrible cold, in which a man could not live for three hours unwarmed, lay over the uniformly drifted swell of the plain.

Around the smoldering peat four men were seated cross-legged. Behind them, traversed by their shadows, was the earth bench, with two old and dirty army blankets, where the owner of the cell slept. In a niche in the opposite wall were a few tin utensils which caught the glint of the coals. The host was rewrapping in a piece of daubed burlap four fine, leather-bound books. He worked slowly and very carefully and at last tied the bundle securely with a piece of grass-woven cord. The other three looked intently upon the process, as if a great significance lay in it. As the host tied the cord he spoke. He was an old man, his long, matted beard and hair gray to nearly white. The shadows made his brows and cheekbones appear gnarled, his eyes and cheeks deeply sunken. His big hands, rough with frost and swollen by rheumatism, were awkward but gentle at their task. He was like a prehistoric priest performing a fateful ceremonial rite. Also his voice had in it a suitable quality of deep, reverent despair, yet perhaps at the moment a sharpness of selfish satisfaction.

"When I perceived what was happening," he said, "I told myself, 'It is the end. I cannot take much; I will take these.'"

"Perhaps I was impractical," he continued. "But for myself, I do not regret, and what do we know of those who will come after us? We are the doddering remnant of a race of mechanical fools. I have saved what I love; the soul of what was good in us is here; perhaps the new ones will make a strong enough beginning not to fall behind when they become clever."

He rose with slow pain and placed the wrapped volumes in the niche with his utensils. The others watched him with the same ritualistic gaze.

"Shakespeare, the Bible, *Moby Dick*, the *Divine Comedy*," one of them said softly, "You might have done worse, much worse."

"You will have a little soul left until you die," said another harshly. "That is more than is true of us. My brain becomes thick, like my hands." He held the big, battered hands, with their black nails, in the glow to be seen.

"I want paper to write on," he said. "And there is none."

The fourth man said nothing. He sat in the shadow farthest from the fire, and sometimes his body jerked in its rags from the cold. Although he was still young, he was sick and coughed often. Writing implied a greater future than he now felt able to consider.

The old man seated himself laboriously and reached out, groaning at the movement, to put another block of peat on the fire. With bowed heads and averted eyes his three guests acknowledged his magnanimity.

"We thank you, Dr. Jenkins, for the reading," said the man who had named the books.

They seemed then to be waiting for

something. Dr. Jenkins understood but was loath to comply. In an ordinary moment he would have said nothing. But the words of *The Tempest*, which he had been reading, and the religious attention of the three made this an unusual occasion.

"You wish to hear the phonograph," he said grudgingly.

The two middle-aged men stared into the fire, unable to formulate and expose the enormity of their desire.

The young man, however, said anxiously, between suppressed coughs, "Oh, please," like an excited child.

The old man rose again in his difficult way and went to the back of the cell. He returned and placed tenderly upon the packed floor, where the firelight might fall upon it, an old portable phonograph in a black case. He smoothed the top with his hand and then opened it. The lovely green-felt-covered disk became visible.

"I have been using thorns as needles," he said. "But tonight, because we have a musician among us"—he bent his head to the young man, almost invisible in the shadow—"I will use a steel needle. There are only three left."

The two middle-aged men stared at him in speechless adoration. The one with the big hands, who wanted to write, moved his lips, but the whisper was not audible.

"Oh, don't," cried the young man, as if he were hurt. "The thorns will do beautifully."

"No," the old man said. "I have become accustomed to the thorns, but they are not really good. For you, my young friend, we will have good music tonight."

"After all," he added generously, and beginning to wind the phonograph, which creaked, "they can't last forever."

"No, nor we," the man who needed to write said harshly. "The needle, by all means."

"Oh, thanks," said the young man. "Thanks," he said again in a low, excited voice, and then stifled his coughing with a bowed head.

"The records, though," said the old man when he had finished winding, "are a different matter. Already they are very worn. I do not play them more than once a week. One, once a week, that is what I allow myself.

"More than a week I cannot stand it; not to hear them," he apologized.

"No, how could you?" cried the young man. "And with them here like this."

"A man can stand anything," said the man who wanted to write, in his harsh, antagonistic voice.

"Please, the music," said the young man.

"Only the one," said the old man. "In the long run, we will remember more that way."

He had a dozen records with luxuriant gold and red seals. Even in that light the others could see that the threads of the records were becoming worn. Slowly he read out the titles and the tremendous, dead names of the composers and the artists and the orchestras. The three worked upon the names in their minds, carefully. It was difficult to select from such a wealth what they would at once most like to remember. Finally the man who wanted to write named Gershwin's "New York."

"Oh, no!" cried the sick young man, and then could say nothing more because he had to cough. The others understood him, and the harsh man withdrew his selection and waited for the musician to choose.

The musician begged Dr. Jenkins to read the titles again, very slowly, so that he could remember the sounds. While they were read he lay back against the wall, his eyes closed, his thin, horny hand pulling at his light beard, and listened to the voices and the orchestras and the single instruments in his mind.

When the reading was done he spoke despairingly. "I have forgotten," he complained. "I cannot hear them clearly.

"There are things missing," he explained.

"I know," said Dr. Jenkins. "I thought

that I knew all of Shelley by heart. I should have brought Shelley."

"That's more soul than we can use," said the harsh man. "*Moby Dick* is better.

"By God, we can understand that," he emphasized.

The Doctor nodded.

"Still," said the man who had admired the books, "we need the absolute if we are to keep a grasp on anything."

"Anything but these sticks and peat clods and rabbit snares," he said bitterly.

"Shelley desired an ultimate absolute," said the harsh man. "It's too much," he said. "It's no good; no earthly good."

The musician selected a Debussy nocturne. The others considered and approved. They rose to their knees to watch the Doctor prepare for the playing, so that they appeared to be actually in an attitude of worship. The peat glow showed the thinness of their bearded faces, and the deep lines in them, and revealed the condition of their garments. The other two continued to kneel as the old man carefully lowered the needle onto the spinning disk, but the musician suddenly drew back against the wall again, with his knees up, and buried his face in his hands.

At the first notes of the piano the listeners were startled. They stared at each other. Even the musician lifted his head in amazement but then quickly bowed it again, strainingly, as if he were suffering from a pain he might not be able to endure. They were all listening deeply, without movement. The wet, blue-green notes tinkled forth from the old machine and were individual, delectable presences in the cell. The individual, delectable presences swept into a sudden tide of unbearably beautiful dissonance and then continued fully the swelling and ebbing of that tide, the dissonant inpourings, and the resolutions, and the diminishments, and the little, quiet wavelets of interlude lapping between. Every sound was piercing and singularly sweet. In all the men except the musician there occurred rapid sequences of tragically heightened recollection. He heard nothing but what was there. At the final, whispering disappearance, but moving quietly so that the others would not hear him and look at him, he let his head fall back in agony, as if it were drawn there by the hair, and clenched the fingers of one hand over his teeth. He sat that way while the others were silent and until they began to breathe again normally. His drawn-up legs were trembling violently.

Quickly Dr. Jenkins lifted the needle off, to save it and not to spoil the recollection with scraping. When he had stopped the whirling of the sacred disk he courteously left the phonograph open and by the fire, in sight.

The others, however, understood. The musician rose last, but then abruptly, and went quickly out at the door without saying anything. The others stopped at the door and gave their thanks in low voices. The Doctor nodded magnificently.

"Come again," he invited, "in a week. We will have the 'New York.'"

When the two had gone together, out towards the rimed road, he stood in the entrance, peering and listening. At first there was only the resonant boom of the wind overhead, and then far over the dome of the dead, dark plain the wolf cry lamenting. In the rifts of clouds the Doctor saw four stars flying. It impressed the Doctor that one of them had just been obscured by the beginning of a flying cloud at the very moment he heard what he had been listening for, a sound of suppressed coughing. It was not near by, however. He believed that down against the pale alders he could see the moving shadow.

With nervous hands he lowered the piece of canvas which served as his door and pegged it at the bottom. Then quickly and quietly, looking at the piece of canvas frequently, he slipped the records into the case, snapped the lid shut, and carried the phonograph to his couch. There, pausing often to stare at the canvas and listen, he dug earth from the wall and disclosed a piece of board. Behind this there was a deep hole in the wall, into which he put the phonograph. After a moment's consideration he went over and reached down his bundle of books and inserted it also. Then, guardedly, he once more sealed up the hole with the board and the earth. He also changed his blankets and the grass-stuffed sack which served as a pillow, so that he could lie facing the entrance. After carefully placing two more blocks of peat upon the fire he stood for a long time watching the stretched canvas, but it seemed to billow naturally with the first gusts of a lowering wind. At last he prayed, and got in under his blankets, and closed his smoke-smarting eyes. On the inside of the bed, next the wall, he could feel with his hand the comfortable piece of lead pipe.

[1941]

For Thought

With "The Portable Phonograph," Clark has written a science-fiction narrative of the days following a great war. His nearly anonymous, flat characters have little to live for. Despite a desperate shortage of necessities such as food, clothing, and shelter, the survivors treasure a few musical and literary masterpieces from the prewar past. The suggested theme is that neither technology nor art is sufficient to avert the human tendency toward individual or mass violence. With the use of the objective point of view, Clark functions as the "camera-eye," abstaining from judgmental comments, relying, instead, on the selective use of language and images to serve as a vehicle of interpretation.

For Discussion

1. At what time and place is the setting of the story?
2. What ironic contrasts emerge between civilization and nature?
3. What values and ideas do the characters represent?
4. How is the value placed on literary and musical masterpieces ironic?

Samuel Clemens (Mark Twain)

The Notorious Jumping Frog of Calaveras County

In compliance with the request of a friend of mine, who wrote me from the East, I called on good-natured, garrulous old Simon Wheeler, and inquired about my friend's friend, Leonidas W. Smiley, as requested to do, and I hereunto append the result. I have a lurking suspicion that *Leonidas* W. Smiley is a myth; that my friend never knew such a personage; and that he only conjectured that if I asked old Wheeler about him, it would remind him of his infamous *Jim* Smiley, and he would go to work and bore me to death with some exasperating reminiscence of him as long and as tedious as it should be useless to me. If that was the design, it succeeded.

I found Simon Wheeler dozing comfortably by the bar-room stove of the dilapidated tavern in the decayed mining camp of Angel's, and I noticed that he was fat and bald-headed, and had an expression of winning gentleness and simplicity upon his tranquil countenance. He roused up, and gave me good day. I told him that a friend of mine had commissioned me to make some inquiries about a cherished companion of his boyhood named *Leonidas* W. Smiley—*Rev. Leonidas* W. Smiley, a young minister of the Gospel, who he had heard was at one time a resident of Angel's Camp. I added that if Mr. Wheeler could tell me anything about this Rev. Leonidas W. Smiley, I would feel under many obligations to him.

Simon Wheeler backed me into a corner and blockaded me there with his chair, and then sat down and reeled off the monotonous narrative which follows this paragraph. He never smiled, he never frowned, he never changed his voice from the gentle-flowing key to which he tuned his initial sentence, he never betrayed the slightest suspicion of enthusiasm; but all through the interminable narrative there ran a vein of impressive earnestness and sincerity, which showed me plainly that, so far from his imagining that there was anything ridiculous or funny about his story, he regarded it as a really important matter, and admired its two heroes as men of transcendent genius in *finesse*. I let him go on his own way, and never interrupted him once.

SOURCE: "The Notorious Jumping Frog of Calaveras County" by Samuel Clemens. Originally published as "Jim Smiley and His Jumping Frog" in the *New York Saturday Press*, November 1865.

"Rev. Leonidas W. H'm, Reverend Le—well, there was a feller here once by the name of *Jim* Smiley, in the winter of '49—or maybe it was the spring of '50—I don't recollect exactly, somehow, though what makes me think it was one or the other is because I remember the big flume warn't finished when he first came to the camp; but anyway, he was the curiousest man about always betting on anything that turned up you ever see, if he could get anybody to bet on the other side; and if he couldn't he'd change sides. Any way that suited the other man would suit *him*—any way just so's he got a bet, *he* was satisfied. But still he was lucky, uncommon lucky; he most always come out winner. He was always ready and laying for a chance; there couldn't be no solit'ry thing mentioned but that feller'd offer to bet on it, and take ary side you please, as I was just telling you. If there was a horse-race, you'd find him flush or you'd find him busted at the end of it; if there was a dog-fight, he'd bet on it; if there was a cat-fight, he'd bet on it; if there was a chicken-fight, he'd bet on it; why, if there was two birds setting on a fence, he would bet you which one would fly first; or if there was a camp-meeting, he would be there reg'lar to bet on Parson Walker, which he judged to be the best exhorter about here, and so he was too, and a good man. If he even see a straddle-bug start to anywheres, he would bet you how long it would take him to get to—to wherever he was going to, and if you took him up, he would foller that straddle-bug to Mexico but what he would find out where he was bound for and how long he was on the road. Lots of the boys here has seen that Smiley, and can tell you about him. Why, it never made no difference to *him*—he'd bet on *any* thing—the dangdest feller. Parson Walker's wife laid very sick once, for a good while, and it seemed as if they warn't going to save her; but one morning he come in, and Smiley up and asked him how she was, and he said she was considerable better—thank the Lord for his inf'nite mercy—and coming on so smart that with the blessing of Prov'dence she'd get well yet; and Smiley, before he thought, says, 'Well, I'll resk two-and-a-half she don't anyway.'

"Thish-yer Smiley had a mare—the boys called her fifteen-minute nag, but that was only in fun, you know, because of course she was faster than that—and he used to win money on that horse, for all she was so slow and always had the asthma, or the distemper, or the consumption, or something of that kind. They used to give her two or three hundred yards' start, and then pass her under way; but always at the fag end of the race she'd get excited and desperate like, and come cavorting and straddling up, and scattering her legs around limber, sometimes in the air, and sometimes out to one side among the fences, and kicking up m-o-r-e dust and raising m-o-r-e racket with her coughing and sneezing and blowing her nose—and *always* fetch up at the stand just about a neck ahead, as near as you could cipher it down.

"And he had a little small bull-pup, that to look at him you'd think he warn't worth a cent but to set around and look ornery and lay for a chance to steal something. But as soon as money was up on him he was a different dog; his under-jaw'd begin to stick out like the fo'castle of a steamboat, and his teeth would uncover and shine like the furnaces. And a dog might tackle him and bully-rag him, and bite him, and throw him over his shoulder two or three times, and Andrew Jackson—which was the name of the pup—Andrew Jackson would never let on but what *he* was satisfied, and hadn't expected nothing else—and the bets being doubled and doubled on the other side all the time, till the money was all up; and then all of a sudden he would grab that other dog jest by the j'int of his hind leg and freeze to it—not chaw, you understand, but only just grip and hang on till they throwed up the sponge, if it was a year. Smiley always come out winner on that pup, till he harnessed a dog once that didn't have no hind legs, because they'd been sawed off in a circular saw, and when the thing had gone along far enough, and the money was all up, and he come to make a snatch for his pet holt, he see in a minute how he'd been imposed on, and how the other dog had him in the door, so to speak, and he 'peared surprised, and then he looked sorter discouraged-like, and didn't try no more to win the fight, and so he got shucked out bad. He give Smiley a look, as much as to say his heart was broke, and it was *his* fault, for putting up a dog that hadn't no hind legs for him to take holt of, which was his main dependence in a fight, and then be limped off a piece and laid down and died. It was a good pup, was that Andrew Jackson, and would have made a name for hisself if he'd lived, for the stuff was in him and he had genius—I know it, because he hadn't no opportunities to speak of, and it don't stand to reason that a dog could make such a fight as he could under them circumstances if he hadn't no talent. It always makes me feel sorry when I think of that last fight of his'n, and the way it turned out.

"Well, thish-yer Smiley had rat-tarriers, and chicken cocks, and tom-cats and all them kind of things, till you couldn' rest, and you couldn't fetch nothing for him to bet on but he'd match you. He ketched a frog one day, and took him home, and said he cal'lated to educate him; and so he never done nothing for three months but set in his back yard and learn that frog to jump. And you bet you he *did* learn him, too. He'd give him a little punch behind, and the next minute you'd see that frog whirling in the air like a doughnut—see him turn one summerset, or maybe a couple, if he got a good start, and come down flat-footed and all right, like a cat. He got him up so in the matter of ketching flies, and kep' him in practice so constant, that he'd nail a fly every time as fur as he could see him. Smiley said all a frog wanted was education, and he could do 'most anything—and I believe him. Why, I've seen him set Dan'l Webster down here on this floor—Dan'l Webster was the name of the frog—and sing out, 'Flies, Dan'l, flies!' and quicker'n you could wink he'd spring straight up and snake a fly off'n the counter there, and flop down on the floor ag'in as solid as a gob of mud, and fall to scratching the side of his head with his hind foot as indifferent as if he hadn't no idea he'd been doin' any more'n any frog might do. You never see a frog so modest and straightfor'ard as he was, for all he was so gifted. And when it come to fair and square jumping on a dead level, he could get over more ground at one straddle than any animal of his breed you ever see. Jumping on a dead level was his strong suit, you understand; and when it come to that, Smiley would ante up money on him as long as he had a red. Smiley was monstrous proud of his frog, and well he might be, for fellers that had traveled and been everywheres, all said he laid over any frog that ever *they* see.

"Well, Smiley kep' the beast in a little lattice box, and he used to fetch him downtown sometimes and lay for a bet. One day a feller—a stranger in the camp, he was—come acrost him with his box, and says:

"'What might it be that you've got in the box?'

"And Smiley says, sorter indifferent-like, 'It might be a parrot, or it might be a canary, maybe, but it ain't—it's only just a frog.'

"And the feller took it, and looked at it careful and turned it round this way and that, and says, 'H'm—so 'tis. Well, what's *he* good for?'

"'Well,' Smiley says, easy and careless, 'he's good enough for *one* thing, I should judge—he can outjump any frog in Calaveras County.'

"The feller took the box again, and took another long, particular look, and give it back to Smiley, and says, very deliberate, 'Well,' he says, 'I don't see no p'ints about that frog that's any better'n any *other* frog.'

"'Maybe you don't,' Smiley says. 'Maybe you understand frogs and maybe you don't understand 'em; maybe you've had experience, and maybe you ain't only a amature, as it were. Anyways, I've got *my* opinion, and I'll resk forty dollars that he can outjump any frog in Calaveras County.'

"And the feller studied a minute, and then says, kinder sadlike 'Well, I'm only a stranger here, and I ain't got no frog; but if I had a frog, I'd bet you.'

"And then Smiley says, 'That's all right—that's all right—if you'll hold my box a minute, I'll go and get you a frog.' And so the feller took the box, and put up his forty dollars along with Smiley's, and set down to wait.

"So he set there a good while thinking and thinking to himself, and then he got the frog out and prized his mouth open and took a teaspoon and filled him full of quail-shot—filled him pretty near up to his chin—and set him on the floor. Smiley he went to the swamp and slopped around in the mud for a long time, and finally he ketched a frog, and fetched him in, and give him to this feller, and says:

"'Now, if you're ready, set him alongside of Dan'l, with his fore paws just even with Dan'l's, and I'll give the word.' Then he says, 'One—two—three—*git!*' and him and the feller touched up the frogs from behind, and the new frog hopped off lively, but Dan'l give a heave, and hysted up his shoulders—so—like a Frenchman, but it warn't no use—he couldn't budge; he was planted as solid as a church, and he couldn't no more stir than if he was anchored out. Smiley was a good deal surprised, and he was disgusted too, but he didn't have no idea what the matter was, of course.

"The feller took the money and started away; and when he was going out at the door, he sorter jerked his thumb over his shoulder—so—at Dan'l, and says again, very deliberate, 'Well,' he says, 'I don't see no p'ints about that frog that's any better'n any other frog.'

"Smiley he stood scratching his head and looking down at Dan'l a long time, and at last he says, 'I do wonder what in the nation that frog throw'd off for—I wonder if there ain't something the matter with him—he 'pears to look mighty baggy, somehow.' And he ketched Dan'l by the nape of the neck, and hefted him, and says, 'Why blame my cats if he don't weigh five pound!' and turned him upside down and he belched out a double handful of shot. And then he see how it was, and he was the maddest man—he set the frog down and took out after that feller, but he never ketched him. And—"

[Here Simon Wheeler heard his name called from the front yard, and got up to see what was wanted.] And turning to me as he moved away, he said: "Just set where you are, stranger, and rest easy—I ain't going to be gone a second."

But, by your leave, I did not think that a continuation of the history of the enterprising vagabond *Jim* Smiley would be likely to afford me much information concerning the Rev. *Leonidas* W. Smiley, and so I started away.

At the door I met the sociable Wheeler returning, and he buttonholed me and recommenced:

"Well, thish-yer Smiley had a yaller one-eyed cow that didn't have no tail, only just a short stump like a bannanner, and—"

However, lacking both time and inclination, I did not wait to hear about the afflicted cow, but took my leave.

[1865]

For Thought

"The Notorious Jumping Frog of Calaveras County" is an episodic and comic tall tale. The seriousness of the narrator stands in conspicuous contrast to the nonsense of the characters. By setting the story in a mining community during the mid-nineteenth century,

Clemens gives the story a rambling Western flavor that is almost mythic. The author has no serious moral or philosophical message to convey. Yet, the story revolves around fate and the unpredictability of life in an unsettled time and place.

For Discussion

1. What contrast does Clemens create between the initial narrator and Simon Wheeler?
2. What do all the anecdotes told by Wheeler have in common?
3. What traits of oral speech emerge in Wheeler's narration? How do they reveal the man himself?
4. How is the frog Dan'l Webster humanized?
5. What universal traits of human nature are suggested by the story?
6. What ironies or comic contradictions emerge from the story?

Joseph Conrad
The Tale

Outside the large single window the crepuscular light was dying out slowly in a great square gleam without colour, framed rigidly in the gathering shades of the room.

It was a long room. The irresistible tide of the night ran into the most distant part of it, where the whispering of a man's voice, passionately interrupted and passionately renewed, seemed to plead against the answering murmurs of infinite sadness.

At last no answering murmur came. His movement when he rose slowly from his knees by the side of the deep, shadowy couch holding the shadowy suggestion of a reclining woman revealed him tall under the low ceiling, and sombre all over except for the crude discord of the white collar under the shape of his head and the faint, minute spark of a brass button here and there on his uniform.

He stood over her a moment, masculine and mysterious in his immobility, before he sat down on a chair near by. He could see only the faint oval of her upturned face and, extended on her black dress, her pale hands, a moment before abandoned to his kisses and now as if too weary to move.

He dared not make a sound, shrinking as a man would do from the prosaic necessities of existence. As usual, it was the woman who had the courage. Her voice was heard first—almost conventional while her being vibrated yet with conflicting emotions.

"Tell me something," she said.

The darkness hid his surprise and then his smile. Had he not just said to her everything worth saying in the world—and that not for the first time!

"What am I to tell you?" he asked, in a voice creditably steady. He was beginning to feel grateful to her for that something final in her tone which had eased the strain.

"Why not tell me a tale?"

"A tale!" He was really amazed.

"Yes. Why not?"

These words came with a slight petulance, the hint of a loved woman's capricious will, which is capricious only because it feels itself to be a law, embarrassing sometimes and always difficult to elude.

"Why not?" he repeated, with a slightly mocking accent, as though he had been asked to give her the moon. But now he was feeling a little angry with her for that feminine mobility that slips out of an emotion as easily as out of a splendid gown.

He heard her say, a little unsteadily with a sort of fluttering intonation which made him think suddenly of a butterfly's flight:

"You used to tell—your—your simple and—and professional—tales very well at one time. Or well enough to interest me. You had a—a sort of art—in the days—the days before the war."

"Really?" he said, with involuntary gloom. "But now, you see, the war is going on," he continued in such a dead, equable tone that she felt a slight chill fall over her shoulders. And yet she persisted. For there's nothing more unswerving in the world than a woman's caprice.

"It could be a tale not of this world," she explained.

"You want a tale of the other, the better world?" he asked, with a matter-of-fact surprise. "You must evoke for that task those who have already gone there."

"No. I don't mean that. I mean another—some other—world. In the universe—not in heaven."

"I am relieved. But you forget that I have only five days' leave."

"Yes. And I've also taken a five days' leave from my duties."

"I like that word."

"What word?"

"Duty."

"It is horrible—sometimes."

"Oh, that's because you think it's narrow. But it isn't. It contains infinities, and—and so—"

"What is this jargon?"

He disregarded the interjected scorn. "An infinity of absolution, for instance," he continued. "But as to this 'another world'—who's going to look for it and for the tale that is in it?"

"You," she said, with a strange, almost rough, sweetness of assertion.

He made a shadowy movement of assent in his chair, the irony of which not even the gathered darkness could render mysterious.

"As you will. In that world, then, there was once upon a time a Commanding Officer and a Northman. Put in the capitals, please, because they had no other names. It was a world of seas and continents and islands—"

"Like the earth," she murmured, bitterly.

"Yes. What else could you expect from sending a man made of our common, tormented clay on a voyage of discovery? What else could he find? What else could you understand or care for, or feel the existence of even? There was comedy in it, and slaughter."

"Always like the earth," she murmured.

"Always. And since I could find in the universe only what was deeply rooted in the fibres of my being there was love in it, too. But we won't talk of that."

"No. We won't," she said, in a neutral tone which concealed perfectly her relief—or her disappointment. Then, after a pause she added: "It's going to be a comic story."

"Well—" he paused, too. "Yes. In a way. In a very grim way. It will be human, and, as you know, comedy is but a matter of the visual angle. And it won't be a noisy story. All the long guns in it will be dumb—as dumb as so many telescopes."

"Ah, there are guns in it, then! And may I ask—where?"

"Afloat. You remember that the world of which we speak had its seas. A war was going on in it. It was a funny world and terribly in earnest. Its war was being carried on over the land, over the water, under the water, up in the air, and even under the ground. And many young men in it, mostly in wardrooms and messrooms, used to say to each other—pardon the unparliamentary word—they used to say, 'It's a damned bad war, but it's better than no war at all.' Sounds flippant, doesn't it?"

He heard a nervous, impatient sigh in the depths of the couch while he went on without a pause.

"And yet there is more in it than meets the eye. I mean more wisdom. Flippancy, like comedy, is but a matter of visual first-impression. That world was not very wise. But there was in it a certain amount of common working sagacity. That, however, was mostly worked by the neutrals in diverse ways, public and private, which had to be watched; watched by acute minds and also by actual sharp eyes. They had to be very sharp indeed, too, I assure you."

"I can imagine," she murmured, appreciatively.

"What is there that you can't imagine?" he pronounced, soberly. "You have the world in you. But let us go back to our commanding officer, who, of course, commanded a ship of a sort. My tales if often professional (as you remarked just now) have never been technical. So I'll just tell you that the ship was of a very ornamental sort once, with lots of grace and elegance and luxury about her. Yes, once! She was like a pretty woman who had suddenly put on a suit of sackcloth and stuck revolvers in her belt. But she floated lightly, she moved nimbly, she was quite good enough."

"That was the opinion of the commanding officer?" said the voice from the couch.

"It was. He used to be sent out with her along certain coasts to see—what he could see. Just that. And sometimes he had some preliminary information to help him, and sometimes he had not. And it was all one, really. It was about as useful as information trying to convey the locality and intentions of a cloud, of a phantom taking shape here and there and impossible to seize, would have been.

"It was in the early days of the war. What at first used to amaze the commanding officer was the unchanged face of the waters, with its familiar expression, neither more friendly nor more hostile. On fine days the sun strikes sparks upon the blue; here and there a peaceful smudge of smoke hangs in the distance, and it is impossible to believe that the familiar clear horizon traces the limit of one great circular ambush.

"Yes, it is impossible to believe, till some day you see a ship not your own ship (that isn't so impressive), but some ship in company, blow up all of a sudden and plop under almost before you know what has happened to her. Then you begin to believe. Henceforth you go out for the work to see—what you can see, and you keep on at it with the conviction that some day you will die from something you have not seen. One envies the soldiers at the end of the day, wiping the sweat and blood from their faces, counting the dead fallen to their hands, looking at the devastated fields, the torn earth that seems to suffer and bleed with them. One does, really. The final brutality of it—the taste of primitive passion—the ferocious frankness of the blow struck with one's hand—the direct call and the straight response. Well, the sea gave you nothing of that, and seemed to pretend that there was nothing the matter with the world."

She interrupted, stirring a little.

"Oh yes. Sincerity—frankness—passion—three words of your gospel. Don't I know them!"

"Think! Isn't it ours—believed in common?" he asked, anxiously, yet without expecting an answer, and went on at once: "Such were the feelings of the commanding officer. When the night came trailing over the sea, hiding what looked like the hypocrisy of an old friend, it was a relief. The night blinds you frankly—and there are circumstances when the sunlight may grow as odious to one as falsehood itself. Night is all right.

"At night the commanding officer could let his thoughts get away—I won't tell you where. Somewhere where there was no choice but between truth and death. But thick weather, though it blinded one, brought no such relief. Mist is deceitful, the dead luminosity of the fog is irritating. It seems that you *ought* to see.

"One gloomy, nasty day the ship was steaming along her beat in sight of a rocky, dangerous coast that stood out intensely black like an India-ink drawing on gray paper. Presently the second in command spoke to his chief. He thought he saw something on the water, to seaward. Small wreckage, perhaps.

"'But there shouldn't be any wreckage here, sir,' he remarked.

"'No,' said the commanding officer. 'The last reported submarined ships were sunk a long way to the westward. But one never knows. There may have been others since then not reported nor seen. Gone with all hands.'

"That was how it began. The ship's course was altered to pass the object close; for it was necessary to have a good look at what one could see. Close, but without touching; for it was not advisable to come in contact with objects of any form whatever floating casually about. Close, but without stopping or even diminishing speed; for in those times it was not prudent to linger on any particular spot, even for a moment. I may tell you at once that the object was not dangerous in itself. No use in describing it. It may have been nothing more remarkable than, say, a barrel of a certain shape and colour. But it was significant.

"The smooth bow-wave hove it up as if for a closer inspection, and then the ship, brought again to her course, turned her back on it with indifference, while twenty pairs of eyes on her deck stared in all directions trying to see—what they could see.

"The commanding officer and his second in command discussed the object with understanding. It appeared to them to be not so much a proof of the sagacity as of the activity of certain neutrals. This activity had in many cases taken the form of replenishing the stores of certain submarines at sea. This was generally believed, if not absolutely known. But the very nature of things in those early days pointed that way. The object, looked at closely and turned away from with apparent indifference, put it beyond doubt that something of the sort had been done somewhere in the neighbourhood.

"The object in itself was more than suspect. But the fact of its being left in evidence roused other suspicions. Was it the result of some deep and devilish purpose? As to that all speculation soon appeared to be a vain thing. Finally the two officers came to the conclusion that it was left there most likely by accident, complicated possibly by some unforseen necessity; such, perhaps, as the sudden need to get away quickly from the spot, or something of that kind.

"Their discussion had been carried on in curt, weighty phrases, separated by long, thoughtful silences. And all the time their eyes roamed about the horizon in an everlasting, almost mechanical effort of vigilance. The younger man summed up grimly:

"'Well, it's evidence. That's what this is. Evidence of what we were pretty certain of before. And plain, too.'

"'And much good it will do to us,' retorted the commanding officer. 'The parties are miles away; the submarine, devil only knows where, ready to kill; and the noble neutral slipping away to the eastward, ready to lie!'

"The second in command laughed a little at the tone. But he guessed that the neutral wouldn't even have to lie very much. Fellows like that, unless caught in the very act, felt themselves pretty safe. They could afford to chuckle. That fellow was probably chuckling to himself. It's very possible he had been before at the game and didn't care a rap for the bit of evidence left behind. It was a game in which practice made one bold and successful, too.

"And again he laughed faintly. But his commanding officer was in revolt against the murderous stealthiness of methods and the atrocious callousness of complicities that seemed to taint the very source of men's deep emotions and noblest activities; to corrupt their imagination which builds up the final conceptions of life and death. He suffered—"

The voice from the sofa interrupted the narrator.

"How well I can understand that in him!"

He bent forward slightly.

"Yes. I, too. Everything should be open in love and war. Open as the day, since both are the call of an ideal which it is so easy, so terribly easy, to degrade in the name of Victory."

He paused; then went on:

"I don't know that the commanding officer delved so deep as that into his feelings. But he did suffer from them—a sort of disenchanted sadness. It is possible, even, that he suspected himself of folly. Man is various. But he had no time for much introspection, because from the southwest a wall of fog had advanced upon his ship. Great convolutions of vapours flew over, swirling about masts and funnel, which looked as if they were beginning to melt. Then they vanished.

"The ship was stopped, all sounds ceased, and the very fog became motionless, growing denser and as if solid in its amazing dumb immobility. The men at their stations lost sight of each other. Footsteps sounded stealthy; rare voices, impersonal and remote, died out without resonance. A blind white stillness took possession of the world.

"It looked, too, as if it would last for days. I don't mean to say that the fog did not vary a little in its density. Now and then it would thin out mysteriously, revealing to the men a more or less ghostly presentment of their ship. Several times the shadow of the coast itself swam darkly before their eyes through the fluctuating opaque brightness of the great white cloud clinging to the water.

"Taking advantage of these moments, the ship had been moved cautiously nearer the shore. It was useless to remain out in such thick weather. Her officers knew every nook and cranny of the coast along their beat. They thought that she would be much better in a certain cove. It wasn't a large place, just ample room for a ship to swing at her anchor. She would have an easier time of it till the fog lifted up.

"Slowly, with infinite caution and patience, they crept closer and closer, seeing no more of the cliffs than an evanescent dark loom with a narrow border of angry foam at its foot. At the moment of anchoring the fog was so thick that for all they could see they might have been a thousand miles out in the open sea. Yet the shelter of the land could be felt. There was a peculiar quality in the stillness of the air. Very faint, very elusive, the wash of the ripple against the encircling land reached their ears, with mysterious sudden pauses.

"The anchor dropped, the leads were laid in. The commanding officer went below into his cabin. But he had not been there very long when a voice outside his door requested his presence on deck. He thought to himself: 'What is it now?' He felt some impatience at being called out again to face the wearisome fog.

"He found that it had thinned again a little and had taken on a gloomy hue from the dark cliffs which had no form, no outline, but asserted themselves as a curtain of shadows all round the ship, except in one bright spot, which was the entrance from the open sea. Several officers were looking that way from the bridge. The second in command met him with the breathlessly whispered information that there was another ship in the cove.

"She had been made out by several pairs

of eyes only a couple of minutes before. She was lying at anchor very near the entrance—a mere vague blot on the fog's brightness. And the commanding officer by staring in the direction pointed out to him by eager hands ended by distinguishing it at last himself. Indubitably a vessel of some sort.

"'It's a wonder we didn't run slap into her when coming in,' observed the second in command.

"'Send a boat on board before she vanishes,' said the commanding officer. He surmised that this was a coaster. It could hardly be anything else. But another thought came into his head suddenly. 'It is a wonder,' he said to his second in command, who had rejoined him after sending the boat away.

"By that time both of them had been struck by the fact that the ship so suddenly discovered had not manifested her presence by ringing her bell.

"'We came in very quietly, that's true,' concluded the younger officer. 'But they must have heard our leadsmen at least. We couldn't have passed her more than fifty yards off. The closest shave! They may even have made us out, since they were aware of something coming in. And the strange thing is that we never heard a sound from her. The fellows on board must have been holding their breath.'

"'Aye,' said the commanding officer, thoughtfully.

"In due course the boarding-boat returned, appearing suddenly alongside, as though she had burrowed her way under the fog. The officer in charge came up to make his report, but the commanding officer didn't give him time to begin. He cried from a distance:

"'Coaster, isn't she?'

"'No, sir. A stranger—a neutral,' was the answer.

"'No. Really! Well, tell us all about it. What is she doing here?'

"The young man stated then that he had been told a long and complicated story of engine troubles. But it was plausible enough from a strictly professional point of view and it had the usual features: disablement, dangerous drifting along the shore, weather more or less thick for days, fear of a gale, ultimately a resolve to go in and anchor anywhere on the coast, and so on. Fairly plausible.

"'Engines still disabled?' inquired the commanding officer.

"'No, sir. She has steam on them.'

"The commanding officer took his second aside. 'By Jove!' he said, 'you were right! They were holding their breaths as we passed them. They were.'

"But the second in command had his doubts now.

"'A fog like this does muffle small sounds, sir,' he remarked. 'And what could his object be, after all?'

"'To sneak out unnoticed,' answered the commanding officer.

"'Then why didn't he? He might have done it, you know. Not exactly unnoticed, perhaps. I don't suppose he could have slipped his cable without making some noise. Still, in a minute or so he would have been lost to view—clean gone before we had made him out fairly. Yet he didn't.'

"They looked at each other. The commanding officer shook his head. Such suspicions as the one which had entered his head are not defended easily. He did not even state it openly. The boarding officer finished his report. The cargo of the ship was of a harmless and useful character. She was bound to an English port. Papers and everything in perfect order. Nothing suspicious to be detected anywhere.

"Then passing to the men, he reported the crew on deck as the usual lot. Engineers of the well-known type, and very full of their achievement in repairing the engines. The mate surly. The master rather a fine specimen of a Northman, civil enough, but appeared to have been drinking. Seemed to be recovering from a regular bout of it.

"'I told him I couldn't give him permission to proceed. He said he wouldn't dare to move his ship her own length out in such weather as this, permission or no permission. I left a man on board, though.'

"'Quite right.'

"The commanding officer, after communing with his suspicions for a time, called his second aside.

"'What if she were the very ship which had been feeding some infernal submarine or other?' he said in an undertone.

"The other started. Then, with conviction:

"'She would get off scot-free. You couldn't prove it, sir.'

"'I want to look into it myself.'

"'From the report we've heard I am afraid you couldn't even make a case for reasonable suspicion, sir.'

"'I'll go on board all the same.'

"He had made up his mind. Curiosity is the great motive power of hatred and love. What did he expect to find? He could not have told anybody—not even himself.

"What he really expected to find there was the atmosphere, the atmosphere of gratuitous treachery, which in his view nothing could excuse; for he thought that even a passion of unrighteousness for its own sake could not excuse that. But could he detect it? Sniff it? Taste it? Receive some mysterious communication which would turn his invincible suspicions into a certitude strong enough to provoke action with all its risks?

"The master met him on the after-deck, looming up in the fog amongst the blurred shapes of the usual ship's fittings. He was a robust Northman, bearded, and in the force of his age. A round leather cap fitted his head closely. His hands were rammed deep into the pockets of his short leather jacket. He kept them there while he explained that at sea he lived in the chart-room, and led the way there, striding carelessly. Just before reaching the door under the bridge he staggered a little, recovered himself, flung it open and stood aside, leaning his shoulder as if involuntarily against the side of the house, and staring vaguely into the fog-filled space. But he followed the commanding officer at once, flung the door to, snapped on the electric light, and hastened to thrust his hands back into his pockets, as though afraid of being seized by them either in friendship or in hostility.

"The place was stuffy and hot. The usual chart-rack overhead was full, and the chart on the table was kept unrolled by an empty cup standing on a saucer half-full of some spilt dark liquid. A slightly nibbled biscuit reposed on the chronometer-case. There were two settees, and one of them had been made up into a bed with a pillow and some blankets, which were now very much tumbled. The Northman let himself fall on it, his hands still in his pockets.

"'Well, here I am,' he said, with a curious air of being surprised at the sound of his own voice.

"The commanding officer from the other settee observed the handsome, flushed face. Drops of fog hung on the yellow beard and moustaches of the Northman. The much darker eyebrows ran together in a puzzled frown, and suddenly he jumped up.

"'What I mean is that I don't know where I am. I really don't,' he burst out, with extreme earnestness. 'Hang it all! I got turned around somehow. The fog has been after me for a week. More than a week. And then my engines broke down. I will tell you how it was.'

"He burst out into loquacity. It was not hurried, but it was insistent. It was not continuous for all that. It was broken by the most queer, thoughtful pauses. Each of these pauses lasted no more than a couple of seconds, and each had the profoundity of an endless meditation. When he began again nothing betrayed in him the slightest consciousness of these intervals. There was the same fixed glance, the same unchanged earnestness of tone. He didn't know. Indeed, more than one of these pauses occurred in the middle of a sentence.

"The commanding officer listened to the tale. It struck him as more plausible than simple truth is in the habit of being. But that, perhaps, was prejudice. All the time the Northman was speaking the commanding officer had been aware of an inward voice, a grave murmur in the depth of his very own self, telling another tale, as if on purpose to keep alive in him his indignation and his anger with that baseness of greed or of mere outlook which lies often at the root of simple ideas.

"It was the story that had been already told to the boarding officer an hour or so before. The commanding officer nodded slightly at the Northman from time to time. The latter came to an end and turned his eyes away. He added, as an afterthought:

"'Wasn't it enough to drive a man out of his mind with worry? And it's my first voyage to this part, too. And the ship's my own. Your officer has seen the papers. She isn't much, as you can see for yourself. Just an old cargo-boat. Bare living for my family.'

"He raised a big arm to point at a row of photographs plastering the bulkhead. The movement was ponderous, as if the arm had been made of lead. The commanding officer said, carelessly:

"'You will be making a fortune yet for your family with this old ship.'

"'Yes, if I don't lose her,' said the Northman, gloomily.

"'I mean—out of this war,' added the commanding officer.

"The Northman stared at him in a curiously unseeing and at the same time interested manner, as only eyes of a particular blue shade can stare.

"'And you wouldn't be angry at it,' he said, 'would you? You are too much of a gentleman. We didn't bring this on you. And suppose we sat down and cried. What good would that be? Let those cry who made the trouble,' he concluded, with energy. 'Time's money, you say. Well—*this* time *is* money. Oh! isn't it!'

"The commanding officer tried to keep under the feeling of immense disgust. He said to himself that it was unreasonable. Men were like that—moral cannibals feeding on each other's misfortunes. He said aloud:

"'You have made it perfectly plain how it is that you are here. Your log-book confirms you very minutely. Of course, a log-book may be cooked. Nothing easier.'

"The Northman never moved a muscle. He was gazing at the floor; he seemed not to have heard. He raised his head after a while.

"'But you can't suspect me of anything,' he muttered, negligently.

"The commanding officer thought: 'Why should he say this?'

"Immediately afterwards the man before him added: 'My cargo is for an English port.'

"His voice had turned husky for the moment. The commanding officer reflected: 'That's true. There can be nothing. I can't suspect him. Yet why was he lying with steam up in this fog—and then, hearing us come in, why didn't he give some sign of life? Why? Could it be anything else but a guilty conscience? He could tell by the leadsmen that this was a man-of-war.'

"Yes—why? The commanding officer went on thinking: 'Suppose I ask him and then watch his face. He will betray himself in some way. It's perfectly plain that the fellow *has* been drinking. Yes, he has been drinking; but he will have a lie ready all the same.' The commanding officer was one of those men who are made morally and almost physically uncomfortable by the mere thought of having to beat down a lie. He shrank from the act in scorn and disgust, which were invincible because more temperamental than moral.

"So he went out on deck instead and had the crew mustered formally for his inspection. He found them very much what the report of the boarding officer had led him to expect. And from their answers to his questions he could discover no flaw in the log-book story.

"He dismissed them. His impression of them was—a picked lot; have been promised a fistful of money each if this came off; all slightly anxious, but not frightened. Not a single one of them likely to give the show away. They don't feel in danger of their life. They know England and English ways too well!

"He felt alarmed at catching himself thinking as if his vaguest suspicions were turning into a certitude. For, indeed, there was no shadow of reason for his inferences. There was nothing to give away.

"He returned to the chart-room. The Northman had lingered behind there; and something subtly different in his bearing, more bold in his blue, glassy stare, induced the commanding officer to conclude that the fellow had snatched at the opportunity to take another swig at the bottle he must have had concealed somewhere.

"He noticed, too, that the Northman on meeting his eyes put on an elaborately surprised expression. At least, it seem elaborated. Nothing could be trusted. And the Englishman felt himself with astonishing conviction faced by an enormous lie, solid like a wall, with no way round to get at the truth, whose ugly murderous face he seemed to see peeping over at him with a cynical grin.

"'I dare say,' he began, suddenly, 'you are wondering at my proceedings, though I am not detaining you, am I? You wouldn't dare to move in this fog?'

"'I don't know where I am,' the Northman ejaculated, earnestly. 'I really don't.'

"He looked around as if the very chart-room fittings were strange to him. The commanding officer asked him whether he had not seen any unusual objects floating about while he was at sea.

"'Objects! What objects? We were groping blind in the fog for days.'

"'We had a few clear intervals,' said the commanding officer. 'And I'll tell you what we have seen and the conclusion I've come to about it.'

"He told him in a few words. He heard the sound of a sharp breath indrawn through closed teeth. The Northman with his hand on the table stood absolutely motionless and dumb. He stood as if thunderstruck. Then he produced a fatuous smile.

"Or at least so it appeared to the commanding officer. Was this significant, or of no meaning whatever? He didn't know, he couldn't tell. All the truth had departed out of the world as if drawn in, absorbed in this monstrous villainy this man was—or was not—guilty of.

"'Shooting's too good for people that conceive neutrality in this pretty way,' remarked the commanding officer, after a silence.

"'Yes, yes, yes,' the Northman assented, hurriedly—then added an unexpected and dreamy-voiced 'Perhaps.'

"Was he pretending to be drunk, or only trying to appear sober? His glance was straight, but it was somewhat glazed. His lips outlined themselves firmly under his yellow moustache. But they twitched. Did they twitch? And why was he drooping like this in his attitude?

"'There's no perhaps about it,' pronounced the commanding officer sternly.

"The Northman had straightened himself. And unexpectedly he looked stern, too.

"'No. But what about the tempters? Better kill that lot off. There's about four, five, six million of them' he said, grimly; but in a moment changed into a whining key. 'But I had better hold my tongue. You have some suspicions.'

"'No, I've no suspicions,' declared the commanding officer.

"He never faltered. At that moment he had the certitude. The air of the chart-room was thick with guilt and falsehood braving the discovery, defying simple right, common decency, all humanity of feeling, every scruple of conduct.

"The Northman drew a long breath. 'Well, we know that you English are gentlemen. But let us speak the truth. Why should we love you so very much? You haven't done anything to be loved. We don't love the other people, of course. They haven't done anything for that either. A fellow comes along with a bag of gold . . . I haven't been in Rotterdam my last voyage for nothing.'

"'You may be able to tell something interesting, then, to our people when you come into port,' interjected the officer.

"I might. But you keep some people in your pay at Rotterdam. Let them report. I am a neutral—am I not? . . . Have you ever seen a poor man on one side and a bag of gold on the other? Of course, I couldn't be tempted. I haven't the nerve for it. Really I haven't. It's nothing to me. I am just talking openly for once.'

"'Yes. And I am listening to you,' said the commanding officer, quietly.

"The Northman leaned forward over the table. 'Now that I know you have no suspicions, I talk. You don't know what a poor man is. I do. I am poor myself. This old ship, she isn't much, and she is mortgaged, too. Bare living, no more. Of course, I wouldn't have the nerve. But a man who has nerve! See. The stuff he takes aboard looks like any other cargo—packages, barrels, tins, copper tubes—what not. He doesn't see it work. It isn't real to him. But he sees the gold. That's real. Of course, nothing could induce me. I suffer from an internal disease. I would either go crazy from anxiety—or—or—take to drink or something. The risk is too great. Why—ruin!'

"'It should be death.' The commanding officer got up, after this curt declaration, which the other received with a hard stare oddly combined with an uncertain smile. The officer's gorge rose at the atmosphere of murderous complicity which surrounded him, denser, more impenetrable, more acrid than the fog outside.

"'It's nothing to me,' murmured the Northman, swaying visibly.

"'Of course not,' assented the commanding officer, with a great effort to keep his voice calm and low. The certitude was strong within him. 'But I am going to clear all you fellows off this coast at once. And I will begin with you. You must leave in half an hour.'

"By that time the officer was walking along the deck with the Northman at his elbow.

"'What! In this fog?' the latter cried out, huskily.

"'Yes, you will have to go in this fog.'

"'But I don't know where I am. I really don't.'

"The commanding officer turned round. A sort of fury possessed him. The eyes of the two men met. Those of the Northman expressed a profound amazement.

"'Oh, you don't know how to get out.' The commanding officer spoke with composure, but his heart was beating with anger and dread. 'I will give you your course. Steer south-by-east-half-east for about four miles and then you will be clear to haul to the eastward for your port. The weather will clear up before very long.'

"'Must I? What could induce me? I haven't the nerve.'

"'And yet you must go. Unless you want to—'

"'I don't want to,' panted the Northman. 'I've enough of it.'

"The commanding officer got over the side. The Northman remained still as if rooted to the deck. Before his boat reached his ship the commanding officer heard the steamer beginning to pick up her anchor. Then, shadowy in the fog, she steamed out on the given course.

"'Yes,' he said to his officers, 'I let him go.'"

The narrator bent forward towards the couch, where no movement betrayed the presence of a living person.

"Listen," he said, forcibly. "That course would lead the Northman straight on a deadly ledge of rock. And the commanding officer gave it to him. He steamed out—ran on it—and went down. So he had spoken the truth. He did not know where he was. But it proves nothing. Nothing either way.

It may have been the only truth in all his story. And yet . . . He seems to have been driven out by a menacing stare—nothing more."

He abandoned all pretence.

"Yes, I gave that course to him. It seemed to me a supreme test. I believe—no, I don't believe. I don't know. At the time I was certain. They all went down; and I don't know whether I have done stern retribution—or murder; whether I have added to the corpses that litter the bed of the unreadable sea the bodies of men completely innocent or basely guilty. I don't know. I shall never know."

He rose. The woman on the couch got up and threw her arms round his neck. Her eyes put two gleams in the deep shadow of the room. She knew his passion for truth, his horror of deceit, his humanity.

"Oh, my poor, poor—"

"I shall never know," he repeated sternly, disengaged himself, pressed her hands to his lips, and went out.

[1918]

For Thought

Conrad's structure for this tale is that of the story-within-a-story. He uses this structure in a way that incorporates the two narratives into an organic unit rather than having one story merely frame the other. In the frame story he employs a third-person scenic point of view, with minor omniscient intrusions in the form of author's asides; in the internal story he employs the central intelligence point of view. He uses the same protagonist in both stories but with a different narrative stance. In the external story, the man is viewed from without in an objective manner; whereas, in the internal story, as the Commanding Officer, he serves as the focus of impressions, but he does not tell the story in the first person. With this device, Conrad imparts an air of detached accuracy to the account of the disturbing events. This note of scrupulous accuracy minimizes any suggestion of self-justification on the part of the Commanding Officer, and at the same time depicts in detail the moral dilemma that still haunts him.

For Discussion

1. What is the physical atmosphere and the accompanying mood in the frame story?
2. What is suggested about the relationship between the man and the woman?
3. Of the two, who seems in better control of the situation and how is this manifested?
4. In the tale, what is the background information about the naval vessel? What is its mission? How does the background and the nature of its mission act as a motivating force influencing the Commanding Officer's actions?
5. What symbols are used in the story?
6. What active role does the fog play in the events of the tale? What irony is there in the role of the fog?
7. What is the irony in the Commanding Officer's remark, "No, I've no suspicions" and his later one, "I let him go?"
8. How are the consequences of his ordering the neutral ship to leave the cove an unresolvable enigma for the Commanding Officer?
9. In what way is the ending of the frame story ironic?

Robert Coover
A Pedestrian Accident

Paul stepped off the curb and got hit by a truck. He didn't know what it was that hit him at first, but now, here on his back, under the truck, there could be no doubt. Is it me? he wondered. Have I walked the earth and come here?

Just as he was struck, and while still tumbling in front of the truck and then under the wheels, in a kind of funhouse gambado of pain and terror, he had thought: this has happened before. His neck had sprung, there was a sudden flash of light and a blaze roaring up in the back of his head. The hot—almost fragrant—pain: that was new. It was the *place* he felt he'd returned to.

He lay perpendicular to the length of the truck, under the trailer, just to the rear of the truck's second of three sets of wheels. All of him was under the truck but his head and shoulders. Maybe I'm being born again, he reasoned. He stared straight up, past the side of the truck, toward the sky, pale blue and cloudless. The tops of skyscrapers closed toward the center of his vision; now that he thought about it, he realized it was the first time in years he had looked up at them, and they seemed inclined to fall. The old illusion; one of them anyway. The truck was red with white letters, but his severe angle of vision up the side kept him from being able to read the letters. A capital "K," he could see that—and a number, yes, it seemed to be a "14." He smiled inwardly at the irony, for he had a private fascination with numbers: fourteen! He thought he remembered having had a green light, but it didn't really matter. No way to prove it. It would have changed by now, in any case. The thought, obscurely, troubled him.

"Crazy goddamn fool he just walk right out in fronta me no respect just burstin for a bustin!"

The voice, familiar somehow, guttural, yet falsetto, came from above and to his right. People were gathering to stare down at him, shaking their heads. He felt like one chosen. He tried to turn his head toward the voice, but his neck flashed hot again.

Things were bad. Better just to lie still, take no chances. Anyway, he saw now, just in the corner of his eye, the cab of the truck, red like the trailer, and poking out its window, the large head of the truckdriver, wagging in the sunshine. The driver wore a small tweed cap—too small, in fact: it sat just on top of his head.

"Boy I seen punchies in my sweet time but this cookie takes the cake God bless the laboring classes I say and preserve us from the humble freak!"

The truckdriver spoke with broad gestures, bulbous eyes rolling, runty body thrusting itself in and out of the cab window, little hands flying wildly about. Paul worried still about the light. It was important, yet how could he ever know? The world was an ephemeral place, it could get away from you in a minute. The driver had a bent red nose and coarse reddish hair that stuck out like straw. A hard shiny chin, too, like a mirror image of the hooked nose. Paul's eyes wearied of the strain, and he had to stop looking.

"Listen lays and gentmens I'm a good Christian by Judy a decent hardworkin fambly man earnin a honest wage and got a dear little woman and seven yearnin younguns all my own seed *a responsible man* and goddamn that boy what he do but walk right into me and my poor ole truck!"

On some faces Paul saw compassion, or at least a neutral curiosity, an idle amusement, but on most he saw reproach. There were those who winced on witnessing his state and seemed to understand, but there were others—a majority—who jeered.

"He asked for it if you ask me!"

"It's the idler plays the fool and the workingman's to hang for it!"

"Shouldn't allow his kind out to walk the streets!"

"What is the use of running when you are on the wrong road?"

It worsened. Their shouts grew louder and ran together. There were orations and the waving of flags. Paul was wondering: had he been carrying anything? No, no. He had only—*wait!* a book? Very likely, but . . . ah well. Perhaps he was carrying it still. There was no feeling in his fingers.

The people were around him like flies, grievances were being aired, sides taken, and there might have been a brawl, but a policeman arrived and broke it up. "All right, everybody! Stand back, please!" he shouted. "Give this man some air! Can't you see he's been injured?"

At last, Paul thought. He relaxed. For a moment, he'd felt himself in a strange and hostile country, but now he felt at home again. He even began to believe he might survive. Though really: had he ever doubted it?

"Everybody back, *back!*" The policeman was effective. The crowd grew quiet, and by the sound of their sullen shuffling, Paul guessed they were backing off. Not that he got more or less air by it, but he felt relieved just the same. "Now," said the policeman, gently but firmly, "what has happened here?"

And with that it all started up again, same as before, the clamor, the outrage, the arguments, the learned quotations, but louder and more discordant than ever. I'm hurt, Paul said. No one heard. The policeman cried out for order, and slowly, with his shouts, with his nightstick, with his threats, he reduced them again to silence.

One lone voice hung at the end: "—for the last time, Mister, *stop goosing me!*" Everybody laughed, released.

"Stop goosing her, sir!" the policeman commanded with his chin thrust firmly forward, and everybody laughed again.

Paul almost laughed, but he couldn't, quite. Besides, he'd just, with that, got the picture, and given his condition, it was not a funny one. He opened his eyes and there was the policeman bent down over him. He had a notebook in his hand.

"Now, tell me, son, what happened here?" The policeman's face was thin and pale, like a student's, and he wore a trim little tuft of black moustache under the pinched peak of his nose.

I've just been hit, Paul explained, by this truck, and then he realized that he probably didn't say it at all, that speech was an art no longer his. He cast his eyes indicatively toward the cab of the truck.

"Listen, I asked you what happened here! Cat got your tongue, young man?"

"Crazy goddam fool he just walk right out in fronta me no respect just burstin for a bustin!"

The policeman remained crouched over Paul, but turned his head up to look at the truckdriver. The policeman wore a brilliant blue uniform with large brass buttons. And gold epaulettes.

"Boy I seen punchies in my sweet time but this cookie takes the cake God bless the laboring classes I say and preserve us from the humble freak!"

The policeman looked down at Paul, then back at the truckdriver. "I know about truckdrivers," Paul heard him say.

"Listen lays and gentmens I'm a good Christian by Judy a decent hardworkin fambly man earnin a honest wage and got a dear little woman and seven yearnin younguns all my own seed *a responsible man* and goddamn that boy what he do but walk right into me and my poor ole trike. Truck, I mean."

There was a loose tittering from the crowd, but the policeman's frown and raised stick contained it. "What's your name, lad?" he asked, turning back to Paul. At first, the policeman smiled, he knew who truckdrivers were and he knew who Pauls were, and there was a salvation of sorts in that smile, but gradually it faded. "Come, come, boy! Don't be afraid!" He winked, nudged him gently. "We're here to help you."

Paul, Paul replied. But, no, no doubt about it, it was jammed up in there and he wasn't getting it out.

"Well, if you won't help me, I can't help you," the policeman said pettishly and tilted his nose up. "Anybody here know this man?" he called out to the crowd.

Again a roar, a threatening tumult of words and sounds, shouts back and forth. It was hard to know if none knew him or if they all did. But then one voice, belted out above the others, came through: "O God in heaven! It's Amory! *Amory Westerman!*" The voice, a woman's, hysterical by the sound of it, drew near. "Amory! What . . . *what* have they *done* to you?"

Paul understood. It was not a mistake. He was astonished by his own acumen.

"Do you know this young man?" the policeman asked, lifting his notebook.

"What? Know him? Did Sarah know Abraham? Did Eve know Cain?"

The policeman cleared his throat uneasily. "Adam," he corrected softly.

"You know who you know, I know who I know," the woman said, and let fly with a low throaty snigger. The crowd responded with a belly laugh.

"But this young man—!" the policeman insisted, flustered.

"Who, you and Amory?" the woman cried. "I can't believe it!" The crowd laughed and the policeman bit his lip. "Amory! What new persecutions are these?" She billowed out above him: old, maybe even seventy, fat and bosomy, pasty-faced with thick red rouges, head haloed by ringlets of sparse orangish hair. "My poor Amory!" And down she came on him. Paul tried to duck, got only a hot flash in his neck for it. Her breath reeked of cheap gin. Help, said Paul.

"Hold, madame! Stop!" the policeman cried, tugging at the woman's sleeve. She stood, threw up her arms before her face, staggered backwards. What more she did, Paul couldn't see, for his view of her face was largely blocked by the bulge of her breasts and belly. There were laughs, though. "Everything in order here," grumped the policeman, tapping his notebook. "Now, what's your name, please . . . uh . . . miss, madame?"

"My name?" She twirled gracelessly on one dropsied ankle and cried to the crowd: "*Shall I tell?*"

"Tell! Tell! Tell!" shouted the spectators, clapping rhythmically. Paul let himself be absorbed by it; there was, after all, nothing else to do.

The policeman, rapping a pencil against his blue notebook to the rhythm of the chant, leaned down over Paul and whispered: ("I think we've got them on our side now!")

Paul, his gaze floating giddily up past the thin white face of the police officer and the red side of the truck into the horizonless blue haze above, wondered if alliance were really the key to it all. What *am* I without them? Could I even die? Suddenly, the whole world seemed to tip: his feet dropped and his head rose. Beneath him the red machine shot grease and muck, the host rioted above his head, the earth pushed him from behind, and out front the skyscrapers pointed, like so many insensate fingers, the path he must walk to oblivion. He squeezed shut his eyes to set right the world again—he was afraid he would slide down beneath the truck to disappear from sight forever.

"*My name—!*" bellowed the woman, and the crowd hushed, tittering softly. Paul opened his eyes. He was on his back again. The policeman stood over him, mouth agape, pencil poised. The woman's puffy face was sequined with sweat. Paul wondered what she'd been doing while he wasn't watching. "My name, officer, is Grundy."

"I beg your pardon?" The policeman, when nervous, had a way of nibbling his moustache with his lowers.

"Mrs. Grundy, dear boy, who did you think I was?" She patted the policeman's thin cheek, tweaked his nose. "But you can call me Charity, handsome!" The policeman blushed. She twiddled her index finger in his little moustache. "Kootchy-kootchy-koo!" There was a roar of laughter from the crowd.

The policeman sneezed. "Please!" he protested.

Mrs. Grundy curtsied and stooped to unzip the officer's fly. "Hello! Anybody home!"

"*Stop that!*" squeaked the policeman through the thunderous laughter and applause. Strange, thought Paul, how much I'm enjoying this.

"Come out, come out, wherever you are!"

"*The story!*" the policeman insisted through the tumult.

"Story? What—?"

"This young fellow," said the policeman, pointing with his pencil. He zipped up, blew his nose. "Mr., uh, Mr. Westerman . . . you said—"

"Mr. *Who?*" The woman shook her jowls, perplexed. She frowned down at Paul, then brightened. "Oh yes! Amory!" She paled, seemed to sicken. Paul, if he could've, would've smiled. "Good God!" she rasped, as though appalled at what she saw. Then, once more, she took an operatic grip on her breasts and staggered back a step. "O mortality! O fatal mischief! Done in! A noble man lies stark and stiff! Delenda est Carthago! *Sic transit glans mundi!*"

Gloria, corrected Paul. No, leave it.

"Squashed like a lousy bug!" she cried. "And at the height of his potency!"

"Now, wait a minute!" the policeman protested.

"The final curtain! The last farewell! The journey's end! Over the hill! The last muster!" Each phrase was answered by a happy shout from the mob. "Across the river! The way of all flesh! The last roundup!" She sobbed, then ballooned down on him again, tweaked his ear and whispered: ("How's Charity's weetsie snotkins, enh? Him fall down and bump his little putsy? Mumsy kiss and make well!") And she let him have it on the—well, sort of on the left side of his nose, left cheek, and part of his left eye: one wet enveloping sour blubbering kiss, and this time, sorrily, the policeman did not intervene. He was busy taking notes. Officer, said Paul.

"Hmmm," the policeman muttered, and wrote. "G-R-U-N-ah, ahem, Grundig, Grundig -D, yes, D-I-G. Now what did you—?"

The woman labored clumsily to her

feet, plodded over behind the policeman, and squinted over his shoulder at the notes he was taking. "That's a 'Y' there, buster, a 'Y.'" She jabbed a stubby ruby-tipped finger at the notebook.

"Grundigy?" asked the policeman in disbelief. "What kind of a name is that?"

"No, no!" the old woman whined, her grand manner flung to the winds. "Grundy! Grundy! Without the '-ig,' don't you see? You take off your—"

"Oh, *Grundy!* Now I have it!" The policeman scrubbed the back end of his pencil in the notebook. "Darned eraser. About shot." The paper tore. He looked up irritably. "Can't we just make it Grundig?"

"Grundy," said the woman coldly.

The policeman ripped the page out of his notebook, rumpled it up angrily, and hurled it to the street. "All right, gosh damn it all!" he cried in a rage, scribbling: "Grundy. I have it. Now get on with it, lady!"

"Officer!" sniffed Mrs. Grundy, clasping a handkerchief to her throat. "Remember your place, or I shall have to speak to your superior!" The policeman shrank, blanched, nibbled his lip.

Paul knew what would come. He could read these two like a book. *I'm* the strange one, he thought. He wanted to watch their faces, but his streetlevel view gave him at best a perspective on their underchins. It was their crotches that were prominent. Butts and bellies: the squashed bug's-eye view. And that was strange, too: that he wanted to watch their faces.

The policeman was begging for mercy, wringing his pale hands. There were faint hissing sounds, wriggling out of the crowd like serpents. "Cut the shit, mac," Charity Grundy said finally, "you're overdoing it." The officer chewed his moustache, stared down at his notebook, abashed. "You wanna know who this poor clown is, right?" The policeman nodded. "Okay, are you ready?" She clasped her bosom again and the crowd grew silent. The police officer held his notebook up, the pencil poised. Mrs. Grundy snuffled, looked down at Paul, winced, turned away and wept. "Officer!" she gasped. "*He was my lover!*"

Halloos and cheers from the crowd, passing to laughter. The policeman started to smile, blinking down at Mrs. Grundy's body, but with a twitch of his moustache, he suppressed it.

"We met . . . just one year ago today. O fateful hour!" She smiled bravely, brushing back a tear, her lower lip quivering. Once, her hands clenched woefully before her face, she winked down at Paul. The wink nearly convinced him. Maybe I'm him after all. Why not? "He was selling seachests, door to door. I can see him now as he was then—" She paused to look down at him as he was now, and wrinkles of revulsion swept over her face. Somehow this brought laughter. She looked away, puckered her mouth and bugged her eyes, shook one hand limply from the wrist. The crowd was really with her.

"Mrs. Grundy," the officer whispered, "please . . ."

"Yes, there he was, chapfallen and misused, orphaned by the rapacious world, yet pure and undefiled, there: there at my door!" With her baggy arm, flung out, quavering, she indicated the door. "Bent nearly double under his impossible seachest, perspiration illuminating his manly brow, wounding his eyes, wrinkling his undershirt—"

"Careful!" cautioned the policeman nervously, glancing up from his notes. He must have filled twenty or thirty pages by now.

"In short, my heart went out to him." Gesture of heart going out. "And though—alas!—my need for seachests was limited—"

The spectators somehow discovered something amusing in this and tittered knowingly. Mainly in the way she said it, he supposed. Her story in truth did not bother Paul so much as his own fascination with it. He knew where it would lead, but it didn't matter. In fact, maybe that *was* what fascinated him.

"—I invited him in. Put down that horrid seachest, dear boy, and come in here, I cried, come in to your warm and obedient Charity, love, come in for a cup of tea, come in and rest, rest your pretty little shoulders, your pretty little back, your pretty little . . ." Mrs. Grundy paused, smiled with a faint arch of one eyebrow, and the crowd responded with another burst of laughter. "And it *was* pretty little, okay," she grumbled, and again they whooped, while she sniggered throatily.

How was it now? he wondered. In fact, he'd been wondering all along.

"And, well, officer, that's what he did, he *did* put down his seachest—alas! sad to tell, right on my unfortunate cat Rasputin, dozing there in the day's brief sun, God rest his soul, his (again, alas!) somewhat homaloidal soul!"

She had a great audience. They never failed her, nor did they now.

The policeman, who had finally squatted down to write on his knee, now stood and shouted for order. "Quiet! *Quiet!*" His moustache twitched. "Can't you see this is a serious matter?" He's the funny one, thought Paul. The crowd thought so, too, for the laughter mounted, then finally died away. "And . . . and then what happened?" the policeman whispered. But they heard him anyway and screamed with delight, throwing up a new clamor in which could be distinguished several coarse paraphrases of the policeman's question. The officer's pale face flushed. He looked down at Paul with a brief commiserating smile, shrugged his shoulders, fluttering the epaulettes. Paul made a try at a never-mind kind of gesture, but, he supposed, without bringing it off.

"What happened next, you ask, you naughty boy?" Mrs. Grundy shook and wriggled. Cheers and whistles. She cupped her plump hands under her breasts and hitched her abundant hips heavily to one side. "You don't understand," she told the crowd. "I only wished to be a mother to the lad." Hoohahs and catcalls. "But I had failed to realize, in that fleeting tragic moment when he unburdened himself upon poor Rasputin, how I was wrenching his young and unsullied heart asunder! Oh yes, I know, I know—"

"This is the dumbest story I ever heard," interrupted the policeman finally, but Mrs. Grundy paid him no heed.

"I know I'm old and fat, that I've crossed the Grand Climacteric!" She winked at the crowd's yowls of laughter. "I know the fragrant flush of first flower is gone forever!" she cried, not letting a good thing go, pressing her wrinkled palms down over the soft swoop of her blimp-sized hips, peeking coyly over one plump shoulder at the shrieking crowd. The policeman stamped his foot, but no one noticed except Paul. "I know, I know—*yet:* somehow, face to face with little Charity, a primitive unnameable urgency welled up in his untaught loins, his pretty little—"

"*Stop it!*" cried the policeman, right on cue. "This has gone far enough!"

"And *you* ask what happened next? I shall tell you, officer! For why conceal the truth . . . from *you* of all people?" Though uneasy, the policeman seemed frankly pleased that she had put it this way. "Yes, without further discourse, he buried his pretty little head in my bosom—" (Paul felt a distressing sense of suffocation, though perhaps it had been with him all the while) "—and he tumbled me there, yes he did, there on the front porch alongside his seachest and my dying Rasputin, there in the sunlight, before God, before the neighbors, before Mr. Dunlevy the mailman who is hard of hearing, before the children from down the block passing on their shiny little—"

"Crazy goddamn fool he just walk right out in fronta me no respect just burstin for a bustin!" said a familiar voice.

Mrs. Grundy's broad face, now streaked with tears and mottled with a tense pink flush, glowered. There was a long and difficult silence. Then she narrowed her eyes, smiled faintly, squared her shoulders, touched a handkerchief to her eye, plunged the handkerchief back down her bosom, and resumed: "—Before, in short, the whole itchy eyes-agog world, a coupling unequaled in the history of Western concupiscence!" Some vigorous applause, which she acknowledged. "Assaulted, but—yes, I confess it—assaulted, but *aglow*, I reminded him of—"

"Boy I seen punchies in my sweet time but this cookie takes the cake God bless the laboring classes I say and preserve us from the humble freak!"

Swiveling his wearying gaze hard right, Paul could see the truckdriver waggling his huge head at the crowd. Mrs. Grundy padded heavily over to him, the back of her thick neck reddening, swung her purse in a great swift arc, but the truckdriver recoiled into his cab, laughing with a taunting cackle. Then, almost in the same instant, he poked his red-beaked head out again, and rolling his eyes, said: "Listen lays and gentmens I'm a good Christian by Judy a decent hardworkin fambly man earnin a honest wage and got a dear little woman and seven yearnin younguns all my own seed *a responsible*—"

"I'll responsible your ass!" hollered Charity Grundy and let fly with her purse again, but once more the driver ducked nimbly inside, cackling obscenely. The crowd, taking sides, was more hysterical than ever. Cheers were raised and bets taken.

Again the driver's waggling head popped out: "—*man* and god—" he began, but this time Mrs. Grundy was waiting for him. Her great lumpish purse caught him square on his bent red nose—*ka*-RAACKK!—and the truckdriver slumped lifelessly over the door of his cab, his stubby little arms dangling limp, reaching just below the top of his head. As best Paul could tell, the tweed cap did not drop off, but since his eyes were cramped with fatigue, he had to stop looking before the truckdriver's head ceased bobbing against the door.

Man and god! he thought. Of course! terrific! What did it mean? Nothing.

The policeman made futile little gestures of interference, but apparently had too much respect for Mrs. Grundy's purse to carry them out. That purse was big enough to hold a bowling ball, and maybe it did.

Mrs. Grundy, tongue dangling and panting furiously, clapped one hand over her heart and, with the handkerchief, fanned herself with the other. Paul saw sweat dripping down her legs. "And so—*foo!*—I . . . I—*puf!*—I reminded him of . . . of the—*whee!*—the cup of tea!" she gasped. She paused, swallowed, mopped her brow, sucked in a deep lungful of air, and exhaled it slowly. She cleared her throat. *"And so I reminded him of the cup of tea!"* she roared with a grand sweep of one powerful arm, the old style recovered. There was a general smattering of complimentary applause, which Mrs. Grundy acknowledged with a short nod of her head. "We went inside. The air was heavy with expectation and the unmistakable aroma of catshit. One might almost be pleased that Rasputin had yielded up the spirit—"

"NOW JUST STOP IT!" cried the policeman. "THIS IS—"

"I poured some tea, we sang the now famous duet, '*¡Ciérrate la bragueta! ¡La bragueta está cerrada!*,' I danced for him, he—"

"ENOUGH, I SAID!" screamed the policeman, his little moustache quivering with indignation. "THIS IS ABSURD!"

You're warm, said Paul. But that's not quite it.

"Absurd?" cried Charity Grundy, aghast. "*Absurd?* You call my dancing *absurd?*"

"I . . . I didn't say—"

"Grotesque, perhaps, and yes, a bit awesome—but *absurd!*" She grabbed him by the lapels, lifting him off the ground. "What do you have against dancing, you worm? *What do you have against grace?*"

"P-please! Put me down!"

"Or is it, you don't believe I *can* dance?" She dropped him.

"N-no!" he squeaked, brushing himself off, straightening his epaulettes. "No! I—"

"Show him! Show him!" chanted the crowd.

The policeman spun on them. "STOP! IN

THE NAME OF THE LAW!" They obeyed. "This man is injured. He may die. He needs help. It's no joking matter. I ask for your cooperation." He paused for effect. "That's better." The policeman stroked his moustache, preening a bit. "Now, ahem, is there a doctor present? A doctor, please?"

"Oh, officer, you're cute! You're *very* cute!" said Mrs. Grundy on a new tack. The crowd snickered. "*Is there a doctor present?*" she mimicked, "*a doctor, please?*"

"Now just cut it out!" the policeman ordered, glaring angrily across Paul's chest at Mrs. Grundy. "Gosh damn it now, you stop it this instant, or . . . or you'll see what'll happen!"

"Aww, you're *jealous!*" cried Mrs. Grundy. "And of poor little supine Rasputin! Amory, I mean." The spectators were in great spirits again, total rebellion threatening, and the police officer was at the end of his rope. "Well, *don't* be jealous, dear boy!" cooed Mrs. Grundy. "Charity tell you a weetsie bitty secret."

"*Stop!*" sobbed the policeman. Be careful where you step, said Paul below.

Mrs. Grundy leaned perilously out over Paul and got a grip on the policeman's ear. He winced, but no longer attempted escape. "That boy," she said, "*he humps terrible!*"

It carried out to the crowd and broke it up. It was her big line and she wambled about gloriously, her rouged mouth stretched in a flabby toothless grin, retrieving the pennies that people were pitching (Paul knew about them from being hit by them; one landed on his upper lip, stayed there, emitting that familiar dead smell common to pennies the world over), thrusting her chest forward to catch them in the cleft of her bosom. She shook and, shaking, jangled. She grabbed the policeman's hand and pulled him forward to share a bow with her. The policeman smiled awkwardly, twitching his moustache.

"You asked for a doctor," said an old but gentle voice.

The crowd noises subsided. Paul opened his eyes and discovered above him a stooped old man in a rumpled gray suit. His hair was shaggy and white, his face dry, lined with age. He wore rimless glasses, carried a black leather bag. He smiled down at Paul, that easy smile of a man who comprehends and assuages pain, then looked back at the policeman. Inexplicably, a wave of terror shook Paul.

"You wanted a doctor," the old man repeated.

"Yes! *Yes!*" cried the policeman, almost in tears. "Oh, thank God!"

"I'd rather you thanked the profession," the doctor said. "Now what seems to be the problem?"

"Oh, doctor, it's awful!" The policeman twisted the notebook in his hands, fairly destroying it. "This man has been struck by this truck, or so it would appear, no one seems to know, it's all a terrible mystery, and there is a woman, but now I don't see—? and I'm not even sure of his name—"

"No matter," interrupted the doctor with a kindly nod of his old head, "who he is. He is a man and that, I assure you, is enough for me."

"Doctor, that's so good of you to say so!" wept the policeman.

I'm in trouble, thought Paul. Oh boy, I'm really in trouble.

"Well, now, let us just see," said the doctor, crouching down over Paul. He lifted Paul's eyelids with his thumb and peered intently at Paul's eyes; Paul, anxious to assist, rolled them from side to side. "Just relax, son," the doctor said. He opened his black bag, rummaged about in it, withdrew a flashlight. Paul was not sure exactly what the doctor did after that, but he seemed to be looking in his ears. I can't move my head, Paul told him, but the doctor only asked: "Why does he have a penny under his nose?" His manner was not such as to insist upon an answer, and he got none. Gently, expertly, he pried Paul's teeth apart, pinned his tongue down with a wooden depressor, and scrutinized his throat. Paul's head was on fire with pain. "Ahh, yes," he mumbled. "Hum, hum."

"How . . . how is he, Doctor?" stammered the policeman, his voice muted with dread and respect. "Will . . . will he . . . ?"

The doctor glared scornfully at the officer, then withdrew a stethoscope from his bag. He hooked it in his ears, slipped the disc inside Paul's shirt and listened intently, his old head inclined to one side like a bird listening for worms. Absolute silence now. Paul could hear the doctor breathing, the policeman whimpering softly. He had the vague impression that the doctor tapped his chest a time or two, but if so, he didn't feel it. His head felt better with his mouth closed. "Hmmm," said the doctor gravely, "yes . . ."

"Oh, please! What *is* it, Doctor?" the policeman cried.

"What is it? *What is it?*" shouted the doctor in a sudden burst of rage. "I'll tell you *what is it!*" He sprang to his feet, nimble for an old man. "I cannot examine this patient while you're hovering over my shoulder and mewling like a goddamn schoolboy, *that's* what *is* it!"

"B-but I only—" stammered the officer, staggering backwards.

"And how do you expect me to examine a man half buried under a damned truck?" The doctor was in a terrible temper.

"But I—"

"Damn it! I'll but-I you, you idiot, if you don't remove this truck from the scene so that I can determine the true gravity of this man's injuries! *Have I made myself clear?*"

"Y-yes! But . . . but wh-what am I to *do?*" wept the police officer, hands clenched before his mouth. "I'm only a simple policeman, Doctor, doing my duty before God and count—"

"Simple, you said it!" barked the doctor. "I *told* you what to do, you God-and-cunt simpleton—*now get moving!*"

God and cunt! Did it again, thought Paul. Now what?

The policeman, chewing wretchedly on the corners of his notebook, stared first at Paul, then at the truck, at the crowd, back at the truck. Paul felt fairly certain now that the letter following the "K" on the truck's side was an "I." "Shall I . . . shall I pull him out from under—?" the officer began tentatively, thin chin aquiver.

"*Good God, no!*" stormed the doctor, stamping his foot. "This man may have a broken neck! Moving him would *kill* him, don't you see that, you sniveling birdbrain? Now, goddamn it, wipe your wretched nose and go wake up your—your accomplice up there, *and I mean right now!* Tell him to back his truck *off* this poor devil!"

"B-back it off—! But . . . but he'd have to run *over* him again! He—"

"Don't by God run-over-him-again *me*, you blackshirt hireling, *or I'll have your badge!*" screamed the doctor, brandishing his stethoscope.

The policeman hesitated but a moment to glance down at Paul's body, then turned and ran to the front of the truck. "Hey! Come on, you!" He whacked the driver on the head with his nightstick. Hollow *thunk!* "Up and at 'em!"

"—DAM THAT BOY WHAT," cried the truckdriver, rearing up wildly and fluttering his head as though lost, "HE DO BUT WALK RIGHT INTO ME AND MY POOR OLE TRICK! TRUCK, I MEAN!" The crowd laughed again, first time in a long time, but the doctor stamped his foot and they quieted right down.

"Now, start up that engine, you, right now! I mean it!" ordered the policeman, stroking his moustache. He was getting a little of his old spit and polish back. He slapped the nightstick in his palm two or three times.

Paul felt the pavement under his back quake as the truckdriver started the motor. The white letters above him joggled in their red fields like butterflies. Beyond, the sky's blue had deepened, but white clouds now flowered in it. The skyscrapers had grayed, as though withdrawing information.

The truck's noise smothered the voices, but Paul did overhear the doctor and the policeman occasionally, the doctor ranting, the policeman imploring, something about mass and weight and vectors and direction. It was finally decided to go forward, since there were two sets of wheels up front and only one to the rear (a decent kind of humanism maintaining, after all, thought Paul), but the truckdriver apparently misunderstood, because he backed up anyway, and the middle set of wheels rolled up on top of Paul.

"Stop! STOP!" shrieked the police officer, and the truck motor coughed and died. "I ordered you to go *forward*, you pighead, not backward!"

The driver popped his head out the window, bulged his ping-pong-ball eyes at the policeman, then waggled his tiny hands in his ears and brayed. The officer took a fast practiced swing at the driver's big head (epaulettes, or no, he had a skill or two), but the driver deftly dodged it. He clapped his runty hands and bobbed back inside the cab.

"What oh *what* shall we ever do *now?*" wailed the officer. The doctor scowled at him with undisguised disgust. Paul felt like he was strangling, but he could locate no specific pain past his neck. "Dear lord above! There's wheels on each side of him and wheels in the middle!"

"Capital!" the doctor snorted. "Figure that out by yourself, or somebody help you?"

"You're making fun," whimpered the officer.

"AND YOU'RE MURDERING THIS MAN!" bellowed the doctor.

The police officer uttered a short anxious cry, then raced to the front of the truck again. Hostility welling in the crowd, Paul could hear it. "Okay, okay!" cried the officer. "Back up or go forward, *please*, I don't care, but hurry! HURRY!"

The motor started up again, there was a jarring grind of gears abrading, then slowly slowly slowly the middle set of wheels backed down off Paul's body. There was a brief tense interim before the next set climbed up on him, hesitated as a ferris wheel hesitates at the top of its ambit, then sank down off him.

Some time passed.

He opened his eyes.

The truck had backed away, out of sight, out of Paul's limited range of sight anyway. His eyelids weighed closed. He remembered the doctor being huddled over him, shreds of his clothing being peeled away.

Much later, or perhaps not, he opened his eyes once more. The doctor and the policeman were standing over him, some other people too, people he didn't recognize, though he felt somehow he ought to know them. Mrs. Grundy, she was there; in fact, it looked for all the world as though she had set up a ticket booth and was charging admission. Some of the people were holding little children up to see, warm faces, tender, compassionate; more or less. Newsmen were taking his picture. "You'll be famous," one of them said.

"His goddamn body is like a mulligan stew," the doctor was telling a reporter.

The policeman shook his head. He was a bit green. "Do you think—?"

"Do I think what?" the doctor asked. Then he laughed, a thin raking old man's laugh. "You mean, do I think he's going to *die?*" He laughed again. "Good God, man, you can see for yourself! There's nothing left of him, he's a goddamn gallimaufry, and hardly an appetizing one at that!" He dipped his fingers into Paul, licked them, grimaced. "Foo!"

"I think we should get a blanket for him," the policeman said weakly.

"Of course you should!" snapped the doctor, wiping his stained hands on a small white towel he had brought out of his black bag. He peered down through his rimless spectacles at Paul, smiled. "Still there, eh?" He squatted beside him. "I'm sorry, son. There's not a damn thing I can do. Well, yes, I suppose I can take this penny off your lip. You've little use for it, eh?" He laughed softly. "Now, let's see, there's no function for it, is there? No, no, there it is." The doctor started to pitch it away, then pocketed it instead. The eyes, don't they use them for the eyes? "Well, that's better, I'm sure. But let's be honest: it doesn't get to the real problem, does it?" Paul's lip tickled where the penny had been. "No, I'm of all too little use to you there, boy. I can't even prescribe a soporific platitude. Leave that to the goddamn priests, eh? Hee hee hee! Oops, sorry, son! Would you like a priest?"

No thanks, said Paul.

"Can't get it out, eh?" The doctor probed Paul's neck. "Hmmm. No, obviously not." He shrugged. "Just as well. What could you possibly have to say, eh?" He chuckled drily, then looked up at the policeman who still had not left to search out a blanket. "Don't just stand there, man! Get this lad a priest!" The police officer, clutching his mouth, hurried away, out of Paul's eye-reach. "I know it's not easy to accept death," the doctor was saying. He finished wiping his hands, tossed the towel into his black bag, snapped the bag shut. "We all struggle against it, boy, it's part and parcel of being alive, this brawl, this meaningless gutterfight with death. In fact, let me tell you, son, it's *all* there is to life." He wagged his finger in punctuation, and ended by pressing the tip of it to Paul's nose. "That's the secret, *that's* my happy paregoric! Hee hee hee!"

KI, thought Paul. KI and 14. What could it have been? Never know now. One of those things.

"But death begets life, there's *that*, my boy, and don't you ever forget it! Survival and murder are synonyms, son, first flaw of the universe! Hee hee h—oh! Sorry, son! No time for puns! Forget I said it!"

It's okay, said Paul. Listening to the doctor had at least made him forget the tickle on his lip and it was gone.

"New life burgeons out of rot, new mouths consume old organisms, father dies a orgasm, mother dies at birth, only old Dame Mass with her twin dugs of Stuff and Tickle persists, suffering her long slow split into pure light and pure carbon! Hee hee hee! A tender thought! Don't you agree, lad?" The doctor gazed off into space, happily contemplating the process.

I tell you what, said Paul. Let's forget it.

Just then, the policeman returned with a big quilted comforter, and he and the doctor spread it gently over Paul's body, leaving only his face exposed. The people pressed closer to watch.

"Back! *Back!*" shouted the policeman. "Have you no respect for the dying? *Back, I say!*"

"Oh, come now," chided the doctor. "Let them watch if they want to. It hardly matters to this poor fellow, and even if it does, it can't matter for much longer. And it will help keep the flies off him."

"Well, doctor, if you think . . ." His voice faded away. Paul closed his eyes.

As he lay there among the curious, several odd questions plagued Paul's mind. He knew there was no point to them, but he couldn't rid himself of them. The book, for example: did he have a book? And if he did, what book, and what had happened to it? And what about the stoplight, that lost increment of what men call history, why had no one brought up the matter of the stoplight? And pure carbon he could understand, but as for light: what could its purity consist of? KI. 14. That impression that it had happened before. Yes, these were mysteries, all right. His head ached from them.

People approached Paul from time to time to look under the blanket. Some only peeked, then turned away, while others stayed to poke around, dip their hands in the mutilations. There seemed to be more interest in them now that they were covered. There were some arguments and some occasional horseplay, but the doctor and policeman kept things from getting out of hand. If someone arrogantly ventured a Latin phrase, the doctor always put him down with some toilet-wall barbarism; on the other hand, he reserved his purest, most mellifluous toponymy for small children and young girls. He made several medical appointments with the latter. The police officer, though queasy, stayed nearby. Once, when Paul happened to open his eyes after having had them closed some while, the policeman smiled warmly down on him and said: "Don't worry, good fellow. I'm still here. Take it as easy as you can. I'll be here to the very end. You can count on me." Bullshit, thought Paul, though not ungratefully, and he thought he remembered hearing the doctor echo him as he fell off to sleep.

When he awoke, the streets were empty. They had all wearied of it, as he had known they would. It had clouded over, the sky had darkened, it was probably night, and it had begun to rain lightly. He could now see the truck clearly, off to his left. Must have been people in the way before.

MAGIC KISS LIPSTICK

IN

14

DIFFERENT SHADES

Never would have guessed. Only in true life could such things happen.

When he glanced to his right, he was surprised to find an old man sitting near him. Priest, no doubt. He had come after all . . . black hat, long grayish beard, sitting in the puddles now forming in the street, legs crossed. Go on, said Paul, don't suffer on my account, don't wait for me, but the old man remained, silent, drawn, rain glistening on his hat, face, beard, clothes: prosopopoeia of patience. The priest. Yet, something about the clothes: well, they were in rags. Pieced together and hanging in tatters. The hat, too, now that he noticed. At short intervals, the old man's head would nod, his eyes would cross, his body would tip, he would catch himself with a start, grunt, glance suspiciously about him, then back down at Paul, would finally relax again and recommence the cycle.

Paul's eyes wearied, especially with the rain splashing into them, so he let them fall closed once more. But he began suffering discomforting visions of the old priest, so he opened them again, squinted off to the left, toward the truck. A small dog, wiry and yellow, padded along in the puddles, hair drooping and bunching up with the rain. It sniffed at the tires of the truck, lifted its legs by one of them, sniffed again, padded on. It circled around Paul, apparently not noticing him, but poking its nose at every object, narrowing the distance between them with every circle. It passed close by the old man, snarled, completed another half-circle, and approached Paul from the left. It stopped near Paul's head—the wet-dog odor was suffocating—and whimpered, licking Paul's face. The old man did nothing, just sat, legs crossed, and passively watched. Of course . . . not a priest at all: an old beggar. Waiting for the clothes when he died. If he still had any. Go ahead and take them now, Paul told him, I don't care. But the beggar only sat and stared. Paul felt a tugging sensation from below, heard the dog growl. His whole body seemed to jerk upwards, sending another hot flash through his neck. The dog's hind feet were planted alongside Paul's head, and now and again the right paw would lose its footing, kick nervously at Paul's face, a buffeting counterpoint to the waves of hot pain behind his throat and eyes. Finally, something gave way. The dog shook water out of its yellow coat, and padded away, a fresh piece of flesh between its jaws. The beggar's eyes crossed, his head dipped to his chest, and he started to topple forward, but again he caught himself, took a deep breath, uncrossed his legs, crossed them again, but the opposite way, reached in his pocket and pulled out an old cigarette butt, molded it between his yellow fingers, put it in his mouth, but did not light it. For an instant, the earth upended again, and Paul found himself hung on the street, a target for the millions of raindarts somebody out in the night was throwing at him.

There's nobody out there, he reminded himself, and that set the earth right again. The beggar spat. Paul shielded his eyes from the rain with his lids. He thought he heard other dogs. How much longer must this go on? he wondered. How much longer?

[1969]

For Thought

The accident at the center of the story is obviously not very pedestrian at all. In fact, Coover takes the reader on a wild flight of fantasy by juxtaposing the total helplessness of the paralyzed victim and the callous interest of the crowd as it is entertained by various caricatures from among its own members. Overall, the entire ludicrous account, with its horrific double accident, emerges as an absurdist parable on human misery and compassion.

For Discussion

1. After the first few paragraphs, the reader realizes that this is not a realistic account of an accident. What details of speech, action, and characterization dispel the initial impression of reality?
2. What is the basic conflict in the story? What makes it comic instead of tragic?
3. How does Coover use the principle of the reversal of stereotypes for comic effect?
4. What do the Latinate and melodramatic words and phrases do for the atmosphere? How are these balanced by contrasting diction in the story?
5. What comment about human existence is Coover making in this absurdist parable?

Stephen Crane
The Bride Comes to Yellow Sky

I

The great pullman was whirling onward with such dignity of motion that a glance from the window seemed simply to prove that the plains of Texas were pouring eastward. Vast flats of green grass, dull-hued spaces of mesquit and cactus, little groups of frame houses, woods of light and tender trees, all were sweeping into the east, sweeping over the horizon, a precipice.

A newly married pair had boarded this coach at San Antonio. The man's face was reddened from many days in the wind and sun, and a direct result of his new black clothes was that his brick-colored hands were constantly performing in a most conscious fashion. From time to time he looked down respectfully at his attire. He sat with a hand on each knee, like a man waiting in a barber's shop. The glances he devoted to other passengers were furtive and shy.

The bride was not pretty, nor was she very young. She wore a dress of blue cashmere, with small reservations of velvet here and there, and with steel buttons abounding. She continually twisted her head to regard her puff sleeves, very stiff, straight, and high. They embarrassed her. It was quite apparent that she had cooked, and that she expected to cook, dutifully. The blushes caused by the careless scrutiny of some passengers as she had entered the car were strange to see upon this plain, under-class countenance, which was drawn in placid, almost emotionless lines.

They were evidently very happy. "Ever been in a parlor car before?" he asked, smiling with delight.

"No," she answered, "I never was. It's fine, ain't it?"

"Great! And then after a while we'll go forward to the diner, and get a big lay-out. Finest meal in the world. Charge a dollar."

"Oh, do they?" cried the bride. "Charge a dollar? Why, that's too much—for us—ain't it, Jack?"

"Not this trip, anyhow," he answered bravely. "We're going to go the whole thing."

Later he explained to her about the trains. "You see, it's a thousand miles from one end of Texas to the other; and this train

SOURCE: "The Bride Comes to Yellow Sky" by Stephen Crane. Originally published in *McClure's Magazine*, February 1898.

runs right across it, and never stops but four times." He had the pride of an owner. He pointed out to her the dazzling fittings of the coach; and in truth her eyes opened wider as she contemplated the sea-green figured velvet, the shining brass, silver, and glass, the wood that gleamed as darkly brilliant as the surface of a pool of oil. At one end a bronze figure sturdily held a support for a separated chamber, and at convenient places on the ceiling were frescoes in olive and silver.

To the minds of the pair, their surroundings reflected the glory of their marriage that morning in San Antonio; this was the environment of their new estate; and the man's face in particular beamed with an elation that made him appear ridiculous to the Negro porter. This individual at times surveyed them from afar with an amused and superior grin. On other occasions he bullied them with skill in ways that did not make it exactly plain to them that they were being bullied. He subtly used all the manners of the most unconquerable kind of snobbery. He oppressed them; but of this oppression they had small knowledge, and they speedily forgot that infrequently a number of travelers covered them with stares of derisive enjoyment. Historically there was supposed to be something infinitely humorous in their situation.

"We are due in Yellow Sky at 3:42," he said, looking tenderly into her eyes.

"Oh, are we?" she said, as if she had not been aware of it. To evince surprise at her husband's statement was part of her wifely amiability. She took from a pocket a little silver watch; and as she held it before her, and stared at it with a frown of attention, the new husband's face shone.

"I bought it in San Anton' from a friend of mine," he told her gleefully.

"It's seventeen minutes past twelve," she said, looking up at him with a kind of shy and clumsy coquetry. A passenger, noting this play, grew excessively sardonic, and winked at himself in one of the numerous mirrors.

At last they went to the dining car. Two rows of Negro waiters, in glowing white suits, surveyed their entrance with the interest, and also the equanimity, of men who had been forewarned. The pair fell to the lot of a waiter who happened to feel pleasure in steering them through their meal. He viewed them with the manner of a fatherly pilot, his countenance radiant with benevolence. The patronage, entwined with the ordinary deference, was not plain to them. And yet, as they returned to their coach, they showed in their faces a sense of escape.

To the left, miles down a long purple slope, was a little ribbon of mist where moved the keening Rio Grande. The train was approaching it at an angle, and the apex was Yellow Sky. Presently it was apparent that, as the distance from Yellow Sky grew shorter, the husband became commensurately restless. His brick-red hands were more insistent in their prominence. Occasionally he was even rather absent-minded and faraway when the bride leaned forward and addressed him.

As a matter of truth, Jack Potter was beginning to find the shadow of a deed weigh upon him like a leaden slab. He, the town marshal of Yellow Sky, a man known, liked, and feared in his corner, a prominent person, had gone to San Antonio to meet a girl he believed he loved, and there, after the usual prayers, had actually induced her to marry him, without consulting Yellow Sky for any part of the transaction. He was now bringing his bride before an innocent and unsuspecting community.

Of course people in Yellow Sky married as it pleased them, in accordance with a general custom; but such was Potter's thought of his duty to his friends, or of their idea of this duty, or of an unspoken form which does not control men in these matters, that he felt he was heinous. He had committed an extraordinary crime. Face to face with this girl in San Antonio, and spurred by his sharp impulse, he had gone headlong over all the social hedges. At San

Antonio he was like a man hidden in the dark. A knife to sever any friendly duty, any form, was easy to his hand in that remote city. But the hour of Yellow Sky—the hour of daylight—was approaching.

He knew full well that his marriage was an important thing to his town. It could only be exceeded by the burning of the new hotel. His friends could not forgive him. Frequently he had reflected on the advisability of telling them by telegraph, but a new cowardice had been upon him. He feared to do it. And now the train was hurrying him toward a scene of amazement, glee, and reproach. He glanced out of the window at the line of haze swinging slowly in toward the train.

Yellow Sky had a kind of brass band, which played painfully, to the delight of the populace. He laughed without heart as he thought of it. If the citizens could dream of his prospective arrival with his bride, they would parade the band at the station and escort them, amid cheers and laughing congratulations, to his adobe home.

He resolved that he would use all the devices of speed and plainscraft in making the journey from the station to his house. Once within the safe citadel, he could issue some sort of vocal bulletin, and then not go among the citizens until they had time to wear off a little of their enthusiasm.

The bride looked anxiously at him. "What's worrying you, Jack?"

He laughed again. "I'm not worrying, girl; I'm only thinking of Yellow Sky."

She flushed in comprehension.

A sense of mutual guilt invaded their minds and developed a finer tenderness. They looked at each other with eyes softly aglow. But Potter often laughed the same nervous laugh; the flush upon the bride's face seemed quite permanent.

The traitor to the feelings of Yellow Sky narrowly watched the speeding landscape. "We're nearly there," he said.

Presently the porter came and announced the proximity of Potter's home. He held a brush in his hand, and, with all his airy superiority gone, he brushed Potter's new clothes as the latter slowly turned this way and that way. Potter fumbled out a coin and gave it to the porter, as he had seen others do. It was a heavy and muscle-bound business, as that of a man shoeing his first horse.

The porter took their bag, and as the train began to slow they moved forward to the hooded platform of the car. Presently the two engines and their long string of coaches rushed into the station of Yellow Sky.

"They have to take water here," said Potter, from a constricted throat and in mournful cadence, as one announcing death. Before the train stopped his eye had swept the length of the platform, and he was glad and astonished to see there was none upon it but the station agent, who, with a slightly hurried and anxious air, was walking toward the water tanks. When the train had halted, the porter alighted first, and placed in position a little temporary step.

"Come on, girl," said Potter, hoarsely. As he helped her down they each laughed on a false note. He took the bag from the Negro, and bade his wife cling to his arm. As they slunk rapidly away, his hangdog glance perceived that they were unloading the two trunks, and also that the station agent, far ahead near the baggage car, had turned and was running toward him, making gestures. He laughed, and groaned as he laughed, when he noted the first effect of his marital bliss upon Yellow Sky. He gripped his wife's arm firmly to his side, and they fled. Behind them the porter stood, chuckling fatuously.

II

The California express on the Southern Railway was due at Yellow Sky in twenty-one minutes. There were six men at the bar of the Weary Gentleman saloon. One was a drummer who talked a great deal and rapidly; three were Texans who did not care to talk at that time; and two were Mexican sheep-herders, who did not talk as a general practice in the Weary Gentleman saloon. The barkeeper's dog lay on the boardwalk that crossed in front of the door. His head was on his paws, and he glanced drowsily here and there with the constant vigilance of a dog that is kicked on occasion. Across the sandy street were some vivid green grassplots, so wonderful in appearance, amid the sands that burned near them in a blazing sun, that they caused a doubt in the mind. They exactly resembled the grass mats used to represent lawns on the stage. At the cooler end of the railway station, a man without a coat sat in a tilted chair and smoked his pipe. The fresh-cut bank of the Rio Grande circled near the town, and there could be seen beyond it a great plum-colored plain of mesquit.

Save for the busy drummer and his companions in the saloon, Yellow Sky was dozing. The newcomer leaned gracefully upon the bar, and recited many tales with the confidence of a bard who has come upon a new field.

"—and at the moment that the old man fell downstairs with the bureau in his arms, the old woman was coming up with two scuttles of coal, and of course—"

The drummer's tale was interrupted by a young man who suddenly appeared in the open door. He cried: "Scratchy Wilson's drunk, and has turned loose with both hands." The two Mexicans at once set down their glasses and faded out of the rear entrance of the saloon.

The drummer, innocent and jocular, answered: "All right, old man. S'pose he has? Come in and have a drink, anyhow."

But the information had made such an obvious cleft in every skull in the room that the drummer was obliged to see its importance. All had become instantly solemn. "Say," said he, mystified, "what is this?" His three companions made the introductory gesture of eloquent speech; but the young man at the door forestalled them.

"It means, my friend," he answered, as he came into the saloon, "that for the next two hours this town won't be a health resort."

The barkeeper went to the door, and locked and barred it; reaching out of the window, he pulled in heavy wooden shutters, and barred them. Immediately a solemn, chapel-like gloom was upon the place. The drummer was looking from one to another.

"But say," he cried, "what is this, anyhow? You don't mean there is going to be a gun fight?"

"Don't know whether there'll be a fight or not," answered one man, grimly, "but there'll be some shootin'—some good shootin'."

The young man who had warned them waved his hand. "Oh, there'll be a fight fast enough, if any one wants it. Anybody can get a fight out there in the street. There's a fight just waiting."

The drummer seemed to be swayed between the interest of a foreigner and a perception of personal danger.

"What did you say his name was?" he asked.

"Scratchy Wilson," they answered in chorus.

"And will he kill anybody? What are you going to do? Does this happen often? Does he rampage around like this once a week or so? Can he break in that door?"

"No, he can't break down that door," replied the barkeeper. "He's tried it three times. But when he comes you'd better lay down on the floor, stranger. He's dead sure to shoot at it, and a bullet may come through."

Thereafter the drummer kept a strict eye upon the door. The time had not yet been called for him to hug the floor, but, as a minor precaution, he sidled near to the wall. "Will he kill anybody?" he said again.

The men laughed low and scornfully at the question.

"He's out to shoot, and he's out for trouble. Don't see any good in experimentin' with him."

"But what do you do in a case like this? What do you do?"

A man responded: "Why, he and Jack Potter—"

"But," in chorus the other men interrupted, "Jack Potter's in San Anton'."

"Well, who is he? What's he got to do with it?"

"Oh, he's the town marshal. He goes out and fights Scratchy when he gets on one of these tears."

"Wow!" said the drummer, mopping his brow. "Nice job he's got."

The voices had toned away to mere whisperings. The drummer wished to ask further questions, which were born of an increasing anxiety and bewilderment; but when he attempted them, the men merely looked at him in irritation and motioned him to remain silent. A tense waiting hush was upon them. In the deep shadows of the room their eyes shone as they listened for sounds from the street. One man made three gestures at the barkeeper; and the latter, moving like a ghost, handed him a glass and a bottle. The man poured a full glass of whisky, and set down the bottle noiselessly. He gulped the whisky in a swallow, and turned again toward the door in immovable silence. The drummer saw that the barkeeper, without a sound, had taken a Winchester from beneath the bar. Later he saw this individual beckoning to him, so he tiptoed across the room.

"You better come with me back of the bar."

"No, thanks," said the drummer, perspiring; "I'd rather be where I can make a break for the back door."

Whereupon the man of bottles made a kindly but peremptory gesture. The drummer obeyed it, and, finding himself seated on a box with his head below the level of the bar, balm was laid upon his soul at sight of various zinc and copper fittings that bore a resemblance to armor plate. The barkeeper took a seat comfortably upon an adjacent box.

"You see," he whispered, "this here Scratchy Wilson is a wonder with a gun—a perfect wonder; and when he goes on the war-trail, we hunt our holes—naturally. He's about the last one of the old gang that used to hang out along the river here. He's a terror when he's drunk. When he's sober he's all right—kind of simple—wouldn't hurt a fly—nicest fellow in town. But when he's drunk—whoo!"

There were periods of stillness. "I wish Jack Potter was back from San Anton'," said the barkeeper. "He shot Wilson up once—in the leg—and he would sail in and pull out the kinks in this thing."

Presently they heard from a distance the sound of a shot, followed by three wild yowls. It instantly removed a bond from the men in the darkened saloon. There was a shuffling of feet. They looked at each other. "Here he comes," they said.

III

A man in a maroon-colored flannel shirt, which had been purchased for purposes of decoration, and made principally by some Jewish women on the East Side of New York, rounded a corner and walked into the middle of the main street of Yellow Sky. In either hand the man held a long, heavy, blue-black revolver. Often he yelled, and these cries rang through a semblance of a deserted village, shrilly flying over the roofs in a volume that seemed to have no relation to the ordinary vocal strength of a man. It was as if the surrounding stillness formed the arch of a tomb over him. These cries of ferocious challenge rang against walls of silence. And his boots had red tops with gilded imprints, of the kind beloved in winter by little sledding boys on the hillsides of New England.

The man's face flamed in a rage begot of whisky. His eyes, rolling, and yet keen for ambush, hunted the still doorways and windows. He walked with the creeping movement of the midnight cat. As it occurred to him, he roared menacing information. The long revolvers in his hands were as easy as straws; they were moved with an electric swiftness. The little fingers of each hand played sometimes in a musician's way. Plain from the low collar of the shirt, the cords of his neck straightened and sank, straightened and sank, as passion moved him. The only sounds were his terrible invitations. The calm adobes preserved their demeanor at the passing of this small thing in the middle of the street.

There was no offer of fight—no offer of fight. The man called to the sky. There were no attractions. He bellowed and fumed and swayed his revolvers here and everywhere.

The dog of the barkeeper of the Weary Gentleman saloon had not appreciated the advance of events. He yet lay dozing in front of his master's door. At sight of the dog, the man paused and raised his revolver humorously. At sight of the man, the dog sprang up and walked diagonally away, with a sullen head, and growling. The man yelled, and the dog broke into a gallop. As it was about to enter an alley, there was a loud noise, a whistling, and something spat the ground directly before it. The dog screamed, and, wheeling in terror, galloped headlong in a new direction. Again there was a noise, a whistling, and sand was kicked viciously before it. Fear-stricken, the dog turned and flurried like an animal in a pen. The man stood laughing, his weapons at his hips.

Ultimately the man was attracted by the closed door of the Weary Gentleman saloon. He went to it and, hammering with a revolver, demanded drink.

The door remaining imperturbable, he picked a bit of paper from the walk, and nailed it to the framework with a knife. He then turned his back contemptuously upon his popular resort and, walking to the opposite side of the street and spinning there on his heel quickly and lithely, fired at the bit of paper. He missed it by a half-inch. He swore at himself, and went away. Later he comfortably fusilladed the windows of his most intimate friend. The man was playing with this town; it was a toy for him.

But still there was no offer of fight. The name of Jack Potter, his ancient antagonist, entered his mind, and he concluded that it would be a glad thing if he should go to Potter's house, and by bombardment induce him to come out and fight. He moved in the direction of his desire, chanting Apache scalp-music.

When he arrived at it, Potter's house presented the same still front as had the other adobes. Taking up a strategic position, the man howled a challenge. But this house regarded him as might a great stone god. It gave no sign. After a decent wait, the man howled further challenges, mingling with them wonderful epithets.

Presently there came the spectacle of a man churning himself into deepest rage over the immobility of a house. He fumed at it as the winter wind attacks a prairie cabin in the North. To the distance there should have gone the sound of a tumult like the fighting of two hundred Mexicans. As necessity bade him, he paused for breath or to reload his revolvers.

IV

Potter and his bride walked sheepishly and with speed. Sometimes they laughed together shamefacedly and low.

"Next corner, dear," he said finally.

They put forth the efforts of a pair walking bowed against a strong wind. Potter was about to raise a finger to point the first appearance of the new home when, as they circled the corner, they came face to face with a man in a maroon-colored shirt, who was feverishly pushing cartridges into a large revolver. Upon the instant the man dropped his revolver to the ground and, like lightning, whipped another from its holster. The second weapon was aimed at the bridegroom's chest.

There was a silence. Potter's mouth seemed to be merely a grave for his tongue. He exhibited an instinct to at once loosen his arm from the woman's grip, and he dropped the bag to the sand. As for the bride, her face had gone as yellow as old cloth. She was a slave to hideous rites, gazing at the apparitional snake.

The two men faced each other at a distance of three paces. He of the revolver smiled with a new and quiet ferocity.

"Tried to sneak up on me," he said. "Tried to sneak up on me!" His eyes grew more baleful. As Potter made a slight movement, the man thrust his revolver venomously forward. "No, don't you do it, Jack Potter. Don't you move a finger toward a gun just yet. Don't you move an eyelash. The time has come for me to settle with you, and I'm goin' to do it my own way, and loaf along with no interferin'. So if you don't want a gun bent on you, just mind what I tell you."

Potter looked at his enemy. "I ain't got a gun on me, Scratchy," he said. "Honest, I ain't." He was stiffening and steadying, but yet somewhere at the back of his mind a vision of the Pullman floated: the sea-green figured velvet, the shining brass, silver, and glass, the wood that gleamed as darkly brilliant as the surface of a pool of oil—all the glory of the marriage, the environment of the new estate. "You know I fight when it comes to fighting, Scratchy Wilson; but I ain't got a gun on me. You'll have to do all the shootin' yourself."

His enemy's face went livid. He stepped forward, and lashed his weapon to and fro before Potter's chest. "Don't you tell me you ain't got no gun on you, you whelp. Don't tell me no lie like that. There ain't a man in Texas ever seen you without no gun. Don't take me for no kid." His eyes blazed with light, and his throat worked like a pump.

"I ain't takin' you for no kid," answered Potter. His heels had not moved an inch backward. "I'm takin' you for a damn fool. I tell you I ain't got a gun, and I ain't. If you're goin' to shoot me up, you better begin now; you'll never get a chance like this again."

So much enforced reasoning had told on Wilson's rage; he was calmer. "If you ain't got a gun, why ain't you got a gun?" he sneered. "Been to Sunday school?"

"I ain't got a gun because I've just come from San Anton' with my wife. I'm married," said Potter. "And if I'd thought there was going to be any galoots like you prowling around when I brought my wife home, I'd had a gun, and don't you forget it."

"Married!" said Scratchy, not at all comprehending.

"Yes, married. I'm married," said Potter, distinctly.

"Married?" said Scratchy. Seemingly for the first time, he saw the drooping, drowning woman at the other man's side. "No!" he said. He was like a creature allowed a glimpse of another world. He moved a pace backward, and his arm, with the revolver, dropped to his side. "Is this the lady?" he asked.

"Yes, this is the lady," answered Potter.

There was another period of silence.

"Well," said Wilson at last, slowly, "I s'pose it's all off now."

"It's all off if you say so, Scratchy. You know I didn't make the trouble." Potter lifted his valise.

"Well, I 'low it's off, Jack," said Wilson. He was looking at the ground. "Married!" He was not a student of chivalry; it was merely that in the presence of this foreign condition he was a simple child of the earlier plains. He picked up his starboard revolver, and, placing both weapons in their holsters, he went away. His feet made funnel-shaped tracks in the heavy sand.

[1898]

For Thought

Crane has inverted the time worn traditions of Western fiction. The hero marries instead of kissing his horse; his antagonist is old and drunken instead of thin and athletic; the duel simply fades out; and the story ends not with a fiery cleansing of evil but with a poignant, backhanded salute to womanhood. By giving up his challenge to Potter, Wilson acknowledges the death of adolescence and irresponsibility, both for him and for the wider community.

For Discussion

1. What point of view does Crane use? What is his attitude toward his characters?
2. What is the tone of the story? How is it achieved?
3. Each part of the story centers around a social ritual: marriage, the alert, the challenge, and the Western shootout. How is each of these ceremonies rendered comic or parodied?
4. How does Crane both foreshadow and build suspense toward the climax of the story?
5. How does Crane represent Potter as a "typical town marshal" in a small western town without making him a stereotyped hero figure?
6. How does Crane ironically invert the stereotype of good guy versus bad guy?
7. How does Crane make Scratchy sympathetic?
8. What is the unnamed traveling salesman's function in the story?
9. What is the unnamed bride's function in the story?
10. What aspects of the story depend on conformity of the characters to a code of the West?
11. How is the conclusion of the story ironic?
12. What is the theme of the story, and how is it unconventional?

Charles Dickens
Hunted Down

I

Most of us see some romances in life. In my capacity as Chief Manager of a Life Assurance Office, I think I have within the last thirty years seen more romances than the generality of men, however unpromising the opportunity may, at first sight, seem.

As I have retired, and live at my ease, I possess the means that I used to want, of considering what I have seen, at leisure. Let me recall one of these Romances of the real world.

II

The partition which separated my own office from our general outer office in the City was of thick plate-glass. I could see through it what passed in the outer office, without hearing a word. I had it put up, in place of a wall that had been there for years,—ever since the house was built. It is no matter whether I did or did not make the change in order that I might derive my first impression of strangers, who came to us on business, from their faces alone, without being influenced by anything they said. Enough to mention that I turned my glass partition to that account, and that a Life Assurance Office is at all times exposed to be practised upon by the most crafty and cruel of the human race.

It was through my glass partition that I first saw the gentleman whose story I am going to tell.

He had come in without my observing it, and had put his hat and umbrella on the broad counter, and was bending over it to take some papers from one of the clerks. He was about forty or so, dark, exceedingly well dressed in black,—being in mourning,—and the hand he extended with a polite air had a particularly well-fitting, black kid glove upon it. His hair, which was elaborately brushed and oiled, was parted straight up the middle; and he presented this parting to the clerk, exactly (to my thinking) as if he had said, in as many words: "You must take me, if you please, my friend, just as I show myself. Come

SOURCE: "Hunted Down" by Charles Dickens. Originally published in the *New York Ledger*, 1859.

straight up here, follow the gravel path, keep off the grass, I allow no trespassing."

I conceived a very great aversion to that man the moment I thus saw him.

He had asked for some of our printed forms, and the clerk was giving them to him and explaining them. An obliged and agreeable smile was on his face, and his eyes met those of the clerk with a sprightly look. (I have known a vast quantity of nonsense talked about bad men not looking you in the face. Don't trust that conventional idea. Dishonesty will stare honesty out of countenance, any day in the week, if there is anything to be got by it.)

I saw, in the corner of his eyelash, that he became aware of my looking at him. Immediately he turned the parting in his hair toward the glass partition, as if he said to me with a sweet smile, "Straight up here, if you please. Off the grass!"

In a few moments he had put on his hat and taken up his umbrella, and was gone.

I beckoned the clerk into my room, and asked, "Who was that?"

He had the gentleman's card in his hand. "Mr. Julius Slinkton, Middle Temple."

"A barrister, Mr. Adams?"

"I think not, sir."

"I should have thought him a clergyman, but for his having no Reverend here," said I.

"Probably, from his appearance," Mr. Adams replied, "he is reading for orders."

I should mention that he wore a dainty white cravat, and dainty linen altogether.

"What did he want, Mr. Adams?"

"Merely a form of proposal, sir, and form of reference."

"Recommended here? Did he say?"

"Yes, he said he was recommended here by a friend of yours. He noticed you, but said that as he had not the pleasure of your personal acquaintance he would not trouble you."

"Did he know my name?"

"O yes, sir! He said, 'There *is* Mr. Sampson, I see!' "

"A well-spoken gentleman, apparently?"

"Remarkably so, sir."

"Insinuating manners, apparently?"

"Very much so, indeed, sir."

"Hah!" said I. "I want nothing at present, Mr. Adams."

Within a fortnight of that day I went to dine with a friend of mine, a merchant, a man of taste who buys pictures and books; and the first man I saw among the company was Mr. Julius Slinkton.

I noticed him ask my friend to introduce him to Mr. Sampson, and my friend did so. Mr. Slinkton was very happy to see me. Not too happy; there was no overdoing of the matter; happy in a thoroughly well-bred, perfectly unmeaning way.

"I thought you had met," our host observed.

"No," said Mr. Slinkton. "I did look in at Mr. Sampson's office, on your recommendation; but I really did not feel justified in troubling Mr. Sampson himself, on a point in the everyday routine of an ordinary clerk."

I said I should have been glad to show him any attention on our friend's introduction.

"You were thinking," said I, "of effecting a policy on your life."

"O dear, no! I am afraid I am not so prudent as you pay me the compliment of supposing me to be, Mr. Sampson. I merely inquired for a friend. But you know what friends are in such matters. Nothing may ever come of it. I have the greatest reluctance to trouble men of business with inquiries for friends, knowing the probabilities to be a thousand to one that the friends will never follow them up. People are so fickle, so selfish, so inconsiderate. Don't you, in your business, find them so every day, Mr. Sampson?"

I was going to give a qualified answer; but he turned his smooth, white parting on me with its "Straight up here, if you please!" and I answered, "Yes."

"I hear, Mr. Sampson," he resumed,

presently, "that your profession has recently suffered a great loss."

"In money!" said I.

He laughed at my ready association of loss with money, and replied, "No, in talent and vigor."

Not at once following out his allusion, I considered for a moment. "*Has* it sustained a loss of that kind?" said I. "I was not aware of it."

"Understand me, Mr. Sampson. I don't imagine that you have retired. It is not so bad as that. But Mr. Meltham—"

"O, to be sure!" said I. "Yes! Mr. Meltham, the young actuary of the 'Inestimable'."

"Just so," he returned in a consoling way.

"He is a great loss. He was at once the most profound, the most original, and the most energetic man I have ever known connected with Life Assurance."

I spoke strongly; for I had a high esteem and admiration for Meltham, and my gentleman had indefinitely conveyed to me some suspicion that he wanted to sneer at him.

"You knew him, Mr. Slinkton."

"Only by reputation. To have known him as an acquaintance, or as a friend, is an honor I should have sought if he had remained in society, though I might never have had the good fortune to attain it, being a man of far inferior mark. He was scarcely above thirty, I suppose?"

"About thirty."

"Ah!" He sighed in his former consoling way. "What creatures we are! To break up, Mr. Sampson, and become incapable of business at that time of life!—Any reason assigned for the melancholy fact?"

("Humph!" thought I, as I looked at him. "But I *won't* go up the track, and I *will* go on the grass.")

"What reason have you heard assigned, Mr. Slinkton?" I asked, point blank.

"Most likely a false one. You know what Rumor is, Mr. Sampson. I never repeat what I hear; it is the only way of paring the nails and shaving the head of Rumor. But, when *you* ask me what reason I have heard assigned for Mr. Meltham's passing away from among men, it is another thing. I am not gratifying idle gossip then. I was told, Mr. Sampson, that Mr. Meltham had relinquished all his avocations and all his prospects, because he was, in fact, broken-hearted. A disappointed attachment I heard,—though it hardly seems probable, in the case of a man so distinguished and so attractive."

"Attractions and distinctions are no armor against death," said I.

"Oh! she died? Pray pardon me. I did not hear that. That, indeed, makes it very, very sad. Poor Mr. Meltham! She died? Ah, dear me! Lamentable, lamentable!"

I still thought his pity was not quite genuine, and I still suspected an unaccountable sneer under all this, until he said, as we were parted, like the other knots of talkers, by the announcement of dinner,—

"Mr. Sampson, you are surprised to see me so moved on behalf of a man whom I have never known. I am not so disinterested as you may suppose. I have suffered, and recently too, from death myself. I have lost one of two charming nieces, who were my constant companions. She died young,—barely three-and-twenty,—and even her remaining sister is far from strong. The world is a grave!"

I took my part in the conversation with him after a time, and we got on remarkably well. In the drawing-room I asked the host how long he had known Mr. Slinkton? He answered, not many months; he had met him at the house of a celebrated painter then present, who had known him well when he was travelling with his nieces in Italy for their health. His plans in life being broken by the death of one of them, he was reading with the intention of going back to college as a matter of form, taking his degree, and going into orders. I could not but argue with myself that here was the true explanation of his interest in poor Meltham, and that I had been almost brutal in my distrust on that simple head.

III

On the very next day but one, I was sitting behind my glass partition, as before, when he came into the outer office as before. The moment I saw him again without hearing him, I hated him worse than ever.

It was only for a moment that I had this opportunity; for he waved his tight-fitting black glove the instant I looked at him, and came straight in.

"Mr. Sampson, good day! I presume, you see, upon your kind permission to intrude upon you. I don't keep my word in being justified by business, for my business here—if I may so abuse the word—is of the slightest nature."

I asked, was it anything I could assist him in?

"I thank you, no. I merely called to inquire outside, whether my dilatory friend had been so false to himself as to be practical and sensible. But, of course, he has done nothing. I gave him your papers with my own hand, and he was hot upon the intention, but of course he has done nothing. You find it like will-making? People are so superstitious, and take it for granted they will die soon afterwards?"

"There is such a feeling sometimes, no doubt," I replied, "but I don't think it obtains to any great extent."

"Well," said he, with a shrug and a smile, "I wish some good angel would influence my friend in the right direction. I rashly promised his mother and sister in Norfolk, to see it done, and he promised them that he would do it. But I suppose he never will."

He spoke for a minute or two on indifferent topics and went away.

I had scarcely unlocked the drawers of my writing-table next morning when he reappeared. I noticed that he came straight to the door in the glass partition, and did not pause a single moment outside.

"Can you spare me two minutes, my dear Mr. Sampson?"

"By all means."

"Much obliged," he said, laying his hat and umbrella on the table; "I came early, not to interrupt you. The fact is, I am taken by surprise, in reference to this proposal my friend has made."

"Has he made one?" said I.

"Ye-es," he answered, deliberately looking at me; and then a bright idea seemed to strike him;—"or he only tells me he has. Perhaps that may be a new way of evading the matter. By Jupiter, I never thought of that!"

Mr. Adams was opening the morning's letters in the outer office. "What is the name, Mr. Slinkton?" I asked.

"Beckwith."

I looked out at the door and requested Mr. Adams, if there were a proposal in that name, to bring it in. He had already laid it out of his hand on the counter. It was easily selected from the rest, and he gave it me. Alfred Beckwith. Proposal to effect a policy with us for two thousand pounds. Dated yesterday.

"From the Middle Temple, I see, Mr. Slinkton."

"Yes. He lives on the same staircase with me; his door is opposite. I never thought he would make me his reference, though."

He took the printed paper from his pocket. "How am I to answer all these questions!"

"According to the truth, of course," said I.

Before answering each question he ran over it aloud, and discussed it. How long had he known Mr. Alfred Beckwith? That he had to calculate by years upon his fingers. What were his habits? No difficulty about them; temperate in the last degree, and took a little too much exercise, if anything. All the answers were satisfactory. When he had written them all, he looked them over, and finally signed them in a very pretty hand. He supposed he had now done with the business? I told him he was not likely to be troubled any further. Should he leave the papers there? If he pleased. Much obliged. Good morning!

I had had one other visitor before him; not at the office, but at my own house. That visitor had come to my bedside when it was not yet daylight, and had been seen by no one else but by my faithful confidential servant.

A second reference paper (for we required always two) was sent down into Norfolk, and was duly received back by post. This, likewise, was satisfactorily answered in every respect. Our forms were all complied with, we accepted the proposal, and the premium for one year was paid.

IV

For six or seven months, I saw no more of Mr. Slinkton. Late in September or early in October, I was down at Scarborough for a breath of sea air, where I met him on the beach. It was a hot evening; he came toward me with his hat in his hand.

He was not alone, but had a young lady on his arm.

She was dressed in mourning, and I looked at her with great interest. She had the appearance of being extremely delicate, and her face was remarkably pale and melancholy; but she was very pretty. He introduced her as his niece, Miss Niner.

"Are you strolling, Mr. Sampson? Is it possible you can be idle?"

It *was* possible, and I *was* strolling.

"Shall we stroll together?"

"With pleasure."

The young lady walked between us, and we walked on the cool sea sand, in the direction of Filey.

"There have been wheels here," said Mr. Slinkton. "And now I look again, the wheels of a hand-carriage! Margaret, my love, your shadow, without doubt!"

"Miss Niner's shadow?" I repeated, looking down at it on the sand.

"Not that one," Mr. Slinkton, returned, laughing. "Margaret, my dear, tell Mr. Sampson."

"Indeed," said the young lady, turning to me, "there is nothing to tell,—except that I constantly see the same invalid old gentleman, at all times, wherever I go. I have mentioned it to my uncle, and he calls the gentleman my shadow."

"Does he live in Scarborough?" I asked.

"He is staying here."

"Do you live in Scarborough?"

"No, I am staying here. My uncle has placed me with a family here, for my health."

"And your shadow?" said I, smiling.

"My shadow," she answered, smiling too, "is—like myself—not very robust, I fear; for I lose my shadow sometimes, as my shadow loses me at other times. We both seem liable to confinement to the house. I have not seen my shadow for days and days; but it does oddly happen, occasionally, that wherever I go, for many days together, this gentleman goes. We have come together in the most unfrequented nooks on this shore."

"Is this he?" said I, pointing before us.

The wheels had swept down to the water's edge, and described a great loop on the sand in turning. Bringing the loop back toward us, and spinning it out as it came, was a hand-carriage drawn by a man.

"Yes," said Miss Niner, "this really is my shadow, uncle!"

As the carriage approached us and we approached the carriage, I saw within it an old man, whose head was sunk on his breast, and who was enveloped in a variety of wrappers. He was drawn by a very quiet but very keen-looking man, with iron-gray hair, who was slightly lame. They had passed us, when the carriage stopped, and the old gentleman within, putting out his arm, called to me by my name. I went back, and was absent from Mr. Slinkton and his niece for about five minutes.

When I rejoined them, Mr. Slinkton was the first to speak. Indeed, he said to me in a raised voice before I came up with him: "It is well you have not been longer, or my niece might have died of curiosity to know who her shadow is, Mr. Sampson."

"An old East India Director," said I. "An intimate friend of our friend's at whose house I first had the pleasure of meeting you. A certain Major Banks. You have heard of him?"

"Never."

"Very rich, Miss Niner; but very old, and very crippled. An amiable man, sensible,—much interested in you. He has just been expatiating on the affection that he has observed to exist between you and your uncle."

Mr. Slinkton was holding his hat again, and he passed his hand up the straight walk, as if he himself went up it serenely, after me.

"Mr. Sampson," he said, tenderly pressing his niece's arm in his, "our affection was always a strong one, for we have had but few near ties. We have still fewer now. We have associations to bring us together, that are not of this world, Margaret."

"Dear uncle!" murmured the young lady, and turned her face aside to hide her tears.

"My niece and I have such remembrances and regrets in common, Mr. Sampson," he feelingly pursued, "that it would be strange indeed if the relations between us were cold or indifferent. If I remember a conversation we once had together, you will understand the reference I make. Cheer up, dear Margaret. Don't droop, don't droop. My Margaret! I cannot bear to see you droop!"

The poor young lady was very much affected, but controlled herself. His feelings, too, were very acute. In a word, he found himself under such great need of a restorative, that he presently went away, to take a bath of seawater, leaving the young lady and me sitting by a point of rock, and probably presuming that she would praise him with all her heart.

She did, poor thing! With all her confiding heart, she praised him to me, for his care of her dead sister, and for his untiring devotion in her last illness. The sister had wasted away very slowly, and wild and terrible fantasies had come over her toward the end, but he had never been impatient with her, or at a loss; had always been gentle, watchful, and self-possessed.

"I shall leave him, Mr. Sampson, very soon," said the young lady; "I know my life is drawing to an end; and when I am gone, I hope he will marry and be happy. I am sure he has lived single so long, only for my sake, and for my poor, poor sister's."

The little-hand carriage had made another great loop on the damp sand, and was coming back again, gradually spinning out a slim figure of eight, half a mile long.

"Young lady," said I, looking around, laying my hand upon her arm, and speaking in a low voice, "time presses. You hear the gentle murmur of that sea?"

She looked at me with the utmost wonder and alarm, saying, "Yes!"

"And you know what a voice is in it when the storm comes?"

"Yes!"

"You see how quiet and peaceful it lies before us, and you know what an awful sight of power without pity it might be, this very night!"

"Yes!"

"But if you had never heard or seen it, or heard of it in its cruelty, could you believe that it beats every inanimate thing in its way to pieces, without mercy, and destroys life without remorse?"

"You terrify me, sir, by these questions!"

"To save you, young lady, to save you! For God's sake, collect your strength and collect your firmness! If you were here alone, and hemmed in by the rising tide on the flow to fifty feet above your head, you could not be in greater danger than the danger you are now to be saved from."

The figure on the sand was spun out, and straggled off into a crooked little jerk that ended at the cliff very near us.

"As I am, before Heaven and the Judge of all mankind, your friend, and your dead sister's friend, I solemnly entreat you, Miss Niner, without one moment's loss of time, to come to this gentleman with me!"

If the little carriage had been less near to us, I doubt if I could have got her away; but it was so near that we were there before she had recovered from the hurry of being urged from the rock. I did not remain there with her two minutes. Certainly within five, I had the inexpressible satisfaction of seeing her—from the point we had sat on, and to which I had returned—half supported and half carried up some rude steps notched in the cliff, by the figure of an active man. With that figure beside her, I knew she was safe anywhere.

I sat alone on the rock, awaiting Mr. Slinkton's return. The twilight was deepening and the shadows were heavy, when he came round the point, with his hat hanging at his buttonhole, smoothing his wet hair with one of his hands, and picking out the old path with the other and a pocket-comb.

"My niece not here, Mr. Sampson?" he said, looking about.

"Miss Niner seemed to feel a chill in the air after the sun was down, and has gone home."

He looked surprised, as though she were not accustomed to do anything without him; even to originate so slight a proceeding. "I persuaded Miss Niner," I explained.

"Ah!" said he. "She is easily persuaded—for her good. Thank you, Mr. Sampson; she is better within doors. The bathing place was farther than I thought, to say the truth."

"Miss Niner is very delicate," I observed.

He shook his head and drew a deep sigh. "Very, very, very. The gloomy shadow that fell upon her sister so early in life seems, in my anxious eyes, to gather over her, ever darker, ever darker. But we must hope."

By this time the carriage, much to my relief, was lost in the darkness. We walked on for a little, side by side over the sand, in silence. After a short while he said, in a voice still affected by the emotion that his niece's state of health had awakened in him,—

"Do you stay here long, Mr. Sampson?"

"Why, no. I am going away to-night."

We left the beach, and our ways diverged. We exchanged good night, and had parted indeed, when he said, returning,—

"Mr. Sampson, *may* I ask? Poor Meltham, whom we spoke of,—dead yet?"

"Not when I last heard of him; but too broken a man to live long, and hopelessly lost to his old calling."

"Dear, dear, dear!" said he, with great feeling. "Sad, sad, sad! The world is a grave!" And so went his way.

V

I had a very particular engagement to breakfast in the Temple.

The appointment took me to some chambers in the Temple. They were at the top of a lonely corner house overlooking the river. The name, Mr. Alfred Beckwith, was painted on the outer door. On the door opposite, on the same landing, the name Mr. Julius Slinkton. The doors of both sets of chambers stood open, so that anything said aloud in one set could be heard in the other.

I had never been in those chambers before. They were dismal, close, unwholesome, and oppressive; the furniture, originally good, and not yet old, was faded and dirty,—the rooms were in great disorder; there was a strong pervading smell of opium, brandy, and tobacco; the grate and fire-irons were splashed all over with unsightly blotches of rust; and on a sofa by the fire, in the room where breakfast had been prepared, lay the host, Mr. Beckwith, a man with all the appearances of the worst kind of drunkard, very far advanced upon his shameful way to death.

"Slinkton is not come yet," said this creature, staggering up when I went in; "I'll call him. Halloa! Julius Cæsar! Come and drink!" As he hoarsely roared this out, he beat the poker and tongs together in a mad way, as if that were his usual manner of summoning his associate.

The voice of Mr. Slinkton was heard through the clatter from the opposite side of the staircase, and he came in. He had not expected the pleasure of meeting me. I have seen several artful men brought to a stand, but I never saw a man so aghast as he was when his eyes rested on mine.

"Julius Cæsar," cried Beckwith, staggering between us, "Mist' Sampson! Mist' Sampson, Julius Cæsar! Julius, Mist' Sampson, is the friend of my soul. Julius keeps me plied with liquor, morning, noon, and night. Julius is a real benefactor. Julius threw the tea and coffee out of window when I used to have any. Julius empties all the water-jugs of their contents, and fills 'em with spirits. Julius winds me up and keeps me going.—Boil the brandy, Julius!"

There was a rusty and furred saucepan in the ashes,—the ashes looked like the accumulation of weeks,—and Beckwith, rolling and staggering between us as if he were going to plunge headlong into the fire, got the saucepan out, and tried to force it into Slinkton's hand.

"Boil the brandy, Julius Cæsar! Come! Do your usual office.—Boil the brandy!"

He became so fierce in his gesticulations with the saucepan, that I expected to see him lay open Slinkton's head with it. I therefore put out my hand to check him. He reeled back to the sofa, and sat there panting, shaking, and red-eyed, in his rags of dressing-gown, looking at us both. I noticed then that there was nothing to drink on the table but brandy, and nothing to eat but salted herrings, and a hot, sickly, highly peppered stew.

"At all events, Mr. Sampson," said Slinkton, offering me the smooth gravel path for the last time, "I thank you for interfering between me and this unfortunate man's violence. However you came here, Mr. Sampson, or with whatever motive you came here, at least I thank you for that."

Without gratifying his desire to know how I came there, I said, quietly, "How is your niece, Mr. Slinkton?"

He looked hard at me, and I looked hard at him.

"I am sorry to say, Mr. Sampson, that my niece has proved treacherous and ungrateful to her best friend. She left me without a word of notice or explanation. She was misled, no doubt, by some designing rascal. Perhaps you may have heard of it?"

"I did hear that she was misled by a designing rascal. In fact, I have proof of it."

"Are you sure of that?" said he.

"Quite."

"Boil the brandy," muttered Beckwith. "Company to breakfast, Julius Cæsar! Do your usual office,—provide the usual breakfast, dinner, tea, and supper.—Boil the brandy!"

The eyes of Slinkton looked from him to me, and he said, after a moment's consideration,—

"Mr. Sampson, you are a man of the world, and so am I. I will be plain with you."

"O no, you won't," said I, shaking my head.

"I tell you, sir, I will be plain with you."

"And I tell you, you will not," said I. "I know all about you. *You* plain with any one? Nonsense, nonsense!"

"I plainly tell you, Mr. Sampson," he went on, with a manner almost composed, "that I understand your object. You want to save your funds, and escape from your liabilities; these are old tricks of trade with you Office-gentlemen. But you will not do it, sir; you will not succeed. You have not an easy adversary to play against, when you play against me. We shall have to inquire, in due time, when and how Mr. Beckwith fell into his present habits. With that remark, sir, I put this poor creature and his incoherent wanderings of speech, aside, and wish you a good morning and a better case next time."

While he was saying this, Beckwith had filled a halfpint glass with brandy. At this moment, he threw the brandy at his face, and threw the glass after it. Slinkton put his hands up, half blinded with the spirit, and cut with the glass across the forehead. At the sound of the breakage, a fourth person came into the room, closed the door, and stood at it; he was a very quiet but very keen-looking man, with iron-gray hair, and slightly lame.

Slinkton pulled out his handkerchief, assuaged the pain in his smarting eyes, and dabbled the blood on his forehead. He was a long time about it, and I saw that, in the doing of it, a tremendous change came over him, occasioned by the change in Beckwith,—who ceased to pant and tremble, sat upright, and never took his eyes off him. I never in my life saw a face in which abhorrence and determination were so forcibly painted, as in Beckwith's then.

"Look at me, you villain," said Beckwith, "and see me as I really am. I took these rooms, to make them a trap for you. I came into them as a drunkard, to bait the trap for you. You fell into the trap, and you will never leave it alive. On the morning when you last went to Mr. Sampson's office, I had seen him first. Your plot has been known to both of us, all along, and you have been counterplotted all along. What? Having been cajoled into putting that prize of two thousand pounds in your power, I was to be done to death with brandy, and, brandy not proving quick enough, with something quicker? Have I never seen you, when you thought my senses gone, pouring from your little bottle into my glass? Why, you Murderer and Forger, alone here with you in the dead of night, as I have so often been, I have had my hand upon the trigger of a pistol, twenty times, to blow your brains out!"

Perfectly consistent with himself, as I believe all such monsters to be, this Slinkton recovered himself, and showed a defiance that was sufficiently cold and quiet. He was white, he was haggard, he was changed; but only as a sharper who had played for a great stake and had been outwitted and had lost the game.

"Listen to me, you villain," said Beckwith," and let every word you hear me say be a stab in your wicked heart. When I took these rooms, to throw myself in your way and lead you on to the scheme that I knew my appearance and supposed character and habits would suggest to such a devil how did I know that? Because you were no stranger to me. I knew you well. And I knew you to be the cruel wretch who, for so much money, had killed one innocent girl while she trusted him implicitly, and who was, by inches killing another."

Slinkton took out a snuff-box, took a pinch of snuff, and laughed.

"That drunkard," said Beckwith, "who had free access to your rooms at all times, that he might drink the strong drinks that you left in his way and be the sooner ended, holding no more terms with you than he would hold with a tiger, has had his master-key for all your locks, his test for all your poisons, his clew to your cipher-writing. He can tell you, as well as you can tell him, how long it took to complete that deed, what doses there were, what intervals, what signs of gradual decay upon mind and body; what distempered fancies were produced, what observable changes, what physical pain. He can tell you, as well as you can tell him, that all this was recorded day by day, as a lesson of experience for future service. He can tell you, better than you can tell him, where that journal is at this moment."

Slinkton stopped the action of his foot, and looked at Beckwith.

"No," said the latter, as if answering a question from him. "Not in the drawer of the writing-desk that opens with the spring; it is not there, and it never will be there again."

"Then you are a thief!" said Slinkton.

"And I am your niece's shadow, too."

Beckwith went on: "Whenever you left here, I left here. Although I understood that you found it necessary to pause in the completion of that purpose, to avert suspicion, still I watched you close, with the poor, confiding girl. When I had the diary, and could read it word by word,—it was only about the night before your last visit to Scarborough,—you remember the night? you slept with a small flat vial tied to your wrist,—I sent to Mr. Sampson, who was kept out of view. This is Mr. Sampson's trusty servant standing by the door. We three saved your niece among us."

Slinkton looked at us all, took an uncertain step or two from the place where he had stood, returned to it, and glanced about him in a very curious way,—as one of the meaner reptiles might, looking for a hole to hide in.

"When you sent the sweet girl whom you murdered to Meltham's office, before taking her abroad to originate the transaction that doomed her to the grave, it fell to Meltham's lot to see her and to speak with her. It did not fall to his lot to save her, though I know he would freely give his own life to have done it. He admired her;—I would say, he loved her deeply, if I thought it possible that you could understand the word. When she was sacrificed, he was thoroughly assured of your guilt. Having lost her, he had but one object left in life, and that was to avenge her and destroy you."

I saw the villain's nostrils rise and fall, convulsively; but I saw no moving at his mouth.

"That man, Meltham," Beckwith steadily pursued, "was as absolutely certain that you could never elude him in this world. I am that man, and I thank God that I have done my work!"

When Meltham had spoken these last words, the miscreant suddenly turned away his face, and seemed to strike his mouth with his open hand. At the same instant, the room was filled with a new and powerful odor, and, almost at the same instant, he broke into a crooked run, leap, start, I have no name for the spasm,—and fell, with a dull weight that shook the heavy old doors and windows in their frames.

That was the fitting end of him.

[1859]

For Thought

"Hunted Down" is a story of genuine detection. The characters are as lifelike as real people; the detectives are as realistic in language, methods, and actions as true-to-life investigators. Charles Dickens lived in London when the first police detective department was formed in 1842. He often wrote articles about various individuals in the department that bordered on hero worship, and he occasionally accompanied the police on their investigations. Dickens even visited the Paris morgue in hopes of seeing a murdered corpse, and he served on a coroner's jury in a case of infanticide. Dickens wrote many detective stories. In fact, he is credited with creating the first fictional English detective—Inspector Bucket—in *Bleak House* (1853).

For Discussion

1. How does the title foreshadow the conclusion of the story?
2. The author uses the first-person point of view, yet he manages to create a somewhat surprising conclusion. How does he do this?
3. What are some of the adjectives the narrator uses to describe Slinkton? How do these adjectives establish character?

4. What initial insights into human character does the narrator have? Do you agree with him?
5. How are the main characters' names indicative of their personality traits?
6. What are the conflicts in the story? How are these typical of mystery fiction?
7. What is the theme of the story?
8. Most mystery writers insist that the detective or mystery story must "play fair." Does Dickens's story follow this rule? Explain.

Fyodor Dostoevsky
A Christmas Tree and a Wedding

The other day I saw a wedding . . . but no, I had better tell you about the Christmas tree. The wedding was nice, I liked it very much; but the other incident was better. I don't know how it was that, looking at that wedding, I thought of that Christmas tree. This was what happened. Just five years ago, on New Year's Eve, I was invited to a children's party. The giver of the party was a well-known and businesslike personage, with connections, with a large circle of acquaintances, and a good many schemes on hand, so that it may be supposed that this party was an excuse for getting the parents together and discussing various interesting matters in an innocent, casual way. I was an outsider; I had no interesting matter to contribute, and so I spent the evening rather independently. There was another gentleman present who was, I fancied, of no special rank or family, and who, like me, had simply turned up at this family festivity. He was the first to catch my eye. He was a tall, lanky man, very grave and very correctly dressed. But one could see that he was in no mood for merrymaking and family festivity; whenever he withdrew into a corner he left off smiling and knitted his bushy black brows. He had not a single acquaintance in the party except his host. One could see that he was fearfully bored, but that he was valiantly keeping up the part of a man perfectly happy and enjoying himself. I learned afterward that this was a gentleman from the provinces, who had a critical and perplexing piece of business in Petersburg, who had brought a letter of introduction to our host, for whom our host was, by no means *con amore*, using his interest, and whom he had invited, out of civility, to his children's party. He did not play cards, cigars were not offered him, everyone avoided entering into conversation with him, most likely recognizing the bird from its feathers: and so my gentleman was forced to sit the whole evening stroking his whiskers simply to have something to do with his hands. His whiskers were certainly very fine. But he stroked them so zealously that, looking at him, one might have supposed that the whiskers were created first and the gentleman only attached to them in order to stroke them.

In addition to this individual who assisted in this way at our host's family festivity (he had five fat, well-fed boys), I was attracted, too, by another gentleman. But he was quite of a different sort. He was a personage. He was called Yulian Mastakovitch. From the first glance one could see that he was an honored guest, and stood in the same relation to our host as our host stood in relation to the gentleman who was stroking his whiskers. Our host and hostess said no end of polite things to him, waited on him hand and foot, pressed him to drink, flattered him, brought their visitors up to be introduced to him, but did not take him to be introduced to anyone else. I noticed that tears glistened in our host's eyes when he remarked about the party that he had rarely spent an evening so agreeably. I felt as it were frightened in the presence of such a personage, and so, after admiring the children, I went away into a little parlor, which was quite empty, and sat down in an arbor of flowers which filled up almost half the room.

The children were all incredibly sweet, and resolutely refused to model themselves on the "grown-ups," regardless of all the admonitions of their governesses and mammas. They stripped the Christmas tree to the last sweetmeat in the twinkling of an eye, and had succeeded in breaking half the playthings before they knew what was destined for which. Particularly charming was a black-eyed, curly-headed boy, who kept trying to shoot me with his wooden gun. But my attention was still more attracted by his sister, a girl of eleven, quiet, dreamy, pale, with big, prominent, dreamy eyes, exquisite as a little Cupid. The children hurt her feelings in some way, and so she came away from them to the same empty parlor in which I was sitting, and played with her doll in the corner. The visitors respectfully pointed out her father, a wealthy contractor, and someone whispered that three hundred thousand rubles were already set aside for her dowry. I turned round to glance at the group who were interested in such a circumstance, and my eye fell on Yulian Mastakovitch, who, with his hands behind his back and his head on one side, was listening with the greatest attention to these gentlemen's idle gossip. Afterward I could not help admiring the discrimination of the host and hostess in the distribution of the children's presents. The little girl, who had already a portion of three hundred thousand rubles, received the costliest doll. Then followed presents diminishing in value in accordance with the rank of the parents of these happy children; finally, the child of lowest degree, a thin, freckled red-haired little boy of ten, got nothing but a book of stories about the marvels of nature and tears of devotion, etc., without pictures or even woodcuts. He was the son of a poor widow, the governess of the children of the house, an oppressed and scared little boy. He was dressed in a short jacket of inferior nankin. After receiving his book he walked round the other toys for a long time; he longed to play with the other children, but did not dare; it was evident that he already felt and understood his position. I love watching children. Their first independent approaches to life are extremely interesting. I noticed that the red-haired boy was so fascinated by the costly toys of the other children, especially by a theater in which he certainly longed to take some part, that he made up his mind to sacrifice his dignity. He smiled and began playing with the other children, he gave away his apple to a fat-faced little boy who had a mass of goodies tied up in a pocket handkerchief already, and even brought himself to carry another boy on his back, simply not to be turned away from the theater, but an insolent youth gave him a heavy thump a minute later. The child did not dare to cry. Then the governess, his mother, made her appearance, and told him not to interfere with the other children's playing. The boy went away to the same room in which was the little girl. She let him join her, and the two set to work very eagerly dressing the expensive doll.

I had been sitting more than half an hour in the ivy arbor, listening to the little prattle of the red-haired boy and the beauty with the dowry of three hundred thousand, who was nursing her doll, when Yulian Mastakovitch suddenly walked into the room. He had taken advantage of the general commotion following a quarrel among the children to step out of the drawing room. I had noticed him a moment before talking very cordially to the future heiress's papa, whose acquaintance he had just made, of the superiority of one branch of the service over another. Now he stood in hesitation and seemed to be reckoning something on his fingers.

"Three hundred . . . three hundred," he was whispering. "Eleven . . . twelve . . . thirteen," and so on. "Sixteen—five years! Supposing it is at four percent—five times twelve is sixty; yes, to that sixty . . . well, in five years we may assume it will be four hundred. Yes! . . . But he won't stick to four percent, the rascal. He can get eight or ten. Well, five hundred, let us say, five hundred at least . . . that's certain; well, say a little more for frills. H'm! . . ."

His hesitation was at an end, he blew his nose and was on the point of going out of the room when he suddenly glanced at the little girl and stopped short. He did not see me behind the pots of greenery. It seemed to me that he was greatly excited. Either his calculations had affected his imagination or something else, for he rubbed his hands and could hardly stand still. This excitement reached its utmost limit when he stopped and bent another resolute glance at the future heiress. He was about to move forward, but first looked round, then moving on tiptoe, as though he felt guilty, he advanced toward the children. He approached with a little smile, bent down and kissed her on the head. The child, not expecting this attack, uttered a cry of alarm.

"What are you doing here, sweet child?" he asked in a whisper, looking round and patting the girl's cheek.

"We are playing."

"Ah! With him?" Yulian Mastakovitch looked askance at the boy. "You had better go into the drawing room, my dear," he said to him.

The boy looked at him open-eyed and did not utter a word. Yulian Mastakovitch looked round him again, and again bent down to the little girl.

"And what is this you've got—a dolly, dear child?" he asked.

"Yes, a dolly," answered the child, frowning, and a little shy.

"A dolly . . . and do you know, dear child, what your dolly is made of?"

"I don't know . . ." the child answered in a whisper, hanging her head.

"It's made of rags, darling. You had better go into the drawing room to your playmates, boy," said Yulian Mastakovitch, looking sternly at the boy. The boy and girl frowned and clutched at each other. They did not want to be separated.

"And do you know why they gave you that doll?" asked Yulian Mastakovitch, dropping his voice to a softer and softer tone.

"I don't know."

"Because you have been a sweet and well-behaved child all the week."

At this point Yulian Mastakovitch, more excited than ever, speaking in most dulcet tones, asked at last, in a hardly audible voice choked with emotion and impatience—

"And will you love me, dear little girl, when I come and see your papa and mamma?"

Saying this, Yulian Mastakovitch tried once more to kiss "the dear little girl," but the red-haired boy, seeing that the little girl was on the point of tears, clutched her hand and began whimpering from sympathy for her. Yulian Mastakovitch was angry in earnest.

"Go away, go away from here, go away!" he said to the boy. "Go into the drawing room! Go in there to your playmates!"

"No, he needn't, he needn't! You go away," said the little girl. "Leave him alone, leave him alone," she said, almost crying.

Someone made a sound at the door. Yulian Mastakovitch instantly raised his majestic person and took alarm. But the red-haired boy was even more alarmed than Yulian Mastakovitch; he abandoned the little girl and, slinking along by the wall, stole out of the parlor into the dining room. To avoid arousing suspicion, Yulian Mastakovitch, too, went into the dining room. He was as red as a lobster, and, glancing into the looking glass, seemed to be ashamed at himself. He was perhaps vexed with himself for his impetuosity and hastiness. Possibly, he was at first so much impressed by his calculations, so inspired and fascinated by them, that in spite of his seriousness and dignity he made up his mind to behave like a boy, and directly approach the object of his attentions, even though she could not be really the object of his attentions for another five years at least. I followed the estimable gentleman into the dining room and there beheld a strange spectacle. Yulian Mastakovitch, flushed with vexation and anger, was frightening the red-haired boy, who, retreating from him, did not know where to run in his terror.

"Go away; what are you doing here? Go away, you scamp; are you after the fruit here, eh? Get along, you naughty boy! Get along, you sniveler, to your playmates!"

The panic-stricken boy in his desperation tried creeping under the table. Then his persecutor, in a fury, took out his large batiste handkerchief and began flicking it under the table at the child, who kept perfectly quiet. It must be observed that Yulian Mastakovitch was a little inclined to be fat. He was a sleek, red-faced, solidly built man, paunchy, with thick legs; what is called a fine figure of a man, round as a nut. He was perspiring, breathless, and fearfully flushed. At last he was almost rigid, so great was his indignation and perhaps—who knows?—his jealousy. I burst into loud laughter. Yulian Mastakovitch turned round and, in spite of all his consequence, was overcome with confusion. At that moment from the opposite door our host came in. The boy crept out from under the table and wiped his elbows and his knees. Yulian Mastakovitch hastened to put to his nose the handkerchief which he was holding in his hand by one end.

Our host looked at the three of us in some perplexity; but as a man who knew something of life, and looked at it from a serious point of view, he at once availed himself of the chance of catching his visitor by himself.

"Here, this is the boy," he said, pointing to the red-haired boy, "for whom I had the honor to solicit your influence."

"Ah!" said Yulian Mastakovitch, who had hardly quite recovered himself.

"The son of my children's governess," said our host, in a tone of a petitioner, "a poor woman, the widow of an honest civil servant; and therefore . . . and therefore, Yulian Mastakovitch, if it were possible . . ."

"Oh, no, no!" Yulian Mastakovitch made haste to answer; "no, excuse me, Filip Alexyevitch, it's quite impossible. I've made inquiries; there's no vacancy, and if there were, there are twenty applicants who have far more claim than he . . . I am very sorry, very sorry. . . ."

"What a pity," said our host. "He is a quiet, well-behaved boy."

"A great rascal, as I notice," answered Yulian Mastakovitch, with a nervous twist of his lip. "Get along, boy; why are you standing there? Go to your playmates," he said, addressing the child.

At that point he could not contain himself, and glanced at me out of one eye. I, too, could not contain myself, and laughed straight in his face. Yulian Mastakovitch turned away at once, and in a voice calculated to reach my ear, asked who was that strange young man? They whispered together and walked out of the room. I saw Yulian Mastakovitch afterward shaking his head incredulously as our host talked to him.

After laughing to my heart's content I returned to the drawing room. There the great man, surrounded by fathers and mothers of families, including the host and hostess, was saying something very warmly to a lady to whom he had just been introduced. The lady was holding by the hand the little girl with whom Yulian Mastakovitch had had the scene in the parlor a little while before. Now he was launching into praises and raptures over the beauty, the talents, the grace, and the charming manners of the charming child. He was unmistakably making up to the mamma. The mother listened to him almost with tears of delight. The father's lips were smiling. Our host was delighted at the general satisfaction. All the guests, in fact, were sympathetically gratified; even the children's games were checked that they might not hinder the conversation: the whole atmosphere was saturated with reverence. I heard afterward the mamma of the interesting child, deeply touched, beg Yulian Mastakovitch, in carefully chosen phrases, to do her the special honor of bestowing upon them the precious gift of his acquaintance, and heard with what unaffected delight Yulian Mastakovitch accepted the invitation, and how afterward the guests, dispersing in different directions, moving away with the greatest propriety, poured out to one another the most touchingly flattering comments upon the contractor, his wife, his little girl, and, above all, upon Yulian Mastakovitch.

"Is that gentleman married?" I asked, almost aloud, of one of my acquaintances, who was standing nearest to Yulian Mastakovitch. Yulian Mastakovitch flung a searching and vindictive glance at me.

"No!" answered my acquaintance, chagrined to the bottom of his heart by the awkwardness of which I had intentionally been guilty. . . .

I passed lately by a certain church; I was struck by the crowd of people in carriages. I heard people talking of the wedding. It was a cloudy day, it was beginning to sleet. I made my way through the crowd at the door and saw the bridegroom. He was a sleek, well-fed, round, paunchy man, very gorgeously dressed up. He was running fussily about, giving orders. At last the news passed through the crowd that the bride was coming. I squeezed my way through the crowd and saw a marvelous beauty, who could scarcely have reached her first season. But the beauty was pale and melancholy. She looked preoccupied; I even fancied that her eyes were red with recent weeping. The classic severity of every feature of her face gave a certain dignity and seriousness to her beauty. But through that sternness and dignity, through that melancholy, could be seen the look of childish innocence; something indescribably naïve, fluid, youthful, which seemed mutely begging for mercy.

People were saying that she was only just sixteen. Glancing attentively at the bridegroom, I suddenly recognized him as Yulian Mastakovitch, whom I had not seen for five years. I looked at her. My God! I began to squeeze my way as quickly as I could out of the church. I heard people saying in the crowd that the bride was an heiress, that she had a dowry of five hundred thousand . . . and a trousseau worth ever so much.

"It was a good stroke of business, though!" I thought as I made my way into the street.

[1848]

For Thought

Selecting a social occasion and a time that normally arouse pleasurable expectations, Dostoevsky ironically creates a mood of helpless despair instead. In a somewhat artificially constructed plot, he relies heavily on coincidence to bring about the narrator's awareness of the tragic situation at both the party and the church where the loveless wedding takes place. The satirically ironic tone, the highly selective descriptions of the characters, and the judgmental comments offered by the narrator make it clear where the reader's sympathies should lie.

For Discussion

1. Using specific examples, comment on Dostoevsky's use of highly selective language as a means of influencing reader attitude toward the characters and events in the story.
2. What is the purpose of having the story told in the first-person point of view and by someone who is an observer at the periphery of the action?
3. Discuss the use of character foils, children and adults, and what they contribute to the story.
4. Comment on the verbal and situational irony in the story. How does situational irony influence mood and atmosphere?
5. Comment on the effectiveness of coincidence or lack of it as an artistic device.

Ralph Ellison
King of the Bingo Game

The woman in front of him was eating roasted peanuts that smelled so good that he could barely contain his hunger. He could not even sleep and wished they'd hurry and begin the bingo game. There, on his right, two fellows were drinking wine out of a bottle wrapped in a paper bag, and he could hear soft gurgling in the dark. His stomach gave a low, gnawing growl. "If this was down South," he thought, "all I'd have to do is lean over and say, 'Lady, gimme a few of those peanuts, please ma'am,' and she'd pass me the bag and never think nothing of it." Or he could ask the fellows for a drink in the same way. Folks down South stuck together that way; they didn't even have to know you. But up here it was different. Ask somebody for something, and they'd think you were crazy. Well, I ain't crazy. I'm just broke, 'cause I got no birth certificate to get a job, and Laura 'bout to die 'cause we got no money for a doctor. But I ain't crazy. And yet a pinpoint of doubt was focused in his mind as he glanced toward the screen and saw the hero stealthily entering a dark room and sending the beam of a flashlight along a wall of bookcases. This is where he finds the trapdoor, he remembered. The man would pass abruptly through the wall and find the girl tied to a bed, her legs and arms spread wide, and her clothing torn to rags. He laughed softly to himself. He had seen the picture three times, and this was one of the best scenes.

On his right the fellow whispered wideeyed to his companion, "Man, look ayonder!"

"Damn!"

"Wouldn't I like to have her tied up like that . . ."

"Hey! That fool's letting her loose!"

"Aw, man, he loves her."

"Love or no love!"

The man moved impatiently beside him, and tried to involve himself in the scene. But Laura was on his mind. Tiring quickly of watching the picture he looked back to where the white beam filtered from the projection room above the balcony. It started small and grew large, specks of dust dancing in its whiteness as it reached the screen. It was strange how the beam always landed right on the screen and didn't mess up and fall somewhere else. But they had it all fixed. Everything was fixed. Now suppose when they showed that girl with her dress torn the girl started taking off the rest of her clothes, and when the guy came in he didn't untie her but kept her there and went to taking off his own clothes? *That* would be something to see. If a picture got out of hand like that those guys up there would go nuts. Yeah, and there'd be so many folks in here you couldn't find a seat for nine months! A strange sensation played over his skin. He shuddered. Yesterday he'd seen a bedbug on a woman's neck as they walked out into the bright street. But exploring his thigh through a hole in his pocket he found only goose pimples and old scars.

The bottle gurgled again. He closed his eyes. Now a dreamy music was accompanying the film and train whistles were sounding in the distance, and he was a boy again walking along a railroad trestle down South, and seeing the train coming, and running back as fast as he could go, and hearing the whistle blowing, and getting off the trestle to solid ground just in time, with the earth trembling beneath his feet, and feeling relieved as he ran down the cinder-strewn embankment onto the highway, and looking back and seeing with terror that the train had left the track and was following him right down the middle of the street, and all the white people laughing as he ran screaming . . .

"Wake up there, buddy! What the hell do you mean hollering like that? Can't you see we trying to enjoy this here picture?"

He stared at the man with gratitude.

"I'm sorry, old man," he said. "I musta been dreaming."

"Well, here, have a drink. And don't be making no noise like that, damn!"

His hands trembled as he tilted his head. It was not wine, but whiskey. Cold rye whiskey. He took a deep swoller, decided it was better not to take another, and handed the bottle back to its owner.

"Thanks, old man," he said.

Now he felt the cold whiskey breaking a warm path straight through the middle of him, growing hotter and sharper as it moved. He had not eaten all day, and it made him light-headed. The smell of the peanuts stabbed him like a knife, and he got up and found a seat in the middle aisle. But no sooner did he sit than he saw a row of intense-faced young girls, and got up again, thinking, "You chicks musta been Lindy-hopping somewhere." He found a seat several rows ahead as the lights came on, and he saw the screen disappear behind a heavy red and gold curtain; then the curtain rising, and the man with the microphone and a uniformed attendant coming on the stage.

He felt for his bingo cards, smiling. The guy at the door wouldn't like it if he knew about his having *five* cards. Well, not everyone played the bingo game; and even with five cards he didn't have much of a chance. For Laura, though, he had to have faith. He studied the cards, each with its different numerals, punching the free center hole in each and spreading them neatly across his lap; and when the lights faded he sat slouched in his seat so that he could look from his cards to the bingo wheel with but a quick shifting of his eyes.

Ahead, at the end of the darkness, the man with the microphone was pressing a button attached to a long cord and spinning the bingo wheel and calling out the number each time the wheel came to rest. And each time the voice rang out his finger raced over the cards for the number. With five cards he had to move fast. He became nervous; there were too many cards, and the man went too fast with his grating voice. Perhaps he should just select one and throw the others away. But he was afraid. He became warm. Wonder how much Laura's doctor would cost? Damn that, watch the cards! And with despair he heard the man call three in a row which he missed on all five cards. This way he'd never win . . .

When he saw the row of holes punched across the third card, he sat paralyzed and heard the man call three more numbers before he stumbled forward, screaming.

"Bingo! Bingo!"

"Let that fool up there," someone called.

"Get up there, man!"

He stumbled down the aisle and up the steps to the stage into a light so sharp and bright that for a moment it blinded him, and he felt that he had moved into the spell of some strange, mysterious power. Yet it was as familiar as the sun, and he knew it was the perfectly familiar bingo.

The man with the microphone was saying something to the audience as he held out his card. A cold light flashed from the man's finger as the card left his hand. His knees trembled. The man stepped closer, checking the card against the numbers chalked on the board. Suppose he had made a mistake? The pomade on the man's hair made him feel faint, and he backed away. But the man was checking the card over the microphone now, and he had to stay. He stood tense, listening.

"Under the O, forty-four," the man chanted. "Under the I, seven. Under the G, three. Under the B, ninety-six. Under the N, thirteen!"

His breath came easier as the man smiled at the audience.

"Yessir, ladies and gentlemen, he's one of the chosen people!"

The audience rippled with laughter and applause.

"Step right up to the front of the stage."

He moved slowly forward, wishing that the light was not so bright.

"To win to-night's jackpot of $36.90 the wheel must stop between the double zero, understand?"

He nodded, knowing the ritual from the many days and nights he had watched the winners march across the stage to press the button that controlled the spinning wheel and receive the prizes. And now he followed the instructions as though he'd crossed the slippery stage a million prize-winning times.

The man was making some kind of a joke, and he nodded vacantly. So tense had he become that he felt a sudden desire to cry and shook it away. He felt vaguely that his whole life was determined by the bingo wheel; not only that which would happen now that he was at last before it, but all that had gone before, since his birth, and his mother's birth and the birth of his father. It had always been there, even though he had not been aware of it, handing out the unlucky cards and numbers of his days. The feeling persisted, and he started quickly away. I better get down from here before I make a fool of myself, he thought.

"Here, boy," the man called. "You haven't started yet."

Someone laughed as he went hesitantly back.

"Are you all reet?"

He grinned at the man's jive talk, but no words would come, and he knew it was not a convincing grin. For suddenly he knew that he stood on the slippery brink of some terrible embarrassment.

"Where are you from, boy?" the man asked.

"Down South."

"He's from down South, ladies and gentlemen," the man said. "Where from? Speak right into the mike."

"Rocky Mont," he said. "Rock' Mont, North Car'lina."

"So you decided to come down off that mountain to the U.S.," the man laughed. He felt that the man was making a fool of him, but then something cold was placed in his hand, and the lights were no longer behind him.

Standing before the wheel he felt alone, but that was somehow right, and he remembered his plan. He would give the wheel a short quick twirl. Just a touch of the button. He had watched it many times, and always it came close to double zero when it was short and quick. He steeled himself; the fear had left, and he felt a profound sense of promise, as though he were about to be repaid for all the things he'd suffered all his life. Trembling, he pressed the button. There was a whirl of lights, and in a second he realized with finality that though he wanted to, he could not stop. It was as though he held a high-powered line in his naked hand. His nerves tightened. As the wheel increased its speed it seemed to draw him more and more into its power, as though it held his fate; and with it came a deep need to submit, to whirl, to lose himself in its swirl of color. He could not stop it now. So let it be.

The button rested snugly in his palm where the man had placed it. And now he became aware of the man beside him, advising him through the microphone, while behind the shadowy audience hummed with noisy voices. He shifted his feet. There was still that feeling of helplessness within him, making part of him desire to turn back, even now that the jackpot was right in his hand. He squeezed the button until his fist ached. Then, like the sudden shriek of a subway whistle, a doubt tore through his head. Suppose he did not spin the wheel long enough? What could he do, and how could he tell? And then he knew, even as he wondered, that as long as he pressed the button, he could control the jackpot. He and only he could determine whether or not it was to be his. Not even the man with the microphone could do anything about it now. He felt drunk. Then, as though he had come down from a high hill into a valley of people, he heard the audience yelling.

"Come down from there, you jerk!"

"Let somebody else have a chance . . ."

"Ole Jack thinks he done found the end of the rainbow . . ."

The last voice was not unfriendly, and he turned and smiled dreamily into the yelling mouths. Then he turned his back squarely on them.

"Don't take too long, boy," a voice said.

He nodded. They were yelling behind him. Those folks did not understand what had happened to him. They had been playing the bingo game day in and night out for years, trying to win rent money or hamburger change. But not one of those wise guys had discovered this wonderful thing. He watched the wheel whirling past the numbers and experienced a burst of exaltation: This is God! This is the really truly God! He said it aloud, "This is God!"

He said it with such absolute conviction that he feared he would fall fainting into the footlights. But the crowd yelled so loud that they could not hear. Those fools, he thought. I'm here trying to tell them the most wonderful secret in the world, and they're yelling like they gone crazy. A hand fell upon his shoulder.

"You'll have to make a choice now, boy. You've taken too long."

He brushed the hand violently away.

"Leave me alone, man. I know what I'm doing!"

The man looked surprised and held on to the microphone for support. And because he did not wish to hurt the man's feelings he smiled, realizing with a sudden pang that there was no way of explaining to the man just why he had to stand there pressing the button forever.

"Come here," he called tiredly.

The man approached, rolling the heavy microphone across the stage.

"Anybody can play this bingo game, right?" he said.

"Sure but . . ."

He smiled, feeling inclined to be patient with this slick looking white man with his blue shirt and his sharp gabardine suit.

"That's what I thought," he said. "Anybody can win the jackpot as long as they get the lucky number, right?"

"That's the rule, but after all . . ."

"That's what I thought," he said. "And the big prize goes to the man who knows how to win it?"

The man nodded speechlessly.

"Well then, go on over there and watch me win like I want to. I ain't going to hurt nobody," he said, "and I'll show you how to win. I mean to show the whole world how it's got to be done."

And because he understood, he smiled again to let the man know that he held nothing against him for being white and impatient. Then he refused to see the man any longer and stood pressing the button, the voices of the crowd reaching him like sounds in distant streets. Let them yell. All the Negroes down there were just ashamed because he was black like them. He smiled inwardly, knowing how it was. Most of the time he was ashamed of what Negroes did himself. Well, let them be ashamed for something this time. Like him. He was like a long thin black wire that was being stretched and wound upon the bingo wheel; wound until he wanted to scream; wound, but this time himself controlling the winding and the sadness and the shame, and because he did, Laura would be all right. Suddenly the lights flickered. He staggered backwards. Had something gone wrong? All this noise. Didn't they know that although he controlled the wheel, it also controlled him, and unless he pressed the button forever and forever and ever it would stop, leaving him high and dry, dry and high on this hard high slippery hill and Laura dead? There was only one chance; he had to do whatever the wheel demanded. And gripping the button in despair, he discovered with surprise that it imparted a nervous energy. His spine tingled. He felt a certain power.

Now he faced the raging crowd with defiance, its screams penetrating his eardrums like trumpets shrieking from a jukebox. The vague faces glowing in the bingo lights gave him a sense of himself that he had never known before. He was running the show, by God! They had to react to him, for he was their luck. This is *me*, he thought. Let the bastards yell. Then someone was laughing inside him, and he realized that somehow he had forgotten his own name. It was a sad, lost feeling to lose your name, and a crazy thing to do. That name had been given him by the white man who had owned his grandfather a long lost time ago down South. But maybe those wise guys knew his name.

"Who am I?" he screamed.

"Hurry up and bingo, you jerk!"

They didn't know either, he thought sadly. They didn't even know their own names, they were all poor nameless bastards. Well, he didn't need that old name; he was reborn. For as long as he pressed the button he was The-man-who-pressed-the-button-who-held-the-prize-who-was-the-King-of-Bingo. That was the way it was, and he'd have to press the button even if nobody understood, even though Laura did not understand.

"Live!" he shouted.

The audience quieted like the dying of a huge fan.

"Live, Laura, baby. I got holt of it now, sugar. Live!"

He screamed it, tears streaming down his face. "I got nobody but YOU!"

The screams tore from his very guts. He felt as though the rush of blood to his head would burst out in baseball seams of small red droplets, like a head beaten by police clubs. Bending over he saw a trickle of blood splashing the toe of his shoe. With his free hand he searched his head. It was his nose. God, suppose something has gone wrong? He felt that the whole audience had somehow entered him and was stamping its feet in his stomach and was unable to throw them out. They wanted the prize, that was it. They wanted the secret for themselves. But they'd never get it; he would keep the bingo wheel whirling forever, and Laura would be safe in the wheel. But would she? It had to be, because if she were not safe the wheel would cease to turn; it could not go on. He had to get away, *vomit* all, and his mind formed an image of himself running with Laura in his arms down the tracks of the subway just ahead of an A train, running desperately *vomit* with people screaming for him to come out but knowing no way of leaving the tracks because to stop would bring the train crushing down upon him and to attempt to leave across the other tracks would mean to run into a hot third rail as high as his waist which threw blue sparks that blinded his eyes until he could hardly see.

He heard singing and the audience was clapping its hands.

> Shoot the liquor to him, Jim, boy!
> Clap-clap-clap
> Well a-calla the cop
> He's blowing his top!
> Shoot the liquor to him, Jim, boy!

Bitter anger grew within him at the singing. They think I'm crazy. Well let 'em laugh. I'll do what I got to do.

He was standing in an attitude of intense listening when he saw that they were watching something on the stage behind him. He felt weak. But when he turned he saw no one. If only his thumb did not ache so. Now they were applauding. And for a moment he thought that the wheel had stopped. But that was impossible, his thumb still pressed the button. Then he saw them. Two men in uniform beckoned from the end of the stage. They were coming toward him, walking in step, slowly, like a tap-dance team returning for a third encore. But their shoulders shot forward, and he backed away, looking wildly about. There was nothing to fight them with. He had only the long black cord which led to a plug somewhere back stage, and he couldn't use that because it operated the bingo wheel. He backed slowly, fixing the men with his eyes as his lips stretched over his teeth in a tight, fixed grin; moved toward the end of the stage and realizing that he couldn't go much further, for suddenly the cord became taut and he couldn't afford to break the cord. But he had to do something. The audience was howling. Suddenly he stopped dead, seeing the men halt, their legs lifted as in an interrupted step of a slow-motion dance. There was nothing to do but run in the other direction and he dashed forward, slipping and sliding. The men fell back, surprised. He struck out violently going past.

"Grab him!"

He ran, but all too quickly the cord tightened, resistingly, and he turned and ran back again. This time he slipped them, and discovered by running in a circle before the wheel he could keep the cord from tightening. But this way he had to flail his arms to keep the men away. Why couldn't they leave a man alone? He ran, circling.

"Ring down the curtain," someone yelled. But they couldn't do that. If they did the wheel flashing from the projection room would be cut off. But they had him before he could tell them so, trying to pry open his fist, and he was wrestling and trying to bring his knees into the fight and holding on to the button, for it was his life. And now he was down, seeing a foot coming down, crushing his wrist cruelly, down, as he saw the wheel whirling serenely above.

"I can't give it up," he screamed. Then quietly, in a confidential tone, "Boys, I really can't give it up."

It landed hard against his head. And in the blank moment they had it away from him, completely now. He fought them trying to pull him up from the stage as he watched the wheel spin slowly to a stop. Without surprise he saw it rest at double-zero.

"You see," he pointed bitterly.

"Sure, boy, sure, it's O.K.," one of the men said smiling.

And seeing the man bow his head to someone he could not see, he felt very, very happy; he would receive what all the winners received.

But as he warmed in the justice of the man's tight smile he did not see the man's slow wink, nor see the bow-legged man behind him step clear of the swiftly descending curtain and set himself for a blow. He only felt the dull pain exploding in his skull, and he knew even as it slipped out of him that his luck had run out on the stage.

[1944]

For Thought

"King of the Bingo Game" is actually a tale that utilizes a gothiclike setting (that of the movie house) and macabre humor. The nameless hero has pitted himself against a spinning wheel of chance. Ellison uses the bingo game as a symbol of America's wheel of fortune, and the American society will never allow the main character to win. Consequently, the central character is overwhelmed by the superior force and his own desperate weakness. Ellison, however, indicates that heroism can spring from unpromising, even commonplace sources.

For Discussion

1. What atmosphere and what mood does Ellison create?
2. What point of view does Ellison use? What are its chief advantages for the story?
3. What does the bingo wheel represent for the protagonist?
4. In what way is the protagonist a tragic rather than merely a pathetic figure?

William Faulkner
A Rose for Emily

I

When Miss Emily Grierson died, our whole town went to her funeral: the men through a sort of respectful affection for a fallen monument, the women mostly out of curiosity to see the inside of her house, which no one save an old manservant—a combined gardener and cook—had seen in at least ten years.

It was a big, squarish frame house that had once been white, decorated with cupolas and spires and scrolled balconies in the heavily lightsome style of the seventies, set on what had once been our most select street. But garages and cotton gins had encroached and obliterated even the august names of that neighborhood; only Miss Emily's house was left, lifting its stubborn and coquettish decay above the cotton wagons and the gasoline pumps—an eyesore among eyesores. And now Miss Emily had gone to join the representatives of those august names where they lay in the cedar-bemused cemetery among the ranked and anonymous graves of Union and Confederate soldiers who fell at the battle of Jefferson.

Alive, Miss Emily had been a tradition, a duty, and a care; a sort of hereditary obligation upon the town, dating from that day in 1894 when Colonel Sartoris, the mayor—he who fathered the edict that no Negro woman should appear on the streets without an apron—remitted her taxes, the dispensation dating from the death of her father on into perpetuity. Not that Miss Emily would have accepted charity. Colonel Sartoris invented an involved tale to the effect that Miss Emily's father had loaned money to the town, which the town, as a matter of business, preferred this way of repaying. Only a man of Colonel Sartoris' generation and thought could have invented it, and only a woman could have believed it.

When the next generation, with its more modern ideas, became mayors and aldermen, this arrangement created some little dissatisfaction. On the first of the year they mailed her a tax notice. February came, and there was no reply. They wrote her a formal letter, asking her to call at the sheriff's office at her convenience. A week later the mayor wrote her himself, offering to call or to send his car for her, and received in reply a note on paper of an archaic shape, in a thin, flowing calligraphy in faded ink, to the effect that she no longer went out at all. The tax notice was also enclosed, without comment.

They called a special meeting of the Board of Aldermen. A deputation waited upon her, knocked at the door through which no visitor had passed since she ceased giving china-painting lessons eight or ten years earlier. They were admitted by the old Negro into a dim hall from which a stairway mounted into still more shadow. It smelled of dust and disuse—a close, dank smell. The Negro led them into the parlor. It was furnished in heavy, leather-covered furniture. When the Negro opened the blinds of one window, they could see that the leather was cracked; and when they sat down, a faint dust rose sluggishly about their thighs, spinning with slow motes in the single sun-ray. On a tarnished gilt easel before the fireplace stood a crayon portrait of Miss Emily's father.

They rose when she entered—a small, fat woman in black, with a thin gold chain descending to her waist and vanishing into her belt, leaning on an ebony cane with a tarnished gold head. Her skeleton was small and spare; perhaps that was why what would have been merely plumpness in another was obesity in her. She looked bloated, like a body long submerged in motionless water, and of that pallid hue. Her eyes, lost in the fatty ridges of her face, looked like two small pieces of coal pressed into a lump of dough as they moved from one face to another while the visitors stated their errand.

She did not ask them to sit. She just stood in the door and listened quietly until the spokesman came to a stumbling halt. Then they could hear the invisible watch ticking at the end of the gold chain.

Her voice was dry and cold. "I have no taxes in Jefferson. Colonel Sartoris explained it to me. Perhaps one of you can gain access to the city records and satisfy yourselves."

"But we have. We are the city authorities, Miss Emily. Didn't you get a notice from the sheriff, signed by him?"

"I received a paper, yes," Miss Emily said. "Perhaps he considers himself the sheriff . . . I have no taxes in Jefferson."

"But there is nothing on the books to show that, you see. We must go by the—"

"See Colonel Sartoris. I have no taxes in Jefferson."

"But, Miss Emily—"

"See Colonel Sartoris." (Colonel Sartoris had been dead almost ten years.) "I have no taxes in Jefferson. Tobe!" The Negro appeared. "Show these gentlemen out."

II

So she vanquished them, horse and foot, just as she had vanquished their fathers thirty years before about the smell. That was two years after her father's death and a short time after her sweetheart—the one we believed would marry her—had deserted her. After her father's death she went out very little; after her sweetheart went away, people hardly saw her at all. A few of the ladies had the temerity to call, but were not received, and the only sign of life about the place was the Negro man—a young man then—going in and out with a market basket.

"Just as if a man—any man—could keep a kitchen properly," the ladies said; so they were not surprised when the smell developed. It was another link between the gross, teeming world and the high and mighty Griersons.

A neighbor, a woman, complained to the mayor, Judge Stevens, eighty years old.

"But what will you have me do about it, madam?" he said.

"Why, send her word to stop it," the woman said. "Isn't there a law?"

"I'm sure that won't be necessary," Judge Stevens said. "It's probably just a snake or a rat that nigger of hers killed in the yard. I'll speak to him about it."

The next day he received two more complaints, one from a man who came in diffident deprecation. "We really must do something about it, Judge. I'd be the last one in the world to bother Miss Emily, but we've got to do something." That night the Board of Aldermen met—three graybeards and one younger man, a member of the rising generation.

"It's simple enough," he said. "Send her word to have her place cleaned up. Give her a certain time to do it in, and if she don't . . ."

"Dammit, sir," Judge Stevens said, "will you accuse a lady to her face of smelling bad?"

So the next night, after midnight, four men crossed Miss Emily's lawn and slunk about the house like burglars, sniffing along the base of the brickwork and at the cellar openings while one of them performed a regular sowing motion with his hand out of a sack slung from his shoulder. They broke open the cellar door and sprinkled lime there, and in all the outbuildings. As they recrossed the lawn, a window that had been dark was lighted and Miss Emily sat in it, the light behind her, and her upright torso motionless as that of an idol. They crept quietly across the lawn and into the shadow of the locusts that lined the street. After a week or two the smell went away.

That was when people had begun to feel really sorry for her. People in our town, remembering how old lady Wyatt, her great-aunt, had gone completely crazy at last, believed that the Griersons held themselves a little too high for what they really were. None of the young men were quite good enough for Miss Emily and such. We had long thought of them as a tableau, Miss Emily a slender figure in white in the background, her father a spraddled silhouette in the foreground, his back to her and clutching a horsewhip, the two of them framed by the back-flung front door. So when she got to be thirty and was still single, we were not pleased exactly, but vindicated; even with insanity in the family she wouldn't have turned down all of her chances if they had really materialized.

When her father died, it got about that the house was all that was left to her; and in a way, people were glad. At last they could pity Miss Emily. Being left alone, and a pauper, she had become humanized. Now she too would know the old thrill and the old despair of a penny more or less.

The day after his death all the ladies prepared to call at the house and offer condolence and aid, as is our custom. Miss Emily met them at the door, dressed as usual and with no trace of grief on her face. She told them that her father was not dead. She did that for three days, with the ministers calling on her, and the doctors, trying to persuade her to let them dispose of the body. Just as they were about to resort to law and force, she broke down, and they buried her father quickly.

We did not say she was crazy then. We believed she had to do that. We remembered all the young men her father had driven away, and we knew that with nothing left, she would have to cling to that which had robbed her, as people will.

III

She was sick for a long time. When we saw her again, her hair was cut short, making her look like a girl, with a vague resemblance to those angels in colored church windows—sort of tragic and serene.

The town had just let the contracts for paving the sidewalks, and in the summer after her father's death they began the work. The construction company came with niggers and mules and machinery, and a foreman named Homer Barron, a Yankee—a big, dark, ready man, with a big voice and eyes lighter than his face. The little boys would follow in groups to hear him cuss the niggers, and the niggers singing in time to the rise and fall of picks.

Pretty soon he knew everybody in town. Whenever you heard a lot of laughing anywhere about the square, Homer Barron would be in the center of the group. Presently we began to see him and Miss Emily on Sunday afternoons driving in the yellow-wheeled buggy and the matched team of bays from the livery stable.

At first we were glad that Miss Emily would have an interest, because the ladies all said, "Of course a Grierson would not think seriously of a Northerner, a day laborer." But there were still others, older people, who said that even grief could not cause a real lady to forget *noblesse oblige*—without calling it *noblesse oblige*. They just said, "Poor Emily. Her kinsfolk should come to her." She had some kin in Alabama; but years ago her father had fallen out with them over the estate of old lady Wyatt, the crazy woman, and there was no communication between the two families. They had not even been represented at the funeral.

And as soon as the old people said, "Poor Emily," the whispering began. "Do you suppose it's really so?" they said to one another. "Of course it is. What else could . . ." This behind their hands; rustling of craned silk and satin behind jalousies closed upon the sun on Sunday afternoon as the thin, swift clop-clop-clop of the matched team passed: "Poor Emily."

She carried her head high enough—even when we believed that she was fallen. It was as if she demanded more than ever the recognition of her dignity as the last Grierson; as if it had wanted that touch of earthiness to reaffirm her imperviousness. Like when she bought the rat poison, the arsenic. That was over a year after they had begun to say "Poor Emily," and while the two female cousins were visiting her.

"I want some poison," she said to the druggist. She was over thirty then, still a slight woman, though thinner than usual, with cold, haughty black eyes in a face the flesh of which was strained across the temples and about the eye-sockets as you imagine a light-house-keeper's face ought to look. "I want some poison," she said.

"Yes, Miss Emily. What kind? For rats and such? I'd recom—"

"I want the best you have. I don't care what kind."

The druggist named several. "They'll kill anything up to an elephant. But what you want is—"

"Arsenic," Miss Emily said. "Is that a good one?"

"Is . . . arsenic? Yes, ma'am. But what you want—"

"I want arsenic."

The druggist looked down at her. She looked back at him, erect, her face like a strained flag. "Why, of course," the druggist said. "If that's what you want. But the law requires you to tell what you are going to use it for."

Miss Emily just stared at him, her head tilted back in order to look him eye for eye, until he looked away and went and got the arsenic and wrapped it up. The Negro delivery boy brought her the package; the druggist didn't come back. When she opened the package at home there was written on the box, under the skull and bones: "For rats."

IV

So the next day we all said, "She will kill herself"; and we said it would be the best thing. When she had first begun to be seen with Homer Barron, we had said, "She will marry him." Then we said, "She will persuade him yet," because Homer himself had remarked—he liked men, and it was known that he drank with the younger men in the Elks' Club—that he was not a marrying man. Later we said, "Poor Emily" behind the jalousies as they passed on Sunday afternoon in the glittering buggy, Miss Emily with her head high and Homer Barron with his hat cocked and a cigar in his teeth, reins and whip in a yellow glove.

Then some of the ladies began to say that it was a disgrace to the town and a bad example to the young people. The men did not want to interfere, but at last the ladies forced the Baptist minister—Miss Emily's people were Episcopal—to call upon her. He would never divulge what happened during that interview, but he refused to go back again. The next Sunday they again drove about the streets, and the following day the minister's wife wrote to Miss Emily's relations in Alabama.

So she had blood-kin under her roof again and we sat back to watch developments. At first nothing happened. Then we were sure that they were to be married. We learned that Miss Emily had been to the jeweler's and ordered a man's toilet set in silver, with the letters H. B. on each piece. Two days later we learned that she had bought a complete outfit of men's clothing, including a nightshirt, and we said, "They are married." We were really glad. We were glad because the two female cousins were even more Grierson than Miss Emily had ever been.

So we were not surprised when Homer Barron—the streets had been finished some time since—was gone. We were a little disappointed that there was not a public blowing-off, but we believed that he had gone on to prepare for Miss Emily's coming, or to give her a chance to get rid of the cousins. (By that time it was a cabal, and we were all Miss Emily's allies to help circumvent the cousins.) Sure enough, after another week they departed. And, as we had expected all along, within three days Homer Barron was back in town. A neighbor saw the Negro man admit him at the kitchen door at dusk one evening.

And that was the last we saw of Homer Barron. And of Miss Emily for some time. The Negro man went in and out with the market basket, but the front door remained closed. Now and then we would see her at a window for a moment, as the men did that night when they sprinkled the lime, but for almost six months she did not appear on the streets. Then we knew that this was to be expected too; as if that quality of her father which had thwarted her woman's life so many times had been too virulent and too furious to die.

When we next saw Miss Emily, she had grown fat and her hair was turning gray. During the next few years it grew grayer and grayer until it attained an even pepper-and-salt iron-gray, when it ceased turning. Up to the day of her death at seventy-four it was still that vigorous iron-gray, like the hair of an active man.

From that time on her front door remained closed, save for a period of six or seven years, when she was about forty, during which she gave lessons in china-painting. She fitted up a studio in one of the downstairs rooms, where the daughters and granddaughters of Colonel Sartoris' contemporaries were sent to her with the same regularity and in the same spirit that they were sent to church on Sundays with a twenty-five-cent piece for the collection plate. Meanwhile her taxes had been remitted.

Then the newer generation became the backbone and the spirit of the town, and the painting pupils grew up and fell away and did not send their children to her with boxes of color and tedious brushes and pictures cut from the ladies' magazines. The front door closed upon the last one and remained closed for good. When the town got free postal delivery, Miss Emily alone refused to let them fasten the metal numbers above her door and attach a mailbox to it. She would not listen to them.

Daily, monthly, yearly we watched the Negro grow grayer and more stooped, going in and out with the market basket. Each December we sent her a tax notice, which would be returned by the post office a week later, unclaimed. Now and then we would see her in one of the downstairs windows—she had evidently shut up the top floor of the house—like the carven torso of an idol in a niche, looking or not looking at us, we could never tell which. Thus she passed from generation to generation—dear, inescapable, impervious, tranquil, and perverse.

And so she died. Fell ill in the house filled with dust and shadows, with only a doddering Negro man to wait on her. We did not even know she was sick; we had long since given up trying to get any information from the Negro. He talked to no one, probably not even to her, for his voice had grown harsh and rusty, as if from disuse.

She died in one of the downstairs rooms, in a heavy walnut bed with a curtain, her gray head propped on a pillow yellow and moldy with age and lack of sunlight.

V

The Negro met the first of the ladies at the front door and let them in, with their hushed, sibilant voices and their quick, curious glances, and then he disappeared. He walked right through the house and out the back and was not seen again.

The two female cousins came at once. They held the funeral on the second day, with the town coming to look at Miss Emily beneath a mass of bought flowers, with the crayon face of her father musing profoundly above the bier and the ladies sibilant and macabre; and the very old men—some in their brushed Confederate uniforms—on the porch and the lawn, talking of Miss Emily as if she had been a contemporary of theirs, believing that they had danced with her and courted her perhaps, confusing time with its mathematical progression, as the old do, to whom all the past is not a diminishing road but, instead, a huge meadow which no winter ever quite touches, divided from them now by the narrow bottle-neck of the most recent decade of years.

Already we knew that there was one room in that region above stairs which no one had seen in forty years, and which would have to be forced. They waited until Miss Emily was decently in the ground before they opened it.

The violence of breaking down the door seemed to fill this room with pervading dust. A thin, acrid pall as of the tomb seemed to lie everywhere upon this room decked and furnished as for a bridal: upon the valance curtains of faded rose color, upon the rose-shaded lights, upon the dressing table, upon the delicate array of crystal and the man's toilet things backed with tarnished silver, silver so tarnished that the monogram was obscured. Among them lay a collar and tie, as if they had just been removed, which, lifted, left upon the surface a pale crescent in the dust. Upon a chair hung the suit, carefully folded; beneath it the two mute shoes and the discarded socks.

The man himself lay in the bed.

For a long while we just stood there, looking down at the profound and fleshless grin. The body had apparently once lain in the attitude of an embrace, but now the long sleep that outlasts love, that conquers even the grimace of love, had cuckolded him. What was left of him, rotted beneath what was left of the nightshirt, had become inextricable from the bed in which he lay; and upon him and upon the pillow beside him lay that even coating of the patient and biding dust.

Then we noticed that in the second pillow was the indentation of a head. One of us lifted something from it, and leaning forward, that faint and invisible dust dry and acrid in the nostrils, we saw a long strand of iron-gray hair.

[1944]

For Thought

Achieving the effect of gothic macabre, the atmosphere dominating the story is one of ruin and decay, starting with the description of the once grand, but now seedy, family home of the Griersons set in deteriorated, grimy surroundings. The images of rottenness and foul odors, repeated at key points, are skillful touches that arouse curiosity and prepare the reader for the climactic evidences of decay in Miss Emily's musty bedroom. Corresponding to this physical decay is a sense of decay in society; the old aristocratic order has passed and is no longer retrievable.

At the end of the story, the reader is shocked by the gruesome defiance of separation and death represented by the strand of iron-gray hair and the indentation on the second pillow. These ghoulish mementoes of intimacy after death offer mute testimony to the unyielding pride of a woman of the Old South who would not let herself become an object of common scorn at having been jilted and abandoned by a faithless lover.

For Discussion

1. What is the point of view? What purpose does it serve?
2. What is the attitude of the narrator toward Miss Emily?
3. What atmosphere is created early in the story and how is this done?
4. What is the significance of Emily's refusal to pay taxes and of her resistance to the burial of her father?
5. Aside from her being divorced from reality, how is Miss Emily characterized by her actions over the payment of taxes and the purchase of arsenic?
6. What events foreshadow the discovery of the skeleton in the upstairs bedroom?
7. What character trait provides the motivation for Miss Emily's central action in the story and how is it used in the action?
8. What is the central conflict in the story? How is it resolved?
9. How is Miss Emily's "victory" over adversity made possible?
10. How does the title relate to the story?

F. Scott Fitzgerald
The Rich Boy

I

Begin with an individual, and before you know it you find that you have created a type; begin with a type, and you find that you have created—nothing. That is because we are all queer fish, queerer behind our faces and voices than we want any one to know or than we know ourselves. When I hear a man proclaiming himself an "average, honest, open fellow," I feel pretty sure that he has some definite and perhaps terrible abnormality which he has agreed to conceal—and his protestation of being average and honest and open is his way of reminding himself of his misprision.

There are no types, no plurals. There is a rich boy, and this is his and not his brothers' story. All my life I have lived among his brothers but this one has been my friend. Besides, if I wrote about his brothers I should have to begin by attacking all the lies that the poor have told about the rich and the rich have told about themselves—such a wild structure they have erected that when we pick up a book about the rich, some instinct prepares us for unreality. Even the intelligent and impassioned reporters of life have made the country of the rich as unreal as fairy-land.

Let me tell you about the very rich. They are different from you and me. They possess and enjoy early, and it does something to them, makes them soft where we are hard, and cynical where we are trustful, in a way that, unless you were born rich, it is very difficult to understand. They think, deep in their hearts, that they are better than we are because we had to discover the compensations and refuges of life for ourselves. Even when they enter deep into our world or sink below us, they still think that they are better than we are. They are different. The only way I can describe young Anson Hunter is to approach him as if he were a foreigner and cling stubbornly to my point of view. If I accept his for a moment I am lost—I have nothing to show but a preposterous movie.

II

Anson was the eldest of six children who would some day divide a fortune of fifteen million dollars, and he reached the age of reason—is it seven?—at the beginning of the century when daring young women were already gliding along Fifth Avenue in electric "mobiles." In those days he and his brother had an English governess who spoke the language very clearly and crisply and well, so that the two boys grew to speak as she did—their words and sentences were all crisp and clear and not run together as ours are. They didn't talk exactly like English children but acquired an accent that is peculiar to fashionable people in the city of New York.

In the summer the six children were moved from the house on 71st Street to a big estate in northern Connecticut. It was not a fashionable locality—Anson's father wanted to delay as long as possible his children's knowledge of that side of life. He was a man somewhat superior to his class, which composed New York society, and to his period, which was the snobbish and formalized vulgarity of the Gilded Age, and he wanted his sons to learn habits of concentration and have sound constitutions and grow up into right-living and successful men. He and his wife kept an eye on them as well as they were able until the two older boys went away to school, but in huge establishments this is difficult—it was much simpler in the series of small and medium-sized houses in which my own youth was spent—I was never far out of the reach of my mother's voice, of the sense of her presence, her approval or disapproval.

Anson's first sense of his superiority came to him when he realized the half-grudging American deference that was paid to him in the Connecticut village. The parents of the boys he played with always inquired after his father and mother, and were vaguely excited when their own children were asked to the Hunters' house. He accepted this as the natural state of things, and a sort of impatience with all groups of which he was not the centre—in money, in position, in authority—remained with him for the rest of his life. He disdained to struggle with other boys for precedence—he expected it to be given him freely, and when it wasn't he withdrew into his family. His family was sufficient, for in the East money is still a somewhat feudal thing, a clan-forming thing. In the snobbish West, money separates families to form "sets."

At eighteen, when he went to New Haven, Anson was tall and thick-set, with a clear complexion and a healthy color from the ordered life he had led in school. His hair was yellow and grew in a funny way on his head, his nose was beaked—these two things kept him from being handsome—but he had a confident charm and a certain brusque style, and the upper-class men who passed him on the street knew without being told that he was a rich boy and had gone to one of the best schools. Nevertheless, his very superiority kept him from being a success in college—the independence was mistaken for egotism, and the refusal to accept Yale standards with the proper awe seemed to belittle all those who had. So, long before he graduated, he began to shift the centre of his life to New York.

He was at home in New York—there was his own house with "the kind of servants you can't get any more"—and his own family, of which, because of his good humor and a certain ability to make things go, he was rapidly becoming the centre, and the débutante parties, and the correct manly world of the men's clubs, and the occasional wild spree with the gallant girls whom New Haven only knew from the fifth row. His aspirations were conventional enough—they included even the irreproachable shadow he would some day marry, but they differed from the aspirations of the majority of young men in that there was no mist over them, none of that quality which is variously known as "idealism" or "illusion." Anson accepted without reservation the world of high finance and high extravagance, of divorce and dissipation, of snobbery and of privilege. Most of our lives end as a compromise—it was as a compromise that his life began.

He and I first met in the late summer of 1917 when he was just out of Yale, and, like the rest of us, was swept up into the systematized hysteria of the war. In the blue-green uniform of the naval aviation he came down to Pensacola, where the hotel orchestras played "I'm sorry, dear," and we young officers danced with the girls. Every one liked him, and though he ran with the drinkers and wasn't an especially good pilot, even the instructors treated him with a certain respect. He was always having long talks with them in his confident, logical voice—talks which ended by his getting himself, or, more frequently, another officer, out of some impending trouble. He was convivial, bawdy, robustly avid for pleasure, and we were all surprised when he fell in love with a conservative and rather proper girl.

Her name was Paula Legendre, a dark, serious beauty from somewhere in California. Her family kept a winter residence just outside of town, and in spite of her primness she was enormously popular; there is a large class of men whose egotism can't endure humor in a woman. But Anson wasn't that sort, and I couldn't understand the attraction of her "sincerity"—that was the thing to say about her—for his keen and somewhat sardonic mind.

Nevertheless, they fell in love—and on her terms. He no longer joined the twilight gathering at the De Soto bar, and whenever they were seen together they were engaged in a long, serious dialogue, which must have gone on several weeks. Long afterward he told me that it was not about anything in particular but was composed on both side of immature and even meaningless statements—the emotional content that gradually came to fill it grew up not out of the words but out of its enormous seriousness. It was a sort of hypnosis. Often it was interrupted, giving way to that emasculated humor we call fun; when they were alone it was resumed again, solemn, low-keyed, and pitched so as to give each other a sense of unity in feeling and thought. They came to resent any interruptions of it, to be unresponsive to facetiousness about life, even to the mild cynicism of their contemporaries. They were only happy when the dialogue was going on, and its seriousness bathed them like the amber glow of an open fire. Toward the end there came an interruption they did not resent—it began to be interrupted by passion.

Oddly enough, Anson was as engrossed in the dialogue as she was and as profoundly affected by it, yet at the same time aware that on his side much was insincere, and on hers much was merely simple. At first, too, he despised her emotional simplicity, as well, but with his love her nature deepened and blossomed, and he could despise it no longer. He felt that if he could enter into Paula's warm safe life he would be happy. The long preparation of the dialogue removed any constraint—he taught her some of what he had learned from more adventurous women, and she responded with a rapt holy intensity. One evening after a dance they agreed to marry, and he wrote a long letter about her to his mother. The next day Paula told him that she was rich, that she had a personal fortune of nearly a million dollars.

III

It was exactly as if they could say "Neither of us has anything: we shall be poor together"—just as delightful that they should be rich instead. It gave them the same communion of adventure. Yet when Anson got leave in April, and Paula and her mother accompanied him North, she was impressed with the standing of his family in New York and with the scale on which they lived. Alone with Anson for the first time in the rooms where he had played as a boy, she was filled with a comfortable emotion, as though she were pre-eminently safe and taken care of. The pictures of Anson in a skull cap at his first school, of Anson on horseback with the sweetheart of a mysterious forgotten summer, of Anson in a gay group of ushers and bridesmaids at a wedding, made her jealous of his life apart from her in the past, and so completely did his authoritative person seem to sum up and typify these possessions of his that she was inspired with the idea of being married immediately and returning to Pensacola as his wife.

But an immediate marriage wasn't discussed—even the engagement was to be secret until after the war. When she realized that only two days of his leave remained, her dissatisfaction crystallized in the intention of making him as unwilling to wait as she was. They were driving to the country for dinner and she determined to force the issue that night.

Now a cousin of Paula's was staying with them at the Ritz, a severe, bitter girl who loved Paula but was somewhat jealous of her impressive engagement, and as Paula was late in dressing, the cousin, who wasn't going to the party, received Anson in the parlor of the suite.

Anson had met friends at five o'clock and drunk freely and indiscreetly with them for an hour. He left the Yale Club at a proper time, and his mother's chauffeur drove him to the Ritz, but his usual capacity was not in evidence, and the impact of the steam-heated sitting-room made him suddenly dizzy. He knew it, and he was both amused and sorry.

Paula's cousin was twenty-five, but she was exceptionally naïve, and at first failed to realize what was up. She had never met Anson before, and she was surprised when he mumbled strange information and nearly fell off his chair, but until Paula appeared it didn't occur to her that what she had taken for the odor of a dry-cleaned uniform was really whiskey. But Paula understood as soon as she appeared; her only thought was to get Anson away before her mother saw him, and at the look in her eyes the cousin understood too.

When Paula and Anson descended to the limousine they found two men inside, both asleep; they were the men with whom he had been drinking at the Yale Club, and they were also going to the party. He had entirely forgotten their presence in the car. On the way to Hempstead they awoke and sang. Some of the songs were rough, and though Paula tried to reconcile herself to the fact that Anson had few verbal inhibitions, her lips tightened with shame and distaste.

Back at the hotel the cousin, confused and agitated, considered the incident, and then walked into Mrs. Legendre's bedroom, saying: "Isn't he funny?"

"Who is funny?"

"Why—Mr. Hunter. He seemed so funny."

Mrs. Legendre looked at her sharply.

"How is he funny?"

"Why, he said he was French. I didn't know he was French."

"That's absurd. You must have misunderstood." She smiled: "It was a joke."

The cousin shook her head stubbornly.

"No. He said he was brought up in France. He said he couldn't speak any English, and that's why he couldn't talk to me. And he couldn't!"

Mrs. Legendre looked away with impatience just as the cousin added thoughtfully, "Perhaps it was because he was so drunk," and walked out of the room.

This curious report was true. Anson, finding his voice thick and uncontrollable, had taken the unusual refuge of announcing that he spoke no English. Years afterwards he used to tell that part of the story, and he invariably communicated the uproarious laughter which the memory aroused in him.

Five times in the next hour Mrs. Legendre tried to get Hempstead on the phone. When she succeeded, there was a ten-minute delay before she heard Paula's voice on the wire.

"Cousin Jo told me Anson was intoxicated."

"On, no. . . ."

"Oh, yes. Cousin Jo says he was intoxicated. He told her he was French, and fell off his chair and behaved as if he was very intoxicated. I don't want you to come home with him."

"Mother, he's all right! Please don't worry about———"

"But I do worry. I think it's dreadful. I want you to promise me not to come home with him."

"I'll take care of it, mother. . . ."

"I don't want you to come home with him."

"All right, mother. Good-by."

"Be sure now, Paula. Ask some one to bring you."

Deliberately Paula took the receiver from her ear and hung it up. Her face was flushed with helpless annoyance. Anson was stretched asleep out in a bedroom up-stairs, while the dinner-party below was proceeding lamely toward conclusion.

The hour's drive had sobered him somewhat—his arrival was merely hilarious—and Paula hoped that the evening was not spoiled, after all, but two imprudent cocktails before dinner completed the disaster. He talked boisterously and somewhat offensively to the party at large for fifteen minutes, and then slid silently under the table; like a man in an old print—but, unlike an old print, it was rather horrible without being at all quaint. None of the young girls present remarked upon the incident—it seemed to merit only silence. His uncle and two other men carried him upstairs, and it was just after this that Paula was called to the phone.

An hour later Anson awoke in a fog of nervous agony, through which he perceived after a moment the figure of his Uncle Robert standing by the door.

". . . I said are you better?"

"What?"

"Do you feel better, old man?"

"Terrible," said Anson.

"I'm going to try you on another bromo-seltzer. If you can hold it down, it'll do you good to sleep."

With an effort Anson slid his legs from the bed and stood up.

"I'm all right," he said dully.

"Take it easy."

"I thin' if you gave me a glassbrandy I could go down-stairs."

"Oh, no———"

"Yes, that's the only thin'. I'm all right now. . . . I suppose I'm in Dutch dow' there."

"They know you're a little under the weather," said his uncle deprecatingly. "But don't worry about it. Schuyler didn't even get here. He passed away in the locker-room over at the Links."

Indifferent to any opinion, except Paula's, Anson was nevertheless determined to have the débris of the evening, but when after a cold bath he made his appearance most of the party had already left. Paula got up immediately to go home.

In the limousine the old serious dialogue began. She had known that he drank, she admitted, but she had never expected anything like this—it seemed to her that perhaps they were not suited to each other, after all. Their ideas about life were too different, and so forth. When she finished speaking, Anson spoke in turn, very soberly. Then Paula said she'd have to think it over; she wouldn't decide to-night; she was not angry but she was terribly sorry. Nor would she let him come into the hotel with her, but just before she got out of the car she leaned and kissed him unhappily on the cheek.

The next afternoon Anson had a long talk with Mrs. Legendre while Paula sat listening in silence. It was agreed that Paula was to brood over the incident for a proper period and then, if mother and daughter thought it best, they would follow Anson to Pensacola. On his part he apologized with sincerity and dignity—that was all; with every card in her hand Mrs. Legendre was unable to establish any advantage over him. He made no promises, showed no humility, only delivered a few serious comments on life which brought him off with rather a moral superiority at the end. When they came South three weeks later, neither

Anson in his satisfaction nor Paula in her relief at the reunion realized that the psychological moment had passed forever.

IV

He dominated and attracted her, and at the same time filled her with anxiety. Confused by his mixture of solidity and self-indulgence, of sentiment and cynicism—incongruities which her gentle mind was unable to resolve—Paula grew to think of him as two alternating personalities. When she saw him alone, or at a formal party, or with his casual inferiors, she felt a tremendous pride in his strong, attractive presence, the paternal, understanding stature of his mind. In other company she became uneasy when what had been a fine imperviousness to mere gentility showed its outer face. The other face was gross, humorous, reckless of everything but pleasure. It startled her mind temporarily away from him, even led her into a short covert experiment with an old beau, but it was no use—after four months of Anson's enveloping vitality there was an anaemic pallor in all other men.

In July he was ordered abroad, and their tenderness and desire reached a crescendo. Paula considered a last-minute marriage—decided against it only because there were always cocktails on his breath now, but the parting itself made her physically ill with grief. After his departure she wrote him long letters of regret for the days of love they had missed by waiting. In August Anson's plane slipped down into the North Sea. He was pulled onto a destroyer after a night in the water and sent to a hospital with pneumonia; the armistice was signed before he was finally sent home.

Then, with every opportunity given back to them, with no material obstacle to overcome, the secret weavings of their temperaments came between them, drying up their kisses and their tears, making their voices less loud to one another, muffling the intimate chatter of their hearts until the old communication was only possible by letters, from far away. One afternoon a society reporter waited for two hours in the Hunters' house for a confirmation of their engagement. Anson denied it; nevertheless an early issue carried the report as a leading paragraph—they were "constantly seen together at Southhampton, Hot Springs, and Tuxedo Park." But the serious dialogue had turned a corner into a long-sustained quarrel, and the affair was almost played out. Anson got drunk flagrantly and missed an engagement with her, whereupon Paula made certain behavioristic demands. His despair was helpless before his pride and his knowledge of himself: the engagement was definitely broken.

"Dearest," said their letters now, "Dearest, Dearest, when I wake up in the middle of the night and realize that after all it was not to be, I feel that I want to die. I can't go on living any more. Perhaps when we meet this summer we may talk things over and decide differently—we were so excited and sad that day, and I don't feel that I can live all my life without you. You speak of other people. Don't you know there are no other people for me, but only you. . . ."

But as Paula drifted here and there around the East she would sometimes mention her gaieties to make him wonder. Anson was too acute to wonder. When he saw a man's name in her letters he felt more sure of her and a little disdainful—he was always superior to such things. But he still hoped that they would some day marry.

Meanwhile he plunged vigorously into all the movement and glitter of post-bellum New York, entering a brokerage house, joining half a dozen clubs, dancing late, and moving in three worlds—his own world, the world of young Yale graduates, and that section of the half-world which rests one end on Broadway. But there was always a thorough and infractible eight hours devoted to his work in Wall Street, where the combination of his influential family connection, his sharp intelligence, and his abundance of sheer physical energy brought him almost immediately forward. He had one of those invaluable minds with partitions in it; sometimes he appeared at his office refreshed by less than an hour's sleep, but such occurrences were rare. So early as 1920 his income in salary and commissions exceeded twelve thousand dollars.

As the Yale tradition slipped into the past he became more and more of a popular figure among his classmates in New York, more popular than he had ever been in college. He lived in a great house, and had the means of introducing young men into other great houses. Moreover, his life already seemed secure, while theirs, for the most part, had arrived again at precarious beginnings. They commenced to turn to him for amusement and escape, and Anson responded readily, taking pleasure in helping people and arranging their affairs.

There were no men in Paula's letters now, but a note of tenderness ran through them that had not been there before. From several sources he heard that she had "a heavy beau," Lowell Thayer, a Bostonian of wealth and position, and though he was sure she still loved him, it made him uneasy to think that he might lose her, after all. Save for one unsatisfactory day she had not been in New York for almost five months, and as the rumors multiplied he became increasingly anxious to see her. In February he took his vacation and went down to Florida.

Palm Beach sprawled plump and opulent between the sparkling sapphire of Lake Worth, flawed here and there by house boats at anchor, and the great turquoise bar of the Atlantic Ocean. The huge bulks of the Breakers and the Royal Poinciana rose as twin paunches from the bright level of the sand, and around them clustered the Dancing Glade, Bradley's House of Chance, and a dozen modistes and milliners with goods at triple prices from New York. Upon the trellised veranda of the Breakers two hundred women stepped right, stepped left, wheeled, and slid in that then celebrated calisthenic known as the double-shuffle, while in half-time to the music two thousand bracelets clicked up and down on two hundred arms.

At the Everglades Club after dark Paula and Lowell Thayer and Anson and a casual fourth played bridge with hot cards. It seemed to Anson that her kind, serious face was wan and tired—she had been around now for four, five, years. He had known her for three.

"Two spades."

"Cigarette? . . . Oh, I beg your pardon. By me."

"By."

"I'll double three spades."

There were a dozen tables of bridge in the room, which was filling up with smoke. Anson's eyes met Paula's, held them persistently even when Thayer's glance fell between them. . . .

"What was bid?" he asked abstractedly.

"Rose of Washington Square"

sang the young people in the corners:

"I'm withering there
In basement air——"

The smoke banked like fog, and the opening of a door filled the room with blown swirls of ectoplasm. Little Bright Eyes streaked past the tables seeking Mr. Conan Doyle among the Englishmen who were posing as Englishmen about the lobby.

"You could cut it with a knife."

" . . . cut it with a knife."

". . . . a knife."

At the end of the rubber Paula suddenly got up and spoke to Anson in a tense, low voice. With scarcely a glance at Lowell Thayer, they walked out the door and descended a long flight of stone steps—in a moment they were walking hand in hand along the moonlit beach.

"Darling, darling. . . ." They embraced recklessly, passionately, in a shadow. . . . Then Paula drew back her face to let his lips say what she wanted to hear—she could feel the words forming as they kissed again. . . . Again she broke away, listening, but as he pulled her close once more she realized that he had said nothing—only *"Darling! Darling!"* in that deep, sad whisper that always made her cry. Humbly, obediently, her emotions yielded to him and the tears streamed down her face, but her heart kept on crying: "Ask me—oh, Anson, dearest, ask me!"

"Paula. . . . *Paula!*"

The words wrung her heart like hands, and Anson, feeling her tremble, knew that emotion was enough. He need say no more, commit their destinies to no practical enigma. Why should he, when he might hold her so, biding his own time, for another year—forever? He was considering them both, her more than himself. For a moment, when she said suddenly that she must go back to her hotel, he hesitated, thinking, first, "This is the moment, after all," and then: "No, let it wait—she is mine. . . ."

He had forgotten that Paula too was worn away inside with the strain of three years. Her mood passed forever in the night.

He went back to New York next morning filled with a certain restless dissatisfaction. Late in April, without warning, he received a telegram from Bar Harbor in which Paula told him that she was engaged to Lowell Thayer, and that they would be married immediately in Boston. What he never really believed could happen had happened at last.

Anson filled himself with whiskey that morning, and going to the office, carried on his work without a break—rather with a fear of what would happen if he stopped. In the evening he went out as usual, saying nothing of what had occurred; he was cordial, humorous, unabstracted. But one thing he could not help—for three days, in any place, in any company, he would suddenly bend his head into his hands and cry like a child.

V

In 1922 when Anson went abroad with the junior partner to investigate some London loans, the journey intimated that he was to be taken into the firm. He was twenty-seven now, a little heavy without being definitely stout, and with a manner older than his years. Old people and young people liked him and trusted him, and mothers felt safe when their daughters were in his charge, for he had a way, when he came into a room, of putting himself on a footing with the oldest and most conservative people there. "You and I," he seemed to say, "we're solid. We understand."

He had an instinctive and rather charitable knowledge of the weaknesses of men and women, and, like a priest, it made him the more concerned for the maintenance of outward forms. It was typical of him that every Sunday morning he taught in a fashionable Episcopal Sunday-school—even though a cold shower and a quick change into a cutaway coat were all that separated him from the wild night before.

After his father's death he was the practical head of his family, and, in effect, guided the destinies of the younger children. Through a complication his authority did not extend to his father's estate, which was administered by his Uncle Robert, who was the horsey member of the family, a good-natured, hard-drinking member of that set which centres about Wheatley Hills.

Uncle Robert and his wife, Edna, had been great friends of Anson's youth, and the former was disappointed when his nephew's superiority failed to take a horsey form. He backed him for a city club which was the most difficult in America to enter—one could only join if one's family had "helped to build up New York" (or, in other words, were rich before 1880)—and when Anson, after his election, neglected it for the Yale Club, Uncle Robert gave him a little talk on the subject. But when on top of that Anson declined to enter Robert Hunter's own conservative and somewhat neglected brokerage house, his manner grew cooler. Like a primary teacher who has taught all he knew, he slipped out of Anson's life.

There were so many friends in Anson's life—scarcely one for whom he had not done some unusual kindness and scarcely one whom he did not occasionally embarrass by his bursts of rough conversation or his habit of getting drunk whenever and however he liked. It annoyed him when any one else blundered in that regard—about his own lapses he was always humorous. Odd things happened to him and he told them with infectious laughter.

I was working in New York that spring, and I used to lunch with him at the Yale Club, which my university was sharing until the completion of our own. I had read of Paula's marriage, and one afternoon, when I asked him about her, something moved him to tell me the story. After that he frequently invited me to family dinners at his house and behaved as though there was a special relation between us, as though with his confidence a little of that consuming memory had passed into me.

I found that despite the trusting mothers, his attitude toward girls was not indiscriminately protective. It was up to the girl—if she showed an inclination toward looseness, she must take care of herself, even with him.

"Life," he would explain sometimes, "has made a cynic of me."

By life he meant Paula. Sometimes, especially when he was drinking, it became a little twisted in his mind, and he thought that she had callously thrown him over.

This "cynicism," or rather his realization that naturally fast girls were not worth sparing, led to his affair with Dolly Karger. It wasn't his only affair in those years, but it came nearest to touching him deeply, and it had a profound effect upon his attitude toward life.

Dolly was the daughter of a notorious "publicist" who had married into society. She herself grew up into the Junior League, came out at the Plaza, and went to the Assembly; and only a few old families like the Hunters could question whether or not she "belonged," for her picture was often in the papers, and she had more enviable attention than many girls who undoubtedly did. She was dark-haired, with carmine lips and a high, lovely color, which she concealed under pinkish-gray powder all through the first year out, because high color was unfashionable—Victorian-pale was the thing to be. She wore black, severe suits and stood with her hands in her pockets leaning a little forward, with a humorous restraint on her face. She danced exquisitely—better than anything she liked to dance—better than anything except making love. Since she was ten she had always been in love, and, usually, with some boy who didn't respond to her. Those who did—and there were many—bored her after a brief encounter, but for her failures she reserved the warmest spot in her heart. When she met them she would always try once more—sometimes she succeeded, more often she failed.

It never occurred to this gypsy of the unattainable that there was a certain resemblance in those who refused to love her—they shared a hard intuition that saw through to her weakness, not a weakness of emotion but a weakness of rudder. Anson perceived this when he first met her, less than a month after Paula's marriage. He was drinking rather heavily, and he pretended for a week that he was falling in love with her. Then he dropped her abruptly and forgot—immediately he took up the commanding position in her heart.

Like so many girls of that day Dolly was slackly and indiscreetly wild. The unconventionality of a slightly older generation had been simply one facet of a post-war movement to discredit obsolete manners—Dolly's was both older and shabbier, and she saw in Anson the two extremes which the emotionally shiftless woman seeks, an abandon to the indulgence alternating with a protective strength. In his character she felt both the sybarite and the solid rock, and these two satisfied every need of her nature.

She felt that it was going to be difficult, but she mistook the reason—she thought that Anson and his family expected a more spectacular marriage, but she guessed immediately that her advantage lay in his tendency to drink.

They met at the large débutante dances, but as her infatuation increased they managed to be more and more together. Like most mothers, Mrs. Karger believed that Anson was exceptionally reliable, so she allowed Dolly to go with him to distant country clubs and suburban houses without inquiring closely into their activities or questioning her explanations when they came in late. At first these explanations might have been accurate, but Dolly's worldly ideas of capturing Anson were soon engulfed in the rising sweep of her emotion. Kisses in the back of taxis and motor-cars were no longer enough; they did a curious thing:

They dropped out of their world for a while and made another world just beneath it where Anson's tippling and Dolly's irregular hours would be less noticed and commented on. It was composed, this world, of varying elements—several of Anson's Yale friends and their wives, two or three young brokers and bond salesmen and a handful of unattached men, fresh from college, with money and a propensity to dissipation. What this world lacked in spaciousness and scale it made up for by allowing them a liberty that it scarcely permitted itself. Moreover, it centred around them and permitted Dolly the pleasure of a faint condescension—a pleasure which Anson, whose whole life was a condescension from the certitudes of his childhood, was unable to share.

He was not in love with her, and in the long feverish winter of their affair he frequently told her so. In the spring he was weary—he wanted to renew his life at some other source—moreover, he saw that either he must break with her now or accept the responsibility of a definite seduction. Her family's encouraging attitude precipitated his decision—one evening when Mr. Karger knocked discreetly at the library door to announce that he had left a bottle of old brandy in the dining-room, Anson felt that life was hemming him in. That night he wrote her a short letter in which he told her that he was going on his vacation, and that in view of all the circumstances they had better meet no more.

It was June. His family had closed up the house and gone to the country, so he was living temporarily at the Yale Club. I had heard about his affair with Dolly as it developed—accounts salted with humor, for he despised unstable women, and granted them no place in the social edifice in which he believed—and when he told me that night that he was definitely breaking with her I was glad. I had seen Dolly here and there, and each time with a feeling of pity at the hopelessness of her struggle, and of shame at knowing so much about her that I had no right to know. She was what is known as "a pretty little thing," but there was a certain recklessness which rather fascinated me. Her dedication to the goddess of waste would have been less obvious had she been less spirited—she would most certainly throw herself away, but I was glad when I heard that the sacrifice would not be consummated in my sight.

Anson was going to leave the letter of farewell at her house next morning. It was one of the few houses left open in the Fifth Avenue district, and he knew that the Kargers, acting upon erroneous information from Dolly, had foregone a trip abroad to give their daughter her chance. As he stepped out the door of the Yale Club into Madison Avenue the postman passed him, and he followed back inside. The first letter that caught his eye was in Dolly's hand.

He knew what it would be—a lonely and tragic monologue, full of the reproaches he knew, the invoked memories, the "I wonder if's"—all the immemorial intimacies that he had communicated to Paula Legendre in what seemed another age. Thumbing over some bills, he brought it on top again and opened it. To his surprise it was a short, somewhat formal note, which said that Dolly would be unable to go to the country with him for the week-end, because Perry Hull from Chicago had unexpectedly come to town. It added that Anson had brought this on himself: "—if I felt that you loved me as I love you I would go with you at any time, any place, but Perry is so nice, and he so much wants me to marry him———"

Anson smiled contemptuously—he had had experience with such decoy epistles. Moreover, he knew how Dolly had labored over this plan, probably sent for the faithful Perry and calculated the time of his arrival—even labored over the note so that it would make him jealous without driving him away. Like most compromises, it had neither force nor vitality but only a timorous despair.

Suddenly he was angry. He sat down in the lobby and read it again. Then he went to the phone, called Dolly and told her in his clear, compelling voice that he had received her note and would call for her at five o'clock as they had previously planned. Scarcely waiting for the pretended uncertainty of her "Perhaps I can see you for an hour," he hung up the receiver and went down to his office. On the way he tore his own letter into bits and dropped it in the street.

He was not jealous—she meant nothing to him—but at her pathetic ruse everything stubborn and self-indulgent in him came to the surface. It was a presumption from a mental inferior and it could not be overlooked. If she wanted to know to whom she belonged she would see.

He was on the door-step at quarter past five. Dolly was dressed for the street, and he listened in silence to the paragraph of "I can only see you for an hour," which she had begun on the phone.

"Put on your hat, Dolly," he said, "we'll take a walk."

They strolled up Madison Avenue and over to Fifth while Anson's shirt dampened upon his portly body in the deep heat. He talked little, scolding her, making no love to her, but before they had walked six blocks she was his again, apologizing for the note, offering not to see Perry at all as an atonement, offering anything. She thought that he had come because he was beginning to love her.

"I'm hot," he said when they reached 71st street. "This is a winter suit. If I stop by the house and change, would you mind waiting for me down-stairs? I'll only be a minute."

She was happy; the intimacy of his being hot, of any physical fact about him, thrilled her. When they came to the iron-grated door and Anson took out his key she experienced a sort of delight.

Down-stairs it was dark, and after he ascended in the lift Dolly raised a curtain and looked out through opaque lace at the houses over the way. She heard the lift machinery stop, and with the notion of teasing him pressed the button that brought it down. Then on what was more than an impulse she got into it and sent it up to what she guessed was his floor.

"Anson," she called, laughing a little.

"Just a minute," he answered from his bedroom . . . then after a brief delay: "Now you can come in."

He had changed and was buttoning his vest.

"This is my room," he said lightly. "How do you like it?"

She caught sight of Paula's picture on the wall and stared at it in fascination, just as Paula had stared at the pictures of Anson's childish sweethearts five years before. She knew something about Paula—sometimes she tortured herself with fragments of the story.

Suddenly she came to Anson, raising her arms. They embraced. Outside the area window a soft artificial twilight already hovered, though the sun was still bright on a back roof across the way. In half an hour the room would be quite dark. The uncalculated opportunity overwhelmed them, made them both breathless, and they clung more closely. It was imminent, inevitable. Still holding one another, they raised their heads—their eyes fell together upon Paula's picture, staring down at them from the wall.

Suddenly Anson dropped his arms, and sitting down at his desk tried the drawer with a bunch of keys.

"Like a drink?" he asked in a gruff voice.

"No, Anson."

He poured himself half a tumbler of whiskey, swallowed it, and then opened the door into the hall.

"Come on," he said.

Dolly hesitated.

"Anson—I'm going to the country with you tonight, after all. You understand that, don't you?"

"Of course," he answered brusquely.

In Dolly's car they rode on to Long Island, closer in their emotions than they had ever been before. They knew what would happen—not with Paula's face to remind them that something was lacking, but when they were alone in the still, hot Long Island night they did not care.

The estate in Port Washington where they were to spend the weekend belonged to a cousin of Anson's who had married a Montana copper operator. An interminable drive began at the lodge and twisted under imported poplar saplings toward a huge, pink Spanish house. Anson had often visited there before.

After dinner they danced at the Linx Club. About midnight Anson assured himself that his cousins would not leave before two—then he explained that Dolly was tired; he would take her home and return to the dance later. Trembling a little with excitement, they got into a borrowed car together and drove to Port Washington. As they reached the lodge he stopped and spoke to the night-watchman.

"When are you making a round, Carl?"

"Right away."

"Then you'll be here till everybody's in?"

"Yes, sir."

"All right. Listen: if any automobile, no matter whose it is, turns in at this gate, I want you to phone the house immediately." He put a five-dollar bill into Carl's hand. "Is that clear?"

"Yes, Mr. Anson." Being of the Old World, he neither winked nor smiled. Yet Dolly sat with her face turned slightly away.

Anson had a key. Once inside he poured a drink for both of them—Dolly left hers untouched—then he ascertained definitely the location of the phone, and found that it was within easy hearing distance of their rooms, both of which were on the first floor.

Five minutes later he knocked at the door of Dolly's room.

"Anson?" He went in, closing the door behind him. She was in bed, leaning up anxiously with elbows on the pillow; sitting beside her he took her in his arms.

"Anson, darling."

He didn't answer.

"Anson. . . . Anson! I love you. . . . Say you love me. Say it now—can't you say it now? Even if you don't mean it?"

He did not listen. Over her head he perceived that the picture of Paula was hanging here upon this wall.

He got up and went close to it. The frame gleamed faintly with thrice-reflected moonlight—within was a blurred shadow of a face that he saw he did not know. Almost sobbing, he turned around and stared with abomination at the little figure on the bed.

"This is all foolishness," he said thickly. "I don't know what I was thinking about. I don't love you and you'd better wait for somebody that loves you. I don't love you a bit, can't you understand?"

His voice broke, and he went hurriedly out. Back in the salon he was pouring himself a drink with uneasy fingers, when the front door opened suddenly, and his cousin came in.

"Why, Anson, I hear Dolly's sick," she began solicitously. "I hear she's sick. . . ."

"It was nothing," he interrupted, raising his voice so that it would carry into Dolly's room. "She was a little tired. She went to bed."

For a long time afterward Anson believed that a protective God sometimes interfered in human affairs. But Dolly Karger, lying awake and staring at the ceiling, never again believed in anything at all.

VI

When Dolly married during the following autumn, Anson was in London on business. Like Paula's marriage, it was sudden, but it affected him in a different way. At first he felt that it was funny, and had an inclination to laugh when he thought of it. Later it depressed him—it made him feel old.

There was something repetitive about it—why, Paula and Dolly had belonged to different generations. He had a foretaste of the sensation of a man of forty who hears that the daughter of an old flame has married. He wired congratulations and, as was not the case with Paula, they were sincere—he had never really hoped that Paula would be happy.

When he returned to New York, he was made a partner in the firm, and, as his responsibilities increased, he had less time on his hands. The refusal of a life-insurance company to issue him a policy made such an impression on him that he stopped drinking for a year, and claimed that he felt better physically, though I think he missed the convivial recounting of those Celliniesque adventures which, in his early twenties, had played such a part in his life. But he never abandoned the Yale Club. He was a figure there, a personality, and the tendency of his class, who were now seven years out of college, to drift away to more sober haunts was checked by his presence.

His day was never too full nor his mind too weary to give any sort of aid to any one who asked it. What had been done at first through pride and superiority had become a habit and a passion. And there was always something—a younger brother in trouble at New Haven, a quarrel to be patched up between a friend and his wife, a position to be found for this man, an investment for that. But his specialty was the solving of problems for young married people. Young married people fascinated him and their apartments were almost sacred to him—he knew the story of their love-affair, advised them where to live and how, and remembered their babies' names. Toward young wives his attitude was circumspect: he never abused the trust which their husbands—strangely enough in view of his unconcealed irregularities—invariably reposed in him.

He came to take a vicarious pleasure in happy marriages, and to be inspired to an almost equally pleasant melancholy by those that went astray. Not a season passed that he did not witness the collapse of an affair that perhaps he himself had fathered. When Paula was divorced and almost immediately remarried to another Bostonian, he talked about her to me all one afternoon. He would never love any one as he had loved Paula, but he insisted that he no longer cared.

"I'll never marry," he came to say; "I've seen too much of it, and I know a happy marriage is a very rare thing. Besides, I'm too old."

But he did believe in marriage. Like all men who spring from a happy and successful marriage, he believed in it passionately—nothing he had seen would change his belief, his cynicism dissolved upon it like air. But he did really believe he was too old. At twenty-eight he began to accept with equanimity the prospect of marrying without romantic love; he resolutely chose a New York girl of his own class, pretty, intelligent, congenial, above reproach—and set about falling in love with her. The things he had said to Paula with sincerity, to other girls with grace, he could no longer say at all without smiling, or with the force necessary to convince.

"When I'm forty," he told his friends, "I'll be ripe. I'll fall for some chorus girl like the rest."

Nevertheless, he persisted in his attempt. His mother wanted to see him married, and he could now well afford it—he had a seat on the Stock Exchange, and his earned income came to twenty-five thousand a year. The idea was agreeable: when his friends—he spent most of his time with the set he and Dolly had evolved—closed themselves in behind domestic doors at night, he no longer rejoiced in his freedom. He even wondered if he should have married Dolly. Not even Paula had loved him more, and he was learning the rarity, in a single life, of encountering true emotion.

Just as this mood began to creep over him a disquieting story reached his ear. His Aunt Edna, a woman just this side of forty, was carrying on an open intrigue with a dissolute, hard-drinking young man named Cary Sloane. Every one knew of it except Anson's Uncle Robert, who for fifteen years had talked long in clubs and taken his wife for granted.

Anson heard the story again and again with increasing annoyance. Something of his old feeling for his uncle came back to him, a feeling that was more than personal, a reversion toward that family solidarity on which he had based his pride. His intuition singled out the essential point of the affair, which was that his uncle shouldn't be hurt. It was his first experiment in unsolicited meddling, but with his knowledge of Edna's character he felt that he could handle the matter better than a district judge or his uncle.

His uncle was in Hot Springs. Anson traced down the sources of the scandal so that there should be no possibility of mistake and then he called Edna and asked her to lunch with him at the Plaza next day. Something in his tone must have frightened her, for she was reluctant, but he insisted, putting off the date until she had no excuse for refusing.

She met him at the appointed time in the Plaza lobby, a lovely, faded, gray-eyed blonde in a coat of Russian sable. Five great rings, cold with diamonds and emeralds, sparkled on her slender hands. It occurred to Anson that it was his father's intelligence and not his uncle's that had earned the fur and the stones, the rich brilliance that buoyed up her passing beauty.

Though Edna scented his hostility, she was unprepared for the directness of his approach.

"Edna, I'm astonished at the way you've been acting," he said in a strong, frank voice. "At first I couldn't believe it."

"Believe what?" she demanded sharply.

"You needn't pretend with me, Edna. I'm talking about Cary Sloane. Aside from any other consideration, I didn't think you could treat Uncle Robert———"

"Now look here, Anson—" she began angrily, but his peremptory voice broke through hers:

"—and your children in such a way. You've been married eighteen years, and you're old enough to know better."

"You can't talk to me like that! You———"

"Yes, I can. Uncle Robert has always been my best friend." He was tremendously moved. He felt a real distress about his uncle, about his three young cousins.

Edna stood up, leaving her crab-flake cocktail untasted.

"This is the silliest thing———"

"Very well, if you won't listen to me I'll go to Uncle Robert and tell him the whole story—he's bound to hear it sooner or later. And afterward I'll go to old Moses Sloane."

Edna faltered back into her chair.

"Don't talk so loud," she begged him. Her eyes blurred with tears. "You have no idea how your voice carries. You might have chosen a less public place to make all these crazy accusations."

He didn't answer.

"Oh, you never liked me, I know," she went on. "You're just taking advantage of some silly gossip to try and break up the only interesting friendship I've ever had. What did I ever do to make you hate me so?"

Still Anson waited. There would be the appeal to his chivalry, then to his pity, finally to his superior sophistication—when he had shouldered his way through all these there would be the admissions, and he could come to grips with her. By being silent, by being impervious, by returning constantly to his main weapon, which was his own true emotion, he bullied her into frantic despair as the luncheon hour slipped away. At two o'clock she took out a mirror and a handkerchief, shined away the marks of her tears and powdered the slight hollows where they had lain. She had agreed to meet him at her own house at five.

When he arrived she was stretched on a *chaise-longue* which was covered with cretonne for the summer, and the tears he had called up at luncheon seemed still to be standing in her eyes. Then he was aware of Cary Sloane's dark anxious presence upon the cold hearth.

"What's this idea of yours?" broke out Sloane immediately. "I understand you invited Edna to lunch and then threatened her on the basis of some cheap scandal."

Anson sat down.

"I have no reason to think it's only scandal."

"I hear you're going to take it to Robert Hunter, and to my father."

Anson nodded.

"Either you break it off—or I will," he said.

"What God damned business is it of yours, Hunter?"

"Don't lose your temper, Cary," said Edna nervously. "It's only a question of showing him how absurd———"

"For one thing, it's my name that's being handed around," interrupted Anson. "That's all that concerns you, Cary."

"Edna isn't a member of your family."

"She most certainly is!" His anger mounted. "Why—she owes this house and the rings on her fingers to my father's brains. When Uncle Robert married her she didn't have a penny."

They all looked at the rings as if they had a significant bearing on the situation. Edna made a gesture to take them from her hand.

"I guess they're not the only rings in the world," said Sloane.

"Oh, this is absurd," cried Edna. "Anson, will you listen to me? I've found out how the silly story started. It was a maid I discharged who went right to the Chilicheffs—all these Russians pump things out of their servants and then put a false meaning on them." She brought down her fist angrily on the table: "And after Robert lent them the limousine for a whole month when we were South last winter———"

"Do you see?" demanded Sloane eagerly. "This maid got hold of the wrong end of the thing. She knew that Edna and I were friends, and she carried it to the Chilicheffs. In Russia they assume that if a man and a woman———"

He enlarged the theme to a disquisition upon social relations in the Caucasus.

"If that's the case it better be explained to Uncle Robert," said Anson dryly, "so that when the rumors do reach him he'll know they're not true."

Adopting the method he had followed with Edna at luncheon he let them explain it all away. He knew that they were guilty and that presently they would cross the line from explanation into justification and convict themselves more definitely than he could ever do. By seven they had taken the desperate step of telling him the truth—Robert Hunter's neglect, Edna's empty life, the casual dalliance that had flamed up into passion—but like so many true stories it had the misfortune of being old, and its enfeebled body beat helplessly against the armor of Anson's will. The threat to go to Sloane's father sealed their helplessness, for the latter, a retired cotton broker out of Alabama, was a notorious fundamentalist who controlled his son by a rigid allowance and the promise that at his next vagary the allowance would stop forever.

They dined at a small French restaurant, and the discussion continued—at one time Sloane resorted to physical threats, a little later they were both imploring him to give them time. But Anson was obdurate.

He saw that Edna was breaking up, and that her spirit must not be refreshed by any renewal of their passion.

At two o'clock in a small night-club on 53d Street, Edna's nerves suddenly collapsed, and she cried to go home. Sloane had been drinking heavily all evening, and he was faintly maudlin, leaning on the table and weeping a little with his face in his hands. Quickly Anson gave them his terms. Sloane was to leave town for six months, and he must be gone within forty-eight hours. When he returned there was to be no resumption of the affair, but at the end of a year Edna might, if she wished, tell Robert Hunter that she wanted a divorce and go about it in the usual way.

He paused, gaining confidence from their faces for his final word.

"Or there's another thing you can do," he said slowly, "if Edna wants to leave her children, there's nothing I can do to prevent your running off together."

"I want to go home!" cried Edna again. "Oh, haven't you done enough to us for one day?"

Outside it was dark, save for a blurred glow from Sixth Avenue down the street. In that light those two who had been lovers looked for the last time into each other's tragic faces, realizing that between them there was not enough youth and strength to avert their eternal parting. Sloane walked suddenly off down the street and Anson tapped a dozing taxi-driver on the arm.

It was almost four; there was a patient flow of cleaning water along the ghostly pavement of Fifth Avenue, and the shadows of two night women flitted over the dark façade of St. Thomas's church. Then the desolate shrubbery of Central Park where Anson had often played as a child, and the mounting numbers, significant as names, of the marching streets. This was his city, he thought, where his name had flourished through five generations. No change could alter the permanence of its place here, for change itself was the essential substratum by which he and those of his name identified themselves with the spirit of New York. Resourcefulness and a powerful will—for his threats in weaker hands would have been less than nothing—had beaten the gathering dust from his uncle's name, from the name of his family, from even this shivering figure that sat beside him in the car.

Cary Sloane's body was found next morning on the lower shelf of a pillar of Queensboro Bridge. In the darkness and in his excitement he had thought that it was the water flowing black beneath him, but in less than a second it made no possible difference—unless he had planned to think one last thought of Edna, and call out her name as he struggled feebly in the water.

VII

Anson never blamed himself for his part in this affair—the situation which brought it about had not been of his making. But the just suffer with the unjust, and he found that his oldest and somehow his most precious friendship was over. He never knew what distorted story Edna told, but he was welcome in his uncle's house no longer.

Just before Christmas Mrs. Hunter retired to a select Episcopal heaven, and Anson became the responsible head of his family. An unmarried aunt who had lived with them for years ran the house, and attempted with helpless inefficiency to chaperone the younger girls. All the children were less self-reliant than Anson, more conventional both in their virtues and in their shortcomings. Mrs. Hunter's death had postponed the début of one daughter and the wedding of another. Also it had taken something deeply material from all of them, for with her passing the quiet, expensive superiority of the Hunters came to an end.

For one thing, the estate, considerably diminished by two inheritance taxes and soon to be divided among six children, was not a notable fortune any more. Anson saw a tendency in his youngest sisters to speak rather respectfully of families that hadn't "existed" twenty years ago. His own feeling of precedence was not echoed in them—sometimes they were conventionally snobbish, that was all. For another thing, this was the last summer they would spend on the Connecticut estate; the clamor against it was too loud: "Who wants to waste the best months of the year shut up in the dead old town?" Reluctantly he yielded—the house would go into the market in the fall, and next summer they would rent a smaller place in Westchester County. It was a step down from the expensive simplicity of his father's idea, and, while he sympathized with the revolt, it also annoyed him; during his mother's lifetime he had gone up there at least every other week-end—even in the gayest summers.

Yet he himself was part of this change, and his strong instinct for life had turned him in his twenties from the hollow obsequies of that abortive leisure class. He did not see this clearly—he still felt that there was a norm, a standard of society. But there was no norm, it was doubtful if there ever had been a true norm in New York. The few who still paid and fought to enter a particular set succeeded only to find that as a society it scarcely functioned—or, what was more alarming, that the Bohemia from which they fled sat above them at table.

At twenty-nine Anson's chief concern was his own growing loneliness. He was sure now that he would never marry. The number of weddings at which he had officiated as best man or usher was past all counting—there was a drawer at home that bulged with the official neckties of this or that wedding-party, neckties standing for romances that had not endured a year, for couples who had passed completely from his life. Scarf-pins, gold pencils, cuff-buttons, presents from a generation of grooms had passed through his jewel-box and been lost—and with every ceremony he was less and less able to imagine himself in the groom's place. Under his hearty good-will toward all those marriages there was despair about his own.

And as he neared thirty he became not a little depressed at the inroads that marriage, especially lately, had made upon his friendships. Groups of people had a disconcerting tendency to dissolve and disappear. The men from his own college—and it was upon them he had expended the most time and affection—were the most elusive of all. Most of them were drawn deep into domesticity, two were dead, one lived abroad, one was in Hollywood writing continuities for pictures that Anson went faithfully to see.

Most of them, however, were permanent commuters with an intricate family life centering around some suburban country club, and it was from these that he felt his estrangement most keenly.

In the early days of their married life they had all needed him; he gave them advice about their slim finances, he exorcised their doubts about the advisability of bringing a baby into two rooms and a bath, especially he stood for the great world outside. But now their financial troubles were in the past and the fearfully expected child had evolved into an absorbing family. They were always glad to see old Anson, but they dressed up for him and tried to impress him with their present importance, and kept their troubles to themselves. They needed him no longer.

A few weeks before his thirtieth birthday the last of his early and intimate friends was married. Anson acted in his usual rôle of best man, gave his usual silver tea-service, and went down to the usual *Homeric* to say good-by. It was a hot Friday afternoon in May, and as he walked from the pier he realized that Saturday closing had begun and he was free until Monday morning.

"Go where?" he asked himself.

The Yale Club, of course; bridge until dinner, then four or five raw cocktails in somebody's room and a pleasant confused evening. He regretted that this afternoon's groom wouldn't be along—they had always been able to cram so much into such nights:

they knew how to attach women and how to get rid of them, how much consideration any girl deserved from their intelligent hedonism. A party was an adjusted thing—you took certain girls to certain places and spent just so much on their amusement; you drank a little, not much more than you ought to drink, and at a certain time in the morning you stood up and said you were going home. You avoided college boys, sponges, future engagements, fights, sentiment, and indiscretions. That was the way it was done. All the rest was dissipation.

In the morning you were never violently sorry—you made no resolutions, but if you had overdone it and your heart was slightly out of order, you went on the wagon for a few days without saying anything about it, and waited until an accumulation of nervous boredom projected you into another party.

The lobby of the Yale Club was unpopulated. In the bar three very young alumni looked up at him, momentarily and without curiosity.

"Hello, there, Oscar," he said to the bartender. "Mr. Cahill been around this afternoon?"

"Mr. Cahill's gone to New Haven."

"Oh . . . that so?"

"Gone to the ball game. Lot of men gone up."

Anson looked once again into the lobby, considered for a moment, and then walked out and over to Fifth Avenue. From the broad window of one of his clubs—one that he had scarcely visited in five years—a gray man with watery eyes stared down at him. Anson looked quickly away—that figure sitting in vacant resignation, in supercilious solitude, depressed him. He stopped and, retracing his steps, started over 47th Street toward Teak Warden's apartment. Teak and his wife had once been his most familiar friends—it was a household where he and Dolly Karger had been used to go in the days of their affair. But Teak had taken to drink, and his wife had remarked publicly that Anson was a bad influence on him. The remark reached Anson in an exaggerated form—when it was finally cleared up, the delicate spell of intimacy was broken, never to be renewed.

"Is Mr. Warden at home?" he inquired.

"They've gone to the country."

The fact unexpectedly cut at him. They were gone to the country and he hadn't known. Two years before he would have known the date, the hour, come up at the last moment for a final drink, and planned his first visit to them. Now they had gone without a word.

Anson looked at his watch and considered a week-end with his family, but the only train was a local that would jolt through the aggressive heat for three hours. And to-morrow in the country, and Sunday—he was in no mood for porch-bridge with polite undergraduates, and dancing after dinner at a rural roadhouse, a diminutive of gaiety which his father had estimated too well.

"Oh, no," he said to himself. . . . "No."

He was a dignified, impressive young man, rather stout now, but otherwise unmarked by dissipation. He could have been cast for a pillar of something—at times you were sure it was not society, at others nothing else—for the law, for the church. He stood for a few minutes motionless on the sidewalk in front of a 47th Street apartment-house; for almost the first time in his life he had nothing whatever to do.

Then he began to walk briskly up Fifth Avenue, as if he had just been reminded of an important engagement there. The necessity of dissimulation is one of the few characteristics that we share with dogs, and I think of Anson on that day as some well-bred specimen who had been disappointed at a familiar back door. He was going to see Nick, once a fashionable bartender in demand at all private dances, and now employed in cooling non-alcoholic champagne among the labyrinthine cellars of the Plaza Hotel.

"Nick," he said, "what's happened to everything?"

"Dead," Nick said.

"Make me a whiskey sour." Anson handed a pint bottle over the counter. "Nick, the girls are different; I had a little girl in Brooklyn and she got married last week without letting me know."

"That a fact? Ha-ha-ha," responded Nick diplomatically. "Slipped it over on you."

"Absolutely," said Anson. "And I was out with her the night before."

"Ha-ha-ha," said Nick, "ha-ha-ha!"

"Do you remember the wedding, Nick, in Hot Springs where I had the waiters and the musicians singing 'God save the King'?"

"Now where was that, Mr. Hunter?" Nick concentrated doubtfully. "Seems to me that was———"

"Next time they were back for more, and I began to wonder how much I'd paid them," continued Anson.

"—seems to me that was Mr. Trenholm's wedding."

"Don't know him," said Anson decisively. He was offended that a strange name should intrude upon his reminiscences; Nick perceived this.

"Na—aw—" he admitted, "I ought to know that. It was one of *your* crowd—Brakins . . . Baker———"

"Bicker Baker," said Anson responsively. "They put me in a hearse after it was over and covered me up with flowers and drove me away."

"Ha-ha-ha," said Nick. "Ha-ha-ha."

Nick's simulation of the old family servant paled presently and Anson went upstairs to the lobby. He looked around—his eyes met the glance of an unfamiliar clerk at the desk, then fell upon a flower from the morning's marriage hesitating in the mouth of a brass cuspidor. He went out and walked slowly toward the blood-red sun over Columbus Circle. Suddenly he turned around and, retracing his steps to the Plaza, immured himself in a telephone-booth.

Later he said that he tried to get me three times that afternoon, that he tried every one who might be in New York—men and girls he had not seen for years, an artist's model of his college days whose faded number was still in his address book—Central told him that even the exchange existed no longer. At length his quest roved into the country, and he held brief disappointing conversations with emphatic butlers and maids. So-and-so was out, riding, swimming, playing golf, sailed to Europe last week. Who shall I say phoned?

It was intolerable that he should pass the evening alone—the private reckonings which one plans for a moment of leisure lose every charm when the solitude is enforced. There were always women of a sort, but the ones he knew had temporarily vanished, and to pass a New York evening in the hired company of a stranger never occurred to him—he would have considered that that was something shameful and secret, the diversion of a travelling salesman in a strange town.

Anson paid the telephone bill—the girl tried unsuccessfully to joke with him about its size—and for the second time that afternoon started to leave the Plaza and go he knew not where. Near the revolving door the figure of a woman, obviously with child, stood sideways to the light—a sheer beige cape fluttered at her shoulders when the door turned and, each time, she looked impatiently toward it as if she were weary of waiting. At the first sight of her a strong nervous thrill of familiarity went over him, but not until he was within five feet of her did he realize that it was Paula.

"Why, Anson Hunter!"

His heart turned over.

"Why, Paula———"

"Why, this is wonderful. I can't believe it, *Anson*!"

She took both his hands, and he saw in the freedom of the gesture that the memory of him had lost poignancy to her. But not to him—he felt that old mood that she evoked in him stealing over his brain, that gentleness with which he had always met her optimism as if afraid to mar its surface.

"We're at Rye for the summer. Pete had to come East on business—you know of course I'm Mrs. Peter Hagerty now—so we brought the children and took a house. You've got to come out and see us."

"Can I?" he asked directly. "When?"

"When you like. Here's Pete." The revolving door functioned, giving up a fine tall man of thirty with a tanned face and a trim mustache. His immaculate fitness made a sharp contrast with Anson's increasing bulk, which was obvious under the faintly tight cut-away coat.

"You oughtn't to be standing," said Hagerty to his wife. "Let's sit down here." He indicated lobby chairs, but Paula hesitated.

"I've got to go right home," she said. "Anson, why don't you—why don't you come out and have dinner with us tonight? We're just getting settled, but if you can stand that———"

Hagerty confirmed the invitation cordially.

"Come out for the night."

Their car waited in front of the hotel, and Paula with a tired gesture sank back against silk cushions in the corner.

"There's so much I want to talk to you about," she said, "it seems hopeless."

"I want to hear about you."

"Well"—she smiled at Hagerty—"that would take a long time too. I have three children—by my first marriage. The oldest is five, then four, then three." She smiled again. "I didn't waste much time having them, did I?"

"Boys?"

"A boy and two girls. Then—oh, a lot of things happened, and I got a divorce in Paris a year ago and married Pete. That's all—except that I'm awfully happy."

In Rye they drove up to a large house near the Beach Club, from which there issued presently three dark, slim children who broke from an English governess and approached them with an esoteric cry. Abstractedly and with difficulty Paula took each one into her arms, a caress which they accepted stiffly, as they had evidently been told not to bump into Mummy. Even against their fresh faces Paula's skin showed scarcely any weariness—for all her physical languor she seemed younger than when he had last seen her at Palm Beach seven years ago.

At dinner she was preoccupied, and afterward, during the homage to the radio, she lay with closed eyes on the sofa, until Anson wondered if his presence at this time were not an intrusion. But at nine o'clock, when Hagerty rose and said pleasantly that he was going to leave them by themselves for a while, she began to talk slowly about herself and the past.

"My first baby," she said—"the one we call Darling, the biggest little girl—I wanted to die when I knew I was going to have her, because Lowell was like a stranger to me. It didn't seem as though she could be my own. I wrote you a letter and tore it up. Oh, you were *so* bad to me, Anson."

It was the dialogue again, rising and falling. Anson felt a sudden quickening of memory.

"Weren't you engaged once?" she asked—"a girl named Dolly something?"

"I wasn't ever engaged. I tried to be engaged, but I never loved anybody but you, Paula."

"Oh," she said. Then after a moment: "This baby is the first one I ever really wanted. You see, I'm in love now—at last."

He didn't answer, shocked at the treachery of her remembrance. She must have seen that the "at last" bruised him, for she continued:

"I was infatuated with you, Anson—you could make me do anything you liked. But we wouldn't have been happy. I'm not smart enough for you. I don't like things to be complicated like you do." She paused. "You'll never settle down," she said.

The phrase struck at him from behind—it was an accusation that of all accusations he had never merited.

"I could settle down if women were different," he said. "If I didn't understand so much about them, if women didn't spoil you for other women, if they had only a little pride. If I could go to sleep for a while and wake up into a home that was really mine—why, that's what I'm made for, Paula, that's what women have seen in me and liked in me. It's only that I can't get through the preliminaries any more."

Hagerty came in a little before eleven; after a whiskey Paula stood up and announced that she was going to bed. She went over and stood by her husband.

"Where did you go, dearest?" she demanded.

"I had a drink with Ed Saunders."

"I was worried. I thought maybe you'd run away."

She rested her head against his coat.

"He's sweet, isn't he, Anson?" she demanded.

"Absolutely," said Anson, laughing.

She raised her face to her husband.

"Well, I'm ready," she said. She turned to Anson: "Do you want to see our family gymnastic stunt?"

"Yes," he said in an interested voice.

"All right. Here we go!"

Hagerty picked her up easily in his arms.

"This is called the family acrobatic stunt," said Paula. "He carries me up-stairs. Isn't it sweet of him?"

"Yes," said Anson.

Hagerty bent his head slightly until his face touched Paula's.

"And I love him," she said. "I've just been telling you, haven't I, Anson?"

"Yes," he said.

"He's the dearest thing that ever lived in this world; aren't you, darling? . . . Well, good night. Here we go. Isn't he strong?"

"Yes," Anson said.

"You'll find a pair of Pete's pajamas laid out for you. Sweet dreams—see you at breakfast."

"Yes," Anson said.

VIII

The older members of the firm insisted that Anson should go abroad for the summer. He had scarcely had a vacation in seven years, they said. He was stale and needed a change. Anson resisted.

"If I go," he declared, "I won't come back any more."

"That's absurd, old man. You'll be back in three months with all this depression gone. Fit as ever."

"No." He shook his head stubbornly. "If I stop, I won't go back to work. If I stop, that means I've given up—I'm through."

"We'll take a chance on that. Stay six months if you like—we're not afraid you'll leave us. Why, you'd be miserable if you didn't work."

They arranged his passage for him. They liked Anson—every one liked Anson—and the change that had been coming over him cast a sort of pall over the office. The enthusiasm that had invariably signalled up business, the consideration toward his equals and his inferiors, the lift of his vital presence—within the past four months his intense nervousness had melted down these qualities into the fussy pessimism of a man of forty. On every transaction in which he was involved he acted as a drag and a strain.

"If I go I'll never come back," he said.

Three days before he sailed Paula Legendre Hagerty died in childbirth. I was with him a great deal then, for we were crossing together, but for the first time in our friendship he told me not a word of how he felt, nor did I see the slightest sign of emotion. His chief preoccupation was with the fact that he was thirty years old—he would turn the conversation to the point where he could remind you of it and then fall silent, as if he assumed that the statement would start a chain of thought sufficient to itself. Like his partners, I was amazed at the change in him, and I was glad when the *Paris* moved off into the wet space between the worlds, leaving his principality behind.

"How about a drink?" he suggested.

We walked into the bar with that defiant feeling that characterizes the day of departure and ordered four Martinis. After one cocktail a change came over him—he suddenly reached across and slapped my knee with the first joviality I had seen him exhibit for months.

"Did you see that girl in the red tam?" he demanded, "the one with the high color who had the two police dogs down to bid her good-by."

"She's pretty," I agreed.

"I looked her up in the purser's office and found out that she's alone. I'm going down to see the steward in a few minutes. We'll have dinner with her to-night."

After a while he left me, and within an hour he was walking up and down the deck with her, talking to her in his strong, clear voice. Her red tam was a bright spot of color against the steel-green sea, and from time to time she looked up with a flashing bob of her head, and smiled with amusement and interest, and anticipation. At dinner we had champagne, and were very joyous—afterward Anson ran the pool with infectious gusto, and several people who had seen me with him asked me his name. He and the girl were talking and laughing together on a lounge in the bar when I went to bed.

I saw less of him on the trip than I had hoped. He wanted to arrange a foursome, but there was no one available, so I saw him only at meals. Sometimes, though, he would have a cocktail in the bar, and he told me about the girl in the red tam, and his adventures with her, making them all bizarre and amusing, as he had a way of doing, and I was glad that he was himself again, or at least the self that I knew, and with which I felt at home. I don't think he was ever happy unless some one was in love with him, responding to him like filings to a magnet, helping him to explain himself, promising him something. What it was I do not know. Perhaps they promised that there would always be women in the world who would spend their brightest, freshest, rarest hours to nurse and protect that superiority he cherished in his heart.

[1925]

For Thought

"The Rich Boy" uses a biographic technique that follows the growth and development of a boy into manhood in a retrospective instead of sequential fashion. At the same time, Fitzgerald employs a dual point of view, one part of which allows him to analyze and pass judgment on his protagonist. With the other side of his approach, he allows the reader to see things through the eyes and mind of Anson and thus be able to make an interpretation of his character based on subjective evidence. In what is essentially an in-depth character study of an individual who also respresents a type, Fitzgerald succeeds in creating a main character possessing strongly contrasting traits of personality which are at war with one another and which lead to unresolvable internal conflicts.

For Discussion

1. How are the title and the events ironic considering the growth and development pattern of Anson Hunter?
2. How does Fitzgerald's description of Anson's love affair with Paula characterize Anson?
3. At Anson's attempted reunion with Paula, how is the card game symbolic? What are the motives for his attempt at renewing their love affair? Why does the attempt fail?
4. Compare and contrast Dolly with Paula.
5. Why does Anson try to end his relationship with Dolly? For what reasons does he force Dolly to see him again?
6. How does Anson's intervention in his aunt's love affair duplicate his previous actions and confirm his ingrained character traits?

7. How is Anson's final meeting with Paula ironic?
8. What is the significance of the girl in the red tam whom Anson meets on shipboard? What pattern will Anson's life follow after the conclusion of the story?
9. What is Fitzgerald's attitude toward Anson?
10. What is the theme of the story?

Keith Fort
The Coal Shoveller

"The clock is ticking."

That's a poor beginning for my short story. The trouble with "clock" is that it symbolizes time, and I don't want to introduce any big ideas into my story. Besides, I actually have an electric clock which whirrs.

It is a snowy day in midwinter. Out of my second-story window I see the street. The snow is so deep that all traffic has stopped. The last vehicle to come by was a truck which dumped five or six tons of coal on the sidewalk beside the red brick Victorian building across the street. It was once a fine mansion, or so my mother told me during her visit. She had lived in Washington in the early 1900's when her father was a senator. She said that a school for young ladies was there, and the "best people" sent their daughters to it. Now the building is divided into small, cheap apartments for government workers. When I walk by, I sometimes see rats in the yard. The land is quite valuable, and in time the grey cupolas, the bay windows, and the portico will come down to be replaced by a new glass and steel office building in the style of the Holiday Inn which is just behind it. On top of the inn is a lattice fence which, I assume, shields some kind of sun porch. At night they turn pink floodlights on the lattice.

A Negro man is shovelling the coal into the basement. I am separated from him by Massachusetts Avenue. The task I have set myself is not a very difficult one. The scene is visually appealing to me. I would like to write a simple short story describing the scene and, perhaps, giving some idea of the rather interesting neighborhood in which I live. I have no theme to draw out of the scene. The thing itself is enough. So it seems that the best style for me would be something on the order of the new novels.

The northeast wind blows the snow almost horizontally down Seventeenth Street. It slaps against the coal shoveller's face, sticks to him briefly, melts and falls. He is wearing a faded green army jacket. A black strip over his left breast has the words "U.S. Army" printed on it in gold letters. The Negro's face is partially muffled by a grey hat with ear flaps and a red scarf wrapped high around his neck. His eyes are turned onto the coal pile in front of him. The lumps are of various sizes, the smaller pieces on the bottom. The head of the coal scoop runs along the snow and enters the coal. The handle is brown with a faded red stripe where it meets the scoop. The shovel comes out. He swings around to the south. The blue flag on the Australian embassy. The white house next to it. The tops of parked cars. The whiteness of Seventeenth Street. The elaborate concrete curves of the B'nai Brith building. The blue fence around the Holiday Inn swimming pool. The red brick building. The black hole into the cellar. The coal clatters down into the chute. Black dust flecks the snow. He continues his movement, turning north into the wind: The apartment building across Massachusetts Avenue. The window on the second floor. Up Seventeenth Street. The flashing red sign "The Bacchus." The coal pile. The shovel goes in. The wood is brown, surrounded by a red stripe where the handle meets the black scoop. A grey glove with a hole in it. The skin beneath the hole is black.

I can't go on like that. Words have a powerful integrity of their own which no amount of authorial intention can eliminate. I could write a hundred essays on how objective I am going to be, but the connotations of "white," "snow," and "black" would still be there. All that I wanted was to describe the scene, but who could fail to see in my story a comment on the white noose that is strangling our black innercity?

You might argue that my objections to continuing my story as I started it are based solely on the assumption of a faulty reader reaction, and that I should be skillful enough to remake the consciousness of my audience as I write. Can someone like Robbe-Grillet actually believe that he is reshaping the mind of man as he writes? I don't have the arrogance to deny reality in the name of an idea of reality.

Nor am I convinced that fiction *should* try to approximate painting (or the films). Prose has been headed in this direction for some time, but like most movements in art this one was begun on ill-defined premises and succeeding writers merely spun out a potential. We have come to a point now where the weaknesses inherent in the original assumptions prevent us from going further. To ask words to make fiction into photographic realism is to demand a performance which they are totally incapable of giving.

Since I cannot escape words and since words are necessarily symbols, I might as well write a more traditional story in which I admit that every time I use a word I am interpreting reality. The only ideas I can draw out of the scene are my own because they are obviously the only ones I know. I have no concept of the way in which the coal shoveller sees the world.

Amelia, who was six, had exhausted every possibility for entertainment she could find in the house. She had played with her dolls, colored the book she had been given at the school Christmas party the day before, and had made two entirely different houses out of the sofa pillows. An unusual inclination to help her mother had resulted in her being ushered out of the kitchen when she had spilled a cup of milk that was to be used for the Christmas cookies. On most holidays she would have gone to visit one of her friends, but the private school she went to was in the suburbs where most of the pupils lived, and her mother wasn't willing to risk driving through the snow. If she were at someone else's house they could at least watch television, but her father allowed only two programs a week and she had squandered her time for two solid hours on Sunday. Amelia had finally settled by the window where she watched the snow and the old colored man across the street who was shovelling the coal. She wanted to go outside and play, but it wasn't allowed because of the traffic.

In desperation she went back to the kitchen and asked her mother to take her out, but "There is too much to be done, darling," was all she got.

"There's not any cars in the street."

"It's still dangerous. Maybe your father will take you out when he's through working."

Amelia went back into the living room and tried to color another picture, but the tiger she was working on didn't interest her. She closed the book and looked at the door which led into her father's study. The rule that "Daddy is not to be bothered when he's working" was, she knew, an absolute one.

Under most circumstances this suited her well enough because she was actually frightened by the room. The study had been built on the side of the house the summer before when her father had published a book and had been given a big raise. To help him in his work the room had no windows and a special control which kept the room at the same temperature all the time. The darkness and the quietness bothered her, but she had reached her limit.

She walked to the door as quietly as she could, turned the knob, and had started in when her mother heard her.

"Don't bother daddy."

Her mother came running from the kitchen and pulled her away. The door was open a crack. She saw her father in the dark room with the bright light over his typewriter making his face look all black and white.

"I'm sorry, Michael," her mother said as she closed the door. "It's snowing and she wanted to go out."

"That's all right," Michael said through the closed door. "I'll take her out in a few minutes. My train of thought is broken now anyway." He had been married for ten years and the way his wife said "snowin'" still bothered him. It was embarrassing for a sociologist, active in the Civil Rights movement, to have a Southern wife.

Michael turned back to his desk. Actually he was pleased with the interruption. He was almost through with the article he had been working on about the problems of urban Negroes in Washington. He had attacked the question from various angles, poking at it first with the intellect then with the emotions. The piece now had about the right amount of feeling and thought to make it acceptable to one of the slick magazines. It would be good to let the manuscript sit overnight. One more polishing tomorrow, and it would be finished. He took the last page out of the typewriter, laid it neatly with the others, leaned back in his chair, and surveyed with satisfaction the day's production.

The bright lights in the living room hurt his eyes. His wife was making more than the usual amount of noise in the kitchen. Out of the window he saw the curtain of snow that was falling over the street. In the distance the old Negro man was shovelling coal.

"Let's go, daddy," Amelia said. "There's lots of snow."

She was dressed in a bright red snow suit.

"Where are your galoshes?" he asked.

"Margaret," he called into the kitchen, "are you trying to make the child sick by letting her go out without her galoshes?"

His wife came out of the kitchen. "Amelia. I told you to put them on."

"I don't want to go out," Amelia said sullenly.

"Now that I've stopped work," her father said, "we are going out into the snow."

Amelia went to the closet, and with her mother's help laboriously pulled on the galoshes. Michael got on his own overshoes and coat.

"I wish I could go with you," his wife said. "The snow is beautiful."

"When I was a boy in Wisconsin, we wouldn't have called this anything but a flurry," he said with a smile.

"I've never seen so much," Amelia said.

From there on the story writes itself. Michael goes into the snow. He gradually discovers the reality of his wife's life and that he has never understood the Negroes at all. Finally, he arrives at some understanding of the emotional sterility of his own life, which is sentimentally compared to his childhood back in Wisconsin.

Sound familiar? Joyce's "The Dead." I didn't deliberately set out to imitate the story, but it was there waiting for me like a trap. I couldn't avoid imitation.

In addition to my feeling that this has been done already better than I could do it, there are other reasons why I don't like my story. The focus is on the main character's movement towards self-understanding. It posits that intellectual and emotional development is all that counts. The reality of the Negro coal shoveller, even the realness of the snow and the house, is not considered important beside the ideas which I have extracted (or perhaps created) from them. My story would end by suggesting the subordination of thing to idea. I am inclined to agree with those who say that literature (no matter how negative the themes) which reinforces the habit of extracting ideas from reality panders to the self-interest of the middle class. You can be sure that both you and I would prefer a few hours of anguish trying to understand the validity of various attitudes that one could take toward the Negro shovelling coal to five minutes of real or fictional exposure to the reality of that man's life and his work.

Not only am I blocked philosophically from writing a Joycean story—I am also incompatible with its style. I lack the necessary innocence. When the symbolic technique was devised, writers must have been able to allow their symbols to emerge "naturally." I have studied fiction too long. Take the "study" in my story. Is that too heavy-handed? How subtle should a symbol be? I honestly don't know. I rather imagine that a good symbol is one that takes an English teacher about two minutes to decipher and one of his students ten. Talk of "organic symbols" that grow out of reality is absolute garbage at this point in the evolution of fictional techniques.

If I use symbols I also depend heavily on my readers' being willing to accept my symbolism for what I intend. For example, I said in my story that Michael laid the last page "neatly" on the others. "Neatly" is a symbol for certain aspects of his character. But what is actually wrong with being neat? If there weren't a general, if ill-defined, prejudice of modern readers in favor of emotional spontaneity, that word might be honorific. If you say that *in the context* the symbol is made meaningful, I reply that my story is nothing but a pastiche of such symbols.

Underlying all of them is a series of romantic values epitomized by the noble Negro coal shoveller, the goodness of nature (represented by the snow), and the joys of childhood. When I draw these values out of my story, as I am doing now, they are subject to attack. But one of the advantages that comes to the fictionalist is that he doesn't have to defend his assumptions. The critics tell us that he doesn't have to defend his assumptions. The critics tell us that we should examine literature from within. This idea has been forced on them by the "creative" writers. Who can blame an author like Henry James for wanting his value assumptions considered "out of bounds"?

Then there is the rather obvious point that I have completely distorted reality in my story. I live in a small apartment. A house on Massachusetts Avenue would cost a fortune. I am the one from the South, not my wife.

Since I am aware of the ideas behind my symbols, why not write an essay instead of a short story? I reject that at once. My first inclination is to explain this rejection by saying something about the "mystery of art." Many writers talk of this mystery, and it seems to me that they do so primarily to convince themselves that they are somehow "special" and belong to a cult of super souls who have powers (and, more importantly, privileges) that ordinary mortals can't understand. The real reason that I prefer fiction is that it gives me a feeling of righteousness which is denied to me in essays. In fiction I redefine reality by style. When

I survey the new world I have created in my story I can say, "Yes, by God, since the world is like that I am completely justified in feeling what I feel." I am quick to admit that I need this kind of self-justification and that I want to use the devices of fiction to make others second my righteousness.

In the fragment of my story on Michael, I disguised, under the illusion of objectivity, my own need to use fiction to justify myself and gain approval of readers. But now that I admit this need, I might as well try an autobiographical story in which I reveal myself more directly and, consequently, make a more overt appeal for approval. I will use the time (mentioned earlier) when my mother came to visit me here.

The woman stands in the small, cramped apartment. She looks down on the oblivious snow in the avenue—not knowing that she or he existed. The woman in front of him—a mother, but not a mother because mothers are associated with home, and here is not home. She, vaguely ashamed to be here—not of him because it is not his fault that he lives here with a Yankee wife, but of herself, of her dead husband, and her dead father and the long line of failures that have reduced the family to the point of living in a small apartment.

He puts her bag on the floor and waits awkwardly for her to do something. She asks for a glass of sherry. It is almost twilight. The snow is falling harder outside—the blanket is making all men equal in cold and misery and accentuating the memory of warm Southern summers with the smell of purple wisteria twisting through honeysuckle when the bright colors differentiated people: blacks from whites and whites from poor whites. And it is all over for her now because there is no more home to live in and no more wooded yards lined with flowers, and she and the son and the Negro servants have all fled north to Washington, where they are equal under the snow but hating that equality—the Negro because the equalness is not real, the son because he is poor, and the Mother because she knows that she is better. She sips sherry in the twilight and the son straight whiskey—waiting.

He has put out on the table a book of family history because it will please her to know that he cares. She looks at it, and the book, like a trigger, explodes the blocks against history, and between sips of sherry there pours out the talk that he has heard so often, but that still can make him desire again to be a child in a world where he could maintain the illusion of a baronial grandeur bequeathed to him by the past—but for him so long away that the memory he had received is like the deformed last of the litter. A tiny final effort from the exhausted womb of the old South. Too twisted and confused to do more than make him wish he had been closer to the source of the myth.

"Do you see that house?" she says as she walks to the window.

"Yes."

"I went to school there when your grandfather was a senator. He was a great man. I drove up every morning to that building in a carriage. All the great people sent their children there. At least I think that's the building. So much has changed."

As she talks, he thinks:

He was a child. It was summer at his grandmother's. The large rambling house with its rows of bedrooms and the porch that ran all around the house high up in the foothills of the Georgia Blue Ridge. "On a clear day," his grandmother said, "you can see to the sea." But even then he knew that was not true. It had been a summer place, but now a few of the downstairs rooms had been insulated so that she could live there—not in isolation but still fighting with the ferocious anger that her mother before her had used to hold the family together after the War, but which had not been able to cope with Yankee businessmen, boll weevils, and resentful Negro workers in South Georgia. Now she lived on the hill surrounded by thick underbrush which kept from her the knowledge of the encroaching townspeople whose squat, white houses lapped at the hill. All that was left outside of the underbrush of what had once been a great estate was the Episcopal church at the foot of the hill which his great-grandfather had built just after the War for the use of the family and the other summer people.

Then the summer when he was seven he came and his grandmother told him that he could no longer play in the church because it had been sold. She said "sold" with an icy pride which made him afraid. On the first Sunday when he was there his grandmother was sitting on the porch reading Sir Walter Scott to him—he not understanding, but made peaceful by the words which flowed in and out of the mimosa trees and the humming of bees. She stopped. "Did you understand that?"

"What, ma'am?"

"What I read to you."

"Not exactly."

"Listen. 'My foot is on my native heath, and my name is MacGregor!' Does that mean anything to you?"

"Yes, ma'am," he lied. But it did. A thousand times since he had said it. When he came home from college and the heath was a quarter-acre yard with an old Ford in it. And even now when he walked into the little apartment on Massachusetts Avenue he said it with bitterness.

Before she started reading again, the church bell sounded from outside of the underbrush. He heard singing coming out of a loudspeaker—cracked twangy accents of country people. He felt his grandmother stiffen.

"Angela," she said.

"Yes'm." The fat old Negro woman came out onto the porch drying her hands on her apron. The enormous kindness of the woman became a natural part of the warm summer morning.

"What is that noise?"

"There's more folks want to go to the church than it'll hold. They put up speakers for those who's outside."

"Thank you, Angela."

Angela went back to fix Sunday dinner.

"I want you to remember," his grandmother said to him, "that Sunday morning is God's gift of Peace. For one as old as I, Peace is sacred."

"Yes, ma'am," he said.

That night as he lay in his bed and watched the moon lie on the state of Georgia he saw a frail woman carrying a big can move like a black shadow away from the house and into the underbrush. He was afraid, too afraid to think, and he waited until the orange light had taken away the silver moonlight, and he slept.

When the vacation was over and he was home he asked his mother and father why it had happened. They pretended not to understand but answered anyway. "Your grandmother is a fine, strong woman," his father said with pride. But he could not understand this because when his father's boss would call on Sunday morning his father would grumble but go to work. "We have to eat," he would say. And his father worked for a Baptist although the boss became an Episcopalian like him later on.

And he could not understand how Sunday mornings could both be sacred and not sacred and he saw that his father loved the strength of his grandmother but also wanted to get a raise from the Baptist. Being a child he could not stand uncertainty and found a third way which he believed could eventually fuse the opposition into oneness—intelligence, which he now knew was the weakest weapon he could have chosen because it compounded, not resolved, the opposition. The more clearly his mind failed to understand why Sundays were sacred the more he longed to share in his grandmother's pride. But unlike his father for whom the beliefs were closer and more real and who lost his life trying to work for the Baptist and live by his grandmother's sureness, the dream of the peace of Sunday mornings was so far removed from him that he was almost denied the pleasure of having it as a dream; and yet at times like this, when his mother was talking, he could almost reach out to the voice of his grandmother ("MY foot is on my native heath") that created in him, for however short a time, the innocence of dreaming, when he could free himself of knowing the inconsistencies, the injustices, the contradictions that were housed in his grandmother's impoverished Eden. Perhaps, he thought, if there is another generation the dream will be taken away and we can function in the Baptists' world (although he did not understand the legitimacy of the Baptist as symbol any more) and the sins of the fathers will be gone. But in the small apartment with its books and its typewriter the disease was all the peace and beauty which he had ever known and the cure seemed worse than the illness. And he watched the coal shoveller—a man without hope, for whom jail and the welfare line are the legacies of a belief in the sanctity of Sunday morning, and the mother's voice, now crumbled into mumbling quests after the ability of words to rebuild a belief in the present reality of the dream, is also the legacy. And he knows that the dream has produced evil, but knowing is, as it always had been for him, a false god.

His mother says: "That old colored man—I suppose you say 'Negro' now—reminds me of old Dick the footman who used to open the carriage door for us when we came to school. Your grandfather sent him money every year. . . ."

I wish that I could honestly see the fall of the Old South as tragic in the way that Faulkner did. Only occasionally do I even care about the fact that I don't care. The story gives a completely false impression of what I actually feel on the subject. I blame the misrepresentation on the style which was so intoxicating that it carried me where I didn't want to go.

And where was I going? Deeper and deeper into my mind or at least into the pseudo-mind which the words were creating as they went along. By the time thinking has become words it has ceased to be self.

Style dominates the piece and focuses the reader's attention on my way of seeing the world. Like most middle-class writers I have a decided anti-middle-class bias, and I don't believe the "I" is worth a sustained story. (Someday I would like to study the strong streak of masochism which runs through or even dominates modern fiction. Middle-class writers take great pleasure in writing about the "emotional bankruptcy" of middle-class writers. And certainly there is no better way to be popular with the general public than to tell them how horrible they are. The way in which this masochism works is obvious in my own story of Michael the sociologist. I have some of my hero's characteristics, and in the story I objectified my own sins and controlled things in such a way that Michael is punished. Having paid for my errors by sticking pins in my image, I can continue to muddle along as usual without feeling the need to take any real action.) I am also interested in the extent to which certain kinds of beliefs control ideas. Does my Faulknerian story depend on my putting myself into a frame of mind where I can believe in the reality of the myth of the Old South? And did the symbolic technique in my first story depend on the romantic values which formed the assumptions on which the story was based? I think the answer to both questions is yes.

At this point I accuse myself of not being able to finish any of these stories because I am a nihilist. But I immediately recognize that nothing is further from the truth. I believe in a great many things—so many in fact that the beliefs tend to cancel each other out. Good writers are successful because they can eliminate (at least in a given work) all but one possible way of seeing the world. They develop styles and structures because they are following through with this single vision. Robbe-Grillet's novels, for example, are the product of one particular way of looking at the world. As he was writing, he was able to block from his mind the knowledge that during most of his life he sees the world in many different ways. If he looked at reality in his daily life as he does in his novels, he would never be able to do a single practical thing like catching a train or showing up for a speaking engagement on time. Is arrogant, spiritual narrowmindedness the essence of the writer?

The scene is still there. The janitor is still shovelling coal. Because the street is quiet, I can hear the shovel as it scrapes into the coal. Do you believe that? You might. But it is cold and the window is closed. Massachusetts Avenue is a big street. I hear nothing. Why did I add the sound to my description? Writers are supposed to "render" and not "report." Writing classes do more harm than good.

That's neither here nor there. Since I am beginning to understand the extent to which masochism is a dominant motivation in all of my stories, perhaps I should try to be more honest and objectify my "anti-self" into an active romantic. I must have bottled up in myself an enormous amount of anti-intellectual, anti-establishment hostility. As I have said before, I know nothing of what the coal shoveller actually thinks, but I can easily make him into whatever I want. I'll make him the rogue hero that I might like to be.

My anti-hero's name is to be Reginald Cowpersmith. He is twenty-eight, married, and unemployed. He finds himself on this particular snowy day walking by the pile of coal, where he sees an angry building superintendent starting to shovel the coal. Reginald, who is broke, asks for the job.

"The boy who is supposed to look after this sort of thing didn't show up," the superintendent said. He was winded from the one or two shovelfuls he had tossed down the chute.

"It's hard to know who to trust these days," Reginald said.

"That's very true. I'm lucky you happened to be passing by."

"I could certainly use the work," Reginald said in his most serious tone.

"I'm surprised a nice-looking young man like yourself has to go around looking for odd jobs."

"I'm at the University, sir," Reginald said. "It's very expensive. I also have a family to support. I try to supplement my income in whatever way I can."

"I wish other people in this city had your ambition."

"*They* need our sympathy, sir."

"Quite right. I know I can trust you. Here's five dollars. Shovel the coal into the cellar. I want to get home while I can." The superintendent shuffled toward Rhode Island Avenue and the bus home.

"Cheerio," Reginald called after him as he waved good-by. "And," he added, when he saw the superintendent was out of earshot, "do me the pleasure of applying thy rosy lips to the gentle curvature of my buttocks."

Reginald imagined the superintendent at home in some place like Hyattsville sitting in front of a fire telling his wife, children, and sad-eyed cocker spaniel how lucky he was to find "this white boy" to shovel his coal instead of "that no-good nigger."

"Cowpersmith," Reginald asked himself, "what would you like for Christmas out of this five dollars?"

"Perhaps, a gift for a needy family," Reginald replied.

"Not likely."

"A bottle of whiskey?"

"It's on the list," Cowpersmith said.

"A fuck in a neighborhood brothel?"

"Agreed."

Reginald stuck the shovel into the pile of coal and retired into the apartment house to contemplate the laws of economics which prevented a five-dollar bill from buying both presents.

He lit a cigarette and leaned against the radiator. Beside him was a row of old mailboxes. He reached into the nearest one and came up with a handful of letters. A hand-addressed one from Des Moines. The writing suggested aged parents. A circular from Catholic Charities, Inc. A request for funds from CORE. An announcement of the January offerings of the Apollo film club and a letter from the Civil Service Commission advertising "New Benefits for Government Employees."

"The poor creature must be lonely," Reginald said.

"It's hard to be away from home at Christmas time," Cowpersmith agreed.

"We might as well give ourselves one of our presents free."

"In what apartment does the lonely young lady live?" Cowpersmith asked.

"In No. three. After you, Mr. Cowpersmith."

"Thank you, Reggie."

Reginald walked up the stairs.

The hall smelled of rotten gentility. Reginald pictured the time when liveried Uncle Toms served great ladies in these halls. He had a fleeting image of himself as a Southern Senator walking down these stairs before the big rooms had been divided up into apartments. "Good evening, Senator Cowpersmith, the ladies are waiting in the drawing room."

He knocked on apartment number three.

The girl who opened the door had four immediately observable characteristics. Two large tits and two wide, frightened eyes.

"Excuse me, ma'am," he said. "I'm the substitute janitor and the superintendent asked me to look at your radiator."

"I didn't know anything was wrong with it."

"It'll only take a second."

"All right."

He went in. The apartment was warm and homey. The living room-bedroom was neat. The convertible couch in the corner, for which he had future plans, seemed adequate to support the two of them, and he was sure that the sheets would be clean, a detail which he had come to insist on since he had been married and had come to appreciate some of the refinements that go with domestic bliss. On the desk in one corner were three pictures. Two were of "mom" and "dad." A third tinted photograph showed an insipid-looking young man in a uniform.

As he fiddled with the radiator he talked to her. "It is certainly a cold day. But then Christmas without snow is like a day without wine, as the French say."

She nodded suspiciously. The use of "French" and "wine" had been a mistake.

"Christmas brings out the best in us," he said, taking a new approach. "Love, charity, the simple virtues that seem so far removed from city life."

"You're an educated man," she said. "It's funny but I've lived in Washington now for almost a year and I haven't really talked to anybody during that time."

"I guess the city isn't what you expected," he said. "It must be very lonely for you."

"Yes."

Any "yes" is a good sign, Reginald thought. Affirm one idea and you will tend to affirm everything.

"How does it happen that you are working as a janitor?" she asked.

"I'm a writer."

"Really?"

"Yes. I have a novel I'm working on. I need the money from odd jobs, but I also want to find out the kind of life the poor people live here, particularly the Negroes."

"I've thought of the same thing," she said excitedly.

"They have a hard time." He stopped fiddling with the radiator and stood up.

"I'll bet you do too," she said.

"Adversity is the trifling burden which man must bear if he is to fulfill the kingdom of God on earth. I do what I can." He was a little anxious about the last statement. It might have been too extreme, but he recognized as he watched her that by adopting the "writer" tag he had adequately prepared her for exaggerated language.

"Would you like some coffee?"

"Thank you, but I have to get back outside to finish shovelling the coal. I think your radiator will be all right now."

"You have time for just a cup."

"I guess so."

She went into the tiny kitchen. Her ass, a fifth characteristic which he had not previously had the opportunity to observe, waved in a friendly way. He followed her. As she put the pot on the stove he moved in on her . . .

God, but I hate bastards who write stories like that. They think that cruelty is cute and justified in the name of their own super souls. Kerouac, Donleavy, Miller, the whole lot of them. Dividing up the world into two parts—themselves and the squares. They condemn with a thoughtless pride grounded in a morality of immorality which is more rigid than the Calvinist code which they profess to hate. Being "right," they are justified in doing anything to the enemy. How many people could Reginald Cowpersmith hurt in the course of one short story? Four or five probably. Maybe two dozen in a novel. When I read *The Catcher in the Rye* my sympathies are with Mr. and Mrs. Caulfield and "old Spencer." I care more about Miss Frost in *The Gingerman* than about the Gingerman.

Does that sound too moral? I would personally be happy with a situation where writers had no effect at all on the immediate existence of readers. But fictionalists have for so long thought of themselves as prophets that they have talked a gullible, freedom-escaping world into believing that they are. Given the function of art in our time, I agree with Bellows when he says that we must have writers who think.

What would happen if the neo-romantics did think? They would find among other things that they are paranoid. They write fiction in which Society tries to destroy them, a theme which serves no other purpose than to inflate their egos. Actually Society cares very little about them. The rôle of the rebel is a self-serving one.

And, furthermore, the rebellion of these anti-heroes is usually much tamer than it seems on the surface because they don't challenge the basic value systems of society. I also feel that my own story (like most of those in the genre) would have ended sentimentally with Reginald showing that at heart he was a swell fellow and that my readers should love him. Behind every romantic hero is a maudlin child.

What is left to me? I seem to lack the necessary emotional commitment to follow through with any of the styles I have tried. Of all writers, the satirist is the closest to being beyond innocence. He accepts, as a given, the futility of self-assertion. Ultimately, of course, no one who bothers to write can be completely un-innocent, but by writing satire I can approach this condition.

I have a perfect scene for my story. There is a little bar around the corner called "The Bacchus." I go there occasionally. It is *the* place for Washington hipsters, so I can ridicule my romantic enemies who hang out there. These habitués are also vaguely associated with the arts, and there is nothing more delightful to one in my position than to attack those who still are committed to the muses.

I need a norm by which the objects of my satire are to be measured. The coal shoveller will do. He is a man who has a job to do and a family to support—a practical, realistic person.

The man was sitting alone in a booth near the bar, drinking beer and watching the scene in front of him. The young hipsters and their older gurus milled around. The door opened. The man turned around. An old Negro was shuffling through the room toward the bar. He wore a "surplus" green jacket. Over his left pocket was a black strip with "U.S. Army" stitched on it in gold. The man in the booth felt suddenly excited. He tried to call the coal shoveller, but he had already taken a seat at the bar. The man watched and listened.

The coal shoveller spoke to the bartender. "I'll have a beer," he said. The bartender gave him a large draft. "I been shovelling coal so long," the coal shoveller said. "I was mighty cold. The boss gone home."

"A cold day," the bartender agreed.

"I wasn't sure about coming in here.

Some places still don't like the colored customers."

"It's okay in here," the bartender laughed.

"I knew it'd be okay. I seen that sign over the door. About Bacchus and all. He's the place kicker for the Cardinals ain't he? Man he sure is a fat fellow. Can you think of gettin' all the money he does without having to stay in shape."

The bartender, who was waiting on another customer, nodded automatically.

"I knew it was okay to come in a place where football fans come. I know a good bit about football. I seen Bacchus kick four field goals on TV against the Browns just last Sunday."

He drank some of his beer. "Lots of Redskin fans in here. But you can carry that football business too far. Letting your hair grow long just for a football team."

The bartender wasn't listening to him, so he spoke to the man beside him.

"I think Jerry Smith's a good tight end"

"*Really?*" said the man. "I don't know him, but I'd like to."

A pretty white girl sat down on the other side of him. "Do you use consciousness expansion drugs?" she asked.

"No, ma'am. I'm a janitor."

"You're cute," she said.

The coal shoveller was embarrassed. Several others were now standing around him. "Do you play an instrument?" one of them asked.

He pulled a harmonica out of his pocket.

"Give us a tune," they said. A crowd had gathered. He began to play "Ole Black Joe."

The man in the booth looked on with disgust at the hipsters.

God, but I hate bastards like that, the man thought. In their arrogant moral sureness. Dividing the world up into two parts—themselves and the squares—and condemning with a thoughtless pride grounded in a morality of immorality which is more rigid than the Calvinist code which they profess to hate. They know nothing of the coal shoveller and they don't care. Poor bastard caught in that stupid conversation.

The coal shoveller had finished his tune.

The crowd standing around him joined in a chorus of praise.

—It's *it.*

—The real thing.

—No Joan Baez crap here.

—Authentic.

—Close to Leadbelly.

—Real Delta Blues.

"Thank you," the shoveller said.

"You must come and give us a concert," the blonde girl said.

"I'll try to," the coal shoveller said. "Right now, I've got to get back to my shovelling."

He got up from the bar stool and shuffled toward the door.

The man in the booth impulsively grabbed his arm as he passed. "Have a beer with me," he said.

"Thank you," the coal shoveller replied, "but I got to get back to my shovelling."

"Please."

The urgency of the request startled the coal shoveller. He sat down. The man ordered two beers. "Those people are all phony," he said. "They don't understand you. They are using you as a symbol."

"I was glad to have a chance to play my harmonica," the coal shoveller said. "My wife don't let me play at home."

"I've been watching you shovel the coal. I live on the second floor of the building across the street."

"Is that a fact."

"I don't come in here often."

"What kind of business you in?"

"I'm a writer," the man said, "but I try to avoid attributing an essence to myself in view of the cultist associations with *the Artist* in our time. I prefer to say, 'I write.'"

"What you write? I like stories on sports."

"That's why it's so important that I talk to you. Right now I'm trying to write a story about you shovelling coal."

"Is that a fact?" the coal shoveller said. He smiled broadly. "Where can I read it?"

"I don't know who'll take it. It's an experimental story."

"Oh." He looked disappointed. "What you experimenting about?"

"With the problems of language," the man said, growing excited. "I am trying to show that literary language is a shifting kaleidoscope of lights and shadows, full at once of absences and replenishments. A word is a door that opens onto the hypocritical and inexact world of idea. The very fact that I must attempt such a story shows that Western tradition has run its course. Art has been dehumanized so that no man can honestly write on anything but the problem of writing. The word as means has become the word as end. But I say to myself, so what? Let's not avoid the reality of this problem, but face it as I am in my story. We can reduce the long history of ideological and bourgeois domination of the arts in which reality has been subordinated by idea . . ." He punctuated his last statement with a violent wave of his arm. He knocked over the bowl of pretzels on the table. The coal shoveller began carefully to replace them.

"You see," the man continued, looking urgently at the shoveller, "words are symbols. Perceiving is not done with words. So when I try to describe you shovelling coal, my story takes on connotations and implications which I don't want and which inevitably reflect my own mind. But if I can help to make both readers and writers question the assumptions on which they work, we will begin to level Western society. The hunger for the word, the nutritive value of idea will be burned out of the literate middle class. And from the courage to criticize the assumptions which have thus far guided our civilization we will reach the zero degree of culture. Of course, I am no fool. I know that the absolute is an abstraction which will never be reached, because you cannot use langauge to destroy language . . ."

"You're right," the shoveller interrupted. "Zero is a little low. I was listening to WOOK a while back and they said it'd be about 15 tonight. Could I have a cigarette?"

"Sure," the man said. He gave a cigarette to the coal shoveller and took one for himself. "Got a light?"

The coal shoveller lit the cigarettes.

"Nor do I think," the man continued, "that destruction of this cultural edifice we have raised would be any great loss. Art has become only another profession. Words are used by people to get ahead in their jobs, to gain prestige. It is not like it must have been with the grand amateurism of my grandfather. But all of these minds working on art with the tools of science eventually will see the emptiness as the center of art. Now literature is a worthless commodity in the market place where it is bartered for money . . ."

"Having money troubles?" the coal shoveller asked sympathetically. "Christmas is a hard time."

"It's not a question of money," the man said irritably. "You see in my business it's publish or . . ." He checked himself. "After all my short story has enormous social overtones as well. You and the other poor people of the world have been hoodwinked by ideas for so long. You will be the ones ultimately benefited by writers' willingness to examine their assumptions."

The man clapped the coal shoveller on the back with such force that he bumped against the table and spilled the pretzels again. "It is for you that I am writing this story."

"I certainly appreciate that," the coal shoveller said as he started replacing the pretzels. "Not many white people think about us colored people. Have a pretzel."

But, good Lord, what has any of this got

to do with the original aim of my short story?

Little has changed. It is darker now. The snow is still falling heavily. The streets are still empty. The streelights are on. The coal shoveller is slowly and steadily shovelling. I don't want to turn on the light because it would prevent me from seeing clearly out the window, but it is too dark for me to continue writing.

[1969]

For Thought

In "The Coal Shoveller," Keith Fort is grappling with a problem that troubles many serious writers of fiction today. These writers have tried to break away from imitating established literary forms in order to discover new ways of expression that would more faithfully reflect the germinal idea behind the work and the times and culture of which it is a part. In the narrator's own short story, done in various styles, he confronts the question of the literary truth of the rendering of what he imagines or perceives as a writer. He also examines the way in which style acts as a tyrannical overseer and peremptory guide, dictating what path the writer must follow to a predestined end beyond his conscious control.

For Discussion

1. What is the main defect Fort sees in the Joycean style he is first trapped into? Why does he think this style is no longer viable?
2. Give examples from the objective or pictorial technique imitation to illustrate what Fort sees as the fundamental weakness in its basic premise.
3. In the Faulkner parody, what verbal and syntactic elements are emphasized? What basic assumption behind the style is Fort rejecting?
4. What is the author's chief objection to the antihero, picaresque form of story?
5. According to Fort, what is the premise of the satirist? What defect in the satirical form is he illustrating in his own sample of the type at the end?

Bruce Jay Friedman
Black Angels

Smothered by debt, his wife and child in flight, Stefano held fast to his old house in the country, a life buoy in a sea of despair. Let him but keep up the house, return to it each day; before long, his wife would come to her senses, fly back to him. Yet he dreaded the approach of spring, which meant large teams of gardeners who would charge him killing prices to keep the place in shape. Cheapest of all had been the Angeluzzi Brothers, who had gotten him off the ground with a two-hundred-and-fifty-dollar cleanup, then followed through with ninety dollars a month for maintenance, April through October, a hundred extra for the leaf-raking fall windup. Meticulous in April, the four Angeluzzis soon began to dog it; for his ninety, Stefano got only a few brisk lawn cuts and a swipe or two at his flower beds. This spring, unable to work, his life in shreds, Stefano held off on the grounds as long as he could. The grass grew to his shins until one day Swansdowne, a next-door neighbor who had won marigold contests, called on another subject, but with much lawn-mowing and fertilizing in his voice. Stefano dialed the Angeluzzis; then, on an impulse, he dropped the phone and reached for the local paper, running his finger along Home Services. A gardener named Please Try Us caught his fancy. He called the number, asked the deep voice at the other end to come by soon and give him an estimate. The following night, a return call came through.

"I have seen and checked out the place," said the voice, the tones, heavy, resonant, solid.

"What'll you take for a cleanup?" asked Stefano. "We'll start there."

Long pause. Lip smack. Then, "Thutty dollars."

"Which address did you go to? I'm at forty-two Spring. Big old place on the corner of Spring and Rooter."

"That's correct. For fertilizing, that'll be eight extra, making thutty-eight."

"Awful lot of work here," said Stefano, confused, tingling with both guilt and relief. "All right, when can you get at it?"

"Tomorrow morning. Eight o'clock."

"You're on."

Stefano watched them arrive the next day, Sunday, a quartet of massive Negroes in two trucks and two sleek private cars. In stifling heat, they worked in checkered shirts and heavy pants, two with fedoras impossibly balanced on the backs of their great shaved heads. Stefano, a free-lance writer of technical manuals, went back to his work, stopping now and then to check the Negroes through the window. How could they possibly make out on thirty-eight dollars, he wondered. Divided four ways it came to nothing. Gas alone for their fleet of cars would kill their nine-fifty each. He'd give them forty-five dollars to salve his conscience, but still, what about their groceries, rent? Late in the afternoon, he ran out with beers for each. "Plenty of leaves, eh?" he said to Cotten, largest of them, the leader, expressionless in dainty steel-rimmed glasses.

"Take about two and a half days," said the Negro.

"I'm giving you forty-five dollars," said Stefano. "What the hell."

The job actually took three full days, two for the cleanup, a third for the lawn and fertilizing the beds. The last day was a bad one for Stefano. Through his window, he watched the black giants trim the lawn, then kneel in winter clothes and lovingly collect what seemed to be each blade of grass so there'd be no mess. He wanted to run out and tell them to do less work; certainly not at those prices. Yet he loved the prices, too. He could take it all out of expense money, not even bother his regular free-lance payments. At the end of the day, he walked up to Cotten, took out his wallet and said, "I'm giving you cash. So you won't have to fool with a check." It had occurred to him that perhaps the Negroes only did cleanups, no maintenance. By doing enough of them, thousands, perhaps they could sneak by, somehow make a living. "What about maintenance?" he asked the head gardener.

The man scratched his ear, shook his head, finally said, "Can't do your place for less than eighteen dollars a month."

"You guys do some work," said Stefano, shivering with glee. "Best I've seen. I think you're too low. I'll give you twenty-two."

The Negroes came back twice a week, turned Stefano's home into a showplace, hacking down dead trees, planting new ones, filling in dead spots, keeping the earth black and loamy. Swansdowne, who usually let Stefano test-run new gardeners and then swooped down to sign them up if they were good, looked on with envy, yet called one day and said, "I would never let a colored guy touch my place."

"They're doing a great job on mine," said Stefano.

May be that explains it, he thought. All of the Swansdownes who won't have Negro gardeners. That's why their rates are low. Otherwise they'd starve. He felt good, a liberal. Why shouldn't he get a slight break on money?

At the end of May, Stefano paid them their twenty-two dollars and distributed four American-cheese sandwiches. The three assistants took them back to a truck where one had mayonnaise. "You guys do other kinds of work?" Stefano asked Cotten, who leaned on a hoe. "What about painting? A house?"

The gardener looked up at Stefano's colonial. "We do," he said.

"How much would you take?" The best estimate on the massive ten-roomer had been seven hundred dollars.

"Fifty-eight dollars," said the huge Negro, neutral in his steel-rims.

"I'll pay for half the paint," said Stefano.

The following day, when Stefano awakened, the four Negroes, on high, buckling ladders, had half the house done, the paint deep brown, rich and gurgling in the sun. Their gardening clothes were wildly spattered. He'd pick up the cleaning bill, thought Stefano. It was only fair.

"It looks great!" he hollered up to Cotten, swaying massively in the wind.

"She'll shape up time we get the fourth coat on."

By mid-June, the four Negroes had cleaned out Stefano's attic for three dollars, waterproofed his basement for another sixteen; an elaborate network of drainage pipes went in for twelve-fifty. One day he came home to find the floors mopped, sanded, shellacked, his cabinets scrubbed, linen closets dizzying in their cleanliness. Irritated for the first time—I didn't order this—he melted quickly when he saw the bill. A slip on the bread box read: "You owes us $2.80." Loving the breaks he was getting, Stefano threw them bonuses, plenty of sandwiches, all his old sports jackets, venetian blinds that had come out of the attic and books of fairly recent vintage on Nova Scotia tourism. Never in the thick of marriage had his place been so immaculate; cars slowed down to admire his dramatically painted home, his shrubs bursting with fertility. Enter any room; its cleanliness would tear your head off. With all these ridiculously cheap home services going for him, Stefano felt at times his luck had turned. Still, a cloak of loneliness rode his shoulders, aggravation clogged his throat. If only to hate her, he missed his wife, a young, pretty woman, circling the globe with her lover, an assistant director on daytime TV. He saw pictures of her, tumbling with lust, in staterooms, inns, the backs of small foreign cars. He missed his son, too, a boy of ten, needing braces. God only knows what shockers he was being exposed to. The pair had fled in haste, leaving behind mementos, toys lined up on shelves, dresses spilling out of chests. Aging quickly, his confidence riddled, Stefano failed in his quest for dates with young girls, speechless and uncertain on the phone. What could he do with himself. At these prices, he could keep his home spotless. But would that make everything all right. Would that haul back a disgruntled wife and son. One night, his heart weighing a ton, he returned from an "Over 28" dance to find the burly Negroes winding up their work. Sweating long into the night, they had rigged up an elaborate network of gas lamps, the better to show off a brilliantly laid out thicket of tea roses and dwarf fruit trees. Total cost for the lighting: five dollars and fifty cents.

"Really lovely," said Stefano, inspecting his grounds, counting out some bills. "Here," he said to the head gardener "take another deuce. In my condition, money means nothing." The huge Negro toweled down his forehead, gathered up his equipment. "Hey," said Stefano. "Come on in for a beer. If I don't talk to someone I'll bust."

"Got to get on," said Cotten. "We got work to do."

"Come on, come on," said Stefano. "What can you do at this hour. Give a guy a break."

The Negro shook his head in doubt, then moved massively toward the house, Stefano clapping him on the back in a show of brotherhood.

Inside, Stefano went for flip-top beers. The gardener sat down in the living room, his great bulk caving deeply into the sofa. For a moment, Stefano worried about gardening clothes, Negro ones to boot, in contact with livingroom furniture, then figured the hell with it, who'd complain.

"I've got the worst kind of trouble," said Stefano, leaning back on a Danish modern slat bench. "Sometimes I don't think I'm going to make it through the night. My wife's checked out on me. You probably figured that out already."

The Negro crossed his great legs, sipped his beer. The steel-rimmed glasses had a shimmer to them and Stefano could not make out his eyes.

"She took the kid with her," said Stefano. "That may be the worst part. You don't know what it's like to have a kid tearing around your house for ten years and then not to hear anything. Or maybe you do?" Stefano asked hopefully. "You probably have a lot of trouble of your own."

Silent, the Negro sat forward and

shoved a cloth inside his flannel shirt to mop his chest.

"Anyway, I'll be goddamned if I know what to do. Wait around? Pretend she's never coming back? I don't know what in the hell to do with myself. Where do I go from here?"

"How long she gone?" asked the guest, working on the back of his neck now.

"What's that got to do with it?" asked Stefano. "About four months, I guess. Just before you guys came. Oh, I see what you mean. If she hasn't come back in four months, she's probably gone for good. I might as well start building a new life. That's a good point."

The Negro put away the cloth and folded his legs again, crossing his heavy, blunted fingers, arranging them on the point of one knee.

"It just happened out of the clear blue sky," said Stefano. "Oh, why kid around. It was never any good." He told the Negro about their courtship, the false pregnancy, how he had been "forced" to get married. Then he really started in on his wife, the constant primping, the thousands of ways she had made him jealous, the in-laws to support. He let it all come out of him, like air from a tire, talking with heat and fury; until he realized he had been talking non-stop for maybe twenty minutes, half an hour. The Negro listened to him patiently, not bothering with his beer. Finally, when Stefano sank back to catch his breath, the gardener asked a question: "You think you any good?"

"What do you mean," said Stefano. "Of course I do. Oh, I get what you're driving at. If I thought I was worth anything, I wouldn't let all of this kill me. I'd just kind of brace myself, dig out and really build something fine for myself. Funny how you make just the right remark. It's really amazing. You know I've done the analysis bit. Never meant a damned thing to me. I've had nice analysts, tough ones, all kinds. But the way you just let me sound off and then asked that one thing. This is going to sound crazy, but what if we just talked this way, couple of times a week. I just sound off and then you come in with the haymaker, the way you just did. Just for fun, what would you charge me? An hour?"

"Fo' hunnid," said the Negro.

"Four hundred. That's really a laugh. You must be out of your head. What are you, crazy? Don't you know I was just kidding around?"

The Negro took a sip of beer and rose to leave. "All right, wait a second," said Stefano. "Hold on a minute. Let's just finish up this hour, all right. Then we'll see about other times. This one doesn't count, does it?"

"It do," said the Negro, sinking into the couch and snapping out a pad and pencil.

"That's not really fair, you know," said Stefano. "To count this one. Anyway, we'll see. Maybe we'll try it for a while. That's some price. Where was I? Whew, all that money. To get back to what I was saying, this girl has been a bitch ever since the day I laid eyes on her. You made me see it tonight. In many ways, I think she's a lot like my mom. . . ."

[1964]

For Thought

In this hilarious parody of "turnabout is fair play," Friedman uses the limited omniscience point of view in a carefully selective fashion to establish the wildly humorous characterization of his protagonist, a middle-class, self-styled liberal. In a smug, self-congratulatory way, Stefano crassly exploits the absurdly low-priced labor of his crew of black gardeners, only to experience a comical reversal of fortune at the end of the story. Here, he abandons the role of exploiter to become the exploited one, ending the action on a fittingly ironic note.

For Discussion

1. In what way is Friedman's use of the limited omniscience point of view highly selective? How is this use appropriate to the author's purpose?
2. Is Stefano characterized as a "flat" or "rounded" character?
3. What is the mood of the story? How is the mood created?
4. How does Friedman employ the literary devices of hyperbole, incredible situations, and self-deception for comic effect?
5. What is both the high point and the low point of Stefano's fortune? What comic reversal is brought about at the end?
6. In spite of the laughable absurdity of the events in the story, what serious comment about human behavior may Friedman be making?

Ernest J. Gaines
The Sky Is Gray

I

Go'n be coming in a few minutes. Coming 'round that bend down there full speed. And I'm go'n get out my hankercher and I'm go'n wave it down, and us go'n get on it and go.

I keep on looking for it, but Mama don't look that way no more. She looking down the road where us jest come from. It's a long old road, and far's you can see you don't see nothing but gravel. You got dry weeds on both sides, and you got trees on both sides, and fences on both sides, too. And you got cows in the pastures and they standing close together. And when us was coming out yer to catch the bus I seen the smoke coming out o' the cow's nose.

I look at my mama and I know what she thinking. I been with Mama so much, jest me and her, I know what she thinking all the time. Right now it's home—Auntie and them. She thinking if they got 'nough wood—if she left 'nough there to keep 'em warm till us get back. She thinking if it go'n rain and if any of 'em go'n have to go out in the rain. She thinking 'bout the hog—if he go'n get out, and if Ty and Val be able to get him back in. She always worry like that when she leave the house. She don't worry too much if she leave me there with the smaller ones 'cause she know I go'n look after 'em and look after Auntie and everything else. I'm the oldest and she say I'm the man.

I look at my mama and I love my mama. She wearing that black coat and that black hat and she looking sad. I love my mama and I want put my arm 'round her and tell her. But I'm no s'pose to do that. She say that's weakness and that's cry-baby stuff, and she don't want no cry-baby 'round her. She don't want you to be scared neither. 'Cause Ty scared of ghosts and she always whipping him. I'm scared of the dark, too. But I make 'tend I ain't. I make 'tend I ain't 'cause I'm the oldest, and I got to set a good sample for the rest. I can't ever be scared and I can't ever cry. And that's the reason I didn't never say nothing 'bout my teef. It been hurting me and hurting me close to a month now. But I didn't say it. I didn't say it 'cause I didn't want act like no cry-baby, and 'cause I know us didn't have 'nough money to have it pulled. But, Lord, it been hurting me. And look like it won't start till at night when you trying to get little sleep. Then soon's you shet your eyes—umm-umm, Lord, look like it go right down to your heart string.

"Hurting, huh?" Ty'd say.

I'd shake my head, but I wouldn't open my mouth for nothing. You open your mouth and let that wind in, and it almost kill you.

I'd just lay there and listen to 'em snore. Ty, there, right 'side me, and Auntie and Val over by the fireplace. Val younger 'an me and Ty, and he sleep with Auntie. Mama sleep 'round the other side with Louis and Walker.

I'd just lay there and listen to 'em, and listen to that wind out there, and listen to that fire in the fireplace. Sometimes it'd stop long enough to let me get little rest. Sometimes it just hurt, hurt, hurt. Lord, have mercy.

II

Auntie knowed it was hurting me. I didn't tell nobody but Ty 'cause us buddies and he ain't go'n tell nobody. But some kind o' way Auntie found out. When she asked me, I told her no, nothing was wrong. But she knowed it all the time. She told me to mash up a piece o' aspirin and wrap it in some cotton and jugg it down in that hole. I did it, but it didn't do no good. It stopped for a little while, and started right back again. She wanted to tell Mama, but I told her Uh-uh. 'Cause I knowed she didn't have no money, and it jest was go'n make her mad again. So she told Monsieur Bayonne, and Monsieur Bayonne came to the house and told me to kneel down 'side him on the fireplace. He put his finger in his mouth and made the Sign of the Cross on my jaw. The tip of Monsieur Bayonne finger is some hard, 'cause he always playing on that guitar. If us sit outside at night us can always hear Monsieur Bayonne playing on his guitar. Sometime us leave him out there playing on the guitar.

He made the Sign of the Cross over and over on my jaw, but that didn't do no good. Even when he prayed and told me to pray some, too, that teef still hurt.

"How you feeling?" he say.

"Same," I say.

He kept on praying and making the Sign of the Cross and I kept on praying, too.

"Still hurting?" he say.

"Yes, sir."

Monsieur Bayonne mashed harder and harder on my jaw. He mashed so hard he almost pushed me on Ty. But then he stopped.

"What kind o' prayers you praying, boy?" he say.

"Baptist," I say.

"Well, I'll be—no wonder that teef still killing him. I'm going one way and he going the other. Boy, don't you know any Catholic prayers?"

"Hail Mary," I say.

"Then you better start saying it."

"Yes, sir."

He started mashing again, and I could hear him praying at the same time. And, sure 'nough, afterwhile it stopped.

Me and Ty went outside where Monsieur Bayonne two hounds was, and us started playing with 'em. "Let's go hunting," Ty say. "All right," I say; and us went on back in the pasture. Soon the hounds got on a trail, and me and Ty followed 'em all cross the pasture and then back in the woods, too. And then they cornered this little old rabbit and killed him, and me and Ty made 'em get back, and us picked up the rabbit and started on back home. But it had started hurting me again. It was hurting me plenty now, but I wouldn't tell Monsieur Bayonne. That night I didn't sleep a bit, and first thing in the morning Auntie told me go back and let Monsieur Bayonne pray over me some more. Monsieur Bayonne was in his kitchen making coffee when I got there. Soon's he seen me, he knowed what was wrong.

"All right, kneel down there 'side that stove," he say. "And this time pray Catholic. I don't know nothing 'bout Baptist, and don't want know nothing 'bout him."

III

Last night Mama say: "Tomorrow us going to town."

"It ain't hurting me no more," I say. "I can eat anything on it."

"Tomorrow us going to town," she say.

And after she finished eating, she got up and went to bed. She always go to bed early now. 'Fore Daddy went in the Army, she used to stay up late. All o' us sitting out on the gallery or 'round the fire. But now, look like soon's she finish eating she go to bed.

This morning when I woke up, her and Auntie was standing 'fore the fireplace. She say: "'Nough to get there and back. Dollar and a half to have it pulled. Twenty-five for me to go, twenty-five for him. Twenty-five for me to come back, twenty-five for him. Fifty cents left. Guess I get a little piece o' salt meat with that."

"Sure can use a piece," Auntie say. "White beans and no salt meat ain't white beans."

"I do the best I can," Mama say.

They was quiet after that, and I made 'tend I was still sleep.

"James, hit the floor," Auntie say.

I still made 'tend I was sleep. I didn't want 'em to know I was listening.

"All right," Auntie say, shaking me by the shoulder. "Come on. Today's the day."

I pushed the cover down to get out, and Ty grabbed it and pulled it back.

"You, too, Ty," Auntie say.

"I ain't getting no teef pulled," Ty say.

"Don't mean it ain't time to get up," Auntie say. "Hit it, Ty."

Ty got up grumbling.

"James, you hurry up and get in your clothes and eat your food," Auntie say. "What time y'all coming back?" she say to Mama.

"That 'leven o'clock bus," Mama say. "Got to get back in that field this evening."

"Get a move on you, James," Auntie say.

I went in the kitchen and washed my face, then I ate my breakfast. I was having bread and syrup. The bread was warm and hard and tasted good. And I tried to make it last a long time.

Ty came back there, grumbling and mad at me.

"Got to get up," he say. "I ain't having no teef pulled. What I got to be getting up for."

Ty poured some syrup in his pan and got a piece of bread. He didn't wash his hands, neither his face, and I could see that white stuff in his eyes.

"You the one getting a teef pulled," he say. "What I got to get up for. I bet you if I was getting a teef pulled, you wouldn't be getting up. Shucks; syrup again. I'm getting tired of this old syrup. Syrup, syrup, syrup. I want me some bacon sometime."

"Go out in the field and work and you can have bacon," Auntie say. She stood in the middle door looking at Ty. "You better be glad you got syrup. Some people ain't got that—hard's time is."

"Shucks," Ty say. "How can I be strong."

"I don't know too much 'bout your strength," Auntie say; "but I know where you go'n be hot, you keep that grumbling up. James, get a move on you; your mama waiting."

I ate my last piece of bread and went in the front room. Mama was standing 'fore the fireplace warming her hands. I put on my coat and my cap, and us left the house.

IV

I look down there again, but it still ain't coming. I almost say, "It ain't coming yet," but I keep my mouth shet. 'Cause that's something else she don't like. She don't like for you to say something just for nothing. She can see it ain't coming, I can see it ain't coming, so why say it ain't coming. I don't say it, and I turn and look at the river that's back o' us. It so cold the smoke just raising up from the water. I see a bunch of pull-doos not too far out—jest on the other side the lilies. I'm wondering if you can eat pull-doos. I ain't too sure, 'cause I ain't never ate none. But I done ate owls and black birds, and I done ate red birds, too. I didn't want kill the red birds, but she made me kill 'em. They had two of 'em back there. One in my trap, one in Ty trap. Me and Ty was go'n play with 'em and let 'em go. But she made me kill 'em 'cause us needed the food.

"I can't," I say. "I can't."

"Here," she say. "Take it."

"I can't," I say. "I can't. I can't kill him, Mama. Please."

"Here," she say. "Take this fork, James."

"Please, Mama, I can't kill him," I say.

I could tell she was go'n hit me. And I jecked back, but I didn't jeck back soon enough.

"Take it," she say.

I took it and reached in for him, but he kept hopping to the back.

"I can't, Mama," I say. The water just kept running down my face. "I can't."

"Get him out o' there," she say.

I reached in for him and he kept hopping to the back. Then I reached in farther, and he pecked me on the hand.

"I can't, Mama," I say.

She slapped me again.

I reached in again, but he kept hopping out my way. Then he hopped to one side, and I reached there. The fork got him on the leg and I heard his leg pop. I pulled my hand out 'cause I had hurt him.

"Give it here," she say, and jecked the fork out of my hand.

She reached and got the little bird right in the neck. I heard the fork go in his neck, and I heard it go in the ground. She brought him out and helt him right in front o' me.

"That's one," she say. She shook him off and gived me the fork. "Get the other one."

"I can't, Mama. I do anything. But I can't do that."

She went to the corner o' the fence and broke the biggest switch over there. I knelt 'side the trap crying.

"Get him out o' there," she say.

"I can't, Mama."

She started hitting me cross the back. I went down on the ground crying.

"Get him," she say.

"Octavia," Auntie say.

'Cause she had come out o' the house and she was standing by the tree looking at us.

"Get him out o' there," Mama say.

"Octavia," Auntie say; "explain to him. Explain to him. Jest don't beat him. Explain to him."

But she hit me and hit me and hit me.

I'm still young. I ain't no more'an eight. But I know now. I know why I had to. (They was so little, though. They was so little. I 'member how I picked the feathers off 'em and cleaned 'em and helt 'em over the fire. Then us all ate 'em. Ain't had but little bitty piece, but us all had little bitty piece, and ever'body jest looked at me, 'cause they was so proud.) S'pose she had to go away? That's why I had to do it. S'pose she had to go away like Daddy went away? Then who was go'n look after us? They had to be somebody left to carry on. I didn't know it then, but I know it now. Auntie and Monsieur Bayonne talked to me and made me see.

V

Time I see it, I get out my hankercher and start waving. It still 'way down there, but I keep waving anyhow. Then it come closer and stop and me and Mama get on. Mama tell me go sit in the back while she pay. I do like she say, and the people look at me. When I pass the little sign that say White and Colored, I start looking for a seat. I jest see one of 'em back there, but I don't take it, 'cause I want my mama to sit down herself. She come in the back and sit down, and I lean on the seat. They got seats in the front, but I know I can't sit there, 'cause I have to sit back o' the sign. Anyhow, I don't want sit there if my mama go'n sit back here.

They got a lady sitting 'side my mama and she look at me and grin little bit. I grin back, but I don't open my mouth, 'cause the wind'll get in and make that teef hurt. The lady take out a pack o' gum and reach me a slice, but I shake my head. She reach Mama a slice, and Mama shake her head. The lady jest can't understand why a little boy'll turn down gum, and she reached me a slice again. This time I point to my jaw. The lady understand and grin little bit, and I grin little bit, but I don't open my mouth, though.

They got a girl sitting 'cross from me. She got on a red overcoat, and her hair plaited in one big plait. First, I make 'tend I don't even see her. But then I start looking at her little bit. She make 'tend she don't see me neither, but I catch her looking that way. She got a cold, and ever' now and then she hist that little hankercher to her nose. She ought to blow it, but she don't. Must think she too much a lady or something.

Ever' time she hist that little hankercher, the lady 'side her say something in her yer. She shake her head and lay her hands in her lap again. Then I catch her kind o' looking where I'm at. I grin at her. But think she'll grin back? No. She turn up her little old nose like I got some snot on my face or something. Well, I show her both o' us can turn us head. I turn mine, too, and look out at the river.

The river is gray. The sky is gray. They have pull-doos on the water. The water is wavey, and the pull-doos go up and down. The bus go 'round a turn, and you got plenty trees hiding the river. Then the bus go 'round another turn, and I can see the river again.

I look to the front where all the white people sitting. Then I look at that little old gal again. I don't look right at her, 'cause I don't want all them people to know I love her. I jest look at her little bit, like I'm looking out that window over there. But she know I'm looking that way, and she kind o' look at me, too. The lady sitting 'side her catch her this time, and she lean over and say something in her yer.

"I don't love him nothing," that little old gal say out loud.

Ever'body back there yer her mouth, and all of 'em look at us and laugh.

"I don't love you, neither," I say. "So you don't have to turn up your nose, Miss."

"You the one looking," she say.

"I wasn't looking at you," I say. "I was looking out that window, there."

"Out that window, my foot," she say. "I seen you. Ever' time I turn 'round you look at me."

"You must o' been looking yourself if you seen me all them times," I say.

"Shucks," she say. "I got me all kind o' boyfriends."

"I got girlfriends, too," I say.

"Well, I just don't want you to get your hopes up," she say.

I don't say no more to that little old gal, 'cause I don't want have to bust her in the mouth. I lean on the seat where Mama sitting, and I don't even look that way no more. When us get to Bayonne, she jugg her little old tongue out at me. I make 'tend I'm go'n hit her, and she duck down side her mama. And all the people laugh at us again.

VI

Me and Mama get off and start walking in town. Bayonne is a little bitty town. Baton Rouge is a hundred times bigger 'an Bayonne. I went to Baton Rouge once—me, Ty, Mama, and Daddy. But that was 'way back yonder—'fore he went in the Army. I wonder when us go'n see him again. I wonder when. Look like he ain't ever coming home. . . . Even the pavement all cracked in Bayonne. Got grass shooting right out the sidewalk. Got weeds in the ditch, too; jest like they got home.

It some cold in Bayonne. Look like it

colder 'an it is home. The wind blow in my face, and I feel that stuff running down my nose. I sniff. Mama say use that hankercher. I blow my nose and put it back.

Us pass a school and I see them white children playing in the yard. Big old red school, and them children jest running and playing. Then us pass a café, and I see a bunch of 'em in there eating. I wish I was in ther 'cause I'm cold. Mama tell me keep my eyes in front where they blonks.

Us pass stores that got dummies, and us pass another café, and then us pass a shoe shop, and that baldhead man in there fixing on a shoe. I look at him and I butt into that white lady, and Mama jeck me in front and tell me stay there.

Us come to the courthouse, and I see the flag waving there. This one yer ain't like the one us got at school. This one yer ain't got but a handful of stars. One at school got a big pile of stars—one for ever' state. Us pass it and us turn and there it is—the dentist office. Me and Mama go in, and they got people sitting ever' where you look. They even got a little boy in there younger 'an me.

Me and Mama sit on that bench, and a white lady come in there and ask me what my name. Mama tell her, and the white lady go back. Then I yer somebody hollering in there. And soon's that little boy hear him hollering, he start hollering, too. His mama pat him and pat him, trying to make him hush up, but he ain't thinking 'bout her.

The man that was hollering in there come out holding his jaw.

"Got it, hanh?" another man say.

The man shake his head.

"Man, I thought they was killing you in there," the older man say. "Hollering like a pig under a gate."

The man don't say nothing. He jest head for the door, and the other man follow him.

"John Lee," the white lady say. "John Lee Williams."

The little boy jugg his head down in his mama lap and holler more now. His mama tell him go with the nurse, but he ain't thinking 'bout her. His mama tell him again, but he don't even yer. His mama pick him up and take him in there, and even when the white lady shet the door I can still hear him hollering.

"I often wonder why the Lord let a child like that suffer," a lady say to my mama. The lady's sitting right in front o' us on another bench. She got on a white dress and a black sweater. She must be a nurse or something herself, I reckoned.

"Not us to question," a man say.

"Sometimes I don't know if we shouldn't," the lady say.

"I know definitely we shouldn't," the man say. The man look like a preacher. He big and fat and he got on a black suit. He got a gold chain, too.

"Why?" the lady say.

"Why anything?" the preacher say.

"Yes," the lady say. "Why anything?"

"Not us to question," the preacher say.

The lady look at the preacher a little while and look at Mama again.

"And look like it's the poor who do most the suffering," she say. "I don't understand it."

"Best not to even try," the preacher say. "He works in mysterious ways. Wonders to perform."

Right then Little John Lee bust out hollering, and ever'body turn they head.

"He's not a good dentist," the lady say. "Dr. Robillard is much better. But more expensive. That's why most of the colored people come here. The white people go to Dr. Robillard. Y'all from Bayonne?"

"Down the river," my mama say. And that's all she go'n say, 'cause she don't talk much. But the lady keep on looking at her, and so she say: "Near Morgan."

"I see," the lady say.

VII

"That's the trouble with the black people in this country today," somebody else say. This one yer sitting on the same side me and Mama sitting, and he kind o'sitting in front of that preacher. He look like a teacher or somebody that go to college. He got on a suit, and he got a book that he been reading. "We don't question is exactly the trouble," he say. "We should question and question and question. Question everything."

The preacher jest look at him a long time. He done put a toothpick or something in his mouth, and he jest keep turning it and turning it. You can see he don't like that boy with that book.

"Maybe you can explain what you mean," he say.

"I said what I meant," the boy say. "Question everything. Every stripe, every star, every word spoken. Everything."

"It 'pears to me this young lady and I was talking 'bout God, young man," the preacher say.

"Question Him, too," the boy say.

"Wait," the preacher say. "Wait now."

"You heard me right," the boy say. "His existence as well as everything else. Everything."

The preacher jest look cross the room at the boy. You can see he getting madder and madder. But mad or no mad, the boy ain't thinking 'bout him. He look at the preacher jest's hard's the preacher look at him.

"Is this what they coming to?" the preacher say. "Is this what we educating them for?"

"You're not educating me," the boy say. "I wash dishes at night to go to school in the day. So even the words you spoke need questioning."

The preacher jest look at him and shake his head.

"When I come in this room and seen you there with your book, I said to myself, There's an intelligent man. How wrong a person can be."

"Show me one reason to believe in the existence of a God," the boy say.

"My heart tell me," the preacher say.

"My heart tells me," the boy say. "My heart tells me. Sure, my heart tells me. And as long as you listen to what your heart tells you, you will have only what the white man gives you and nothing more. Me, I don't listen to my heart. The purpose of the heart is to pump blood throughout the body, and nothing else."

"Who's your paw, boy?" the preacher say.

"Why?"

"Who is he?"

"He's dead."

"And your mom?"

"She's in Charity Hospital with pneumonia. Half killed herself working for nothing."

"And 'cause he's dead and she sick, you mad at the world?"

"I'm not mad at the world. I'm questioning the world. I'm questioning it with cold logic, sir. What do words like Freedom, Liberty, God, White, Colored mean? I want to know. That's why *you* are sending us to school, to read and to ask questions. And because we ask these questions, you call us mad. No, sir, it is not us who are mad."

"You keep saying 'us'?"

"'Us' . . . why not? I'm not alone."

The preacher jest shake his head. Then he look at ever'body in the room—ever'body. Some of the people look down at the floor, keep from looking at him. I kind o' look 'way myself, but soon's I know he done turn his head, I look that way again.

"I'm sorry for you," he say.

"Why?" the boy say. "Why not be sorry for yourself? Why are you so much better off than I am? Why aren't you sorry for these other people in here? Why not be sorry for the lady who had to drag her child into the dentist office? Why not be sorry for the lady sitting on that bench over there? Be sorry for them. Not for me. Some way or other I'm going to make it."

"No, I'm sorry for you," the preacher say.

"Of course. Of course," the boy say, shaking his head. "You're sorry for me because I rock that pillar you're leaning on."

"You can't ever rock the pillar I'm leaning on, young man. It's stronger than anything man can ever do."

"You believe in God because a man told you to believe in God. A white man told you to believe in God. And why? To keep you ignorant, so he can keep you under his feet."

"So now, we the ignorant?"

"Yes," the boy say. "Yes." And he open his book again.

The preacher jest look at him there. The boy done forgot all about him. Ever'body else make 'tend they done forgot 'bout the squabble, too.

Then I see that preacher getting up real slow. Preacher a great big old man, and he got to brace hisself to get up. He come 'cross the room where the boy is. He jest stand there looking at him, but the boy don't raise his head.

"Stand up, boy," preacher say.

The boy looked up at him, then he shet his book real slow and stand up. Preacher jest draw back and hit him in the face. The boy fall 'gainst the wall, but he straighten hisself up and look right back at that preacher.

"You forgot the other check," he say.

The preacher hit him again on the other side. But this time the boy don't fall.

"That hasn't changed a thing," he say.

The preacher jest look at the boy. The preacher breathing real hard like he jest run up a hill. The boy sit down and open his book again.

"I feel sorry for you," the preacher say. "I never felt so sorry for a man before."

The boy make 'tend he don't even hear that preacher. He keep on reading his book. The preacher go back and get his hat off the chair.

"Excuse me," he say to us. "I'll come back some other time. Y'all, please excuse me."

And he look at the boy and go out the room. The boy hist his hand up to his mouth one time, to wipe 'way some blood. All the rest o' the time he keep on reading.

VIII

The lady and her little boy come out the dentist, and the nurse call somebody else in. Then little bit later they come out, and the nurse call another name. But fast's she call somebody in there, somebody else come in the place where we at, and the room stay full.

The people coming in now, all of 'em wearing big coats. One of 'em say something 'bout sleeting, and another one say he hope not. Another one say he think it ain't nothing but rain. 'Cause, he say, rain can get awful cold this time o' year.

All 'cross the room they talking. Some of 'em talking to people right by 'em, some of 'em talking to people clare 'cross the room, some of 'em talking to anybody'll listen. It's a little bitty room, no bigger 'an us kitchen, and I can see ever'body in there. The little old room's full of smoke, 'cause you got two old men smoking pipes. I think I feel my teef thumping me some, and I hold my breath and wait. I wait and wait, but it don't thump me no more. Thank God for that.

I feel like going to sleep, and I lean back 'gainst the wall. But I'm scared to go to sleep: Scared 'cause the nurse might call my name and I won't hear her. And Mama might go to sleep, too, and she be mad if neither us heard the nurse.

I look up at Mama. I love my mama. I love my mama. And when cotton come I'm go'n get her a newer coat. And I ain't go'n get a black one neither. I think I'm go'n get her a red one.

"They got some books over there," I say. "Want read one of 'em?"

Mama look at the books, but she don't answer me.

"You got yourself a little man there," the lady say.

Mama don't say nothing to the lady, but she must 'a' grin a little bit, 'cause I seen the lady grinning back. The lady look at me a little while, like she feeling sorry for me.

"You sure got that preacher out here in a hurry," she say to that other boy.

The boy look up at her and look in his book again. When I grow up I want be jest like him. I want clothes like that and I want keep a book with me, too.

"You really don't believe in God?" the lady say.

"No," he say.

"But why?" the lady say.

"Because the wind is pink," he say.

"What?" the lady say.

The boy don't answer her no more. He jest read in his book.

"Talking 'bout the wind is pink," that old lady say. She sitting on the same bench with the boy, and she trying to look in his face. The boy make 'tend the old lady ain't even there. He jest keep reading. "Wind is pink," she say again. "Eh, Lord, what children go'n be saying next?"

The lady 'cross from us bust out laughing.

"That's a good one," she say. "The wind is pink. Yes, sir, that's a good one."

"Don't you believe the wind is pink?" the boy say. He keep his head down in the book.

"Course I believe it, Honey," the old lady say. "Course I do." She look at us and wink her eye. "And what color is grass, Honey?"

"Grass? Grass is black."

She bust out laughing again. The boy look at her.

"Don't you believe grass is black?" he say.

The lady quit laughing and look at him. Ever'body else look at him now. The place quiet, quiet.

"Grass is green, Honey," the lady say. "It was green yesterday, it's green today, and it's go'n be green tomorrow."

"How do you know it's green?"

"I know because I know."

"You don't know it's green. You believe it's green because someone told you it was green. If someone had told you it was black you'd believe it was black."

"It's green," the lady say. "I know green when I see green."

"Prove it's green."

"Surely, now," the lady say. "Don't tell me it's coming to that?"

"It's coming to just that," the boy say. "Words mean nothing. One means no more than the other."

"That's what it all coming to?" that old lady say. That old lady got on a turban and she got on two sweaters. She got a green sweater under a black sweater. I can see the green sweater 'cause some of the buttons on the other sweater missing.

"Yes, ma'am," the boy say. "Words mean nothing. Action is the only thing. Doing. That's the only thing."

"Other words, you want the Lord to come down here and show Hisself to you?" she say.

"Exactly, ma'am."

"You don't mean that, I'm sure?"

"I do, ma'am."

"Done, Jesus," the old lady say, shaking her head.

"I didn't go 'long with that preacher at first," the other lady say; "but now—I don't know. When a person say the grass is black, he's either a lunatic or something wrong."

"Prove to me that it's green."

"It's green because the people say it's green."

"Those same people say we're citizens of the United States."

"I think I'm a citizen."

"Citizens have certain rights. Name me one right that you have. One right, granted by the Constitution, that you can exercise in Bayonne."

The lady don't answer him. She jest look at him like she don't know what he talking 'bout. I know I don't.

"Things changing," she say.

"Things are changing because some black men have begun to follow their brains instead of their hearts."

"You trying to say these people don't believe in God?"

"I'm sure some of them do. Maybe most of them do. But they don't believe that God is going to touch these white people's hearts and change them tomorrow. Things change through action. By no other way."

Ever'body sit quiet and look at the boy. Nobody say a thing. Then the lady 'cross from me and Mama jest shake her head.

"Let's hope that not all your generation feel the same way you do," she say.

"Think what you please, it doesn't matter," the boy say. "But it will be men who listen to their heads and not their hearts who will see that your children have a better chance than you had."

"Let's hope they ain't all like you, though," the old lady say. "Done forgot the heart absolutely."

"Yes, ma'am, I hope they aren't all like me," the boy say. "Unfortunately I was born too late to believe in your God. Let's hope that the ones who come after will have your faith—if not in your God, then in something else, something definitely that they can lean on. I haven't anything. For me, the wind is pink; the grass is black."

IX

The nurse come in the room where us all sitting and waiting and say the doctor won't take no more patients till one o'clock this evening. My mama jump up off the bench and go up to the white lady.

"Nurse, I have to go back in the field this evening," she say.

"The doctor is treating his last patient now," the nurse say. "One o'clock this evening."

"Can I at least speak to the doctor?" my mama say.

"I'm his nurse," the lady say.

"My little boy sick," my mama say. "Right now his teef almost killing him."

The nurse look at me. She trying to make up her mind if to let me come in. I look at her real pitiful. The teef ain't hurting me a tall, but Mama say it is, so I make 'tend for her sake.

"This evening," the nurse say, and go back in the office.

"Don't feel 'jected, Honey," the lady say to Mama. "I been 'round 'em a long time—they take you when they want to. If you was white, that's something else; but you the wrong shade."

Mama don't say nothing to the lady, and me and her go outside and stand 'gainst the wall. It's cold out there. I can feel that wind going through my coat. Some of the other people come out of the room and go up the street. Me and Mama stand there a little while and start to walking. I don't know where us going. When us come to the other street us jest stand there.

"You don't have to make water, do you?" Mama say.

"No, ma'am," I say.

Us go up the street. Walking real slow. I can tell Mama don't know where she going. When us come to a store us stand there and look at the dummies. I look at a little boy with a brown overcoat. He got on brown shoes, too. I look at my old shoes and look at his'n again. You wait till summer, I say.

Me and Mama walk away. Us come up to another stores and us stop and look at them dummies, too. Then us go again. Us pass a café where the white people in there eating. Mama tell me keep my eyes in front where they blonks, but I can't help from seeing them people eat. My stomach start to growling 'cause I'm hungry. When I see people eating, I get hungry; when I see a coat, I get cold.

A man whistle at my mama when us go by a filling station. She make 'tend she don't even see him. I look back and I feel like hitting him in the mouth. If I was bigger, I say. If I was bigger, you see.

Us keep on going. I'm getting colder and colder, but I don't say nothing. I feel that stuff running down my nose and I sniff.

"That rag," she say.

I git it out and wipe my nose. I'm getting cold all over now—my face, my hands, my feet, ever'thing. Us pass another little café, but this'n for white people, too, and us can't go in there neither. So us jest walk. I'm so cold now, I'm 'bout ready to say it.

If I knowed where us was going, I wouldn't be so cold, but I don't know where us going. Us go, us go, us go. Us walk clean out o' Bayonne. Then us cross the street and us come back. Same thing I seen when I got off the bus. Same old trees, same old walk, same old weeds, same old cracked pave—same old ever'thing.

I sniff again.

"That rag," she say.

I wipe my nose real fast and jugg that hankercher back in my pocket 'fore my hand get too cold. I raise my head and I can see David hardware store. When us come up to it, us go in. I don't know why, but I'm glad.

It warm in there. It so warm in there you don't want ever leave. I look for the heater, and I see it over by them ba'ls. Three white men standing 'round the heater talking in Creole. One of 'em come to see what Mama want.

"Got any ax handle?" she say.

Me, Mama, and the white man start to the back, but Mama stop me when us come to the heater. Her and the white man go on. I hold my hand over the heater and look at 'em. They go all the way in the back, and I see the white man point to the ax handle 'gainst the wall. Mama take one of 'em and shake it like she trying to figure how much it weigh. Then she rub her hand over it from one end to the other end. She turn over and look at the other side, then she shake it again, and shake her head and put it back. She get another one and she do it jest like she did the first one, then she shake her head. Then she get a brown one and do it that, too. But she don't like this one neither. Then she get another one, but 'fore she shake it or anything, she look at me. Look like she trying to say something to me, but I don't know what it is. All I know is I done got warm now and I'm feeling right smart better. Mama shake this ax handle jest like she done the others, and shake her head and say something to the white man. The white man jest look at his pile of ax handle, and when Mama pass by him to come to the front, the white man jest scratch his head and follow her. She tell me come on, and us go on out and start walking again.

Us walk and walk, and no time at all I'm cold again. Look like I'm colder now 'cause I can still remember how good it was back there. My stomach growl and I suck it in to keep Mama from yering it. She walking right 'side me, and it growl so loud you can yer it a mile. But Mama don't say a word.

X

When us come up to the courthouse, I look at the clock. It got quarter to twelve. Mean us got another hour and a quarter to be out yer in the cold. Us go and stand side a building. Something hit my cap and I look up at the sky. Sleet falling.

I look at Mama standing there. I want stand close 'side her, but she don't like that. She say that's cry-baby stuff. She say you got to stand for yourself, by yourself.

"Let's go back to that office," she say.

Us cross the street. When us get to the dentist I try to open the door, but I can't. Mama push me on the side and she twist the knob. But she can't open it neither. She twist it some more, harder, but she can't open it. She turn 'way from the door. I look at her, but I don't move and I don't say nothing. I done seen her like this before and I'm scared.

"You hungry?" she say. She say it like she mad at me, like I'm the one cause of ever'thing.

"No, ma'am," I say.

"You want eat and walk back, or you rather don't eat and ride?"

"I ain't hungry," I say.

I ain't jest hungry, but I'm cold, too. I'm so hungry and I'm so cold I want cry. And look like I'm getting colder and colder. My feet done got numb. I try to work my toes, but I can't. Look like I'm go'n die. Look like I'm go'n stand right here and freeze to death. I think about home. I think about

Val and Auntie and Ty and Louis and Walker. It 'bout twelve o'clock and I know they eating dinner. I can hear Ty making jokes. That's Ty. Always trying to make some kind o' joke. I wish I was right there listening to him. Give anything in the world if I was home 'round the fire.

"Come on," Mama say.

Us start walking again. My feet so numb I can't hardly feel 'em. Us turn the corner and go back up the street. The clock start hitting for twelve.

The sleet's coming down plenty now. They hit the pave and bounce like rice. Oh, Lord; oh, Lord, I pray. Don't let me die. Don't let me die. Don't let me die, Lord.

XI

Now I know where us going. Us going back o' town where the colored people eat. I don't care if I don't eat. I been hungry before. I can stand it. But I can't stand the cold.

I can see us go'n have a long walk. It 'bout a mile down there. But I don't mind. I know when I get there I'm go'n warm myself. I think I can hold out. My hands numb in my pockets and my feet numb, too, but if I keep moving I can hold out. Jest don't stop no more, that's all.

The sky's gray. The sleet keep falling. Falling like rain now—plenty, plenty. You can hear it hitting the pave. You can see it bouncing. Sometime it bounce two times 'fore it settle.

Us keep going. Us don't say nothing. Us jest keep going, keep going.

I wonder what Mama thinking. I hope she ain't mad with me. When summer come I'm go'n pick plenty cotton and get her a coat. I'm go'n get her a red one.

I hope they make it summer all the time. I be glad if it was summer all the time—but it ain't. Us got to have winter, too. Lord, I hate the winter. I guess ever'body hate the winter.

I don't sniff this time. I get out my hankercher and wipe my nose. My hand so cold I can hardly hold the hankercher.

I think us getting close, but us ain't there yet. I wonder where ever'body is. Can't see nobody but us. Look like us the only two people moving 'round today. Must be too cold for the rest of the people to move 'round.

I can hear my teefes. I hope they don't knock together too hard and make that bad one hurt. Lord, that's all I need, for that bad one to start off.

I hear a church bell somewhere. But today ain't Sunday. They must be ringing for a funeral or something.

I wonder what they doing at home. They must be eating. Monsieur Bayonne might be there with his guitar. One day Ty played with Monsieur Bayonne guitar and broke one o' the string. Monsieur Bayonne got some mad with Ty. He say Ty ain't go'n never 'mount to nothing. Ty can go jest like him when he ain't there. Ty can make ever'body laugh mocking Monsieur Bayonne.

I used to like to be with Mama and Daddy. Us used to be happy. But they took him in the Army. Now, nobody happy no more. . . . I be glad when he come back.

Monsieur Bayonne say it wasn't fair for 'em to take Daddy and give Mama nothing and give us nothing. Auntie say, Shhh, Etienne. Don't let 'em yer you talk like that. Monsieur Bayonne say, It's God truth. What they giving his children? They have to walk three and a half mile to school hot or cold. That's anything to give for a paw? She got to work in the field rain or shine jest to make ends meet. That's anything to give for a husband? Auntie say, Shhh, Etienne, shhh. Yes, you right, Monsieur Bayonne say. Best don't say it in front of 'em now. But one day they go'n find out. One day. Yes, s'pose so, Auntie say. Then what, Rose Mary? Monsieur Bayonne say. I don't know, Etienne, Auntie say. All us can do is us job, and leave ever'thing else in His hand. . . .

Us getting closer, now. Us getting closer. I can see the railroad tracks.

Us cross the tracks, and now I see the café. Jest to get in there, I say. Jest to get in there. Already I'm starting to feel little better.

XII

Us go in. Ahh, it good. I look for the heater; there 'gainst the wall. One of them little brown ones. I jest stand there and hold my hand over it. I can't open my hands too wide 'cause they almost froze.

Mama standing right 'side me. She done unbuttoned her coat. Smoke rise out the coat, and the coat smell like a wet dog.

I move to the side so Mama can have more room. She open out her hands and rub 'em together. I rub mine together, too, 'cause this keep 'em from hurting. If you let 'em warm too fast, they hurt you sure. But if you let 'em warm jest little bit at a time, and you keep rubbing 'em they be all right ever' time.

They got jest two more people in the café. A lady back o' the counter, and a man on this side the counter. They been watching us ever since us come in.

Mama get out the hankercher and count the money. Both o' us know how much money she got there. Three dollars. No, she ain't got three dollars. 'Cause she had to pay us way up here. She ain't got but two dollars and a half left. Dollar and a half to get my teef pulled, and fifty cents for us to go back on, and fifty cents worse o' salt meat.

She stir the money 'round with her finger. Most o' the money is change 'cause I can hear it rubbing together. She stir it and stir it. Then she look at the door. It still sleeting. I can yer it hitting 'gainst the wall like rice.

"I ain't hungry, Mama," I say.

"Got to pay 'em something for they heat," she say.

She take a quarter out the hankercher and tie the hankercher up again. She look over her shoulder at the people, but she still don't move. I hope she don't spend the money. I don't want her spend it on me. I'm hungry, I'm almost starving I'm so hungry, but I don't want her spending the money on me.

She flip the quarter over like she thinking. She must be thinking 'bout us walking back home. Lord, I sure don't want walk home. If I thought it done any good to say something, I say it. But my mama make up her own mind.

She turn way from the heater right fast, like she better hurry up and do it 'fore she change her mind. I turn to look at her go to the counter. The man and the lady look at her, too. She tell the lady something and the lady walk away. The man keep on looking at her. Her back turn to the man, and Mama don't even know he standing there.

The lady put some cakes and a glass o' milk on the counter. Then she pour up a cup o' coffee and set it side the other stuff. Mama pay her for the things and come back where I'm at. She tell me sit down at that table 'gainst the wall.

The milk and the cakes for me. The coffee for my mama. I eat slow, and I look at her. She looking outside at the sleet. She looking real sad. I say to myself, I'm go'n make all this up one day. You see, one day, I'm go'n make all this up. I want to say it now. I want to tell how I feel right now. But Mama don't like for us to talk like that.

"I can't eat all this," I say.

They got just three little cakes there. And I'm so hungry right now, the Lord know I can eat a hundred times three. But I want her to have one.

She don't even look my way. She know I'm hungry. She know I want it. I let it stay there a while, then I get it and eat it. I eat jest on my front teefes, 'cause if it tech that back teef I know what'll happen. Thank God it ain't hurt me a tall today.

After I finish eating I see the man go to the juke box. He drop a nickel in it, then he jest stand there looking at the record.

Mama tell me keep my eyes in front where they blonks. I turn my head like she say, but then I yer the man coming towards us.

"Dance, Pretty?" he say.

Mama get up to dance with him. But 'fore you know it, she done grabbed the little man and done throwed him 'side the wall. He hit the wall so hard he stop the juke box from playing.

"Some pimp," the lady back o' the counter say. "Some pimp."

The little man jump up off the floor and start towards my mama. 'Fore you know it, Mama done sprung open her knife and she waiting for him.

"Come on," she say. "Come on. I'll cut you from your neighbo to your throat. Come on."

I go up to the little man to hit him, but Mama make me come and stand 'side her. The little man look at me and Mama and go back to the counter.

"Some pimp," the lady back o' the counter say. "Some pimp." She start laughing and pointing at the little man. "Yes, sir, you a pimp, all right. Yes, sir."

XIII

"Fasten that coat. Let's go," Mama say.

"You don't have to leave," the lady say.

Mama don't answer the lady, and us right out in the cold again. I'm warm right now—my hands, my yers, my feet—but I know this ain't go'n last too long. It done sleet so much now you got ice ever'where.

Us cross the railroad tracks, and soon's us do, I get cold. That wind go through this little old coat like it ain't nothing. I got a shirt and a sweater under it, but that wind don't pay 'em no mind. I look up and I can see us got a long way to go. I wonder if us go'n make it 'fore I get too cold.

Us cross over to walk on the sidewalk. They got jest one sidewalk back here. It's over there.

After us go jest a little piece, I smell bread cooking. I look, then I see a baker shop. When us get closer, I can smell it more better. I shet my eyes and make 'tend I'm eating. But I keep 'em shet too long and I butt up 'gainst a telephone post. Mama grab me and see if I'm hurt. I ain't bleeding or nothing and she turn me loose.

I can feel I'm getting colder and colder, and I look up to see how far us still got to go. Uptown is 'way up yonder. A half mile, I reckoned. I try to think of something. They say think and you won't get cold. I think of that poem, *Annabel Lee*. I ain't been to school in so long—this bad weather—I reckoned they done passed *Annabel Lee*. But passed it or not, I'm sure Miss Walker go'n make me recite it when I get there. That woman don't never forget nothing. I ain't never seen nobody like that.

I'm still getting cold. *Annabel Lee* or no *Annabel Lee*, I'm still getting cold. But I can see us getting closer. Us getting there gradually.

Soon's us turn the corner, I see a little old white lady up in front o' us. She the only lady on the street. She all in black and she got a long black rag over her head.

"Stop," she say.

Me and Mama stop and look at her. She must be crazy to be out in all this sleet. Ain't got but a few other people out there, and all of 'em men.

"Yall done ate?" she say.

"Jest finished," Mama say.

"Yall must be cold then?" she say.

"Us headed for the dentist," Mama say. "Us'll warm up when us get there."

"What dentist?" the old lady say. "Mr. Bassett?"

"Yes, ma'am," Mama say.

"Come on in," the old lady say. "I'll telephone him and tell him yall coming."

Me and Mama follow the old lady in the store. It's a little bitty store, and it don't have much in there. The old lady take off her head piece and fold it up.

"Helena?" somebody call from the back.

"Yes, Alnest?" the old lady say.

"Did you see them?"

"They're here. Standing beside me."

"Good. Now you can stay inside."

The old lady look at Mama. Mama waiting to hear what she brought us in here for. I'm waiting for that, too.

"I saw yall each time you went by," she say. "I came out to catch you, but you were gone."

"Us went back o' town," Mama say.

"Did you eat?"

"Yes, ma'am."

The old lady look at Mama a long time, like she thinking Mama might be jest saying that. Mama look right back at her. The old lady look at me to see what I got to say. I don't say nothing. I sure ain't going 'gainst my mama.

"There's food in the kitchen," she say to Mama. "I've been keeping it warm."

Mama turn right around and start for the door.

"Just a minute," the old lady say. Mama stop. "The boy'll have to work for it. It isn't free."

"Us don't take no handout," Mama say.

"I'm not handing out anything," the old lady say. "I need my garbage moved to the front. Ernest has a bad cold and can't go out there."

"James'll move it for you," Mama say.

"Not unless you eat," the old lady say. "I'm old, but I have my pride, too, you know."

Mama can see she ain't go'n beat this old lady down, so she jest shake her head.

"All right," the old lady say. "Come into the kitchen."

She lead the way with that rag in her hand. The kitchen is a little bitty little thing, too. The table and the stove jest about fill it up. They got a little room to the side. Somebody in there laying cross the bed. Must be the person she was talking with: Alnest or Ernest—I forget what she call him.

"Sit down," the old lady say to Mama. "Not you," she say to me. "You have to move the cans."

"Helena?" somebody say in the other room.

"Yes, Alnest?" the old lady say.

"Are you going out there again?"

"I must show the boy where the garbage is," the old lady say.

"Keep that shawl over your head," the old man say.

"You don't have to remind me. Come, boy," the old lady say.

Us go out in the yard. Little old back yard ain't no bigger 'an the store or the kitchen. But it can sleet here jest like it can sleet in any big back yeard. And 'fore you know it I'm trembling.

"There," the old lady say, pointing to the cans. I pick up one of the cans. The can so light I put it back down to look inside o' it.

"Here," the old lady say. "Leave that cap alone."

I look at her in the door. She got that black rag wrapped 'round her shoulders, and she pointing one of her fingers at me.

"Pick it up and carry it to the front," she say. I go by her with the can. I'm sure the thing's empty. She could 'a' carried the thing by herself, I'm sure. "Set it on the sidewalk by the door and come back for the other one," she say.

I go and come back, Mama look at me when I pass her. I get the other can and take it to the front. It don't feel no heavier 'an the other one. I tell myself to look inside and see just what I been hauling. First, I look up and down the street. Nobody coming. Then I look over my shoulder. Little old lady done slipped there jest's quiet's mouse, watching me. Look like she knowed I was go'n try that.

"Ehh, Lord," she say. "Children, children. Come in here, boy, and go wash your hands."

I follow her into the kitchen, and she point, and I go to the bathroom. When I come out, the old lady done dished up the food. Rice, gravy, meat, and she even got some lettuce and tomato in a saucer. She even got a glass o' milk and a piece o' cake there, too. It look so good. I almost start eating 'fore I say my blessing.

"Helena?" the old man say.

"Yes, Alnest?" she say.

"Are they eating?"

"Yes," she say.

"Good," he say. "Now you'll stay inside."

The old lady go in there where he is and I can hear 'em talking. I look at Mama. She eating slow like she thinking. I wonder what 's the matter now. I reckoned she think 'bout home.

The old lady come back in the kitchen.

"I talked to Dr. Bassett's nurse," she say. "Dr. Bassett will take you as soon as you get there."

"Thank you, ma'am," Mama say.

"Perfectly all right," the old lady say. "Which one is it?"

Mama nod towards me. The old lady look at me real sad. I look sad, too.

"You're not afraid, are you?" she say.

"No'm," I say.

"That's a good boy," the old lady say. "Nothing to be afraid of."

When me and Mama get through eating, us thank the old lady again.

"Helena, are they leaving?" the old man say.

"Yes, Alnest."

"Tell them I say good-by."

"They can hear you, Alnest."

"Good-by both mother and son," the old man say. "And may God be with you."

Me and Mama tell the old man good-by, and us follow the old lady in the front. Mama open the door to go out, but she stop and come back in the store.

"You sell salt meat?" she say.

"Yes."

"Give me two bits worse."

"That isn't very much salt meat," the old lady say.

"That's all I have," Mama say.

The old lady go back o' the counter and cut a big piece off the chunk. Then she wrap it and put it in a paper bag.

"Two bits," she say.

"That looks like awful lot of meat for a quarter," Mama say.

"Two bits," the old lady say. "I've been selling salt meat behind this counter twenty-five years. I think I know what I'm doing."

"You got a scale there," Mama say.

"What?" the old lady say.

"Weigh it," Mama say.

"What?" the old lady say. "Are you telling me how to run my business?"

"Thanks very much for the food," Mama say.

"Just a minute," the old lady say.

"James," Mama say to me. I move towards the door.

"Just one minute, I said," the old lady say.

Me and Mama stop again and look at her. The old lady take the meat out the bag and unwrap it and cut 'bout half o' it off. Then she wrap it up again and jugg it back in the bag and give it to Mama. Mama lay the quarter on the counter.

"Your kindness will never be forgotten," she say. "James," she say to me.

Us go out, and the old lady come to the door to look at us. After us go a little piece I look back, and she still there watching us.

The sleet's coming down heavy, heavy now, and I turn up my collar to keep my neck warm. My mama tell me turn it right back down.

"You not a bum," she say. "You a man."

[1963]

For Thought

In an atmosphere of financial privation, wintry cold, and racial discrimination, Gaines establishes the close relationship between mother and son and the hardships they endure as a result of their poverty, the weather, and the indifferent or hostile treatment they encounter. At the same time that he does this, he also balances the hardships by showing the kind treatment they receive from the old white woman and her husband in an episode marked by the exact reverse of discrimination. As a central idea, Gaines makes clear the fierce pride possessed by the mother, which is being passed on to her son to help shape him into a man who will be able to cope with whatever life brings him. Although Gaines incorporates signs of coming social change in the South in the person of the iconoclastic young black student with the book, he does not make this the theme, or even a dominant element, in his story.

For Discussion

1. What is the advantage of using the boy as the narrator instead of the mother?
2. Even though the point of view is not omniscient, how does Gaines manage to achieve some of the omniscient effect in parts of the story?
3. What attitude does the author have toward the boy? How does he convey it?
4. How is the relationship between mother and son revealed in the encounters they have with other characters in the story?
5. Mother and son might be said to be mirror images of one another; how does each exhibit the same traits in different events in the story?
6. What is the central conflict in the story? What is the resolution? How is it brought about?
7. Why is the regional language so effective in terms of description, introspection, and dialogue?
8. What evidence of racial discrimination is found in the story? How does the author handle this?
9. How do the encounters between Octavia and the dentist's nurse, and between Octavia and the little old lady act as dramatic counterparts?
10. What is the significance of the title?

John Galsworthy
Ultima Thule

Ultima Thule! The words come into my head this winter night. That is why I write down the story, as I know it, of a little old friend.

I used to see him first in Kensington Gardens, where he came in the afternoons, accompanied by a very small girl. One would see them silent before a shrub or flower, or with their heads inclined to heaven before a tree, or leaning above water and the ducks, or stretched on their stomachs watching a beetle, or on their backs watching the sky. Often they would stand holding crumbs out to the birds, who would perch about them, and even drop on their arms little white marks of affection and esteem. They were admittedly a noticeable couple. The child, who was fair-haired and elfinlike, with dark eyes and a pointed chin, wore clothes that seemed somewhat hard put to it. And, if the two were were not standing still, she went along pulling at his hand, eager to get there; and, since he was a very little, light old man, he seemed always in advance of his own feet. He was garbed, if I remember, in a daverdy brown overcoat and broad-brimmed soft grey hat, and his trousers, what was visible of them, were tucked into half-length black gaiters which tried to join with very old brown shoes. Indeed, his costume did not indicate any great share of prosperity. But it was his face that riveted attention. Thin, cherry-red, and wind-dried as old wood, it had a special sort of brightness, with its spikes and waves of silvery hair, and blue eyes which seemed to shine. Rather mad, I used to think. Standing by the rails of an enclosure, with his withered lips pursed and his cheeks drawn in till you would think the wind might blow through them, he would emit the most enticing trills and pipings, exactly imitating various birds.

Those who rouse our interest are generally the last people we speak to, for interest seems to set up a kind of special shyness; so it was long before I made his acquaintance. But one day by the Serpentine, I saw him coming along alone, looking sad, but still with that queer brightness about him. He sat down on my bench with his little dried hands on his thin little knees, and began talking to himself in a sort of whisper. Presently I caught the words: "God cannot be like us." And for fear that he might go on uttering such precious remarks that were obviously not intended to be heard, I had either to go away or else address him. So, on an impulse, I said:

"Why?"

He turned without surprise.

"I've lost my landlady's little girl," he said. "Dead! And only seven years old."

"That little thing I used to watch you with?"

"Did you? Did you? I'm glad you saw her."

"I used to see you looking at flowers, and trees, and those ducks."

His face brightened wistfully. "Yes; she was a great companion to an old man like me." And he relapsed into his contemplation of the water. He had a curious, precise way of speaking, that matched his pipchinesque little old face. At last he again turned to me those blue youthful eyes which seemed to shine out of a perfect little nest of crow's-feet.

"We were great friends! But I couldn't expect it. Things don't last, do they?" I was glad to notice that his voice was getting cheerful. "When I was in the orchestra at the Harmony Theatre, it never used to occur to me that some day I shouldn't play there any more. One felt like a bird. That's the beauty of music, sir. You lose yourself; like that blackbird there." He imitated the note of a blackbird so perfectly that I could have sworn the bird started.

"Birds and flowers! Wonderful things; wonderful! Why, even a buttercup———!" He pointed at one of those little golden flowers with his toe. "Did you ever see such a marvellous thing?" And he turned his face up at me. "And yet, somebody told me once that they don't agree with cows. Now can that be? I'm not a countryman—though I was born at Kingston."

"The cows do well enough on them," I said, "in my part of the world. In fact, the farmers say they like to see buttercups."

"I'm glad to hear you say that. I was always sorry to think they disagreed."

When I got up to go, he rose, too.

"I take it as very kind of you," he said, "to have spoken to me."

"The pleasure was mine. I am generally to be found hereabouts in the afternoons any time you like a talk."

"Delighted," he said; "delighted. I make friends of the creatures and flowers as much as possible, but they can't always make us understand." And after we had taken off our respective hats, he reseated himself, with his hands on his knees.

Next time I came across him standing by the rails of an enclosure, and, in his arms, an old and really wretched-looking cat.

"I don't like boys," he said, without preliminary of any sort. "What do you think they were doing to this poor old cat? Dragging it along by a string to drown it; see where it's cut into the fur! I think boys despise the old and weak!" He held it out to me. At the ends of those little sticks of arms the beast looked more dead than alive; I had never seen a more miserable creature.

"I think a cat," he said, "is one of the most marvellous things in the world. Such a depth of life in it."

And, as he spoke, the cat opened its mouth as if protesting at that assertion. It *was* the sorriest-looking beast.

"What are you going to do with it?"

"Take it home; it looks to me as if it might die."

"You don't think that might be more merciful?"

"It depends; it depends. I shall see. I fancy a little kindness might do a great deal for it. It's got plenty of spirit. I can see from its eye."

"May I come along with you a bit?"

"Oh!" he said; "delighted."

We walked on side by side, exciting the derision of nearly everyone we passed—his face looked so like a mother's when she is feeding her baby!

"You'll find this'll be quite a different cat to-morrow," he said. "I shall have to get in, though, without my landlady seeing; a funny woman! I have two or three strays already."

"Can I help in any way?"

"Thank you," he said. "I shall ring the area bell, and as she comes out below I shall go in above. She'll think it's boys. They *are* like that."

"But doesn't she do your rooms, or anything?"

A smile puckered his face. "I've only one; I do it myself. Oh, it'd never do to have her about, even if I could afford it. But," he added, "if you're so kind as to come with me to the door, you might engage her by asking where Mr. Thompson lives. That's me. In the musical world my name was Moronelli; not that I have Italian blood in me, of course."

"And shall I come up?"

"Honoured; but I live very quietly."

We passed out of the gardens at Lancaster Gate, where all the house fronts seem so successful, and out of it into a little street that was extremely like a grubby child trying to hide under its mother's skirts. Here he took a newspaper from his pocket and wrapped it round the cat.

"She's a funny woman," he repeated; "Scotch descent, you know." Suddenly he pulled an area bell and scuttled up the steps.

When he had opened the door, however, I saw before him in the hall a short, thin woman dressed in black, with a sharp and bumpy face. Her voice sounded brisk and resolute.

"What have you got there, Mr. Thompson?"

"Newspaper, Mrs. March."

"Oh, indeed! Now, you're not going to take that cat upstairs!"

The little old fellow's voice acquired a sudden shrill determination. "Stand aside, please. If you stop me, I'll give you notice. The cat is going up. It's ill, and it is going up."

It was then I said:

"Does Mr. Thompson live here?"

In that second he shot past her, and ascended.

"That's him," she said; "and I wish it wasn't, with his dirty cats. Do you want him?"

"I do."

"He lives at the top." Then, with a grudging apology: "I can't help it; he tries me—he's very trying."

"I am sure he is."

She looked at me. The longing to talk that comes over those who answer bells all day, and the peculiar Scottish desire to justify oneself, rose together in that face which seemed all promontories dried by an east wind.

"Ah!" she said; "he is. I don't deny his heart; but he's got no sense of anything. Goodness knows what he hasn't got up there. I wonder I keep him. An old man like that ought to know better; half-starving himself to feed them." She paused, and her eyes, which had a cold and honest glitter, searched me closely.

"If you're going up," she said, "I hope you'll give him good advice. He never lets me in. I wonder I keep him."

There were three flights of stairs, narrow, clean, and smelling of oilcloth. Selecting one of two doors at random, I knocked. His silvery head and bright, pinched face were cautiously poked out.

"Ah!" he said; "I thought it might be her!"

The room, which was fairly large, had a bare floor with little on it save a camp-bed and chest of drawers with jug and basin. A large bird-cage on the wall hung wide open. The place smelt of soap and a little of beasts and birds. Into the walls, whitewashed over a green wall-paper which stared through in places, were driven nails with their heads knocked off, on to which bits of wood had been spiked, so that they stood out as bird-perches high above the ground. Over the open window a piece of wire-netting had been fixed. A little spirit-stove and an old dressing-gown hanging on a peg completed the accoutrements of a room which one entered with a certain diffidence. He had not exaggerated. Besides the new cat, there were three other cats and four birds, all—save one, a bullfinch—invalids. The cats kept close to the walls, avoiding me, but wherever my little old friend went they followed him with their eyes. The birds were in the cage, except the bullfinch, which had perched on his shoulder.

"How on earth," I said, "do you manage to keep cats and birds in one room?"

"There is danger," he answered, "but I have not had a disaster yet. Till their legs or wings are mended, they hardly come out of the cage; and after that they keep up on my perches. But they don't stay long, you know, when they're once well. That wire is only put over the window while they're mending; it'll be off to-morrow for this lot."

"And then they'll go?"

"Yes. The sparrow first, and then the two thrushes."

"And this fellow?"

"Ask him," he said. "Would *you* go, bully?" But the bullfinch did not deign to answer.

"And were all those cats, too, in trouble?"

"Yes," he said. "They wouldn't want me if they weren't."

Thereupon he began to warm some blue-looking milk, contemplating the new cat, which he had placed in a round basket close to the little stove, while the bullfinch sat on his head. It seemed time to go.

"Delighted to see you, sir," he said, "any day." And, pointing up at the bullfinch on his head, he added: "Did you ever see anything so wonderful as that bird? The size of its heart! Really marvellous."

To the rapt sound of that word marvellous, and full of the memory of his mysterious brightness while he stood pointing upward to the bird perched on his thick, silvery hair, I went.

The landlady was still at the bottom of the stairs, and began at once. "So you found him! I don't know why I keep him. Of course, he was kind to my little girl." I saw tears gather in her eyes.

"With his cats and his birds, I wonder I keep him! But where would he go? He's no relations, and no friends—not a friend in the world, I think! He's a character. Lives on air—feeding them cats! I've no patience with them, eating him up. He never lets me in. Cats and birds! I wonder I keep him. Losing himself for those rubbishy things! It's my belief he was always like that; and that's why he never got on. He's no sense of anything."

And she gave me a shrewd look, wondering, no doubt, what the deuce I had come about.

I did not come across him again in the gardens for some time, and went at last to pay him a call. At the entrance to a mews just round the corner of his grubby little street, I found a knot of people collected round one of those bears that are sometimes led through the less conspicuous streets of our huge towns. The yellowish beast was sitting up in deference to its master's rod, uttering little grunts, and moving its uplifted snout from side to side, in the way bears have. But it seemed to be extracting more amusement than money from its audience.

"Let your bear down off its hind legs and I'll give you a penny." And suddenly I saw my little old friend under his flopping grey hat, amongst the spectators, all taller than himself. But the bear's master only grinned and prodded the animal in the chest. He evidently knew a good thing when he saw it.

"I'll give you twopence to let him down."

Again the bear-man grinned. "More!" he said, and again prodded the bear's chest. The spectators were laughing now.

"Threepence! And if you don't let him down for that, I'll hit you in the eye."

The bear-man held out his hand. "All a-right," he said, "threepence: I let him down."

I saw the coins pass and the beast dropping on his forefeet; but just then a policeman coming in sight, the man led his bear off, and I was left alone with my little old friend.

"I wish I had that poor bear," he said: "I could teach him to be happy. But, even if I could buy him, what could I do with him up there? She's such a funny woman."

He looked quite dim, but brightened as we went along.

"A bear," he said, "is really an extraordinary animal. What wise little eyes he has! I do think he's a marvellous creation! My cats will have to go without their dinner, though. I was going to buy it with that threepence."

I begged to be allowed the privilege.

"Willingly!" he said. "Shall we go in here? They like cod's head best."

While we stood waiting to be served I saw the usual derisive smile pass over the fishmonger's face. But my little old friend by no means noticed it; he was too busy looking at the fish. "A fish is a marvellous thing, when you come to think of it," he murmured. "Look at its scales. Did you ever see such mechanism?"

We bought five cod's heads, and I left him carrying them in a bag, evidently lost in the anticipation of five cats eating them.

After that I saw him often, going with him sometimes to buy food for his cats, which seemed ever to increase in numbers. His talk was always of his strays, and the marvels of creation, and that time of his life when he played the flute at the Harmony Theatre. He had been out of a job, it seemed, for more than ten years; and, when questioned, only sighed and answered: "Don't talk about it, please!"

His bumpy landlady never failed to favour me with a little conversation. She was one of those women who have terrific consciences, and terrible grudges against them.

"I never get out," she would say.

"Why not?"

"Couldn't leave the house."

"It won't run away!"

But she would look at me as if she thought it might, and repeat:

"Oh! I never get out."

An extremely Scottish temperament.

Considering her descent, however, she was curiously devoid of success, struggling on apparently from week to week, cleaning, and answering the bell, and never getting out, and wondering why she kept my little old friend; just as he struggled on from week to week, getting out and collecting strays, and discovering the marvels of creation, and finding her a funny woman. Their hands were joined, one must suppose, by that dead child.

One July afternoon, however, I found her very much upset. He had been taken dangerously ill three days before.

"There he is," she said; "can't touch a thing. It's my belief he's done for himself, giving his food away all these years to those cats of his. I shooed 'em out to-day, the nasty creatures; they won't get in again."

"Oh!" I said, "you shouldn't have done that. It'll only make him miserable."

She flounced her head up. "Hoh!" she said: "I wonder I've kept him all this time, with his birds and his cats dirtying my house. And there he lies, talking gibberish about them. He made me write to a Mr. Jackson, of some theatre or other—I've no patience with him. And that little bullfinch all the time perching on his pillow, the dirty little thing! I'd have turned it out, too, only it wouldn't let me catch it."

"What does the doctor say?"

"Double pneumonia—caught it getting his feet wet, after some stray, I'll be bound. I'm nursing him. There has to be someone with him all the time."

He was lying very still when I went up, with the sunlight falling across the foot of his bed, and, sure enough, the bullfinch perching on his pillow. In that high fever he looked brighter than ever. He was not exactly delirious, yet not exactly master of his thoughts.

"Mr. Jackson! He'll be here soon. Mr. Jackson! He'll do it for me. I can ask him, if I die. A funny woman. I don't want to eat; I'm not a great eater—I want my breath, that's all."

At sound of his voice the bullfinch fluttered off the pillow and flew round and round the room, as if alarmed at something new in the tones that were coming from its master.

Then he seemed to recognise me. "I think I'm going to die," he said; "I'm very weak. It's lucky there's nobody to mind. If only he'd come soon. I wish"—and he raised himself with feeble excitement—"I wish you'd take that wire off the window; I want my cats. She turned them out. I want him to promise me to take them, and bully-boy, and feed them with my money, when I'm dead."

Seeing that excitement was certainly worse for him than cats, I took the wire off. He fell back, quiet at once; and presently, first one and then another cat came stealing in, till there were four or five seated against the walls. The moment he ceased to speak the bullfinch, too, came back to his pillow. His eyes looked most supernaturally bright, staring out of his little, withered-up old face at the sunlight playing on his bed; he said just audibly: "Did you ever see anything more wonderful than that sunlight? It's really marvellous!" After that he fell into a sort of doze or stupor. And I continued to sit there in the window, relieved, but rather humiliated, that he had not asked me to take care of his cats and bullfinch.

Presently there came the sound of a motor-car in the little street below. And almost at once the landlady appeared. For such an abrupt woman, she entered very softly.

"Here he is," she whispered.

I went out and found a gentleman, perhaps sixty years of age, in a black coat, buff waistcoat, gold watch-chain, light trousers, patent-leather boots, and a wonderfully shining hat. His face was plump and red, with a glossy grey moustache; indeed, he seemed to shine everywhere, save in the eyes, which were of a dull and somewhat liverish hue.

"Mr. Jackson?"

"The same. How is the little old chap?"

Opening the door of the next room, which I knew was always empty, I beckoned Mr. Jackson in.

"He's really very ill; I'd better tell you what he wants to see you about."

He looked at me with that air of "You can't get at me—whoever you may be," which belongs to the very successful.

"Right-o!" he said. "Well?"

I described the situation. "He seems to think," I ended, "that you'll be kind enough to charge yourself with his strays, in case he should die."

Mr. Jackson prodded the unpainted washstand with his gold-headed cane.

"Is he really going to kick it?"

"I'm afraid so; he's nothing but skin, bone, and spirit, as it is."

"H'm! Stray cats, you say, and a bird! Well, there's no accounting. He was always a cracky little chap. So that's it! When I got the letter I wondered what the deuce! We pay him his five quid a quarter regular to this day. To tell truth, he deserved it. Thirty years he was at our shop; never missed a night. First-rate flute he was. He ought never to have given it up, though I always thought it showed a bit of heart in him. If a man don't look after number one, he's as good as gone; that's what I've always found. Why, I was no more than he was when I started. Shouldn't have been worth a plum if I'd gone on his plan, that's certain." And he gave that profound chuckle which comes from the very stomach of success. "We were having a rocky time at the Harmony; had to cut down everything we could—music, well, that came about first. Little old Moronelli, as we used to call him—old Italian days before English names came in, you know—he was far the best of the flutes; so I went to him and said: 'Look here, Moronelli, which of these other boys had better go?' 'Oh!' he said—I remember his funny little old mug now—'has one of them to go, Mr. Jackson? Timminsa'—that was the elder—'he's a wife and family; and Smetoni'—Smith, you know—'he's only a boy. Times are bad for flutes.' 'I know it's a bit hard,' I said, 'but this theatre's goin' to be run much cheaper; one of 'em's got to get.' 'Oh!' he said, 'dear me!' he said. What a funny little old chap it was! Well—what do you think? Next day I had his resignation. Give you my word I did my best to turn him. Why, he was sixty then if he was a day—at sixty a man don't get jobs in a hurry. But not a bit of it! All he'd say was: 'I shall get a place all right!' But that's it, you know—he never did. Too long in one shop. I heard by accident he was on the rocks; that's how I make him that allowance. But that's the sort of hopeless little old chap he is—no idea of himself. Cats! Why not? I'll take his old cats on; don't you let him worry about that. I'll see to his bird, too. If I can't give 'em a better time than ever they have here, it'll be funny!" And, looking round the little empty room, he again uttered that profound chuckle: "Why, he was with us at the Harmony thirty years—that's time, you know; I made my fortune in it."

"I'm sure," I said, "it'll be a great relief to him."

"Oh! Ah! That's all right. You come down to my place"—he handed me a card: 'Mr. Cyril Porteous Jackson, Ultima Thule, Wimbledon'—"and see how I fix 'em up. But if he's really going to kick it, I'd like to have a look at the little old chap, just for old times' sake."

We went, as quietly as Mr. Jackson's bright boots would permit, into his room, where the landlady was sitting gazing angrily at the cats. She went out without noise, flouncing her head as much as to say: "Well, now you can see what I have to go through, sitting up here. I never get out."

Our little old friend was still in that curious stupor. He seemed unconscious, but his blue eyes were not closed, staring brightly out before them at things we did not see. With his silvery hair and his flushed frailty, he had an unearthly look. After standing perhaps three minutes at the foot of the bed, Mr. Jackson whispered:

"Well, he does look queer. Poor little old chap! You tell him from me I'll look after his cats and bird; he needn't worry. And now, I think I won't keep the car. Makes me feel a bit throaty, you know. Don't move; he might come to."

And, leaning all the weight of his substantial form on those bright and creaking toes, he made his way to the door, flashed at me a diamond ring, whispered hoarsely: "So long! That'll be all right!" and vanished. And soon I heard the whirring of his car and just saw the top of his shiny hat travelling down the little street.

Some time I sat on there, wanting to deliver that message. An uncanny vigil in the failing light, with those five cats—yes, five at least—lying or sitting against the walls, staring like sphinxes at their motionless protector. I could not make out whether it was he in his stupor with his bright eyes that fascinated them, or the bullfinch perched on his pillow, who they knew perhaps might soon be in their power. I was glad when the landlady came up and I could leave the message with her.

When she opened the door to me next day at six o'clock I knew that he was gone. There was about her that sorrowful, unmistakable importance, that peculiar mournful excitement, which hovers over houses where death has entered.

"Yes," she said, "he went this morning. Never came round after you left. Would you like to see him?"

We went up.

He lay, covered with a sheet, in the darkened room. The landlady pulled the window-curtains apart. His face, as white now almost as his silvery head, had in the sunlight a radiance like that of a small, bright angel gone to sleep. No growth of hair, such as comes on most dead faces, showed on those frail cheeks that were now smooth and lineless as porcelain. And on the sheet above his chest the bullfinch sat, looking into his face.

The landlady let the curtains fall, and we went out.

"I've got the cats in here"—she pointed to the room where Mr. Jackson and I had talked—"all ready for that gentleman when he sends. But that little bird, I don't know what to do; he won't let me catch him, and there he sits. It makes me feel all funny."

It had made me feel all funny, too.

"He hasn't left the money for his funeral. Dreadful, the way he never thought about himself. I'm glad I kept him, though." And, not to my astonishment, she suddenly began to cry.

A wire was sent to Mr. Jackson, and on the day of the funeral I went down to "Ultima Thule," Wimbledon, to see if he had carried out his promise.

He had. In the grounds, past the vinery, an outhouse had been cleaned and sanded, with cushions placed at intervals against the wall, and a little trough of milk. Nothing could have been more suitable or luxurious.

"How's that?" he said. "I've done it thoroughly." But I noticed that he looked a little glum.

"The only thing," he said, "is the cats. First night they seemed all right; and the second, there were three of 'em left. But today the gardener tells me there's not the ghost of one anywhere. It's not for want of feeding. They've had tripe, and liver, and milk—as much as ever they liked. And cod's heads, you know—they're very fond of them. I must say it's a bit of a disappointment to me."

As he spoke, a sandy cat which I perfectly remembered, for it had only half of its left ear, appeared in the doorway, and stood, crouching, with its green eyes turned on us; then, hearing Mr. Jackson murmur, "Puss, puss!" it ran for its life, slinking almost into the ground, and vanished among some shrubs.

Mr. Jackson sighed. "Perversity of the brutes!" he said. He led me back to the house through a conservatory full of choice orchids. A gilt bird-cage was hanging there, one of the largest I had ever seen, replete with every luxury the heart of bird could want.

"Is that for the bullfinch?" I asked him.

"Oh!" he said; "didn't you know? The little beggar wouldn't let himself be caught, and the second morning, when they went up, there he lay on the old chap's body, dead. I thought it was very touchin'. But I kept the cage hung up for you to see that I should have given him a good time here. Oh, yes, 'Ultima Thule' would have done him well!"

And from a bright leather case Mr. Jackson offered me a cigar.

The question I had long been wishing to ask him slipped out of me then:

"Do you mind telling me why you called your house 'Ultima Thule?'"

"Why?" he said. "Found it on the gate. Think it's rather distingué, don't you?" and he uttered his profound chuckle.

"First-rate. The whole place is the last word in comfort."

"Very good of you to say so," he said. "I've laid out a goodish bit on it. A man must have a warm corner to end his days in. 'Ultima Thule,' as you say—it isn't bad. There's success about it, somehow."

And with that word in my ears, and in my eyes a vision of the little old fellow in his "Ultima Thule," with the bullfinch lying dead on a heart that had never known success, I travelled back to town.

[1914]

For Thought

Galsworthy's attitude assumed toward his main character in "Ultima Thule" is that of a saintly hero. Thompson uses the motif "a marvellous thing" whenever he refers to anything that is "weak," "old," or threatened; the motif helps establish his characterization. Thompson reveals an unworldly concern for helpless outcasts. He befriends damaged cats and birds. Thompson's compassionate treatment of victims seems to express a wish that someone would treat him the same way. In death as in life, he achieves an uncomplaining dignity free of self-pity and bitterness.

For Discussion

1. What leads the narrator to befriend Thompson? How does Thompson's characterization reveal his past as a musician?
2. How does Galsworthy maintain Thompson's dignity without surrounding his situation with excessive pathos?
3. How is Thompson's landlady humanized? What role does Jackson play in the story?

John Gardner
Queen Louisa

I

Mad Queen Louisa awakened feeling worried and irritable. That was by no means unusual for her. It had been happening since she was a little girl, or, as she sometimes clearly remembered, a lizard. She fanned herself with the fingers of one hand, anxiously searching, as she always did for the first few minutes, for the deeply buried secret of her soul's unrest. She was not afraid of rape or poverty or death. She'd established these facts beyond a shadow of a doubt many years ago—she'd long since forgotten precisely how, but one cannot keep plowing the same old ground. As for lesser fears, suffice it to say that she'd read all the books in the royal palace—not only those in Slavonic and Latin, but those in German and French as well, and one in English, sometimes reading in her character as queen, sometimes as a huge and sleepy-eyed toad in spectacles—and she'd systematically crossed off all possible causes of distress from anorexy to zygomatic fever. Despite that, she always woke up worried and irritable. Her solution, which was simple and brilliantly effective, once she was awake to remember it, was to find little nothings to attach her deep, vague worry to. The lady-in-waiting seemed peaked, out of sorts; some trouble with her husband? Or the castle's north wall had moss on it. Do moss roots run deep? Could they loosen the stones?

She opened the curtains of her huge gold bed. (The king always slept alone these days. He said it was the wars. Had he taken some mistress?) Already the chamber was alive with light—the chambermaid always threw the windows wide open at six o'clock. Orderly details make orderly days, Queen Louisa believed. Also, toads like the early morning damp. Every surface, every plane or flange or lozenge of the furniture gleamed, almost sang, with light. The combs and brushes on her dressing table were so bright she had to blink.

Carefully, she slipped her toes into the cold, then her shins and knees. The floor, when she reached it, was deliciously icy.

She'd catch her death of pneumonia, she realized, and hurriedly felt left and right for her slippers.

The door flew open, and the chambermaid rushed in. She was supposed to be here when the queen awakened. Queen Louisa felt a catch and thoughtfully narrowed her large and luminous (she knew) eyes. What had the chambermaid been up to? she wondered. The girl looked flushed. She was fourteen, no older. She looked—the queen touched her bosom in alarm—she looked pregnant!

At Queen Louisa's moan, the child rushed to her and seized her hands.

"Are you ill, your majesty?" On her cheeks, two bright roses. Her eyes were gray.

"*I'm* well enough," the queen said very cautiously. Her mind raced over whom it might be. Not the page, certainly. He was fat as a pig and reeked of old cider. She did hope not one of those trumpet players! It couldn't be one of the knights, of course, because of the wars—unless perhaps one of the wounded ones. Her mind fixed with horrible and vaguely pleasurable fascination on the thought of the chambermaid creeping to the infirmary, slipping into bed with some great gored creature with a six-month beard. She secretly whispered a prayer to protect her from salacious thoughts.

"I just stepped out for a minute, your majesty," the chambermaid said.

Queen Louisa was sick with worry now. Perhaps it was no one from the castle at all. Perhaps the girl's father, some peasant from the village.

"Help me with my dressing-gown," the queen said weakly.

"Of course, your majesty!" She bowed very low and went pale for an instant. A sign of pregnancy if ever there was one! But the queen said nothing. Mad she might be—so everyone maintained, though they did not seem so all right themselves, in her opinion—but she was not a person who poked into other people's business. A little cry escaped her. The lady-in-waiting who'd been fighting with her husband should be here now too. Was she off with the great dog, the chambermaid's father? The girl was studying her, alarmed by the cry. Queen Louisa smiled gently, and the girl was reassured. Queen Louisa extended her arms for the golden sleeves.

"Is his majesty at breakfast?" Queen Louisa asked. It was important to keep one's servants at ease, keep their minds occupied.

"He left in the middle of the night, my lady. The wars, you know." The child's voice sounded so apologetic you'd have thought the wars were all her fault.

"Well, no matter, my dear," Queen Louisa said. "I'm sure we'll manage."

"I do *hope* so, your majesty!"

Queen Louisa froze. There was no mistaking the distress in the voice of her chambermaid. It was something beyond any personal distress. (Mad Queen Louisa had a sense about these things.) She moved toward her gold and ivory mirror, lacing up the front of her dressing gown. Very casually, she said, "Is something wrong, my dear?"

Suddenly, touched off by the tender concern in her majesty's voice, the chambermaid burst into tears. "Oh, my lady, my lady, how dare I reveal it?"

Queen Louisa frowned, profoundly worried, then hurriedly smiled, for fear she might shake the child's foundations, and lightly patted the chambermaid's hand. "Tell me everything," she said, "and Queen Louisa will fix it."

The child required no further encouragement. Clinging to her majesty's hand, she said, "A witch has appeared on the mountain and put all the hermits to flight. The peasants are so frightened they can hardly speak for shuddering. What are we to do? Oh, your majesty, your majesty! The king and his knights are a hundred miles away!"

Queen Louisa sighed but refused to tremble. She put her arm gently around the poor girl and sadly gazed into the mirror. Her great heavy-lidded eyes gazed back at her, and her wide, sad toad's mouth. The golden dressing-gown clung tightly to her thick, rough, swampgreen torso, though the sleeves were loose and a little too long. "Never mind," she said. "Queen Louisa will fix it." And she would. No question. All the same, it was inconsiderate and irrational of the king to leave his kingdom in the hands of a queen who was insane. Fleetingly, she wondered who his mistress might be. *Not* her own lady-in-waiting, surely! But the moment the thought occurred to her, she was certain she was right. (These hunches of hers were infallible.)—But if so, then his majesty was the chambermaid's fat peasant father, who was sleeping with the lady-in-waiting because of her troubles with her husband; and the peasant's child, that is, the king's, her little chambermaid, could be only—her own lost daughter! Queen Louisa smiled, feeling wildly happy, but said nothing for the moment, biding her time. She felt warm all over, and strangely majestic. She was soon to be a grandmother.

II

"The Court is now in session," Queen Louisa said.

The judges looked befuddled and a trifle annoyed, which she could well understand. But the facts were simple, and nothing makes a trial run more smoothly than simple facts. It was not, of course, the business of royalty to explain itself to mere judges of the realm. ("Never complain, never explain" was Queen Louisa's motto.) And the facts were these: that the king and his knights were all far away, except for the knights in the infirmary, and there was no one at home to deal with the troubles but the Royal Court. Therefore Queen Louisa had assembled the Court.

The chief justice looked over the tops of his spectacles, holding his wig away with the backs of the fingers of his hands, partly for the sake of seeing better, partly for the sake of hearing. He looked from the empty defendant's chair to the empty benches where the various lawyers and their witnesses should be. It was a tense moment, and the chambermaid glanced in alarm at the queen. The lower justices, one on each side of the chief justice, pretended to study their copious notes and copy them over more legibly, though the queen suspected they had nothing written down in the first place. Queen Louisa could easily forgive them, however. Indeed, she'd have done the same herself. Surely they'd never encountered a case quite like this before.

Timidly, but with a hint of irritation, the chief justice said, "Where is the defendant?"

The lower justices smiled as they always smiled at every question he asked, as if saying to themselves, "Very shrewdly put!" Their smiles emboldened him to ask it again, even letting out a little smile himself: "*Your majesty, where is the defendant?*"

Queen Louisa smiled too, though she pitied them, really: dependent as children, hopelessly shackled in rules and procedures, wholly unprepared for the rich and strange. In their long white wigs they looked like sheep. In fact, when she saw how they held their pencils—poked between their pointed hooves—she became half-convinced that they *were* sheep. With the greatest possible dignity—to set a good example for the chambermaid, since a kingdom where the honor of courts is forgotten is a kingdom in trouble, and also because sheep are people, too, whose feelings can be hurt—but mainly because she had a vague suspicion that only by speaking with the greatest possible dignity could she prevent her words from seeming ridiculous, even to a sheep—Queen Louisa said: "You ask me where the defendant is. *That,* my lord justices"—she paused dramatically—"I leave to the wisdom of this Court."

They looked at each other, and the chief of the justices paled a little and glanced at the clock. Again he peered down at the empty benches where the defendant, witnesses, and lawyers should be. He cleaned his spectacles. "Your majesty," he said at last, like a creature completely baffled . . . but he let his words trail off.

Queen Louisa said nothing, merely patted the chambermaid's knee to show that all was well. The child, of course, never having been in a court before, had no idea how long these things took. She too kept glancing anxiously at the clock, wringing her hands, and pulling at her kerchief till it was so twisted around one could hardly see her face.

Meekly, the justices began to make guesses. "Is the defendant somewhere else?" asked the one on the left.

Queen Louisa pursed her lips and thought. "You're warm," she said at last. She exchanged winks with the chambermaid.

"Somewhere outside the castle?" asked the one on the right.

"Warmer!" said the queen, and squeezed her hands together.

"He's having his coffee!" the chief justice cried.

"Cold," snapped the queen.

"Poor devil!" they moaned. They had no real understanding of trials, she saw, or else they weren't really trying.

"In my opinion," the chambermaid whispered, "this Court's getting *nowhere*."

"Trials are like that, my dear," said Queen Louisa. "But if you insist, I'll give their honors a hint."

"Would you?" begged the girl.

Queen Louisa rose and extended her long-sleeved arms for silence. "My lord justices," she said, "let me give you a hint."

They accepted eagerly, all three of them waiting with their pencils poised.

"Our business, I think you'll agree," said the queen, "is justice."

The justices furtively glanced at each other, as self-conscious and timid as newts. For no clear reason, she was suddenly filled with a profound sadness. Still the justices waited, hoping for something more and scratching their foreheads with their chewed-down eraser ends. ("Justice," the chief justice kept mumbling, picking at his lip. He wrote down: "Just Ice?")

Queen Louisa continued, watching them carefully for a sign they'd got it: "You've perhaps heard that our hermits have been frightened from the mountain by an alleged witch." She paused, startled, rather pleased that she'd thought to say *alleged*. It was the first real clue. The witch was perhaps in fact *not* a witch, in which case, of course, the whole trial . . . She glanced suspiciously at the chambermaid, then remembered, in confusion, that the child was her daughter. The child glanced suspiciously back at her. But still the judges' faces were blank. Queen Louisa sighed and worried that she might be spoiling everything by revealing too much. She continued, however: "Since the king and his knights are all away, it seems to me our bounden duty to investigate this matter. I therefore suggest that we ride to the mountain and investigate."

"Hear, hear!" the judges cried wildly, all three of them at once, and glanced at each other.

That must have been the answer (though Queen Louisa had to admit she'd gotten lost somewhere), because the poor little chambermaid was trembling all over and clapping her hands and weeping.

III

There was some difficulty with the queen's horse. In the end, they all rode in the royal carriage. The chambermaid huddled in the shadow of the queen, contributing nothing to the conversation, no doubt partly because, sitting with the queen, she was wedged in tight.

"I was born of simple, honest stock," the queen narrated. The chambermaid looked up at her eagerly, from the seat beside her. Outside, the landscape was glittering white. On the castle wall, now far in the distance, the gored knights from the infirmary were all waving colored banners and shouting. The three old sheep sat leaning far forward, for Queen Louisa was speaking very softly, harkening back. All three had their thin hooves folded on their knees and their bowlers in their laps, for the ceiling of the carriage was strangely low. She was reminded, and spoke of, the ceiling of the cottage at the edge of the forest where her parents lived. (She sat with her knees pulled tightly together, despite cramp and discomfort, but even so she could give no more room to the chambermaid. As she spoke, Queen Louisa kept her hands carefully in front of her great green wattles, merely as a kindness to the others. Personally, she rather enjoyed her appearance. "A queen with a *difference*," she liked to say, winking coyly.)

"It was a marriage no one believed would work. Mother was Irish, and Father was a dragon. Except for a very few dear friends, they were cut off by both communities. But the cruelty of people who had supposedly loved them served only to intensify their love and deep respect for one another. I was the youngest of the children, of whom there were sometimes seven and sometimes four, depending."

"Depending on what?" the chief justice broke in, not at all urgently—in fact tears were streaming from his large, pink eyes.

"Depending on our parents," Queen Louisa explained, and realized now for perhaps the first time how profoundly true that was. "We were poor but extremely proud, you see.—Of course it was difficult for Father to get work." She remembered with a pang how he'd sit by the fireplace pretending to read the evening paper, though in fact, as everyone in the family knew, it was a paper from last year. A tear ran down the side of Queen Louisa's nose. "It was difficult," she said once more—merely to find her place again—"for Father to get work."

"It would be, yes," said the sheep on the left, "being married to a Catholic."

Queen Louisa brightened. "But poor as we were, we had each other!"

"Perhaps that's why sometimes there were only four," the chief justice said.

She had a curious feeling, which she couldn't in the least explain to herself, that the conversation was losing direction. She decided to leap forward. "When I was nine, there was a fire in the old wooden church in the nearby village. Naturally, Father was blamed for it." She paused, frowning, though she was secretly flattered. "Excuse me," she said to the chief justice, "are you writing all this down?"

He looked up, startled, still weeping profusely, then immediately blushed. He held the paper toward her, on which he'd been writing, in large block letters, with the greatest imaginable concentration. The paper said: JUSTICE ST. JUICE CUTE JEST [crossed off] SUITE SITE TIE IS US USE

Queen Louisa mused, the chambermaid peeking around past her elbow. "IST!" Queen Louisa said suddenly in German.

"TU ES," cried the chambermaid in French.

"JE SUIS," cried the sheep on the left.

They merely looked at him.

Queen Louisa sighed. "Well," she said, "they took Father away. I remember his parting words to us. He was a poet at heart, I've always felt. It was a wintry morning very like this one." She gazed sadly out the window. "He gazed sadly out the window, a policeman standing at each side of him—he had only his old singed overcoat on, and I remember the tears were coursing down his cheeks—and he said:

"'My loves, do not blame the authorities for
this. Who can swear
that his own apprehension of reality is valid?
There are certain insects—
I forget which ones—that have no apparatus
for determining
that other insects of their own same kind exist.
Such is
our lot. Have faith! Love even those who bring
sorrow to you!'"

"Hexameters—loosely," the chief justice said.

She looked at him with new respect.

There, unfortunately, she was forced to

discontinue her narrative. They'd arrived at their destination.

IV

The monastery gates were open wide. Queen Louisa discovered, descending from the carriage and keeping the chambermaid's hand in hers to give the poor child courage, that in the monastery yard there was no one at all, not even a footprint in the snow to suggest that possibly someone had been there, or at least someone's shoe. She tiptoed softly to the monastery door, leading the child, and the three old sheep came audiculously behind her, huddled close together and holding their bowlers on with both hands, as people would do in a windstorm. There was, of course, not a breath of wind, but logic was not their strong point (she thought fondly) and, also, the bowlers were new. The inside of the monastery was also empty. She tried the back door.

"I'm frightened," said the chambermaid.

"Call me Mother, if you like," Queen Louisa said.

The chambermaid looked at her, then looked away, sucked in her lower lip, and seemed to think about it.

Queen Louisa laughed gently. "You young people!" she said.

In the snowy back garden they encountered a truly amazing sight.

The garden's stone walls were encased in ice, as was every tree and shrub and left-over flower stalk. But in the center of the garden there was a glorious rosebush in triumphant bloom, such bloom as would hardly be natural on even the warmest summer day. And beside the bush there was a horrible ugly old witchlike person who was trying to cut down the rosebush with an axe. With every swipe she took, the trunk of the bush grew wider and stronger, and the roses bloomed more brightly. At the feet of the ugly witchlike person, an old red hound lay whimpering and whining.

Queen Louisa stared in astonishment, believing for an instant that her whole life had been a terrible mistake. But somehow or other she collected her wits and called out in a stern and commanding voice, "Stop!"—for she was capable of such things, if driven too far.

At once both the witchlike person and the dog looked up at her. For an instant the witchlike person was thrown, but only for an instant. "Never!" she cried, her lean lips trembling and her eyes so ferociously green with evil that Queen Louisa was fearful that the chambermaid might faint. Immediately the witchlike person began swinging the axe like someone in a drunken rage, and the old dog whimpered and whined in such awful and unspeakable misery that even the Royal Court was moved to tears. The rosebush, of course, grew stronger by leaps and bounds.

"Stop her! Do something!" the chambermaid hissed, clinging to Queen Louisa with trembling hands.

But Queen Louisa thoughtfully narrowed her eyes, pursed her lips, and calmed the chambermaid by patting her hand. "Be quiet, Muriel," she said very softly. "I don't think we've quite understood this situation."

"Muriel?" said the chambermaid.

"My dear," said Queen Louisa in a stern but not unfriendly voice, signifying by a look that she was addressing the person swinging the axe, "every stroke you strike makes the rosebush stronger."

"Good point!" said the judges, frantically searching through their trouser pockets for their notebooks.

"Get away! Be gone!" said the witchlike person.

Queen Louisa smiled. She said. "Dog, come here."

With an awful groan, the old red hound got up and came timidly toward her. It settled at her feet and closed its eyes like a creature enormously embarrassed.

"Muriel," Queen Louisa said out of the side of her mouth, "meet your ridiculous father."

The chambermaid looked at the dog,

touching her chin with three fingers. "How do you do," she said at last.

The witchlike person was perspiring now. Her black robe clung to her armpits and back, and her nose and chin (which were as blue and as pointed as icicles) dripped. She stopped swinging and leaned on her axe, panting. "I'm not beaten," she whispered.

Immediately, as if at a signal, a hundred wolves in the robes of pious monks came bounding over the garden wall and crouched, growling, with their ghastly fangs bared, in a semicircle around Queen Louisa and her friends.

The witchlike person laughed. "You see, my ancient enemy," she cried, "your whole life has been a terrible mistake! The forces of evil do exist! Ha, ha!" Words cannot describe the unearthly horror of that final "Ha ha!" She raised the axe in one hand and brandished it. "We're cosmic accidents!" cried the witchlike person. "Life is gratuitous, it has no meaning till we make one up by our intensity. That is why these gentle monks have joined me in seeking to wreak havoc on the kingdom. Not for personal gain. Ha ha! Ha ha! But to end the boredom! To end all those mornings of waking up vaguely irritable! Ha ha!" She sidled toward the queen. "I have seduced your husband. What do you think of that? I have filled him with the feeling that life *is* meaningful, if only because it can be thrown away. I have—"

Suddenly Queen Louisa heard, behind her in the formerly empty monastery, a thrilling crashing and clanking of armor. The witchlike person went pale with fear. "Strike now!" she exclaimed to the wolves. "Strike now, and quickly, before it's too late!"

But the wolves stood trembling and wringing their paws, too terrified to move an inch. And before you could say Jack Robinson, the door behind Queen Louisa opened and a thousand gory wounded knights came out, pushing into every available space in the garden, saying "Excuse me" as they passed Queen Louisa and her friends, and they raised their swords to execute the wolves.

"Stop!" cried Queen Louisa.

Everybody stopped.

Queen Louisa walked with great dignity and calm to the miraculous rosebush, her webbed hands gracefully crossed across her wattles.

"You've all misunderstood everything," she said. "Or else I have. But no matter, since I'm the queen." She could have explained, if she wanted to, how sorry she felt for the wicked of this world, who couldn't even cut a rosebush down. Though she'd admit, in all fairness, that perhaps the rosebush *was* cut down, since she was insane and could never know anything for sure, and perhaps the whole story was taking place in a hotel in Philadelphia.

"Watch!" said Queen Louisa. She closed her large and luminous eyes and concentrated. A gasp went through the monastery garden, for behold, Queen Louisa had changed from an enormous toad to a magnificently beautiful redheaded woman with a pale, freckled nose. Her white, white arms were so delicately dimpled at the elbows that neither knight nor wolf could refrain from licking his lips with desire. "Mother!" cried the chambermaid. "My beloved!" cried the king—changed that same instant from the dog he was before. The witchlike person was reduced in a flash to the lady-in-waiting. She sat weeping and groaning at her monstrous betrayal of everybody, and especially her husband. The leader of the wolves said, "Let us pray." The rosebush, being of no further use, withered to an ice-clad stick.

Queen Louisa extended her soft white arm to the chambermaid. "My sweet," she said, "it's natural that youth should be rebellious. I was rebellious myself. But I want you to know that if you want to come home, your father and I agree, you're welcome."

Neither demanding nor expecting that the others would follow her, lovely Queen

Louisa turned, with a gentle bow, and went back into the monastery and through it to the yard and on to the carriage. She got in and, with a thoughtful frown, turned back into a toad. Immediately the three sheep got in, and after them Queen Louisa's daughter, Muriel, and then His Majesty the King and Her Majesty's lady-in-waiting. The wounded knights lined up behind the carriage to follow it home. With two extra people beside them now, the three sheep were so crowded they could hardly breathe. Yet they smiled like madmen in their joy at the king's proximity.

Queen Louisa said—the child looked up at her with admiration like a gasp—"Don't blame yourself, my sweet. It's true, of course, that your dramatic leaving gave your father ideas. The poor old fool was in his forties then, and, I'm sorry to say, all people in their thirties and early forties have this awful lust—this ridiculous hunger for experience, so to speak. And the pretty way you mocked him, of course, and flirted with him—"

"*I* did all this?" the chambermaid said.

Queen Louisa smiled sadly at the look of dismay and bafflement in little Muriel's eyes. Then, with the carriage gently swaying and the snow falling softly from the pitchdark sky, Mad Queen Louisa told her beautiful newfound daughter the story of her life.

The boy beside the coachman said: "Isn't this a marvelous tale to be in?"

The coachman, who was silver-haired and wise, gave his nephew a wink. "You barely made it, laddie!"

[1974]

For Thought

In this inspired bit of make-believe, Gardner freely borrows clichés of situation and plot from Graustarkian romance to involve the reader in the characters and events of a zany fairy tale set in a world of amiable toads, judicial sheep, and ineffectual witches. Through the use of comic transformations, gross incongruities, and whimsical logic, Gardner cleverly manipulates the conventions he employs to amuse and delight rather than to perplex the reader with subtle profundities. In so doing, he makes use of the salutary, laugh-provoking nonsense that preserves our sanity by liberating the child in our consciousness, which needs an occasional escape from humdrum reality and cold logic.

For Discussion

1. How does the way in which Queen Louisa's mind works make her a comic figure? How does the author render her an amiably comic figure?
2. In the court scene, what elements of action and characterization are comic?
3. What conventions from costume romance and fairy tales does Gardner rely on his reader knowing? How does he change the conventions to make them comic?
4. What tone does he adopt in telling his tale? How is this accomplished?

William H. Gass

In the Heart of the Heart of the Country

A PLACE

So I have sailed the seas and come . . .
to B . . .
a small town fastened to a field in Indiana. Twice there have been twelve hundred people here to answer to the census. The town is outstandingly neat and shady, and always puts its best side to the highway. On one lawn there's even a wood or plastic iron deer.

You can reach us by crossing a creek. In the spring the lawns are green, the forsythia is singing, and even the railroad that guts the town has straight bright rails which hum when the train is coming, and the train itself has a welcome horning sound.

Down the back streets the asphalt crumbles into gravel. There's Westbrook's, with the geraniums, Horsefall's, Mott's. The sidewalk shatters. Gravel dust rises like breath behind the wagons. And I am in retirement from love.

WEATHER

In the Midwest, around the lower Lakes, the sky in the winter is heavy and close, and it is a rare day, a day to remark on, when the sky lifts and allows the heart up. I am keeping count, and as I write this page, it is eleven days since I have seen the sun.

MY HOUSE

There's a row of headless maples behind my house, cut to free the passage of electric wires. High stumps, ten feet tall, remain, and I climb these like a boy to watch the country sail away from me. They are ordinary fields, a little more uneven than they should be, since in the spring they puddle. The topsoil's thin, but only moderately stony. Corn is grown one year, soybeans another. At dusk starlings darken the single tree—a larch—which stands in the middle. When the sky moves, fields move under it. I feel, on my perch, that I've lost my years. It's as though I were living at last in my eyes, as I have always dreamed of doing, and I think then I know why I've come here: to see, and so to go out against new things—oh god how easily—like air in a breeze. It's true there are moments—foolish moments, ecstasy on a tree stump—

when I'm all but gone, scattered I like to think like seed, for I'm the sort now in the fool's position of having love left over which I'd like to lose; what good is it now to me, candy ungiven after Halloween?

A PERSON

There are vacant lots on either side of Billy Holsclaw's house. As the weather improves, they fill with hollyhocks. From spring through fall, Billy collects coal and wood and puts the lumps and pieces in piles near his door, for keeping warm is his one work. I see him most often on mild days sitting on his doorsill in the sun. I notice he's squinting a little, which is perhaps the reason he doesn't cackle as I pass. His house is the size of a single garage, and very old. It shed its paint with its youth, and its boards are a warped and weathered gray. So is Billy. He wears a short lumpy faded black coat when it's cold, otherwise he always goes about in the same loose, grease-spotted shirt and trousers. I suspect his galluses were yellow once, when they were new.

WIRES

These wires offend me. Three trees were maimed on their account, and now these wires deface the sky. They cross like a fence in front of me, enclosing the crows with the clouds. I can't reach in, but like a stick, I throw my feelings over. What is it that offends me? I am on my stump, I've built a platform there and the wires prevent my going out. The cut trees, the black wires, all the beyond birds therefore anger me. When I've wormed through a fence to reach a meadow, do I ever feel the same about the field?

THE CHURCH

The church has a steeple like the hat of a witch, and five birds, all doves, perch in its gutters.

MY HOUSE

Leaves move in the windows. I cannot tell you yet how beautiful it is, what it means. But they do move. They move in the glass.

POLITICS

. . . for all those not in love.

I've heard Batista described as a Mason. A farmer who'd seen him in Miami made this claim. He's as nice a fellow as you'd ever want to meet. Of Castro, of course, no one speaks.

For all those not in love there's law: to rule . . . to regulate . . . to rectify. I cannot write the poetry of such proposals, the poetry of politics, though sometimes—often—always now—I am in that uneasy peace of equal powers which makes a State; then I communicate by passing papers, proclamations, orders, through my bowels. Yet I was not a State with you, nor were we both together any Indiana. A squad of Pershing Rifles at the moment, I make myself Right Face! Legislation packs the screw of my intestines. Well, king of the classroom's king of the hill. You used to waddle when you walked because my sperm between your legs was draining to a towel. Teacher, poet, folded lover—like the politician, like those drunkards, ill, or those who faucet-off while pissing heartily to preach upon the force and fullness of that stream, or pause from vomiting to praise the purity and passion of their puke—I chant, I beg, I orate, I command, I sing—

Come back to Indiana—not too late!
(Or will you be a ranger to the end?)
Good-bye . . . Good-bye . . . oh, I shall
always wait
You, Larry, traveler—
stranger,
son,
—my friend—

my little girl, my poem by heart, my self, my childhood.

But I've heard Batista described as a Mason. That dries up my pity, melts my hate. Back from the garage where I have overhead it, I slap the mended fender of my car to laugh, and listen to the metal stinging tartly in my hand.

PEOPLE

Their hair in curlers and their heads wrapped in loud scarves, young mothers, fattish in trousers, lounge about in the speedwash, smoking cigarettes, eating candy, drinking pop, thumbing magazines, and screaming at their children above the whir and rumble of the machines.

At the bank a young man freshly pressed is letting himself in with a key. Along the street, delicately teetering, many grandfathers move in a dream. During the murderous heat of summer, they perch on window ledges, their feet dangling just inside the narrow shelf of shade the store has made, staring steadily into the street. Where their consciousness has gone I can't say. It's not in the eyes. Perhaps it's diffuse, all temperature and skin, like an infant's, though more mild. Near the corner there are several large overalled men employed in standing. A truck turns to be weighed on the scales at the Feed and Grain. Images drift on the drugstore window. The wind has blown the smell of cattle into town. Our eyes have been driven in like the eyes of the old men. And there's no one to have mercy on us.

VITAL DATA

There are two restaurants here and a tearoom, two bars, one bank, three barbers, one with a green shade with which he blinds his window, two groceries, a dealer in Fords, one drug, one hardware, and one appliance store, several that sell feed, grain, and farm equipment, an antique shop, a poolroom, a laundromat, three doctors, a dentist, a plumber, a vet, a funeral home in elegant repair the color of a buttercup, numerous beauty parlors which open and shut like night-blooming plants, a tiny dime and department store of no width but several floors, a hutch, home-made, where you can order, after lying down or squirming in, furniture that's been fashioned from bent lengths of stainless tubing, glowing plastic, metallic thread, and clear shellac, an American Legion Post and a root beer stand, little agencies for this and that: cosmetics, brushes, insurance, greeting cards and garden produce—anything—sample shoes—which do their business out of hats and satchels, over coffee cups and dissolving sugar, a factory for making paper sacks and pasteboard boxes that's lodged in an old brick building bearing the legend OPERA HOUSE, still faintly golden, on its roof, a library given by Carnegie, a post office, a school, a railroad station, fire station, lumberyard, telephone company, welding shop, garage . . . and spotted through the town from one end to the other in a line along the highway, gas stations to the number five.

EDUCATION

In 1833, Colin Goodykoontz, an itinerant preacher with a name from a fairytale, summed up the situation in one Indiana town this way:

> Ignorance and her squalid brood. A universal dearth of intellect. Total abstinence from literature is very generally practiced. . . . There is not a scholar in grammar or geography, or a *teacher capable* of *instructing* in them, to my knowledge. . . . Others are supplied a few months of the year with the most antiquated & unreasonable forms of teaching reading, writing & cyphering. . . . Need I stop to remind you of the host of loathsome reptiles such a stagnant pool is fitted to breed! Croaking jealousy; bloated bigotry; coiling suspicion; wormish blindness; crocodile malice!

Things have changed since then, but in none of the respects mentioned.

BUSINESS

One side section of street is blocked off with sawhorses. Hard, thin, bitter men in blue jeans, cowboy boots and hats, untruck a dinky carnival. The merchants are promoting themselves. There will be free rides, raucous music, parades and coneys, pop, popcorn, candy, cones, awards and drawings, with all you can endure of pinch, push, bawl, shove, shout, scream, shriek, and bellow. Children pedal past on decorated bicycles, their wheels a blur of color, streaming crinkled paper and excited dogs. A little later, there's a pet show for a prize—dogs, cats, birds, sheep, ponies, goats—none of which wins. The whirlabouts whirl about. The Ferris wheel climbs dizzily into the sky as far as a tall man on tiptoe might be persuaded to reach, and the irritated operators measure the height and weight of every child with sour eyes to see if they are safe for the machines. An electrical megaphone repeatedly trumpets the names of the generous sponsors. The following day they do not allow the refuse to remain long in the street.

MY HOUSE, THIS PLACE AND BODY

I have met with some mischance, wings withering, as Plato says obscurely, and across the breadth of Ohio, like heaven on a table, I've fallen as far as the poet, to the sixth sort of body, this house in B, in Indiana, with its blue and gray bewitching windows, holy magical insides. Great thick evergreens protect its entry. And I live *in*.

Lost in the corn rows, I remember feeling just another stalk, and thus this country takes me over in the way I occupy myself when I am well . . . completely—to the edge of both my house and body. No one notices, when they walk by, that I am brimming in the doorways. My house, this place and body, I've come in mourning to be born in. To anybody else it's pretty silly: love. Why should I feel a loss? How am I bereft? She was never mine; she was a fiction, always a golden tomgirl, barefoot, with an adolescent's slouch and a boy's taste for sports and fishing, a figure out of Twain, or worse, in Riley. Age cannot be kind.

There's little hand-in-hand here . . . not in B. No one touches except in rage. Occasionally girls will twine their arms about each other and lurch along, school out, toward home and play. I dreamed my lips would drift down your back like a skiff on a river. I'd follow a vein with the point of my finger, hold your bare feet in my naked hands.

THE SAME PERSON

Billy Holsclaw lives alone—how alone it is impossible to fathom. In the post office he talks greedily to me about the weather. His head bobs on a wild flood of words, and I take this violence to be a measure of his eagerness for speech. He badly needs a shave, coal dust has layered his face, he spits when he speaks, and his fingers pick at his tatters. He wobbles out in the wind when I leave him, a paper sack mashed in the fold of his arm, the leaves blowing past him, and our encounter drives me sadly home to poetry—where there's no answer. Billy closes his door and carries coal or wood to his fire and closes his eyes, and there's simply no way of knowing how lonely and empty he is or whether he's as vacant and barren and loveless as the rest of us are—here in the heart of the country.

WEATHER

For we're always out of luck here. That's just how it is—for instance in the winter. The sides of the buildings, the roofs, the limbs of the trees are gray. Streets, sidewalks, faces, feelings—they are gray. Speech is gray, and the grass where it shows. Every flank and front, each top is gray. Everything is gray: hair, eyes, window glass, the hawkers' bills and touters' posters, lips, teeth, poles and metal signs—they're gray, quite gray. Cars are gray. Boots, shoes, suits, hats, gloves are gray. Horses, sheep, and cows, cats killed in the road, squirrels in the same way, sparrows, doves, and pigeons, all are gray, everything is gray, and everyone is out of luck who lives here.

A similar haze turns the summer sky milky, and the air muffles your head and shoulders like a sweater you've got caught in. In the summer light, too, the sky darkens a moment when you open your eyes. The heat is pure distraction. Steeped in our fluids, miserable in the folds of our bodies, we can scarcely think of anything but our sticky parts. Hot cyclonic winds and storms of dust crisscross the country. In many places, given an indifferent push, the wind will still coast for miles, gathering resource and edge as it goes, cunning and force. According to the season, paper, leaves, field litter, seeds, snow, fill up the fences. Sometimes I think the land is flat because the winds have leveled it, they blow so constantly. In any case, a gale can grow in a field of corn that's as hot as a draft from hell, and to receive it is one of the most dismaying experiences of this life, though the smart of the same wind in winter is more humiliating, and in that sense even worse. But in the spring it rains as well, and the trees fill with ice.

PLACE

Many small Midwestern towns are nothing more than rural slums, and this community could easily become one. Principally, during the first decade of the century, though there were many earlier instances, well-to-do farmers moved to town and built fine homes to contain them in their retirement. Others desired a more social life, and so lived in, driving to their fields like storekeepers to their businesses. These houses are now dying like the bereaved who inhabit them; they are slowly losing their senses—deafness, blindness, forgetfulness, mumbling, an insecure gait, an uncontrollable trembling has overcome them. Some kind of Northern Snopes will occupy them next: large-familied, Catholic, Democratic, scrambling, vigorous, poor; and since the parents will work in larger, nearby towns, the children will be loosed upon themselves and upon the hapless neighbors much as the fabulous Khan loosed his legendary horde. These Snopes will undertake makeshift repairs with materials that other people have thrown away; paint halfway round their house, then quit; almost certainly maintain an ugly loud cantankerous dog and underfeed a pair of cats to keep the rodents down. They will collect piles of possibly useful junk in the back yard, park their cars in the front, live largely leaning over engines, give not a hoot for the land, the old community, the hallowed ways, the established clans. Weakening widow ladies have already begun to hire large rude youths from families such as these to rake and mow and tidy the grounds they will inherit.

PEOPLE

In the cinders at the station boys sit smoking steadily in darkened cars, their arms bent out the windows, white shirts glowing behind the glass. Nine o'clock is the best time. They sit in a line facing the highway—two or three or four of them—idling their engines. As you walk by a machine may growl at you or a pair of headlights flare up briefly. In a moment one will pull out, spinning cinders behind it, to stalk impatiently up and down the dark streets or roar half a mile into the country before returning to its place in line and pulling up.

MY HOUSE, MY CAT, MY COMPANY

I must organize myself. I must, as they say, pull myself together, dump this cat from my lap, stir—yes, resolve, move, do. But do what? My will is like the rosy dustlike light in this room: soft, diffuse, and gently comforting. It lets me do . . . anything . . . nothing. My ears hear what they happen to; I eat what's put before me; my eyes see what blunders into them; my thoughts are not thoughts, they are dreams. I'm empty or I'm full . . . depending; and I cannot choose. I sink my claws in Tick's fur and scratch the bones of his back until his rear rises amorously. Mr. Tick, I murmur, I must organize myself. I must pull myself together. And Mr. Tick rolls over on his belly, all ooze.

I spill Mr. Tick when I've rubbed his stomach. Shoo. He steps away slowly, his long tail rhyming with his paws. How beautifully he moves, I think; how beautifully he accepts. So I rise and wander from room to room, up and down, gazing through most of my forty-one windows. How well this house receives its loving too. Let out like Mr. Tick, my eyes sink in the shrubbery. I am not here; I've passed the glass, passed second-story spaces, flown by branches, brilliant berries, to the ground, grass high in seed and leafage every season; and it is the same as when I passed above you in my aged, ardent body; it's, in short, a kind of love; and I am learning to restore myself, my house, my body, by paying court to gardens, cats, and running water, and with neighbors keeping company.

Mrs. Desmond is my right-hand friend; she's eighty-five. A thin white mist of hair, fine and tangled, manifests the climate of her mind. She is habitually suspicious, fretful, nervous. Burglars break in at noon. Children trespass. Even now they are shaking the pear tree, stealing rhubarb, denting lawn. Flies caught in the screen and numbed by frost awake in the heat to buzz and scrape the metal cloth and frighten her, though she is deaf to me, and consequently cannot hear them. Boards creak, the wind whistles across the chimney mouth, drafts cruise like fish through the hollow rooms. It is herself she hears, her own flesh failing, for only death will preserve her from those daily chores she climbs like stairs, and all that anxious waiting. Is it now, she wonders. No? Then: is it now?

We do not converse. She visits me to talk. My task to murmur. She talks about her grandson, her daughter who lives in Delphi, her sister or her husband—both gone—obscure friends—dead—obscurer aunts and uncles—lost—ancient neighbors, members of her church or of her clubs—passed or passing on; and in this way she brings the ends of her life together with a terrifying rush: she is a girl, a wife, a mother, widow, all at once. All at once—appalling—but I believe it; I wince in expectation of the clap. Her talk's a fence—a shade drawn, window fastened, door that's locked—for no one dies taking tea in a kitchen; and as her years compress and begin to jumble, I really believe in the brevity of life; I sweat in my wonder; death is the dog down the street, the angry gander, bedroom spider, goblin who's come to get her; and it occurs to me that in my listening posture I'm the boy who suffered the winds of my grandfather with an exactly similar politeness, that I am, right now, all my ages, out in elbows, as angular as badly stacked cards. Thus was I, when I loved you, every man I could be, youth and child—far from enough—and you, so strangely ambiguous a being, met me, heart for spade, play after play, the whole run of our suits.

Mr. Tick, you do me honor. You not only lie in my lap, but you remain alive there, coiled like a fetus. Through your deep nap, I feel you hum. You are, and are not, a machine. You are alive, alive exactly, and it means nothing to you—much to me. You are a cat—you cannot understand—you are a cat so easily. Your nature is not something you must rise to. You, not I, live in: in house, in skin, in shrubbery. Yes. I think I shall hat my head with a steeple; turn church; devour people. Mr. Tick, though, has a tail he can twitch, he need not fly his Fancy. Claws, not metrical schema, poetry his paws; while smoothing . . . smoothing . . . smoothing roughly, his tongue laps its neatness. O Mr. Tick, I know you; you are an electrical penis. Go on now, shoo. Mrs. Desmond doesn't like you. She thinks you will tangle yourself in her legs and she will fall. You murder her birds, she knows, and walk upon her roof with death in your jaws. I must gather myself together for a bound. What age is it I'm at right now. I wonder. The heart, don't they always say, keeps the true time. Mrs. Desmond is knocking. Faintly, you'd think, but she pounds. She's brought me a cucumber. I believe she believes I'm a woman. Come in, Mrs. Desmond, thank you, be my company, it looks lovely, and have tea. I'll slice it, crisp, with cream, for luncheon, each slice as thin as me.

POLITICS

O all ye isolate and separate powers, Sing! Sing, and sing in such a way that from a distance it will seem a harmony, a a Strindberg play, a friendship ring . . . so happy—happy, happy, happy—as here we go hand in handling, up and down. Our union was a singing, though we were silent in the songs we sang like single notes are silent in a symphony. In no sense sober, we barbershopped together and never heard the discords in our music or saw ourselves as dirty, cheap, or silly. Yet cats have worn out better shoes than those thrown through our love songs at us. Hush. Be patient—prudent—politic. Still, Cleveland killed you, Mr. Crane. Were you not politic enough and fond of being beaten? Like a piece of sewage, the city shat you from its stern three hundred miles from history—beyond the loving reach of sailors. Well, I'm not a poet who puts Paris to his temple in his youth to blow himself from Idaho, or—fancy that—Missouri. My god, I said, this is my country, but must my country go so far as Terre Haute or Whiting, go so far as Gary?

When the Russians first announced the launching of their satellite, many people naturally refused to believe them. Later others were outraged that they had sent a dog around the earth. I wouldn't want to take that mutt from out that metal flying thing if he's still living when he lands, our own dog catcher said; anybody knows you shut a dog up by himself to toss around the first thing he'll be setting on to do you let him out is bite somebody.

This Midwest. A dissonance of parts and people, we are a consonance of Towns. Like a man grown fat in everything but heart, we overlabor; our outlook never really urban, never rural either, we enlarge and linger at the same time. As Alice both changed and remained in her story. You are a blond. I put my hand upon your belly; feel it tremble from my trembling. We always drive large cars in my section of the country. How could you be a comfort to me now?

MORE VITAL DATA

The town is exactly fifty houses, trailers, stores, and miscellaneous buildings long, but in places no streets deep. It takes on width as you drive south, always adding to the east. Most of the dwellings are fairly spacious farm houses in the customary white, with wide wraparound porches and tall narrow windows, though there are many of the grander kind—fretted, scalloped, turreted, and decorated with clapboards set at angles or on end, with stained-glass windows at the stair landings and lots of wrought iron full of fancy curls—and a few of these look like castles in their rarer brick. Old stables serve as garages now, and the lots are large to contain them and the vegetable and flower gardens which, ultimately, widows plant and weed and then entirely disappear in. The shade is ample, the grass is good, the sky a glorious fall violet; the apple trees are heavy and red, the roads are calm and empty; corn has sifted from the chains of tractored wagons to speckle the streets with gold and with the russet fragments of the cob, and a man would be a fool who wanted, blessed with this, to live anywhere else in the world.

EDUCATION

Buses like great orange animals move through the early light to school. There the children will be taught to read and warned against Communism. By Miss Janet Jakes. That's not her name. Her name is Helen something—Scott or James. A teacher twenty years. She's now worn fine and smooth, and has a face, Wilfred says, like a mail-order ax. Her voice is hoarse, and she has a cough. For she screams abuse. The children stare, their faces blank. This is the thirteenth week. They are used to it. You will all, she shouts, you will all draw pictures of me. No. She is a Mrs.—someone's missus. And in silence they set to work while Miss Jakes jabs hairpins in her hair. Wilfred says an ax, but she has those rimless tinted glasses, graying hair, an almost dimpled chin. I must concentrate. I must stop making up things. I must give myself to life; let it mold me: that's what they say in *Wisdom's Monthly Digest* every day. Enough, enough—you've been at it long enough; and the children rise formally a row at a time to present their work to her desk. No, she wears rims; it's her chin that's dimpleless. Well, it will take more than a tablespoon of features to sweeten that face. So she grimly shuffles their sheets, examines her reflection crayoned on them. I would not dare . . . allow a child . . . to put a line around me. Though now and then she smiles like a nick in the blade, in the end these drawings depress her. I could not bear it—how can she ask?—that anyone . . . draw me. Her anger's lit. That's why she does it: flame. There go her eyes; the pink in her glasses brightens, dims. She is a pumpkin, and her rage is breathing like the candle in. No, she shouts, no—the cartoon trembling—no, John Mauck, John Stewart Mauck, this will not do. The picture flutters from her fingers. You've made me too muscular.

I work on my poetry. I remember my friends, associates, my students, by their names. Their names are Maypop, Dormouse, Upsydaisy. Their names are Gladiolus, Callow Bladder, Prince and Princess Oleo, Hieronymus, Cardinal Mummum, Mr. Fitchew, The Silken Howdah, Spot. Sometimes you're Tom Sawyer, Huckleberry Finn; it is perpetually summer; your buttocks are my pillow; we are adrift on a raft; your back is our river. Sometimes you are Major Barbara, sometimes a goddess who kills men in battle, sometimes you are soft like a shower of water; you are bread in my mouth.

I do not work on my poetry. I forget my friends, associates, my students, and their names: Gramophone, Blowgun, Pickle, Serenade . . . Marge the Barge, Arena, Uberhaupt . . . Doctor Dildoe, The Fog Machine. For I am now in B, in Indiana: out of job and out of patience, out of love and time and money, out of bread and out of body, in a temper, Mrs. Desmond, out of tea. So shut your fist up, bitch, you bag of death; go bang another door; go die, my dearie. Die, life-deaf old lady. Spill your breath. Fall over like a frozen board. Gray hair grows from the nose of your mind. You are a skull already—*memento mori*—the foreskin retracts from your teeth. Will your plastic gums last longer than your bones, and color their grinning? And is your twot still hazel-hairy, or are you bald as a ditch? . . . bitch. . . . . . bitch. . . . . bitch. I wanted to be famous, but you bring me age—my emptiness. Was it *that* which I thought would balloon me above the rest? Love? where are you? . . . love me. I want to rise so high, I said, that when I shit I won't miss anybody.

BUSINESS

For most people, business is poor. Nearby cities have siphoned off all but a neighborhood trade. Except for feed and grain and farm supplies, you stand a chance to sell only what runs out to buy. Chevrolet has quit, and Frigidaire. A locker plant has left its afterimage. The lumberyard has been, so far, six months about its going. Gas stations change hands clumsily, a restaurant becomes available, a grocery closes. One day they came and knocked the cornices from the watch repair and pasted campaign posters on the windows. Torn across, by now, by boys, they urge you still to vote for half an orange beblazoned man who as a whole one failed two years ago to win at his election. Everywhere, in this manner, the past speaks, and it mostly speaks of failure. The empty stores, the old signs and dusty fixtures, the debris in alleys, the flaking paint and rusty gutters, the heavy locks and sagging boards: they say the same disagreeable things. What do the sightless windows see, I wonder, when the sun throws a passerby against them? Here a stair unfolds toward the street—dark, rickety, and treacherous—and I always feel, as I pass it, that if I just went carefully up and turned the corner at the landing. I would find myself out of the world. But I've never had the courage.

THAT SAME PERSON

The weeds catch up with Billy. In pursuit of the hollyhocks, they rise in coarse clumps all around the front of his house. Billy has to stamp down a circle by his door like a dog or cat does turning round to nest up, they're so thick. What particularly troubles me is that winter will find the weeds still standing stiff and tindery to take the sparks which Billy's little mortarless chimney spouts. It's true that fires are fun here. The town whistle, which otherwise only blows for noon (and there's no noon on Sunday), signals the direction of the fire by the length and number of its blasts, the volunteer firemen rush past in their cars and trucks, houses empty their owners along the street every time like an illustration in a children's book. There are many bikes, too, and barking dogs, and sometimes—halleluiah—the fire's right here in town—a vacant lot of weeds and stubble flaming up. But I'd rather it weren't Billy or Billy's lot or house. Quite selfishly, I want him to remain the way he is—counting his sticks and logs, sitting on his sill in the soft early sun—though I'm not sure what his presence means to me . . . or to anyone. Nevertheless, I keep wondering whether, given time, I might not someday find a figure in our language which would serve him faithfully, and furnish his poverty and loneliness richly out.

WIRES

Where sparrows sit like fists. Doves fly the steeple. In mist the wires change perspective, rise and twist. If they led to you, I would know what they were. Thoughts passing often, like the starlings who flock these fields at evening to sleep in the trees beyond, would form a family of paths like this; they'd foot down the natural height of air to just about a bird's perch. But they do not lead to you.

Of whose beauty it was sung
She shall make the old man young

They fasten me.

If I walked straight on, in my present mood, I would reach the Wabash. It's not a mood in which I'd choose to conjure you. Similes dangle like baubles from me. This time of year the river is slow and shallow, the clay banks crack in the sun, weeds surprise the sandbars. The air is moist and I am sweating. It's impossible to rhyme in this dust. Everything—sky, the cornfield, stump, wild daisies, my old clothes and pressless feelings—seem fabricated for installment purchase. Yes. Christ. I am suffering a summer Christmas; and I cannot walk under the wires. The sparrows scatter like handfuls of gravel. Really, wires are voices in thin strips. They are words wound in cables. Bars of connection.

WEATHER

I would rather it were the weather that was to blame for what I am and what my friends and neighbors are—we who live here in the heart of the country. Better the weather, the wind, the pale dying snow . . . the snow—why not the snow? There's never much really, not around the lower Lakes anyway, not enough to boast about, not enough to be useful. My father tells how the snow in the Dakotas would sweep to the roofs of the barns in the old days, and he and his friends could sled on the crust that would form because the snow was so fiercely driven. In Bemidji trees have been known to explode. That would be something—if the trees in Davenport or Francisville or Carbondale or Niles were to go blam some winter—blam! blam! blam! all the way down the gray, cindery, snow-sick streets.

A cold fall rain is blackening the trees or the air is like lilac and full of parachuting seeds. Who cares to live in any season but his own? Still I suspect the secret's in this snow, the secret of our sickness, if we could only diagnose it, for we are all dying like the elms in Urbana. This snow—like our skin it covers the country. Later dust will do it. Right now—snow. Mud presently. But it is snow without any laughter in it, a pale gray pudding thinly spread on stiff toast, and if that seems a strange description, it's accurate all the same. Of course soot blackens everything, but apart from that, we are never sufficiently cold here. The flakes as they come, alive and burning, we cannot retain, for if our temperatures fall, they rise promptly again, just as, in the summer, they bob about in the same feckless way. Suppose though . . . suppose they were to rise some August, climb and rise, and then hang in the hundreds like a hawk through December, what a desert we could make of ourselves—from Chicago to Cairo, from Hammond to Columbus—what beautiful Death Valleys.

PLACE

I would rather it were the weather. It drives us in upon ourselves—an unlucky fate. Of course there is enough to stir our wonder anywhere: there's enough to love, anywhere, if one is strong enough, if one is diligent enough, if one is perceptive, patient, kind enough—whatever it takes; and surely it's better to live in the country, to live on a prairie by a drawing of rivers, in Iowa or Illinois or Indiana, say, than in any city, in any stinking fog of human beings, in any blooming orchard of machines. It ought to be. The cities are swollen and poisonous with people. It ought to be better. Man has never been a fit environment for man—for rats, maybe, rats do nicely, or for dogs or cats and the household beetle.

And how long the street is, nowadays. These endless walls are fallen to keep back the tides of earth. Brick could be beautiful but we have covered it gradually with gray industrial vomits. Age does not make concrete genial, and asphalt is always—like America—twenty-one, until it breaks up in crumbs like stale cake. The brick, the asphalt, the concrete, the dancing signs and garish posters, the feed and excrement of the automobile, the litter of its inhabitants: they compose, they decorate, they line our streets, and there is nowhere, nowadays, our streets can't reach.

A man in the city has no natural thing by which to measure himself. His parks are potted plants. Nothing can live and remain free where he resides but the pigeon, starling, sparrow, spider, cockroach, mouse, moth, fly and weed, and he laments the existence of even these and makes his plans to poison them. The zoo? There *is* the zoo. Through its bars the city man stares at the great cats and dully sucks his ice. Living, alas, among men and their marvels, the city man supposes that his happiness depends on establishing, somehow, a special kind of harmonious accord with others. The novelists of the city, of slums and crowds, they call it love—and break their pens.

Wordsworth feared the accumulation of men in cities. He foresaw their "degrading thirst after outrageous stimulation," and some of their hunger for love. Living in a city, among so many, dwelling in the heat and tumult of incessant movement, a man's affairs are touch and go—that's all. It's not surprising that the novelists of the slums, the cities, and the crowds, should find that sex is but a scratch to ease a tickle, that we're most human when we're sitting on the john, and that the justest image of our life is in full passage through the plumbing.

> That man, immur'd in cities, still retains
> His inborn inextinguishable thirst
> Of rural scenes, compensating his loss
> By supplemental shifts, the best he may.

Come into the country, then. The air nimbly and sweetly recommends itself unto our gentle senses. Here, growling tractors tear the earth. Dust roils up behind them. Drivers sit jouncing under bright umbrellas. They wear refrigerated hats and steer by looking at the tracks they've cut behind them, their transistors blaring. Close to the land, are they? good companions to the soil? Tell me: do they live in harmony with the alternating seasons?

It's a lie of old poetry. The modern husbandman uses chemicals from cylinders and sacks, spike-ball-and-claw machines, metal sheds, and cost accounting. Nature in the old sense does not matter. It does not exist. Our farmer's only mystical attachment is to parity. And if he does not realize that cows and corn are simply different kinds of chemical engine, he cannot expect to make a go of it.

It isn't necessary to suppose our cows have feelings; our neighbor hasn't as many as he used to have either; but think of it this way a moment, you can correct for the human imputations later: how would it feel to nurse those strange tentacled calves with their rubber, glass, and metal lips, their stainless eyes?

PEOPLE

Aunt Pet's still able to drive her car—a high square Ford—even though she walks with difficulty and a stout stick. She has a watery gaze, a smooth plump face despite her age, and jet black hair in a bun. She has the slowest smile of anyone I ever saw, but she hates dogs, and not very long ago cracked the back of one she cornered in her garden. To prove her vigor she will tell you this, her smile breaking gently while she raises the knob of her stick to the level of your eyes.

HOUSE, MY BREATH AND WINDOW

My window is a grave, and all that lies within it's dead. No snow is falling. There's no haze. It is not still, not silent. Its images are not an animal that waits, for movement is no demonstration. I have seen the sea slack, life bubble through a body without a trace, its spheres impervious as soda's. Downwound, the whore at wagtag clicks and clacks. Leaves wiggle. Grass sways. A bird chirps, pecks the ground. An auto wheel in penning circles keeps its rigid spokes. These images are stones; they are memorials. Beneath this sea lies sea: god rest it . . . rest the world beyond my window, me in front of my reflection, above this page, my shade. Death is not so still, so silent, since silence implies a falling quiet, stillness a stopping, containing, holding in; for death is time in a clock, like Mr. Tick, electric . . . like wind through a windup poet. And my blear floats out to visible against the glass, befog its country and bespill myself. The mist lifts slowly from the fields in the morning. No one now would say: the Earth throws back its covers; it is rising from sleep. Why is the feeling foolish? The image is too Greek. I used to gaze at you so wantonly your body blushed. Imagine: wonder: that my eyes could cause such flowering. Ah, my friend, your face is pale, the weather cloudy; a street has been felled through your chin, bare trees do nothing, houses take root in their rectangles, a steeple stands up in your head. You speak of loving; then give me a kiss. The pane is cold. On icy mornings the fog rises to greet me (as you always did); the barns and other buildings, rather than ghostly, seem all the more substantial for looming, as if they grew in themselves while I watched (as you always did). Oh my approach, I suppose, was like breath in a rubber monkey. Nevertheless, on the road along the Wabash in the morning, though the trees are sometimes obscured by fog, their reflection floats serenely on the river, reasoning the banks, the sycamores in French rows. Magically, the world tips. I'm led to think that only those who grow down live (which will scarcely win me twenty-five from *Wisdom's Monthly Digest*), but I find I write that only those who live down grow; and what I write, I hold, whatever I really know. My every word's inverted, or reversed—or I am. I held you, too, that way. You were so utterly provisional, subject to my change. I could inflate your bosom with a kiss, disperse your skin with gentleness, enter your vagina from within, and make my love emerge like a fresh sex. The pane is cold. Honesty is cold, my inside lover. The sun looks, through the mist, like a plum on the tree of heaven, or a bruise on the slope of your belly. Which? The grass crawls with frost. We meet on this window, the world and I, inelegantly, swimmers of the glass; and swung wrong way round to one another, the world seems in. The world—how grand, how monumental, grave and deadly, that word is: the world, my house and poetry. All poets have their inside lovers. Wee penis does not belong to me, or any of this foggery. It is *his* property which he's thrust through what's womanly of me to set down this. These wooden houses in their squares, gray streets and fallen sidewalks, standing trees, your name I've written sentimentally across my breath into the whitening air, pale birds: they exist in me now because of him. I gazed with what intensity . . . A bush in the excitement of its roses could not have bloomed so beautifully as you did then. It was a look I'd like to give this page. For that is poetry: to bring within about, to change.

POLITICS

Sports, politics, and religion are the three passions of the badly educated. They are the Midwest's open sores. Ugly to see, a source of constant discontent, they sap the body's strength. Appalling quantities of money, time, and energy are wasted on them. The rural mind is narrow, passionate, and reckless on these matters. Greed, however shortsighted and direct, will not alone account for it. I have known men, for instance, who for years have voted squarely against their interests. Nor have I ever noticed that their surly Christian views prevented them from urging forward the smithereening, say, of Russia, China, Cuba, or Korea. And they tend to back their country like they back their local team: they have a fanatical desire to win; yelling is their forte; and if things go badly, they are inclined to sack the coach. All in all, then, Birch is a good name. It stands for the bigot's stick, the wild-child-tamer's cane.

Forgetfulness—is that their object?

Oh, I was new, I thought. A fresh start; new cunt, new climate, and new country—there you were, and I was pioneer, and had no history. That language hurts me, too, my dear. You'll never hear it.

FINAL VITAL DATA

The Modern Homemakers' Demonstration Club. The Prairie Home Demonstration Club. The Night-outer's Home Demonstration Club. The IOOF, FFF, VFW, WCTU, WSCS, 4-H, 40 and 8, Psi Iota Chi, and PTA. The Boy and Girl Scouts, Rainbows, Masons, Indians and Rebekah Lodge. Also the Past Noble Grand Club of the Rebekah Lodge. As well as the Moose and the Ladies of the Moose. The Elks, the Eagles, the Jaynettes and the Eastern Star. The Women's Literary Club, the Hobby Club, the Art Club, the Sunshine Society, the Dorcas Society, the Pythian Sisters, the Pilgrim Youth Fellowship, the American Legion, the American Legion Auxiliary, the American Legion Junior Auxiliary, the Garden Club, the Bridge for Fun Club, the What-can-you-do? Club, the Get Together Club, the Coterie Club, the Worthwhile Club, the Let's Help Our Town Club, the No Name Club, the Forget-me-not Club, the Merry-go-round Club . . .

EDUCATION

Has a quarter disappeared from Paula Frosty's pocket book? Imagine the landscape of that face: no crayon could engender it; soft wax is wrong; thin wire in trifling snips might do the trick. Paula Frosty and Christopher Roger accuse the pale and splotchy Cheryl Pipes. But Miss Jakes, I *saw* her. Miss Jakes is so extremely vexed she snaps her pencil. What else is missing? I appoint you a detective, John: search her desk. Gum, candy, paper, pencils, marble, round eraser—whose? A thief. I can't watch her all the time, I'm here to teach. Poor pale fossetted Cheryl, it's determined, can't return the money because she took it home and spent it. Cindy, Janice, John, and Pete—you four who sit around her—you will be detectives this whole term to watch her. A thief. In all my time. Miss Jakes turns, unfists, and turns again. I'll handle you, she cries. To think. A thief. In all my years. Then she writes on the blackboard the name of Cheryl Pipes and beneath that the figure twenty-five with a large sign for cents. Now Cheryl, she says, this won't be taken off until you bring that money out of home, out of home straight up to here, Miss Jakes says, tapping her desk.

Which is three days.

ANOTHER PERSON

I was raking leaves when Uncle Halley introduced himself to me. He said his name came from the comet, and that his mother had borne him prematurely in her fright of it. I thought of Hobbes, whom fear of the Spanish Armada had hurried into birth, and so I believed Uncle Halley to honor the philosopher, though Uncle Halley is a liar, and neither the one hundred twenty-nine nor the fifty-three he ought to be. That fall the leaves had burned themselves out on the trees, the leaf lobes had curled, and now they flocked noisily down the street and were broken in the wires of my rake. Uncle Halley was himself (like Mrs. Desmond and history generally) both deaf and implacable, and he shooed me down his basement stairs to a room set aside there for stacks of newspapers reaching to the ceiling, boxes of leaflets and letters and programs, racks of photo albums, scrapbooks, bundles of rolled-up posters and maps, flags and pennants and slanting piles of dusty magazines devoted mostly to motoring and the Christian ethic. I saw a bird cage, a tray of butterflies, a bugle, a stiff straw boater and all kinds of tassels tied to a coat tree. He still possessed and had on display the steering lever from his first car, a linen duster, driving gloves and goggles, photographs along the wall of himself, his friends, and his various machines, a shell from the first war, a record of "Ramona" nailed through its hole to a post, walking sticks and fanciful umbrellas, shoes of all sorts (his baby shoes, their counters broken, were held in sorrow beneath my nose—they had not been bronzed, but he might have them done someday before he died, he said), countless boxes of medals, pins, beads, trinkets, toys, and keys (I scarcely saw—they flowed like jewels from his palms), pictures of downtown when it was only a path by the railroad station, a brightly colored globe of the world with a dent in Poland, antique guns, belt buckles, buttons, souvenir plates and cups and saucers (I can't remember all of it—I won't), but I recall how shamefully, how rudely, how abruptly, I fled, a good story in my mouth but death in my nostrils; and how afterward I busily, righteously, burned my leaves as if I were purging the world of its years. I still wonder if this town—its life, and mine now—isn't really a record like the one of "Ramona" that I used to crank around on my grandmother's mahogany Victrola through lonely rainy days as a kid.

THE FIRST PERSON

Billy's like the coal he's found: spilled, mislaid, discarded. The sky's no comfort. His house and his body are dying together. His windows are boarded. And now he's reduced to his hands. I suspect he has glaucoma. At any rate he can scarcely see, and weeds his yard of rubble on his hands and knees. Perhaps he's a surgeon cleansing a wound or an ardent and tactile lover. I watch, I must say, apprehensively. Like mine-war detectors, his hands graze in circles ahead of him. Your nipples were the color of your eyes. Pebble. Snarl of paper. Length of twine. He leans down closely, picks up something silvery, holds it near his nose. Foil? cap? coin? He has within him—what, I wonder? Does he know more now because he fingers everything and has to sniff to see? It would be romantic cruelty to think so. He bends the down on your arms like a breeze. You wrote me: something is strange when we don't understand. I write in return: I think when I loved you I fell to my death.

Billy, I could read to you from Beddoes; he's your man perhaps; he held with dying, freed his blood of its arteries; and he said that there were many wretched love-ill fools like me lying alongside the last bone of their former selves, as full of spirit and speech, nonetheless, as Mrs. Desmond, Uncle Halley and the Ferris wheel, Aunt Pet, Miss Jakes, Ramona or the megaphone; yet I reverse him finally, Billy, on no evidence but braggadocio, and I declare that though my inner organs were devoured long ago, the worm which swallowed down my parts still throbs and glows like a crystal palace.

Yes, you were younger. I was Uncle Halley, the museum man and infrequent meteor. Here is my first piece of ass. They weren't so flat in those days, had more round, more juice. And over here's the sperm I've spilled, nicely jarred and clearly labeled. Look at this tape like lengths of intestine where I've stored my spew, the endless worm of words I've written, a hundred million emissions or more: oh I was quite a man right from the start; even when unconscious in my cradle, from crotch to cranium, I was erectile tissue; though mostly, after the manner approved by Plato, I had intercourse by eye. Never mind, old Holsclaw, you are blind. We pull down darkness when we go to bed; put out like Oedipus the actually offending organ, and train our touch to lies. All cats are gray, says Mr. Tick; so under cover of glaucoma you are sack gray too, and cannot be distinguished from a stallion.

I must pull myself together, get a grip, just as they say, but I feel spilled, bewildered, quite mislaid. I did not restore my house to its youth, but to its age. Hunting you hitch through the hollyhocks. I'm inclined to say you aren't half the cripple I am, for there is nothing left of me but mouth. However, I resist the impulse. It is another lie of poetry. My organs are all there, though it's there where I fail—at the roots of my experience. Poet of the spiritual, Rilke, weren't you? yet that's what you said. Poetry, like love, is—in and out—a physical caress. I can't tolerate any more of my sophistries about spirit, mind, and breath. Body equals being, and if your weight goes down, you are the less.

HOUSEHOLD APPLES

I knew nothing about apples. Why should I? My country came in my childhood, and I dreamed of sitting among the blooms like the bees. I failed to spray the pear tree too. I doubled up under them at first, admiring the sturdy low branches I should have pruned, and later I acclaimed the blossoms. Shortly after the fruit formed there were falls—not many—apples the size of goodish stones which made me wobble on my ankles when I walked about the yard. Sometimes a piece crushed by a heel would cling on the shoe to track the house. I gathered a few and heaved them over the wires. A slingshot would have been splendid. Hard, an unattractive green, the worms had them. Before long I realized the worms had them all. Even as the apples reddened, lit their tree, they were being swallowed. The birds preferred the pears, which were small—sugar pears I think they're called—with thick skins of graying green that ripen on toward violet. So the fruit fell, and once I made some applesauce by quartering and paring hundreds; but mostly I did nothing, left them, until suddenly, overnight it seemed, in that ugly late September heat we often have in Indiana, my problem was upon me.

My childhood came in the country. I remember, now, the flies on our snowy luncheon table. As we cleared away they would settle, fastidiously scrub themselves and stroll to the crumbs to feed where I would kill them in crowds with a swatter. It was quite a game to catch them taking off. I struck heavily since I didn't mind a few stains; they'd wash. The swatter was a square of screen bound down in red cloth. It drove no air ahead of it to give them warning. They might have thought they'd flown headlong into a summered window. The faint pink dot where they had died did not rub out as I'd supposed, and after years of use our luncheon linen would faintly, pinkly, speckle.

The country became my childhood. Flies braided themselves on the flypaper in my grandmother's house. I can smell the bakery and the grocery and the stables and the dairy in that small Dakota town I knew as a kid; knew as I dreamed I'd know your body, as I've known nothing, before or since; knew as the flies knew, in the honest, unchaste sense: the burned house, hose-wet, which drew a mist of insects like the blue smoke of its smolder, and gangs of boys, moist-lipped, destructive as its burning. Flies have always impressed me; they are so persistently alive. Now they were coating the ground beneath my trees. Some were ordinary flies; there were the large blue-green ones; there were swarms of fruit flies too, and the red-spotted scavenger beetle; there were a few wasps, several sorts of bees and butterflies—checkers, sulphurs, monarchs, commas, question marks—and delicate dragonflies . . . but principally houseflies and horseflies and bottleflies, flies and more flies in clusters around the rotting fruit. They loved the pears. Inside, they fed. If you picked up a pear, they flew, and the pear became skin and stem. They were everywhere the fruit was: in the tree still—apples like a hive for them—or where the fruit littered the ground, squashing itself as you stepped . . . there was no help for it. The flies droned, feasting on the sweet juice. No one could go near the trees; I could not climb; so I determined at last to labor like Hercules. There were fruit baskets in the barn. Collecting them and kneeling under the branches, I began to gather remains. Deep in the strong rich smell of the fruit, I began to hum myself. The fruit caved in at the touch. Glistening red apples, my lifting disclosed, had families of beetles, flies, and bugs, devouring their rotten undersides. There were streams of flies; there were lakes and cataracts and rivers of flies, seas and oceans. The hum was heavier, higher, than the hum of the bees when they came to the blooms in the spring, though the bees were there, among the flies, ignoring me—ignoring everyone. As my work went on and juice covered my hands and arms, they would form a sleeve, black and moving, like knotty wool. No caress could have been more indifferently complete. Still I rose fearfully, ramming my head in the branches, apples bumping against me before falling, bursting with bugs. I'd snap my hand sharply but the flies would cling to the sweet. I could toss a whole cluster into a basket from several feet. As the pear or apple lit, they would explosively rise, like monads for a moment, windowless, certainly, with respect to one another, sugar their harmony. I had to admit, though, despite my distaste, that my arm had never been more alive, oftener or more gently kissed. Those hundreds of feet were light. In washing them off, I pretended the hose was a pump. What have I missed? Childhood is a lie of poetry.

THE CHURCH

Friday night. Girls in dark skirts and white blouses sit in ranks and scream in concert. They carry funnels loosely stuffed with orange and black paper which they shake wildly, and small megaphones through which, as drilled, they direct and magnify their shouting. Their leaders, barely pubescent girls, prance and shake and whirl their skirts above their bloomers. The young men, leaping, extend their arms and race through puddles of amber light, their bodies glistening. In a lull, though it rarely occurs, you can hear the squeak of tennis shoes against the floor. Then the yelling begins again, and then continues: fathers, mothers, neighbors joining in to form a single pulsing ululation—a cry of the whole community—for in this gymnasium each body becomes the bodies beside it, pressed as they are together, thigh to thigh, and the same shudder runs through all of them, and runs toward the same release. Only the ball moves serenely through this dazzling din. Obedient to law it scarcely speaks but caroms quietly and lives at peace.

BUSINESS

It is the week of Christmas and the stores, to accommodate the rush they hope for, are remaining open in the evening. You can see snow falling in the cones of the street lamps. The roads are filling—undisturbed. Strings of red and green lights droop over the principal highway, and the water tower wears a star. The windows of the stores have been bedizened. Shamelessly they beckon. But I am alone, leaning against a pole—no . . . there is no one in sight. They're all at home, perhaps by their instruments, tuning in on their evenings, and like Romana, tirelessly playing and replaying themselves. There's a speaker perched in the tower, and through the boughs of falling snow and over the vacant streets, it drapes the twisted and metallic strains of a tune that can barely be distinguished—yes, I believe it's one of the jolly ones, it's "Joy to the World." There's no one to hear the music but myself, and though I'm listening, I'm no longer certain. Perhaps the record's playing something else.

[1968]

For Thought

William Gass has cataloged the anatomy of a small Indiana town into a seemingly random series of sections—thirty-two of them. Following in Walt Whitman's footsteps, the author immerses himself in the ebb and flow of a community. Gass's title, with its repeated "hearts," hints at the inner, poetic thrust of his fictional ramblings. The author suggests that even the commonplace and unremarkable people of a Midwestern village have a universal interest when filtered through a sensitive and poetic sensibility.

For Discussion

1. How is the narrator self-characterized? What motivated the narrator's move to the dying village in Indiana? What mood or combination of moods is reflected in his outlook?
2. How is the town described? What parallels could be drawn between the town and the narrator?
3. Why is the story organized in labeled segments? What unified image emerges from the segments?
4. Can the story be said to be "about" something? How is the title of the story symbolic?

Caroline Gordon
The Ice House

Doug was waiting where the paths forked as Raeburn came through the woods. He had his Barlow out and was whittling a stick, but he threw it away and started striding along the path as soon as he saw Raeburn.

"I thought you wasn't coming," he said. "I thought you'd just about give it out and decided you wasn't coming."

"I had to get my breakfast," Raeburn told him. "I ain't going to work for nobody on a empty stomach." He cast an eye at the sun. "'Tain't more'n six o'clock anyhow."

Doug slackened his pace a little. "Well," he said, "the way I look at it if you going to work for a man you ought to work for him. We don't know nothin' about this man. If we get there late he may not pay us what he said he would."

Raeburn watched his own skinny shadow racing with him, over the new green shoots of pokeberry and sassafras. It occurred to him that it was the middle of April. The dogwoods were in full flower. Channel cat ought to be biting.

"Wilmer was over to our house last night," he said. "He wanted to know if that man had asked us to work for him. He said *he* wouldn't tech it. He said he wouldn't tech it for *no* amount of money."

Doug laughed. "I don't reckon he would," he said. "I don't reckon anybody that once took a look at Wilmer would hire him for *this* job. He couldn't hold out to handle a pick . . ."

"You reckon we'll have to use a pick, Doug?"

Doug stopped short in the path. "You know who's in that ice house?" he asked.

"I don't know none of their names."

"I reckon you don't. They's Yankees. Every last one of 'em's Yankees. Course now if you don't want to you don't have to do it. I can git somebody else. Handlin' a dead Yankee ain't no more to *me* than handlin' a dead hawg, but of course now you don't have to go if you don't want to."

"Oh, I'll go," Raeburn said. "It ain't nothin' to me."

They emerged from the woods into the

clearing. A hundred yards away the ice house stood, with around it the black, straight trunks of half a dozen oak trees. There were no leaves as yet on any of their branches, but a sugar tree at one corner of the house cast its yellowish green tassels low on the sloping roof.

The man was standing before the ice house door looking down into the pit. A short man, so plump that the waistband of his trousers seemed on the verge of bursting. He heard them coming and turned around. His eyes were gray. They looked pale in the creases of his red, round face.

"Well, boys," he said affably, "I see you're like me. Early risers."

He waved his hands at the unpainted pine coffins that curved in a long glistening line around one whole side of the ice house and back behind the sugar tree. "Now what we got to do is fill them boxes up. The sooner we get them boxes filled up the sooner we get done and the sooner we get done the sooner you get your money. . . . Ain't that right, Bud?"

"That's right," Doug said. He took a pick and stepped over the threshold of the ice house onto the little ledge of earth that ran all around the circular pit. Raeburn followed him.

The skeletons were level with the earth. There was a man's skull on top of the pile. The eye sockets turned towards the door, the ribs and long leg bones slanting away diagonally across the heap, as if the man had flung himself down face forward to look out over the field. Where the light from the open door fell the bones were pale, almost white, but the bones that showed here and there underneath were darker. There was moss on some of them.

Doug picked up one of the fingers. The joints still stuck together. But as he held them in his hand the little joint dropped from its socket and a wisp of dried tendon fell out on the heap.

Doug stooped and with both hands lifted the curved grayish ribs where they were joined to the backbone. "Here," he said, "I'll give 'em to you and you put 'em outside. That's the best way to do it."

Raeburn laid the ribs in the wheelbarrow that the contractor had drawn up to the door. When he turned around Doug had more bones ready to hand him. They worked there that way for a long while. When the barrow was full the contractor wheeled it around the corner and deposited the load in the pine boxes. Raeburn could hear the light clatter as the more fragile bones fell from the barrow into the coffin and could hear the contractor whistling as he went the rounds of the boxes arranging the skeletons.

Once when he knew the contractor was at the creek getting a drink Raeburn called down into the pit cautiously:

"Doug, how you reckon he knows when he's got a whole skeleton in one of them coffins?"

Doug raised a face curiously striped by the greenish light that filtered down through cracks in the planking. "I'd know," he said. "He can put a skull in each box, I reckon, even if he don't know where all them little bones belong. . . . Naw, he can't, either. Some of them fellers was put in here without any head!"

"Some of 'em was blowed clean to pieces," Raeburn said.

He looked out over the field where the new green was creeping up through clumps of brown sedge grass. They had fought all over that field, and in the woods. In December. In the snow. When they went to bury the dead the next day the ground was frozen. A foot deep. They had to dig them out with pickaxes. They had buried a lot of them on the battlefield. In two big trenches. And then they had put all the rest in this ice house. . . . In 1862 that had been. Four years ago. . . .

The contractor's round, red face showed in the doorway. "Well, boys," he said, "time for a little snack, ain't it?"

Doug had heard him and was clambering up the side of the pit. Raeburn gave him a hand and pulled him up beside him.

They walked around the side of the ice house and down the path to the creek. Both boys stretched themselves on the ground and lowered their faces into the water. It was clear and very cold. Raeburn gulped some down, then thrust his hands in wrist deep and let the cold water run over them. Doug was wiping his on some water grasses. "Wish I'd brought some soap," he said. He looked at Raeburn. "It ain't so hard when you just have to stand there and let me hand 'em up to you. It's getting 'em dug out and getting 'em loose from each other that's so hard."

"I'll get down in the pit after dinner," Raeburn told him.

The contractor was on his knees in the shade of the sugar tree when they came up the path. He had a trash fire going and was boiling coffee in a little bucket. Doug and Raeburn took their cold meat and biscuits and sat down on the grass. The contractor poured coffee into tin cups.

Raeburn drank the hot coffee down at a gulp. It warmed his insides and invigorated him. He decided that he would be able to eat something, after all, and bit into a biscuit, but the sick feeling swept over him again and he had to put it down quickly. He stretched out in the grass, supporting his head on one hand. Through a rift in the bushes he could see the creek shining in the noonday sun. It ran swiftly along here just above the falls, but there were good pools, all along here and higher up, too.

Doug was asking the man questions about his business. Had he ever worked for the government before? And how was he paid? By the day or so much for the job?

The contractor had finished eating his lunch and was lighting his pipe. "I ain't had much experience working for the government. Fact is, this is the first job I ever did fer 'em. Now on this job they pay me every time I take in a load of them boxes. Every time I take in a load of them boxes they count 'em and pay me so much a head." He took his pipe out of his mouth. "So much a head," he repeated meditatively.

"Channel cat ought to be biting now," Raeburn said. His voice that was not through changing yet, though he was nearly sixteen, broke unexpectedly into a deep bass. "I know a way to catch channel cat till the world looks level."

The contractor had got up and was standing beside one of the boxes. He had his stubby fingers spread out as if he were counting. "How's that?" he asked.

"Well," Raeburn said, "you have to do it at night." He fixed his large brown eyes intently on the man's face. "The channel cat, he's a night feeder, so you have to fix for him at night. . . ."

The contractor was looking at the boxes again, but he nodded politely. "What do you have to do, Son?"

"Well, you fix you some limb lines. Get you a tree that has a branch over the creek and just tie half a dozen lines on the limbs and leave 'em. Don't use too much sinker, because the channel cat he feeds on top of the water. Just fix 'em and leave 'em there and in the morning you'll have all the fish you can eat for breakfast."

The contractor came back and sat down. "Now that's right noticing, for a boy your age," he said.

"I'm fifteen," Raeburn told him. "I'm fifteen and Doug'll be sixteen next month."

"Well now . . ." the contractor said, "and what do you boys aim to do when you get through with this job?"

"Work for Mr. Foster out on the aidge of town here," Doug said, "if he needs any hands. Folks ain't hirin' many hands now, though."

The contractor shook his head. "Farm work's all right," he said. "Farm work's all right if you can't get nothing else to do, but a smart young feller like you wants to be looking out fer oppertunity. . . . Ain't everybody knows oppertunity when they see it. The folks at home all thought I was mighty foolish when I come down in this country, but I knew they was oppertunity in the South . . . bound to be." He put out his pipe and rose briskly. "Well," he said,

"I reckon we better be gettin' back to work."

Doug stood up. "One thing," he said, "we got to have a ladder. They're way down in there now. I don't know as I can get 'em up to Raeburn without a ladder."

The contractor looked at the Porter house, just visible through the trees. "Maybe them folks would lend us a ladder. . . . Supposing I walk over and see if they'd lend us a ladder."

"You reckon they'll lend him a ladder?" Raeburn asked when he was gone.

"Shore they will," Doug said. "'Tain't nothin' to lend anybody a ladder."

Raeburn watched the rotund figure disappear in the bushes that fringed the slope. "Mrs. Porter hates Yankees," he said. "They was three of her boys killed by the Yankees."

Doug laughed. "This feller never killed no Confederates."

He stepped back into the ice house and slid quickly down into the pit.

Raeburn protested as he took his stand on the ledge. "I told you I was going to get down there after dinner."

Doug shook his head. "I'm used to it now. You have to kind of get the hang of it. It'd just be wasting time now if we changed places."

He stirred the bones vigorously with his pick and a rank odor rose and floated in the chill air. Raeburn drew it into his nostrils, wondering. It was several minutes before he knew where he had smelled it before—in the wooden walls and flooring of an abandoned slaughter house that had stood for a long time in one of Foster's fields.

The bones that Doug was piling up on the ledge now were different from the ones on top, grayish-green, matted, some of them, with strange fungus growths. Water had stood in the ice house a good deal of the time, it seemed. Doug had to keep shifting about to find a dry place to stand on.

He did not like it if Raeburn kept his face turned away from the pit to look over the field. He talked incessantly:

"You know what that Yankee done? . . . He went down there in Blue Gum Hollow and asked Uncle Hooser's boys to work for him." He laughed. "Uncle Hooser told him them boys sho would be glad to make that money, but every one of them was away from home." He laughed again, so hard that he shook all over. "Every last one of them niggers was away from home!"

"Niggers is funny," Raeburn agreed. "When my Uncle Rod was killed . . . over in Caroline County . . . killed right there on his front porch . . . there was a old nigger man standing there in the front yard. Old Uncle Lias Sims. And he wouldn't even help my mother carry Uncle Rod in the house. Naw, sir, he just turned around and ran. Niggers don't like to have nothin' to do with dead people."

"How come your Uncle Rod to get killed settin' on his front porch?" Doug enquired.

"He was so deaf he couldn't hear 'em shelling. The rest of the folks they all got down in the cellar, then somebody got to asking where Uncle Rod was. After it was over they went out on the front porch and there he was, settin' bolt up in his chair . . ."

"Dead?"

"Dead as a herring." Raeburn looked off across the field. "There's that man coming," he said, "but he ain't got no ladder. How long you reckon he expects us to work? It'll be gettin' dark pretty soon."

"Must be past seven o'clock," Doug said. "I ain't going to work no longer."

The man came up just as Doug was climbing out of the ice house. He was panting and his round face wore a harassed look. "Them folks didn't have no ladder," he said; "more'n that they sent me off on a fool errant . . . said the Widow Hickman might have a ladder. And when I get to where they say the Widow Hickman lives there ain't nothing but an old house looks like nobody ain't lived in it these thirty years. . . . Either you boys ever hear of the Widow Hickman?"

"I don't know many folks over this way," Doug said. He laid his pick up against a tree. "Well," he said, "I reckon it's about quittin' time."

The man took a leather wallet from his pocket and counted silver out into their hands. "I don't believe I'll be needin' you boys tomorrow, after all," he said.

Doug stood looking at him a minute as if he wasn't sure he'd heard right, then he said, "Suit yourself," and started off across the field. Raeburn ran and caught up with him at the edge of the woods.

"I thought you said he wanted us to work three, four days, Doug. I thought you said he wanted us to get *all* of them skeletons out of that ice house."

"Hunh," Doug said.

He stopped and looked about him a minute, then turned off into the woods. Raeburn stood there waiting. When Doug did not come back he whistled, the soft, low whistle that they used for calling each other. Doug's head appeared suddenly over a clump of buckberry bushes. "Shh!" he said and beckoned Raeburn to come.

Raeburn made his way through the bushes. Doug was lying flat on his stomach behind the buckberries. Raeburn lay down beside him.

"What you doing this for?" he whispered.

Doug pushed a spray of buckberry a little to one side. "Look at that," he said.

The man was standing with his back to them. In front of the coffins. He had his hat off. They could see his bald head and the fringe of gray hair that came down on his blue shirt collar. He put his hand up and scratched his bald head, then he leaned over and lifted some bones out of one of the coffins. He held them in his hands a minute as if he didn't know what to do with them, then he laid them in one of the boxes farther down the line. He kept on doing this until he had put some bones in each of the empty boxes. Then he began fastening the lids and hammering them down.

"What you reckon he's doing, Doug?" Raeburn said.

Doug put his lips up close to Raeburn's ear. "He's dividing up them skeletons," he whispered. "He's dividing up them skeletons so he can git paid double."

He got to his feet and slipped off silently through the underbrush. Raeburn followed him. When they came to where the paths forked Doug stopped. "There ain't a whole man in ary one of them boxes," he said. He slapped his leg and rocked with laughter.

"If that ain't a Yankee fer ye!"

[1932]

For Thought

"The Ice House" has an unusual setting: a house where frozen corpses of dead Union soldiers are buried in a common grave. Despite the gruesome nature of their task, the three workers hired to place the corpses into coffins treat their duties rather routinely. Gordon uses the underlying motif of eating food to help establish her theme: for most people, the passions of war cool quickly. Little is left to mark the momentous issues of the Civil War but the humdrum tasks of counting and burying the unnamed dead.

For Discussion

1. How does the author create a sharp contrast between the unidentifiable, dismembered dead and the renewal of nature?
2. How are the boys of the story characterized? How and why do they minimize the horror of their task?

3. How is the contractor characterized? What is his attitude toward the job he has taken?
4. What point of view do the boys take toward the recent conflict? How does the humor with which they view particular incidents of violence affect the reader's attitude toward the events of the story?
5. In what way is the conclusion of the story ironic?

Nathaniel Hawthorne
The Minister's Black Veil —A Parable[1]

The sexton stood in the porch of Milford meeting-house, pulling busily at the bell-rope. The old people of the village came stooping along the street. Children, with bright faces, tripped merrily beside their parents, or mimicked a graver gait, in the conscious dignity of their Sunday clothes. Spruce bachelors looked sidelong at the pretty maidens, and fancied that the Sabbath sunshine made them prettier than on week days. When the throng had mostly streamed into the porch, the sexton began to toll the bell, keeping his eyes on the Reverend Mr. Hooper's door. The first glimpse of the clergyman's figure was the signal for the bell to cease its summons.

"But what has good Parson Hooper got upon his face?" cried the sexton in astonishment.

All within hearing immediately turned about, and beheld the semblance of Mr. Hooper, pacing slowly his meditative ways towards the meeting-house. With one accord they started, expressing more wonder than if some strange minister were coming to dust the cushions of Mr. Hooper's pulpit.

"Are you sure it is our parson?" inquired Goodman Gray of the sexton.

"Of a certainty it is good Mr. Hooper," replied the sexton. "He was to have exchanged pulpits with Parson Shute, of Westbury; but Parson Shute sent to excuse himself yesterday, being to preach a funeral sermon."

The cause of so much amazement may appear sufficiently slight. Mr. Hooper, a gentlemanly person, of about thirty, though still a bachelor, was dressed with due clerical neatness, as if a careful wife had starched his band, and brushed the weekly dust from his Sunday's garb. There was but one thing remarkable in his appearance. Swathed about his forehead, and hanging down over his face, so low as to be shaken

---

[1]Another clergyman in New England, Mr. Joseph Moody, of York, Maine, who died about eighty years since, made himself remarkable by the same eccentricity that is here related of the Reverend Mr. Hooper. In his case, however, the symbol had a different import. In early life he had accidentally killed a beloved friend; and from that day till the hour of his own death, he hid his face from men. [Hawthorne's note]

SOURCE: "The Minister's Black Veil" by Nathaniel Hawthorne. Reprinted from *Twice Told Tales*, vol. 1 of *The Complete Writings of Nathaniel Hawthorne*, Houghton Mifflin, 1900.

by his breath, Mr. Hooper had on a black veil. On a nearer view it seemed to consist of two folds of crape, which entirely concealed his features, except the mouth and chin, but probably did not intercept his sight, further than to give a darkened aspect to all living and inanimate things. With this gloomy shade before him, good Mr. Hooper walked onward, at a slow and quiet pace, stooping somewhat, and looking on the ground, as is customary with abstracted men, yet nodding kindly to those of his parishioners who still waited on the meeting-house steps, But so wonder-struck were they that his greeting hardly met with a return.

"I can't really feel as if good Mr. Hooper's face was behind that piece of crape," said the sexton.

"I don't like it," muttered an old woman, as she hobbled into the meeting-house. "He has changed himself into something awful, only by hiding his face."

"Our parson has gone mad!" cried Goodman Gray, following him across the threshold.

A rumor of some unaccountable phenomenon had preceded Mr. Hooper into the meeting-house, and set all the congregation astir. Few could refrain from twisting their heads towards the door; many stood upright, and turned directly about; while several little boys clambered upon the seats, and came down again with a terrible racket. There was a general bustle, a rustling of the women's gowns and shuffling of the men's feet, greatly at variance with that hushed repose which should attend the entrance of the minister. But Mr. Hooper appeared not to notice the perturbation of his people. He entered with an almost noiseless step, bent his head mildly to the pews on each side, and bowed as he passed his oldest parishioner, a white-haired great-grandsire, who occupied an armchair in the centre of the aisle. It was strange to observe how slowly this venerable man became conscious of something singular in the appearance of his pastor. He seemed not fully to partake of the prevailing wonder, till Mr. Hooper had ascended the stairs, and showed himself in the pulpit, face to face with his congregation, except for the black veil. That mysterious emblem was never once withdrawn. It shook with his measured breath as he gave out the psalm; it threw its obscurity between him and the holy page, as he read the Scriptures; and while he prayed, the veil lay heavily on his uplifted countenance. Did he seek to hide it from the dread Being whom he was addressing?

Such was the effect of this simple piece of crape, that more than one woman of delicate nerves was forced to leave the meeting-house. Yet perhaps the pale-faced congregation was almost as fearful a sight to the minister, as his black veil to them.

Mr. Hooper had the reputation of a good preacher, but not an energetic one: he strove to win his people heavenward by mild, persuasive influences, rather than to drive them thither by the thunders of the Word. The sermon which he now delivered was marked by the same characteristics of style and manner as the general series of his pulpit oratory. But there was something, either in the sentiment of the discourse itself, or in the imagination of the auditors, which made it greatly the most powerful effort that they had ever heard from their pastor's lips. It was tinged, rather more darkly than usual, with the gentle gloom of Mr. Hooper's temperament. The subject had reference to secret sin, and those sad mysteries which we hide from our nearest and dearest, and would fain conceal from our own consciousness, even forgetting that the Omniscient can detect them. A subtle power was breathed into his words. Each member of the congregation, the most innocent girl, and the man of hardened breast, felt as if the preacher had crept upon them, behind his awful veil, and discovered their hoarded iniquity of deed or thought. Many spread their clasped hands on their bosoms. There was nothing terrible in what Mr. Hooper said, at least, no violence; and yet, with every tremor of his melancholy voice, the hearers quaked. An unsought pathos came hand in hand with awe. So sensible were the audience of some unwonted attribute in their minister, that they longed for a breath of wind to blow aside the veil, almost believing that a stranger's visage would be discovered, though the form, gesture, and voice were those of Mr. Hooper.

At the close of the services, the people hurried out with indecorous confusion, eager to communicate their pent-up amazement, and conscious of lighter spirits the moment they lost sight of the black veil. Some gathered in little circles, huddled closely together, with their mouths all whispering in the centre; some went homeward alone, wrapt in silent meditation; some talked loudly, and profaned the Sabbath-day with ostentatious laughter. A few shook their sagacious heads, intimating that they could penetrate the mystery; while one or two affirmed that there was no mystery at all, but only that Mr. Hooper's eyes were so weakened by the midnight lamp, as to require a shade. After a brief interval, forth came good Mr. Hooper also, in the rear of his flock. Turning his veiled face from one group to another, he paid due reverence to the hoary heads, saluted the middle aged, with kind dignity as their friend and spiritual guide, greeted the young with mingled authority and love, and laid his hands on the little children's heads to bless them. Such was always his custom on the Sabbath-day. Strange and bewildered looks repaid him for his courtesy. None, as on former occasions, aspired to the honor of walking by their pastor's side. Old Squire Saunders, doubtless by an accidental lapse of memory, neglected to invite Mr. Hooper to his table, where the good clergyman had been wont to bless the food, almost every Sunday since his settlement. He returned, therefore, to the parsonage, and, at the moment of closing the door, was observed to look back upon the people, all of whom had their eyes fixed upon the minister. A sad smile gleamed faintly from beneath the black veil, and flickered about his mouth, glimmering as he disappeared.

"How strange," said a lady, "that a simple black veil, such as any woman might wear on her bonnet, should become such a terrible thing on Mr. Hooper's face!"

"Something must surely be amiss with Mr. Hooper's intellects," observed her husband, the physician of the village. "But the strangest part of the affair is the effect of this vagary, even on a sober-minded man like myself. The black veil, though it covers only our pastor's face, throws its influence over his whole person, and makes him ghostlike from head to foot. Do you not feel it so?"

"Truly do I," replied the lady; "and I would not be alone with him for the world. I wonder he is not afraid to be alone with himself!"

"Men sometimes are so," said her husband.

The afternoon service was attended with similar circumstances. At its conclusion, the bell tolled for the funeral of a young lady. The relatives and friends were assembled in the house, and the more distant acquaintances stood about the door, speaking of the good qualities of the deceased, when their talk was interrupted by the appearance of Mr. Hooper, still covered with his black veil. It was not an appropriate emblem. The clergyman stepped into the room where the corpse was laid, and bent over the coffin, to take a last farewell of his deceased parishioner. As he stooped, the veil hung straight from his forehead, so that, if her eyelids had not been closed forever, the dead maiden might have seen his face. Could Mr. Hooper be fearful of her glance, that he so hastily caught back the black veil? A person who watched the interview between the dead and living, scrupled not to affirm, that, at the instant when the clergyman's features were disclosed, the corpse had slightly shuddered, rustling the shroud and muslin cap, though the countenance retained the composure of death. A superstitious old woman was the only witness of this prodigy. From the coffin Mr. Hooper passed into the chamber of the mourners, and thence to the head of the staircase, to make the funeral prayer. It was a tender and heart-dissolving prayer, full of sorrow, yet so imbued with celestial hopes, that the music of a heavenly harp, swept by the fingers of the dead, seemed faintly to be heard among the saddest accents of the minister. The people trembled, though they but darkly understood him, when he prayed that they, and himself, and all of mortal race, might be ready, as he trusted this young maiden had been, for the dreadful hour that should snatch the veil from their faces. The bearers went heavily forth, and the mourners followed, saddening all the street,with the dead before them, and Mr. Hooper in his black veil behind.

"Why do you look back?" said one in the procession of his partner.

"I had a fancy," replied she, "that the minister and the maiden's spirit were walking hand in hand."

"And so had I, at the same moment," said the other.

That night, the handsomest couple in Milford village were to be joined in wedlock. Though reckoned a melancholy man, Mr. Hooper had a placid cheerfulness for such occasions, which often excited a sympathetic smile where livelier merriment would have been thrown away. There was no quality of his disposition which made him more beloved than this. The company at the wedding awaited his arrival with impatience, trusting that the strange awe, which had gathered over him throughout the day, would now be dispelled. But such was not the result. When Mr. Hooper came, the first thing that their eyes rested on was the same horrible black veil, which had added deeper gloom to the funeral, and could portend nothing but evil to the wedding. Such was its immediate effect on the guests that a cloud seemed to have rolled duskily from beneath the black crape, and dimmed the light of the candles. The bridal pair stood up before the minister. But the bride's cold fingers quivered in the tremulous hand of the bridegroom, and her deathlike paleness caused a whisper that the maiden who had been buried a few hours before was come from her grave to be married. If ever another wedding were so dismal, it was that famous one where they tolled the wedding knell. After performing the ceremony, Mr. Hooper raised a glass of wine to his lips, wishing happiness to the new-married couple in a strain of mild pleasantry that ought to have brightened the features of the guests, like a cheerful gleam from the heart. At that instant, catching a glimpse of his figure in the looking-glass, the black veil involved his own spirit in the horror with which it overwhelmed all others. His frame shuddered, his lips grew pale, he spilt the untasted wine upon the carpet, and rushed forth into the darkness. For the Earth, too, had on her Black Veil.

The next day, the whole village of Milford talked of little else than Parson Hooper's black veil. That, and the mystery concealed behind it, supplied a topic for discussion between acquaintances meeting in the street, and good women gossiping at their open windows. It was the first item of news that the tavern-keeper told to his guests. The children babbled of it on their way to school. One imitative little imp covered his face with an old black handkerchief, thereby so affrighting his playmates that the panic seized himself, and he well-nigh lost his wits by his own waggery.

It was remarkable that of all the busybodies and impertinent people in the parish, not one ventured to put the plain question to Mr. Hooper, wherefore he did this thing. Hitherto, whenever there appeared the slightest call for such interference, he had never lacked advisers, nor shown himself averse to be guided by their judgment. If he erred at all, it was by so painful a degree of self-distrust, that even the mildest censure would lead him to consider an indifferent action as a crime. Yet, though so well acquainted with this amiable weakness, no individual among his parishioners chose to make the black veil a subject of friendly remonstrance. There was a feeling of dread, neither plainly confessed nor carefully concealed, which caused each to shift the responsibility upon another, till at length it was found expedient to send a deputation of the church, in order to deal with Mr. Hooper about the mystery, before it should grow into a scandal. Never did an embassy so ill discharge its duties. The minister received them with friendly courtesy, but became silent, after they were seated, leaving to his visitors the whole burden of introducing their important business. The topic, it might be supposed, was obvious enough. There was the black veil swathed round Mr. Hooper's forehead, and concealing every feature above his placid mouth, on which, at times, they could perceive the glimmering of a melancholy smile. But that piece of crape, to their imagination, seemed to hang down before his heart, the symbol of a fearful secret between him and them. Were the veil but cast aside, they might speak freely of it, but not till then. Thus they sat a considerable time, speechless, confused, and shrinking uneasily from Mr. Hooper's eye, which they felt to be fixed upon them with an invisible glance. Finally, the deputies returned abashed to their constituents, pronouncing the matter too weighty to be handled except by a council of the churches, if, indeed, it might not require a general synod.

But there was one person in the village unappalled by the awe with which the black veil had impressed all beside herself. When the deputies returned without an explanation, or even venturing to demand one, she, with the calm energy of her character, determined to chase away the strange cloud that appeared to be settling round Mr. Hooper, every moment more darkly than before. As his plighted wife, it should be her privilege to know what the black veil concealed. At the minister's first visit, therefore, she entered upon the subject, with a direct simplicity, which made the task easier both for him and her. After he had seated himself, she fixed her eyes steadfastly upon the veil, but could discern nothing of the dreadful gloom that had so overawed the multitude; it was but a double fold of crape, hanging down from his forehead to his mouth, and slightly stirring with his breath.

"No," said she aloud, and smiling, "there is nothing terrible in this piece of crape, except that it hides a face which I am always glad to look upon. Come, good sir, let the sun shine from behind the cloud. First lay aside your black veil: then tell me why you put it on."

Mr. Hooper's smile glimmered faintly.

"There is an hour to come," said he, "when all of us shall cast aside our veils. Take it not amiss, beloved friend, if I wear this piece of crape till then."

"Your words are a mystery, too," returned the young lady. "Take away the veil from them, at least."

"Elizabeth, I will," said he, "so far as my vow may suffer me. Know, then, this veil is a type and a symbol, and I am bound to wear it ever, both in light and darkness, in solitude and before the gaze of multitudes, and as with strangers, so with my familiar friends. No mortal eye will see it withdrawn. This dismal shade must separate me from the world: even you, Elizabeth, can never come behind it!"

"What grievous affliction hath befallen you," she earnestly inquired, "that you should thus darken your eyes forever?"

"If it be a sign of mourning," replied Mr. Hooper, "I perhaps, like most other mortals, have sorrows dark enough to be typified by a black veil."

"But what if the world will not believe that it is the type of an innocent sorrow?" urged Elizabeth. "Beloved and respected as you are, there may be whispers that you hide your face under the consciousness of secret sin. For the sake of your holy office, do away this scandal!"

The color rose into her cheeks as she intimated the nature of the rumors that were already abroad in the village. But Mr. Hooper's mildness did not forsake him. He even smiled again—that same sad smile, which always appeared like a faint glimmering of light, proceeding from the obscurity beneath the veil.

"If I hide my face for sorrow, there is cause enough," he merely replied; "and if I cover it for secret sin, what mortal might not do the same?"

And with this gentle, but unconquerable obstinacy did he resist all her entreaties. At length Elizabeth sat silent. For a few moments she appeared lost in thought, considering, probably, what new methods might be tried to withdraw her lover from so dark a fantasy, which, if it had no other meaning, was perhaps a symptom of mental disease. Though of a firmer character than his own, the tears rolled down her cheeks. But, in an instant, as it were, a new feeling took the place of sorrow: her eyes were fixed insensibly on the black veil, when, like a sudden twilight in the air, its terrors fell around her. She arose, and stood trembling before him.

"And do you feel it then, at last?" said he mournfully.

She made no reply, but covered her eyes with her hand, and turned to leave the room. He rushed forward and caught her arm.

"Have patience with me, Elizabeth!" cried he, passionately. "Do not desert me, though this veil must be between us here on earth. Be mine, and hereafter there shall be no veil over my face, no darkness between our souls! It is but a mortal veil—it is not for eternity! O! you know not how lonely I am, and how frightened to be alone behind my black veil. Do not leave me in this miserable obscurity forever!"

"Lift the veil but once, and look me in the face," said she.

"Never! It cannot be!" replied Mr. Hooper.

"Then farewell!" said Elizabeth.

She withdrew her arm from his grasp, and slowly departed, pausing at the door, to give one long, shuddering gaze, that seemed almost to penetrate the mystery of the black veil. But, even amid his grief, Mr. Hooper smiled to think that only a material emblem had separated him from happiness, though the horrors, which it shadowed forth, must be drawn darkly between the fondest of lovers.

From that time no attempts were made to remove Mr. Hooper's black veil, or, by a direct appeal, to discover the secret which it was supposed to hide. By persons who claimed a superiority to popular prejudice, it was reckoned merely an eccentric whim, such as often mingles with the sober actions of men otherwise rational, and tinges them all with its own semblance of insanity. But with the multitude good Mr. Hooper was irreparably a bugbear. He could not walk the street with any peace of mind, so conscious was he that the gentle and timid would turn aside to avoid him, and that others would make it a point of hardihood to throw themselves in his way. The impertinence of the latter class compelled him to give up his customary walk at sunset to the burial ground; for when he leaned pensively over the gate, there would always be faces behind the gravestones, peeping at his black veil. A fable went the rounds that the stare of the dead people drove him thence. It grieved him, to the very depth of his kind heart, to observe how the children fled from his approach, breaking up their merriest sports, while his melancholy figure was yet afar off. Their instinctive dread caused him to feel more strongly than aught alse, that a preter-natural horror was interwoven with the threads of the black crape. In truth, his own antipathy to the veil was known to be so great, that he never willingly passed before a mirror, nor stooped to drink at a still fountain, lest, in its peaceful bosom, he should be affrighted by himself. This was what gave plausibility to the whispers, that Mr. Hooper's conscience tortured him for some great crime too horrible to be entirely concealed, or otherwise than so obscurely intimated. Thus, from beneath the black veil, there rolled a cloud into the sunshine, an ambiguity of sin or sorrow, which enveloped the poor minister, so that love or sympathy could never reach him. It was said, that ghost and fiend consorted with him there. With self-shudderings and outward terrors, he walked continually in its shadow, groping darkly within his own soul, or gazing through a medium that saddened the whole world. Even the lawless wind, it was believed, respected his dreadful secret, and never blew aside the veil. But still good Mr. Hooper sadly smiled at the pale visages of the worldly throng as he passed by.

Among all its bad influences, the black veil had the one desirable effect, of making its wearer a very efficient clergyman. By the aid of his mysterious emblem—for there was no other apparent cause—he became a man of awful power, over souls that were in agony for sin. His converts always regarded him with a dread peculiar to themselves, affirming, though but figuratively, that, before he brought them to celestial light, they had been with him behind the black veil. Its gloom, indeed, enabled him to sympathize with all dark affections. Dying sinners cried aloud for Mr. Hooper, and would not yield their breath till he appeared; though ever, as he stooped to whisper consolation, they shuddered at the veiled face so near their own. Such were the terrors of the black veil, even when Death had bared his visage! Strangers came long distances to attend service at his church, with the mere idle purpose of gazing at his figure, because it was forbidden them to behold his face. But many were made to quake ere they departed! Once, during Governor Belcher's administration, Mr. Hooper was appointed to preach the election sermon. Covered with his black veil, he stood before the chief magistrate, the council, and the representatives, and wrought so deep an impression, that the legislative measures of that year were characterized by all the gloom and piety of our earliest ancestral sway.

In this manner Mr. Hooper spent a long life, irreproachable in outward act, yet shrouded in dismal suspicions; kind and loving, though unloved, and dimly feared; man apart from men, shunned in their health and joy, but ever summoned to their aid in mortal anguish. As years wore on, shedding their snows above his sable veil, he acquired a name throughout the New England churches, and they called him Father Hooper. Nearly all his parishioners, who were of mature age when he was settled, had been borne away by many a funeral: he had one congregation in the church, and a more crowded one in the churchyard; and having wrought so late into the evening, and done his work so well, it was now good Father Hooper's turn to rest.

Several persons were visible by the shaded candlelight, in the death chamber of the old clergyman. Natural connections he had none. But there was the decorously grave, though unmoved physician, seeking only to mitigate the last pangs of the patient whom he could not save. There were the deacons, and other eminently pious members of his church. There, also, was the Reverend Mr. Clark, of Westbury, a young and zealous divine, who had ridden in haste to pray by the bedside of the expiring minister. There was the nurse, no hired handmaiden of death, but one whose calm affection had endured thus long in secrecy, in solitude, amid the chill of age, and would not perish, even at the dying hour. Who, but Elizabeth! And there lay the hoary head of good Father Hooper upon the death pillow, with the black veil still swathed about his brow, and reaching down over his face, so that each more difficult gasp of his faint breath caused it to stir. All through life that piece of crape had hung between him and the world; it had separated him from cheerful brotherhood and woman's love, and kept him in that saddest of all prisons, his own heart; and still it lay upon his face, as if to deepen the gloom of his darksome chamber, and shade him from the sunshine of eternity.

For some time previous, his mind had been confused, wavering doubtfully between the past and the present, and hovering forward, as it were, at intervals, into the indistinctness of the world to come. There had been feverish turns, which tossed him from side to side, and wore away what little strength he had. But in his most convulsive struggles, and in the wildest vagaries of his intellect, when no other thought retains its sober influence, he still showed an awful solicitude lest the black veil should slip aside. Even if his bewildered soul could have forgotten, there was a faithful woman at his pillow, who, with averted eyes, would have covered that aged face, which she had last beheld in the comeliness of manhood. At length the death-stricken old man lay quietly in the torpor of mental and bodily exhaustion, with an imperceptible pulse, and breath that grew fainter and fainter, except when a long, deep, and irregular inspiration seemed to preclude the flight of his spirit.

The minister of Westbury approached the bedside.

"Venerable Father Hooper," said he, "the moment of your release is at hand. Are you ready for the lifting of the veil that shuts in time from eternity?"

Father Hooper at first replied merely by a feeble motion of his head; then, apprehensive, perhaps, that his meaning might be doubtful, he exerted himself to speak.

"Yea," said he, in faint accents, "my soul hath a patient weariness until that veil be lifted."

"And is it fitting," resumed the Reverend Mr. Clark, "that a man so given to prayer, of such a blameless example, holy in deed and thought, so far as mortal judgment may pronounce; is it fitting that a father in the church should leave a shadow in his memory, that may seem to blacken a life so pure? I pray you, my venerable brother, let not this thing be! Suffer us to be gladdened by your triumphant aspect, as you go to your reward. Before the veil of eternity be lifted, let me cast aside this black veil from your face!"

And thus speaking, the Reverend Mr. Clark bent forward to reveal the mystery of so many years. But, exerting a sudden energy, that made all the beholders stand aghast, Father Hooper snatched both his hands from beneath the bedclothes, and pressed them strongly on the black veil, resolute to struggle, if the minister of Westbury would contend with a dying man.

"Never!" cried the veiled clergyman. "On earth, never!"

"Dark old man!" exclaimed the affrighted minister, "with what horrible crime upon your soul are you now passing to the judgment?"

Father Hooper's breath heaved; it rattled in his throat but, with a mighty effort, grasping forward with his hands, he caught hold of life, and held it back till he should speak. He even raised himself in bed; and there he sat, shivering with the arms of death around him, while the black veil hung down, awful, at that last moment, in the gathered terrors of a lifetime. And yet the faint, sad smile, so often there, now seemed to glimmer from its obscurity, and linger on Father Hooper's lips.

"Why do you tremble at me alone?" cried he, turning his veiled face round the circle of pale spectators. "Tremble also at each other! Have men avoided me, and women shown no pity, and children screamed and fled, only for my black veil? What, but the mystery which it obscurely typifies, has made this piece of crape so awful? When the friend shows his inmost heart to his friend; the lover to his best beloved; when man does not vainly shrink from the eye of his Creator, loathsomely treasuring up the secret of his sin; then deem me a monster; for the symbol beneath which I have lived, and die! I look around me, and lo! on every visage a Black Veil!"

While his auditors shrank from one another, in mutual affright, Father Hooper fell back upon his pillow, a veiled corpse with a faint smile lingering on the lips. Still veiled, they laid him in his coffin, and a veiled corpse they bore him to the grave.

The grass of many years has sprung up and withered on that grave, the burial stone is moss-grown, and good Mr. Hooper's face is dust; but awful is still the thought that it mouldered beneath the Black Veil!

[1837]

For Thought

Hawthorne takes the motif of the scapegoat victimized by society and veils it in the form of a puritan parable. In his version, however, he has the scapegoat establish the conditions of his own ostracism. The alienation Hooper creates is counterbalanced by the spiritual fascination he exerts on dying sinners who seek his help in their passage from life into eternity. Thus, the minister serves as both an outcast and a revered Promethean figure, with the gift he brings being deathbed consolation.

For Discussion

1. What does the opening paragraph do to create a motivating setting and atmosphere for the subsequent action?
2. How does Hawthorne use the third-person point of view to deepen the mystery and suspense?
3. Why would not the minister himself or one of the villagers as narrator suit the purposes of the story?
4. What conflict is at the heart of the story? What is the resolution of the conflict?
5. What ironic transformation is brought about by the minister's wearing the veil?
6. What paradox is there in the characterization of the minister?
7. What parallels and dissimilarities exist between Hooper and Christ?
8. What elements of the comic are there in the story?
9. What symbolic value does the veil assume at Hooper's deathbed?
10. What ambiguities exist in the tone and form of the story?

Ernest Hemingway
The Killers

The door of Henry's lunch-room opened and two men came in. They sat down at the counter.

"What's yours?" George asked them.

"I don't know," one of the men said. "What do you want to eat, Al?"

"I don't know," said Al. "I don't know what I want to eat."

Outside it was getting dark. The street-light came on outside the window. The two men at the counter read the menu. From the other end of the counter Nick Adams watched them. He had been talking to George when they came in.

"I'll have a roast pork tenderloin with apple sauce and mashed potatoes," the first man said.

"It isn't ready yet."

"What the hell do you put it on the card for?"

"That's the dinner," George explained. "You can get that at six o'clock."

George looked at the clock on the wall behind the counter.

"It's five o'clock."

"The clock says twenty minutes past five," the second man said.

"It's twenty minutes fast."

"Oh, to hell with the clock," the first man said. "What have you got to eat?"

"I can give you any kind of sandwiches," George said. "You can have ham and eggs, bacon and eggs, liver and bacon, or a steak."

"Give me chicken croquettes with green peas and cream sauce and mashed potatoes."

"That's the dinner."

"Everything we want's the dinner, eh? That's the way you work it."

"I can give you ham and eggs, bacon and eggs, liver—"

"I'll take ham and eggs," the man called Al said. He wore a derby hat and a black overcoat buttoned across the chest. His face was small and white and he had tight lips. He wore a silk muffler and gloves.

"Give me bacon and eggs," said the other man. He was about the same size as Al. Their faces were different, but they were dressed like twins. Both wore overcoats too tight for them. They sat leaning forward, their elbows on the counter.

"Got anything to drink?" Al asked.

"Silver beer, bevo, ginger-ale," George said.

"I mean you got anything to *drink?*"

"Just those I said."

"This is a hot town," said the other. "What do they call it?"

"Summit."

"Ever hear of it?" Al asked his friend.

"No," said the friend.

"What do you do here nights?" Al asked.

"They eat the dinner," his friend said. "They all come here and eat the big dinner."

"That's right," George said.

"So you think that's right?" Al asked George.

"Sure," said George.

"You're a pretty bright boy, aren't you?"

"Sure," said George.

"Well, you're not," said the other little man. "Is he, Al?"

"He's dumb," said Al. He turned to Nick. "What's your name?"

"Adams."

"Another bright boy," Al said. "Ain't he a bright boy, Max?"

"The town's full of bright boys," Max said.

George put the two platters, one of ham and eggs, the other of bacon and eggs, on the counter. He set down two sidedishes of fried potatoes and closed the wicket into the kitchen.

"Which is yours?" he asked Al.

"Don't you remember?"

"Ham and eggs."

"Just a bright boy," Max said. He leaned forward and took the ham and eggs. Both men ate with their gloves on. George watched them eat.

"What are *you* looking at?" Max looked at George.

"Nothing."

"The hell you were. You were looking at me."

"Maybe the boy meant it for a joke, Max," Al said.

George laughed.

"You don't have to laugh," Max said to him. "*You* don't have to laugh at all, see?"

"All right," said George.

"So he thinks it's all right." Max turned to Al. "He thinks it's all right. That's a good one."

"Oh, he's a thinker," Al said. They went on eating.

"What's the bright boy's name down the counter?" Al asked Max.

"Hey, bright boy," Max said to Nick. "You go around on the other side of the counter with your boy friend."

"What's the idea?" Nick asked.

"There isn't any idea."

"You better go around, bright boy," Al said. Nick went around behind the counter.

"What's the idea?" George asked.

"None of your damn business," Al said. "Who's out in the kitchen?"

"The nigger."

"What do you mean the nigger?"

"The nigger that cooks."

"Tell him to come in."

"What's the idea?"

"Tell him to come in."

"Where do you think you are?"

"We know damn well where we are," the man called Max said. "Do we look silly?"

"You talk silly," Al said to him. "What the hell do you argue with this kid for? Listen," he said to George, "tell the nigger to come out here."

"What are you going to do to him?"

"Nothing. Use your head, bright boy. What would we do to a nigger?"

George opened the slit that opened back into the kitchen. "Sam," he called. "Come in here a minute."

The door to the kitchen opened and the

nigger came in. "What was it?" he asked. The two men at the counter took a look at him.

"All right, nigger. You stand right there," Al said.

Sam, the nigger, standing in his apron, looked at the two men sitting at the counter. "Yes, sir," he said. Al got down from his stool.

"I'm going back to the kitchen with the nigger and bright boy," he said. "Go on back to the kitchen, nigger. You go with him, bright boy." The little man walked after Nick and Sam, the cook, back into the kitchen. The door shut after them. The man called Max sat at the counter opposite George. He didn't look at George but looked in the mirror that ran along back of the counter. Henry's had been made over from a saloon into a lunch-counter.

"Well, bright boy," Max said, looking into the mirror, "why don't you say something?"

"What's it all about?"

"Hey, Al," Max called, "bright boy wants to know what it's all about."

"Why don't you tell him?" Al's voice came from the kitchen.

"What do you think it's all about?"

"I don't know."

"What do you think?"

Max looked into the mirror all the time he was talking.

"I wouldn't say."

"Hey, Al, bright boy says he wouldn't say what he thinks it's all about."

"I can hear you, all right," Al said from the kitchen. He had propped open the slit that dishes passed through into the kitchen with a catsup bottle. "Listen, bright boy," he said from the kitchen to George. "Stand a little further along the bar. You move a little to the left, Max." He was like a photographer arranging for a group picture.

"Talk to me, bright boy," Max said. "What do you think's going to happen?"

George did not say anything.

"I'll tell you," Max said. "We're going to kill a Swede. Do you know a big Swede named Ole Andreson?"

"Yes."

"He comes here to eat every night, don't he?"

"Sometimes he comes here."

"He comes here at six o'clock, don't he?"

"If he comes."

"We know all that, bright boy," Max said. "Talk about something else. Ever go to the movies?"

"Once in a while."

"You ought to go to the movies more. The movies are fine for a bright boy like you."

"What are you going to kill Ole Andreson for? What did he ever do to you?"

"He never had a chance to do anything to us. He never even seen us."

"And he's only going to see us once," Al said from the kitchen.

"What are you going to kill him for, then?" George asked.

"We're killing him for a friend. Just to oblige a friend, bright boy."

"Shut up," said Al from the kitchen. "You talk too goddam much."

"Well, I got to keep bright boy amused. Don't I, bright boy?"

"You talk too damn much," Al said. "The nigger and my bright boy are amused by themselves. I got them tied up like a couple of girl friends in the convent."

"I suppose you were in a convent."

"You never know."

"You were in a kosher convent. That's where you were."

George looked up at the clock.

"If anybody comes in you tell them the cook is off, and if they keep after it, you tell them you'll go back and cook yourself. Do you get that, bright boy?"

"All right," George said. "What you going to do with us afterward?"

"That'll depend," Max said. "That's one of those things you never know at the time."

George looked up at the clock. It was a quarter past six. The door from the street opened. A streetcar motorman came in.

"Hello, George," he said. "Can I get supper?"

"Sam's gone out," George said. "He'll be back in about half an hour."

"I'd better go up the street," the motorman said. George looked at the clock. It was twenty minutes past six.

"That was nice, bright boy," Max said. "You're a regular little gentleman."

"He knew I'd blow his head off," Al said from the kitchen.

"No," said Max. "It ain't that. Bright boy is nice. He's a nice boy. I like him."

At six-fifty-five George said: "He's not coming."

Two other people had been in the lunchroom. Once George had gone out to the kitchen and made a ham-and-egg sandwich "to go" that a man wanted to take with him. Inside the kitchen he saw Al, his derby hat tipped back, sitting on a stool beside the wicket with the muzzle of a sawed-off shotgun resting on the ledge. Nick and the cook were back to back in the corner, a towel tied in each of their mouths. George had cooked the sandwich, wrapped it up in oiled paper, put in in a bag, brought it in, and the man had paid for it and gone out.

"Bright boy can do everything," Max said. "He can cook and everything. You'd make some girl a nice wife, bright boy."

"Yes?" George said. "Your friend, Ole Andreson, isn't going to come."

"We'll give him ten minutes," Max said.

Max watched the mirror and the clock. The hands of the clock marked seven o'clock, and then five minutes past seven.

"Come on, Al," said Max. "We better go. He's not coming."

"Better give him five minutes," Al said from the kitchen.

In the five minutes a man came in, and George explained that the cook was sick.

"Why the hell don't you get another cook?" the man asked. "Aren't you running a lunch-counter?" He went out.

"Come on, Al," Max said.

"What about the two bright boys and the nigger?"

"They're all right."

"You think so?"

"Sure. We're through with it."

"I don't like it," said Al. "It's sloppy. You talk too much."

"Oh, what the hell," said Max. "We got to keep amused, haven't we?"

"You talk too much, all the same," Al said. He came out from the kitchen. The cut-off barrels of the shotgun made a slight bulge under the waist of his too tight-fitting overcoat. He straightened his coat with his gloved hands.

"So long, bright boy," he said to George. "You got a lot of luck."

"That's the truth," Max said. "You ought to play the races, bright boy."

The two of them went out the door. George watched them, through the window, pass under the arc-light and cross the street. In their tight overcoats and derby hats they looked like a vaudeville team. George went back through the swinging-door into the kitchen and untied Nick and the cook.

"I don't want any more of that," said Sam, the cook. "I don't want any more of that."

Nick stood up. He had never had a towel in his mouth before.

"Say," he said. "What the hell?" He was trying to swagger it off.

"They were going to kill Ole Andreson," George said. "They were going to shoot him when he came in to eat."

"Ole Andreson?"

"Sure."

The cook felt the corners of his mouth with his thumbs.

"They all gone?" he asked.

"Yeah," said George. "They're gone now."

"I don't like it," said the cook. "I don't like any of it at all."

"Listen," George said to Nick. "You better go see Ole Andreson."

"All right."

"You better not have anything to do with it at all," Sam, the cook said, "You better stay way out of it."

"Don't go if you don't want to," George said.

"Mixing up in this ain't going to get you anywhere," the cook said. "You stay out of it."

"I'll go see him," Nick said to George. "Where does he live?"

The cook turned away.

"Little boys always know what they want to do," he said.

"He lives up at Hirsch's rooming-house," George said to Nick.

"I'll go up there."

Outside the arc-light shone through the bare branches of a tree. Nick walked up the street beside the car-tracks and turned at the next arc-light down a side-street. Three houses up the street was Hirsch's rooming-house. Nick walked up the two steps and pushed the bell. A woman came to the door.

"Is Ole Andreson here?"

"Do you want to see him?"

"Yes, if he's in."

Nick followed the woman up a flight of stairs and back to the end of a corridor. She knocked on the door.

"Who is it?"

"It's somebody to see you, Mr. Andreson," the woman said.

"It's Nick Adams."

"Come in."

Nick opened the door and went into the room. Ole Andreson was lying on the bed with all his clothes on. He had been a heavyweight prizefighter and he was too long for the bed. He lay with his head on two pillows. He did not look at Nick.

"What was it?" he asked.

"I was up at Henry's," Nick said, "and two fellows came in and tied up me and the cook, and they said they were going to kill you."

It sounded silly when he said it. Ole Andreson said nothing.

"They put us out in the kitchen," Nick went on. "They were going to shoot you when you came in to supper."

Ole Andreson looked at the wall and did not say anything.

"George thought I better come and tell you about it."

"There isn't anything I can do about it," Ole Andreson said.

"I'll tell you what they were like."

"I don't want to know what they were like," Ole Andreson said. He looked at the wall. "Thanks for coming to tell me about it."

"That's all right."

Nick looked at the big man lying on the bed.

"Don't you want me to go and see the police?"

"No," Ole Andreson said. "That wouldn't do any good."

"Isn't there something I could do?"

"No. There ain't anything to do."

"Maybe it was just a bluff."

"No. It ain't just a bluff."

Ole Andreson rolled over toward the wall.

"The only thing is," he said, talking toward the wall, "I just can't make up my mind to go out. I been in here all day."

"Couldn't you get out of town?"

"No," Ole Andreson said. "I'm through with all that running around."

He looked at the wall.

"There ain't anything to do now."

"Couldn't you fix it up some way?"

"No, I got in wrong." He talked in the same flat voice. "There ain't anything to do. After a while I'll make up my mind to go out."

"I better go back and see George," Nick said.

"So long," said Ole Andreson. He did not look toward Nick. "Thanks for coming around."

Nick went out. As he shut the door he saw Ole Andreson with all his clothes on, lying on the bed looking at the wall.

"He's been in his room all day," the

landlady said downstairs. "I guess he don't feel well. I said to him: 'Mr. Andreson, you ought to go out and take a walk on a nice fall day like this,' but he didn't feel like it."

"He doesn't want to go out."

"I'm sorry he don't feel well," the woman said. "He's an awfully nice man. He was in the ring, you know."

"I know it."

"You'd never know it except from the way his face is," the woman said. They stood talking just inside the street door. "He's just as gentle."

"Well, good-night, Mrs. Hirsch," Nick said.

"I'm not Mrs. Hirsch," the woman said. "She owns the place. I just look after it for her. I'm Mrs. Bell."

"Well, good-night, Mrs. Bell," Nick said.

"Good-night," the woman said.

Nick walked up the dark street to the corner under the arc-light, and then along the car-tracks to Henry's eating-house. George was inside, back of the counter.

"Did you see Ole?"

"Yes," said Nick. "He's in his room and he won't go out."

The cook opened the door from the kitchen when he heard Nick's voice.

"I don't even listen to it," he said and shut the door.

"Did you tell him about it?" George asked.

"Sure. I told him but he knows what it's all about."

"What's he going to do?"

"Nothing."

"They'll kill him."

"I guess they will."

"He must have got mixed up in something in Chicago."

"I guess so," said Nick.

"It's a hell of a thing."

"It's an awful thing," Nick said.

They did not say anything. George reached down for a towel and wiped the counter.

"I wonder what he did?" Nick said.

"Double-crossed somebody. That's what they kill them for."

"I'm going to get out of this town," Nick said.

"Yes," said George. "That's a good thing to do."

"I can't stand to think about him waiting in the room and knowing he's going to get it. It's too damned awful."

"Well," said George, "you better not think about it."

[1927]

For Thought

Language plays an especially important role in "The Killers." It is used to create a tense, intimidating atmosphere and give the action a sense of urgency and imminent danger. The short sentences, terse dialogue, and curt repetition of phrases set a pace and rhythm that allow the story to be told economically and swiftly. With this fast-moving technique, Hemingway concentrates on the discovery by an inexperienced, idealistic youth of the presence and power of evil in life. By the end of the story, this discovery exerts an overwhelmingly disillusioning effect upon the young protagonist, who previously had naively assumed that evil could be thwarted and right would prevail over wrong.

For Discussion

1. From what point of view is the story told? What advantages does this point of view possess in this story for action and characterization?
2. What are the major conflicts in the story?

3. How does the title of the story help to set the tone?
4. How do the locale, time of day, and historical period help create a motivating atmosphere?
5. By what means and by the use of what details does Hemingway characterize the killers?
6. How does Max's boasting of the murder plan add to the atmosphere and theme?
7. What is significant about the intended murder weapon being a shotgun?
8. What comic elements, if any, are there in the story?
9. How do George and Sam's reactions differ from each other's and from Nick's?
10. What theme arises out of the action and its resolution?

Langston Hughes
On the Road

He was not interested in the snow. When he got off the freight, one early evening during the depression, Sargeant never even noticed the snow. But he must have felt it seeping down his neck, cold, wet, sopping in his shoes. But if you had asked him, he wouldn't have known it was snowing. Sargeant didn't see the snow, not even under the bright lights of the main street, falling white and flaky against the night. He was too hungry, too sleepy, too tired.

The Reverend Mr. Dorset, however, saw the snow when he switched on his porch light, opened the front door of his parsonage, and found standing there before him a big black man with snow on his face, a human piece of night with snow on his face—obviously unemployed.

Said the Reverend Mr. Dorset before Sargeant even realized he'd opened his mouth: "I'm sorry. No! Go right on down this street four blocks and turn to your left, walk up seven and you'll see the Relief Shelter. I'm sorry. No!" He shut the door.

Sargeant wanted to tell the holy man that he had already been to the Relief Shelter, been to hundreds of relief shelters during the depression years, the beds were always gone and supper was over, the place was full, and they drew the color line anyhow. But the minister said, "No," and shut the door. Evidently he didn't want to hear about it. And he *had* a door to shut.

The big black man turned away. And even yet he didn't see the snow, walking right into it. Maybe he sensed it, cold, wet, sticking to his jaws, wet on his black hands, sopping in his shoes. He stopped and stood on the sidewalk hunched over—hungry, sleepy, cold—looking up and down. Then he looked right where he was—in front of a church. Of course! A church! Sure, right next to a parsonage, certainly a church.

It had *two* doors.

Broad white steps in the night all snowy white. Two high arched doors with slender stone pillars on either side. And way up, a round lacy window with a stone crucifix in the middle and Christ on the crucifix in stone. All this was pale in the street lights, solid and stony pale in the snow.

Sargeant blinked. When he looked up, the snow fell into his eyes. For the first time that night he *saw* the snow. He shook his head. He shook the snow from his coat sleeves, felt hungry, felt lost, felt not lost, felt cold. He walked up the steps of the church. He knocked at the door. No answer. He tried the handle. Locked. He put his shoulder against the door and his long black body slanted like a ramrod. He pushed. With loud rhythmic grunts, like the grunts in a chain-gang song, he pushed against the door.

"I'm tired . . . Huh! . . . Hongry . . . Uh! . . . I'm sleepy . . . Huh! I'm cold . . . I got to sleep somewheres," Sargeant said. "This here is a church, ain't it? Well, uh!"

He pushed against the door.

Suddenly, with an undue cracking and screaking the door began to give way to the tall black Negro who pushed ferociously against it.

By now two or three white people had stopped in the street, and Sargeant was vaguely aware of some of them yelling at him concerning the door. Three or four more came running, yelling at him.

"Hey!" they said. "Hey!"

"Uh-huh," answered the big tall Negro, "I know it's a white folks' church, but I got to sleep somewhere." He gave another lunge at the door. "Huh!"

And the door broke open.

But just when the door gave way, two white cops arrived in a car, ran up the steps with their clubs, and grabbed Sargeant. But Sargeant for once had no intention of being pulled or pushed away from the door.

Sargeant grabbed, but not for anything so weak as a broken door. He grabbed for one of the tall stone pillars beside the door, grabbed at it and caught it. And held it. The cops pulled and Sargeant pulled. Most of the people in the street got behind the cops and helped them pull.

"A big black unemployed Negro holding onto our church!" thought the people. "The idea!"

The cops began to beat Sargeant over the head, and nobody protested. But he held on.

And then the church fell down.

Gradually, the big stone front of the church fell down, the walls and the rafters, the crucifix and the Christ. Then the whole thing fell down, covering the cops and the people with bricks and stones and debris. The whole church fell down in the snow.

Sargeant got out from under the church and went walking on up the street with the stone pillar on his shoulder. He was under the impression that he had buried the parsonage and the Reverend Mr. Dorset who said, "No!" So he laughed, and threw the pillar six blocks up the street and went on.

Sargeant thought he was alone, but listening to the *crunch, crunch, crunch* on the snow of his own footsteps, he heard other footsteps, too, doubling his own. He looked around, and there was Christ walking along beside him, the same Christ that had been on the cross on the church—still stone with a rough stone surface, walking along beside him just like he was broken off the cross when the church fell down.

"Well, I'll be dogged," said Sargeant. "This here's the first time I ever seed you off the cross."

"Yes," said Christ, crunching his feet in the snow. "You had to pull the church down to get me off the cross."

"You glad?" said Sargeant.

"I sure am," said Christ.

They both laughed.

"I'm a hell of a fellow, ain't I?" said Sargeant. "Done pulled the church down!"

"You did a good job," said Christ. "They have kept me nailed on a cross for nearly two thousand years."

"Whee-ee-e!" said Sargeant. "I know you are glad to get off."

"I sure am," said Christ.

They walked on in the snow. Sargeant looked at the man of stone.

"And you have been up there two thousand years?"

"I sure have," Christ said.

"Well, if I had a little cash," said Sargeant, "I'd show you around a bit."

"I been around," said Christ.

"Yeah, but that was a long time ago."

"All the same," said Christ, "I've been around."

They walked on in the snow until they came to the railroad yards. Sargeant was tired, sweating and tired.

"Where you goin'?" Sargeant said, stopping by the tracks. He looked at Christ. Sargeant said, "I'm just a bum on the road. How about you? Where you goin'?"

"God knows," Christ said, "but I'm leavin' here."

They saw the red and green lights of the railroad yard half veiled by the snow that fell out of the night. Away down the track they saw a fire in a hobo jungle.

"I can go there and sleep," Sargeant said.

"You can?"

"Sure," said Sargeant. "That place ain't got no doors."

Outside the town, along the tracks, there were barren trees and bushes below the embankment, snow-gray in the dark. And down among the trees and bushes there were makeshift houses made out of boxes and tin and old pieces of wood and canvas. You couldn't see them in the dark, but you knew they were there if you'd ever been on the road, if you had ever lived with the homeless and hungry in a depression.

"I'm side-tracking," Sargeant said. "I'm tired."

"I'm gonna make it on to Kansas City," said Christ.

"O.K.," Sargeant said. "So long!"

He went down into the hobo jungle and found himself a place to sleep. He never did see Christ no more. About 6:00 A.M. a freight came by. Sargeant scrambled out of the jungle with a dozen or so more hobos and ran along the track, grabbing at the freight. It was dawn, early dawn, cold and gray.

"Wonder where Christ is by now?" Sargeant thought. "He musta gone on way on down the road. He didn't sleep in this jungle."

Sargeant grabbed the train and started to pull himself up into a moving coal car, over the edge of a wheeling coal car. But strangely enough, the car was full of cops. The nearest cop rapped Sargeant soundly across the knuckles with his night stick. Wham! Rapped his big black hands for clinging to the top of the car. Wham! But Sargeant did not turn loose. He clung on and tried to pull himself into the car. He hollered at the top of his voice, "Damn it, lemme in this car!"

"Shut up," barked the cop. "You crazy coon!" He rapped Sargeant across the knuckles and punched him in the stomach. "You ain't out in no jungle now. This ain't no train. You in jail."

Wham! Across his bare black fingers clinging to the bars of his cell. Wham! between the steel bars low down against his shins.

Suddenly Sargeant realized that he really was in jail. He wasn't on no train. The blood of the night before had dried on his face, his head hurt terribly, and a cop outside in the corridor was hitting him across the knuckles for holding onto the door, yelling and shaking the cell door.

"They musta took me to jail for breaking down the door last night," Sargeant thought, "that church door."

Sargeant went over and sat on a wooden bench against the cold stone wall. He was emptier than ever. His clothes were wet, clammy cold wet, and shoes sloppy with snow water. It was just about dawn. There he was, locked up behind a cell door, nursing his bruised fingers.

The bruised fingers were his, but not the *door*.

Not the *club*, but the fingers.

"You wait," mumbled Sargeant, black against the jail wall. "I'm gonna break down this door, too."

"Shut up—or I'll paste you one," said the cop.

"I'm gonna break down this door," yelled Sargeant as he stood up in his cell.

Then he must have been talking to himself because he said, "I wonder where Christ's gone? I wonder if he's gone to Kansas City?"

[1934]

For Thought

Hughes has created a black tramp for the downtrodden hero of "On the Road." Sargeant moves through a half-real, half-fantastic world of the American Depression era in search of food, lodging, and dignity. Like the Biblical hero Samson, Sargeant, a stranger in a cruel land, pulls down the pillars of a church that has rejected him. Hughes suggests that Sargeant's partnership with Christ is a startling reminder of the kinship of all people.

For Discussion

1. How does Hughes characterize Sargeant? How are Sargeant's fantasies of his destruction of the church and his partnership with a living Christ "realistic," considering Sargeant's state of mind?
2. What elements of the story suggest the American Depression era? How does the story avoid being "dated," taking on universal implications that go beyond a particular place and time?
3. What comment does Hughes seem to make regarding comtemporary Christianity? (Consider the minister's response to Sargeant, the symbolism of the church, and Christ's appearance and comments.)
4. What is the theme of the story?

Shirley Jackson
The Lottery

The morning of June 27th was clear and sunny, with the fresh warmth of a full-summer day; the flowers were blossoming profusely and the grass was richly green. The people of the village began to gather in the square, between the post office and the bank, around ten o'clock; in some towns there were so many people that the lottery took two days and had to be started on June 26th, but in this village, where there were only about three hundred people, the whole lottery took less than two hours, so it could begin at ten o'clock in the morning and still be through in time to allow the villagers to get home for noon dinner.

The children assembled first, of course. School was recently over for the summer, and the feeling of liberty sat uneasily on most of them; they tended to gather together quietly for a while before they broke into boisterous play, and their talk was still of the classroom and the teacher, of books and reprimands. Bobby Martin had already stuffed his pockets full of stones, and the other boys soon followed his example, selecting the smoothest and roundest stones; Bobby and Harry Jones and Dickie Delacroix—the villagers pronounced this name "Dellacroy"—eventually made a great pile of stones in one corner of the square and guarded it against the raids of the other boys. The girls stood aside, talking among themselves, looking over their shoulders at the boys, and the very small children rolled in the dust or clung to the hands of their older brothers or sisters.

Soon the men began to gather, surveying their own children, speaking of planting and rain, tractors and taxes. They stood together, away from the pile of stones in the corner, and their jokes were quiet and they smiled rather than laughed. The women, wearing faded house dresses and sweaters, came shortly after their menfolk. They greeted one another and exchanged bits of gossip as they went to join their husbands. Soon the women, standing by their husbands, began to call to their children, and the children came reluctantly, having to be called four or five times. Bobby Martin ducked under his mother's grasping hand and ran, laughing, back to the pile of stones. His father spoke up sharply, and Bobby came quickly and took his place between his father and his oldest brother.

The lottery was conducted—as were the square dances, the teen-age club, the Halloween program—by Mr. Summers, who had time and energy to devote to civic activities. He was a round-faced, jovial man and he ran the coal business, and people were sorry for him, because he had no children and his wife was a scold. When he arrived in the square, carrying the black wooden box, there was a murmur of conversation among the villagers, and he waved and called, "Little late today, folks." The postmaster, Mr. Graves, followed him, carrying a three-legged stool, and the stool was put in the center of the square and Mr. Summers set the black box down on it. The villagers kept their distance, leaving a space between themselves and the stool, and when Mr. Summers said, "Some of you fellows want to give me a hand?" there was a hesitation before two men, Mr. Martin and his oldest son, Baxter, came forward to hold the box steady on the stool while Mr. Summers stirred up the papers inside it.

The original paraphernalia for the lottery had been lost long ago, and the black box now resting on the stool had been put into use even before Old Man Warner, the oldest man in town, was born. Mr. Summers spoke frequently to the villagers about making a new box, but no one liked to upset even as much tradition as was represented by the black box. There was a story that the present box had been made with some pieces of the box that had preceded it, the one that had been constructed when the first people settled down to make a village here. Every year, after the lottery, Mr. Summers began talking again about a new box, but every year the subject was allowed to fade off without anything's being done. The black box grew shabbier each year; by now it was no longer completely black but splintered badly along one side to show the original wood color, and in some places faded or stained.

Mr. Martin and his oldest son, Baxter, held the black box securely on the stool until Mr. Summers had stirred the papers thoroughly with his hand. Because so much of the ritual had been forgotten or discarded, Mr. Summers had been successful in having slips of paper substituted for the chips of wood that had been used for generations. Chips of wood, Mr. Summers had argued, had been all very well when the village was tiny, but now that the population was more than three hundred and likely to keep on growing, it was necessary to use something that would fit more easily into the black box. The night before the lottery, Mr. Summers and Mr. Graves made up the slips of paper and put them in the box, and it was then taken to the safe of Mr. Summers' coal company and locked up until Mr. Summers was ready to take it to the square next morning. The rest of the year, the box was put away, sometimes one place, sometimes another; it had spent one year in Mr. Grave's barn and another year underfoot in the post office, and sometimes it was set on a shelf in the Martin grocery and left there.

There was a great deal of fussing to be done before Mr. Summers declared the lottery open. There were the lists to make up—of heads of families, heads of households in each family, members of each household in each family. There was the proper swearing-in of Mr. Summers by the postmaster, as the official of the lottery; at one time, some people remembered, there had been a recital of some sort, performed by the official of the lottery, a perfunctory, tuneless chant that had been rattled off duly each year; some people believed that the official of the lottery used to stand just so when he said or sang it, others believed that he was supposed to walk among the people, but years and years ago this part of the ritual had been allowed to lapse. There had been, also, a ritual salute, which the official of the lottery had had to use in addressing each person who came up to draw from the box, but this also had changed with time, until now it was felt necessary only for the official to speak to each person approaching. Mr. Summers was very good at all this; in his clean white shirt and blue jeans, with one hand resting carelessly on the black box, he seemed very proper and important as he talked interminably to Mr. Graves and the Martins.

Just as Mr. Summers finally left off talking and turned to the assembled villagers, Mrs. Hutchinson came hurriedly along the path to the square, her sweater thrown over her shoulders, and slid into place in the back of the crowd. "Clean forgot what day it was," she said to Mrs. Delacroix, who stood next to her, and they both laughed softly. "Thought my old man was out back stacking wood," Mrs. Hutchinson went on, "and then I looked out the window and the kids were gone, and then I remembered it was the twenty-seventh and came a-running." She dried her hands on her apron, and Mrs. Delacroix said, "You're in time, though. They're still talking away up there."

Mrs. Hutchinson craned her neck to see through the crowd and found her husband and children standing near the front. She tapped Mrs. Delacroix on the arm as a farewell and began to make her way through the crowd. The people separated good-humoredly to let her through; two or three people said, in voices just loud enough to be heard across the crowd, "Here comes your Missus, Hutchinson," and "Bill, she made it after all." Mrs. Hutchinson reached her husband, and Mr. Summers, who had been waiting, said cheerfully, "Thought we were going to have to get on without you, Tessie." Mrs. Hutchinson said, grinning, "Wouldn't have me leave m'dishes in the sink, now, would you, Joe?" and soft laughter ran through the crowd as the people stirred back into position after Mrs. Hutchinson's arrival.

"Well, now," Mr. Summers said soberly, "guess we better get started, get this over with, so's we can go back to work. Anybody ain't here?"

"Dunbar," several people said. "Dunbar, Dunbar."

Mr. Summers consulted his list. "Clyde Dunbar," he said. "That's right. He's broke his leg, hasn't he? Who's drawing for him?"

"Me, I guess," a woman said, and Mr. Summers turned to look at her. "Wife draws for her husband," Mr. Summers said. "Don't you have a grown boy to do it for you, Janey?" Although Mr. Summers and everyone else in the village knew the answer perfectly well, it was the business of the official of the lottery to ask such questions formally. Mr. Summers waited with an expression of polite interest while Mrs. Dunbar answered.

"Horace's not but sixteen yet," Mrs. Dunbar said regretfully. "Guess I gotta fill in for the old man this year."

"Right," Mr. Summers said. He made a note on the list he was holding. Then he asked, "Watson boy drawing this year?"

A tall boy in the crowd raised his hand. "Here," he said. "I'm drawing for m'mother and me." He blinked his eyes nervously and ducked his head as several voices in the crowd said things like "Good fellow, Jack," and "Glad to see your mother's got a man to do it."

"Well," Mr. Summers said, "guess that's everyone. Old Man Warner make it?"

"Here," a voice said, and Mr. Summers nodded.

A sudden hush fell on the crowd as Mr. Summers cleared his throat and looked at the list. "All ready?" he called. "Now, I'll read the names—heads of families first—and the men come up and take a paper out of the box. Keep the paper folded in your hand without looking at it until everyone has had a turn. Everything clear?"

The people had done it so many times that they only half listened to the directions; most of them were quiet, wetting their lips, not looking around. Then Mr.

Summers raised one hand high and said, "Adams." A man disengaged himself from the crowd and came forward. "Hi, Steve," Mr. Summers said, and Mr. Adams said, "Hi, Joe." They grinned at one another humorlessly and nervously. Then Mr. Adams reached into the black box and took out a folded paper. He held it firmly by one corner as he turned and went hastily back to his place in the crowd, where he stood a little apart from his family, not looking down at his hand.

"Allen," Mr. Summers said. "Anderson. . . . Bentham."

"Seems like there's no time at all between lotteries any more," Mrs. Delacroix said to Mrs. Graves in the back row. "Seems like we got through with the last one only last week."

"Time sure goes fast," Mrs. Graves said.

"Clark. . . . Delacroix."

"There goes my old man," Mrs. Delacroix said. She held her breath while her husband went forward.

"Dunbar," Mr. Summers said, and Mrs. Dunbar went steadily to the box while one of the women said, "Go on, Janey," and another said, "There she goes."

"We're next," Mrs. Graves said. She watched while Mr. Graves came around from the side of the box, greeted Mr. Summers gravely, and selected a slip of paper from the box. By now, all through the crowd there were men holding the small folded papers in their large hands, turning them over and over nervously. Mrs. Dunbar and her two sons stood together, Mrs. Dunbar holding the slip of paper.

"Harburt. . . . Hutchinson."

"Get up there, Bill," Mrs. Hutchinson said, and the people near her laughed.

"Jones."

"They do say," Mr. Adams said to Old Man Warner, who stood next to him, "that over in the north village they're talking of giving up the lottery."

Old Man Warner snorted. "Pack of crazy fools," he said. "Listening to the young folks, nothing's good enough for *them.* Next thing you know, they'll be wanting to go back to living in caves, nobody work any more, live *that* way for a while. Used to be a saying about 'Lottery in June, corn be heavy soon.' First thing you know, we'd all be eating stewed chickweed and acorns. There's *always* been a lottery," he added petulantly. "Bad enough to see young Joe Summers up there joking with everybody."

"Some places have already quit lotteries," Mrs. Adams said.

"Nothing but trouble in *that,*" Old Man Warner said stoutly. "Pack of young fools."

"Martin." And Bobby Martin watched his father go forward. "Overdyke. . . . Percy."

"I wish they'd hurry," Mrs. Dunbar said to her older son. "I wish they'd hurry."

"They're almost through," her son said.

"You get ready to run tell Dad," Mrs. Dunbar said.

Mr. Summers called his own name and then stepped forward precisely and selected a slip from the box. Then he called, "Warner."

"Seventy-seventh year I been in the lottery," Old Man Warner said as he went through the crowd. "Seventy-seventh time."

"Watson." The tall boy came awkwardly through the crowd. Someone said, "Don't be nervous, Jack," and Mr. Summers said, "Take your time, son."

"Zanini."

After that, there was a long pause, a breathless pause, until Mr. Summers, holding his slip of paper in the air, said "All right, fellows." For a minute, no one moved, and then all the slips of paper were opened. Suddenly, all the women began to speak at once, saying, "Who is it?" "Who's got it?" "Is it the Dunbars?" "Is it the Watsons?" Then the voices began to say, "It's Hutchinson. It's Bill," "Bill Hutchinson's got it."

"Go tell your father," Mrs. Dunbar said to her older son.

People began to look around to see the Hutchinsons. Bill Hutchinson was standing quiet, staring down at the paper in his hand. Suddenly, Tessie Hutchinson shouted to Mr. Summers, "You didn't give him time enough to take any paper he wanted. I saw you. It wasn't fair."

"Be a good sport, Tessie," Mrs. Delacroix called, and Mrs. Graves said, "All of us took the same chance."

"Shut up, Tessie," Bill Hutchinson said.

"Well, everyone," Mr. Summers said, "that was done pretty fast, and now we've got to be hurrying a little more to get done in time." He consulted his next list. "Bill," he said, "you draw for the Hutchinson family. You got any other households in the Hutchinsons?"

"There's Don and Eva," Mrs. Hutchinson yelled. "Make *them* take their chance!"

"Daughters draw with their husbands' families, Tessie," Mr. Summers said gently. "You know that as well as anyone else.

"It wasn't *fair*," Tessie said.

"I guess not, Joe," Bill Hutchinson said regretfully. "My daughter draws with her husband's family, that's only fair. And I've got no other family except the kids."

"Then, as far as drawing for families is concerned, it's you," Mr. Summers said in explanation, "and as far as drawing for households is concerned, that's you, too. Right?"

"Right," Bill Hutchinson said.

"How many kids, Bill?" Mr. Summers asked formally.

"Three," Bill Hutchinson said. "There's Bill, Jr., and Nancy, and little Dave. And Tessie and me."

"All right, then," Mr. Summers said. "Harry, you got their tickets back?"

Mr. Graves nodded and held up the slips of paper. "Put them in the box, then," Mr. Summers directed. "Take Bill's and put it in."

"I think we ought to start over," Mrs. Hutchinson said, as quietly as she could. "I tell you it wasn't *fair*. You didn't give him time enough to choose. *Every*body saw that."

Mr. Graves had selected the five slips and put them in the box, and he dropped all the papers but those onto the ground, where the breeze caught them and lifted them off.

"Listen, everybody," Mrs. Hutchinson was saying to the people around her.

"Ready, Bill?" Mr. Summers asked, and Bill Hutchinson, with one quick glance around at his wife and children, nodded.

"Remember," Mr. Summers said, "take the slips and keep them folded until each person has taken one. Harry, you help little Dave." Mr. Graves took the hand of the little boy, who came willingly with him up to the box. "Take a paper out of the box, Davy," Mr. Summers said. Davy put his hand into the box and laughed. "Take just *one* paper," Mr. Summers said. "Harry, you hold it for him." Mr. Graves took the child's hand and removed the folded paper from the tight fist and held it while little Dave stood next to him and looked up at him wonderingly.

"Nancy next," Mr. Summers said. Nancy was twelve, and her school friends breathed heavily as she went forward, switching her skirt, and took a slip daintily from the box. "Bill, Jr.," Mr. Summers said, and Billy, his face red and his feet overlarge, nearly knocked the box over as he got a paper out. "Tessie," Mr. Summers said. She hesitated for a minute, looking around defiantly, and then set her lips and went up to the box. She snatched a paper out and held it behind her.

"Bill," Mr. Summers said, and Bill Hutchinson reached into the box and felt around, bringing his hand out at last with the slip of paper in it.

The crowd was quiet. A girl whispered, "I hope it's not Nancy," and the sound of the whisper reached the edges of the crowd.

"It's not the way it used to be," Old Man Warner said clearly. "People ain't the way they used to be."

"All right," Mr. Summers said. "Open the papers. Harry, you open little Dave's."

Mr. Graves opened the slip of paper and

there was a general sigh through the crowd as he held it up and everyone could see that it was blank. Nancy and Bill, Jr., opened theirs at the same time, and both beamed and laughed, turning around to the crowd and holding their slips of paper above their heads.

"Tessie," Mr. Summers said. There was a pause, and then Mr. Summers looked at Bill Hutchinson, and Bill unfolded his paper and showed it. It was blank.

"It's Tessie," Mr. Summers said, and his voice was hushed. "Show us her paper, Bill."

Bill Hutchinson went over to his wife and forced the slip of paper out of her hand. It had a black spot on it, the black spot Mr. Summers had made the night before with the heavy pencil in the coal-company office. Bill Hutchinson held it up, and there was a stir in the crowd.

"All right, folks," Mr. Summers said. "Let's finish quickly."

Although the villagers had forgotten the ritual and lost the original black box, they still remembered to use stones. The pile of stones the boys had made earlier was ready; there were stones on the ground with the blowing scraps of paper that had come out of the box. Mrs. Delacroix selected a stone so large she had to pick it up with both hands and turned to Mrs. Dunbar. "Come on," she said. "Hurry up."

Mrs. Dunbar had small stones in both hands, and she said, gasping for breath, "I can't run at all. You'll have to go ahead and I'll catch up with you."

The children had stones already, and someone gave little Davy Hutchinson a few pebbles.

Tessie Hutchinson was in the center of a cleared space by now, and she held her hands out desperately as the villagers moved in on her. "It isn't fair," she said. A stone hit her on the side of the head.

Old Man Warner was saying, "Come on, come on, everyone." Steve Adams was in the front of the crowd of villagers, with Mrs. Graves beside him.

"It isn't fair, it isn't right," Mrs. Hutchinson screamed, and then they were upon her.

[1943]

For Thought

The story-telling technique used in "The Lottery" involves turning the outwardly normal and innocent into the chillingly macabre and barbaric. The action is set in a disarmingly folksy small town whose ordinariness lulls the reader's perceptions to sleep until one is rudely awakened by the conclusion of the ritual lottery, at which point one's curiosity is transformed into horrified surprise and disbelief.

For Discussion

1. What is the atmosphere and mood at the beginning of the story? How are they established?
2. What is the first sinister element in the story? How is its true nature disguised?
3. What point of view is used and what purpose does it serve? What other points of view might the author have used and with what losses and what gains?
4. How does the dialogue help to create the mood of the story?
5. How are the arrival of Mrs. Hutchinson, her joining the crowd, and her conversation with Mr. Summers used as an element of parody to heighten the irony?
6. Of what is Mr. Warner symbolic? Of what are Mr. and Mrs. Adams symbolic?
7. What is the climax of the story and what mood shifts occur with it?
8. What is the fundamental irony in the story? What is the central symbol?
9. What is the main conflict in the story? What meaning emerges from its resolution?

Henry James
The Real Thing

I

When the porter's wife, who used to answer the house-bell, announced "A gentleman and a lady, sir," I had, as I often had in those days—the wish being father to the thought—an immediate vision of sitters. Sitters my visitors in this case proved to be; but not in the sense I should have preferred. There was nothing at first however to indicate that they mightn't have come for a portrait. The gentleman, a man of fifty, very high and very straight, with a moustache slightly grizzled and a dark gray walking-coat admirably fitted, both of which I noted professionally—I don't mean as a barber or yet as a tailor—would have struck me as a celebrity if celebrities often were striking. It was a truth of which I had for some time been conscious that a figure with a good deal of frontage was, as one might say, almost never a public institution. A glance at the lady helped to remind me of this paradoxical law: she also looked too distinguished to be a "personality." Moreover one would scarcely come across two variations together.

Neither of the pair immediately spoke—they only prolonged the preliminary gaze suggesting that each wished to give the other a chance. They were visibly shy; they stood there letting me take them in—which, as I afterwards perceived, was the most practical thing they could have done. In this way their embarrassment served their cause. I had seen people painfully reluctant to mention that they desired anything so gross as to be represented on canvas; but the scruples of my new friends appeared almost insurmountable. Yet the gentleman might have said, "I should like a portrait of my wife," and the lady might have said "I should like a portrait of my husband." Perhaps they weren't husband and wife—this naturally would make the matter more delicate. Perhaps they wished to be done together—in which case they ought to have brought a third person to break the news.

"We come from Mr. Rivet," the lady finally said with a dim smile that had the effect of a moist sponge passed over a "sunk" piece of painting, as well as of a vague al-

SOURCE: "The Real Thing" by Henry James. Originally published in 1890. Reprinted from *The Novels and Tales of Henry James*, vol. 18.

lusion to vanished beauty. She was as tall and straight, in her degree, as her companion, and with ten years less to carry. She looked as sad as a woman could look whose face was not charged with expression; that is her tinted oval mask showed waste as an exposed surface shows friction. The hand of time had played over her freely, but to an effect of elimination. She was slim and stiff, and so well-dressed, in dark blue cloth, with lappets and pockets and buttons, that it was clear she employed the same tailor as her husband. The couple had an indefinable air of prosperous thrift—they evidently got a good deal of luxury for their money. If I was to be one of their luxuries it would behoove me to consider my terms.

"Ah Claude Rivet recommended me?" I echoed; and I added that it was very kind of him, though I could reflect that, as he only painted landscape, this wasn't a sacrifice.

The lady looked very hard at the gentleman, and the gentleman looked round the room. Then staring at the floor a moment and stroking his moustache, he rested his pleasant eye on me with the remark: "He said you were the right one."

"I try to be, when people want to sit."

"Yes, we should like to," said the lady anxiously.

"Do you mean together?"

My visitors exchanged a glance. "If you could do anything with *me* I suppose it would be double," the gentleman stammered.

"Oh yes, there's naturally a higher charge for two figures than for one."

"We should like to make it pay," the husband confessed.

"That's very good of you," I returned, appreciating so unwonted a sympathy—for I supposed he meant pay the artist.

A sense of strangeness seemed to dawn on the lady. "We mean for the illustrations—Mr. Rivet said you might put one in."

"Put in—an illustration?" I was equally confused.

"Sketch her off, you know," said the gentleman, colouring.

It was only then that I understood the service Claude Rivet had rendered me; he had told them how I worked in black-and-white, for magazines, for storybooks, for sketches of contemporary life, and consequently had copious employment for models. These things were true, but it was not less true—I may confess it now; whether because the aspiration was to lead to everything or to nothing I leave the reader to guess—that I couldn't get the honours, to say nothing of the emoluments, of a great painter of portraits out of my head. My "illustrations" were my potboilers; I looked to a different branch of art—far and away the most interesting it had always seemed to me—to perpetuate my fame. There was no shame in looking to it also to make my fortune; but that fortune was by so much further from being made from the moment my visitors wished to be "done" for nothing. I was disappointed; for in the pictorial sense I had immediately *seen* them. I had seized their type—I had already settled what I would do with it. Something that wouldn't absolutely have pleased them, I afterwards reflected.

"Ah you're—you're—a?" I began as soon as I had mastered my surprise. I couldn't bring out the dingy word "models": it seemed so little to fit the case.

"We haven't had much practice," said the lady.

"We've got to *do* something, and we've thought that an artist in your line might perhaps make something of us," her husband threw off. He further mentioned that they didn't know many artists and that they had gone first, on the off-chance—he painted views of course, but sometimes put in figures; perhaps I remembered—to Mr. Rivet, whom they had met a few years before at a place in Norfolk where he was sketching.

"We used to sketch a little ourselves," the lady hinted.

"It's very awkward, but we absolutely *must* do something," her husband went on.

"Of course we're not so *very* young," she admitted with a wan smile.

With the remark that I might as well know something more about them the husband had handed me a card extracted from a neat new pocket-book—their appurtenances were all of the freshest—and inscribed with the words "Major Monarch." Impressive as these words were they didn't carry my knowledge much further; but my visitor presently added: "I've left the army and we've had the misfortune to lose our money. In fact our means are dreadfully small."

"It's awfully trying—a regular strain," said Mrs. Monarch.

They evidently wished to be discreet—to take care not to swagger because they were gentlefolk. I felt them willing to recognise this as something of a drawback, at the same time that I guessed at an underlying sense—their consolation in adversity—that they *had* their points. They certainly had; but these advantages struck me as preponderantly social; such for instance as would help to make a drawing-room look well. However, a drawing room was always, or ought to be, a picture.

In consequence of his wife's allusion to their age Major Monarch observed: "Naturally it's more for the figure that we thought of going in. We can still hold ourselves up." On the instant I saw that the figure was indeed their strong point. His "naturally" didn't sound vain, but it lighted up the question. "*She* has the best one," he continued, nodding at his wife with a pleasant after-dinner absence of circumlocution. I could only reply, as if we were in fact sitting over our wine, that this didn't prevent his own from being very good; which led him in turn to make answer: "We thought that if you ever have to do people like us we might be something like it. *She* particularly—for a lady in a book, you know."

I was so amused by them that, to get more of it, I did my best to take their point of view; and though it was an embarrassment to find myself appraising physically, as if they were animals on hire or useful blacks, a pair whom I should have expected to meet only in one of the relations in which criticism is tacit, I looked at Mrs. Monarch judicially enough to be able to exclaim after a moment with conviction: "Oh yes, a lady in a book!" She was singularly like a bad illustration.

"We'll stand up, if you like," said the Major; and he raised himself before me with a really grand air.

I could take his measure at a glance—he was six feet two and a perfect gentleman. It would have paid any club in process of formation and in want of a stamp to engage him at a salary to stand in the principal window. What struck me at once was that in coming to me they had rather missed their vocation; they could surely have been turned to better account for advertising purposes. I couldn't of course see the thing in detail, but I could see them make somebody's fortune—I don't mean their own. There was something in them for a waistcoat-maker, an hotel-keeper or a soap-vendor. I could imagine "We always use it" pinned on their bosoms with the greatest effect; I had a vision of the brilliancy with which they would launch a table d'hôte.

Mrs. Monarch sat still, not from pride but from shyness, and presently her husband said to her: "Get up, my dear, and show how smart you are." She obeyed, but she had no need to get up to show it. She walked to the end of the studio and then came back blushing, her fluttered eyes on the partner of her appeal. I was reminded of an incident I had accidentally had a glimpse of in Paris—being with a friend there, a dramatist about to produce a play, when an actress came to him to ask to be entrusted with a part. She went through her paces before him, walked up and down as Mrs. Monarch was doing. Mrs. Monarch did it quite as well, but I abstained from applauding. It was very odd to see such people apply for such poor pay. She looked as if she had ten thousand a year. Her husband had used the word that described her: she was in the London current jargon essentially and typically "smart." Her figure was, in the same order of ideas, conspicuously and irreproachably "good." For a woman of her age her waist was surprisingly small; her elbow moreover had the orthodox crook. She held her head at the conventional angle, but why did she come to *me?* She ought to have tried on jackets at a big shop. I feared my visitors were not only destitute but "artistic"—which would be a great complication. When she sat down again I thanked her, observing that what a draughtsman most valued in his model was the faculty of keeping quiet.

"Oh *she* can keep quiet," said Major Monarch. Then he added jocosely: "I've always kept her quiet."

"I'm not a nasty fidget, am I?" It was going to wring tears from me, I felt, the way she hid her head, ostrich-like, in the other broad bosom.

The owner of this expanse addressed his answer to me. "Perhaps it isn't out of place to mention—because we ought to be quite business-like, oughtn't we?—that when I married her she was known as the Beautiful Statue."

"Oh dear!" said Mrs. Monarch ruefully.

"Of course I should want a certain amount of expression," I rejoined.

"Of *course!*"—and I had never heard such unanimity.

"And then I suppose you know that you'll get awfully tired."

"Oh we *never* get tired!" they eagerly cried.

"Have you had any kind of practice?"

They hesitated—they looked at each other. "We've been photographed—*immensely*," said Mrs. Monarch.

"She means the fellows have asked us themselves," added the Major.

"I see—because you're so good-looking."

"I don't know what they thought, but they were always after us."

"We always got our photographs for nothing," smiled Mrs. Monarch.

"We might have brought some, my dear," her husband remarked.

"I'm not sure we have any left. We've given quantities away," she explained to me.

"With our autographs and that sort of thing," said the Major.

"Are they to be got in the shops?" I enquired as a harmless pleasantry.

"Oh yes, *hers*—they used to be."

"Not now," said Mrs. Monarch, with her eyes on the floor.

II

I could fancy the "sort of thing" they put on the presentation copies of their photographs, and I was sure they wrote a beautiful hand. It was odd how quickly I was sure of everything that concerned them. If they were now so poor as to have to earn shillings and pence they could never have had much of a margin. Their good looks had been their capital, and they had good-humouredly made the most of the career that this resource marked out for them. It was in their faces, the blankness, the deep intellectual repose of the twenty years of country-house visiting that had given them pleasant intonations. I could see the sunny drawing-rooms, sprinkled with periodicals she didn't read, in which Mrs. Monarch had continuously sat; I could see the wet shrubberies in which she had walked, equipped to admiration for either exercise. I could see the rich covers the Major had helped to shoot and the wonderful garments in which, late at night, he repaired to the smoking-room to talk about them. I could imagine their leggings and waterproofs, their knowing tweeds and rugs, their rolls of sticks and cases of tackle and neat umbrellas; and I could evoke the exact appearance of their servants and the compact variety of their luggage on the platforms of country stations.

They gave small tips, but they were liked; they didn't do anything themselves, but they were welcome. They looked so well everwhere; they gratified the general relish for stature, complexion and "form."

They knew it without fatuity or vulgarity, and they respected themselves in consequence. They weren't superficial; they were thorough and kept themselves up—it had been their line. People with such a taste for activity had to have some line. I could feel how even in a dull house they could have been counted on for the joy of life. At present something had happened—it didn't matter what, their little income had grown less, it had grown least—and they had to do something for pocket-money. Their friends could like them, I made out, without liking to support them. There was something about them that represented credit—their clothes, their manners, their type; but if credit is a large empty pocket in which an occasional chink reverberates, the chink at least must be audible. What they wanted of me was to help to make it so. Fortunately they had no children—I soon divined that. They would also perhaps wish our relations to be kept secret: this was why it was "for the figure"—the reproduction of the face would betray them.

I liked them—I felt, quite as their friends must have done—they were so simple; and I had no objection to them if they would suit. But somehow with all their perfections I didn't easily believe in them. After all they were amateurs, and the ruling passion of my life was the detestation of the amateur. Combined with this was another perversity—an innate preference for the represented subject over the real one: the defect of the real one was so apt to be a lack of representation. I like things that appeared; then one was sure. Whether they *were* or not was subordinate and almost always a profitless question. There were other considerations, the first of which was that I already had two or three recruits in use, notably a young person with big feet, in alpaca, from Kilburn, who for a couple of years had come to me regularly for my illustrations and with whom I was still—perhaps ignobly—satisfied. I frankly explained to my visitors how the case stood, but they had taken more precautions than I supposed. They had reasoned out their opportunity, for Claude Rivet had told them of the projected *édition de luxe* of one of the writers of our day—the rarest of the novelists—who, long neglected by the multitudinous vulgar and dearly prized by the attentive (need I mention Philip Vincent?), had had the happy fortune of seeing, late in life, the dawn and then the full light of a higher criticism; an estimate in which on the part of the public there was something really of expiation. The edition preparing, planned by a publisher of taste, was practically an act of high reparation; the woodcuts with which it was to be enriched were the homage of English art to one of the most independent representatives of English letters. Major and Mrs. Monarch confessed to me they had hoped I might be able to work *them* into my branch of the enterprise. They knew I was to do the first of the books, "Rutland Ramsay," but I had to make clear to them that my participation in the rest of the affair—this first book was to be a test—must depend on the satisfaction I should give. If this should be limited my employers would drop me with scarce common forms. It was therefore a crisis for me, and naturally I was making special preparations, looking about for new people, should they be necessary, and securing the best types. I admitted however that I should like to settle down to two or three good models who would do everything.

"Should we have often to—a—put on special clothes?" Mrs. Monarch timidly demanded.

"Dear yes—that's half the business."

"And should we be expected to supply our own costumes?"

"Oh no; I've got a lot of things. A painter's models put on—or put off—anything he likes."

"And you mean—a—the same?"

"The same?"

"Oh she was just wondering," he exclaimed, "if the costumes are in *general* use." I had to confess that they were, and

I mentioned further that some of them—I had a lot of genuine greasy last-century things—had served their time, a hundred years ago, on living world-stained men and women; on figures not perhaps so far removed, in that vanished world from *their* type, the Monarchs' *quoi!* of a breeched and bewigged age. "We'll put on anything that *fits*," said the Major.

"Oh I arrange that—they fit in the pictures."

"I'm afraid I should do better for the modern books. I'd come as you like," said Mrs. Monarch.

"She has got a lot of clothes at home: they might do for contemporary life," her husband continued.

"Oh I can fancy scenes in which you'd be quite natural." And indeed I could see the slipshod rearrangements of stale properties—the stories I tried to produce pictures for without the exasperation of reading them—whose sandy tracts the good lady might help to people. But I had to return to the fact that for this sort of work—the daily mechanical grind—I was already equipped: the people I was working with were fully adequate.

"We only thought we might be more like *some* characters," said Mrs. Monarch mildly, getting up.

Her husband also rose; he stood looking at me with a dim wistfulness that was touching in so fine a man. "Wouldn't it be rather a pull sometimes to have—a—to have—?" He hung fire; he wanted me to help him by phrasing what he meant. But I couldn't—I didn't know. So he brought it out awkwardly: "The *real* thing; a gentleman, you know, or a lady." I was quite ready to give a general assent—I admitted that there was a great deal in that. This encouraged Major Monarch to say, following up his appeal with an unacted gulp: "It's awfully hard—we've tried everything." The gulp was communicative; it proved too much for his wife. Before I knew it Mrs. Monarch had dropped again upon a divan and burst into tears. Her husband sat down beside her, holding one of her hands; whereupon she quickly dried her eyes with the other, while I felt embarrassed as she looked up at me. "There isn't a confounded job I haven't applied for—waited for—prayed for. You can fancy we'd be pretty bad first. Secretaryships and that sort of thing? You might as well ask for a peerage. I'd be *anything*—I'm strong; a messenger or a coalheaver. I'd put on a gold-laced cap and open carriage-doors in front of the haberdasher's; I'd hang about a station to carry portmanteaux; I'd be a postman. But they won't *look* at you; there are thousands as good as yourself already on the ground. *Gentlemen*, poor beggars, who've drunk their wine, who've kept their hunters!"

I was as reassuring as I knew how to be, and my visitors were presently on their feet again while, for the experiment, we agreed on an hour. We were discussing it when the door opened and Miss Churm came in with a wet umbrella. Miss Churm had to take the omnibus to Maida Vale and then walk half a mile. She looked a trifle blowsy and slightly splashed. I scarcely ever saw her come in without thinking afresh how odd it was that, being so little in herself, she should yet be so much in others. She was a meagre little Miss Churm, but was such an ample heroine of romance. She was only a freckled cockney, but she could represent everything, from a fine lady to a shepherdess; she had the faculty as she might have had a fine voice or long hair. She couldn't spell and she loved beer, but she had two or three "points," and practice, and a knack, and mother-wit, and a whimsical sensibility, and a love of the theatre, and seven sisters, and not an ounce of respect, especially for the *h*. The first thing my visitors saw was that her umbrella was wet, and in their spotless perfection they visibly winced at it. The rain had come on since their arrival.

"I'm all in a soak; there was a mess of people in the 'bus. I wish you lived near a stytion," said Miss Churm. I requested her to get ready as quickly as possible, and she passed into the room in which she always changed her dress. But before going out she asked me what she was to get into this time.

"It's the Russian princess, don't you know?" I answered; "the one with the 'golden eyes,' in black velvet, for the long thing in the *Cheapside*."

"Golden eyes? I say!" cried Miss Churm, while my companions watched her with intensity as she withdrew. She always arranged herself, when she was late, before I could turn round; and I kept my visitors a little on purpose, so that they might get an idea, from seeing her, what would be expected of themselves. I mentioned that she was quite my notion of an excellent model—she was really very clever.

"Do you think she looks like a Russian princess?" Major Monarch asked with lurking alarm.

"When I make her, yes."

"Oh if you have to *make her*—!" he reasoned, not without point.

"That's the most you can ask. There are so many who are not makeable."

"Well now, *here's* a lady"—and with a persuasive smile he passed his arm into his wife's—"who's already made!"

"Oh I'm not a Russian princess," Mrs. Monarch protested a little coldly. I could see she had known some and didn't like them. There at once was a complication of a kind I never had to fear with Miss Churm.

This young lady came back in black velvet—the gown was rather rusty and very low on her lean shoulders—and with a Japanese fan in her red hands. I reminded her that in the scene I was doing she had to look over some one's head. "I forget whose it is; but it doesn't matter. Just look over a head."

"I'd rather look over a stove," said Miss Churm; and she took her station near the fire. She fell into position, settled herself into a tall attitude, gave a certain backward inclination to her head and a certain forward droop to her fan, and looked, at least to my prejudiced sense, distinguished and charming, foreign and dangerous. We lefther looking so while I went downstairs with Major and Mrs. Monarch.

"I believe I could come about as near it as that," said Mrs. Monarch.

"Oh you think she's shabby, but you must allow for the alchemy of art."

However, they went off with an evident increase of comfort founded on their demonstrable advantage in being the real thing. I could fancy them shuddering over Miss Churm. She was very droll about them when I went back, for I told her what they wanted.

"Well, if *she* can sit I'll tyke to book-keeping," said my model.

"She's very ladylike," I replied as an innocent form of aggravation.

"So much the worse for *you*. That means she can't turn round."

"She'll do for the fashionable novels."

"Oh yes, she'll *do* for them!" my model humorously declared. "Ain't they bad enough without her?" I had often sociably denounced them to Miss Churm.

III

It was for the elucidation of a mystery in one of these works that I first tried Mrs. Monarch. Her husband came with her, to be useful if necessary—it was sufficiently clear that as a general thing he would prefer to come with her. At first I wondered if this were for "propriety's" sake—if he were going to be jealous and meddling. The idea was too tiresome, and if it had been confirmed it would speedily have brought our acquaintance to a close. But I soon saw there was nothing in it and that if he accompanied Mrs. Monarch it was—in addition to the chance of being wanted—simply because he had nothing else to do. When they were separate his occupation was gone and they never *had* been separate. I judged rightly that in their awkward situation their close union was their main comfort and that this union had no weak spot. It was a real marriage, an encouragement to the hesitating, a nut for pessimists to crack. Their address was humble—I remember afterwards thinking it had been the only thing about them that was really professional—and I could fancy the lamentable lodgings in which the Major would have been left alone. He could sit there more or less grimly with his wife—he couldn't sit there anyhow without her.

He had too much tact to try and make himself agreeable when he couldn't be useful; so when I was too absorbed in my work to talk he simply sat and waited. But I liked to hear him talk—it made my work, when not interrupting it, less mechanical, less special. To listen to him was to combine the excitement of going out with the economy of staying at home. There was only one hindrance—that I seemed not to know any of the people this brilliant couple had known. I think he wondered extremely, during the term of our intercourse, whom the deuce I *did* know. He hadn't a stray sixpence of an idea to fumble for, so we didn't spin it very fine; we confined ourselves to questions of leather and even of liquor—saddlers and breeches-makers and how to get excellent claret cheap—and matters like "good trains" and the habits of small game. His lore on these last subjects was astonishing—he managed to interweave the station-master with the ornithologist. When he couldn't talk about greater things he could talk cheerfully about smaller, and since I couldn't accompany him into reminiscences of the fashionable world he could lower the conversation without a visible effort to my level.

So earnest a desire to please was touching in a man who could so easily have knocked one down. He looked after the fire and had an opinion on the draught of the stove without my asking him, and I could see that he thought many of my arrangements not half knowing. I remember telling him that if I were only rich I'd offer him a salary to come and teach me how to live. Sometimes he gave a random sigh of which the essence might have been: "Give me even such a bare old barrack as *this*, and I'd do something with it!" When I wanted to use him he came alone; which was an illustration of the superior courage of women. His wife could bear her solitary second floor, and she was in general more discreet; showing by various small reserves that she was alive to the propriety of keeping our relations markedly professional—not letting them slide into sociability. She wished it to remain clear that she and the Major were employed, not cultivated, and if she approved of me as a superior, who could be kept in his place, she never thought me quite good enough for an equal.

She sat with great intensity, giving the whole of her mind to it, and was capable of remaining for an hour almost as motionless as before a photographer's lens. I could see she had been photographed often, but somehow the very habit that made her good for that purpose unfitted her for mine. At first I was extremely pleased with her ladylike air, and it was a satisfaction, on coming to follow her lines, to see how good they were and how far they could lead the pencil. But after a little skirmishing I began to find her too insurmountably stiff; do what I would with it my drawing looked like a photograph or a copy of a photograph. Her figure had no variety of expression—she herself had no sense of variety. You may say that this was my business and was only a question of placing her. Yet I placed her in every conceivable position and she managed to obliterate their differences. She was always a lady certainly, and into the bargain was always the same lady. She was the real thing, but always the same thing. There were moments when I rather writhed under the serenity of her confidence that she was the real thing. All her dealings with me and all her husband's were an implication that this was lucky for *me*. Meanwhile I found myself trying to invent types that approached her own, instead of making her own transform itself—in the clever way that was not impossible for instance to poor Miss Churm. Arrange as I would and take the precautions I would, she always came out, in my pictures, too tall—landing me in the dilemma of having represented a fascinating woman as seven feet high, which (out of respect perhaps to my own very much scantier inches) was far from my idea of such a personage.

The case was worse with the Major—nothing I could do would keep *him* down, so that he became useful only for the representation of brawny giants. I adored variety and range, I cherished human accidents, the illustrative note; I wanted to characterise closely, and the thing in the world I most hated was the danger of being ridden by a type. I had quarreled with some of my friends about it; I had parted company with them for maintaining that one *had* to be, and that if the type was beautiful—witness Raphael and Leonardo—the servitude was only a gain. I was neither Leonardo nor Raphael—I might only be a presumptuous young modern searcher; but I held that everything was to be sacrificed sooner than character. When they claimed that the obsessional form could easily *be* character I retorted, perhaps superficially, "Whose?" It couldn't be everybody's—it might end in being nobody's.

After I had drawn Mrs. Monarch a dozen times I felt surer even than before that the value of such a model as Miss Churm resided precisely in the fact that she had no positive stamp, combined of course with the other fact that what she did have was a curious and inexplicable talent for imitation. Her usual appearance was like a curtain which she could draw up at request for a capital performance. This performance was simply suggestive; but it was a word to the wise—it was vivid and pretty. Sometimes even I thought it, though she was plain herself, too insipidly pretty; I made it a reproach to her that the figures drawn from her were monotonously (*bêtement*, as we used to say) graceful. Nothing made her more angry; it was so much her pride to feel she could sit for characters that had nothing in common with each other. She would accuse me at such moments of taking away her "reputytion."

It suffered a certain shrinkage, this queer quantity, from the repeated visits of my new friends. Miss Churm was greatly in demand, never in want of employment, so I had no scruple in putting her off occasionally, to try them more at my ease. It was certainly amusing at first to do the real thing—it was amusing to do Major Monarch's trousers. They *were* the real thing, even if he did come out colossal. It was amusing to do his wife's back hair—it was so mathematically neat—and the particular "smart" tension of her tight stays. She lent herself especially to positions in which the face was somewhat averted or blurred; she abounded in ladylike back views and *profils perdus*. When she stood erect she took naturally one of the attitudes in which court-painters represent queens and princesses; so that I found myself wondering whether, to draw out this accomplishment, I couldn't get the editor of the *Cheapside* to publish a really royal romance, "A Tale of Buckingham Palace." Sometimes however the real thing and the make-believe came into contact; by which I mean that Miss Churm, keeping an appointment or coming to make one on days when I had much work in hand, encountered her invidious rivals. The encounter was not on their part, for they noticed her no more than if she had been the housemaid; not from intentional loftiness, but simply because as yet, professionally, they didn't know how to fraternise, as I could imagine they would have liked—or at least that the Major would. They couldn't talk about the omnibus—they always walked; and they didn't know what else to try—she wasn't interested in good trains or cheap claret. Besides, they must have felt—in the air—that she was amused at them, secretly derisive of their ever knowing how. She wasn't a person to conceal the limits of her faith if she had had a chance to show them. On the other hand Mrs. Monarch didn't think her tidy; for why else did she take pains to say to me—it was going out of the way, for Mrs. Monarch—that she didn't like dirty women?

One day when my young lady happened to be present with my other sitters—she even dropped in, when it was convenient, for a chat—I asked her to be so good as to lend a hand in getting tea, a service with which she was familiar and which was one of a class that, living as I did in a small way, with slender domestic resources, I often appealed to my models to render. They liked to lay hands on my property, to break the sitting, and sometimes the china—it made them feel Bohemian. The next time I saw Miss Churm after this incident she surprised me greatly by making a scene about it—she accused me of having wished to humiliate her. She hadn't resented the outrage at the time, but had seemed obliging and amused, enjoying the comedy of asking Mrs. Monarch, who sat vague and silent, whether she would have cream and sugar, and putting an exaggerated simper into the question. She had tried intonations—as if she too wished to pass for the real thing—till I was afraid my other visitors would take offence.

Oh they were determined not to do this, and their touching patience was the measure of their great need. They would sit by the hour, uncomplaining, till I was ready to use them; they would come back on the chance of being wanted and would walk away cheerfully if it failed. I used to go to the door with them to see in what magnificent order they retreated. I tried to find other employment for them—I introduced them to several artists. But they didn't "take," for reasons I could appreciate, and I became rather anxiously aware that after such disappointments they fell back upon me with a heavier weight. They did me the honour to think me most *their* form. They weren't romantic enough for the painters, and in those days there were few serious workers in black-and-white. Besides, they had an eye to the great job I had mentioned to them—they had secretly set their hearts on supplying the right essence for my pictorial vindication of our fine novelist. They knew that for this undertaking I should want no costume-effects, none of the frippery of past ages—that it was a case in which everything would be contemporary and satirical and presumably genteel. If I could work them into it their future would be assured, for the labour would of course be long and the occupation steady.

One day Mrs. Monarch came without her husband—she explained his absence by his having had to go to the City. While she sat there in her usual relaxed majesty there came at the door a knock which I immediately recognised as the subdued appeal of a model out of work. It was followed by the entrance of a young man whom I at once saw to be a foreigner and who proved in fact an Italian acquainted with no English word but my name, which he uttered in a way that made it seem to include all others. I hadn't then visited his country, nor was I proficient in his tongue; but as he was not so meanly constituted—what Italian is?—as to depend only on that member for expression he conveyed to me, in familiar but graceful mimicry, that he was in search of exactly the employment in which the lady before me was engaged. I was not struck with him at first, and while I continued to draw I dropped few signs of interest or encouragement. He stood his ground however—not importunately, but with a dumb dog-like fidelity in his eyes that amounted to innocent impudence, the manner of a devoted servant—he might have been in the house for years—unjustly suspected. Suddenly it struck me that this very attitude and expression made a picture; whereupon I told him to sit down and wait till I should be free. There was another picture in the way he obeyed me, and I observed as I worked that there were others still in the way he looked wonderingly, with his head thrown back, about the high studio. He might have been crossing himself in Saint Peter's. Before I finished I said to myself "The fellow's a bankrupt orange-monger, but a treasure."

When Mrs. Monarch withdrew he passed across the room like a flash to open the door for her, standing there with the rapt pure gaze of the young Dante spell-bound by the young Beatrice. As I never insisted, in such situations, on the blankness of the British domestic, I reflected that he had the making of a servant—and I needed one, but couldn't pay him to be only that—as well as of a model; in short I resolved to adopt my bright adventurer if he would agree to officiate in the double capacity. He jumped at my offer, and in the event my rashness—for I had really known nothing about him—wasn't brought home to me. He proved a sympathetic though a desultory ministrant, and had in a wonderful degree the *sentiment de la pose*. It was uncultivated, instinctive, a part of the happy instinct that had guided him to my door and helped him to spell out my name on the card nailed to it. He had had no other introduction to me than a guess, from the shape of my high north window, seen outside, that my place was a studio and that as a studio it would contain an artist. He had wandered to England in search of fortune, like other itinerants, and had embarked, with a partner and a small green hand-cart, on the sale of penny ices. The ices had melted away, and the partner had dissolved in their train. My young man wore tight yellow trousers with reddish stripes and his name was Oronte. He was sallow but fair, and when I put him into some old clothes of my own he looked like an Englishman. He was as good as Miss Churm, who could look, when requested, like an Italian.

IV

I thought Mrs. Monarch's face slightly convulsed when, on her coming back with her husband, she found Oronte installed. It was strange to have to recognise in a scrap of a lazzarone a competitor to her magnificent Major. It was she who scented danger first, for the Major was anecdotically unconscious. But Oronte gave us tea, with a hundred eager confusions—he had never been concerned in so queer a process—and I think she thought better of me for having at least an "establishment." They saw a couple of drawings that I had made of the establishment, and Mrs. Monarch hinted that it never would have struck her he had sat for them. "Now the drawings you make from *us*, they look exactly like us," she reminded me, smiling in triumph; and I recognised that this was indeed just their defect. When I drew the Monarchs I couldn't anyhow get away from them—get into the character I wanted to represent; and I hadn't the least desire my model should be discoverable in my picture. Miss Churm never was, and Mrs. Monarch thought I hid her, very properly, because she was vulgar; whereas if she was lost it was only as the dead who got to heaven are lost—in the gain of an angel the more.

By this time I had got a certain start with "Rutland Ramsay," the first novel in the great projected series; that is I had produced a dozen drawings, several with the help of the Major and his wife, and I had sent them in for approval. My understanding with the publishers, as I have already hinted, had been that I was to be left to do my work, in this particular case, as I liked, with the whole book committed to me; but my connexion with the rest of the series was only contingent. There were moments when, frankly, it was a comfort to have the real thing under one's hand; for there were characters in "Rutland Ramsay" that were very much like it. There were people presumably as erect as the Major and women of as good a fashion as Mrs. Monarch. There was a great deal of country-house life—treated, it is true, in a fine fanciful ironical generalised way—and there was a considerable implication of knickerbockers and kilts. There were certain things I had to settle at the outset; such things for instance as the exact appearance of the hero and the particular bloom and figure of the heroine. The author of course gave me a lead, but there was a margin for interpretation. I took the Monarchs into my confidence, I told them frankly what I was about, I mentioned my embarrassments and alternatives. "Oh take *him!*" Mrs. Monarch murmured sweetly, looking at her husband; and "What could you want better than my wife?" the Major enquired with the comfortable candour that now prevailed between us.

I wasn't obliged to answer these remarks—I was only obliged to place my sitters. I wasn't easy in mind, and I postponed a little timidly perhaps the solving of my question. The book was a large canvas, the other figures were numerous, and I worked off at first some of the episodes in which the hero and the heroine were not concerned. When once I had set *them* up I should have to stick to them—I couldn't make my young man seven feet high in one place and five feet nine in another. I inclined on the whole to the latter measurement, though the Major more than once reminded me that *he* looked about as young as any one. It was indeed quite possible to arrange him, for the figure, so that it would have been difficult to detect his age. After the spontaneous Oronte had been with me a month, and after I had given him to understand several times over that his native exuberance would presently constitute an insurmountable barrier to our further intercourse, I waked to a sense of his heroic capacity. He was only five feet seven, but the remaining inches were latent. I tried him almost secretly at first, for I was really rather afraid of the judgement my other models would pass on such a choice. If they regarded Miss Churm as little better than a snare what would they think of the representation by a person so little the real thing as an Italian street-vendor of a protagonist formed by a public school?

If I went a little in fear of them it wasn't because they bullied me, because they had got an oppressive foothold, but because in their really pathetic decorum and mysteriously permanent newness they counted on me so intensely. I was therefore very glad when Jack Hawley came home: he was always of such good counsel. He painted badly himself, but there was no one like him for putting his finger on the place. He had been absent from England for a year; he had been somewhere—I don't remember where—to get a fresh eye. I was in a good deal of dread of any such organ, but we were old friends; he had been away for months and a sense of emptiness was creeping into my life. I hadn't dodged a missile for a year.

He came back with a fresh eye, but with the same old black velvet blouse, and the first evening he spent in my studio we smoked cigarettes till the small hours. He had done no work himself, he had only got the eye; so the field was clear for the production of my little things. He wanted to see what I had produced for the *Cheapside*, but he was disappointed in the exhibition. That at least seemed the meaning of two or three comprehensive groans which, as he lounged on my big divan, his leg folded under him, looking at my latest drawings, issued from his lips with the smoke of the cigarette.

"What's the matter with you?" I asked.

"What's the matter with *you?*"

"Nothing save that I'm mystified."

"You are indeed. You're quite off the hinge. What's the meaning of this new fad?" And he tossed me, with visible irreverance, a drawing in which I happened to have depicted both my elegant models. I asked if he didn't think it good, and he replied that it struck him as execrable, given the sort of thing I had always represented myself to him as wishing to arrive at; but I let that pass—I was so anxious to see exactly what he meant. The two figures in the picture looked colossal, but I supposed this was *not* what he meant, inasmuch as, for aught he knew to the contrary, I might have been trying for some such effect. I maintained that I was working exactly in the same way as when he last had done me the honour to tell me I might do something some day.

"Well, there's a screw loose somewhere," he answered; "wait a bit and I'll discover it." I depended upon him to do so: where else was the fresh eye? But he produced at last nothing more luminous than "I don't know—I don't like your types." This was lame for a critic who had never consented to discuss with me anything but the question of execution, the direction of strokes and the mystery of values.

"In the drawings you've been looking at I think my types are very handsome."

"Oh they won't do!"

"I've been working with new models."

"I see you have. They won't do."

"Are you very sure of that?"

"Absolutely—they're stupid."

"You mean *I* am—for I ought to get round that."

"You can't—with such people. Who are they?"

I told him, so far as was necessary, and he concluded heartlessly: "Ce sont des gens qu'il faut mettre à la porte."

"You've never seen them; they're awfully good"—I flew to their defence.

"Not seen them? Why all this recent work of yours drops to pieces with them. It's all I want to see of them."

"No one else has said anything against it—the *Cheapside* people are pleased."

"Everyone else is an ass, and the *Cheapside* people the biggest asses of all. Come, don't pretend at this time of day to have pretty illusions about the public, especially about publishers and editors. It's not for such animals you work—it's for those you know, *coloro che sanno;* so keep straight for me if you can't keep straight for yourself. There was a certain sort of thing you used to try for—and a very good thing it was. But this twaddle isn't *in* it." When I talked with Hawley later about "Rutland Ramsay" and its possible successors he declared that I must get back into my boat again or I should go to the bottom. His voice in short was the voice of warning.

I noted the warning, but I didn't turn my friends out of doors. They bored me a good deal; but the very fact that they bored me admonished me not to sacrifice them—if there was anything to be done with them—simply to irritation. As I look back at this phase they seem to me to have pervaded my life not a little. I have a vision of them as most of the time in my studio, seated against the wall on an old velvet bench to be out of the way, and resembling the while a pair of patient courtiers in a royal ante-chamber. I'm convinced that during the coldest weeks of the winter they held their ground because it saved them fire. Their newness was losing its gloss, and it was impossible not to feel them objects of charity. Whenever Miss Churm arrived they went away, and after I was fairly launched in "Rutland Ramsay" Miss Churm arrived pretty often. They managed to express to me tacitly that they supposed I wanted her for the low life of the book and I let them suppose it, since they had attempted to study the work—it was lying about the studio—without discovering that it dealt only with the highest circles. They had dipped into the most brilliant of our novelists without deciphering many passages. I still took an hour from them, now and again, in spite of Jack Hawley's warning: it would be time enough to dismiss them, if dismissal should be necessary, when the rigour of the season was over. Hawley had made their acquaintance—he had met them at my fireside—and thought them a ridiculous pair. Learning that he was a painter they tried to approach him, to show him too that they were the real thing; but he looked at them, across the big room, as if they were miles away: they were a compendium of everything he most objected to in the social system of his country. Such people as that, all convention and patent-leather, with ejaculations that stopped conversation, had no business in a studio. A studio was a place to learn to see, and how could you see through a pair of feather-beds?

The main inconvenience I suffered at their hands was that at first I was shy of letting it break upon them that my artful little servant had begun to sit for me for "Rutland Ramsay." They knew I had been odd enough—they were prepared by this time to allow oddity to artists—to pick a foreign vagabond out of the streets when I might have had a person with whiskers and credentials; but it was some time before they learned how high I rated his accomplishments. They found him in an attitude more than once, but they never doubted I was doing him as an organ-grinder. There were several things they never guessed, and one of them was that for a striking scene in the novel, in which a footman briefly figured, it occurred to me to make use of Major Monarch as the menial. I kept putting this off, I didn't like to ask him to don the livery—besides the difficulty of finding a livery to fit him. At last, one day late in the winter, when I was at work on the despised Oronte, who caught one's idea on the wing, and was in the glow of feeling myself go very straight, they came in, the Major and his wife, with their society laugh about nothing (there was less and less to laugh at); came in like country-callers—they always reminded me of that—who have walked across the park after church and are presently persuaded to stay to luncheon. Luncheon was over, but they could stay to tea—I knew they wanted it. The fit was on me, however, and I couldn't let my ardour cool and my work wait, with the fading daylight, while my model prepared it. So I asked Mrs. Monarch if she would mind laying it out—a request which for an instant brought all the blood to her face. Her eyes were on her husband's for a second, and some mute telegraphy passed between them. Their folly was over the next instant; his cheerful shrewdness put an end to it. So far from pitying their wounded pride, I must add, I was moved to give it as complete a lesson as I could. They bustled about together and got out the cups and saucers and made the kettle boil. I know they felt as if they were waiting on my servant, and when the tea was prepared I said: "He'll have a cup, please—he's tired." Mrs. Monarch brought him one where he stood and he took it from her as if he had been a gentleman at a party squeezing a crush-hat with an elbow.

Then it came over me that she had made a great effort for me—made it with a kind of nobleness—and that I owed her a compensation. Each time I saw her after this I wondered what the compensation could be. I couldn't go on doing the wrong thing to oblige them. Oh it was the wrong thing, the stamp of the work for which they sat—Hawley was not the only person to say it now. I sent in a large number of the drawings I had made for "Rutland Ramsay," and I received a warning that was more to the point than Hawley's. The artistic adviser of the house for which I was working was of opinion that many of my illustrations were not what had been looked for. Most of these illustrations were the subjects in which the Monarchs had figured. Without going into the question of what *had* been looked for, I had to face the fact that at this rate I shouldn't get the other books to do. I hurled myself in despair on Miss Churm—I put her through all her paces. I not only adopted Oronte publicly as my hero, but one morning when the Major looked in to see if I didn't require him to finish a *Cheapside* figure for which he had begun to sit the week before, I told him I had changed my mind—I'd do the drawing from my man. At this my visitor turned pale and stood looking at me. "Is *he* your idea of an English gentleman?" he asked.

I was disappointed, I was nervous, I wanted to get on with my work; so I replied with irritation: "Oh my dear Major—I can't be ruined for you!"

It was a horrid speech, but he stood another moment—after which, without a word, he quitted the studio. I drew a long breath, for I said to myself that I shouldn't see him again. I hadn't told him definitely that I was in danger of having my work rejected, but I was vexed at his not having felt the catastrophe in the air, read with me the moral of our fruitless collaboration, the lesson that in the deceptive atmosphere of art even the highest respectability may fail of being plastic.

I didn't owe my friends money, but I did see them again. They reappeared together three days later, and, given all the other facts, there was something tragic in that one. It was a clear proof they could find nothing else in life to do. They had threshed the matter out in a dismal conference—they had digested the bad news that they were not in for the series. If they weren't useful to me even for the *Cheapside* their function seemed difficult to determine, and I could only judge at first that they had come, forgivingly, decorously, to take a last leave. This made me rejoice in secret that I had little leisure for a scene; for I had placed both my other models in position together and I was pegging away at a drawing from which I hoped to derive glory. It had been suggested by the passage in which Rutland Ramsay, drawing up a chair to Artemisia's piano-stool, says extraordinary things to her while she ostensibly fingers out a difficult piece of music. I had done Miss Churm at the piano before—it was an attitude in which she knew how to take on an absolutely poetic grace. I wished the two figures to "compose" together with intensity, and my little Italian had entered perfectly into my conception. The pair were vividly before me, the piano had been pulled out; it was a charming show of blended youth and murmured love, which I had only to catch and keep. My visitors stood and looked at it, and I was friendly to them over my shoulder.

They made no response, but I was used to silent company and went on with my work, only a little disconcerted—even though exhilarated by the sense that *this* was at least the ideal thing—at not having got rid of them after all. Presently I heard Mrs. Monarch's sweet voice beside or rather above me: "I wish her hair were a little better done." I looked up and she was staring with a strange fixedness at Miss Churm, whose back was turned to her. "Do you mind my just touching it?" she went on—a question which made me spring up for an instant as with the instinctive fear that she might do the young lady a harm. But she quieted me with a glance I shall never forget—I confess I should like to have been able to paint *that*—and went for a moment to my model. She spoke to her softly, laying a hand on her shoulder and bending over her; and as the girl, understanding, gratefully assented, she disposed her rough curls, with a few quick passes, in such a way as to make Miss Churm's head twice as charming. It was one of the most heroic personal services I've ever seen rendered. Then Mrs. Monarch turned away with a low sigh and, looking about her as if for something to do, stooped to the floor with a noble humility and picked up a dirty rag that had dropped out of my paint-box.

The Major meanwhile had also been looking for something to do, and, wandering to the other end of the studio, saw before him my breakfast-things neglected, unremoved. "I say, can't I be useful *here?*" he called out to me with an irrepressible quaver. I assented with a laugh that I fear was awkward, and for the next ten minutes, while I worked, I heard the light clatter of china and the tinkle of spoons and glass. Mrs. Monarch assisted her husband—they washed up my crockery, they put it away. They wandered off into my little scullery, and I afterwards found that they had cleaned my knives and that my slender stock of plate had an unprecendented surface. When it came over me, the latent eloquence of what they were doing, I confess that my drawing was blurred for a moment—the picture swam. They had accepted their failure, but they couldn't accept their fate. They had bowed their heads in bewilderment to the perverse and cruel law in virtue of which the real thing could be so much less precious than the unreal; but they didn't want to starve. If my servants were my models, then my models might be my servants. They would reverse the parts—the others would sit for the ladies and gentlemen and *they* would do the work. They would still be in the studio—it was an intense dumb appeal to me not to turn them out. "Take us on," they wanted to say—"we'll do *anything*."

My pencil dropped from my hand; my sitting was spoiled and I got rid of my sitters, who were also evidently rather mystified and awestruck. Then, alone with the Major and his wife I had a most uncomfortable moment. He put their prayer into a single sentence: "I say, you know—just let *us* do for you, can't you?" I couldn't—it was dreadful to see them emptying my slops; but I pretended I could, to oblige them, for about a week. Then I gave them a sum of money to go away, and I never saw them again. I obtained the remaining books, but my friend Hawley repeats that Major and Mrs. Monarch did me a permanent harm, got me into false ways. If it be true I'm content to have paid the price—for the memory.

[1890]

For Thought

James plays a variation upon the Pygmalion story with his tale of the unfortunate Monarchs. His painter hopes that models who resemble the epitome of style will turn him into a great painter. Ironically, they debase his talent and must be replaced by more mercurial and pliant models. James suggests that real artistic ability works best with airy and flimsy materials. It is too often paralyzed by subjects too firmly rooted in reality.

For Discussion

1. The development of a short story conventionally involves a complication, a reversal, and the denouement, ending with insight into one's predicament. At what point in "The Real Thing" does each of these variations occur?
2. What virtues are evident from James's characterization of the Monarchs? What shortcomings do the Monarchs possess?
3. To what extent are the Monarchs not "the real thing" at all, but spurious copies?
4. In what ways are the characters paired, with what ironic contrasts?
5. Although the story's point of view is established as first person, all the events being registered on the mind of the painter (James's central intelligence), the painter actually plays several roles: actor, stage manager, and audience. What actions or impressions of the narrator support his fulfillment of each of these roles?
6. To what extent do all the characters face the problem of adjusting personal values to public roles?
7. The painter faces a series of dilemmas which are partly moral and social, but primarily aesthetic (e.g., he must certainly react to people's moods, but he must also be able to assess his emotions while he experiences them). What other difficult choices confront him?
8. What does the painter learn or recognize from the action he has viewed? What factors determine his degree of free will? How is his extent of choice related to the theme?

James Joyce
Araby

North Richmond Street, being blind, was a quiet street except at the hour when the Christian Brothers' School set the boys free. An uninhabited house of two stories stood at the blind end, detached from its neighbours in a square ground. The other houses of the street, conscious of decent lives within them, gazed at one another with brown imperturbable faces.

The former tenant of our house, a priest, had died in the back drawing-room. Air, musty from having been long enclosed, hung in all the rooms, and the waste-room behind the kitchen was littered with old useless papers. Among these I found a few paper-covered books, the pages of which were curled and damp: *The Abbot*, by Walter Scott, *The Devout Communicant*, and *The Memoirs of Vidocq*. I liked the last best because its leaves were yellow. The wild garden behind the house contained a central apple tree and a few straggling bushes under one of which I found the late tenant's rusty bicycle pump. He had been a very charitable priest; in his will he had left all his money to institutions and the furniture of his house to his sister.

When the short days of winter came dusk fell before we had well eaten our dinners. When we met in the street the houses had grown sombre. The space of sky above us was the colour of ever-changing violet and towards it the lamps of the street lifted their feeble lanterns. The cold air stung us and we played till our bodies glowed. Our shouts echoed in the silent street. The career of our play brought us through the dark muddy lanes behind the houses where we ran the gauntlet of the rough tribes from the cottages, to the back doors of the dark dripping gardens where odours arose from the ash-pits, to the dark odorous stables where a coachman smoothed and combed the horse or shook music from the buckled harness. When we returned to the street, light from the kitchen windows had filled the areas. If my uncle was seen turning the corner we hid in the shadow until we had seen him safely housed. Or if Mangan's sister came out on the doorstep to call her brother in to his tea we watched her from our shadow peer up and down the street. We waited to see whether she would remain or go in and, if she remained, we left our shadow and walked up to Mangan's steps resignedly. She was waiting for us, her figure defined by the light from the half-opened door. Her brother always teased her before he obeyed and I stood by the railings looking at her. Her dress swung as she moved her body and the soft rope of her hair tossed from side to side.

Every morning I lay on the floor in the front parlor watching her door. The blind was pulled down to within an inch of the sash so that I could not be seen. When she came out on the doorstep my heart leaped. I ran to the hall, seized my books and followed her. I kept her brown figure always in my eye and, when we came near the point at which our ways diverged, I quickened my pace and passed her. This happened morning after morning. I had never spoken to her, except for a few casual words, and yet her name was like a summons to all my foolish blood.

Her image accompanied me even in places the most hostile to romance. On Saturday evenings when my aunt went marketing I had to go to carry some of the parcels. We walked through the flaring streets, jostled by drunken men and bargaining women, amid the curses of labourers, the shrill litanies of shop boys who stood on guard by the barrels of pigs' cheeks, the nasal chanting of street singers, who sang a *come-all-you* about O'Donavan Rossa, or a ballad about the troubles in our native land. These noises converged in a single sensation of life for me: I imagined that I bore my chalice safely through a throng of foes. Her name sprang to my lips at moments in strange prayers and praises which I myself did not understand. My eyes were often full of tears (I could not tell why) and at times a flood from my heart seemed to pour itself out into my bosom. I thought little of the future. I did not know whether I would ever speak to her or not or, if I spoke to her, how I could tell her of my confused adoration. But my body was like a harp and her words and gestures were like fingers running upon the wires.

One evening I went into the back drawing-room in which the priest had died. It was a dark rainy evening and there was no sound in the house. Through one of the broken panes I heard the rain impinge upon the earth, the fine incessant needles of water playing in the sodden beds. Some distant lamp or lighted window gleamed below me. I was thankful that I could see so little. All my senses seemed to desire to veil themselves and, feeling that I was about to slip from them, I pressed the palms of my hands together until they trembled, murmuring: "*O love! O love!*" many times.

At last she spoke to me. When she addressed the first words to me I was so confused that I did not know what to answer. She asked me was I going to *Araby*. I forgot whether I answered yes or no. It would be a splendid bazaar, she said; she would love to go.

"And why can't you?" I asked.

While she spoke she turned a silver bracelet round and round her wrist. She could not go, she said, because there would be a retreat that week in her convent. Her brother and two other boys were fighting for their caps and I was alone at the railings. She held one of the spikes, bowing her head towards me. The light from the lamp opposite our door caught the white curve of her neck, lit up her hair that rested there and, falling, lit up the hand upon the railing. It fell over one side of her dress and caught the white border of a petticoat, just visible as she stood at ease.

"It's well for you," she said.

"If I go," I said, "I will bring you something."

What innumerable follies laid waste my waking and sleeping thoughts after that evening! I wished to annihilate the tedious intervening days. I chafed against the work of school. At night in my bedroom and by day in the classroom her image came between me and the page I strove to read. The syllables of the word *Araby* were called to me through the silence in which my soul luxuriated and cast an Eastern enchantment over me. I asked for leave to go the bazaar on Saturday night. My aunt was surprised and hoped it was not some Freemason affair. I answered few questions in class. I watched my master's face pass from amiability to sternness; he hoped I was not beginning to idle. I could not call my wandering thoughts together. I had hardly any patience with the serious work of life which, now that it stood between me and my desire, seemed to me child's play, ugly monotonous child's play.

On Saturday morning I reminded my uncle that I wished to go to the bazaar in the evening. He was fussing at the hallstand, looking for the hat brush, and answered me curtly:

"Yes, boy, I know."

As he was in the hall I could not go into the front parlour and lie at the window. I left the house in bad humour and walked slowly towards the school. The air was pitilessly raw and already my heart misgave me.

When I came home to dinner my uncle had not yet been home. Still it was early. I sat staring at the clock for some time and, when its ticking began to irritate me, I left the room. I mounted the staircase and gained the upper part of the house. The high cold empty gloomy rooms liberated me and I went from room to room singing. From the front window I saw my companions playing below in the street. Their cries reached me weakened and indistinct and, leaning my forehead against the cool glass, I looked over at the dark house where she lived. I may have stood there for an hour, seeing nothing but the brown-clad figure cast by my imagination, touched discreetly by the lamplight at the curved neck, at the hand upon the railings and at the border below the dress.

When I came downstairs again I found Mrs. Mercer sitting at the fire. She was an old garrulous woman, a pawnbroker's widow, who collected used stamps for some pious purpose. I had to endure the gossip of the tea table. The meal was prolonged beyond an hour and still my uncle did not come. Mrs. Mercer stood up to go: she was sorry she couldn't wait any longer, but it was after eight o'clock and she did not like to be out late, as the night air was bad for her. When she had gone I began to walk up and down the room, clenching my fists. My aunt said:

"I'm afraid you may put off your bazaar for this night of Our Lord."

At nine o'clock I heard my uncle's latchkey in the hall door. I heard him talking to himself and heard the hall-stand rocking when it had received the weight of his overcoat. I could interpret these signs. When he was midway through his dinner I asked him to give me the money to go the bazaar. He had forgotten.

"The people are in bed and after their first sleep now," he said.

I did not smile. My aunt said to him energetically:

"Can't you give him the money and let him go? You've kept him late enough as it is."

My uncle said he was very sorry he had forgotten. He said he believed in the old saying: "All work and no play makes Jack a dull boy." He asked me where I was going and, when I told him a second time he asked me did I know *The Arab's Farewell to His Steed*. When I left the kitchen he was about to recite the opening lines of the piece to my aunt.

I held a florin tightly in my hand as I strode down Buckingham Street towards the station. The sight of the streets thronged with buyers and glaring with gas recalled to me the purpose of my journey. I took my seat in a third-class carriage of a deserted train. After an intolerable delay the train moved out of the station slowly. It crept onward among ruinous houses and over the twinkling river. At Westland Row Station a crowd of people pressed to the carriage doors; but the porters moved them back, saying that it was a special train for the bazaar. I remained alone in the bare carriage. In a few minutes the train drew up beside an improvised wooden platform. I passed out on to the road and saw by the lighted dial of a clock that it was ten minutes to ten. In front of me was a large building which displayed the magical name.

I could not find any sixpenny entrance and, fearing that the bazaar would be closed, I passed in quickly through a turnstile, handing a shilling to a weary-looking man. I found myself in a big hall girdled at half its height by a gallery. Nearly all the stalls were closed and the greater part of the hall was in darkness. I recognised a silence like that which pervades a church after a service. I walked into the center of the bazaar timidly. A few people were gathered about the stalls which were still open. Before a curtain, over which the words *Café Chantant* were written in coloured lamps, two men were counting money on a salver. I listened to the fall of the coins.

Remembering with difficulty why I had come I went over to one of the stalls and examined porcelain vases and flowered teasets. At the door of the stall a young lady was talking and laughing with two young gentlemen. I remarked their English accents and listened vaguely to their conversation.

"O, I never said such a thing!"

"O, but you did!"

"O, but I didn't!"

"Didn't she say that?"

"Yes, I heard her."

"O, there's a . . . fib!"

Observing me, the young lady came over and asked me did I wish to buy anything. The tone of her voice was not encouraging; she seemed to have spoken to me out of a sense of duty. I looked humbly at the great jars that stood like the eastern guards at either side of the dark entrance to the stall and murmured:

"No, thank you."

The young lady changed the position of one of the vases and went back to the two young men. They began to talk of the same subject. Once or twice the young lady glanced at me over her shoulder.

I lingered before her stall, though I knew my stay was useless, to make my interest in her wares seem the more real. Then I turned away slowly and walked down the middle of the bazaar. I allowed the two pennies to fall against the sixpence in my pocket. I heard a voice call from one end of the gallery that the light was out. The upper part of the hall was now completely dark.

Gazing up into the darkness I saw myself as a creature driven and derided by vanity; and my eyes burned with anguish and anger.

[1905]

For Thought

In an atmosphere of drabness, morbidity, and decay, Joyce sets up a conflict between the lofty, naive idealism of a sensitive adolescent and the shabby reality that lies behind the facade of romantic allure represented by the bazaar, Araby. The closer the boy comes to the place of his dreams, the farther away he is from them. On leaving the tawdry bazaar, after waiting all week to get there, he is left standing among the shards of his ruined hopes and with the bitter choice between illusions that are no longer tenable and a shabby reality that deadens the soul.

For Discussion

1. What kind of environment does the boy wish to escape? How is the environment represented?
2. How is the action of the story complicated, brought to a crisis, and then resolved?

3. How is the boy characterized by his thoughts, his actions, and his relation to others?
4. How does the boy's inner conflict group and contrast the other characters?
5. In what way does the language stress the conflict between reality and illusion?
6. What motif emerges from the progression of the action and how is it rendered ironic?
7. What theme emerges from a consideration of the overall structure, the plot, the characterization, and the underlying motif?
8. What are the advantages of the point of view used in the story?
9. How does Joyce make use of symbols in the story?

James Joyce
Counterparts

The bell rang furiously and, when Miss Parker went to the tube, a furious voice called out in a piercing North of Ireland accent:

"Send Farrington here!"

Miss Parker returned to her machine, saying to a man who was writing at a desk:

"Mr. Alleyne wants you upstairs."

The man muttered "*Blast* him!" under his breath and pushed back his chair to stand up. When he stood up he was tall and of great bulk. He had a hanging face, dark wine-coloured, with fair eyebrows and moustache: his eyes bulged forward slightly and the whites of them were dirty. He lifted up the counter and, passing by the clients, went out of the office with a heavy step.

He went heavily upstairs until he came to the second landing, where a door bore a brass plate with the inscription *Mr. Alleyne*. Here he halted, puffing with labour and vexation, and knocked. The shrill voice cried:

"Come in!"

The man entered Mr. Alleyne's room. Simultaneously Mr. Alleyne, a little man wearing gold-rimmed glasses on a clean-shaven face, shot his head up over a pile of documents. The head itself was so pink and hairless it seemed like a large egg reposing on the papers. Mr. Alleyne did not lose a moment:

"Farrington? What is the meaning of this? Why have I always to complain of you? May I ask you why you haven't made a copy of that contract between Bodley and Kirwan? I told you it must be ready by four o'clock."

"But Mr. Shelley said, sir—"

"*Mr. Shelley said, sir*. . . . Kindly attend to what I say and not to what *Mr. Shelley says, sir*. You have always some excuse or another for shirking work. Let me tell you that if the contract is not copied before this evening I'll lay the matter before Mr. Crosbie. . . . Do you hear me now?"

"Yes, sir."

"Do you hear me now? . . . Ay and another little matter! I might as well be talking to the wall as talking to you. Understand once for all that you get a half an hour for your lunch and not an hour and a half. How many courses do you want, I'd like to know. . . . Do you mind me now?"

"Yes, sir."

Mr. Alleyne bent his head again upon his pile of papers. The man stared fixedly at the polished skull which directed the affairs of Crosbie & Alleyne, gauging its fragility. A spasm of rage gripped his throat for a few moments and then passed, leaving after it a sharp sensation of thirst. The man recognized the sensation and felt that he must have a good night's drinking. The middle of the month was passed and, if he could get the copy done in time, Mr. Alleyne might give him an order on the cashier. He stood still, gazing fixedly at the head upon the pile of papers. Suddenly Mr. Alleyne began to upset all the papers, searching for something. Then, as if he had been unaware of the man's presence till that moment, he shot up his head again, saying:

"Eh? Are you going to stand there all day? Upon my word, Farrington, you take things easy!"

"I was waiting to see . . ."

"Very good, you needn't wait to see. Go downstairs and do your work."

The man walked heavily towards the door and, as he went out of the room, he heard Mr. Alleyne cry after him that if the contract was not copied by evening Mr. Crosbie would hear of the matter.

He returned to his desk in the lower office and counted the sheets which remained to be copied. He took up his pen and dipped it in the ink but he continued to stare stupidly at the last words he had written: *In no case shall the said Bernard Bodley be* . . . The evening was falling and in a few minutes they would be lighting the gas: then he could write. He felt that he must slake the thirst in his throat. He stood up from his desk and, lifting the counter as before, passed out of the office. As he was passing out the chief clerk looked at him inquiringly.

"It's all right, Mr. Shelley," said the man, pointing with his finger to indicate the objective of his journey.

The chief clerk glanced at the hat-rack, but, seeing the row complete, offered no remark. As soon as he was on the landing the man pulled a shepherd's plaid cap out of his pocket, put it on his head and ran quickly down the rickety stairs. From the street door he walked on furtively on the inner side of the path towards the corner and all at once dived into a doorway. He was now safe in the dark snug of O'Neill's shop, and, filling up the little window that looked into the bar with his inflamed face, the colour of dark wine or dark meat, he called out:

"Here, Pat, give us a g.p., like a good fellow."

The curate brought him a glass of plain porter. The man drank it at a gulp and asked for a caraway seed. He put his penny on the counter and, leaving the curate to grope for it in the gloom, retreated out of the snug as furtively as he had entered it.

Darkness, accompanied by a thick fog, was gaining upon the dusk of February and the lamps in Eustace Street had been lit. The man went up by the houses until he reached the door of the office, wondering whether he could finish his copy in time. On the stairs a moist pungent odour of perfumes saluted his nose: evidently Miss Delacour had come while he was out in O'Neill's. He crammed his cap back again into his pocket and re-entered the office, assuming an air of absent-mindedness.

"Mr. Alleyne has been calling for you," and the chief clerk severely. "Where were you?"

The man glanced at the two clients who were standing at the counter as if to intimate that their presence prevented him from answering. As the clients were both male the chief clerk allowed himself a laugh.

"I know that game," he said. "Five times in one day is a little bit. . . . Well, you better look sharp and get a copy of our correspondence in the Delacour case for Mr. Alleyne."

This address in the presence of the public, his run upstairs and the porter he had gulped down so hastily confused the man and, as he sat down at his desk to get what was required, he realised how hopeless was the task of finishing his copy of the contract before half past five. The dark damp night was coming and he longed to spend it in the bars, drinking with his friends amid the glare of gas and the clatter of glasses. He got out the Delacour correspondence and passed out of the office. He hoped Mr. Alleyne would not discover that the last two letters were missing.

The moist pungent perfume lay all the way up to Mr. Alleyne's room. Miss Delacour was a middle-aged woman of Jewish appearance. Mr. Alleyne was said to be sweet on her or on her money. She came to the office often and stayed a long time when she came. She was sitting beside his desk now in an aroma of perfumes, smoothing the handle of her umbrella and nodding the great black feather in her hat. Mr. Alleyne had swivelled his chair round to face her and thrown his right foot jauntily upon his left knee. The man put the correspondence on the desk and bowed respectfully but neither Mr. Alleyne nor Miss Delacour took any notice of his bow. Mr. Alleyne tapped a finger on the correspondence and then flicked it towards him as if to say: "*That's all right: you can go.*"

The man returned to the lower office and sat down again at his desk. He stared intently at the incomplete phrase: *In no case shall the said Bernard Bodley be . . .* and thought how strange it was that the last three words began with the same letter. The chief clerk began to hurry Miss Parker, saying she would never have the letters typed in time for post. The man listened to the clicking of the machine for a few minutes and then set to work to finish his copy. But his head was not clear and his mind wandered away to the glare and rattle of the public-house. It was a night for hot punches. He struggled on with his copy, but when the clock struck five he had still fourteen pages to write. Blast it! He couldn't finish it in time. He longed to execrate aloud, to bring his fist down on something violently. He was so enraged that he wrote *Bernard Bernard* instead of *Bernard Bodley* and had to begin again on a clean sheet.

He felt strong enough to clear out the whole office single-handed. His body ached to do something, to rush out and revel in violence. All the indignities of his life enraged him. . . . Could he ask the cashier privately for an advance? No, the cashier was no good, no damn good: he wouldn't give an advance. . . . He knew where he would meet the boys: Leonard and O'Halloran and Nosey Flynn. The barometer of his emotional nature was set for a spell of riot.

His imagination had so abstracted him that his name was called twice before he answered. Mr. Alleyne and Miss Delacour were standing outside the counter and all the clerks had turned round in anticipation of something. The man got up from his desk. Mr. Alleyne began a tirade of abuse, saying that two letters were missing. The man answered that he knew nothing about them, that he had made a faithful copy. The tirade continued: it was so bitter and violent that the man could hardly restrain his fist from descending upon the head of the manikin before him:

"I know nothing about any other two letters," he said stupidly.

"*You—know—nothing.* Of course you know nothing," said Mr. Alleyne. "Tell me," he added, glancing first for approval to the lady beside him, "do you take me for a fool? Do you think me an utter fool?"

The man glanced from the lady's face to the little egg-shaped head and back again; and, almost before he was aware of it, his tongue had found a felicitous moment:

"I don't think, sir" he said, "that that's a fair question to put to me."

There was a pause in the very breathing of the clerks. Everyone was astounded (the author of the witticism no less than his neighbours) and Miss Delacour, who was a stout amiable person, began to smile broadly. Mr. Alleyne flushed to the hue of a wild rose and his mouth twitched with a dwarf's passion. He shook his fist in the man's face till it seemed to vibrate like the knob of some electric machine:

"You impertinent ruffian! You impertinent ruffian! I'll make short work of you! Wait till you see! You'll apologise to me for your impertinence or you'll quit the office instanter! You'll quit this, I'm telling you, or you'll apologise to me!"

He stood in a doorway opposite the office watching to see if the cashier would come out alone. All the clerks passed out and finally the cashier came out with the chief clerk. It was no use trying to say a word to him when he was with the chief clerk. The man felt that his position was bad enough. He had been obliged to offer an abject apology to Mr. Alleyne for his impertinence but he knew what a hornet's nest the office would be for him. He could remember the way in which Mr. Alleyne had hounded little Peake out of the office in order to make room for his own nephew. He felt savage and thirsty and revengeful, annoyed with himself and with everyone else. Mr. Alleyne would never give him an hour's rest; his life would be a hell to him. He had made a proper fool of himself this time. Could he not keep his tongue in his cheek? But they had never pulled together from the first, he and Mr. Alleyne, ever since the day Mr. Alleyne had overheard him mimicking his North of Ireland accent to amuse Higgins and Miss Parker; that had been the beginning of it. He might have tried Higgins for the money, but sure Higgins never had anything for himself. A man with two establishments to keep up, of course he couldn't . . .

He felt his great body again aching for the comfort of the public-house. The fog had begun to chill him and he wondered could he touch Pat in O'Neill's. He could not touch him for more than a bob—and a bob was no use. Yet he must get money somewhere or other: he had spent his last penny for the g.p. and soon it would be too late for getting money anywhere. Suddenly, as he was fingering his watch-chain, he thought of Terry Kelly's pawn-office in Fleet Street. That was the dart! Why didn't he think of it sooner?

He went through the narrow alley of Temple Bar quickly, muttering to himself that they could all go to hell because he was going to have a good night of it. The clerk in Terry Kelly's said *A crown!* but the consignor held out for six shillings; and in the end the six shillings was allowed him literally. He came out of the pawn-office joyfully, making a little cylinder of the coins between his thumb and fingers. In Westmoreland Street the footpaths were crowded with young men and women returning from business and ragged urchins ran here and there yelling out the names of the evening editions. The man passed through the crowd, looking on the spectacle generally with proud satisfaction and staring masterfully at the office-girls. His head was full of the noises of tram-gongs and swishing trolleys and his nose already sniffed the curling fumes of punch. As he walked on he preconsidered the terms in which he would narrate the incident to the boys:

"So, I just looked at him—coolly, you know, and looked at her. Then I looked back at him again—taking my time, you know. 'I don't think that that's a fair question to put to me,' says I."

Nosey Flynn was sitting up in his usual corner of Davy Byrne's and, when he heard the story, he stood Farrington a half-one, saying it was as smart a thing as ever he heard. Farrington stood a drink in his turn. After a while O'Halloran and Paddy Leonard came in and the story was repeated to them. O'Halloran stood tailors of malt hot all round and told the story of the retort he had made to the chief clerk when he was in Callan's of Fownes's Street; but, as the retort was after the manner of the liberal shepherds in the eclogues, he had to admit that it was not as clever as Farrington's retort. At this Farrington told the boys to polish off that and have another.

Just as they were naming their poisons who should come in but Higgins! Of course he had to join in with the others. The men asked him to give his version of it, and he did so with great vivacity for the sight of five small hot whiskies was very exhilarating. Everyone roared laughing when he showed the way in which Mr. Alleyne shook his fist in Farrington's face. Then he imitated Farrington, saying, "*And here was my nabs, as cool as you please,*" while Farrington looked at the company out of his heavy dirty eyes, smiling and at times drawing forth stray drops of liquor from his moustache with the aid of his lower lip.

When that round was over there was a pause. O'Halloran had money but neither of the other two seemed to have any; so the whole party left the shop somewhat regretfully. At the corner of Duke Street Higgins and Nosey Flynn bevelled off to the left while the other three turned back towards the city. Rain was drizzling down on the cold streets and, when they reached the Ballast Office, Farrington suggested the Scotch House. The bar was full of men and loud with the noise of tongues and glasses. The three men pushed past the whining match-sellers at the door and formed a little party at the corner of the counter. They began to exchange stories. Leonard introduced them to a young fellow named Weathers who was performing at the Tivoli as an acrobat and knockabout *artiste*. Farrington stood a drink all round. Weathers said he would take a small Irish and Apollinaris. Farrington, who had definite notions of what was what, asked the boys would they have an Appolinaris too; but the boys told Tim to make theirs hot. The talk became theatrical. O'Halloran stood a round and then Farrington stood another round, Weathers protesting that the hospitality was too Irish. He promised to get them in behind the scenes and introduce them to some nice girls. O'Halloran said that he and Leonard would go, but that Farrington wouldn't go because he was a married man; and Farrington's heavy dirty eyes leered at the company in token that he understood he was being chaffed. Weathers made them all have just one little tincture at his expense and promised to meet them later on at Mulligan's in Poolbeg Street.

When the Scotch House closed they went round to Mulligan's. They went into the parlour at the back and O'Halloran ordered small hot specials all around. They were all beginning to feel mellow. Farrington was just standing another round when Weathers came back. Much to Farrington's relief he drank a glass of bitter this time. Funds were getting low but they had enough to keep them going. Presently two young women with big hats and a young man in a check suit came in and sat at a table close by. Weathers saluted them and told the company that they were out of the Tivoli. Farrington's eyes wandered at every moment in the direction of one of the young women. There was something striking in her appearance. An immense scarf of peacock-blue muslin was wound round her hat and knotted in a great bow under her chin; and she wore bright yellow gloves, reaching to the elbows. Farrington gazed admiringly at the plump arm which she moved very often and with much grace; and when, after a little time, she answered his gaze he admired still more her large dark brown eyes. The oblique staring expression in them fascinated him. She glanced at him once or twice and, when the party was leaving the room, she brushed against his chair and said "*O, pardon!*" in a London accent. He watched her leave the room in the hope that she would look back at him, but he was disappointed. He cursed his want of money and cursed all the rounds he had stood, particularly all the whiskies and Apollinaris which he had stood to Weathers. If there was one thing that he hated it was a sponge. He was so angry that he lost count of the conversation of his friends.

When Paddy Leonard called him he found that they were talking about feats of strength. Weathers was showing his biceps muscle to the company and boasting so much that the other two had called on Farrington to uphold the national honour. Farrington pulled up his sleeve accordingly and showed his biceps muscle to the company. The two arms were examined and compared and finally it was agreed to have a trial of strength. The table was cleared and the two men rested their elbows on it, clasping hands. When Paddy Leonard said "*Go!*" each was to try to bring down the other's hand on to the table. Farrington looked very serious and determined.

The trial began. After about thirty seconds Weathers brought his opponent's hand slowly down on to the table. Farrington's dark wine-coloured face flushed darker still with anger and humiliation at having been defeated by such a stripling.

"You're not to put the weight of your body behind it. Play fair," he said.

"Who's not playing fair?" said the other.

"Come on again. The two best out of three."

The trial began again. The veins stood out on Farrington's forehead, and the pallor of Weathers' complexion changed to peony. Their hands and arms trembled under the stress. After a long struggle Weathers again brought his opponent's hand slowly on to the table. There was a murmur of applause from the spectators. The curate, who was standing beside the table, nodded his red head towards the victor and said with stupid familiarity:

"Ah! that's the knack!"

"What the hell do you know about it?" said Farrington fiercely, turning on the man. "What do you put in your gab for?"

"Sh, sh!" said O'Halloran, observing the violent expression of Farrington's face. "Pony up, boys. We'll have just one little smahan more and then we'll be off."

A very sullen-faced man stood at the corner of O'Connell Bridge waiting for the little Sandymount tram to take him home. He was full of smouldering anger and revengefulness. He felt humiliated and discontented; he did not even feel drunk; and he had only two-pence in his pocket. He cursed everything. He had done for himself in the office, pawned his watch, spent all his money; and he had not even got drunk. He began to feel thirsty again and he longed to be back again in the hot reeking publichouse. He had lost his reputation as a strong man, having been defeated twice by a mere boy. His heart swelled with fury and, when he thought of the woman in the big hat who had brushed against him and said *Pardon!* his fury nearly choked him.

His tram let him down at Shelbourne Road and he steered his great body along the shadow of the wall of the barracks. He loathed returning to his home. When he went in by the side-door he found the kitchen empty and the kitchen fire nearly out. He bawled upstairs:

"Ada! Ada!"

His wife was a little sharp-faced woman who bullied her husband when he was sober and was bullied by him when he was drunk. They had five children. A little boy came running down the stairs.

"Who is that?" said the man, peering through the darkness.

"Me, pa."

"Who are you? Charlie?"

"No, pa. Tom."

"Where's your mother?"

"She's out at the chapel."

"That's right. . . . Did she think of leaving any dinner for me?"

"Yes, pa. I—"

"Light the lamp. What do you mean by having the place in darkness? Are the other children in bed?"

The man sat down heavily on one of the chairs while the little boy lit the lamp. He began to mimic his son's flat accent, saying half to himself: "*At the chapel. At the chapel, if you please!*" When the lamp was lit he banged his fist on the table and shouted:

"What's for my dinner?"

"I'm going . . . to cook it, pa," said the little boy.

The man jumped up furiously and pointed to the fire.

"On that fire! You let the fire out! By God, I'll teach you to do that again!"

He took a step to the door and seized the walking-stick which was standing behind it.

"I'll teach you to let the fire out!" he said, rolling up his sleeve in order to give his arm free play.

The little boy cried *"O, pa!"* and ran whimpering round the table, but the man followed him and caught him by the coat. The little boy looked about him wildly, but, seeing no way to escape, fell upon his knees.

"Now, you'll let the fire out the next time!" said the man, striking at him vigorously with the stick. "Take that, you little whelp!"

The boy uttered a squeal of pain as the stick cut his thigh. He clasped his hands together in the air and his voice shook with fright.

"O, pa!" he cried. "Don't beat me, pa! And I'll . . . I'll say a *Hail Mary* for you. . . . I'll say a *Hail Mary* for you, pa, if you don't beat me. . . . I'll say a *Hail Mary*. . . ."

[1905]

For Thought

Throughout "Counterparts," from the first sentence, with its emphasis on the word "furious," to the last paragraph, with its repetition of the word "beat," Joyce stresses the constant presence of violent emotions in the life of his main character. The reader is able to feel the presence of the violence smoldering in Farrington through Joyce's tone and skillful use of descriptive language. By incorporating highly suggestive images (such as the fragile, egg-shaped head of Mr. Alleyne), motifs (such as repeated references to darkness and recurring confrontations), and details that stress the chronic thirst bedevilling "the man," Joyce characterizes Farrington as someone who turns to drink repeatedly throughout the day to escape the frustration created in his life by his incompetence and lack of any sense of responsibility. The barely suppressed violence at the core of his nature finally erupts into an unprovoked attack on his innocent, terrified son, who begs not to be beaten, offering to say a Hail Mary on his father's behalf as a pathetic quid pro quo.

For Discussion

1. Trace the characterization of Farrington through key incidents in the story.
2. Comment on Joyce's attitude toward his protagonist. How is it displayed?
3. Explain how the title is a fit comment on the action and how it contributes to the meaning of the story.
4. Examine three encounters in the story with regard to mood. Comment on the cause and effect of each mood.
5. Discuss how Joyce effectively uses realistic details as a backdrop for the tone and characterization in the story.
6. Discuss the details of Farrington's consciousness that Joyce chooses to reveal. Comment on the purpose lying behind the selection process.

James Joyce
A Little Cloud

Eight years before he had seen his friend off at the North Wall and wished him godspeed, Gallaher had got on. You could tell that at once by his travelled air, his well-cut tweed suit, and fearless accent. Few fellows had talents like his and fewer still could remain unspoiled by such success. Gallaher's heart was in the right place and he had deserved to win. It was something to have a friend like that.

Little Chandler's thoughts ever since lunch-time had been of his meeting with Gallaher, of Gallaher's invitation and of the great city London where Gallaher lived. He was called Little Chandler because, though he was but slightly under the average stature, he gave one the idea of being a little man. His hands were white and small, his frame was fragile, his voice was quiet and his manners were refined. He took the greatest care of his fair silken hair and moustache and used perfume discreetly on his handkerchief. The half-moons of his nails were perfect and when he smiled you caught a glimpse of a row of childish white teeth.

As he sat at his desk in the King's Inns he thought what changes those eight years had brought. The friend whom he had known under a shabby and necessitous guise had become a brilliant figure on the London Press. He turned often from his tiresome writing to gaze out of the office window. The glow of a late autumn sunset covered the grass plots and walks. It cast a shower of kindly golden dust on the untidy nurses and decrepit old men who drowsed on the benches; it flickered upon all the moving figures—on the children who ran screaming along the gravel paths and on everyone who passed through the gardens. He watched the scene and thought of life; and (as always happened when he thought of life) he became sad. A gentle melancholy took possession of him. He felt how useless it was to struggle against fortune, this being the burden of wisdom which the ages had bequeathed to him.

He remembered the books of poetry upon his shelves at home. He had bought them in his bachelor days and many an evening, as he sat in the little room off the hall, he had been tempted to take one down from the bookshelf and read out something to his wife. But shyness had always held him back; and so the books had remained on their shelves. At times he repeated lines to himself and this consoled him.

When his hour had struck he stood up and took leave of his desk and of his fellow-clerks punctiliously. He emerged from under the feudal arch of the King's Inns, a neat modest figure, and walked swiftly down Henrietta Street. The golden sunset was waning and the air had grown sharp. A horde of grimy children populated the street. They stood or ran in the roadway or crawled up the steps before the gaping doors or squatted like mice upon the thresholds. Little Chandler gave them no thought. He picked his way deftly through all that minute vermin-like life and under the shadow of the gaunt spectral mansions in which the old nobility of Dublin had roystered. No memory of the past touched him, for his mind was full of a present joy.

He had never been in Corless's but he knew the value of the name. He knew that people went there after the theatre to eat oysters and drink liqueurs; and he had heard that the waiters there spoke French and German. Walking swiftly by at night he had seen cabs drawn up before the door and richly dressed ladies, escorted by cavaliers, alight and enter quickly. They wore noisy dresses and many wraps. Their faces were powdered and they caught up their dresses, when they touched earth, like alarmed Atalantas. He had always passed without turning his head to look. It was his habit to walk swiftly in the street even by day and whenever he found himself in the city late at night he hurried on his way apprehensively and excitedly. Sometimes, however, he courted the causes of his fear. He chose the darkest and narrowest streets and, as he walked boldly forward, the silence that was spread about his footsteps troubled him, the wandering, silent figures troubled him; and at times a sound of low fugitive laughter made him tremble like a leaf.

He turned to the right towards Capel Street. Ignatius Gallaher on the London Press! Who would have thought it possible eight years before? Still, now that he reviewed the past, Little Chandler could remember many signs of future greatness in his friend. People used to say that Ignatius Gallaher was wild. Of course, he did mix with a rakish set of fellows at that time, drank freely and borrowed money on all sides. In the end he had got mixed up in some shady affair, some money transaction: at least, that was one version of his flight. But nobody denied him talent. There was always a certain . . . something in Ignatius Gallaher that impressed you in spite of yourself. Even when he was out at elbows and at his wits' end for money he kept up a bold face. Little Chandler remembered (and the remembrance brought a slight flush of pride to his cheek) one of Ignatius Gallaher's sayings when he was in a tight corner:

"Half time now, boys," he used to say light-heartedly. "Where's my considering cap?"

That was Ignatius Gallaher all out; and, damn it, you couldn't but admire him for it.

Little Chandler quickened his pace. For the first time in his life he felt himself superior to the people he passed. For the first time his soul revolted against the dull inelegance of Capel Street. There was no doubt about it: if you wanted to succeed you had to go away. You could do nothing in Dublin. As he crossed Grattan Bridge he looked down the river towards the lower quays and pitied the poor stunted houses. They seemed to him a band of tramps, huddled together along the river-banks, their old coats covered with dust and soot, stupefied by the panorama of sunset and waiting for the first chill of night to bid them arise, shake themselves and begone. He wondered whether he could write a poem to express his idea. Perhaps Gallaher might be able to get it into some London paper for him. Could he write something original? He was not sure what idea he wished to express but the thought that a poetic moment had touched him took life within him like an infant hope. He stepped onward bravely.

Every step brought him nearer to London, farther from his own sober inartistic life. A light began to tremble on the horizon of his mind. He was not so old—thirty-two. His temperament might be said to be just at the point of maturity. There were so many different moods and impressions that he wished to express in verse. He felt them within him. He tried to weigh his soul to see if it was a poet's soul. Melancholy was the dominant note of his temperament, he thought, but it was a melancholy tempered by recurrences of faith and resignation and simple joy. If he could give expression to it in a book of poems perhaps men would listen. He would never be popular: he saw that. He could not sway the crowd but he might appeal to a little circle of kindred minds. The English critics, perhaps, would recognise him as one of the Celtic school by reason of the melancholy tone of his poems; besides that, he would put in allusions. He began to invent sentences and phrases from the notice which his book would get. "*Mr. Chandler has the gift of easy and graceful verse.*" . . . "*A wistful sadness pervades these poems.*" . . . "*The Celtic note.*" It was a pity his name was not more Irish-looking. Perhaps it would be better to insert his mother's name before the surname: Thomas Malone Chandler, or better still: T. Malone Chandler. He would speak to Gallaher about it.

He pursued his revery so ardently that he passed his street and had to turn back. As he came near Corless's his former agitation began to overmaster him and he halted before the door in indecision. Finally he opened the door and entered.

The light and noise of the bar held him at the doorways for a few moments. He looked about him, but his sight was confused by the shining of many red and green wine-glasses. The bar seemed to him to be full of people and he felt that the people were observing him curiously. He glanced quickly to right and left (frowning slightly to make his errand appear serious), but when his sight cleared a little he saw that nobody had turned to look at him: and there, sure enough, was Ignatius Gallaher leaning with his back against the counter and his feet planted far apart.

"Hallo, Tommy, old hero, here you are! What is it to be? What will you have? I'm taking whisky: better stuff than we get across the water. Soda? Lithia? No mineral? I'm the same. Spoils the flavour. . . . Here, *garçon*, bring us two halves of malt whisky, like a good fellow. . . . Well, and how have you been pulling along since I saw you last? Dear God, how old we're getting! Do you see any signs of aging in me—eh, what? A little grey and thin on the top—what?"

Ignatius Gallaher took off his hat and displayed a large closely cropped head. His face was heavy, pale and clean-shaven. His eyes, which were of bluish slate-colour, relieved his unhealthy pallor and shone out plainly above the vivid orange tie he wore. Between these rival features the lips appeared very long and shapeless and colourless. He bent his head and felt with two sympathetic fingers the thin hair at the crown. Little Chandler shook his head as a denial. Ignatius Gallaher put on his hat again.

"It pulls you down," he said. "Press life. Always hurry and scurry, looking for copy and sometimes not finding it: and then, always to have something new in your stuff. Damn proofs and printers, I say, for a few days. I'm deuced glad, I can tell you, to get back to the old country. Does a fellow good, a bit of a holiday. I feel a ton better since I landed again in dear dirty Dublin. . . . Here you are, Tommy. Water? Say when."

Little Chandler allowed his whisky to be very much diluted.

"You don't know what's good for you, my boy," said Ignatius Gallaher. "I drink mine neat."

"I drink very little as a rule," said Little Chandler modestly. "An odd half-one or so when I meet any of the old crowd: that's all."

"Ah, well," said Ignatius Gallaher, cheerfully, "here's to us and to old times and old acquaintance."

They clinked glasses and drank the toast.

"I met some of the old gang to-day," said Ignatius Gallaher. "O'Hara seems to be in a bad way. What's he doing?"

"Nothing," said Little Chandler. "He's gone to the dogs."

"But Hogan has a good sit, hasn't he?"

"Yes; he's in the Land Commission."

"I met him one night in London and he seemed to be very flush. . . . Poor O'Hara! Boose, I suppose?"

"Other things, too," said Little Chandler shortly.

Ignatius Gallaher laughed.

"Tommy," he said, "I see you haven't changed an atom. You're the very same serious person that used to lecture me on Sunday mornings when I had a sore head and a fur on my tongue. You'd want to knock about a bit in the world. Have you never been anywhere even for a trip?"

"I've been to the Isle of Man," said Little Chandler.

Ignatius Gallaher laughed.

"The Isle of Man!" he said. "Go to London or Paris: Paris, for choice. That'd do you good."

"Have you seen Paris?"

"I should think I have! I've knocked about there a little."

"And is it really so beautiful as they say?" asked Little Chandler.

He sipped a little of his drink while Ignatius Gallaher finished his boldly.

"Beautiful?" said Ignatius Gallaher, pausing on the word and on the flavour of his drink. "It's not so beautiful, you know. Of course, it is beautiful. . . . But it's the life of Paris; that's the thing. Ah, there's no city like Paris for gaiety, movement, excitement. . . ."

Little Chandler finished his whisky and, after some trouble, succeeded in catching the barman's eye. He ordered the same again.

"I've been to the Moulin Rouge," Ignatius Gallaher continued when the barman had removed their glasses, "and I've been to all the Bohemian cafés. Hot stuff! Not for a pious chap like you, Tommy."

Little Chandler said nothing until the barman returned with two glasses: then he touched his friend's glass lightly and reciprocated the former toast. He was beginning to feel somewhat disillusioned. Gallaher's accent and way of expressing himself did not please him. There was something vulgar in his friend which he had not observed before. But perhaps it was only the result of living in London amid the bustle and competition of the Press. The old personal charm was still there under this new gaudy manner. And, after all, Gallaher had lived, he had seen the world. Little Chandler looked at his friend enviously.

"Everything in Paris is gay," said Ignatius Gallaher. "They believe in enjoying life and don't you think they're right? If you want to enjoy yourself properly you must go to Paris. And, mind you, they've a great feeling for the Irish there. When they heard I was from Ireland they were ready to eat me, man."

Little Chandler took four or five sips from his glass.

"Tell me," he said, "is it true that Paris is so . . . immoral as they say?"

Ignatius Gallaher made a catholic gesture with his right arm.

"Every place is immoral," he said. "Of course you do find spicy bits in Paris. Go to one of the students' balls, for instance. That's lively, if you like, when the *cocottes* begin to let themselves loose. You know what they are, I suppose?"

"I've heard of them," said Little Chandler.

Ignatius Gallaher drank off his whisky and shook his head.

"Ah," he said, "you may say what you

like. There's no woman like the Parisienne—for style, for go."

"Then it is an immoral city," said Little Chandler, with timid insistence—"I mean, compared with London or Dublin?"

"London!" said Ignatius Gallaher. "It's six of one and half-a-dozen of the other. You ask Hogan, my boy. I showed him a bit about London when he was over there. He'd open your eye. . . . I say, Tommy, don't make punch of that whisky: liquor up."

"No, really. . . ."

"O, come on, another one won't do you any harm. What is it? The same again, I suppose?"

"Well . . . all right."

"*François*, the same again. . . . Will you smoke, Tommy?"

Ignatius Gallaher produced his cigar-case. The two friends lit their cigars and puffed at them in silence until their drinks were served.

"I'll tell you my opinion," said Ignatius Gallaher, emerging after some time from the clouds of smoke in which he had taken refuge, "it's a rum world. Talk of immorality! I've heard of cases—what am I saying?—I've known them: cases of . . . immorality. . . ."

Ignatius Gallaher puffed thoughtfully at his cigar and then, in a calm historian's tone, he proceeded to sketch for his friend some pictures of the corruption which was rife abroad. He summarised the vices of many capitals and seemed inclined to award the palm to Berlin. Some things he could not vouch for (his friends had told him), but of others he had had personal experience. He spared neither rank nor caste. He revealed many of the secrets of religious houses on the Continent and described some of the practices which were fashionable in high society and ended by telling, with details, a story about an English duchess—a story which he knew to be true. Little Chandler was astonished.

"Ah, well," said Ignatius Gallaher, "here we are in old jog-along Dublin where nothing is known of such things."

"How dull you must find it," said Little Chandler, "after all the other places you've seen!"

"Well," said Ignatius Gallaher, "it's a relaxation to come over here, you know. And, after all, it's the old country, as they say, isn't it? You can't help having a certain feeling for it. That's human nature. . . . But tell me something about yourself. Hogan told me you had . . . tasted the joys of connubial bliss. Two years ago, wasn't it?"

Little Chandler blushed and smiled.

"Yes," he said. "I was married last May twelve months."

"I hope it's not too late in the day to offer my best wishes," said Ignatius Gallaher. "I didn't know your address or I'd have done so at the time."

He extended his hand, which Little Chandler took.

"Well, Tommy," he said, "I wish you and yours every joy in life, old chap, and tons of money, and may you never die till I shoot you. And that's the wish of a sincere friend, an old friend. You know that?"

"I know that," said Little Chandler.

"Any youngsters?" said Ignatius Gallaher.

Little Chandler blushed again.

"We have one child," he said.

"Son or daughter?"

"A little boy."

Ignatius Gallaher slapped his friend sonorously on the back.

"Bravo," he said, "I wouldn't doubt you, Tommy."

Little Chandler smiled, looked confusedly at his glass and bit his lower lip with three childishly white front teeth.

"I hope you'll spend an evening with us," he said, "before you go back. My wife will be delighted to meet you. We can have a little music and——"

"Thanks awfully, old chap," said Ignatius Gallaher, "I'm sorry we didn't meet earlier. But I must leave to-morrow night."

"To-night, perhaps . . .?"

"I'm awfully sorry, old man. You see I'm over here with another fellow, clever young chap he is too, and we arranged to go to a little card party. Only for that . . ."

"O, in that case. . . ."

"But, who knows?" said Ignatius Gallaher considerately. "Next year I may take a little skip over here now that I've broken the ice. It's only a pleasure deferred."

"Very well," said Little Chandler, "the next time you come we must have an evening together. That's agreed now, isn't it?"

"Yes, that's agreed," said Ignatius Gallaher. "Next year if I come, *parole d'honneur*."

"And to clinch the bargain," said Little Chandler, "we'll just have one more now."

Ignatius Gallaher took out a large gold watch and looked at it.

"Is it to be the last?" he said. "Because you know, I have an a.p."

"O, yes, positively," said Little Chandler.

"Very well, then," said Ignatius Gallaher "let us have another one as a *deoc an doruis*—that's good vernacular for a small whisky, I believe."

Little Chandler ordered the drinks. The blush which had risen to his face a few moments before was establishing itself. A trifle made him blush at any time: and now he felt warm and excited. Three small whiskies had gone to his head and Gallaher's strong cigar had confused his mind, for he was a delicate and abstinent person. The adventure of meeting Gallaher after eight years, of finding himself with Gallaher in Corless's surrounded by lights and noise, of listening to Gallaher's stories and of sharing for a brief space Gallaher's vagrant and triumphant life, upset the equipoise of his sensitive nature. He felt acutely the contrast between his own life and his friend's, and it seemed to him unjust. Gallaher was his inferior in birth and education. He was sure that he could do something better than his friend had ever done, or could ever do, something higher than mere tawdry journalism if he only got the chance. What was it that stood in his way? His unfortunate timidity! He wished to vindicate himself in some way, to assert his manhood. He saw behind Gallaher's refusal of his invitation. Gallaher was only patronising him by his friendliness just as he was patronising Ireland by his visit.

The barman brought their drinks. Little Chandler pushed one glass towards his friend and took up the other boldly.

"Who knows?" he said, as they lifted their glasses. "When you come next year I may have the pleasure of wishing long life and happiness to Mr. and Mrs. Ignatius Gallaher."

Ignatius Gallaher in the act of drinking closed one eye expressively over the rim of his glass. When he had drunk he smacked his lips decisively, set down his glass and said:

"No blooming fear of that, my boy. I'm going to have my fling first and see a bit of life and the world before I put my head in the sack—if I ever do."

"Some day you will," said Little Chandler calmly.

Ignatius Gallaher turned his orange tie and slate-blue eyes full upon his friend.

"You think so?" he said.

"You'll put your head in the sack," repeated Little Chandler stoutly, "like everyone else if you can find the girl."

He had slightly emphasised his tone and he was aware that he had betrayed himself; but, though the colour had heightened in his cheek, he did not flinch from his friend's gaze. Ignatius Gallaher watched him for a few moments and then said:

"If ever it occurs, you may bet your bottom dollar there'll be no mooning and spooning about it. I mean to marry money. She'll have a good fat account at the bank or she won't do for me."

Little Chandler shook his head.

"Why, man alive," said Ignatius Gallaher, vehemently, "do you know what it is? I've only to say the word and to-morrow I can have the woman and the cash. You don't believe it? Well, I know it. There are hundreds—what am I saying?—thousands of rich Germans and Jews, rotten with money, that'd only be too glad. . . . You wait a while, my boy. See if I don't play my cards properly. When I go about a thing I mean business, I tell you. You just wait."

He tossed his glass to his mouth, finished his drink and laughed loudly. Then he looked thoughtfully before him and said in a calmer tone:

"But I'm in no hurry. They can wait. I don't fancy tying myself up to one woman, you know."

He imitated with his mouth the act of tasting and made a wry face.

"Must get a bit stale, I should think," he said.

Little Chandler sat in the room off the hall, holding a child in his arms. To save money they kept no servant but Annie's young sister Monica came for an hour or so in the morning and an hour or so in the evening to help. But Monica had gone home long ago. It was a quarter to nine. Little Chandler had come home late for tea and, moreover, he had forgotton to bring Annie home the parcel of coffee from Bewley's. Of course she was in a bad humour and gave him short answers. She said she would do without any tea but when it came near the time at which the shop at the corner closed she decided to go out herself for a quarter of a pound of tea and two pounds of sugar. She put the sleeping child deftly in his arms and said:

"Here. Don't waken him."

A little lamp with a white china shade stood upon the table and its light fell over a photograph which was enclosed in a frame of crumped horn. It was Annie's photograph. Little Chandler looked at it, pausing at the thin tight lips. She wore the pale blue summer blouse which he had brought her home as a present one Saturday. It had cost him ten and elevenpence; but what an agony of nervousness it had cost him! How he had suffered that day, waiting at the shop door until the shop was empty, standing at the counter and trying to appear at his ease while the girl piled ladies' blouses before him, paying at the desk and forgetting to take up the odd penny of his change, being called back by the cashier, and finally, striving to hide his blushes as he left the shop by examining the parcel to see if it was securely tied. When he brought the blouse home Annie kissed him and said it was very pretty and stylish; but when she heard the price she threw the blouse on the table and said it was a regular swindle to charge ten and elevenpence for it. At first she wanted to take it back but when she tried it on she was delighted with it, especially with the make of the sleeves, and kissed him and said he was very good to think of her.

Hm! . . .

He looked coldly into the eyes of the photograph and they answered coldly. Certainly they were pretty and the face itself was pretty. But he found something mean in it. Why was it so unconscious and ladylike? The composure of the eyes irritated him. They repelled him and defied him: there was no passion in them, no rapture. He thought of what Gallaher had said about rich Jewesses. Those dark Oriental eyes, he thought, how full they are of passion, of voluptuous longing! . . . Why had he married the eyes in the photograph?

He caught himself up at the question and glanced nervously round the room. He found something mean in the pretty furniture which he had bought for his house on the hire system. Annie had chosen it herself and it reminded him of her. It too was prim and pretty. A dull resentment against his life awoke within him. Could he not escape from his little house? Was it too late for him to live bravely like Gallaher? Could he go to London? There was the furniture still to be paid for. If he could only write a book and get it published, that might open the way for him.

A volume of Byron's poems lay before him on the table. He opened it cautiously with his left hand lest he should waken the child and began to read the first poem in the book:

> "Hushed are the winds and still the evening
> gloom,
> Not e'en a Zephyr wanders through the
> grove,
> Whilst I return to view my Margaret's tomb
> And scatter flowers on the dust I love."

He paused. He felt the rhythm of the verse about him in the room. How melancholy it was! Could he, too, write like that, express the melancholy of his soul in verse? There were so many things he wanted to describe: his sensation of a few hours before on Grattan Bridge, for example. If he could get back again into that mood. . . .

The child awoke and began to cry. He turned from the page and tried to hush it: but it would not be hushed. He began to rock it to and fro in his arms but its wailing cry grew keener. He rocked it faster while his eyes began to read the second stanza:

> "Within this narrow cell reclines her clay,
> That clay where once. . . ."

It was useless. He couldn't read. He couldn't do anything. The wailing of the child pierced the drum of his ear. It was useless, useless! He was a prisoner for life. His arms trembled with anger and suddenly bending to the child's face he shouted:

"Stop!"

The child stopped for an instant, had a spasm of fright and began to scream. He jumped up from his chair and walked hastily up and down the room with the child in his arms. It began to sob piteously, losing its breath for four or five seconds, and then bursting out anew. The thin walls of the room echoed the sound. He tried to soothe it but it sobbed more convulsively. He looked at the contracted and quivering face of the child and began to be alarmed. He counted seven sobs without a break between them and caught the child to his breast in fright. If it died! . . .

The door was burst open and a young woman ran in, panting.

"What is it? What is it?" she cried.

The child, hearing its mother's voice, broke out into a paroxysm of sobbing.

"It's nothing, Annie . . . it's nothing. . . . He began to cry . . ."

She flung her parcels on the floor and snatched the child from him.

"What have you done to him?" she cried, glaring into his face.

Little Chandler sustained for one moment the gaze of her eyes and his heart closed together as he met the hatred in them. He began to stammer:

"It's nothing. . . . He . . . he began to cry. . . . I couldn't . . . I didn't do anything. . . . What?"

Giving no heed to him she began to walk up and down the room, clasping the child tightly in her arms and murmuring:

"My little man! My little mannie! Was 'ou frightened, love? . . . There now, love! There now! . . . Lambabaun! Mamma's little lamb of the world! . . . There now!"

Little Chandler felt his cheeks suffused with shame and he stood back out of the lamplight. He listened while the paroxysm of the child's sobbing grew less and less; and tears of remorse started to his eyes.

[1905]

For Thought

In "A Little Cloud," Joyce encapsulates the life of his protagonist in the events of an afternoon and evening. He focuses on Little Chandler's attempt at revived camaraderie with his old friend, Gallaher, now a "brilliant figure of the London Press," and on his troubles when he returns home. The author contrasts Chandler's character to Gallaher's by depicting the little law clerk as a would-be poet who feels the stirrings of rebellion against the constraints of marriage and life in provincial Dublin, both of which Gallaher has escaped. Given the characterization of Chandler, however, the story ends not with the protagonist taking any action that might lead to fulfillment of his dreams and vague ambitions but, ironically, with him weeping tears of guilt, remorse, and despair in the face of an angry attack from his wife.

For Discussion

1. What is Joyce's attitude toward Chandler? Toward Gallaher? Select details from the story that establish the attitude toward each.
2. Joyce often uses realistic details with symbolic overtones. Find evidence of this practice in the story.
3. What insight or discovery, if any, does Chandler experience? Does it coincide with any insight the reader might have?
4. Discuss Joyce's use of mood shifts to convey meaning.
5. How is the climactic moment in the action prepared for? What irony is inherent in the circumstances of Little Chandler's life?
6. How is the title related to the meaning of the story and to the characterization of Chandler?

Franz Kafka
In the Penal Colony

"It's a remarkable piece of apparatus," said the officer to the explorer and surveyed with a certain air of admiration the apparatus which was after all quite familiar to him. The explorer seemed to have accepted merely out of politeness the Commandant's invitation to witness the execution of a soldier condemned to death for disobedience and insulting behavior to a superior. Nor did the colony itself betray much interest in this execution. At least, in the small sandy valley, a deep hollow surrounded on all sides by naked crags, there was no one present save the officer, the explorer, the condemned man, who was a stupid-looking wide-mouthed creature with bewildered hair and face, and the soldier who held the heavy chain controlling the small chains locked on the prisoner's ankles, wrists and neck chains which were themselves attached to each other by communicating links. In any case, the condemned man looked so like a submissive dog that one might have thought he could be left to run free on the surrounding hills and would only need to be whistled for when the execution was due to begin.

The explorer did not much care about the apparatus and walked up and down behind the prisoner with almost visible indifference while the officer made the last adjustments, now creeping beneath the structure, which was bedded deep in the earth, now climbing a ladder to inspect its upper parts. These were tasks that might well have been left to a mechanic, but the officer performed them with great zeal, whether because he was a devoted admirer of the apparatus or because of other reasons the work could be entrusted to no one else. "Ready now!" he called at last and climbed down from the ladder. He looked uncommonly limp, breathed with his mouth wide open and had tucked two fine ladies' handkerchiefs under the collar of his uniform. "These uniforms are too heavy for the tropics, surely," said the explorer, instead of making some inquiry about the apparatus, as the officer had expected. "Of course," said the officer, washing his oily and greasy hands in a bucket of water that stood ready, "but they mean home to us; we don't want to forget about home. Now just have a look at this machine," he added at once, simultaneously drying his hands on a towel and indicating the apparatus. "Up till now a few things still had to be set by hand, but from this moment it works all by itself." The explorer nodded and followed him. The officer, anxious to secure himself against all contingencies, said: "Things sometimes go wrong, of course; I hope that nothing goes wrong today, but we have to allow for the possibility. The machinery should go on working continuously for twelve hours. But if anything does go wrong it will only be some small matter that can be set right at once."

"Won't you take a seat?" he asked finally, drawing a cane chair out from among a heap of them and offering it to the explorer, who could not refuse it. He was now sitting at the edge of a pit, into which he glanced for a fleeting moment. It was not very deep. On one side of the pit the excavated soil had been piled up in a rampart, on the other side of it stood the apparatus. "I don't know," said the officer, "if the Commandant has already explained this apparatus to you." The explorer waved one hand vaguely; the officer asked for nothing better, since now he could explain the apparatus himself. "This apparatus," he said, taking hold of a crank handle and leaning against it, "was invented by our former Commandant. I assisted at the very earliest experiments and had a share in all the work until its completion. But the credit of inventing it belongs to him alone. Have you ever heard of our former Commandant? No? Well, it isn't saying too much if I tell you that the organization of the whole penal colony is his work. We who were his friends knew even before he died that the organization of the colony was so perfect that his successor, even with a thousand new schemes in his head, would find it impossible to alter anything, at least for many years to come. And our prophecy has come true; the new Commandant has had to acknowledge the truth. A pity you never met the old Commandant!—But," the officer interrupted himself, "I am rambling on, and here stands his apparatus before us. It consists, as you see, of three parts. In the course of time each of these parts has acquired a kind of popular nickname. The lower one is called the 'Bed,' the upper one the 'Designer,' and this one here in the middle that moves up and down is called the 'Harrow.'" "The Harrow?" asked the explorer. He had not been listening very attentively, the glare of the sun in the shadeless valley was altogether too strong, it was difficult to collect one's thoughts. All the more did he admire the officer, who in spite of his tight-fitting full-dress uniform coat, amply befrogged and weighed down by epaulettes, was pursuing his subject with such enthusiasm and, besides talking, was still tightening a screw here and there with a spanner. As for the soldier, he seemed to be in much the same condition as the explorer. He had wound the prisoner's chain round both his wrists, propped himself on his rifle, let his head hang and was paying no attention to anything. That did not surprise the explorer, for the officer was speaking French, and certainly neither the soldier nor the prisoner understood a word of French. It was all the more remarkable, therefore, that the prisoner was none the less making an effort to follow the officer's explanations. With a kind of drowsy persistence he directed his gaze wherever the officer pointed a finger, and at the interruption of the explorer's question he, too, as well as the officer, looked round.

"Yes, the Harrow," said the officer, "a good name for it. The needles are set in like the teeth of a harrow and the whole thing works something like a harrow, although its action is limited to one place and contrived with much more artistic skill. Anyhow, you'll soon understand it. On the Bed here the condemned man is laid—I'm going to describe the apparatus first before I set it in motion. Then you'll be able to follow the proceedings better. Besides, one of the cog wheels in the Designer is badly worn; it creaks a lot when it's working; you can hardly hear yourself speak; spare parts, unfortunately, are difficult to get here.— Well, here is the Bed, as I told you. It is completely covered with a layer of cotton wool; you'll find out why later. On this cotton wool the condemned man is laid, face down, quite naked, of course; here are straps for the hands, here for the feet, and here for the neck, to bind him fast. Here at the head of the bed, where the man, as I said, first lays down his face, is this little gag of felt, which can be easily regulated to go straight into his mouth. It is meant to keep him from screaming and biting his tongue. Of course the man is forced to take the felt into his mouth, for otherwise his neck would be broken by the strap." "Is that cotton wool?" asked the explorer, bending forward. "Yes, certainly," said the officer, with a smile, "feel it for yourself." He took the explorer's hand and guided it over the bed. "It's specially prepared cotton wool, that's why it looks so different; I'll tell you presently what it's for." The explorer already felt a dawning interest in the apparatus; he sheltered his eyes from the sun with one hand and gazed up at the structure. It was a huge affair. The Bed and the Designer were of the same size and looked like two dark wooden chests. The Designer hung about two meters above the Bed; each of them was bound at the corners with four rods of brass that almost flashed out rays in the sunlight. Between the chests shuttled the Harrow on a ribbon of steel.

The officer had scarcely noticed the explorer's previous indifference, but he was now well aware of his dawning interest; so he stopped explaining in order to leave a space of time for quiet observation. The condemned man imitated the explorer; since he could not use a hand to shelter his eyes he gazed upwards without shade.

"Well, the man lies down," said the explorer, leaning back in his chair and crossing his legs.

"Yes," said the officer, pushing his cap back a little and passing one hand over his heated face, "now listen! Both the Bed and the Designer have an electric battery each; the Bed needs one for itself, the Designer for the Harrow. As soon as the man is strapped down, the Bed is set in motion. It quivers in minute, very rapid vibrations, both from side to side and up and down. You will have seen similar apparatus in hospitals; but in our Bed the movements are all precisely calculated; you see, they have to correspond very exactly to the movements of the Harrow. And the Harrow is the instrument for the actual execution of the sentence."

"And how does the sentence run?" asked the explorer.

"You don't know that either?" said the officer in amazement, and bit his lips. "Forgive me if my explanations seem rather incoherent. I do beg your pardon. You see, the Commandant always used to do the explaining; but the new Commandant shirks this duty; yet that such an important visitor"—the explorer tried to deprecate the honor with both hands, the officer, however, insisted—"that such an important visitor should not even be told about the kind of sentence we pass is a new development, which—" He was just on the point of using strong language but checked himself and said only: "I was not informed, it is not my fault. In any case, I am certainly the best person to explain our procedure, since I have here"—he patted his breast pocket—"the relevant drawings made by our former Commandant."

"The Commandant's own drawings?" asked the explorer. "Did he combine everything in himself, then? Was he soldier, judge, mechanic, chemist and draughtsman?"

"Indeed he was," said the officer, nodding assent, with a remote, glassy look. Then he inspected his hands critically; they did not seem clean enough to him for touching the drawings; so he went over to the bucket and washed them again. Then he drew out a small leather wallet and said: "Our sentence does not sound severe. Whatever commandment the prisoner has disobeyed is written upon his body by the

Harrow. This prisoner, for instance"—the officer indicated the man—"will have written on his body; HONOR THY SUPERIORS!"

The explorer glanced at the man; he stood, as the officer pointed him out, with bent head, apparently listening with all his ears in an effort to catch what was being said. Yet the movement of his blubber lips, closely pressed together, showed clearly that he could not understand a word. Many questions were troubling the explorer, but at the sight of the prisoner he asked only: "Does he know his sentence?" "No," said the officer, eager to go on with his exposition, but the explorer interrupted him: "He doesn't know the sentence that has been passed on him?" "No," said the officer again, pausing a moment as if to let the explorer elaborate his question, and then said: "There would be no point in telling him. He'll learn it on his body." The explorer intended to make no answer, but he felt the prisoner's gaze turned on him; it seemed to ask if he approved such ongoings. So he bent forward again, having already leaned back in his chair, and put another question: "But surely he knows that he has been sentenced?" "Nor that either," said the officer, smiling at the explorer as if expecting him to make further surprising remarks. "No," said the explorer, wiping his forehead, "then he can't know either whether his defense was effective?" "He has had no chance of putting up a defense," said the officer, turning his eyes away as if speaking to himself and so sparing the explorer the shame of hearing self-evident matters explained. "But he must have had some chance of defending himself," said the explorer, and rose from his seat.

The officer realized that he was in danger of having his exposition of the apparatus held up for a long time; so he went up to the explorer, took him by the arm, waved a hand towards the condemned man, who was standing very straight now that he had so obviously become the center of attention—the soldier had also given the chain a jerk—and said: "This is how the matter stands. I have been appointed judge in this penal colony. Despite my youth. For I was the former Commandant's assistant in all penal matters and know more about the apparatus than anyone. My guiding principle is this: Guilt is never to be doubted. Other courts cannot follow that principle, for they consist of several opinions and have higher courts to scrutinize them. That is not the case here, or at least, it was not the case in the former Commandant's time. The new man has certainly shown some inclination to interfere with my judgments, but so far I have succeeded in fending him off and will go on succeeding. You wanted to have the case explained; it is quite simple, like all of them. A captain reported to me this morning that this man, who had been assigned to him as a servant and sleeps before his door, had been asleep on duty. It is his duty, you see, to get up every time the hour strikes and salute the captain's door. Not an exacting duty, and very necessary, since he has to be a sentry as well as a servant, and must be alert in both functions. Last night the captain wanted to see if the man was doing his duty. He opened the door as the clock struck two and there was his man curled up asleep. He took his riding whip and lashed him across the face. Instead of getting up and begging pardon, the man caught hold of his master's legs, shook him and cried: 'Throw that whip away or I'll eat you alive.'—That's the evidence. The captain came to me an hour ago, I wrote down his statement and appended the sentence to it. Then I had the man put in chains. That was all quite simple. If I had first called the man before me and interrogated him, things would have got into a confused tangle. He would have told lies, and had I exposed these lies he would have backed them up with more lies, and so on and so forth. As it is, I've got him and I won't let him go.—Is that quite clear now? But we're wasting time, the execution should be beginning and I haven't finished explaining the apparatus yet." He pressed the explorer back into his chair, went up again to the apparatus and began: "As you see, the shape of the Harrow corresponds to the human form; here is the harrow for the torso, here are the harrows for the legs. For the head there is only this one small spike. Is that quite clear?" He bent amiably forward towards the explorer, eager to provide the most comprehensive explanations.

The explorer considered the Harrow with a frown. The explanation of the judicial procedure had not satisfied him. He had to remind himself that this was in any case a penal colony where extraordinary measures were needed and that military discipline must be enforced to the last. He also felt that some hope might be set on the new Commandant, who was apparently of a mind to bring in, although gradually, a new kind of procedure which the officer's narrow mind was incapable of understanding. This train of thought prompted his next question: "Will the Commandant attend the execution?" "It is not certain," said the officer, wincing at the direct question, and his friendly expression darkened. "That is just why we have to lose no time. Much as I dislike it, I shall have to cut my explanations short. But of course tomorrow, when the apparatus has been cleaned—its one drawback is that it gets so messy—I can recapitulate all the details. For the present, then, only the essentials.—When the man lies down on the Bed and it begins to vibrate, the Harrow is lowered onto his body. It regulates itself automatically so that the needles barely touch his skin; once contact is made the steel ribbon stiffens immediately into a rigid band. And then the performance begins. An ignorant onlooker would see no difference between one punishment and another. The Harrow appears to do its work with uniform regularity. As it quivers, its points pierce the skin of the body which is itself quivering from the vibration of the Bed. So that the actual progress of the sentence can be watched, the Harrow is made of glass. Getting the needles fixed in the glass was a technical problem, but after many experiments we overcame the difficulty. No trouble was too great for us to take, you see. And now anyone can look through the glass and watch the inscription taking form on the body. Wouldn't you care to come a little nearer and have a look at the needles?"

The explorer got up slowly, walked across and bent over the Harrow. "You see," said the officer, "there are two kinds of needles arranged in multiple patterns. Each long needle has a short one beside it. The long needle does the writing, and the short needle sprays a jet of water to wash away the blood and keep the inscription clear. Blood and water together are then conducted here through small runnels into this main runnel and down a waste pipe into the pit." With his finger the officer traced the exact course taken by the blood and water. To make the picture as vivid as possible he held both hands below the outlet of the waste pipe as if to catch the outflow, and when he did this the explorer drew back his head and feeling behind him with one hand sought to return to his chair. To his horror he found that the condemned man too had obeyed the officer's invitation to examine the Harrow at close quarters and had followed him. He had pulled forward the sleepy soldier with the chain and was bending over the glass. One could see that his uncertain eyes were trying to perceive what the two gentlemen had been looking at, but since he had not understood the explanation he could not make head or tail of it. He was peering this way and that way. He kept running his eyes along the glass. The explorer wanted to drive him away, since what he was doing was probably culpable. But the officer firmly restrained the explorer with one hand and with the other took a clod of earth from the rampart and threw it at the soldier. He opened his eyes with a jerk, saw what the comdemned man had dared to do, let his rifle fall, dug his heels into the ground, dragged his prisoner back so that he stumbled and fell immediately, and then stood looking down at him, watching him struggling and rattling in his chains. "Set him on his feet!" yelled the officer, for he noticed that the explorer's attention was being too much distracted by the prisoner. In fact he was even leaning right across the Harrow, without taking any notice of it, intent only on finding out what was happening to the prisoner. "Be careful with him!" cried the officer again. He ran round the apparatus, himself caught the condemned man under the shoulders and with the soldier's help got him up on his feet, which kept slithering from under him.

"Now I know all about it," said the explorer as the officer came back to him. "All except the most important thing," he answered, seizing the explorer's arm and pointing upwards: "In the Designer are all the cogwheels that control the movements of the Harrow, and this machinery is regulated according to the inscription demanded by the sentence. I am still using the guiding plans drawn by the former Commandant. Here they are"—he extracted some sheets from the leather wallet—"but I'm sorry I can't let you handle them, they are my most precious possessions. Just take a seat and I'll hold them in front of you like this, then you'll be able to see everything quite well." He spread out the first sheet of paper. The explorer would have liked to say something appreciative, but all he could see was a labyrinth of lines crossing and re-crossing each other, which covered the paper so thickly that it was difficult to discern the blank spaces between them. "Read it," said the officer. "I can't," said the explorer. "Yet it's clear enough," said the officer. "It's very ingenious," said the explorer evasively, "but I can't make it out." "Yes," said the officer with a laugh, putting the paper away again, "it's no calligraphy for school children. It needs to be studied closely. I'm quite sure that in the end you would understand it too. Of course the script can't be a simple one; it's not supposed to kill a man straight off, but only after an interval of, on an average, twelve hours; the turning point is reckoned to come at the sixth hour. So there have to be lots and lots of flourishes around the actual script; the script itself runs round the body only in a narrow girdle; the rest of the body is reserved for the embellishments. Can you appreciate now the work accomplished by the Harrow and the whole apparatus?—Just watch it!" He ran up the ladder, turned a wheel, called down: "Look out, keep to one side!" and everything started working. If the wheel had not creaked, it would have been marvelous. The officer, as if surprised by the noise of the wheel, shook his fist at it, then spread out his arms in excuse to the explorer and climbed down rapidly to peer at the working of the machine from below. Something perceptible to no one save himself was still not in order; he clambered up again, did something with both hands in the interior of the Designer, then slid down one of the rods, instead of using the ladder, so as to get down quicker, and with the full force of his lungs, to make himself heard at all in the noise, yelled in the explorer's ear: "Can you follow it? The Harrow is beginning to write; when it finishes the first draft of the inscription on the man's back, the layer of cotton wool begins to roll and slowly turns the body over, to give the Harrow fresh space for writing. Meanwhile the raw part that has been written on lies on the cotton wool, which is specially prepared to staunch the bleeding and so makes all ready for a new deepening of the script. Then these teeth at the edge of the Harrow, as the body turns further round, tear the cotton wool away from the wounds, throw it into the pit, and there is more work for the Harrow. So it keeps on writing deeper and deeper for the whole twelve hours. The first six hours the condemned man stays alive almost as before, he suffers only pain. After two hours the felt gag is taken away, for he has no longer strength to scream. Here, into this electrically heated basin at the head of the bed, some warm rice pap is poured, from which the man, if he feels like it, can take as much as his tongue can lap. Not one of them ever misses the chance. I can remember none, and my experience is extensive. Only about the sixth hour does the man lose all desire to eat. I usually kneel down here at that moment and observe what happens. The man rarely swallows his last mouthful, he only rolls it round his mouth and spits it out into the pit. I have to duck just then or he would spit it in my face. But how quiet he grows at just about the sixth hour! Enlightenment comes to the most dull-witted. It begins around the eyes. From there it radiates. A moment that might tempt one to get under the Harrow oneself. Nothing more happens than that the man begins to understand the inscription, he purses his mouth as if he were listening. You have seen how difficult it is to decipher the script with one's eyes; but our man deciphers it with his wounds. To be sure, that is a hard task; he needs six hours to accomplish it. By that time the Harrow has pierced him quite through and casts him into the pit, where he pitches down upon the blood and water and the cotton wool. Then the judgment has been fulfilled, and we, the soldier and I, bury him."

The explorer had inclined his ear to the officer and with his hands in his jacket pockets watched the machine at work. The condemned man watched it too, but uncomprehendingly. He bent forward a little and was intent on the moving needles when the soldier, at a sign from the officer, slashed through his shirt and trousers from behind with a knife, so that they fell off; he tried to catch at his falling clothes to cover his nakedness, but the soldier lifted him into the air and shook the last remnants from him. The officer stopped the machine, and in the sudden silence the condemned man was laid under the Harrow. The chains were loosened and the straps fastened on instead; in the first moment that seemed almost a relief to the prisoner. And now the Harrow was adjusted a little lower, since he was a thin man. When the needle points touched him a shudder ran over his skin; while the soldier was busy strapping his right hand, he flung out his left hand blindly; but it happened to be in the direction towards where the explorer was standing. The officer kept watching the explorer sideways, as if seeking to read from his face the impression made on him by the execution, which had been at least cursorily explained to him.

The wrist strap broke; probably the soldier had drawn it too tight. The officer had to intervene, the soldier held up the broken piece of strap to show him. So the officer went over to him and said, his face still turned towards the explorer: "This is a very complex machine, it can't be helped that things are breaking or giving way here and there; but one must not thereby allow oneself to be diverted in one's general judgment. In any case, this strap is easily made good; I shall simply use a chain; the delicacy of the vibrations for the right arm will of course be a little impaired." And while he fastened the chains, he added: "The resources for maintaining the machine are now very much reduced. Under the former Commandant I had free access to a sum of money set aside entirely for this purpose. There was a store, too, in which spare parts were kept for repairs of all kinds. I confess I have been almost prodigal with them, I mean in the past, not now as the new Commandant pretends, always looking for an excuse to attack our old way of doing things. Now he has taken charge of the machine money himself, and if I send for a new strap they ask for the broken old strap as evidence, and the new strap takes ten days to appear and then is of shoddy material and not much good. But how I am supposed to work the machine without a strap, that's something nobody bothers about."

The explorer thought to himself: It's always a ticklish matter to intervene decisively in other people's affairs. He was neither a member of the penal colony nor a citizen of the state to which it belonged. Were he to denounce this execution or actually try to stop it, they could say to him:

You are a foreigner, mind your own business. He could make no answer to that, unless he were to add that he was amazed at himself in this connection, for he traveled only as an observer, with no intention at all of altering other people's methods of administering justice. Yet here he found himself strongly tempted. The injustice of the procedure and the inhumanity of the execution were undeniable. No one could suppose that he had any selfish interest in the matter, for the condemned man was a complete stranger, not a fellow countryman or even at all sympathetic to him. The explorer himself had recommendations from high quarters, had been received here with great courtesy, and the very fact that he had been invited to attend the execution seemed to suggest that his views would be welcome. And this was all the more likely since the Commandant, as he had heard only too plainly, was no upholder of the procedure and maintained an attitude almost of hostility to the officer.

At that moment the explorer heard the officer cry out in rage. He had just, with considerable difficulty, forced the felt gag into the condemned man's mouth when the man in an irresistible access of nausea shut his eyes and vomited. Hastily the officer snatched him away from the gag and tried to hold his head over the pit; but it was too late, the vomit was running all over the machine. "It's all the fault of that Commandant!" cried the officer, senselessly shaking the brass rods in front, "the machine is befouled like a pigsty." With trembling hands he indicated to the explorer what had happened. "Have I not tried for hours at a time to get the Commandant to understand that the prisoner must fast for a whole day before the execution. But our new, mild doctrine thinks otherwise. The Commandant's ladies stuff the man with sugar candy before he's led off. He has lived on stinking fish his whole life long and now he has to eat sugar candy! But it could still be possible, I should have nothing to say against it, but why won't they get me a new felt gag, which I have been begging for the last three months. How should a man not feel sick when he takes a felt gag into his mouth which more than a hundred men have already slobbered and gnawed in their dying moments?"

The condemned man had laid his head down and looked peaceful, the soldier was busy trying to clean the machine with the prisoner's shirt. The officer advanced towards the explorer, who in some vague presentiment fell back a pace, but the officer seized him by the hand, and drew him to one side. "I should like to exchange a few words with you in confidence," he said, "may I?" "Of course," said the explorer, and listened with downcast eyes.

"This procedure and method of execution, which you are now having the opportunity to admire, has at the moment no longer any open adherents in our colony. I am its sole advocate, and at the same time the sole advocate of the old Commandant's tradition. I can no longer reckon on any further extension of the method, it takes all my energy to maintain it as it is. During the old Commandant's lifetime the colony was full of his adherents; his strength of conviction I still have in some measure, but not an atom of his power; consequently the adherents have skulked out of sight, there are still many of them but none of them will admit it. If you were to go into the teahouse today, on execution day, and listen to what is being said, you would perhaps hear only ambiguous remarks. These would all be made by adherents, but under the present Commandant and his present doctrines they are of no use to me. And now I ask you: because of this Commandant and the women who influence him, is such a piece of work, the work of a lifetime"—he pointed to the machine—"to perish? Ought one to let that happen? Even if one has only come as a stranger to our island for a few days? But there's no time to lose, an attack of some kind is impending on my function as judge; conferences are already being held in the Commandant's office from which I am excluded; even your coming here today seems to me a significant move; they are cowards and use you as a screen, you, a stranger.—How different an execution was in the old days! A whole day before the ceremony the valley was packed with people; they all came only to look on; early in the morning the Commandant appeared with his ladies; fanfares roused the whole camp; I reported that everything was in readiness; the assembled company—no high official dared to absent himself—arranged itself round the machine; this pile of cane chairs is a miserable survival from that epoch. The machine was freshly cleaned and glittering. I got new spare parts for almost every execution. Before hundreds of spectators—all of them standing on tiptoe as far as the heights there—the condemned man was laid under the Harrow by the Commandant himself. What is left today for a common soldier to do was then my task, the task of the presiding judge, and was an honor for me. And then the execution began! No discordant noise spoilt the working of the machine. Many did not care to watch it but lay with closed eyes in the sand; they all knew: Now Justice is being done. In the silence one heard nothing but the condemned man's sighs, half muffled by the felt gag. Nowadays the machine can no longer wring from anyone a sigh louder than the felt gag can stifle; but in those days the writing needles let drop an acid fluid, which we're no longer permitted to use. Well, and then came the sixth hour! It was impossible to grant all the requests to be allowed to watch it from near by. The Commandant in his wisdom ordained that the children should have the preference; I, of course, because of my office had the privilege of always being at hand; often enough I would be squatting there with a small child in either arm. How we all absorbed the look of transfiguration on the face of the sufferer, how we bathed our cheeks in the radiance of that justice, achieved at last and fading so quickly! What times these were, my comrade!" The officer had obviously forgotten whom he was addressing; he had embraced the explorer and laid his head on his shoulder. The explorer was deeply embarrassed, impatiently he stared over the officer's head. The soldier had finished his cleaning job and was now pouring rice pap from a pot into the basin. As soon as the condemned man, who seemed to have recovered entirely, noticed this action he began to reach for the rice with his tongue. The soldier kept pushing him away, since the rice pap was certainly meant for a later hour, yet it was just as unfitting that the soldier himself should thrust his dirty hands into the basin and eat out of it before the other's avid face.

The officer quickly pulled himself together. "I didn't want to upset you," he said, "I know it is impossible to make those days credible now. Anyhow, the machine is still working and it is still effective in itself. It is effective in itself even though it stands alone in this valley. And the corpse still falls at the last into the pit with an incomprehensively gentle wafting motion, even although there are no hundreds of people swarming round like flies as formerly. In those days we had to put a strong fence round the pit, it has long since been torn down."

The explorer wanted to withdraw his face from the officer and looked round him at random. The officer thought he was surveying the valley's desolation; so he seized him by the hands, turned him round to meet his eyes, and asked: "Do you realize the shame of it?"

But the explorer said nothing. The officer left him alone for a little; with legs apart, hands on hips, he stood very still, gazing at the ground. Then he smiled encouragingly at the explorer and said: "I was quite near you yesterday when the Commandant gave you the invitation. I heard him giving it. I know the Commandant. I divined at once what he was after. Although he is powerful enough to take measures against me, he doesn't dare to do it yet, but he certainly means to use your verdict against me, the verdict of an illustrious foreigner. He has calculated it carefully: this is your second day on the island, you did not know the old Commandant and his ways, you are conditioned by European ways of thought, perhaps you object on principle to capital punishment in general and to such mechanical instruments of death in particular, besides you will see that the execution has no support from the public, a shabby ceremony—carried out with a machine already somewhat old and worn—now, taking all that into consideration, would it not be likely (so thinks the Commandant) that you might disapprove of my methods? And if you disapprove, you wouldn't conceal the fact (I'm still speaking from the Commandant's point of view), for you are a man to feel confidence in your own well-tried conclusions. True, you have seen and learned to appreciate the peculiarities of many peoples, and so you would not be likely to take a strong line against our proceedings, as you might do in your own country. But the Commandant has no need of that. A casual, even an unguarded remark will be enough. It doesn't even need to represent what you really think, so long as it can be used speciously to serve his purpose. He will try to prompt you with sly questions, of that I am certain. And his ladies will sit around you and prick up their ears; you might be saying something like this: 'In our country we have a different criminal procedure,' or 'In our country the prisoner is interrogated before he is sentenced,' or 'We haven't used torture since the Middle Ages.' All these statements are as true as they seem natural to you, harmless remarks that pass no judgment on my methods. But how would the Commandant react to them? I can see him, our good Commandant, pushing his chair away immediately and rushing on to the balcony, I can see his ladies streaming out after him, I can hear his voice—the ladies call it a voice of thunder—well, and this is what he says: 'A famous Western investigator, sent out to study criminal procedure in all the countries of the world, has just said that our old tradition of administering justice is inhumane. Such a verdict from such a personality makes it impossible for me to countenance these methods any longer. Therefore from this very day I ordain . . .' and so on. You may want to interpose that you never said any such thing, that you never called my methods inhumane, on the contrary your profound experience leads you to believe they are most humane and most in consonance with human dignity, and you admire the machine greatly—but it will be too late; you won't even get onto the balcony, crowded as it will be with ladies; you may try to draw attention to yourself; you may want to scream out; but a lady's hand will close your lips—and I and the work of the old Commandant will be done for.'"

The explorer had to suppress a smile; so easy, then, was the task he had felt to be so difficult. He said evasively: "You overestimate my influence; the Commandant has read my letters of recommendation, he knows that I am no expert in criminal procedure. If I were to give an opinion, it would be as a private individual, an opinion no more influential than that of any ordinary person, and in any case much less influential than that of the Commandant, who, I am given to understand, has very extensive powers in this penal colony. If his attitude to your procedure is as definitely hostile as you believe, then I fear the end of your tradition is at hand, even without any humble assistance from me."

Had it dawned on the officer at last? No, he still did not understand. He shook his head emphatically, glanced briefly round at the condemned man and the soldier, who both flinched away from the rice, came close up to the explorer and without looking at his face but fixing his eye on some spot on his coat said in a lower voice than before: "You don't know the Commandant; you feel yourself—forgive the expression—a kind of outsider so far as all of us are concerned; yet, believe me, your influence cannot be rated too highly. I was simply delighted when I heard that you were to attend the execution all by yourself. The Commandant arranged it to aim a blow at me, but I shall turn it to my advantage. Without being distracted by lying whispers and contemptuous glances—which could not have been avoided had a crowd of people attended the execution—you have heard my explanations, seen the machine and are now in course of watching the execution. You have doubtless already formed your own judgment; if you still have some small uncertainties the sight of the execution will resolve them. And now I make this request to you: help me against the Commandant!"

The explorer would not let him go on. "How could I do that," he cried, "it's quite impossible. I can neither help nor hinder you."

"Yes, you can," the officer said. The explorer saw with a certain apprehension that the officer had clenched his fists. "Yes, you can," repeated the officer, still more insistently. "I have a plan that is bound to succeed. You believe your influence is insufficient. I know that it is sufficient. But even granted that you are right, is it not necessary, for the sake of preserving this tradition, to try even what might prove insufficient? Listen to my plan, then. The first thing necessary for you to carry it out is to be as reticent as possible today regarding your verdict on these proceedings. Unless you are asked a direct question you must say nothing at all; but what you do say must be brief and general; let it be remarked that you would prefer not to discuss the matter, that you are out of patience with it, that if you are to let yourself go you would use strong language. I don't ask you to tell any lies; by no means; you should only give curt answers, such as: 'Yes, I saw the execution,' or 'Yes, I had it explained to me.' Just that, nothing more. There are grounds enough for any impatience you betray, although not such as will occur to the Commandant. Of course, he will mistake your meaning and interpret it to please himself. That's what my plan depends on. Tomorrow in the Commandant's office there is to be a large conference of all the high administrative officials, the Commandant presiding. Of course the Commandant is the kind of man to have turned these conferences into public spectacles. He has had a gallery built that is always packed with spectators. I am compelled to take part in the conferences, but they make me sick with disgust. Now, whatever happens, you will certainly be invited to this conference; if you behave today as I suggest the invitation will become an urgent request. But if for some mysterious reason you're not invited, you'll have to ask for an invitation; there's no doubt of your getting it then. So tomorrow you're sitting in the Commandant's box with the ladies. He keeps looking up to make sure you're there. After various trivial and ridiculous matters, brought in merely to impress the audience—mostly harbor works, nothing but harbor works!—our judicial procedure comes up for discussion too. If the Commandant doesn't introduce it, or not soon enough, I'll see that it's mentioned. I'll stand up and report that today's execution has taken place. Quite briefly, only a statement. Such a statement is not usual, but I shall make it. The Commandant thanks me, as always, with an amiable smile, and then he can't restrain himself, he seizes the excellent opportunity. 'It has just been reported,' he will say, or words to that effect, 'that an execution has taken place. I should like merely to add that this execution was witnessed by the famous explorer who has, as you all know, honored our colony so greatly by his visit to us. His presence at today's session of our conference also contributes to the importance of this occasion. Should we not now ask the famous explorer to give us his verdict on our traditional mode of execution and the procedure that leads up to it?' Of course there is loud applause, general agreement, I am more insistent than anyone. The Commandant bows to you and says: 'Then in the name of the assembled company, I put the question to you.' And now you advance to the front of the box. Lay your hands where everyone can see them, or the ladies will catch them and press your fingers.—And then at last you can speak out. I don't know how I'm going to endure the tension of waiting for that moment. Don't put any restraint on yourself when you make your speech, publish the truth aloud, lean over the front of the box, shout, yes indeed, shout your verdict, your unshakable conviction, at the Commandant. Yet perhaps you wouldn't care to do that, it's not in keeping with your character, in your country perhaps people do these things differently, well, that's all right too, that will be quite as effective, don't even stand up, just say a few words, even in a whisper, so that only the officials beneath you will hear them, that will be quite enough, you don't even need to mention the lack of public support for the execution, the creaking wheel, the broken strap, the filthy gag of felt, no, I'll take all that upon me, and, believe me, if my indictment doesn't drive him out of the conference hall, it will force him to his knees to make the acknowledgment: Old Commandant, I humble myself before you.—That is my plan; will you help me to carry it out? But of course you are willing, what is more, you must." And the officer seized the explorer by both arms and gazed, breathing heavily, into his face. He had shouted the last sentence so loudly that even the soldier and the condemned man were startled into attending; they had not understood a word but they stopped eating and looked over at the explorer, chewing their previous mouthfuls.

From the very beginning the explorer had no doubt about what answer he must give; in his lifetime he had experienced too much to have any uncertainty here; he was fundamentally honorable and unafraid. And yet now, facing the soldier and the condemned man, he did hesitate, for as long as it took to draw one breath. At last, however, he said, as he had to: "No." The officer blinked several times but did not turn his eyes away. "Would you like me to explain?" asked the explorer. The officer nodded wordlessly. "I do not approve of your procedure," said the explorer then, "even before you took me into your confidence—of course, I shall never in any circumstances betray your confidence—I was already wondering whether it would be my duty to intervene and whether my intervention would have the slightest chance of success. I realized to whom I ought to turn: to the Commandant, of course. You have made that fact even clearer, but without having strengthened my resolution, on the contrary, your sincere conviction has touched me, even though it cannot influence my judgment."

The officer remained mute, turned to the machine, caught hold of a brass rod, and then, leaning back a little, gazed at the Designer as if to assure himself that all was in order. The soldier and the condemned man seemed to have come to some understanding; the condemned man was making signs to the soldier, difficult though his movements were because of the tight straps; the soldier was bending down to him; the condemned man whispered something and the soldier nodded.

The explorer followed the officer and said: "You don't know yet what I mean to do. I shall tell the Commandant what I think of the procedure, certainly, but not at a public conference, only in private; nor shall I stay here long enough to attend any conference; I am going away early tomorrow morning, or at least embarking on my ship."

It did not look as if the officer had been listening. "So you did not find the procedure convincing," he said to himself and smiled, as an old man smiles at childish nonsense and yet pursues his own meditations behind the smile.

"Then the time has come," he said at last, and suddenly looked at the explorer with bright eyes that held some challenge, some appeal for co-operation. "The time for what?" asked the explorer uneasily, but got no answer.

"You are free," said the officer to the condemned man in the native tongue. The man did not believe it at first. "Yes, you are set free," said the officer. For the first time the condemned man's face woke to real animation. Was it true? Was it only a caprice of the officer's, that might change again? Had the foreign explorer begged him off? What was it? One could read these questions on his face. But not for long. Whatever it might be, he wanted to be really free if he might, and he began to struggle so far as the Harrow permitted him.

"You'll burst my straps," cried the officer, "lie still! We'll soon loosen them." And signing the soldier to help him, he set about doing so. The condemned man laughed wordlessly to himself, now he turned his face left towards the officer, now right towards the soldier, nor did he forget the explorer.

"Draw him out," ordered the officer. Because of the Harrow this had to be done with some care. The condemned man had already torn himself a little in the back through his impatience.

From now on, however, the officer paid hardly any attention to him. He went up to the explorer, pulled out the small leather wallet again, turned over the papers in it, found the one he wanted and showed it to the explorer. "Read it," he said. "I can't," said the explorer, "I told you before that I can't make out these scripts." "Try taking a close look at it," said the officer and came quite near to the explorer so that they might read it together. But when even that proved useless, he outlined the script with his little finger, holding it high above the paper as if the surface dared not be sullied by touch, in order to help the explorer to follow the script in that way. The explorer did make an effort, meaning to please the officer in this respect at least, but he was quite unable to follow. Now the officer began to spell it, letter by letter, and then read out the words. " 'BE JUST!' is what is written there," he said, "surely you can read it now." The explorer bent so close to the paper that the officer feared he might touch it and drew it farther away; the explorer made no remark, yet it was clear that he still could not decipher it. " 'BE JUST!' is what is written there," said the officer once more. "Maybe," said the explorer, "I am prepared to believe you." "Well, then," said the officer, at least partly satisfied, and climbed up the ladder with the paper; very carefully he laid it inside the Designer and seemed to be changing the disposition of all the cogwheels; it was a troublesome piece of work and must have involved wheels that were extremely small, for sometimes the officer's head vanished altogether from sight inside the Designer, so precisely did he have to regulate the machinery.

The explorer, down below, watched the labor uninterruptedly, his neck grew stiff and his eyes smarted from the glare of sunshine over the sky. The soldier and the condemned man were now busy together. The man's shirt and trousers, which were already lying in the pit, were fished out by the point of the soldier's bayonet. The shirt was abominably dirty and its owner washed it in the buckets of water. When he put on the shirt and trousers both he and the soldier could not help guffawing, for the garments were of course slit up behind. Perhaps the condemned man felt it incumbent on him to amuse the soldier, he turned round and round in his slashed garments before the soldier, who squatted on the ground beating his knees with mirth. All the same, they presently controlled their mirth out of respect for the gentlemen.

When the officer had at length finished his task aloft, he surveyed the machinery in all its details once more, with a smile, but this time shut the lid of the Designer, which had stayed open till now, climbed down, looked into the pit and then at the condemned man, noting with satisfaction that the clothing had been taken out, then went over to wash his hands in the water bucket, perceived too late that it was disgustingly dirty, was unhappy because he could not wash his hands, in the end thrust them into the sand—this alternative did not please him, but he had to put up with it—then stood upright and began to unbutton his uniform jacket. As he did this, the two ladies' handkerchiefs he had tucked under his collar fell into his hands. "Here are your handkerchiefs," he said, and threw them to the condemned man. And to the explorer he said in explanation: "A gift from the ladies."

In spite of the obvious haste with which he was discarding first his uniform jacket and then all his clothing, he handled each garment with loving care, he even ran his fingers caressingly over the silver lace on the jacket and shook a tassel into place. This loving care was certainly out of keeping with the fact that as soon as he had a garment off he flung it at once with a kind of unwilling jerk into the pit. The last thing left to him was his short sword with the sword belt. He drew it out of the scabbard, broke it, then gathered all together, the bits of the sword, the scabbard and the belt, and flung them so violently down that they clattered into the pit.

Now he stood naked there. The explorer bit his lips and said nothing. He knew very well what was going to happen, but he had no right to obstruct the officer in anything. If the judicial procedure which the officer cherished were really so near its end—possibly as a result of his own intervention, as to which he felt himself pledged—then the officer was doing the right thing; in his place the explorer would not have acted otherwise.

The soldier and the condemned man did not understand at first what was happening, at first they were not even looking on. The condemned man was gleeful at having got the handkerchiefs back, but he was not allowed to enjoy them for long, since the soldier snatched them with a sudden, unexpected grab. Now the condemned man in turn was trying to twitch them from under the belt where the soldier had tucked them, but the soldier was on his guard. So they were wrestling, half in jest. Only when the officer stood quite naked was their attention caught. The condemned man especially seemed struck with the notion that some great change was impending. What had happened to him was now going to happen to the officer. Perhaps even to the very end. Apparently the foreign explorer had given the order for it. So this was revenge. Although he himself had not suffered to the end, he was to be revenged to the end. A broad, silent grin now appeared on his face and stayed there all the rest of the time.

The officer, however, had turned to the machine. It had been clear enough previously that he understood the machine well, but now it was almost staggering to see how he managed it and how it obeyed him. His hand had only to approach the Harrow for it to rise and sink several times till it was adjusted to the right position for receiving him; he touched only the edge of the Bed and already it was vibrating; the felt gag came to meet his mouth, one could see that the officer was really reluctant to take it but he shrank from it only a moment, soon he submitted and received it. Everything was ready, only the straps hung down at the sides, yet they were obviously unnecessary, the officer did not need to be fastened down. Then the condemned man noticed the loose straps, in his opinion the execution was incomplete unless the straps were buckled, he gestured eagerly to the soldier and they ran together to strap the officer down. The latter had already stretched out one foot to push the lever that started the Designer; he saw the two men coming up; so he drew his foot back and let himself be buckled in. But now he could not reach the lever; neither the soldier nor the condemned man would be able to find it, and the explorer was determined not to lift a finger. It was not necessary; as soon as the straps were fastened the machine began to work; the Bed vibrated, the needles flickered above the skin, the Harrow rose and fell. The explorer had been staring at it quite a while before he remembered that a wheel in the Designer should have been creaking; but everything was quiet, not even the slightest hum could be heard.

Because it was working so silently the machine simply escaped one's attention. The explorer observed the soldier and the condemned man. The latter was the more animated of the two, everything in the machine interested him, now he was bending down and now stretching up on tiptoe, his forefinger was extended all the time pointing out details to the soldier. This annoyed the explorer. He was resolved to stay till the end, but he could not bear the sight of these two. "Go back home," he said. The soldier would have been willing enough, but the condemned man took the order as a punishment. With clasped hands he implored to be allowed to stay, and when the explorer shook his head and would not relent, he even went down on his knees. The explorer saw that it was no use merely giving orders, he was on the point of going over and driving them away. At that moment he heard a noise above him in the Designer. He looked up. Was that cogwheel going to make trouble after all? But it was something quite different. Slowly the lid of the Designer rose up and then clicked wide open. The teeth of a cogwheel showed themselves and rose higher, soon the whole wheel was visible, it was as if some enormous force were squeezing the Designer so that there was no longer room for the wheel, the wheel moved up till it came to the very edge of the Designer, fell down, rolled along the sand a little on its rim and then lay flat. But a second wheel was already rising after it, followed by many others, large and small and indistinguishably minute, the same thing happened to all of them, at every moment one imagined the Designer must now really be empty, but another complex of numerous wheels was already rising into sight, falling down, trundling along the sand and lying flat. This phenomenon made the condemned man completely forget the explorer's command, the cogwheels fascinated him, he was always trying to catch one and at the same time urging the soldier to help, but always drew back his hand in alarm, for another wheel always came hopping along which, at least on its first advance, scared him off.

The explorer, on the other hand, felt greatly troubled; the machine was obviously going to pieces; its silent working was a delusion; he had a feeling that he must now stand by the officer, since the officer was no longer able to look after himself. But while the tumbling cogwheels absorbed his whole attention he had forgotten to keep an eye on the rest of the machine; now that the last cogwheel had left the Designer, however, he bent over the Harrow and had a new and still more unpleasant surprise. The Harrow was not writing, it was only jabbing, and the bed was not turning the body over but only bringing it up quivering against the needles. The explorer wanted to do something, if possible, to bring the whole machine to a standstill, for this was no exquisite torture such as the officer desired, this was plain murder. He stretched out his hands. But at that moment the Harrow rose with the body spitted on it and moved to the side, as it usually did only when the twelfth hour had come. Blood was flowing in a hundred streams, not mingled with water, the water jets too had failed to function. And now the last action failed to fulfil itself, the body did not drop off the long needles, streaming with blood it went on hanging over the pit without falling into it. The Harrow tried to move back to its old position, but as if it had itself noticed that it had not yet got rid of its burden it stuck after all where it was, over the pit. "Come and help!" cried the explorer to the other two, and himself seized the officer's feet. He wanted to push against the feet while the others seized the head from the opposite side and so the officer might be slowly eased off the needles.

But the other two could not make up their minds to come; the condemned man actually turned away; the explorer had to go over to them and force them into position at the officer's head. And here, almost against his will, he had to look at the face of the corpse. It was as it had been in life; no sign was visible of the promised redemption; what the others had found in the machine the officer had not found; the lips were firmly pressed together, the eyes were open, with the same expression as in life, the look was calm and convinced, through the forehead went the point of the great iron spike.

As the explorer, with the soldier and the condemned man behind him, reached the first houses of the colony, the soldier pointed to one of them and said, "There is the teahouse."

In the ground floor of the house was a deep, low, cavernous space, its walls and ceiling blackened with smoke. It was open to the road all along its length. Although this teahouse was very little different from the other houses of the colony, which were all very dilapidated, even up to the Commandant's palatial headquarters, it made on the explorer the impression of a historic tradition of some kind, and he felt the power of past days. He went near to it, followed by his companions, right up between the empty tables which stood in the street before it, and breathed the cool, heavy air that came from the interior. "The old man's buried here," said the soldier, "the priest wouldn't let him die in the churchyard. Nobody knew where to bury him for a while, but in the end they buried him here. The officer never told you about that, for sure, because of course that's what he was most ashamed of. He even tried several times to dig the old man up by night, but he was always chased away." "Where is the grave?" asked the explorer, who found it impossible to believe the soldier. At once both of them, the soldier and the condemned man, ran before him pointing with outstretched hands in the direction where the grave should be. They led the explorer right up to the back wall, where guests were sitting at a few tables. They were apparently dock laborers, strong men with short, glistening, full black beards. None had a jacket, their shirts were torn, they were poor, humble creatures. As the explorer drew near, some of them got up, pressed close to the wall, and stared at him. "It's a foreigner," ran the whisper around him, "he wants to see the grave." They pushed one of the tables aside, and under it there was really a gravestone. It was a simple stone, low enough to be covered by a table. There was an inscription on it in very small letters, the explorer had to kneel down to read it. This was what it said: "Here rests the old Commandant. His adherents, who now must be nameless, have dug this grave and set up this stone. There is a prophecy that after a certain number of years the Commandant will rise again and lead his adherents from this house to recover the colony. Have faith and wait!" When the explorer had read this and risen to his feet he saw all the bystanders around him smiling, as if they too had read the inscription, had found it ridiculous and were expecting him to agree with them. The explorer ignored this, distributed a few coins among them, waiting till the table was pushed over the grave again, quitted the teahouse and made for the harbor.

The soldier and the condemned man had found some acquaintances in the teahouse, who detailed them. But they must have soon shaken them off, for the explorer was only halfway down the long flight of steps leading to the boats when they came rushing after him. Probably they wanted to force him at the last minute to take them with him. While he was bargaining below with a ferryman to row him to the steamer, the two of them came headlong down the steps, in silence, for they did not dare to shout. But by the time they reached the foot of the steps the explorer was already in the boat, and the ferryman was just casting off from the shore. They could have jumped into the boat, but the explorer lifted a heavy knotted rope from the floor boards, threatened them with it and so kept them from attempting the leap.

[1919]

For Thought

"In the Penal Colony" is a fantasy that employs nightmarish images, irony of situation and language, and the quest motif in a cryptic and complex allegorical pattern. The abstract concepts represented by the characters and events derive from the Judaeo-Christian tradition, which has played a major role in shaping the religious and ethical systems of Western civilization. In Kafka's surrealistic vision, the tradition is shown to be so arbitrary, contradiction ridden, and irrational as to be of no real use to the genuine seeker-of-truth in the realm of ethical behavior.

For Discussion

1. What is the tone of the story? How is it created?
2. Despite the realistic detail, how does Kafka manage to create an atmosphere of fantasy?
3. What purpose is served by the point of view Kafka uses?
4. What early indications are there that the story is intended to be taken allegorically instead of literally?
5. What or whom might the Old Commandant represent? The new Commandant?
6. What or whom might the officer supervising the execution represent?
7. What or whom might the condemned man represent?
8. What or whom might the explorer represent?
9. What is the significance of the disintegration of the execution apparatus?
10. What is the central conflict in the story? How is it resolved?
11. What meaning arises out of the story?

D. H. Lawrence
The Rocking-Horse Winner

There was a woman who was beautiful, who started with all the advantages, yet she had no luck. She married for love, and the love turned to dust. She had bonny children, yet she felt they had been thrust upon her, and she could not love them. They looked at her coldly, as if they were finding fault with her. And hurriedly she felt she must cover up some fault in herself. Yet what it was that she must cover up she never knew. Nevertheless, when her children were present, she always felt the centre of her heart go hard. This troubled her, and in her manner she was all the more gentle and anxious for her children, as if she loved them very much. Only she herself knew that at the centre of her heart was a hard little place that could not feel love, no, not for anybody. Everybody else said of her: "She is such a good mother. She adores her children." Only she herself, and her children themselves, knew it was not so. They read it in each other's eyes.

There were a boy and two little girls. They lived in a pleasant house, with a garden, and they had discreet servants, and felt themselves superior to anyone in the neighbourhood.

Although they lived in style, they felt always an anxiety in the house. There was never enough money. The mother had a small income, and the father had a small income, but not nearly enough for the social position which they had to keep up. The father went in to town to some office. But though he had good prospects, these prospects never materialised. There was always the grinding sense of the shortage of money, though the style was always kept up.

At last the mother said, "I will see if *I* can't make something." But she did not know where to begin. She racked her brains, and tried this thing and the other, but could not find anything successful. The failure made deep lines come into her face. Her children were growing up, they would have to go to school. There must be more money, there must be more money. The father, who was always very handsome and expensive in his tastes, seemed as if he never *would* be able to do anything worth doing. And the mother, who had a great belief in herself, did not succeed any better, and her tastes were just as expensive.

And so the house came to be haunted by the unspoken phrase: *There must be more money! There must be more money!* The children could hear it all the time, though nobody said it aloud. They heard it at Christmas, when the expensive and splendid toys filled the nursery. Behind the shining modern rocking-horse, behind the smart doll's-house, a voice would start whispering: "There *must* be more money. There *must* be more money!" And the children would stop playing, to listen for a moment. They would look into each other's eyes, to see if they had all heard. And each one saw in the eyes of the other two that they too had heard. "There *must* be more money! There *must* be more money!"

It came whispering from the springs of the still-swaying rocking-horse, and even the horse, bending his wooden, champing head, heard it. The big doll, sitting so pink and smirking in her new pram, could hear it quite plainly, and seemed to be smirking all the more self-consciously because of it. The foolish puppy, too, that took the place of the teddybear, he was looking so extraordinarily foolish for no other reason but that he heard the secret whisper all over the house: "There *must* be more money!"

Yet nobody ever said it aloud. The whisper was everywhere, and therefore no one spoke it. Just as no one ever says: "We are breathing!" in spite of the fact that breath is coming and going all the time.

"Mother," said the boy Paul one day, "why don't we keep a car of our own? Why do we always use uncle's, or else a taxi?"

"Because we're the poor members of the family," said the mother.

"But why *are* we, mother?"

"Well,—I suppose," she said slowly and bitterly, "it's because your father has no luck."

The boy was silent for some time.

"Is luck money, mother?" he asked, rather timidly.

"No, Paul. Not quite. It's what causes you to have money."

"Oh!" said Paul vaguely. "I thought when Uncle Oscar said *filthy lucker*, it meant money."

"*Filthy lucre* does mean money," said the mother. "But it's lucre, not luck."

"Oh!" said the boy. "Then what *is* luck, mother?"

"It's what causes you to have money. If you're lucky you have money. That's why it's better to be born lucky than rich. If you're rich, you may lose your money. But if you're lucky, you will always get more money."

"Oh! Will you? And is father not lucky?"

"Very unlucky, I should say," she said bitterly.

The boy watched her with unsure eyes.

"Why?" he asked.

"I don't know. Nobody ever knows why one person is lucky and another unlucky."

"Don't they? Nobody at all? Does nobody know?"

"Perhaps God. But He never tells."

"He ought to, then. And aren't you lucky either, mother?"

"I can't be, if I married an unlucky husband."

"But by yourself, aren't you?"

"I used to think I was, before I married. Now I think I am very unlucky indeed."

"Why?"

"Well—never mind! Perhaps I'm not really," she said.

The child looked at her, to see if she meant it. But he saw, by the lines of her mouth, that she was only trying to hide something from him.

"Well, anyhow," he said stoutly, "I'm a lucky person."

"Why?" said his mother, with a sudden laugh.

He stared at her. He didn't even know why he had said it.

"God told me," he asserted, brazening it out.

"I hope He did, dear!" she said, again with a laugh, but rather bitter.

"He did, mother!"

"Excellent!" said the mother, using one of her husband's exclamations.

The boy saw she did not believe him; or rather, that she paid no attention to his assertion. This angered him somewhat, and made him want to compel her attention.

He went off by himself, vaguely, in a childish way, seeking for the clue to "luck." Absorbed, taking no heed of other people, he went about with a sort of stealth, seeking inwardly for luck. He wanted luck, he wanted it, he wanted it. When the two girls were playing dolls in the nursery, he would sit on his big rocking-horse, charging madly into space, with a frenzy that made the little girls peer at him uneasily. Wildly the horse careered, the waving dark hair of the boy tossed, his eyes had a strange glare in them. The little girls dared not speak to him.

When he had ridden to the end of his mad little journey, he climbed down and stood in front of his rocking-horse, staring fixedly into its lowered face. Its red mouth was slightly open, its big eye was wide and glassy-bright.

"Now!" he would silently command the snorting steed. "Now, take me to where there is luck! Now take me!"

And he would slash the horse on the neck with the little whip he had asked Uncle Oscar for. He *knew* the horse could take him to where there was luck, if only he forced it. So he would mount again, and start on his furious ride, hoping at last to get there. He knew he could get there.

"You'll break your horse, Paul!" said the nurse.

"He's always riding like that! I wish he'd leave off!" said his elder sister Joan.

But he only glared down on them in silence. Nurse gave him up. She could make nothing of him. Anyhow he was growing beyond her.

One day his mother and his Uncle Oscar came in when he was on one of his furious rides. He did not speak to them.

"Hallo, you young jockey! Riding a winner?" said his uncle.

"Aren't you growing too big for a rocking horse? You're not a very little boy any longer, you know," said his mother.

But Paul only gave a blue glare from his big, rather close-set eyes. He would speak to nobody when he was in full tilt. His mother watched him with an anxious expression on her face.

At last he suddenly stopped forcing his horse into the mechanical gallop, and slid down.

"Well, I got there!" he announced fiercely, his blue eyes still flaring, and his sturdy long legs straddling apart.

"Where did you get to?" asked his mother.

"Where I wanted to go," he flared back to her.

"That's right, son!" said Uncle Oscar. "Don't you stop till you get there. What's the horse's name?"

"He doesn't have a name," said the boy.

"Gets on without all right?" asked the uncle.

"Well, he has different names. He was called Sansovino last week."

"Sansovino, eh? Won the Ascot. How did you know his name?"

"He always talks about horse-races with Bassett," said Joan.

The uncle was delighted to find that his small nephew was posted with all the racing news. Bassett, the young gardener, who had been wounded in the left foot in the war and had got his present job through Oscar Cresswell, whose batman he had been, was a perfect blade of the "turf." He lived in the racing events, and the small boy lived with him.

Oscar Cresswell got it all from Bassett.

"Master Paul comes and asks me, so I can't do more than tell him, sir," said Bassett, his face terribly serious, as if he were speaking of religious matters.

"And does he ever put anything on a horse he fancies?"

"Well—I don't want to give him away—he's a young sport, a fine sport, sir.

Would you mind asking him himself? He sort of takes a pleasure in it, and perhaps he'd feel I was giving him away, sir, if you don't mind."

Bassett was serious as a church.

The uncle went back to his nephew, and took him off for a ride in the car.

"Say, Paul, old man, do you ever put anything on a horse?" the uncle asked.

The boy watched the handsome man closely.

"Why, do you think I oughtn't to?" he parried.

"Not a bit of it! I thought perhaps you might give me a tip for the Lincoln."

The car sped on into the country, going down to Uncle Oscar's place in Hampshire.

"Honour bright?" said the nephew.

"Honour bright, son!" said the uncle.

"Well, then Daffodil."

"Daffodil! I doubt it, sonny. What about Mirza?"

"I only know the winner," said the boy. "That's Daffodil."

"Daffodil, eh?"

There was a pause. Daffodil was an obscure horse comparatively.

"Uncle!"

"Yes, son?"

"You won't let it go any further, will you? I promised Bassett."

"Bassett be damned, old man! What's he got to do with it?"

"We're partners. We've been partners from the first. Uncle, he lent me my first five shillings, which I lost. I promised him, honour bright, it was only between me and him; only you gave me that ten-shilling note I started winning with, so I thought you were lucky. You won't let it go any further, will you?"

The boy gazed at his uncle from those big, hot, blue eyes, set rather close together. The uncle stirred and laughed uneasily.

"Right you are, son! I'll keep your tip private. Daffodil, eh? How much are you putting on him?"

"All except twenty pounds," said the boy. "I keep that in reserve."

The uncle thought it a good joke.

"You keep twenty pounds in reserve, do you, you young romancer? What are you betting, then?"

"I'm betting three hundred," said the boy gravely. "But it's between you and me, Uncle Oscar! Honour bright?"

The uncle burst into a roar of laughter.

"It's between you and me all right, you young Nat Gould," he said, laughing. "But where's your three hundred?"

"Bassett keeps it for me. We're partners."

"You are, are you! And what is Bassett putting on Daffodil?"

"He won't go quite as high as I do, I expect. Perhaps he'll go a hundred and fifty."

"What, pennies?" laughed the uncle.

"Pounds," said the child, with a surprised look at his uncle. "Bassett keeps a bigger reserve than I do."

Between wonder and amusement Uncle Oscar was silent. He pursued the matter no further, but he determined to take his nephew with him to the Lincoln races.

"Now, son," he said, "I'm putting twenty on Mirza, and I'll put five for you on any horse you fancy. What's your pick?"

"Daffodil, uncle."

"No, not the fiver on Daffodil!"

"I should if it were my own fiver," said the child.

"Good! Good! Right you are! A fiver for me and a fiver for you on Daffodil."

The child had never been to a race-meeting before, and his eyes were blue fire. He pursed his mouth tight, and watched. A Frenchman just in front had put his money on Lancelot. Wild with excitement, he flayed his arms up and down, yelling "*Lancelot! Lancelot!*" in his French accent.

Daffodil came in first, Lancelot second, Mirza third. The child, flushed and with eyes blazing, was curiously serene. His uncle brought him four five-pound notes, four to one.

"What am I to do with these?" he cried, waving them before the boy's eyes.

"I suppose we'll talk to Bassett," said the boy. "I expect I have fifteen hundred now; and twenty in reserve; and this twenty."

His uncle studied him for some moments.

"Look here, son! You're not serious about Bassett and that fifteen hundred, are you?"

"Yes, I am. But it's between you and me, uncle. Honour bright!"

"Honour bright all right, son! But I must talk to Bassett."

"If you'd like to be a partner, uncle, with Bassett and me, we could all be partners. Only, you'd have to promise, honour bright, uncle, not to let it go beyond us three. Bassett and I are lucky, and you must be lucky, because it was your ten shillings I started winning with. . . ."

Uncle Oscar took both Bassett and Paul into Richmond Park for an afternoon, and there they talked.

"It's like this, you see, sir," Bassett said. "Master Paul would get me talking about racing events, spinning yarns, you know, sir. And he was always keen on knowing if I'd made or if I'd lost. It's about a year since, now, that I put five shillings on Blush of Dawn for him: and we lost. Then the luck turned, with that ten shllings he had from you: that we put on Singhalese. And since that time, it's been pretty steady, all things considering. What do you say, Master Paul?"

"We're all right when we're sure," said Paul. "It's when we're not quite sure that we go down."

"Oh, but we're careful then," said Bassett.

"But when are you *sure*?" smiled Uncle Oscar.

"It's Master Paul, sir," said Bassett, in a secret, religious voice. "It's as if he had it from heaven. Like Daffodil, now, for the Lincoln. That was as sure as eggs."

"Did you put anything on Daffodil?" asked Oscar Cresswell.

"Yes, sir. I made my bit."

"And my nephew?"

Bassett was obstinately silent, looking at Paul.

"I made twelve hundred, didn't I, Bassett? I told uncle I was putting three hundred on Daffodil."

"That's right," said Bassett, nodding.

"But where's the money?" asked the uncle.

"I keep it safe locked up, sir. Master Paul he can have it any minute he likes to ask for it."

"What, fifteen hundred pounds?"

"And twenty! And *forty*, that is, with the twenty he made on the course."

"It's amazing!" said the uncle.

"If Master Paul offers you to be partners, sir, I would, if I were you: if you'll excuse me," said Bassett.

Oscar Cresswell thought about it.

"I'll see the money," he said.

They drove home again, and, sure enough, Bassett came round to the garden-house with fifteen hundred pounds in notes. The twenty pounds reserve was left with Joe Glee, in the Turf Commission deposit.

"You see, it's all right, uncle, when I'm *sure!* Then we go strong, for all we're worth. Don't we, Bassett?"

"We do that, Master Paul."

"And when are you sure?" said the uncle, laughing.

"Oh, well, sometimes I'm *absolutely* sure, like about Daffodil," said the boy; "and sometimes I have an idea; and sometimes I haven't even an idea, have I, Bassett? Then we're careful, because we mostly go down."

"You do, do you! And when you're sure, like about Daffodil, what makes you sure, sonny?"

"Oh, well, I don't know," said the boy uneasily. "I'm sure, you know, uncle; that's all."

"It's as if he had it from heaven, sir," Bassett reiterated.

"I should say so!" said the uncle.

But he became a partner. And when the Leger was coming on, Paul was "sure" about Lively Spark, which was a quite inconsiderable horse. The boy insisted on putting a thousand on the horse, Bassett went for five hundred, and Oscar Cresswell two hundred. Lively Spark came in first, and the betting had been ten to one against him. Paul had made ten thousand.

"You see," he said, "I was absolutely sure of him."

Even Oscar Cresswell had cleared two thousand.

"Look here, son," he said, "this sort of thing makes me nervous."

"It needn't, uncle! Perhaps I shan't be sure again for a long time."

"But what are you going to do with your money?" asked the uncle.

"Of course," said the boy. "I started it for mother. She said she had no luck, because father is unlucky, so I thought if *I* was lucky, it might stop whispering."

"What might stop whispering?"

"Our house. I *hate* our house for whispering."

"What does it whisper?"

"Why—why"—the boy fidgeted—"why, I don't know. But it's always short of money, you know, uncle."

"I know it, son, I know it."

"You know people send mother writs, don't you, uncle?"

"I'm afraid I do," said the uncle.

"And then the house whispers, like people laughing at you behind your back. It's awful, that is! I thought if I was lucky—"

"You might stop it," added the uncle.

The boy watched him with big blue eyes, that had an uncanny cold fire in them, and he said never a word.

"Well, then!" said the uncle. "What are we doing?"

"I shouldn't like mother to know I was lucky," said the boy.

"Why not, son?"

"She'd stop me."

"I don't think she would."

"Oh!"—and the boy writhed in an odd way—"I *don't* want her to know, uncle."

"All right, son! We'll manage it without her knowing."

They managed it very easily. Paul, at the other's suggestion, handed over five thousand pounds to his uncle, who deposited it with the family lawyer, who was then to inform Paul's mother that a relative had put five thousand pounds into his hands, which sum was to be paid out a thousand pounds at a time, on the mother's birthday, for the next five years.

"So she'll have a birthday present of a thousand pounds for five successive years," said Uncle Oscar. "I hope it won't make it all the harder for her later."

Paul's mother had her birthday in November. The house had been "whispering," worse than ever lately, and, even in spite of his luck, Paul could not bear up against it. He was very anxious to see the effect of the birthday letter, telling his mother about the thousand pounds.

When there were no visitors, Paul now took his meals with his parents, as he was beyond the nursery control. His mother went into town nearly every day. She had discovered that she had an odd knack of sketching furs and dress materials, so she worked secretly in the studio of a friend who was the chief "artist" for the leading drapers. She drew the figures of ladies in furs and ladies in silk and sequins for the newspaper advertisements. This young woman artist earned several thousand pounds a year, but Paul's mother only made several hundreds, and she was again dissatisfied. She so wanted to be first in something, and she did not succeed, even in making sketches for drapery advertisements.

She was down to breakfast on the morning of her birthday. Paul watched her face as she read her letters. He knew the lawyer's letter. As his mother read it, her face hardened and became more expressionless. Then a cold, determined look came on her mouth. She hid the letter under the pile of others, and said not a word about it.

"Didn't you have anything nice in the post for your birthday, mother?" said Paul.

"Quite moderately nice," she said, her voice cold and absent.

She went away to town without saying more.

But in the afternoon Uncle Oscar appeared. He said Paul's mother had had a long interview with the lawyer, asking if the whole five thousand could not be advanced at once, as she was in debt.

"What do you think, uncle?" said the boy.

"I leave it to you, son."

"Oh, let her have it, then! We can get some more with the other," said the boy.

"A bird in the hand is worth two in the bush, laddie!" said Uncle Oscar.

"But I'm sure to *know* for the Grand National; or the Lincolnshire; or else the Derby. I'm sure to know for one of them," said Paul.

So Uncle Oscar signed the agreement, and Paul's mother touched the whole five thousand. Then something very curious happened. The voices in the house suddenly went mad, like a chorus of frogs on a spring evening. There were certain new furnishings, and Paul had a tutor. He was *really* going to Eton, his father's school, in the following autumn. There were flowers in the winter, and a blossoming of the luxury Paul's mother had been used to. And yet the voices in the house, behind the sprays of mimosa and almond-blossom, and from under the piles of irridescent cushions, simply trilled and screamed in a sort of ecstasy: "There *must* be more money! Oh-h-h; there *must* be more money. Oh, now, now-w! Now-w-w—there *must* be more money!—more than ever! More than ever!"

It frightened Paul terribly. He studied away at his Latin and Greek with his tutors. But his intense hours were spent with Bassett. The Grand National had gone by: he had not "known," and had lost a hundred pounds. Summer was at hand. He was in agony for the Lincoln. But even for the Lincoln he didn't "know," and he lost fifty pounds. He became wild-eyed and strange, as if something were going to explode in him.

"Let it alone, son! Don't you bother about it!" urged Uncle Oscar. But it was as if the boy couldn't really hear what his uncle was saying.

"I've got to know for the Derby! I've got to know for the Derby!" the child reiterated, his big blue eyes blazing with a sort of madness.

His mother noticed how overwrought he was.

"You'd better go to the seaside. Wouldn't you like to go now to the seaside, instead of waiting? I think you'd better," she said, looking down at him anxiously, her heart curiously heavy because of him.

But the child lifted his uncanny blue eyes.

"I couldn't possibly go before the Derby, mother!" he said. "I couldn't possibly!"

"Why not?" she said, her voice becoming heavy when she was opposed. "Why not? You can still go from the seaside to see the Derby with your Uncle Oscar, if that's what you wish. No need for you to wait here. Besides, I think you care too much about these races. It's a bad sign. My family has been a gambling family, and you won't know till you grow up how much damage it has done. But it has done damage. I shall have to send Bassett away, and ask Uncle Oscar not to talk racing to you, unless you promise to be reasonable about it: go away to the seaside and forget it. You're all nerves!"

"I'll do what you like, mother, so long as you don't send me away till after the Derby," the boy said.

"Send you away from where? Just from this house?"

"Yes," he said, gazing at her.

"Why, you curious child, what makes you care about this house so much, suddenly? I never knew you loved it."

He gazed at her without speaking. He had a secret within a secret, something he had not divulged, even to Bassett or to his Uncle Oscar.

But his mother, after standing undecided and a little bit sullen for some moments, said:

"Very well, then! Don't go to the seaside till after the Derby, if you don't wish it. But promise me you won't let your nerves go to pieces. Promise you won't think so much about horseracing and *events*, as you call them!"

"Oh, no," said the boy casually. "I won't think much about them, mother. You needn't worry. I wouldn't worry, mother, if I were you."

"If you were me and I were you," said his mother, "I wonder what we *should* do!"

"But you know you needn't worry, mother, don't you?" the boy repeated.

"I should be awfully glad to know it," she said wearily.

"Oh, well, you *can*, you know. I mean, you *ought* to know you needn't worry," he insisted.

"Ought I? Then I'll see about it," she said.

Paul's secret of secrets was his wooden horse, that which had no name. Since he was emancipated from a nurse and a nursery-governess, he had had his rocking-horse removed to his own bedroom at the top of the house.

"Surely, you're too big for a rocking-horse!" his mother had remonstrated.

"Well, you see, mother, till I can have a *real* horse, I like to have some sort of animal about," had been his quaint answer.

"Do you feel he keeps you company?" she laughed.

"Oh, yes! He's very good, he always keeps me company, when I'm there," said Paul.

So the horse, rather shabby, stood in an arrested prance in the boy's bedroom.

The Derby was drawing near, and the boy grew more and more tense. He hardly heard what was spoken to him, he was very frail, and his eyes were really uncanny. His mother had sudden strange seizures of uneasiness about him. Sometimes, for half-an-hour, she would feel a sudden anxiety about him that was almost anguish. She wanted to rush to him at once, and know he was safe.

Two nights before the Derby, she was at a big party in town, when one of her rushes of anxiety about her boy, her firstborn, gripped her heart till she could hardly speak. She fought with the feeling, might and main, for she believed in common-sense. But it was too strong. She had to leave the dance and go downstairs to telephone to the country. The children's nursery-governess was terribly surprised and startled at being rung up in the night.

"Are the children all right, Miss Wilmot?"

"Oh, yes, they are quite all right."

"Master Paul? Is he all right?"

"He went to bed as right as a trivet. Shall I run up and look at him?"

"No," said Paul's mother reluctantly. "No! Don't trouble. It's all right. Don't sit up. We shall be home fairly soon." She did not want her son's privacy intruded upon.

"Very good," said the governess.

It was about one o'clock when Paul's mother and father drove up to their house. All was still. Paul's mother went to her room and slipped off her white fur cloak. She had told her maid not to wait up for her. She heard her husband downstairs, mixing a whisky-and-soda.

And then, because of the strange anxiety at her heart, she stole upstairs to her son's room. Noiselessly she went along the upper corridor. Was there a faint noise? What was it?

She stood, with arrested muscles, outside his door, listening. There was a strange, heavy, and yet not loud noise. Her heart stood still. It was a soundless noise, yet rushing and powerful. Something huge, in violent, hushed motion. What was it? What in God's name was it? She ought to know. She felt that she knew the noise. She knew what it was.

Yet she could not place it. She couldn't say what it was. And on and on it went, like a madness.

Softly, frozen with anxiety and fear, she turned the doorhandle.

The room was dark. Yet in the space

near the window, she heard and saw something plunging to and fro. She gazed in fear and amazement.

Then suddenly she switched on the light, and saw her son, in his green pyjamas, madly surging on the rocking-horse. The blaze of light suddenly lit him up, as he urged the wooden horse, and lit her up, as she stood, blonde, in her dress of pale green and crystal, in the doorway.

"Paul!" she cried. "Whatever are you doing?"

"It's Malabar!" he screamed, in a powerful, strange voice. "It's Malabar!"

His eyes blazed at her for one strange and senseless second, as he ceased urging his wooden horse. Then he fell with a crash to the ground, and she, all her tormented motherhood flooding upon her, rushed to gather him up.

But he was unconscious, and unconscious he remained, with some brain-fever. He talked and tossed, and his mother sat stonily by his side.

"Malabar! It's Malabar! Bassett, Bassett, I *know!* It's Malabar!"

So the child cried, trying to get up and urge the rocking-horse that gave him his inspiration.

"What does he mean by Malabar?" asked the heart-frozen mother.

"I don't know," said the father stonily.

"What does he mean by Malabar?" she asked her brother Oscar.

"It's one of the horses running for the Derby," was the answer.

And, in spite of himself, Oscar Cresswell spoke to Bassett, and himself put a thousand on Malabar: at fourteen to one.

The third day of the illness was critical: they were waiting for a change. The boy, with his rather long, curly hair, was tossing ceaselessly on the pillow. He neither slept nor regained consciousness, and his eyes were like blue stones. His mother sat, feeling her heart had gone, turned actually into a stone.

In the evening, Oscar Cresswell did not come, but Bassett sent a message, saying could he come up for one moment, just one moment? Paul's mother was very angry at the intrusion, but on second thoughts she agreed. The boy was the same. Perhaps Bassett might bring him to consciousness.

The gardener, a shortish fellow with a little brown moustache, and sharp little brown eyes, tiptoed into the room, touched his imaginary cap to Paul's mother, and stole to the bedside, staring with glittering, smallish eyes at the tossing, dying child.

"Master Paul!" he whispered, "Master Paul! Malabar came in first all right, a clean win. I did as you told me. You've made over seventy thousand pounds, you have; you've got over eighty thousand. Malabar came in all right, Master Paul."

"Malabar! Malabar! Did I say Malabar, mother? Did I say Malabar? Do you think I'm lucky, mother? I knew Malabar, didn't I? Over eighty thousand pounds! I call that lucky, don't you, mother? Over eighty thousand pounds! I knew, didn't I know I knew? Malabar came in all right. If I ride my horse till I'm sure, then I tell you, Bassett, you can go as high as you like. Did you go for all you were worth, Bassett?"

"I went a thousand on it, Master Paul."

"I never told you, mother, that if I can ride my horse, and get *there,* then I'm absolutely sure—oh, absolutely! Mother, did I ever tell you? I *am* lucky!"

"No, you never did," said the mother.

But the boy died in the night.

And even as he lay dead, his mother heard her brother's voice saying to her: "My God, Hester, you're eighty-odd thousand to the good, and a poor devil of a son to the bad. But, poor devil, poor devil, he's best gone out of a life where he rides his rocking-horse to find a winner."

[1932]

For Thought

Behind Lawrence's tale of a compulsive young boy is the fairy tale motif of the young peasant lad who discovers a magic charm and turns straw (or whatever) into gold. Ironically, the boy's uncanny knack for guessing winners of horse races is a terrible curse. He becomes like Midas—all he touches turns to cold, unsatisfying wealth. He buys love, he thinks, but by paying the highest price of all—his life.

For Discussion

1. What is the significance of the title?
2. What is the significance of the opening words, "There was a woman who was beautiful, who started with all the advantages, yet she had no luck"?
3. What is the point of view?
4. How is Paul characterized? What are the conflicts which surround him?
5. Why is the mother not named until the end?
6. How does the mother's bitterness toward her husband undermine the basis of the family?
7. What is Paul's mother's basic flaw?
8. Can it be said that the story is also a parody of the romantic rescue of a lady by a knight from danger?
9. What is Uncle Oscar's function in the story?
10. What religious aspects are introduced into the story?
11. What do Paul's glittering eyes symbolize?
12. What is the theme of the story?

Ursula Le Guin
April in Paris

Professor Barry Pennywither sat in a cold, shadowy garret and stared at the table in front of him, on which lay a book and a breadcrust. The bread had been his dinner, the book had been his lifework. Both were dry. Dr. Pennywither sighed, and then shivered. Though the lower-floor apartments of the old house were quite elegant, the heat was turned off on April 1st, come what may; it was now April 2nd, and sleeting. If Dr. Pennywither raised his head a little he could see from his window the two square towers of Notre Dame de Paris, vague and soaring in the dusk, almost near enough to touch: for the Island of Saint-Louis, where he lived, is like a little barge being towed downstream behind the Island of the City, where Notre Dame stands. But he did not raise his head. He was too cold.

The great towers sank into darkness. Dr. Pennywither sank into gloom. He stared with loathing at his book. It had won him a year in Paris—publish or perish, said the Dean of Faculties, and he had published, and been rewarded with a year's leave from teaching, without pay. Munson College could not afford to pay unteaching teachers. So on his scraped-up savings he had come back to Paris, to live again as a student in a garret, to read fifteenth-century manuscripts at the Library, to see the chestnuts flower along the avenues. But it hadn't worked. He was forty, too old for lonely garrets. The sleet would blight the budding chestnut flowers. And he was sick of his work. Who cared about his theory, the Pennywither Theory, concerning the mysterious disappearance of the poet François Villon in 1463? Nobody. For after all his Theory about poor Villon, the greatest juvenile delinquent of all time, was only a theory and could never be proved, not across the gulf of five hundred years. Nothing could be proved. And besides, what did it matter if Villon died on Montfaucon gallows or (as Pennywither thought) in a Lyons brothel on the way to Italy? Nobody cared. Nobody else loved Villon enough.

Nobody loved Dr. Pennywither, either; not even Dr. Pennywither. Why should he? An unsocial, unmarried, underpaid pedant, sitting here alone in an unheated attic in an unrestored tenement trying to write another unreadable book. "I'm unrealistic," he said aloud with another sigh and another shiver. He got up and took the blanket off his bed, wrapped himself in it, sat down thus bundled at the table, and tried to light a Gauloise Bleue. His lighter snapped vainly. He sighed once more, got up, fetched a can of vile-smelling French lighter fluid, sat down, rewrapped his cocoon, filled the lighter, and snapped it. The fluid had spilled around a good bit. The lighter lit, so did Dr. Pennywither, from the wrists down. "Oh hell!" he cried, blue flames leaping from his knuckles, and jumped up batting his arms wildly, shouting "Hell!" and raging against Destiny. Nothing ever went right. What was the use? It was then 8:12 on the night of April 2nd, 1961.

A man sat hunched at a table in a cold, high room. Through the window behind him the two square towers of Notre Dame loomed in the Spring dusk. In front of him on the table lay a hunk of cheese and a huge, iron-latched, handwritten book. The book was called (in Latin) *On the Primacy of the Element Fire over the Other Three Elements*. Its author stared at it with loathing. Nearby on a small iron stove a small alembic simmered. Jehan Lenoir mechanically inched his chair nearer the stove now and then, for warmth, but his thoughts were on deeper problems. "Hell!" he said finally (in Late Mediaeval French), slammed the book shut, and got up. What if his theory was wrong? What if water were the primal element? How could you prove these things? There must be some way—some method—so that one could be sure, absolutely sure, of one single fact! But each fact led into others, a monstrous tangle, and the Authorities conflicted, and anyway no one would read his book, not even the wretched pedants at the Sorbonne. They smelled heresy. What was the use? What good this life spent in poverty and alone, when he had learned nothing, merely guessed and theorized? He strode about the garret, raging, and then stood still. "All right!" he said to Destiny. "Very good! You've given me nothing, so I'll take what I want!" He went to one of the stacks of books that covered most of the floorspace, yanked out a bottom volume (scarring the leather and bruising his knuckles when the overlying folios avalanched), slapped it on the table and began to study one page of it. Then, still with a set cold look of rebellion, he got things ready: sulfur, silver, chalk. . . . Though the room was dusty and littered, his little workbench was neatly and handily arranged. He was soon ready. Then he paused. "This is ridiculous," he muttered, glancing out the window into the darkness where now one could only guess at the two square towers. A watchman passed below calling out the hour, eight o'clock of a cold clear night. It was so still he could hear the lapping of the Seine. He shrugged, frowned, took up the chalk and drew a neat pentagram on the floor near his table, then took up the book and began to read in a clear but self-conscious voice: "Haere, haere, audi me . . ." It was a long spell, and mostly nonsense. His voice sank. He stood bored and embarrassed. He hurried through the last words, shut the book, and then fell backwards against the door, gap-mouthed, staring at the enormous, shapeless figure that stood within the pentagram, lit only by the blue flicker of its waving, fiery claws.

Barry Pennywither finally got control of himself and put out the fire by burying his hands in the folds of the blanket wrapped around him. Unburned but upset, he sat down again. He looked at his book. Then he stared at it. It was no longer thin and grey and titled *The Last Years of Villon: an Investigation of Possibilities*. It was thick and brown and titled *Incantatoria*

Magna. On his table? A priceless manuscript dating from 1407 of which the only extant undamaged copy was in the Ambrosian Library in Milan. He looked slowly around. His mouth dropped slowly open. He observed a stove, a chemist's workbench, two or three dozen heaps of unbelievable leatherbound books, the window, the door. His window, his door. But crouching against his door was a little creature, black and shapeless, from which came a dry rattling sound.

Barry Pennywither was not a very brave man, but he was rational. He thought he had lost his mind, and so he said quite steadily, "Are you the Devil?"

The creature shuddered and rattled.

Experimentally, with a glance at invisible Notre Dame, the professor made the sign of the Cross.

At this the creature twitched; not a flinch, a twitch. Then it said something, feebly, but in perfectly good English—no, in perfectly good French—no, in rather odd French: "Mais vous estes de Dieu," it said.

Barry got up and peered at it. "Who are you?" he demanded, and it lifted up a quite human face and answered meekly, "Jehan Lenoir."

"What are you doing in my room?"

There was a pause. Lenoir got up from his knees and stood straight, all five foot two of him. "This is *my* room," he said at last, though very politely.

Barry looked around at the books and alembics. There was another pause. "Then how did I get here?"

"I brought you."

"Are you a doctor?"

Lenoir nodded, with pride. His whole air had changed. "Yes, I'm a doctor," he said. "Yes, I brought you here. If Nature will yield me no knowledge, then I can conquer Nature herself, I can work a miracle! To the Devil with science, then. I was a scientist—" he glared at Barry. "No longer! They call me a fool, a heretic, well by God I'm worse! I'm a sorcerer, a black magician, Jehan the Black! Magic works, does it? Then science is a waste of time. Ha!" he said, but he did not really look triumphant. "I wish it hadn't worked," he said more quietly, pacing up and down between folios.

"So do I," said the guest.

"Who are you?" Lenoir looked up challengingly at Barry, though there was nearly a foot difference in their heights.

"Barry A. Pennywither, I'm a professor of French at Munson College, Indiana, on leave in Paris to pursue my studies of Late Mediaeval Fr—" He stopped. He had just realized what kind of accent Lenoir had. "What year is this? What century? Please, Dr. Lenoir—" The Frenchman looked confused. The meanings of words change, as well as their pronunciations. "Who rules this country?" Barry shouted.

Lenoir gave a shrug, a French shrug (some things never change).

"Louis is king," he said. "Louis the Eleventh. The dirty old spider."

They stood staring at each other like wooden Indians for some time. Lenoir spoke first. "Then you're a man?"

"Yes. Look, Lenoir, I think you—your spell—you must have muffed it a bit."

"Evidently," said the alchemist. "Are you French?"

"No."

"Are you English?" Lenoir glared. "Are you a filthy Goddam?"

"No. No. I'm from America. I'm from the—from your future. From the twentieth century A.D." Barry blushed. It sounded silly, and he was a modest man. But he knew this was no illusion. The room he stood in, his room, was new. Not five centuries old. Unswept, but new. And the copy of Albertus Magnus by his knee was new, bound in soft supple calfskin, the gold lettering gleaming. And there stood Lenoir in his black gown, not in costume, at home. . . .

"Please sit down, sir," Lenoir was saying. And he added, with the fine though absent courtesy of the poor scholar, "Are you tired from the journey? I have bread and cheese, if you'll honor me by sharing it."

They sat at the table munching bread and cheese. At first Lenoir tried to explain why he had tried black magic. "I was fed up," he said. "Fed up! I've slaved in solitude since I was twenty, for what? For knowledge. To learn some of Nature's secrets. They are not to be learned." He drove his knife half an inch into the table, and Barry jumped. Lenoir was a thin little fellow, but evidently a passionate one. It was a fine face, though pale and lean: intelligent, alert, vivid. Barry was reminded of the face of a famous atomic physicist, seen in newspaper pictures up until 1953. Somehow this likeness prompted him to say, "Some are, Lenoir; we've learned a good bit, here and there. . . ."

"What?" said the alchemist, skeptical but curious.

"Well, I'm no scientist—"

"Can you make gold?" He grinned as he asked.

"No, I don't think so, but they do make diamonds."

"How?"

"Carbon—coal, you know—under great heat and pressure, I believe. Coal and diamond are both carbon, you know, the same element."

"Element?"

"Now as I say, I'm no—"

"Which is the primal element?" Lenoir shouted, his eyes fiery, the knife poised in his hand.

"There are about a hundred elements," Barry said coldly, hiding his alarm.

Two hours later, having squeezed out of Barry every dribble of the remnants of his college chemistry course, Lenoir rushed out into the night and reappeared shortly with a bottle. "O my master," he cried, "to think I offered you only bread and cheese!" It was a pleasant burgundy, vintage 1477, a good year. After they had drunk a glass together Lenoir said, "If somehow I could repay you . . ."

"You can. Do you know the name of the poet François Villon?"

"Yes," Lenoir said with some surprise, "but he wrote only French trash, you know, not in Latin."

"Do you know how or when he died?"

"Oh, yes; hanged at Montfaucon here in '64 or '65, with a crew of no-goods like himself. Why?"

Two hours later the bottle was dry, their throats were dry, and the watchman had called three o'clock of a cold clear morning. "Jehan, I'm worn out," Barry said, "you'd better send me back." The alchemist was too polite, too grateful, and perhaps also too tired to argue. Barry stood stiffly inside the pentagram, a tall bony figure muffled in a brown blanket, smoking a Gauloise Bleue. "Adieu," Lenoir said sadly. "Au revoir," Barry replied. Lenoir began to read the spell backwards. The candle flickered, his voice softened. "Me audi, haere, haere," he read, sighed, and looked up. The pentagram was empty. The candle flickered. "But I learned so little!" Lenoir cried out to the empty room. Then he beat the open book with his fists and said, "And a friend like that—a real friend—" He smoked one of the cigarettes Barry had left him—he had taken to tobacco at once. He slept, sitting at his table, for a couple of hours. When he woke he brooded a while, relit his candle, smoked the other cigarette, then opened the *Incantatoria* and began to read aloud: "Haere, haere . . ."

"Oh, thank God," Barry said, stepping quickly out of the pentagram and grasping Lenoir's hand. "Listen, I got back there—this room, this same room, Jehan! but old, horribly old, and empty, you weren't there—I thought, my God, what have I done? I'd sell my soul to get back there, to him—What can I do with what I've learned? Who'll believe it? How can I prove it? And who the devil could I tell it to anyhow? Who cares? I couldn't sleep, I sat and cried for an hour—"

"Will you stay?"

"Yes. Look, I brought these—in case you did invoke me." Sheepishly he exhibited eight packs of Gauloises, several books, and a gold watch. "It might fetch a price," he explained. "I knew paper francs wouldn't do much good."

At sight of the printed books Lenoir's eyes gleamed with curiosity, but he stood still. "My friend," he said, "you said you'd sell your soul . . . you know . . . so would I. Yet we haven't. How—after all—how did this happen? That we're both men. No devils. No pacts in blood. Two men who've lived in this room . . ."

"I don't know," said Barry. "We'll think that out later. Can I stay with you, Jehan?"

"Consider this your home," Lenoir said with a gracious gesture around the room, the stacks of books, the alembics, the candle growing pale. Outside the window, grey on grey, rose up the two great towers of Notre Dame. It was the dawn of April 3rd.

After breakfast (bread crusts and cheese rinds) they went out and climbed the south tower. The cathedral looked the same as always, though cleaner than in 1961, but the view was rather a shock to Barry. He looked down upon a little town. Two small islands covered with houses; on the right bank more houses crowded inside a fortified wall; on the left bank a few streets twisting around the college; and that was all. Pigeons chortled on the sun-warmed stone between gargoyles. Lenoir, who had seen the view before, was carving the date (in Roman numerals) on a parapet. "Let's celebrate," he said. "Let's go out into the country. I haven't been out of the city for two years. Let's go clear over there—" he pointed to a misty green hill on which a few huts and a windmill were just visible—"to Montmartre, eh? There are some good bars there, I'm told."

Their life soon settled into an easy routine. At first Barry was a little nervous in the crowded streets, but, in a spare black gown of Lenoir's, he was not noticed as outlandish except for his height. He was probably the tallest man in fifteenth-century France. Living standards were low and lice were unavoidable, but Barry had never valued comfort much; the only thing he really missed was coffee at breakfast. When they had bought a bed and a razor—Barry had forgotten his—and introduced him to the landlord as M. Barrie, a cousin of Lenoir's from the Auvergne, their housekeeping arrangements were complete. Barry's watch brought a tremendous price, four gold pieces, enough to live on for a year. They sold it as a wondrous new timepiece from Illyria, and the buyer, a Court chamberlain looking for a nice present to give the king, looked at the inscription—Hamilton Bros., New Haven, 1881—and nodded sagely. Unfortunately he was shut up in one of King Louis's cages for naughty courtiers at Tours before he had presented his gift, and the watch may still be there behind some brick in the ruins of Plessis; but this did not affect the two scholars. Mornings they wandered about sightseeing the Bastille and the churches, or visiting various minor poets in whom Barry was interested; after lunch they discussed electricity, the atomic theory, physiology, and other matters in which Lenoir was interested, and performed minor chemical and anatomical experiments, usually unsuccessfully; after supper they merely talked. Endless, easy talks that ranged over the centuries but always ended here, in the shadowy room with its window open to the Spring night, in their friendship. After two weeks they might have known each other all their lives. They were perfectly happy. They knew they would do nothing with what they had learned from each other. In 1961 how could Barry ever prove his knowledge of old Paris, in 1482 how could Lenoir ever prove the validity of the scientific method? It did not bother them. They had never really expected to be listened to. They had merely wanted to learn.

So they were happy for the first time in their lives; so happy, in fact, that certain desires always before subjugated to the desire for knowledge, began to awaken. "I don't suppose," Barry said one night across the table, "that you ever thought much about marrying?"

"Well, no," his friend answered, doubtfully. "That is, I'm in minor orders . . . and it seemed irrelevant. . . ."

"And expensive. Besides, in my time, no self-respecting woman would want to share my kind of life. American women are so damned poised and efficient and glamorous, terrifying creatures. . . ."

"And women here are little and dark, like beetles, with bad teeth," Lenoir said morosely.

They said no more about women that night. But the next night they did; and the next; and on the next, celebrating the successful dissection of the main nervous system of a pregnant frog, they drank two bottles of Montrachet '74 and got soused. "Let's invoke a woman, Jehan," Barry said in a lascivious bass, grinning like a gargoyle.

"What if I raised a devil this time?"

"Is there really much difference?"

They laughed wildly, and drew a pentagram. "Haere, haere," Lenoir began; when he got the hiccups, Barry took over. He read the last words. There was a rush of cold, marshy-smelling air, and in the pentagram stood a wild-eyed being with long black hair, stark naked, screaming.

"Woman, by God," said Barry.

"Is it?"

It was. "Here, take my cloak," Barry said, for the poor thing now stood gawping and shivering. He put the cloak over her shoulders. Mechanically she pulled it round her, muttering, "Gratias ago, domine."

"Latin!" Lenoir shouted. "A woman speaking Latin?" It took him longer to get over that shock than it did Bota to get over hers. She was, it seemed, a slave in the household of the Sub-Prefect of North Gaul, who lived on the smaller island of the muddy island town called Lutetia. She spoke Latin with a thick Celtic brogue, and did not even know who was emperor in Rome in her day. A real barbarian, Lenoir said with scorn. So she was, an ignorant, taciturn, humble barbarian with tangled hair, white skin, and clear grey eyes. She had been waked from a sound sleep. When they convinced her that she was not dreaming, she evidently assumed that this was some prank of her foreign and all-powerful master the Sub-Prefect, and accepted the situation without further question. "Am I to serve you, my masters?" she inquired timidly but without sullenness, looking from one to the other.

"Not me," Lenoir growled, and added in French to Barry, "Go on; I'll sleep in the store-room." He departed.

Bota looked up at Barry. No Gauls, and few Romans, were so magnificently tall; no Gauls and no Romans ever spoke so kindly. "Your lamp" (it was a candle, but she had never seen a candle) "is nearly burnt out," she said, "Shall I blow it out?"

For an additional two sols a year the landlord let them use the store-room as a second bedroom, and Lenoir now slept alone again in the main room of the garret. He observed his friend's idyll with a brooding, unjealous interest. The professor and the slave-girl loved each other with delight and tenderness. Their pleasure overlapped Lenoir in waves of protective joy. Bota had led a brutal life, treated always as a woman but never as a human. In one short week she bloomed, she came alive, evincing beneath her gentle passiveness a cheerful, clever nature. "You're turning out a regular Parisienne," he heard Barry accuse her one night (the attic walls were thin). She replied, "If you knew what it is for me not to be always defending myself, always afraid, always alone . . ."

Lenoir sat up on his cot and brooded. About midnight, when all was quiet, he rose and noiselessly prepared the pinches of sulfur and silver, drew the pentagram, opened the book. Very softly he read the spell. His face was apprehensive.

In the pentagram appeared a small white dog. It cowered and hung its tail, then came shyly forward, sniffed Lenoir's hand, looked up at him with liquid eyes and gave a modest, pleading whine. A lost puppy . . . Lenoir stroked it. It licked his hands and jumped all over him, wild with relief. On its white leather collar was a silver plaque engraved, "Jolie. Dupont, 36 rue de Seine, Paris VIe."

Jolie went to sleep, after gnawing a crust, curled up under Lenoir's chair. And the alchemist opened the book again and read, still softly, but this time without self-consciousness, without fear, knowing what would happen.

Emerging from his store-room-bedroom-honeymoon in the morning, Barry stopped short in the doorway. Lenoir was sitting up in bed, petting a white puppy, and deep in conversation with the person sitting on the foot of the bed, a tall red-haired woman dressed in silver. The puppy barked. Lenoir said, "Good morning!" The woman smiled wondrously.

"Jumping Jesus," Barry muttered (in English). Then he said, "Good morning. When are you from?" The effect was Rita Hayworth, sublimated—Hayworth plus the Mona Lisa, perhaps?

"From Altair, about seven thousand years from now," she said, smiling still more wondrously. Her French accent was worse than that of a football-scholarship freshman. "I'm an archaeologist. I was excavating the ruins of Paris III. I'm sorry I speak the language so badly; of course we know it only from inscriptions."

"From Altair? The star? But you're human—I think—"

"Our planet was colonized from Earth about four thousand years ago—that is, three thousand years from now." She laughed, most wondrously, and glanced at Lenoir. "Jehan explained it all to me, but I still get confused."

"It was a dangerous thing to try it again, Jehan!" Barry accused him. "We've been awfully lucky, you know."

"No," said the Frenchman. "Not lucky."

"But after all it's black magic you're playing with—Listen—I don't know your name, madame."

"Kislk," she said.

"Listen, Kislk," Barry said without even a stumble, "your science must be fantastically advanced—is there any magic? Does it exist? Can the laws of Nature really be broken, as we seem to be doing?"

"I've never seen nor heard of an authenticated case of magic."

"Then what goes on?" Barry roared. "Why does that stupid old spell work for Jehan, for us, that one spell, and here, nowhere else, for nobody else, in five—no, eight—no, fifteen thousand years of recorded history? Why? Why? And where did that damn puppy come from?"

"The puppy was lost," Lenoir said, his dark face grave. "Somewhere near this house, on the Ile Saint-Louis."

"And I was sorting potsherds," Kislk said, also gravely, "in a house-site, Island 2, Pit 4, Section D. A lovely Spring day, and I hated it. Loathed it. The day, the work, the people around me." Again she looked at the gaunt little alchemist, a long, quiet look. "I tried to explain it to Jehan last night. We have improved the race, you see. We're all very tall, healthy, and beautiful. No fillings in our teeth. All skulls from Early America have fillings in the teeth. . . . Some of us are brown, some white, some gold-skinned. But all beautiful, and healthy, and well-adjusted, and aggressive, and successful. Our professions and degree of success are preplanned for us in the State Pre-School Homes. But there's an occasional genetic flaw. Me, for instance. I was trained as an archaeologist because the Teachers saw that I really didn't like people, live people. People bored me. All like me on the outside, all alien to me on the inside. When everything's alike, which place is home? . . . But now I've seen an unhygienic room with insufficient heating. Now I've seen a cathedral not in ruins. Now I've met a living man who's shorter than me, with bad teeth and a short temper. Now I'm home, I'm where I can be myself, I'm no longer alone!"

"Alone," Lenoir said gently to Barry. "Loneliness, eh? Loneliness is the spell, loneliness is stronger. . . . Really it doesn't seem unnatural."

Bota was peering round the doorway, her face flushed between the black tangles of her hair. She smiled shyly and said a polite Latin good-morning to the newcomer.

"Kislk doesn't know Latin," Lenoir said with immense satisfaction. "We must teach Bota some French. French is the language of love, anyway, eh? Come along, let's go out and buy some bread. I'm hungry."

Kislk hid her silver tunic under the useful and anonymous cloak, while Lenoir pulled on his moth-eaten black gown. Bota combed her hair, while Barry thoughtfully scratched a louse-bite on his neck. Then they set forth to get breakfast. The alchemist and the interstellar archaeologist went first, speaking French; the Gaulish slave and the professor from Indiana followed, speaking Latin, and holding hands. The narrow streets were crowded, bright with sunshine. Above them Notre Dame reared its two square towers against the sky. Beside them the Seine rippled softly. It was April in Paris, and on the banks of the river the chestnuts were in bloom.

[1962]

For Thought

In this comically offbeat love story, Le Guin has selected two contrasting settings (twentieth-century France and late-medieval France) to complement the two contrasting moods which dominate the action. According to this light-hearted fantasy, magic does exist; but in a way that is more mundane and yet more marvelous than we might think. For, above all, it is the overpowering human need for companionship and love that works the greatest feats of magic, especially when it is April in Paris.

For Discussion

1. What is the mood at the beginning of the story? What details are given to establish it?
2. What is the mood at the end of the story, and how is this mood established?
3. What ironic contrast exists between each pair of lovers, between the two men, and between the two women? What purpose do these contrasts serve in the story?
4. What elements of characterization and action, along with rhetorical devices, create the comic tone?
5. Of what is the title symbolic? What theme arises out of the characterization and action?

Ursula Le Guin
The Masters

In darkness a man stood alone, naked, holding a smoking torch. The reddish glow lit air and ground for only a few feet; beyond that was the darkness, the immeasurable. From moment to moment there was a rush of wind, a half-glimpsed glitter of eyes, a vast muttering: "Hold it higher!" The man obeyed, though the torch shook in his shaking hands. He raised it clear above his head, while the darkness rushed and jabbered around him, closing in. The wind blew colder, the red flame guttered. His rigid arms began to quiver, then to jerk a little; his face was oily with sweat; he barely heard the soft, huge jabbering, "Hold it up, up, hold it up. . . ." The current of time had stopped; only the whispering grew and grew till it was a howling, and still, horribly, nothing touched him, nothing came within the circle of light. "Now walk!" the great voice howled. "Walk forward!"

The torch above his head, he stepped forward on the ground he could not see. It was not there. With a scream for help, he fell, darkness and thunder about him, the torch he would not let go flaming backward into his eyes.

Time . . . time, and light, and pain, they had all started again. He was crouching in some kind of ditch, on all fours in the mud. His face stung and his eyes, in this bright light, were full of fog. He looked up from his mud-blotched nakedness to a blurred, radiant figure standing above him. Light fell in glory on white hair, the long folds of a white cloak. The eyes gazed at Ganil, the voice spoke to him: "You lie in the Grave. You lie in the Grave of Knowledge. So lie your forefathers forever beneath the ashes of the fires of Hell." The voice swelled out: "O fallen Man, arise!" Ganil managed to get to his feet. The white figure was pointing: "That is the Light of Human Reason. It guided you to the grave. Drop it." Ganil realized he was still holding a mud sodden black stick, the torch; he let it fall. "Now rise," the white figure cried in a slow exaltation, "rise from darkness and walk in the Light of Common Day!" Hands reached to Ganil, helping and hauling him up. Men knelt offering him basins and sponges, others towelled him, rubbed him down till he stood clean and warm, a grey cloak round his shoulders, amid the chatting and laughter, coming and going, in the bright spacious hall. A bald man clapped his shoulder. "Come on, time for the Oath."

"Did I—did I do all right?"

"Fine! Only you held up that damn fool torch so long. thought you'd keep us growling around in the dark all day. Come on." They led him over black pavement and under the very lofty, white-beamed ceiling, to a curtain that dropped, pure white, in a few straight folds, thirty feet from roof to floor. "Curtain of Mystery," somebody said to Ganil in a matter-of-fact tone. Laughing and talking had died away; they stood all round him, silent. In silence the white curtain parted. Ganil stared foggily at what was revealed: a high altar, a long table, and an old man in white.

"Postulant, will you swear our Oath with us?"

Somebody nudged Ganil, whispering, "I will." "I will," Ganil stuttered.

"Swear then, Masters of the Rite!" The old man raised up a shape of silver: an X-cross, supported by an iron shaft. "Under the Cross of the Common Day I swear never to reveal the rites and mysteries of my Lodge—"

"Under the Cross . . . I swear . . . the rites . . ." muttered all the men around Ganil, and propelled by another nudge he muttered with them.

"To live well, to work well, to think well—" As Ganil finished repeating this a voice whispered in his ear, "Don't swear."

"To avoid all heresies, to betray all necromancers to the Courts of College, and to obey the High Masters of my Lodge from now forth till my death—" Mutter, mutter. Some seemed to be repeating the long passage, some not; Ganil, confused, muttered a word or two and then stood silent. "And I swear never to teach the Mysteries of Machinery to any gentile. I swear this beneath the Sun." A grating rumble almost drowned their voices. Slowly, crankily, a section of the roof was swinging back to reveal the yellow-grey, cloud-covered sky of summer. "Behold the Light of Common Day!" the old man in white cried out, triumphant, and Ganil stared up at it. The machinery apparently stuck before the skylight was fully open; there was a loud clanking of gears, then silence. The old man came forward, kissed Ganil on both cheeks, and said, "Welcome, Master Ganil, to the Inner Rite of the Mystery of the Machine." The initiation was over. Ganil was a Master of his Lodge.

"Mean burn you got there," the bald fellow said as they all walked back down the hall. Ganil put up his hand and found that his left cheek and temple were raw and sore. "Lucky it missed your eye."

"Just missed being blinded by the light of Reason, eh?" said a soft voice. Glancing round Ganil saw a fair man, with brown hair and blue eyes, actually blue, like those of an albino cat or a blind horse. He looked away from the deformity at once, but the fair man went on in his soft voice, the voice that had whispered "Don't swear" during the taking of the Oath, "I'm Mede Fairman. I'll be your Co-Master in Lee's shop. Feel like getting a beer when we're out of here?"

The dank beer-dreggy warmth of the tavern was a queer change from all the terror and ceremony of the day. Ganil felt dizzy. Mede Fairman drank off half a tankard, wiped foam pleasurably off his mouth, and inquired, "What d'you think of the initiation?"

"It was—it was—"

"Humbling?"

"Yes," Ganil agreed. "Really humbling."

"Humiliating, even," the blue-eyed man suggested.

"Yes. A—a great mystery." Perplexed, Ganil stared down into his beer. Mede smiled and said in his soft voice, "I know. Drink up, now. I think you ought to have an Apothecary look at that burn." Ganil obediently followed him out into the evening, into the narrow streets thronged with pedestrians, horse-carts, ox-carts, chuffing motor-carts. In the Merchantsplace the booths of the artisans were being closed for the night, and down High Street the great doors of the Shops and Lodges were already barred. Here and there the overhung, elbowing houses were parted by the blank yellow façade of a temple, marked with one plain circle of polished brass. In the dull, brief summer twilight under the unmoving clouds the black-haired, bronze-skinned people of the Common Day crowded and idled and pushed and talked and cursed and laughed, and Ganil, dizzy from fatigue and pain and strong beer, kept close beside Mede as if, for all his own new Masterhood, this blue-eyed stranger were his only guide.

"XVI plus IXX," Ganil said impatiently, "what the devil, boy, can't you add?" The apprentice flushed red. "Isn't it XXXVI, then, Master Ganil?" he asked feebly. For answer Ganil jammed one of the rods the boy had been machining into its place in the steam engine that was being repaired; it was too long by an inch.

"It's because my rule of thumb's so long, sir," the boy said, displaying his knobby hands. The distance between first and second thumb-joint was in fact unusually long. "So it is," Ganil said. His dark face darkened. "Very interesting. But it doesn't matter how long your inch is so long as you use it consistently. And what matters, you blockhead, is that XVI and IXX don't make XXXVI, never have, never can, never will till the world ends—you incompetent gentile!"

"Yes, sir. It's so hard to remember, sir."

"It's intended to be hard to remember, Wanno Prentice," said a deep voice: Lee the Shopmaster, a fat deep-chested man with bright black eyes. "Come over here a minute, Ganil." Leading him to a quieter corner of the great workshop, Lee went on cheerfully, "You're a bit impatient, Master Ganil."

"Wanno should know his addition-tables."

"Even Masters forget an addition now and then, you know." Lee patted Ganil's shoulder in a fatherly way. "Why, you sounded for a moment there as if you expected him to compute it!" He laughed aloud, a fine bass laugh through which his eyes gleamed merrily and with infinite shrewdness. "Take it easy, that's all. . . . I understand you're coming for dinner next Altarday Eve?"

"I took the liberty—"

"Fine, fine! More power to you. Wish she'd take on a good steady fellow like you. But I give you fair warning. My daughter's a willful hussy." Again the Master laughed, and Ganil grinned, a little ruefully. The Shopmaster's daughter Lani had not only most of the young men of the Shop, but also her father, twisted right round her little finger. A clever, quicksilver girl, she had at first rather scared Ganil. It took him a while to notice that she spoke, to him only, with a certain shyness, a hint almost of pleading. He had finally got up courage to ask a dinner invitation from her mother, the recognized first step of a courtship. He stood now where Lee had left him, thinking of Lani's smile.

"Ganil, have you ever seen the Sun?"

It was a low voice, dry and easy. He turned, meeting his friend's blue eyes.

"The Sun? Yes, of course I have."

"When was the last time?"

"Let's see, I was twenty-six; four years ago. Weren't you here in Edun then? It came out in late afternoon, and that night there were stars. I counted eighty-one, I remember, before the sky closed."

"I was up north in Keling then in my first Mastership." Mede leaned against the wooden guard rail of the model heavy steam engine as he spoke. His light eyes looked away from the busy shop, out the windows at the fine, steady rain of late autumn. "Heard you telling off young Wanno just now . . . 'What matters is that XVI and IXX don't make XXXVI. . . .' 'When I was twenty-six, four years ago . . . I counted eighty-one stars . . .' A little more and you'd be computing, Ganil."

Ganil frowned, unconsciously rubbing the whitish scar on his temple. "Well, hell, Mede! even gentiles know IV from XXX!"

Mede smiled faintly. He had his Comparing Stick in his hand, and lowering it he drew on the dusty floor a round shape. "What's that?" he asked.

"The Sun."

"Right. It's also a . . . a figure. A number. The figure for Nothing."

"The figure for Nothing?"

"Yes. You could use it in the subtraction-tables, for instance. I from II leaves I, right? But what does II from II leave?" A pause. He tapped the circle with his stick. "That."

"Yes, of course." Ganil stared down at the circle, the sacred image of the Sun, the Hidden Light, the Face of God. "Is that priest-knowledge?"

"No." Mede drew an X-cross over the circle. "That is."

"Then what—whose knowledge is the—the figure for Nothing?"

"No one's. Anyone's. It's not a mystery." Ganil frowned in surprise at this statement. They spoke in low voices, standing close as if discussing a measurement on Mede's Comparing Stick. "Why did you count the stars, Ganil?"

"I . . . I wanted to know. I've always liked counting, numbers, the tables. That's why I'm a Mechanic."

"Yes. You're thirty, aren't you, you've been a Master for four months now. Did you ever think, Ganil, that to be a Master means you have learned everything your trade can teach? From now on until your death you'll learn nothing more. There is no more."

"But the Shopmasters—"

"Shopmasters learn some secret signals and passwords," Mede said in his soft, dry voice, "and of course they have power. But they know no more than you. . . . You thought perhaps they were allowed to compute, didn't you? They aren't."

Ganil was silent.

"And yet there are things to be learned, Ganil."

"Where?"

"Outside."

There was a long pause.

"I can't listen to this, Mede. Don't speak of it again. I won't betray you." Ganil turned and walked away, his face harsh with anger. With all his will he turned that confused and struggling anger against Mede, a man as deformed of mind as of body, an evil counsellor, a lost friend.

It had been a pleasant evening: Lee jovial, his fat wife motherly, and Lani shy and radiant. Ganil's youthful gravity made her tease him, but even in her teasing was that pleading, yielding note; another moment, it seemed, and all her verve would turn to tenderness. Passing a dish at table once her hand had for an instant touched his. He still knew exactly where, there, the side of his right hand near the wrist, one soft touch. He moaned luxuriously as he lay in bed in his room over the Shop in the utter blackness of the city night. O Lani, soft touch of a hand, of lips—O Lord, Lord! Courtship was a long business, eight months at least, going from step to step as one must with a Master's daughter. Ganil had to get his mind off this unendurable sweetness. Think of nothing, he told himself firmly, go to sleep. Think of nothing. . . . And he thought of nothing. The circle. The round empty circle. What was I times 0? The same as II times 0. What if you put I beside 0, what would that figure, be, I0?

Mede Fairman sat up in bed, brown hair lank over groggy blue eyes, and tried to focus on the person crashing around his room. The first dirty-yellow light of dawn showed at the window. "This is Altarday," he growled, "go away, I'm sleepy." The vague figure resolved into Ganil, the crashing into a whisper. "Mede!" Ganil kept whispering, "look!" He stuck a slat slate under Mede's nose. "Look, look what you can do with that figure for Nothing—"

"Oh, that," said Mede. He pushed Ganil and the slate away, went and dunked his head in the basin of icy water on his clothes-chest, and kept it there a while. He returned dripping to sit on the bed. "Let's see."

"See, you can use any number for a base, I used XII because it's handy. XII becomes I-0, see, and XIII is I-I, then when you get up to XXIV—"

"Sh."

Mede studied the slate. Finally he said, "Will you remember this?" and at Ganil's nod, wiped the neat crowded figures off the slate with a rub of his sleeve. "I hadn't realized that one could use any base. . . . But look, use the base X, I'll tell you why in a minute, and here's a device that makes it easier. Now X will be I0, and XI will be II, but for XII, write this," and he wrote on the slate, 12.

Ganil stared at the figure. At last he said in a peculiar struggling voice, "Isn't that one of the black numbers?"

"Yes, it is. All you've done, Ganil, is to come at the black numbers by the back door."

Ganil sat beside him, silent.

"What's CXX times MCC?" Mede inquired.

"The tables don't go that high."

"Watch." Mede wrote on the slate:

$$
\begin{array}{r}
1200 \\
120 \\
\hline
\end{array}
$$

and then as Ganil watched,

$$
\begin{array}{r}
0000 \\
2400 \\
1200 \\
\hline
144000
\end{array}
$$

Another long pause. "Three Nothings . . . XII times itself . . . Give me the slate," Ganil muttered. Then after a silence broken only by the patter of rain and the squeak of chalk on slate, "What's the black number for VIII?"

By twilight of that cold Altarday they had gone as far as Mede could take Ganil. Indeed Ganil had gone farther than Mede could follow him. "You must meet Yin," the fair man said. "He can teach you what you need. Yin works with angles, triangles, measurements. He can measure the distance between any two points, points you can't reach, using his triangles. He is a great Learner. Numbers are the heart of this knowledge, the language of it."

"And my own language."

"Yes, it is. Not mine. I don't love numbers for themselves. I want to use them. To explain things . . . For instance, if you throw a ball, what makes the ball move?"

"Your throwing it." Ganil grinned. White as a sheet—much whiter than Mede's sheets—his head ringing with sixteen straight hours of mathematics minus meals or sleep, he had lost all fear, all humility. His smile was that of a king come home from exile.

"Fine," said Mede. "Why does it *keep on* moving?"

"Because . . . because the air holds it up?"

"Then why does it ever fall? Why does it follow a curve? What kind of curve is it? Do you see how I need your numbers?" It was Mede who now looked like a king, an angry king with an empire too immense to control. "And they talk about Mysteries," he snorted, "in their little shuttered shops!—Here, come on, let's get some dinner and go see Yin."

Built right up against the city wall, the tall old house peered from leaded windows at the two young Masters down in the street. Sulfurous late-autumn twilight hung over the steep slate roofs shining with rain. "Yin was a Machine-Master like us," Mede told Ganil as they waited at the iron-barred door, "retired now, you'll see why. Men from all the Lodges come here, apothecaries, weavers, masons. Even some artisans. One butcher. He cuts up dead cats." Mede spoke with amused tolerance, as physicists generally speak of biologists. Now the door swung open, and a servant took them upstairs to a room where logs glowed on a great hearth, and a man rose from a high-backed oaken chair to greet them.

Ganil thought at once of the Overmaster of his Lodge, the figure that had cried down to him in his grave, "Arise." Yin too was old and tall, and wore the white cloak of the High Masters. But he stooped, and his face was creased and weary as an old hound's. He held out his left hand to greet them. His right arm ended in a long healed, shiny stump at the wrist.

"This is Ganil," Mede was saying. "He invented the duodecimal system last night. Get him working on the mathematics of curves for me, Master Yin."

Yin laughed, an old man's short, soft laugh. "Welcome, Ganil. From now on, come here when you please. We're all necromancers here, we practice the black arts. Or try to . . . Come freely, day or night. And go freely. If we're betrayed, so be it. We must trust one another. Mystery belongs to no man; we're not keeping a secret, but practicing an art. Does that make sense to you?"

Ganil nodded. Words never came easily to him, only numbers. And he found himself very moved, which embarrassed him. This was no solemn symbolic Initiation and Oath, but only an old man talking quietly.

"Good," said Yin, as if Ganil's nod had been quite sufficient. "Some wine, young Masters, or ale? My dark ale came out first-rate this year. So you like numbers, do you, Ganil?"

In early spring Ganil stood in the shop supervising Wanno as the prentice took measurements onto his Comparing Stick from the model of the hauling-cart engine. Ganil's face was grim. He had changed over these few months, looked older, more resolute, harder. Four hours' sleep a night plus the invention of algebra might well change a man.

"Master Ganil?" said a shy voice.

"Repeat that measurement," he told Wanno, and then turned questioningly to the girl. Lani too had changed. Her face looked a little cross, a little forlorn, and she spoke to Ganil with real timidity. He had taken the second step of courtship, the three evening calls, and then becoming absorbed in his work with Yin, had gone no further. No man had ever dropped Lani in the middle of a courtship. No man had ever looked right through her, as he was doing now. What was it he saw, when he looked through her? She was wild to know that, to get at his secret, to get at him. In a vague, unquantifiable way he knew this, and was sorry for Lani, and a little afraid of her.

She was watching Wanno. "Do they . . . do you ever change those measurements?" she asked, trying to make conversation.

"To change a Model is the heresy of Invention."

That ended that. "My father wanted me to tell you the Shop will be shut tomorrow."

"Shut? Why's that?"

"The College has announced there's a west wind rising, and the Sun may come out tomorrow."

"Good! A good beginning for the spring, eh? Thanks." And he turned back to the model.

The Priests of the College had for once been right. Weather prediction, on which they spent most of their waking hours, was a thankless task. But once in ten tries or so they caught a Sun, and this was one of the times. By noon the rains had ceased and the cloud-cover was paling, beginning to boil and flow slowly eastward. By mid-afternoon all the people of Edun were out on the streets and squares, on chimneypots and roof-trees, on the wall and the fields beyond the wall, watching; the Priests of the College had begun their ceremonial dance, bowing and interweaving on the great forecourt of the College; priests stood ready in every temple to pull chains that would open the roofs so that the Sun's light might strike the altar-stones. And in late afternoon at last the sky opened. Between ragged smoking edges of yellow-grey appeared a streak of blue. A sigh, a soft tremendous murmur rose up from the streets, squares, windows, roofs, walls of the city of Edun: "Heaven, heaven . . ."

The rent in the sky widened. A shower of rain spattered over the city, blown aslant on the fresh wind, and suddenly the raindrops glittered, as at night in torchlight; but this glory they reflected was the glory of the Sun. To westward it stood, all alone in heaven, blinding.

Ganil stood with the others, face lifted. On his face, on the scar of his burn, he felt the heat of the Sun. He stared at it till his eyes swam with tears, the Circle of Fire, the face of God. . . .

"What is the Sun?"

That was Mede's soft voice, remembered. A cold midwinter night, he and Mede and Yin and the others talking before the fire in Yin's house. "Is it a circle, or a sphere? Why does it cross the sky? And how big is it—how far away is it? Ah, to think that once all a man had to do to see the Sun was lift up his head. . . ."

Flutes and drums throbbed, a gay faint sound, away off at the College. Sometimes cloud-fragments blew across the intolerable face and the world turned grey and chill again, the flutes stopped; but the west wind blew, the clouds passed and the Sun reappeared, always a little lower. Just before it sank into the heavy cloud-rack in the west it was growing red and one could look at it without pain. In those moments it certainly looked to Ganil's eyes not like a disk but like an enormous, haze-warped, slowly falling ball.

It fell, was gone.

Overhead through the torn sky glimpses of heaven still shone, clear and deep, blue-green. Then westward near where the Sun had set, at the edge of a mounting cloud, gleamed one bright point: the evening star. "Look!" Ganil cried, but few turned to look. The Sun was set, what did stars matter. The yellowish haze, part of the single windingsheet of cloud that had covered earth with its mantle of dust and rain ever since Hellfire fourteen generations ago, moved up over the star, erased it. Ganil sighed, rubbed his neck that was stiff with craning, and started home along with all the other people of the Common Day.

He was arrested that night. From guards and fellow-prisoners (all his shop was in jail with him except the Shopmaster Lee) he learned that his crime was that of knowing Mede Fairman. Mede stood accused of heresy. He had been seen out on the fields pointing an instrument at the Sun, a device, they said, for measuring distances. He had been trying to measure the distance between the earth and God.

The prentices were soon let go. On the third day guards came for Ganil, bringing him out into one of the enclosed courts of the College, into the soft, fine rain of early spring. Priests lived almost wholly out of doors, and the great complex of Edun College was only a series of meager barracks surrounding the roofless sleeping-courts, writing-courts, prayer-courts, eating-courts, and courts of law. Into one of these they brought Ganil, forcing him on between the ranks of men robed in white and yellow that filled it, until he stood in front of them all. He saw a clear space, an altar, a long table shining wet with rain, and behind it a priest in the golden robe of the High Mystery. At the far end of the table was another man who like Ganil was flanked by guards. This man was looking at Ganil, a straight look, cold and blank; yet they were blue eyes, the same blue as heaven above the clouds.

"Ganil Kalson of Edun, you are suspect

as an acquaintance of Mede Fairman, accused of the heresies of Invention and Computation. You were this man's friend?"

"We were Co-Masters—"

"Yes. Did he ever speak to you of measurements made without Comparing Sticks?"

"No."

"Of black numbers?"

"No."

"Of the black arts?"

"No."

"Master Ganil, you've answered No three times. Do you know the Order of the Priest-Masters of the Mystery of the Law concerning suspects in heresy?"

"No, I don't—"

"The Order says: 'If the suspect shall deny the questions four times, the questions may be repeated with use of the handpress until answered.' I shall now repeat, unless you wish to retract one of your denials."

"No," Ganil said, confused, looking round him at the crowded blank faces, the high walls. When they had brought out a squat wooden machine of some kind and had locked his right hand into it, he was still more confused than scared. What was all this mumbo-jumbo? It was like his initiation, when they had worked so hard to frighten him; that time they had succeeded.

"As a Mechanic," the golden priest was saying, "you know the use of the lever, Master Ganil. Will you retract?"

"No," Ganil said, frowning a little. He had noticed that his right arm now seemed to end at the wrist, like Yin's.

"Very well." One of the guards put his hands on the lever sticking out of the wooden box, and the golden priest said, "Were you a friend of Mede Fairman?"

"No," Ganil said. He said No to each question even after he had ceased to hear the priest's voice; he went on saying No till he heard his own voice mixed with the clapping echo from the walls above the courtyard, No, no, no, no.

The light came and went, the rain fell cold on his face and ceased, somebody kept trying to help him stand up. His grey cloak stank, he had been sick with pain. At the thought, he was sick again. "Take it easy, now," a guard was whispering to him. The motionless white and yellow ranks were still crowded there, the faces set, the eyes staring . . . but not at him now.

"Heretic, do you know this man?"

"He is my Co-Master."

"Did you speak to him of the black arts?"

"Yes."

"Did you teach him the black arts?"

"No. I tried to." The voice cracked a little; even in the silence of the courtyard, over only the whisper of the rain, it was hard to hear Mede speak. "He was too stupid. He dared not and could not learn. He'll make a fine Shopmaster." The cold blue eyes looked straight at Ganil without pity or appeal.

The golden priest turned to face the court again. "There is no evidence against the suspect Ganil. You may go, suspect. Come here at noon tomorrow to witness the execution of judgment. Failure to come will be taken as proof of your guilt." Before he understood, the guards had led Ganil out of the courtyard. They left him at a side door of the College, barring the door behind him with a clang. He stood there a while, then crouched down on the pavement, pressing his blackened, blood-caked hand against his side under his cloak. Rain whispered around him. No one passed. It was not till dusk that he pulled himself up and walked, street by street, house by house, step by step, across the city to Yin's house.

In the shadows of the doorway a shadow moved, spoke: "Ganil!" He stopped. "Ganil, I don't care if you're suspect. It's all right. Come back home with me. My father will take you back into the shop. He will if I ask him."

Ganil was silent.

"Come with me. I waited for you, I knew you'd come here, I've followed you before." Her nervous, jubilant laugh died away.

"Let me by, Lani."

"No. Why do you come to old Yin's house? Who lives here? Who is she? Come back with me, you have to, my father won't take a suspect back into his shop, unless I—"

Yin's door was never locked. Ganil brushed past her and went in, shutting it behind him. No servant came; the house was dark, silent. They had all been taken, all the Learners, they would all be questioned and tortured and killed.

"Who's that?"

Yin stood on the stair-landing, lamplight bright on his white hair. He came to Ganil and helped him up the stairs. Ganil spoke very fast: "I was followed here, a girl from the shop, Lee's daughter, if she tells him he'll recognize your name, he'll send the guards here—"

"I sent the others away three days ago." At the sound of Yin's voice Ganil stopped, stared at the old man's creased, quiet face, and then said childishly, "Look," holding out his right hand, "look, like yours."

"Yes. Come sit down, Ganil."

"They condemned him. Not me, they let me go. He said he couldn't teach me, I couldn't learn. To save me—"

"And your mathematics. Come here now, sit down."

Ganil got control of himself, and obeyed. Yin made him lie down, then did what he could about cleaning and bandaging his hand. Then, sitting down between Ganil and the glowing fire, he gave a wheezy sigh. "Well," he said, "now you're a heresy suspect. I've been one for twenty years. You get used to it. . . . Don't worry about our friends. But if the girl tells Lee and your name gets linked with mine . . . We'd better leave Edun. Separately. But tonight."

Ganil said nothing. To leave his shop without the Overmaster's permission meant excommunication, the loss of his Mastership. He would be barred from his own trade. What could he do, with his crippled hand, where could he go? He had never been out of Edun in his life.

The silence of the house spread out above and below them. Ganil strained to hear sounds down in the street, the tramping of a troop of guards come to re-arrest him. He had to get out, to get away, tonight—"I can't," he said, abruptly. "I have to be—to be at the College tomorrow, at noon."

Yin knew what he meant. Again the silence closed round them. The old man's voice was very dry and weary when he finally spoke. "That's the condition of your release, eh? All right; go do it; you don't want them hunting you through the Forty Towns as a condemned heretic. A suspect isn't hunted, merely outcast. It's preferable. Get some sleep, now, Ganil. Before I go I'll tell you where to meet me. Leave as soon as you can; and travel light. . . ."

When Ganil left the house late in the morning, however, he carried something with him, a roll of papers hidden under his cloak, each sheet covered edge to edge with Mede Fairman's clear writing: "Trajectories," "Speed of Falling Bodies," "The Nature of Motion . . ." Yin had left before daybreak, jogging calmly out of town on a grey donkey. "I'll see you in Keling" had been his only parting with Ganil. Ganil had seen none of the other Learners. Only serfs, servants, beggars, truant schoolboys, and women with their nursemaids and whining children stood with him now in the dull light of noon on the great forecourt of the College. Only riffraff and the idle gathered to see a heretic die. A priest had ordered Ganil to stand at the very front of the crowd. Many people glanced curiously at him, standing there alone in his Master's cloak.

On the other side of the square, in the front of the crowd, he saw a girl in a violet gown. He was not sure it was Lani. Why would she be here to see Mede die? She did not know what it was she hated; or what it was she loved. Love that wants only to get, to possess, is a monstrous thing, Ganil thought. She loved him, she stood separated from him only by the width of that square. She would never be willing to see that she was separated from him by her own act, by ignorance, by exile, by death.

They brought Mede out just before noon. Ganil glimpsed his face; it was very white, all his deformity exposed, the atavistic pallor of skin, hair, eyes. There was no drawing-out of the scene; a gold-robed priest raised his crossed arms in invocation to the Sun that stood, unseen, at noon behind the pall of clouds, and as he lowered his arms torches were set to the stacks of wood round the stake. Smoke curled up, the same grey-yellow as the clouds. Ganil stood with his injured hand in its sling pressed hard against the roll of papers under his cloak, repeating silently, "Let the smoke suffocate him first. . . ." But the wood was dry and caught quickly. He felt the heat on his face, on his fire-scarred temple. Beside him a young priest tried to draw back, could not because of the pressing, staring, sighing crowd, and stood still, swaying a little and breathing in gasps. The smoke was thick now, hiding the flames and the figure among them. But Ganil could hear his voice, not soft now, loud, very loud. He heard it, he forced himself to hear it, but at the same time he listened in his spirit to a steady voice, soft, continuing: "What is the Sun:? Why does it cross the sky? . . . Do you see how I need your numbers? . . . For XII, write 12. . . . This is also a figure, the figure for Nothing."

The screaming had stopped, but the soft voice had not.

Ganil raised his head. The crowd was drifting away; the young priest knelt on the pavement by him, praying and sobbing aloud. Ganil glanced up at the heavy sky and then set off alone through the streets of the city and out through the city gate, northward, into exile and towards his home.

[1963]

For Thought

In the setting of a neomedieval culture, "The Masters" explores the human race's need to exercise the mind in free and independent inquiry. The need is presented as being so overpowering that it compels the nonconformist thinker to resist, at whatever cost, the repressive controls and punishments of a society that puts arbitrary limits on the right to seek and to learn. Instead of social acceptance and security in return for intellectual submission, Ganil chooses to quest after knowledge even at the price of exile and the precarious existence that looms beyond the pale of orthodoxy.

For Discussion

1. Compare and contrast the two initiations that Ganil undergoes.
2. What evidence is there to indicate that Common Day is a society at a lower level than the preexisting society?
3. What is the conflict in the story? What elements of suspense or surprise are there in the complications and resolution of the conflict?
4. Science fiction writing oftens suffers from shallow characterization. Comment on the depth or lack of depth of the characterizations in this story. What purpose would there be for the depth or lack of depth of the characterizations?
5. Of what is mathematics symbolic in the story? How is it incorporated into the theme?

Ursula Le Guin
The Rule of Names

Mr. Underhill came out from under his hill, smiling and breathing hard. Each breath shot out of his nostrils as a double puff of steam, snow-white in the morning sunshine. Mr. Underhill looked up at the bright December sky and smiled wider than ever, showing snow-white teeth. Then he went down to the village.

"Morning, Mr. Underhill," said the villagers as he passed them in the narrow street between houses with conical, overhanging roofs like the fat red caps of toadstools. "Morning, morning!" he replied to each. (It was of course bad luck to wish anyone a *good* morning; a simple statement of the time of day was quite enough, in a place so permeated with Influences as Sattins Island, where a careless adjective might change the weather for a week.) All of them spoke to him, some with affection, some with affectionate disdain. He was all the little island had in the way of a wizard, and so deserved respect—but how could you respect a little fat man of fifty who waddled along with his toes turned in, breathing steam and smiling? He was no great shakes as a workman either. His fireworks were fairly elaborate but his elixirs were weak. Warts he charmed off frequently reappeared after three days; tomatoes he enchanted grew no bigger than canteloupes; and those rare times when a strange ship stopped at Sattins Harbor, Mr. Underhill always stayed under his hill—for fear, he explained, of the evil eye. He was, in other words, a wizard the way walleyed Gan was a carpenter: by default. The villagers made do with badly-hung doors and inefficient spells, for this generation, and relieved their annoyance by treating Mr. Underhill quite familiarly, as a mere fellow-villager. They even asked him to dinner. Once he asked some of them to dinner, and served a splendid repast, with silver, crystal, damask, roast goose, sparkling Andrades '639, and plum pudding with hard sauce; but he was so nervous all through the meal that it took the joy out of it, and besides, everybody was hungry again half an hour afterward. He did not like anyone to visit his cave, not even the anteroom, beyond which in fact nobody had ever got. When he saw people approaching the hill he always came trotting out to meet them. "Let's sit out here under the pine trees!" he would say, smiling and waving towards the fir grove, or if it was raining, "Let's go have a drink at the inn, eh?" though everybody knew he drank nothing stronger than well-water.

Some of the village children, teased by that locked cave, poked and pried and made raids while Mr. Underhill was away; but the small door that led into the inner chamber was spell-shut, and it seemed for once to be an effective spell. Once a couple of boys, thinking the wizard was over on the West Shore curing Mrs. Ruuna's sick donkey, brought a crowbar and a hatchet up there, but at the first whack of the hatchet on the door there came a roar of wrath from inside, and a cloud of purple steam. Mr. Underhill had got home early. The boys fled. He did not come out, and the boys came to no harm, though they said you couldn't believe what a huge hooting howling hissing horrible bellow that little fat man could make unless you'd heard it.

His business in town this day was three dozen fresh eggs and a pound of liver; also a stop at Seacaptain Fogeno's cottage to renew the seeing-charm on the old man's eyes (quite useless when applied to a case of detached retina, but Mr. Underhill kept trying), and finally a chat with old Goody Guld, the concertina-maker's widow. Mr. Underhill's friends were mostly old people. He was timid with the strong young men of the village, and the girls were shy of him. "He makes me nervous, he smiles so much," they all said, pouting, twisting silky ringlets round a finger. "Nervous" was a newfangled word, and their mothers all replied grimly, "Nervous my foot, silliness is the word for it. Mr. Underhill is a very respectable wizard!"

After leaving Goody Guld, Mr. Underhill passed by the school, which was being held this day out on the common. Since no one on Sattins Island was literate, there were no books to learn to read from and no desks to carve initials on and no blackboards to erase, and in fact no schoolhouse. On rainy days the children met in the loft of the Communal Barn, and got hay in their pants; on sunny days the schoolteacher, Palani, took them anywhere she felt like. Today, surrounded by thirty interested children under twelve and forty uninterested sheep under five, she was teaching an important item on the curriculum: the Rules of Names. Mr. Underhill, smiling shyly, paused to listen and watch. Palani, a plump, pretty girl of twenty, made a charming picture there in the wintry sunlight, sheep and children around her, a leafless oak above her, and behind her the dunes and sea and clear, pale sky. She spoke earnestly, her face flushed pink by wind and words. "Now you know the Rules of Names already, children. There are two, and they're the same on every island in the world. What's one of them?"

"It ain't polite to ask anybody what his name is," shouted a fat, quick boy, interrupted by a little girl shrieking, "You can't never tell your own name to nobody my ma says!"

"Yes, Suba. Yes, Popi dear, don't screech. That's right. You never ask anybody his name. You never tell your own. Now think about that a minute and then tell me why we call our wizard Mr. Underhill." She smiled across the curly heads and the woolly backs at Mr. Underhill, who beamed, and nervously clutched his sack of eggs.

"'Cause he lives under a hill!" said half the children.

"But is it his truename?"

"No!" said the fat boy, echoed by little Popi shrieking, "No!"

"How do you know it's not?"

"'Cause he came here all alone and so there wasn't anybody knew his truename so they couldn't tell us, and *he* couldn't—"

"Very good, Suba. Popi, don't shout. That's right. Even a wizard can't tell his truename. When you children are through school and go through the Passage, you'll leave your childnames behind and keep only your truenames, which you must never ask for and never give away. Why is that the rule?"

The children were silent. The sheep bleated gently. Mr. Underhill answered the question: "Because the name is the thing," he said in his shy, soft, husky voice, "and the truename is the true thing. To speak the name is to control the thing. Am I right, Schoolmistress?"

She smiled and curtseyed, evidently a little embarrassed by his participation. And he trotted off towards his hill, clutching his eggs to his bosom. Somehow the minute spent watching Palani and the children had made him very hungry. He locked his inner door behind him with a hasty incantation, but there must have been a leak or two in the spell, for soon the bare anteroom of the cave was rich with the smell of frying eggs and sizzling liver.

The wind that day was light and fresh out of the west, and on it at noon a little boat came skimming the bright waves into Sattins Harbor. Even as it rounded the point a sharp-eyed boy spotted it, and knowing, like every child on the island, every sail and spar of the forty boats of the fishing fleet, he ran down the street calling out, "A foreign boat, a foreign boat!" Very seldom was the lonely isle visited by a boat from some equally lonely isle of the East Reach, or an adventurous trader from the Archipelago. By the time the boat was at the pier half the village was there to greet it, and fishermen were following it homewards, and cowherds and clam diggers and herb-hunters were puffing up and down all the rocky hills, heading towards the harbor.

But Mr. Underhill's door stayed shut.

There was only one man aboard the boat. Old Seacaptain Fogeno, when they told him that, drew down a bristle of white brows over his unseeing eyes. "There's only one kind of man," he said, "that sails the Outer Reach alone. A wizard, or a warlock, or a Mage. . ."

So the villagers were breathless hoping to see for once in their lives a Mage, one of the mighty White Magicians of the rich, towered, crowded inner islands of the Archipelago. They were disappointed, for the voyager was quite young, a handsome black-bearded fellow who hailed them cheerfully from his boat, and leaped ashore like any sailor glad to have made port. He introduced himself at once as a sea-peddlar. But when they told Seacaptain Fogeno that he carried an oaken walking-stick around with him, the old man nodded. "Two wizards in one town," he said. "Bad!" And his mouth snapped shut like an old carp's.

As the stranger could not give them his name, they gave him one right away: Blackbeard. And they gave him plenty of attention. He had a small mixed cargo of cloth and sandals and piswi feathers for trimming cloaks and cheap incense and levity stones and fine herbs and great glass beads from Venway—the usual peddlar's lot. Everyone on Sattins Island came to look, to chat with the voyager, and perhaps to buy something—"Just to remember him by!" cackled Goody Guld, who like all the women and girls of the village was smitten with Blackbeard's bold good looks. All the boys hung round him too, to hear him tell of his voyages to far, strange islands of the Reach or describe the great rich islands of the Archipelago, the Inner Lanes, the roadsteads white with ships, and the golden roofs of Havnor. The men willingly listened to his tales; but some of them wondered why a trader should sail alone, and kept their eyes thoughtfully upon his oaken staff.

But all this time Mr. Underhill stayed under his hill.

"This is the first island I've ever seen that had no wizard," said Blackbeard one evening to Goody Guld, who had invited him and her nephew and Palani in for a cup of rushwash tea. "What do you do when you get a toothache, or the cow goes dry?"

"Why, we've got Mr. Underhill!" said the old woman.

"For what that's worth," muttered her nephew Birt, and then blushed purple and spilled his tea. Birt was a fisherman, a large, brave, wordless young man. He loved the schoolmistress, but the nearest he had come to telling her of his love was to give baskets of fresh mackerel to her father's cook.

"Oh, you do have a wizard?" Blackbeard asked. "Is he invisible?"

"No, he's just very shy," said Palani. "You've only been here a week, you know, and we see so few strangers here . . ." She also blushed a little, but did not spill her tea.

Blackbeard smiled at her. "He's a good Sattinsman, then, eh?"

"No," said Goody Guld, "no more than you are. Another cup, nevvy? keep it in the cup this time. No, my dear, he came in a little bit of a boat, four years ago was it? just a day after the end of the shad run, I recall, for they was taking up the nets over in East Creek, and Pondi Cowherd broke his leg that very morning—five years ago it must be. No, four. No, five it is, 'twas the year the garlic didn't sprout. So he sails in on a bit of a sloop loaded full up with great chests and boxes and says to Seacaptain Fogeno, who wasn't blind then, though old enough goodness knows to be blind twice over, 'I hear tell,' he says, 'you've got no wizard nor warlock at all, might you be wanting one?' 'Indeed, if the magic's white!' says the Captain, and before you could say cuttlefish Mr. Underhill had settled down in the cave under the hill and was charming the mange off Goody Beltow's cat. Though the fur grew in grey, and 'twas an orange cat. Queer-looking thing it was after that. It died last winter in the cold spell. Goody Beltow took on so at the cat's death, poor thing, worse than when her man was drowned on the Long Banks, the year of the long herring-runs, when nevvy Birt here was but a babe in petticoats." Here Birt spilled his tea again, and Blackbeard grinned, but Goody Guld proceeded undismayed, and talked on till nightfall.

Next day Blackbeard was down at the pier, seeing after the sprung board in his boat which he seemed to take a long time fixing, and as usual drawing the taciturn Sattinsmen into talk. "Now which of these is your wizard's craft?" he asked. "Or has he got one of those the Mages fold up into a walnut shell when they're not using it?"

"Nay," said a stolid fisherman. "She's oop in his cave, under hill."

"He carried the boat he came in up to his cave?"

"Aye. Clear oop. I helped. Heavier as lead she was. Full oop with great boxes, and they full oop with books o' spells, he says. Heavier as lead she was." And the stolid fisherman turned his back, sighing stolidly. Goody Guld's nephew, mending a net nearby, looked up from his work and asked with equal stolidity, "Would ye like to meet Mr. Underhill, maybe?"

Blackbeard returned Birt's look. Clever black eyes met candid blue ones for a long moment; then Blackbeard smiled and said, "Yes. Will you take me up to the hill, Birt?"

"Aye, when I'm done with this," said the fisherman. And when the net was mended, he and the Archipelagan set off up the village street towards the high green hill above it. But as they crossed the common Blackbeard said, "Hold on a while, friend Birt. I have a tale to tell you, before we meet your wizard."

"Tell away," says Birt, sitting down in the shade of a live-oak.

"It's a story that started a hundred years ago, and isn't finished yet—though it soon will be, very soon. . . . In the very heart of the Archipelago, where the islands crowd thick as flies on honey, there's a little isle called Pendor. The sealords of Pendor were mighty men, in the old days of war before the League. Loot and ransom and tribute came pouring into Pendor, and they gathered a great treasure there, long ago. Then from somewhere away out in the West Reach, where dragons breed on the lava isles, came one day a very mighty dragon. Not one of those overgrown lizards most of you Outer Reach folk call dragons, but a big, black, winged, wise, cunning monster, full of strength and subtlety, and like all dragons loving gold and precious stones above all things. He killed the Sealord and his soldiers, and the people of Pendor fled in their ships by night. They all fled away and left the dragon coiled up in Pendor Towers. And there he stayed for a hundred years, dragging his scaly belly over the emeralds and sapphires and coins of gold, coming forth only once in a year or two when he must eat. He'd raid nearby islands for his food. You know what dragons eat?"

Birt nodded and said in a whisper, "Maidens."

"Right," said Blackbeard. "Well, that couldn't be endured forever, nor the thought of him sitting on all that treasure. So after the League grew strong, and the Archipelago wasn't so busy with wars and piracy, it was decided to attack Pendor, drive out the dragon, and get the gold and jewels for the treasury of the League. They're forever wanting money, the League is. So a huge fleet gathered from fifty islands, and seven Mages stood in the prows of the seven strongest ships, and they sailed towards Pendor. . . . They got there. They landed. Nothing stirred. The houses all stood empty, the dishes on the tables full of a hundred years' dust. The bones of the old Sealord and his men lay about in the castle courts and on the stairs. And the Tower rooms reeked of dragon. But there was no dragon. And no treasure, not a diamond the size of a poppyseed, not a single silver bead . . . Knowing that he couldn't stand up to seven Mages, the dragon had skipped out. They tracked him, and found he'd flown to a deserted island up north called Udrath; they followed his trail there, and what did they find? Bones again. His bones—the dragon's. But no treasure. A wizard, some unknown wizard from somewhere, must have met him single-handed, and defeated him—and then made off with the treasure, right under the League's nose!"

The fisherman listened, attentive and expressionless.

"Now that must have been a powerful wizard and a clever one, first to kill a dragon, and second to get off without leaving a trace. The lords and Mages of the Archipelago couldn't track him at all, neither where he'd come from nor where he'd made off to. They were about to give up. That was last spring; I'd been off on a three-year voyage up in the North Reach, and got back about that time. And they asked me to help them find the unknown wizard. That was clever of them. Because I'm not only a wizard myself, as I think some of the oafs here have guessed, but I am also a descendant of the Lords of Pendor. That treasure is mine. It's mine, and knows that it's mine. Those fools of the League couldn't find it, because it's not theirs. It belongs to the House of Pendor, and the great emerald, the star of the hoard, Inalkil the Greenstone, knows its master. Behold!" Blackbeard raised his oaken staff and cried aloud, "Inalkil!" The tip of the staff began to glow green, a fiery green radiance, a dazzling haze the color of April grass, and at the same moment the staff tipped in the wizard's hand, leaning, slanting till it pointed straight at the side of the hill above them.

"It wasn't so bright a glow, far away in Havnor," Blackbeard murmured, "but the staff pointed true. Inalkil answered when I called. The jewel knows its master. And I know the thief, and I shall conquer him. He's a mighty wizard, who could overcome a dragon. But I am mightier. Do you want to know why, oaf? Because I know his name!"

As Blackbeard's tone got more arrogant, Birt had looked duller and duller, blanker and blanker; but at this he gave a twitch, shut his mouth, and stared at the Archipelagan. "How did you . . . learn it?" he asked very slowly.

Blackbeard grinned, and did not answer.

"Black magic?"

"How else?"

Birt looked pale, and said nothing.

"I am the Sealord of Pendor, oaf, and I will have the gold my fathers won, and the jewels my mothers wore, and the Greenstone! For they are mine. —Now, you can tell your village boobies the whole story after I have defeated this wizard and gone. Wait here. Or you can come and watch, if you're not afraid. You'll never get the chance again to see a great wizard in all his power." Blackbeard turned, and without a backward glance strode off up the hill towards the entrance to the cave.

Very slowly, Birt followed. A good distance from the cave he stopped, sat down under a hawthorn tree, and watched. The Archipelagan had stopped; a stiff, dark figure alone on the green swell of the hill before the gaping cave-mouth, he stood perfectly still. All at once he swung his staff up over his head, and the emerald radiance shone about him as he shouted, "Thief, thief of the Hoard of Pendor, come forth!"

There was a crash, as of dropped crockery, from inside the cave, and a lot of dust came spewing out. Scared, Birt ducked. When he looked again he saw Blackbeard still standing motionless, and at the mouth of the cave, dusty and dishevelled, stood Mr. Underhill. He looked small and pitiful, with his toes turned in as usual, and his little bowlegs in black tights, and no staff—he never had had one, Birt suddenly thought. Mr. Underhill spoke. "Who are you?" he said in his husky little voice.

"I am the Sealord of Pendor, thief, come to claim my treasure!"

At that, Mr. Underhill slowly turned pink, as he always did when people were rude to him. But he then turned something else. He turned yellow. His hair bristled out, he gave a coughing roar—and was a yellow lion leaping down the hill at Blackbeard, white fangs gleaming.

But Blackbeard no longer stood there. A gigantic tiger, color of night and lightning, bounded to meet the lion. . . .

The lion was gone. Below the cave all of a sudden stood a high grove of trees, black in the winter sunshine. The tiger, checking himself in mid-leap just before he entered the shadow of the trees, caught fire in the air, became a tongue of flame lashing out at the dry black branches. . . .

But where the trees had stood a sudden cataract leaped from the hillside, an arch of silvery crashing water, thundering down upon the fire. But the fire was gone. . . .

For just a moment before the fisherman's staring eyes two hills rose—the green one he knew, and a new one, a bare, brown hillock ready to drink up the rushing waterfall. That passed so quickly it made Birt blink, and after blinking he blinked again, and moaned, for what he saw now was a great deal worse. Where the cataract had been there hovered a dragon. Black wings darkened all the hill, steel claws reached groping, and from the dark, scaly, gaping lips fire and steam shot out.

Beneath the monstrous creature stood Blackbeard, laughing.

"Take any shape you please, little Mr. Underhill!" he taunted. "I can match you. But the game grows tiresome. I want to look upon my treasure, upon Inalkil. Now, big dragon, little wizard, take your true shape. I command you by the power of your true name—Yevaud!"

Birt could not move at all, not even to blink. He cowered, staring whether he would or not. He saw the black dragon hang there in the air above Blackbeard. He saw the fire lick like many tongues from the scaly mouth, the steam jet from the red nostrils. He saw Blackbeard's face grow white, white as chalk, and the beard-fringed lips trembling.

"Your name is Yevaud!"

"Yes," said a great, husky, hissing voice. "My truename is Yevaud, and my true shape is this shape."

"But the dragon was killed—they found dragon-bones on Udrath Island—"

"That was another dragon," said the dragon, and then stopped like a hawk, talons outstretched. And Birt shut his eyes.

When he opened them the sky was clear, the hillside empty, except for a reddish-blackish trampled spot, and a few talon-marks in the grass.

Birt the fisherman got to his feet and ran. He ran across the common, scattering sheep to right and left, and straight down the village street to Palani's father's house. Palani was out in the garden weeding the nasturtiums. "Come with me!" Birt gasped. She stared. He grabbed her wrist and dragged her with him. She screeched a little, but did not resist. He ran with her straight to the pier, pushed her into his fishing-sloop the *Queenie*, untied the painter, took up the oars and set off rowing like a demon. The last that Sattins Island saw of him and Palani was the *Queenie's* sail vanishing in the direction of the nearest island westward.

The villagers thought they would never stop talking about it, how Goody Guld's nephew Birt had lost his mind and sailed off with the schoolmistress on the very same day that the peddlar Blackbeard disappeared without a trace, leaving all his feathers and beads behind. But they did stop talking about it, three days later. They had other things to talk about, when Mr. Underhill finally came out of his cave.

Mr. Underhill had decided that since his truename was no longer a secret, he might as well drop his disguise. Walking was a lot harder than flying, and besides, it was a long, long time since he had had a real meal.

[1964]

For Thought

The fire breathing dragon with its gleaming treasure hoard is a stock figure in folk literature, as is the valiant young champion who slays the beast and wins a beautiful damsel along with untold wealth. However, with tongue-in-cheek, LeGuin takes these elements of legend and turns them into a light-hearted comic variation of the old heroic pattern. Also, in this kind of story involving a trick denouement, the author inserts early hints as to the real nature of the mysterious protagonist. In addition, LeGuin creates an atmosphere of magic to serve as a conditioning device to prepare the reader for the final outcome of events.

For Discussion

1. List some of the hints given as to the real nature of the mysterious protagonist and discuss what hidden evidence these hints point to.
2. What elements in the character of Mr. Underhill are stressed and what irony is inherent in his characterization?
3. What is the attitude of the townspeople toward Mr. Underhill? How is this attitude used as comic preparation?
4. How are the details of setting used to set up a light-hearted tone and comic mood?
5. What conflict is established with the arrival of Blackbeard? What is the inciting force, the crisis, and the resolution?
6. How is the atmosphere of "magic in the air" created?
7. How is Birt used in the resolution of the action? How does Birt's role in the resolution create irony?

Doris Lessing
The Nuisance

Two narrow tracks, one of them deepened to a smooth dusty groove by the incessant padding of bare feet, wound from the farm compound to the old well through half a mile of tall blond grass that was soiled and matted because of the nearness of the clustering huts: the compound had been on that ridge for twenty years.

The native women with their children used to loiter down the track, and their shrill laughter and chattering sounded through the trees as if one might suddenly have come on a flock of brilliant noisy parrots. It seemed as if fetching water was more of a social event to them than a chore. At the well itself they would linger half the morning, standing in groups to gossip, their arms raised in that graceful, eternally moving gesture to steady glittering or rusted petrol tins balanced on head-rings woven of grass; kneeling to slap bits of bright cloth on slabs of stone blasted long ago from the depths of earth. Here they washed and scolded and dandled their children. Here they scrubbed their pots. Here they sluiced themselves and combed their hair.

Coming upon them suddenly there would be sharp exclamations; a glimpse of soft brown shoulders and thighs withdrawing to the bushes, or annoyed and resentful eyes. It was their well. And while they were there, with their laughter, and gossip and singing, their folded draperies, bright armbands, earthenware jars and metal combs, grouped in attitudes of head-slowed indolence, it seemed as if the bellowing of distant cattle, drone of tractor, all the noises of the farm, were simply lending themselves to form a background to this antique scene: Women, drawing water at the well.

When they left the ground would be scattered with the bright-pink, fleshy skins of the native wild-plum which contracts the mouth shudderingly with its astringency, or with the shiny green fragments of the shells of kaffir oranges.

Without the women the place was ugly, paltry. The windlass, coiled with greasy rope, propped for safety with a forked stick, was sheltered by a tiny cock of thatch that threw across the track a long, intensely black shadow. For the rest, veld; the sere, flattened, sun-dried veld.

They were beautiful, these women. But she whom I thought of vaguely as "The cross-eyed one," offended the sight. She used to lag behind the others on the road, either by herself, or in charge of the older children. Not only did she suffer from a painful squint, so that when she looked towards you it was with a confused glare of white eyeball; but her body was hideous. She wore the traditional dark-patterned blue stuff looped at the waist, and above it her breasts were loose, flat crinkling triangles.

She was a solitary figure at the well, doing her washing unaided and without laughter. She would strain at the windlass during the long slow ascent of the swinging bucket that clanged sometimes, far below, against the sides of naked rock until at that critical moment when it hung vibrating at the mouth of the well, she would set the weight of her shoulder in the crook of the handle and with a fearful snatching movement bring the water to safety. It would slop over, dissolving in a shower of great drops that fell tinkling to disturb the surface of that tiny, circular, dully-gleaming mirror which lay at the bottom of the plunging rock tunnel. She was clumsy. Because of her eyes her body lumbered.

She was the oldest wife of "The Long One," who was our most skilful driver.

"The Long One" was not so tall as he was abnormally thin. It was the leanness of those driven by inner restlessness. He could never keep still. His hands plucked at pieces of grass, his shoulder twitched to a secret rhythm of the nerves. Set a-top of that sinewy, narrow, taut body was a narrow head, with wide-pointed ears, which gave him an appearance of alert caution. The expression of the face was always violent, whether he was angry, laughing, or—most usually—sardonically critical. He had a tongue that was feared by every labourer of the farm. Even my father would smile ruefully after an altercation with his driver and say: "He's a man, that native. One must respect him, after all. He never lets you get away with anything."

In his own line he was an artist—his line being cattle. He handled oxen with a delicate brutality that was fascinating and horrifying to watch. Give him a bunch of screaming, rearing three-year-olds, due to take their first taste of the yoke, and he would fight them for hours under a blistering sun with the sweat running off him, his eyes glowing with a wicked and sombre satisfaction. Then he would use his whip. grunting savagely as the lash cut down into flesh, his tongue stuck calculatingly between his teeth as he measured the exact weight of the blow. But to watch him handle a team of sixteen fat tamed oxen was a different thing. It was like watching a circus act; there was the same suspense in it: it was a matter of pride to him that he did not need to use the whip. This did not by any means imply that he wished to spare the beasts pain, not at all; he liked to feed his pride on his own skill. Alongside the double line of ponderous cattle that strained across acres of heavy clods, danced, raved and screamed the Long One, with his twelve-foot-long lash circling in black patterns over their backs; and though his threatening yells were the yells of an inspired madman, and the heavy whip could be heard clean across the farm, so that on a moonlight night when they were ploughing late it sounded like the crack and whine of a rifle, never did the dangerous metal-tipped lash so much as touch a hair of their hides. If you examined the oxen as they were outspanned, they might be exhausted, driven to staggering-point, so that my father had to remonstrate, but there was never a mark on them.

"He knows how to handle oxen, but he can't handle his women."

We gave our natives labels such as that, since it was impossible ever to know them as their fellows knew them, in the round. That phrase summarised for us what the Long One offered in entertainment during the years he was with us. Coming back to the farm, after an absence, one would say in humorous anticipation: "And what has the Long One been up to now, with his harem?"

There was always trouble with his three wives. He used to come up to the house to discuss with my father, man to man, how the youngest wife was flirting with the boss-boy from the neighbouring compound, six miles off; or how she had thrown a big pot of smoking mealie-pap at the middle wife, who was jealous of her.

We grew accustomed to the sight of the Long One standing at the back door, at the sunset hour, when my father held audience after work. He always wore long khaki trousers that slipped down over thin bony hips and went bare-chested, and there would be a ruddy gleam on his polished black skin, and his spindly gesticulating form would be outlined against a sea of fiery colours. At the end of his tale of complaint he would relapse suddenly into a pose of resignation that was self-consciously weary. My father used to laugh until his face was wet and say: "That man is a natural-born comedian. He would have been on the stage if he had been born another colour."

But he was no buffoon. He would play up to my father's appreciation of the comic, but he would never play the ape, as some Africans did, for our amusement. And he was certainly no figure of fun to his fellows. That same thing in him that sat apart, watchfully critical, even of himself, gave his humour its mordancy, his tongue its sting. And he was terribly attractive to his women. I have seen him slouch down the road on his way from one team to another, his whip trailing behind in the dust, his trousers sagging in folds from hip-bone to ankle, his eyes broodingly directed in front of him, merely nodding as he passed a group of women among whom might be his wives. And it was as if he had lashed them with that whip. They would bridle and writhe; and then call provocatively after him, but with a note of real anger, to make him notice them. He would not so much as turn his head.

When the real trouble started, though, my father soon got tired of it. He liked to be amused, not seriously implicated in his labourers' problems. The Long One took to coming up not occasionally, as he had been used to do, but every evening. He was deadly serious, and very bitter. He wanted my father to persuade the old wife, the cross-eyed one, to go back home to her own people. The woman was driving him crazy. A nagging woman in your house was like having a flea on your body; you could scratch but it always moved to another place, and there was no peace till you killed it.

"But you can't send her back, just because you are tired of her."

The Long One said his life had become insupportable. She grumbled, she sulked, she spoilt his food.

"Well, then your other wives can cook for you."

But it seemed there were complications. The two younger women hated each other, but they were united in one thing, that the old wife should stay, for she was so useful. She looked after the children; she did the hoeing in the garden; she picked relishes from the veld. Besides, she provided endless amusement with her ungainliness. She was the eternal butt, the fool, marked by fate for the entertainment of the whole-limbed and the comely.

My father referred at this point to a certain handbook on native lore, which stated definitively that an elder wife was entitled to be waited on by a young wife, perhaps as compensation for having to give up the pleasures of her lord's favour. The Long One and his ménage cut clean across the amiable theory. And my father, being unable to find a prescribed remedy (as one might look for a cure of a disease in a pharmacopoeia), grew angry. After some weeks of incessant complaint from the Long One he was told to hold his tongue and manage his women himself. That evening the man stalked furiously down the path, muttering to himself between teeth clenched on a grass-stem, on his way home to his two giggling younger wives and the ugly sour-faced old woman, the mother of his elder children, the drudge of his household and the scourge of his life.

It was some weeks later that my father asked casually one day: "And by the way, Long One, how are things with you? All right again?"

And the Long One answered simply: "Yes, baas. She's gone away."

"What do you mean, gone away?"

The Long One shrugged. She had just gone. She had left suddenly, without saying anything to anyone.

Now, the woman came from Nyasaland, which was days and days of weary walking away. Surely she hadn't gone by herself? Had a brother or an uncle come to fetch her? Had she gone with a band of passing Africans on their way home?

My father wondered a little, and then forgot about it. It wasn't his affair. He was pleased to have his most useful native back at work with an unharassed mind. And he was particularly pleased that the whole business was ended before the annual trouble over the water-carrying.

For there were two wells. The new one, used by ourselves, had fresh sparkling water that was sweet in the mouth; but in July of each year it ran dry. The water of the old well had a faintly unpleasant taste and was pale brown, but there was always plenty of it. For three or four months of the year, depending on the rains, we shared that well with the compound.

Now, the Long One hated fetching water three miles, four times a week, in the water-cart. The women of the compound disliked having to arrange their visits to the well so as not to get in the way of the water-carriers. There was always grumbling.

This year we had not even begun to use the old well when complaints started that the water tasted bad. The big baas must get the well cleaned.

My father said vaguely that he would clean the well when he had time.

Next day there came a deputation from the women of the compound. Half a dozen of them stood at the back door, arguing that if the well wasn't cleaned soon, all their children would be sick.

"I'll do it next week," he promised, with bad grace.

The following morning the Long One brought our first load of the season from the old well; and as we turned the taps on the barrels a foetid smell began to pervade the house. As for drinking it, that was out of the question.

"Why don't you keep the cover on the well?" my father said to the women, who were still loitering resentfully at the back door. He was really angry. "Last time the well was cleaned there were fourteen dead rats and a dead snake. We never get things in our well because we remember to keep the lid on."

But the women appeared to consider the lid being on, or off, was an act of God, and nothing to do with them.

We always went down to watch the well-emptying, which had the fascination of a ritual. Like a mealie-shelling, or the first rains, it marked a turning-point in the year. It seemed as if a besieged city were laying plans for the conservation of supplies. The sap was falling in tree and grass-root; the sun was withdrawing high, high, behind a veil of smoke and dust; the fierce dryness of the air was a new element, parching foliage as the heat cauterized it. The well-emptying was an act of faith, and of defiance. For a whole afternoon there would be no water on the farm at all. One well was completely dry. And this one would be drained, dependent on the mysterious ebbing and flowing of underground rivers. What if they should fail us? There was an anxious evening, every year; and in the morning, when the Long One stood at the back door and said, beaming, that the bucket was bringing up fine new water, it was like a festival.

But this afternoon we could not stick it out. The smell was intolerable. We saw the usual complement of bloated rats, laid out on the stones around the well, and there was even the skeleton of a small buck that must have fallen in the dark. Then we left, along the road that was temporarily a river whose source was that apparently endless succession of buckets filled by greyish, evil water.

It was the Long One himself that came to tell us the news. Afterwards we tried to remember what look that always expressive face wore as he told it.

It seemed that in the last bucket but one had floated a human arm, or rather the fragments of one. Piece by piece they had fetched her up, the Cross-eyed Woman, his own first wife. They recognised her by her bangles. Last of all, the Long One went down to fetch up her head, which was missing.

"I thought you said your wife had gone home?" said my father.

"I thought she had. Where else could she have gone?"

"Well," said my father at last, disgusted by the whole thing, "if she had to kill herself, why couldn't she hang herself on a tree, instead of spoiling the well?"

"She might have slipped and fallen," said the Long One.

My father looked up at him suddenly. He started for a few moments. Then: "Ye-yes," he said, "I suppose she might."

Later, we talked about the thing, saying how odd it was that natives should commit suicide; it seemed almost like an impertinence, as if they were claiming to have the same delicate feelings as ours.

But later still, apropos of nothing in particular, my father was heard to remark: "Well, I don't know, I'm damned if I know, but in any case he's a damned good driver."

[1951]

For Thought

Lessing's story focuses on marital disharmony. An African driver has become deeply irritated with his first wife, but can find no basis for sending her away. When she suddenly disappears, the water of a well is spoiled and the old wife's dismembered body is discovered. It is ironic that the life of a human being can be snuffed out with so little concern and reduced to no more than a nuisance.

For Discussion

1. What persona is adopted by the author in telling the story? How is this useful?
2. What is established about the Long One in the ox-training episode?
3. What two major conflicts are there in the story?
4. How are the two conflicts resolved?
5. What is the narrator's attitude toward the native women?
6. What is the narrator's attitude toward the Long One?
7. What is the tone of the story? How does it add to the effect?
8. Why are the gruesome details at the well elaborated upon?
9. Does the narrator have any insight?
10. What is the theme of the story?

Doris Lessing
One off the Short List

When he had first seen Barbara Coles, some years before, he only noticed her because someone said: "That's Johnson's new girl." He certainly had not used of her the private erotic formula: *Yes, that one*. He even wondered what Johnson saw in her. "She won't last long," he remembered thinking, as he watched Johnson, a handsome man, but rather flushed with drink, flirting with some unknown girl while Barbara stood by a wall looking on. He thought she had a sullen expression.

She was a pale girl, not slim, for her frame was generous, but her figure could pass as good. Her straight yellow hair was parted on one side in a way that struck him as gauche. He did not notice what she wore. But her eyes were all right, he remembered: large, and solidly green, square-looking because of some trick of the flesh at their corners. Emeraldlike eyes in the face of a schoolgirl, or young schoolmistress who was watching her lover flirt and would later sulk about it.

Her name sometimes cropped up in the papers. She was a stage decorator, a designer, something on those lines.

Then a Sunday newspaper had a competition for stage design and she won it. Barbara Coles was one of the "names" in the theatre, and her photograph was seen about. It was always serious. He remembered having thought her sullen.

One night he saw her across the room at a party. She was talking with a well-known actor. Her yellow hair was still done on one side, but now it looked sophisticated. She wore an emerald ring on her right hand that seemed deliberately to invite comparison with her eyes. He walked over and said: "We have met before, Graham Spence." He noted, with discomfort, that he sounded abrupt. "I'm sorry, I don't remember, but how do you do?" she said, smiling. And continued her conversation.

He hung around a bit, but soon she went off with a group of people she was inviting to her home for a drink. She did not invite Graham. There was about her an assurance, a carelessness, that he recognised as the signature of success. It was then, watching her laugh as she went off with her friends, that he used the formula: *"Yes, that one."* And he went home to his wife with enjoyable expectation, as if his date with Barbara Coles were already arranged.

His marriage was twenty years old. At first it had been stormy, painful, tragic—full of partings, betrayals, and sweet reconciliations. It had taken him at least a decade to realise that there was nothing remarkable about this marriage that he had lived through with such surprise of the mind and the senses. On the contrary, the marriages of most of the people he knew, whether they were first, second or third attempts, were just the same. His had run true to form even to the serious love affair with the young girl for whose sake he had *almost* divorced his wife—yet at the last moment had changed his mind, letting the girl down so that he must have her for always (not unpleasurably) on his conscience. It was with humiliation that he had understood that this drama was not at all the unique thing he had imagined. It was nothing more than the experience of everyone in his circle. And presumbly in everybody else's circle too?

Anyway, round about the tenth year of his marriage he had seen a good many things clearly, a certain kind of emotional adventure went from his life, and the marriage itself changed.

His wife had married a poor youth with a great future as a writer. Sacrifices had been made, chiefly by her, for that future. He was neither unaware of them, nor ungrateful; in fact he felt permanently guilty about it. He at last published a decently successful book, then a second which now, thank God, no one remembered. He had drifted into radio, television, book reviewing.

He understood he was not going to make it; that he had become—not a hack, no one could call him that—but a member of that army of people who live by their wits on the fringes of the arts. The moment of realisation was when he was in a pub one lunchtime near the B.B.C. where he often dropped in to meet others like himself: he understood that was why he went there—they *were* like him. Just as that melodramatic marriage had turned out to be like everyone else's—except that it had been shared with one woman instead of two or three—so it had turned out that his unique talent, his struggles as a writer had led him here, to this pub and the half dozen pubs like it, where all the men in sight had the same history. They all had their novel, their play, their book of poems, a moment of fame, to their credit. Yet here they were, running television programmes about which they were cynical (to each other or to their wives) or writing reviews about other people's books. Yes, that's what he had become, an impresario of other people's talent. These two moments of clarity, about his marriage and about his talent, had roughly coincided; and (perhaps not by chance) had coincided with his wife's decision to leave him for a man younger than himself who had a future, she said, as a playwright. Well, he had talked her out of it. For her part she had to understand he was not going to be the T. S. Eliot or Graham Greene of our time—but after all, how many were? She must finally understand this, for he could no longer bear her awful bitterness. For his part he must stop coming home drunk at five in the morning, and starting a new romantic affair every six months which he took so seriously that he made her miserable because of her implied deficiencies. In short he was to be a good husband. (He had always been a dutiful father.) And she was a good wife. And so it was; the marriage became stable, as they say.

The formula: *Yes, that one* no longer implied a necessarily sexual relationship. In its more mature form, it was far from being something he was ashamed of. On the contrary, it expressed a humorous respect for what he was, for his real talents and flair, which had turned out to be not artistic after all, but to do with emotional life, hard-earned experience. It expressed an ironical dignity, a proving to himself not only: I can be honest about myself, but also: I have earned the best in *that* field whenever I want it.

He watched the field for the women who were well known in the arts, or in politics; looked out for photographs, listened for bits of gossip. He made a point of going to see them act, or dance, or orate. He built up a not unshrewd picture of them. He would either quietly pull strings to meet her or—more often, for there was a gambler's pleasure in waiting—bide his time until he met her in the natural course of events, which was bound to happen sooner or later. He would be seen out with her a few times in public, which was in order, since his work meant he had to entertain well-known people, male and female. His wife always knew, he told her. He might have a brief affair with this woman, but more often than not it was the appearance of an affair. Not that he didn't get pleasure from other people envying him—he would make a point, for instance, of taking this woman into the pubs where his male colleagues went. It was that his real pleasure came when he saw her surprise at how well she was understood by him. He enjoyed the atmosphere he was able to set up between an intelligent woman and himself: a humorous complicity which had in it much that was unspoken, and which almost made sex irrelevant.

Onto the list of women with whom he planned to have this relationship went Barbara Coles. There was no hurry. Next week, next month, next year, they would meet at a party. The world of well-known people in London is a small one. Big and little fishes, they drift around, nose each other, flirt their fins, wriggle off again. When he bumped into Barbara Coles, it would be time to decide whether or not to sleep with her.

Meanwhile he listened. But he didn't discover much. She had a husband and children, but the husband seemed to be in the background. The children were charming and well brought up, like everyone else's children. She had affairs, they said; but while several men he met sounded familiar with her, it was hard to determine whether they had slept with her, because none directly boasted of her. She was spoken of in terms of her friends, her work, her house, a party she had given, a job she had found someone. She was liked, she was respected, and Graham Spence's self-esteem was flattered because he had chosen her. He looked forward to saying in just the same tone: "Barbara Coles asked me what I thought about the set and I told her quite frankly. . . ."

Then by chance he met a young man who did boast about Barbara Coles; he claimed to have had the great love affair with her, and recently at that; and he spoke of it as something generally known. Graham realised how much he had already become involved with her in his imagination because of how perturbed he was now on account of the character of this youth, Jack Kennaway. He had recently become successful as a magazine editor—one of those young men who, not as rare as one might suppose in the big cities, are successful from sheer impertinence, effrontery. Without much talent or taste, yet he had the charm of his effrontery. "Yes, I'm going to succeed, because I've decided to; yes, I may be stupid, but not so stupid that I don't know my deficiencies. Yes, I'm going to be successful because you people with integrity, etc., etc., simply don't believe in the possibility of people like me. You are too cowardly to stop me. Yes, I've taken your measure and I'm going to succeed because I've got the courage, not only to be unscrupulous, but to be quite frank about it. And besides, you admire me, you must, or otherwise you'd stop me. . . ." Well, that was young Jack Kennaway, and he shocked Graham. He was a tall, languishing young man, handsome in a dark melting way, and, it was quite clear, he was either asexual or homosexual. And this youth boasted of the favours of Barbara Coles; boasted, indeed, of her love. Either she was a raving neurotic with a taste for neurotics; or Jack Kennaway was a most accomplished liar; or she slept with anyone. Graham was intrigued. He took Jack Kennaway out to dinner in order to hear him talk about Barbara Coles. There was no doubt the two were pretty close—all those dinners, theatres, weekends in the country—Graham Spence felt he had put his finger on the secret pulse of Barbara Coles; and it was intolerable that he must wait to meet her; he decided to arrange it.

It became unnecessary. She was in the news again, with a run of luck. She had done a successful historical play, and immediately afterwards a modern play, and then a hit musical. In all three, the sets were remarked on. Graham saw some interviews in newspapers and on television. These all centered around the theme of her being able to deal easily with so many different styles of theatre; but the real point was, of course, that she was a woman, which naturally added piquancy to the thing. And now Graham Spence was asked to do a half-hour radio interview with her. He planned the questions he would ask her with care, drawing on what people had said of her, but above all on his instinct and experience with women. The interview was to be at nine-thirty at night; he was to pick her up at six from the theatre where she was currently at work, so that there would be time, as the letter from the B.B.C. had put it, "for you and Miss Coles to get to know each other."

At six he was at the stage door, but a message from Miss Coles said she was not quite ready, could he wait a little. He hung about, then went to the pub opposite for a quick one, but still no Miss Coles. So he made his way backstage, directed by voices, hammering, laughter. It was badly lit, and the group of people at work did not see him. The director, James Poynter, had his arm around Barbara's shoulders. He was newly well-known, a carelessly good-looking young man reputed to be intelligent. Barbara Coles wore a dark blue overall, and her flat hair fell over her face so that she kept pushing it back with the hand that had the emerald on it. These two stood close, side by side. Three young men, stagehands, were on the other side of a trestle which had sketches and drawings on it. They were studying some sketches. Barbara said, in a voice warm with energy: "Well, so I thought if we did *this*—do you see, James? What do you think, Steven?" "Well, love," said the young man she called Steven, "I see your idea, but I wonder if . . ." "I think you're right, Babs," said the director. "Look," said Barbara, holding one of the sketches towards Steven, "look, let me show you." They all leaned forward, the five of them, absorbed in the business.

Suddenly Graham couldn't stand it. He understood he was shaken to his depths. He went off stage, and stood with his back against a wall in the dingy passage that led to the dressing rooms. His eyes were filled with tears. He was seeing what a long way he had come from the crude, uncompromising, admirable young egomaniac he had been when he was twenty. That group of people there—working, joking, arguing, yes, that's what he hadn't known for years. What bound them was the democracy of respect for each other's work, a confidence in themselves and in each other. They looked like people banded together against a world which they—no, not despised, but which they measured, understood, would fight to the death, out of respect for what *they* stood for, for what *it* stood for. It was a long time since he felt part of that balance. And he understood that he had seen Barbara Coles when she was most herself, at ease with a group of people she worked with. It was then, with the tears drying on his eyelids, which felt old and ironic, that he decided he would sleep with Barbara Coles. It was a necessity for him. He went back through the door onto the stage, burning with this single determination.

The five were still together. Barbara had a length of blue gleaming stuff which she was draping over the shoulder of Steven, the stagehand. He was showing it off, and the others watched. "What do you think, James?" she asked the director. "We've got that sort of dirty green, and I thought . . ." "Well," said James, not sure at all, "well, Babs, well . . ."

Now Graham went forward so that he stood beside Barbara, and said: "I'm Graham Spence, we've met before." For the second time she smiled socially and said: "Oh I'm sorry, I don't remember." Graham nodded at James, whom he had known, or at least had met off and on, for years. But it was obvious James didn't remember him either.

"From the B.B.C.," said Graham to Barbara again sounding abrupt, against his will. "Oh I'm sorry, I'm so sorry, I forgot all about it. I've got to be interviewed," she said to the group. "Mr. Spence is a journalist." Graham allowed himself a small smile ironical of the word journalist, but she was not looking at him. She was going on with her work. "We should decide tonight," she said. "Steven's right." "Yes, I am right," said the stagehand. "She's right, James, we need that blue with that sludge-green everywhere." "James," said Barbara, "James, what's wrong with it? You haven't said." She moved forward to James, passing Graham. Remembering him again, she became contrite. "I'm sorry," she said "we can none of us agree. Well, look"—she turned to Graham—"you advise us, we've got so involved with it that . . ." At which James laughed, and so did the stagehands. "No, Babs," said James, "of course Mr. Spence can't advise. He's just this moment come in. We've got to decide. Well I'll give you till tomorrow morning. Time to go home, it must be six by now."

"It's nearly seven," said Graham, taking command.

"It isn't!" said Barbara, dramatic. "My God, how terrible, how appalling, how could I have done such a thing. . . ." She was laughing at herself. "Well, you'll have to forgive me, Mr. Spence, because you haven't got any alternative."

They began laughing again: this was clearly a group joke. And now Graham took his chance. He said firmly, as if he were her director, in fact copying James Poynter's manner with her: "No, Miss Coles, I won't forgive you, I've been kicking my heels for nearly an hour." She grimaced, then laughed and accepted it. James said: "There, Babs, that's how you ought to be treated. We spoil you." He kissed her on the cheek, she kissed him on both his, the stagehands moved off. "Have a good evening, Babs," said James, going, and nodding to Graham, who stood concealing his pleasure with difficulty. He knew, because he had had the courage to be firm, indeed, peremptory, with Barbara, that he had saved himself hours of maneuvering. Several drinks, a dinner—perhaps two or three evenings of drinks and dinners—had been saved because he was now on this footing with Barbara Coles, a man who could say: "No, I won't forgive you, you've kept me waiting."

She said: "I've just got to . . ." and went ahead of him. In the passage she hung her overall on a peg. She was thinking, it seemed, of something else, but seeing him watching her, she smiled at him, companionably: he realised with triumph it was the sort of smile she would offer one of the stagehands, or even James. She said again: "Just one second . . ." and went to the stage-door office. She and the stage doorman conferred. There was some problem. Graham said, taking another chance: "What's the trouble, can I help?"—as if he could help, as if he expected to be able to. "Well . . ." she said, frowning. Then, to the man: "No, it'll be all right. Good night." She came to Graham. "We've got ourselves into a bit of a fuss because half the set's in Liverpool and half's here and—but it will sort itself out." She stood, at ease, chatting to him, one colleague to another. All this was admirable, he felt; but there would be a bad moment when they emerged from the special atmosphere of the theatre into the street. He took another decision, grasped her arm firmly, and said: "We're going to have a drink before we do anything at all, it's a terrible evening out." Her arm felt resistant, but remained within his. It was raining outside, luckily. He directed her, authoritative: "No, not that pub, there's a nicer one around the corner." "Oh, but I like this pub," said Barbara, "we always use it."

"Of course you do," he said to himself. But in that pub there would be the stagehands, and probably James, and he'd lose contact with her. He'd become a *journalist* again. He took her firmly out of danger around two corners, into a pub he picked at random. A quick look around—no, they weren't there. At least, if there were people from the theatre, she showed no sign. She asked for a beer. He ordered her a double Scotch, which she accepted. Then, having won a dozen preliminary rounds already, he took time to think. Something was bothering him—what? Yes, it was what he had observed backstage, Barbara and James Poynter. Was she having an affair with him? Because if so, it would all be much more difficult. He made himself see the two of them together, and thought with a jealousy surprisingly strong: *Yes, that's it.* Meantime he sat looking at her, seeing himself look at her, *a man gazing in calm appreciation at a woman:* waiting for her to feel it and respond. She was examining the pub. Her white woolen suit was belted, and had a not unprovocative suggestion of being a uniform. Her flat yellow hair, hastily pushed back after work, was untidy. Her clear white skin, without any colour, made her look tired. Not very exciting, at the moment, thought Graham, but maintaining his appreciative pose for when she would turn and see it. He knew what she would see: he was relying not only on the "warm kindly" beam of his gaze, for this was merely a reinforcement of the impression he knew he made. He had black hair, a little greyed. His clothes were loose and bulky—masculine. His eyes were humorous and appreciative. He was not, never had been, concerned to lessen the impression of being settled, dependable: the husband and father. On the contrary, he knew women found it reassuring.

When she at last turned she said, almost apologetic: "Would you mind if we sat down? I've been lugging great things around all day." She had spotted two empty chairs in a corner. So had he, but he rejected them, because there were other people at the table. "But my dear, of course!" They took the chairs, and then Barbara said: "If you'll excuse me a moment." She had remembered she needed makeup. He watched her go off, annoyed with himself. She was tired; and he could have understood, protected, sheltered. He realised that in the other pub, with the people she had worked with all day, she would not have thought: "I must make myself up, I must be on show." That was for outsiders. She had not, until now, considered Graham an outsider, because of his taking his chance to seem one of the working group in the theatre; but now he had thrown this opportunity away. She returned armoured. Her hair was sleek, no longer defenceless. And she had made up her eyes. Her eyebrows were untouched, pale gold streaks above the brilliant green eyes whose lashes were blackened. Rather good, he thought, the contrast. Yes, but the moment had gone when he could say: Did you know you had a smudge on your cheek? Or—my dear girl!—pushing her hair back with the edge of a brotherly hand. In fact, unless he was careful, he'd be back at starting point.

He remarked: "That emerald is very cunning"—smiling into her eyes.

She smiled politely, and said: "It's not cunning, it's an accident, it was my grandmother's." She flirted her hand lightly by her face, though, smiling. But that was something she had done before, to a compliment she had had before, and often. It was all social, she had become social entirely. She remarked: "Didn't you say it was half past nine we had to record?"

"My dear Barbara, we've got two hours. We'll have another drink or two, then I'll ask you a couple of questions, then we'll drop down to the studio and get it over, and then we'll have a comfortable supper."

"I'd rather eat now, if you don't mind. I had no lunch, and I'm really hungry."

"But my dear, of course." He was angry. Just as he had been surprised by his real jealousy over James, so now he was thrown off balance by his anger: he had been counting on the long quiet dinner afterwards to establish intimacy. "Finish your drink and I'll take you to Nott's." Nott's was expensive. He glanced at her assessingly as he mentioned it. She said: "I wonder if you know Butler's? It's good and it's rather close." Butler's was good, and it was cheap, and he gave her a good mark for liking it. But Nott's it was going to be. "My dear, we'll get into a taxi and be at Nott's in a moment, don't worry."

She obediently got to her feet: the way she did it made him understand how badly he had slipped. She was saying to herself: Very well, he's like that, then all right, I'll do what he wants and get it over with. . . .

Swallowing his own drink he followed her, and took her arm in the pub doorway. It was polite within his. Outside it drizzled. No taxi. He was having bad luck now. They walked in silence to the end of the street. There Barbara glanced into a side street where a sign said: BUTLER's. Not to remind him of it, on the contrary, she concealed the glance. And here she was, entirely at his disposal, they might never have shared the comradely moment in the theatre.

They walked half a mile to Nott's. No taxis. She made conversation: this was, he saw, to cover any embarrassment he might feel because of a half-mile walk through rain when she was tired. She was talking about some theory to do with the theatre, with designs for theatre building. He heard himself saying, and repeatedly: Yes, yes, yes. He thought about Nott's, how to get things right when they reached Nott's. There he took the headwaiter aside, gave him a pound, and instructions. They were put in a corner. Large Scotches appeared. The menus were spread. "And now, my dear," he said, "I apologise for dragging you here, but I hope you'll think it's worth it."

"Oh, it's charming, I've always liked it. It's just that . . ." She stopped herself saying: it's such a long way. She smiled at him, raising her glass, and said: "It's one of my very favourite places, and I'm glad you dragged me here." Her voice was flat with tiredness. All this was appalling; he knew it; and he sat thinking how to retrieve his position. Meanwhile she fingered the menu. The headwaiter took the order, but Graham made a gesture which said: Wait a moment. He wanted the Scotch to take effect before she ate. But she saw his silent order; and, without annoyance or reproach, leaned forward to say, sounding patient: "Graham, please, I've got to eat, you don't want me drunk when you interview me, do you?"

"They are bringing it as fast as they can," he said, making it sound as if she were greedy. He looked neither at the headwaiter nor at Barbara. He noted in himself, as he slipped further and further away from contact with her, a cold determination growing in him; one apart from, apparently, any conscious act of will, that come what may, if it took all night, he'd be in her bed before morning. And now, seeing the small pale face with the enormous green eyes, it was for the first time that he imagined her in his arms. Although he had said: *Yes, that one*, weeks ago, it was only now that he imagined her as a sensual experience. Now he did, so strongly that he could only glance at her, and then away towards the waiters who were bringing food.

"Thank the Lord," said Barbara, and all at once her voice was gay and intimate. "Thank heavens. Thank every power that is. . . ." She was making fun of her own exaggeration; and, as he saw, because she wanted to put him at ease after his boorishness over delaying the food. (She hadn't been taken in, he saw, humiliated, disliking her.) "Thank all the gods of Nott's," she went on, "because if I hadn't eaten inside five minutes I'd have died, I tell you." With which she picked up her knife and fork and began on her steak. He poured wine, smiling with her, thinking that *this* moment of closeness he would not throw away. He watched her frank hunger as she ate, and thought: Sensual—it's strange I hadn't wondered whether she would be or not.

"Now," she said, sitting back, having taken the edge off her hunger: "Let's get to work."

He said: "I've thought it over carefully—how to present you. The first thing seems to me, we must get away from that old chestnut: Miss Coles, how extraordinary for a woman to be so versatile in her work . . . I hope you agree?" This was trump card. He had noted, when he had seen her on television, her polite smile when this note was struck. (The smile he had seen so often tonight.) This smile said: All right, if you *have* to be stupid, what can I do?

Now she laughed and said: "What a relief. I was afraid you were going to do the same thing."

"Good, now you eat and I'll talk."

In his carefully prepared monologue he spoke of the different styles of theatre she had shown herself mistress of, but not directly: he was flattering her on the breadth of her experience; the complexity of her character, as shown in her work. She ate, steadily, her face showing nothing. At last she asked: "And how did you plan to introduce this?"

He had meant to spring that on her as a surprise, something like: Miss Coles, a surprisingly young woman for what she has accomplished (she was thirty? thirty-two?) and a very attractive one. . . . "Perhaps I can give you an idea of what she's like if I say she could be taken for the film star Marie Carletta. . . ." The Carletta was a strong earthy blonde, known to be intellectual. He now saw he could not possibly say this : he could imagine her cool look if he did. She said: "Do you mind if we get away from all that—my manifold talents, et cetera. . . ." He felt himself stiffen with annoyance: particularly because this was not an accusation, he saw she did not think him worth one. She had assessed him: This is the kind of man who uses this kind of flattery and therefore. . . . It made him angrier that she did not even trouble to say: Why did you do exactly what you promised you wouldn't? She was being invincibly polite, trying to conceal her patience with his stupidity.

"After all," she was saying, "it is a stage designer's job to design what comes up. Would anyone take, let's say Johnnie Cranmore (another stage designer) onto the air or television and say: How very versatile you are because you did that musical about Java last month and a modern play about Irish labourers this?"

He battened down his anger. "My dear Barbara, I'm sorry. I didn't realise that what I said would sound just like the mixture as before. So what shall we talk about?"

"What I was saying as we walked to the restaurant: can we get away from the personal stuff?"

Now he almost panicked. Then, thank God, he laughed from nervousness, for she laughed and said: "You didn't hear one word I said."

"No, I didn't. I was frightened you were going to be furious because I made you walk so far when you were tired."

They laughed together, back to where they had been in the theatre. He leaned over, took her hand, kissed it. He said: "Tell me again." He thought: Damn, now she's going to be earnest and intellectual.

But he understood he had been stupid. He had forgotten himself at twenty—or, for that matter, at thirty; forgotten one could live inside an idea, a set of ideas, with enthusiasm. For in talking about her ideas (also the ideas of the people she worked with) for a new theatre, a new style of theatre, she was as she had been with her colleagues over the sketches or the blue material. She was easy, informal, almost chattering. This was how, he remembered, one talked about ideas that were a breath of life. The ideas, he thought, were intelligent enough; and he would agree with them, with her, if he believed it mattered a damn one way or another, if any of these enthusiasms mattered a damn. But at least he now had the key, he knew what to do. At the end of not more than half an hour, they were again two professionals, talking about ideas they shared, for he remembered caring about all this himself once. *When? How many years ago was it that he had been able to care?*

At last he said: "My dear Barbara, do you realise the impossible position you're putting me in? Margaret Ruyen who runs this programme is determined to do you personally, the poor woman hasn't got a serious thought in her head."

Barbara frowned. He put his hand on hers, teasing her for the frown: "No, wait, trust me, we'll circumvent her." She smiled. In fact Margaret Ruyen had left it all to him, had said nothing about Miss Coles.

"They aren't very bright—the brass," he said. "Well, never mind: we'll work out what we want, do it, and it'll be a *fait accompli.*"

"Thank you, what a relief. How lucky I was to be given you to interview me." She was relaxed now, because of the whisky, the food, the wine, above all because of this new complicity against Margaret Ruyen. It would all be easy. They worked out five or six questions, over coffee, and took a taxi through rain to the studios. He noted that the cold necessity to have her, to make her, to beat her down, had left him. He was even seeing himself, as the evening ended, kissing her on the cheek and going home to his wife. This comradeship was extraordinarily pleasant. It was balm to the wound he had not known he carried until that evening, when he had had to accept the justice of the word *journalist*. He felt he could talk forever about the state of the theatre, its finances, the stupidity of the government, the philistinism of . . .

At the studios he was careful to make a joke so that they walked in on the laugh. He was careful that the interview began at once, without conversation with Margaret Ruyen; and that from the moment the green light went on, his voice lost its easy familiarity. He made sure that not one personal note was struck during the interview. Afterwards, Margaret Ruyen, who was pleased, came forward to say so; but he took her aside to say that Miss Coles was tired and needed to be taken home at once; for he knew this must look to Barbara as if he were squaring a producer who had been expecting a different interview. He led Barbara off, her hand held tight in his against his side. "Well," he said, "we've done it, and I don't think she knows what hit her."

"Thank you," she said, "it really was pleasant to talk about something sensible for once."

He kissed her lightly on the mouth. She returned it, smiling. By now he felt sure that the mood need not slip again, he could hold it.

"There are two things we can do," he said. "You can come to my club and have a drink. Or I can drive you home and you can give me a drink. I have to go past you."

"Where do you live?"

"Wimbledon." He lived, in fact, at Highgate; but she lived in Fulham. He was taking another chance, but by the time she found out, they would be in a position to laugh over his ruse.

"Good," she said, "You can drop me home then. I have to get up early." He made no comment. In the taxi he took her hand; it was heavy in his, and he asked: "Does James slave-drive you?"

"I didn't realize you knew him—no, he doesn't."

"Well I don't know him intimately. What's he like to work with?"

"Wonderful," she said at once. "There's no one I enjoy working with more."

Jealousy spurted in him. He could not help himself: "Are you having an affair with him?"

She looked: what's it to do with you? but said: "No, I'm not."

"He's very attractive," he said with a chuckle of wordly complicity. She said nothing, and he insisted: "If I were a woman I'd have an affair with James."

It seemed she might very well say nothing. But she remarked: "He's married."

His spirits rose in a swoop. It was the first stupid remark she had made. It was a remark of such staggering stupidity that . . . he let out a humoring snort of laughter, put his arm around her, kissed her, said: "My dear little Babs."

She said: "Why Babs?"

"Is that the prerogative of James. And of the stagehands?" he could not prevent himself adding.

"I'm only called that at work." She was stiff inside his arm.

"My dear Barbara, then . . ." He waited for her to enlighten and explain, but she said nothing. Soon she moved out of his arm, on the pretext of lighting a cigarette. He lit it for her. He noted that his determination to lay her, and at all costs, had come back. They were outside her house. He said quickly: "And now, Barbara, you can make me a cup of coffee and give me a brandy." She hesitated; but he was out of the taxi, paying, opening the door for her. The house had no lights on, he noted. He said: "We'll be very quiet as not to wake the children."

She turned her head slowly to look at him. She said, flat, replying to his real question: "My husband is away. As for the children, they are visiting friends tonight." She now went ahead of him to the door of the house. It was a small house, in a terrace of small and not very pretty houses. Inside a little, bright, intimate hall, she said: "I'll go and make some coffee. Then, my friend, you must go home because I'm very tired."

The *my friend* struck him deep, because he had become vulnerable during their comradeship. He said, gabbling: "You're annoyed with me—oh, please don't, I'm sorry."

She smiled, from a cool distance. He saw, in the small light from the ceiling, her extraordinary eyes. "Green" eyes are hazel, are brown with green flecks, are even blue. Eyes are chequered, flawed, changing. Hers were solid green, but really, he had never seen anything like them before. They were like very deep water. They were like—well, emeralds; or the absolute clarity of green in the depths of a tree in summer. And now, as she smiled almost perpendicularly up at him, he saw a darkness come over them. Darkness swallowed the clear green. She said: "I'm not in the least annoyed." It was as if she had yawned with boredom. "And now I'll get the things . . . in there." She nodded at a white door and left him. He went into a long, very tidy white room, that had a narrow bed in one corner, a table covered with drawings, sketches, pencils. Tacked to the walls with drawing pins were swatches of coloured stuffs. Two small chairs stood near a low round table: an area of comfort in the working room. He was thinking: I wouldn't like it if my wife had a room like this. I wonder what Barbara's husband . . .? He had not thought of her till now in relation to her husband, or to her children. Hard to imagine her with a frying pan in her hand, or for that matter, cosy in the double bed.

A noise outside: he hastily arranged himself, leaning with one arm on the mantelpiece. She came in with a small tray that had cups, glasses, brandy, coffeepot. She looked abstracted. Graham was on the whole flattered by this: it probably meant she was at ease in his presence. He realised he was a little tight and rather tired. Of course, she was tired too, that was why she was vague. He remembered that earlier that evening he had lost a chance by not using her tiredness. Well now, if he were intelligent . . . She was about to pour coffee. He firmly took the coffeepot out of her hand, and nodded at a chair. Smiling, she obeyed him. "That's better," he said. He poured coffee, poured brandy, and pulled the table towards her. She watched him. Then he took her hand, kissed it, patted it, laid it down gently. Yes, he thought, I did that well.

Now, a problem. He wanted to be closer to her, but she was fitted into a damned silly little chair that had arms. If he were to sit by her on the floor . . . ? But no, for him, the big bulky reassuring man, there could be no casual gestures, no informal postures. Suppose I scoop her out of the chair onto the bed? He drank his coffee as he plotted. Yes, he'd carry her to the bed, but not yet.

"Graham," she said, setting down her cup. She was, he saw with annoyance, looking tolerant. "Graham, in about half an hour I want to be in bed and asleep."

As she said this, she offered him a smile of amusement at this situation—man and woman maneuvering, the great comic situation. And with part of himself he could have shared it. Almost, he smiled with her, laughed. (Not till days later he exclaimed to himself: Lord what a mistake I made, not to share the joke with her then: that was where I went seriously wrong.) But he could not smile. His face was frozen, with a stiff pride. Not because she had been watching him plot; the amusement she now offered him took the sting out of that; but because of his revived determination that he was going to have his own way, he was going to have her. He was not going home. But he felt that he held a bunch of keys, and did not know which one to choose.

He lifted the second small chair opposite to Barbara, moving aside the coffee table for this purpose. He sat in this chair, leaned forward, took her two hands, and said: "My dear, don't make me go home yet, don't, I beg you." The trouble was, nothing had happened all evening that could be felt to lead up to these words and his tone—simple, dignified, human being pleading with human being for surcease. He saw himself leaning forward, his big hands swallowing her small ones; he saw his face, warm with the appeal. And he realised he had meant the words he used. They were nothing more than what he felt. He wanted to stay with her because she wanted him to, because he was her colleague, a fellow worker in the arts. He needed this desperately. But she was examining him, curious rather than surprised, and from a critical distance. He heard himself saying: "If James were here, I wonder what you'd do?" His voice was aggrieved; he saw the sudden dark descent over her eyes, and she said: "Graham, would you like some more coffee before you go?"

He said: "I've been wanting to meet you for years. I know a good many people who know you."

She leaned forward, poured herself a little more brandy, sat back, holding the glass between her two palms on her chest. An odd gesture: Graham felt that this vessel she was cherishing between her hands was herself. A patient, long-suffering gesture. He thought of various men who had mentioned her. He thought of Jack Kennaway, wavered, panicked, said: "For instance, Jack Kennaway."

And now, at the name, an emotion lit her eyes—what was it? He went on deliberately testing this emotion, adding to it: "I had dinner with him last week—oh, quite by chance!—and he was talking about you."

"Was he?"

He remembered he had thought her sullen, all those years ago. Now she seemed defensive, and she frowned. He said: "In fact he spent most of the evening talking about you."

She said in short, breathless sentences, which he realised were due to anger: "I can very well imagine what he says. But surely you can't think I enjoy being reminded that . . ." She broke off, resenting him, he saw, because he forced her down onto a level she despised. But it was not his level either: it was all her fault, all hers! He couldn't remember not being in control of a situation with a woman for years. Again he felt like a man teetering on a tightrope. He said, trying to make good use of Jack Kennaway, even at this late hour: "Of course, he's a charming boy, but not a man at all."

She looked at him, silent, guarding her brandy glass against her breasts.

"Unless appearances are totally deceptive, of course." He could not resist probing, even though he knew it was fatal.

She said nothing.

"Do you know you are supposed to have had the great affair with Jack Kennaway?" he exclaimed, making this an amused expostulation against the fools who could believe it.

"So I am told." She set down her glass. "And now," she said, standing up, dismissing him. He lost his head, took a step forward, grabbed her in his arms, and groaned: "Barbara!"

She turned her face this way and that under his kisses. He snatched a diagnostic look at her expression—it was still patient. He placed his lips against her neck, groaned "Barbara" again, and waited. She would have to do something. Fight free, respond, something. She did nothing at all. At last she said: "For the Lord's sake, Graham!" She sounded amused: he was again being offered amusement. But if he shared it with her, it would be the end of this chance to have her. He clamped his mouth over hers, silencing her. She did not fight him off so much as blow him off. Her mouth treated his attacking mouth as a woman blows and laughs in water, puffing off waves or spray with a laugh, turning aside her head. It was a gesture half annoyance, half humour. He continued to kiss her while she moved her head and face about under the kisses as if they were small attacking waves.

And so began what, when he looked back on it afterwards, was the most embarrassing experience of his life. Even at the time he hated her for his ineptitude. For he held her there for what must have been nearly half an hour. She was much shorter than he, he had to bend, and his neck ached. He held her rigid, his thighs on either side of hers, her arms clamped to her side in a bear's hug. She was unable to move, except for her head. When his mouth ground hers open and his tongue moved and writhed inside it, she still remained passive. And he could not stop himself. While with his intelligence he watched this ridiculous scene, he was determined to go on, because sooner or later her body must soften in wanting his. And he could not stop because he could not face the horror of the moment when he set her free and she looked at him. And he hated her more, every moment. Catching glimpses of her great green eyes, open and dismal beneath his, he knew he had never disliked anything more than those "jeweled" eyes. They were repulsive to him. It occurred to him at last that even if by now she wanted him, he wouldn't know it, because she was not able to move at all. He cautiously loosened his hold so that she had an inch or so leeway. She remained quite passive. As if, he thought derisively, she had read or been told that the way to incite men maddened by lust was to fight them. He found he was thinking: Stupid cow, so you imagine I find you attractive, do you? You've got the conceit to think that!

The sheer, raving insanity of this thought hit him, opened his arms, his thighs, and lifted his tongue out of her mouth. She stepped back, wiping her mouth with the back of her hand, and stood dazed with incredulity. The embarrassment that lay in wait for him nearly engulfed him, but he let anger postpone it. She said positively apologetic, even, at this moment, humorous: "You're crazy, Graham. What's the matter, are you drunk? You don't seem drunk. You don't even find me attractive."

The blood of hatred went to his head and he gripped her again. Now she had got her face firmly twisted away so that he could not reach her mouth, and she repeated steadily as he kissed the parts of her cheeks and neck that were available to him: "Graham, let me go, do let me go, Graham." She went on saying this; he went on squeezing, grinding, kissing and licking. It might go on all night: it was a sheer contest of wills, nothing else. He thought: It's only a really masculine woman who wouldn't have given in by now out of sheer decency of the flesh! One thing he knew, however: that she would be in that bed, in his arms, and very soon. He let her go, but said: "I'm going to sleep with you tonight, you know that, don't you?"

She leaned with hand on the mantelpiece to steady herself. Her face was colourless, since he had licked all the makeup off. She seemed quite different: small and defenceless with her large mouth pale now, her smudged green eyes fringed with gold. And now, for the first time, he felt what it might have been supposed (certainly by her) he felt hours ago. Seeing the small damp flesh of her face, he felt kinship, intimacy with her, he felt intimacy of the flesh, the affection and good humour of sensuality. He felt she was flesh of his flesh, his sister in the flesh. He felt desire for her, instead of the will to have her; and because of this, was ashamed of the farce he had been playing. Now he desired simply to take her into bed in the affection of his senses.

She said: "What on earth am I supposed to do? Telephone for the police, or what?" He was hurt that she still addressed the man who had ground her into sulky apathy; she was not addressing *him* at all.

She said: "Or scream for the neighbours, is that what you want?"

The gold-fringed eyes were almost black, because of the depth of the shadow of boredom over them. She was bored and weary to the point of falling to the floor, he could see that.

He said: "'I'm going to sleep with you."

"But how can you possibly want to?"—a reasonable, a civilised demand addressed to a man who (he could see) she believed would respond to it. She said: "You know I don't want to, and I know you don't really give a damn one way or the other."

He was stung back into being the boor because she had not the intelligence to see that the boor no longer existed; because she could not see that this was a man who wanted her in a way which she must respond to.

There she stood, supporting herself with one hand, looking small and white and exhausted, and utterly incredulous. She was going to turn and walk off out of simple incredulity, he could see that. "Do you think I don't mean it?" he demanded, grinding this out between his teeth. She made a movement—she was on the point of going away. His hand shot out on its own volition and grasped her wrist. She frowned. His other hand grasped her other wrist. His body hove up against hers to start the pressure of a new embrace. Before it could, she said: "Oh Lord, no, I'm not going through all that again. Right, then."

"What do you mean—right, then?" he demanded.

She said: "You're going to sleep with me. O.K. Anything rather than go through that again. Shall we get it over with?"

He grinned, saying in silence: "No darling, oh no you don't, I don't care what words you use, I'm going to have you now and that's all there is to it."

She shrugged. The contempt, the weariness of it, had no effect on him, because he was now again hating her so much that wanting her was like needing to kill something or someone.

She took her clothes off, as if she were going to bed by herself: her jacket, skirt, petticoat. She stood in white bra and panties, a rather solid girl, brown-skinned still from the summer. He felt a flash of affection for the brown girl with her loose yellow hair as she stood naked. She got into bed and lay there, while the green eyes looked at him in civilised appeal: Are you really going through with this? Do you have to? Yes, his eyes said back: I do have to. She shifted her gaze aside, to the wall, saying silently: Well, if you want to take me without any desire at all on my part, then go ahead, if you're not ashamed. He was not ashamed, because he was maintaining the flame of hate for her which he knew quite well was all that stood between him and shame. He took off his clothes, and got into bed beside her. As he did so, knowing he was putting himself in the position of raping a woman who was making it elaborately clear he bored her, his flesh subsided completely, sad, and full of reproach because a few moments ago it was reaching out for his sister whom he could have made happy. He lay on his side by her, secretly at work on himself, while he supported himself across her body on his elbow, using the free hand to manipulate her breasts. He saw that she gritted her teeth against his touch. At least she could not know that after all this fuss he was not potent.

In order to incite himself, he clasped her again. She felt his smallness, writhed free of him, sat up and said: "Lie down."

While she had been lying there, she had been thinking: The only way to get this over with is to make him big again, otherwise I've got to put up with him all night. His hatred of her was giving him a clairvoyance: he knew very well what went on through her mind. She had switched on, with the determination to *get it all over with,* a sensual good humour, a patience. He lay down. She squatted beside him, the light from the ceiling blooming on her brown shoulders, her flat fair hair falling over her face. But she would not look at his face. Like a bored, skilled wife, she was; or like a prostitute. She administered to him, she was setting herself to please him. Yes, he thought, she's sensual, or she could be. Meanwhile she was succeeding in defeating the reluctance of his flesh, which was the tender token of a possible desire for her, by using a cold skill that was the result of her contempt for him. Just as he decided: Right, it's enough, now I shall have her properly, she made him come. It was not a trick, to hurry or cheat him, what defeated him was her transparent thought: Yes, that's what he's worth.

Then, having succeeded, and waited for a moment or two, she stood up, naked, the fringes of gold at her loins and in her armpits speaking to him a language quite different from that of her green, bored eyes. She looked at him and thought, showing it plainly: What sort of man is it who . . . ? He watched the slight movement of her shoulders: a just-checked shrug. She went out of the room, then the sound of running water. Soon she came back in a white dressing gown, carrying a yellow towel. She handed him the towel, looking away in politeness as he used it. "Are you going home now?" she enquired hopefully, at this point.

"No, I'm not." He believed that now he would have to start fighting her again, but she lay down beside him, not touching him (he could feel the distaste of her flesh for his) and he thought: Very well, my dear, but there's a lot of the night left yet. He said aloud: "I'm going to have you properly tonight." She said nothing, lay silent, yawned. Then she remarked consolingly, and he could have laughed outright from sheer surprise: "Those were hardly conducive circumstances for making love." She was *consoling* him. He hated her for it. A proper little slut: I force her into bed, she doesn't want me, but she still has to make me feel good, like a prostitute. But even while he hated her he responded in kind, from the habit of sexual generosity. "It's because of my admiration for you, because . . . after all, I was holding in my arms one of the thousand women."

A pause. "The thousand?" she enquired, carefully.

"The thousand especial women."

"In Britain or in the world? You choose

them for their brains, their beauty—what?"

"Whatever it is that makes them outstanding," he said, offering her a compliment.

"Well," she remarked at last, inciting him to be amused again: "I hope that at least there's a short list you can say I am on, for politeness' sake."

He did not reply for he understood he was sleepy. He was still telling himself that he must stay awake when he was slowly waking and it was morning. It was about eight. Barbara was not there. He thought: My God! What on earth shall I tell my wife? Where was Barbara? He remembered the ridiculous scenes of last night and nearly succumbed to shame. Then he thought, reviving anger: If she didn't sleep beside me I'll never forgive her . . . He sat up, quietly, determined to go through the house until he found her and, having found her, to possess her, when the door opened and she came in. She was fully dressed in a green suit, her hair done, her eyes made up. She carried a tray of coffee, which she set down beside the bed. He was conscious of his big loose hairy body, half uncovered. He said to himself that he was not going to lie in bed, naked, while she was dressed. He said: "Have you got a gown of some kind?" She handed him, without speaking, a towel, and said: "The bathroom's second on the left." She went out. He followed, the towel around him. Everything in this house was gay, intimate—not at all like her efficient working room. He wanted to find out where she had slept, and opened the first door. It was the kitchen, and she was in it, putting a brown earthenware dish into the oven. "The next door," said Barbara. He went hastily past the second door, and opened (he hoped quietly) the third. It was a cupboard full of linen. "This door," said Barbara, behind him.

"So all right then, where did you sleep?"

"What's it to do with you? Upstairs, in my own bed. Now, if you have everything, I'll say goodbye, I want to get to the theatre."

"I'll take you," he said at once.

He saw again the movement of her eyes, the dark swallowing the light in deadly boredom. "I'll take you," he insisted.

"I'd prefer to go by myself," she remarked. Then she smiled: "However, you'll take me. Then you'll make a point of coming right in, so that James and everyone can see—that's what you want to take me for, isn't it?"

He hated her, finally, and quite simply, for her intelligence; that not once had he got away with anything, that she had been watching, since they had met yesterday, every movement of his campaign for her. However, some fate of inner urge over which he had no control made him say sentimentally: "My dear, you must see that I'd like at least to take you to your work."

"Not at all, have it on me," she said, giving him the lie direct. She went past him to the room he had slept in. "I shall be leaving in ten minutes," she said.

He took a shower, fast. When he returned, the workroom was already tidied, the bed made, all signs of the night gone. Also, there were no signs of the coffee she had brought in for him. He did not like to ask for it, for fear of an outright refusal. Besides, she was ready, her coat on, her handbag under her arm. He went, without a word, to the front door, and she came after him, silent.

He could see that ever fibre of her body signalled a simple message: Oh God, for the moment when I can be rid of this boor! She was nothing but a slut, he thought.

A taxi came. In it she sat as far away from him as she could. He thought of what he should say to his wife.

Outside the theatre she remarked: "You could drop me here, if you liked." It was not a plea, she was too proud for that. "I'll take you in," he said, and saw her thinking: Very well, I'll go through with it to shame him. He was determined to take her in and hand her over to her colleagues, he was afraid she would give him the slip. But far from playing it down, she seemed determined to play it his way. At the stage door, she said to the doorman: "This is Mr. Spence, Tom—do you remember, Mr. Spence from last night?" "Good morning, Babs," said the man, examining Graham, politely, as he had been ordered to do.

Barbara went to the door to the stage, opened it, held it open for him. He went in first, then held it open for her. Together they walked into the cavernous, littered, badly lit place and she called out: "James, James!" A man's voie called out from the front of the house: "Here, Babs, why are you so late?"

The auditorium opened before them darkish, silent, save for an early-morning busyness of charwomen. A vacuum cleaner roared, smally, somewhere close. A couple of stagehands stood looking up at a drop which had a design of blue and green spirals. James stood with his back to the auditorium, smoking. "You're late, Babs," he said again. He saw Graham behind her, and nodded. Barbara and James kissed. Barbara said, giving allowance to every syllable: "You remember Mr. Spence from last night?" James nodded: How do you do? Barbara stood beside him, and they looked together up at the blue-and-green backdrop. Then Barbara looked again at Graham, asking silently: All right now, isn't that enough? He could see her eyes, sullen with boredom.

He said: "Bye, Babs. Bye, James. I'll ring you, Babs." No response, she ignored him. He walked off slowly, listening for what might be said. For instance: "Babs, for God's sake, what are you doing with him?" Or she might say: "Are you wondering about Graham Spence? Let me explain."

Graham passed the stagehands who, he could have sworn, didn't recognise him. Then at last he heard James's voice to Barbara: "It's no good, Babs, I know you're enamoured of that particular shade of blue, but do have another look at it, there's a good girl. . . ." Graham left the stage, went past the office where the stage doorman sat reading a newspaper. He looked up, nodded, went back to his paper. Graham went to find a taxi, thinking: I'd better think up something convincing, then I'll telephone my wife.

Luckily he had an excuse not to be at home that day, for this evening he had to interview a young man (for television) about his new novel.

[1963]

For Thought

"One off the Short List" treats a short love affair with a devastating twist: neither one of the lovers cares, in the least, for the other. Both are highly intelligent, sensitive, married, and—to outsiders at least—enviably successful in their professions. Lessing builds tension and suspense in the reader's mind by forcing one to ask: Will Spence continue to press his conquest from stage to stage despite Barbara's fatigue and deep distaste for him? And: Will she, can she, somehow free herself from his repulsive embraces? It is an open question in the end as to which of the lovers is most damaged by the encounter.

For Discussion

1. What point of view has Lessing chosen for the story? How does this point of view enhance the reader's sense of Spence's intelligence and at the same time, debase the reader's estimate of his stability and moral standards?
2. How is Spence characterized? What motivates him to choose Barbara Coles as the ob-

ject of his attention? Why is he more interested in an endless series of conquests than in a warm, affectionate relationship with one person?

3. What segment of English society has Lessing chosen to deal with? How does she distinguish between those at the center of this society and those lingering at the fringes of it?
4. What stages does Spence's seduction of Barbara move through? Why does she repeatedly surrender the initiative in the situation to him?
5. What ironies emerge from the story? Which of the characters is most damaged by the encounter and which is least damaged?

Doris Lessing
Our Friend Judith

I stopped inviting Judith to meet people when a Canadian woman remarked, with the satisfied fervour of one who has at last pinned a label on a rare specimen: "She is, of course, one of your typical English spinsters."

This was a few weeks after an American sociologist, having elicited from Judith the facts that she was forty-ish, unmarried, and living alone, had inquired of me: "I suppose she has given up?" "Given up what?" I asked; and the subsequent discussion was unrewarding.

Judith did not easily come to parties. She would come after pressure, not so much—one felt—to do one a favour, but in order to correct what she believed to be a defect in her character. "I really ought to enjoy meeting new people more than I do," she said once. We reverted to an earlier pattern of our friendship: odd evenings together, an occasional visit to the cinema, or she would telephone to say: "I'm on my way past you to the British Museum. Would you care for a cup of coffee with me? I have twenty minutes to spare."

It is characteristic of Judith that the word spinster, used of her, provoked fascinated speculation about other people. There are my aunts, for instance: aged seventy-odd, both unmarried, one an exmissionary from China, one a retired matron of a famous London hospital. These two old ladies live together under the shadow of the Cathedral in a country town. They devote much time to the Church, to good causes, to letter writing with friends all over the world, to the grandchildren and the great-grand-children of relatives. It would be a mistake, however, on entering a house in which nothing has been moved for fifty years, to diagnose a condition of fossilized late-Victorian integrity. They read every book reviewed in the *Observer* or *The Times*, so that I recently got a letter from Aunt Rose inquiring whether I did not think that the author of *On the Road* was not perhaps?—exaggerating his difficulties. They know a good deal about music, and write letters of encouragement to young composers they feel are being neglected—"You must understand that anything new and original takes time to be understood." Well-informed and critical Tories, they are as likely to dispatch telegrams of protest to the Home Secretary as letters of support. These ladies, my aunts Emily and Rose, are surely what is meant by the phrase *English spinster*. And yet, once the connection had been pointed out, there is no doubt that Judith and they are spiritual cousins, if not sisters. Therefore it follows that one's pitying admiration for women who have supported manless and uncomforted lives needs a certain modification?

One will, of course, never know; and I feel now that it is entirely my fault that I shall never know. I had been Judith's friend for upwards of five years before the incident occurred which I involuntarily thought of—stupidly enough—as "the first time Judith's mask slipped."

A mutual friend, Betty, had been given a cast-off Dior dress. She was too short for it. Also she said: "It's not a dress for a married woman with three children and a talent for cooking. I don't know why not, but it isn't." Judith was the right build. Therefore one evening the three of us met by appointment in Judith's bedroom, with the dress. Neither Betty nor I were surprised at the renewed discovery that Judith was beautiful. We had both too often caught each other, and ourselves, in moments of envy when Judith's calm and severe face, her undemonstratively perfect body, succeeded in making everyone else in a room or a street look cheap.

Judith is tall, small-breasted, slender. Her light brown hair is parted in the centre and cut straight around her neck. A high straight forehead, straight nose, a full grave mouth are a setting for her eyes, which are green, large and prominent. Her lids are very white, fringed with gold, and moulded close over the eyeball, so that in profile she has the look of a staring gilded mask. The dress was of dark green glistening stuff, cut straight, with a sort of loose tunic. It opened simply at the throat. In it Judith could of course evoke nothing but classical images. Diana, perhaps, back from the hunt, in a relaxed moment? A rather intellectual wood nymph who had opted for an afternoon in the British Museum reading-room? Something like that. Neither Betty nor I said a word, since Judith was examining herself in a long mirror, and must know she looked magnificent.

Slowly she drew off the dress and laid it aside. Slowly she put on the old cord skirt and woollen blouse she had taken off. She must have surprised a resigned glance between us, for she then remarked, with the smallest of mocking smiles: "One surely ought to stay in character, wouldn't you say?" She added, reading the words out of some invisible book, written not by her, since it was a very vulgar book, but perhaps by one of us: "It does everything *for* me, I must admit."

"After seeing you in it," Betty cried out, defying her, "I can't bear for anyone else to have it. I shall simply put it away." Judith shrugged, rather irritated. In the shapeless skirt and blouse, and without make-up, she stood smiling at us, a woman at whom forty-nine out of fifty people would not look twice.

A second revelatory incident occurred soon after. Betty telephoned me to say that Judith had a kitten. Did I know that Judith adored cats? "No, but of course she would," I said.

Betty lived in the same street as Judith and saw more or her than I did. I was kept posted about the growth and habits of the cat and its effect on Judith's life. She remarked, for instance, that she felt it was good for her to have a tie and some responsibility. But no sooner was the cat out of kittenhood than all the neighbours complained. It was a tomcat, ungelded, and making every night hideous. Finally the landlord said that either the cat or Judith must go, unless she was prepared to have the cat "fixed." Judith wore herself out trying to find some person, anywhere in Britain, who would be prepared to take the cat. This person would, however, have to sign a written statement not to have the cat "fixed." When Judith took the cat to the vet to be killed, Betty told me she cried for twenty-four hours.

"She didn't think of compromising? After all, perhaps the cat might have preferred to live, if given the choice?"

"Is it likely I'd have the nerve to say anything so sloppy to Judith? It's the nature of a male cat to rampage lustfully about, and therefore it would be morally wrong for Judith to have the cat fixed, simply to suit her own convenience."

"She said that?"

"She wouldn't have to *say* it, surely?"

A third incident was when she allowed a visiting young American, living in Paris, the friend of a friend and scarcely known to her, to use her flat while she visited her parents over Christmas. The young man and his friends lived it up for ten days of alcohol and sex and marijuana, and when Judith came back it took a week to get the place clean again and the furniture mended. She telephoned twice to Paris, the first time to say that he was a disgusting young thug and if he knew what was good for him he would keep out of her way in the future; the second time to apologize for losing her temper. "I had a choice either to let someone use my flat, or to leave it empty. But having chosen that you should have it, it was clearly an unwarrantable infringement of your liberty to make any conditions at all. I do most sincerely ask your pardon." The moral aspects of the matter having been made clear, she was irritated rather than not to receive letters of apology from him—fulsome, embarrassed, but above all, baffled.

It was the note of curiosity in the letters—he even suggested coming over to get to know her better—that irritated her most. "What do you suppose he means?" she said to me. "He lived in my flat for ten days. One would have thought that should be enough, wouldn't you?"

The facts about Judith, then, are all in the open, unconcealed, and plain to anyone who cares to study them; or, as it became plain she feels—to anyone with the intelligence to interpret them.

She has lived for the last twenty years in a small two-roomed flat high over a busy West London street. The flat is shabby and badly heated. The furniture is old, was never anything but ugly, is now rickety and fraying. She has an income of £200 a year from a dead uncle. She lives on this and what she earns from her poetry, and from lecturing on poetry to night classes and extra-mural University classes.

She does not smoke or drink, and eats very little, from preference, not self-discipline.

She studied poetry and biology at Oxford, with distinction.

She is a Castlewell. That is, she is a member of one of the academic upper-middle-class families, which have been producing for centuries a steady supply of brilliant but sound men and women who are the backbone of the arts and sciences in Britain. She is on cool good terms with her family who respect her and leave her alone.

She goes on long walking tours, by herself, in such places as Exmoor or West Scotland.

Every three or four years she publishes a volume of poems.

The walls of her flat are completely lined with books. They are scientific, classical and historical; there is a great deal of poetry and some drama. There is not one novel. When Judith says: "Of course I don't read novels," this does not mean that novels have no place, or a small place, in literature; or that people should not read novels; but that it must be obvious that she can't be expected to read novels.

I had been visiting her flat for years before I noticed two long shelves of books, under a window, each shelf filled with the works of a single writer. The two writers are not, to put it at the mildest, the kind one would associate with Judith. They are mild, reminiscent, vague and whimsical. Typical English *belles-lettres*, in fact, and by definition abhorrent to her. Not one of the books in the two shelves has been read; some of the pages are still uncut. Yet each book is inscribed or dedicated to her: gratefully, admiringly, sentimentally and, more than once, amorously. In short, it is open to anyone who cares to examine these two shelves, and to work out dates, to conclude that Judith from the age of fifteen to twenty-five had been the beloved young companion of one elderly literary gentleman, and from twenty-five to thirty-five, the inspiration of another.

During all that time she had produced her own poetry, and the sort of poetry, it is quite safe to deduce, not at all likely to be admired by her two admirers. Her poems are always cool and intellectual; that is their form, which is contradicted or supported by a gravely sensuous texture. They are poems to read often; one has to, to understand them.

I did not ask Judith a direct question about these two eminent but rather fusty lovers. Not because she would not have answered, or because she would have found the question impertinent, but because such questions are clearly unnecessary. Having those two shelves of books where they are, and books she could not conceivably care for, for their own sake, is publicly giving credit where credit is due. I can imagine her thinking the thing over, and deciding it was only fair, or perhaps honest, to place the books there; and this despite the fact that she would not care at all for the same attention to be paid to her. There is something almost contemptuous in it. For she certainly despises people who feel they need attention.

For instance, more than once a new emerging wave of "modern" young poets have discovered her as the only "modern" poet among their despised and well-credited elders. This is because, since she began writing at fifteen, her poems have been full of scientific, mechanical and chemical imagery. This is how she thinks, or feels.

More than once has a young poet hastened to her flat, to claim her as an ally, only to find her totally and by instinct unmoved by words like modern, new, contemporary. He has been outraged and wounded by her principle, so deeply rooted as to be unconscious, and to need no expression but a contemptuous shrug of the shoulders, that publicity seeking or to want critical attention is despicable. It goes without saying that there is perhaps one critic in the world she has any time for. He has sulked off, leaving her on her shelf, which she takes it for granted is her proper place, to be read by an appreciative minority.

Meanwhile she gives her lectures, walks alone through London, writes her poems, and is seen sometimes at a concert or a play with a middle-aged professor of Greek who has a wife and two children.

Betty and I speculated about this Professor, with such remarks as: Surely she must sometimes be lonely? Hasn't she ever wanted to marry? What about that awful moment when one comes in from somewhere at night to an empty flat?

It happened recently that Betty's husband was on a business trip, her children visiting, and she was unable to stand the empty house. She asked Judith for a refuge until her own home filled again.

Afterwards Betty rang me up to report: "Four of the five nights Professor Adams came in about ten or so."

"Was Judith embarrassed?"

"Would you expect her to be?"

"Well if not embarrassed at least conscious there was a situation?"

"No, not at all. But I must say I don't think he's good enough for her. He can't possibly understand her. He calls her Judy."

"Good God."

"Yes. But I was wondering. Suppose the other two called her Judy —'little Judy'— imagine it! Isn't it awful! But it does rather throw a light on Judith?"

"It's rather touching."

"I suppose it's touching. But *I* was embarrassed—oh, not because of the situation.

Because of how she was, with him. 'Judy, is there another cup of tea in that pot?' And she, rather daughterly and demure, pouring him one."

"Well yes, I can see how you felt."

"Three of the nights he went to her bedroom with her—very casual about it, because she was being. But he was not there in the mornings. So I asked her. You know how it is when you ask her a question. As if you've been having long conversations on that very subject for years and years, and she is merely continuing where you left off last. So when she says something surprising, one feels such a fool to be surprised?"

"Yes. And then?"

"I asked her if she was sorry not to have children. She said yes, but one couldn't have everything."

"One can't have everything, she said?"

"Quite clearly feeling she *has* nearly everything. She said she thought it was a pity, because she would have brought up children very well."

"When you come to think of it, she would, too."

"I asked about marriage, but she said on the whole the role of a mistress suited her better."

"She used the word mistress?"

"You must admit it's the accurate word."

"I suppose so."

"And then she said that while she liked intimacy and sex and everything, she enjoyed waking up in the morning alone and *her own person*."

"Yes, *of course*."

"Of course. But now she's bothered because the Professor would like to marry her. Or he feels he ought. At least, he's getting all guilty and obsessive about it. She says she doesn't see the point of divorce, and anyway, surely it would be very hard on his poor old wife after all these years particularly after bringing up two children so satisfactorily. She talks about his wife as if she's a kind of nice old charwoman, and it wouldn't be *fair* to sack her, you know. Anyway. What with one thing and another Judith's going off to Italy soon in order *to collect herself*."

"But how's she going to pay for it?"

"Luckily the Third Programme's commissioning her to do some arty programmes. They offered her a choice of the Cid—El Thid, you know—and the Borgias. Well, the Borghese, then. And Judith settled for the Borgias."

"The Borgias," I said, "*Judith?*"

Yes quite. I said that too, in that tone of voice. She saw my point. She says the epic is right up her street, whereas the Renaissance has never been on her wavelength. Obviously it couldn't be, all the magnificence and cruelty and *dirt*. But of course chivalry and a high moral code and all those idiotically noble goings-on are right on her wavelength."

"Is the money the same?"

"Yes. But is it likely Judith would let money decide? No, she said that one should always choose something new, that isn't up one's street. Well, because it's better for her character, and so on, to get herself unsettled by the Renaissance. She didn't say *that*, of course."

"Of course not."

Judith went to Florence; and for some months postcards informed us tersely of her doings. Then Betty decided she must go by herself for a holiday. She had been appalled by the discovery that if her husband was away for a night she couldn't sleep; and when he went to Australia for three weeks, she stopped living until he came back. She had discussed this with him, and he had agreed that, if she really felt the situation to be serious, he would dispatch her by air, to Italy, in order to recover her self-respect. As she put it.

I got this letter from her: "It's no use, I'm coming home. I might have known. Better face it, once you're really married you're not fit for man nor beast. And if you remember what I used to be like! *Well!* I moped around Milan. I sun-bathed in Venice, then I thought my tan was surely worth something, so I was on the point of starting an affair with another lonely soul, but I lost heart, and went to Florence to see Judith. She wasn't there. She'd gone to the Italian Riviera. I had nothing better to do, so I followed her. When I saw the place I wanted to laugh, it's so much not Judith, you know, all those palms and umbrellas and gaiety at all costs and ever such an ornamental blue sea. Judith is in an enormous stone room up on the hillside above the sea, with grapevines all over the place. You should see her, she's got beautiful. It seems for the last fifteen years she's been going to Soho every Saturday morning to buy food at an Italian shop. I must have looked surprised, because she explained she liked Soho. I suppose because all that dreary vice and nudes and prositutes and everything prove how right she is to be as she is? She told the people in the shop she was going to Italy, and the signora said what a coincidence, she was going back to Italy too, and she did hope an old friend like Miss Castlewell would visit her there. Judith said to me: "I felt lacking, when she used the word friend. Our relations have always been formal. Can you understand it?" she said to me. "For fifteen years," I said to her. She said: "I think I must feel it's a kind of imposition, don't you know, expecting people to feel friendship for one." *Well.* I said: "You ought to understand it, because you're like that yourself." "Am I?" she said. "Well, think about it," I said. But I could see she didn't want to think about it. Anyway, she's here, and I've spent a week with her. The widow Maria Rineiri inherited her mother's house, so she came home, from Soho. On the ground floor is a tatty little Rosticcheria patronized by the neighbours. They are all working people. This isn't tourist country, up on the hill. The widow lives above the shop with her little boy, a nasty little brat of about ten. Say what you like, the English are the only people who know how to bring up children, I don't care if that's insular. Judith's room is at the back, with a balcony. Underneath her room is the barber's shop, and the barber is Luigi Rineiri, the widow's younger brother. Yes, I was keeping him until the last. He is about forty, tall dark handsome, a great *bull*, but rather a sweet fatherly bull. He has cut Judith's hair and made it lighter. Now it looks like a sort of gold helmet. Judith is all brown. The widow Rineiri has made her a white dress and a green dress. They fit, for a change. When Judith walks down the street to the lower town, all the Italian males take one look at the golden girl and melt in their own oil like ice-cream. Judith takes all this in her stride. She sort of acknowledges the homage. Then she strolls into the sea and vanishes into the foam. She swims five miles every day. *Naturally.* I haven't asked Judith whether she has collected herself, because you can see she hasn't. The widow Rineiri is match-making. When I noticed this I wanted to laugh, but luckily I didn't, because Judith asked me, really wanting to know, Can you see me married to an Italian barber? (Not being snobbish, but stating the position, so to speak.) "Well yes," I said, "you're the only woman I know who I can see married to an Italian barber." Because it wouldn't matter who she married, she'd always be her *own person*. "At any rate, for a time," I said. At which she said, asperously: "You can use phrases like for a time in England but not in Italy." Did you ever see England, at least London, as the home of licence, liberty and free love? No, neither did I, but of course she's right. Married to Luigi it would be the family, the neighbours, the church and the bambini. All the same she's thinking about it, believe it or not. Here she's quite different, all relaxed and free. She's melting in the attention she gets. The widow mothers her and makes her coffee all the time, and listens to a lot of good advice about how to bring up that nasty brat of hers. Unluckily she doesn't take it. Luigi is crazy for her. At mealtimes she goes to the trattoria in the upper square and all the workmen treat her like a goddess. Well, a film-star then. I said to her, you're mad to come here. For one thing her rent is ten bob a week, and you eat pasta and drink red wine till you bust for about one and sixpence. No, she said, it would be nothing but self-indulgence to stay. Why? I said. She said, she's got nothing to stay for. (Ho ho!) And besides, she's done her research on the Borghese, though so far she can't see her way to an honest presentation of the facts. What made these people tick? she wants to know. And so she's only staying because of the cat. I forgot to mention the cat. This is a town of cats. The Italians here love their cats. I wanted to feed a stray cat at the table, but the waiter said no; and after lunch, all the waiters came with trays crammed with left-over food and stray cats came from everywhere to eat. And at dark when the tourists go in to feed and the beach is empty—you know how empty and forlorn a beach is at dusk?—well, cats appear from everywhere. The beach seems to move, then you see it's cats. They go stalking along the thin inch of grey water at the edge of the sea, shaking their paws crossly at each step, snatching at the dead little fish, and throwing them with their mouths up on the dry sand. Then they scamper after them. You've never seen such a snarling and fighting. At dawn when the fishing-boats come in to the empty beach, the cats are there in dozens. The fishermen throw them bits of fish. The cats snarl and fight over it. Judith gets up early and goes down to watch. Sometimes Luigi goes too, being tolerant. Because what he really likes is to join the evening promenade with Judith on his arm around and around the square of the upper town. Showing her off. Can you *see* Judith? But she does it. Being tolerant. But she smiles and enjoys the attention she gets, there's no doubt of it.

"She has a cat in her room. It's a kitten really, but it's pregnant. Judith says she can't leave until the kittens are born. The cat is too young to have kittens. Imagine Judith. She sits on her bed in that great stone room, with her bare feet on the stone floor and watches the cat, and tries to work out why a healthy uninhibited Italian cat always fed on the best from the Rosticcheria should be neurotic. Because it is. When it sees Judith watching it gets nervous and starts licking at the roots of its tail. But Judith goes on watching, and says about Italy that the reason why the English love the Italians is because the Italians make the English feel superior. They have no discipline. And that's a despicable reason for one nation to love another. Then she talks about Luigi and says he has no sense of guilt, but a sense of sin; whereas she has no sense of sin but she has guilt. I haven't asked her if this has been an insuperable barrier, because judging from how she looks, it hasn't. She says she would rather have a sense of sin, because sin can be atoned for, and if she understood sin, perhaps she would be more at home with the Renaissance. Luigi is very healthy, she says, and not neurotic. He is a Catholic, of course. He doesn't mind that she's an atheist. His mother has explained to him that the English are all pagans, but good people at heart. I suppose he thinks a few smart sessions with the local priest would set Judith on the right path for good and all. Meanwhile, the cat walks nervously around the room, stopping to lick, and when it can't stand Judith watching it another second, it rolls over on the floor, with its paws tucked up, and rolls up its eyes, and Judith scratches its lumpy pregnant stomach and tells it to relax. It makes *me* nervous to see her, it's not like her, I don't know why. Then Luigi shouts from the barber's shop, then he comes up and stands at the door laughing, and Judith laughs, and the widow says: Children enjoy yourselves. And off they go, walking down to the town eating ice-cream. The cat follows them. It won't let Judith out of its sight, like a dog. When she swims miles out to sea, the cat hides under a beach-hut until she comes back. Then she carries it back up the hill, because that nasty little boy chases it. *Well.* I'm coming home tomorrow, thank God, to my dear old Billy, I was mad to ever leave him. There is something about Judith and Italy that has upset me, I don't know what. The point is, what on earth can Judith and Luigi *talk* about? Nothing. How can they? And, of course, it doesn't matter. So I turn out to be a prude as well. See you next week."

It was my turn for a dose of the sun, so I didn't see Betty. On my way back from Rome I stopped off in Judith's resort and walked up through narrow streets to the upper town, where, in the square with the vine-covered trattoria at the corner, was a house with Rosticcheria written in black print on a cracked wooden board over a low door. There was a door-curtain of red beads, and flies settled on the beads. I opened the beads with my hands and looked in to a small dark room with a stone counter. Loops of salami hung from metal hooks. A glass bell covered some plates of cooked meats. There were flies on the salami and on the glass bell. A few tins on the wooden shelves, a couple of pale loaves, some wine-casks and an open case of sticky pale green grapes covered with fruit flies, seemed to be the only stock. A single wooden table with two chairs stood in a corner, and two workmen sat there, eating lumps of sausage and bread. Through another bead curtain at the back came a short, smoothly fat, slender limbed woman with greying hair. I asked for Miss Castlewell, and her face changed. She said in an offended, offhand way: "Miss Castlewell left last week." She took a white cloth from under the counter, and flicked at the flies on the glass bell. "I'm a friend of hers," I said, and she said "Si," and put her hands, palm down, on the counter and looked at me, expressionless. The workmen got up, gulped down the last of their wine, nodded and went. She ciao'd them; and looked back at me. Then, since I didn't go, she called "Luigi!" A shout came from the back room, there was a rattle of beads, and in came first a wiry sharp-faced boy, and then Luigi. He was tall, heavy shouldered, and his black rough hair was like a cap, pulled low over his brows. He looked good-natured, but at the moment, uneasy. His sister said something, and he stood beside her, an ally, and confirmed: "Miss Castlewell went away." I was on the point of giving up, when through the bead curtain that screened off a dazzling light eased a thin, tabby cat. It was ugly and it walked uncomfortably, with its back quarters bunched up. The child suddenly let out a 'Sssss' through his teeth, and the cat froze. Luigi said something sharp to the child, and something encouraging to the cat, which sat down, looked straight in front of it, then began frantically licking at its flanks. "Miss Castlewell was offended with us," said Mrs Rineiri suddenly, and with dignity. "She left early one morning. We did not expect her to go." I said: "Perhaps she had to go home and finish some work."

Mrs Rineiri shrugged, then sighed. Then she exchanged a hard look with her brother. Clearly the subject had been discussed, and closed for ever.

"I've known Judith a long time," I said, trying to find the right note. "She's a remarkable woman. She's a poet." But there was no response to this at all. Meanwhile the child, with a fixed bared-teeth grin, was staring at the cat, narrowing his eyes. Suddenly he let out another "Sssssss," and added a short, high yelp. The cat shot backwards, hit the wall, tried desperately to claw its way up the wall, came to its senses and again sat down and began its urgent, undirected licking at its fur. This time Luigi cuffed the child, who yelped in earnest, and then ran out into the street past the cat. Now that the way was clear the cat shot across the floor, up on to the counter, and bounded past Luigi's shoulder and straight through the bead curtain into the barber's shop, where it landed with a thud.

"Judith was sorry when she left us," said Mrs Rineiri uncertainly. "She was crying."

"I'm sure she was."

"And so," said Mrs Rineiri, with finality, laying her hands down again, and looking past me at the bead curtain. That was the end. Luigi nodded brusquely at me, and went into the back. I said goodbye to Mrs

Rineiri and walked back to the lower town. In the square I saw the child, sitting on the running-board of a lorry parked outside the trattoria, drawing in the dust with his bare toes, and directing in front of him a blank, unhappy stare.

I had to go through Florence, so I went to the address Judith had been at. No, Miss Castlewell had not been back. Her papers and books were still here. Would I take them back with me to England? I made a great parcel and brought them back to England.

I telephoned Judith and she said she had already written for the papers to be sent, but it was kind of me to bring them. There had seemed to be no point, she said, in returning to Florence.

"Shall I bring them over?"

"I would be very grateful, of course."

Judith's flat was chilly, and she wore a bunchy sage-green woolen dress. Her hair was still a soft gold helmet, but she looked pale and rather pinched. She stood with her back to a single bar of electric fire—lit because I demanded it—with her legs apart and her arms folded. She contemplated me.

"I went to the Rineiris' house."

"Oh. Did you?"

"They seemed to miss you."

She said nothing.

"I saw the cat too."

"Oh. Oh, I suppose you and Betty discussed it?" This was with a small unfriendly smile.

"Well, Judith, you must see we were likely to?"

She gave this her consideration and said: "I don't understand why people discuss other people. Oh—I'm not criticizing you. But I don't see why you are so interested. I don't understand human behaviour and I'm not particularly interested."

"I think you should write to the Rineiris."

"I wrote and thanked them, of course."

"I don't mean that."

"You and Betty have worked it out?"

"Yes, we talked about it. We thought we should talk to you, so you should write to the Rineiris."

"Why?"

"For one thing, they are both very fond of you."

"Fond," she said smiling.

"Judith, I've never in my life felt such an atmosphere of being let down."

Judith considered this. "When something happens that shows one there is really a complete gulf in understanding, what is there to say?"

"It could scarcely have been a complete gulf in understanding. I suppose you are going to say we are being interfering?"

Judith showed distaste. "That is a very stupid word. And it's a stupid idea. No one can interfere with me if I don't let them. No, it's that I don't understand people. I don't understand why you or Betty should care. Or why the Rineiris should, for that matter," she added with the small tight smile.

"Judith!"

"If you've behaved stupidly, there's no point in going on. You put an end to it."

"What happened? Was it the cat?"

"Yes, I suppose so. But it's not important." She looked at me, saw my ironical face, and said: "The cat was too young to have kittens. That is all there was to it."

"Have it your way. But that is obviously not all there is to it."

"What upsets me is that I don't understand at all why I was so upset then."

"What happened? Or don't you want to talk about it?"

"I don't give a damn whether I talk about it or not. You really do say the most extraordinary things, you and Betty. If you want to know, I'll tell you, what does it matter?"

"I would like to know of course."

"*Of course!*" she said. "In your place I wouldn't care. Well, I think the essence of the thing was that I must have had the wrong attitude to that cat. Cats are supposed to be independent. They are supposed to go off by themselves to have their kittens. This one didn't. It was climbing up on to my bed all one night and crying for attention. I don't like cats on my bed. In the morning I saw she was in pain. I stayed with her all that day. Then Luigi—he's the brother, you know."

"Yes."

"Did Betty mention him? Luigi came up to say it was time I went for a swim. He said the cat should look after itself. I blame myself very much. That's what happens when you submerge yourself in somebody else."

Her look at me was now defiant; and her body showed both defensiveness and aggression. "Yes. It's true. I've always been afraid of it. And in the last few weeks I've behaved badly. It's because I let it happen."

"Well, go on."

"I left the cat and swam. It was late, so it was only for a few minutes. When I came out of the sea the cat had followed me and had had a kitten on the beach. That little beast Michele—the son, you know?—Well, he always teased the poor thing, and now he had frightened her off the kitten. It was dead, though. He held it up by the tail and waved it at me as I came out of the sea. I told him to bury it. He scooped two inches of sand away and pushed the kitten in—on the beach, where people are all day. So I buried it properly. He had run off. He was chasing the poor cat. She was terrified and running up the town. I ran too. I caught Michele and I was so angry I hit him. I don't believe in hitting children. I've been feeling beastly about it ever since."

"You were angry."

"It's no excuse. I would never have believed myself capable of hitting a child. I hit him very hard. He went off, crying. The poor cat had got under a big lorry parked in the square. Then she screamed. And then a most remarkable thing happened. She screamed just once, and all at once cats just materialized. One minute there was just one cat, lying under a lorry, and the next, dozens of cats. They sat in a big circle around the lorry, all quite still, and watched my poor cat."

"Rather moving," I said.

"Why?"

"There is no evidence one way or the other," I said in inverted commas, "that the cats were there out of concern for a friend in trouble."

"No," she said energetically. "There isn't. It might have been curiosity. Or anything. How do we know? However, I crawled under the lorry. There were two paws sticking out of the cat's back end. The kitten was the wrong way round. It was stuck. I held the cat down with one hand and I pulled the kitten out with the other." She held out her long white hands. They were still covered with fading scars and scratches. "She bit and yelled, but the kitten was alive. She left the kitten and crawled across the square into the house. Then all the cats got up and walked away. It was the most extraordinary thing I've ever seen. They vanished again. One minute they were all there, and then they had vanished. I went after the cat, with the kitten. Poor little thing, it was covered with dust—being wet, don't you know. The cat was on my bed. There was another kitten coming, but it got stuck too. So when she screamed and screamed I just pulled it out. The kittens began to suck. One kitten was very big. It was a nice fat black kitten. It must have hurt her. But she suddenly bit out—snapped, don't you know, like a reflex action, at the back of the kitten's head. It died just like that. Extraordinary, isn't it?" she said, blinking hard, her lips quivering. "She was its mother, but she killed it. Then she ran off the bed and went downstairs into the shop under the counter. I called to Luigi. You know, he's Mrs. Rineiri's brother."

"Yes, I know."

"He said, she was too young, and she was badly frightened and very hurt. He took the alive kitten to her but she got up and walked away. She didn't want it. Then Luigi told me not to look. But I followed him. He held the kitten by the tail and he banged it against the wall twice. Then he dropped it into the rubbish heap. He moved aside some rubbish with his toe, and put the kitten here and pushed rubbish over it. Then Luigi said the cat should be destroyed. He said she was badly hurt and it would always hurt her to have kittens."

"He hasn't destroyed her. She's still alive. But it looks to me as if he were right."

"Yes, I expect he was."

"What upset you—that he killed the kitten?"

"Oh no, I expect the cat would if he hadn't. But that isn't the point, is it?"

"What is the point?"

"I don't think I really know." She had been speaking breathlessly, and fast. Now she said slowly: "It's not a question of right or wrong is it? Why should it be? It's a question of what one is. That night Luigi wanted to go promenading with me. For him, that was *that*. Something had to be done, and he'd done it. But I felt ill. He was very nice to me. He's a very good person," she said, defiantly.

"Yes, he looks it."

"That night I couldn't sleep. I was blaming myself. I should never have left the cat to go swimming. Well, and then I decided to leave the next day. And I did. And that's all. The whole thing was a mistake, from start to finish."

"Going to Italy at all?"

"Oh, to go for a holiday would have been all right."

"You've done all that work for nothing? You mean you aren't going to make use of all that research?"

"No. It was a mistake."

"Why don't you leave it a few weeks and see how things are then?"

"Why?"

"You might feel differently about it."

"What an extraordinary thing to say. Why should I? Oh, you mean, time passing, healing wounds—that sort of thing? What an extraordinary idea. It's always seemed to me an extraordinary idea. No, right from the beginning I've felt ill at ease with the whole business, not myself at all."

"Rather irrationally, I should have said."

Judith considered this, very seriously. She frowned while she thought it over. Then she said: "But if one cannot rely on what one feels, what can one rely on?"

"On what one thinks, I should have expected you to say."

"Should you? Why? Really, you people are all very strange. I don't understand you." She turned off the electric fire, and her face closed up. She smiled, friendly and distant and said: "I don't really see any point at all in discussing it."

[1958]

For Thought

Judith is an English woman who is highly educated, a professional poet with an independent income, the female scion of a centuries old distinguished family. Her friendships and sexual relationships are equally casual. On a trip to Italy, she forms close ties with a barber and a maladjusted, pregnant cat. Her sudden, impetuous flight from Italy after her cat's disastrous birthing reveals a shocking side of her that her friends have never glimpsed before. Though considered cool and rational by others, Judith believes herself to be warm and sympathetic. She uses thought, Lessing suggests, to protect herself from lasting attachments and the anxieties they produce.

For Discussion

1. What is Judith's familial and educational background? How do her friends and acquaintances perceive her?

2. What evidence is there in the story to indicate that Judith craves emotional responsiveness from others, yet cannot commit herself to anyone or anything in any lasting way?
3. Why does Judith prefer temporary sexual and personal relationships to anything permanent?
4. From what point of view is the story told? Why is this choice effective?
5. What contrasts between the English and the Italians, between Luigi Rineiri and Judith, emerge from the story?
6. Why is Judith so loyal to her maladjusted cat? Why does she find her experience in Italy so unnerving and unpleasant?
7. What theme emerges from the story?

Mary McCarthy
"Cruel and Barbarous Treatment"

She could not bear to hurt her husband. She impressed this on the Young Man, on her confidantes, and finally on her husband himself. The thought of Telling Him actually made her heart turn over in a sudden and sickening way, she said. This was true, and yet she knew that being a potential divorcee was deeply pleasurable in somewhat the same way that being an engaged girl had been. In both cases, there was at first a subterranean courtship, whose significance it was necessary to conceal from outside observers. The concealment of the original, premarital courtship had, however, been a mere superstitious gesture, briefly sustained. It had also been, on the whole, a private secretiveness, not a partnership of silence. One put one's family and one's friends off the track because one was still afraid that the affair might not come out right, might not lead in a clean, direct line to the altar. To confess one's aspirations might be, in the end, to publicize one's failure. Once a solid understanding had been reached, there followed a short intermission of ritual bashfulness, in which both parties awkwardly participated, and then came the Announcement.

But with the extramarital courtship, the deception was prolonged where it had been ephemeral, necessary where it had been frivolous, conspiratorial where it had been lonely. It was, in short, serious where it had been dilettantish. That it was accompanied by feelings of guilt, by sharp and genuine revulsions, only complicated and deepened its delights, by abrading the sensibilities, and by imposing a sense of outlawry and consequent mutual dependence upon the lovers. But what this interlude of deception gave her, above all, she recognized, was an opportunity, unparalleled in her experience, for exercising feelings of superiority over others. For her husband she had, she believed, only sympathy and compunction. She got no fun, she told the Young Man, out of putting horns on her darling's head, and never for a moment, she said, did he appear to her as the comic figure of the cuckolded husband that one saw on the stage. (The

Young Man assured her that his own sentiments were equally delicate, that for the wronged man he felt the most profound respect, tinged with consideration.) It was as if by the mere act of betraying her husband, she had adequately bested him; it was supererogatory for her to gloat, and, if she gloated at all, it was over her fine restraint in not-gloating, over the integrity of her moral sense, which allowed her to preserve even while engaged in sinfulness the acute realization of sin and shame. Her overt superiority feelings she reserved for her friends. Lunches and teas, which had been time-killers, matters of routine, now became perilous and dramatic adventures. The Young Man's name was a bright, highly explosive ball which she bounced casually back and forth in these feminine tête-à-têtes. She would discuss him in his status of friend of the family, speculate on what girls he might have, attack him or defend him, anatomize him, keeping her eyes clear and impersonal, her voice empty of special emphasis, her manner humorously detached. *While all the time . . . !*

Three times a week or oftener, at lunch or tea, she would let herself tremble thus on the exquisite edge of self-betrayal, involving her companions in a momentous game whose rules and whose risks only she herself knew. The Public Appearances were even more satisfactory. To meet at a friend's house by design and to register surprise, to strike just the right note of young-matronly affection at cocktail parties, to treat him formally as "my escort" at the theater during intermissions—these were triumphs of stage management, more difficult of execution, more nerve-racking than the lunches and teas, because *two* actors were involved. His overardent glance must be hastily deflected; his too-self-conscious reading of his lines must be entered in the debit side of her ledger of love, in anticipation of an indulgent accounting in private.

The imperfections of his performance were, indeed, pleasing to her. Not, she thought, because his impetuosities, his gaucheries, demonstrated the sincerity of his passion for her, nor because they proved him a new hand at this game of intrigue, but rather because the high finish of her own acting showed off well in comparison. "I should have gone on the stage," she could tell him gaily, "or been a diplomat's wife or an international spy," while he would admiringly agree. Actually, she doubted whether she could ever have been an actress, acknowledging that she found it more amusing and more gratifying to play herself than to interpret any character conceived by a dramatist. In these private theatricals it was her own many-faceted nature that she put on exhibit, and the audience, in this case unfortunately limited to two, could applaud both her skill of projection and her intrinsic variety. Furthermore, this was a play in which the donnée was real, and the penalty for a missed cue or an inopportune entrance was, at first anyway, unthinkable.

She loved him, she knew, for being a bad actor, for his docility in accepting her tender, mock-impatient instruction. Those superiority feelings were fattening not only on the gullibility of her friends, but also on the comic flaws of her lover's character, and on the vulnerability of her lover's passion. In this particular hive she was undoubtedly queen bee.

The Public Appearances were not exclusively duets. They sometimes took the form of a trio. On these occasions the studied and benevolent carefulness which she always showed for her husband's feelings served a double purpose. She would affect a conspicuous domesticity, an affectionate conjugal demonstrativeness, would sprinkle her conversation with "Darlings," and punctuate it with pats and squeezes till her husband would visibly expand and her lover plainly and painfully shrink. For the Young Man no retaliation was possible. These endearments of hers were sanctioned by law, usage, and habit; they belonged to her rôle of wife and could not be condemned or paralleled by a young man who was himself unmarried. They were clear provocations, but they could not be called so, and the Young Man preferred not to speak of them. *But she knew....* Though she was aware of the sadistic intention of these displays, she was not ashamed of them, as she was sometimes twistingly ashamed of the hurt she was preparing to inflict on her husband. Partly she felt that they were punishments which the Young Man richly deserved for the wrong he was doing her husband, and that she herself in contriving them was acting, quite fittingly, both as judge and accused. Partly, too, she believed herself justified in playing the fond wife, whatever the damage to her lover's ego, because, in a sense, she actually was a fond wife. She *did* have these feelings, she insisted, whether she was exploiting them or not.

Eventually, however, her reluctance to wound her husband and her solicitude for his pride were overcome by an inner conviction that her love affair must move on to its next preordained stage. The possibilities of the subterranean courtship had been exhausted; it was time for the Announcement. She and the Young Man began to tell each other in a rather breathless and literary style that the Situation Was Impossible, and Things Couldn't Go On This Way Any Longer. The ostensible meaning of these flurried laments was that, under present conditions, they were not seeing enough of each other, that their hours together were too short and their periods of separation too dismal, that the whole business of deception had become morally distasteful to them. Perhaps the Young Man really believed these things; she did not. For the first time, she saw that the virtue of marriage as an institution lay in its public character. Private cohabitation, long continued, was, she concluded, a bore. Whatever the coziness of isolation, the warm delights of having a secret, a love affair finally reached the point where it needed the glare of publicity to revive the interest of its protagonists. Hence, she thought, the engagement parties, the showers, the big church weddings, the presents, the receptions. These were simply socially approved devices by which the lovers got themselves talked about. The gossip-value of a divorce and remarriage was obviously far greater than the gossip-value of a mere engagement, and she was now ready, indeed hungry, to hear What People Would Say.

The lunches, the teas, the Public Appearances were getting a little flat. It was not, in the end, enough to be a Woman With A Secret, if to one's friends one appeared to be a woman without a secret. The bliss of having a secret required, in short, the consummation of telling it, and she looked forward to the My-dear-I-had-no-idea's, the I-thought-you-and-Bill-were-so-happy-together's, the How-did-you-keep-it-so-dark's with which her intimates would greet her announcement. The audience of two no longer sufficed her; she required a larger stage. She tried it first, a little nervously, on two or three of her closest friends, swearing them to secrecy. "Bill must hear it first from me," she declared. "It would be too terrible for his pride if he found out afterwards that the whole town knew it before he did. So you mustn't tell, even later on, that I told you about this today. I felt I had to talk to someone." After these lunches she would hurry to a phone booth to give the Young Man the gist of the conversation, just as a reporter, sent to cover a fire, telephones in to the city desk. "She certainly was surprised," she could always say with a little gush of triumph. "But she thinks it's fine." *But did they actually?* She could not be sure. Was it possible that she sensed in these luncheon companions, her dearest friends, a certain reserve, a certain unexpressed judgment?

It was a pity, she reflected, that she was so sensitive to public opinion. "I couldn't really love a man," she murmured to herself once, "if everybody didn't think he was wonderful." Everyone seemed to like the Young Man, of course. *But still....* She was getting panicky, she thought. Surely it was only common sense that nobody is admired by everybody. And even if a man were universally despised, would there not be a kind of defiant nobility in loving him in the teeth of the whole world? There would, certainly, but it was a type of heroism that she would scarcely be called upon to practice, for the Young Man was popular, he was invited everywhere, he danced well, his manners were ingratiating, he kept up intellectually. But was he not perhaps *too* amiable, *too* accommodating? Was it for this that her friends seemed silently to criticize him?

At this time a touch of acridity entered into her relations with the Young Man. Her indulgent scoldings had an edge to them now, and it grew increasingly difficult for her to keep her make-believe impatience from becoming real. She would look for dark spots in his character and drill away at them as relentlessly as a dentist at a cavity. A compulsive didacticism possessed her: no truism of his, no cliché, no ineffectual joke could pass the rigidity of her censorship. And, hard as she tried to maintain the character of charming schoolmistress, the Young Man, she saw, was taking alarm. She suspected that, frightened and puzzled, he contemplated flight. She found herself watching him with scientific interest, speculating as to what course he would take, and she was relieved but faintly disappointed when it became clear that he ascribed her sharpness to the tension of the situation and had decided to stick it out.

The moment had come for her to tell her husband. By this single, cathartic act, she would, she believed, rid herself of the doubts and anxieties that beset her. If her husband were to impugn the Young Man's character, she could answer his accusations and at the same time discount them as arising from jealousy. From her husband, at least, she might expect the favor of an open attack to which she could respond with the prepared defense that she carried, unspoken, about with her. Further, she had an intense, childlike curiosity as to How Her Husband Would Take It, a curiosity which she disguised for decency's sake as justifiable apprehension. The confidences already imparted to her friends seemed like pale dress rehearsals of the supreme confidence she was about to make. Perhaps it was toward this moment that the whole affair had been tending, for this moment that the whole affair had been designed. This would be the ultimate testing of her husband's love, its final, rounded, quintessential expression. Never, she thought, when you live with a man do you feel the full force of his love. It is gradually rationed out to you in an impure state, compounded with all the other elements of daily existence, so that you are hardly sensible of receiving it. There is no single point at which it is concentrated; it spreads out into the past and the future until it appears as a nearly imperceptible film over the surface of your life. Only face to face with its own annihilation could it show itself wholly, and, once shown, drop into the category of completed experiences.

She was not disappointed. She told him at breakfast in a fashionable restaurant, because, she said, he would be better able to control his feelings in public. When he called at once for the check, she had a spasm of alarm lest in an access of brutality or grief he leave her there alone, conspicuous, and, as it were, unfulfilled. But they walked out of the restaurant together and through the streets, hand in hand, tears streaming, "unchecked," she whispered to herself, down their faces. Later they were in the Park, by an artificial lake, watching the ducks swim. The sun was very bright, and she felt a kind of superb pathos in the careful and irrelevant attention they gave to the pastoral scene. This was, she knew, the most profound, the most subtle, the most idyllic experience of her life. All the strings of her nature were, at last, vibrant. She was both doer and sufferer: she inflicted pain and participated in it. And she was, at the same time, physician, for, as she was the weapon that dealt the wound, she was also the balm that could assuage it. Only she could know the hurt that engrossed him, and it was to her that he turned for the sympathy she had ready for him. Finally, though she offered him his discharge slip with one hand, with the other she beckoned him to approach. She was wooing him all over again, but wooing him to a deeper attachment than he had previously experienced, to an unconditional surrender. She was demanding his total understanding of her, his compassion, and his forgiveness. When at last he answered her repeated and agonized I-love-you's by grasping her hand more tightly and saying gently, "I know," she saw that she had won him over. She had drawn him into a truly mystical union. Their marriage was complete.

Afterwards everything was more prosaic. The Young Man had to be telephoned and summoned to a conference á trois, a conference, she said, of civilized, intelligent people. The Young Man was a little awkward, even dropped a tear or two, which embarrassed everyone else, but what after all, she thought, could you expect? He was in a difficult position; his was a thankless part. With her husband behaving so well, indeed, so gallantly, the Young Man could not fail to look a trifle inadequate. The Young Man would have preferred it, of course, if her husband had made a scene, had bullied or threatened her, so that he himself might have acted the chivalrous protector. She, however, did not hold her husband's heroic courtesy against him: in some way, it reflected credit on herself. The Young Man, apparently, was expecting to Carry Her Off, but this she would not allow. "It would be too heartless," she whispered when they were alone for a moment. "We must all go somewhere together."

So the three went out for a drink, and she watched with a sort of desperation her husband's growing abstraction, the more and more perfunctory attention he accorded the conversation she was so bravely sustaining. "He is bored," she thought. "He is going to leave." The prospect of being left alone with the Young Man seemed suddenly unendurable. If her husband were to go now, he would take with him the third dimension that had given the affair depth, and abandon her to a flat and vulgar love scene. Terrified, she wondered whether she had not already prolonged the drama beyond its natural limits, whether the confession in the restaurant and the absolution in the Park had not rounded off the artistic whole, whether the sequel of divorce and remarriage would not, in fact, constitute an anticlimax. Already she sensed that behind her husband's good manners an ironical attitude toward herself had sprung up. Was it possible that he had believed that they would return from the Park and all would continue as before? It was conceivable that her protestations of love had been misleading, and that his enormous tenderness toward her had been based, not on the idea that he was giving her up, but rather on the idea that he was taking her back—with no questions asked. If that were the case, the telephone call, the conference, and the excursion had in his eyes been a monstrous gaffe, a breach of sensibility and good taste, for which he would never forgive her. She blushed violently. Looking at him again, she thought he was watching her with an expression which declared: I have found you out: now I know what you are like. For the first time, she felt him utterly alienated.

When he left them she experienced the let-down she had feared but also a kind of relief. She told herself that it was as well that he had cut himself off from her: it made her decision simpler. There was now nothing for her to do but to push the love affair to its conclusion, whatever that might be, and this was probably what she most deeply desired. Had the poignant intimacy of the Park persisted, she might have been tempted to drop the adventure she had begun and return to her routine. But that was, looked at coldly, unthinkable. For if the adventure would seem a little flat after the scene in the Park, the resumption of her marriage would seem even flatter. If the drama of the triangle had been amputated by her confession, the curtain had been brought down with a smack on the drama of wedlock.

And, as it turned out, the drama of the triangle was not quite ended by the superficial rupture of her marriage. Though she had left her husband's apartment and been offered shelter by a confidante, it was still necessary for her to see him every day. There were clothes to be packed, and possessions to be divided, love letters to be reread and mementos to be wept over in common. There were occasional passionate, unconsummated embraces; there were endearments and promises. And though her husband's irony remained, it was frequently vulnerable. It was not, as she had at first thought, an armor against her, but merely a sword, out of *Tristan and Isolde*, which lay permanently between them and enforced discretion.

They met often, also, at the houses of friends, for, as she said, "What can I do? I know it's not tactful, but we all know the same people. You can't expect me to give up my friends." These Public Appearances were heightened in interest by the fact that these audiences, unlike the earlier ones, had, as it were, purchased librettos, and were in full possession of the intricacies of the plot. She preferred, she decided, the evening parties to the cocktail parties, for there she could dance alternately with her lover and her husband to the accompaniment of subdued gasps on the part of the bystanders.

This interlude was at the same time festive and heart-rending: her only dull moments were the evenings she spent alone with the Young Man. Unfortunately, the Post-Announcement period was only too plainly an interlude and its very nature demanded that it be followed by something else. She could not preserve her anomalous status indefinitely. It was not decent, and, besides, people would be bored. From the point of view of one's friends, it was all very well to entertain a Triangle as a novelty; to cope with it as a permanent problem was a different matter. Once they had all three gotten drunk, and there was a scene, and, though everyone talked about it afterwards, her friends were, she thought, a little colder, a little more critical. People began to ask her when she was going to Reno. Furthermore, she noticed that her husband was getting a slight edge in popularity over the Young Man. It was natural, of course, that everyone should feel sorry for him, and be especially nice. *But yet. . . .*

When she learned from her husband that he was receiving invitations from members of her own circle, invitations in which she and the Young Man were unaccountably not included, she went at once to the station and bought her ticket. Her goodbye to her husband, which she had privately allocated to her last hours in town, took place prematurely, two days before she was to leave. He was rushing off to what she inwardly feared was a Gay Weekend in the country; he had only a few minutes; he wished her a pleasant trip; and he would write, of course. His highball was drained while her glass still stood half full; he sat forward nervously on his chair; and she knew herself to be acting the Ancient Mariner, but her dignity would not allow her to hurry. She hoped that he would miss his train for her, but he did not. He left her sitting in the bar, and that night the Young Man could not, as he put it, do a thing with her. There was nowhere, absolutely nowhere, she said passionately, that she wanted to go, nobody she wanted to see, nothing she wanted to do. "You need a drink," he said with the air of a diagnostician. "A drink," she answered bitterly. "I'm sick of the drinks we've been having. Gin, whiskey, rum, what else is there?" He took her into a bar, and she cried, but he bought her a fancy mixed drink, something called a Ramos gin fizz, and she was a little appeased because she had never had one before. Then some friends came in, and they all had another drink together, and she felt better. "There," said the Young Man, on the way home, "don't I know what's good for you? Don't I know how to handle you?" "Yes," she answered in her most humble and feminine tones, but she knew that they had suddenly dropped into a new pattern, that they were no longer the cynosure of a social group, but merely another young couple with an evening to pass, another young couple looking desperately for entertainment, wondering whether to call on a married couple or to drop in somewhere for a drink. This time the Young Man's prescription had worked, but it was pure luck that they had chanced to meet someone they knew. A second or a third time they would scan the faces of the other drinkers in vain, would order a second drink and surreptitiously watch the door, and finally go out alone, with a quite detectable air of being unwanted.

When, a day and a half later, the Young Man came late to take her to the train, and they had to run down the platform to catch it, she found him all at once detestable. He would ride to 125th Street with her, he declared in a burst of gallantry, but she was angry all the way because she was afraid there would be trouble with the conductor. At 125th Street, he stood on the platform blowing kisses to her and shouting something that she could not hear through the glass. She made a gesture of repugnance, but, seeing him flinch, seeing him weak and charming and incompetent, she brought her hand reluctantly to her lips and blew a kiss back. The other passengers were watching, she was aware, and though their looks were doting and not derisive, she felt herself to be humiliated and somehow vulgarized. When the train began to move, and the Young Man began to run down the platform after it, still blowing kisses and shouting alternately, she got up, turned sharply away from the window and walked back to the club car. There she sat down and ordered a whiskey and soda.

There were a number of men in the car, who looked up in unison as she gave her order, but, observing that they were all the middle-aged, small-business-men who "belonged" as inevitably to the club car as the white-coated porter and the leather-bound *Saturday Evening Post*, she paid them no heed. She was now suddenly overcome by a sense of depression and loss that was unprecedented for being in no way dramatic or pleasurable. In the last half hour she had seen clearly that she would never marry the Young Man, and she found herself looking into an insubstantial future with no signpost to guide her. Almost all women, she thought, when they are girls never believe that they will get married. The terror of spinsterhood hangs over them from adolescence on. Even if they are popular they think that no one really interesting will want them enough to marry them. Even if they get engaged they are afraid that something will go wrong, something will intervene. When they do get married it seems to them a sort of miracle, and, after they have been married for a time, though in retrospect the whole process looks perfectly natural and inevitable, they retain a certain unarticulated pride in the wonder they have performed. Finally, however, the terror of spinsterhood has been so thoroughly exorcised that they forget ever having been haunted by it, and it is at this stage that they comtemplate divorce. "How could I have forgotten?" she said to herself and began to wonder what she would do.

She could take an apartment by herself in the Village. She would meet new people. She would entertain. But, she thought, if I have people in for cocktails, there will always come the moment when they have to leave, and I will be alone and have to pretend to have another engagement in order to save embarrassment. If I have them to dinner, it will be the same thing, but at least I will not have to pretend to have an engagement. I shall give dinners. Then, she thought, there will be the cocktail parties, and, if I go alone, I shall always stay a little too late, hoping that a young man or even a party of people will ask me to dinner. And if I fail, if no one asks me, I shall have the ignominy of walking out alone, trying to look as if I had somewhere to go. Then there will be the evenings at home with a good book when there will be no reason at all for going to bed, and I shall perhaps sit up all night. And the mornings when there will be no point in getting up, and I shall perhaps stay in bed till dinnertime. There will be the dinners in tea rooms with other unmarried women, tea rooms because women alone look conspicuous and forlorn in good restaurants. And then, she thought, I shall get older.

She would never, she reflected angrily, have taken this step, had she felt that she was burning her bridges behind her. She would never have left one man unless she had had another to take his place. But the Young Man, she now saw, was merely a sort of mirage which she had allowed herself to mistake for an oasis. "If the Man," she muttered, "did not exist, the Moment would create him." This was what had happened to her. She had made herself the victim of an imposture. But, she argued, with an access of cheerfulness, if this were true, if out of the need of a second, a new, husband she had conjured up the figure of one, she had possibly been impelled by unconscious forces to behave more intelligently than appearances would indicate. She was perhaps acting out in a sort of hypnotic trance a ritual whose meaning had not yet been revealed to her, a ritual which required that, first of all, the Husband be eliminated from the cast of characters. Conceivably, she was designed for the rôle of *femme fatale,* and for such a personage considerations of safety, provisions against loneliness and old age, were not only Philistine but irrelevant. She might marry a second, a third, a fourth time, or she might never marry again. But, in any case, for the thrifty bourgeois love-insurance, with its daily payments of patience, forbearance, and resignation, she was no longer eligible. She would be, she told herself delightedly, a bad risk.

She was, or soon would be, a Young Divorcee, and the term still carried glamor. Her divorce decree would be a passport conferring on her the status of citizeness of the world. She felt gratitude toward the Young Man for having unwittingly effected her transit into a new life. She looked about her at the other passengers. Later she would talk to them. They would ask, of course, where she was bound for; that was the regulation opening move of train conversations. But it was a delicate question what her reply shoud be. To say "Reno" straight out would be vulgar; it would smack of confidences too cheaply given. Yet to lie, to say "San Francisco" for instance, would be to cheat herself, to minimize her importance, to mislead her interlocutor into believing her an ordinary traveler with a commonplace destination. There must be some middle course which would give information without appearing to do so, which would hint at a *vie galante* yet indicate a barrier of impeccable reserve. It would probably be best, she decided, to say "West" at first, with an air of vagueness and hesitation. Then, when pressed, she might go so far as to say "Nevada." But no farther.

[1939]

For Thought

McCarthy's heroine is a shallow, desperate woman who lives life as though it were a play. She mistakenly treats her husband and lover like bit players, whose roles are designed mainly to show off her dazzling talents. However, as her scenario takes on a life of its own, she finds herself trapped by her role as "Woman with A Secret." In the end, she has still failed to learn that life lived without commitment or risk is as unsatisfying as a bad play.

For Discussion

1. Why is the title in quotes?
2. Why are certain expressions, such as "the Young Man," "Telling Him," and "the Announcement," capitalized throughout the story?
3. How is the protagonist characterized by phrases that indicate ambivalence in her emotions?
4. What is the attitude of the author toward the protagonist, and how does she convey this?
5. What is ironic about the protagonist's pride in her "acting ability"?
6. From what point of view is the story told? How does this suit the author's purpose?
7. How is the love intrigue between the protagonist and the Young Man made to appear shallow and tawdry?
8. What is the conflict in the story?
9. How does the protagonist's choice of a place to tell her husband about her love affair characterize her?
10. What is ironic about the climax of the story (that is, about the disclosure of her secret to her husband)?
11. What ironic reversal of roles occurs after the separation from her husband?
12. What ironic contrast exists between the scene in the park where she tells her husband of her divorce plans and the scene in the bar where she says goodbye to her husband prior to her departure for Reno?
13. What is the irony in the allusion to *Tristan and Isolde?*
14. What is the significance of the Ramos gin fizz that the Young Man orders for her?
15. Why does her fear of loneliness and old age arouse no pity?
16. Does the protagonist gain any insight? Does the reader?

Carson McCullers
The Sojourner

The twilight border between sleep and waking was a Roman one this morning: splashing fountains and arched, narrow streets, the golden lavish city of blossoms and age-soft stone. Sometimes in this semiconsciousness he sojourned again in Paris, or war German rubble, or Swiss skiing and a snow hotel. Sometimes, also, in a fallow Georgia field at hunting dawn. Rome it was this morning in the yearless region of dreams.

John Ferris awoke in a room in a New York hotel. He had the feeling that something unpleasant was awaiting him—what it was, he did not know. The feeling, submerged by matinal necessities, lingered even after he had dressed and gone downstairs. It was a cloudless autumn day and the pale sunlight sliced between the pastel skyscrapers. Ferris went into the next-door drugstore and sat at the end booth next to the window glass that overlooked the sidewalk. He ordered an American breakfast with scrambled eggs and sausage.

Ferris had come from Paris to his father's funeral which had taken place the week before in his home town in Georgia. The shock of death had made him aware of youth already passed. His hair was receding and the veins in his now naked temples were pulsing and prominent and his body was spare except for an incipient belly bulge. Ferris had loved his father and the bond between them had once been extraordinarily close—but the years had somehow unraveled this filial devotion; the death, expected for a long time, had left him with an unforeseen dismay. He had stayed as long as possible to be near his mother and brothers at home. His plane for Paris was to leave the next morning.

Ferris pulled out his address book to verify a number. He turned the pages with growing attentiveness. Names and addresses from New York, the capitals of Europe, a few faint ones from his home state in the South. Faded, printed names, sprawled drunken ones. Betty Wills: a random love, married now. Charlie Williams: wounded in the Hürtgen Forest, unheard of since. Grand old Williams—did he live or die? Don Walker: a B.T.O. in television, getting rich. Henry Green: hit the skids after the war, in a sanitarium now, they say. Cozie Hall: he had heard that she was dead. Heedless, laughing Cozie—it was strange to think that she too, silly girl, could die. As Ferris closed the address book, he suffered a sense of hazard, transience, almost of fear.

It was then that his body jerked suddenly. He was staring out of the window when there, on the sidewalk, passing by, was his ex-wife. Elizabeth passed quite close to him, walking slowly. He could not understand the wild quiver of his heart, nor the following sense of recklessness and grace that lingered after she was gone.

Quickly Ferris paid his check and rushed out to the sidewalk. Elizabeth stood on the corner waiting to cross Fifth Avenue. He hurried toward her meaning to speak, but the lights changed and she crossed the street before he reached her. Ferris followed. On the other side he could easily have overtaken her, but he found himself lagging unaccountably. Her fair brown hair was plainly rolled, and as he watched her Ferris recalled that once his father had remarked that Elizabeth had a "beautiful carriage." She turned at the next corner and Ferris followed, although by now his intention to overtake her had disappeared. Ferris questioned the bodily disturbance that the sight of Elizabeth aroused in him, the dampness of his hands, the hard heartstrokes.

It was eight years since Ferris had last seen his ex-wife. He knew that long ago she had married again. And there were children. During recent years he had seldom thought of her. But at first, after the divorce, the loss had almost destroyed him. Then after the anodyne of time, he had loved again, and then again. Jeannine, she was now. Certainly his love for his ex-wife was long since past. So why the unhinged body, the shaken mind? He knew only that his clouded heart was oddly dissonant with the sunny, candid autumn day. Ferris wheeled suddenly and, walking with long strides, almost running, hurried back to the hotel.

Ferris poured himself a drink, although it was not yet eleven o'clock. He sprawled out in an armchair like a man exhausted, nursing his glass of bourbon and water. He had a full day ahead of him as he was leaving by plane the next morning for Paris. He checked over his obligations: take luggage to Air France, lunch with his boss, buy shoes and an overcoat. And something—wasn't there something else? Ferris finished his drink and opened the telephone directory.

His decision to call his ex-wife was impulsive. The number was under Bailey, the husband's name, and he called before he had much time for self-debate. He and Elizabeth had exchanged cards at Christmastime, and Ferris had sent a carving set when he received the announcement of her wedding. There was not reason *not* to call. But as he waited, listening to the ring at the other end, misgiving fretted him.

Elizabeth answered; her familiar voice was a fresh shock to him. Twice he had to repeat his name, but when he was identified, she sounded glad. He explained he was only in town for that day. They had a theater engagement, she said—but she wondered if he would come by for an early dinner. Ferris said he would be delighted.

As he went from one engagement to another, he was still bothered at odd moments by the feeling that something necessary was forgotten. Ferris bathed and changed in the late afternoon, often thinking about Jeannine: he would be with her the following night. "Jeannine," he would say, "I happened to run into my ex-wife when I was in New York. Had dinner with her. And her husband, of course. It was strange seeing her after all these years."

Elizabeth lived in the East Fifties, and as Ferris taxied uptown he glimpsed at intersections the lingering sunset, but by the time he reached his destination it was already autumn dark. The place was a building with a marquee and a doorman, and the apartment was on the seventh floor.

"Come in, Mr. Ferris."

Braced for Elizabeth or even the unimagined husband, Ferris was astonished by the freckled red-haired child; he had known of the children, but his mind had failed somehow to acknowledge them. Surprise made him step back awkwardly.

"This is our apartment," the child said politely. "Aren't you Mr. Ferris? I'm Billy. Come in."

In the living room beyond the hall, the husband provided another surprise; he too had not been acknowledged emotionally. Bailey was a lumbering red-haired man with a deliberate manner. He arose and extended a welcoming hand.

"I'm Bill Bailey. Glad to see you. Elizabeth will be in, in a minute. She's finishing dressing."

The last words struck a gliding series of vibrations, memories of the other years. Fair Elizabeth, rosy and naked before her bath. Half-dressed before the mirror of her dressing table, brushing her fine, chestnut hair. Sweet, casual intimacy, the soft-fleshed loveliness indisputably possessed. Ferris shrank from the unbidden memories and compelled himself to meet Bill Bailey's gaze.

"Billy, will you please bring that tray of drinks from the kitchen table?"

The child obeyed promptly, and when he was gone Ferris remarked conversationally, "Fine boy you have there."

"We think so."

Flat silence until the child returned with a tray of glasses and a cocktail shaker of Martinis. With the priming drinks they pumped up conversation: Russia, they spoke of, and the New York rain-making, and the apartment situation in Manhattan and Paris.

"Mr. Ferris is flying all the way across the ocean tomorrow," Bailey said to the little boy who was perched on the arm of his chair, quiet and well behaved. "I bet you would like to be a stowaway in his suitcase."

Billy pushed back his limp bangs. "I want to fly in an airplane and be a newspaperman like Mr. Ferris." He added with sudden assurance, "That's what I would like to do when I am big."

Bailey said, "I thought you wanted to be a doctor."

"I do!" said Billy. "I would like to be both. I want to be a atom-bomb scientist too."

Elizabeth came in carrying in her arms a baby girl.

"Oh, John!" she said. She settled the baby in the father's lap. "It's grand to see you. I'm awfully glad you could come."

The little girl sat demurely on Bailey's knees. She wore a pale pink crepe de Chine frock, smocked around the yoke with rose, and a matching silk hair ribbon tying back her pale soft curls. Her skin was summer tanned and her brown eyes flecked with gold and laughing. When she reached up and fingered her father's horn-rimmed glasses, he took them off and let her look through them a moment. "How's my old Candy?"

Elizabeth was very beautiful, more beautiful perhaps than he had ever realized. Her straight clean hair was shining. Her face was softer, glowing and serene. It was a madonna loveliness, dependent on the family ambiance.

"You've hardly changed at all," Elizabeth said, "but it has been a long time."

"Eight years." His hand touched his thinning hair self-consciously while further amenities were exchanged.

Ferris felt himself suddenly a spectator—an interloper among these Baileys. Why had he come? He suffered. His own life seemed so solitary, a fragile column supporting nothing amidst the wreckage of the years. He felt he could not bear much longer to stay in the family room.

He glanced at his watch. "You're going to the theater?"

"It's a shame," Elizabeth said, "but

we've had this engagement for more than a month. But surely, John, you'll be staying home one of these days before long. You're not going to be an expatriate, are you?"

"Expatriate," Ferris repeated. "I don't much like the word."

"What's a better word?" she asked.

He thought for a moment. "Sojourner might do."

Ferris glanced at his watch, and again Elizabeth apologized. "If only we had known ahead of time—"

"I just had this day in town. I came home unexpectedly. You see, Papa died last week."

"Papa Ferris is dead?"

"Yes, at Johns-Hopkins. He had been sick there nearly a year. The funeral was down home in Georgia."

"Oh, I'm so sorry, John. Papa Ferris was always one of my favorite people."

The little boy moved from behind the chair so that he could look into his mother's face. He asked, "Who is dead?"

Ferris was oblivious to apprehension; he was thinking of his father's death. He saw again the outstretched body on the quilted silk within the coffin. The corpse flesh was bizarrely rouged and the familiar hands lay massive and joined above a spread of funeral roses. The memory closed and Ferris awakened to Elizabeth's calm voice.

"Mr. Ferris's father, Billy. A really grand person. Somebody you didn't know."

"But why did you call him *Papa* Ferris?"

Bailey and Elizabeth exchanged a trapped look. It was Bailey who answered the questioning child. "A long time ago," he said, "your mother and Mr. Ferris were once married. Before you were born—a long time ago."

"Mr. Ferris?"

The little boy stared at Ferris, amazed and unbelieving. And Ferris's eyes, as he returned the gaze, were somehow unbelieving too. Was it indeed true that at one time he had called this stranger, Elizabeth, Little Butterduck during nights of love, that they had lived together, shared perhaps a thousand days and nights and—finally—endured in the misery of sudden solitude the fiber by fiber (jealousy, alcohol and money quarrels) destruction of the fabric of married love.

Bailey said to the children, "It's somebody's suppertime. Come on now."

"But Daddy! Mama and Mr. Ferris—I—"

Billy's everlasting eyes—perplexed and with a glimmer of hostility—reminded Ferris of the gaze of another child. It was the young son of Jeannine—a boy of seven with a shadowed little face and knobby knees whom Ferris avoided and usually forgot.

"Quick, march!" Bailey gently turned Billy toward the door. "Say good night now, son."

"Good night, Mr. Ferris." He added resentfully, "I thought I was staying up for the cake."

"You can come in afterward for the cake," Elizabeth said. "Run along now with Daddy for your supper."

Ferris and Elizabeth were alone. The weight of the situation descended on those first moments of silence. Ferris asked permission to pour himself another drink and Elizabeth set the cocktail shaker on the table at his side. He looked at the grand piano and noticed the music on the rack.

"Do you still play as beautifully as you used to?"

"I still enjoy it."

"Please play, Elizabeth."

Elizabeth arose immediately. Her readiness to perform when asked had always been one of her amiabilities; she never hung back, apologized. Now as she approached the piano there was the added readiness of relief.

She began with a Bach prelude and fugue. The prelude was as gaily iridescent as a prism in a morning room. The first voice of the fugue, an announcement pure and solitary, was repeated intermingling with a second voice, and again repeated within an elaborated frame, the multiple music, horizontal and serene, flowed with unhurried majesty. The principal melody was woven with two other voices, embellished with countless ingenuities—now dominant, again submerged, it had the sublimity of a single thing that does not fear surrender to the whole. Toward the end, the density of the material gathered for the last enriched insistence on the dominant first motif and with a chorded final statement the fugue ended. Ferris rested his head on the chair back and closed his eyes. In the following silence a clear, high voice came from the room down the hall.

"Daddy, how *could* Mama and Mr. Ferris—" A door was closed.

The piano began again—what was this music? Unplaced, familiar, the limpid melody had lain a long while dormant in his heart. Now it spoke to him of another time, another place—it was the music Elizabeth used to play. The delicate air summoned a wilderness of memory. Ferris was lost in the riot of past longings, conflicts, ambivalent desires. Strange that the music, catalyst for this tumultuous anarchy, was so serene and clear. The singing melody was broken off by the appearance of the maid.

"Miz Bailey, dinner is out on the table now."

Even after Ferris was seated at the table between his host and hostess, the unfinished music still overcast his mood. He was a little drunk.

"*L'improvisation de la vie humaine*," he said. "There's nothing that makes you so aware of the improvisation of human existence as a song unfinished. Or an old address book."

"Address book?" repeated Bailey. Then he stopped, noncommittal and polite.

"You're still the same old boy, Johnny," Elizabeth said with a trace of the old tenderness.

It was a Southern dinner that evening, and the dishes were his old favorites. They had fried chicken and corn pudding and rich, glazed candied sweet potatoes. During the meal Elizabeth kept alive a conversation when the silences were overlong. And it came about that Ferris was led to speak of Jeannine.

"I first knew Jeannine last autumn—about this time of the year—in Italy. She's a singer and she had an engagement in Rome. I expect we will be married soon."

The words seemed so true, inevitable, that Ferris did not at first acknowledge to himself the lie. He and Jeannine had never in that year spoken of marriage. And indeed, she was still married—to a White Russian moneychanger in Paris from whom she had been separated for five years. But it was too late to correct the lie. Already Elizabeth was saying: "This really makes me glad to know. Congratulations, Johnny."

He tried to make amends with truth. "The Roman autumn is so beautiful. Balmy and blossoming." He added, "Jeannine has a little boy of six. A curious trilingual little fellow. We go to the Tuileries sometimes."

A lie again. He had taken the boy once to the gardens. The sallow foreign child in shorts that bared his spindly legs and sailed his boat in the concrete pond and ridden the pony. The child had wanted to go in to the puppet show. But there was not time, for Ferris had an engagement at the Scribe Hotel. He had promised they would go to the guignol another afternoon. Only once had he taken Valentin to the Tuileries.

There was a stir. The maid brought in a white-frosted cake with pink candles. The children entered in their night clothes. Ferris still did not understand.

"Happy birthday, John," Elizabeth said. "Blow out the candles."

Ferris recognized his birthday date. The candles blew out lingeringly and there was the smell of burning wax. Ferris was thirty-eight years old. The veins in his temples darkened and pulsed visibly.

"It's time you started for the theater."

Ferris thanked Elizabeth for the birthday dinner and said the appropriate good-byes. The whole family saw him to the door.

A high, thin moon shone above the jagged, dark skyscrapers. The streets were windy, cold. Ferris hurried to Third Avenue and hailed a cab. He gazed at the nocturnal city with the deliberate attentiveness of departure and perhaps farewell. He was alone. He longed for flighttime and the coming journey.

The next day he looked down on the city from the air, burnished in sunlight, toylike, precise. Then America was left behind and there was only the Atlantic and the distant European shore. The ocean was milky pale and placid beneath the clouds. Ferris dozed most of the day. Toward dark he was thinking of Elizabeth and the visit of the previous evening. He thought of Elizabeth among her family with longing, gentle envy and inexplicable regret. He sought the melody, the unfinished air, that had so moved him. The cadence, some unrelated tones, were all that remained; the melody itself evaded him. He found instead the first voice of the fugue that Elizabeth had played—it came to him, inverted mockingly and in a minor key. Suspended above the ocean the anxieties of transience and solitude no longer troubled him and he thought of his father's death with equanimity. During the dinner hour the plane reached the shore of France.

At midnight Ferris was in a taxi crossing Paris. It was a clouded night and mist wreathed the lights of the Place de la Concorde. The midnight bistros gleamed on the wet pavements. As always after a trans-ocean flight the change of continents was too sudden. New York at morning, this midnight Paris. Ferris glimpsed the disorder of his life: the succession of cities, of transitory loves; and time, the sinister glissando of the years, time always.

"*Vite! Vite!*" he called in terror. "*Dépêchez-vous.*"

Valentin opened the door to him. The little boy wore pajamas and an outgrown red robe. His grey eyes were shadowed and, as Ferris passed into the flat, they flickered momentarily.

"*J'attends Maman.*"

Jeannine was singing in a night club. She would not be home before another hour. Valentin returned to a drawing, squatting with his crayons over the paper on the floor. Ferris looked down at the drawing—it was a banjo player with notes and wavy lines inside a comic-strip balloon.

"We will go again to the Tuileries."

The child looked up and Ferris drew him closer to his knees. The melody, the unfinished music that Elizabeth had played, came to him suddenly. Unsought, the load of memory jettisoned—this time bringing only recognition and sudden joy.

"Monsieur Jean," the child said, "did you see him?"

Confused, Ferris thought only of another child—the freckled, family-loved boy. "See who, Valentin?"

"Your dead papa in Georgia." The child added, "Was he okay?"

Ferris spoke with rapid urgency: "We will go often to the Tuileries. Ride the pony and we will go into the guignol. We will see the puppet show and never be in a hurry any more."

"Monsieur Jean," Valentin said. "The guignol is now closed."

Again, the terror, the acknowledgement of wasted years and death. Valentin, responsive and confident, still nestled in his arms. His cheek touched the soft cheek and felt the brush of the delicate eyelashes. With inner desperation he pressed the child close—as though an emotion as protean as his love could dominate the pulse of time.

[1955]

For Thought

In Ferris, McCullers creates a protagonist engaged in a futile, one-man war against the inexorable passage of time by simply attempting to ignore its consequences. Through incidents that impress upon him the ephemeral nature of human life—in his return to

America for his father's funeral, in his seeing the new life his former wife Elizabeth has moved on to, and in his learning that the Guignol is now closed in his conversation with Valentin—he is forced to come to grips with the frightening realization that time goes on remorselessly and that life is rapidly running its course without his having anything to cling to or to give a stable basis to his emotions.

For Discussion

1. What are the implications in the use of the word "sojourner" as it applies to Ferris?
2. What is the atmosphere of the story? How does the author establish it?
3. What is the central conflict in the story?
4. How are the address book and the birthday cake used symbolically?
5. What is the importance of the conversation over cocktails at the Bailey's?
6. What is the thematic significance of the details describing the Bailey family?
7. How is the characterization of Ferris developed further by his recollection of and attitude toward Jeannine's son Valentin?
8. What theme arises out of the resolution of the conflict?

Bernard Malamud
Take Pity

Davidov, the census-taker, opened the door without knocking, limped into the room and sat wearily down. Out came his notebook and he was on the job. Rosen, the ex-coffee salesman, wasted, eyes despairing, sat motionless, cross-legged, on his cot. The square, clean but cold room, lit by a dim globe, was sparsely furnished: the cot, a folding chair, small table, old unpainted chests—no closets but who needed them?—and a small sink with a rough piece of green, institutional soap on its holder—you could smell it across the room. The worn black shade over the single narrow window was drawn to the ledge, surprising Davidov.

"What's the matter you don't pull the shade up?" he remarked.

Rosen ultimately sighed. "Let it stay."

"Why? Outside is light."

"Who needs light?"

"What then you need?"

"Light I don't need," replied Rosen.

Davidov, sour-faced, flipped through the closely scrawled pages of his notebook until he found a clean one. He attempted to scratch in a word with his fountain pen but it had run dry, so he fished a pencil stub out of his vest pocket and sharpened it with a cracked razor blade. Rosen paid no attention to the feathery shavings falling to the floor. He looked restless, seemed to be listening to or for something, although Davidov was convinced there was absolutely nothing to listen to. It was only when the census-taker somewhat irritably and with increasing loudness repeated a question, that Rosen stirred and identified himself. He was about to furnish an address but caught himself and shrugged.

Davidov did not comment on the salesman's gesture. "So begin," he nodded.

"Who knows where to begin?" Rosen stared at the drawn shade. "Do they know here where to begin?"

"Philosophy we are not interested," said Davidov. "Start in how you met her."

"Who?" pretended Rosen.

"Her," he snapped.

"So if I got to begin, how you know

about her already?" Rosen asked triumphantly.

Davidov spoke wearily, "You mentioned before."

Rosen remembered. They had questioned him upon his arrival and he now recalled blurting out her name. It was perhaps something in the air. It did not permit you to retain what you remembered. That was part of the cure, if you wanted a cure.

"Where I met her—?" Rosen murmured. "I met her where she always was—in the back room there in that hole in the wall that it was a waste of time for me I went there. Maybe I sold them a bag of coffee a month. This is not business."

"In business we are not interested."

"What then you are interested?" Rosen mimicked Davidov's tone.

Davidov clammed up coldly.

Rosen knew they had him where it hurt, so he went on: "The husband was maybe forty, Axel Kalish, a Polish refugee. He worked like a blind horse when he got to America, and saved maybe two—three thousand dollars that he bought with the money this pisher grocery in a dead neighborhood where he didn't have a chance. He called my company up for credit and they sent me I should see. I recommended okay because I felt sorry. He had a wife, Eva, you know already about her, and two darling girls, one five and one three, little dolls, Fega and Surale, that I didn't want them to suffer. So right away I told him, without tricks, 'Kiddo, this is a mistake. This place is a grave. Here they will bury you if you don't get out quick!'"

Rosen sighed deeply.

"So?" Davidov had thus far written nothing, irking the ex-salesman.

"So?—Nothing. He didn't get out. After a couple months he tried to sell but nobody bought, so he stayed and starved. They never made expenses. Every day they got poorer you couldn't look in their faces. 'Don't be a damn fool,' I told him, 'go in bankruptcy.' But he couldn't stand it to lose all his capital, and he was also afraid it would be hard to find a job. 'My God,' I said, 'do anything. Be a painter, a janitor, a junk man, but get out of here before everybody is a skeleton.'

"This he finally agreed with me, but before he could go in auction he dropped dead."

Davidov made a note. "How did he die?"

"On this I am not an expert," Rosen replied. "You know better than me."

"How did he die?" Davidov spoke impatiently. "Say in one word."

"From what he died?—he died, that's all."

"Answer, please, this question."

"Broke in him something. That's how."

"Broke what?"

"Broke what breaks. He was talking to me how bitter was his life, and he touched me on my sleeve to say something else, but the next minute his face got small and he fell down dead, the wife screaming, the little girls crying that it made in my heart pain. I am myself a sick man and when I saw him laying on the floor, I said to myself, 'Rosen, say goodbye, this guy is finished.' So I said it."

Rosen got up from the cot and strayed despondently around the room, avoiding the window. Davidov was occupying the only chair, so the ex-salesman was finally forced to sit on the edge of the bed again. This irritated him. He badly wanted a cigarette but disliked asking for one.

Davidov permitted him a short interval of silence, then leafed impatiently through his notebook. Rosen, to needle the census-taker, said nothing.

"So what happened?" Davidov finally demanded.

Rosen spoke with ashes in his mouth. "After the funeral—" he paused, tried to wet his lips, then went on, "He belonged to a society that they buried him, and he also left a thousand dollars insurance, but after the funeral I said to her, 'Eva, listen to me. Take the money and your children and run away from here. Let the creditors take the store. What will they get?—Nothing.'

"But she answered me, 'Where will I go,

where, with my two orphans that their father left them to starve?'

"'Go anywhere,' I said. 'Go to your relatives.'

"She laughed like laughs somebody who hasn't got no joy. 'My relatives Hitler took away from me.'

"'What about Axel—surely an uncle somewheres?'

"'Nobody,' she said. 'I will stay here like my Axel wanted. With the insurance I will buy new stock and fix up the store. Every week I will decorate the window, and in this way gradually will come in new customers—'

"'Eva, my darling girl—'

"'A millionaire I don't expect to be. All I want is I should make a little living and take care on my girls. We will live in the back here like before, and in this way I can work and watch them, too.'

"'Eva,' I said, 'you are a nice-looking young woman, only thirty-eight years. Don't throw away your life here. Don't flush in the toilet—you should excuse me—the thousand poor dollars from your dead husband. Believe me, I know from such stores. After thirty-five years' experience I know a graveyard when I smell it. Go better some place and find a job. You're young yet. Sometime you will meet somebody and get married.'

"'No, Rosen, not me,' she said. 'With marriage I am finished. Nobody wants a poor widow with two children.'

"'This I don't believe it.'

"'I know,' she said.

"Never in my life I saw so bitter a woman's face.

"'No,' I said. 'No.'

"'Yes, Rosen, yes. In my whole life I never had anything. In my whole life I always suffered. I don't expect better. This is my life.'

"I said no and she said yes. What could I do? I am a man with only one kidney, and worse than that, that I won't mention it. When I talked she didn't listen, so I stopped to talk. Who can argue with a widow?"

The ex-salesman glanced up at Davidov but the census-taker did not reply. "What happened then?" he asked.

"What happened?" mocked Rosen. "Happened what happens."

Davidov's face grew red.

"What happened, happened," Rosen said hastily. "She ordered from the wholesalers all kinds goods that she paid for them cash. All week she opened boxes and packed on the shelves cans, jars, packages. Also she cleaned, and she washed, and she mopped with oil the floor. With tissue paper she made new decorations in the window, everything should look nice—but who came in? Nobody except a few poor customers from the tenement around the corner. And when they came? When was closed the supermarkets and they needed some little item that they forgot to buy, like a quart milk, fifteen cents' cheese, a small can sardines for lunch. In a few months was again dusty the cans on the shelves, and her thousand was gone. Credit she couldn't get except from me, and from me she got because I paid out of my pocket the company. This she didn't know. She worked, she dressed clean, she waited that the store should get better. Little by little the shelves got empty, but where was the profit? They ate it up. When I looked on the little girls I knew what she didn't tell me. Their faces were white, they were thin, they were hungry. She kept the little food that was left, on the shelves. One night I brought in a nice piece sirloin, but I could see from her eyes that she didn't like that I did it. So what else could I do? I have a heart and I am human."

Here the ex-salesman wept.

Davidov pretended not to see though once he peeked.

Rosen blew his nose, then went on more calmly, "When the children were sleeping we sat in the dark there, in the back, and not once in four hours opened the door should come in a customer. 'Eva, for Godsakes, *run away*,' I said.

"'I have no place to go,' she said.

"'I will give you where you can go, and please don't say to me no. I am a bachelor, this you know. I got whatever I need and more besides. Let me help you and the children. Money don't interest me. Interests me good health, but I can't buy it. I'll tell you what I will do. Let this place go to the creditors and move into a two-family house that I own, which the top floor is now empty. Rent will cost you nothing. In the meantime you can go and find a job. I will also pay the downstairs lady to take care of the girls—God bless them—until you will come home. With your wages you will buy the food, if you need clothes, and also save a little. This you can use when you get married someday. What do you say?'

"She didn't answer me. She only looked on me in such a way, with such burning eyes, like I was small and ugly. For the first time I thought to myself, 'Rosen, this woman don't like you.'

"'Thank you very kindly, my friend Mr. Rosen,' she answered me, 'but charity we are not needing. I got yet a paying business, and it will get better when times are better. Now is bad times. When comes again good times will get better the business.'

"'Who charity?' I cried to her. 'What charity? Speaks to you your husband's friend.'

"'Mr. Rosen, my husband didn't have no friends.'

"'Can't you see that I want to help the children?'

"'The children have their mother.'

"'Eva, what's the matter with you?' I said. 'Why do you make sound bad something that I mean it should be good?'

"This she didn't answer. I felt sick in my stomach, and was coming also a headache so I left.

"All night I didn't sleep, and then all of a sudden I figured out a reason why she was worried. She was worried I would ask for some kind payment except cash. She got the wrong man. Anyway, this made me think of something that I didn't think about before. I thought now to ask her to marry me. What did she have to lose? I could take care of myself without any trouble to them. Fega and Surale would have a father he could give them for the movies, or sometime to buy a little doll to play with, and when I died, would go to them my investments and insurance policies.

"The next day I spoke to her.

"'For myself, Eva, I don't want a thing. Absolutely not a thing. For you and your girls—everything. I am not a strong man, Eva. In fact, I am sick. I tell you this you should understand. I don't expect to live long. But even for a few years would be nice to have a little family.'

"She was with her back to me and didn't speak.

"When she turned around again her face was white but the mouth was like iron.

"'No, Mr. Rosen.'

"'Why not, tell me?'

"'I had enough with sick men.' She began to cry. 'Please, Mr. Rosen. Go home.'

"I didn't have strength I should argue with her, so I went home. I went home but hurt me my mind. All day long and all night I felt bad. My back pained me where was missing my kidney. Also too much smoking. I tried to understand this woman but I couldn't. Why should somebody that her two children were starving always say no to a man that he wanted to help her? What did I do to her bad? Am I maybe a murderer she should hate me so much? All that I felt in my heart was pity for her and the children, but I couldn't convince her. Then I went back and begged her she should let me help them, and once more she told me no.

"'Eva,' I said, 'I don't blame you that you don't want a sick man. So come with me to a marriage broker and we will find you a strong, healthy husband that he will support you and your girls. I will give the dowry.'

"She screamed, 'On this I don't need your help, Rosen!'

"I didn't say no more. What more could I say? All day long, from early in the morning till late in the night she worked like an animal. All day she mopped, she washed with soap and a brush the shelves, the few cans she polished, but the store was still rotten. The little girls I was afraid to look at. I could see in their faces their bones. They were tired, they were weak. Little Surale held with her hand all the time the dress of Fega. Once when I saw them in the street I gave them some cakes, but when I tried the next day to give them something else, the mother shouldn't know, Fega answered me, 'We can't take, Momma says today is a fast day.'

"I went inside. I made my voice soft. 'Eva, on my bended knee, I am a man with nothing in this world. Allow me that I should have a little pleasure before I die. Allow me that I should help you to stock up once more the store.'

"So what did she do? She cried, it was terrible to see. And after she cried, what did she say? She told me to go away and I shouldn't come back. I felt like to pick up a chair and break her head.

"In my house I was too weak to eat. For two days I took in my mouth nothing except maybe a spoon of chicken noodle soup, or maybe a glass of tea without sugar. This wasn't good for me. My health felt bad.

"Then I made up a scheme that I was a friend of Axel's who lived in Jersey. I said I owed Axel seven hundred dollars that he lent me this money fifteen years ago, before he got married. I said I did not have the whole money now, but I would send her every week twenty dollars till it was paid up the debt. I put inside the letter two tens and gave it to a friend of mine, also a salesman, he should mail it in Newark so she would not be suspicious who wrote the letters."

To Rosen's surprise Davidov had stopped writing. The book was full, so he tossed it onto the table, yawned, but listened amiably. His curiosity had died.

Rosen got up and fingered the notebook. He tried to read the small distorted handwriting but could not make out a single word.

"It's not English and it's not Yiddish," he said. "Could it be in Hebrew?"

"No," answered Davidov. "It's an old-fashioned language that they don't use it nowadays."

"Oh?" Rosen returned to the cot. He saw no purpose to going on now that it was not required, but he felt he had to.

"Came back all the letters," he said dully. "The first she opened it, then pasted back again the envelope, but the rest she didn't even open."

"'Here,' I said to myself, 'is a very strange thing—a person that you can never give her anything.—*But I will give*.'

"I went then to my lawyer and we made out a will that everything I had—all my investments, my two houses that I owned, also furniture, my car, the checking account—every cent would go to her, and when she died, the rest would be left for the two girls. The same with my insurance. They would be my beneficiaries. Then I signed and went home. In the kitchen I turned on the gas and put my head in the stove.

"Let her say now no."

Davidov, scratching his stubbed cheek, nodded. This was the part he already knew. He got up and before Rosen could cry no, idly raised the window shade.

It was twilight in space but a woman stood before the window.

Rosen with a bound was off his cot to see.

It was Eva, staring at him with haunted, beseeching eyes. She raised her arms to him.

Infuriated, the ex-salesman shook his fist.

"Whore, bastard, bitch," he shouted at her. "Go 'way from here. Go home to your children."

Davidov made no move to hinder him as Rosen rammed down the window shade.

[1956]

For Thought

"Take Pity" is a strongly ethnic story in which Malamud skillfully combines the element of absurdist fantasy with the familiar technique of the story-within-a-story. To create the fantasy, he uses paradoxically mundane, realistic details to set up a starkly institutional-type processing room in some kind of after-life. The story-within-a-story arises out of Rosen being questioned by an overworked functionary in the celestial bureaucracy. In his bored interrogation, the census taker extracts the grimly comic details of Rosen's despairing struggle, while alive, to assist the implacably proud, young widow. It is a struggle that continues in ludicrous pantomime, but with roles reversed, as Eva's vision is seen through the window inaudibly beseeching forgiveness for driving him to suicide.

For Discussion

1. What is the mood of the story? How is it established?
2. What is the point of view and what purpose does it serve?
3. What is the narrator's attitude toward the reader? Toward his characters?
4. What is the tone and how is it established?
5. What does the Yiddish dialect contribute to the story?
6. What is the inciting force, the complication, and the resolution in the frame story?
7. What is the conflict in the main story, how is it brought to a crisis, and how is it resolved?
8. What stage props are used and to what purpose?
9. What is the significance of the title?
10. What is the theme of the story?

Katherine Mansfield
Miss Brill

Although it was so brilliantly fine—the blue sky powdered with gold and great spots of light like white wine splashed over the Jardins Publiques—Miss Brill was glad that she had decided on her fur. The air was motionless, but when you opened your mouth there was just a faint chill, like a chill from a glass of iced water before you sip, and now and again a leaf came drifting—from nowhere, from the sky. Miss Brill put up her hand and touched her fur. Dear little thing! It was nice to feel it again. She had taken it out of its box that afternoon, shaken out the moth powder, given it a good brush, and rubbed the life back into the dim little eyes. "What has been happening to me?" said the sad little eyes. Oh, how sweet it was to see them snap at her again from the red eider-down! . . . But the nose, which was of some black composition, wasn't at all firm. It must have had a knock, somehow. Never mind—a little dab of black sealing-wax when the time came—when it was absolutely necessary. . . . Little rogue! Yes, she really felt like that about it. Little rogue biting its tail just by her left ear. She could have taken it off and laid it on her lap and stroked it. She felt a tingling in her hands and arms, but that came from walking, she supposed. And when she breathed, something light and sad—no, not sad, exactly—something gentle seemed to move in her bosom.

There were a number of people out this afternoon, far more than last Sunday. And the band sounded louder and gayer. That was because the Season had begun. For although the band played all the year round on Sundays, out of season it was never the same. It was like some one playing with only the family to listen; it didn't care how it played if there weren't any strangers present. Wasn't the conductor wearing a new coat, too? She was sure it was new. He scraped with his foot and flapped his arms like a rooster about to crow, and the bandsmen sitting in the green rotunda blew out their cheeks and glared at the music. Now there came a little "flutey" bit—very pretty!—a little chain of bright drops. She was sure it would be repeated. It was; she lifted her head and smiled.

Only two people shared her "special" seat: a fine old man in a velvet coat, his hands clasped over a huge carved walking stick, and a big old woman, sitting upright, with a roll of knitting on her embroidered apron. They did not speak. This was disappointing, for Miss Brill always looked forward to the conversation. She had become really quite expert, she thought, at listening as though she didn't listen, at sitting in other people's lives just for a minute while they talked round her.

She glanced, sideways, at the old couple. Perhaps they would go soon. Last Sunday, too, hadn't been as interesting as usual. An Englishman and his wife, he wearing a dreadful Panama hat and she button boots. And she'd gone on the whole time about how she ought to wear spectacles; she knew she needed them; but that it was no good getting any; they'd be sure to break and they'd never keep on. And he'd been so patient. He'd suggest everything—gold rims, the kind that curved round your ears, little pads inside the bridge. No, nothing would please her. "They'll always be sliding down my nose!" Miss Brill had wanted to shake her.

The old people sat on the bench, still as statues. Never mind, there was always the crowd to watch. To and fro, in front of the flower beds and the band rotunda, the couples and groups paraded, stopped to talk, to greet, to buy a handful of flowers from the old beggar who had his tray fixed to the railings. Little children ran among them, swooping and laughing; little boys with big white silk bows under their chins, little girls, little French dolls, dressed up in velvet and lace. And sometimes a tiny staggerer came suddenly rocking into the open from under the trees, stopped, stared, as suddenly sat down "flop," until its small high-stepping mother, like a young hen, rushed scolding to its rescue. Other people sat on the benches and green chairs, but they were nearly always the same, Sunday after Sunday, and—Miss Brill had often noticed—there was something funny about nearly all of them. They were odd, silent, nearly all old, and from the way they stared they looked as though they'd just come from dark little rooms or even—even cupboards!

Behind the rotunda the slender trees with yellow leaves down drooping, and through them just a line of sea, and beyond the blue sky with gold-veined clouds.

Tum-tum-tum tiddle-um! tiddle-um! tum tiddley-um tum ta! blew the band.

Two young girls in red came by and two young soldiers in blue met them, and they laughed and paired and went off arm-in-arm. Two peasant women with funny straw hats passed, gravely, leading beautiful smoke-colored donkeys. A cold, pale nun hurried by. A beautiful woman came along and dropped her bunch of violets, and a little boy ran after to hand them to her, and she took them and threw them away as if they'd been poisoned. Dear me! Miss Brill didn't know whether to admire that or not! And now an ermine toque and a gentleman in gray met just in front of her. He was tall, stiff, dignified, and she was wearing the ermine toque she'd bought when her hair was yellow. Now everything, her hair, her face, even her eyes, was the same color as the shabby ermine, and her hand, in its cleaned glove, lifted to dab her lips, was a tiny yellowish paw. Oh, she was so pleased to see him—delighted! She rather thought they were going to meet that afternoon. She described where she'd been—everywhere, here, there, along by the sea. The day was so charming—didn't he agree? And wouldn't he, perhaps? . . . But he shook his head, lighted a cigarette, slowly breathed a great deep puff into her face, and, even while she was still talking and laughing, flicked the match away and walked on. The ermine toque was alone; she smiled more brightly than ever. But even the band seemed to know what she was feeling and played more softly, played tenderly, and the drum beat, "The Brute! The Brute!" over and over. What would she do? What was going to happen now? But as Miss Brill wondered, the ermine toque turned, raised her hand as though she'd seen some one else, much nicer, just over there, and pattered away. And the band changed again and played more quickly, more gayly than ever, and the old couple on Miss Brill's seat got up and marched away, and such a funny old man with long whiskers hobbled along in time to the music and was nearly knocked over by four girls walking abreast.

Oh, how fascinating it was! How she enjoyed it! How she loved sitting here, watching it all! It was like a play. It was exactly like a play. Who could believe the sky at the back wasn't painted? But it wasn't till a little brown dog trotted on solemn and then slowly trotted off, like a little "theater" dog, a little dog that had been drugged, that Miss Brill discovered what it was that made it so exciting. They were all on the stage. They weren't only the audience, not only looking on; they were acting. Even she had a part and came every Sunday. No doubt somebody would have noticed if she hadn't been there; she was part of the performance after all. How strange she'd never thought of it like that before! And yet it explained why she made such a point of starting from home at just the same time each week—so as not to be late for the performance—and it also explained why she had quite a queer, shy feeling at telling her English pupils how she spent her Sunday afternoons. No wonder! Miss Brill nearly laughed out loud. She was on the stage. She thought of the old invalid gentleman to whom she read the newspaper four afternoons a week while he slept in the garden. She had got quite used to the frail head on the cotton pillow, the hollowed eyes, the open mouth and the high pinched nose. If he'd been dead she mightn't have noticed for weeks; she wouldn't have minded. But suddenly he knew he was having the paper read to him by an actress! "An actress!" The old head lifted; two points of light quivered in the old eyes. "An actress—are ye?" And Miss Brill smoothed the newspaper as though it were the manuscript of her part and said gently: "Yes, I have been an actress for a long time."

The band had been having a rest. Now they started again. And what they played was warm, sunny, yet there was just a faint chill—a something, what was it?—not sadness—no, not sadness—a something that made you want to sing. The tune lifted, the light shone; and it seemed to Miss Brill that in another moment all of them, all the whole company, would begin singing. The young ones, the laughing ones who were moving together, they would begin, and the men's voices very resolute and brave, would join them. And then she too, she too, and the others on the benches—they would come in with a kind of accompaniment—something low, that scarcely rose or fell, something so beautiful—moving. . . . And Miss Brill's eyes filled with tears and she looked smiling at all the other members of the company. Yes, we understand, we understand, she thought—though what they understood she didn't know.

Just at that moment a boy and a girl came and sat down where the old couple had been. They were beautifully dressed; they were in love. The hero and heroine, of course, just arrived from his father's yacht. And still soundlessly singing still with that trembling smile, Miss Brill prepared to listen.

"No, not now," said the girl. "Not here, I can't."

"But why? Because of that stupid old thing at the end there?" asked the boy. "Why does she come here at all—who wants her? Why doesn't she keep her silly old mug at home?"

"It's her fu-fur which is so funny," giggled the girl. "It's exactly like a fried whiting."

"Ah, be off with you!" said the boy in

an angry whisper. Then: "Tell me, ma petite chère—"

"No, not here," said the girl. "Not *yet*."

On her way home she usually bought a slice of honeycake at the baker's. It was her Sunday treat. Sometimes there was an almond in her slice, sometimes not. It made a great difference. If there was an almond it was like carrying home a tiny present—a surprise—something that might very well not have been there. She hurried on the almond Sundays and struck the match for the kettle in quite a dashing way.

But today she passed the baker's by, climbed the stairs, went into the little dark room—her room like a cupboard—and sat down on the red eiderdown. She sat there for a long time. The box that the fur came out of was on the bed. She unclasped the necklet quickly; quickly, without looking, laid it inside. But when she put the lid on she thought she heard something crying.

[1922]

For Thought

On a regular Sunday outing to listen to the band concert in the park and to observe and participate in the lives of others by her customary, discreet eavesdropping, the fantasy life of Miss Brill is shattered beyond repair before the day is over. With a series of carefully constructed, short scenes, both from the past and in the present, Mansfield characterizes Miss Brill by her reactions to what she sees and hears. Then, in a climactic scene, the author arranges an ironic reversal at a time when the protagonist is at a high point in her vicarious existence. With great economy and force, Mansfield produces a catastrophic denouement that seems inevitable in retrospect, rather than merely surprising or clever.

For Discussion

1. What point of view does Mansfield use? What are its advantages for this story?
2. How is the action of the story moved forward and complicated? How is the action brought to a turning point, a climax, and then resolved?
3. How does the discussion between the Englishman and his wife over her spectacles help prepare for the story's conclusion?
4. How is the meeting of the "ermine toque" with the "gentleman in gray" preparatory?
5. In what way is the climax anticipated, considering the other elements in the story, such as tone and atmosphere?
6. How is the reversal of the story ironic, considering Miss Brill's sensitivity, alertness, and source of happiness?
7. How is the fox fur used symbolically, both to represent feelings or ideas and to move the action forward?
8. What is symbolized by the honeycake?
9. How are minor, technically flat characters used as symbols and as props?
10. How is Miss Brill's role as observer reversed, or negated, by the remarks made by the young couple?

W. Somerset Maugham
The Outstation

The new assistant arrived in the afternoon. When the Resident, Mr. Warburton, was told that the prahu was in sight he put on his solar topee and went down to the landing-stage. The guard, eight little Dyak soldiers, stood to attention as he passed. He noted with satisfaction that their bearing was martial, their uniforms neat and clean, and their guns shining. They were a credit to him. From the landing-stage he watched the bend of the river round which in a moment the boat would sweep. He looked very smart in his spotless ducks and white shoes. He held under his arm a gold-headed Malacca cane which had been given him by the Sultan of Perak. He awaited the newcomer with mingled feelings. There was more work in the district than one man could properly do, and during his periodical tours of the country under his charge it had been inconvenient to leave the station in the hands of a native clerk, but he had been so long the only white man there that he could not face the arrival of another without misgiving. He was accustomed to loneliness. During the war he had not seen an English face for three years; and once when he was instructed to put up an afforestation officer he was seized with panic, so that when the stranger was due to arrive, having arranged everything for his reception, he wrote a note telling him he was obliged to go up-river, and fled; he remained away till he was informed by a messenger that his guest had left.

Now the prahu appeared in the broad reach. It was manned by prisoners, Dyaks under various sentences, and a couple of warders were waiting on the landing-stage to take them back to jail. They were sturdy fellows, used to the river, and they rowed with a powerful stroke. As the boat reached the side a man got out from under the attap awning and stepped on shore. The guard presented arms.

"Here we are at last. By God, I'm as cramped as the devil. I've brought you your mail."

He spoke with exuberant joviality. Mr. Warburton politely held out his hand.

"Mr. Cooper, I presume?"

"That's right. Were you expecting any one else?"

The question had a facetious intent, but the Resident did not smile.

"My name is Warburton. I'll show you your quarters. They'll bring your kit along."

He preceded Cooper along the narrow pathway and they entered a compound in which stood a small bungalow.

"I've had it made as habitable as I could, but of course no one has lived in it for a good many years."

It was built on piles. It consisted of a long living-room which opened on to a broad verandah, and behind, on each side of a passage, were two bedrooms.

"This'll do me all right," said Cooper.

"I daresay you want to have a bath and a change. I shall be very much pleased if you'll dine with me tonight. Will eight o'clock suit you?"

"Any old time will do for me."

The Resident gave a polite, but slightly disconcerted, smile and withdrew. He returned to the Fort where his own residence was. The impression which Allen Cooper had given him was not very favorable, but he was a fair man, and he knew that it was unjust to form an opinion on so brief a glimpse. Cooper seemed to be about thirty. He was a tall, thin fellow, with a sallow face in which there was not a spot of color. It was a face all in one tone. He had a large, hooked nose and blue eyes. When, entering the bungalow, he had taken off his topee and flung it to a waiting boy, Mr. Warburton noticed that his large skull, covered with short, brown hair, contrasted somewhat oddly with a weak, small chin. He was dressed in khaki shorts and a khaki shirt, but they were shabby and soiled; and his battered topee had not been cleaned for days. Mr. Warburton reflected that the young man had spent a week on a coasting steamer and had passed the last forty-eight hours lying in the bottom of a prahu.

"We'll see what he looks like when he comes in to dinner."

He went into his room where his things were as neatly laid out as if he had an English valet, undressed, and, walking down the stairs to the bathhouse, sluiced himself with cool water. The only concession he made to the climate was to wear a white dinner-jacket; but otherwise, in a boiled shirt and a high collar, silk socks and patent-leather shoes, he dressed as formally as though he were dining at his club in Pall Mall. A careful host, he went into the dining-room to see that the table was properly laid. It was gay with orchids and the silver shone brightly. The napkins were folded into elaborate shapes. Shaded candles in silver candlesticks shed a soft light. Mr. Warburton smiled his approval and returned to the sitting-room to await his guest. Presently he appeared. Cooper was wearing the khaki shorts, the khaki shirt, and the ragged jacket in which he had landed. Mr. Warburton's smile of greeting froze on his face.

"Hulloa, you're all dressed up," said Cooper. "I didn't know you were going to do that. I very nearly put on a sarong."

"It doesn't matter at all. I daresay your boys were busy."

"You needn't have bothered to dress on my account, you know."

"I didn't. I always dress for dinner."

"Even when you're alone?"

"Especially when I'm alone," replied Mr. Warburton, with a frigid stare.

He saw a twinkle of amusement in Cooper's eyes, and he flushed an angry red. Mr. Warburton was a hot-tempered man; you might have guessed that from his red face with its pugnacious features and from his red hair, now growing white; his blue eyes, cold as a rule and observing, could flush with sudden wrath; but he was a man of the world and he hoped a just one. He must do his best to get on with this fellow.

"When I lived in London I moved in circles in which it would have been just as eccentric not to dress for dinner every night as not to have a bath every morning. When I came to Borneo I saw no reason to discontinue so good a habit. For three years, during the war, I never saw a white man. I never omitted to dress on a single occasion on which I was well enough to come in to dinner. You have not been very long in this country; believe me, there is no better way to maintain the proper pride which you should have in yourself. When a white man surrenders in the slightest degree to the influences that surround him he very soon loses his self-respect, and when he loses his self-respect you may be quite sure that the natives will soon cease to respect him."

"Well, if you expect me to put on a boiled shirt and a stiff collar in this heat I'm afraid you'll be disappointed."

"When you are dining in your own bungalow you will, of course, dress as you think fit, but when you do me the pleasure of dining with me, perhaps you will come to the conclusion that it is only polite to wear the costume usual in civilized society."

Two Malay boys, in sarongs and songkoks, with smart white coats and brass buttons, came in, one bearing gin pahits, and the other a tray on which were olives and anchovies. Then they went in to dinner. Mr. Warburton flattered himself that he had the best cook, a Chinese, in Borneo, and he took great trouble to have as good food as in the difficult circumstances was possible. He exercised much ingenuity in making the best of his materials.

"Would you care to look at the menu?" he said, handing it to Cooper.

It was written in French and the dishes had resounding names. They were waited on by the two boys. In opposite corners of the room two more waved immense fans, and so gave movement to the sultry air. The fare was sumptuous and the champagne excellent.

"Do you do yourself like this every day?" said Cooper.

Mr. Warburton gave the menu a careless glance.

"I have not noticed that the dinner is any different from usual," he said. "I eat very little myself, but I make a point of having a proper dinner served to me every night. It keeps the cook in practice and it's good discipline for the boys."

The conversation proceeded with effort. Mr. Warburton was elaborately courteous, and it may be that he found a slightly malicious amusement in the embarrassment which he thereby occasioned in his companion. Cooper had not been more than a few months in Sembulu, and Mr. Warburton's inquiries about friends of his in Kuala Solor were soon exhausted.

"By the way," he said presently, "did you meet a lad called Hennerley? He's come out recently, I believe."

"Oh, yes, he's in the police. A rotten bounder."

"I should hardly have expected him to be that. His uncle is my friend Lord Barraclough. I had a letter from Lady Barraclough only the other day asking me to look out for him."

"I heard he was related to somebody or other. I suppose that's how he got the job. He's been to Eton and Oxford and he doesn't forget to let you know it."

"You surprise me," said Mr. Warburton. "All his family have been at Eton and Oxford for a couple of hundred years. I should have expected him to take it as a matter of course."

"I thought him a damned prig."

"To what school did you go?"

"I was born in Barbados. I was educated there."

"Oh, I see."

Mr. Warburton managed to put so much offensiveness into his brief reply that Cooper flushed. For a moment he was silent.

"I've had two or three letters from Kuala Solor," continued Mr. Warburton, "and my impression was that young Hennerley was a great success. They say he's a first-rate sportsman."

"Oh, yes, he's very popular. He's just the sort of fellow they would like in K.S. I haven't got much use for the first-rate sportsman myself. What does it amount to in the long run that a man can play golf and tennis better than other people? And who cares if he can make a break of seventy-five at billiards? They attach a damned sight too much importance to that sort of thing in England."

"Do you think so? I was under the impression that the first-rate sportsman had come out of the war certainly no worse than any one else."

"Oh, if you're going to talk of the war then I do know what I'm talking about. I was in the same regiment as Hennerley and I can tell you that the men couldn't stick him at any price."

"How do you know?"

"Because I was one of the men."

"Oh, you hadn't got a commission."

"A fat chance I had of getting a commission. I was what was called a Colonial. I hadn't been to a public school and I had no influence. I was in the ranks the whole damned time."

Cooper frowned. He seemed to have difficulty in preventing himself from breaking into violent invective. Mr. Warburton watched him, his little blue eyes narrowed, watched him and formed his opinion. Changing the conversation, he began to speak to Cooper about the work that would be required of him, and as the clock struck ten he rose.

"Well, I won't keep you any more. I daresay you're tired by your journey."

They shook hands.

"Oh, I say, look here," said Cooper, "I wonder if you can find me a boy. The boy I had before never turned up when I was starting from K.S. He took my kit on board and all that and then disappeared. I didn't know he wasn't there till we were out of the river."

"I'll ask my head-boy. I have no doubt he can find you some one."

"All right. Just tell him to send the boy along and if I like the look of him I'll take him."

There was a moon, so that no lantern was needed. Cooper walked across from the Fort to his bungalow.

"I wonder why on earth they've sent me a fellow like that?" reflected Mr. Warburton. "If that's the kind of man they're going to get out now I don't think much of it."

He strolled down his garden. The Fort was built on the top of a little hill and the garden ran down to the river's edge; on the bank was an arbor, and hither it was his habit to come after dinner to smoke a cheroot. And often from the river that flowed below him a voice was heard, the voice of some Malay too timorous to venture into the light of day, and a complaint or an accusation was softly wafted to his ears, a piece of information was whispered to him or a useful hint, which otherwise would never have come into his official ken. He threw himself heavily into a long rattan chair. Cooper! An envious, ill-bred fellow, bumptious, self-assertive and vain. But Mr. Warburton's irritation could not withstand the silent beauty of the night. The air was scented with the sweet-smelling flowers of a tree that grew at the entrance to the arbor, and the fireflies, sparkling dimly, flew with their slow and silvery flight. The moon made a pathway on the broad river for the light feet of Siva's bride, and on the further bank a row of palm trees was delicately silhouetted against the sky. Peace stole into the soul of Mr. Warburton.

He was a queer creature and he had had a singular career. At the age of twenty-one he had inherited a considerable fortune, a hundred thousand pounds, and when he left Oxford he threw himself into the gay life which in those days (now Mr. Warburton was a man of four and fifty) offered itself to the young man of good family. He had his flat in Mount Street, his private hansom, and his hunting-box in Warwickshire. He went to all the places where the fashionable congregate. He was handsome, amusing and generous. He was a figure in the society of London in the early nineties, and society then had not lost its exclusiveness nor its brilliance. The Boer War which shook it was unthought of; the Great War which destroyed it was prophesied only by the pessimists. It was no unpleasant thing to be a rich young man in those days, and Mr. Warburton's chimney-piece during the season was packed with cards for one great function after another. Mr. Warburton displayed them with complacency. For Mr. Warburton was a snob. He was not a timid snob, a little ashamed of being impressed by his betters, nor a snob who sought the intimacy of persons who had acquired celebrity in politics or notoriety in the arts, nor the snob who was dazzled by riches; he was the naked, unadulterated common snob who dearly loved a lord. He was touchy and quick-tempered, but he would much rather have been snubbed by a person of quality than flattered by a commoner. His name figured insignificantly in *Burke's Peerage*, and it was marvelous to watch the ingenuity he used to mention his distant relationship to the noble family he belonged to; but never a word did he say of the honest Liverpool manufacturer from whom, through his mother, a Miss Gubbins, he had come by his fortune. It was the terror of his fashionable life that at Cowes, maybe, or at Ascot, when he was with a duchess or even with a prince of the blood, one of these relatives would claim acquaintance with him.

His failing was too obvious not soon to become notorious, but its extravagance saved it from being merely despicable. The great whom he adored laughed at him, but in their hearts felt his adoration not unnatural. Poor Warburton was a dreadful snob, of course, but after all he was a good fellow. He was always ready to back a bill for an impecunious nobleman, and if you were in a tight corner you could safely count on him for a hundred pounds. He gave good dinners. He played whist badly, but never minded how much he lost if the company was select. He happened to be a gambler, an unlucky one, but he was a good loser, and it was impossible not to admire the coolness with which he lost five hundred pounds at a sitting. His passion for cards, almost as strong as his passion for titles, was the cause of his undoing. The life he led was expensive and his gambling losses were formidable. He began to plunge more heavily, first on horses, and then on the Stock Exchange. He had a certain simplicity of character and the unscrupulous found him an ingenuous prey. I do not know if he ever realized that his smart friends laughed at him behind his back, but I think he had an obscure instinct that he could not afford to appear other than careless of his money. He got into the hands of money-lenders. At the age of thirty-four he was ruined.

He was too much imbued with the spirit of his class to hesitate in the choice of his next step. When a man in his set had run through his money he went out to the colonies. No one heard Mr. Warburton repine. He made no complaint because a noble friend had advised a disastrous speculation, he pressed nobody to whom he had lent money to repay it, he paid his debts (if he had only known it, the despised blood of the Liverpool manufacturer came out in him there), sought help from no one, and, never having done a stroke of work in his life, looked for a means of livelihood. He remained cheerful, unconcerned and full of humor. He had no wish to make any one with whom he happened to be uncomfortable by the recital of his misfortune. Mr. Warburton was a snob, but he was also a gentleman.

The only favor he asked of any of the great friends in whose daily company he had lived for years was a recommendation. The able man who was at that time Sultan of Sembulu took him into his service. The night before he sailed he dined for the last time at his club.

"I hear you're going away, Warburton," the old Duke of of Hereford said to him.

"Yes, I'm going to Borneo."

"Good God, what are you going there for?"

"Oh, I'm broke."

"Are you? I'm sorry. Well, let us know when you come back. I hope you have a good time."

"Oh, yes. Lots of shooting, you know."

The Duke nodded and passed on. A few hours later Mr. Warburton watched the coast of England recede into the mist, and he left behind everything which to him made life worth living.

Twenty years had passed sinced then. He kept up a busy correspondence with various great ladies and his letters were amusing and chatty. He never lost his love for titled persons and paid careful attention to the announcements in *The Times* (which reached him six weeks after publication) of their comings and goings. He perused the column which records births, deaths, and marriages, and he was always ready with his letter of congratulation or condolence. The illustrated papers told him how people looked and on his periodical visits to England, able to take up the threads as though they had never been broken, he knew all about any new person who might have appeared on the social surface. His interest in the world of fashion was as vivid as when he himself had been a figure in it. It still seemed to him the only thing that mattered.

But insensibly another interest had entered into his life. The position he found himself in flattered his vanity; he was no longer the sycophant craving the smiles of the great, he was the master whose word was law. He was gratified by the guard of Dyak soldiers who presented arms as he passed. He liked to sit in judgment on his fellow men. It pleased him to compose quarrels between rival chiefs. When the head-hunters were troublesome in the old days he set out to chastise them with a thrill of pride in his own behavior. He was too vain not to be of dauntless courage, and a pretty story was told of his coolness in adventuring singlehanded into a stockaded village and demanding the surrender of a blood-thirsty pirate. He became a skilful administrator. He was strict, just and honest.

And little by little he conceived a deep love for the Malays. He interested himself in their habits and customs. He was never tired of listening to their talk. He admired their virtues, and with a smile and a shrug of the shoulders condoned their vices.

"In my day," he would say, "I have been on intimate terms with some of the greatest gentlemen in England, but I have never known finer gentlemen than some well-born Malays whom I am proud to call my friends."

He liked their courtesy and their distinguished manner, their gentleness and their sudden passions. He knew by instinct exactly how to treat them. He had a genuine tenderness for them. But he never forgot that he was an English gentleman and he had no patience with the white men who yielded to native customs. He made no surrenders. And he did not imitate so many of the white men in taking a native woman to wife, for an intrigue of this nature, however sanctified by custom, seemed to him not only shocking but undignified. A man who had been called George by Albert Edward, Prince of Wales, could hardly be expected to have any connection with a native. And when he returned to Borneo from his visits to England it was now with something like relief. His friends, like himself, were no longer young, and there was a new generation which looked upon him as a tiresome old man. It seemed to him that the England of today had lost a good deal of what he had loved in the England of his youth. But Borneo remained the same. It was home to him now. He meant to remain in the service as long as was possible, and the hope in his heart was that he would die before at last he was forced to retire. He had stated in his will that wherever he died he wished his body to be brought back to Sembulu and buried among the people he loved within sound of the softly flowing river.

But these emotions he kept hidden from the eyes of men; and no one, seeing this spruce, stout, well-set-up man, with his clean-shaven strong face and his whitening hair, would have dreamed that he cherished so profound a sentiment.

He knew how the work of the station should be done, and during the next few days he kept a suspicious eye on his assistant. He saw very soon that he was painstaking and competent. The only fault he had to find with him was that he was brusque with the natives.

"The Malays are shy and very sensitive," he said to him. "I think you will find that you will get much better results if you take care always to be polite, patient and kindly."

Cooper gave a short grating laugh.

"I was born in Barbados and I was in Africa in the war. I don't think there's much about niggers that I don't know."

"I know nothing," said Mr. Warburton acidly. "But we were not talking of them. We were talking of Malays."

"Aren't they niggers?"

"You are very ignorant," replied Mr. Warburton.

He said no more.

On the first Sunday after Cooper's arrival he asked him to dinner. He did everything ceremoniously, and though they had met on the previous day in the office and later, on the Fort verandah where they drank a gin and bitters together at six o'clock, he sent a polite note across to the bungalow by a boy. Cooper, however unwillingly, came in evening dress and Mr. Warburton, though gratified that his wish was respected, noticed with disdain that the young man's clothes were badly cut and his shirt ill-fitting. But Mr. Warburton was in a good temper that evening.

"By the way," he said to him, as he shook hands, "I've talked to my head-boy about finding you some one and he recommends his nephew. I've seen him and he seems a bright and willing lad. Would you like to see him?"

"I don't mind."

"He's waiting now."

Mr. Warburton called his boy and told him to send for his nephew. In a moment a tall, slender youth of twenty appeared. He had large dark eyes and a good profile. He was very neat in his sarong, a little white coat, and a fez, without a tassel, of plum-colored velvet. He answered to the name of Abas. Mr. Warburton looked on him with approval, and his manner insensibly softened as he spoke to him in fluent and idiomatic Malay. He was inclined to be sarcastic with white people, but with the Malays he had a happy mixture of condescension and kindliness. He stood in the place of the Sultan. He knew perfectly how to preserve his own dignity, and at the same time put a native at his ease.

"Will he do?" said Mr. Warburton, turning to Cooper.

"Yes, I daresay he's no more of a scoundrel than any of the rest of them."

Mr. Warburton informed the boy that he was engaged and dismissed him.

"You're very lucky to get a boy like that," he told Cooper. "He belongs to a very good family. They came over from Malacca nearly a hundred years ago."

"I don't much mind if the boy who cleans my shoes and brings me a drink when I want it has blue blood in his veins or not. All I ask is that he should do what I tell him and look sharp about it."

Mr. Warburton pursed his lips, but made no reply.

They went in to dinner. It was excellent, and the wine was good. Its influence presently had its effect on them and they talked not only without acrimony, but even with friendliness. Mr. Warburton liked to do himself well, and on Sunday night he made it a habit to do himself even a little better than usual. He began to think he was unfair to Cooper. Of course he was not a gentleman, but that was not his fault, and when you got to know him it might be that he would turn out a very good fellow. His faults, perhaps, were faults of manner. And he was certainly good at his work, quick, conscientious and thorough. When they reached the dessert Mr. Warburton was feeling kindly disposed towards all mankind.

"This is your first Sunday and I'm going to give you a very special glass of port. I've only got about two dozen of it left and I keep it for special occasions."

He gave his boy instructions and presently the bottle was brought. Mr. Warburton watched the boy open it.

"I got this port from my old friend Charles Hollington. He'd had it for forty years and I've had it for a good many. He was well known to have the best cellar in England."

"Is he a wine merchant?"

"Not exactly," smiled Mr. Warburton. "I was speaking of Lord Hollington of Castle Reagh. He's one of the richest peers in England. A very old friend of mine. I was at Eton with his brother."

This was an opportunity that Mr. Warburton could never resist and he told a little anecdote of which the only point seemed to be that he knew an earl. The port was certainly very good; he drank a glass and then a second. He lost all caution. He had not talked to a white man for months. He began to tell stories. He showed himself in the company of the great. Hearing him you would have thought that at one time ministries were formed and policies decided on his suggestion whispered into the ear of a duchess or thrown over the dinner-table to be gratefully acted on by the confidential adviser of the sovereign. The old days at Ascot, Goodwood and Cowes lived again for him. Another glass of port. There were the great house-parties in Yorkshire and in Scotland to which he went every year.

"I had a man called Foreman then, the best valet I ever had, and why do you think he gave me notice? You know in the Housekeeper's Room the ladies' maids and the gentlemen's gentlemen sit according to the precedence of their masters. He told me he was sick of going to party after party at which I was the only commoner. It meant that he always had to sit at the bottom of the table and all the best bits were taken before a dish reached him. I told the story to the Duke of Hereford and he roared. 'By God, sir,' he said, 'if I were King of England I'd make you a viscount just to give your man a chance.' 'Take him yourself, Duke,' I said. 'He's the best valet I've ever had.' 'Well, Warburton,' he said, 'if he's good enough for you he's good enough for me. Send him along.'"

Then there was Monte Carlo, where Mr. Warburton and the Grand Duke Fyodor, playing in partnership, had broken the bank one evening; and there was Marienbad. At Marienbad Mr. Warburton had played baccarat with Edward VII.

"He was only Prince of Wales then, of course. I remember him saying to me, 'George, if you draw on a five you'll lose your shirt.' He was right; I don't think he ever said a truer word in his life. He was a wonderful man. I always said he was the greatest diplomatist in Europe. But I was a young fool in those days, I hadn't the sense to take his advice. If I had, if I'd never drawn on a five, I daresay I shouldn't be here today."

Cooper was watching him. His brown eyes, deep in their sockets, were hard and supercilious, and on his lips was a mocking smile. He had heard a good deal about Mr. Warburton in Kuala Solor. Not a bad sort, and he ran his district like clockwork, they said, but by heaven, what a snob! They laughed at him good-naturedly, for it was impossible to dislike a man who was so generous and so kindly, and Cooper had already heard the story of the Prince of Wales and the game of baccarat. But Cooper listened without indulgence. From the beginning he had resented the Resident's manner. He was very sensitive and he writhed under Mr. Warburton's polite sarcasms. Mr. Warburton had a knack of receiving a remark of which he disapproved with a devastating silence. Cooper had lived little in England and he had a peculiar dislike of the English. He resented especially the public-school boy since he always feared that he was going to patronize him. He was so much afraid of others putting on airs with him that, in order as it were to get in first, he put on such airs as to make every one think him insufferably conceited.

"Well, at all events the war has done one good thing for us," he said at last. "It's smashed up the power of the aristocracy. The Boer War started it, and 1914 put the lid on."

"The great families of England are doomed," said Mr. Warburton with the complacent melancholy of an *émigré* who remembered the court of Louis XV. "They cannot afford any longer to live in their splendid palaces and their princely hospitality will soon be nothing but a memory."

"And a damned good job too in my opinion."

"My poor Cooper, what can you know of the glory that was Greece and the grandeur that was Rome?"

Mr. Warburton made an ample gesture. His eyes for an instant grew dreamy with a vision of the past.

"Well, believe me, we're fed up with all that rot. What we want is a business government by business men. I was born in a Crown Colony and I've lived practically all my life in the colonies. I don't give a row of pins for a lord. What's wrong with England is snobbishness. And if there's anything that gets my goat it's a snob."

A snob! Mr. Warburton's face grew purple and his eyes blazed with anger. That was a word that had pursued him all his life. The great ladies whose society he had enjoyed in his youth were not inclined to look upon his appreciation of themselves as unworthy, but even great ladies are sometimes out of temper and more than once Mr. Warburton had had the dreadful word flung in his teeth. He knew, he could not help knowing, that there were odious people who called him a snob. How unfair it was! Why, there was no vice he found so detestable as snobbishness. After all, he liked to mix with people of his own class, he was only at home in their company, and how in heaven's name could any one say that was snobbish? Birds of a feather.

"I quite agree with you," he answered. "A snob is a man who admires or despises another because he is of a higher social rank than his own. It is the most vulgar failing of our English middle class."

He saw a flicker of amusement in Cooper's eyes. Cooper put up his hand to hide the broad smile that rose to his lips, and so made it more noticeable. Mr. Warburton's hands trembled a little.

Probably Cooper never knew how greatly he had offended his chief. A sensitive man himself, he was strangely insensitive to the feeling of others.

Their work forced them to see one another for a few minutes now and then during the day, and they met at six to have a drink on Mr. Warburton's verandah. This was an old-established custom of the country which Mr. Warburton would not for the world have broken. But they ate their meals separately, Cooper in his bungalow and Mr. Warburton at the Fort. After the office work was over they walked till dusk fell, but they walked apart. There were but few paths in this country, where the jungle pressed close upon the plantations of the village, and when Mr. Warburton caught sight of his assistant passing along with his loose stride, he would make a circuit in order to avoid him. Cooper, with his bad manners, his conceit in his own judgment and his intolerance, had already got on his nerves; but it was not till Cooper had been on the station for a couple of months that an incident happened which turned the Resident's dislike into bitter hatred.

Mr. Warburton was obliged to go up-country on a tour of inspection, and he left the station in Cooper's charge with more confidence, since he had definitely come to the conclusion that he was a capable fellow. The only thing he did not like was that he had no indulgence. He was honest, just and painstaking, but he had no sympathy for the natives. It bitterly amused Mr. Warburton to observe that this man, who looked upon himself as every man's equal, should look upon so many men as his own inferiors. He was hard, he had no patience with the native mind, and he was a bully. Mr. Warburton very quickly realized that the Malays disliked and feared him. He was not altogether displeased. He would not have liked it very much if his assistant had enjoyed a popularity which might rival his own. Mr. Warburton made his elaborate preparations, set out on his expedition, and in three weeks returned. Meanwhile the mail had arrived. The first thing that struck his eyes when he entered his sitting-room was a great pile of open newspapers. Cooper had met him, and they went into the room together. Mr. Warburton turned to one of the servants who had been left behind and sternly asked him what was the meaning of those open papers. Cooper hastened to explain.

"I wanted to read all about the Wolverhampton murder and so I borrowed your *Times*. I brought them back again. I knew you wouldn't mind."

Mr. Warburton turned on him, white with anger.

"But I do mind. I mind very much."

"I'm sorry," said Cooper, with composure. "The fact is, I simply couldn't wait till you came back."

"I wonder you didn't open my letters as well."

Cooper, unmoved, smiled at his chief's exasperation.

"Oh, that's not quite the same thing. After all, I couldn't imagine you'd mind my looking at your newspapers. There's nothing private in them."

"I very much object to any one reading my paper before me." He went up to the pile. There were nearly thirty numbers there. "I think it extremely impertinent of you. They're all mixed up."

"We can easily put them in order," said Cooper, joining him at the table.

"Don't touch them," cried Mr. Warburton.

"I say, it's childish to make a scene about a little thing like that."

"How dare you speak to me like that?"

"Oh, go to hell," said Cooper, and he flung out of the room.

Mr. Warburton, trembling with passion, was left contemplating his papers. His greatest pleasure in life had been destroyed by those callous, brutal hands. Most people living in out-of-the-way places when the mail comes tear open impatiently their papers and taking the last ones first glance at the latest news from home. Not so Mr. Warburton. His newsagent had instructions to write on the outside of the wrapper the date of each paper he despatched and when the great bundle arrived Mr. Warburton looked at these dates and with his blue pencil numbered them. His headboy's orders were to place one on the table every morning in the verandah with the early cup of tea, and it was Mr. Warburton's especial delight to break the wrapper as he sipped his tea, and read the morning paper. It gave him the illusion of living at home. Every Monday morning he read the Monday *Times* of six weeks back and so went through the week. On Sunday he read *The Observer*. Like his habit of dressing for dinner it was a tie to civilization. And it was his pride that no matter how exciting the news was he had never yielded to the temptation of opening a paper before its allotted time. During the war the suspense sometimes had been intolerable, and when he read one day that a push was begun he had undergone agonies of suspense which he might have saved himself by the simple expedient of opening a later paper which lay waiting for him on a shelf. It had been the severest trial to which he had ever exposed himself, but he victoriously surmounted it. And that clumsy fool had broken open those neat tight packages because he wanted to know whether some horrid woman had murdered her odious husband.

Mr. Warburton sent for his boy and told him to bring wrappers. He folded up the papers as neatly as he could, placed a wrapper round each and numbered it. But it was a melancholy task.

"I shall never forgive him," he said. "Never."

Of course his boy had been with him on his expedition; he never traveled without him, for his boy knew exactly how he liked things, and Mr. Warburton was not the kind of jungle traveler who was prepared to dispense with his comforts; but in the interval since their arrival he had been gossiping in the servants' quarters. He had learnt that Cooper had had trouble with his boys. All but the youth Abas had left him. Abas had desired to go too, but his uncle had placed him there on the instructions of the Resident, and he was afraid to leave without his uncle's permission.

"I told him he had done well, Tuan," said the boy. "But he is unhappy. He says it is not a good house and he wishes to know if he may go as the others have gone."

"No, he must stay. The tuan must have servants. Have those who went been replaced?"

"No, Tuan, no one will go."

Mr. Warburton frowned. Cooper was an insolent fool, but he had an official position and must be suitably provided with servants. It was not seemly that his house should be improperly conducted.

"Where are the boys who ran away?"

"They are in the kampong, Tuan."

"Go and see them tonight and tell them that I expect them to be back in Tuan Cooper's house at dawn to-morrow."

"They say they will not go, Tuan."

"On my order?"

The boy had been with Mr. Warburton for fifteen years, and he knew every intonation of his master's voice. He was not afraid of him, they had gone through too much together, once in the jungle the Resident had saved his life and once, upset in some rapids, but for him the Resident would have been drowned; but he knew when the Resident must be obeyed without question.

"I will go to the kampong," he said.

Mr. Warburton expected that his subordinate would take the first opportunity to apologize for his rudeness, but Cooper had the ill-bred man's inability to express regret; and when they met next morning in the office he ignored the incident. Since Mr. Warburton had been away for three weeks it was necessary for them to have a somewhat prolonged interview. At the end of it Mr. Warburton dismissed him.

"I don't think there's anything else, thank you." Cooper turned to go, but Mr. Warburton stopped him. "I understand you've been having some trouble with your boys."

Cooper gave a harsh laugh.

"They tried to blackmail me. They had the damned cheek to run away, all except that incompetent Abas—he knew when he was well off—but I just sat tight. They've all come to heel again."

"What do you mean by that?"

"This morning they were all back on their jobs, the Chinese cook and all. There they were, as cool as cucumbers; you would have thought they owned the place. I suppose they'd come to the conclusion that I wasn't such a fool as I looked."

"By no means. They came back on my express order."

Cooper flushed slightly.

"I should be obliged if you wouldn't interfere with my private concerns."

"They're not your private concerns. When your servants run away it makes you ridiculous. You are perfectly free to make a fool of yourself, but I cannot allow you to be made a fool of. It is unseemly that your house should not be properly staffed. As soon as I heard that your boys had left you, I had them told to be back in their places at dawn. That'll do."

Mr. Warburton nodded to signify that

the interview was at an end. Cooper took no notice.

"Shall I tell you what I did? I called them and gave the whole bally lot the sack. I gave them ten minutes to get out of the compound."

Mr. Warburton shrugged his shoulders.

"What makes you think you can get others?"

"I've told my own clerk to see about it."

Mr. Warburton reflected for a moment.

"I think you behaved very foolishly. You will do well to remember in future that good masters make good servants."

"Is there anything else you want to teach me?"

"I should like to teach you manners, but it would be an arduous task, and I have not the time to waste. I will see that you get boys."

"Please don't put yourself to any trouble on my account. I'm quite capable of getting them for myself."

Mr. Warburton smiled acidly. He had an inkling that Cooper disliked him as much as he disliked Cooper, and he knew that nothing is more galling than to be forced to accept the favors of a man you detest.

"Allow me to tell you that you have no more chance of getting Malay or Chinese servants here now than you have of getting an English butler or a French chef. No one will come to you except on an order from me. Would you like me to give it?"

"No."

"As you please. Good morning."

Mr. Warburton watched the development of the situation with acrid humor. Cooper's clerk was unable to persuade Malay, Dyak or Chinese to enter the house of such a master. Abas, the boy who remained faithful to him, knew how to cook only native food, and Cooper, a coarse feeder, found his gorge rise against the everlasting rice. There was no watercarrier, and in that great heat he needed several baths a day. He cursed Abas, but Abas opposed him with sullen resistance and would not do more than he chose. It was galling to know that the lad stayed with him only because the Resident insisted. This went on for a fortnight and then, one morning, he found in his house the very servants whom he had previously dismissed. He fell into a violent rage, but he had learnt a little sense, and this time, without a word, he let them stay. He swallowed his humiliation, but the impatient contempt he had felt for Mr. Warburton's idiosyncrasies changed into a sullen hatred; the Resident with this malicious stroke had made him the laughing-stock of all the natives.

The two men now held no communication with one another. They broke the time-honored custom of sharing, notwithstanding personal dislike, a drink at six o'clock with any white man who happened to be at the station. Each lived in his own house as though the other did not exist. Now that Cooper had fallen into the work, it was necessary for them to have little to do with one another in the office. Mr. Warburton used his orderly to send any message he had to give his assistant, and his instructions he sent by formal letter. They saw one another constantly, that was inevitable, but did not exchange half a dozen words in a week. The fact that they could not avoid catching sight of one another got on their nerves. They brooded over their antagonism and Mr. Warburton, taking his daily walk, could think of nothing but how much he detested his assistant.

And the dreadful thing was that in all probability they would remain thus, facing each other in deadly enmity, till Mr. Warburton went on leave. It might be three years. He had no reason to send in a complaint to headquarters: Cooper did his work very well, and at that time men were hard to get. True, vague complaints reached him and hints that the natives found Cooper harsh. There was certainly a feeling of dissatisfaction among them. But when Mr. Warburton looked into specific cases, all he could say was that Cooper had shown severity where mildness would not have been misplaced and had been unfeeling when himself would have been sympathetic. He had done nothing for which he could be taken to task. But Mr. Warburton watched him. Hatred will often make a man clear-sighted, and he had a suspicion that Cooper was using the natives without consideration, yet keeping within the law, because he felt that thus he could exasperate his chief. One day perhaps he would go too far. None knew better than Mr. Warburton how irritable the incessant heat could make a man and how difficult it was to keep one's self-control after a sleepless night. He smiled softly to himself. Sooner or later Cooper would deliver himself into his hand.

When at last the opportunity came Mr. Warburton laughed aloud. Cooper had charge of the prisoners; they made roads, built sheds, rowed when it was necessary to send the prahu up- or down-stream, kept the town clean and otherwise usefully employed themselves. If well-behaved they even on occasion served as house-boys. Cooper kept them hard at it. He liked to see them work. He took pleasure in devising tasks for them; and seeing quickly enough that they were being made to do useless things the prisoners worked badly. He punished them by lengthening their hours. This was contrary to the regulations, and as soon as it was brought to the attention of Mr. Warburton, without referring the matter back to his subordinate, he gave instructions that the old hours should be kept; Cooper, going out for his walk, was astounded to see the prisoners strolling back to the jail; he had given instructions that they were not to knock off till dusk. When he asked the warder in charge why they had left off work he was told that it was the Resident's bidding.

White with rage he strode to the Fort. Mr. Warburton, in his spotless white ducks and his neat topee, with a walking-stick in his hand, followed by his dogs, was on the point of starting out on his afternoon stroll. He had watched Cooper go and knew that he had taken the road by the river. Cooper jumped up the steps and went straight up to the Resident.

"I want to know what the hell you mean by countermanding my order that the prisoners were to work till six," he burst out, beside himself with fury.

Mr. Warburton opened his cold blue eyes very wide and assumed an expression of great surprise.

"Are you out of your mind? Are you so ignorant that you do not know that that is not the way to speak to your official superior?"

"Oh, go to hell. The prisoners are my pidgin and you've got no right to interfere. You mind your business and I'll mind mine. I want to know what the devil you mean by making a damned fool of me. Every one in the place will know that you've countermanded my order."

Mr. Warburton kept very cool.

"You had no power to give the order you did. I countermanded it because it was harsh and tyrannical. Believe me, I have not made half such a damned fool of you as you have made of yourself."

"You disliked me from the first moment I came here. You've done everything you could to make the place impossible for me because I wouldn't lick your boots for you. You got your knife into me because I wouldn't flatter you."

Cooper, sputtering with rage, was nearing dangerous ground, and Mr. Warburton's eyes grew on a sudden colder and more piercing.

"You are wrong. I thought you were a cad, but I was perfectly satisfied with the way you did your work."

"You snob. You damned snob. You thought me a cad because I hadn't been to Eton. Oh, they told me in K.S. what to expect. Why, don't you know that you're the laughing-stock of the whole country? I could hardly help bursting into a roar of laughter when you told your celebrated story about the Prince of Wales. My God, how they shouted at the club when they told it. By God, I'd rather be the cad I am than the snob you are."

He got Mr. Warburton on the raw.

"If you don't get out of my house this minute I shall knock you down," he cried.

The other came a little closer to him and put his face in his.

"Touch me, touch me," he said. "By God, I'd like to see you hit me. Do you want me to say it again? Snob. Snob."

Cooper was three inches taller than Mr. Warburton, a strong, muscular young man. Mr. Warburton was fat and fifty-four. His clenched fist shot out. Cooper caught him by the arm and pushed him back.

"Don't be a damned fool. Remember I'm not a gentleman. I know how to use my hands."

He gave a sort of hoot, and, grinning all over his pale, sharp face, jumped down the verandah steps. Mr. Warburton, his heart in his anger pounding against his ribs, sank exhausted into a chair. His body tingled as though he had prickly heat. For one horrible moment he thought he was going to cry. But suddenly he was conscious that his head-boy was on the verandah and instinctively regained control of himself. The boy came forward and filled him a glass of whisky and soda. Without a word Mr. Warburton took it and drank it to the dregs.

"What do you want to say to me?" asked Mr. Warburton, trying to force a smile on to his strained lips.

"Tuan, the assistant tuan is a bad man. Abas wishes again to leave him."

"Let him wait a little. I shall write to Kuala Solor and ask that Tuan Cooper should go elsewhere."

"Tuan Cooper is not good with the Malays."

"Leave me."

The boy silently withdrew. Mr. Warburton was left alone with his thoughts. He saw the club at Kuala Solor, the men sitting round the table in the window in their flannels, when the night had driven them in from golf and tennis, drinking whiskies and gin pahits and laughing when they told the celebrated story of the Prince of Wales and himself at Marienbad. He was hot with shame and misery. A snob! They all thought him a snob. And he had always thought them very good fellows, he had always been gentleman enough to let it make no difference to him that they were of very second-rate position. He hated them now. But his hatred for them was nothing compared with his hatred for Cooper. And if it had come to blows Cooper could have thrashed him. Tears of mortification ran down his red, fat face. He sat there for a couple of hours smoking cigarette after cigarette, and he wished he were dead.

At last the boy came back and asked him if he would dress for dinner. Of course! He always dressed for dinner. He rose wearily from his chair and put on his stiff shirt and the high collar. He sat down at the prettily decorated table and was waited on as usual by the two boys while two others waved their great fans. Over there in the bungalow, two hundred yards away, Cooper was eating a filthy meal clad only in a sarong and a baju. His feet were bare and while he ate he probably read a detective story. After dinner Mr. Warburton sat down to write a letter. The Sultan was away, but he wrote, privately and confidentially, to his representative. Cooper did his work very well, he said, but the fact was that he couldn't get on with him. They were getting dreadfully on each other's nerves and he would look upon it as a very great favor if Cooper could be transferred to another post.

He despatched the letter next morning by special messenger. The answer came a fortnight later with the month's mail. It was a private note and ran as follows:

"My Dear Warburton:

"I do not want to answer your letter officially and so I am writing you a few lines myself. Of course if you insist I will put the matter up to the Sultan, but I think you would be much wiser to drop it. I know Cooper is a rough diamond, but he is capable, and he had a pretty thin time in the war, and I think he should be given every chance. I think you are a little too much inclined to attach importance to a man's social position. You must remember that times have changed. Of course it's a very good thing for a man to be a gentleman, but it's better that he should be competent and hard-working. I think if you'll exercise a little tolerance you'll get on very well with Cooper.

"Yours very sincerely,
"RICHARD TEMPLE."

The letter dropped from Mr. Warburton's hand. It was easy to read between the lines. Dick Temple, whom he had known for twenty years, Dick Temple, who came from quite a good county family, thought him a snob and for that reason had no patience with his request. Mr. Warburton felt on a sudden discouraged with life. The world of which he was a part had passed away, and the future belonged to a meaner generation. Cooper represented it and Cooper he hated with all his heart. He stretched out his hand to fill his glass and at the gesture his head-boy stepped forward.

"I didn't know you were there."

The boy picked up the official letter. Ah, that was why he was waiting.

"Does Tuan Cooper go, Tuan?"

"No."

"There will be a misfortune."

For a moment the words conveyed nothing to his lassitude. But only for a moment. He sat up in his chair and looked at the boy. He was all attention.

"What do you mean by that?"

"Tuan Cooper is not behaving rightly with Abas."

Mr. Warburton shrugged his shoulders. How should a man like Cooper know how to treat servants? Mr. Warburton knew the type: he would be grossly familiar with them at one moment and rude and inconsiderate the next.

"Let Abas go back to his family."

"Tuan Cooper holds back his wages so that he may not run away. He has paid him nothing for three months. I tell him to be patient. But he is angry, he will not listen to reason. If the tuan continues to use him ill there will be a misfortune."

"You were right to tell me."

The fool! Did he know so little of the Malays as to think he could safely injure them? It would serve him damned well right if he got a kris in his back. A kris. Mr. Warburton's heart seemed on a sudden to miss a beat. He had only to let things take their course and one fine day he would be rid of Cooper. He smiled faintly as the phrase, a masterly inactivity, crossed his mind. And now his heart beat a little quicker, for he saw the man he hated lying on his face in a pathway of the jungle with a knife in his back. A fit end for the cad and the bully. Mr. Warburton sighed. It was his duty to warn him and of course he must do it. He wrote a brief and formal note to Cooper asking him to come to the Fort at once.

In ten minutes Cooper stood before him. They had not spoken to one another since the day when Mr. Warburton had nearly struck him. He did not now ask him to sit down.

"Did you wish to see me?" Cooper asked.

He was untidy and none too clean. His face and hands were covered with little red blotches where mosquitoes had bitten him and he had scratched himself till the blood came. His long, thin face bore a sullen look.

"I understand that you are again having trouble with your servants. Abas, my head-boy's nephew, complains that you have held back his wages for three months. I consider it a most arbitrary proceeding. The lad wishes to leave you, and I certainly do not blame him. I must insist on your paying what is due to him."

"I don't choose that he should leave me. I am holding back his wages as a pledge of his good behavior."

"You do not know the Malay character. The Malays are very sensitive to injury and ridicule. They are passionate and revengeful. It is my duty to warn you that if you drive this boy beyond a certain point you run a great risk."

Cooper gave a contemptuous chuckle.

"What do you think he'll do?"

"I think he'll kill you."

"Why should you mind?"

"Oh, I wouldn't," replied Mr. Warburton, with a faint laugh. "I should bear it with the utmost fortitude. But I feel the official obligation to give you a proper warning."

"Do you think I'm afraid of a damned nigger?"

"It's a matter of entire indifference to me."

"Well, let me tell you this, I know how to take care of myself; that boy Abas is a dirty, thieving rascal, and if he tries any monkey tricks on me, by God, I'll wring his bloody neck."

"That was all I wished to say to you," said Mr. Warbuton. "Good evening."

Mr. Warburton gave him a little nod of dismissal. Cooper flushed, did not for a moment know what to say or do, turned on his heel and stumbled out of the room. Mr. Warburton watched him go with an icy smile on his lips. He had done his duty. But what would he have thought had he known that when Copper got back to his bungalow, so silent and cheerless, he threw himself down on his bed and in his bitter loneliness on a sudden lost all control of himself? Painful sobs tore his chest and heavy tears rolled down his thin cheeks.

After this Mr. Warburton seldom saw Cooper, and never spoke to him. He read his *Times* every morning, did his work at the office, took his exercise, dressed for dinner, dined and sat by the river smoking his cheroot. If by chance he ran across Cooper he cut him dead. Each, though never for a moment unconscious of the propinquity, acted as though the other did not exist. Time did nothing to assuage their animosity. They watched one another's actions and each knew what the other did. Though Mr. Warburton had been a keen shot in his youth, with age he had acquired a distaste for killing the wild things of the jungle, but on Sundays and holidays Cooper went out with his gun: if he got something it was a triumph over Mr. Warburton; if not, Mr. Warburton shrugged his shoulders and chuckled. These counter-jumpers trying to be sportsmen! Christmas was a bad time for both of them: they ate their dinners alone, each in his own quarters, and they got deliberately drunk. They were the only white men within two hundred miles and they lived within shouting distance of each other. At the beginning of the year Cooper went down with fever, and when Mr. Warburton caught sight of him again he was surprised to see how thin he had grown. He looked ill and worn. The solitude, so much more unnatural because it was due to no necessity, was getting on his nerves. It was getting on Mr. Warburton's too, and often he could not sleep at night. He lay awake brooding. Cooper was drinking heavily and surely the breaking point was near; but in his dealings with the natives he took care to do nothing that might expose him to his chief's rebuke. They fought a grim and silent battle with one another. It was a test of endurance. The months passed, and neither gave sign of weakening. They were like men dwelling in regions of eternal night, and their souls were oppressed with the knowledge that never would the day dawn for them. It looked as though their lives would continue for ever in this dull and hideous monotony of hatred.

And when at last the inevitable happened it came upon Mr. Warburton with all the shock of the unexpected. Cooper accused the boy Abas of stealing some of his clothes, and when the boy denied the theft took him by the scruff of the neck and kicked him down the steps of the bungalow. The boy demanded his wages, and Cooper flung at his head every word of abuse he knew. If he saw him in the compound in an hour he would hand him over to the police. Next morning the boy waylaid him outside the Fort when he was walking over to his office, and again demanded his wages. Cooper struck him in the face with his clenched fist. The boy fell to the ground and got up with blood streaming from his nose.

Cooper walked on and set about his work. But he could not attend to it. The blow had calmed his irritation, and he knew that he had gone too far. He was worried. He felt ill, miserable and discouraged. In the adjoining office sat Mr. Warburton, and his impulse was to go and tell him what he had done; he made a movement in his chair, but he knew with what icy scorn he would listen to the story. He could see his patronizing smile. For a moment he had an uneasy fear of what Abas might do. Warburton had warned him all right. He sighed. What a fool he had been! But he shrugged his shoulders impatiently. He did not care; a fat lot he had to live for. It was all Warburton's fault; if he hadn't put his back up nothing like this would have happened. Warburton had made life a hell for him from the start. The snob. But they were all like that: it was because he was a Colonial. It was a damned shame that he had never got his commission in the war; he was as good as any one else. They were a lot of dirty snobs. He was damned if he was going to knuckle under now. Of course Warburton would hear of what had happened; the old devil knew everything. He wasn't afraid. He wasn't afraid of any Malay in Borneo, and Warburton could go to blazes.

He was right in thinking that Mr. Warburton would know what had happened. His head-boy told him when he went in to tiffin.

"Where is your nephew now?"

"I do not know, Tuan. He has gone."

Mr. Warburton remained silent. After luncheon as a rule he slept a little, but today he found himself very wide awake. His eyes involuntarily sought the bungalow where Cooper was now resting.

The idiot! Hesitation for a little was in Mr. Warburton's mind. Did the man know in what peril he was? He supposed he ought to send for him. But each time he had tried to reason with Cooper, Cooper had insulted him. Anger, furious anger welled up suddenly in Mr. Warburton's heart, so that the veins on his temples stood out and he clenched his fists. The cad had had his warning. Now let him take what was coming to him. It was no business of his and if anything happened it was not his fault. But perhaps they would wish in Kuala Solor that they had taken his advice and transferred Cooper to another station.

He was strangely restless that night. After dinner he walked up and down the verandah. When the boy went away to his own quarters, Mr. Warburton asked him whether anything had been seen of Abas.

"No, Tuan, I think maybe he has gone to the village of his mother's brother."

Mr. Warburton gave him a sharp glance, but the boy was looking down and their eyes did not meet. Mr. Warburton went down to the river and sat in his arbor. But peace was denied him. The river flowed ominously silent. It was like a great serpent gliding with sluggish movement towards the sea. And the trees of the jungle over the water were heavy with a breathless meanace. No bird sang. No breeze ruffled the leaves of the cassias. All around him it seemed as though something waited.

He walked across the garden to the road. He had Cooper's bungalow in full view from there. There was a light in his sitting-room and across the road floated the sound of rag-time. Cooper was playing his gramophone. Mr. Warburton shuddered; he had never got over his instinctive dislike of that instrument. But for that he would have gone over and spoken to Cooper. He turned and went back to his own house. He read late into the night, and at last he slept. But he did not sleep very long, he had terrible dreams, and he seemed to be awakened by a cry. Of course that was a dream too, for no cry—from the bungalow for instance—could be heard in his room. He lay awake till dawn. Then he heard hurried steps and the sound of voices, his head-boy burst into the room without his fez, and Mr. Warburton's heart stood still.

"Tuan, Tuan."

Mr. Warburton jumped out of bed.

"I'll come at once."

He put on his slippers; and in his sarong

and pyjama-jacket walked across his compound and into Cooper's. Cooper was lying in bed, with his mouth open, and a kris sticking in his heart. He had been killed in his sleep. Mr. Warburton started, but not because he had not expected to see just such a sight, he started because he felt in himself a sudden glow of exultation. A great burden had been lifted from his shoulders.

Cooper was quite cold. Mr. Warburton took the kris out of the wound, it had been thrust in with such force that he had to use an effort to get it out, and looked at it. He recognized it. It was a kris that a dealer had offered him some weeks before and which he knew Cooper had bought.

"Where is Abas?" he asked sternly.

"Abas is at the village of his mother's brother."

The sergeant of the native police was standing at the foot of the bed.

"Take two men and go to the village and arrest him."

Mr. Warburton did what was immediately necessary. With set face he gave orders. His words were short and peremptory. Then he went back to the Fort. He shaved and had his bath, dressed and went into the diningroom. By the side of his plate *The Times* in its wrapper lay waiting for him. He helped himself to some fruit. The head-boy poured out his tea while the second handed him a dish of eggs. Mr. Warburton ate with a good appetite. The head-boy waited.

"What is it?" asked Mr. Warburton.

"Tuan, Abas, my nephew, was in the house of his mother's brother all night. It can be proved. His uncle will swear that he did not leave the kampong."

Mr. Warburton turned upon him with a frown.

"Tuan Cooper was killed by Abas. You know it as well as I know it. Justice must be done."

"Tuan, you would not hang him?"

Mr. Warburton hesitated an instant, and though his voice remained set and stern a change came into his eyes. It was a flicker which the Malay was quick to notice and across his own eyes flashed an answering look of understanding.

"The provocation was very great. Abas will be sentenced to a term of imprisonment." There was a pause while Mr. Warburton helped himself to marmalade. "When he has served a part of his sentence in prison I will take him into this house as a boy. You can train him in his duties. I have no doubt that in the house of Tuan Cooper he got into bad habits."

"Shall Abas give himself up, Tuan?"

"It would be wise of him."

The boy withdrew. Mr. Warburton took his *Times* and neatly slit the wrapper. He loved to unfold the heavy, rustling pages. The morning, so fresh and cool, was delicious and for a moment his eyes wandered out over his garden with a friendly glance. A great weight had been lifted from his mind. He turned to the columns in which were announced the births, deaths, and marriages. That was what he always looked at first. A name he knew caught his attention. Lady Ormskirk had had a son at last. By George, how pleased the old dowager must be! He would write her a note of congratulation by the next mail.

Abas would made a very good houseboy.

That fool Cooper!

[1924]

For Thought

"The Outstation" explores the contrasting social prejudices of two British colonial officials stationed in the Far East shortly after World War I. Maugham develops the characterization of Warburton and Cooper in several ways: by the use of polarizing dialogue, by the creation of totally different backgrounds for the two men (Edwardian London for one, colonial Barbados for the other), by a balanced presentation of their virtues and vices, and by the use of the third-person limited omniscient and omniscient points of view, with occasional scene setting tactics. These elements work together to produce a rounded characterization for both the chief resident and his assistant. Provided with this varied approach, the reader is able to see how the two characters are destined to clash, with each being a prisoner to his own set of fixed ideas. It seems inevitable, therefore, that when the deepening hostility between the two leads to murder of the unacceptable newcomer, it is achieved with the passive connivance and gratification of his social adversary.

For Discussion

1. In what way are the characters of Warburton and Cooper each made up of moral and emotional opposites?
2. List the characteristics of the Malays as Warburton sees them; as Cooper describes them; and as Maugham (as objective narrator) presents them.
3. By what stages does the action of the story develop from hidden personal and professional irritations to open animosity, then to complete alienation?
4. What factors determine Warburton's degree of responsibility for Cooper's death? How is Cooper's death foreshadowed through language and action?
5. To what extent is it possible to sympathize with one character to the exclusion of the other?
6. How do the figurative descriptions of nature extend or modify Warburton's moods?
7. Find evidence of stage directions, gestures, and dialogue in the story that support the observation that Maugham uses techniques borrowed from the stage.
8. How are the title, location, and setting of the story symbolic, often ironically so?
9. What elements in the story satirize English social life, education, sportsmanship, and the military?
10. What theme arises out of the conflict and its resolution?

Alberto Moravia
The Fetish

Immediately after the wedding they had gone to live in a penthouse flat in the Parioli district of Rome which Livio's father-in-law had made over to his daughter as a dowry. The flat was almost empty, except for such pieces of furniture as were indispensable; but the bride declared she was in no hurry: she wished to furnish it her own way. And so, in a leisurely manner, she started to acquire, here and there, furniture, fittings, ornaments and pictures, all in a very "modern" taste which to Livio, convinced that she was following the fashion rather than a reasoned preference, seemed at the same time both conceited and snobbish. The fetish was discovered by his wife in the back shop of a rather special kind of antique-dealer, an elderly American who had set up a small shop in order to liquidate the stuff he had accumulated, in a villa belonging to him, during twenty years of travel all over the world. It—the fetish—was a cylinder of grey stone of the most ordinary kind, as tall as a man but much broader, terminating in a head shaped like a pointed cone, with strongly stylized features: all that was indicated was the arches of the eyebrows, the septum of the nose, and the chin. At each side of the cylinder, where the junctions of the arms should have been, two round bosses, like two buttons, were carved in the stone. The figure, rough and imprecise though evilly expressive, at once aroused extreme antipathy in Livio. He did not admit it to himself, but the reason for this antipathy lay, in truth, in his wife's infatuation for the fetish—one infatuation amongst many that he disapproved of because he did not understand it.

Livio took to calling the figure "The Martian"; it did in fact somewhat resemble the clumsy puppets by which the illustrators of comic papers usually represent those imaginary celestial creatures. "I'm not going to kiss you good-morning today," he would say; "the Martian is watching us." "The Martian seems more than usually ill-humoured to-day; d'you see how sulky he looks?" "Last night I went into the bathroom and what did I see? The Martian brushing his teeth." "Don Giovanni had the statue of the Commendatore, I have the

Martian. That's an idea: why don't we invite him to supper?"

This last remark, contrary to what was usual, elicited a response. They were eating in the living-room, right in front of the fetish, which appeared to be watching them intently from its half-dark corner. "I'm almost inclined," she said, "to take you at your word and leave you to finish eating with *him*."

She spoke calmly, pronouncing each syllable distinctly, her head lowered. But with so obvious a hostility that Livio had almost a feeling of fear. Nevertheless, carried away by his own joke he persisted: "The first thing to do is to see whether he'll accept the invitation."

"In fact," she went on, as though she had not heard him, "I'll leave you anyhow. Enjoy your meal." She put down her napkin on the table, rose and left the room.

Livio remained seated and tried for a little to imagine how the fetish would manage to leave its corner, roll on its circular base up to the table, and then sit down and eat. A few days before he had been to a performance of *Don Giovanni* at the Opera; and the coincidence amused him. But what sort of a voice would the fetish have? In what language would it speak? To what Papuan or Polynesian hell would it drag him down at the end of the supper-party?

These fancies, however, did not suffice to distract him from his wife's gesture. He hoped it was a piece of momentary ill-humour, he expected to see her reappear in the doorway; but nothing happened. Now, after his previous amusement, the idea of the fetish coming to dine with him disgusted him. And the fetish itself, looking at him from its dark corner, filled him with embarrassment. Finally he called out in a loud voice: "Alina!"; but no one answered, the flat seemed empty. The maid had come in with the dishes on a tray. Livio told her to put it down on the table, then rose and went out.

The bedroom was at the far end of the passage; the door was ajar; Livio pushed it and went in. This room, too, contained no furniture apart from the bed and two chairs. There was a suitcase on the bed, open. His wife, standing in front of the wide-open wall-cupboard, was taking a dress off its hanger.

For a moment Livio was dumbfounded, not knowing what to say. Then he realized that his wife was on the point of leaving him, two months after their wedding; and an icy chill ran up his spine. "Why Alina," he said, "what in the world are you doing?"

At the sound of his voice she at once let go of the coathanger and sat down on the bed. Livio also sat down, put his arm round her waist and murmured: "But why, Alina, why? What's come over you?"

He expected a conciliatory reply but, when he looked at her, he saw that he was mistaken. His wife's face, round, massive, of a livid pallor in which her pale blue eyes stood out conspicuously, was darkened by a settled hostility. "What has come over me," she said, "is that you make jokes about everything and that I can't stand your jokes any longer."

"But it's my nature; I like making jokes—and what's the harm in it?"

"There may not be any harm in it, but I can't stand it any longer."

"But why, my love?"

"Don't call me 'my love.' You never talk seriously, you have to be witty about everything, you always have to show that you're superior to everything."

"Come, come, Alina, don't you think you're exaggerating?"

"I'm not exaggerating at all. Every time you make a joke, I feel my heart sink. One would think . . ."

"What would one think?"

"One would think that, since you can't bring yourself up to the level of certain things, you try, by means of sarcasm, to bring them down to *your* level. Besides, it's not only that . . ."

"What is it, then?"

"You even make jokes at moments when

no man would make jokes. During our honeymoon you said something that I shall remember all my life."

"What was that?"

"That I shall never tell you."

Silence followed. Livio was still clasping her round the waist, as he sat beside her. Then, as he looked at her, he realized, with the feeling that he was making an important discovery, that it was the first time since they had come to know each other that he had spoken to her seriously, in a sincere, affectionate way, without hiding behind a mask of jokes. He reflected that it had needed nothing less than a threat of abandonment to induce him to change his tone, and suddenly he felt remorseful. "Now Alina," he said, "let's consider what it is that has really happened. You bought that fetish, which I didn't like, and brought it home. Why did I begin to make jokes about the fetish? Not, certainly, because it's ugly or ridiculous or clumsy; there are already plenty of clumsy, ugly, ridiculous things in this flat. No, it was because you became infatuated with it to such a degree . . ."

His wife sat listening to him with an attentiveness that seemed to emanate from the whole of her compact, heavy body and become concentrated in the small, fleshy ear which peeped out from beneath her black hair. All of a sudden she clapped her hands and turned towards Livio: "You've said it, you've said it, once and for all."

"What d'you mean?"

"You can't endure what you call my infatuations."

"No, of course not; and so . . . ?"

"But don't you realize that what you call my infatuations are my feelings, my affections, myself, in fact?"

"Have you then a feeling, an affection for that stone puppet?"

"I might have—who knows? I have—or rather, I had—a feeling for you, certainly. And you've treated it as an infatuation, you've thrown your icy shower-bath of jokes over it."

"When have I ever done that?"

"I've already told you, during our honeymoon."

"I made jokes about your feeling for me during our honeymoon?"

"Yes, in Venice, to be precise, in the hotel room, the first night. And you didn't make jokes only about my feeling but also about my physical appearance, and just at a moment when no man—and mind, I say this with the utmost seriousness—when no man would have dared to do so."

"I made jokes about your physical appearance?"

"Yes, about one detail of my appearance."

Livio suddenly blushed up to his ears, although he was quite unable to recall having made a joke on that occasion. At last he said: "It may be true, but I don't remember. Anyhow I should like to know what the joke was. It may have been an innocent thing, like the remark I made about your fetish this evening."

"Certainly it was an innocent thing, inasmuch as you weren't conscious of it. However, it had the same effect on me as if you had put a piece of ice down my neck. It was our first night after our wedding and you didn't realize that I hated you."

"You hated me?"

"Yes, with all my soul."

"And do you hate me now?"

"Now—I don't know."

Livio again remained silent, looking intently at her. Then suddenly he had the feeling that he was face to face with a complete stranger, about whom he knew nothing, neither past nor present, neither feelings nor thoughts. This feeling of estrangement had arisen from her remark: "You didn't realize that I hated you." And indeed he had not realized that he was holding in his arms a woman who hated him. About that night he remembered everything, even the wind that from time to time caused the curtain to swell out slightly over the window wide-open on to the Lagoon; but not her hatred. Moreover, if he had not been aware of so important a feeling, how many other things had escaped his notice, how much of her had remained unknown to him? But it was clear by now that his wife did not intend to leave; that the suitcase open on the bed formed part of a kind of ritual of matrimonial dispute; that he himself must now initiate the reconciliation, however strange and unknown she might seem to him. With an effort, he took her hand and said: "You must forgive me. I am what is generally called an impious man."

"What does impious mean?"

"The opposite of pious. A man for whom sacred things do not exist. But from now onwards I shall try and mend my ways, I promise you."

His wife looked at him, she contemplated him, in fact, with her pale blue, rather sullen eyes; as one looks at a singular and incomprehensible object. Finally she said, quite simply: "Well, go on back, I'll be with you in a moment"; and, leaning forward, she gave him a smacking kiss on the cheek.

Livio would have liked to say something but he could not find anything to say. He rose, went back into the living-room and sat down again at the table. He took a cutlet from the tray, put it on his plate and prepared to start eating. Then he dropped his knife and fork and looked in front of him.

The fetish, as before, was right opposite him; its brow low above its eyes like a vizor, it seemed to be staring at him with a menacing, demanding air. As though it wished to say to him: "This is only the beginning. There will be all too many other things about which you will have to stop making jokes."

Livio remembered Don Giovanni and reflected that he at least had had the consolation of being punished for mocking at the principles of a recognized and respected religion. But he himself had to pay respect to an unconsecrated world, without hell and without paradise, a world that was mute and absurd, like the stone fetish.

A rustling sound made him start. His wife had come back and was now seated opposite to him again. Livio noticed that, in perspective, his wife's face appeared to be closely coupled with the stupid, ferocious face of the fetish. And he shuddered anxiously.

[1964]

For Thought

"The Fetish" treats a striking twist on the eternal love triangle. That is, Moravia makes the husband's rival an inanimate statue. Moreover, it is he who becomes obsessed with the fetish, not his wife. Through Livio's belief in the statue's powers, the fetish takes on the status of a near deity. In truth, Livio's wife's affections have been alienated and Livio will have to learn to live with a growing feeling of despair and futility.

For Discussion

1. How is the story divided into four consecutive sequences?
2. The psychologist Otto Fenichel has defined a fetish as "an object with little intrinsic value" that "takes on immense importance through over valuation." In what way has the fetish been given exaggerated significance?
3. What is the significance of Livio's nickname for the fetish?
4. How has the wife, Alina, in demanding seriousness from her husband, required a sort of unspoken collusion or game-playing from him?
5. What is the significance of having the couple newly married?
6. What symbols does the author use to amplify the emptiness of the marriage?

7. In the opera *Don Giovanni*, the Commendatore, while trying to defend his daughter's honor, is murdered by Don Giovanni in a duel. Don Giovanni later invites the Commendatore's statue to dinner as a joke. To his surprise and regret, the statue arrives and summons him to hell for his crimes of murder and lust. How does the husband's situation ironically parallel that of Don Giovanni?
8. How is Livio characterized?
9. What insight does Livio achieve?
10. What is the central conflict?
11. The climax of the story is the highest point in the action from the standpoint of tension and decision. It represents the termination of the character's opportunity to choose; from this point on, he progresses to an inevitable resolution brought about by his decision at the climactic moment. When does this moment occur in "The Fetish"?
12. What is the point of view of the story, and what is its advantage?
13. What is the theme of the story?

Vladimir Nabokov
The Vane Sisters

I might never have heard of Cynthia's death, had I not run, that night, into D., whom I had also lost track of for the last four years or so; and I might never have run into D., had I not got involved in a series of trivial investigations.

The day, a compunctious Sunday after a week of blizzards, had been part jewel, part mud. In the midst of my usual afternoon stroll through the small hilly town attached to the girls' college where I taught French literature, I had stopped to watch a family of brilliant icicles drip-dripping from the eaves of a frame house. So clear-cut were their pointed shadows on the white boards behind them that I was sure the shadows of the falling drops should be visible too. But they were not. The roof jutted too far out, perhaps, or the angle of vision was faulty, or, again, I did not chance to be watching the right icicle when the right drop fell. There was a rhythm, an alternation in the dripping that I found as teasing as a coin trick. It led me to inspect the corners of several house blocks, and this brought me to Kelly Road, and right to the house where D. used to live when he was instructor here. And as I looked up at the eaves of the adjacent garage with its full display of transparent stalactites backed by their blue silhouettes, I was rewarded at last, upon choosing one, by the sight of what might be described as the dot of an exclamation mark leaving its ordinary position to glide down very fast—a jot faster than the thaw-drop it raced. This twinned twinkle was delightful but not completely satisfying; or rather it only sharpened my appetite for other tidbits of light and shade, and I walked on in a state of raw awareness that seemed to transform the whole of my being into one big eyeball rolling in the world's socket.

Through peacocked lashes I saw the dazzling diamond reflection of the low sun on the round back of a parked automobile. To all kinds of things a vivid pictorial sense had been restored by the sponge of the thaw. Water in overlapping festoons flowed down one sloping street and turned gracefully into another. With ever so slight a note of meretricious appeal, narrow passages between buildings revealed treasures of brick and purple. I remarked for the first time the humble fluting—last echoes of grooves on the shafts of columns—ornamenting a garbage can, and I also saw the rippling upon its lid—circles diverging from a fantastically ancient center. Erect, dark-headed shapes of dead snow (left by the blades of a bulldozer last Friday) were lined up like rudimentary penguins along the curbs, above the brilliant vibration of live gutters.

I walked up, and I walked down, and I walked straight into a delicately dying sky, and finally the sequence of observed and observant things brought me, at my usual eating time, to a street so distant from my usual eating place that I decided to try a restaurant which stood on the fringe of the town. Night had fallen without sound or ceremony when I came out again. The lean ghost, the elongated umbra cast by a parking meter upon some damp snow, had a strange ruddy tinge; this I made out to be due to the tawny red light of the restaurant sign above the sidewalk; and it was then—as I loitered there, wondering rather wearily if in the course of my return tramp I might be lucky enough to find the same in neon blue—it was then that a car crunched to a standstill near me and D. got out of it with an exclamation of feigned pleasure.

He was passing, on his way from Albany to Boston, through the town he had dwelt in before, and more than once in my life have I felt that stab of vicarious emotion followed by a rush of personal irritation against travelers who seem to feel nothing at all upon revisiting spots that ought to harass them at every step with wailing and writhing memories. He ushered me back into the bar that I had just left, and after the usual exchange of buoyant platitudes came the inevitable vacuum which he filled with the random words: "Say, I never thought there was anything wrong with Cynthia Vane's heart. My lawyer tells me she died last week."

He was still young, still brash, still shifty, still married to the gentle, exquisitely pretty woman who had never learned or suspected anything about his disastrous affair with Cynthia's hysterical young sister, who in her turn had known nothing of the interview I had had with Cynthia when she suddenly summoned me to Boston to make me swear I would talk to D. and get him "kicked out" if he did not stop seeing Sybil at once—or did not divorce his wife (whom incidentally she visualized through the prism of Sybil's wild talk as a termagant and a fright). I had cornered him immediately. He had said there was nothing to worry about—had made up his mind, anyway, to give up his college job and move with his wife to Albany where he would work in his father's firm; and the whole matter, which had threatened to become one of those hopelessly entangled situations that drag on for years, with peripheral sets of well-meaning friends endlessly discussing it in universal secrecy—and even founding, among themselves, new intimacies upon its alien woes—came to an abrupt end.

I remember sitting next day at my raised desk in the large classroom where a midyear examination in French Lit was being held on the eve of Sybil's suicide. She came in on high heels, with a suitcase, dumped it in a corner where several other bags were stacked, with a single shrug slipped her fur coat off her thin shoulders, folded it on her bag, and with two or three other girls stopped before my desk to ask when would I mail them their grades. It would take me a week, beginning from tomorrow, I said, to read the stuff. I also remember wondering whether D. had already informed her of his decision—and I felt acutely unhappy about my dutiful little student as during one hundred and fifty minutes my gaze kept reverting to her, so childishly slight in closefitting gray, and kept observing that carefully waved dark hair, that small, small-flowered hat with a little hyaline veil as worn that season and under it her small face broken into a cubist pattern by scars due to a skin disease, pathetically masked by a sunlamp tan that hardened her features whose charm was further impaired by her having painted everything that could be painted, so that the pale gums of her teeth between cherry-red chapped lips and the diluted blue ink of her eyes under darkened lids were the only visible openings into her beauty.

Next day, having arranged the ugly copybooks alphabetically, I plunged into their chaos of scripts and came prematurely to Valevsky and Vane whose books I had somehow misplaced. The first was dressed up for the occasion in a semblance of legibility, but Sybil's work displayed her usual combination of several demon hands. She had begun in very pale, very hard pencil which had conspicuously embossed the blank verso, but had produced little of permanent value on the upperside of the page. Happily the tip soon broke, and Sybil continued in another, darker, lead, gradually lapsing into the blurred thickness of what looked almost like charcoal, to which, by sucking the blunt point, she had contributed some traces of lipstick. Her work, although even poorer than I had expected, bore all the signs of a kind of desperate conscientiousness, with underscores, transposes, unnecessary footnotes, as if she were intent upon rounding up things in the most respectable manner possible. Then she had borrowed Mary Valevsky's fountain pen and added: "*Cette examain est finie ainsi que ma vie. Adieu, jeunes filles!* Please, *Monsieur le Professeur*, contact *ma soeur* and tell her that Death was not better than D minus, but definitely better than Life minus D."

I lost no time in ringing up Cynthia who told me it was all over—had been all over since eight in the morning—and asked me to bring her the note, and when I did, beamed through her tears with proud admiration for the whimsical use ("Just like her!") Sybil had made of an examination in French literature. In no time she "fixed" two highballs, while never parting with Sybil's notebook—by now splashed with soda water and tears—and went on studying the death message, whereupon I was impelled to point out to her the grammatical mistakes in it and to explain the way "girl" is translated in American colleges lest students innocently bandy around the French equivalent of "wench," or worse. These rather tasteless trivialities pleased Cynthia hugely as she rose, with gasps, above the heaving surface of her grief. And then, holding that limp notebook as if it were a kind of passport to a casual Elysium (where pencil points do not snap and a dreamy young beauty with an impeccable complexion winds a lock of her hair on a dreamy forefinger, as she meditates over some celestial test), Cynthia led me upstairs, to a chilly little bedroom just to show me, as if I were the police or a sympathetic Irish neighbor, two empty pill bottles and the tumbled bed from which a tender, inessential body, that D. must have known down to its last velvet detail, had been already removed.

It was four or five months after her sister's death that I began seeing Cynthia fairly often. By the time I had come to New York for some vocational research in the Public Library she had also moved to that city where for some odd reason (in vague connection, I presume, with artistic motives) she had taken what people, immune to gooseflesh, term a "cold water" flat, low down in the scale of the city's transverse streets. What attracted me were neither her ways, which I thought repulsively vivacious, nor her looks, which other men thought striking. She had wide-spaced eyes very much like her sister's, of a frank, frightened blue with dark points in a radial arrangement. The interval between her thick black eyebrows was always shiny, and shiny too were the fleshy volutes of her nostrils. The coarse texture of her epiderm looked almost masculine, and, in the stark lamplight of her studio, you could see the pores of her thirty-two-year-old face fairly gaping at you like something in an aquarium. She used cosmetics with as much zest as her little sister had, but with an additional slovenliness that would result in her big front teeth getting some of the rouge. She was handsomely dark, wore a not too tasteless mixture of fairly smart heterogenous things, and had a so-called good figure; but all of her was curiously frowsy, after a way I obscurely associated with left-wing enthusiasms in politics and "advanced" banalities in art, although, actually, she cared for neither. Her coily hairdo, on a part-and-bun basis, might have looked feral and bizarre had it not been thoroughly domesticated by its own soft unkemptness at the vulnerable nape. Her fingernails were gaudily painted, but badly bitten and not clean. Her lovers were a silent young photographer with a sudden laugh and two older men, brothers, who owned a small printing establishment across the street. I wondered at their tastes whenever I glimpsed, with a secret shudder, the higgledy-piggledy striation of black hairs that showed all along her pale shins through the nylon of her stockings with the scientific distinctness of a preparation flattened under glass; or when I felt, at her every movement, the dullish, stalish, not particularly conspicuous but all-pervading and depressing emanation that her seldom-bathed flesh spread from under weary perfumes and creams.

Her father had gambled away the greater part of a comfortable fortune, and her mother's first husband had been of Slav origin, but otherwise Cynthia Vane belonged to a good, respectable family. For aught we know, it may have gone back to kings and soothsayers in the mists of ultimate islands. Transferred to a newer world, to a landscape of doomed, splendid deciduous trees, her ancestry presented, in one of its first phases, a white churchful of farmers against a black thunderhead, and then an imposing array of townsmen engaged in mercantile pursuits, as well as a number of learned men, such as Dr. Jonathan Vane, the gaunt bore (1780–1839), who perished in the conflagration of the steamer "Lexington" to become later an habitué of Cynthia's tilting table. I have always wished to stand genealogy on its head, and here I have an opportunity to do so, for it is the last scion, Cynthia, and Cynthia alone, who will remain of any importance in the Vane dynasty. I am alluding of course to her artistic gift, to her delightful, gay, but not very popular paintings which the friends of her friends bought at long intervals—and I dearly should like to know where they went after her death, those honest and poetical pictures that illuminated her living room—the wonderfully detailed images of metallic things, and my favorite "Seen Through a Windshield"—a windshield partly covered with rime, with a brilliant trickle (from an imaginary car roof) across its transparent part and, through it all, the sapphire flame of the sky and a green and white fir tree.

Cynthia had a feeling that her dead sister was not altogether pleased with her—had discovered by now that she and I had conspired to break her romance; and so, in order to disarm her shade, Cynthia reverted to a rather primitive type of sacrificial offering (tinged, however, with something of Sybil's humor), and began to send to D.'s business address, at deliberately unfixed dates, such trifles as snapshots of Sybil's tomb in a poor light; cuttings of her own hair which was indistinguishable from Sybil's; a New England sectional map with an inked-in cross, midway between two chaste towns, to mark the spot where D. and Sybil had stopped on October the twenty-third, in broad daylight, at a lenient motel, in a pink and brown forest; and, twice, a stuffed skunk.

Being as a conversationalist more voluble than explicit, she never could describe in full the theory of intervenient auras that she had somehow evolved. Fundamentally there was nothing particularly new about her private creed since it presupposed a fairly conventional hereafter, a silent solarium of immortal souls (spliced with mortal antecedents) whose main recreation consisted of periodical hoverings over the dear quick. The interesting point was a curious practical twist that Cynthia gave to her tame metaphysics. She was sure that her existence was influenced by all sorts of dead friends each of whom took turns in directing her fate much as if she were a stray kitten which a schoolgirl in passing gathers up, and presses to her cheek, and carefully puts down again, near some suburban hedge—to be stroked presently by another transient hand or carried off to a world of doors by some hospitable lady.

For a few hours, or for several days in a row, and sometimes recurrently, in an irregular series, for months or years, anything that happened to Cynthia, after a given person had died, would be, she said, in the manner and mood of that person. The event might be extraordinary, changing the course of one's life; or it might be a string of minute incidents just sufficiently clear to stand out in relief against one's usual day and then shading off into still vaguer trivia as the aura gradually faded. The influence might be good or bad; the main thing was that its source could be identified. It was like walking through a person's soul, she said. I tried to argue that she might not always be able to determine the exact source since not everybody has a recognizable soul; that there are anonymous letters and Christmas presents which anybody might send; that, in fact, what Cynthia called "a usual day" might be itself a weak solution of mixed auras or simply the routine shift of a humdrum guardian angel. And what about God? Did or did not people who would resent any omnipotent dictator on earth look forward to one in heaven? And wars? What a dreadful idea—dead soldiers still fighting with living ones, or phantom armies trying to get at each other through the lives of crippled old men.

But Cynthia was above generalities as she was beyond logic. "Ah, that's Paul," she would say when the soup spitefully boiled over, or: "I guess good Betty Brown is dead"—when she won a beautiful and very welcome vacuum cleaner in a charity lottery. And, with Jamesian meanderings that exasperated my French mind, she would go back to a time when Betty and Paul had not yet departed, and tell me of the showers of well-meant, but odd and quite unacceptable bounties—beginning with an old purse that contained a check for three dollars which she picked up in the street and, of course, returned (to the aforesaid Betty Brown—this is where she first comes in—a decrepit colored woman hardly able to walk), and ending with an insulting proposal from an old beau of hers (this is where Paul comes in) to paint "straight" pictures of his house and family for a reasonable remuneration—all of which followed upon the demise of a certain Mrs. Page, a kindly but petty old party who had pestered her with bits of matter-of-fact advice since Cynthia had been a child.

Sybil's personality, she said, had a rainbow edge as if a little out of focus. She said that had I known Sybil better I would have at once understood how Sybil-like was the aura of minor events which, in spells, had suffused her, Cynthia's, existence after Sybil's suicide. Ever since they had lost their mother they had intended to give up their Boston home and move to New York, where Cynthia's paintings, they thought, would have a chance to be more widely admired; but the old home had clung to them with all its plush tentacles. Dead Sybil, however, had proceeded to separate the house from its view—a thing that affects fatally the sense of home. Right across the narrow street a building project had come into loud, ugly, scaffolded life. A pair of familiar poplars died that spring, turning to blond skeletons. Workmen came and broke up the warm-colored lovely old sidewalk that had a special violet sheen on wet April days and had echoed so memorably to the morning footsteps of museum-bound Mr. Lever, who upon retiring from the business at sixty had devoted a full quarter of a century exclusively to the study of snails.

Speaking of old men, one should add that sometimes these posthumous auspices and interventions were in the nature of parody. Cynthia had been on friendly terms with an eccentric librarian called Porlock who in the last years of his dusty life had been engaged in examining old books for miraculous misprints such as the substitution of "l" for the second "h" in the word "hither." Contrary to Cynthia, he cared nothing for the thrill of obscure predictions; all he sought was the freak itself, the chance that mimics choice, the flaw that looks like a flower; and Cynthia, a much more perverse amateur of misshapen or illicitly connected words, puns, logogriphs, and so on, had helped the poor crank to pursue a quest that in the light of the example she cited struck me as statistically insane. Anyway, she said, on the third day after his death she was reading a magazine and had just come across a quotation from an imperishable poem (that she, with other gullible readers, believed to have been really composed in a dream) when it dawned upon her that "Alph" was a prophetic sequence of the initial letters of Anna Livia Plurabelle (another sacred river running through, or rather around, yet another fake dream), while the additional "h" modestly stood, as a private signpost, for the word that had so hypnotized Mr. Porlock. And I wish I could recollect that novel or short story (by some contemporary writer, I believe) in which, unknown to its author, the first letters of the words in its last paragraph formed, as deciphered by Cynthia, a message from his dead mother.

I am sorry to say that not content with these ingenious fancies Cynthia showed a ridiculous fondness for spiritualism. I refused to accompany her to sittings in which paid mediums took part: I knew too much about that from other sources. I did consent, however, to attend little farces rigged up by Cynthia and her two poker-faced gentlemen-friends of the printing shop. They were podgy, polite and rather eerie old fellows, but I satisfied myself that they possessed considerable wit and culture. We sat down at a light little table, and crackling tremors started almost as soon as we laid our fingertips upon it. I was treated to an assortment of ghosts who rapped out their reports most readily though refusing to elucidate anything that I did not quite catch. Oscar Wilde came and in rapid garbled French, with the usual anglicisms, obscurely accused Cynthia's dead parents of what appeared in my jottings as "*plagiatisme*." A brisk spirit contributed the unsolicited information that he, John Moore, and his borther Bill had been coal miners in Colorado and had perished in an avalanche at "Crested Beauty" in January 1883. Frederic Myers, an old hand at the game, hammered out a piece of verse (oddly resembling Cynthia's own fugitive productions) which in part reads in my notes:

> What is this—a conjuror's rabbit,
> Or a flawy but genuine gleam—
> Which can check the perilous habit
> And dispel the dolorous dream?

Finally, with a great crash and all kinds of shudderings and jig-like movements on the part of the table, Leo Tolstoy visited our little group and, when asked to identify himself by specific traits of terrene habitation, launched upon a complex description of what seemed to be some Russian type of architectural woodwork ("figures on boards—man, horse, cock, man, horse, cock"), all of which was difficult to take down, hard to understand and impossible to verify.

I attended two or three other sittings which were even sillier but I must confess that I preferred the childish entertainment they afforded and the cider we drank

(Podgy and Pudgy were teetotalers) to Cynthia's awful house parties.

She gave them at the Wheelers' nice flat next door—the sort of arrangement dear to her centrifugal nature, but then, of course, her own living room always looked like a dirty old palette. Following a barbaric, unhygienic, and adulterous custom, the guests' coats, still warm on the inside, were carried by quiet baldish Bob Wheeler into the sanctity of a tidy bedroom and heaped on the conjugal bed. It was also he who poured out the drinks which were passed around by the young photographer while Cynthia and Mrs. Wheeler took care of the canapés.

A late arrival had the impression of lots of loud people unnecessarily grouped within a smoke-blue space between two mirrors gorged with reflections. Because, I suppose, Cynthia wished to be the youngest in the room, the women she used to invite, married or single, were, at the best, in their precarious forties; some of them would bring from their homes, in dark taxis, intact vestiges of good looks, which, however, they lost as the party progressed. It has always amazed me—the capacity sociable weekend revelers have of finding almost at once, by a purely empiric but very precise method, a common denominator of drunkenness, to which everybody loyally sticks before descending, all together, to the next level. The rich friendliness of the matrons was marked by tomboyish overtones, while the fixed inward look of amiably tight men was like a sacrilegious parody of pregnancy. Although some of the guests were connected in one way or another with the arts, there was no inspired talk, no wreathed, elbow-propped heads, and of course no flute girls. From some vantage point where she had been sitting in a stranded mermaid pose on the pale carpet with one or two younger fellows, Cynthia, her face varnished with a film of beaming sweat, would creep up on her knees, a proffered plate of nuts in one hand, and crisply tap with the other the athletic leg of Cochran or Corcoran, an art dealer, ensconced, on a pearl-gray sofa, between two flushed, happily disintegrating ladies.

At a further state there would come spurts of more riotous gaiety. Corcoran or Coransky would grab Cynthia or some other wandering woman by the shoulder and lead her into a corner to comfort her with a grinning embroglio of private jokes and rumors, whereupon, with a laugh and a toss of her head, she would break away. And still later there would be flurries of intersexual chumminess, jocular reconciliations, a bare fleshy arm flung around another woman's husband (he standing very upright in the midst of a swaying room), or a sudden rush of flirtatious anger, of clumsy pursuit—and the quiet half smile of Bob Wheeler picking up glasses that grew like mushrooms in the shade of chairs.

After one last party of that sort, I wrote Cynthia a perfectly harmless and, on the whole, well-meant note, in which I poked a little Latin fun at some of her guests. I also apologized for not having touched her whiskey, saying that as a Frenchman I preferred the grape to the grain. A few days later I met her on the steps of the Public Library, in the broken sun, under a weak cloudburst, opening her amber umbrella, struggling with a couple of armpitted books (of which I relieved her for a moment), "Footfalls on the Boundary of Another World," by Robert Dale Owen, and something on "Spiritualism and Christianity"; when, suddenly, with no provocation on my part, she blazed out at me with vulgar vehemence, using poisonous words, saying—through pear-shaped drops of sparse rain—that I was a prig and a snob; that I only saw the gestures and disguises of people; that Corcoran had rescued from drowning, in two different oceans, two men—by an irrelevant coincidence both called Corcoran; that romping and screeching Joan Winter had a little girl doomed to grow completely blind in a few months; and that the woman in green with the freckled chest whom I had snubbed in some way or other had written a national best seller in 1932. Strange Cynthia! I had been told she could be thunderously rude to people whom she liked and respected; one had, however, to draw the line somewhere and since I had by then sufficiently studied her interesting auras and other odds and ids, I decided to stop seeing her altogether.

The night D. informed me of Cynthia's death I returned after eleven to the two-storied house I shared, in horizontal section, with an emeritus professor's widow. Upon reaching the porch I looked with the apprehension of solitude at the two kinds of darkness in the two rows of windows: the darkness of absence and the darkness of sleep.

I could do something about the first but could not duplicate the second. My bed gave me no sense of safety; its springs only made my nerves bounce. I plunged into Shakespeare's sonnets—and found myself idiotically checking the first letters of the lines to see what sacramental words they might form. I got FATE (LXX), ATOM (CXX) and, twice, TAFT (LXXXVIII, CXXI). Every now and then I would glance around to see how the objects in my room were behaving. It was strange to think that if bombs began to fall I would feel little more than a gambler's excitement (and a great deal of earthy relief) whereas my heart would burst if a certain suspiciously tense-looking little bottle on yonder shelf moved a fraction of an inch to one side. The silence, too, was suspiciously compact as if deliberately forming a black backdrop for the nerve flash caused by any small sound of unknown origin. All traffic was dead. In vain did I pray for the groan of a truck up Perkins Street. The woman above who used to drive me crazy by the booming thuds occasioned by what seemed monstrous feet of stone (actually, in diurnal life, she was a small dumpy creature resembling a mummified guinea pig) would have earned my blessings had she now trudged to her bathroom. I put out my light and cleared my throat several times so as to be responsible for at least *that* sound. I thumbed a mental ride with a very remote automobile but it dropped me before I had a chance to doze off. Presently a crackle (due, I hoped, to a discarded and crushed sheet of paper opening like a mean, stubborn night flower)—started and stopped in the wastepaper basket, and my bed-table responded with a little click. It would have been just like Cynthia to put on right then a cheap poltergeist show.

I decided to fight Cynthia. I reviewed in thought the modern era of raps and apparitions, beginning with the knockings of 1848, at the hamlet of Hydesville, N.Y., and ending with grotesque phenomena at Cambridge, Mass.; I evoked the anklebones and other anatomical castanets of the Fox sisters (as described by the sages of the University of Buffalo); the mysteriously uniform type of delicate adolescent in bleak Epworth or Tedworth, radiating the same disturbances as in old Peru; solemn Victorian orgies with roses falling and accordions floating to the strains of sacred music; professional impostors regurgitating moist cheesecloth; Mr. Duncan, a lady medium's dignified husband, who, when asked if he would submit to a search, excused himself on the ground of soiled underwear; old Alfred Russel Wallace, the naïve naturalist, refusing to believe that the white form with bare feet and unperforated earlobes before him, at a private pandemonium in Boston, could be prim Miss Cook whom he had just seen asleep, in her curtained corner, all dressed in black, wearing laced-up boots and earrings; two other investigators, small, puny, but reasonably intelligent and active men, closely clinging with arms and legs about Eusapia, a large plump elderly female reeking of garlic, who still managed to fool them; and Dingwall, the sceptical and embarrassed magician, instructed by charming young Margery's "control" not to get lost in the bathrobe's lining but to follow up the left stocking until he reached the bare thigh—upon the warm skin of which he felt a "teleplastic" mass that appeared to the touch uncommonly like cold uncooked liver.

I was appealing to flesh, and the corruption of flesh, to refute and defeat the possible persistence of discarnate life. Alas, these conjurations only enhanced my fear of Cynthia's phantom. Atavistic peace came with dawn, and when I slipped into sleep, the sun through the tawny window shades penetrated a dream that somehow was full of Cynthia.

This was disappointing. Secure in the fortress of daylight, I said to myself that I had expected more. She, a painter of glass-bright minutiae—and now so vague! I lay in bed, thinking my dream over and listening to the sparrows outside: Who knows, if recorded and then run backward, those bird sounds might not become human speech, voiced words, just as the latter become a twitter when reversed? I set myself to reread my dream—backward, diagonally, up, down—trying hard to unravel something Cynthia-like in it, something strange and suggestive that must be there.

I could isolate, consciously, little. Everything seemed blurred, yellow-clouded, yielding nothing tangible. Her inept acrostics, maudlin evasions, theopathies—every recollection formed ripples of mysterious meaning. Everything seemed yellowly blurred, illusive, lost.

[1975]

For Thought

"The Vane Sisters" takes the form of a long, rambling monologue. The narrator purports to be a professor of French literature who dissects the characters of two eccentric, oddly attractive sisters. Through the main character, Cynthia, who experiments with spiritualism and house parties, Nabokov's narrator explores the fascination and muffled horror of a life apart from physical reality. In the end, the author suggests, all memory becomes illusive and difficult to recapture.

For Discussion

1. How does the narrator view his own personality? How do the views of other characters modify his opinion of himself and the reader's opinion of his character, sometimes unfavorably?
2. What do the Vane sisters have in common with regard to the ways they maintain themselves, choose lovers, and express their beliefs? Why does the narrator take an interest in them?
3. Describe Cynthia's interest in spiritualism. Why is the narrator alternately attracted to and repelled by it?
4. Why does Cynthia treat Sybil's one-time lover as she does? How do Cynthia's house parties reflect her own temperament, her likes and dislikes?
5. How is spiritualism related to the narrator's view of the sisters and the creative process?

R. K. Narayan
Lawley Road

The Talkative Man said:

For years people were not aware of the existence of a Municipality in Malgudi. The town was none the worse for it. Diseases, if they started, ran their course and disappeared, for even diseases must end some day. Dust and rubbish were blown away by the wind out of sight; drains ebbed and flowed and generally looked after themselves. The Municipality kept itself in the background, and remained so till the country got its independence on the 15th of August, 1947. History holds few records of such jubilation as was witnessed on that day from the Himalayas to Cape Comorin. Our Municipal Council caught the inspiration. They swept the streets, cleaned the drains and hoisted flags all over the place. Their hearts warmed up when processions with flags and music passed through their streets.

The Municipal Chairman looked down benignly from his balcony, muttering, 'We have done our bit for this great occasion.' I believe one or two members of the Council who were with him saw tears in his eyes. He was a man who had done himself well as a supplier of blankets to the army during the War, later spending a great deal of his gains in securing the Chairmanship. That's an epic by itself and does not concern us now. My present story is different. The satisfaction the Chairman now felt was, however, short-lived. In about a week, when the bunting was torn off, he became quite dispirited. I used to visit him almost every day, trying to make a living out of news-reports to an upcountry paper which paid me two rupees for every inch of published news. Every month I could measure out about ten inches of news in that paper, which was mostly a somewhat idealised account of municipal affairs. This made me a great favourite there. I walked in and out of the Municipal Chairman's office constantly. Now he looked so unhappy that I was forced to ask, 'What is wrong, Mr. Chairman?'

'I feel we have not done enough,' he replied.

'Enough of what?' I asked.

'Nothing to mark off the great event.' He sat brooding and then announced,

'Come what may, I am going to do something great!' He called up an Extraordinary Meeting of the Council, and harangued them; and at once they decided to nationalize the names of all the streets and parks, in honour of the birth of Independence. They made a start with the park at the Market Square. It used to be called The Coronation Park—whose coronation God alone knew; it might have been the coronation of Victoria or of Asoka. No one bothered about it. Now the old board was uprooted and lay on the lawn, and a brand new sign stood up in its place declaring it henceforth to be 'Hamara Hindusthan Park'.

The other transformations, however, could not be so smoothly worked out. 'Mahatma Gandhi Road' was the most sought-after name. Eight different Ward Councillors were after it. There were six others who wanted to call the roads in front of their houses 'Nehru Road' or 'Netaji Subash Bose Road'. Tempers were rising and I feared they might come to blows. There came a point when, I believe, the Council just went mad. It decided to give the same name to four different streets. Well, sir, even in the most democratic or patriotic town it is not feasible to have two roads bearing the same name. The result was seen within a fortnight. The town became unrecognisable with new names. Gone were the 'Market Road', 'North Road', 'Chitra Road', 'Vinayak Mudali Street', and so on. In their place appeared the names, repeated in four different places, of all the ministers, deputy ministers, and the members of the Congress Working Committee. Of course, it created a lot of hardship—letters went where they were not wanted, people were not able to say where they lived or direct others there. The town became a wilderness with all its landmarks gone.

The Chairman was gratified with his inspired work—but not for long. He became restless again and looked for fresh fields of action.

At the corner of Lawley Extension and Market there used to be a statue. People had got so used to it that they never bothered to ask whose it was or even look up. It was generally used by the birds as a perch. The Chairman suddenly remembered that it was the statue of Sir Frederick Lawley. The extension had been named after him. Now it was changed to 'Gandhi Nagar', and it seemed impossible to keep Lawley's statue any longer there. The Council unanimously resolved to remove it. The Council with the Chairman sallied forth triumphantly next morning and circumambulated the statue. They now realized their mistake. The statue towered 20 feet above them and seemed to arise from a pedestal of molten lead. In their imagination they had thought that a vigorous resolution would be enough to topple down the statue of this satrap, but now they found that it stood with the firmness of a mountain. They realized that Britain, when she was here, had attempted to raise herself on no mean foundation. But it made them only firmer in their resolve. If it was going to mean blasting up that part of the town for the purpose, they would do it. For they unearthed a lot of history about Sir Frederick Lawley. He was a combination of Attila, the scourge of Europe, and Nadir Shah, with the craftiness of a Machiavelli. He subjugated Indians with the sword and razed to the ground the villages from which he heard the slightest murmur of protest. He never countenanced Indians except when they approached him on their knees.

People dropped their normal occupations and loitered around the statue, wondering how they could have tolerated it for so many years. The gentleman seemed to smile derisively at the nation now, with his arms locked behind and sword dangling from his belt. There could be no doubt that he must have been the worst tyrant imaginable: the true picture—with breeches and wig and white waistcoat and that hard determined look—of all that has been hatefully familiar in the British period of Indian history. They shuddered when they thought of the fate of their ancestors who had to bear the tyrannies of this man.

Next the Municipality called for tenders. A dozen contractors sent in their estimates, the lowest standing at fifty thousand rupees, for removing the statue and carting it to the Municipal office where they were already worried about the housing of it. The Chairman thought over it and told me, 'Why don't you take it yourself? I will give you the statue free if you do not charge us anything for removing it.' I had thought till then that only my municipal friends were mad, but now I found I could be just as mad as they. I began to calculate the whole affair as a pure investment. Suppose it cost me five thousand rupees to dislodge and move the statue (I knew the contractors were overestimating), and I sold it as metal for six thousand . . . About three tons of metal might fetch anything. Or I could probably sell it to the British Museum or Westminster Abbey. I saw myself throwing up the upcountry paper job.

The Council had no difficulty in passing a resolution permitting me to take the statue away. I made elaborate arrangements for the task . . . I borrowed money from my father-in-law, promising him a fantastic rate of interest. I recruited a team of fifty coolies to hack the pedestal. I stoood over them like a slave-driver and kept shouting instructions. They put down their implements at six in the evening, and returned to their attack early next day. They were specially recruited from Koppal, where the men's limbs were hardened by generations of teak-cutting in Mempi forest. We hacked for ten days. No doubt we succeeded in chipping the pedestal here and there, but that was all; the statue showed no sign of moving. At this rate I feared I might become bankrupt in a fortnight. I took permission from the District Magistrate to acquire a few sticks of dynamite, cordoned off the area, and lighted the fuse. I brought down the Knight from his pedestal without injuring any limb. Then it took me three days to reach the house with my booty. It was stretched out on a specially designed carriage drawn by several bullocks. The confusion brought about by my passage along Market Road, the crowd that followed uttering jokes, the incessant shouting and instructions I had to be giving, the blinding heat of the day, Sir F.'s carriage coming to a halt at every inconvenient spot and angle, neither moving forward nor backward, holding up the traffic on all sides, and darkness coming on suddenly with the statue nowhere near my home—all this was a nightmare I wish to pass over. I mounted guard over him on the roadside at night. As he lay on his back staring at the stars I felt sorry for him and said, 'Well, this is what you get for being such a haughty imperialist. It never pays.' In due course, he was safely lodged in my small house. His head and shoulders were in my front hall and the rest of him stretched out into the street through the doorway. It was an obliging community there at Kabir Lane and nobody minded this obstruction.

The Municipal Council passed a resolution thanking me for my services. I wired this news to my paper, tacking on to it a ten-inch story of the statue. A week later the Chairman came to my house in a state of agitation. I seated him on the chest of the tyrant. He said, 'I have bad news for you. I wish you had not sent up that news item about the statue. See these . . .' He held out a sheaf of telegrams. They were from every kind of historical society in India, all protesting against the removal of the statue. We had all been misled about Sir F. All the present history pertained to a different Lawley of the time of Warren Hastings. This Frederick Lawley (of the statue) was a Military Governor who settled down here after the Mutiny. He cleared the jungles and almost built the town of Malgudi. He established here the first co-operative society for the whole of India, and the first canal system by which thousands of acres of land were irrigated from the Sarayu, which had been dissipating itself till then. He established this, he established that, and he died in the great Sarayu floods while attempting to save the lives of villagers living on its banks. He was the first Englishman to advise the British Parliament to associate more and more Indians in all Indian affairs. In one of his despatches he was said to have declared, 'Britain must quit India some day for her own good.'

The Chairman said, 'The Government have ordered us to reinstate the statue.' 'Impossible!' I cried. 'This is my statue and I shall keep it. I like to collect statues of national heroes.' This heroic sentiment impressed no one. Within a week all the newspapers in the country were full of Sir Frederick Lawley. The public caught the enthusiasm. They paraded in front of my house, shouting slogans. They demanded the statue back. I offered to abandon it if the Municipality at least paid my expenses in bringing it here. The public viewed me as their enemy. 'This man is trying to blackmarket even a statue . . .' they remarked. Stung by it I wrote a placard and hung it on my door: 'Statue For Sale. Two and a half tons of excellent metal. Ideal gift for a patriotic friend. Offers above ten thousand will be considered.' It infuriated them and made them want to kick me, but they had been brought up in a tradition of non-violence and so they picketed my house; they lay across my door in relays holding a flag and shouting slogans. I had sent away my wife and children to the village in order to make room for the statue in my house, and so this picketing did not bother me—only I had to use the backdoor a great deal. The Municipality sent me a notice of prosecution under the Ancient Monuments Act, which I repudiated in suitable terms. We were getting into bewildering legalities—a battle of wits between me and the municipal lawyer. The only nuisance about it was that an abnormal quantity of correspondence developed and choked up an already congested household.

I clung to my statue, secretly despairing how it was ever going to end. I longed to be able to stretch myself fully in my own house.

Six months later relief came. The Government demanded a report from the Municipality on the question of the statue, and this together with other lapses on the part of the Municipality made them want to know why the existing Council should not be dissolved and re-elections ordered. I called on the Chairman and said, 'You will have to do something grand now. Why not acquire my house as a National Trust?'

'Why should I?' he asked.

'Because,' I said, 'Sir F. is here. You will never be able to cart him to his old place. It'll be a waste of public money. Why not put him up where he is now? He has stayed in the other place too long, I'm prepared to give you my house for a reasonable price.'

'But our funds don't permit it,' he wailed.

'I'm sure you have enough funds of your own. Why should you depend upon the municipal funds? It'll indeed be a grand gesture on your part, unique in India . . .' I suggested he ought to relieve himself of some of his old blanket gains. 'After all . . . how much more you will have to spend if you have to fight another election!' It appealed to him. We arrived at a figure. He was very happy when he saw in the papers a few days later; 'The Chairman of Malgudi Municipality has been able to buy back as a present for the nation the statue of Sir Frederick Lawley. He proposes to instal it in a newly acquired property which is shortly to be converted into a park. The Municipal Council have resolved that Kabir Lane shall be changed to Lawley Road.'

[1969]

For Thought

The plot of "Lawley Road" appears to deal with the rehabilitation of a former imperial governor, Frederick Lawley. As a group of India's townspeople assert their independence from past British domination, they wipe out all reminders of English rule. These actions are taken hastily and passionately, with severe dislocation of their daily lives. Narayan, however, is most interested in the uses and abuses of history to gain power and to form a national sense of identity. Truth about the past is totally dependent on the stability and good sense of those who make use of it, the author suggests.

For Discussion

1. How does the narrator combine practical and impractical traits? How are his motives mixed?
2. How do the people of Malgudi combine a highly emotional temperament with a strong sense of realism? Why do they hold such contradictory views of the British?
3. What views of Lawley are presented by the story? What ironies emerge from these conflicting views?
4. How is the Chairman of the Council characterized? Does Narayan's picture of him appear comic or realistic or some of both?
5. What is the theme of the story?

Joyce Carol Oates
Four Summers

It is some kind of special day. "Where's Sissie?" Ma says. Her face gets sharp, she is frightened. When I run around her chair she laughs and hugs me. She is pretty when she laughs. Her hair is long and pretty.

We are sitting at the best table of all, out near the water. The sun is warm and the air smells nice. Daddy is coming back from the building with some glasses of beer held in his arms. He makes a grunting noise when he sits down.

"Is the lake deep?" I ask them.

They don't hear me, they're talking. A woman and a man are sitting with us. The man marched in the parade we saw just a while ago; he is a volunteer fireman and is wearing a uniform. Now his shirt is pulled open because it is hot. I can see the dark curly hair way up by his throat.

A man in a soldier's uniform comes over to us. They are all friends, but I can't remember him. We used to live around here, Ma told me, and then we moved away. The men are laughing. The man in the uniform leans back against the railing, laughing, and I am afraid it will break and he will fall into the water.

"Can we go out in a boat? Dad?" says Jerry.

He and Frank keep running back and forth. I don't want to go with them, I want to stay by Ma. She smells nice. Frank's face is dirty with sweat. "Dad," he says, whining, "can't we go out in a boat? Them kids are going out."

A big lake is behind the building and the open part where we are sitting. Some people are rowing on it. This tavern is noisy and everyone is laughing; it is too noisy for Dad to think about what Frank said.

"Harry," says Ma, "the kids want a boat-ride. Why don't you leave off drinking and take them?"

"What?" says Dad.

He looks up from laughing with the men. His face is damp with sweat and he is happy. "Yeah, sure, in a few minutes. Go over there and play and I'll take you out in a few minutes."

The boys run out back by the rowboats,

and I run after them. I have a bag of potato chips.

An old man with a white hat pulled down over his forehead is sitting by the boats, smoking. "You kids be careful," he says.

Frank is leaning over and looking at one of the boats. "This here is the best one," he says.

"Why's this one got water in it?" says Jerry.

"You kids watch out. Where's your father?"the man says.

"He's gonna take us for a ride," says Frank.

"Where is he?"

The boys run along, looking at the boats that are tied up. They don't bother with me. The boats are all painted dark green, but the paint is peeling off some of them in little pieces. There is water inside some of them. We watch two people come in, a man and a woman. The woman is giggling. She has on a pink dress and she leans over to touch one finger in the water. "What's all this filthy stuff by the shore?" she says. There is some scum in the water. It is colored a light brown, and there are little seeds and twigs and leaves in it.

The man helps the woman out of the boat. They laugh together. Around their rowboat little waves are still moving; they make a churning noise that I like.

"Where's Dad?" Frank says.

"He ain't coming," says Jerry.

They are tossing pebbles out into the water. Frank throws his sideways, twisting his body. He is ten and very big. "I bet he ain't coming," Jerry says, wiping his nose with the back of his hand.

After a while we go back to the table. Behind the table is the white railing, and then the water, and then the bank curves out so that the weeping willow trees droop over the water. More men in uniforms, from the parade, are walking by.

"Dad," says Frank, "can't we go out? Can't we? There's a real nice boat there—"

"For Christ's sake, get them off me," Dad says. He is angry with Ma. "Why don't you take them out?"

"Honey, I can't row."

"Should we take out a boat, us two?" the other woman says. She has very short wet-looking hair. It is curled in tiny little curls close to her head and is very bright. "We'll show them, Lenore. Come on, let's give your kids a ride. Show these guys how strong we are."

"That's all you need, to sink a boat," her husband says.

They all laugh.

The table is filled with brown beer bottles and wrappers of things. I can feel how happy they all are together, drawn together by the round table. I lean against Ma's warm leg and she pats me without looking down. She lunges forward and I can tell even before she says something that she is going to be loud.

"You guys're just jealous! Afraid we'll meet some soldiers!" she says.

"Can't we go out, Dad? Please?" Frank says. "We won't fight . . ."

"Go and play over there. What're those kids doing—over there?" Dad says, frowning. His face is damp and loose, the way it is sometimes when he drinks. "In a little while, okay? Ask your mother."

"She can't do it," Frank says.

"They're just jealous," Ma says to the other woman, giggling. "They're afraid we might meet somebody somewhere."

"Just who's gonna meet this one here?" the other man says, nodding with his head at his wife.

Frank and Jerry walk away. I stay by Ma. My eyes burn and I want to sleep, but they won't be leaving for a long time. It is still daylight. When we go home from places like this it is always dark and getting chilly and the grass by our house is wet.

"Duane Dorsey's in jail," Dad says. "You guys heard about that?"

"Duane? Yeah, really?"

"It was in the newspaper. His mother-in-law or somebody called the police, he was breaking windows in her house."

"That Duane was always a nut!"

"Is he out now, or what?"

"I don't know, I don't see him these days. We had a fight," Dad says.

The woman with the short hair looks at me. "She's a real cute little thing," she says, stretching her mouth. "She drink beer, Lenore?"

"I don't know."

"Want some of mine?"

She leans toward me and holds the glass by my mouth. I can smell the beer and the warm stale smell of perfume. There are pink lipstick smudges on the glass.

"Hey, what the hell are you doing?" her husband says.

When he talks rough like that I remember him: we were with him once before.

"Are you swearing at me?" the woman says.

"Leave off the kid, you want to make her a drunk like yourself?"

"It don't hurt, one little sip . . ."

"It's okay," Ma says. She puts her arm around my shoulders and pulls me closer to the table.

"Let's play cards. Who wants to?" Dad says.

"Sissie wants a little sip, don't you?" the woman says. She is smiling at me and I can see that her teeth are darkish, not nice like Ma's.

"Sure, go ahead," says Ma.

"I said leave off that, Sue, for Christ's sake," the man says. He jerks the table. He is a big man with a thick neck; he is bigger than Dad. His eyebrows are blond, lighter than his hair, and are thick and tufted. Dad is staring at something out on the lake without seeing it. "Harry, look, my goddam wife is trying to make your kid drink beer."

"Who's getting hurt?" Ma says angrily.

Pa looks at me all at once and smiles. "Do you want it, baby?"

I have to say yes. The woman grins and holds the glass down to me, and it clicks against my teeth. They laugh. I stop swallowing right away because it is ugly, and some of the beer drips down on me. "Honey, you're so clumsy," Ma says, wiping me with a napkin.

"She's a real cute girl," the woman says, sitting back in her chair. "I wish I had a nice little girl like that."

"Lay off of that," says her husband.

"Hey, did you bring any cards?" Dad says to the soldier.

"They got some inside."

"Look, I'm sick of cards," Ma says.

"Yeah, why don't we all go for a boatride?" says the woman. "Be real nice, something new. Every time we get together we play cards. How's about a boatride?"

"It better be a big boat, with you in it," her husband says. He is pleased when everyone laughs, even the woman. The soldier lights a cigarette and laughs. "How come your cousin here's so skinny and you're so fat?"

"She isn't fat," says Ma. "What the hell do you want? Look at yourself."

"Yes, the best days of my life are behind me," the man says. He wipes his face and then presses a beer bottle against it. "Harry, you're lucky you moved out. It's all going downhill, back in the neighborhood."

"You should talk, you let our house look like hell," the woman says. Her face is blotched now, some parts pale and some red. "Harry don't sit out in his back yard all weekend, drinking. He gets something done."

"Harry's younger than me."

Ma reaches over and touches Dad's arm. "Harry, why don't you take the kids out? Before it gets dark."

Dad lifts his glass and finishes his beer. "Who else wants more?" he says.

"I'll get them, you went last time," the soldier says.

"Get a chair for yourself," says Dad. "We can play poker."

"I don't want to play poker, I want to play rummy," the woman says.

"At church this morning Father Reilly was real mad," says Ma. "He said some kids or somebody was out in the cemetery and left some beer bottles. Isn't that awful?"

"Duane Dorsey used to do worse than that," the man says, winking.

"Hey, who's that over there?"

"You mean that fat guy?"

"Isn't that the guy at the lumberyard that owes all that money?"

Dad turns around. His chair wobbles and he almost falls; he is angry.

"This goddam place is too crowded," he says.

"This is a real nice place," the woman says. She is taking something out of her purse. "I always liked it, didn't you, Lenore?"

"Sue and me used to come here a lot," says Ma. "And not just with you two, either."

"Yeah, we're real jealous," the man says.

"You should be," says the woman.

The soldier comes back. Now I can see that he is really a boy. He runs to the table with the beer before he drops anything. He laughs.

"Jimmy, your ma wouldn't like to see you drinking!" the woman says happily.

"Well, she ain't here."

"Are they still living out in the country?" Ma says to the woman.

"Sure. No electricity, no running water, no bathroom—same old thing. What can you do with people like that?"

"She always talks about going back to the old country," the soldier says. "Thinks she can save up money and go back."

"Poor old bastards don't know there was a war," Dad says. He looks as if something tasted bad in his mouth. "My old man died thinking he could go back in a year or two. Stupid old bastards!"

"Your father was real nice . . ." Ma says.

"Yeah, real nice," says Dad. "Better off dead."

Everybody is quiet.

"June Dieter's mother's got the same thing," the woman says in a low voice to Ma. "She's had it a year now and don't weigh a hundred pounds—you remember how big she used to be."

"She was big, all right," Ma says.

"Remember how she ran after June and slapped her? We were there—some guys were driving us home."

"Yeah. So she's got it too."

"Hey," says Dad, "why don't you get a chair, Jimmy? Sit down here."

The soldier looks around. His face is raw in spots, broken out. But his eyes are nice. He never looks at me.

"Get a chair from that table," Dad says.

"Those people might want it."

"Hell, just take it. Nobody's sitting on it."

"They might—"

Dad reaches around and yanks the chair over. The people look at him but don't say anything. Dad is breathing hard. "Here, sit here," he says. The soldier sits down.

Frank and Jerry come back. They stand by Dad, watching him. "Can we go out now?" Frank says.

"What?"

"Out for a boatride."

"What? No, next week. Do it next week. We're going to play cards."

"You said—"

"Shut up ,we'll do it next week." Dad looks up and shades his eyes. "The lake don't look right, anyway."

"Lots of people are out there—"

"I said shut up."

"Honey," Ma whispers, "let him alone. Go and play by yourselves."

"Can we sit in the car?"

"Okay, but don't honk the horn."

"Ma, can't we go for a ride?"

"Go and play by yourselves, stop bothering us," she says. "Hey, will you take Sissie?"

They look at me. They don't like me, I can see it, but they take me with them. We run through the crowd and somebody spills a drink—he yells at us. "Oops, got to watch it!" Frank giggles.

We run along the walk by the boat. A

woman in a yellow dress is carrying a baby. She looks at us like she doesn't like us.

Down at the far end some kids are standing together.

"Hey, lookit that," Frank says.

A blackbird is caught in the scum, by one of the boats. It can't fly up. One of the kids, a long-legged girl in a dirty dress, is poking at it with a stick.

The bird's wings keep fluttering but it can't get out. If it could get free it would fly and be safe, but the scum holds it down.

One of the kids throws a stone at it. "Stupid old goddam bird," somebody says. Frank throws a stone. They are all throwing stones. The bird doesn't know enough to turn away. Its feathers are all wet and dirty. One of the stones hits the bird's head.

"Take that!" Frank says, throwing a rock. The water splashes up and some of the girls scream.

I watch them throwing stones. I am standing at the side. If the bird dies then everything can die, I think. Inside the tavern there is music from the jukebox.

We are at the boathouse tavern again. It is a mild day, a Sunday afternoon. Dad is talking with some men; Jerry and I are waiting by the boats. Mommy is at home with the new baby. Frank went off with some friends of his, to a stock car race. There are some people here, sitting out at the tables, but they don't notice us.

"Why doesn't he hurry up?" Jerry says.

Jerry is twelve now. He has pimples on his forehead and chin.

He pushes one of the rowboats with his foot. He is wearing sneakers that are dirty. I wish I could get in that boat and sit down, but I am afraid. A boy not much older than Jerry is squatting on the board walk, smoking. You can tell he is in charge of the boats.

"Daddy, come on. Come on," Jerry says, whining. Daddy can't hear him.

I have mosquito bites on my arms and legs. There are mosquitoes and flies around here; the flies crawl around the sticky mess left on tables. A car over in the parking lot has its radio on loud. You can hear the music all this way. "He's coming," I tell Jerry, so he won't be mad. Jerry is like Dad, the way his eyes look.

"Oh, that fat guy keeps talking to him," Jerry says.

The fat man is one of the bartenders; he has on a dirty white apron. All these men are familiar. We have been seeing them for years. He punches Dad's arm, up by the shoulder, and Dad pushes him. They are laughing, though. Nobody is mad.

"I'd sooner let a nigger—" the bartender says. We can't hear anything more, but the men laugh again.

"All he does is drink," Jerry says. "I hate him."

At school, up on the sixth-grade floor, Jerry got in trouble last month. The principal slapped him. I am afraid to look at Jerry when he's mad.

"I hate him, I wish he'd die," Jerry says.

Dad is trying to come to us, but every time he takes a step backward and gets ready to turn, one of the men says something. There are three men beside him. Their stomachs are big, but Dad's isn't. He is wearing dark pants and a white shirt; his tie is in the car. He wears a tie to church, then takes it off. He has his shirtsleeves rolled up and you can see how strong his arms must be.

Two women cross over from the parking lot. They are wearing high-heeled shoes and hats and bright dresses—orange and yellow—and when they walk past, the men look at them. They go into the tavern. The men laugh about something. The way they laugh makes my eyes focus on something away from them—a bird flying in the sky—and it is hard for me to look anywhere else. I feel as if I'm falling asleep.

"Here he comes," Jerry says.

Dad walks over to us, with his big steps. He is smiling and carrying a bottle of beer. "Hey, kid," he says to the boy squatting on the walk, "how's about a boat?"

"This one is the best," Jerry says.

"The best, huh? Great." Dad grins at us. "Okay, Sissie, let's get you in. Be careful now." He picks me up even though I am too heavy for it, and sets me in the boat. It hurts a little where he held me, under the arms, but I don't care.

Jerry climbs in. Dad steps in and something happens—he almost slips, but he catches himself. With the wet oar he pushes us off from the boardwalk.

Dad can row fast. The sunlight is gleaming on the water. I sit very still, facing him, afraid to move. The boat goes fast, and Dad is leaning back and forth and pulling on the oars, breathing hard, doing everything fast like he always does. He is always in a hurry to get things done. He has set the bottle of beer down by his leg, pressed against the side of the boat so it won't fall.

"There's the guys we saw go out, before," Jerry says. Coming around the island is a boat with three boys in it, older than Jerry. "They went on the island. Can we go there too?"

"Sure," says Dad. His eyes squint in the sun. He is suntanned, and there are freckles on his forehead. I am sitting close to him, facing him, and it surprises me what he looks like—he is like a stranger, with his eyes narrowed. The water beneath the boat makes me feel funny. It keeps us up now, but if I fell over the side I would sink and drown.

"Nice out here, huh?" Dad says. He is breathing hard.

"We should go over that way, to get on the island," Jerry says.

"This goddam oar has splinters in it," Dad says. He hooks the oar up and lets us glide. He reaches down to get the bottle of beer. Though the lake and some trees and the buildings back on shore are in front of me, what makes me look at it is my father's throat, the way it bobs when he swallows. He wipes his forehead. "Want to row, Sissie?" he says.

"Can I?"

"Let me do it," says Jerry.

"Naw, I was just kidding," Dad says.

"I can do it. It ain't hard."

"Stay where you are," Dad says.

He starts rowing again, faster. Why does he go so fast? His face is getting red, the way it does at home when he has trouble with Frank. He clears his throat and spits over the side; I don't like to see that but I can't help but watch. The other boat glides past us, heading for shore. The boys don't look over at us.

Jerry and I look to see if anyone else is on the island, but no one is. The island is very small. You can see around it.

"Are you going to land on it, Dad?" Jerry says.

"Sure okay." Dad's face is flushed and looks angry.

The boat scrapes bottom and bumps. "Jump out and pull it in," Dad says. Jerry jumps out. His shoes and socks are wet now, but Dad doesn't notice. The boat bumps; it hurts me. I am afraid. But then we're up on the land and Dad is out and lifting me. "Nice ride, sugar?" he says.

Jerry and I run around the island. It is different from what we thought, but we don't know why. There are some trees on it, some wild grass, and then bare caked mud that goes down to the water. The water looks dark and deep on the other side, but when we get there it's shallow. Lily pads grow there; everything is thick and tangled. Jerry wades in the water and gets his pants legs wet. "There might be money in the water," he says.

Some napkins and beer cans are nearby. There is part of a hotdog bun, with flies buzzing around it.

When we go back by Dad, we see him squatting over the water doing something. His back jerks. Then I see that he is being sick. He is throwing up in the water and making a noise like coughing.

Jerry turns around right away and runs back. I follow him, afraid. On the other side we can look back at the boathouse and wish we were there.

Marian and Betty went to the show, but I couldn't. She made me come along here with them. "And cut out that snippy face," Ma said, to let me know she's watching. I have to help her take care of Linda—poor fat Linda, with her runny nose! So here we are inside the tavern. There's too much smoke, I hate smoke. Dad is smoking a cigar. I won't drink any more root beer, it's flat, and I'm sick of potato chips. Inside me there is something that wants to run away, that hates them. How loud they are, my parents! My mother spilled something on the front of her dress, but does she notice? And my Aunt Lucy and Uncle Joe, they're here. Try to avoid them. Lucy has false teeth that makes everyone stare at her. I know that everyone is staring at us. I could hide my head in my arms and turn away, I'm so tired and my legs hurt from sunburn and I can't stand them any more.

"So did you ever hear from them? That letter you wrote?" Ma says to Lucy.

"I'm still waiting. Somebody said you got to have connections to get on the show. But I don't believe it. That Howie Masterson that's the m.c., he's a real nice guy. I can tell."

"It's all crap," Dad says. "You women believe anything."

"I don't believe it," I say.

"Phony as hell," says my uncle.

"You do too believe it, Sissie," says my mother. "Sissie thinks he's cute. I know she does."

"I hate that guy," I tell her, but she and my aunt are laughing. "I said I hate him! He's greasy."

"All that stuff is phony as hell," says my Uncle Joe. He is tired all the time, and right now he sits with his head bowed. I hate his bald head with the little fringe of gray hair on it. At least my father is still handsome. His jaws sag and there are lines in his neck—edged with dirt, I can see, embarrassed—and his stomach is bulging a little against the table, but still he is a handsome man. In a place like this, women look at him. What's he see in *her?* they think. My mother had her hair cut too short last time; she looks queer. There is a photograph taken of her when she was young, standing by someone's motorcycle, with her hair long. In the photograph she was pretty, almost beautiful, but I don't believe it. Not really. I can't believe it, and I hate her. Her forehead gathers itself up in little wrinkles whenever she glances down at Linda, as if she can't remember who Linda is.

"Well, nobody wanted you, kid," she once said to Linda. Linda was a baby then, one year old. Ma was furious, standing in the kitchen where she was washing the floor, screaming: "Nobody wanted you, it was a goddam accident! A accident!" That surprised me so I didn't know what to think, and I didn't know if I hated Ma or not; but I kept it all a secret . . . only my girl friends know, and I won't tell the priest either. Nobody can make me tell. I narrow my eyes and watch my mother leaning forward to say something—it's like she's going to toss something out on the table—and think that maybe she isn't my mother, after all, and she isn't that pretty girl in the photograph, but someone else.

"A woman was on the show last night that lost two kids in a fire. Her house burned down," my aunt says loudly. "And she answered the questions right off and got a lot of money and the audience went wild. You could see she was a real lady. I love that guy, Howie Masterson. He's real sweet."

"He's a bastard," Dad says.

"Harry, what the hell? You never even seen him," Ma says.

"I sure as hell never did. Got better things to do at night." Dad turns to my uncle and his voice changes. "I'm on the night shift, now."

"Yeah, I hate that, I . . ."

"I can sleep during the day. What's the difference?"

"I hate those night shifts."

"What's there to do during the day?"

Dad says flatly. His eyes scan us at the table as if he doesn't see anything, then they seem to fall off me and go behind me, looking at nothing.

"Not much," says my uncle, and I can see his white scalp beneath his hair. Both men are silent.

Dad pours beer into his glass and spills some of it. I wish I could look away. I love him, I think, but I hate to be here. Where would I rather be? With Marian and Betty at the movies, or in my room, lying on the bed and staring at the photographs of movie stars on my walls—those beautiful people that never say anything—while out in the kitchen my mother is waiting for my father to come home, so they can continue their quarrel. It never stops, that quarrel. Sometimes they laugh together, kid around, they kiss. Then the quarrel starts up again in a few minutes.

"Ma, can I go outside and wait in the car?" I say. "Linda's asleep."

"What's so hot about the car?" she says, looking at me.

"I'm tired. My sunburn hurts."

Linda is sleeping in Ma's lap, with her mouth open and drooling on the front of her dress. "Okay, go on," Ma says. "But we're not going to hurry just for you." When she has drunk too much there is a struggle in her between being angry and being affectionate; she fights both of them, as if standing with her legs apart and her hands on her hips, bracing a strong wind.

When I cross through the crowded tavern I'm conscious of people looking at me. My hair lost its curl because it was so humid today, my legs are too thin, my figure is flat and not nice like Marian's—I want to hide somewhere, hide my face from them. I hate this noisy place and these people. Even the music is ugly because it belongs to them. Then, when I'm outside, the music gets faint right away and it doesn't sound so bad. It's cooler out here. No one is around. Out back, the old rowboats are tied up. Nobody's on the lake. There's no moon, the sky is overcast, it was raining earlier.

When I turn around, a man is standing by the door watching me.

"What're you doing?" he says.

"Nothing."

He has dark hair and a tanned face, I think, but everything is confused because the light from the door is pinkish—there's a neon sign there. My heart starts to pound. The man leans forward to stare at me. "Oh, I thought you were somebody else," he says.

I want to show him I'm not afraid. "Yeah, really? Who did you think I was?" When we ride on the schoolbus we smile out the windows at strange men, just for fun. We do that all the time. I'm not afraid of any of them.

"You're not her," he says.

Some people come out the door and he has to step out of their way. I say to him, "Maybe you seen me around here before. We come here pretty often."

"Who do you come with?" He is smiling as if he thinks I'm funny. "Anybody I know?"

"That's my business."

It's a game. I'm not afraid. When I think of my mother and father inside, something makes me want to step closer to this man—why should I be afraid? I could be wild like some of the other girls. Nothing surprises me.

We keep on talking. At first I can tell he wants me to come inside the tavern with him, but then he forgets about it; he keeps talking. I don't know what we say, but we talk in drawling voices, smiling at each other but in a secret knowing way, as if each one of us knew more than the other. My cheeks start to burn. I could be wild like Betty is sometimes—like some of the other girls. Why not? Once before I talked with a man like this, on the bus. We were both sitting in the back. I wasn't afraid. This man and I keep talking and we talk about nothing, he wants to know how old I am, but it makes my heart pound so hard that I want to touch my chest to calm it. We are walking along the old boardwalk and I say:

"Somebody took me out rowing once, here."

"Is that so?" he says. "You want me to take you out?"

He has a hard, handsome face. I like that face. Why is he alone? When he smiles I know he's laughing at me, and this makes me stand taller, walk with my shoulders raised.

"Hey, are you with somebody inside there?" he says.

"I left them."

"Have a fight?"

"A fight, yes."

He looks at me quickly. "How old are you, anyway?"

"That's none of your business."

"Girls your age are all alike."

"We're not all alike!" I arch my back and look at him in a way I must have learned somewhere—where?—with my lips not smiling but ready to smile, and my eyes narrowed. One leg is turned as if I'm ready to jump away from him. He sees all this. He smiles.

"Say, you're real cute."

We're walking over by the parking lot now. He touches my arm. Right away my heart trips, but I say nothing, I keep walking. High above us the tree branches are moving in the wind. It's cold for June. It's late—after eleven. The man is wearing a jacket, but I have on a sleeveless dress and there are goose pimples on my arms.

"Cold, huh?" he says.

He takes hold of my shoulders and leans toward me. This is to show me he's no kid, he's grown-up, this is how they do things; when he kisses me his grip on my shoulders gets tighter. "I better go back," I say to him. My voice is queer.

"What?" he says.

I am wearing a face like one of those faces pinned up in my room, and what if I lose it? This is not my face. I try to turn away from him.

He kisses me again. His breath smells like beer, maybe, it's like my father's breath, and my mind is empty; I can't think what to do. Why am I here? My legs feel numb, my fingers are cold. The man rubs my arms and says, "You should have a sweater or something . . ."

He is waiting for me to say something, to keep on the way I was before. But I have forgotten how to do it. Before, I was Marian or one of the older girls; now I am just myself. I am fourteen. I think of Linda sleeping in my mother's lap, and something frightens me.

"Hey, what's wrong?" the man says.

He sees I'm afraid but pretends he doesn't. He comes to me again and embraces me, his mouth presses against my neck and shoulder, I feel as if I'm suffocating. "My car's over here," he says, trying to catch his breath. I can't move. Something dazzling and icy rises up in me, an awful fear, but I can't move and can't say anything. He is touching me with his hands. His mouth is soft but wants too much from me. I think: What is he doing? Do they all do this? Do I have to have it done to me too?

"You cut that out," I tell him.

He steps away. His chest is heaving and his eyes look like a dog's eyes, surprised and betrayed. The last thing I see of him is those eyes, before I turn and run back to the tavern.

Jesse says, "Let's stop at this place. I been here a few times before."

It's the "Lakeside Bar." That big old building with the grubby siding, and a big pink neon sign in front, and the cinder driveway that's so bumpy. Yes, everything the same. But different, too—smaller, dirtier. There is a custard stand nearby with a glaring orange roof, and people are crowded around it. That's new. I haven't been here for years.

"I feel like a beer," he says.

He smiles at me and caresses my arm. He treats me as if I were something that might break; in my cheap-linen maternity dress I feel ugly and heavy. My flesh is so soft and thick that nothing could hurt it.

"Sure, honey, Pa used to stop in here too."

We cross through the parking lot to the tavern. Wild grass grows along the sidewalk and in the cracks of the sidewalk. Why is this place so ugly to me? I feel as if a hand were pressing against my chest, shutting off my breath. Is there some secret here? Why am I afraid?

I catch sight of myself in a dusty window as we pass. My hair is long, down to my shoulders. I am pretty, but my secret is that I am pretty like everyone is. My husband loves me for this but doesn't know it. I have a pink mouth and plucked darkened eyebrows and soft bangs over my forehead; I know everything, I have no need to learn from anyone else now. I am one of those girls younger girls study closely, to learn from. On buses, in five-and-tens, thirteen-year-old girls must look at me solemnly, learning, memorizing.

"Pretty Sissie!" my mother likes to say when we visit, though I told her how I hate that name. She is proud of me for being pretty, but thinks I'm too thin. "You'll fill out nice, after the baby," she says. Herself, she is fat and veins have begun to darken on her legs; she scuffs around the house in bedroom slippers. Who is my mother? When I think of her I can't think of anything—do I love her or hate her, or is there nothing there?

Jesse forgets and walks ahead of me, I have to walk fast to catch up. I'm wearing pastel blue high heels—that must be because I am proud of my legs. I have little else. Then he remembers and turns to put out his hand for me, smiling to show he is sorry. Jesse is the kind of young man thirteen-year-old girls stare at, secretly; he is not a man, not old enough, but not a boy either. He is a year older than I am, twenty. When I met him he was wearing a navy uniform and he was with a girl friend of mine.

Just a few people sitting outside at the tables. They're afraid of rain—the sky doesn't look good. And how bumpy the ground is here, bare spots and little holes and pataches of crabgrass, and everywhere napkins and junk. Too many flies, outside. Has this place changed hands? The screens at the windows don't fit right; you can see why flies get inside. Jesse opens the door for me and I go in. All bars smell alike. There is a damp, dark odor of beer and something indefinable—spilled soft drinks, pretzels getting stale? This bar is just like any other. Before we were married we went to places like this, Jesse and me and other couples. We had to spend a certain amount of time doing things like that—and going to movies, playing miniature golf, bowling, dancing, swimming—and then we got married, now we're going to have a baby. I think of the baby all the time, because my life will be changed then; everything will be different. Four months from now. I should be frightened, but a calm laziness has come over me. It was so easy for my mother . . . But it will be different with me because my life will be changed by it, and nothing ever changed my mother. You couldn't change her! Why should I think? Why should I be afraid? My body is filled with love for this baby, and I will never be the same again.

We sit down at a table near the bar. Jesse is in a good mood. My father would have liked him, I think; when he laughs Jesse reminds me of him. Why is a certain kind of simple, healthy, honest man always destined to lose everything? Their souls are as clean and smooth as the muscular line of their arms. At night I hold Jesse, thinking of my father and what happened to him—all that drinking, then the accident at the factory—and I pray that Jesse will be different. I hope that his quick, open, loud way of talking is just a disguise, that really he is someone else—slower and calculating. That kind of man grows old without jerks and spasms. Why did I marry Jesse, then?

Someone at the bar turns around, and it's a man I think I know—I have known. Yes. That man outside, the man I met outside. I stare at him, my heart pounding, and he doesn't see me. He is dark, his hair is neatly combed but is thinner than before; he is wearing a cheap gray suit. But is it the same man? He is standing with a friend and looking around, as if he doesn't like what he sees. He is tired, too. He has grown years older.

Our eyes meet. He glances away. He doesn't remember—that frightened girl he held in his arms.

I am tempted to put my hand on Jesse's arm and tell him about that man, but how can I? Jesse is talking about trading in our car for a new one . . . I can't move, my mind seems to be coming to a stop. Is that the man I kissed, or someone else? A feeling of angry loss comes over me. Why should I lose everything? Everything? Is it the same man, and would he remember? My heart bothers me, it's stupid to be like this: here I sit, powdered and sweet, a girl safely married, pregnant and secured to the earth, with my husband beside me. He still loves me. Our love keeps on. Like my parents' love, it will subside someday, but nothing surprises me because I have learned everything.

The man turns away, talking to his friend. They are weary, tired of something. He isn't married yet, I think, and that pleases me. Good. But why are these men always tired? Is it the jobs they hold, the kind of men who stop in at this tavern? Why do they flash their teeth when they smile, but stop smiling so quickly? Why do their children cringe from them sometimes—an innocent upraised arm a frightening thing? Why do they grow old so quickly, sitting at kitchen tables with bottles of beer? They are everywhere, in every house. All the houses in this neighborhood and all neighborhoods around here. Jesse is young, but the outline of what he will be is already in his face; do you think I can't see it? Their lives are like hands dealt out to them in their innumerable card games. You pick up the sticky cards, and there it is: there it is. Can't change anything, all you can do is switch some cards around, stick one in here, one over here . . . pretend there is some sense, a secret scheme.

The man at the bar tosses some coins down and turns to go. I want to cry out to him, "Wait, wait!" But I cannot. I sit helplessly and watch him leave. Is it the same man? If he leaves I will be caught here, what can I do? I can almost hear my mother's shrill laughter, coming in from outside, and some drawling remark of my father's—lifting for a moment above the music. Those little explosions of laughter, the slap of someone's hand on the damp table, in anger, the clink of bottles accidentally touching—and there, there, my drunken aunt's voice, what is she saying? I am terrified at being left with them. I watch the man at the door and think that I could have loved him, I know it.

He has left, he and his friend. He is nothing to me, but suddenly I feel tears in my eyes. What's wrong with me? I hate everything that springs upon me and seems to draw itself down and oppress me in a way I could never explain to anyone . . . I am crying because I am pregnant but not with that man's child. It could have been his child, I could have gone with him to his car; but I did nothing, I ran away, I was afraid, and now I'm sitting here with Jesse, who is picking the label off his beer bottle with his thick squarish fingernails. I did nothing. I was afraid. Now he has left me here and what can I do?

I let my hand fall onto my stomach to remind myself that I am in love: with this baby, with Jesse, with everything. I am in love with our house and our life and the future and even this moment—right now—that I am struggling to live through.

[1967]

For Thought

With careful attention to the creation of atmosphere and mood, Joyce Carol Oates shows the developing character of a girl from early childhood to late adolescence, from innocence to sad wisdom. By using vivid sensory details, the author establishes the shabby dreariness of the surroundings in which the ritualized events take place. By skillful use of the central intelligence point of view, Oates reveals the emotions and perceptions of her main character in the course of four summer days spread out over approximately fourteen years. The author emphasizes the strong mixture of love and hate, fascination and revulsion, that dominate Sissie's attitude toward the people in her life. By means of this episodic, but integrated, approach, Oates evokes in the reader a poignant awareness of blighted lives filled with regret over what might have been and burdened with sadness at what the future inevitably will bring.

For Discussion

1. What emotions does Oates concentrate on in each of the four sections?
2. What is the girl's attitude toward her father? Toward her mother? What changes do these feelings undergo from one age level to the next?
3. Discuss Sissie's characterization, both as an individual and as a type.
4. What details of dialogue and description create the atmosphere and the mood of the lakeside tavern and the area around it?
5. What symbols are used in the story? What do they point to collectively?

Grace Paley
Wants

I saw my ex-husband in the street. I was sitting on the steps of the new library.

Hello, my life, I said. We had once been married for twenty-seven years, so I felt justified.

He said, What? What life? No life of mine.

I said, O.K. I don't argue when there's real disagreement. I got up and went into the library to see how much I owed them.

The librarian said $32 even and you've owed it for eighteen years. I didn't deny anything. Because I don't understand how time passes. I have had those books. I have often thought of them. The library is only two blocks away.

My ex-husband followed me to the Books Returned desk. He interrupted the librarian, who had more to tell. In many ways, he said, as I look back, I attribute the dissolution of our marriage to the fact that you never invited the Bertrams to dinner.

That's possible, I said. But really, if you remember: first, my father was sick that Friday, then the children were born, then I had those Tuesday night meetings, then the war began. Then we didn't seem to know them any more. But you're right. I should have had them to dinner.

I gave the librarian a check for $32. Immediately she trusted me, put my past behind her, wiped the record clean, which is just what most other municipal and/or state bureaucracies will *not* do.

I checked out the two Edith Wharton books I had just returned because I'd read them so long ago and they are more apropos now than ever. They were *The House of Mirth* and *The Children*, which is about how life in the United States in New York changed in twenty-seven years fifty years ago.

A nice thing I do remember is breakfast, my ex-husband said. I was surprised. All we ever had was coffee. Then I remembered there was a hole in the back of the kitchen closet which opened into the apartment next door. There, they always ate sugar-cured smoked bacon. It gave us a very grand feeling about breakfast, but we never got stuffed and sluggish.

That was when we were poor, I said.

When were we ever rich? he asked.

Oh, as time went on, as our responsibilities increased, we didn't go in need. You took adequate financial care, I reminded him. The children went to camp four weeks a year and in decent ponchos with sleeping bags and boots, just like everyone else. They looked very nice. Our place was warm in winter, and we had nice red pillows and things.

I wanted a sailboat, he said. But you didn't want anything.

Don't be bitter, I said. It's never too late.

No, he said with a great deal of bitterness. I may get a sailboat. As a matter of fact I have money down on an eighteen-foot two-rigger. I'm doing well this year and can look forward to better. But as for you, it's too late. You'll always want nothing.

He had had a habit throughout the twenty-seven years of making a narrow remark which, like a plumber's snake, could work its way through the ear down the throat, halfway to my heart. He would then disappear, leaving me choking with equipment. What I mean is, I sat down on the library steps and he went away.

I looked through *The House of Mirth*, but lost interest. I felt extremely accused. Now, it's true, I'm short of requests and absolute requirements. But I do want *something.*

I want, for instance, to be a different person. I want to be the woman who brings these two books back in two weeks. I want to be the effective citizen who changes the school system and addresses the Board of Estimate on the troubles of this dear urban center.

I *had* promised my children to end the war before they grew up.

I wanted to have been married forever to one person, my ex-husband or my present one. Either has enough character for a whole life, which as it turns out is really not such a long time. You couldn't exhaust either man's qualities or get under the rock of his reasons in one short life.

Just this morning I looked out the window to watch the street for a while and saw that the little sycamores the city had dreamily planted a couple of years before the kids were born had come that day to the prime of their lives.

Well! I decided to bring those two books back to the library. Which proves that when a person or an event comes along to jolt or appraise me I *can* take some appropriate action, although I am better known for my hospitable remarks.

[1971]

For Thought

"Wants" compresses the communal life of a family from beginning to end into a vignette. In a chance encounter with her ex-husband, the narrator is forced to recollect the memories, mostly trivial, that emerge from their 27 years together. She views their past life together with detachment and acceptance. However, her ex-husband is bitter, accusing her of destroying both of their chances for happiness through wanting nothing. In the end, the narrator retrieves her self-esteem by a reminder that she *can* act if jolted strongly enough.

For Discussion

1. What kind of person does the narrator consider herself to be? How is her self-concept contrasted to the portrait her ex-husband draws of her?

2. How is the narrator's husband characterized? Are there any clues as to why their marriage finally failed?
3. Why were the events in the narrator's marriage both so unremarkable and memorable? How do these events help locate the marriage as to time and place?
4. Why is the narrator so deeply hurt by her ex-husband's criticisms? How does she come to terms with his anger and restore her self-esteem?

Dorothy Parker
Big Blonde

I

Hazel Morse was a large, fair woman of the type that incites some men when they use the word "blonde" to click their tongues and wag their heads roguishly. She prided herself upon her small feet and suffered for her vanity, boxing them in snub-toed, high-heeled slippers of the shortest bearable size. The curious thing about her were her hands, strange terminations to the flabby white arms splattered with pale tan spots—long, quivering hands with deep and convex nails. She should not have disfigured them with little jewels.

She was not a woman given to recollections. At her middle thirties, her old days were a blurred and flickering sequence, an imperfect film, dealing with the actions of strangers.

In her twenties, after the deferred death of a hazy widowed mother, she had been employed as a model in a wholesale dress establishment—it was still the day of the big woman, and she was then prettily colored and erect and high-breasted. Her job was not onerous, and she met numbers of men and spent numbers of evenings with them, laughing at their jokes and telling them she loved their neckties. Men liked her, and she took it for granted that the liking of many men was a desirable thing. Popularity seemed to her to be worth all the work that had to be put into its achievement. Men liked you because you were fun, and when they liked you they took you out, and there you were. So, and successfully, she was fun. She was a good sport. Men like a good sport.

No other form of diversion, simpler or more complicated, drew her attention. She never pondered if she might not be better occupied doing something else. Her ideas, or, better, her acceptances, ran right along with those of the other substantially built blondes in whom she found her friends.

When she had been working in the dress establishment some years she met Herbie Morse. He was thin, quick, attractive, with shifting lines about his shiny, brown eyes and a habit of fiercely biting at the skin around his fingers nails. He drank largely; she found that entertaining. Her habitual greeting to him was an allusion to his state of the previous night.

"Oh, what a peach you had," she used to say, through her easy laugh. "I thought I'd die, the way you kept asking the waiter to dance with you."

She liked him immediately upon their meeting. She was enormously amused at his fast, slurred sentences, his interpolations of apt phrases from vaudeville acts and comic strips; she thrilled at the feel of his lean arm tucked firm beneath the sleeve of her coat; she wanted to touch the wet, flat surface of his hair. He was as promptly drawn to her. They were married six weeks after they had met.

She was delighted at the idea of being a bride; coquetted with it, played upon it. Other offers of marriage she had had, and not a few of them, but it happened that they were all from stout, serious men who had visited the dress establishment as buyers; men from Des Moines and Houston and Chicago and, in her phrase, even funnier places. There was always something immensely comic to her in the thought of living elsewhere than New York. She could not regard as serious proposals that she share a western residence.

She wanted to be married. She was nearing thirty now, and she did not take the years well. She spread and softened, and her darkening hair turned her to inexpert dabblings with peroxide. There were times when she had little flashes of fear about her job. And she had had a couple of thousand evenings of being a good sport among her male acquaintances. She had come to be more conscientious than spontaneous about it.

Herbie earned enough, and they took a little apartment far uptown. There was a Mission-furnished dining-room with a hanging central light globed in liver-colored glass; in the living-room were an "over-stuffed suite," a Boston fern, and a reproduction of the Henner "Magdalene" with the red hair and the blue draperies; the bedroom was in gray enamel and old rose, with Herbie's photograph on Hazel's dressing-table and Hazel's likeness on Herbie's chest of drawers.

She cooked—and she was a good cook—and marketed and chatted with the delivery boys and the colored laundress. She loved the flat, she loved her life, she loved Herbie. In the first months of their marriage, she gave him all the passion she was ever to know.

She had not realized how tired she was. It was a delight, a new game, a holiday, to give up being a good sport. If her head ached or her arches throbbed, she complained piteously, babyishly. If her mood was quiet, she did not talk. If tears came to her eyes, she let them fall.

She fell readily into the habit of tears during the first year of her marriage. Even in her good sport days, she had been known to weep lavishly and disinterestedly on occasion. Her behavior at the theater was a standing joke. She could weep at anything in a play—tiny garments, love both unrequited and mutual, seduction, purity, faithful servitors, wedlock, the triangle.

"There goes Haze," her friends would say, watching her. "She's off again."

Wedded and relaxed, she poured her tears freely. To her who had laughed so much, crying was delicious. All sorrows became her sorrows; she was Tenderness. She would cry long and softly over newspaper accounts of kidnaped babies, deserted wives, unemployed men, strayed cats, heroic dogs. Even when the paper was no longer before her, her mind revolved upon these things and the drops slipped rhythmically over her plump cheeks.

"Honestly," she would say to Herbie, "all the sadness there is in the world when you stop to think about it!"

"Yeah," Herbie would say.

She missed nobody. The old crowd, the people who had brought her and Herbie together, dropped from their lives, lingeringly at first. When she thought of this at all, it was only to consider it fitting. This was marriage. This was peace.

But the thing was that Herbie was not amused.

For a time, he had enjoyed being alone with her. He found the voluntary isolation novel and sweet. Then it palled with a ferocious suddenness. It was as if one night, sitting with her in the steam-heated living-room, he would ask no more; and the next night he was through and done with the whole thing.

He became annoyed by her misty melancholies. At first, when he came home to find her softly tired and moody, he kissed her neck and patted her shoulder and begged her to tell her Herbie what was wrong. She loved that. But time slid by, and he found that there was never anything really, personally, the matter.

"Ah, for God's sake," he would say. "Crabbing again. All right, sit here and crab your head off. I'm going out."

And he would slam out of the flat and come back late and drunk.

She was completely bewildered by what happened to their marriage. First they were lovers; and then, it seemed without transition, they were enemies. She never understood it.

There were longer and longer intervals between his leaving his office and his arrival at the apartment. She went through agonies of picturing him run over and bleeding, dead and covered with a sheet. Then she lost her fears for his safety and grew sullen and wounded. When a person wanted to be with a person, he came as soon as possible. She desperately wanted him to want to be with her; her own hours only marked the time till he would come. It was often nearly nine o'clock before he came home to dinner. Always he had had many drinks, and their effect would die in him, leaving him loud and querulous and bristling for affronts.

He was too nervous, he said, to sit and do nothing for an evening. He boasted, probably not in all truth, that he had never read a book in his life.

"What am I expected to do—sit around this dump on my tail all night?" he would ask, rhetorically. And again he would slam out.

She did not know what to do. She could not manage him. She could not meet him.

She fought him furiously. A terrific domesticity had come upon her, and she would bite and scratch to guard it. She wanted what she called "a nice home." She wanted a sober, tender husband, prompt at dinner, punctual at work. She wanted sweet, conforting evenings. The idea of intimacy with other men was terrible to her; the thought that Herbie might be seeking entertainment in other women set her frantic.

It seemed to her that almost everything she read—novels from the drug-store lending library, magazine stories, women's pages in the papers—dealt with wives who lost their husbands' love. She could bear those, at that, better than accounts of neat, companionable marriage and living happily ever after.

She was frightened. Several times when Herbie came home in the evening, he found her determinedly dressed—she had had to alter those of her clothes that were not new, to make them fasten—and rouged.

"Let's go wild tonight, what do you say?" she would hail him. "A person's got lots of time to hang around and do nothing when they're dead."

So they would go out, to chop houses and the less expensive cabarets. But it turned out badly. She could no longer find amusement in watching Herbie drink. She could not laugh at his whimsicalities, she was so tensely counting his indulgences. And she was unable to keep back her remonstrances—"Ah, come on, Herb, you've had enough, haven't you? You'll feel something terrible in the morning."

He would be immediately enraged. All right, crab; crab, crab, crab, crab, that was all she ever did. What a lousy sport *she* was!

There would be scenes, and one or the other of them would rise and stalk out in fury.

She could not recall the definite day that she started drinking, herself. There was nothing separate about her days. Like drops upon a window-pane, they ran together and trickled away. She had been married six months; then a year; then three years.

She had never needed to drink, formerly. She could sit for most of a night at a table where the others were imbibing earnestly and never droop in looks or spirits, nor be bored by the doings of those about her. If she took a cocktail, it was so unusual as to cause twenty minutes or so of jocular comment. But now anguish was in her. Frequently, after a quarrel, Herbie would stay out for the night, and she could not learn from him where the time had been spent. Her heart felt tight and sore in her breast, and her mind turned like an electric fan.

She hated the taste of liquor. Gin, plain or in mixtures, made her promptly sick. After experiment, she found that Scotch whisky was best for her. She took it without water, because that was the quickest way to its effect.

Herbie pressed it on her. He was glad to see her drink. They both felt it might restore her high spirits, and their good times together might again be possible.

"'Atta girl," he would approve her. "Let's see you get boiled, baby."

But it brought them no nearer. When she drank with him, there would be a little while of gaiety and then, strangely without beginning, they would be in a wild quarrel. They would wake in the morning not sure what it had all been about, foggy as to what had been said and done, but each deeply injured and bitterly resentful. There would be days of vengeful silence.

There had been a time when they had made up their quarrels, usually in bed. There would be kisses and little names and assurances of fresh starts. . . . "Oh, it's going to be great now, Herb. We'll have swell times. I was a crab. I guess I must have been tired. But everything's going to be swell. You'll see."

Now there were no gentle reconciliations. They resumed friendly relations only in the brief magnanimity caused by liquor, before more liquor drew them into new battles. The scenes became more violent. There were shouted invectives and pushes, and sometimes sharp slaps. Once she had a black eye. Herbie was horrified next day at sight of it. He did not go to work; he followed her about, suggesting remedies and heaping dark blame on himself. But after they had had a few drinks—"to pull themselves together"—she made so many wistful references to her bruise that he shouted at her and rushed out and was gone for two days.

Each time he left the place in a rage, he threatened never to come back. She did not believe him, nor did she consider separation. Somewhere in her head or her heart was the lazy, nebulous hope that things would change and she and Herbie settle suddenly into soothing married life. Here were her home, her furniture, her husband, her station. She summoned no alternatives.

She could no longer bustle and potter. She had no more vicarious tears; the hot drops she shed were for herself. She walked ceaselessly about the rooms, her thoughts running mechanically round and round Herbie. In those days began the hatred of being alone that she was never to overcome. You could be by yourself when things were all right, but when you were blue you got the howling horrors.

She commenced drinking alone, little, short drinks all through the day. It was only with Herbie that alcohol made her nervous and quick in offense. Alone, it blurred sharp things for her. She lived in a haze of it. Her life took on a dream-like quality. Nothing was astonishing.

A Mrs. Martin moved into the flat across the hall. She was a great blonde woman of forty, a promise in looks of what Mrs. Morse was to be. They made acquaintance, quickly became inseparable. Mrs. Morse spent her days in the opposite apartment. They drank together, to brace themselves after the drinks of the nights before.

She never confided her troubles about Herbie to Mrs. Martin. The subject was too bewildering to her to find comfort in talk. She let it be assumed that her husband's business kept him much away. It was not regarded as important; husbands, as such, played but shadowy parts in Mrs. Martin's circle.

Mrs. Martin had no visible spouse; you were left to decide for yourself whether he was or was not dead. She had an admirer, Joe, who came to see her almost nightly. Often he brought several friends with him—"The Boys," they were called. The Boys were big, red, good-humored men, perhaps forty-five, perhaps fifty. Mrs. Morse was glad of invitations to join the parties—Herbie was scarcely ever at home at night now. If he did come home, she did not visit Mrs. Martin. An evening alone with Herbie meant inevitably a quarrel, yet she would stay with him. There was always her thin and worthless idea that, maybe, this night, things would begin to be all right.

The Boys brought plenty of liquor along with them whenever they came to Mrs. Martin's. Drinking with them, Mrs. Morse became lively and good-natured and audacious. She was quickly popular. When she had drunk enough to cloud her most recent battle with Herbie, she was excited by their approbation. Crab, was she? Rotten sport, was she? Well, there were some that thought different.

Ed was one of the The Boys. He lived in Utica—had "his own business" there, was the awed report—but he came to New York almost every week. He was married. He showed Mrs. Morse the then current photographs of Junior and Sister, and she praised them abundantly and sincerely. Soon it was accepted by the others that Ed was her particular friend.

He staked her when they all played poker; sat next her and occasionally rubbed his knee against hers during the game. She was rather lucky. Frequently she went home with a twenty-dollar bill or a ten-dollar bill or a handful of crumpled dollars. She was glad of them. Herbie was getting, in her words, something awful about money. To ask him for it brought an instant row.

"What the hell do you do with it?" he would say. "Shoot it all on Scotch?"

"I try to run this house half-way decent," she would retort. "Never thought of that, did you? Oh, no, his lordship couldn't be bothered with that."

Again, she could not find a definite day, to fix the beginning of Ed's proprietorship. It became his custom to kiss her on the mouth when he came in, as well as for farewell, and he gave her little quick kisses of approval all through the evening. She liked this rather more than she disliked it. She never thought of his kisses when she was not with him.

He would run his hand lingeringly over her back and shoulders.

"Some dizzy blonde, eh?" he would say "Some doll."

One afternoon she came home from Mrs. Martin's to find Herbie in the bedroom. He had been away for several nights, evidently on a prolonged drinking bout. His face was gray, his hands jerked as if they were on wires. On the bed were two old suitcases, packed high. Only her photograph remained on his bureau, and the wide doors of his closet disclosed nothing but coat-hangers.

"I'm blowing," he said, "I'm through with the whole works. I got a job in Detroit."

She sat down on the edge of the bed. She had drunk much the night before, and the four Scotches she had had with Mrs. Martin had only increased her fogginess.

"Good job?" she said.

"Oh, yeah," he said. "Looks all right."

He closed a suitcase with difficulty, swearing at it in whispers.

"There's some dough in the bank," he said. "The bank book's in your top drawer. You can have the furniture and stuff."

He looked at her, and his forehead twitched.

"God damn it, I'm through, I'm telling you," he cried. "I'm through."

"All right, all right," she said. "I heard you, didn't I?"

She saw him as if he were at one end of a cannon and she at the other. Her head was beginning to ache bumpingly, and her voice had a dreary, tiresome tone. She could not have raised it.

"Like a drink before you go?" she asked.

Again he looked at her, and a corner of his mouth jerked up.

"Cockeyed again for a change, aren't you?" he said. "That's nice. Sure, get a couple of shots, will you?"

She went to the pantry, mixed him a stiff highball, poured herself a couple of inches of whisky and drank it. Then she gave herself another portion and brought the glasses into the bedroom. He had strapped both suitcases and had put on his hat and overcoat.

He took his highball.

"Well," he said, and he gave a sudden, uncertain laugh. "Here's mud in your eye."

"Mud in your eye," she said.

They drank. He put down his glass and took up the heavy suitcases.

"Got to get a train around six," he said.

She followed him down the hall. There was a song, a song that Mrs. Martin played doggedly on the phonograph, running loudly through her mind. She had never liked the thing.

> "Night and daytime,
> Always playtime.
> Ain't we got fun?"

At the door he put down the bags and faced her.

"Well," he said. "Well, take care of yourself. You'll be all right, will you?"

"Oh, sure," she said.

He opened the door, then came back to her, holding out his hand.

"'By, Haze," he said. "Good luck to you."

She took his hand and shook it.

"Pardon my wet glove," she said.

When the door had closed behind him, she went back to the pantry.

She was flushed and lively when she went into Mrs. Martin's that evening. The Boys were there, Ed among them. He was glad to be in town, frisky and loud and full of jokes. But she spoke quietly to him for a minute.

"Herbie blew today," she said. "Going to live out west."

"That so?" he said. He looked at her and played with the fountain pen clipped to his waistcoat pocket.

"Think he's gone for good, do you?" he asked.

"Yeah," she said. "I know he is. I know. Yeah."

"You going to live on across the hall just the same?" he said. "Know what you're going to do?"

"Gee, I don't know," she said. "I don't give much of a damn."

"Oh, come on, that's no way to talk," he told her. "What you need—you need a little snifter. How about it?"

"Yeah," she said. "Just straight."

She won forty-three dollars at poker. When the game broke up, Ed took her back to her apartment.

"Got a little kiss for me?" he asked.

He wrapped her in his big arms and kissed her violently. She was entirely passive. He held her away and looked at her.

"Little tight, honey?" he asked, anxiously. "Not going to be sick, are you?"

"Me?" she said. "I'm swell."

II

When Ed left in the morning, he took her photograph with him. He said he wanted her picture to look at, up in Utica. "You can have that one on the bureau," she said.

She put Herbie's picture in a drawer, out of her sight. When she could look at it, she meant to tear it up. She was fairly successful in keeping her mind from racing around him. Whisky slowed it for her. She was almost peaceful, in her mist.

She accepted her relationship with Ed without question or enthusiasm. When he was away, she seldom thought definitely of him. He was good to her; he gave her frequent presents and a regular allowance. She was even able to save. She did not plan ahead of any day, but her wants were few, and you might as well put money in the bank as have it lying around.

When the lease of her apartment neared its end, it was Ed who suggested moving. His friendship with Mrs. Martin and Joe had become strained over a dispute at poker; a feud was impending.

"Let's get the hell out of here," Ed said. "What I want you to have is a place near the Grand Central. Make it easier for me."

So she took a little flat in the Forties. A colored maid came in every day to clean and to make coffee for her—she was "through with that housekeeping stuff," she said, and Ed, twenty years married to a passionately domestic woman, admired this romantic uselessness and felt doubly a man of the world in abetting it.

The coffee was all she had until she went out to dinner, but alcohol kept her fat. Prohibition she regarded only as a basis for jokes. You could always get all you wanted. She was never noticeably drunk and seldom nearly sober. It required a larger daily allowance to keep her misty-minded. Too little, and she was achingly melancholy.

Ed brought her to Jimmy's. He was proud, with the pride of the transient who would be mistaken for a native, in his knowledge of small, recent restaurants occupying the lower floors of shabby brownstone houses; places where, upon mentioning the name of an habitué friend, might be obtained strange whisky and fresh gin in many of their ramifications. Jimmy's place was the favorite of his acquaintances.

There, through Ed, Mrs. Morse met many men and women, formed quick friendships. The men often took her out when Ed was in Utica. He was proud of her popularity.

She fell into the habit of going to Jimmy's alone when she had no engagement. She was certain to meet some people she knew, and join them. It was a club for her friends, both men and women.

The women at Jimmy's looked remarkably alike, and this was curious, for, through feuds, removals, and opportunities of more profitable contacts, the personnel of the group changed constantly. Yet always the newcomers resembled those whom they replaced. They were all big women and stout, broad of shoulder and abundantly breasted, with faces thickly clothed in soft, high-colored flesh. They laughed loud and often, showing opaque and lusterless teeth like squares of crockery. There was about them the health of the big, yet a slight, unwholesome suggestion of stubborn preservation. They might have been thirty-six or forty-five or anywhere between.

They composed their titles of their own first names with their husbands' surnames—Mrs. Florence Miller, Mrs. Vera Riley, Mrs. Lilian Block. This gave at the same time the solidity of marriage and the glamour of freedom. Yet only one or two were actually divorced. Most of them never referred to their dimmed spouses; some, a shorter time separated, described them in terms of great biological interest. Several were mothers, each of an only child—a boy at school somewhere, or a girl being cared for by a grandmother. Often, well on towards morning, there would be displays of kodak portraits and of tears.

They were comfortable women, cordial and friendly and irrepressibly matronly.

Theirs was the quality of ease. Become fatalistic, especially about money matters, they were unworried. Whenever their funds dropped alarmingly, a new donor appeared; this had always happened. The aim of each was to have one man, permanently, to pay all her bills, in return for which she would have immediately given up other admirers and probably would have become exceedingly fond of him; for the affections of all of them were, by now, unexacting, tranquil, and easily arranged. This end, however, grew increasingly difficult yearly. Mrs. Morse was regarded as fortunate.

Ed had a good year, increased her allowance and gave her a sealskin coat. But she had to be careful of her moods with him. He insisted upon gaiety. He would not listen to admissions of aches or weariness.

"Hey, listen," he would say, "I got worries of my own, and plenty. Nobody wants to hear other people's troubles, sweetie. What you got to do, you got to be a sport and forget it. See? Well, slip us a little smile, then. That's my girl."

She never had enough interest to quarrel with him as she had with Herbie, but she wanted the privilege of occasional admitted sadness. It was strange. The other women she saw did not have to fight their moods. There was Mrs. Florence Miller who got regular crying jags, and the men sought only to cheer and comfort her. The others spent whole evenings in grieved recitals of worries and ills; their escorts paid them deep sympathy. But she was instantly undesirable when she was low in spirits. Once, at Jimmy's, when she could not make herself lively, Ed had walked out and left her.

"Why the hell don't you stay home and not go spoiling everybody's evening?" he had roared.

Even her slightest acquaintances seemed irritated if she were not conspicuously light-hearted.

"What's the matter with you, anyway?" they would say. "Be your age, why don't you? Have a little drink and snap out of it."

When her relationship with Ed had continued nearly three years, he moved to Florida to live. He hated leaving her; he gave her a large check and some shares of a sound stock, and his pale eyes were wet when he said good-by. She did not miss him. He came to New York infrequently, perhaps two or three times a year, and hurried directly from the train to see her. She was always pleased to have him come and never sorry to see him go.

Charley, an acquaintance of Ed's that she had met at Jimmy's, had long admired her. He had always made opportunities of touching her and leaning close to talk to her. He asked repeatedly of all their friends if they had ever heard such a fine laugh as she had. After Ed left, Charley became the main figure in her life. She classified him and spoke of him as "not so bad." There was nearly a year of Charley; then she divided her time between him and Sydney, another frequenter of Jimmy's; then Charley slipped away altogether.

Sydney was a little, brightly dressed, clever Jew. She was perhaps nearest contentment with him. He amused her always; her laughter was not forced.

He admired her completely. Her softness and size delighted him. And he thought she was great, he often told her, because she kept gay and lively when she was drunk.

"Once I had a gal," he said, "used to try and throw herself out of the window every time she got a can on. *Jee-zuss*," he added, feelingly.

Then Sydney married a rich and watchful bride, and then there was Billy. No—after Sydney came Ferd, then Billy. In her haze, she never recalled how men entered her life and left it. There were no surprises. She had no thrill at their advent, nor woe at their departure. She seemed to be always able to attract men. There was never another as rich as Ed, but they were all generous to her, in their means.

Once she had news of Herbie. She met Mrs. Martin dining at Jimmy's, and the old friendship was vigorously renewed. The still admiring Joe, while on a business trip, had seen Herbie. He had settled in Chicago, he looked fine, he was living with some woman—seemed to be crazy about her. Mrs. Morse had been drinking vastly that day. She took the news with mild interest, as one hearing of the sex peccadilloes of somebody whose name is, after a moment's groping, familiar.

"Must be damn near seven years since I saw him," she commented. "Gee. Seven years."

More and more, her days lost their individuality. She never knew dates, nor was sure of the day of the week.

"My God, was that a year ago!" she would exclaim, when an event was recalled in conversation.

She was tired so much of the time. Tired and blue. Almost everything could give her the blues. Those old horses she saw on Sixth Avenue—struggling and slipping along the car-tracks, or standing at the curb, their heads dropped level with their worn knees. The tightly stored tears would squeeze from her eyes as she teetered past on her aching feet in the stubby, champagne-colored slippers.

The thought of death came and stayed with her and lent her a sort of drowsy cheer. It would be nice, nice and restful, to be dead.

There was no settled, shocked moment when she first thought of killing herself; it seemed to her as if the idea had always been with her. She pounced upon all the accounts of suicides in the newspapers. There was an epidemic of self-killings—or maybe it was just that she searched for the stories of them so eagerly that she found many. To read of them roused reassurance in her; she felt a cozy solidarity with the big company of the voluntary dead.

She slept, aided by whisky, till deep into the afternoons, then lay abed, a bottle and glass at her hand, until it was time to dress to go out for dinner. She was beginning to feel towards alcohol a little puzzled distrust, as toward an old friend who has refused a simple favor. Whisky could still soothe her for most of the time, but there were sudden, inexplicable moments when the cloud fell treacherously away from her, and she was sawed by the sorrow and bewilderment and nuisance of all living. She played voluptuously with the thought of cool, sleepy retreat. She had never been troubled by religious belief and no vision of an after-life intimidated her. She dreamed by day of never again putting on tight shoes, of never having to laugh and listen and admire, of never more being a good sport. Never.

But how would you do it? It made her sick to think of jumping from heights. She could not stand a gun. At the theater, if one of the actors drew a revolver, she crammed her fingers into her ears and could not even look at the stage until after the shot had been fired. There was no gas in her flat. She looked long at the bright blue veins in her slim wrists—a cut with a razor blade, and there you'd be. But it would hurt, hurt like hell, and there would be blood to see. Poison—something tasteless and quick and painless—was the thing. But they wouldn't sell it to you in drugstores, because of the law.

She had few other thoughts.

There was a new man now—Art. He was short and fat and exacting and hard on her patience when he was drunk. But there had been only occasionals for some time before him, and she was glad of a little stability. Too, Art must be away for weeks at a stretch, selling silks, and that was restful. She was convincingly gay with him, though the effort shook her.

"The best sport in the world," he would murmur, deep in her neck. "The best sport in the world."

One night, when he had taken her to Jimmy's, she went into the dressing-room with Mrs. Florence Miller. There, while designing curly mouths on their faces with lip-rouge, they compared experiences of insomnia.

"Honestly," Mrs. Morse said, "I wouldn't close an eye if I didn't go to bed full of Scotch. I lie there and toss and turn and toss and turn. Blue! Does a person get blue lying awake that way!"

"Say, listen, Hazel," Mrs. Miller said, impressively, "I'm telling you I'd be awake for a year if I didn't take veronal. That stuff makes you sleep like a fool."

"Isn't it poison, or something?" Mrs. Morse asked.

"Oh, you take too much and you're out for the count!" said Mrs. Miller. "I just take five grains—they come in tablets. I'd be scared to fool around with it. but five grains, and you cork off pretty."

"Can you get it anywhere?" Mrs. Morse felt superbly Machiavellian.

"Get all you want in Jersey," said Mrs. Miller. "They won't give it to you here without you have a doctor's prescription. Finished? We'd better go back and see what the boys are doing."

That night, Art left Mrs. Morse at the door of her apartment; his mother was in town. Mrs. Morse was still sober, and it happened that there was no whisky left in her cupboard. She lay in bed, looking up at the black ceiling.

She rose early, for her, and went to New Jersey. She had never taken the tube, and did not understand it. So she went to the Pennsylvania Station and bought a railroad ticket to Newark. She thought of nothing in particular on the trip out. She looked at the uninspired hats of the women about her and gazed through the smeared window at the flat, gritty scene.

In Newark, in the first drug-store she came to, she asked for a tin of talcum powder, a nailbrush, and a box of veronal tablets. The powder and the brush were to make the hypnotic seem also a casual need. The clerk was entirely unconcerned. "We only keep them in bottles," he said, and wrapped up for her a little glass vial containing ten white tablets, stacked one on another.

She went to another drug-store and bought a face-cloth, an orange-wood stick, and a bottle of veronal tablets. The clerk was also uninterested.

"Well, I guess I got enought to kill an ox," she thought, and went back to the station.

At home, she put the little vials in the drawer of her dressingtable and stood looking at them with a dreamy tenderness.

"There they are, God bless them," she said, and she kissed her finger-tip and touched each bottle.

The colored maid was busy in the living-room.

"Hey. Nettie," Mrs. Morse called. "Be an angel, will you? Run around to Jimmy's and get me a quart of Scotch."

She hummed while she awaited the girl's return.

During the next few days, whisky ministered to her as tenderly as it had done when she first turned to its aid. Alone, she was soothed and vague, at Jimmy's she was the gayest of the groups. Art was delighted with her.

Then one night, she had an appointment to meet Art at Jimmy's for an early dinner. He was to leave afterward on a business excursion, to be away for a week. Mrs. Morse had been drinking all the afternoon; while she dressed to go out, she felt herself rising pleasurably from drowsiness to high spirits. But as she came out into the street the effects of the whisky deserted her completely, and she was filled with a slow, grinding wretchedness so horrible that she stood swaying on the pavement, unable for a moment to move forward. It was a gray night with spurts of mean, thin snow, and the streets shone with dark ice. As she slowly crossed Sixth Avenue, consciously dragging one foot past the other, a big, scarred horse pulling a rickety express-wagon crashed to his knees before her. The driver swore and screamed and lashed the beast insanely, bringing the whip back over his shoulder for every blow, while the horse struggled to get a footing on the slippery asphalt. A group gathered and watched with interest.

Art was waiting, when Mrs. Morse reached Jimmy's.

"What's the matter with you, for God's sake?" was his greeting to her.

"I saw a horse," she said. "Gee, I—a person feels sorry for horses. I—it isn't just horses. Everything's kind of terrible, isn't it? I can't help getting sunk."

"Ah, sunk, me eye," he said. "What's the idea of all the bellyaching? What have you got to be sunk about?"

"I can't help it," she said.

"Ah, help it, me eye," he said. "Pull yourself together, will you? Come on and sit down, and take that face off you."

She drank industriously and she tried hard, but she could not overcome her melancholy. Others joined them and commented on her gloom, and she could do no more for them than smile weakly. She made little dabs at her eyes with her handkerchief, trying to time her movements so they would be unnoticed, but several times Art caught her and scowled and shifted impatiently in his chair.

When it was time for him to go to his train, she said she would leave, too, and go home.

"And not a bad idea, either," he said. "See if you can't sleep yourself out of it. I'll see you Thursday. For God's sake, try and cheer up by then, will you?"

"Yeah," she said. "I will."

In her bedroom, she undressed with a tense speed wholly unlike her usual slow uncertainty. She put on her nightgown, took off her hair-net and passed the comb quickly through her dry, vari-colored hair. Then she took the two little vials from the drawer and carried them into the bathroom. The splintering misery had gone from her, and she felt the quick excitement of one who is about to receive an anticipated gift.

She uncorked the vials, filled a glass with water and stood before the mirror, a table between her fingers. Suddenly she bowed graciously to her reflection, and raised the glass to it.

"Well, here's mud in your eye," she said.

The tablets were unpleasant to take, dry and powdery and sticking obstinately halfway down her throat. It took her a long time to swallow all twenty of them. She stood watching her reflection with deep, impersonal interest, studying the movements of the gulping throat. Once more she spoke aloud.

"For God's sake, try and cheer up by Thursday, will you?" she said. "Well, you know what he can do. He and the whole lot of them."

She had no idea how quickly to expect effect from the veronal. When she had taken the last tablet, she stood uncertainly, wondering, still with a courteous, vicarious interest, if death would strike her down then and there. She felt in no way strange, save for a slight stirring of sickness from the effort of swallowing the tablets, nor did her reflected face look at all different. It would not be immediate, then; it might even take an hour or so.

She stretched her arms high and gave a vast yawn.

"Guess I'll go to bed," she said. "Gee, I'm nearly dead."

That struck her as comic, and she turned out the bathroom light and went in and laid herself down in her bed, chuckling softly all the time.

"Gee, I'm nearly dead," she quoted. "That's a hot one!"

III

Nettie, the colored maid, came in late the next afternoon to clean the apartment, and found Mrs. Morse in her bed. But then, that was not unusual. Usually, though, the sounds of cleaning waked her, and she did not like to wake up. Nettie, an agreeable girl, had learned to move softly about her work.

But when she had done the living-room and stolen in to tidy the little square bedroom, she could not avoid a tiny clatter as she arranged the objects on the dressing-table. Instinctively, she glanced over her shoulder at the sleeper, and without warning a sickly uneasiness crept over her. She came to the bed and stared down at the woman lying there.

Mrs. Morse lay on her back, one flabby, white arm flung up, the wrist against her forehead. Her stiff hair hung untenderly along her face. The bed covers were pushed down, exposing a deep square of soft neck and a pink nightgown, its fabric worn uneven by many launderings; her great breasts, freed from their tight confiner, sagged beneath her arm-pits. Now and then she made knotted, snoring sounds, and from the corner of her opened mouth to the blurred turn of her jaw ran a lane of crusted spittle.

"Mis' Morse," Nettie called. "Oh, Mis' Morse! It's terrible late."

Mrs. Morse made no move.

"Mis' Morse," said Nettie. "Look, Mis' Morse. How'm I goin' get this bed made?"

Panic sprang upon the girl. She shook the woman's hot shoulder.

"Ah, wake up, will yuh?" she whined. "Ah, please wake up."

Suddenly the girl turned and ran out in the hall to the elevator door, keeping her thumb firm on the black, shiny button until the elderly car and its Negro attendant stood before her. She poured a jumble of words over the boy, and led him back to the apartment. He tiptoed creakingly in to the bedside; first gingerly, then so lustily that he left marks in the soft flesh, he prodded the unconscious woman.

"Hey, there!" he cried, and listened intently, as for an echo.

"Jeez. Out like a light," he commented.

At his interest in the spectacle, Nettie's panic left her. Importance was big in both of them. They talked in quick, unfinished whispers, and it was the boy's suggestion that he fetch the young doctor who lived on the ground floor. Nettie hurried along with him. They looked forward to the limelit moment of breaking their news of something untoward, something pleasurably unpleasant. Mrs. Morse had become the medium of drama. With no ill wish to her, they hoped that her state was serious, that she would not let them down by being awake and normal on their return. A little fear of this determined them to make the most, to the doctor, of her present condition. "Matter of life and death," returned to Nettie from her thin store of reading. She considered startling the doctor with the phrase.

The doctor was in and none too pleased at interruption. He wore a yellow and blue striped dressing-gown, and he was lying on his sofa, laughing with a dark girl, her face scaly with inexpensive powder, who perched on the arm. Half-emptied highball glasses stood beside them, and her coat and hat were neatly hung up with the comfortable implication of a long stay.

Always something, the doctor grumbled. Couldn't let anybody alone after a hard day. But he put some bottles and instruments into a case, changed his dressing-gown for his coat and started out with the Negroes.

"Snap it up there, big boy," the girl called after him. "Don't be all night."

The doctor strode loudly into Mrs. Morse's flat and on to the bedroom, Nettie and the boy right behind him. Mrs. Morse had not moved; her sleep was as deep, but soundless, now. The doctor looked sharply at her, then plunged his thumbs into the lidded pits above her eyeballs and threw his weight upon them. A high, sickened cry broke from Nettie.

"Look like he tryin' to push her right on th'ough the bed," said the boy. He chuckled.

Mrs. Morse gave no sign under the pressure. Abruptly the doctor abandoned it, and with one quick movement swept the covers down to the foot of the bed. With another he flung her nightgown back and lifted the thick, white legs, cross-hatched with blocks of tiny, iris-colored veins. He pinched them repeatedly, with long, cruel nips, back of the knees. She did not awaken.

"What's she been drinking?" he asked Nettie, over his shoulder.

With the certain celerity of one who knows just where to lay hands on a thing, Nettie went into the bathroom, bound for the cupboard where Mrs. Morse kept her whisky. But she stopped at the sight of the two vials, with their red and white labels, lying before the mirror. She brought them to the doctor.

"Oh, for the Lord Almighty's sweet sake!" he said. He dropped Mrs. Morse's legs, and pushed them impatiently across the bed. "What did she want to go taking that tripe for? Rotten yellow trick, that's what a thing like that is. Now we'll have to pump her out, and all that stuff. Nuisance, a thing like that is; that's what it amounts to. Here, George, take me down in the elevator. You wait here, maid. She won't do anything."

"She won't die on me, will she?" cried Nettie.

"No," said the doctor. "God, no. You couldn't kill her with an ax."

IV

After two days, Mrs. Morse came back to consciousness, dazed at first, then with a comprehension that brought with it the slow, saturating wretchedness.

"Oh, Lord, oh, Lord," she moaned, and tears for herself and for life striped her cheeks.

Nettie came in at the sound. For two days she had done the ugly, incessant tasks in the nursing of the unconscious, for two nights she had caught broken bits of sleep on the living-room couch. She looked coldly at the big, blown woman in the bed.

"What you been tryin' to do, Mis' Morse?" she said. "What kine o' work is that, takin' all that stuff?"

"Oh, Lord," moaned Mrs. Morse, again, and she tried to cover her eyes with her arms. But the joints felt stiff and brittle, and she cried out at their ache.

"Tha's no way to ack, takin' them pills," said Nettie. "You can thank you' stars you heah at all. How you feel now?"

"Oh, I feel great," said Mrs. Morse. "Swell, I feel."

Her hot, painful tears fell as if they would never stop.

"Tha's no way to take on, cryin' like that," Nettie said. "After what you done. The doctor, he says he could have you arrested, doin' a thing like that. He was fit to be tied, hear."

"Why couldn't he let me alone?" wailed Mrs. Morse. "Why the hell couldn't he have?"

"Tha's terr'ble, Mis' Morse, swearin' an' talkin' like that," said Nettie, "after what people done for you. Here I ain' had no sleep at all for two nights, an' had to give up goin' out to my other ladies!"

"Oh, I'm sorry, Nettie," she said. "You're a peach. I'm sorry I've given you so much trouble. I couldn't help it. I just got sunk. Didn't you ever feel like doing it? When everything looks just lousy to you?"

"I wouldn't think o' no such thing," declared Nettie. "You got to cheer up. Tha's what you got to do. Everybody's got their troubles."

"Yeah," said Mrs. Morse. "I know."

"Come a pretty picture card for you," Nettie said. "Maybe that will cheer you up."

She handed Mrs. Morse a post-card. Mrs. Morse had to cover one eye with her hand, in order to read the message; her eyes were not yet focusing correctly.

It was from Art. On the back of a view of the Detroit Athletic Club he had written: "Greeting and salutations. Hope you have lost the gloom. Cheer up and don't take any rubber nickles. See you on Thursday."

She dropped the card to the floor. Misery crushed her as if she were between great smooth stones. There passed before her a slow, slow pageant of days spent lying in her flat, of evenings at Jimmy's being a good sport, making herself laugh and coo at Art and other Arts; she saw a long parade of weary horses and shivering beggars and all beaten, driven, stumbling things. Her feet throbbed as if she had crammed them into the stubby champagne-colored slippers. Her heart seemed to swell and harden.

"Nettie," she cried, "for heaven's sake pour me a drink, will you?"

The maid looked doubtful.

"Now you know, Mis' Morse," she said, "you been near daid. I don' know if the doctor he let you drink nothing yet."

"Oh, never mind him," she said. "You get me one, and bring in the bottle. Take one yourself."

"Well," said Nettie.

She poured them each a drink, deferentially leaving hers in the bathroom to be taken in solitude, and brought Mrs. Morse's glass in to her.

Mrs. Morse looked into the liquor and shuddered back from its odor. Maybe it would help. Maybe, when you had been knocked cold for a few days, your very first drink would give you a lift. Maybe whisky would be her friend again. She prayed without addressing a God, without knowing a God. Oh, please, please, let her be able to get drunk, please keep her always drunk.

She lifted the glass.

"Thanks, Nettie," she said. "Here's mud in your eye."

The maid giggled. "Tha's the way, Mis' Morse," she said. "You cheer up, now."

"Yeah," said Mrs. Morse. "Sure."

[1929]

For Thought

Setting "Big Blonde" during Prohibition, Parker chronicles a compliant woman's downward progress from the halcyon days of her twenties to a liquor sodden, flabby middle age, with no prospect of happiness and one suicide attempt already behind her. The author establishes an air of realism throughout the story by the use of catch phrases of the period, careful description of the physical surroundings, the rounded characterization of Hazel, and pinpoint accuracy in her delineation of the flat characters in the way they relate to her main character.

For Discussion

1. What is the dominant mood of the story? How is it established?
2. How does each of the four sections of the story contribute to the sense of inevitable disaster?
3. How is Hazel characterized by her furnishings, her reading habits, and her propensity to shed tears easily?
4. How is the setting, in regard to time and place, important in the story?
5. Discuss the effect of the judgmental comments made by the narrator at various points in the story.
6. How does the attitude of the men with regard to the role they feel women should assume play a part in the story?
7. What is the central irony in the story with regard to Hazel's character and fate?
8. What is the author's attitude toward Hazel—sympathetic and forgiving, disapproving and hostile, or objective and nonjudgmental? Give evidence to support the interpretation chosen.

Ann Petry

Has Anybody Seen Miss Dora Dean?

One afternoon last winter, when the telephone rang in my house in Wheeling, New York, I started not to answer it; it was snowing, I was reading a book I had been waiting for weeks to get hold of, and I did not want to be disturbed. But it seemed to me that the peals of the bell were longer, more insistent than usual, so I picked up the phone and said, "Hello."

It was Peter Forbes—and neither that name nor any other is the actual one—and he was calling from Bridgeport. He said abruptly, and wheezily, for he is an asthmatic, "Ma is terribly ill. Really awfully sick."

He paused, and I said I was very sorry. His mother, Sarah Forbes, and my mother had grown up together in a black section of Bridgeport.

Peter said, "She's got some dishes she wants you to have. So will you come as soon as you can? Because she is really very sick."

I had heard that Sarah, who was in her seventies, was not well, but I was startled to learn that she was "terribly ill," "really very sick." I said, "I'll come tomorrow. Will that be all right?"

"No, no," he said "Please come today. Ma keeps worrying about these dishes. So will you please come—well, right away? She is really terribly, terribly ill."

Knowing Sarah as well as I did, I could understand his insistence. Sarah had an unpleasant voice; it was a querulous, peevish voice. When she was angry or irritated, or wanted you to do something that you did not want to do, she talked and talked and talked, until finally her voice seemed to be pursuing you. It was like a physical pursuit from which there was no escape.

I said, "I'll leave right away," and hung up.

It took me three hours to drive from Wheeling to Bridgeport, though the distance is only forty-five miles. But it is forty-five miles of winding road—all hills and sharp curves. The slush in the road was beginning to freeze, and the windshield wiper kept getting stuck; at frequent intervals I had to stop the car and get out and push the snow away so that the wiper could function again.

During that long, tedious drive, I kept thinking about Sarah and remembering things about her. It was at least two years since I had seen her. But before that, over a period of twenty years, I had seen her almost every summer, because Peter drove over to Wheeling to go fishing, and his mother came too. She usually accompanied him whenever he went out for a ride. He would leave her at my house, so that she could visit with me while he and his two boys went fishing.

I thoroughly enjoyed these visits, for Sarah could be utterly charming when she was so minded. She was a tall woman with rather bushy black hair that had a streak of gray near the front. Her skin was a wonderful reddish brown color and quite unwrinkled, in spite of her age. She would have been extremely attractive if she hadn't grown so fat. All this fat was deposited on her abdomen and behind. Her legs had stayed thin, and her feet were long and thin, and her head, neck, and shoulders were small, but she was huge from waist to knee. In silhouette, she looked rather like a pouter pigeon in reverse. Her legs were not sturdy enough to support so much weight, and she was always leaning against doors, or against people, for support. This gave her an air of helplessness, which was completely spurious. She had a caustic sense of humor, and though she was an old woman, if something struck her as being funny, she would be seized by fits of giggling just as if she were a very young and silly girl.

I knew a great deal about Sarah Forbes. This knowledge stemmed from a long-distance telephone call that she made to my mother thirty-three years ago, when I was nine years old. I overheard my mother's side of the conversation. I can still repeat what she said, word for word, even imitating the intonation, the inflection of her voice.

In those days we lived in the building that housed my father's drugstore, in Wheeling. Our kitchen was on the ground floor, behind the store, and the bedrooms were upstairs, above it. Just as other children sat in the family living room, I sat in the drugstore—right near the front window on a bench when the weather was cold, outside on the wooden steps that extended across the front of the building when the weather was warm. Sitting outside on those splintery steps, I could hear everything that went on inside. In summer, the big front door of the store stayed wide open all day, and there was a screen door with fancy scrollwork on all the wooden parts. There were windows on either side of the door. On each window my father had painted his name in white letters with the most wonderful curlicues and flourishes, and under it the word "Druggist." On one window it said "Cold Soda," and on the other window "Ice Cream," and over the door it said "Drug Store."

Whether I sat inside the store or outside it, I had a long, sweeping view of the church, the church green, and the street. The street was as carefully composed as a painting: tall elm trees, white fences, Federal houses.

If I was sitting outside on the steps, listening to what went on in the store, no one paid any attention to me, but if I was sitting inside on the bench near the window, my mother or my father would shoo me out whenever a customer reached the really interesting part of the story he was telling. I was always being shooed out until I discovered that if I sat motionless on the bench, with a book held open in front of me, and did not glance up, everyone forgot about me. Occasionally, someone would stop right in the middle of a hair-raising story, and then my father would say, "Oh, she's got her nose in a book. She's just like she's deaf when she's got her nose in a book. You can say anything you want to and she won't hear a word." It was like having a permanent season ticket in a theater where there was a continuous performance and the same play was never given twice.

My special interest in Sarah dates from a rainy afternoon when I was sitting inside the store. It was a dull afternoon—no customers, nothing, just the busy sound of rain dripping from the eaves, hitting the wooden steps. The wall telephone rang, and my mother, wiping her hands on her apron, came to answer it from the kitchen, which was just behind the prescription room of the store. Before she picked up the receiver, she said, "That's a long-distance call. I can tell by the way the operator is ringing. That's a long-distance call."

I sat up straight, I picked up my book and I heard the tinkling sound of money being dropped in at the other end. Then I heard my mother saying, "Why, Sarah, how are you? . . . What? What did you say? . . . Found him? Found him where?" She listened. "Oh, *no!*" She listened again. "Oh my dear! Why, how dreadful! Surely an accident. You think—!" A longer period of listening: "Oh, no. Why that's impossible. Nobody would deliberately—" She didn't finish what she was going to say, and listened again. "A letter? Forbes left a letter? Tear it up! You mustn't let any one know that—" There was a long pause. "But you must think of Peter. These things have an effect on—Excuse me."

She turned and looked at me. I had put the book down on the bench, and I was staring straight at her, breathing quite fast and listening so intently that my mouth was open.

She said, "Go out and play."

I kept staring at her, not moving, because I was trying to figure out what in the world she and Sarah Forbes had been discussing. What had happened that no one must know about?

She said again, her voice rising slightly, "Go out and play."

So I went the long way, through the back of the store and the prescription room and the kitchen, and I slammed the back door, and then I edged inside the prescription room again, very quietly, and I heard my mother say, "He must have had a heart attack and fallen right across the railroad tracks just as the train was due. That's the only possible explanation. And, Sarah, burn that letter. Burn it up!" She hung up the phone, and then she said to herself, "How dreadful. How perfectly dreadful!"

Whether Sarah took my mother's advice and burned Forbes' letter I do not know, but it became common knowledge that he had committed suicide, and his death was so reported in the Bridgeport newspapers. His body had been found on the railroad tracks near Shacktown, an outlying, poverty-stricken section of Bridgeport, where the white riffraff lived and the lowest brothels were to be found. He was the only person that my father and my mother and my aunts had ever known who had killed himself, and they talked about him endlessly—not his suicide but his life as they had known it. His death seemed to have put them on the defensive. They sounded as though he had said to them, "This life all of us black folk lead is valueless; it is disgusting, it is cheap, it is contemptible, and I am throwing it away, so that every one will know exactly what I think of it." They did not say this, but they sounded perplexed and uneasy whenever they spoke of Forbes, and they seemed to feel that if they could pool their knowledge of him they might be able to reach some acceptable explanation of why he had killed himself. I heard Forbes and Sarah discussed, off and on, all during the period of my growing up.

I never saw Forbes. The Wingates, an enormously wealthy white family for whom he worked, had stopped coming to Wheeling before I was born, and he had stopped coming there too. But I heard him described so often that I knew exactly what he looked like, how he sounded when he talked, what kind of clothes he wore. He was a tall, slender black man. He was butler, social secretary, gentleman's gentleman. When Mr. Wingate became ill, he played the role of male nurse. Then, after Mr. Wingate's death, he ran the house for Mrs. Wingate. He could cook, he could sew, he could act as coachman if necessary; he did all the buying and all the hiring.

The Wingates were summer residents of Wheeling. Their winter home was in Bridgeport. In Wheeling, they owned what they called a cottage; it was an exact replica of an old Southern mansion—white columns, long graveled driveways, carefully maintained lawns, brick stables, and all within six hundred feet of Long Island Sound.

During the summer, Forbes rode a bicycle over to my father's drugstore every pleasant afternoon. He said he needed the exercise. Whenever I heard my family describing Forbes, I always thought how dull and uninteresting he must have been. There would never be anything unexpected about him, never anything unexplained. He would always move exactly as he was supposed to when someone pulled the proper strings. He was serious, economical, extremely conservative—a tall, elegant figure in carefully pressed black clothes and polished shoes. His voice was slightly effeminate, his speech very precise. Mrs. Wingate was an Episcopalian and so was Forbes.

But one day when my father was talking about Forbes, some six months after his death, he suddenly threw his head back and laughed. He said, "I can see him now, bicycling down the street, with those long legs of his pinched up in those straight tight pants he wore, pumping his legs up down, and whistling 'Has Anybody Seen Miss Dora Dean?' with his coattails flying in the wind. I can see him now." And he laughed again.

At the time, I could not understand why my father should have found this funny. Years later, I learned that the tune Forbes whistled was one that Bert Williams and George Walker, a memorable team of black comedians, had made famous along with their cakewalk. They were singing "Dora Dean" in New York in about 1896. Dora Dean, the girl of the song, played the lead in a hit show called "The Creole Show," which was notable for a chorus of sixteen beautiful brown girls. I suppose it amused my father to think that Forbes, who seemed to have silver polish in his veins instead of good red blood, should be whistling a tune that suggested cakewalks, beautiful brown girls, and ragtime.

Mrs. Wingate's name entered into the discussions of Forbes because he worked for her. It was usually my mother who spoke of Mrs. Wingate, and she said the same thing so often that I can quote her: "Mrs. Wingate always said she simply couldn't live without Forbes. She said he planned the menus, he checked the guest lists, he supervised the wine cellar—he did everything. Remember how she used to come into the store and say he was her mind, her heart, her hands? That was a funny thing to say, wasn't it?" There would be a pause, and then she would say, "Wasn't it too bad that she let herself get so fat?"

It was from my mother that I learned what Mrs. Wingate looked like. She was short and blond, and her face looked like the face of a fat china doll—pink and white and round. She used rice powder and rouge to achieve this effect. She bought these items in our drugstore. The powder came wrapped in thin white paper with a self stripe, and the rouge came in little round cardboard boxes, and inside there was a round, hard cake of reddish powder and a tiny powder puff to apply it with. She must have used a great deal of rouge, because at least once during the summer she would send Forbes up to the drugstore with a carton filled with these little empty rouge boxes. He would put them on the counter, saying, in his careful, precise, high-pitched voice, "Mrs. Wingate thought you might be able to use these." My father said he dumped them on the pile of rubbish in back of the store, to be burned, wondering what in the world she thought he would or could use them for. They smelled of perfume, and the reddish powder had discolored them, even on the outside.

Mrs. Wingate grew fatter and fatter, until, finally, getting her in and out of carriages, and then, during a later period, in and out of cars—even cars that were specially built—was impossible unless Forbes was on hand.

Forbes was lean, but he was wiry and tremendously strong. He could get Mrs. Wingate in and out of a carriage or a car without effort; at least he gave the illusion of effortlessness. My father said it was Mrs. Wingate who panted, who frowned, whose flesh quivered, whose forehead was dampened with sweat.

My father always ended his description of this performance by saying, "Remember how he used to have that white woman practically on his back? Yes, sir, practically on his back."

After I heard my father say that, I retained a curious mental picture of Forbes—a lean, wiry black man carrying an enormously fat pink and white woman piggyback. He did not lean over or bend over under the woman's weight; he stood straight, back unbent, so that she kept sliding down, down, down, and as he carried this quivering, soft-fleshed Mrs. Wingate, he was whistling "Has Anybody Seen Miss Dora Dean?"

I don't know that Forbes was actually looking for a reasonable facsimile of Dora Dean, but he found one, and he fell in love with her when he was forty years old. That was in 1900. He was so completely the perfect servant, with no emotional ties of his own and no life of his own, that my family seemed to think it was almost shocking that his attention should have been diverted from his job long enough to let him fall in love.

But it must have been inevitable from the first moment he saw Sarah Trumbull. I have a full-length photograph of her taken before she was married. She might well have been one of those beautiful girls in "The Creole Show." In the photograph she has a young, innocent face—lovely eyes, and a pointed chin, and a very pretty mouth with a quirk at the corner that suggests a sense of humor. Her hair is slightly frizzy, and it is worn in a high, puffed-out pompadour, which serves as a frame for the small, exquisite face. She is wearing a shirtwaist with big, stiff sleeves, and a tight choker of lace around her throat. This costume makes her waist look tiny and her neck long and graceful.

My mother had been born in Bridgeport, and though she was older than Sarah, she had known her quite well. Sarah was the only child of a Baptist minister, and, according to my mother's rather severe standards, she was a silly, giggling girl with a reputation for being fast. She was frivolous, flirtatious. She liked to play cards, and played pinochle for money. She played the violin very well, and she used to wear a ring with a diamond in it on her little finger, and just before she started to play, she would polish it on her skirt, so that it would catch the light and wink at the audience. She had scandalized the people in her father's church because she played ragtime on the piano at dances, parties, and cakewalks. (I overheard my father say that he had always heard this called "whorehouse music"; he couldn't understand how it got to be "ragtime.")

Anyway, one night in 1900 Forbes had a night off and went to a dance in New Haven, and there was Sarah Trumbull in a white muslin dress with violet ribbons, playing ragtime on the piano. And there was a cakewalk that night, and Forbes and Sarah were the winners. I found a yellowed clipping about it in one of my mother's scrapbooks—that's how I know what Sarah was wearing.

I have never seen a cakewalk but I have heard it described. About fourteen couples took part, and they walked in time to music—not in a circle but in a square, with the men on the inside. The participants were always beautifully dressed, and they walked with grace and style. It was a strutting kind of walk. The test of their skill lay in the way they pivoted when they turned the corners . The judges stopped the music at intervals and eliminated possibly three couples at a time. The most graceful couple was awarded a beautifully decorated cake, so that they had literally walked to win a cake.

In those days, Sarah Trumbull was tall, slender, and graceful, and John Forbes was equally tall, slender, and graceful. He was probably very solemn and she was probably giggling as they turned the corners in a cakewalk.

A year later, they were married in the Episcopal Church (colored) in Bridgeport. Sarah was a Baptist and her father was a Baptist minister, but she was married in an Episcopal church. If this had been a prize fight, I would say that Mrs. Wingate won the first round on points.

When my family discussed Forbes, they skipped the years after his marriage and went straight from his wedding to Sarah Trumbull in an Episcopal church (colored) to his death, twenty-four years later. Because I knew so little of the intervening years, I pictured him as being as ageless as a highly stylized figure in a marionette show—black, erect, elegantly dressed, effeminate, temperamental as a cat. I had never been able to explain why our cats did the things they did, and since there did not seem to be any reasonable explanation for Forbes' suicide, I attributed to him the unreasonableness of a cat.

The conversations in which my parents conjectured why Forbes killed himself were inconclusive and repetitive. My mother would sigh and say that she really believed Forbes killed himself because Sarah was such a slovenly housekeeper—that he just couldn't bear the dirt and the confusion in which he had to live, because, after all, he was accustomed to the elegance of the Wingate mansion.

My father never quite agreed. He said, "Well, yes, except that he'd been married to Sarah for twenty years or so. Why should he suddenly get upset about dirt after all that time.?"

Once, my mother pressed him for his point of view, and he said, "Maybe he was the type that never should have married."

"What do you mean by that?"

"Well, he'd worked for that Mrs. Wingate, and he waited too long to get married, and then he married a younger girl. How old was Sarah—twenty, wasn't she? And he was forty at the time, and—"

"Yes, yes," my mother said impatiently. "But what did you mean when you said he was a type that never should have married?"

"Well, if he'd been another type of man, I would have said there was more than met the eye between him and Mrs. Wingate. But he was so ladylike there couldn't have been. Mrs. Wingate thought a lot of him, and he thought a lot of Mrs. Wingate. That's all there was to it—it was just like one of those lifetime friendships between two ladies."

"'Between two ladies'!" my mother said indignantly. "Why, what a wicked thing to say! Forbes was—Well, I've never seen another man, white or black, with manners like his. He was a perfect gentleman."

"Too perfect," my father said dryly. "That type don't make good husbands."

"But something must have *happened* to make him kill himself. He was thrifty and hard-working and intelligent and honest. Why should he kill himself?"

My father tried to end the conversation. "It isn't good to keep talking about the dead like this, figuring and figuring about why they did something—it's like you were pulling at them, trying to pull them back. After all, how do you know but you might succeed in bringing them back? It's best to let them alone. Let Forbes alone. It isn't for nothing that they have that saying about let them rest in peace."

There was silence for a while. Then my mother said softly, "But I do wish I knew why he killed himself."

My father said, "Sarah told you he said in the letter he was tired of living. I don't believe that. But I guess we have to accept it. There's just one thing I'd like to know."

"What's that?"

"I keep wondering what he was doing in Shacktown. That seems a strange place for a respectable married man like Forbes. That's where all those barefooted foreign women live, and practically every one of those orange-crate houses they live in has a red light in the window. It seems like a strange part of the city for a respectable married man like Forbes to have been visiting."

By the time I was ten, Forbes' death had for me a kind of reality of its own—a theatrical reality. I used to sit on the steps in front of the drugstore, and half close my eyes so that I could block out the church green and the picket fences and the elm trees and the big old houses, and I would pretend that I was looking at a play instead. I set it up in my mind's eye. The play takes place on the wrong side of the railroad tracks, where the land is all cinders, in a section where voluptuous, big-hipped foreign women go barefooted, wrap their heads and shoulders in brilliant red and green shawls, and carry bundles on their heads—that is, those who work. Those who do not work wear hats with so many feathers on them they look as if they had whole turkeys on their heads. The houses in this area are built entirely of packing cases and orange crates. There is the sound of a train in the distance, and a thin, carefully dressed black man, in a neat black suit and polished shoes, walks swiftly onstage and up the slight incline toward the railroad tracks—no path there, no road. It is a winter's night and cold. This is Forbes and he is not wearing an overcoat.

As narrator for an imaginary audience, I used to say, "What is he doing in this part of town in his neat black suit and his starched white shirt? He could not possibly know anyone here in Shacktown, a place built of cinders and packing cases. Bleak. Treeless. No road here. What is he doing here? Where is he going?"

The train whistles, and Forbes walks up the embankment and lies down across the tracks. The train comes roaring into sight and it slices him in two—quickly, neatly. And the curtain comes down as a telephone rings in a drugstore miles away.

This picture of Forbes remained with me, unchanged; I still see him like that. but in the intervening years Sarah changed. My first distinct recollection of her was of a stout middle-aged woman with a querulous voice, which was always lifted in complaint. Her complaint centered on money—the lack of it, the importance of it. But even in middle age there were vestigial remains of the girl who scandalized the religious black folk of Bridgeport by pounding out whorehouse music on the piano, and who looked as though she had just stepped out of the chorus line of "The Creole Show": the wonderful smooth reddish brown skin, the giggle over which she seemed to have no control, and the flirtatious manner of a Gay Nineties beauty. The coyness and the fits of giggling she had as an old woman were relics of these mannerisms.

I got to Bridgeport just at dusk. As I rang the bell of the two-story frame house where Sarah lived, I remembered something. This was the house that Mrs. Wingate had given to Forbes and Sarah as a wedding present. They had lived in it together exactly three weeks, and then Forbes went back to live at the Wingate mansion. Mrs. Wingate had asked him to come back because she might want to go out at night, and how could she get in and out of a car without him? It would be very inconvenient to have to wait for him to come all the way from the other side of town. (The Wingate mansion was at the south end of the city, and the dark brown, two-story taxpayer was at the north end of the city.) Mrs. Wingate had said that Sarah would, of course, stay where she was. She increased Forbes' wages and promised to remember him most generously in her will.

"It was a funny thing," my mother once said. "You know, Sarah used to call Forbes by his first name, John, when he was courting her, and when they were first marreid. After he went back to live at Mrs. Wingate's, she called him Forbes. All the rest of his life, she called him by his last name, just as though she was talking to Mrs. Wingate's butler."

One of Peter Forbes' gangling boys—Sarah's younger grandson—opened the door, and I stopped thinking about the past. He was a nice-mannered, gentle-looking boy, tall and thin, his face shaped rather like Sarah's in the old photograph—a small-boned face. His skin was the same wonderful reddish brown color. I wondered why he wasn't in school, and immediately asked him.

"I've finished," he said. "I finished last June. I'm eighteen and I'm going in the Army."

I said what most people say when confronted by evidence of the passage of time. "It doesn't seem possible."

He said, "Yeah, that's right," took a deep breath, and said. "Nana's in the bedroom. You'd better come right in."

He seemed to be affected by the same need for haste that had made his father urge me to come see Sarah right away. I did not pause even long enough to take my coat off; I followed him down a dark hall, trying to remember what his real name was. Sarah had brought Peter's children up. Peter had been married to a very nice girl, and they had two boys. The very nice girl left Peter after the second baby was born and never came back. Sarah had given nicknames to the boys; the older was called Boodie, and the younger was Lud. It was Lud who had answered the door. I could not remember anything but the nickname—Lud.

We entered a bedroom at the back of the house. The moment I saw Sarah, I knew that she was dying. She was sitting slumped over in a wheelchair. In the two years since I had seen her, she had become a gaunt old woman with terrible bruised shadows under her eyes and she was so thin that she looked like a skeleton. Her skin, which had been that rich reddish brown, was now overlaid with gray.

Lud said, "Nana, she's here. She's come, Nana."

Sarah opened her eyes and nodded. The eyes that I had remembered as black and penetrating were dull and their color had changed; they were light brown. I bent over and kissed her.

"I'm not so bright today," she said, and the words came out slowly, as though she had to think about using the muscles of her throat, her tongue, her lips—had to think, even, before she breathed. After she finished speaking, she closed her eyes and she looked as though she were already dead.

"She isn't asleep," Lud said. "You just say something to her. She'll answer—won't you, Nana?"

Sarah did not answer. I took off my coat, for the heat in the room was unbearable, and I looked around for a place to put it and laid it on a chair, thinking that the room had not changed. It was exactly as I remembered it, and I had not been in it for twenty years. There was too much furniture, the windows were heavily curtained, there was a figured carpet on the floor, and a brass bed, a very beautiful brass bed; one of the walls was covered with framed photographs.

A white cat darted through the room, and I jumped, startled, remembering another white cat that used to dart throught these same rooms—but that was twenty years ago. "That's surely not the same cat, Lud? The one you've always had?"

"We've had this one about three years."

"Oh. But the other cat was white, too, wasn't it? It was deaf and it had never been outside the house—isn't that right? And it had blue eyes."

"So's this one. He doesn't go outside. He's deaf and he's got blue eyes." Lud grinned and his face was suddenly lively and very young. "And he's white," he said, and then laughed out loud. "Nana calls him our white folks."

"What's the cat's name?"

"Willie."

That was the name of the other cat, the one I had known. And Willie, so Sarah Forbes had said (boasted, perhaps?)—Willie did not like men. I wondered if this cat did.

"Is he friendly?"

"No," Lud said.

"Doesn't like men," Sarah Forbes said. Her voice was strong and clear, and it had its old familiar querulousness. The boy and I looked at her in surprise. She seemed about to say something more, and I wondered what it was going to be, for there was a kind of malevolence in her expression.

But Peter Forbes came into the room and she did not say anything. We shook hands and talked about the weather, and I thought how little he had changed during the years I had known him. He is a tall, slender man, middle-aged now, with a shaggy head and a petulant mouth that has deeply etched lines at the corners.

At the sight of Peter, Sarah seemed to grow stronger. She sat up straight. "Wheel me out to the dining room," she ordered.

"Yes, Ma," he said obediently. The wheelchair made no sound. "You come, too," he said to me.

"There's some china . . . " Sarah's voice trailed off, and she was slumping again, almost onto one arm of the wheelchair, her arms, head, and neck absolutely limp. She looked like a discarded rag doll.

We stood in the dining room and looked at her, all three of us. I said, "I'd better go. She's not well enough to be doing this. She hasn't the strength."

"You can't go," Peter said, with a firmness that surprised me. "Ma has some dishes she wants you to have. She's been talking about them for days now. She won't give us a minute's peace until you have them. You've got to stay until she gives them to you." Then he added, very politely and quite winningly, "Please don't go."

So I stayed. The dining room was just as hot as the bedroom. It, too, was filled with furniture—a dining room set, three cabinets filled with china and glassware, a studio couch, and in a bay window, a big aquarium with fish in it.

Willie, the white cat, ran into the room from the hall, clawed his way up the draperies at the bay window and sat crouched on the cornice, staring into the fish tank. His round blue eyes kept following the movements of the fish, back and forth, back and forth.

"Doesn't he try to catch the fish?" I asked.

Lud said, "That's what he wants to do. But he can't get at them. So he just watches them."

"Why, that's terrible," I said. "Can't you—"

Sarah had straightened up again. "Open those doors," she said.

"Yes, Ma." Peter opened one of the china cabinets.

"Get my cane."

"Yes, Ma." He went into the bedroom and came back with a slender Malacca cane. She took it from him in a swift snatching movement, and holding it and pointing with it, was transformed. She was no longer a hideous old woman dying slowly but an arrogant, commanding figure.

"That," she said, "and that," pointing imperiously to a shelf in the china cabinet where a tall chocolate pot stood, with matching cups and saucers, covered thick with dust.

"Get a carton and some newspapers." She pointed at Lud, and she jabbed him viciously in the stomach with the cane. He jumped, and said, "Oh, oo-ooh!" pain and outrage in his voice.

"Go get the carton," Peter said matter-of-factly.

While we waited for Lud to come back, Sarah seemed to doze. Finally, Peter sat down and motioned to me to sit down. He picked up a newspaper and began to read.

Something about the way Sarah had ordered him around set me to wondering what kind of childhood Peter had had. He must have been about twelve years old when Mrs. Wingate died and left thirty-five thousand dollars to Forbes.

With this money, Forbes took what he called a flyer in real estate; he acquired an equity in six tenement houses. My mother had disapproved. She distrusted the whole idea of mortgages and loans, and she felt that Forbes was gambling with his inheritance; if his tenants were unable to pay the rent, he would be unable to meet the interest on his notes and would lose everything.

During this period, Mother went to see Sarah fairly often and she always came away from these visits quite disturbed. She said that Sarah, who had at one time cared too much about her looks, now did not seem to care at all. The house was dreadful—confused and dusty. She said that Forbes had changed. He was still immaculate, but he was now too thin—bony—and his movements were jerky. He seemed to have a dreadful, almost maniacal urge to keep moving, and he would sit down, stand up, walk about the room, sit down again, get up, walk about again. At first she used to say that he was nervous, and then she amended this and enlarged it by saying he was distraught.

Mrs. Wingate had been dead exactly two years when Forbes committed suicide. Immediately, all of Sarah's friends predicted financial disaster for her. Forbes' money was tied up in heavily mortgaged real estate, and shortly after his death the depression came along, with its eviction notices and foreclosures.

I glanced at Sarah, dozing in the wheelchair, her chin resting on her chest. At twenty, she had been a silly, giggling girl. And yet somewhere under the surface there must have been the makings of a cold, shrewd property owner, a badgering, browbeating fishwife of a woman who could intimidate drunks, evict widows and orphans—a woman capable of using an umbrella or a hatpin as a weapon. She had made regular weekly collections of rent, because she soon learned that if she went around only once a month, the rent money would have gone for food or for liquor or for playing the numbers. Peter went with her when she made her collections. He was tall, thin, and asthmatic, and wore tweed knee pants and long stockings—a ridiculous costume for a boy in his teens.

It was during those years that Sarah perfected her technique of leaning against people, and began to develop a whining voice. She began to get fat. Her behind seemed to swell up, but her legs stayed thin, like pipestems, so that she walked carefully. She was what my father called spindle-shanked.

I suppose she had to whine, to threaten, to cajole, perhaps cry, in order to screw the rent money out of her tenants; at any rate, she succeeded. Years later, she told Mother that she had not lost a single piece of property. She finally sold all of it except the two-story taxpayer where they lived. She said that the bank that held the mortgages and notes had congratulated her; they told her that no real estate operator in Bridgeport had been able to do what she had done—bring all his property through the depression intact.

Sarah straightened up in the wheelchair and pointed with her cane. "That," she said. Peter hesitated. "That" seemed to be some white cups and saucers with no adornment of any kind. Sarah threatened Peter with the cane, and he took them out of the cabinet and put them on the table.

"Perfect," she said to me. "Six of them. All perfect. Belonged to my grandmother. Handed down. They're yours now. You hand them down."

I shook my head. "Wait a minute," I said, slowly and distinctly, in order to be sure she understood. "What about your grandsons? What about Lud and Boodie? These cups should belong to Lud and Boodie."

"They will run with whores," she said coldly. "Just like Peter does. Just like Forbes kept trying to do, only he couldn't. That's what he was after in Shacktown that time, and when he found he couldn't—just wasn't able to—he laid himself down on the railroad track." She paused for a moment. "I cried for three days afterward. For three whole days." She paused again. "I wasn't crying because of what happened to him. I was crying because of what had happened to me. To my whole life. My whole life."

I could not look at Peter. I heard him take a deep breath.

Sarah said, "Those cups are yours. I'm giving them to you so that I'll know where they are. I'll know who owns them. If they should stay here . . . " She shrugged.

Lud came back with the carton and a pile of newspapers and Sarah did not even glance in his direction. She said, "The chocolate cups belonged to a French king. Mrs. Wingate gave them to me for a wedding present when I married her Forbes. I want you to have them so that I'll know who owns them."

We wrapped the pieces of china separately, and put wads of crumpled newspaper in between as we packed the carton. Sarah watched us. Sometimes she half closed her eyes, but she kept looking until we had finished. After that, her head slumped and her breathing changed. It was light, shallow, with pauses in between. I could hear the thumping of her heart way across the room.

I said "Good-bye, Sarah," and kissed the back of her neck, but she did not answer or move.

It was still snowing when Lud carried the carton out to the car for me, held the door open, and closed it after I got in. I thought he did it with a kind of gracefulness that he couldn't possibly have acquired from Peter; perhaps it was something inherited from Forbes, his grandfather.

Lud said, "Did those cups really belong to one of the kings of France?"

"Maybe. I really don't know. I wish you'd put them back in the house. This whole carton of china is more yours than it is mine. These things belonged to your grandmother and they should stay in your family."

"Oh, no," he said hastily, and he stepped away from the car. "I don't want them. What would I do with them? Besides, Nana's ghost would come back and bug me." He laughed uneasily. "And if Nana's ghost bugged anybody, they'd flip for sure."

When I got home, I washed the chocolate set, and having got rid of the accumulated dust of fifty years, I decided that it could easily have belonged to one of the kings of France. It was of the very old, soft-paste type of porcelain. It had been made in the Sèvres factory and it was exquisitely decorated in the lovely color known as rose pompadour.

I was admiring the shape of the cups when the telephone rang. It was Peter Forbes. He said, "Ma died in her sleep just a few minutes after you left."

[1971]

For Thought

"Has Anybody Seen Miss Dora Dean?" is told as a personal reminiscence of something that happened 30 years in the past, when the narrator was a little girl. Petry uses the motif of the invited outsider confronted with an old mystery, remembered from childhood, concerning the question of death by accident or suicide of someone she knew only by hearsay. Recalling bits of information, some of it helpful and some of it misleading, the narrator finally learns the truth, not by active discovery but by a deathbed revelation that is still somewhat ambiguous and incomplete.

For Discussion

1. Trace the trail of evidence by which Petry leads the reader to the final revelation made by Sarah on her deathbed.
2. What purpose does the story-within-a-story technique serve? How are the two stories related?
3. Discuss the ironies in the characters of Forbes and Sarah.
4. What ironies of situation does Petry use to enrich the narrative in both stories?
5. How does Petry use understatement, ambiguity, and figurative language as part of the structure of the story? Give specific examples and explain the purpose and appropriateness of each instance.
6. What questions and ambiguities are left unresolved at the end of the story?

Luigi Pirandello
The Medals

All that morning, Sciarame' had been pacing his little room like a lion in a cage.

On more than one occasion Roro', his stepdaughter, had peeped through the door to ask him:

"What are you looking for?"

Whereupon Sciarame', trying to hide his worry, had answered at first that he was searching for his stick.

"But there it is, can't you see it? There, in that corner."

And Roro' had handed it to him. Then, a little later, he had asked for a handkerchief. Roro' had given him a clean one, but still Sciarame' would not leave the room.

The truth was that Sciarame' was summoning up his courage to speak to his stepdaughter about something very important but, so far, he had failed. He had failed because he was as shy of her as he had always been of his wife, now dead for the last seven years, dead "from a broken heart"—Roro' used to say—"due to her husband's stupidity."

A succession of bad years had forced Sciarame'—at one time comfortably off—to sell first his small lemon and orange orchards and then the house, so that, at sixty-eight years of age, he had been compelled to turn a middleman, selling on commission those very oranges and lemons which were once his own.

Poor Sciarame'! He who had always looked upon middlemen as thieves was now finding himself one of them; tramping from morning to night at his age, weak and ailing, dragging his swollen feet buried in a pair of ragged felt shoes, fighting for a small commission which dealers would throw at him more as a charity than as a due.

Those who had known him before felt sorry for him. Yet everyone was certain that all these trials were more than made up for on national holidays when—dressed up in a faded red shirt, with the large handkerchief tied round his neck and the pointed hat well over his eyes—he would join the Garibaldian veterans in their procession, with his fine row of medals shining on his breast.

Seven medals!

And yet, when walking with his old companions behind the Garibaldian flag, he looked almost like a lost dog. He would constantly lift his left arm tugging at his beard or stroking his mustache, as though shy and anxious to hide those very medals of which he was so proud.

Many of his friends, seeing him pass by, would shout:

"Long live the Fatherland, Sciarame'! Long live Italy!"

Shy and smiling, he would lower his bald little eyes, answering in a low voice:

"Long live Italy! Hurrah! Hurrah!"

The headquarters of the Garibaldian Veterans' Society occupied a ground-floor room of the last shanty left in Sciarame's possession. A steep wooden staircase led to two rooms upstairs, one for his stepdaughter and one for himself. On the front door, half covered by a stray branch of jasmine gracefully stretching from Roro's window, was a large inscription in bold red lettering:

GARIBALDIAN VETERANS' SOCIETY

The room was scantily furnished: a large table, covered with a green cloth, specially reserved for the Council; a smaller table for the display of newspapers and magazines; an old and dusty bookcase stuffed with volumes mostly uncut. On the walls hung a life-size color-print of Garibaldi; a portrait of Mazzini—of smaller size; a portrait of Carlo Cattaneo—still smaller; and—surrounded by ribbons, paper lanterns and flags—a print commemorating the "Death of the Hero of the Two Worlds."

Every morning Roro', having tidied up the two rooms upstairs, would put on her famous flaming red blouse and would go down to the ground-floor room where, sitting by the door, she would talk to her neighbors while carrying on with her sewing. She was a beautiful girl, dark and healthy, and they called her "La Garibaldina."

It so happened that, that very day, Sciarame' had to ask his stepdaughter not to come down to that room any more and to remain upstairs instead. For Amilcare Bellone, the President of the Association, had complained to him, not because of this habit of Roro's who, after all, was mistress in her own home, but because of a certain young fellow, Rosalino La Rosa, who—with the excuse of coming to read the papers—would go there every morning and pretend to be a Garibaldian veteran when, in fact, he had merely fought in Greece against the Turks.

This La Rosa, rich and lazy, was so proud of his youthful adventure that it had almost become an obsession with him and he could speak of nothing else. One of the three companions who had fought with him—Gasperi—had been slightly wounded at Domokos and Rosalino spoke of this almost as though the wound had been his own. Tall, slender, with a long square-cut, reddish beard and a generous turned-up mustache which, if properly stretched, could easily have been tied into a knot at the back of his neck, Rosalino La Rosa was certainly a handsome young fellow.

It was not difficult to realize that his visits to the headquarters were not so much for the purpose of reading the papers as for the double purpose of letting everyone know that he was quite at home with the Garibaldians and of taking the opportunity for a little flirtation with Roro', the girl with the red blouse.

Sciarame' had noticed it too, but he also knew that Roro' was a level-headed girl and that the young man was comfortably off. Could he, in all consciousness, rule out the possibility of a profitable wedding for his stepdaughter? He was old and poor; what would happen to the girl if he died and she had not found a husband? Besides, he wasn't her real father and hadn't sufficient authority to forbid her a thing which he not only considered harmless but eventually profitable to her.

On the other hand, he could not say that

the President was altogether wrong. These were family matters which it was wiser to keep away from the Veterans' Society. Neighbors were already gossiping, some of them speaking of an intrigue between La Rosa and Roro' under the shadow of the Society and which the President—rightly jealous of the Society's good name—could not allow. What was Sciarame' to do? How should he approach Roro' on the subject?

The poor old man had been puzzling himself for over an hour, when Roro' herself gave him the lead.

Wearing her flaming red blouse, she bounced into her stepfather's room:

"Still here? Are you or are you not going out this morning? I haven't even had an opportunity of tidying your room. I'm going downstairs."

"Wait . . . Roro' . . . listen," started Sciarame', mustering up his courage. "That's just what I wanted to tell you."

"What?"

"That you . . . well, you see . . . I mean, couldn't you . . . wouldn't you prefer to work here, upstairs in your room, rather than downstairs?"

"And may I ask why?"

"Well . . . well, you see, because . . . because downstairs, you see, the members . . ."

Roro' raised her eyebrows in surprise.

"A new idea is it? Have the honorable gentlemen decided to pay you for the rent of the room, then?"

Sciarame' grinned, as though amused by Roro's remark.

"Of course," he said, "it's true that they don't . . . they don't pay for the room."

"Then what do they want?" asked Roro' haughtily. "Are they going to dictate terms in our house?"

"No! that has nothing to do with it!" Sciarame' tried to explain. "It was my own offer. . . ."

"Yes, but for the evenings only," agreed Roro'. "They are free to do as they like in the evenings, since you had the bright idea of offering them a free shelter, here. I alone know how difficult it is for me to get to sleep with all that talking, shouting and mad singing going on downstairs! Now, on top of all this, they would want me . . ."

"It isn't you," Sciarame' interrupted, "not really you, my dear. . . ."

"I see!" said Roro' becoming serious. "I knew what you meant even before you began to speak. You can tell the honorable gentlemen to mind their own business and to let me look after my own; and if this doesn't suit them let them find another place and I shall not be sorry. In my house I meet whom I like. I have to ask nobody's permission but yours. Now tell me: have you by any chance lost trust in me?"

"Of course not, my dear! Of course not!"

"Then that's enough! I have nothing further to tell you."

And Roro', her face as red as her blouse, turned her shoulders on him and went downstairs, fuming with rage.

Sciarame' gulped, then, standing in the center of the room, he rubbed his lips, worried and angry with himself, with Roro' and with the veterans. Something he must do, but what? Better go out, perhaps. Some fresh air! In the open, who knows, some bright idea might occur to him.

Hobbling carefully down the stairs, one hand leaning on the wall and the other on the stick, dragging down on one swollen foot after another and panting at each step, he crossed the ground-floor room, leaving the house without a word. Roro'—sitting at her usual place—was too fully absorbed in conversation with one of the neighbors to take any notice of him.

Oh, what a relief it would have been for him if that blessed child were married! A marriage with La Rosa was—all things considered—unlikely: first of all because Roro' was poor, and then because she was known as "La Garibaldina," while La Rosa's family wanted—for their lightheaded son—a steady, sensible young woman, without patriotic vagaries. Not that Roro' had ever had any such vagaries, but having got the name for them she was perhaps using it now, like a spider with his web, to entangle that young butterfly—La Rosa.

"After all, why not?" sighed Sciarame', thinking how entangled the butterfly seemed already to be.

In all fairness, how could he destroy that cobweb just now, merely to satisfy the honorable veterans who did not even pay any rent? And, after all, what was the President's grievance? He had complained that, in Greece, La Rosa had worn a red shirt. Silly jealousy! The red shirt on that young man's back was a sacrilege to the President's eyes: making him as wild as a bull. If it had been any other young man he could have gone to the Society to read the papers and Bellone would have taken no notice of him, but La Rosa. . . .

Deeply absorbed with his thoughts, Sciarame' reached the main square of the village and seated himself, as he did each day, at one of the small tables outside the café.

There he would stop for hours, waiting for someone to find him an odd job, and eventually falling asleep from boredom, never ordering anything, not even a glass of water with a taste of kummel. Yet the proprietor welcomed him, knowing that clients liked to hear his tales of Garibaldi and of his battles. Sciarame' would speak of them with touching sadness, shaking his head and half closing his bald little eyes. He would describe painful episodes, the dead, the wounded, without a trace of boasting, so that—in the end—those who had expected to be amused by his talk became gloomy and distressed at this little old man whose poverty and misery seemed to have killed even the enthusiasm and the fire of the past.

That morning one of the customers, seeing him more depressed than ever, had tried to cheer him up:

"Don't worry, Sciarame'! The King's birthday will soon be here: a fine chance for an airing to the old red shirt!"

Sciarame', without moving from his seat, had made a quick gesture with his hands as if to say that far different thoughts were in his head. He was about to rest his chin on the knob of his stick when he heard the President yelling his name from across the piazza: "Sciarame', Sciarame'!" Sciarame' jumped to his feet to inform him:

"I have told her. . . . I have told her all right!"

But Bellone, seizing him by the arm and advancing a fist under his nose shouted:

"Liar! He is there again!"

"Who?"

"La Rosa."

"There?"

"Yes, and now I'll show you what I'll do with him. I'll kick him out myself."

"For heaven's sake!" begged Sciarame', "don't start a row. Let *me* go. I promise that he will never set foot in there again. I thought Roro' would tell him. . . . But leave it to me. . . ."

The President jeered at him; then, without releasing his grip, he asked:

"Shall I tell you what you are?"

Sciarame' smiled bitterly, shrugging his shoulders.

"A blockhead?" he said. "I know it, but did you only find it out now?"

And off he went, stooping, shaking his head, leaning heavily on his stick.

When Roro'—sitting by the door—saw him approaching, she made a hasty sign for La Rosa to move away and to sit at the table covered with newspapers. In a stride La Rosa was there, at once opening a magazine and engrossed in reading it.

"Back so soon?" she asked her stepfather, trying to look indifferent. "What's wrong?"

Sciarame' glanced first at La Rosa who, his elbows on the table and his head sunk between his hands, was pretending to read, and then turned to his stepdaughter:

"I had asked you to stop upstairs."

"And I had told you that in my house . . ." began Roro'. But Sciarame' cut her short, raising his stick and pointing to the staircase:

"Go upstairs and don't argue! I have a few words to say to Signor La Rosa."

"To me?" said the young man, as though falling from the clouds and pulling at his fine mustache. "To me?" he repeated.

He rose to his feet, and, moving close to Sciarame', stretched himself to his full height, making him look smaller than ever.

"Yes, to you," he stammered, "but pray, be seated. . . . All I wanted to tell you was . . . You can go, Roro'; leave us alone, please."

Rosalino La Rosa bent himself in two to bid Roro' good-by, and when she had gone Sciarame'—turning to him with a smile—began:

"I know you are a good fellow, my dear Don Rosalino. . . ."

"My deepest thanks!"

"No, it is true," resumed Sciarame', "and I, for one, feel honored . . ."

"My deepest thanks!"

"No, no, it is true, I tell you. I am deeply honored, my dear Don Rosalino, that you should come here to . . . to read the papers. But, well, how can I explain? I am the master here and yet I am not the master. You see: these are the Headquarters of the Society of Veterans and I have certain responsibilities toward my fellow members. . . . Perhaps you don't understand. . . ."

"No, I don't," said La Rosa abruptly.

"Well," continued Sciarame', "I will put it in another way; you are a good fellow who comes here to read the papers; as far as I am concerned you are welcome, but these papers . . . well, these papers, unfortunately, do not belong to me. . . . If they were mine . . . Why, you could have them all, of course! But as you are not a member . . ."

"Stop," shouted La Rosa, furious and raising his hand. "Stop. I knew you would say this; I was waiting for it. I am not a member, am I? And now answer this: Have I been to Greece, yes or no?"

"But of course you have been to Greece! Who would doubt it?"

"Very well! And now the red shirt: did I wear it, yes or no?"

"But of course you did," repeated Sciarame'.

"Therefore I have been to Greece, I have fought, I have come back. I have documents, mind you, Sciarame', written documents to prove all this. And now, then, according to you, what am I?"

"Why, you are a good fellow, a nice young man, I have already said so."

"Many thanks!" hissed La Rosa. "But that isn't what I want to know. According to you am I, or am I not, a Garibaldian?"

"A Garibaldian? Er . . . yes . . . why not?" replied Sciarame', quite dazed and not knowing where La Rosa was leading him to.

"And a veteran?" resumed the latter. "I am also a veteran because I am not dead and have come back. Is that right? And yet these veterans here do not allow me to come and read the papers of the Association because I am not a member, isn't that so? You said it yourself. Well, I'm going right away to find my three veteran comrades of Domokos and the four of us will, this very evening, make our formal application for membership."

"What? . . . What do you say?" replied Sciarame', opening his eyes in amazement. "You, a member here?"

"And why not?" asked Rosalino La Rosa, with a frown. "Aren't we worthy?"

"Yes, yes . . . I did not mean that. . . . Personally, I assure you, it would be an honor, a pleasure!" exclaimed Sciarame'. "But the others, you see . . . my . . . comrades . . ."

"I am not afraid of them, don't worry. I know that I am better entitled to be a member of this Association than someone else, do you understand, Sciarame'? And I will prove it, if they force me to do it."

Seizing him by the lapel of his coat, La Rosa gave him a good shaking; then, looking deep into his eyes, he added:

"Tonight, Sciarame', do you understand?"

Stunned and shivering, Sciarame' was left standing in the center of the room, scratching his head.

The Veterans' Association had only a little over a dozen members left, none of whom was a native of the village. Amilcare Bellone, the President, was a native of Brescia; Nardi and Navetta were from Ravenna, and in fact all of them were born in different parts of Italy, but had come to Sicily to trade in fruit or sulphur.

The Association had been formed by Bellone many years ago. At the news that Garibaldi himself was coming to Sicily to celebrate the independence of the island from foreign domination, the few Garibaldians living in the village had gathered at the café with the idea of discussing a joint trip to Palermo in order to meet—perhaps for the last time—their glorious Leader. Bellone's proposal to get together, there and then, a deputation of veterans who would—under their own flag—take part in the official procession had been greeted with genuine enthusiasm. Some of the customers at the café had brought to Bellone's notice Sciarame'—dozing as usual at one of the tables—introducing him as the old patriot of the village, a Garibaldian veteran, too. Bellone, warmed by the memory of his youthful enthusiasm and perhaps also by the wine, had gone to him, shaking him from his sleep and urging him to join the newly born Society. "Picciotto! Picciotto!"

Enthusiasm was running high, everybody toasting and cheering. Sciarame'—amid the general shouting—had made an offer. To help the newly born Association he would allow them to install their headquarters on the ground floor of his house, free of charge, at least temporarily, until they were able to pay their own rent. The offer had been accepted amidst general enthusiasm and from that day—forgetting that it had been merely a temporary arrangement—the veterans had stayed there for good, and paid no rent, while Sciarame', in his turn, had saved the monthly contribution of three lire paid by the others toward the cost of newspapers, magazines, light, etc. Apart from them meeting in the evening to play cards, read the papers, talk politics or share a drink, these veterans were really giving him no trouble.

It was only now—after the President's request about Roro'—that Sciarame' had found himself between the hammer and the anvil; between an impulsive and noisy President who would hear of no contradiction, and an obstinate girl who would listen to no reason.

"Mere children! Mere children!" shouted the President that evening, having read the application for membership from La Rosa and his friends. "Mere children, gentlemen, mere children! These brand-new red shirts of recent make at three lire a yard, have only been worn once in Greece and have been brought back as clean and spotless as if they had never been used. Sit down, sit down. We shall forgo all formalities. Let the meeting decide at once; let us get rid of these children right away, with a stroke of the pen! Sit down, sit down."

But the members—all except Sciarame'—had gathered round him, asking to see the application, as though unable to believe it, and firing questions at him, especially the fat and toothless Navetta who was slightly deaf and whose wooden leg—a kind of stump round which flapped the trouser—he dragged along with almost dull, repulsive thuds.

Bellone swept them back with his arms and resumed his seat at the conference table where, ringing the bell for silence, he began to read the application aloud with endless grimaces and with comic twisting of his nose and of his lips, which sent the audience into fits of laughter.

Sciarame' alone sat quiet, his chin resting on the knob of his stick, his eyes staring at the paraffin lamp.

Having finished reading the letter, the President became solemn and dignified.

Sciarame', who had stood up to speak, was quickly called to order.

"Sit down!" shouted the President.

"The lamp is smoking," retorted Sciarame', humble.

"Let it smoke! Now, gentlemen, I consider that it is idle, almost humiliating for us even to discuss such a ridiculous application" (cheers). "By a unanimous vote we shall reject—with a mere stroke of the pen—this incredible . . . this unqualifiable . . . this. . . . How shall I call it! . . ." (Bursts of applause.)

Presently Nardi asked to be allowed to speak, saying that in his opinion, it was necessary and imperative to state, once and for all, that Garibaldians were only and exclusively those who had actually followed Garibaldi. (Hear, hear! Hurrah! Well spoken!) Giuseppe Garibaldi, and nobody else.

"And nobody else, yes, nobody else!"

"And let us add . . ." said Navetta, suddenly springing from his seat, "let us add, gentlemen, that the . . . the, what do you call it? . . . the unfortunate war between Greece and . . . and, what's the name? . . . and Turkey cannot, must not be taken seriously, in view of the . . . yes, exactly, of the . . . the dreadful impression created by that nation which . . . which . . ."

"By that degenerate nation," interrupted the President, rising to his feet.

"That's the word. *Delgenerate, delgenerate,*" shouted Navetta amongst the general approval.

At this moment Sciarame', who had been listening from his seat, lifted his chin from the knob of his stick and raised a hand.

"May I? . . ." he asked timidly.

Everybody turned round, frowning, while the President could not help showing his disapproval.

"You? What have *you* to say?"

Poor Sciarame' felt lost, gulped and raised his hand once more.

"You see, I should like to point out that . . . when all's said and done . . . these . . . these four young men . . ."

"Bluffers!" snapped Bellone. "They are bluffers and nothing else. Why, would you try to stick up for them?"

"No," Sciarame' hastened to reply. "No . . . but you see, I should like to point out, as I was saying, that . . . when all's said and done they . . . they *have* fought, these four young men: they actually *have* been in the war . . . and have shown that they were brave and fearless . . . one of them, in fact, was even wounded . . . what more do you want? That they should have all been killed? If Garibaldi, our great Leader, was not there, it was merely because he was dead, but his son was there, and it seems to me that nobody better than he had the right to wear the red shirt and to allow it to be worn by those who followed him to Greece. Therefore . . ."

To his surprise, Sciarame' had so far been allowed to speak without interruptions but now he was beginning to feel less sure of himself and less confident at the ominous silence which greeted his words. He knew quite well what it meant. He was sure that his comrades—by remaining silent—were far from approving his arguments and merely daring him to go on in order to test his stupidity or his impudence, ready to attack him at the first ill-chosen word. He became panicky and tried to soften, little by little, the expression on his face and the tone of his voice. But soon, the words failed him as if he had said enough and the last word had been spoken in defense of those boys.

"And therefore, having regard to all this . . . I believe . . . I believe . . ."

"What do you believe?" the President interrupted at last, leaving his seat and going up to him.

"Trash! Trash!" shouted the others, also rising from their seats to hem him in, pulling him right and left and trying to convince him that he was sticking up for an unworthy cause. How could he say that those children were Garibaldians? He should be ashamed of himself—they said—for defending those four lazy rascals! Did he imagine that epics—real epics like that of Garibaldi—could have extensions and additions? Greece, he should know, had covered herself with the ridicule of the world.

They were all talking at the same time and poor Sciarame' was unable to answer them all. At random he stuck to what Nardi was saying and shouted:

"You say that the expedition was not a national one? But, allow me, did Garibaldi, by any chance, fight exclusively for our independence? He also fought in America and even in France, always at the service of Humanity!"

"Will you be quiet, Sciarame'?" thundered Bellone at this point, with a loud bang of his fist on the conference table. "Don't make insulting comparisons! How dare you compare the Garibaldian epic with the farcical expedition to Greece? Shame! Shame! I know why you want to uphold those four buffoons, but we here tonight, you understand, with a unanimous decision will render you a service too by freeing you of a pest which threatens the honor of your family. The application of these fellows must be rejected without a single dissenting voice. Do you understand?"

"Allow me at least to stand aside . . ." begged Sciarame', joining his hands as if in prayer.

But such was their pressure and so loud were their shouts that poor Sciarame' at last agreed to cast his vote with theirs. The application was "unanimously" rejected.

Two days later, the following letter appeared in the local newspaper under the signature of Gaspari, the young fellow who had been wounded at Domokos:

NEW AND OLD GARIBALDIANS:

Sir,

In my own name and on behalf of my comrades La Rosa, Betti and Marcolini, I beg to inform you of a unanimous decision arrived at by the Garibaldian Veterans' Association in reply to our application for membership.

The Association has refused our application. According to them, our red shirts are not authentic. Just so. . . . And do you know why? Because—as we were neither born nor even babies when Giuseppe Garibaldi—the REAL the ONLY one (to use the words of the Association)—decided to fight for the freedom of the Fatherland, we, poor fellows, could not—together with our nurses and our mothers—follow him at the time and we have made the mistake of following to the sacred land of the Hellenes, his son, who (it would appear from the resolution of the above-praised veterans) is not a Garibaldi. Moreover, we are held responsible for the sad and humiliating end of the Greco-Turkish war, as if we had not fought and won at Domokos, leaving on the field the heroic Fratti and several others.

You will therefore realize, sir, how difficult it is for us to defend our Leader, as well as the great ideal which made us answer his call, our fallen comrades and the survivors, against the cruel offense embodied in the unqualifiable decision of these Veterans; we have no remedy because we are, unfortunately, faced by old men obviously in their dotage. These words may seem hard, Sir, but are justified by the fact that these men have rejected our application while harboring amongst their members, *a man who has not only never been a Garibaldian and has never taken part in any actual fighting, but actually wears a red shirt and pins to his breast no less than seven medals which do not belong to him but to his brother, heroically killed at Dijon.*

Having said this much, I deem it superfluous to make any further comment on the Association's decision. I am ready to prove, with the support of undeniable evidence, all I have written above. If necessary, I shall also give the name of this false Garibaldian who even had the audacity of voting with the others against our admission.

In the meantime, I beg to remain, Sir,

Yours, etc.

ALESSANDRO GASPARI.

The letter was followed by a short note by the Editor.

We have been aware for some considerable time that one of the members of the Association of Garibaldi Veterans had never fought with Garibaldi or even seen him. We have always refrained from revealing this fact out of pity for an old man, but owing to the incredible step taken by the above-mentioned Association in refusing the application of Signor Gaspari and his brave companions who fought in Greece, we consider that the Association should at least give some satisfaction to these young men and safeguard its own reputation by urging the resignation of a member who appears to be totally unworthy of belonging to it.

The entire village was puzzled, everyone commenting on Gaspari's unexpected protest. Sciarame' was about to leave his home for the piazza, when Bellone—a copy of the paper in his hand—rushed to him, pushing him into a chair and holding the paper under his nose.

"Have you read it?" he asked. "Read this!"

"No . . . what . . . what has happened?" muttered Sciarame', unable to understand the outburst.

"Read! Read!" yelled Bellone, clenching his fists to control himself, and pacing the room like a lion.

Sciarame' fumbled for his glasses, placing them on the tip of his nose and wondering what he was supposed to read in that paper. Bellone came up to him, tearing it from his hands and pointing to the letter which appeared on the second page.

"Here! here! Read here!"

"Ah!" said the other sadly, after a quick glance at the headline and the signature. "Didn't I tell you?"

"Go on! go on! Read!" again yelled Bellone, more furious than ever.

Sciarame' began to read, at times knitting his brows, at times smoothing them out again, then staring with his mouth wide open as if staggered. The paper nearly fell from his hands. He grasped it more firmly bringing it closer to his eyes as though his sight had suddenly failed him. The President was now watching him, his eyes flaming, his arms folded, waiting for a protest, a denial or an explanation.

"What have you to say about it? Lift up your head! Look at me!"

Sciarame', his face deadly pale and his eyelids hanging heavily over his weary eyes, shook his head slowly, unable to speak: he placed the paper on the table and brought a hand to his heart.

"Wait . . ." he finally said, more with his gesture than with his voice.

He tried hard to swallow, but his tongue was dry and swollen. His breathing had become heavy.

"I . . ." he feebly murmured, "I . . . I *was* there . . . at . . . at Calatafimi . . . and at . . . at . . . Palermo . . . at Millazo . . . and in Calabria at . . . at Melito . . . then right up to . . . to Naples . . . and the Volturno. . . ."

"But how were you there? What proofs can you give?"

"Wait . . . I . . . together with my brother . . . I followed him with the donkey. . . ."

"What are you raving about? The medals, I want to know, whose are they? Yours or your brother's? Speak up!"

"I was . . . let me explain. . . . At Marsala . . . we were there together, my little brother Stefanuccio and I . . . I had been acting as a father to him. . . . He was barely fifteen, you see? He ran way from me when . . . when the glorious 'Thousand' landed there . . . to follow him, Garibaldi, along with the other volunteers. . . . I came home; I found my brother had gone. . . . So I hired a donkey . . . I made up my mind to bring Stefanuccio back. . . . I caught him up before he had reached Calatafimi. . . . At fifteen years of age of what good could he have been to the Leader, I ask you? . . . But he threatened to . . . to blow his own head off with an old rifle—twice his size—which they had given him, if I forced him to return. . . . Yes, his own head. . . . Then, listening to the advice of the other volunteers, I let the donkey free . . . for which I had to pay later on . . . and . . . and I decided to join them too."

"As a volunteer also? And did you fight?"

"I . . . I hadn't a rifle."

"And in fact you hadn't the courage?"

"No . . . no . . . I would have rather died than leave my brother."

"So you followed him."

"Yes, everywhere."

And Sciarame', feeling a shiver down his back, pressed his hand a little firmer against his heart.

"But the medals? The red shirt?" resumed Bellone, trembling with rage. "Whose are they? Yours or your brother's? Answer me!"

Sciarame' extended his arms without daring to lift his head; then he said:

"My brother was dead . . . and could not enjoy them any more . . . so I thought . . ."

"You decided to show them off, instead!" The President finished the sentence for him. "Oh, you wretched imposter! Cheat! I could spit at your face! You deserve to be . . . But I will have pity on you. Out you go from the Association; out you go, at once!"

"What? You want to turn me out of my own house?"

"No, we shall go away ourselves, right now! Have the plate removed! How blind I was not to see that a fool like you could never have seen Garibaldi—even at a distance!"

"Never seen him, you say?" shouted Sciarame' with a jerk. "Never seen him? I'll tell you whether I saw him or not! I even kissed his hands! I kissed them on the piazza Pretorio at Palermo, where he had set his camp."

"Shut up, scoundrel. I don't want to listen to you any longer. I don't want to see you any more! Remove the plate and heaven help you if I ever see you wearing the red shirt again."

He made for the door, but once more turned round to yell:

"Cheat! Cheat!"

Left alone, Sciarame' tried to rise to his feet, but his legs were unsteady and trembling. Clinging first to the table, then to the chair and to the railing, he carried himself heavily upstairs.

Roro', seeing him in such a state, gave a cry: but he motioned to her to be quiet: then, pointing to the chest of drawers in the room, he begged her in a half-choked voice: "The papers?"

"What papers?" implored Roro', trying to help him.

"My papers . . . my brother's . . ." muttered Sciarame', dragging himself to the chest of drawers. "Open it. . . . Let me look. . . ."

Roro' opened the drawer. Sciarame' laid a trembling hand on a bundle of soiled, faded documents tied together with a string, and then turned to his stepdaughter with lifeless eyes:

"Did you . . . did you show them to . . . to La Rosa?" he asked. At first Roro' could make no reply: then, anxious and scared, she said:

"He asked me to see them. . . . What harm have I done?"

Breaking into wild sobs, Sciarame' collapsed in her arms. With difficulty Roro' dragged him to the chair at the foot of the bed and made him sit down.

"Daddy! Daddy!" she implored. "What is it? What have I done? Why are you crying? What has happened?"

"Go . . . go away . . . leave me alone!" gasped Sciarame', choking. "And to think that I stood up for them . . . I alone . . . and this is their gratitude! I *was* there . . . with him. . . . He was only fifteen. . . . There was the donkey, too . . . then at the first shots . . . my legs . . . my legs. . . . No, I was not afraid. . . . And later at Milazzo . . . concealed amongst the vineyards . . ."

Roro' was watching him, unable to understand.

"Daddy . . . Daddy . . . what are you saying?"

But Sciarame', his eyes wide and lifeless, his face contorted, a hand pressed on his heart, no longer heard her words.

He was looking back, far back, into the past.

He really *had* followed him, that little brother of his to whom he had been a second father; he really *had* caught him up, on his donkey, before they had reached Calatafimi, imploring him with joined hands to come back home, and not to make him die of sorrow at the thought of leaving him alone in such grave danger. It had all been in vain, so that he had had to give way and little by little, fired by the general enthusiasm—he had himself followed the others. Then, when the first shots had been fired . . . No, no, even then he was never really sorry to have let the donkey go. Would he have ever gone back knowing that his young brother was in the thick of a battle and perhaps on the verge of being mercilessly killed? On the contrary, he had felt like rushing to his help and throwing himself into the battle too, but his legs, his legs had failed him. What can a poor man do when he is no longer master of his legs? Nothing but wait and suffer. God alone knew how much he had suffered. He had suffered for two: for himself and for his brother. . . . Then, when the battle was over, he had searched the field trying to find his little Stefanuccio amongst the dead and the wounded. . . . But no. . . . Stefanuccio was alive and well! From that day, he had followed him everywhere, first to Palermo, as far as Gibilrossa, where he had waited for him, more dead than alive, for endless days: an eternity! At Palermo, Stefanuccio—as a reward for his bravery—had been allowed to join the Carabineers, a famous regiment which was later almost annihilated in the Battle of Milazzo. It was really a miracle that he too—Sciarame'—had not been killed on that day: Squatting in a vineyard he could occasionally hear—on all sides—strange thuds among the foliage; but never once had it dawned on him that they might be bullets, when suddenly, amongst the branches of the vines he was crouching against . . . Ah! that dreadful hiss before the thud! Flattened on the ground, shivering with fear, he had tried to move away, but in vain; and he had stopped there, in agony, amid the deluge of bullets, facing death at every thud.

Who could dare to say that he had not known all the horrors of war? Who could dare to say that the stories he was so fond to relate had not been seen and lived by him? Yes, he *had* been in the war even if he had not actually fought in it. Back in his village, after Garibaldi's gift of the Two Sicilies to King Victor-Emmanuel, he had been hailed as a hero along with his brother Stefanuccio. As to the medals, however, his brother alone had received them, but in a way didn't they belong to them both? . . . Besides, he had never boasted about them: when he had been asked to speak, he had always talked on something he had actually seen, nothing else. Never—never indeed—would he have dreamt of joining the Association had he not been almost forced to do so on that eventful night at the café, when he had found himself a member almost against his will. He had reciprocated the honor bestowed upon him (an honor of which he was really not altogether unworthy) by giving them shelter, rent free, during all those years. Yes, perhaps it was wrong to wear his brother's shirt and to decorate his breast with medals which—strictly speaking—were not his own; but, having once made the first step, how could he possibly withdraw? He simply had to keep on, being satisfied at the thought that—at all events—he was representing his poor little brother, now dead, killed in battle at Dijon, his poor little Stefanuccio who so well deserved those medals and yet had never been able to wear them at a single ceremony.

This—if a sin it was—had been his only one. Those new Garibaldians had been the cause of all the trouble; they had quarreled with the old ones; and *he* had been their victim, he who had stood up for them, one against them all. Ah, the ungrateful creatures! They had killed him!

Roro', frightened at the ghastly, lifeless expression of his face, rushed to the window shouting for help.

A few of the neighbors hurried to her assistance.

"What is it? What is it?"

At the sight of Sciarame', sunk in his chair, they stood still.

Two of them, bolder than the others, took him by his shoulders and feet, trying to lift him on his bed. They had only just laid him down when . . .

"God! . . ." said one.

"Look! . . ." said the other.

"Dead? . . ." asked someone from behind.

For a second Roro' was stunned, her wide eyes staring at him, helplessly. Then, turning to the neighbors who had answered her call, she muttered:

"God! . . . Dead? . . . Really *dead?*"

And, throwing herself over her stepfather's body, her head bent low and her arms stretched out over the corpse, she knelt by the bed.

"Forgive me, Daddy! Forgive me! . . ."

The neighbors were puzzled. Forgive her? Why? What had she done? Why—in her sobs—was she speaking of papers and documents? What documents? They tore her away from the bed and dragged her into her own room. While some of them went to fetch the President others remained to watch beside the bed.

When the President arrived—dark and concerned—with Navetta, Nardi and the other members, old Sciarame' was lying on his little bed, wearing his red shirt, with the seven medals pinned to his breast.

The neighbors had thought it right to bury the old man in the red shirt of which he was so proud. It didn't belong to him? What then? Worse lies than this have been written on many graves. On with the medals! Let all seven of them be pinned to his breast!

Thud, thud, thud. Navetta—the man with the wooden leg—came near the corpse. For a while he stood by in silence, then turning to his comrades and in a hollow voice:

"Shall we take them off?" he said.

The President—who had retired to confabulate with the others in a corner of the room—called him with a sign of his hand. Then, shrugging his shoulders as if to show that he was merely expressing the opinion of his members, he ordered:

"Leave them on. . . . He is dead. . . ."

They gave him a magnificent funeral.

[1939]

For Thought

"The Medals" is a tale of conflict between different views of reality in a Sicilian village during the late 1800s. Centering on the troubles besetting an ingenuous imposter, the story is told through a combination of the third-person peripheral observer and central intelligence point of view. In working out the complications of the plot to arrive at a resolution, Pirandello makes use of situational irony to convey his observation on life regarding the elastic nature of reality.

For Discussion

1. How does Pirandello use each of the two points of view employed in the story?
2. What is the inciting incident in the plot?
3. What is the immediate or superficial conflict? What is the deeper, more significant one?
4. What does the expository information about the reduced financial status of Sciarame' set up in the way of ironic contradiction? How is this important to the story?
5. What is the crisis, or turning point, in the action? What is ironic about it?
6. What is the climax of the action?
7. What is the author's attitude toward Bellone? Toward Rosolino? Toward Roro'?
8. Does what the reader learns about the actual role of Sciarame' in the Garibaldi campaigns affect the reader's estimation of his worth? In what way?
9. What is the irony in the burial of Sciarame' in the red shirt with the medals pinned to his breast?
10. How is the conflict between illusion and reality in the story resolved?

Luigi Pirandello
The Soft Touch of Grass

They went into the next room, where he was sleeping in a big chair, to ask if he wanted to look at her for the last time before the lid was put on the coffin.

"It's dark. What time is it?" he asked.

It was nine-thirty in the morning, but the day was overcast and the light dim. The funeral had been set for ten o'clock.

Signor Pardi stared up at them with dull eyes. It hardly seemed possible that he could have slept so long and well all night. He was still numb with sleep and the sorrow of these last days. He would have liked to cover his face with his hands to shut out the faces of his neighbors grouped about his chair in the thin light; but sleep had weighted his body like lead, and although there was a tingling in his toes urging him to rise, it quickly went away. Should he still give way to his grief? He happened to say aloud, "Always . . ." but he said it like someone settling himself under the covers to go back to sleep. They all looked at him questioningly. Always what?

Always dark, even in the daytime, he had wanted to say, but it made no sense. The day after her death, the day of her funeral, he would always remember this wan light and his deep sleep, too, with her lying dead in the next room. Perhaps the windows . . .

"The windows?"

Yes, they were still closed. They had not been opened during the night, and the warm glow of those big dripping candles lingered. The bed had been taken away and she was there in her padded casket, rigid and ashen against the creamy satin.

No. Enough. He had seen her.

He closed his eyes, for they burned from all the crying he had done these past few days. Enough. He had slept and everything had been washed away with that sleep. Now he was relaxed, with a sense of sorrowful emptiness. Let the casket be closed and carried away with all it held of his past life.

But since she was still there . . .

He jumped to his feet and tottered. They caught him and, with eyes still closed, he allowed himself to be led to the open casket. When he opened his eyes and saw her, he called her by name, her name that lived for him alone, the name in which he saw her and knew her in all the fullness of the life they had shared together. He glared resentfully at the others daring to stare at her lying still in death. What did they know about her? They could not even imagine what it meant to him to be deprived of her. He felt like screaming, and it must have been apparent, for his son hurried over to take him away. He was quick to see the meaning of this and felt a chill as though he were stripped bare. For shame—those foolish ideas up to the very last, even after his night-long sleep. Now they must hurry so as not to keep the friends waiting who had come to follow the coffin to the church.

"Come on, Papa. Be reasonable."

With angry, piteous eyes, the bereaved man turned back to his big chair.

Reasonable, yes; it was useless to cry out the anguish that welled within him and that could never be expressed by words or deeds. For a husband who is left a widower at a certain age, a man still yearning for his wife, can the loss be the same as that of a son for whom—at a certain point—it is almost timely to be left an orphan? Timely, since he was on the point of getting married and would, as soon as the three months' mourning were passed, now that he had the added excuse that it was better for both of them to have a woman to look after the house.

"Pardi! Pardi!" they shouted from the entrance hall.

His chill became more intense when he understood clearly for the first time that they were not calling him but his son. From now on their surname would belong more to his son than to him. And he, like a fool, had gone in there to cry out the living name of his mate, like a profanation. For shame! Yes, useless, foolish ideas, he now realized, after that long sleep which had washed him clean of everything.

Now the one vital thing to keep him going was his curiosity as to how their new home would be arranged. Where, for example, were they going to have him sleep? The big double bed had been removed. Would he have a small bed? he wondered. Yes, probably his son's single bed. Now he would have the small bed. And his son would soon be lying in a big bed, his wife beside him within arm's reach. He, alone, in his little bed, would stretch out his arms into thin air.

He felt torpid, perplexed, with a sensation of emptiness inside and all around him. His body was numb from sitting so long. If he tried now to get up he felt sure that he would rise light as a feather in all that emptiness, now that his life was reduced to nothing. There was hardly any difference between himself and the big chair. Yet that chair appeared secure on its four legs, whereas he no longer knew where his feet and legs belonged nor what to do with his hands. What did he care about his life? He did not care particularly about the lives of others, either. Yet as he was still alive he must go on. Begin again—some sort of life which he could not yet conceive and which he certainly would never have contemplated if things had not changed in his own world. Now, deposed like this all of a sudden, not old and yet no longer young . . .

He smiled and shrugged his shoulders. For his son, all at once, he had become a child. But after all, as everyone knows, fathers are children to their grown sons who are full of worldly ambition and have successfully outdistanced them in positions of importance. They keep their fathers in idleness to repay all they have received when they themselves were small, and their fathers in turn become young again.

The single bed . . .

But they did not even give him the little room where his son had slept. Instead, they said, he would feel more independent in another, almost hidden on the courtyard; he would feel free there to do as he liked. They refurnished it with all the best pieces, so it would not occur to anyone that it had once been a servant's room. After the marriage, all the front rooms were pretentiously decorated and newly furnished, even to the luxury of carpets. Not a trace remained of the way the old house had looked. Even with his own furniture relegated to that little dark room, out of the mainstream of the young people's existence, he did not feel at home. Yet, oddly enough, he did not resent the disregard he seemed to have reaped along with the old furniture, because he admired the new rooms and was satisfied with his son's success.

But there was another deeper reason, not too clear as yet, a promise of another life, all shining and colorful, which was erasing the memory of the old one. He even drew a secret hope from it that a new life might begin for him too. Unconsciously, he sensed the luminous opening of a door at his back whence he might escape at the right moment, easy enough now that no one bothered about him, leaving him as if on holiday in the sanctuary of his little room "to do as he pleased." He felt lighter than air. His eyes had a gleam in them that colored everything, leading him from marvel to marvel, as though he really were a child again. He had the eyes of a child—lively and open wide on a world which was still new.

He took the habit of going out early in the morning to begin his holiday which was to last as long as his life lasted. Relieved of all responsibilities, he agreed to pay his son so much every month out of his pension for his maintenance. It was very little. Though he needed nothing, his son thought he should keep some money for himself to satisfy any need he might have. But need for what? He was satisfied now just to look on at life.

Having shaken off the weight of experience, he no longer knew how to get along with oldsters. He avoided them. And the younger people considered him too old, so he went to the park where the children played.

That was how he started his new life—in the meadow among the children in the grass. What an exhilarating scent the grass had, and so fresh where it grew thick and high. The children played hide-and-seek there. The constant trickle of some hidden stream outpurled the rustle of the leaves. Forgetting their game, the children pulled off their shoes and stockings. What a delicious feeling to sink into all that freshness of soft new grass with bare feet!

He took off one shoe and was stealthily removing the other when a young girl appeared before him, her face flaming. "You, pig!" she cried, her eyes flashing.

Her dress was caught up in front on a bush, and she quickly pulled it down over her legs, because he was looking up at her from where he sat on the ground.

He was stunned. What had she imagined? Already she had disappeared. He had wanted to enjoy the children's innocent fun. Bending down, he put his two hands over his hard, bare feet. What had she seen wrong? Was he too old to share a child's delight in going barefoot in the grass? Must one immediately think evil because he was old? Ah, he knew that he could change in a flash from being a child to becoming a man again, if he must. He was still a man, after all, but he didn't want to think about it. He refused to think about it. It was really as a child that he had taken off his shoes. How wrong it was of that wretched girl to insult him like that! He threw himself face down on the grass. All his grief, his loss, his daily loneliness had brought about this gesture, interpreted now in the light of vulgar malice. His gorge rose in disgust and bitterness. Stupid girl! If he had wanted that—even his son admitted he might have "some desires"—he had plenty of money in his pocket for such needs.

Indignant, he pulled himself upright. Shamefacedly, with trembling hands, he put on his shoes again. All the blood had gone to his head and the pulse now beat hot behind his eyes. Yes, he knew where to go for that. He knew.

Calmer now, he got up and went back to the house. In the welter of furniture which seemed to have been placed there on purpose to drive him mad, he threw himself on the bed and turned his face to the wall.

[1939]

For Thought

What starts out as a mood piece on grief and despair over the death of a loved one turns into an ironic tale depicting a pathetically aborted attempt on the part of the bereaved widower to create a new life for himself on a different, more simple level. In one brief, innocently cruel encounter, however, the main character in "The Soft Touch of Grass" is denied escape and turns away from life to an angry hopelessness that is overwhelming and final.

For Discussion

1. What is the dominant mood in the first part of the story? How is the mood established?
2. What mood shifts occur in the second part and how are they created?
3. In the second part, what is the inciting factor, the crisis, and the resolution of the action?
4. Discuss Pirandello's use of irony in the title, in the characterization, and in the action of the story.
5. Discuss the use of symbols and what they contribute to the effect of the story.

Luigi Pirandello
War

The passengers who had left Rome by the night express had had to stop until dawn at the small station of Fabriano in order to continue their journey by the small old-fashioned "local" joining the main line with Sulmona.

At dawn, in a stuffy and smoky second-class carriage in which five people had already spent the night, a bulky woman in deep mourning was hoisted in—almost like a shapeless bundle. Behind her—puffing and moaning, followed her husband—a tiny man, thin and weakly, his face death-white, his eyes small and bright and looking shy and uneasy.

Having at last taken a seat he politely thanked the passengers who had helped his wife and who had made room for her; then he turned round to the woman trying to pull down the collar of her coat and politely inquired:

"Are you all right, dear?"

The wife, instead of answering, pulled up her collar again to her eyes, so as to hide her face.

"Nasty world," muttered the husband with a sad smile.

And he felt it his duty to explain to his traveling companions that the poor woman was to be pitied, for the war was taking away from her her only son, a boy of twenty to whom both had devoted their entire life, even breaking up their home at Sulmona to follow him to Rome, where he had to go as a student, then allowing him to volunteer for war with an assurance, however, that at least for six months he would not be sent to the front and now, all of a sudden, receiving a wire saying that he was due to leave in three days' time and asking them to go and see him off.

The woman under the big coat was twisting and wriggling, at times growling like a wild animal, feeling certain that all those explanations would not have aroused even a shadow of sympathy from those people who—most likely—were in the same plight as herself. One of them, who had been listening with particular attention, said:

"You should thank God that your son is only leaving now for the front. Mine has been sent there the first day of the war. He has already come back twice wounded and been sent back again to the front."

"What about me? I have two sons and three nephews at the front," said another passenger.

"Maybe, but in our case it is our *only* son," ventured the husband.

"What difference can it make? You may spoil your only son with excessive attentions, but you cannot love him more than you would all your other children if you had any. Paternal love is not like bread that can be broken into pieces and split amongst the children in equal shares. A father gives *all* his love to each one of his children without discrimination, whether it be one or ten, and if I am suffering now for my two sons, I am not suffering half for each of them but double . . ."

"True . . . true . . ." sighed the embarrassed husband, "but suppose (of course we all hope it will never be your case) a father has two sons at the front and he loses one of them, there is still one left to console him . . . while . . ."

"Yes," answered the other, getting cross, "a son left to console him but also a son left for whom he must survive, while in the case of the father of an only son, if the son dies the father can die too and put an end to his distress. Which of the two positions is the worse? Don't you see how my case would be worse than yours?"

"Nonsense," interrupted another traveler, a fat, redfaced man with bloodshot eyes of the palest gray.

He was panting. From his bulging eyes seemed to spurt inner violence of an uncontrolled vitality which his weakened body could hardly contain.

"Nonsense," he repeated, trying to cover his mouth with his hand so as to hide the two missing front teeth. "Nonsense. Do we give life to our children for our own benefit?"

The other travelers stared at him in distress. The one who had had his son at the front since the first day of the war sighed: "You are right. Our children do not belong to us, they belong to the Country. . . ."

"Bosh," retorted the fat traveler. "Do we think of the Country when we give life to our children? Our sons are born because . . . well, because they must be born and when they come to life they take our own life with them. This is the truth. We belong to them but they never belong to us. And when they reach twenty they are exactly what we were at their age. We too had a father and mother, but there were so many other things as well . . . girls, cigarettes, illusions, new ties . . . and the Country, of course, whose call we would have answered—when we were twenty—even if father and mother had said no. Now, at our age, the love of our Country is still great, of course, but stronger than it is the love for our children. Is there any one of us here who wouldn't gladly take his son's place at the front if he could?"

There was a silence all round, everybody nodding as to approve.

"Why then," continued the fat man, "shouldn't we consider the feelings of our children when they are twenty? Isn't it natural that at their age they should consider the love for their Country (I am speaking of decent boys, of course) even greater than the love for us? Isn't it natural that it should be so, as after all they must look upon us as upon old boys who cannot move any more and must stay at home? If Country exists, if Country is a natural necessity, like bread, of which each of us must eat in order not to die of hunger, somebody must go to defend it. And our sons go, when they are twenty, and they don't want tears, because if they die, they die inflamed and happy (I am speaking, of course, of decent boys). Now, if one dies young and happy, without having the ugly sides of life, the boredom of it, the pettiness, the bitterness of disillusion . . . what more can we ask for him? Everyone should stop crying; everyone should laugh, as I do . . . or at least thank God—as

I do—because my son, before dying, sent me a message saying that he was dying satisfied at having ended his life in the best way he could have wished. That is why, as you see, I do not even wear mourning. . . ."

He shook his light fawn coat as to show it; his livid lip over his missing teeth was trembling, his eyes were watery and motionless, and soon after he ended with a shrill laugh which might well have been a sob.

"Quite so . . . quite so . . ." agreed the others.

The woman who, bundled in a corner under her coat, had been sitting and listening had—for the last three months—tried to find in the words of her husband and her friends something to console her in her deep sorrow, something that might show her how a mother should resign heself to send her son not even to death but to a probably dangerous life. Yet not a word had she found amongst the many which had been said . . . and her grief had been greater in seeing that nobody—as she thought—could share her feelings.

But now the words of the traveler amazed and almost stunned her. She suddenly realized that it wasn't the others who were wrong and could not understand her but herself who could not rise up to the same height of those fathers and mothers willing to resign themselves, without crying, not only to the departure of their sons but even to their death.

She lifted her head, she bent over from her corner trying to listen with great attention to the details which the fat man was giving to his companions about the way his son had fallen as a hero, for his King and his Country, happy and without regrets. It seemed to her that she had stumbled into a world she had never dreamt of, a world so far unknown to her, and she was so pleased to hear everyone joining in congratulating that brave father who could so stoically speak of his child's death.

Then suddenly, just as if she had heard nothing of what had been said and almost as if waking up from a dream, she turned to the old man, asking him:

"Then . . . is your son really dead?"

Everybody stared at her. The old man, too, turned to look at her, fixing his great, bulging, horribly watery light gray eyes, deep in her face. For some little time he tried to answer, but words failed him. He looked and looked at her, almost as if only then—at that silly, incongruous question—he had suddenly realized at last that his son was really dead—gone forever—forever. His face contracted, became horribly distorted, then he snatched in haste a handkerchief from his pocket and, to the amazement of everyone, broke into harrowing heart-rending, uncontrollable sobs.

[1939]

For Thought

On a night train from Rome during World War I, the flimsy cocoon of platitudes and abstractions that one parent has spun to make the death of young men in war personally acceptable is pierced and torn to shreds in a moment of bitter truth. Relying heavily upon dialogue and a stage setting technique, Pirandello depicts how parents, through indoctrination and self-deception, have been conditioned to accept as truth the dictum, *Dulce et decorum . . .*

For Discussion

1. What atmosphere is created on the train? How does it serve as a motivating force in the action?

2. What is the inciting factor in the plot? What are the complication, the crisis, and the resolution?
3. How is the crisis ironic for both the man in the light fawn coat and the woman?
4. How is the title both an overstatement and an understatement?

Edgar Allan Poe
The Fall of the House of Usher

Son coeur est un luth suspendu; Sitôt qu'on le touche il résonne.

De Béranger

During the whole of a dull, dark, and soundless day in the autumn of the year, when the clouds hung oppressively low in the heavens, I had been passing alone, on horseback, through a singularly dreary tract of country; and at length found myself, as the shades of the evening drew on, within view of the melancholy House of Usher. I know not how it was—but, with the first glimpse of the building, a sense of insufferable gloom pervaded my spirit. I say insufferable; for the feeling was unrelieved by any of that half-pleasurable, because poetic, sentiment with which the mind usually receives even the sternest natural images of the desolate or terrible. I looked upon the scene before me—upon the mere house, and the simple landscape features of the domain—upon the bleak walls—upon the vacant eye-like windows—upon a few rank sedges—and upon a few white trunks of decayed trees—with an utter depression of soul which I can compare to no earthly sensation more properly than to the after-dream of the reveller upon opium—the bitter lapse into everyday life—the hideous dropping off of the veil. There was an iciness, a sinking, a sickening of the heart—an unredeemed dreariness of thought, which no goading of the imagination could torture into aught of the sublime. What was it—I paused to think—what was it that so unnerved me in the contemplation of the House of Usher? It was a mystery all insoluble; nor could I grapple with the shadowy fancies that crowded upon me as I pondered. I was forced to fall back upon the unsatisfactory conclusion, that while, beyond doubt, there are combinations of very simple natural objects which have the power of thus affecting us, still the analysis of this power lies among considerations beyond our depth. It was possible, I reflected, that a mere different arrangement of the particulars of the scene, of the details of the picture, would be sufficient to modify, or perhaps to annihilate, its capacity for sorrowful impression; and, acting upon this idea, I reined my horse to the precipitous brink of a black and lurid tarn that lay in unruffled lustre by the dwelling, and gazed down—but with a

SOURCE: "The Fall of the House of Usher" by Edgar Allan Poe. Originally published in *Burton's Gentleman's Magazine*, September 1839.

shudder even more thrilling than before—upon the remodeled and inverted images of the gray sedge, and the ghastly tree-stems, and the vacant and eye-like windows.

Nevertheless, in this mansion of gloom I now proposed to myself a sojourn of some weeks. Its proprietor, Roderick Usher, had been one of my boon companions in boyhood; but many years had elapsed since our last meeting. A letter, however, had lately reached me in a distant part of the country—a letter from him—which, in its wildly importunate nature, had admitted of no other than a personal reply. The MS. gave evidence of nervous agitation. The writer spoke of acute bodily illness—of a mental disorder which oppressed him—and of an earnest desire to see me, as his best, and indeed his only personal friend, with a view of attempting, by the cheerfulness of my society, some alleviation of his malady. It was the manner in which all this, and much more, was said—it was the apparent *heart* that went with his request—which allowed me no room for hesitation; and I accordingly obeyed forthwith what I still considered a very singular summons.

Although, as boys, we had been even intimate associates, yet I really knew little of my friend. His reserve had been always excessive and habitual. I was aware, however, that his very ancient family had been noted, time out of mind, for a peculiar sensibility of temperament, displaying itself, through long ages, in many works of exalted art, and manifested, of late, in repeated deeds of munificent yet unobtrusive charity, as well as in a passionate devotion to the intricacies, perhaps even more than to the orthodox and easily recognisable beauties, of musical science. I had learned, too, the very remarkable fact, that the stem of the Usher race, all time-honored as it was, had put forth, at no period, any enduring branch; in other words, that the entire family lay in the direct line of descent, and had always, with a very trifling and very temporary variation, so lain. It was this deficiency, I considered, while running over in thought the perfect keeping of the character of the premises with the accredited character of the people, and while speculating upon the possible influence which the one, in the long lapse of centuries, might have exercised upon the other—it was this deficiency, perhaps, of collateral issue, and the consequent undeviating transmission, from sire to son, of the patrimony with the name, which had, at length, so identified the two as to merge the original title of the estate in the quaint and equivocal appellation of the "House of Usher"—an appellation which seemed to include, in the minds of the peasantry who used it, both the family and the family mansion.

I have said that the sole effect of my somewhat childish experiment—that of looking down within the tarn—had been to deepen the first singular impression. There can be no doubt that the consciousness of the rapid increase of my superstition—for why should I not so term it?—served mainly to accelerate the increase itself. Such, I have long known, is the paradoxical law of all sentiments having terror as a basis. And it might have been for this reason only, that, when I again uplifted my eyes to the house itself, from its image in the pool, there grew in my mind a strange fancy—a fancy so ridiculous, indeed, that I but mention it to show the vivid force of the sensations which oppressed me. I had so worked upon my imagination as really to believe that about the whole mansion and domain there hung an atmosphere peculiar to themselves and their immediate vicinity—an atmosphere which had no affinity with the air of heaven, but which had reeked up from the decayed trees, and the gray wall, and the silent tarn—a pestilent and mystic vapour, dull, sluggish, faintly discernible, and leaden-hued.

Shaking off from my spirit what *must* have been a dream, I scanned more narrowly the real aspect of the building. Its principal feature seemed to be that of an excessive antiquity. The discoloration of ages had been great. Minute *fungi* overspread the whole exterior, hanging in a fine tangled web-work from the eaves. Yet all this was apart from any extraordinary dilapidation. No portion of the masonry had fallen; and there appeared to be a wild inconsistency between its still perfect adaptation of parts, and the crumbling condition of the individual stones. In this there was much that reminded me of the specious totality of old woodwork which has rotted for long years in some neglected vault, with no disturbance from the breath of the external air. Beyond this indication of extensive decay, however, the fabric gave little token of instability. Perhaps the eye of a scrutinising observer might have discovered a barely perceptible fissure, which, extending from the roof of the building in front, made its way down the wall in a zigzag direction, until it became lost in the sullen waters of the tarn.

Noticing these things, I rode over a short causeway to the house. A servant in waiting took my horse, and I entered the Gothic archway of the hall. A valet, of stealthy step, thence conducted me, in silence, through many dark and intricate passages in my progress to the *studio* of his master. Much that I encountered on the way contributed, I know not how, to heighten the vague sentiments of which I have already spoken. While the objects around me—while the carvings of the ceiling, the sombre tapestries of the walls, the ebon blackness of the floors, and the phantasmagoric armorial trophies which rattled as I strode, were but matters to which, or to such as which, I had been accustomed from my infancy—while I hesitated not to acknowledge how familiar was all this—I still wondered to find how unfamiliar were the fancies which ordinary images were stirring up. On one of the staircases, I met the physician of the family. His countenance, I thought, wore a mingled expression of low cunning and perplexity. He accosted me with trepidation and passed on. The valet now threw open a door and ushered me into the presence of his master.

The room in which I found myself was very large and lofty. The windows were long, narrow, and pointed, and at so vast a distance from the black oaken floor as to be altogether inaccessible from within. Feeble gleams of encrimsoned light made their way through the trellised panes, and served to render sufficiently distinct the more prominent objects around; the eye, however, struggled in vain to reach the remoter angles of the chamber, or the recesses of the vaulted and fretted ceiling. Dark draperies hung upon the walls. The general furniture was profuse, comfortless, antique, and tattered. Many books and musical instruments lay scattered about, but failed to give any vitality to the scene. I felt that I breathed an atmosphere of sorrow. An air of stern, deep, and irredeemable gloom hung over and pervaded all.

Upon my entrance, Usher arose from a sofa on which he had been lying at full length, and greeted me with a vivacious warmth which had much in it, I at first thought, of an overdone cordiality—of the constrained effort of the *ennuyé* man of the world. A glance, however, at his countenance, convinced me of his perfect sincerity. We sat down; and for some moments, while he spoke not, I gazed upon him with a feeling half of pity, half of awe. Surely, man had never before so terribly altered, in so brief a period, as had Roderick Usher! It was with difficulty that I could bring myself to admit the identity of the wan being before me with the companion of my early boyhood. Yet the character of his face had been at all times remarkable. A cadaverousness of complexion; an eye large, liquid, and luminous beyond comparison; lips somewhat thin and very pallid, but of a surpassingly beautiful curve; a nose of a delicate Hebrew model, but with a breadth of nostril unusual in similar formations; a finely moulded chin, speaking, in its want of prominence, of a want of moral energy; hair of a more than web-like softness and tenuity; these features, with an inordinate expansion above the regions of the temple, made up altogether a countenance not easily to be forgotten. And now in the mere exaggeration of the prevailing character of these features, and of the expression they were wont to convey, lay so much of change that I doubted to whom I spoke. The now ghastly pallor of the skin, and the now miraculous lustre of the eye, above all things startled and even awed me. The silken hair, too, had been suffered to grow all unheeded, and as, in its wild gossamer texture, it floated rather than fell about the face, I could not, even with effort, connect its Arabesque expression with any idea of simple humanity.

In the manner of my friend I was at once struck with an incoherence—an inconsistency; and I soon found this to arise from a series of feeble and futile struggles to overcome an habitual trepidancy—an excessive nervous agitation. For something of this nature I had indeed been prepared, no less by his letter, than by reminiscences of certain boyish traits, and by conclusions deduced from his peculiar physical conformation and temperament. His action was alternately vivacious and sullen. His voice varied rapidly from a tremulous indecision (when the animal spirits seemed utterly in abeyance) to that species of energetic concision—that abrupt, weighty, unhurried, and hollow-sounding enunciation, that leaden, self-balanced, and perfectly modulated guttural utterance, which may be observed in the lost drunkard, or the irreclaimable eater of opium, during the periods of his most intense excitement.

It was thus that he spoke of the object of my visit, of his earnest desire to see me, and of the solace he expected me to afford him. He entered, at some length, into what he conceived to be the nature of his malady. It was, he said, a constitutional and a family evil, and one for which he despaired to find a remedy—a mere nervous affection, he immediately added, which would undoubtedly soon pass off. It displayed itself in a host of unnatural sensations. Some of these, as he detailed them, interested and bewildered me; although, perhaps, the terms and the general manner of the narration had their weight. He suffered much from a morbid acuteness of the senses; the most insipid food was alone endurable; he could wear only garments of certain texture; the odors of all flowers were oppressive; his eyes were tortured by even faint light; and there were but peculiar sounds, and these from stringed instruments, which did not inspire him with horror.

To an anomalous species of terror I found him a bounden slave. "I shall perish," said he, "I *must* perish in this deplorable folly. Thus, thus, and not otherwise, shall I be lost. I dread the events of the future, not in themselves, but in their results. I shudder at the thought of any, even the most trivial, incident, which may operate upon this intolerable agitation of soul. I have, indeed, no abhorrence of danger, except in its absolute effect—in terror. In this unnerved—in this pitiable condition—I feel that the period will sooner or later arrive when I must abandon life and reason together in some struggle with the grim phantasm, FEAR."

I learned, moreover, at intervals, and through broken and equivocal hints, another singular feature of his mental condition. He was enchained by certain superstitious impressions in regard to the dwelling which he tenanted, and whence, for many years, he had never ventured forth—in regard to an influence whose supposititious force was conveyed in terms too shadowy here to be re-stated—an influence which some peculiarities in the mere form and substance of his family mansion, had, by dint of long sufferance, he said, obtained over his spirit—an effect which the *physique* of the gray walls and turrets, and of the dim tarn into which they all looked down, had, at length, brought about upon the *morale* of his existence.

He admitted, however, although with hesitation, that much of the peculiar gloom which thus afflicted him could be traced to a more natural and far more palpable origin—to the severe and long-continued illness—indeed to the evidently approaching dissolution—of a tenderly beloved sister—his sole companion for long years—his last and only relative on earth. "Her decease," he said, with a bitterness which I can never forget, "would leave him (him the hopeless and the frail) the last of the ancient race of the Ushers." While he spoke, the lady Madeline (for so was she called) passed slowly through a remote portion of the apartment, and without having noticed my presence, disappeared. I regarded her with an utter astonishment not unmingled with dread—and yet I found it impossible to account for such feelings. A sensation of stupor oppressed me, as my eyes followed her retreating steps. When a door, at length, closed upon her, my glance sought instinctively and eagerly the countenance of the brother—but he had buried his face in his hands, and I could only perceive that a far more than ordinary wanness had overspread the emaciated fingers through which trickled many passionate tears.

The disease of the lady Madeline had long baffled the skill of her physicians. A settled apathy, a gradual wasting away of the person, and frequent although transient affections of a partially cataleptical character, were the unusual diagnosis. Hitherto she had steadily borne up against the pressure of her malady, and had not betaken herself finally to bed; but, on the closing in of the evening of my arrival at the house, she succumbed (as her brother told me at night with inexpressible agitation) to the prostrating power of the destroyer; and I learned that the glimpse I had obtained of her person would thus probably be the last I should obtain—that the lady, at least while living, would be seen by me no more.

For several days ensuing, her name was unmentioned by either Usher or myself: and during this period I was busied in earnest endeavours to alleviate the melancholy of my friend. We painted and read together; or I listened, as if in a dream, to the wild improvisations of his speaking guitar. And thus, as a closer and still closer intimacy admitted me more unreservedly into the recesses of his spirit, the more bitterly did I perceive the futility of all attempts at cheering a mind from which darkness, as if an inherent positive quality, poured forth upon all objects of the moral and physical universe, in one unceasing radiation of gloom.

I shall ever bear about me a memory of the many solemn hours I thus spent alone with the master of the House of Usher. Yet I should fail in my attempt to convey an idea of the exact character of the studies, or of the occupations, in which he involved me, or led me the way. An excited and highly distempered ideality threw a sulphureous lustre over all. His long improvised dirges will ring forever in my ears. Among other things, I hold painfully in mind a certain singular perversion and amplification of the wild air of the last waltz of Von Weber. From the paintings over which his elaborate fancy brooded, and which grew, touch by touch, into vaguenesses at which I shuddered the more thrillingly, because I shuddered knowing not why;—from these paintings (vivid as their images now are before me) I would in vain endeavour to educe more than a small portion which should lie within the compass of merely written words. By the utter simplicity, by the nakedness of his designs, he arrested and overawed attention. If ever mortal painted an idea, that mortal was Roderick Usher. For me at least—in the circumstances then surrounding me—there arose out of the pure abstractions which the hypochondriac contrived to throw upon his canvas, an intensity of intolerable awe, no shadow of which felt I ever yet in the contemplation of the certainly glowing yet too concrete reveries of Fuseli.

One of the phantasmagoric conceptions of my friend, partaking not so rigidly of the spirit of abstraction, may be shadowed forth, although feebly, in words. A small picture presented the interior of an immensely long and rectangular vault or tunnel, with low walls, smooth, white, and without interruption or device. Certain accessory points of the design served well to convey the idea that this excavation lay at an exceeding depth below the surface of the earth. No outlet was observed in any portion of its vast extent, and no torch, or other artificial source of light was discernible; yet a flood of intense rays rolled throughout, and bathed the whole in a ghastly and inappropriate splendour.

I have just spoken of that morbid condition of the auditory nerve which rendered all music intolerable to the sufferer, with the exception of certain effects of stringed instruments. It was, perhaps, the narrow limits to which he thus confined himself upon the guitar, which gave birth, in great measure, to the fantastic character of his performances. But the fervid facility of his impromptus could not be so accounted for. They must have been, and were, in the notes, as well as in the words of his wild fantasies (for he not unfrequently accompanied himself with rhymed verbal improvisations), the result of that intense mental collectedness and concentration to which I have previously alluded as observable only in particular moments of the highest artificial excitement. The words of one of these rhapsodies I have easily remembered. I was, perhaps, the more forcibly impressed with it, as he gave it, because, in the under or mystic current of its meaning, I fancied that I perceived, and for the first time, a full consciousness on the part of Usher, of the tottering of his lofty reason upon her throne. The verses, which were entitled "The Haunted Palace," ran very nearly, if not accurately, thus:

I

In the greenest of our valleys,
  By good angels tenanted,
Once a fair and stately palace—
  Radiant palace—reared its head.
In the monarch Thought's dominion—
  It stood there!
Never seraph spread a pinion
  Over fabric half so fair.

II

Banners yellow, glorious, golden,
  On its roof did float and flow;
(This—all this—was in the olden
  Time long ago)
And every gentle air that dallied,
  In that sweet day,
Along the ramparts plumed and pallid,
  A winged odour went away.

III

Wanderers in that happy valley
  Through two luminous windows saw
Spirits moving musically
  To a lute's well-tuned law,
Round about a throne, where sitting,
  (Porphyrogene!)
In state of his glory well befitting,
  The ruler of the realm was seen.

IV

And all with pearl and ruby glowing
  Was the fair palace door,
Through which came flowing, flowing, flowing,
  And sparkling evermore,
A troop of Echoes whose sweet duty
  Was but to sing,
In voices of surpassing beauty,
  The wit and wisdom of their king.

V

But evil things, in robes of sorrow,
  Assailed the monarch's high estate;
(Ah, let us mourn, for never morrow)
  Shall dawn upon him, desolate!)
And, round about his home, the glory
  That blushed and bloomed
Is but a dim-remembered story
  Of the old time entombed.

VI

And travellers now within that valley,
  Through the red-litten windows, see
Vast forms that move fantastically
  To a discordant melody;
While, like a ghastly rapid river,
  Through the pale door,
A hideous throng rush out forever,
  And laugh—but smile no more.

I well remember that suggestions arising from this ballad, led us into a train of thought wherein there became manifest an opinion of Usher's which I mention, not so much on account of its novelty, (for other men[1] have thought thus,) as on account of the pertinacity with which he maintained it. This opinion, in its general form, was that of the sentience of all vegetable things. But, in his disordered fancy, the idea had assumed a more daring character, and trespassed, under certain conditions, upon the kingdom of inorganization. I lack words to express the full extent, or the earnest *abandon* of his persuasion. The belief, however, was connected (as I have previously hinted) with the gray stones of the home of his forefathers. The conditions of the sentience had been here, he imagined, fulfilled in the method of collocation of these stones—in the order of their arrangement, as well as in that of the many *fungi* which overspread them, and of the decayed trees which stood around—above all, in the long undisturbed endurance of this arrangement, and in its reduplication in the still waters of the tarn. Its evidence—the evidence of the sentience—was to be seen, he said (and I here started as he spoke,) in the gradual yet certain condensation of an atmosphere of their own about the waters and the walls. The result was discoverable, he added, in that silent yet importunate and terrible influence which for centuries had moulded the destinies of his family, and which made *him* what I now saw him—what he was. Such opinions need no comment, and I will make none.

Our books—the books which for years had formed no small portion of the mental existence of the invalid—were, as might be supposed, in strict keeping with this character of phantasm. We pored together over such works as the Ververt and Chartreuse of Gresset; the Belphegor of Machiavelli; the Heaven and Hell of Swedenborg; the Subterranean Voyage of Nicholas Klimm by Holberg; the Chiromancy of Robert Flud, of Jean D'Indaginé, and of De la Chambre; the Journey into the Blue Distance of Tieck; and the City of the Sun of Campanella. One favourite volume was a small octavo edition of the *Directorium Inquisitorum*, by the Dominican Eymeric de Gironne; and there were passages in Pomponius Mela, about the old African Satyrs and Aegipans, over which Usher would sit dreaming for hours. His chief delight, however, was found in the perusal of an exceedingly rare and curious book in quarto Gothic—the manual of a forgotten church—the *Vigilae Mortuorum secundum Chorum Ecclessiae Maguntinae.*

I could not help thinking of the wild ritual of this work, and of its probable influence upon the hypochondriac, when one evening, having informed me abruptly that the lady Madeline was no more, he stated his intention of preserving her corpse for a fortnight, (previously to its final interment,) in one of the numerous vaults within the main walls of the building. The worldly reason, however, assigned for this singular proceeding, was one which I did not feel at liberty to dispute. The brother had been led to his resolution (so he told me) by consideration of the unusual character of the malady of the deceased, of certain obtrusive and eager inquiries on the part of her medical men, and of the remote and exposed situation of the burial-ground of the family. I will not deny that when I called to mind the sinister countenance of the person whom I met upon the staircase, on the day of my arrival at the house, I had no desire to oppose what I regarded as at best but a harmless, and by no means an unnatural, precaution.

At the request of Usher, I personally aided him in the arrangement for the temporary entombment. The body having been encoffined, we two alone bore it to its rest. The vault in which we placed it (and which had been so long unopened that our torches, half smothered in its oppressive at-

[1] Watson, Dr. Percival, Spallanzani, and especially the Bishop of Landaff.—See "Chemical Essays," vol. v.

mosphere, gave us little opportunity for investigation) was small, damp, and entirely without means of admission for light; lying, at great depth, immediately beneath that portion of the building in which was my own sleeping apartment. It had been used, apparently, in remote feudal times, for the worst purposes of a donjon-keep, and, in later days, as a place of deposit for powder, or some other highly combustible substance, as a portion of its floor, and the whole interior of a long archway through which we reached it, were carefully sheathed with copper. The door, of massive iron, had been, also, similarly protected. Its immense weight caused an unusually sharp grating sound, as it moved upon its hinges.

Having deposited our mournful burden upon tressels within this region of horror, we partially turned aside the yet unscrewed lid of the coffin, and looked upon the face of the tenant. A striking similitude between the brother and sister now first arrested my attention; and Usher, divining, perhaps, my thoughts, murmured out some few words from which I learned that the deceased and himself had been twins, and that sympathies of a scarcely intelligible nature had always existed between them. Our glances, however, rested not long upon the dead—for we could not regard her unawed. The disease which had thus entombed the lady in the maturity of youth, had left, as usual in all maladies of a strictly cataleptical character, the mockery of a faint blush upon the bosom and the face, and that suspiciously lingering smile upon the lip which is so terrible in death. We replaced and screwed down the lid, and having secured the door of iron, made our way, with toil, into the scarcely less gloomy apartments of the upper portion of the house.

And now, some days of bitter grief having elapsed, an observable change came over the features of the mental disorder of my friend. His ordinary manner had vanished. His ordinary occupations were neglected or forgotten. He roamed from chamber to chamber with hurried, unequal, and objectless step. The pallor of his countenance had assumed, if possible, a more ghastly hue—but the luminousness of his eye had utterly gone out. The once occasional huskiness of his tone was heard no more; and a tremulous quaver, as if of extreme terror, habitually characterized his utterance. There were times, indeed, when I thought his unceasingly agitated mind was labouring with some oppressive secret, to divulge which he struggled for the necessary courage. At times, again, I was obliged to resolve all into the mere inexplicable vagaries of madness, for I beheld him gazing upon vacancy for long hours, in an attitude of the profoundest attention, as if listening to some imaginary sound. It was no wonder that his condition terrified—that it infected me. I felt creeping upon me, by slow yet certain degrees, the wild influences of his own fantastic yet impressive superstitions.

It was, especially, upon retiring to bed late in the night of the seventh or eighth day after the placing of the lady Madeline within the donjon, that I experienced the full power of such feelings. Sleep came not near my couch—while the hours waned and waned away. I struggled to reason off the nervousness which had dominion over me. I endeavoured to believe that much, if not all of what I felt, was due to the bewildering influence of the gloomy furniture of the room—of the dark and tattered draperies, which, tortured into motion by the breath of a rising tempest, swayed fitfully to and fro upon the walls, and rustled uneasily about the decorations of the bed. But my efforts were fruitless. An irrepressible tremour gradually pervaded my frame; and, at length, there sat upon my very heart an incubus of utterly causeless alarm. Shaking this off with a gasp and a struggle, I uplifted myself upon the pillows, and, peering earnestly within the intense darkness of the chamber, hearkened—I know not why, except that an instinctive spirit prompted me—to certain low and indefinite sounds which came, through the pauses of the storm, at long intervals, I knew not whence. Overpowered by an intense sentiment of horror, unaccountable yet unendurable, I threw on my clothes with haste (for I felt that I should sleep no more during the night), and endeavoured to arouse myself from the pitiable condition into which I had fallen, by pacing rapidly to and fro through the apartment.

I had taken but few turns in this manner, when a light step on an adjoining staircase arrested my attention. I presently recognized it as that of Usher. In an instant afterward he rapped, with a gentle touch, at my door, and entered, bearing a lamp. His counteance was, as usual, cadaverously wan—but, moreover, there was a species of mad hilarity in his eyes—an evidently restrained *hysteria* in his whole demeanour. His air appalled me—but anything was preferable to the solitude which I had so long endured, and I even welcomed his presence as a relief.

"And you have not seen it?" he said abruptly, after having stared about him for some moments in silence—"you have not then seen it?—but, stay! you shall." Thus speaking, and having carefully shaded his lamp, he hurried to one of the casements, and threw it freely open to the storm.

The impetuous fury of the entering gust nearly lifted us from our feet. It was, indeed, a tempestuous yet sternly beautiful night, and one wildly singular in its terror and its beauty. A whirlwind had apparently collected its force in our vicinity; for there were frequent and violent alterations in the direction of the wind; and the exceeding density of the clouds (which hung so low as to press upon the turrets of the house) did not prevent our perceiving the life-like velocity with which they flew careering from all points against each other, without passing away into the distance. I say that even their exceeding density did not prevent our perceiving this—yet we had no glimpse of the moon or stars—nor was there any flashing forth of the lightning. But the under surfaces of the huge masses of agitated vapour, as well as all terrestrial objects immediately around us, were glowing in the unnatural light of a faintly luminous and dinstinctly visible gaseous exhalation which hung about and enshrouded the mansion.

"You must not—you shall not behold this!" said I, shudderingly, to Usher, as I led him with a gentle violence, from the window to a seat. "These appearances, which bewilder you, are merely electrical phenomena not uncommon—or it may be that they have their ghastly origin in the rank miasma of the tarn. Let us close this casement;—the air is chilling and dangerous to your frame. Here is one of your favorite romances. I will read, and you shall listen;—and so we will pass away this terrible night together."

The antique volume which I had taken up was the "Mad Trist" of Sir Launcelot Canning; but I had called it a favourite of Usher's more in sad jest than in earnest; for, in turn, there is little in its uncouth and unimaginative prolixity which could have had interest for the lofty and spiritual ideality of my friend. It was, however, the only book immediately at hand; and I indulged a vague hope that the excitement which now agitated the hypochondriac, might find relief (for the history of mental disorder is full of similar anomalies) even in the extremeness of the folly which I should read. Could I have judged, indeed, by the wild, overstrained air of vivacity with which he hearkened, or apparently hearkened, to the words of the tale, I might well have congratulated myself upon the success of my design.

I had arrived at that well-known portion of the story where Ethelred, the hero of the Trist, having sought in vain for peaceable admission into the dwelling of the hermit, proceeds to make good an entrance by force. Here, it will be remembered, the words of the narrative run thus:

"And Ethelred, who was by nature of a doughty heart, and who was now mighty withal, on account of the powerfulness of the wine which he had drunken, waited no longer to hold parley with the hermit, who, in sooth, was of an obstinate and maliceful turn, but, feeling the rain upon his shoulders, and fearing the rising of the tempest, uplifted his mace outright, and, with blows, made quickly room in the plankings of the door for his gauntleted hand; and now, pulling therewith sturdily, he so cracked, and ripped, and tore all asunder, that the noise of the dry and hollow-sounding wood alarumed and reverberated throughout the forest."

At the termination of this sentence I started, and for a moment, paused; for it appeared to me (although I at once concluded that my excited fancy had deceived me)—it appeared to me that, from some very remote portion of the mansion, there came, indistinctly, to my ears, what might have been, in its exact similarity of character, the echo (but a stifled and dull one certainly) of the very cracking and ripping sound which Sir Launcelot had so particularly described. It was, beyond doubt, the coincidence alone which had arrested my attention; for, amid the rattling of the sashes of the casements, and the ordinary commingled noises of the still increasing storm, the sound, in itself, had nothing, surely, which should have interested or disturbed me. I continued the story:

"But the good champion Ethelred, now entering within the door, was sore enraged and amazed to perceive no signal of the maliceful hermit; but, in the stead thereof, a dragon of a scaly and prodigious demeanour, and of a fiery tongue, which sate in guard before a palace of gold, with a floor of silver; and upon the wall there hung a shield of shining brass with this legend enwritten—

> Who entereth herein, a conqueror hath bin;
> Who slayeth the dragon, the shield he shall
> win;

And Ethelred uplifted his mace, and struck upon the head of the dragon, which fell before him, and gave up his pesty breath, with a shriek so horrid and harsh, and withal so piercing, that Ethelred had fain to close his ears with his hands against the dreadful noise of it, the like whereof was never before heard."

Here again I paused abruptly, and now with a feeling of wild amazement—for there could be no doubt whatever that, in this instance, I did actually hear (although from what direction it proceeded I found it impossible to say) a low and apparently distant, but harsh, protracted, and most unusual screaming or grating sound—the exact counterpart of what my fancy had already conjured up for the dragon's unnatural shriek as described by the romancer.

Oppressed, as I certainly was, upon the occurrence of this second and most extraordinary coincidence, by a thousand conflicting sensations, in which wonder and extreme terror were predominant, I still retained sufficient presence of mind to avoid exciting, by any observation, the sensitive nervousness of my companion. I was by no means certain that he had noticed the sounds in question; although, assuredly, a strange alteration had, during the last few minutes, taken place in his demeanour. From a position fronting my own, he had gradually brought round his chair, so as to sit with his face to the door of the chamber; and thus I could but partially perceive his features, although I saw that his lips trembled as if he were murmuring inaudibly. His head had dropped upon his breast—yet I knew that he was not asleep, from the wide rigid opening of the eye as I caught a glance of it in profile. The motion of his body, too, was at variance with this idea—for he rocked from side to side with a gentle yet constant and uniform sway. Having rapidly taken notice of all this, I resumed the narrative of Sir Launcelot, which thus proceeded:

"And now, the champion, having escaped from the terrible fury of the dragon, bethinking himself of the brazen shield, and of the breaking up of the enchantment which was upon it, removed the carcass from out of the way before him, and approached valorously over the silver pavement of the castle to where the shield was upon the wall; which in sooth tarried not for his full coming, but fell down at his feet upon the silver floor, with a mighty great and terrible ringing sound."

No sooner had these syllables passed my lips, than—as if a shield of brass had indeed, at the moment, fallen heavily upon a floor of silver—I became aware of a distinct, hollow, metallic, and clangorous yet apparently muffled reverberation. Completely unnerved, I leaped to my feet; but the measured rocking movement of Usher was undisturbed. I rushed to the chair in which he sat. His eyes were bent fixedly before him, and throughout his whole countenace there reigned a stony rigidity. But, as I placed my hand upon his shoulder, there came a strong shudder over his whole person; a sickly smile quivered about his lips; and I saw that he spoke in a low, hurried, and gibbering murmur, as if unconscious of my presence. Bending closely over him, I at length drank in the hideous import of his words.

"Not hear it?—yes, I hear it, and *have* heard it. Long—long—long—many minutes, many hours, many days, have I heard it—yet I dared not—oh, pity me, miserable wretch that I am!—I dared not—I *dared* not speak! *We have put her living in the tomb!* Said I not that my senses were acute? I *now* tell you that I heard her first feeble movements in the hollow coffin. I heard them—many, many days ago—yet I dared not—*I dared not speak!* And now—to-night—Ethelred—ha! ha!—the breaking of the hermit's door, and the death-cry of the dragon, and the clangour of the shield!—say, rather, the rending of her coffin, and the grating of the iron hinges of her prison, and her struggles within the coppered archway of the vault! Oh whither shall I fly? Will she not be here anon? Is she not hurrying to upbraid me for my haste? Have I not heard her footsteps on the stair? Do I not distinguish that heavy and horrible beating of her heart? MADMAN!" here he sprang furiously to his feet, and shrieked out his syllables, as if in the effort he were giving up his soul—"MADMAN! I TELL YOU THAT SHE NOW STANDS WITHOUT THE DOOR!"

As if in the superhuman energy of his utterance there had been found the potency of a spell—the huge antique panels to which the speaker pointed, threw slowly back, upon the instant, their ponderous and ebony jaws. It was the work of the rushing gust—but then without those doors there DID stand the lofty and enshrouded figure of the lady Madeline of Usher. There was blood upon her white robes, and the evidence of some bitter struggle upon every portion of her emaciated frame. For a moment she remained trembling and reeling to and fro upon the threshold, then, with a low moaning cry, fell heavily inward upon the person of her brother, and in her violent and now final death-agonies, bore him to the floor a corpse, and a victim to the terrors he had anticipated.

From that chamber, and from that mansion, I fled aghast. The storm was still abroad in all its wrath as I found myself crossing the old causeway. Suddenly there shot along the path a wild light, and I turned to see whence a gleam so unusual could have issued; for the vast house and its shadows were alone behind me. The radiance was that of the full, setting, and blood-red moon, which now shone vividly through that once barely discernible fissure of which I have before spoken as extending from the roof of the building, in a zigzag direction, to the base. While I gazed, this fissure rapidly widened—there came a fierce breath of the whirlwind—the entire orb of the satellite burst at once upon my sight—my brain reeled as I saw the mighty walls rushing asunder—there was a long tumultuous shouting sound like the voice of a thousand waters—and the deep and dark tarn at my feet closed sullenly and silently over the fragments of the "House of Usher."

[1839]

For Thought

Poe's story follows the traditions of Gothic fiction. Within a crumbling mansion hidden in a remote and deserted area, a high-strung intellectual slowly deteriorates in mind and body. When Roderick Usher's sister bursts from the tomb in which he had placed her, the two die, and their "house" collapses. Poe's use of an apparently objective observer as reporter magnifies the story's horrors.

For Discussion

1. How does Poe suggest that the setting is isolated, decaying, and extremely gloomy?
2. How is the narrator characterized and what is his function in relation to the reader?
3. How are the heart-lute images of the epigraph echoed by the story?
4. What kinds of doubling or counterparts can be found in the story?
5. What are the parallels in physical appearance between Roderick and the house?
6. How is the character of Roderick used as a gothic symbol of physical and psychological isolation?
7. How does the tarn possess symbolic meaning?
8. How does Roderick's abstract painting serve both foreshadowing and symbolic functions?
9. What contrasts involved in the ballad "The Haunted Palace" also appear in the story itself?
10. What part does suspense play in the total effect of the story?

Katherine Anne Porter
Flowering Judas

Braggioni sits heaped upon the edge of a straight-backed chair much too small for him, and sings to Laura in a furry, mournful voice. Laura has begun to find reasons for avoiding her own house until the latest possible moment, for Braggioni is there almost every night. No matter how late she is, he will be sitting there with a surly, waiting expression, pulling at his kinky yellow hair, thumbing the strings of his guitar, snarling a tune under his breath. Lupe the Indian maid meets Laura at the door, and says with a flicker of a glance towards the upper room, "He waits."

Laura wishes to lie down, she is tired of her hairpins and the feel of her long tight sleeves, but she says to him, "Have you a new song for me this evening?" If he says yes, she asks him to sing it. If he says no, she remembers his favorite one, and asks him to sing it again. Lupe brings her a cup of chocolate and a plate of rice, and Laura eats at the small table under the lamp, first inviting Braggioni, whose answer is always the same: "I have eaten, and besides, chocolate thickens the voice."

Laura says, "Sing, then," and Braggioni heaves himself into song. He scratches the guitar familiarly as though it were a pet animal, and sings passionately off key, taking the high notes in a prolonged painful squeal. Laura, who haunts the markets listening to the ballad singers, and stops every day to hear the blind boy playing his reed-flute in Sixteenth of September Street, listens to Braggioni with pitiless courtesy, because she dares not smile at his miserable performance. Nobody dares to smile at him. Braggioni is cruel to everyone, with a kind of specialized insolence, but he is so vain of his talents, and so sensitive to slights, it would require a cruelty and vanity greater than his own to lay a finger on the vast cureless wound of his self-esteem. It would require courage, too, for it is dangerous to offend him, and nodody has this courage.

Braggioni loves himself with such tenderness and amplitude and eternal charity that his followers—for he is a leader of men, a skilled revolutionist, and his skin has been punctured in honorable warfare—

warm themselves in the reflected glow, and say to each other: "He has a real nobility, a love of humanity raised above mere personal affections." The excess of this self-love has flowed out, inconveniently for her, over Laura, who, with so many others, owes her comfortable situation and her salary to him. When he is in a very good humor, he tells her, "I am tempted to forgive you for being a *gringa, Gringita!*" and Laura, burning, imagines herself leaning forward suddenly, and with a sound backhanded slap wiping the suety smile from his face. If he notices her eyes at these moments he gives no sign.

She knows what Braggioni would offer her, and she must resist tenaciously without appearing to resist, and if she could avoid it she would not admit even to herself the slow drift of his intention. During these long evenings which have spoiled a long month for her, she sits in her deep chair with an open book on her knees, resting her eyes on the consoling rigidity of the printed page when the sight and sound of Braggioni singing threaten to identify themselves with all her remembered afflictions and to add their weight to her uneasy premonitions of the future. The gluttonous bulk of Braggioni has become a symbol of her many disillusions, for a revolutionist should be lean, animated by heroic faith, a vessel of abstract virtues. This is nonsense, she knows it now and is ashamed of it. Revolution must have leaders, and leadership is a career for energetic men. She is, her comrades tell her, full of romantic error, for what she defines as cynicism in them is merely "a developed sense of reality." She is almost too willing to say, "I am wrong, I suppose I don't really understand the principles," and afterward she makes a secret truce with herself, determined not to surrender her will to such expedient logic. But she cannot help feeling that she had been betrayed irreparably by the disunion between her way of living and her feeling of what life should be, and at times she is almost contented to rest in this sense of grievance as a private store of consolation. Sometimes she wishes to run away, but she stays. Now she longs to fly out of this room, down the narrow stairs, and into the street where the houses lean together like conspirators under a single mottled lamp, and leave Braggioni singing to himself.

Instead she looks at Braggioni, frankly and clearly, like a good child who understands the rules of behavior. Her knees cling together under sound blue serge, and her round white collar is not purposely nun-like. She wears the uniform of an idea, and has renounced vanities. She was born Roman Catholic, and in spite of her fear of being seen by someone who might make a scandal of it, she slips now and again into some crumbling little church, kneels on the chilly stone, and says a Hail Mary on the gold rosary she bought in Tehuantepec. It is no good and she ends by examining the altar with its tinsel flowers and ragged brocades, and feels tender about the battered doll-shape of some male saint whose white, lace-trimmed drawers hang limply around his ankles below the hieratic dignity of his velvet robe. She has encased herself in a set of principles derived from her early training, leaving no detail of gesture or of personal taste untouched, and for this reason she will not wear lace made on machines. This is her private heresy, for in her special group the machine is sacred, and will be the salvation of the workers. She loves fine lace, and there is a tiny edge of fluted cobweb on this collar, which is one of twenty precisely alike, folded in blue tissue paper in the upper drawer of her clothes chest.

Braggioni catches her glance solidly as if he had been waiting for it, leans forward, balancing his paunch between his spread knees, and sings with tremendous emphasis, weighing his words. He has, the song relates, no father and no mother, nor even a friend to console him; lonely as a wave of the sea he comes and goes, lonely as a wave. His mouth opens round and yearns sideways, his balloon cheeks grow oily with the labor of song. He bulges marvelously in his expensive garments. Over his lavender collar, crushed upon a purple necktie, held by a diamond hoop: over his ammunition belt of tooled leather worked in silver, buckled cruelly around his gasping middle: over the tops of his glossy yellow shoes Braggioni swells with ominous ripeness, his mauve silk hose stretched taut, his ankles bound with the stout leather thongs of his shoes.

When he stretches his eyelids at Laura she notes again that his eyes are the true tawny yellow cat's eyes. He is rich, not in money, he tells her, but in power, and this power brings with it the blameless ownership of things, and the right to indulge his love of small luxuries. "I have a taste for the elegant refinements," he said once, flourishing a yellow silk handkerchief before her nose. "Smell that? It is Jockey Club, imported from New York." Nonetheless he is wounded by life. He will say so presently. "It is true everything turns to dust in the hand, to gall on the tongue." He sighs and his leather belt creaks like a saddle girth. "I am disappointed in everything as it comes. Everything." He shakes his head. "You, poor thing, you will be disappointed too. You are born for it. We are more alike than you realize in some things. Wait and see. Some day you will remember what I have told you, you will know that Braggioni was your friend."

Laura feels a slow chill, a purely physical sense of danger, a warning in her blood that violence, mutilation, a shocking death, wait for her with lessening patience. She has translated this fear into something homely, immediate, and sometimes hesitates before crossing the street. "My personal fate is nothing, except as the testimony of a mental attitude," she reminds herself, quoting from some forgotten philosophic primer, and is sensible enough to add, "Anyhow, I shall not be killed by an automobile if I can help it."

"It may be true I am as corrupt, in another way, as Braggioni," she thinks in spite of herself, "as callous, as incomplete," and if this is so, any kind of death seems preferable. Still she sits quietly, she does not run. Where could she go? Uninvited she has promised herself to this place; she can no longer imagine herself as living in another country, and there is no pleasure in remembering her life before she came here.

Precisely what is the nature of this devotion, its true motives, and what are its obligations? Laura cannot say. She spends part of her days in Xochimilco, near by, teaching Indian children to say in English, "The cat is on the mat." When she appears in the classroom they crowd about her with smiles on their wise, innocent, clay-colored faces, crying, "Good morning, my titcher!" in immaculate voices, and they make of her desk a fresh garden of flowers every day.

During her leisure she goes to union meetings and listens to busy important voices quarreling over tactics, methods, internal politics. She visits the prisoners of her own political faith in their cells, where they entertain themselves with counting cockroaches, repenting of their indiscretions, composing their memoirs, writing out manifestoes and plans for their comrades who are still walking about free, hands in pockets, sniffing fresh air. Laura brings them food and cigarettes and a little money, and she brings messages disguised in equivocal phrases from the men outside who dare not set foot in the prison for fear of disappearing into the cells kept empty for them. If the prisoners confuse night and day, and complain, "Dear little Laura, time doesn't pass in this infernal hole, and I won't know when it is time to sleep unless I have a reminder," she brings them their favorite narcotics, and says in a tone that does not wound them with pity, "Tonight will really be night for you," and though her Spanish amuses them, they find her comforting, useful. If they lose patience and all faith, and curse the slowness of their friends in coming to their rescue with money and influence, they trust her not to repeat everything, and if she inquires, "Where do you think we can find money, or influence?"

they are certain to answer, "Well, there is Braggioni, why doesn't he do something?"

She smuggles letters from headquarters to men hiding from firing squads in back streets in mildewed houses, where they sit in tumbled beds and talk bitterly as if all Mexico were at their heels, when Laura knows positively they might appear at the band concert in the Alameda on Sunday morning, and no one would notice them. But Braggioni says, "Let them sweat a little. The next time they may be careful. It is very restful to have them out of the way for a while." She is not afraid to knock on any door in any street after midnight, and enter in the darkness, and say to one of these men who is really in danger: "They will be looking for you—seriously—tomorrow morning after six. Here is some money from Vincente. Go to Vera Cruz and wait."

She borrows money from the Roumanian agitator to give to his bitter enemy the Polish agitator. The favor of Braggioni is their disputed territory, and Braggioni holds the balance nicely, for he can use them both. The Polish agitator talks love to her over café tables, hoping to exploit what he believes is her secret sentimental preference for him, and he gives her misinformation which he begs her to repeat as the solemn truth to certain persons. The Roumanian is more adroit. He is generous with his money in all good causes, and lies to her with an air of ingenuous candor, as if he were her good friend and confidant. She never repeats anything they may say. Braggioni never asks questions. He has other ways to discover all that he wishes to know about them.

Nobody touches her, but all praise her gray eyes, and the soft, round under lip which promises gayety, yet is always grave, nearly always firmly closed: and they cannot understand why she is in Mexico. She walks back and forth on her errands, with puzzled eyebrows, carrying her little folder of drawings and music and school papers. No dancer dances more beautifully than Laura walks, and she inspires some amusing, unexpected ardors, which cause little gossip, because nothing comes of them. A young captain who had been a soldier in Zapata's army attempted, during a horseback ride near Cuernavaca, to express his desire for her with the noble simplicity befitting a rude folk-hero: but gently, because he was gentle. This gentleness was his defeat, for when he alighted, and removed her foot from the stirrup, and essayed to draw her down into his arms, her horse, ordinarily a tame one, shied fiercely, reared and plunged away. The young hero's horse careered blindly after his stablemate, and the hero did not return to the hotel until rather late that evening. At breakfast he came to her table in full charro dress, gray buckskin jacket and trousers with strings of silver buttons down the leg, and he was in a humorous, careless mood. "May I sit with you?" and "You are a wonderful rider. I was terrified that you might be thrown and dragged. I should never have forgiven myself. But I cannot admire you enough for your riding!"

"I learned to ride in Arizona," said Laura.

"If you will ride with me again this morning, I promise you a horse that will not shy with you," he said. But Laura remembered that she must return to Mexico City at noon.

Next morning the children made a celebration and spent their playtime writing on the blackboard. "We lov ar ticher," and with tinted chalks they drew wreaths of flowers around the words. The young hero wrote her a letter: "I am a very foolish, wasteful, impulsive man. I should have first said I love you, and then you would not have run away. But you shall see me again." Laura thought, "I must send him a box of colored crayons," but she was trying to forgive herself for having spurred her horse at the wrong moment.

A brown, shock-haired youth came and stood in her patio one night and sang like a lost soul for two hours, but Laura could think of nothing to do about it. The moonlight spread a wash of gauzy silver over the clear spaces of the garden, and the shadows were cobalt blue. The scarlet blossoms of the Judas tree were dull purple, and the names of the colors repeated themselves automatically in her mind, while she watched not the boy, but his shadow, fallen like a dark garment across the fountain rim, trailing in the water. Lupe came silently and whispered expert counsel in her ear: "If you will throw him one little flower, he will sing another song or two and go away." Laura threw the flower, and he sang a last song and went away with the flower tucked in the band of his hat. Lupe said, "He is one of the organizers of the Typographers Union, and before that he sold corridos in the Merced market, and before that, he came from Guanajuato, where I was born. I would not trust any man, but I trust least those from Guanajuato."

She did not tell Laura that he would be back again the next night, and the next, nor that he would follow her at a certain fixed distance around the Merced market, through Zócola, up Francisco I. Madero Avenue, and so along the Paseo de la Reforma to Chapultepec Park, and into the Philosopher's Footpath, still with that flower withering in his hat, and an indivisible attention in his eyes.

Now Laura is accustomed to him, it means nothing except that he is nineteen years old and is observing a convention with all propriety, as though it were founded on a law of nature, which in the end it might well prove to be. He is beginning to write poems which he prints on a wooden press, and he leaves them stuck like handbills in her door. She is pleasantly disturbed by the abstract, unhurried watchfulness of his black eyes which will in time turn easily towards another object. She tells herself that throwing the flower was a mistake, for she is twenty-two years old and knows better; but she refuses to regret it, and persuades herself that her negation of all external events as they occur is a sign that she is gradually perfecting herself in the stoicism she strives to cultivate against that disaster she fears, though she cannot name it.

She is not at home in the world. Every day she teaches children who remain strangers to her, though she loves their tender round hands and their charming opportunist savagery. She knocks at unfamiliar doors not knowing whether a friend or a stranger shall answer, and even if a known face emerges from the sour gloom of that unknown interior, still it is the face of a stranger. No matter what this stranger says to her, nor what her message to him, the very cells of her flesh reject knowledge and kinship in one monotonous word. No. No. No. She draws her strength from this one holy talismanic word which does not suffer her to be led into evil. Denying everything, she may walk anywhere in safety, she looks at everything without amazement.

No, repeats this firm unchanging voice of her blood; and she looks at Braggioni without amazement. He is a great man, he wishes to impress this simple girl who covers her great round breasts with thick dark cloth, and who hides long, invaluably beautiful legs under a heavy skirt. She is almost thin except for the incomprehensible fullness of her breasts, like a nursing mother's, and Braggioni, who considers himself a judge of women, speculates again on the puzzle of her notorious virginity, and takes the liberty of speech which she permits without a sign of modesty, indeed, without any sort of sign, which is disconcerting.

"You think you are so cold, *gringita!* Wait and see. You will surprise yourself some day! May I be there to advise you!" He stretches his eyelids at her, and his ill-humored cat's eyes waver in a separate glance for the two points of light marking the opposite ends of a smoothly drawn path between the swollen curve of her breasts. He is not put off by that blue serge, nor by her resolutely fixed gaze. There is all the time in the world. His cheeks are bellying with the wind of song. "O girl with the dark eyes," he sings, and reconsiders. "But yours are not dark. I can change all that O girl with the green eyes, you have stolen my heart away!" then his mind wanders to the song, and Laura feels the weight of his attention being shifted elsewhere. Singing thus, he seems harmless, he is quite harmless, there is nothing to do but sit patiently and say "No," when the moment comes. She draws a full breath, and her mind wanders also, but not far. She dares not wander too far.

Not for nothing has Braggioni taken pains to be a good revolutionist and a professional lover of humanity. He will never die of it. He has the malice, the cleverness, the wickedness, the sharpness of wit, the hardness of heart, stipulated for loving the world profitably. *He will never die of it.* He will live to see himself kicked out from his feeding trough by other hungry world-saviors. Traditionally he must sing in spite of his life which drives him to bloodshed, he tells Laura, for his father was a Tuscany peasant who drifted to Yucatan and married a Maya woman: a woman of race, an aristocrat. They gave him the love and knowledge of music, thus: and under the rip of his thumbnail, the strings of the instrument complain like exposed nerves.

Once he was called Delgadito by all the girls and married women who ran after him; he was so scrawny all his bones showed under his thin cotton clothing, and he could squeeze his emptiness to the very backbone with his two hands. He was a poet and the revolution was only a dream then; too many women loved him and sapped away his youth, and he could never find enough to eat anywhere, anywhere! Now he is a leader of men, crafty men who whisper in his ear, hungry men who wait for hours inside his office for a word with him, emaciated men with wild faces who waylay him at the street gate with a timid, "Comrade, let me tell you . . ." and they blow the foul breath from their empty stomachs in his face.

He is always sympathetic. He gives them handfuls of small coins from his own pocket, he promises them work, there will be demonstrations, they must join the unions and attend the meetings, above all they must be on the watch for spies. They are closer to him than his own brothers, without them he can do nothing—until tomorrow, comrade!

Until tomorrow. "They are stupid, they are lazy, they are treacherous, they would cut my throat for nothing," he says to Laura. He has good food and abundant drink, he hires an automobile and drives in the Paseo on Sunday morning, and enjoys plenty of sleep in a soft bed beside a wife who dares not disturb him; and he sits pampering his bones in easy billows of fat, singing to Laura, who knows and thinks these things about him. When he was fifteen, he tried to drown himself because he loved a girl, his first love, and she laughed at him. "A thousand women have paid for that," and his tight little mouth turns down at the corners. Now he perfumes his hair with Jockey Club, and confides to Laura: "One woman is really as good as another for me, in the dark. I prefer them all."

His wife organizes unions among the girls in the cigarette factories, and walks in picket lines, and even speaks at meetings in the evening. But she cannot be brought to acknowledge the benefits of true liberty. "I tell her I must have my freedom, nyet. She does not understand my point of view." Laura has heard this many times. Braggioni scratches the guitar and meditates. "She is an instinctively virtuous woman, pure gold, no doubt of that. If she were not, I should lock her up, and she knows it."

His wife, who works so hard for the good of the factory girls, employs part of her leisure lying on the floor weeping because there are so many women in the world, and only one husband for her, and she never knows where nor when to look for him. He told her: "Unless you can learn to cry when I am not here, I must go away for good." That day he went away and took a room at the Hotel Madrid.

It is this month of separation for the sake of higher principles that has been spoiled not only for Mrs. Braggioni, whose sense of reality is beyond criticism, but for Laura, who feels herself bogged in a nightmare. Tonight Laura envies Mrs. Braggioni, who is alone, and free to weep as much as she pleases about a concrete wrong. Laura has just come from a visit to the prison, and she is waiting for tomorrow with a bitter anxiety as if tomorrow may not come, but time may be caught immovably in this hour, with herself transfixed, Braggioni singing on forever, and Eugenio's body not yet discovered by the guard.

Braggioni says: "Are you going to sleep?" Almost before she can shake her head, he begins telling her about the May day disturbances coming on in Morelia, for the Catholics hold a festival in honor of the Blessed Virgin, and the Socialists celebrate their martyrs on that day. "There will be two independent processions, starting from either end of town, and they will march until they meet, and the rest depends . . ." He asks her to oil and load his pistols. Standing up, he unbuckles his ammunition belt, and spreads it laden across her knees. Laura sits with the shells slipping through the cleaning cloth dipped in oil, and he says again he cannot understand why she works so hard for the revolutionary idea unless she loves some man who is in it. "Are you not in love with someone?" "No," says Laura. "And no one is in love with you?" "No." "Then it is your own fault. No woman need go begging. Why, what is the matter with you? The legless beggar woman in the Alameda has a perfectly faithful lover. Did you know that?"

Laura peers down the pistol barrel and says nothing, but a long, slow faintness rises and subsides in her; Braggioni curves his swollen fingers around the throat of the guitar and softly smothers the music out of it, and when she hears him again he seems to have forgotten her, and is speaking in the hypnotic voice he uses when talking in small rooms to a listening, close-gathered crowd. Some day this world, now seemingly so composed and eternal, to the edges of every sea shall be merely a tangle of gaping trenches, of crashing walls and broken bodies. Everything must be torn from its accustomed place where it has rotted for centuries, hurled skyward and distributed, cast down again clean as rain, without separate identity. Nothing shall survive that the stiffened hands of poverty have created for the rich and no one shall be left alive except the elect spirits destined to procreate a new world cleansed of cruelty and injustice, ruled by benevolent anarchy: "Pistols are good, I love them, cannon are even better, but in the end I pin my faith to good dynamite," he concludes, and strokes the pistol lying in her hands. "Once I dreamed of destroying this city, in case it offered resistence to General Ortíz, but it fell into his hands like an overripe pear."

He is made restless by his own words, rises and stands waiting. Laura holds up the belt to him: "Put that on, and go kill somebody in Morelia, and you will be happier," she says softly. The presence of death in the room makes her bold. "Today, I found Eugenio going into a stupor. He refused to allow me to call the prison doctor. He had taken all the tablets I brought him yesterday. He said he took them because he was bored."

"He is a fool, and his death is his own business," says Braggioni, fastening his belt carefully.

"I told him if he had waited only a little while longer, you would have got him set free," says Laura. "He said he did not want to wait."

"He is a fool and we are well rid of him," says Braggioni, reaching for his hat.

He goes away. Laura knows his mood has changed, she will not see him any more for a while. He will send word when he needs her to go on errands into strange streets, to speak to the strange faces that will appear, like clay masks with the power of human speech, to mutter their thanks to Braggioni for his help. Now she is free, and she thinks, I must run while there is time. But she does not go.

Braggioni enters his own house where for a month his wife has spent many hours every night weeping and tangling her hair upon her pillow. She is weeping now, and she weeps more at the sight of him, the cause of all her sorrows. He looks about the room. Nothing is changed, the smells are good and familiar, he is well acquainted with the woman who comes toward him with no reproach except grief on her face. He says to her tenderly: "You are so good, please don't cry any more, you dear good creature." She says, "Are you tired, my angel? Sit here and I will wash your feet." She brings a bowl of water, and kneeling, unlaces his shoes, and when from her knees she raises her sad eyes under her blackened lids, he is sorry for everything, and bursts into tears. "Ah, yes, I am hungry, I am tired, let us eat something together," he says, between sobs. His wife leans her head on his arm and says, "Forgive me!" and this time he is refreshed by the solemn, endless rain of her tears.

Laura takes off her serge dress and puts on a white linen nightgown and goes to bed. She turns her head a little to one side, and lying still, reminds herself that it is time to sleep. Numbers tick in her brain like little clocks, soundless doors close of themselves around her. If you would sleep, you must not remember anything, the children will say tomorrow, good morning, my teacher, the poor prisoners who come every day bringing flowers to their jailor. 1-2-3-4-5—it is monstrous to confuse love with revolution, night with day, life with death—ah, Eugenio!

The tolling of the midnight bell is a signal, but what does it mean? Get up, Laura, and follow me: come out of your sleep, out of your bed, out of this strange house. What are you doing in this house? Without a word, without fear she rose and reached for Eugenio's hand, but he eluded her with a sharp, sly smile and drifted away. This is not all, you shall see—Murderer, he said, follow me, I will show you a new country, but it is far away and we must hurry. No, said Laura, not unless you take my hand, no; and she clung first to the stair rail and then to the topmost branch of the Judas tree that bent down slowly and set her upon the earth, and then to the rocky ledge of a cliff, and then to the jagged wave of a sea that was not water but a desert of crumbling stone. Where are you taking me, she asked in wonder but without fear. To death, and it is a long way off, and we must hurry, said Eugenio. No, said Laura, not unless you take my hand. Then eat these flowers, poor prisoner, said Eugenio in a voice of pity, take and eat: and from the Judas tree he stripped the warm bleeding flowers, and held them to her lips. She saw that his hand was fleshless, a cluster of small white petrified branches, and his eye sockets were without light, but she ate the flowers greedily for they satisfied both hunger and thirst. Murderer! said Eugenio, and Cannibal! This is my body and my blood. Laura cried No! and at the sound of her own voice, she awoke trembling, and was afraid to sleep again.

[1930]

For Thought

Porter has placed her young heroine, Laura, in the unsettled Mexico of the 1920s. The slight action deals with the revolutionary leader Braggioni, now gone complacent and cynical, and his unsuccessful siege upon her virtue. Laura is torn between her youthful fervor and the unavoidable messiness of humanity. She also struggles between her virginal self-esteem and her desire for a powerful emotional release. Finally, Porter is most interested in the girl's sensitive, if confused, exploration of her own internal psychic landscape.

For Discussion

1. What is Laura's emotional state at the beginning of the story? What is it at the end of the story?
2. How is Braggioni's name ironically suggestive?
3. How are his size and shape ironically symbolic?
4. What does Braggioni mean when he says, "I am tempted to forgive you for being a *gringa, gringita*?"
5. How is Laura's style of dress symbolic?
6. Of what is Braggioni's attire symbolic?
7. What does the business about Laura's trafficking with the Roumanian and Polish agitators establish?
8. What is the significance of the episode involving the Captain?
9. What is ironic about the stoicism Laura prides herself in?
10. As Laura listens to Braggioni play and sing, what is the structural purpose of the long section analyzing Braggioni's nature?
11. How is Laura's nightmare related to the theme of the story?
12. Does Laura gain any insight? To what extent?

Katherine Anne Porter
The Jilting of Granny Weatherall

She flicked her wrist neatly out of Doctor Harry's pudgy careful fingers and pulled the sheet up to her chin. The brat ought to be in knee breeches. Doctoring around the country with spectacles on his nose! "Get along now, take your schoolbooks and go. There's nothing wrong with me."

Doctor Harry spread a warm paw like a cushion on her forehead where the forked green vein danced and made her eyelids twitch. "Now, now, be a good girl, and we'll have you up in no time."

"That's no way to speak to a woman nearly eighty years old just because she's down. I'd have you respect your elders, young man."

"Well, Missy, excuse me." Doctor Harry patted her cheek. "But I've got to warn you, haven't I? You're a marvel, but you must be careful or you're going to be good and sorry."

"Don't tell me what I'm going to be. I'm on my feet now, morally speaking. It's Cornelia. I had to go to bed to get rid of her."

Her bones felt loose, and floated around in her skin, and Doctor Harry floated like a balloon around the foot of the bed. He floated and pulled down his waistcoat and swung his glasses on a cord. "Well, stay where you are, it certainly can't hurt you."

"Get along and doctor your sick," said Granny Weatherall. "Leave a well woman alone. I'll call for you when I want you. . . . Where were you forty years ago when I pulled through milk-leg and double pneumonia? You weren't even born. Don't let Cornelia lead you on," she shouted, because Doctor Harry appeared to float up to the ceiling and out. "I pay my own bills, and I don't throw my money away on nonsense!"

She meant to wave good-by, but it was too much trouble. Her eyes closed of themselves, it was like a dark curtain drawn around the bed. The pillow rose and floated under her, pleasant as a hammock in a light wind. She listened to the leaves rustling outside the window. No, somebody was swishing newspapers: no, Cornelia and Doctor Harry were whispering together. She leaped broad awake, thinking they whispered in her ear.

"She was never like this, *never* like

this!" "Well, what can we expect?" "Yes, eighty years old. . . ."

Well, and what if she was? She still had ears. It was like Cornelia to whisper around doors. She always kept things secret in such a public way. She was always being tactful and kind. Cornelia was dutiful; that was the trouble with her. Dutiful and good: "So good and dutiful," said Granny, "that I'd like to spank her." She saw herself spanking Cornelia and making a fine job of it.

"What'd you say, Mother?"

Granny felt her face tying up in hard knots.

"Can't a body think, I'd like to know?"

"I thought you might want something."

"I do. I want a lot of things. First off, go away and don't whisper."

She lay and drowsed, hoping in her sleep that the children would keep out and let her rest a minute. It had been a long day. Not that she was tired. It was always pleasant to snatch a minute now and then. There was always so much to be done, let me see: tomorrow.

Tomorrow was far away and there was nothing to trouble about. Things were finished somehow when the time came; thank God there was always a little margin over for peace: then a person could spread out the plan of life and tuck in the edges orderly. It was good to have everything clean and folded away, with the hair brushes and tonic bottles sitting straight on the white embroidered linen: the day started without fuss and the pantry shelves laid out with rows of jelly glasses and brown jugs and white stone-china jars with blue whirligigs and words painted on them: coffee, tea, sugar, ginger, cinnamon, allspice: and the bronze clock with the lion on top nicely dusted off. The dust that lion could collect in twenty-four hours! The box in the attic with all those letters tied up, well, she'd have to go through that tomorrow. All those letters—George's letters and John's letters and her letters to them both—lying around for the children to find afterwards made her uneasy. Yes, that would be tomorrow's business. No use to let them know how silly she had been once.

While she was rummaging around she found death in her mind and it felt clammy and unfamiliar. She had spent so much time preparing for death there was no need for bringing it up again. Let it take care of itself now. When she was sixty she had felt very old, finished, and went around making farewell trips to see her children and grandchildren, with a secret in her mind: This is the very last of your mother, children! Then she made her will and came down with a long fever. That was all just a notion like a lot of other things, but it was lucky too, for she had once for all got over the idea of dying for a long time. Now she couldn't be worried. She hoped she had better sense now. Her father had lived to be one hundred and two years old and had drunk a noggin of strong hot toddy on his last birthday. He told the reporters it was his daily habit, and he owed his long life to that. He had made quite a scandal and was very pleased about it. She believed she'd just plague Cornelia a little.

"Cornelia! Cornelia!" No footsteps, but a sudden hand on her cheek. "Bless you, where have you been?"

"Here, Mother."

"Well, Cornelia, I want a noggin of hot toddy."

"Are you cold, darling?"

"I'm chilly, Cornelia. Lying in bed stops the circulation. I must have told you that a thousand times."

Well, she could just hear Cornelia telling her husband that Mother was getting a little childish and they'd have to humor her. The thing that most annoyed her was that Cornelia thought she was deaf, dumb, and blind. Little hasty glances and tiny gestures tossed around her and over her head saying, "Don't cross her, let her have her way, she's eighty years old," and she sitting there as if she lived in a thin glass cage. Sometimes Granny almost made up her mind to pack up and move back to her own house where nobody could remind her every minute that she was old. Wait, wait, Cornelia, till your own children whisper behind your back!

In her day she had kept a better house and had got more work done. She wasn't too old yet for Lydia to be driving eighty miles for advice when one of the children jumped the track, and Jimmy still dropped in and talked things over: "Now, Mammy, you've a good business head, I want to know what you think of this? . . ." Old. Cornelia couldn't change the furniture around without asking. Little things, little things! They had been so sweet when they were little. Granny wished the old days were back again with the children young and everything to be done over. It had been a hard pull, but not too much for her. When she thought of all the food she had cooked, and all the clothes she had cut and sewed, and all the gardens she had made—well, the children showed it. There they were, made out of her, and they couldn't get away from that. Sometimes she wanted to see John again and point to them and say, Well, I didn't do so badly, did I? But that would have to wait. That was for tomorrow. She used to think of him as a man, but now all the children were older than their father, and he would be a child beside her if she saw him now. It seemed strange and there was something wrong in the idea. Why, he couldn't possibly recognize her. She had fenced in a hundred acres once, digging the post holes herself and clamping the wires with just a negro boy to help. That changed a woman. John would be looking for a young woman with the peaked Spanish comb in her hair and the painted fan. Digging post holes changed a woman. Riding country roads in the winter when women had their babies was another thing: sitting up nights with sick horses and sick negroes and sick children and hardly ever losing one. John, I hardly ever lost one of them! John would see that in a minute, that would be something he could understand, she wouldn't have to explain anything!

It made her feel like rolling up her sleeves and putting the whole place to rights again. No matter if Cornelia was determined to be everywhere at once, there were a great many things left undone on this place. She would start tomorrow and do them. It was good to be strong enough for everything, even if all you made melted and changed and slipped under your hands, so that by the time you finished you almost forgot what you were working for. What was it I set out to do? she asked herself intently, but she could not remember. A fog rose over the valley, she saw it marching across the creek swallowing the trees and moving up the hill like an army of ghosts. Soon it would be at the near edge of the orchard, and then it was time to go in and light the lamps. Come in, children, don't stay out in the night air.

Lighting the lamps had been beautiful. The children huddled up to her and breathed like little calves waiting at the bars in the twilight. Their eyes followed the match and watched the flame rise and settle in a blue curve, then they moved away from her. The lamp was lit, they didn't have to be scared and hang on to mother any more. Never, never, never more. God, for all my life I thank Thee. Without Thee, my God, I could never have done it. Hail, Mary, full of grace.

I want you to pick all the fruit this year and see that nothing is wasted. There's always someone who can use it. Don't let good things rot for want of using. You waste life when you waste good food. Don't let things get lost. It's bitter to lose things. Now, don't let me get to thinking, not when I am tired and taking a little nap before supper. . . .

The pillow rose about her shoulders and pressed against her heart and the memory was being squeezed out of it: oh, push down the pillow, somebody: it would smother her if she tried to hold it. Such a fresh breeze blowing and such a green day with no threats in it. But he had not come, just the same. What does a woman do when she has put on the white veil and set out the white cake for a man and he doesn't come? She tried to remember. No, I swear he never harmed me but in that. He never harmed me but in that . . . and what if he did? There was the day, the day, but a whirl of dark smoke rose and covered it, crept up and over into the bright field where everything was planted so carefully in orderly rows. That was hell, she knew hell when she saw it. For sixty years she had prayed against remembering him and against losing her soul in the deep pit of hell, and now the two things were mingled in one and the thought of him was a smoky cloud from hell that moved and crept in her head when she had just got rid of Doctor Harry and was trying to rest a minute. Wounded vanity, Ellen, said a sharp voice in the top of her mind. Don't let your wounded vanity get the upper hand of you. Plenty of girls get jilted. You were jilted, weren't you? Then stand up to it. Her eyelids wavered and let in streamers of blue-gray light like tissue paper over her eyes. She must get up and pull the shades down or she'd never sleep. She was in bed again and the shades were not down. How could that happen? Better turn over, hide from the light, sleeping in the light gave you nightmares. "Mother, how do you feel now?" and a stinging wetness on her forehead. But I don't like having my face washed in cold water!

Hapsy? George? Lydia? No, Cornelia, and her features were swollen and full of little puddles. "They're coming, darling, they'll all be here soon." Go wash your face, child, you look funny.

Instead of obeying, Cornelia knelt down and put her head on the pillow. She seemed to be talking but there was no sound. "Well, are you tongue-tied? Whose birthday is it? Are you going to give a party?"

Cornelia's mouth moved urgently in strange shapes. "Don't do that, you bother me, daughter."

"Oh, no, Mother. Oh, no. . . ."

Nonsense. It was strange about children. They disputed your every word. "No what, Cornelia?"

"Here's Doctor Harry."

"I won't see that boy again. He just left five minutes ago."

"That was this morning, Mother. It's night now. Here's the nurse."

"This is Doctor Harry, Mrs. Weatherall. I never saw you look so young and happy!"

"Ah, I'll never be young again—but I'd be happy if they'd let me lie in peace and get rested."

She thought she spoke up loudly, but no one answered. A warm weight on her forehead, a warm bracelet on her wrist, and a breeze went on whispering, trying to tell her something. A shuffle of leaves in the everlasting hand of God, He blew on them and they danced and rattled. "Mother, don't mind, we're going to give you a little hypodermic." "Look here, daughter, how do ants get in this bed? I saw sugar ants yesterday." Did you send for Hapsy too?

It was Hapsy she really wanted. She had to go a long way back through a great many rooms to find Hapsy standing with a baby on her arm. She seemed to herself to be Hapsy also, and the baby on Hapsy's arm was Hapsy and himself and herself, all at once, and there was no surprise in the meeting. Then Hapsy melted from within and turned flimsy as gray gauze and the baby was a gauzy shadow, and Hapsy came up close and said, "I thought you'd never come," and looked at her very searchingly and said, "You haven't changed a bit!" They leaned forward to kiss, when Cornelia began whispering from a long way off, "Oh, is there anything you want to tell me? Is there anything I can do for you?"

Yes, she had changed her mind after sixty years and she would like to see George. I want you to find George. Find him and be sure to tell him I forgot him. I want him to know I had my husband just the same and my children and my house like any other woman. A good house too and a good husband that I loved and fine children out of him. Better than I hoped for even. Tell him I was given back everything he took away and more. Oh, no, oh, God, no, there was something else besides the house and the man and the children. Oh, surely they were not all? What was it? Something not given back. . . . Her breath crowded down under her ribs and grew into a monstrous frightening shape with cutting edges; it bored up into her head, and the agony was unbelievable: Yes, John, get the Doctor now, no more talk, my time has come.

When this one was born it should be the last. The last. It should have been born first, for it was the one she had truly wanted. Everything came in good time. Nothing left out, left over. She was strong, in three days she would be as well as ever. Better. A woman needed milk in her to have her full health.

"Mother, do you hear me?"

"I've been telling you—"

"Mother, Father Connolly's here."

"I went to Holy Communion only last week. Tell him I'm not so sinful as all that."

"Father just wants to speak to you."

He could speak as much as he pleased. It was like him to drop in and inquire about her soul as if it were a teething baby, and then stay on for a cup of tea and a round of cards and gossip. He always had a funny story of some sort, usually about an Irishman who made his little mistakes and confessed them, and the point lay in some absurd thing he would blurt out in the confessional showing his struggles between native piety and original sin. Granny felt easy about her soul. Cornelia, where are your manners? Give Father Connolly a chair. She had her secret comfortable understanding with a few favorite saints who cleared a straight road to God for her. All as surely signed and sealed as the papers for the new Forty Acres. Forever . . . heirs and assigns forever. Since the day the wedding cake was not cut, but thrown out and wasted. The whole bottom dropped out of the world, and there she was blind and sweating with nothing under her feet and the walls falling away. His hand had caught her under the breast, she had not fallen, there was the freshly polished floor with the green rug on it, just as before. He had cursed like a sailor's parrot and said, "I'll kill him for you." Don't lay a hand on him, for my sake leave something to God. "Now, Ellen, you must believe what I tell you. . . ."

So there was nothing, nothing to worry about any more, except sometimes in the night one of the children screamed in a nightmare, and they both hustled out shaking and hunting for the matches and calling, "There, wait a minute, here we are!" John, get the doctor now, Hapsy's time has come. But there was Hapsy standing by the bed in a white cap. "Cornelia, tell Hapsy to take off her cap. I can't see her plain."

Her eyes opened very wide and the room stood out like a picture she had seen somewhere. Dark colors with the shadows rising towards the ceiling in long angles. The tall black dresser gleamed with nothing on it but John's picture, enlarged from a little one, with John's eyes very black when they should have been blue. You never saw him, so how do you know how he looked? But the man insisted the copy was perfect, it was very rich and handsome. For a picture, yes, but it's not my husband. The table by the bed had a linen cover and a candle and a crucifix. The light was blue from Cornelia's silk lampshades. No sort of light at all, just frippery. You had to live forty years with kerosene lamps to appreciate honest electricity. She felt very strong and she saw Doctor Harry with a rosy nimbus around him.

"You look like a saint, Doctor Harry, and I vow that's as near as you'll ever come to it."

"She's saying something."

"I heard you, Cornelia. What's all this carrying-on?"

"Father Connolly's saying—"

Cornelia's voice staggered and bumped like a cart in a bad road. It rounded corners and turned back again and arrived nowhere. Granny stepped up in the cart very lightly and reached for the reins, but a man sat beside her and she knew him by his hands, driving the cart. She did not look in his face, for she knew without seeing, but looked instead down the road where the trees leaned over and bowed to each other and a thousand birds were singing a Mass. She felt like singing too, but she put her hand in the bosom of her dress and pulled out a rosary, and Father Connolly murmured Latin in a very solemn voice and tickled her feet. My God, will you stop that nonsense? I'm a married woman. What if he did run away and leave me to face the priest by myself? I found another a whole world better. I wouldn't have exchanged my husband for anybody except St. Michael himself, and you may tell him that for me with a thank you in the bargain.

Light flashed on her closed eyelids, and a deep roaring shook her. Cornelia, is that lightning? I hear thunder. There's going to be a storm. Close all the windows. Call the children in. . . . "Mother, here we are, all of us." "Is that you, Hapsy?" "Oh, no, I'm Lydia. We drove as fast as we could." Their faces drifted above her, drifted away. The rosary fell out of her hands and Lydia put it back. Jimmy tried to help, their hands fumbled together, and Granny closed two fingers around Jimmy's thumb. Beads wouldn't do, it must be something alive. She was so amazed her thoughts ran round and round. So, my dear Lord, this is my death and I wasn't even thinking about it. My children have come to see me die. But I can't, it's not time. Oh, I always hated surprises. I wanted to give Cornelia the amethyst set—Cornelia, you're to have the amethyst set, but Hapsy's to wear it when she wants, and, Doctor Harry, do shut up. Nobody sent for you. Oh, my dear Lord, do wait a minute. I meant to do something about the Forty Acres, Jimmy doesn't need it and Lydia will later on, with that worthless husband of hers. I meant to finish the altar cloth and send six bottles of wine to Sister Borgia for her dyspepsia. I want to send six bottles of wine to Sister Borgia, Father Connolly, now don't let me forget.

Cornelia's voice made short turns and tilted over and crashed. "Oh, Mother, oh, Mother, oh, Mother. . . ."

"I'm not going, Cornelia. I'm taken by surprise. I can't go."

You'll see Hapsy again. What about her? "I thought you'd never come." Granny made a long journey outward, looking for Hapsy. What if I don't find her? What then? Her heart sank down and down, there was no bottom to death, she couldn't come to the end of it. The blue light from Cornelia's lampshade drew into a tiny point in the center of her brain, it flickered and winked like an eye, quietly it fluttered and dwindled. Granny lay curled down within herself, amazed and watchful, staring at the point of light that was herself; her body was now only a deeper mass of shadow in an endless darkness and this darkness would curl around the light and swallow it up. God, give a sign!

For the second time there was no sign. Again no bridegroom and the priest in the house. She could not remember any other sorrow because this grief wiped them all away. Oh, no, there's nothing more cruel than this—I'll never forgive it. She stretched herself with a deep breath and blew out the light.

[1944]

For Thought

With "The Jilting of Granny Weatherall," Porter has written an unusually fresh and vivid narrative of the last hours of a dying woman. Her lively memories contrast sharply with her physical weakness and the sadness evidently felt by her relatives. Through it all runs the deep resentment and shame that a suitor had failed to appear for their wedding 60 years before. Porter has chosen an unusual twist to the old saying, "Hell hath no fury like a woman scorn'd."

For Discussion

1. How is the title ironic? What is suggested by the play of words on her name, "Weather-all?"
2. What point of view has Porter chosen to tell the story from and why?
3. How has Porter characterized Granny Weatherall? What thoughts are uppermost in her mind? Consider the influence of religion on her attitudes toward the past.
4. What use does Porter make of light-dark symbolism? Consider matters of vision as well as light-giving objects.
5. What contrasts does Porter create between the constricted time and place of the story and the range of Granny's memories?

Katherine Anne Porter
Theft

She had the purse in her hand when she came in. Standing in the middle of the floor, holding her bathrobe around her and trailing a damp towel in one hand, she surveyed the immediate past and remembered everything clearly. Yes, she had opened the flap and spread it out on the bench after she had dried the purse with her handkerchief.

She had intended to take the Elevated, and naturally she looked in her purse to make certain she had the fare, and was pleased to find forty cents in the coin envelope. She was going to pay her own fare, too, even if Camilo did have the habit of seeing her up the steps and dropping a nickel in the machine before he gave the turnstile a little push and sent her through it with a bow. Camilo by a series of compromises had managed to make effective a fairly complete set of smaller courtesies, ignoring the larger and more troublesome ones. She had walked with him to the station in a pouring rain, because she knew he was almost as poor as she was, and when he insisted on a taxi, she was firm and said, "You know it simply will not do." He was wearing a new hat of a pretty biscuit shade, for it never occurred to him to buy anything of a practical color; he had put it on for the first time and the rain was spoiling it. She kept thinking, "But this is dreadful, where will he get another?" She compared it with Eddie's hats that always seemed to be precisely seven years old and as if they had been quite purposely left out in the rain, and yet they sat with a careless and incidental rightness on Eddie. But Camilo was far different; if he wore a shabby hat it would be merely shabby on him, and he would lose his spirits over it. If she had not feared Camilo would take it badly, for he insisted on the practice of his little ceremonies up to the point he had fixed for them, she would have said to him as they left Thora's house, "Do go home. I can surely reach the station by myself."

"It is written that we must be rained upon tonight," said Camilo, "so let it be together."

At the foot of the platform stairway she staggered slightly—they were both nicely set up on Thora's cocktails—and said: "At least, Camilo, do me the favor not to climb these stairs in your present state, since for you it is only a matter of coming down again at once, and you'll certainly break your neck."

He made three quick bows, he was Spanish, and leaped off through the rainy darkness. She stood watching him, for he was a very graceful young man, thinking that tomorrow morning he would gaze soberly at his spoiled hat and soggy shoes and possibly associate her with his misery. As she watched, he stopped at the far corner and took off his hat and hid it under his overcoat. She felt she had betrayed him by seeing, because he would have been humiliated if he thought she even suspected him of trying to save his hat.

Roger's voice sounded over her shoulder above the clang of the rain falling on the stairway shed, wanting to know what she was doing out in the rain at this time of night, and did she take herself for a duck? His long, imperturbable face was streaming with water, and he tapped a bulging spot on the breast of his buttoned-up overcoat: "Hat," he said. "Come on, let's take a taxi."

She settled back against Roger's arm which he laid around her shoulders, and with the gesture they exchanged a glance full of long amiable associations, then she looked through the window at the rain changing the shapes of everything, and the colors. The taxi dodged in and out between the pillars of the Elevated, skidding slightly on every curve, and she said: "The more it skids the calmer I feel, so I really must be drunk."

"You must be," said Roger. "This bird is a homicidal maniac, and I could do with a cocktail myself this minute."

They waited on the traffic at Fortieth Street and Sixth Avenue, and three boys walked before the nose of the taxi. Under the globes of light they were cheerful scarecrows, all very thin and all wearing very seedy snappy-cut suits and gay neckties. They were not very sober either, and they stood for a moment wobbling in front of the car, and there was an argument going on among them. They leaned toward each other as if they were getting ready to sing, and the first one said: "When I get married it won't be jus' for getting married, I'm gonna marry for *love*, see?" and the second one said, "Aw, gwan and tell that stuff to *her*, why n't yuh?" and the third one gave a kind of hoot, and said, "Hell, dis guy? Wot the hell's he got?" and the first one said: "Aaah, shurrup yuh mush, I got plenty." Then they all squealed and scrambled across the street beating the first one on the back and pushing him around.

"Nuts," commented Roger, "pure nuts."

Two girls went skittering by in short transparent raincoats, one green, one red, their heads tucked against the drive of the rain. One of them was saying to the other, "Yes, I know all about *that*. But what about me? You're always so sorry for *him* . . ." and they ran on with their little pelican legs flashing back and forth.

The taxi backed up suddenly and leaped forward again, and after a while Roger said: "I had a letter from Stella today, and she'll be home on the twenty-sixth, so I suppose she's made up her mind and it's all settled."

"I had a sort of letter today too," she said, "making up my mind for me. I think it is time for you and Stella to do something definite."

When the taxi stopped on the corner of West Fifty-third Street, Roger said, "I've just enough if you'll add ten cents," so she opened her purse and gave him a dime, and he said, "That's beautiful, that purse."

"It's a birthday present," she told him, "and I like it. How's your show coming?"

"Oh, still hanging on, I guess. I don't go near the place. Nothing sold yet. I mean to keep right on the way I'm going and they can take it or leave it. I'm through with the argument."

"It's absolutely a matter of holding out, isn't it?"

"Holding out's the tough part."

"Good night, Roger."

"Good night, you should take aspirin and push yourself into a tub of hot water, you look as though you're catching cold."

"I will."

With the purse under her arm she went upstairs, and on the first landing Bill heard her step and poked his head out with his hair tumbled and his eyes red, and he said: "For Christ's sake, come in and have a drink with me. I've had some bad news."

"You're perfectly sopping," said Bill, looking at her drenched feet. They had two drinks, while Bill told how the director had thrown his play out after the cast had been picked over twice, and had gone through three rehearsals. "I said to him, 'I didn't say it was a masterpiece, I said it would make a good show.' And he said, 'It just doesn't *play,* do you see? It needs a doctor.' So I'm stuck, absolutely stuck," said Bill, on the edge of weeping again. "I've been crying," he told her, "in my cups." And he went on to ask her if she realized his wife was ruining him with her extravagance. "I send her ten dollars every week of my unhappy life, and I don't really have to. She threatens to jail me if I don't, but she can't do it. God, let her try it after the way she treated me! She's no right to alimony and she knows it. She keeps on saying she's got to have it for the baby and I keep on sending it because I can't bear to see anybody suffer. So I'm way behind on the piano and the victrola, both—"

"Well, this is a pretty rug, anyhow," she said.

Bill stared at it and blew his nose. "I got it at Ricci's for ninety-five dollars," he said. "Ricci told me it once belonged to Marie Dressler, and cost fifteen hundred dollars, but there's a burnt place on it, under the divan. Can you beat that?"

"No," she said. She was thinking about her empty purse and that she could not possibly expect a check for her latest review for another three days, and her arrangement with the basement restaurant could not last much longer if she did not pay something on account. "It's no time to speak of it," she said, "but I've been hoping you would have by now that fifty dollars you promised for my scene in the third act. Even if it doesn't play. You were to pay me for the work anyhow out of your advance."

"Weeping Jesus," said Bill, "you, too?" He gave a loud sob, or hiccough, in his moist handkerchief. "Your stuff was no better than mine, after all. Think of that."

"But you got something for it," she said. "Seven hundred dollars."

Bill said, "Do me a favor, will you? Have another drink and forget about it. I can't, you know I can't, I would if I could, but you know the fix I'm in."

"Let it go, then," she found herself saying almost in spite of herself. She had meant to be quite firm about it. They drank again without speaking, and she went to her apartment on the floor above.

There, she now remembered distinctly, she had taken the letter out of the purse before she spread the purse out to dry.

She had sat down and read the letter over again: but there were phrases that insisted on being read many times, they had a life of their own separate from the others, and when she tried to read past and around them, they moved with the movement of her eyes, and she could not escape them . . . "thinking about you more than I mean to . . . yes, I even talk about you . . . why were you so anxious to destroy . . . even if I could see you now I would not . . . not worth all this abominable . . . the end . . ."

Carefully she tore the letter into narrow strips, and touched a lighted match to them in the coal grate.

Early the next morning she was in the bathtub when the janitress knocked and then came in, calling out that she wished to examine the radiators before she started the furnace going for the winter. After moving about the room for a few minutes, the janitress went out, closing the door very sharply.

She came out of the bathroom to get a cigarette from the package in the purse.

The purse was gone. She dressed and made coffee, and sat by the window while she drank it. Certainly the janitress had taken the purse, and certainly it would be impossible to get it back without a great deal of ridiculous excitement. Then let it go. With this decision of her mind, there rose coincidentally in her blood a deep almost murderous anger. She set the cup carefully in the center of the table, and walked steadily downstairs, three long flights and a short hall and a steep short flight into the basement, where the janitress, her face streaked with coal dust, was shaking up the furnace. "Will you please give me back my purse? There isn't any money in it. It was a present, and I don't want to lose it."

The janitress turned without straightening up and peered at her with hot flickering eyes, a red light from the furnace reflected in them. "What do you mean, your purse?"

"The gold cloth purse you took from the wooden bench in my room," she said. "I must have it back."

"Before God I never laid eyes on your purse, and that's the holy truth," said the janitress.

"Oh, well then, keep it," she said, but in a very bitter voice; "keep it if you want it so much." And she walked away.

She remembered how she had never locked a door in her life, on some principle of rejection in her that made her uncomfortable in the ownership of things, and her paradoxical boast before the warnings of her friends, that she had never lost a penny by theft; and she had been pleased with the bleak humility of this concrete example designed to illustrate and justify a certain fixed, otherwise baseless and general faith which ordered the movements of her life without regard to her will in the matter.

In this moment she felt that she had been robbed of an enormous number of valuable things, whether material or intangible: things lost or broken by her own fault, things she had forgotten and left in houses when she moved: books borrowed from her and not returned, journeys she had planned and had not made, words she had waited to hear spoken to her and had not heard, and the words she had meant to answer with; bitter alternatives and intolerable substitutes worse than nothing, and yet inescapable: the long patient suffering of dying friendships and the dark inexplicable death of love—all that she had had, and all that she had missed, were lost together, and were twice lost in this landslide of remembered losses.

The janitress was following her upstairs with the purse in her hand and the same deep red fire flickering in her eyes. The janitress thrust the purse towards her while they were still a half dozen steps apart, and said: "Don't never tell on me. I musta been crazy. I get crazy in the head sometimes, I swear I do. My son can tell you."

She took the purse after a moment, and the janitress went on: "I got a niece who is going on seventeen, and she's a nice girl and I thought I'd give it to her. She needs a pretty purse. I musta been crazy; I thought maybe you wouldn't mind, you leave things around and don't seem to notice much."

She said: "I missed this because it was a present to me from someone . . ."

The janitress said: "He'd get you another if you lost this one. My niece is young and needs pretty things, we oughta give the young ones a chance. She's got young men after her maybe will want to marry her. She oughta have nice things. She needs them bad right now. You're a grown woman, you've had your chance, you ought to know how it is!"

She held the purse out to the janitress saying: "You don't know what you're talking about. Here, take it, I've changed my mind. I really don't want it."

The janitress looked up at her with hatred and said: "I don't want it either now. My niece is young and pretty, she don't need fixin' up to be pretty, she's young and pretty anyhow! I guess you need it worse than she does!"

"It wasn't really yours in the first place," she said, turning away. "You mustn't talk as if I had stolen it from you."

"It's not from me, it's from her you're stealing it," said the janitress, and went back downstairs.

She laid the purse on the table and sat down with the cup of chilled coffee, and thought: I was right not to be afraid of any thief but myself, who will end by leaving me nothing.

[1930]

For Thought

Porter has chosen a group of theater people in New York for her characters. All of them are struggling artists and writers, except for the janitress. Rather than portray the romance and glitter that the public associates with playacting, the author depicts the rather humdrum difficulties people have when dealing with disappointment and humiliation. The theft of the unnamed heroine's purse is a poignant hint to her that she has only herself to depend upon.

For Discussion

1. What do the characters in the story have in common?
2. How does Porter characterize her unnamed heroine? How do people's treatment of her enhance the reader's impression of her? Is she sympathetic?
3. How does Porter foreshadow the theft of the purse and her heroine's reaction to its loss?
4. From what point of view is the story told? Why is it effective?
5. What are the apparent and actual types of conflict that break out between the heroine and the janitress, as well as within the mind of the heroine?
6. How does the theme of the story develop from the various reminders of loss received by the heroine?

J. F. Powers
The Valiant Woman

They had come to the dessert in a dinner that was a shambles. "Well, John," Father Nulty said, turning away from Mrs. Stoner and to Father Firman, long gone silent at his own table. "You've got the bishop coming for confirmations next week."

"Yes," Mrs. Stoner cut in, "and for dinner. And if he don't eat any more than he did last year—"

Father Firman, in a rare moment, faced it. "Mrs. Stoner, the bishop is not well. You know that."

"And after I fixed that fine dinner and all." Mrs. Stoner pouted in Father Nulty's direction.

"I wouldn't feel bad about it, Mrs. Stoner," Father Nulty said. "He never eats much anywhere."

"It's funny. And that new Mrs. Allers said he ate just fine when he was there," Mrs. Stoner argued, and then spit out, "but she's a damned liar!"

Father Nulty, unsettled but trying not to show it, said, "Who's Mrs. Allers?"

"She's at Holy Cross," Mrs. Stoner said.

"She's the housekeeper," Father Firman added, thinking Mrs. Stoner made it sound as though Mrs. Allers were the pastor there.

"I swear I don't know what to do about the dinner this year," Mrs. Stoner said.

Father Firman moaned. "Just do as you've always done, Mrs. Stoner."

"Huh! And have it all to throw out! Is that any way to do?"

"Is there any dessert?" Father Firman asked coldly.

Mrs. Stoner leaped up from the table and bolted into the kitchen, mumbling. She came back with a birthday cake. She plunged it in the center of the table. She found a big wooden match in her apron pocket and thrust it at Father Firman.

"I don't like this bishop," she said. "I never did. And the way he went and cut poor Ellen Kennedy out of Father Doolin's will!"

She went back into the kitchen.

"Didn't they talk a lot of filth about Doolin and the housekeeper?" Father Nulty asked.

"I should think they did," Father Firman said. "All because he took her to the movies on Sunday night. After he died and the bishop cut her out of the will, though I hear he gives her a pension privately, they talked about the bishop."

"I don't like this bishop at all," Mrs. Stoner said, appearing with a cake knife. "Bishop Doran—there was the man!"

"We know," Father Firman said. "All man and all priest."

"He did know real estate," Father Nulty said.

Father Firman struck the match.

"Not on the chair!" Mrs. Stoner cried, too late.

Father Firman set the candle burning—it was suspiciously large and yellow, like a blessed one, but he could not be sure. They watched the fluttering flame.

"I'm forgetting the lights!" Mrs. Stoner said, and got up to turn them off. She went into the kitchen again.

The priests had a moment of silence in the candle-light.

"Happy birthday, John," Father Nulty said softly, "Is it fifty-nine you are?"

"As if you didn't know, Frank," Father Firman said, "and you the same but one."

Father Nulty smiled, the old gold of his incisors shining in the flickering light, his collar whiter in the dark, and raised his glass of water, which would have been wine or better in the bygone days, and toasted Father Firman.

"Many of 'em, John."

"Blow it out," Mrs. Stoner said, returning to the room. She waited by the light switch for Father Firman to blow out the candle.

Mrs. Stoner, who ate no desserts, began to clear the dishes into the kitchen, and the priests, finishing their cake and coffee in a hurry, went to sit in the study.

Father Nulty offered a cigar.

"John?"

"My ulcers, Frank."

"Ah, well, you're better off." Father Nulty lit the cigar and crossed his long black legs. "Fish Frawley has got him a Filipino, John. Did you hear?"

Father Firman leaned forward, interested. "He got rid of the woman he had?"

"He did. It seems she snooped."

"Snooped, eh?"

"She did. And gossiped. Fish introduced two town boys to her, said, 'Would you think these boys were my nephews?' That's all, and the next week the paper had it that his two nephews were visiting him from Erie. After that, he let her believe he was going East to see his parents, though both are dead. The paper carried the story. Fish returned and made a sermon out of it. Then he got the Filipino."

Father Firman squirmed with pleasure in his chair. "That's like Fish, Frank. He can do that." He stared at the tips of his fingers bleakly. "You could never get a Filipino to come to a place like this."

"Probably not," Father Nulty said. "Fish is pretty close to Minneapolis. Ah, say, do you remember the trick he played on us all in Marmion Hall!"

"That I'll not forget!" Father Firman's eyes remembered. "Getting up New Year's morning and finding the toilet seats all painted!"

"*Happy Circumcision*! Hah!" Father Nulty had a coughing fit.

When he had got himself together again, a mosquito came and sat on his wrist. He watched it a moment before bringing his heavy hand down. He raised his hand slowly, viewed the dead mosquito, and sent it spinning with a plunk of his middle finger.

"Only the female bites," he said.

"I didn't know that," Father Firman said.

"Ah, yes . . ."

Mrs. Stoner entered the study and sat down with some sewing—Father Firman's black socks.

She smiled pleasantly at Father Nulty. "And what do you think of the atom bomb, Father?"

"Not much," Father Nulty said.

Mrs. Stoner had stopped smiling. Father Firman yawned.

Mrs. Stoner served up another: "Did you read about this communist convert, Father?"

"He's been in the Church before," Father nulty said, "and so it's not a conversion, Mrs. Stoner."

"No? Well, I already got him down on my list of Monsignor's converts."

"It's better than a conversion, Mrs. Stoner, for there is more rejoicing in heaven over the return of . . . uh, he that was lost, Mrs. Stoner, is found."

"And that congresswoman, Father?"

"Yes. A convert—she."

"And Henry Ford's grandson, Father. I got him down."

"Yes, to be sure."

Father Firman yawned, this time audibly, and held his jaw.

"But he's one only by marriage, Father," Mrs. Stoner said. "I always say you got to watch those kind."

"Indeed you do, but a convert nonetheless, Mrs. Stoner. Remember, Cardinal Newman himself was one."

Mrs. Stoner was unimpressed. "I see where Henry Ford's making steering wheels out of soybeans, Father."

"I didn't see that."

"I read it in the Reader's Digest or some place."

"Yes, well . . ." Father Nulty rose and held his hand out to Father Firman. "John," he said. "It's been good."

"I hear Hirohito's next," Mrs. Stoner said, returning to converts.

"Let's wait and see, Mrs. Stoner," Father Nulty said.

The priests walked to the door.

"You know where I live, John."

"Yes. Come again, Frank. Good night."

Father Firman watched Father Nulty go down the walk to his car at the curb. He hooked the screen door and turned off the porch light. He hesitated at the foot of the stairs, suddenly moved to go to bed. But he went back into the study.

"Phew!" Mrs. Stoner said. "I thought he'd never go. Here it is after eight o'clock."

Father Firman sat down in his rocking chair. "I don't see him often," he said.

"I give up!" Mrs. Stoner exclaimed, flinging the holey socks upon the horsehair sofa. "I'd swear you had a nail in your shoe."

"I told you I looked."

"Well, you ought to look again. And cut your toenails, why don't you? Haven't I got enough to do?"

Father Firman scratched in his coat pocket for a pill, found one, swallowed it. He let his head sink back against the chair and closed his eyes. He could hear her moving about the room, making the preparations; and how he knew them—the fumbling in the drawer for a pencil with a point, the rip of the page from his daily calendar, and finally the leg of the card table sliding up against his leg.

He opened his eyes. She yanked the floor lamp alongside the table, setting the bead fringe tinkling on the shade, and pulled up her chair on the other side. She sat down and smiled at him for the first time that day. Now she was happy.

She swept up the cards and began to shuffle with the abandoned virtuosity of an old riverboat gambler, standing them on end, fanning them out, whirling them through her fingers, dancing them halfway up her arms, cracking the whip over them. At last they lay before him tamed into a neat deck.

"Cut?"

"Go ahead," he said. She liked to go first.

She gave him her faint, avenging smile and drew a card, cast it aside for another which he thought must be an ace from the way she clutched it face down.

She was getting all the cards, as usual, and would have been invincible if she had possessed his restraint and if her cunning had been of a higher order. He knew a few things about leading and lying back that she would never learn. Her strategy was attack, forever attack, with one baffling departure: she might sacrifice certain tricks as expendable if only she could have the last ones, the heartbreaking ones, if she could slap them down one after another, shatteringly.

She played for blood, no bones about it, but for her there was no other way; it was her nature, as it was the lion's, and for this reason he found her ferocity pardonable, more a defect of the flesh, venial, while his own trouble was all in the will, mortal. He did not sweat and pray over each card as she must, but he did keep an eye out for reneging and demanded a cut now and then just to aggravate her, and he was always secretly hoping for aces.

With one card left in her hand, the telltale trick coming next, she delayed playing it, showing him first the smile, the preview of defeat. She laid it on the table—so! She held one more trump than he had reasoned possible. Had she palmed it from somewhere? No, she would not go that far; that would not be fair, was worse than reneging, which so easily and often happened accidentally, and she believed in being fair. Besides he had been watching her.

God smote the vines with hail, the sycamore trees with frost, and offered up the flocks to the lightning—but Mrs. Stoner! What a cross Father Firman had from God in Mrs. Stoner! There were other housekeepers as bad, no doubt, walking the rectories of the world, yes, but . . . yes. He could name one and maybe two priests who were worse off. One, maybe two. Cronin. His scraggly blonde of sixty—take her, with her everlasting banging on the grand piano, the gift of the pastor; her proud talk about the goiter operation at the Mayo Brothers', also a gift; her honking the parish Buick at passing strange priests because they were all in the game together. She was worse. She was something to keep the home fires burning. Yes sir. And Cronin said she was not a bad person really, but what was he? He was quite a freak himself.

For that matter, could anyone say that Mrs. Stoner was a bad person? No. He could not say it himself, and he was no freak. She had her points, Mrs. Stoner. She was clean. And though she cooked poorly, could not play the organ, would not take up the collection in an emergency, and went to card parties, and told all—even so, she was clean. She washed everything. Sometimes her underwear hung down beneath her dress like a paratrooper's pants, but it and everything she touched was clean. She washed constantly. She was clean.

She had her other points, to be sure—her faults, you might say. She snooped—no mistake about it—but it was not snooping for snooping's sake; she had a reason. She did other things, always with a reason. She overcharged on rosaries and prayer books, but that was for the sake of the poor. She censored the pamphlet rack, but that was to prevent scandal. She pried into the baptismal and matrimonial records, but there was no other way if Father was out, and in this way she had once uncovered a bastard and flushed him out of the rectory, but that was the perverted decency of the times. She held her nose over bad marriages in the presence of the victims, but that was her sorrow and came from having her husband buried in a mine. And he had caught her telling a bewildered young couple that there was only one good reason for their wanting to enter into a mixed marriage—the child had to have a name, and that—that was what?

She hid his books, kept him from smoking, picked his friends (usually the pastors of her colleagues), bawled out people for calling after dark, had no humor, except at cards, and then it was grim, very grim, and she sat hatchet-faced every morning at Mass. But she went to Mass, which was all that kept the church from being empty some mornings. She did annoying things all day long. She said annoying things into the night. She said she had given him the best years of her life. Had she? Perhaps—for the miner had her only a year. It was too bad, sinfully bad, when he thought of it like that. But all talk of best years and life was nonsense. He had to consider the heart of the matter, the essence. The essence was that housekeepers were hard to get, harder to get than ushers, than willing workers, than organists, than secretaries—yes, harder to get than assistants or vocations.

And she was a *saver*—saved money, saved electricity, saved string, bags, sugar, saved—him. That's what she did. That's what she said she did, and she was right, in a way. In a way, she was usually right. In fact, she was always right—in a way. And you could never get a Filipino to come way out here and live. Not a young one anyway, and he had never seen an old one. Not a Filipino. They liked to dress up and live.

Should he let it drop about Fish having one, just to throw a scare into her, let her know he was doing some thinking? No. It would be a perfect cue for the one about a man needing a woman to look after him. He was not up to that again, not tonight.

Now she was doing what she liked most of all. She was making a grand slam, playing it out card for card, though it was in the bag, prolonging what would have been cut short out of mercy in gentle company. Father Firman knew the agony of losing.

She slashed down the last card, a miserable deuce trump, and did in the hapless king of hearts he had been saving.

"Skunked you!"

She was awful in victory. Here was the bitter end of their long day together, the final murderous hour in which all they wanted to say—all he wouldn't and all she couldn't—came out in the cards. Whoever won at honeymoon won the day, slept on the other's scalp, and God alone had to help the loser.

"We've been at it long enough, Mrs. Stoner," he said, seeing her assembling the cards for another round.

"Had enough, huh!"

Father Firman grumbled something.

"No?"

"Yes."

She pulled the table away and left it against the wall for the next time. She went out of the study carrying the socks, content and clucking. He closed his eyes after her and began to get under way in the rocking chair, the nightly trip to nowhere. He could hear her brewing a cup of tea in the kitchen and conversing with the cat. She made her way up the stairs, carrying the tea, followed by the cat, purring.

He waited, rocking out to sea, until she would be sure to be through in the bathroom. Then he got up and locked the front door (she looked after the back door) and loosened his collar going upstairs.

In the bathroom he mixed a glass of antiseptic, always afraid of pyorrhea, and gargled to ward off pharyngitis.

When he turned on the light in his room, the moths and beetles began to batter against the screens, the lighter insects humming. . . .

Yes, and she had the guest room. How did she come to get that? Why wasn't she in the back room, in her proper place? He knew, if he cared to remember. The screen in the back room—it let in mosquitoes, and if it didn't do that she'd love to sleep back there, Father, looking out at the steeple and the blessed cross on top, Father, if it just weren't for the screen, Father. Very well, Mrs. Stoner, I'll get it fixed or fix it myself. Oh, could you now, Father? I could, Mrs. Stoner, and I will. In the meantime you take the guest room. Yes, Father, and thank you, Father, the house ringing with amenities then. Years ago, all that. She was a pie-faced girl then, not really a girl perhaps, but not too old to marry again. But she never had. In fact, he could not remember that she had even tried for a husband since coming to the rectory, but, of course, he could be wrong, not knowing how they went about it. God! God save us! Had she got her wires crossed and mistaken him all these years for that? *That*! Him! Suffering

God! No. That was going too far. That was getting morbid. No. He must not think of that again, ever. No.

But just the same she had got the guest room and she had it yet. Well, did it matter? Nobody ever came to see him any more, nobody to stay overnight anyway, nobody to stay very long . . . not any more. He knew how they laughed at him. He had heard Frank humming all right—before he saw how serious and sad the situation was and took pity—humming. "Wedding Bells Are Breaking Up That Old Gang of Mine." But then they'd always laughed at him for something—for not being an athlete, for wearing glasses, for having kidney trouble . . . and mail coming addressed to Rev. and Mrs. Stoner.

Removing his shirt, he bent over the table to read the volume left open from last night. He read, translating easily, "Eisdem licet cum illis . . . Clerics are allowed to reside only with women about whom there can be no suspicion, either because of a natural bond (as mother, sister, aunt) or of advanced age, combined in both cases with good repute."

Last night he had read it, and many nights before, each time as though this time to find what was missing, to find what obviously was not in the paragraph, his problem considered, a way out. She was not mother, not sister, not aunt, and *advanced* age was a relative term (why, she was younger than he was) and so, eureka, she did not meet the letter of the law—but, alas, how she fulfilled the spirit! And besides it would be a slimy way of handling it after all her years of service. He could not afford to pension her off, either.

He slammed the book shut. He slapped himself fiercely on the back, missing the wily mosquito, and whirled to find it. He took a magazine and folded it into a swatter. Then he saw it—oh, the preternatural cunning of it!—poised in the beard of St. Joseph on the bookcase. He could not hit it there. He teased it away, wanting it to light on the wall, but it knew his thoughts and flew high away. He swung wildly, hoping to stun it, missed, swung back, catching St. Joseph across the neck. The statue fell to the floor and broke.

Mrs. Stoner was panting in the hall outside his door.

"What is it!"

"Mosquitoes!"

"What is it, Father? Are you hurt?"

"Mosquitoes—damn it! And only the female bites!"

Mrs. Stoner, after a moment, said, "Shame on you, Father. She needs the blood for her eggs."

He dropped the magazine and lunged at the mosquito with his bare hand.

She went back to her room, saying, "Pshaw, I thought it was burglars murdering you in your bed."

He lunged again.

[1947]

For Thought

In "The Valiant Woman," Powers uses language to characterize the two main characters. Powers's priest has all the disadvantages of marriage with none of the advantages. He is dominated and intimidated by his housekeeper, Mrs. Stoner. Her aggressive meddling and nagging are a parody of the good wife described in the Bible in Proverbs. Finally, the priest takes his frustration out on a statue of St. Joseph, another alleged victim of female deception.

For Discussion

1. What point of view does Powers adopt?
2. In farce, institutions are satirized with marriage as a favored target, with flat char-

acters who repeat violent, mechanical gestures. What verbal and mechanical repetitions appear in the story?

3. How is the action of the story complicated, brought to a climax, reversed, and resolved?
4. Many readers feel that the central situation of Father Firman resembles a marriage, with all its responsibilities and disadvantages and with none of its compensating pleasures. What factors combine to trap Father Firman into this state?
5. How is the ending of the story ironic?
6. What is the significance of Mrs. Stoner's name?
7. How is Father Firman's name indicative of character?
8. What contrast appears between Father Firman's thoughts and his words?
9. Although Firman's vocation should place a barrier between him and his housekeeper, how does Mrs. Stoner contrive to undermine his self-respect and dignity?
10. Are Mrs. Stoner's faults only a passive "defect of the flesh, venial," as Firman believes, or active "in the will, mortal" as well?
11. How are Mrs. Stoner's traits revealed in loaded language, particularly Powers's early choice of verbs?
12. The "valiant woman" of the title alludes to the Biblical description of a good wife in Proverbs 31, reprinted here for comparison with Powers's story. How are Mrs. Stoner's traits ironically contrasted with these virtues?

    Who shall find a valiant woman? Far from the uttermost coasts is the price of her.

    The heart of her husband trusteth in her, and he shall have no need of spoils.

    She will render him good, and not evil, all the days of her life.

    She hath sought wool and flax, and hath wrought by the counsel of her hands.

    She is like the merchant's ship, she bringeth her bread from afar.

    And she hath risen in the night, and given a prey to her household, and victuals to her maidens.

    She hath considered a field, and bought it: with the fruit of her hands she hath planted a vineyard.

    She hath girded her loins with strength, and hath strengthened her arm.

    She hath tasted and seen that her traffic is good. Her lamp shall not be put out in the night.

    She hath put out her hand to strong things, and her fingers have taken hold of the spindle.

    She hath opened her hand to the needy, and stretched out her hands to the poor.

    She shall not fear for her house in the cold of snow, for all her domestics are clothed with double garments.

    She hath made for herself clothing of tapestry: fine linen and purple are her covering.

    Her husband is honorable in the gates, when he sitteth among the senators of the land.

    She made fine linen, and sold it and delivered a girdle to the Canaanite.

    Strength and beauty are her clothing, and she shall laugh in the latter day.

    She hath opened her mouth to wisdom, and the law of clemency is on her tongue.

    She hath looked well to the paths of her house, and hath not eaten her bread idle.

    Her children rose up, and called her blessed; her husband, and he praised her.

13. How are the two priests paralleled and contrasted?
14. What symbolism is involved in the following: (a) The game of cards (consider especially "She played for blood")? (b) The mosquito? (c) The bust of St. Joseph?
15. What is the theme of the story?

James Purdy
Don't Call Me by My Right Name

Her new name was Mrs. Klein. There was something in the meaning that irritated her. She liked everything about her husband except his name and that had never pleased her. She had fallen in love with him before she found out what his name was. Once she knew he was Klein, her disappointment had been strong. Names do make a great difference, and after six months of marriage she found herself still not liking her name. She began using more and more her maiden name. Then she always called herself on her letters Lois McBane. Her husband seldom saw the mail arrive so perhaps he did not know, and had he known she went by her old name he might not have cared enough to feel any particular hurt.

Lois Klein, she often thought as she lay next to her husband in bed. It is not the name of a woman like myself. It does not reflect my character.

One evening at a party when there had been more drinking for her than usual, she said offhand to him in the midst of some revelry: "I would like you to change your name."

He did not understand. He thought that it was a remark she was making in drink which did not refer to anything concrete, just as once she had said to him, "I want you to begin by taking your head off regularly." The remark had meant nothing, and he let it pass.

"Frank," she said, "you must change your name, do you hear? I cannot go on being Mrs. Klein."

Several people heard what it was she said, and they laughed loudly so that Lois and Frank would hear them appreciating the remark.

"If you were all called Mrs. Klein," she said turning to the men who were laughing, "you would not like to be Mrs. Klein either."

Being all men, they laughed harder.

"Well, you married him, didn't you," a man said, "and we guess you will have to keep his name."

"If he changed his name," another of

the men said, "what name would you have him change it to?"

Frank put his hand on her glass, as though to tell her they must go home, but she seized the glass with his hand on it and drank quickly out of it.

"I hadn't thought what name I did want," she said, puzzled.

"Well, you aren't going to change your name," Frank said. "The gentlemen know that."

"The gentlemen do?" she asked him. "Well, I don't know what name I would like it changed to," she admitted to the men.

"You don't look much like Mrs. Klein," one of the men said and began to laugh again.

"You're not friends!" she called back at them.

"What are we, then?" they asked.

"Why don't I look like Mrs. Klein?" she wanted to know.

"Don't you ever look in the mirror?" one of the men replied.

"We ought to go, Lois," her husband said.

She sat there as though she had heard the last of the many possible truths she could hear about herself.

"I wonder how I will get out of here, Frank," she said.

"Out of where, dear?" he wondered. He was suddenly sad enough himself to be dead, but he managed to say something to her at this point.

"Out of where I seem to have got into," she told him.

The men had moved off now and were laughing among themselves. Frank and Lois did not notice this laughter.

"I'm not going to change my name," he said, as though to himself. Then turning to her: "I know it's supposed to be wrong to tell people when they're drunk the insane whim they're having is insane, but I am telling you now and I may tell the whole room of men."

"I have to have my name changed, Frank," she said. "You know I can't stand to be tortured. It is too painful and I am not young anymore. I am getting old and fat."

"No wife of mine would ever be old or fat," he said.

"I just cannot be Mrs. Klein and face the world."

"Anytime you want me to pull out is all right," he said. "Do you want me to pull out?"

"What are you saying?" she wanted to know. "What did you say about pulling out?"

"I don't want any more talk about your changing your name or I intend to pull up stakes."

"I don't know what you're talking about. You know you can't leave me. What would I do, Frank, at my age?"

"I told you no wife of mine is old."

"I couldn't find anybody now, Frank, if you went."

"Then quit talking about changing our name."

"*Our* name? I don't know what you mean by *our* name."

He took her drink out of her hand and when she coaxed and whined he struck her not too gently over the mouth.

"What was the meaning of that?" she wanted to know.

"Are you coming home, Mrs. Klein?" he said, and he hit her again. Her lip was cut against her teeth so that you could see it beginning to bleed.

"Frank, you're abusing me," she said, white and wide-eyed now, and as though tasting the blood slightly with the gin and soda mix.

"Mrs. Klein," he said idiotically.

It was one of those fake dead long parties where nobody actually knows anybody and where people could be pushed out of windows without anybody's being sure until the morrow.

"I'm not going home as Mrs. Klein," she said.

He hit her again.

"Frank, you have no right to hit me just because I hate your name."

"If you hate my name what do you feel then for me? Are you going to act like my wife or not."

"I don't want to have babies, Frank. I will not go through that at my age. Categorically not."

He hit her again so that she fell on the floor, but this did not seem to surprise either her or him because they both continued the conversation.

"I can't make up my mind what to do," she said, weeping a little. "I know of course what the safe thing is to do."

"Either you come out of here with me as Mrs. Klein, or I go to a hotel room alone. Here's the key to the house," he said, and he threw it on the floor at her.

Several of the men at the party had begun to notice what was really going on now. They thought that it was married clowning at first and they began to gather around in a circle, but what they saw had something empty and stiff about it that did not interest and yet kept one somehow watching. For one thing, Mrs. Klein's dress had come up and exposed her legs, which were not beautiful.

"I can't decide if I can go on with his name," she explained from the floor position to the men.

"Well, it's a little late, isn't it, Mrs. Klein," one of the men said in a sleepy voice.

"It's never too late, I don't suppose, is it?" she inquired. "Oh, I can't believe it is even though I feel old."

"Well, you're not young," the same man ventured. "You're too old to be lying there."

"My husband can't see my point of view," she explained. "And that is why he can't understand why his name doesn't fit me. I was unmarried too long, I suppose, to suddenly surrender my own name. I have always been known professionally and socially under my own name and it is hard to change now, I can tell you. I don't think I can go home with him unless he lets me change my name."

"I will give you just two minutes," Mr. Klein said.

"For what? Only two minutes for what?" she cried.

"To make up your mind what name you are going out of here with."

"I know, men," she said, "what the sensible decision is, and tomorrow, of course, when I'm sober I will wish I had taken it."

Turning to Frank Klein, she said simply, "You will have to go your way without me."

He looked hurriedly around as though looking for an exit to leave by, and then he looked back to her on the floor as though he could not come to a decision.

"Come to your senses," Frank Klein said unemphatically.

"There were hundreds of Kleins in the telephone directory," she went on, "but when people used to come to my name they recognized at once that I was the only woman going under my own special name."

"For Jesus Christ's sake, Lois," he said, turning a peculiar green color.

"I can't go with you as Mrs. Klein," she said.

"Well, let me help you up," he said.

She managed to let him help her up.

"I'm not going home with you, but I will send you in a cab," he informed her.

"Are you leaving me?" she wanted to know.

He did not know what to say. He felt anything he said might destroy his mind. He stood there with an insane emptiness on his eyes and lips.

Everyone had moved off from them. There was a silence from the phonograph and from the TV set which had both been going at the same time. The party was over and people were calling down to cabs from all the windows.

"Why won't you come home with me?" she said in a whisper.

Suddenly he hurried out the door without waiting for her. "Frank!" she called after him, and a few of the men from the earlier group came over and joked with her.

"He went out just like a boy, without any sense of responsibility," she said to them without any expression in her voice.

She hurried on out too, not waiting to put her coat on straight.

She stood outside in the fall cold and shivered. Some children went by dressed in Hallowe'en costumes.

"Is she dressed as anybody?" one of the children said pointlessly.

"Frank!" she began calling. "I don't know what is happening really," she said to herself.

Suddenly he came up to her from behind a hedge next to where she was standing.

"I couldn't quite bring myself to go off," he said.

She thought for a minute of hitting him with her purse which she had remembered to bring, but she did nothing now but watch him.

"Will you change your name?" she said.

"We will live together the way we have been," he said not looking at her.

"We can't be married, Frank, with that name between us."

Suddenly he hit her and knocked her down to the pavement.

She lay there for a minute before anything was said.

"Are you conscious?" he said crouching down beside her. "Tell me if you are suffering," he wanted to know.

"You have hurt something in my head, I think," she said, getting up slightly on one elbow.

"You have nearly driven me out of my mind," he said, and he was making funny sounds in his mouth. "You don't know what it means to have one's name held up to ridicule like this. You are such a cruel person, Lois."

"We will both change our names, if you like," she said.

"Why do you torture me?" he said. "Why is it you can't control your power to torture?"

"Then we won't think about it, we will go home," she said, in a cold comforting voice. "Only I think I am going to be sick," she warned.

"We will go home," he said in a stupid voice.

"I will let you call me Mrs. Klein this one evening, then tomorrow we will have a good talk." At the same moment she fell back on the walk.

Some young men from the delicatessen who had been doing inventory came by and asked if there was anything they could do.

"My wife fell on the walk," he said. "I thought she was all right. She was talking to me just a moment ago."

"Was it your wife, did you say?" the younger man leaned down to look at her.

"Mrs. Klein," Frank replied.

"You are Mr. Klein, then?"

"I don't understand," the older of the two young men said. "You don't look somehow like her husband."

"We have been married six months."

"I think you ought to call a doctor," the younger man said. "She is bleeding at the mouth."

"I hit her at a party," Frank said.

"What did you say your name was?" the older man asked.

"Mr. Klein. She is Mrs. Klein," Frank told them.

The two men from the delicatessen exchanged looks

"Did you push her?" the one man asked.

"Yes," Frank said. "I hit her. She didn't want to be Mrs. Klein."

"You're drunk," the one man ventured an opinion.

Lois suddenly came to. "Frank, you will have to take me home," she said. "There is something wrong with my head. My God," she began to scream, "I am in awful pain."

Frank helped her up again.

"Is this your husband?" the one man asked.

She nodded.

"What is your name?" he wanted to know.

"It's none of your business," she said.

"Are you Mrs. Klein?" he asked.

"No," Lois replied, "I don't happen to be Mrs. Klein."

"Come on, J. D., we can't get mixed up in this," the younger man said. "Whatever the hell their names are."

"Well, I'm not Mrs. Klein, whoever you are," she said.

Immediately then she struck Frank with the purse and he fell back in surprise against the building wall.

"Call me a cab, you cheap son of a bitch," she said. "Can't you see I'm bleeding?"

[1956]

For Thought

In "Don't Call Me by My Right Name," Purdy practices the art of black humor by taking the Rule of Names (the "name" is the "thing") and applying it literally to a husband and wife brawl arising out of a clash of wills at a cocktail party. The humor in the story derives from the protagonist's stubborn elevation of the inconsequential to the monumentally important and from her mock-heroic endurance in the face of the physical and verbal abuse she suffers.

For Discussion

1. How does Purdy use non sequiturs, shifts in meaning, and conversations at cross-purposes for comic effect?
2. What two points of view does Purdy use? Why does he shift from one point of view to the other in the course of the story?
3. What elements of black humor does the story possess?
4. What is the critical point in the action? How is its effect comically defused?
5. What do the other men at the party and the two men from the delicatessen contribute to the structure of the story?

Philip Roth
The Conversion of the Jews

"You're a real one for opening your mouth in the first place," Itzie said. "What do you open your mouth all the time for?"

"I didn't bring it up, Itz, I didn't," Ozzie said.

"What do you care about Jesus Christ for anyway?"

"I didn't bring up Jesus Christ. He did. I didn't even know what he was talking about. Jesus is historical, he kept saying. Jesus is historical." Ozzie mimicked the monumental voice of Rabbi Binder.

"Jesus was a person that lived like you and me," Ozzie continued. "That's what Binder said—"

"Yeah? . . . So what! What do I give two cents whether he lived or not. And what do you gotta open your mouth!" Itzie Lieberman favored closed-mouthedness, especially when it came to Ozzie Freedman's questions. Mrs. Freedman had to see Rabbi Binder twice before about Ozzie's questions and this Wednesday at four-thirty would be the third time. Itzie preferred to keep *his* mother in the kitchen; he settled for behind-the-back subtleties such as gestures, faces, snarls and other less delicate barnyard noises.

"He was a real person, Jesus, but he wasn't like God, and we don't believe he is God." Slowly, Ozzie was explaining Rabbi Binder's position to Itzie, who had been absent from Hebrew School the previous afternoon.

"The Catholics," Itzie said helpfully, "they believe in Jesus Christ, that he's God." Itzie Lieberman used "the Catholics" in its broadest sense—to include the Protestants.

Ozzie received Itzie's remark with a tiny head bob, as though it were a footnote, and went on. "His mother was Mary, and his father probably was Joseph," Ozzie said. "But the New Testament says his real father was God."

"His *real* father?"

"Yeah," Ozzie said, "that's the big thing, his father's supposed to be God."

"Bull."

"That's what Rabbi Binder says, that it's impossible—"

"Sure it's impossible. That stuff's all

bull. To have a baby you gotta get laid," Itzie theologized. "Mary hadda get laid."

"That's what Binder says: 'The only way a woman can have a baby is to have intercourse with a man.'"

"He said *that*, Ozz?" For a moment it appeared that Itzie had put the theological question aside. "He said that, intercourse?" A little curled smile shaped itself in the lower half of Itzie's face like a pink mustache. "What you guys do, Ozz, you laugh or something?"

"I raised my hand."

"Yeah? Whatja say?"

"That's when I asked the question."

Itzie's face lit up. "Whatja ask about—intercourse?"

"No, I asked the question about God, how if He could create the heaven and earth in six days, and make all the animals and the fish and the light in six days—the light especially, that's what always gets me, that He could make the light. Making fish and animals, that's pretty good—"

"That's damn good." Itzie's appreciation was honest but unimaginative: it was as though God had just pitched a one-hitter.

"But making light . . . I mean when you think about it, it's really something," Ozzie said. "Anyway, I asked Binder if He could make all that in six days, and He could *pick* the six days he wanted right out of nowhere, why couldn't He let a woman have a baby without having intercourse."

"You said intercourse, Ozz, to Binder?"

"Yeah."

"Right in class?"

"Yeah."

Itzie smacked the side of his head.

"I mean, no kidding around," Ozzie said, "that'd really be nothing. After all that other stuff, that'd practically be nothing."

Itzie considered a moment. "What'd Binder say?"

"He started all over again explaining how Jesus was historical and how he lived like you and me but he wasn't God. So I said I under*stood* that. What I wanted to know was different."

What Ozzie wanted to know was always different. The first time he had wanted to know how Rabbi Binder could call the Jews "The Chosen People" if the Declaration of Independence claimed all men to be created equal. Rabbi Binder tried to distinguish for him between political equality and spiritual legitimacy, but what Ozzie wanted to know, he insisted vehemently, was different. That was the first time his mother had to come.

Then there was the plane crash. Fifty-eight people had been killed in a plane crash at La Guardia. In studying a casualty list in the newspaper his mother had discovered among the list of those dead eight Jewish names (his grandmother had nine but she counted Miller as a Jewish name): because of the eight she said the plane crash was "a tragedy." During free-discussion time on Wednesday Ozzie had brought to Rabbi Binder's attention this matter of "some of his relations" always picking out the Jewish names. Rabbi Binder had begun to explain cultural unity and some other things when Ozzie stood up at his seat and said that what he wanted to know was different. Rabbi Binder insisted that he sit down and it was then that Ozzie shouted that he wished all fifty-eight were Jews. That was the second time his mother came.

"And he kept explaining about Jesus being historical, and so I kept asking him. No kidding, Itz, he was trying to make me look stupid."

"So what he finally do?"

"Finally he starts screaming that I was deliberately simpleminded and a wise guy, and that my mother had to come, and this was the last time. And that I'd never get bar-mitzvahed if he could help it. Then, Itz, then he starts talking in that voice like a statue, real slow and deep, and he says that I better think over what I said about the Lord. He told me to go to his office and think it over." Ozzie leaned his body towards Itzie. "Itz, I thought it over for a solid hour, and now I'm convinced God could do it."

Ozzie had planned to confess his latest transgression to his mother as soon as she came home from work. But it was a Friday night in November and already dark, and when Mrs. Freedman came through the door she tossed off her coat, kissed Ozzie quickly on the face, and went to the kitchen table to light the three yellow candles, two for the Sabbath and one for Ozzie's father.

When his mother lit the candles she would move her two arms slowly towards her, dragging them through the air, as though persuading people whose minds were half made up. And her eyes would get glassy with tears. Even when his father was alive Ozzie remembered that her eyes had gotten glassy, so it didn't have anything to do with his dying. It had something to do with lighting the candles.

As she touched the flaming match to the unlit wick of a Sabbath candle, the phone rang, and Ozzie, standing only a foot from it, plucked it off the receiver and held it muffled to his chest. When his mother lit candles Ozzie felt there should be no noise; even breathing, if you could manage it, should be softened. Ozzie pressed the phone to his breast and watched his mother dragging whatever she was dragging, and he felt his own eyes get glassy. His mother was a round, tired, gray-haired penguin of a woman whose gray skin had begun to feel the tug of gravity and the weight of her own history. Even when she was dressed up she didn't look like a chosen person. But when she lit candles she looked like something better; like a woman who knew momentarily that God could do anything.

After a few mysterious minutes she was finished. Ozzie hung up the phone and walked to the kitchen table where she was beginning to lay the two places for the four-course Sabbath meal. He told her that she would have to see Rabbi Binder next Wednesday at four-thirty, and then he told her why. For the first time in their life together she hit Ozzie across the face with her hand.

All through the chopped liver and chicken soup part of the dinner Ozzie cried; he didn't have any appetite for the rest.

On Wednesday, in the largest of the three basement classrooms of the synagogue, Rabbi Marvin Binder, a tall, handsome, broad-shouldered man of thirty with thick strong-fibered black hair, removed his watch from his pocket and saw that it was four o'clock. At the rear of the room Yakov Blotnik, the seventy-one-year-old custodian, slowly polished the large window, mumbling to himself, unaware that it was four o'clock or six o'clock, Monday or Wednesday. To most of the students Yakov Blotnik's mumbling, along with his brown curly beard, scythe nose, and two heel-trailing black cats, made of him an object of wonder, a foreigner, a relic, towards whom they were alternately fearful and disrespectful. To Ozzie the mumbling had always seemed a monotonous, curious prayer; what made it curious was that old Blotnik had been mumbling so steadily for so many years, Ozzie suspected he had memorized the prayers and forgotten all about God.

"It is now free-discussion time," Rabbi Binder said. "Feel free to talk about any Jewish matter at all—religion, family, politics, sports—"

There was silence. It was a gusty, clouded November afternoon and it did not seem as though there ever was or could be a thing called baseball. So nobody this week said a word about that hero from the past, Hank Greenberg—which limited free discussion considerably.

And the soul-battering Ozzie Freedman had just received from Rabbi Binder had imposed its limitation. When it was Ozzie's turn to read aloud from the Hebrew book the rabbi had asked him petulantly why he didn't read more rapidly. He was showing no progress. Ozzie said he could read faster but that if he did he was sure not to understand what he was reading. Nevertheless, at the rabbi's repeated suggestion Ozzie tried, and showed a great talent, but in the midst of a long passage he stopped short and said he didn't understand a word he was reading, and started in again at a drag-footed pace. Then came the soul-battering.

Consequently when free-discussion time rolled around none of the students felt too free. The rabbi's invitation was answered only by the mumbling of feeble old Blotnik.

"Isn't there anything at all you would like to discuss?" Rabbi Binder asked again, looking at his watch. "No questions or comments?"

There was a small grumble from the third row. The rabbi requested that Ozzie rise and give the rest of the class the advantage of his thought.

Ozzie rose. "I forget it now," he said, and sat down in his place. Rabbi Binder advanced a seat towards Ozzie and poised himself on the edge of the desk. It was Itzie's desk and the rabbi's frame only a dagger's length away from his face snapped him to sitting attention.

"Stand up again, Oscar," Rabbi Binder said calmly, "and try to assemble your thoughts."

Ozzie stood up. All his classmates turned in their seats and watched as he gave an unconvincing scratch to his forehead.

"I can't assemble any," he announced, and plunked himself down.

"Stand up!" Rabbi Binder advanced from Itzie's desk to the one directly in front of Ozzie; when the rabbinical back was turned Itzie gave it five-fingers off the tip of his nose, causing a small titter in the room. Rabbi Binder was too absorbed in squelching Ozzie's nonsense once and for all to bother with titters. "Stand up, Oscar. What's your question about?"

Ozzie pulled a word out of the air. It was the handiest word. "Religion."

"Oh, now you remember?"

"Yes."

"What is it?"

Trapped, Ozzie blurted the first thing that came to him. "Why can't He make anything He wants to Make!"

As Rabbi Binder prepared an answer, a final answer, Itzie, ten feet behind him, raised one finger on his left hand, gestured it meaningfully towards the rabbi's back, and brought the house down.

Binder twisted quickly to see what had happened and in the midst of the commotion Ozzie shouted into the rabbi's back what he couldn't have shouted to his face. It was a loud, toneless sound that had the timbre of something stored inside for about six days.

"You don't know! You don't know anything about God!"

The rabbi spun back towards Ozzie. "What?"

"You don't know—you don't—"

"Apologize, Oscar, apologize!" It was a threat.

"You don't—"

Rabbi Binder's hand flicked out at Ozzie's cheek. Perhaps it had only been meant to clamp the boy's mouth shut, but Ozzie ducked and the palm caught him sqaurely on the nose.

The blood came in a short, red spurt on to Ozzie's shirt front.

The next moment was all confusion. Ozzie screamed, "You bastard, you bastard!" and broke for the classroom door. Rabbi Binder lurched a step backwards, as though his own blood had started flowing violently in the opposite direction, then gave a clumsy lurch forward and bolted out the door after Ozzie. The class followed after the rabbi's huge blue-suited back, and before old Blotnik could turn from his window, the room was empty and everyone was headed full speed up the three flights leading to the roof.

If one should compare the light of day to the life of man: sunrise to birth, sunset—the dropping down over the edge—to death; then as Ozzie Freedman wiggled through the trapdoor of the synagogue roof, his feet kicking backwards bronco-style at Rabbi Binder's outstretched arms—at that moment the day was fifty years old. As a rule, fifty or fifty-five reflects accurately the age of late afternoons in November, for its is in that month, during those hours, that one's awareness of light seems no longer a matter of seeing, but of hearing: light begins clicking away. In fact, as Ozzie locked shut the trapdoor in the rabbi's face, the sharp click of the bolt into the lock might momentarily have been mistaken for the sound of the heavier gray that has just throbbed through the sky.

With all his weight Ozzie kneeled on the locked door; any instant he was certain that Rabbi Binder's shoulder would fling it open, splintering the wood into shrapnel and catapulting his body into the sky. But the door did not move and below him he heard only the rumble of feet, first loud then dim, like thunder rolling away.

A question shot through his brain. "Can this be *me*?" For a thirteen-year-old who had just labeled his religious leader a bastard, twice, it was not an improper question. Louder and louder the question came to him—"Is it me? It is me?"—until he discovered himself no longer kneeling, but racing crazily towards the edge of the roof, his eyes crying, his throat screaming, and his arms flying everywhichway as though not his own.

"Is it me? Is it me Me Me Me Me! It has to be me—but is it!"

It is the question a thief must ask himself the night he jimmies open his first window, and it is said to be the question with which bridegrooms quiz themselves before the altar.

In the few wild seconds it took Ozzie's body to propel him to the edge of the roof, his self-examination began to grow fuzzy. Gazing down at the street, he became confused as to the problem beneath the question: was it, is-it-me-who-called-Binder-a-bastard? or, is-it-me-prancing-around-on-the-roof? However, the scene below settled all, for there is an instant in any action when whether it is you or somebody else is academic. The thief crams the money in his pockets and scoots out the window. The bridegroom signs the hotel register for two. And the boy on the roof finds a streetful of people gaping at him, necks stretched backwards, faces up, as though he were the ceiling of the Hayden Planetarium. Suddenly you know it's you.

"Oscar! Oscar Freedman!" A voice rose from the center of the crowd, a voice that, could it have been seen, would have looked like the writing on scroll. "Oscar Freedman, get down from there. Immediately!" Rabbi Binder was pointing one arm stiffly up at him; and at the end of that arm, one finger aimed menacingly. It was the attitude of a dictator, but one—the eyes confessed all—whose personal valet had spit neatly in his face.

Ozzie didn't answer. Only for a blink's length did he look towards Rabbi Binder. Instead his eyes began to fit together the world beneath him, to sort out people from places, friends from enemies, participants from spectators. In little jagged starlike clusters his friends stood around Rabbi Binder, who was still pointing. The topmost point on a star compounded not of angels but of five adolescent boys was Itzie. What a world it was, with those stars below, Rabbi Binder below . . . Ozzie, who a moment earlier hadn't been able to control his own body, started to feel the meaning of the word control: he felt Peace and he felt Power.

"Oscar Freedman, I'll give you three to come down."

Few dictators give their subjects three to do anything; but, as always, Rabbi Binder only looked dictatorial.

"Are you ready, Oscar?"

Ozzie nodded his head yes, although he had no intention in the world—the lower one of the celestial one he'd just entered—of coming down even if Rabbi Binder should give him a million.

"All right then," said Rabbi Binder. He ran a hand through his black Samson hair as though it were the gesture prescribed for uttering the first digit. Then, with his other hand cutting a circle out of the small piece of sky around him, he spoke. "One!"

There was no thunder. On the contrary, at that moment, as though "one" was the cue for which he had been waiting, the world's least thunderous person appeared on the synagogue steps. He did not so much come out the synagogue door as lean out, onto the darkening air. He clutched at the doorknob with one hand and looked up at the roof.

"Oy!"

Yakov Blotnik's old mind hobbled slowly, as if on crutches, and though he couldn't decide precisely what the boy was doing on the roof, he knew it wasn't good—that is, it wasn't-good-for-the-Jews. For Yakov Blotnik life had fractionated itself simply: things were either good-for-the-Jews or no-good-for-the-Jews.

He smacked his free hand to his in-sucked cheek, gently. "Oy, Gut!" And then quickly as he was able, he jacked down his head and surveyed the street. There was Rabbi Binder (like a man at an auction with only three dollars in his pocket, he had just delivered a shaky "Two!"); there were the students, and that was all. So far it-wasn't-so-bad-for-the-Jews. But the boy had to come down immediately, before anybody saw. The problem: how to get the boy off the roof?

Anybody who has ever had a cat on the roof knows how to get him down. You call the fire department. Or first you call the operator and you ask her for the fire department. And the next thing there is great jamming of brakes and clanging of bells and shouting of instructions. And then the cat is off the roof. You do the same thing to get a boy off the roof.

That is, you do the same thing if you are Yakov Blotnik and you once had a cat on the roof.

When the engines, all four of them, arrived, Rabbi Binder had four times given Ozzie the count of three. The big hook-and-ladder swung around the corner and one of the firemen leaped from it, plunging headlong towards the yellow fire hydrant in front of the synagogue. With a huge wrench he began to unscrew the top nozzle. Rabbi Binder raced over to him and pulled at his shoulder.

"There's no fire . . ."

The fireman mumbled back over his shoulder and, heatedly, continued working at the nozzle.

"But there's no fire, there's no fire . . ." Binder shouted. When the fireman mumbled again, the rabbi grasped his face with both his hands and pointed it up at the roof.

To Ozzie it looked as though Rabbi Binder was trying to tug the fireman's head out of his body, like a cork from a bottle. He had to giggle at the picture they made: it was a family portrait—rabbi in black skullcap, fireman in red fire hat, and the little yellow hydrant squatting beside like a kid brother, bareheaded. From the edge of the roof Ozzie waved at the portrait, a one-handed, flapping, mocking wave; in doing it his right foot slipped from under him. Rabbi Binder covered his eyes with his hands.

Firemen work fast. Before Ozzie had even regained his balance, a big, round, yellowed net was being held on the synagogue lawn. The firemen who held it looked up at Ozzie with stern, feelingless faces.

One of the firemen turned his head towards Rabbi Binder. "What, is the kid nuts or something?"

Rabbi Binder unpeeled his hands from his eyes, slowly, painfully, as if they were tape. Then he checked: nothing on the sidewalk, no dents in the net.

"Is he gonna jump, or what?" the fireman shouted.

In a voice not at all like a statue, Rabbi Binder finally answered. "Yes, Yes, I think so . . . He's been threatening to . . ."

Threatening to? Why, the reason he was on the roof, Ozzie remembered, was to get away; he hadn't even thought about jumping. He had just run to get away, and the truth was that he hadn't really headed for the roof as much as he'd been chased there.

"What's his name, the kid?"

"Freedman," Rabbi Binder answered. "Oscar Freedman."

The fireman looked up at Ozzie. "What is it with you, Oscar? You gonna jump, or what?"

Ozzie did not answer. Frankly, the question had just arisen.

"Look, Oscar, if you're gonna jump, jump—and if you're not gonna jump, don't jump. But don't waste our time, will ya?"

Ozzie looked at the fireman and then at Rabbi Binder. He wanted to see Rabbi Binder cover his eyes one more time.

"I'm going to jump."

And then he scampered around the edge of the roof to the corner, where there was no net below, and he flapped his arms at his sides, swishing the air and smacking his palms to his trousers on the downbeat. He began screaming like some kind of engine. "Wheeeee . . . wheeeeee," and leaning way out over the edge with the upper half of his body. The firemen whipped around to cover the ground with the net. Rabbi Binder mumbled a few words to Somebody and covered his eyes. Everything happened quickly, jerkily, as in a silent movie. The crowd, which had arrived with the fire engines, gave out a long, Fourth-of-July fireworks oooh-aahhh. In the excitement no one had paid the crowd much heed, except, of course, Yakov Blotnik, who swung from the doorknob counting heads. "Fier und tsvansik . . . finf und tsvantsik . . . Oy, Gut!" It wasn't like this with the cat.

Rabbi Binder peeked through his fingers, checked the sidewalk and net. Empty. But there was Ozzie racing to the other corner. The firemen raced with him but were unable to keep up. Whenever Ozzie wanted to he might jump and splatter himself upon the sidewalk, and by the time the firemen scooted to the spot all they could do with their net would be to cover the mess.

"Wheeeee . . . wheeeee . . ."

"Hey, Oscar," the winded fireman yelled, "What the hell is this, a game or something?"

"Wheeeee . . . wheeeee . . ."

"Hey, Oscar—"

But he was off now to the other corner, flapping his wings fiercely. Rabbi Binder couldn't take it any longer—the fire engines from nowhere, the screaming suicidal boy, the net. He fell to his knees, exhausted, and with his hands curled together in front of his chest like a little dome, he pleaded, "Oscar, stop it, Oscar. Don't jump, Oscar. Please come down . . . Please don't jump."

And further back in the crowd a single voice, a single young voice, shouted a lone word to the boy on the roof.

"Jump!"

It was Itzie. Ozzie momentarily stopped flapping.

"Go ahead, Ozz—jump!" Itzie broke off his point of the star and courageously, with the inspiration not of a wise-guy but of a disciple, stood alone. "Jump, Ozz, jump!"

Still on his knees, his hand still curled, Rabbi Binder twisted his body back. He looked at Itzie, then, agonizingly, back to Ozzie.

"OSCAR, DON'T JUMP! PLEASE, DON'T JUMP . . . please please . . ."

"Jump!" This time it wasn't Itzie but another point of the star. By the time Mrs. Freedman arrived to keep her four-thirty appointment with Rabbi Binder, the whole little upside down heaven was shouting and pleading for Ozzie to jump, and Rabbi Binder no longer was pleading with him not to jump, but was crying into the dome of his hands.

Understandably Mrs. Freedman couldn't figure out what her son was doing on the roof. So she asked.

"Ozzie, my Ozzie, what are you doing? My Ozzie, what is it?"

Ozzie stopped wheeeeeing and slowed his arms down to a cruising flap, the kind birds use in soft winds, but he did not answer. He stood against the low, clouded, darkening sky—light clicked down swiftly now, as on a small gear—flapping softly and gazing down at the small bundle of a woman who was his mother.

"What are you doing, Ozzie?" She turned towards the kneeling Rabbi Binder and rushed so close that only a paper-thickness of dusk lay between her stomach and his shoulders.

"What is my baby doing?"

Rabbi Binder gaped up at her but he too was mute. All that moved was the dome of his hands; it shook back and forth like a weak pulse.

"Rabbi, get him down! He'll kill himself. Get him down, my only baby . . ."

"I can't," Rabbi Binder said, "I can't . . ." and he turned his handsome head towards the crowd of boys behind him. "It's them. Listen to them."

And for the first time Mrs. Freedman saw the crowd of boys, and she heard what they were yelling.

"He's doing it for them. He won't listen to me. It's them." Rabbi Binder spoke like one in a trance.

"For them?"

"Yes."

"Why for them?"

"They want him to . . ."

Mrs. Freedman raised her two arms upward as though she were conducting the sky. "For them he's doing it!" And then in a gesture older than pyramids, older than prophets and floods, her arms came slapping down to her sides. "A martyr I have. Look!" She tilted her head to the roof. Ozzie was still flapping softly. "My martyr."

"Oscar, come down, *please*," Rabbi Binder groaned.

In a startlingly even voice Mrs. Freedman called to the boy on the roof. "Ozzie, come down, Ozzie. Don't by a martyr, my baby."

As though it were a litany, Rabbi Binder repeated her words. "Don't be a martyr, my baby. Don't be a martyr."

"Gawhead, Ozz—*be* a Martin!" It was Itzie. "Be a Martin, be a Martin," and all the voices joined in singing for Martindom, whatever *it* was. "Be a Martin, be a Martin . . ."

Somehow when you're on a roof the darker it gets the less you can hear. All Ozzie knew was that two groups wanted two new things: his friends were spirited and musical about what they wanted; his mother and the rabbi were even-toned, chanting, about what they didn't want. The rabbi's voice was without tears now and so was his mother's.

The big net stared up at Ozzie like a slightless eye. The big, clouded sky pushed down. From beneath it looked like a gray corrugated board. Suddenly, looking up into that unsympathetic sky, Ozzie realized all the strangeness of what these people, his friends, were asking: they wanted him to jump, to kill himself; they were singing about it now—it made them that happy. And there was an even greater strangeness: Rabbi Binder was on his knees, trembling. If there was a question to be asked now it was not "Is it me?" but rather "Is it us? . . . Is it us?"

Being on the roof, it turned out, was a serious thing. If he jumped would the singing become dancing? Would it? What would jumping stop? Yearningly, Ozzie wished he could rip open the sky, plunge his hands through, and pull out the sun; and on the sun, like a coin, would be stamped JUMP OR DON'T JUMP.

Ozzie's knees rocked and sagged a little under him as though they were setting him for a dive. His arms tightened, stiffened, froze, from shoulders to fingernails. He felt as if each part of his body were going to vote as to whether he should kill himself or not—and each part as though it were independent of *him*.

The light took an unexpected click down and the new darkness, like a gag, hushed the friends singing for this and the mother and rabbi chanting for that.

Ozzie stopped counting votes, and in a curiously high voice, like one who wasn't prepared for speech, he spoke.

"Mamma?"

"Yes, Oscar."

"Mamma, get down on your knees, like Rabbi Binder."

"Oscar—"

"Get down on your knees," he said, "or I'll jump."

Ozzie heard a whimper, then a quick rustling, and when he looked down where his mother had stood he saw the top of a head and beneath that a circle of dress. She was kneeling beside Rabbi Binder.

He spoke again. "Everybody kneel." There was the sound of everybody kneeling.

Ozzie looked around. With one hand he pointed towards the synagogue entrance. "Make *him* kneel."

There was a noise, not of kneeling, but of body-and-cloth stretching. Ozzie could hear Rabbi Binder saying in a gruff whisper, " . . . or he'll *kill* himself," and when next he looked there was Yakov Blotnik off the doorknob and for the first time in his life upon his knees in the Gentile posture of prayer.

As for the firemen—it is not as difficult as one might imagine to hold a net taut while you are kneeling.

Ozzie looked around again; and then he called to Rabbi Binder.

"Rabbi?"

"Yes, Oscar."

"Rabbi Binder, do you believe in God."

"Yes."

"Do you believe God can do Anything?" Ozzie leaned his head out into the darkness. "Anything?"

"Oscar, I think—"

"Tell me you believe God can do Anything."

There was a second's hesitation. Then: "God can do Anything."

"Tell me you believe God can make a child without intercourse."

"He can."

"Tell me!"

"God," Rabbi Binder admitted, "can make a child without intercourse."

"Mamma, you tell me."

"God can make a child without intercourse," his mother said.

"Make *him* tell me." There was no doubt who *him* was.

In a few moments Ozzie heard an old comical voice say something to the increasing darkness about God.

Next, Ozzie made everybody say it. And then he made them all say they believed in Jesus Christ—first one at a time, then all together.

When the catechizing was through it was the beginning of evening. From the street it sounded as if the boy on the roof might have sighed.

"Ozzie?" A woman's voice dared to speak. "You'll come down now?"

There was no answer, but the woman waited, and when a voice finally did speak it was thin and crying, and exhausted as that of an old man who has just finished pulling the bells.

"Mamma, don't you see—you shouldn't hit me. He shouldn't hit me. You shouldn't hit me about God, Mamma. You should never hit anybody about God—"

"Ozzie, please come down now."

"Promise me, promise me you'll never hit anybody about God."

He had asked only his mother, but for some reason everyone kneeling in the street promised he would never hit anybody about God.

Once again there was silence.

"I can come down now, Mamma," the boy on the roof finally said. He turned his head both ways as though checking the traffic lights. "Now I can come down . . ."

And he did, right into the center of the yellow net that glowed in the evening's edge like an overgrown halo.

[1959]

For Thought

"The Conversion of the Jews" tells of a wild escapade involving a bedeviled boy's flight to the rooftop of a synagogue and his subsequent flying leap into a net stretched out below by firemen. Roth has his main character, a naive rebel, engage in a parody of the indoctrination process he has been subjected to in his class in religious instruction. In the parody, the boy, not the adult, has the power to demand unquestioning compliance with certain set beliefs. The conflict is resolved by having the boy's former tormentor, and those gathered about him, forced to avow belief publicly in a contrary and equally arbitrary religious dispensation.

For Discussion

1. What is the tone of the story and how is it achieved?
2. What is the emotional atmosphere of the story? How is it brought about?
3. What is the author's attitude toward Ozzie in his conflict with the rabbi and with the system of indoctrination?
4. What methods does Roth use to characterize Ozzie?
5. How is Ozzie's antagonist, Rabbi Binder, characterized?
6. How do Ozzie's mother and Yakov Blotnik fit into the story?
7. What role do Itzie and the other boys play in the events?
8. What is the effect of the author's asides and descriptions?
9. What is the inciting action, the turning point, the climax, and the resolution of the plot?
10. What is the basic pattern of the story?

William Saroyan
Seventy Thousand Assyrians

I hadn't had a haircut in forty days and forty nights, and I was beginning to look like several violinists out of work. You know the look: genius gone to pot, and ready to join the Communist Party. We barbarians from Asia Minor are hairy people: when we need a haircut, we *need* a haircut. It was so bad, I had outgrown my only hat. (I am writing a serious story, perhaps one of the most serious I shall ever write. That is why I am being flippant. Readers of Sherwood Anderson will begin to understand what I am saying after a while; they will know that my laughter is rather sad.) I was a young man in need of a haircut, so I went down to Third Street (San Francisco), to the Barber College, for a fifteen-cent haircut.

Third Street, below Howard, is a district; think of the Bowery in New York, Main Street in Los Angeles: think of old men and boys, out of work, hanging around, smoking Bull Durham, talking about the government, waiting for something to turn up, simply waiting. It was a Monday morning in August and a lot of the tramps had come to the shop to brighten up a bit. The Japanese boy who was working over the free chair had a waiting list of eleven; all the other chairs were occupied. I sat down and began to wait. Outside, as Hemingway *(The Sun Also Rises; A Farewell to Arms; Death in the Afternoon; Winner Take Nothing)* would say, haircuts were four bits. I had twenty cents and a half pack of Bull Durham. I rolled a cigarette, handed the pack to one of my contemporaries who looked in need of nicotine, and inhaled the dry smoke, thinking of America, what was going on politically, economically, spiritually. My contemporary was a boy of sixteen. He looked Iowa; splendid potentially, a solid American, but down, greatly down in the mouth. Little sleep, no change of clothes for several days, a little fear, etc. I wanted very much to know his name. A writer is always wanting to get the reality of faces and figures. Iowa said, 'I just got in from Salinas. No work in the lettuce fields. Going north now, to Portland; try to ship out.' I wanted to tell him how it was with me: rejected story from *Scribner's*, rejected essay from *The Yale Review*, no money for decent cigarettes, worn shoes, old shirts, but I was afraid to make something of my own troubles. A writer's troubles are always boring, a bit unreal. People are apt to feel, *Well, who asked you to write in the first place?* A man must pretend not to be a writer. I said, 'Good luck, north.' Iowa shook his head. 'I know better. Give it a try, anyway. Nothing to lose.' Fine boy, hope he isn't dead, hope he hasn't frozen, mighty cold these days (December, 1933), hope he hasn't gone down; he deserved to live. Iowa, I hope you got work in Portland; I hope you are earning money; I hope you have rented a clean room with a warm bed in it; I hope you are sleeping nights, eating regularly, walking along like a human being, being happy. Iowa, my good wishes are with you. I have said a number of prayers for you. (All the same, I think he is dead by this time. It was in him the day I saw him, the low malicious face of the beast, and at the same time all the theatres in America were showing, over and over again, an animated film-cartoon in which there was a song called 'Who's Afraid of the Big Bad Wolf?', and that's what it amounts to: people with money laughing at the death that is crawling slyly into boys like young Iowa, pretending that it isn't there, laughing in warm theatres. I have prayed for Iowa, and I consider myself a coward. By this time he must be dead, and I am sitting in a small room, talking about him, only talking.)

I began to watch the Japanese boy who was learning to become a barber. He was shaving an old tramp who had a horrible face, one of those faces that emerge from years and years of evasive living, years of being unsettled, of not belonging anywhere, of owning nothing, and the Japanese boy was holding his nose back (his own nose), so that he would not smell the old tramp. A trivial point in a story, a bit of data with no place in a work of art, nevertheless, I put it down. A young writer is always afraid some significant fact may escape him. He is always wanting to put in everything he sees. I wanted to know the name of the Japanese boy. I am profoundly interested in names. I have found that those that are unknown are the most genuine. Take a big name like Andrew Mellon. I was watching the Japanese boy very closely. I wanted to understand from the way he was keeping his sense of smell away from the mouth and nostrils of the old man what he was thinking, how he was feeling. Years ago, when I was seventeen, I pruned vines in my uncle's vineyard, north of Sanger, in the San Joaquin Valley, and there were several Japanese working with me, Yoshio Enomoto, Hideo Suzuki, Katsumi Sujimoto, and one or two others. These Japanese taught me a few simple phrases, *hello, how are you, fine day, isn't it, good-bye,* and so on. I said in Japanese to the barber student, 'How are you?' He said in Japanese, 'Very well, thank you.' Then, in impeccable English, 'Do you speak Japanese? Have you lived in Japan?' I said, 'Unfortunately, no. I am able to speak only one or two words. I used to work with Yoshio Enomoto, Hideo Suzuki, Katsumi Sujimoto; do you know them?' He went on with his work, thinking of the names. He seemed to be whispering, 'Enomoto, Suzuki, Sujimoto.' He said, 'Suzuki. Small man?' I said, 'Yes.' He said, 'I know him. He lives in San José now. He is married now.'

I want you to know that I am deeply interested in what people remember. A young writer goes out to places and talks to people. He tries to find out what they remember. I am not using great material for a short story. Nothing is going to happen in this work. I am not fabricating a fancy plot. I am not creating memorable characters. I am not using a slick style of writing. I am not building up a fine atmosphere. I have no desire to sell this story or any story to *The Saturday Evening Post* or to *Cosmopolitan* or to *Harper's*. I am not trying to compete with the great writers of short stories, men like Sinclair Lewis and Joseph

Hergesheimer and Zane Grey, men who really know how to write, how to make up stories that will sell. Rich men, men who understand all the rules about plot and character and style and atmosphere and all that stuff. I have no desire for fame. I am not out to win the Pulitzer Prize or the Nobel Prize or any other prize. I am out here in the far West, in San Francisco, in a small room on Carl Street, writing a letter to common people, telling them in simple language things they already know. I am merely making a record, so if I wander around a little, it is because I am in no hurry and because I do not know the rules. If I have any desire at all, it is to show the brotherhood of man. This is a big statement and it sounds a little precious. Generally a man is ashamed to make such a statement. He is afraid sophisticated people will laugh at him. But I don't mind. I'm asking sophisticated people to laugh. That is what sophistication is for. I do not believe in races. I do not believe in governments. I see life as one life at one time, so many million simultaneously, all over the earth. Babies who have not yet been taught to speak any language are the only race of the earth, the race of man: all the rest is pretence, what we call civilization, hatred, fear, desire for strength. . . . But a baby is a baby. And the way they cry, there you have the brotherhood of man, babies crying. We grow up and we learn the words of a language and we see the universe through the language we know, we do not see it through all languages or through no language at all, through silence, for example, and we isolate ourselves in the language we know. Over here we isolate ourselves in English, or American as Mencken calls it. All the eternal things, in our words. If I want to do anything, I want to speak a more universal language. The heart of man, the unwritten part of man, that which is eternal and common to all races.

Now I am beginning to feel guilty and incompetent. I have used all this language and I am beginning to feel that I have said nothing. This is what drives a young writer out of his head, this feeling that nothing is being said. Any ordinary journalist would have been able to put the whole business into a three-word caption. Man is man, he would have said. Something clever, with any number of implications. But I want to use language that will create a single implication. I want the meaning to be precise, and perhaps that is why the language is so imprecise, I am walking around my subject, the impression I want to make, and I am trying to see it from all angles, so that I will have a whole picture, a picture of wholeness. It is the heart of man that I am trying to imply in this work.

Let me try again: I hadn't had a haircut in a long time and I was beginning to look seedy, so I went down to the Barber College on Third Street, and I sat in a chair. I said, 'Leave it full in the back. I have a narrow head and if you do not leave it full in the back, I will go out of this place looking like a horse. Take as much as you like off the top. No lotion, no water, comb it dry.' Reading makes a full man, writing a precise one, as you see. This is what happened. It doesn't make much of a story, and the reason is that I have left out the barber, the young man who gave me the haircut.

He was tall, he had a dark serious face, thick lips, on the verge of smiling, but melancholy, thick lashes, sad eyes, a large nose. I saw his name on the card that was pasted on the mirror, Theodore Badal. A good name, genuine, a good young man, genuine. Theodore Badal began to work on my head. A good barber never speaks until he has been spoken to, no matter how full his heart may be.

'That name,' I said, 'Badal. Are you an Armenian?' I am an Armenian. I have mentioned this before. People look at me and begin to wonder, so I come right out and tell them. 'I am an Armenian,' I say. Or they read something I have written and begin to wonder, so I let them know. 'I am an Armenian,' I say. It is a meaningless remark, but they expect me to say it, so I do.

I have no idea what it is like to be an Armenian or what it is like to be an Englishman or a Japanese or anything else. I have a faint idea what it is like to be alive. This is the only thing that interests me greatly. This and tennis. I hope some day to write a great philosophical work on tennis, something of the order of *Death in the Afternoon,* but I am aware that I am not yet ready to undertake such a work. I feel that the cultivation of tennis on a large scale among the peoples of the earth will do much to annihilate racial differences, prejudices, hatred, etc. Just as soon as I have perfected my drive and my lob, I hope to begin my outline of this great work. (It may seem to some sophisitcated people that I am trying to make fun of Hemingway. I am not. *Death in the Afternoon* is a pretty sound piece of prose. I could never object to it as prose. I cannot even object to it as philosophy. I think it is finer philosophy than that of Will Durant and Walter Pitkin. Even when Hemingway is a fool, he is at least an accurate fool. He tells you what actually takes place and he doesn't allow the speed of an occurence to make his exposition of it hasty. This is a lot. It is some sort of advancement for literature. To relate leisurely the nature and meaning of that which is very brief in duration.)

'Are you an Armenian?' I asked.

We are a small people and whenever one of us meets another, it is an event. We are always looking around for someone to talk to in our language. Our most ambitious political party estimates that there are nearly two million of us living on the earth, but most of us don't think so. Most of us sit down and take a pencil and a piece of paper and we take one section of the world at a time and imagine how many Armenians at the most are likely to be living in that section and we put the highest number on the paper, and then we go on to another section, India, Russia, Soviet Armenia, Egypt, Italy, Germany, France, America, South America, Australia, and so on, and after we add up our most hopeful figures the total comes to something a little less than a million. Then we start to think how big our families are, how high our birthrate and how low our deathrate (except in times of war when massacres increase the deathrate), and we begin to imagine how rapidly we will increase if we are left alone a quarter of a century, and we feel pretty happy. We always leave out earthquakes, wars, massacres, famines, etc., and it is a mistake. I remember the Near East Relief drives in my home town. My uncle used to be our orator and he used to make a whole auditorium full of Armenians weep. He was an attorney and he was a great orator. Well, at first the trouble was war. Our people were being destroyed by the enemy. Those who hadn't been killed were homeless and they were starving, *our own flesh and blood,* my uncle said, and we all wept. And we gathered money and sent it to our people in the old country. Then after the war, when I was a bigger boy, we had another Near East Relief drive and my uncle stood on the stage of the Civic Auditroium of my home town and he said, 'Thank God this time it is not the enemy, but an earthquake. God has made us suffer. We have worshipped Him through trial and tribulation, through suffering and disease and torture and horror and (my uncle began to weep, began to sob) through the madness of despair, and now He has done this thing, and still we praise Him, still we worship Him. We do not understand the ways of God.' And after the drive I went to my uncle and I said, 'Did you mean what you said about God?' And he said, 'That was oratory. We've got to raise money. What God? It is nonsense.' 'And when you cried?' I asked, and my uncle said, 'That was real. I could not help it. I had to cry. Why, for God's sake, why must we go through all this God damn hell? What have we done to deserve all this torture? Man won't let us alone. God won't let us alone. Have we done something? Aren't we supposed to be pious people? What is our sin? I am disgusted with God. I am sick of man. The only reason I am willing to get up and talk is that I don't dare keep my mouth shut. I can't bear the thought of more of our people dying. Jesus Christ, have we done something?'

I asked Theodore Badal if he was an Armenian.

He said, 'I am an Assyrian.'

Well, it was something. They, the Assyrians, came from our part of the world, they had noses like our noses, eyes like our eyes, hearts like our hearts. They had a different language. When they spoke we couldn't understand them, but they were a lot like us. It wasn't quite as pleasing as it would have been if Badal had been an Armenian, but it was something.

'I am an Armenian,' I said. 'I used to know some Assyrian boys in my home town, Joseph Sargis, Nito Elia, Tony Saleh. Do you know any of them?'

'Joseph Sargis, I know him,' said Badal. 'The others I do not know. We lived in New York until five years ago, then we came out west to Turlock. Then we moved up to San Francisco.'

'Nito Elia,' I said, 'is a Captain in the Salvation Army.' (I don't want anyone to imagine that I am making anything up, or that I am trying to be funny.) 'Tony Saleh,' I said, 'was killed eight years ago. He was riding a horse and he was thrown and the horse began to run. Tony couldn't get himself free, he was caught by a leg, and the horse ran around and around for a half hour and then stopped, and when they went up to Tony he was dead. He was fourteen at the time. I used to go to school with him. Tony was a very clever boy, very good at arithmetic.'

We began to talk about the Assyrian language and the Armenian language, about the old world, conditions over there, and so on. I was getting a fifteen-cent haircut and I was doing my best to learn something at the same time, to acquire some new truth, some new appreciation of the wonder of life, the dignity of man. (Man has great dignity, do not imagine that he has not.)

Badal said, 'I cannot read Assyrian. I was born in the old country, but I want to get over it.'

He sounded tired, not physically but spiritually.

'Why?' I said. 'Why do you want to get over it?'

'Well,' he laughed, 'simply because everything is washed up over there.' I am repeating his words, precisely, putting in nothing of my own. 'We were a great people once,' he went on. 'But that was yesterday, the day before yesterday. Now we are a topic in ancient history. We had a great civilization. They're still admiring it. Now I am in America learning to cut hair. We're washed up as a race, we're through, it's all over, why should I learn to read the language? We have no writers, we have no news—well, there is a little news: once in a while the English encourage the Arabs to massacre us, that is all. It's an old story, we know all about it. The news comes over to us through the Associated Press, anyway.'

These remarks were painful to me, an Armenian. I had always felt badly about my own people being destroyed. I had never heard an Assyrian speaking in English about such things. I felt great love for this young fellow. Don't get me wrong. There is a tendency these days to think in terms of pansies whenever a man says that he has affection for man. I think now that I have affection for all people, even for the enemies of Armenia, whom I have so tactfully not named. Everyone knows who they are. I have nothing against any of them because I think of them as one man living one life at a time, and I know, I am positive, that one man at a time is incapable of the monstrosities performed by mobs. My objection is to mobs only.

'Well,' I said, 'it is much the same with us. We, too, are old. We still have our church. We still have a few writers, Aharonian, Isahakian, a few others, but it is much the same.'

'Yes,' said the barber. 'I know. We went in for the wrong things. We went in for the simple things, peace and quiet and families. We didn't go in for machinery and conquest and militarism. We didn't go in for diplomacy and deceit and the invention of machine-guns and poison gases. Well, there is no use being disappointed. We had our day, I suppose.'

'We are hopeful,' I said. 'There is no Armenian living who does not still dream of an independent Armenia.'

'Dream?' said Badal. 'Well, that is something. Assyrians cannot even dream any more. Why, do you know how many of us are left on earth?'

'Two or three million,' I suggested.

'Seventy thousand,' said Badal. 'That is all. Seventy thousand Assyrians in the world, and the Arabs are still killing us. They killed seventy of us in a little uprising last month. There was a small paragraph in the paper. Seventy more of us destroyed. We'll be wiped out before long. My brother is married to an American girl and he has a son. There is no more hope. We are trying to forget Assyria. My father still reads a paper that comes from New York, but he is an old man. He will be dead soon.'

Then his voice changed, he ceased speaking as an Assyrian and began to speak as a barber: 'Have I taken enough off the top?' he asked.

The rest of the story is pointless. I said *so long* to the young Assyrian and left the shop. I walked across town, four miles, to my room on Carl Street. I thought about the whole business: Assyria and this Assyrian. Theodore Badal, learning to be a barber, the sadness of his voice, the hopelessness of his attitude. This was months ago, in August, but ever since I have been thinking about Assyria, and I have been wanting to say something about Theodore Badal, a son of an ancient race, himself youthful and alert, yet hopeless. Seventy thousand Assyrians, a mere seventy thousand of that great people, and all the others quiet in death and all the greatness crumbled and ignored, and a young man in America learning to be a barber, and a young man lamenting bitterly the course of history.

Why don't I make up plots and write beautiful love stories that can be made into motion pictures? Why don't I let these unimportant and boring matters go hang? Why don't I try to please the American reading public?

Well, I am an Armenian. Michael Arlen is an Armenian, too. He is pleasing the public. I have great admiration for him, and I think he has perfected a very fine style of writing and all that, but I don't want to write about the people he likes to write about. Those people were dead to begin with. You take Iowa and the Japanese boy and Theodore Badal, the Assyrian; well, they may go down physically, like Iowa, to death, or spiritually, like Badal, to death, but they are of the stuff that is eternal in man and it is this stuff that interests me. You don't find them in bright places, making witty remarks about sex and trivial remarks about art. You find them where I found them, and they will be there forever, the race of man, the part of man, of Assyria as much as of England, that cannot be destroyed, the part that massacre does not destroy, the part that earthquake and war and famine and madness and everything else cannot destroy.

This work is in tribute to Iowa, to Japan, to Assyria, to Armenia, to the race of man everywhere, to the dignity of that race, the brotherhood of things alive. I am not expecting Paramount Pictures to film this work. I am thinking of seventy thousand Assyrians, one at a time, alive, a great race. I am thinking of Theodore Badal, himself seventy thousand Assyrians and seventy million Assyrians, himself Assyria, and man, standing in a barber's shop, in San Francisco, in 1933, and being, still, himself, the whole race.

[1934]

For Thought

"Seventy Thousand Assyrians" is more of an impressionistic discourse that is fortuitously connected with getting a haircut than a short story in any formal sense of the term. In this discourse, Saroyan sees a universal human principle in a seemingly trivial encounter. The young Assyrian apprentice barber is viewed as an individual in his own right and as a mournful symbol of a once-proud race and great civilization of the past.

For Discussion

1. What is the narrator's attitude toward the people in his story?
2. What seems to be the narrator's philosophy of life as judged by this account?
3. How does the background of the Great Depression of the 1930s serve as an active force in the story?
4. In his system of literary values, what does the narrator regard highly and what does he dislike?
5. How is the title deliberately ironic and misleading?

Dorothy L. Sayers
The Unprincipled Affair of the Practical Joker

The *Zambesi,* they said, was expected to dock at six in the morning. Mrs Ruyslaender booked a bedroom at the Magnifical, with despair in her heart. A bare nine hours and she would be greeting her husband. After that would begin the sickening period of waiting—it might be days, it might be weeks, possibly even months—for the inevitable discovery.

The reception-clerk twirled the register towards her. Mechanically, as she signed it, she glanced at the preceding entry:

'Lord Peter Wimsey and valet—London—suite 24.'

Mrs Ruyslaender's heart seemed to stop for a second. Was it possible that, even now, God had left a loophole? She expected little from Him—all her life He had shown Himself a sufficiently stern creditor. It was fantastic to base the frailest hope on this signature of a man she had never even seen.

Yet the name remained in her mind while she dined in her own room. She dismissed her maid presently, and sat for a long time looking at her own haggard reflection in the mirror. Twice she rose and went to the door—then turned back, calling herself a fool. The third time she turned the handle quickly and hurried down the corridor, without giving herself time to think.

A large golden arrow at the corner directed her to Suite 24. It was eleven o'clock, and nobody was within view. Mrs Ruyslaender gave a sharp knock on Lord Peter Wimsey's door and stood back, waiting, with the sort of desperate relief one experiences after hearing a dangerous letter thump the bottom of the pillar-box. Whatever the adventure, she was committed to it.

The manservant was of the imperturbable sort. He neither invited nor rejected, but stood respectfully upon the threshold.

'Lord Peter Wimsey?' murmured Mrs Ruyslaender.

'Yes, madam.'

'Could I speak to him for a moment?'

'His lordship has just retired, madam. If you will step in, I will inquire.'

Mrs Ruyslaender followed him into one of those palatial sitting-rooms which the Magnifical provides for the wealthy pilgrim.

'Will you take a seat, madam?'

The man stepped noiselessly to the bedroom door and passed in, shutting it behind him. The lock, however, failed to catch, and Mrs Ruyslaender caught the conversation.

'Pardon me, my lord, a lady has called. She mentioned no appointment, so I considered it better to acquaint your lordship.'

'Excellent discretion,' said a voice. It had a slow, sarcastic intonation, which brought a painful flush to Mrs Ruyslaender's cheek. 'I never make appointments. Do I know the lady?'

'No, my lord. But—hem—I know her by sight, my lord. It is Mrs Ruyslaender.'

'Oh, the diamond merchant's wife. Well, find out tactfully what it's all about, and, unless it's urgent, ask her to call tomorrow.'

The valet's next remark was inaudible, but the reply was:

'Don't be coarse, Bunter.'

The valet returned.

'His lordship desires me to ask you, madam, in what way he can be of service to you?'

'Will you say to him that I have heard of him in connexion with the Attenbury diamond case, and am anxious to ask his advice.'

'Certainly, madam. May I suggest that, as his lordship is greatly fatigued, he would be better able to assist you after he has slept.'

'If tomorrow would have done, I would not have thought of disturbing him tonight. Tell him, I am aware of the trouble I am giving—'

'Excuse me one moment, madam.'

This time the door shut properly. After a short interval Bunter returned to say, 'His lordship will be with you immediately, madam,' and to place a decanter of wine and a box of Sobranies beside her.

Mrs Ruyslaender lit a cigarette, but had barely sampled its flavour when she was aware of a soft step beside her. Looking round, she perceived a young man, attired in a mauve dressing gown of great splendour, from beneath the hem of which peeped coyly a pair of primrose silk pyjamas.

'You must think it very strange of me, thrusting myself on you at this hour,' she said, with a nervous laugh.

Lord Peter put his head on one side.

'Don't know the answer to that,' he said. 'If I say, "Not at all," it sounds abandoned. If I say, "Yes, very," it's rude. Supposin' we give it a miss, what? and you tell me what I can do for you.'

Mrs Ruyslaender hesitated. Lord Peter was not what she had expected. She noted the sleek, straw-coloured hair, brushed flat back from a rather sloping forehead, the ugly, lean, arched nose, and the faintly foolish smile, and her heart sank within her.

'I—I'm afraid it's ridiculous of me to suppose you can help me,' she began.

'Always my unfortunate appearance,' moaned Lord Peter, with such alarming acumen as to double her discomfort. 'Would it invite confidence more, d'you suppose, if I dyed my hair black an' grew a Newgate fringe? It's very tryin', you can't think, always to look as if one's name was Algy.'

'I only meant,' said Mrs Ruyslaender, 'that I don't think *anybody* could possibly help. But I saw your name in the hotel book, and it seemed just a chance.'

Lord Peter filled the glasses and sat down.

'Carry on,' he said cheerfully; 'it sounds interestin'.'

Mrs Ruyslaender took the plunge.

'My husband,' she explained, 'is Henry Ruyslaender, the diamond merchant. We came over from Kimberley ten years ago, and settled in England. He spends several months in Africa every year on business, and I am expecting him back on the *Zambesi* tomorrow morning. Now, this is the trouble. Last year he gave me a magnificent diamond necklace of a hundred and fifteen stones—'

'The Light of Africa—I know,' said Wimsey.

She looked a little surprised, but assented. 'The necklace has been stolen from me, and I can't hope to conceal the loss from him. No duplicate would deceive him for an instant.'

She paused, and Lord Peter prompted gently;

'You have come to me, I presume, because it is not to be a police matter. Will you tell me quite frankly why?'

'The police would be useless. I know who took it.'

'Yes?'

'There is a man we both know slightly—a man called Paul Melville.'

Lord Peter's eyes narrowed. 'M'm, yes, I fancy I've seen him about the clubs. New Army, but transferred himself into the Regulars. Dark. Showy. Bit of an ampelopsis, what?'

'Ampelopsis?'

'Suburban plant that climbs by suction. *You* know—first year, tender little shoots—second year, fine show—next year, all over the shop. Now tell me I am rude.'

Mrs Ruyslaender giggled. 'Now you mention it, he is *exactly* like an ampelopsis. What a relief to be able to think of him as that. . . . Well, he is some sort of distant relation of my husband's. He called one evening when I was alone. We talked about jewels, and I brought down my jewel-box and showed him the Light of Africa. He knows a good deal about stones. I was in and out of the room two or three times, but didn't think to lock up the box. After he left, I was putting the things away, and I opened the jeweller's case the diamonds were in—and they had gone!'

'H'm—pretty barefaced. Look here, Mrs Ruyslaender, you agree he's an ampelopsis, but you won't call in the police. Honestly, now—forgive me; you're askin' my advice, you know—is he worth botherin' about?'

'It's not that,' said the woman in a low tone. 'Oh, no! But he took something else as well. He took—a portrait—a small painting set with diamonds.'

'Oh!'

'Yes. It was in a secret drawer in the jewel-box. I can't imagine how he knew it was there, but the box was an old casket, belonging to my husband's family, and I fancy he must have known about the drawer and—well, thought that investigation might prove profitable. Anyway, the evening the diamonds went the portrait went too, and he knows I daren't try to get the necklace back because they'd both be found together.'

'Was there something more than just the portrait, then? A protrait in itself isn't necessarily hopeless of explantaion. It was given you to take care of, say.'

'The names were on it—and—and an inscription which nothing, *nothing* could ever explain away. A—a passage from Petronius.'

'Oh, dear!' said Lord Peter, 'dear me, yes. Rather a lively author.'

'I was married very young,' said Mrs Ruyslaender, 'and my husband and I have never got on well. Then one year, when he was in Africa, it all happened. We were wonderful—and shameless. It came to an end. I was bitter. I wish I had not been. He left me, you see, and I couldn't forgive it. I prayed day and night for revenge. Only now—I don't want it to be through me!'

'Wait a moment,' said Wimsey, 'you mean that, if the diamonds are found and the protrait is found too, all this story is bound to come out.'

'My husband would get a divorce. He would never forgive me—or him. It is not so much that I mind paying the price myself, but—'

She clenched her hands.

'I have cursed him again and again, and the clever girl who married him. She played her cards so well. This would ruin them both.'

'But if *you* were the instrument of vengeance,' said Wimsey gently, 'you would hate yourself. And it would be terrible to you because he would hate you. A woman like you couldn't stoop to get your own back. I see that. If God makes a thunderbolt, how awful and satisfying—if you help to make a beastly row, what a rotten business it would be.'

'You seem to understand,' said Mrs Ruyslaender. 'How unusual.'

'I understand perfectly. Though let me tell you,' said Wimsey, with a wry little twist of the lips. 'that it's sheer foolsihness for a woman to have a sense of honour in such matters. It only gives her excruciating pain, and nobody expects it, anyway. Look here, don't let's get all worked up. You certainly shan't have your vengeance thrust upon you by an ampelopsis. Why should you? Nasty fellow. We'll have him up—root, branch and little suckers. Don't worry. Let's see. My business here will only take a day. Then I've got to get to know Melville—say a week. Then I've got to get the doings—say another week, provided he hasn't sold them yet, which isn't likely. Can you hold your husband off 'em for a fortnight, d'you think?'

'Oh, yes. I'll say they're in the country, or being cleaned, or something. But do you really think you can—?'

'I'll have a jolly good try, anyhow, Mrs Ruyslaender. Is the fellow hard up, to start stealing diamonds?'

'I fancy he has got into debt over horses lately. And possibly poker.'

'Oh! Poker player, is he? That makes an excellent excuse for gettin' to know him. Well, cheer up—we'll get the goods, even if we have to buy 'em. But we won't, if we can help it. Bunter!'

'My lord?' The valet appeared from the inner room.

'Just go an' give the "All Clear," will you?'

Mr Bunter accordingly stepped into the passage, and, having seen an old gentleman safely away to the bathroom and a young lady in a pink kimono pop her head out of an adjacent door and hurriedly pop it back on beholding him, blew his nose with a loud, trumpeting sound.

'Good night,' said Mrs Ruyslaender, 'and thank you.'

She slipped back to her room unobserved.

'Whatever has induced you, my dear boy,' said Colonel Marchbanks, 'To take up with that very objectionable fellow Melville?'

'Diamonds,' said Lord Peter. 'Do you find him so, really?'

'Perfectly dreadful man,' said the Hon. Frederick Arbuthnot. 'Hearts. What did you want to go and get him a room here for? This used to be quite a decent club.'

'Two clubs?' said Sir Impey Biggs, who had been ordering a whisky, and had only caught the last word.

'No, no, one heart.'

'I beg your pardon. Well, partner, how about spades? Perfectly good suit.'

'Pass,' said the Colonel. 'I don't know what the Army's coming to nowadays.'

'No trumps,' said Wimsey. 'It's all right, children. Trust your Uncle Pete. Come on, Freddy, how many of those hearts are you going to shout for?'

'None, the Colonel havin' let me down so 'orrid,' said the Hon. Freddy.

'Cautious blighter. All content? Righty-ho! Bring out your dead, partner. Oh, very pretty indeed. We'll make it a slam this time. I'm rather glad to hear that expression of opinion from you, Colonel, because I particularly want you and Biggy to hang on this evening and take a hand with Melville and me.'

'What happens to me?' inquired the Hon. Freddy.

'You have an engagement and go home early, dear old thing. I've specially invited friend Melville to meet the redoubtable Colonel Marchbanks and our greatest criminal lawyer. Which hand am I supposed to be playin' this from? Oh, yes. Come on, Colonel—you've got to hike that old king out some time, why not now?'

'It's a plot,' said Mr Arbuthnot, with an exagerated expression of mystery. 'Carry on, don't mind me.'

'I take it you have your own reasons for cultivating the man,' said Sir Impey.

'The rest are mine, I fancy. Well, yes, I have. You and the Colonel would really do me a favour by letting Melville cut in tonight.'

'If you wish it,' growled the Colonel, 'but I hope the impudent young beggar won't presume on the acquaintance.'

'I'll see to that,' said his lordship. 'Your cards, Freddy. Who had the ace of hearts? Oh! I had it myself, of course. Our honours.... Hullo! Evenin', Melville.'

The ampelopsis was rather a good-looking creature in his own way. Tall and bronzed, with a fine row of very persuasive teeth. He greeted Wimsey and Arbuthnot heartily, the Colonel with a shade too much familiarity, and expressed himself delighted to be introduced to Sir Impey Biggs.

'You're just in time to hold Freddy's hand,' said Wimsey; 'he's got a date. Not his little paddy-paw, I don't mean—but the dam' rotten hand he generally gets dealt him. Joke.'

'Oh, well,' said the obedient Freddy, rising, 'I s'pose I'd better make a noise like a hoop and roll away. Night, night, everybody.'

Melville took his place, and the game continued with varying fortunes for two hours, at the end of which time Colonel Marchbanks, who had suffered much under his partner's eloquent theory of the game, was beginning to wilt visibly.

Wimsey yawned.

'Gettin' a bit bored, Colonel? Wish they'd invent somethin' to liven this game up a bit.'

'Oh, bridge is a one-horse show, anyway,' said Melville. 'Why not have a little flutter at poker, Colonel? Do you all the good in the world. What d'you say, Biggs?'

Sir Impey turned on Wimsey a thoughtful eye, accustomed to the sizing-up of witnesses. Then he replied:

'I'm quite willing, if the others are.'

'Damn good idea,' said Lord Peter. 'Come now, Colonel, be a sport. You'll find the chips in that drawer I think. I always lose money at poker, but what's the odds so long as you're happy. Let's have a new pack.'

'Any limit?'

'What do *you* say, Colonel?'

The Colonel proposed a twenty-shilling limit. Melville, with a grimace, amended this to one-tenth of the pool. The amendment was carried and the cards cut, the deal falling to the Colonel.

Contrary to his own prophecy, Wimsey began by winning considerably, and grew so garrulously imbecile in the process that even the experienced Melville began to wonder whether this indescribable fatuity was the cloak of ignorance or the mask of the hardened poker-player. Soon, however, he was reassured. The luck came over to his side, and he found himself winning hands down, steadily from Sir Impey and the Colonel, who played cautiously and took little risk—heavily from Wimsey, who appeared reckless and slightly drunk, and was staking foolishly on quite impossible cards.

'I never knew such luck as yours, Melville,' said Sir Impey, when that young man had scooped in the proceeds from a handsome straight-flush.

'My turn tonight, yours tomorrow,' said Melville, pushing the cards across to Biggs, whose deal it was.

Colonel Marchbanks required one card. Wimsey laughed vacantly and demanded an entirely fresh hand; Biggs asked for three; and Melville, after a pause for consideration, took one.

It seemed as though everybody had

something respectable this time—though Wimsey was not to be depended upon, frequently going the limit upon a pair of jacks in order, as he expressed it, to keep the pot a-boiling. He became peculiarly obstinate now, throwing his chips in with a flushed face, in spite of Melville's confident air.

The Colonel got out, and after a short time Biggs followed his example. Melville held on till the pool mounted to something under a hundred pounds, when Wimsey suddenly turned restive and demanded to see him.

'Four kings,' said Melville.

'Blast you!' said Lord Peter, laying down four queens. 'No holdin' this feller tonight, is there? Here, take the ruddy cards, Melville, and give somebody else a look in, will you.'

He shuffled them as he spoke, and handed them over. Melville dealt, satisfied the demands of the other three players, and was in the act of taking three new cards for himself, when Wimsey gave a sudden exclamation, and shot a swift hand across the table.

'Hullo! Melville,' he said, in a chill tone which bore no resemblance to his ordinary speech, 'what exactly does this mean?'

He lifted Melville's left arm clear of the table and, with a sharp gesture, shook it. From the sleeve something fluttered to the table and glided away to the floor. Colonel Marchbanks picked it up, and in a dreadful silence laid the joker on the table.

'Good God!' said Sir Impey.

'You young blackguard!' gasped the Colonel, recovering speech.

'What the hell do you mean by this?' gasped Melville, with a face like chalk. 'How dare you! This is a trick—a plant—' A horrible fury gripped him. 'You dare to say that I have been cheating. You liar! You filthy sharper. You put it there. I tell you, gentlemen,' he cried, looking desperately round the table, 'he must have put it there.'

'Come, come,' said Colonel Marchbanks, 'no good carryin' on that way, Melville. Dear me, no good at all. Only makes matters worse. We all saw it, you know. Dear, dear, I don't know what the Army's coming to.'

'Do you mean you believe it?' shrieked Melville. 'For God's sake, Wimsey, is this a joke or what? Biggs—you've got a head on your shoulders—are you going to believe this half-drunk fool and this doddering old idiot who ought to be in his grave?'

'That language won't do you any good, Melville,' said Sir Impey. 'I'm afraid we all saw it clearly enough.'

'I've been suspectin' this some time, y'know,' said Wimsey. 'That's why I asked you two to stay tonight. We don't want to make a public row, but—'

'Gentlemen,' said Melville more soberly, 'I swear to you that I am absolutely innocent of this ghastly thing. Can't you believe me?'

'I can believe the evidence of my own eyes, sir,' said the Colonel, with some heat.

'For the good of the club,' said Wimsey, 'this couldn't go on, but—also for the good of the club—I think we should all prefer the matter to be quietly arranged. In the face of what Sir Impey and the Colonel can witness, Melville, I'm afraid your protestations are not likely to be credited.'

Melville looked from the soldier's face to that of the great criminal lawyer.

'I don't know what your game is,' he said sullenly to Wimsey, 'but I can see you've laid a trap and pulled it off all right.'

'I think, gentlemen,' said Wimsey, 'that if I might have a word in private with Melville in his own room, I could get the thing settled satisfactorily, without undue fuss.'

'He'll have to resign his commission,' growled the Colonel.

'I'll put it to him in that light,' said Peter. 'May we go to your room for a minute, Melville?'

With a lowering brow, the young soldier led the way. Once alone with Wimsey, he turned furiously on him.

'What do you want? What do you mean

by making this monstrous charge? I'll take action for libel!'

'Do,' said Wimsey coolly, 'if you think anybody is likely to believe your story.'

He lit a cigarette, and smiled lazily at the angry young man.

'Well, what's the meaning of it, anyway?'

'The meaning,' said Wimsey, 'is simply that you, an officer and a member of this club, have been caught red-handed cheating at cards while playing for money, the witnesses being Sir Impey Biggs, Colonel Marchbanks, and myself. Now, I suggest to you, Captain Melville, that your best plan is to let me take charge of Mrs Ruyslaender's diamond necklace and portrait, and then just to trickle away quiet-like from these halls of dazzlin' light—without any questions asked.'

Melville leapt to his feet.

'My God!' he cried. 'I can see it now. It's blackmail.'

'You may certainly call it blackmail, and theft too,' said Lord Peter, with a shrug. 'But why use ugly names? I hold five aces, you see. Better chuck in your hand.'

'Suppose I say I never heard of the diamonds?'

'It's a bit late now, isn't it?' said Wimsey affably. 'But, in that case, I'm beastly sorry and all that, of course, but we shall have to make tonight's business public.'

'Damn you!' muttered Melville, 'you sneering devil.'

He showed all his white teeth, half springing, with crouched shoulders. Wimsey waited quietly, his hands in his pockets.

The rush did not come. With a furious gesture, Melville pulled out his keys and unlocked his dressing-case.

'Take them,' he growled, flinging a small parcel on the table; 'you've got me. Take 'em and go to hell.'

'Eventually—why not now?' murmured his lordship. 'Thanks frightfully. Man of peace myself, you know—hate unpleasantness and all that.' He scrutinized his booty carefully, running the stones expertly between his fingers. Over the portrait he pursed up his lips. 'Yes,' he murmured, 'that *would* have made a row.' He replaced the wrapping and slipped the parcel into his pocket.

'Well, good night, Melville—and thanks for a pleasant game.'

'I say, Biggs,' said Wimsey, when he had returned to the cardroom. 'You've had a lot of experience. What tactics d'you think one's justified in usin' with a blackmailer?'

'Ah!' said the K.C. 'There you've put your finger on Society's sore place, where the Law is helpless. Speaking as a man, I'd say nothing could be too bad for the brute. It's a crime crueller and infinitely worse in its results than murder. As a lawyer, I can only say that I have consistently refused to defend a blackmailer or to prosecute any poor devil who does away with his tormentor.'

'H'm,' replied Wimsey. 'What do you say, Colonel?'

'A man like that's a filthy pest,' said the little warrior stoutly. 'Shootin's too good for him. I knew a man—close personal friend, in fact—hounded to death—blew his brains out—one of the best. Don't like to talk about it.'

'I want to show you something,' said Wimsey.

He picked up the pack which still lay scattered on the table, and shuffled it together.

'Catch hold of these, Colonel, and lay 'em out face downwards. That's right. First of all you cut 'em at the twentieth card—you'll see the seven of diamonds at the bottom. Correct? Now I'll call 'em. Ten of hearts, ace of spades, three of clubs, five of clubs, king of diamonds, nine, jack, two of hearts. Right? I could pick 'em all out, you see, except the ace of hearts, and that's here.'

He leaned forward and produced it dexterously from Sir Impey's breast-pocket.

'I learnt it from a man who shared my dug-out near Ypres,' he said. 'You needn't mention tonight's business, you two. There are crimes which the Law cannot reach.'

[1928]

For Thought

"The Unprincipled Affair of the Practical Joker" casts Lord Peter Wimsey as the nemesis of a young and desperate blackmailer. Approached by a woman compromised by the loss of an incriminating portrait, Peter turns the tables on his villain with a brilliant card trick. His device is a clever instance of an old-story tale device, "the biter bitten." Sayers suggests that motives count far more than actions when dealing with unscrupulous thieves.

For Discussion

1. Sayers arouses suspense in the first paragraph by posing a number of unanswered questions. What are these questions?
2. Sometimes, detectives are not physically impressive. How does Wimsey's description seem appropriate for a detective? What makes him likable?
3. Why does Mrs. Ruyslaender not want the story about her affair to come out?
4. The story is divided into three parts. What happens in each part?
5. What conflicts emerge from the story?
6. Why does Wimsey call Melville an ampelopsis?
7. An old saying goes, "one must set a thief to catch a thief." Is this applicable to Wimsey's situation?
8. What is the significance of the title?
9. In what way is the story a version of a romance?

Irwin Shaw
The Girls in Their Summer Dresses

Fifth Avenue was shining in the sun when they left the Brevoort. The sun was warm, even though it was February, and everything looked like Sunday morning—the buses and the well-dressed people walking slowly in couples and the quiet buildings with the windows closed.

Michael held Frances' arm tightly as they walked toward Washington Square in the sunlight. They walked lightly, almost smiling, because they had slept late and had a good breakfast and it was Sunday. Michael unbuttoned his coat and let it flap around him in the mild wind.

"Look out," Frances said as they crossed Eighth Street. "You'll break your neck." Michael laughed and Frances laughed with him.

"She's not so pretty," Frances said. "Anyway, not pretty enough to take a chance of breaking your neck."

Michael laughed again. "How did you know I was looking at her?"

Frances cocked her head to one side and smiled at her husband under the brim of her hat. "Mike, darling," she said.

"O.K.," he said. "Excuse me."

Frances patted his arm lightly and pulled him along a little faster toward Washington Square. "Let's not see anybody all day," she said. "Let's just hang around with each other. You and me. We're always up to our neck in people, drinking their Scotch or drinking our Scotch; we only see each other in bed. I want to go out with my husband all day long. I want him to talk only to me and listen only to me."

"What's to stop us?" Michael asked.

"The Stevensons. They want us to drop by around one o'clock and they'll drive us into the country."

"The cunning Stevensons," Mike said. "Transparent. They can whistle. They can go driving in the country by themselves."

"Is it a date?"

"It's a date."

Frances leaned over and kissed him on the tip of the ear.

"Darling," Michael said, "this is Fifth Avenue."

"Let me arrange a program," Frances said. "A planned Sunday in New York for a young couple with money to throw away."

"Go easy."

"First let's go to the Metropolitan Museum of Art," Frances suggested, because Michael had said during the week he wanted to go. "I haven't been there in three years and there're at least ten pictures I want to see again. Then we can take the bus down to Radio City and watch them skate. And later we'll go down to Cavanagh's and get a steak as big as a blacksmith's apron, with a bottle of wine, and after that there's a French picture at the Filmarte that everybody says—say, are you listening to me?"

"Sure," he said. He took his eyes off the hatless girl with the dark hair, cut dancer-style like a helmet, who was walking past him.

"That's the program for the day," Frances said flatly. "Or maybe you'd just rather walk up and down Fifth Avenue."

"No," Michael said. "Not at all."

"You always look at other women," Frances said. "Everywhere. Every damned place we go."

"No, darling," Michael said, "I look at everything. God gave me eyes and I look at women and men in subway excavations and moving pictures and the little flowers of the field. I casually inspect the universe."

"You ought to see the look in your eye," Frances said, "as you casually inspect the universe on Fifth Avenue."

"I'm a happily married man." Michael pressed her elbow tenderly. "Example for the whole twentieth century—Mr. and Mrs. Mike Loomis. Hey, let's have a drink," he said, stopping.

"We just had breakfast."

"Now listen, darling," Mike said, choosing his words with care, "it's a nice day and we both feel good and there's no reason why we have to break it up. Let's have a nice Sunday."

"All right. I don't know why I started this. Let's drop it. Let's have a good time."

They joined hands consciously and walked without talking among the baby carriages and the old Italian men in their Sunday clothes and the young women with Scotties in Washington Square Park.

"At least once a year everyone should go to the Metropolitan Museum of Art," Frances said after a while, her tone a good imitation of the tone she had used at breakfast and at the beginning of their walk. "And it's nice on Sunday. There're a lot of people looking at the pictures and you get the feeling maybe Art isn't on the decline in New York City, after all—"

"I want to tell you something," Michael said very seriously. "I have not touched another woman. Not once. In all the five years."

"All right," Frances said.

"You believe that, don't you?"

"All right."

They walked between the crowded benches, under the scrubby city-park trees.

"I try not to notice it," Frances said, "but I feel rotten inside, in my stomach, when we pass a woman and you look at her and I see that look in your eye and that's the way you looked at me the first time. In Alice Maxwell's house. Standing there in the living room, next to the radio, with a green hat on and all those people."

"I remember the hat," Michael said.

"The same look," Frances said. "And it makes me feel bad. It makes me feel terrible."

"Sh-h-h, please, darling, sh-h-h."

"I think I would like a drink now," Frances said.

They walked over to a bar on Eighth Street, not saying anything, Michael automatically helping her over curbstones and guiding her past automobiles. They sat near a window in the bar and the sun streamed in and there was a small, cheerful fire in the fireplace. A little Japanese waiter came over and put down some pretzels and smiled happily at them.

"What do you order after breakfast?" Michael asked.

"Brandy, I suppose," Frances said.

"Courvoisier," Michael told the waiter. "Two Courvoisiers."

The waiter came with the glasses and they sat drinking the brandy in the sunlight. Michael finished half his and drank a little water.

"I look at women," he said. "Correct. I don't say it's wrong or right. I look at them. If I pass them on the street and I don't look at them, I'm fooling you, I'm fooling myself."

"You look at them as though you want them," Frances said, playing with her brandy glass. "Every one of them."

"In a way," Michael said, speaking softly and not to his wife, "in a way that's true. I don't do anything about it, but it's true."

"I know it. That's why I feel bad."

"Another brandy," Michael called. "Waiter, two more brandies." He sighed and closed his eyes and rubbed them gently with his fingertips. "I love the way women look. One of the things I like best about New York is the battalions of women. When I first came to New York from Ohio that was the first thing I noticed, the million wonderful women, all over the city. I walked around with my heart in my throat."

"A kid," Frances said. "That's a kid's feeling."

"Guess again," Michael said. "Guess again. I'm older now. I'm a man getting near middle age, putting on a little fat, and I still love to walk along Fifth Avenue at three o'clock on the east side of the street between Fiftieth and Fifty-seventh Streets. They're all out then, shopping, in their furs and their crazy hats, everything all concentrated from all over the world into seven blocks—the best furs, the best clothes, the handsomest women, out to spend money and feeling good about it."

The Japanese waiter put the two drinks down, smiling with great happiness.

"Everything is all right?" he asked.

"Everything is wonderful," Michael said.

"If it's just a couple of fur coats," Frances said, "and forty-five dollar hats—"

"It's not the fur coats. Or the hats. That's just the scenery for that particular kind of woman. Understand," he said, "you don't have to listen to this."

"I want to listen."

"I like the girls in the offices. Neat, with their eyeglasses, smart, chipper, knowing what everything is about. I like the girls on Forty-fourth Street at lunchtime, the actresses, all dressed up on nothing a week. I like the salesgirls in the stores, paying attention to you first because you're a man, leaving lady customers waiting. I got all this stuff accumulated in me because I've been thinking about it for ten years and now you've asked for it and here it is."

"Go ahead," Frances said.

"When I think of New York City, I think of all the girls on parade in the city. I don't know whether it's something special with me or whether every man in the city walks around with the same feeling inside him, but I feel as though I'm at a picnic in this city. I like to sit near the women in the theatres, the famous beauties who've taken six hours to get ready and look it. And the young girls at the football games, with the red cheeks, and when the warm weather comes, the girls in their summer dresses." He finished his drink. "That's the story."

Frances finished her drink and swallowed two or three times extra. "You say you love me?"

"I love you."

"I'm pretty, too," Frances said. "As pretty as any of them."

"You're beautiful," Michael said.

"I'm good for you," Frances said, pleading. "I've made a good wife, a good housekeeper, a good friend. I'd do any damn thing for you."

"I know," Michael said. He put his hand out and grasped hers.

"You'd like to be free to—" Frances said.

"Sh-h-h."

"Tell the truth." She took her hand away from under his.

Michael flicked the edge of his glass with his finger. "O.K.," he said gently. "Sometimes I feel I would like to be free."

"Well," Frances said, "any time you say."

"Don't be foolish." Michael swung his chair around to her side of the table and patted her thigh.

She began to cry silently into her handkerchief, bent over just enough so that nobody else in the bar would notice. "Someday," she said crying, "you're going to make a move."

Michael didn't say anything. He sat watching the bartender slowly peel a lemon.

"Aren't you?" Frances asked harshly. "Come on, tell me. Talk. Aren't you?"

"Maybe," Michael said. He moved his chair back again. "How the hell do I know?"

"You know," Frances persisted. "Don't you know?"

"Yes," Michael said after a while, "I know."

Frances stopped crying then. Two or three snuffles into the handerchief and she put it away and her face didn't tell anything to anybody. "At least do me one favor," she said.

"Sure."

"Stop talking about how pretty this woman is or that one. Nice eyes, nice breasts, a pretty figure, good voice." She mimicked his voice. "Keep it to yourself. I'm not interested."

Machael waved to the waiter. "I'll keep it to myself," he said.

Frances flicked the corners of her eyes. "Another brandy," she told the waiter.

"Two," Michael said.

"Yes, Ma'am, yes, sir," said the waiter, backing away.

Frances regarded Michael coolly across the table. "Do you want me to call the Stevensons?" she asked. "It'll be nice in the country."

"Sure," Michael said. "Call them."

She got up from the table and walked across the room toward the telephone. Michael watched her walk, thinking what a pretty girl, what nice legs.

[1939]

For Thought

Rather than a fully developed short story, "The Girls in Their Summer Dresses" is a very clever vignette involving essentially flat characters in a critical situation in their life together. Shaw shows Michael and Frances in a single, germinal episode that determines the nature of their future relationship. Because of the extreme compression required by the literary form he has chosen, the author is limited to those details of setting, characterization, and action that directly contribute to his central purpose—to bring to light, in a dramatic fashion and with a startling reversal of mood, the hitherto hidden problem that profoundly affects the relationship between Michael and Frances as husband and wife.

For Discussion

1. What is the tone of the conversation at the beginning of the story? What atmosphere prevails?
2. What "conspiracy" does Michael pretend to be foiling with his comment containing the words "cunning" and "transparent"?
3. What is the first indication of the discord that will displace the apparent harmony of the couple's relationship?
4. What is the symbolic value of the title?

5. What device does Shaw use to indicate an attempt on Frances's part to declare a truce?
6. What is the ironic effect of their stopping for a drink as originally suggested by Michael? What is ironic about Michael helping Frances over curbstones and guiding her past automobiles on their way to the bar?
7. What is ironic about Michael's protestations of fidelity?
8. What fundamental conflict is there between Michael and Frances as expressed in their different attitudes toward his girl watching?
9. What is the irony in their agreement to call the Stevensons?
10. What is the ironic effect of the last paragraph?
11. What is the author's attitude toward his two characters?

Michael Sholokhov
During the Retreat

The majority of the men settled down to sleep in the yard near the shed. The woman of the house made a bed for herself in the kitchen, while the sergeant, together with Streltzov, Lopahin, Khmyz and Kopitovsky, as well as four others, lay down in a room separated by a small passage from the kitchen.

Khmyz and a long-necked soldier, to whom the nickname of "crabcatcher" had firmly stuck, talked for a long time in whispers. Kopitovsky kept blindly catching fleas and swearing in a low voice. Lopahin smoked two cigarettes, one after the other, and then grew still. After a while, the sergeant called to him in a whisper:

"Lopahin, are you asleep?"

"No."

"Make sure you don't fall asleep!"

"Don't worry!"

"You need a shot or two of vodka to bolster your courage, but where the devil's father can we get it?"

Lopahin laughed quietly in the darkness and replied:

"I'll manage without that poison."

His bones could be heard cracking as he stretched himself and then got up.

"Are you going then?" the sergeant whispered.

"And why should I lose time?" Lopahin answered without restraining his voice.

"May you be successful!" the crabcatcher earnestly exclaimed. Lopahin kept silent. Tiptoeing, he groped his way in the infernal darkness towards the door leading to the passage.

"All the hungriest men are sleeping in the house, the rest—in the yard," said Khmyz in an undertone, and then boyishly put his hand over his mouth and blew a raspberry.

"What's got into you?" Kopitovsky asked in astonishment.

"*No passaran!* He'll not get through!" Khmyz answered in a voice shaking with laughter.

He was immediately rebuffed by Akimov, a sniper of the third batallion, a bilious and irritable man, who had worked before the war as an accountant in a large construction plant in Siberia:

SOURCE: "During the Retreat" by Michael Sholokhov. Translation by George Reavey. Translation © by George Reavey. Originally published in *Collected Works*, Belles Lettres Publishers, Moscow. Reprinted by permission of Jean Reavey.

"I would ask you, comrade Khmyz, to be more careful with words that are precious to humanity. An intelligent young man, with ten years of schooling behind him as far as I know, and here you are falling into the bad habit of using words carelessly. . ."

"He'll not get through!" Khmyz repeated, choking with laughter.

"What are you croaking about, you flaplip?" the crabcatcher inquired indignantly. "'He'll not get through, not get through,' but he is advancing quietly. Do you hear the board creak, and here you keep saying he won't get through. What do you mean by won't? He'll get through easily enough!"

"Quiet there! Silence and snoring is what we need most. If hunger won't let you snooze, pretend at least to sleep."

"How can we camouflage ourselves if the belly rumbles loud enough to be heard in the street," the crabcatcher commented dismally. "These damned cannibals! Not to feed a soldier, how do you like that? In the old days in the province of Smolensk, a peasant woman would give you her last potato; but from these people you wouldn't even get a helping of snow in the winter. Their collective farm here must be made up entirely of former kulaks, most likely. . . . How is he getting on there? There isn't a sound."

"He's got within range, but he won't get through all the same!" Khmyz jovially whispered.

"The situation at the front has completely spoiled you. You are incorrigible, I see," Akimov protested in disgust.

"Hey there, stop chattering," the sergeant whispered hoarsely.

"What's he hissing for, like a goose at a dog? He's got his own old man's business to attend to, so why doesn't he snore both ways. . . . It's no sergeant we have, but a beast on a chain."

"I'll give you beast tomorrow! You think I don't know your voice, Nekrasov? You can alter your voice as much as you like, but I'll know you anyhow!"

There was a minute's silence in the room, interrupted by a variety of snores; then the crabcatcher spoke out with unconcealed disappointment:

"He's not advancing! What's he marking time for? Oh, contagion! He'll wear the soul out of us before he gets into the line of fire! O Lord, what a lumpkin you sent! By the morning, maybe, he'll reach the passage."

There was silence again for a while, and then the crabcatcher spoke again, with despair this time in his voice:

"No, he's not advancing! Hugging the ground, is he? What's keeping him down? Has she set up barbed wire in front of the kitchen, or what?"

Finally losing his patience, the sergeant raised himself:

"Will you shut up now, you sons of Satan?"

"O Lord, as it is we're lying here as if under a German rocket . . ." the crabcatcher whispered almost inaudibly and then stopped:

Kopitovsky had clapped his outsized hand to his mouth. . . .

Several more minutes passed in harrassing expectation; then came the sound of a woman's indignant voice in the kitchen, the noise of brief scuffling, the crash of something as the fragments of a broken dish scattered over the floor; and then the door hit the wall with such a bang that the plaster fell rustling from the walls and, with a mournful wail, the fussy pendulum clock above the chest came to a stop.

Pushing the door with his back, Lopahin tumbled into the room and, walking backwards, took several quick, unsteady steps and, hardly keeping his feet, finally halted in the middle of the room. . . .

The sergeant leapt up with youthful zest and, lighting the kerosene lamp, raised it above his head. Lopahin stood there, his legs straddled. His right eye was glossily black and blue; but the left eye glittered with bright exultation. All the men lying on the floor raised themselves as if by command. Sitting up on their spread out army coats, they stared in silence at Lopahin and asked no questions. And there was nothing to ask: the black eye and the swelling lump the size of an egg, on his forehead, spoke more eloquently than any words. . . .

"Alexander the Great! Petty flea! Well, and did you have your unexpected fill?" the sergeant, pale with anger, ground annihilatingly through his teeth.

Lopahin fingered the still growing lump above his right eyebrow and casually waved his hand:

"An unforseen hitch! But, brothers, you should have seen the strength of that woman! She's not a woman, but beauty itself! I haven't seen the like of her before. A first rate boxer, a wrestler of the highest category! Thank God, I had my training beaten into me. I've got strength in my hands, I can lift up a hundred-weight from the ground and carry it where you will, but she seized me by the leg above the knee and by the shoulder, raised me up and said. 'Go and get some sleep, Pyotr Feodorovich, or I'll throw you out of the window!'—'Well,' I said, 'we shall see about that!' Well, and I did see. . . . I displayed some superfluous activity, and that's it, if you please. . . ." Lopahin, wrinkling his forehead from the pain, fingered again the knobbly, purple patch above his brow, and said: "Yes, lucky it was that I hit the door with my back or the whole doorway might have come away on my shoulders. Well, do as you like, but—if I survive the war—I shall return to this village after the war and take this woman away from her lieutenant of a husband. She's a real find, not a woman!"

"And what about the sheep now?" Nekrasov asked in a dispirited tone.

He was answered with such an explosion of deafening laughter that Streltzov jumped up in alarm and, in his drowsy state, stretched his arm out for the automatic rifle which lay where his head had been.

"But will your 'find' feed us tomorrow?" the sergeant asked, containing his rage.

Lopahin, after emptying a flask of tepid water, answered quietly.

"I doubt it."

"So what were you messing about and bothering us for?"

"And what do you want from me, comrade sergeant? That I should try another pass? I prefer the German tanks. But if you are so impatient—go yourself. I have earned one bump, but she'd plant a whole dozen of them on you, that's sure! Well, shall I accompany you as far as the kitchen?"

The sergeant spat, swore under his breath and began to pull on his tunic. Having dressed and speaking to no one in particular, he said grimly:

"I'll go to the chairman of the collective farm. We shan't leave without breakfast. I can't turn up before the commander and ask to be fed at once: 'Please feed us tramps.' You just stay quiet here, I'll be back soon."

Lopahin lay down in his place, put his hands behind his head and said with a feeling of duty well executed:

"Well, we can sleep now. My attack was repulsed. I retreated in order but with some loss, and, in view of the enemy's obvious superiority, I shall not renew my advance in this section. I know you will laugh at me, lads, for a month or two—those of you who will survive two months. But one thing I ask of you: begin doing so tomorrow morning, and now let's sleep!"

Without waiting for an answer, Lopahin turned over on his side and, within a few minutes, fell into a unawakening, childlike sleep.

Early next morning Kopitovsky awakened Lopahin.

"Get up for breakfast, you petty flea!"

"What is he for a flea? He's Alexander the Great," said Akimov who was conscientiously rubbing an aluminum spoon with a clean rag.

"He's a conqueror of peoples and a menace to women," Khmyz put in. "But yesterday, he didn't go through even though I warned you all."

"Rely on such a conqueror and you'll die of hunger!" Nekrasov exclaimed.

Lopahin opened his eyes and raised himself. His left eye looked as bold and sparkling as always; the right one, bordered with puffy purple, was hardly visible except for a glimmer through a narrow slit.

"She struck you all purple, didn't she!" Kopitov smirked, turning away for fear of laughing out loud.

Lopahin knew that his only salvation from his comrades' derision lay in silence. Whistling to himself and looking absolutely indifferent, he took a towel and a tiny piece of soap and went out on the steps. The soldiers were washing themselves, crowding round the well, and in the garden of the house some weatherproof tent-cloaks had been spread out, and upon them in close array stood kettles, plates and mugs. Nearby a bonfire blazed hotly. On an iron bar above the fire hung a large army cauldron. The woman of the house, attractively dressed, was keeping the fire going as she bent her mighty body and stirred the cauldron with a wooden spoon.

It was all like a dream. Lopahin blinked in a daze and rubbed his eyes. "The devil's own work!" he thought, but then his nostrils caught the smell of boiled meat; shrugging his shoulders, Lopahin descended the steps. Stopping by the bonfire, he gallantly bowed:

"Good morning, Natalia Stepanovna!"

The woman straightened herself, threw a quick look at him and bent over the cauldron again. A rosy flush spread over her cheeks, and red spots even appeared on her full white neck.

"Good day to you," she said gently. "You must excuse me, Pyotr Feodorovich. . . . Your bruise doesn't look good. . . . I fear your comrades may have heard the noise in the night?"

"That's nothing," Lopahin generously said. "Bruises adorn men's faces. Of course, you should use your fists more accurately, but there's nothing to be done now. And don't worry about me, it'll heal beautifully. A dog will leave no stone unturned to find a bone. But I sought you by ruse only to find a purple bruise. It's a marriageable affair we have between us, Natalia Stepanovna."

The woman straightened herself, looked at him with clear eyes, and severely knitted her heavy, auburn eyebrows.

"The trouble is you fancy yourself as a bridegroom. You believe that, if her husband is away in the army, a wife must be a bitch. So I have to show you with my fists, Pyotr Feodorovich, what we are like, and God did not stint me strength."

Lopahin squinted with his seeing eye at the woman's clenched fists and then inquired:

"I apologize, of course, for my immodesty, but tell me all the same what sort of man was your husband? Well, how tall, for example?"

The woman measured Lopahin with her eyes and smiled:

"About your height, Pyotr Feodorovich, only a little more solid."

"I'm sure you bullied him? He must have been like a brother-in-law to you?"

"Don't say that! How can you, Pyotr Feodorovich! We lived lovey-dovey!"

The woman's full rosy lips quivered. She turned away and with the tip of her handkerchief wiped a tear from her cheek, but then in a twinkling she smiled archly and, looking at Lopahin with moist eyes, said:

"There's no better man than mine in the whole world! He was a good man, hardworking and quiet, but as soon as he had his fill of vodka, he'd turn hard. But I never went complaining to the local militia. He'd start raising hell, but I'd manage him soon enough; I wouldn't hurt him beating him, but just do it lovingly, so to speak. . . . Now he's in Kuibyshev, in the hospital, after being wounded. Maybe they'll let him come home afterwards to recuperate?"

"Of course they will," Lopahin assured her. "But tell me, Natalia Stepanovna, what makes you prepare this breakfast for the whole band of us? There's something I don't understand. . . ."

"There's nothing to understand here. If you had only explained soundly yesterday to our chairman that it was your company that fought the Germans the day before at the Pod'yemsk village, why, we would have fed you yesterday. But we, women, thought that you were taking to your heels and didn't want to defend us from the enemy, so we got together and decided among us as follows: such as are running away to the rear from the river Don were to get not a morsel of bread, not a mug of milk, and might they perish of hunger, the damned runaways! But as for those going towards the Don, in our defense, they were to be fed with anything they asked. And that's what we did. We didn't know about you, that you had been fighting at Pod'yemsk. The day before yesterday our collective farm girls had been carting shells to the Don and they told us when they got back: a lot of our dear ones, they said, had been killed on the other side of the Don, but they had piled the Germans up too on the mound and they lay there like logs in a wood stack. Had we known it was you battling out there, we'd have greeted you otherwise. Your sergeant, the red-haired one, the graying old man, he went to the chairman this night and told him how hard you'd been fighting. Well, I looked—and there at dawn was the chairman hurrying almost at a run towards my yard. 'We got it wrong, Natalia,' he said. 'These aren't runaways, but heroes. Slaughter the chickens and make a noodle soup for them, so that these lads may be well fed.' He told me how you defended yourselves in Pod'yemsk, and what losses you suffered, and I at once prepared the dough for the noodles and killed eight chickens and threw them into the pot. Surely we are not sorry to part with these wretched chickens for the sake of our dear defenders. Surely we'll give up everything if only you don't let the Germans in here! And well we might ask how long you will go on retreating? Time you stuck your heels in. . . . Don't let a harsh word hurt you, but it's shameful to look at you. . . ."

"Seems we hadn't picked the right little key for your lock?" Lopahin inquired.

"Seems like it," the woman confirmed with a smile.

Lopahin groaned with disappointment, made a gesture with his hand and walked off towards the well. "It's bad luck I'm having with love latterly," he grieved to admit as he strode along the path.

[1956]

For Thought

Sholokhov's story of a group of Russian soldiers is antiheroic. The soldiers are thought to be deserters by the local peasantry and are, therefore, left unfed, until the mistake is corrected. It is ironic that Lopahin is forced into retreat by the sturdy wife he attempts to seduce. Sholokhov implies that, far from being glorious and soul stirring, war is more often a matter of boredom, fatigue, hunger, and vermin.

For Discussion

1. What is the significance of the title?
2. How is the story structured?
3. What is the tone of the story?

4. How does the author create his humor?
5. What is the conflict?
6. How are the men characterized?
7. How is Lopahin characterized?
8. How is Lopahin's trip to the kitchen ironic in its outcome?
9. How does the battle scene between the woman and Lopahin parody the main situation?
10. How is the woman characterized?
11. Does the story conform in any way to the demands of Soviet communistic propaganda?
12. What use does the author make of symbolism?
13. What is the point of view and its advantage?
14. What is the theme?
15. If the theme of a story can be summed up in a single sentence, the story lacks the complexity of fiction. Does the explanation of the woman at the end deepen or over-simplify the story's ironies?
16. What view of human nature emerges from the story?

Alan Sillitoe
Mr. Raynor the School-Teacher

Now that the boys were relatively quiet Mr. Raynor looked out of the classroom window, across the cobbled road and into the window of Harrison's the draper's shop. With sight made keener by horn-rimmed spectacles he observed the new girl lift her arm above her head to reach some small drawers of cotton, an action which elongated the breasts inside her dark blue dress until she looked almost flat-chested. Mr. Raynor rasped his shoes slightly on the bar of his tall stool, a stool once the subject of a common-room joke, which said that he had paid the caretaker well to put on longer legs so that he could see better out of the window and observe with more ease the girls in Harrison's shop across the road. Most of the boys before him had grown so used to his long periods of distraction—freedom for them—that they no longer found inclination or time to sneer, at the well-known reason for it.

When the flat-chested girl went upstairs into the Men's Suits, another girl, small, heavy, and with a satisfyingly larger bosom, came into the centre span of the counter and spread out a box of coloured ties like wheel-spokes before a man who had just come in. But her appeal to his taste was still at an unpalatable extreme, and he again regretted the departure of a girl who had been, to him, perfect in every way. Against a background of road and shop, the movements between the two that his fixed stare kept easily in a state of insignificance, he recalled her image, a difficult thing because faces did not linger clearly for a long time in his memory, even though she had been dead only ten days.

Eighteen, he remembered her, and not too tall, with almost masculine features below short chestnut hair: brown eyes, full cheeks and proportionate lips, like Aphrodite his inward eye had commented time and time again, only a little sweeter. She wore brown sweater and brown cardigan, a union that gave only tormenting glimpses of her upper figure, until one summer's day when the cardigan was set aside, revealing breasts on the same classical style, hips a trifle broad, complementing nevertheless her somewhat stocky legs and fleshy redeeming calves. She had only to move from the counter to the foot of the stairs that led to the upper part of the shop, and Mr. Raynor's maxims of common arithmetic became stale phrases of instruction to be given out quickly, leaving his delighted class with an almost free session.

What memory could not accomplish, imagination did, and he recreated a tangible image, moved by long-cultivated preoccupations of sensuality in which his wife and family took no part. He adjusted his spectacles, rolled his tongue around the dry back of his teeth, and grated his feet once more on the bar of the chair. As she walked she had carried her whole body in a sublime movement conducive to the attraction of every part of it, so that he was even aware of heels inside her shoes and fingertips buried perhaps beneath a bolt of opulent cloth. A big trolley-bus bundled its green-fronted track along the road, and carried his vision away on the coloured advertisements decorating the band between top and bottom deck.

Deprived so suddenly he felt for a cigarette, but there was half an hour yet for the playtime break. And he still had to deal with the present class before they went to geography at ten o'clock. The noise broke into him, sunk him down to reality like cold water entering a ship. They were the eldest rag-mob of the school, and the most illiterate, a C stream of fourteen-year-old louts rearing to leave and start work at the factories round about. Bullivant the rowdiest subsided only after his head was well turned from the window; but the noise went on. The one feasible plan was to keep them as quiet as possible for the remaining months, then open the gates and let them free, allow them to spill out into the big wide world like the young animals they were, eager for fags and football, beer and women and a forest of streets to roam in. The responsibility would be no longer his, once they were packed away with the turned pages of his register into another, more incorrigible annex than the enclave of jungle he ruled for his living. He would have done whatever could be done with such basically unsuitable and unwilling scholars.

"All right," he called out in a loud clear voice, "let's have a little quietness in the room." Though the noise persisted, an air of obedience reigned. Mr. Raynor was not a strict disciplinarian, but he had taught for twenty-five years, and so acquired a voice of authority that was listened to. Even if he didn't hit them very often, it was realized that he was not a young man and could easily do so. And it was consciously felt that there was more force behind a middle-aged fist than a young and inexperienced one. Consequently when he told them to keep quiet, they usually did.

"Take out your Bibles," he said, "and open them at Exodus, chapter six."

He watched forty-five hands, few of them clean, unaccountably opening the Bible, as they did all books, from the back and working to the front. Now and again he caught the flicker of brightly coloured illustrations at different points in the class, on their way through a welter of pages. He leaned forward on the high desk, one elbow supporting his forehead, seeing Bullivant whisper to the boy next to him, and hearing the boy giggle.

"Handley," Mr. Raynor demanded with a show of sternness, "who was Aaron?"

A small boy from the middle of the class stood up: "Aaron from the Bible, sir?"

"Yes. Who else, you ass?"

"Don't know, sir," the boy answered, either because he really didn't, Mr. Raynor told himself, or by way of revenge for being called an ass.

"Didn't you read the chapter yesterday I told you to read?"

Here was a question he could answer. "Yes, sir," came the bright response.

"Well then who was Aaron?"

His face was no longer bright. It became clouded as he admitted: "I've forgot, sir."

Mr. Raynor ran a hand slowly over his forehead. He changed tack. "NO!" he yelled, so loudly that the boy jumped. "Don't sit down yet, Handley." He stood up again. "We've been reading this part of the Bible for a month, so you should be able to answer my question. Now: Who was the brother of Moses?"

Bullivant chanted from behind:

> "Then the Lord said unto Moses
> All the Jews shall have long noses
> Exceptin' Aaron
> He shall 'ave a square 'un
> And poor old Peter
> He shall 'ave a gas-meter!"

The low rumble reached Mr. Raynor, and he saw several half-tortured faces around Bullivant trying not to laugh. "Tell me, Handley," he said again, "who was the brother of Moses?"

Handley's face became happy, almost recognizable under the unfamiliar light of inspiration, for the significance of the chanted verse had eaten its way through to his understanding. "Aaron, sir," he said.

"And so"—Mr. Raynor assumed he was getting somewhere at last—"who was Aaron?"

Handley, who had considered his ordeal to be over on hearing a subdued cheer of irony from Bullivant, lifted a face blank in defeat. "Don't know, sir."

A sigh of frustration, not allowed to reach the boys, escaped Mr. Raynor. "Sit down," he said to Handley, who did so with such alacrity that the desk lid rattled. Duty had been done as far as Handley was concerned, and now it was Robinson's turn, who stood up from his desk a few feet away. "Tell us who Aaron was," Mr. Raynor ordered.

Robinson was a brighter boy, who had thought to keep a second Bible open beneath his desk lid for reference. "A priest, sir," he answered sharply, "the brother of Moses."

"Sit down, then," Mr. Raynor said. "Now, remember that, Handley. What House are you in, Robinson?"

He stood up again, grinning respectfully. "Buckingham, sir."

"Then take a credit star."

After the green star had been fixed to the chart he set one of the boys to read, and when the monotonous drone of his voice was well under way he turned again to span the distance between his high stool and the draper's window. By uniting the figures and faces of the present assistants, and then by dissolving them, he tried to recapture the carnal vision of the girl who had recently died, a practice of reconstruction that had been a mainstay of his sojourn at this school, a line of sight across the cobbled road into Harrison's shop, beamed on to the girls who went to work there when they were fifteen and left at twenty to get married. He had become a connoisseur of young suburban womanhood, and thus the fluctuating labour and marriage market made Mr. Raynor a fickle lover, causing him too often to forget each great passion as another one walked in to take its place. Each 'good' one was credit-starred upon his mind, left behind a trail of memories when it went, until a new 'good' one came like a solid fiscal stamp of spiritual currency that drove the other one out. Each memory was thus renewed, so that none of them died.

But the last one was the best of all, an unexpected beauty back-dropped against the traffic artery of squalid streets. He had watched her work and talk or on wet afternoons stand at the counter as if in a trance. The boy on the front row was reading like a prophet, and an agitated muttering sea began to grow about him, and the curtain of Mr. Raynor's memory drew back upon the runners of a line recalled from Baudelaire: "*Timide et libertine, et fragile et robuste*"—revealing the secret of her classical beauty and nubility, which vanished when the blood-filled phrase was dragged away by the top deck of a trolley-bus laden with rigid staring faces. A tea-boy carrying a white jug slipped out of the estate agents' offices, dodged deftly through a line of cars and lorries that had stopped for the traffic-lights, and walked whistling a tune into a café further down the road.

The sea of noise surrounding the prophet-like monotonous voice of the reading boy increased to a higher magnitude than discipline would permit, until a wave carried his sonorous words away and another sound dominated the scene. He looked, and saw Bullivant on his feet thumping the boy at the desk in front with all his might. The boy raised his fists to hit back.

Mr. Raynor roared with such fury that there was instant silence, his ageing pink face thrust over his desk towards them. "Come out, Bullivant," he cried. *Libertine et robuste:* the phrase fought and died, was given a white cross and packed away.

Bullivant slouched out between rows of apprehensive boys " 'e 'it me first," he said, nearing the blackboard.

"And now I'm going to hit you," Mr. Raynor retorted, lifting the lid of his desk and taking out a stick. His antagonist eyed him truculently, displaying his contempt of the desperate plight he was supposed to be in by turning around and winking at his friends. He was a big boy of fourteen, wearing long drainpipe trousers and a grey jersey.

"Y'aren't gooin' ter 'it me," he said. "I ain't dun owt ter get 'it, yer know."

"Hold out your hand," Mr. Raynor said, his face turning a deep crimson. *Timide.* No, he thought, not likely. This is the least I can do. I'll get these Teddy-boy ideas out of his head for a few seconds.

No hand was extended towards him as it should have been. Bullivant stood still, and Mr. Raynor repeated his order. The class looked on, and moving traffic on the road hid some of the smaller mutterings that passed for silence. Bullivant still wouldn't lift his hand, and time enough had gone by that could be justified by Mr. Raynor as patience.

"Y'aren't gooin' ter 'it me wi' that," Bullivant said again, a gleam just showing from his blue half-closed eyes.

Robust. An eye for an eye. The body of the girl, the bottom line of the sweater spreading over her hips, was destroyed in silence. His urge for revenge was checked, but was followed by a rage that nevertheless hit hard and forced him to action. In the passing of a bus he stepped to Bullivant's side and struck him several times across the shoulders with the stick, crashing each blow down with all his force. "Take that," he cried out, "you stupid defiant oaf."

Bullivant shied away, and before any more blows could fall, and before Mr. Raynor realized that such a thing was possible, Bullivant lashed back with his fists, and they were locked in a battle of strength, both trying to push the other away, to get clear and strike. Mr. Raynor took up a stance with legs apart, trying to push Bullivant back against the desks, but Bullivant foresaw such a move from his stronger adversary and moved his own body so that they went scuffling between the desks. "Yo' ain't 'ittin' me like that," Bullivant gasped between his teeth. "Oo do yo' think yo' are?" He unscrewed his head that was suddenly beneath Mr. Raynor's arm, threw out his fists that went wide of the mark, and leapt like a giraffe over a row of desks. Mr. Raynor moved quickly and blocked his retreat, grabbed his arm firmly and glowered at him with blood-red face, twisted the captive limb viciously, all in a second, then pushed him free, though he stood with the stick ready in case Bullivant should come for him again.

But Bullivant recognized the dispensation of a truce, and merely said: "I'll bring our big kid up to settle yo'," and sat down. Experience was Mr. Raynor's friend; he saw no point in spinning out trouble to its logical conclusion, which meant only more trouble. He was content to warn Bullivant to behave himself, seeing that no face had been lost by either side in the equal contest. He sat again on the high stool behind his desk. What did it matter, really? Bullivant and most of the others would be leaving in two months, and he could keep them in check for that short time. And after the holidays more Bullivants would move up into his classroom from the scholastic escalator.

It was five minutes to ten, and to ensure that the remaining time was peaceful he took out his Bible and began reading in a clear steady voice:

"Then the Lord said unto Moses (titters here), now shalt thou see what I will do to Pharaoh: for with a strong hand shall he let them go, and with a strong hand shall he drive them out of his land."

The class that came in at half past ten was for arithmetic, and they were told to open their books and do the exercises on page fifty-four. He observed the leaves of many books covered with ink-scrawls, and obscene words written across the illustrations and decorating the 'answer' margins like tattooing on the arms of veteran sailors, pages that would be unrecognizable in a month, but would have to last for another twelve. This was a younger class, whose rebellion had so far reached only the pages of their books.

But that, too, was only something to accept and, inclining his head to the right, he forgot the noise of his class and looked across the road at the girls working in the draper's shop. Oh yes, the last one had been the best he could remember, and the time had come when he decided to cure his madness by speaking to her one evening as she left the shop. It was a good idea. But it was too late, for a young man had begun meeting her and seeing her safely, it seemed, to the bus stop. Most of the girls who gave up their jobs at the shop did so because they met some common fate or other. ("*Timide et libertine, et fragile et robuste*"—he could not forget the phrase.) Some were married, others, he had noticed, became pregnant and disappeared; a few had quarrelled with the manager and appeared to have been sacked. But the last one, he had discovered, on opening the newspaper one evening by the trafficlights at the corner, had been murdered by the young man who came to meet her.

Three double-decker trolley-buses trundled by in a line, but he still saw her vision by the counter.

"Quiet!" he roared, to the forty faces before him. "The next one to talk gets the stick."

And there was quiet.

[1959]

For Thought

Sillitoe's choice of a schoolroom for the setting of "Mr. Raynor the School-Teacher" points up a dual irony. Both teacher and students are trapped by one another and the system. While Raynor seeks relief in sexual fantasies, the boys ridicule and attack their school materials and one another. The murder of the shop girl who was watched by Raynor implies a violent and unstable core beneath the facade of modern society.

For Discussion

1. A teacher is usually stereotyped as kindly, moral, and only occasionally incompetent. How is Mr. Raynor characterized?
2. What is Sillitoe's attitude toward Mr. Raynor, and how is it conveyed to the reader?
3. Does the fact that Raynor is a teacher make his obsession more—or less—acceptable?
4. How do other people, especially the students, respond to Mr. Raynor?
5. What makes him so angry with Bullivant?
6. What parallels and contrasts could be drawn between Mr. Raynor and Bullivant?

7. What does Mr. Raynor symbolize?
8. The author uses the sentence, "The curtain of Mr. Raynor's memory drew back upon the runners of a line recalled from Baudelaire: *timide et libertine et fragile et robust*." What is the significance of this?
9. What point of view has the author chosen, and what are its advantages?
10. How is the story structured?
11. The Biblical references in the story form a sort of mythical underpattern that adds complexity to the theme. What are the various quests, and what parallels exist to Moses's search for the Promised Land?
12. What is the significance of the references to Aaron?
13. What are the conflicts? How do they reflect the theme?

Isaac Bashevis Singer
Gimpel the Fool

I

I am Gimpel the fool. I don't think myself a fool. On the contrary. But that's what folks call me. They gave me the name while I was still in school. I had seven names in all: imbecile, donkey, flax-head, dope, glump, ninny, and fool. The last name stuck. What did my foolishness consist of? I was easy to take in. They said, "Gimpel, you know the rabbi's wife has been brought to childbed?" So I skipped school. Well, it turned out to be a lie. How was I supposed to know? She hadn't had a big belly. But I never looked at her belly. Was that really so foolish? The gang laughed and hee-hawed, stomped and danced and chanted a good-night prayer. And instead of the raisins they give when a woman's lying in, they stuffed my hand full of goat turds. I was no weakling. If I slapped someone he'd see all the way to Cracow. But I'm really not a slugger by nature. I think to myself, Let it pass. So they take advantage of me.

I was coming home from school and heard a dog barking. I'm not afraid of dogs, but of course I never want to start up with them. One of them may get mad, and if he bites there's not a Tartar in the world who can help you. So I made tracks. Then I looked around and saw the whole market place wild with laughter. It was no dog at all but Wolf-Leib the chief. How was I supposed to know it was he? It sounded like a howling bitch.

When the pranksters and leg-pullers found that I was easy to fool, every one of them tried his luck with me. "Gimpel, the Czar is coming to Frampol; Gimpel, the moon fell down in Turbeen; Gimpel, little Hodel Furpiece found a treasure behind the bathhouse." And I like a *golem* believed everyone. In the *first* place, everything is possible, as it is written in the Wisdom of the Fathers, I've forgotten just how. Second, I had to believe when the whole town came down on me! If I ever dared to say, "Ah, you're kidding!" there was trouble. People got angry. "What do you mean! You want to call everyone a liar?" What was I to do? I believed them, and I hope at least that did them some good.

I was an orphan. My grandfather who brought me up was already bent toward the grave. So they turned me over to a baker, and what a time they gave me there! Every woman or girl who came to bake a pan of cookies or dry a batch of noodles had to fool me at least once. "Gimpel, there's a fair in heaven; Gimpel, the rabbi gave birth to a calf in the seventh month; Gimpel, a cow flew over the roof and laid brass eggs." A student from the yeshiva came once to buy a roll, and he said, "You, Gimpel, while you stand here scraping with your baker's shovel the Messiah has come. The dead have arisen." "What do you mean?" I said. "I heard no one blowing the ram's horn!" He said "Are you deaf?" And all began to cry, "We heard it, we heard!" Then in came Reitze, the candledipper and called out in her hoarse voice, "Gimpel, your father and mother have stood up from the grave. They're looking for you."

To tell the truth, I knew very well that nothing of the sort had happened, but all the same, as folks were talking, I threw on my wool vest and went out. Maybe something had happened. What did I stand to lose by looking? Well, what a cat music went up! And then I took a vow to believe nothing more. But that was no go either. They confused me so that I didn't know the big end from the small.

I went to the rabbi to get some advice. He said, "It is written, better to be a fool all your days than for one hour to be evil. You are not a fool. They are the fools. For he who causes his neighbor to feel shame loses Paradise himself." Nevertheless the rabbi's daughter took me in. As I left the rabbinical court she said, "Have you kissed the wall yet?" I said, "No; what for?" She answered, "It's a law; you've got to do it after every visit." Well, there didn't seem to be any harm in it. And she burst out laughing. It was a fine trick. She put one over on me, all right.

I wanted to go off to another town, but then everyone got busy matchmaking, and they were after me so they nearly tore my coat tails off. They talked at me and talked until I got water on the ear. She was no chaste maiden, but they told me she was virgin pure. She had a limp, and they said it was deliberate, from coyness. She had a bastard, and they told me the child was her little brother. I cried, "You're wasting your time. I'll never marry that whore." But they said indignantly, "What a way to talk! Aren't you ashamed of yourself? We can take you to the rabbi and have you fined for giving her a bad name." I saw then that I wouldn't escape them so easily and I thought, They're set on making me their butt. But when you're married the husband's the master, and if that's all right with her it's agreeable to me too. Besides, you can't pass through life unscathed, nor expect to.

I went to her clay house, which was built on the sand, and the whole gang, hollering and chorusing, came after me. They acted like bear-baiters. When we came to the well they stopped all the same. They were afraid to start anything with Elka. Her mouth would open as if it were on a hinge, and she had a fierce tongue. I entered the house. Lines were strung from wall to wall and clothes were drying. Barefoot she stood by the tub, doing the wash. She was dressed in a worn hand-me-down gown of plush. She had her hair put up in braids and pinned across her head. It took my breath away, almost, the reek of it all.

Evidently she knew who I was. She took a look at me and said, "Look who's here! He's come, the drip. Grab a seat."

I told her all; I denied nothing. "Tell me the truth," I said, "are you really a virgin, and is that mischievous Yechiel actually your little brother? Don't be deceitful with me, for I'm an orphan."

"I'm an orphan myself," she answered, "and whoever tries to twist you up, may the end of his nose take a twist. But don't let them think they can take advantage of me. I want a dowry of fifty guilders, and let them take up a collection besides. Otherwise they can kiss my you-know-what." She was very plainspoken. I said, "It's the bride and not the groom who gives a dowry." Then she said, "Don't bargain with me. Either a flat 'yes' or a flat 'no'—go back where you came from."

I thought. No bread will ever be baked from *this* dough. But ours is not a poor town. They consented to everything and proceeded with the wedding. It so happened that there was a dysentery epidemic at the time. The ceremony was held at the cemetery gates, near the little corpse-washing hut. The fellows got drunk. While the marriage contract was being drawn up I heard the most pious high rabbi ask, "Is the bride a widow or a divorced woman?" And the sexton's wife answered for her, "Both a widow and divorced." It was a black moment for me. But what was I to do, run away from under the marriage canopy?

There was singing and dancing. An old granny danced opposite me, hugging a braided white *chalah*. The master of revels made a "God 'a mercy" in memory of the bride's parents. The schoolboys threw burrs, as on *Tishe b'Av* fast day. There were a lot of gifts after the sermon: a noodle board, a kneading trough, a bucket, brooms, ladles, household articles galore. Then I took a look and saw two strapping young men carrying a crib. "What do we need this for?" I asked. So they said, "Don't rack your brains about it. It's all right, it'll come in handy." I realized I was going to be rooked. Take it another way though, what did I stand to lose? I reflected, I'll see what comes of it. A whole town can't go altogether crazy.

II

At night I came where my wife lay, but she wouldn't let me in. "Say, look here, is this what they married us for?" I said. And she said, "My monthly has come." But yesterday they took you to the ritual bath, and that's afterward, isn't it supposed to be?" "Today isn't yesterday," said she, "and yesterday's not today. You can beat it if you don't like it." In short, I waited.

Not four months later she was in childbed. The townsfolk hid their laughter with their knuckles. But what could I do? She suffered intolerable pains and clawed at the walls. "Gimpel," she cried, "I'm going. Forgive me!" The house filled with women. They were boiling pans of water. The screams rose to the welkin.

The thing to do was to go to the House of Prayer to repeat Psalms, and that was what I did.

The townsfolk liked that, all right. I stood in a corner saying Psalms and prayers, and they shook their heads at me. "Pray, pray!" they told me. "Prayer never made any woman pregnant." One of the congregation put a straw to my mouth and said, "Hay for the cows." There was something to that too, by God!

She gave birth to a boy. Friday at the synagogue the sexton stood up before the Ark, pounded on the reading table, and announced, "The wealthy Reb Gimpel invites the congregation to a feast in honor of the birth of a son." The whole House of Prayer rang with laughter. My face was flaming. But there was nothing I could do. After all, I was the one responsible for the circumcision honors and rituals.

Half the town came running. You couldn't wedge another soul in. Women brought peppered chick-peas, and there was a keg of beer from the tavern. I ate and drank as much as anyone, and they all congratulated me. Then there was a circumcision, and I named the boy after my father, may he rest in peace. When all were gone and I was left with my wife alone, she thrust her head through the bed-curtain and called me to her.

"Gimpel," said she, "why are you silent? Has your ship gone and sunk?"

"What shall I say?" I answered. "A fine thing you've done to me! If my mother had known of it she'd have died a second time."

She said, "Are you crazy, or what?"

"How can you make such a fool," I said,

"of one who should be the lord and master?"

"What's the matter with you?" she said. "What have you taken it into your head to imagine?"

I saw that I must speak bluntly and openly. "Do you think this is the way to use an orphan?" I said. "You have borne a bastard."

She answered, "Drive this foolishness out of your head. The child is yours."

"How can he be mine?" I argued. "He was born seventeen weeks after the wedding."

She told me then that he was premature. I said, "Isn't he a little too premature?" She said she had had a grandmother who carried just as short a time and she resembled this grandmother of hers as one drop of water does another. She swore to it with such oaths that you would have believed a peasant at the fair if he had used them. To tell the plain truth, I didn't believe her; but when I talked it over the next day with the schoolmaster he told me that the very same thing had happened to Adam and Eve. Two they went up to bed, and four they descended.

"There isn't a woman in the world who is not the granddaughter of Eve," he said.

That was how it was—they argued me dumb. But then, who really knows how such things are?

I began to forget my sorrow. I loved the child madly, and he loved me too. As soon as he saw me he'd wave his little hands and want me to pick him up, and when he was colicky I was the only one who could pacify him. I bought him a little bone teething ring and a little gilded cap. He was forever catching the evil eye from someone, and then I had to run to get one of those abracadabras for him that would get him out of it. I worked like an ox. You know how expenses go up when there's an infant in the house. I don't want to lie about it; I didn't dislike Elka either, for that matter. She swore at me and cursed, and I couldn't get enough of her. What strength she had! One of her looks could rob you of the power of speech. And her orations! Pitch and sulphur, that's what they were full of, and yet somehow also full of charm. I adored her every word. She gave me bloody wounds though.

In the evening I brought her a white loaf as well as a dark one, and also poppyseed rolls I baked myself. I thieved because of her and swiped everything I could lay hands on, macaroons, raisins, almonds, cakes. I hope I may be forgiven for stealing from the Saturday pots the women left to warm in the baker's oven. I would take out scraps of meat, a chunk of pudding, a chicken leg or head, a piece of tripe, whatever I could nip quickly. She ate and became fat and handsome.

I had to sleep away from home all during the week, at the bakery. On Friday nights when I got home she always made an excuse of some sort. Either she had heartburn, or a stitch in the side, or hiccups, or headaches. You know what women's excuses are. I had a bitter time of it. It was rough. To add to it, this little brother of hers, the bastard, was growing bigger. He'd put lumps on me, and when I wanted to hit back she'd open her mouth and curse so powerfully I saw a green haze floating before my eyes. Ten times a day she threatened to divorce me. Another man in my place would have taken French leave and disappeared. But I'm the type that bears it and says nothing. What's one to do? Shoulders are from God, and burdens too.

One night there was a calamity in the bakery; the oven burst, and we almost had a fire. There was nothing to do but go home, so I went home. Let me, I thought, also taste the joy of sleeping in bed in midweek. I didn't want to wake the sleeping mite and tiptoed into the house. Coming in, it seemed to me that I heard not the snoring of one but, as it were, a double snore, one a thin enough snore and the other like the snoring of a slaughtered ox. Oh, I didn't like that! I didn't like it at all. I went up to the bed, and things suddenly turned black.

Next to Elka lay a man's form. Another in my place would have made an uproar, and enough noise to rouse the whole town, but the thought occurred to me that I might wake the child. A little thing like that—why frighten a little swallow like that, I thought. All right then, I went back to the bakery and stretched out on a sack of flour, and till morning I never shut an eye. I shivered as if I had had malaria. "Enough of being a donkey," I said to myself. "Gimpel isn't going to be a sucker all his life. There's a limit even to the foolishness of a fool like Gimpel."

In the morning I went to the rabbi to get advice, and it made a great commotion in town. They sent the beadle for Elka right away. She came, carrying the child. And what do you think she did? She denied it, denied everything, bone and stone! "He's out of his head," she said. "I know nothing of dreams or divinations." They yelled at her, warned her, hammered on the table, but she stuck to her guns: it was a false accusation, she said.

The butchers and the horse traders took her part. One of the lads from the slaughterhouse came by and said to me, "We've got our eye on you, you're a marked man." Meanwhile the child started to bear down and soiled itself. In the rabbinical court there was an Ark of the Covenant, and they couldn't allow that, so they sent Elka away.

I said to the rabbi, "What shall I do?"

"You must divorce her at once," said he.

"And what if she refuses?" I asked.

He said, "You must serve the divorce, that's all you'll have to do."

I said, "Well, all right, Rabbi. Let me think about it."

"There's nothing to think about," said he. "You mustn't remain under the same roof with her."

"And if I want to see the child?" I asked.

"Let her go, the harlot," said he, "and her brood of bastards with her."

The verdict he gave was that I mustn't even cross her threshold—never again, as long as I should live.

During the day it didn't bother me so much. I thought, it was bound to happen, the abscess had to burst. But at night when I stretched out upon the sacks I felt it all very bitterly. A longing took me, for her and for the child. I wanted to be angry, but that's my misfortune exactly, I don't have it in me to be really angry. In the first place—this was how my thoughts went—there's bound to be a slip sometimes. You can't live without errors. Probably that lad who was with her led her on and gave her presents and what not, and women are often long on hair and short on sense, and so he got around her. And then since she denies it so, maybe I was only seeing things? Hallucinations do happen. You see a figure or a mannikin or something, but when you come up closer it's nothing, there's not a thing there. And if that's so, I'm doing her an injustice. And when I got so far in my thoughts I started to weep. I sobbed so that I wet the flour where I lay. In the morning I went to the rabbi and told him that I had made a mistake. The rabbi wrote on with his quill, and he said that if that were so he would have to reconsider the whole case. Until he had finished I wasn't to go near my wife, but I might send her bread and money by messenger.

III

Nine months passed before all the rabbis could come to an agreement. Letters went back and forth. I hadn't realized that there could be so much erudition about a matter like this.

Meantime Elka gave birth to still another child, a girl this time. On the Sabbath I went to the synagogue and invoked a blessing on her. They called me up to the Torah, and I named the child for my mother-in-law, may she rest in peace. The louts and loudmouths of the town who came into the bakery gave me a going over. All Frampol refreshed its spirits because of my trouble and grief. However, I resolved that I would always believe what I was told. What's the good of *not* believing? Today it's your wife you don't believe; tomorrow it's God Himself you won't take stock in.

By an apprentice who was her neighbor I sent her daily a corn or a wheat loaf, or a piece of pastry, rolls or bagels, or when I got the chance, a slab of pudding, a slide of honeycake, or wedding strudel—whatever came my way. The apprentice was a good-hearted lad, and more than once he added something on his own. He had formerly annoyed me a lot, plucking my nose and digging me in the ribs, but when he started to be a visitor to my house he became kind and friendly. "Hey, you, Gimpel," he said to me, "you have a very decent little wife and two fine kids. You don't deserve them."

"But the things people say about her," I said.

"Well, they have long tongues," he said, "and nothing to do with them but babble. Ignore it as you ignore the cold of last winter."

One day the rabbi sent for me and said, "Are you certain, Gimpel, that you were wrong about your wife?"

I said, "I'm certain."

"Why, but look here! You yourself saw it."

"It must have been a shadow," I said.

"The shadow of what?"

"Just of one of the beams, I think."

"You can go home then. You owe thanks to the Yanover rabbi. He found an obscure reference in Maimonides that favored you."

I seized the rabbi's hand and kissed it.

I wanted to run home immediately. It's no small thing to be separated for so long a time from wife and child. Then I reflected, I'd better go back to work now, and go home in the evening. I said nothing to anyone, although as far as my heart was concerned it was like one of the Holy Days. The women teased and twitted me as they did every day, but my thought was, Go on, with your loose talk. The truth is out, like the oil upon the water. Maimonides says it's right, and therefore it is right!

At night, when I had covered the dough to let it rise, I took my share of bread and a little sack of flour and started homeward. The moon was full and the stars were glistening, something to terrify the soul. I hurried onward, and before me darted a long shadow. It was winter, and a fresh snow had fallen. I had a mind to sing, but it was growing late and I didn't want to wake the householders. Then I felt like whistling, but remembered that you don't whistle at night because it brings the demons out. So I was silent and walked as fast as I could.

Dogs in the Christian yards barked at me when I passed, but I thought, Bark your teeth out! What are you but mere dogs? Whereas I am a man, the husband of a fine wife, the father of promising children.

As I approached the house my heart started to pound as though it were the heart of a criminal. I felt no fear, but my heart went thump! thump! Well, no drawing back. I quietly lifted the latch and went in. Elka was asleep. I looked at the infant's cradle. The shutter was closed, but the moon forced its way through the cracks. I saw the newborn child's face and loved it as soon as I saw it—immediately—each tiny bone.

Then I came nearer to the bed. And what did I see but the apprentice lying there beside Elka. The moon went out all at once. It was utterly black, and I trembled. My teeth chattered. The bread fell from my hands and my wife waked and said, "Who is that, ah?"

I muttered, "It's me."

"Gimpel?" she asked. "How come you're here? I thought it was forbidden."

"The rabbi said," I answered and shook as with a fever.

"Listen to me, Gimpel," she said, "go out to the shed and see if the goat's all right. It seems she's been sick." I have forgotten to say that we had a goat. When I heard she was unwell I went into the yard. The nannygoat was a good little creature. I had a nearly human feeling for her.

With hesitant steps I went up to the shed and opened the door. The goat stood there on her four feet. I felt her everwhere, drew her by the horns, examined her udders, and found nothing wrong. She had probably eaten too much bark. "Good night, little goat," I said. "Keep well." And the little beast answered with a "Maa" as though to thank me for the good will.

I went back. The apprentice had vanished.

"Where," I asked, "is the lad?"

"What lad?" my wife answered.

"What do you mean?" I said. "The apprentice. You were sleeping with him.

"The things I have dreamed this night and the night before," she said, "may they come true and lay you low, body and soul! An evil spirit has taken root in you and dazzles your sight." She screamed out, "You hateful creature! You moon calf! You spook! You uncouth mane! Get out, or I'll scream all Frampol out of bed!"

Before I could move, her brother sprang out from behind the oven and struck me a blow on the back of the head. I thought he had broken my neck. I felt that something about me was deeply wrong, and I said, "Don't make a scandal. All that's needed now is that people should accuse me of raising spooks and *dybbuks*." For that was what she had meant. "No one will touch bread of my baking."

In short, I somehow calmed her.

"Well," she said, "that's enough. Lie down, and be shattered by wheels."

Next morning I called the apprentice aside. "Listen here, brother!" I said. And so on and so forth. "What do you say?" He stared at me as though I had dropped from the roof or something.

"I swear," he said, "you'd better go to an herb doctor or some healer. I'm afraid you have a screw loose, but I'll hush it up for you." And that's how the thing stood.

To make a long story short, I lived twenty years with my wife. She bore me six children, four daughters and two sons. All kinds of things happened, but I neither saw nor heard. I believed, and that's all. The rabbi recently said to me, "Belief in itself is beneficial. It is written that a good man lives by his faith."

Suddenly my wife took sick. It began with a trifle, a little growth upon the breast. But she evidently was not destined to live long; she had no years. I spent a fortune on her. I have forgotten to say that by this time I had a bakery of my own and in Frampol was considered to be something of a rich man. Daily the healer came, and every witch doctor in the neighborhood was brought. They decided to use leeches, and after that to try cupping. They even called a doctor from Lublin, but it was too late. Before she died she called me to her bed and said, "Forgive me, Gimpel."

I said, "What is there to forgive? You have been a good and faithful wife."

"Woe, Gimpel!" she said. "It was ugly how I deceived you all these years. I want to go clean to my Maker, and so I have to tell you that the children are not yours."

If I had been clouted on the head with a piece of wood it couldn't have bewildered me more.

"Whose are they?" I asked.

"I don't know," she said. "There were a lot . . . but they're not yours." And as she spoke she tossed her head to the side, her eyes turned glassy, and it was all up with Elka. On her whitened lips there remained a smile.

I imagined that, dead as she was, she was saying, "I deceived Gimpel. That was the meaning of my brief life."

IV

One night, when the period of mourning was done, as I lay dreaming on the flour sacks, there came the Spirit of Evil himself and said to me, "Gimpel, why do you sleep?"

I said, "What should I be doing? Eating *kreplach?*"

"The whole world deceives you," he said, "and you ought to deceive the world in your turn."

"How can I deceive all the world?" I asked him.

He answered, "You might accumulate a bucket of urine every day and at night pour it into the dough. Let the sages of Frampol eat filth."

"What about the judgment in the world to come?" I said.

"There is no world to come," he said. "They've sold you a bill of goods and talked you into believing you carried a cat in your belly. What nonsense!"

"Well then," I said, "and is there a God?"

He answered, "There is no God either."

"What," I said, "*is* there, then?"

"A thick mire."

He stood before my eyes with a goatish beard and horn, long-toothed, and with a tail. Hearing such words, I wanted to snatch him by the tail, but I tumbled from the flour sacks and nearly broke a rib. Then it happened that I had to answer the call of nature, and, passing, I saw the risen dough, which seemed to say to me, "Do it." In brief, I let myself be persuaded.

At dawn the apprentice came. We kneaded the bread, scattered caraway seeds on it, and set it to bake. Then the apprentice went away, and I was left sitting in the little trench by the oven, on a pile of rags. Well, Gimpel, I thought, you've revenged yourself on them for all the shame they've put on you. Outside the frost glittered, but it was warm beside the oven. The flames heated my face. I bent my head and fell into a doze.

I saw in a dream, at once, Elka in her shroud. She called to me, "What have you done, Gimpel?"

I said to her, "It's all your fault," and started to cry.

"You fool!" she said. "You fool! Because I was false is everything false too? I never deceived anyone but myself. I'm paying for it all, Gimpel. They spare you nothing here."

I looked at her face. It was black. I was startled and waked, and remained sitting dumb. I sensed that everything hung in the balance. A false step now and I'd lose Eternal life. But God gave me His help. I seized the long shovel and took out the loaves, carried them into the yard, and started to dig a hole in the frozen earth.

My apprentice came back, as I was doing it. "What are you doing, boss?" he said, and grew pale as a corpse.

"I know what I'm doing," I said, and buried it all before his very eyes.

Then I went home, took my hoard from its hiding place, and divided it among the children. "I saw your mother tonight," I said. "She's turning black, poor thing."

They were so astounded they couldn't speak a word.

"Be well," I said, "and forget that such a one as Gimpel ever existed." I put on my short coat, a pair of boots, took the bag that held my prayer shawl in one hand, my stick in the other, and kissed the *mezzuzah*. When people saw me in the street they were greatly surprised.

"Where are you going?" they said.

I answered, "Into the world." And so I departed from Frampol.

I wandered over the land, and good people did not neglect me. After many years I became old and white; I heard a great deal, many lies and falsehoods, but the longer I lived the more I understood that there were really no lies. Whatever doesn't really happen is dreamed at night. It happens to one if it doesn't happen to another, tomorrow if not today, or a century hence if not next year. What difference can it make? Often I heard tales of which I said, "Now this is a thing that cannot happen." But before a year had elapsed I heard that it actually had come to pass somewhere.

Going from place to place, eating at strange tables, it often happens that I spin yarns—improbable things that could never have happened—about devils, magicians, windmills, and the like. The children run after me, calling, "Grandfather, tell us a story." Sometimes they ask for particular stories, and I try to please them. A fat young boy once said to me, "Grandfather, it's the same story you told us before." The little rogue, he was right.

So it is with dreams too. It is many years since I left Frampol, but as soon as I shut my eyes I am there again. And whom do you think I see? Elka. She is standing by the washtub, as at our first encounter, but her face is shining and her eyes are as radiant as the eyes of a saint, and she speaks outlandish words to me, strange things. When I wake I have forgotten it all. But while the dream lasts I am comforted. She answers all my queries, and what comes out is that all is right. I weep and implore, "Let me be with you." And she consoles me and tells me to be patient. The time is nearer than it is far. Sometimes she strokes and kisses me and weeps upon my face. When I awaken I feel her lips and taste the salt of her tears.

No doubt the world is entirely an imaginary world, but it is only once removed from the true world. At the door of the hovel where I lie, there stands the plank on which the dead are taken away. The gravedigger jew has his spade ready. The grave waits and the worms are hungry; the shrouds are prepared—I carry them in my beggar's sack. Another *schnorrer* is waiting to inherit my bed of straw. When the time comes I will go joyfully. Whatever may be there, it will be real, without complication, without ridicule, without deception. God be praised: there even Gimpel cannot be deceived.

[1953]

For Thought

The setting for "Gimpel the Fool" is a Polish village in the nineteenth century. Singer's main character is Gimpel, whom the author has characterized as saintly. Gimpel is the butt of the townspeople's jokes, the greatest of which is his marriage to a shrewish harridan. Despite Elka's repeated infidelities, Gimpel honors her and loves her children. He finally gives up his worldly goods to wander as a sort of holy man. Singer implies that though a readiness to forgive personal wrongs may be highly unusual, the ability to forgive is a virtue to be prized, despite the world's ridicule.

For Discussion

1. The Yiddish word "nebech" refers to an ineffectual, innocuous, gullible misfit. In what ways is Gimpel a nebech?
2. Is Gimpel really a fool?
3. What is ironic about having the wedding ceremony at the cemetery gates?
4. What is the symbolic significance of Gimpel's job?
5. Though Gimpel steals from the bakery for Elka, this does not seem to be a serious sin. Yet, when he is tempted to defile the loaves, it is made clear that the fires of Hell await him. Why?
6. How is Gimpel's encounter with Satan prepared for?
7. What recognition does Gimpel achieve?
8. Singer's saints and godly people are often more plausible than his demons or evildoers. How is this true of "Gimpel the Fool"?
9. Does Singer make a judgment on the actions of his characters?
10. The story takes place in nineteenth-century Poland. With this setting, what significance, other than an historical one, does the story have for the modern reader?
11. What are the conflicts in the story?
12. The plot itself has the potentiality of melodramatic tragedy. How does Singer avoid this pitfall?
13. What is the point of view?
14. How is the story structured?
15. What is the theme?
16. How does the author use symbols to amplify his theme?

Muriel Spark
Come Along, Marjorie

Not many days had passed since my arrival at Watling Abbey when I realized that most of us were recovering from nerves. The Abbey, a twelfth-century foundation, lies in Worcestershire on the site of an ancient Temple of Mithras. It had recently been acquired and restored by its original religious Order at that time, just after the war, when I went to stay there and found after a few days that most of us were nervous cases.

By "most of us" I mean the lay visitors who resided in the pilgrims' quarters on two sides of the Annexe. We were all known as pilgrims. Apart from us, there was a group of permanent lay residents known as the Cloisters, because they lived in rooms above the cloisters.

Neurotics are awfully quick to notice other people's mentalities, everyone goes into an exaggerated category. I placed four categories at the Abbey. First ourselves, the visiting neurotic pilgrims. Second the Cloisters, they were cranks on the whole. Third the monks; they seemed not to have nerves, but non-individualized, non-neurotic, so I thought then, they billowed about in their white habits under the gold of that October, or swung out from the cloisters in processions on Feast Days. Into the fourth category I placed Miss Marjorie Pettigrew.

Indeed, she did seem sane. I got the instant impression that she alone among the lay people, both pilgrims and Cloisters, understood the purpose of the place. I did get that impression.

Three of us had arrived at Watling together. It was dark when I got off the train, but under the only gas bracket on the platform I saw the two women standing. They looked about them in that silly manner of women unused to arriving at strange railway stations. They heard me asking the ticket man the way to the Abbey and chummed up with me immediately. As we walked along with our suitcases I made note that there was little in common between them and me except Catholicism, and then only in the mystical sense, for their religious apprehensions were different from mine. "Different from" is the form my neurosis takes. I do like the differentiation of things, but it is apt to lead to nerve-racking pursuits. On the other hand, life led on the different-from level is always an adventure.

Those were quite nice women. One was Squackle-wackle, so I called her to myself, for she spoke like that, squackle-wackle, squackle-wackle—it was her neurosis—all about her job as a nurse in a London hospital. She had never managed to pass an exam but was content, squackle-wackle, to remain a subordinate, though thirty-three in December. All this in the first four minutes. The other woman would be nearer forty. She was quieter, but not much. As we approached the Abbey gates she said, "My name's Jennifer, what's yours?"

"Gloria Deplores-you," I answered. It is true my Christian name is Gloria.

"Gloria what?"

"It's a French name," I said, inventing in my mind the spelling "des Pleuresyeux" in case I should be pressed for it.

"We'll call you Gloria," she said. I had stopped in the Abbey gateway, wondering if I should turn back after all. "Come along, Gloria," she said.

It was not till some days later that I found that Jennifer's neurosis took the form of "same as." We are all the same, she would assert, infuriating me because I knew that God had made everyone unique. "We are all the same" was her way of saying we were all equal in the sight of God. Still, the inaccuracy irritated me. And still, like Squackle-wackle, she was quite an interesting person. It was only in my more vibrant moments that I deplored them.

Oh, the trifles, the people, that get on your nerves when you have a neurosis!

Don't I remember the little ginger man with the bottle-green cloak? He was one of the Cloisters, having been resident at Watling for over three years. He was compiling a work called *The Monkish Brooke of Brewes*. Once every fortnight he would be absent at the British Museum and I suppose other record houses, from where he would return with a great pad of notes on the methods and subleties of brewing practised in ancient monasteries, don't I remember? And he, too, was a kindly sort in between his frightful fumes against the management of Watling Abbey. When anything went wrong he blamed the monks, unlike the Irish who blamed the Devil. This sometimes caused friction between the ginger man and the Irish, for which the monks blamed the Devil.

There were ladies from Cork and thereabouts, ladies from Tyrone and Londonderry, all having come for a rest or a Retreat, and most being those neurotic stigmata of South or North accordingly. There were times when bitter bits of meaning would whistle across the space between North and South when they were gathered together outside of their common worship. Though all were Catholics, "Temperament tells," I told myself frequently. I did so often tell myself remarks like that to still my own nerves.

I joined Squackle-wackle and Jennifer each morning to recite the Fifteen Mysteries. After that we went to the town for coffee. Because I rested in the afternoons Jennifer guessed I was recovering from nerves. She asked me outright, "Is it nerves?" I said "Yes," outright.

Squackle-wackle had also been sent away with nervous exhaustion, she made no secret of it, indeed no.

Jennifer was delighted. "I've got the same trouble. Fancy, all three of us. That makes us *all the same*."

"It makes us," I said, "more different from each other than other people are."

"But, all the same," she said, "we're all *the same*."

But there was Miss Marjorie Pettigrew. Miss Pettigrew's appearance and bearing attracted me with a kind of consolation. I learned that she had been at Watling for about six months and from various hints and abrupt silences I gathered that she was either feared or disliked. I put this down to the fact that she wasn't a neurotic. Usually, neurotics take against people whose nerves they can't jar upon. So I argued to myself; and that I myself rather approved of Miss Pettigrew was a sign that I was a different sort of neurotic from the others.

Miss Pettigrew was very tall and stick-like, with very high shoulders and a square face. She seemed to have a lot of bones. Her eyes were dark, her hair black; it was coiled in the earphone style but she was not otherwise unfashionable.

I thought at first she must be in Retreat, for she never spoke at mealtimes, though she always smiled faintly when passing anything at table. She never joined the rest of the community except for meals and prayers. She was often in the chapel praying. I envied her resistance, for though I too wanted solitude I often hadn't the courage to refuse to join the company, and so make myself unpopular like Miss Pettigrew. I hoped she would speak to me when she came out of her Retreat.

One day in that first week a grand-looking north-countrywoman said to me at table, nodding over to where Miss Pettigrew sat in her silence.

"There's nothing wrong with *her* at all."

"Wrong with her?"

"It's pretence, she's clever, that's it."

By clever she meant cunning, I realized that much.

"How do you mean, pretence?" I said.

"Her silence. She won't speak to anyone."

"But she's in Retreat, isn't she?"

"Not her," said this smart woman. "She's been living here for over six months and for the past four she hasn't opened her mouth. It isn't mental trouble, it is not."

"Has she taken some religious vow, perhaps?"

"Not her; she's clever, She won't open her mouth. They brought a doctor, but she wouldn't open her mouth to him."

"I'm glad she's quiet, anyhow," I said, "Her room's next door to mine and I like quietness."

Not all the pilgrims regarded Miss Pettigrew as "clever." She was thought to be genuinely touched in the head. And it was strange how she was disapproved of by the Cloisters, for they were kind—only too intrusively kind—towards obvious nervous sufferers like me. Their disapproval of Miss Pettigrew was almost an admission that they believed nothing wrong with her. If she had gone untidy, made grotesque faces, given jerks and starts and twitches, if she had in some way lost their respect I do not think she would have lost their approval.

I began to notice her more closely in the hope of finding out more about her mental aberration; such things are like a magnet to neurotics. I would meet her crossing the courtyard, or come upon her kneeling in the lonely Lady Chapel. Always she inclined her coiled head towards me, ceremonious as an Abbess greeting a nun. Passing her in a corridor I felt the need to stand aside and make way for her confident quiet progress. I could not believe she was insane.

I could not believe she was practising some crude triumphant cunning, enduring from day to day, with her silence and prayers. It was said she had money. Perhaps she was very mystical. I wondered how long she would be able to remain hermitted so within herself. The monks were in a difficult position. It was against their nature to turn her out; maybe it was against their Rule; certainly it would cause a bad impression in the neighbourhood which was not at all Abbey-minded. One after another the monks had approached her, tactful monks, sympathetic, firm, and curious ones.

"Well, Miss Pettigrew, I hope you've benefited from your stay at the Abbey? I suppose you have plans for the winter?"

No answer, only a mild gesture of acknowledgement.

No answer, likewise, to another monk, "Now, Miss Pettigrew, dear child, you simply can't go on like this. It isn't that we don't want to keep you. Glory be to God, we'd never turn you out of doors, nor any soul. But we need the room, d'you see, for another pilgrim."

And again, "Now tell us what's the trouble, open your heart, poor Miss Pettigrew. This isn't the Catholic way at all. You've got to communicate with your fellows."

"Is it a religious vow you've taken all on your own? That's very unwise, it's . . ."

"See, Miss Pettigrew, we've found you a lodging in the town. . . ."

Not a word. She was seen to go weekly to Confession so evidently she was capable of speech. But she would not talk, even to do her small bits of shopping. Every week or so she would write on a piece of paper,

Please get me a Snowdrop Shampoo, 1s 6d encl.

or some such errand, handing it to the laundry-girl who was much attached to her, and who showed me these slips of paper as proudly as if they were the relics of a saint.

"Gloria, are you coming for a walk?"

No, I wasn't going for a trudge. It was my third week. Squackle-wackle was becoming most uninteresting.

I sat by my window and thought how happy I would be if I wasn't waiting uncertainly for a telephone call. I still have in mind the blue and green and gold of that October afternoon which was spoiled for me at the time. The small ginger man with his dark-green cloak slipping off his shoulders crossed the grass in the courtyard below. Two lay brothers in blue workmen's overalls were manipulating a tractor away in the distance. From the Lady Chapel came the chant of the monks at their office. There is nothing like plainsong to eternalize a memory, it puts a seal on whatever is happening at the time. I thought it a pity that my appreciation of this fact should be vitiated by an overwhelmning need for the telephone call.

I had hoped, in fact, that the ginger man had crossed the courtyard to summon me to the telephone, but he disappeared beneath my window and his footsteps faded out somewhere round the back. Everything's perfect, I told myself, and I can't enjoy it. Brown, white, and purples, I distinguished the pigeons on the grass.

Everyone else seemed to be out of doors. My room was on the attic floor, under the dusty beams of the roof. All along this top floor the rooms were separated by thin partitions which allowed transit to every sound. Even silent Miss Pettigrew, my immediate neighbour, could not lie breathing on her still bed without my knowing it. That afternoon she too was out, probably over in the chapel.

The telephone call was to be from Jonathan, my very best friend. I had returned from my coffee session in the town that morning to find a letter from him which had been delayed in the post. "I'll ring you at 11:30," he had written, referring to that very day. It was then past twelve. At eleven thirty I had been drinking coffee with unutterable Squackle-wackle and Jennifer.

"Has there been a call for me?" I inquired.

"Not that I know," said the secretary vaguely. "I've been away from the phone all morning, of course, so there may have been, I don't know."

Not that there was anything important to discuss with Jonathan; the idea was only to have a chat. But at that moment I felt imperatively dependent on his voice over the telephone. I stopped everyone, monks and brothers and pilgrims. "Did you take a telephone message for me? I should have received a very urgent call. It should have come at eleven-thirty."

"Sorry, I've been out," or "Sorry, I haven't been near the phone."

"Doesn't anyone attend to your telephone?" I demanded.

"Hardly ever, dear. We're too busy."

"I've missed an important telephone call, a vital—"

"Can't you telephone to your friend from here?"

"No," I said. "It's impossible, it's too bad."

Jonathan did not have a telephone in his studio. I wondered whether I should send him a wire and even drafted one, "Sorry love your letter arrived too late was out, please ring at once love Gloria." I tore this up on the grounds that I couldn't afford the expense. And something about the torment of the affair attracted me, it was better than boredom. I decided that Jonathan would surely ring again during the afternoon. I prepared, even, to sit in the little office by the telephone with my sense of suspense and vigilance, all afternoon. But "I'll be here till five o'clock," said the secretary; "of course, of course, I'll send for you if the call comes."

And so there I was by the window waiting for the summons. At three o'clock I washed and made up my face and changed my frock as if this were a propitiation to whatever stood between Jonathan's telephone call and me. I decided to stroll round the green-gold courtyard where I could not fail to miss any messenger. Once round, and still no one came. Only Miss Pettigrew emerged from the cloisters, crossing the courtyard towards me.

I was so bemused by my need to talk to Jonathan that I thought, as she approached, "Perhaps they've sent her to call me." Immediately I remembered, that was absurd, for she carried no messages ever. But she continued so directly towards me that I thought again, "She's going to speak." She had her dark eyes on my face.

I made as if to pass her, not wishing to upset her by inviting approach. But she stopped me. "Excuse me," she said, "I have a message for you."

I was so relieved that I forgot to be surprised by her speaking.

"Am I wanted on the telephone?" I said, half ready to run across to the office.

"No, I have a message for you," she said.

"What's the message?"

"The Lord is risen," she said.

It was not until I had got over my disappointment that I felt the shock of her having spoken, and recalled an odd focus of her eyes that I had not seen before. "After all," I thought "she has a religious mania. She *is* different from the neurotics, but not because she is sane."

"Gloria!"—this was the girl from the repository poking her head round the door. She beckoned to me, and, still disturbed, I idled over to her.

"I say, did I see Miss Pettigrew actually speaking to you, or was I dreaming?"

"You were dreaming." If I had said otherwise the news would have bristled round the monastery. It would have seemed a betrayal to reveal this first crack in Miss Pettigrew's control. The pilgrims would have pitied her more if they had known it, they would have respected her less. I could not bear to think of their heads shaking sorrowfully over Miss Pettigrew's vital "The Lord is risen."

"But surely," this girl pursued, "she stopped beside you just now."

"You've got Miss Pettigrew on the brain," I said. "Leave her alone, poor soul."

"Poor soul!" said the girl. "I don't know about poor soul. There's nothing wrong with that one. She's got foolish medieval ideas, that's all."

"There's nothing to be done with her," I said.

And yet it was not long before something had to be done with Miss Pettigrew. From the Sunday of the fourth week of my stay she went off food. It was not till suppertime on the Monday that her absence was noticed from the refectory.

"Anyone seen Miss Pettigrew?"

"No, she hasn't been down here for two days."

"Does she eat in the town, perhaps?"

"No, she hasn't left the Abbey."

A deputation with a tray of food was

sent to her room. There was no answer. The door was bolted from the inside. But I heard her moving calmly as ever in her room that evening.

Next morning she came in to breakfast after Mass, looking distant and gray, but still very neat. She took up a glass of milk, lifted the crust end of the bread from the board and carried them shakily off to her room. When she did not appear for lunch the cook tried her room again, without success. The door was bolted, there was no answer.

I saw Miss Pettigrew again at Mass next morning, kneeling a little in front of me, resting her head upon her missal as if she could not bear the weight of head on neck. When at last she left the chapel she walked extremely slowly but without halting in her measure. Squackle-wackle ran to help her down the steps. Miss Pettigrew stopped and looked at her, inclining her head in recognition, but clearly rejecting her help.

The doctor was waiting in her room. I heard later that he asked her many questions, used many persuasives, but she simply stared right through him. The Abbot and several of the monks visited her, but by then she had bolted the door again, and though they tempted her with soups and beef broth, Miss Pettigrew would not open.

News went round that her relatives had been sent for. The news went round that she had no relatives to send for. It was said she had been certified insane and was to be taken away.

She did not rise next morning at her usual seven o'clock. It was not till after twelve that I heard her first movement, and the protracted sounds of her slow rising and dressing. A tiny clatter—that would be her shoe falling out of her weak hands; I knew she was bending down, trying again. My pulse was pattering so rapidly that I had to take more of my sedative than usual, as I listened to this slow deliberated performance. Heavy rhythmic rain had started to ping on the roof.

"Neurotics never go mad," my friends had always told me. Now I realized the distinction between neurosis and madness, and in my agitation I half envied the woman beyond my bedroom wall, the sheer cool sanity of her behaviour within the limits of her impracticable mania. Only the very mad, I thought, can come out with the information "The Lord is risen," in the same factual way as one might say, "You are wanted on the telephone," regardless of the time and place.

A knock at my door. I opened it, still shaking with my nerves. It was Jennifer. She whispered, with an eye on the partition dividing me from Miss Pettigrew,

"Come along, Gloria. They say you are to come away for half an hour. The nurses are coming to fetch *her*."

"What nurses?"

"From the asylum. And there will be men with a stretcher. We haven't to distress ourselves, they say."

I could see that Jennifer was agog. She was more transparent than I was. I could see she was longing to stay and overhear, watch out of the windows, see what would happen. I was overcome with disgust and indignation. Why should Jennifer want to satisfy her curiosity? She believed everyone was "the same," she didn't acknowledge the difference of things, what right had she to possess curiosity? My case was different.

"I shall stay here," I said in a normal voice, signifying that I wasn't going to participate in any whispering. Jennifer disappeared, annoyed.

Insanity was my great sort of enemy at that time. And here, clothed in the innocence and dignity of Miss Pettigrew, was my next-door enemy being removed by ambulance. I would not miss it. Afterwards I learned that Jennifer too was lurking around when the ambulance arrived. So were most of the neurotics.

The ambulance came round the back. My window looked only on the front but my ears were windows. I heard a woman's voice, then in reply the voice of one of our priests. Heavy footsteps and something bumping on the stairs and strange men's voices ascending.

"What's her name, did you say?"

"Marjorie Pettigrew."

The hauling and bumping up the stairs continued.

"Ain't no key. Bolt from the inside."

Whenever they paused I could hear Miss Pettigrew's tiny movements. She was continuing to do what she was doing.

They knocked at the door. I pulled like mad at the rosary which I was telling for Miss Pettigrew. A man's voice said, kindly but terribly loud,

"Open up the door, dear. Else we shall have to force it dear."

She opened the door.

"That's a good girl," said the man. "What was the name again?"

The other man replied, "Marjorie Pettigrew."

"Well, come on, Marjorie dear. You just follow me and you won't go wrong. Come along, Marjorie."

I knew she must have been following, though I could not hear her footsteps. I heard the heavy men's boots descending the stairs, and their unnecessary equipment bumping behind them.

"That's right Marjorie. That's a good girl."

Down below the nurse said something, and I heard no more till the ambulance drove off.

"Oh, I saw her!" This was the laundry-girl who had been fond of Miss Pettigrew. "She must have been combing her hair," she said, "when they came for her. It was all loose and long, not at all like Miss Pettigrew. She was always just so. And that going out in the rain, I hope she doesn't catch cold. But they'll be good to her."

Everyone was saying, "They will be kind to her." "They will look after her." "They might cure her."

I never saw them so friendly with each other.

After supper someone said, "I had a respect for Miss Pettigrew."

"So did I," said another.

"They will be very kind. Those men—they sounded all right."

"They meant well enough."

Suddenly the ginger man came out with that one thing which stood at the core of this circuitous talk.

"Did you hear them," he said, "call her Marjorie?"

"My God, yes!"

"Yes, it made me feel funny."

"Same here. Fancy calling her Marjorie."

After that the incident was little discussed. But the community was sobered and united for a brief time, contemplating with fear and pity the calling of Miss Pettigrew Marjorie.

[1960]

For Thought

"Come Along, Marjorie" deals with the gradual deterioration of a woman's mind. The plot is intertwined with ironic situations. And, irony is closely related to the theme. It is ironic that Marjorie Pettigrew should slowly slip into incompetence in a religious institution that is dedicated to restoring people's stability. Moreover, it is ironic that the final, forced departure of Marjorie from the Abbey briefly unites the previously divided guests. Spark suggests that despite attempts to force people into simplified categories, such attempts are neither Christian nor humane: each individual should be viewed as unique.

For Discussion

1. How is the narrator characterized? Why has the narrator joined a retreat at Watling Abbey?

2. What conflicts separate the permanent from the temporary inhabitants of the abbey?
3. What generally accepted views about mental instability are called into question by the story?
4. How is Marjorie characterized? Why is she so powerful a magnet for the interest of others?
5. What point of view has the author adopted for her narrator? Why is it so effective?
6. How is Marjorie's forced departure foreshadowed? Why are the other pilgrims drawn together by Marjorie's plight?
7. What is the theme of the story?

Wallace Stegner
Goin' to Town

After the night's rain the yard was spongy and soft under the boy's bare feet. He stood at the edge of the packed dooryard in the flat thrust of sunrise looking at the ground washed clean and smooth and trackless, feeling the cool firm mud under his toes. Experimentally he lifted his right foot and put it down in a new place, pressed, picked it up again to look at the neat imprint of straight edge and curving instep and the five round dots of toes. The air was so fresh that he sniffed at it as he would have sniffed at the smell of cinnamon.

Lifting his head backward, he saw how the prairie beyond the fireguard looked darker than in dry times, healthier with green-brown tints, smaller and more intimate somehow than it did when the heat waves crawled over scorched grass and carried the horizons backward into dim and unseeable distances. And standing in the yard above his one clean sharp footprint, feeling his own verticality in all that spread of horizontal land, he sensed how the prairie shrank on this morning and how he himself grew. He was immense. A little jump would crack his head on the sky; a few strides would take him to any horizon.

His eyes turned south, into the low south sky, cloudless, almost colorless in the strong light. Just above the brown line of the horizon, faint as a watermark on pale blue paper, was the wavering tracery of the mountains, tenuous and far off, but today accessible for the first time. His mind had played among those ghostly summits for uncountable lost hours; today, in a few strides, they were his. And more: under the shadow of those peaks, under those Bearpaws that he and his mother privately called the Mountains of the Moon, was Chinook; and in Chinook, on this Fourth of July, were the band, the lemonade stands, the crowds, the parade, the ball game, the fireworks, that his mind had hungered toward in anticipation for three weeks.

His shepherd pup lay watching, belly down on the damp ground. In a gleeful spasm the boy stooped down to flap the pup's ears, then bent and spun like an Indian in a war dance while the wide-mouthed dog raced around him. And when his father came to the door in his undershirt, yawning, running a hand up the back of his head and through his hair, peering out from gummed eyes to see how the weather looked, the boy watched him, and his voice was one deep breathing relief from yesterday's rainy fear.

"It's clear as a bell," he said.

His father yawned again, clopped his jaws, rubbed his eyes, mumbled something from a mouth furry with sleep. He stood on the doorstep scratching himself comfortably, looking down at the boy and the dog.

"Gonna be hot," he said slyly. "Might be too hot to drive."

"Aw, Pa!"

"Gonna be a scorcher, Melt you right down to axle grease riding in that car."

The boy regarded him doubtfully, saw the lurking sly droop of his mouth. "Aw, we are too going!"

At his father's laugh he burst from his immobility like a sprinter starting, raced one complete circle of the house with the dog after him. When he flew around past his father again his voice trailed out behind him at the corner of the house. "Gonna feed the hens," he said. His father looked after him, scratched himself, laughed suddenly, and went back indoors.

Through chores and breakfast the boy moved with the dream of a day's rapture haunting his eyes, but that did not keep him from swift and agile helpfulness. He didn't even wait for commands. He scrubbed himself twice, slicked down his hair, hunted up clean clothes, wiped the mud from his shoes with a wet rag and put them on. While his mother packed the shoe box of lunch he stood at her elbows proffering aid. He flew to stow things in the topless old Ford. He got a cloth and polished the brass radiator. Once or twice, jumping around to help, he looked up to catch his parents watching him, or looking at each other with the knowing, smiling expression in the eyes that said they were calling each other's attention to him.

"Just like a race horse," his father said once, and the boy felt foolish, swaggered, twisted his mouth down in a leer, said "Awww!" But in a moment he was hustling them again. They ought to get going, with fifty miles to drive. And long before they were ready he was standing beside the Ford, licked and immaculate and so excited that his feet jumped him up and down without his volition or knowledge.

It was eight o'clock before his father came out, lifted off the front seat, poked the flat stick down into the gas tank, and pulled it out again dripping. "Pretty near full," he said. "If we're gonna drive up to the mountains we better take a can along, though. Fill that two-gallon one with the spout."

The boy ran, dug the can out of the shed, filled it from the spigot of the sixty-gallon drum that stood on a plank support to the north of the farmhouse. When he came back, his left arm stuck straight out and the can knocking against his legs, his mother was settling herself into the back seat among the parcels and water bags.

"Goodness!" she said. "This is the first time I've been the first ready since I don't know when. I should think you'd have got all this done last night."

"Plenty time." The father stood looking down at the boy, grinning. "All right, race horse. You want to go to this shindig, you better hop in."

The boy was up into the front seat like a squirrel. His father walked around in front of the car. "Okay," he said. "You look sharp now. When she kicks over, switch her onto magneto and pull the spark down."

The boy said nothing. He looked upon the car, as his father did, with respect and a little awe. They didn't use it much, and starting it was a ritual like a fire drill. The father unscrewed the four-eared brass plug, looked down into the radiator, screwed the cap back on, and bent to take hold of the crank. "Watch it now," he said.

The boy felt the gentle heave of the springs, up and down, as his father wound the crank. He heard the gentle hiss in the bowels of the engine as the choke wire was pulled out, and his nostrils filled with the strong volatile odor of gasoline. Over the slope of the radiator his father's brown strained face lifted up. "Is she turned on all right?"

"Yup. She's on battery."

"Must of flooded her. Have to let her rest a minute."

They waited—and then after a few minutes the wavelike heaving of the springs again, the rise and fall of the blue shirt and bent head over the radiator, the sighing swish of the choke, a stronger smell of gasoline. The motor had not even coughed.

The two voices came simultaneously from the car. "What's the matter with it?"

His brow puckered in an intent and serious scowl, the father stood blowing mighty breaths. "Son of a gun," he said. Coming around, he pulled at the switch to make sure it was clear over, adjusted the spark and gas levers. A fine mist of sweat made his face shine like oiled leather in the sun.

"There isn't anything really wrong with it, is there?" the mother said, and her voice wavered uncertainly on the edge of fear.

"I don't see how there could be," he said. "She's always started right off, and she was running all right when I drove her in here."

The boy looked at his mother where she sat erect among the things in the seat. She looked all dressed up, a flowered dress, a hat with hard red varnished cherries on it pinned to her red hair. For a moment she sat, stiff and nervous. "What'll you have to do?" she said.

"I don't know. Look into the motor."

"Well, I guess I'll get in out of the sun while you do it," she said, and, opening the door, she fumbled her way out of the clutter.

The boy felt her exodus like a surrender, a betrayal. If they didn't hurry up they'd miss the parade. In one motion he bounced out of the car. "Gee whiz!" he said. "Let's do something. We got to get started."

"Keep your shirt on," his father grunted. Lifting the hood, he bent his head inside, studying the engine. His hand went out to test wires, wiggle spark-plus connections, make tentative pulls at the choke. The weakly hinged hood slipped and came down across his wrist, and he swore, pushing it back. "Get me the pliers," he said.

For ten minutes he probed and monkeyed. "Might be the spark plugs," he said. "She don't seem to be getting any fire through her."

The mother, sitting on a box in the shade, smoothed her flowered voile dress nervously. "Will it take long?"

"Half-hour."

"Any day but this!" she said. "I don't see why you didn't make sure last night."

He breathed through his nose and bent over the engine again. "Don't go laying on any blame," he said. "It was raining last night."

One by one the plugs came out, were squinted at, scraped with a knife blade, the gap tested with a thin dime. The boy stood on one foot, then on the other, time pouring like a flood of uncatchable silver dollars through his hands. He kept looking at the sun, estimating how much time there was left. If they got it started right away they might still make it for the parade, but it would be close. Maybe they'd drive right up the street while the parade was on, and be part of it. . . .

"Is she ready?" he said.

"Pretty quick."

He wandered over by his mother, and she reached out and put an arm around his shoulders, hugging him quickly. "Well, anyway we'll get there for the band and the ball game and the fireworks," he said. "If she doesn't start till noon we c'n make it for those."

"Sure," she said. "Pa'll get it going in a minute. We won't miss anything, hardly."

"You ever seen skyrockets, Ma?"

"Once."

"Are they fun?" "Wonderful," she said.

"Just like a million stars, all colors, exploding all at once."

His feet took him back to his father, who straightened up with a belligerent grunt. "Now!" he said. "If the sucker doesn't start now . . ."

And once more the heaving of the springs, the groaning of the turning engine, the hiss of choke. He tried short, sharp half-turns, as if to catch the motor off guard. Then he went back to the stubborn laboring spin. The back of his blue shirt was stained darkly, the curving dikes of muscle along the spine's hollow showing cleanly where the cloth stuck. Over and over, heaving, stubborn at first, then furious, until he staggered back panting.

"God damn!" he said. "What you suppose is the matter with the damn thing?"

"She didn't even cough once," the boy said, and, staring up at his father's face full of angry bafflement, he felt the cold fear touch him. What if it didn't start at all? What if they never got to any of it? What if, all ready to go, they had to turn around and unload the Ford and not even get out of the yard? His mother came over and they stood close together, looking at the Ford and avoiding each other's eyes.

"Maybe something got wet last night," she said.

"Well, it's had plenty time to dry out," said his father.

"Isn't there anything else you could try?" "We can jack up the hind wheel, I guess. But there's no damn reason we ought to have to."

"Well, if you have to, you'll have to," she said briskly. "After planning it for three weeks we can't just get stuck like this. Can we, son?"

His answer was mechanical, his eyes steady on his father. "Sure not," he said.

The father opened his mouth to say something, saw the boy's lugubrious face, and shut his lips again. Without a word he pulled off the seat and got out the jack.

The sun climbed steadily while they jacked up one hind wheel and blocked the car carefully so that it wouldn't run over anybody when it started. The boy helped, and when they were ready again he sat in the front seat so full of hope and fear that his whole body was one taut concentration. His father stooped, his cheek pressed against the radiator as a milker's cheek touches the flank of a cow. His shoulder dropped, jerked up. Nothing. Another jerk. Nothing. Then he was rolling in a furious spasm of energy, the wet dark back of his shirt rising and falling. And inside the motor only the futile swish of the choke and the half sound, half feel of cavernous motion as the crankshaft turned over. The Ford bounced on its springs as if the front wheels were coming off the ground on every upstroke. Then it stopped, and the boy's father was hanging on the radiator, breathless, dripping wet, swearing: "Son of a dirty, lousy, stinking, corrupted . . ."

The boy, his eyes dark, stared from his father's angry wet face to his mother's, pinched with worry. The pup lay down in the shade and put his head on his paws. "Gee whiz," the boy said. "Gee whiz!" He looked at the sky, and the morning was half gone.

His shoulders jerking with anger, the father threw the crank halfway across the yard and took a step or two toward the house. "The hell with the damn thing!"

"Harry, you can't!"

He stopped, glared at her, took an oblique look at the boy, bared his teeth in an irresolute, silent swearword. "Well, God, if it won't go!"

"Maybe if you hitched the horses to it," she said.

His laugh was short and choppy. "That'd be fine!" he said. "Why don't we just hitch up and let the team haul this damned old boat into Chinook?"

"But we've got to get it started! Why wouldn't it be all right to let them pull it around? You push it sometimes on a hill and it starts."

He looked at the boy again, jerked his eyes away with an exasperated gesture, as if he held the boy somehow accountable. The boy stared, mournful, defeated, ready to cry, and his father's head swing back unwillingly. Then abruptly he winked, mopped his head and neck, and grinned. "Think you want to go, uh?"

The boy nodded. "All right!" his father's voice snapped crisply. "Fly up in the pasture and get the team. Hustle!"

On the high lope the boy was off up the coulee bank. Just down under the lip of the swale, a quarter-mile west, the bay backs of the horses and the black dot of the colt showed. Usually he ran circumspectly across that pasture, because of the cactus, but now he flew. With shoes it was all right, and even without shoes he would have run—across burnouts, over stretches so undermined with gopher holes that sometimes he broke through to the ankle, staggering. Skimming over patches of cactus, soaring over a badger hole, plunging down into the coulee and up the other side, he ran as if bears were after him. The black colt, spotting him, hoisted his tail and took off in a spectacular, stiff-legged sprint across the flats, but the bays merely lifted their heads to watch him. He slowed, came up walking, laid a hand on the mare's neck and untied the looped halter rope. She stood for him while he scrambled and wriggled and kicked his way to her back, and then they were off, the mare in an easy lope, the gelding trotting after, the colt stopping his wild showoff career and wobbling hastily and ignominiously after his departing mother.

They pulled up before the Ford, the boy sliding off to throw the halter rope to his father. "Shall I get the harness?" he said, and before anyone could answer he was off running, to come back lugging one heavy harness, tugs trailing little furrows in the damp bare earth. He dropped it, turned to run again, his breath laboring in his lungs. "I'll get the other'n," he said.

With a short, almost incredulous laugh his father looked at his mother and shook his head before he threw the harness on the mare. When the second one came he laid it over the gelding, pushed against the heavy shoulder to get the horse into place. The gelding resisted, pranced a little, got a curse and a crack with the rope across his nose, jerked back and trembled and lifted his feet nervously, and set one shod hoof on his owner's instep. The father, unstrung by the hurry and the heat and the labor and the exasperation of a morning when nothing went right, kicked the horse savagely in the belly. "Get in there, you damned big blundering ox! Back! Back, you bastard! Whoa! Whoa, now!"

With a heavy rope for a towline he hitched the now-skittish team to the axle. Without a word he stooped and lifted the boy to the mare's back. "All right," he said, and his face relaxed in a quick grin. "This is where we start her. Ride 'em around in a circle, not too fast."

Then he climbed into the Ford, turned on the switch to magneto, fussed with the levers. "Let her go!" he said.

The boy kicked the mare ahead, twisting as he rode to watch the Ford heave forward as a tired, heavy man heaves to his feet, begin rolling after him, lurching on the uneven ground, jerking and kicking and making growling noises when his father let the emergency brake off and put it in gear. The horses settled as the added pull came on them, flattened into their collars, swung in a circle, bumped each other, skittered. The mare reared, and the boy shut his eyes and clung. When he came down, her leg was entangled in the towline and his father was climbing cursing out of the Ford to straighten it out. His father was mad again, and yelled at him. "Keep 'em apart! There ain't any tongue. You got to keep Dick kicked over on his own side."

And again the start, the flattening into the collars, the snapping tight of the tugs under his legs. This time it went smoothly, the Ford galloped after the team in lumbering, plunging jerks. The mare's eyes rolled white, and she broke into a trot, pulling the gelding after her. Desperately the boy clung to the knotted and shortened reins, his ears alert for the grumble of the Ford starting behind him. The pup ran beside the team yapping in a high, falsetto, idiot monotone, crazy with excitement.

They made three complete circles of the back yard between house and chicken coop before the boy looked back again. "Won't she start?" he shouted. He saw his father rigid behind the wheel, heard his ripping burst of swearwords, saw him bend and glare down into the mysterious inwards of the engine through the pulled-up floorboards. Guiding the car with one hand, he fumbled down below, one glaring eye just visible over the cowl.

"Shall I stop?" the boy shouted. Excitement and near-despair made his voice a tearful scream. But his father's wild arm waved him on. "Go on, go on! Gallop 'em! Pull the guts out of this thing. Run 'em, run 'em!"

And the galloping—the furious, mud-flinging, rolling-eyed galloping around the circle already rutted like a road, the Ford, now in savagely held low, growling and surging and plowing behind; the mad yapping of the dog, the erratic scared bursts of runaway from the colt, the mother in sight briefly for a quarter of each circle, her hands to her mouth and her eyes hurt, and behind him in the Ford his father in a strangling rage, yelling him on, his lips back over his teeth and his face purple.

Until finally they stopped, the horses blown, the boy white and tearful and still, the father dangerous with unexpended wrath. The boy slipped off, his lip bitten between his teeth, not crying now but ready to at any moment, the corners of his eyes prickling with it, and his teeth tight on his misery. His father climbed over the side of the car and stood looking as if he wanted to tear the thing apart with his bare hands.

Shoulders sagging, tears trembling to fall, his jaw aching with the need to cry, the boy started toward his mother. As he came near his father he looked up, their eyes met, and he saw his father's blank with impotent rage. Dull hopelessness swallowed him. Not any of it, his mind said. Not even any of it—no parade, no ball game, no band, no fireworks. No lemonade or ice cream or paper horns or firecrackers. No close sight of the mountains that throughout every summer called like a legend from his horizons. No trip, no adventure—none of it, nothing.

Everything he was feeling was in that one still look. In spite of him his lip trembled, and he choked off a sob, his eyes on his father's face, on the brows pulling down and the eyes narrowing.

"Well, don't blubber!" his father shouted at him. "Don't stand there looking at me as if it was me that was keeping you from your picnic!"

"I can't —help it," the boy said, and with a kind of terror he felt the grief swelling up, overwhelming him, driving the voice out of him in a wail. Through the blur of his crying he saw the convulsive tightening of his father's face, and then all the fury of a maddening morning concentrated itself in a swift backhand blow that knocked the boy staggering.

He bawled aloud, from pain, from surprise, from outrage, from pure desolation, and ran to bury his face in his mother's skirts. From that muffled sanctuary he heard her angry voice. "No," she said. "It won't do any good to try to make up to him now. Go on away somewhere till he gets over it."

She rocked him against her, but the voice she had for his father was bitter with anger. "As if he wasn't hurt enough already!" she said.

He heard the heavy, quick footsteps going away, and for a long time he lay crying into the voile flowers. And when he had cried himself out, and had listened apathetically to his mother's soothing promises that they would go in the first chance they got, go to the mountains, have a picnic under some waterfall, maybe be able to find a ball game going on in town, some Saturday—when he had listened and become quiet, wanting to believe it but not believing it at all, he went inside to take off his good clothes and his shoes and put on his old overalls again.

It was almost noon when he came out to stand in the front yard looking southward toward the impossible land where the

Mountains of the Moon lifted above the plains, and where, in the town at the foot of the peaks, crowds would now be eating picnic lunches, drinking pop, getting ready to go out to the ball field and watch heroes in real uniforms play ball. The band would be braying now from a bunting-wrapped stand, kids would be tossing firecrackers, playing in a cool grove. . . .

In the still heat his face went sorrowful and defeated, and his eyes searched the horizon for the telltale watermark. But there was nothing but waves of heat crawling and lifting like invisible flames; the horizon was a blurred and writhing flatness where earth and sky met in an indistinct band of haze. This morning two strides would have taken him there; now it was gone.

Looking down, he saw at his feet the clean footprint that he had made in the early morning. Aimlessly he put his right foot down and pressed. The mud was drying, but in a low place he found a spot that would still take an imprint. Very carefully, as if he were performing some ritual for his life, he went around, stepping and leaning, stepping and leaning, until he had a circle six feet in diameter of delicately exact footprints, straight edge and curving instep and the five round dots of toes.

[1940]

For Thought

In "Goin' to Town," Stegner captures the sense of eagerness and anticipatory high spirits a little boy experiences over a longed-for trip to town on a very special day in the middle of a long, hot summer on a prairie farm in the early part of the twentieth century. Against this, he poignantly balances the feelings of crushing disappointment and dull hopelessness that arise from the failure of the dream to be realized.

For Discussion

1. What is the mood at the beginning of the story? What is the mood at the end? What details are provided to establish the mood?
2. What is the inciting force, the complication, the crisis, and the resolution in the plot? How does Stegner create a sense of inevitability about the progression of events?
3. What influence does the setting have on the characters and on the action in the story?
4. How is the boy characterized by his actions and reactions, and by his parents' attitude toward him?
5. What is Stegner's attitude toward the boy, the mother, and the father? How does he establish his attitude?

John Steinbeck
The Chrysanthemums

The high grey-flannel fog of winter closed off the Salinas Valley from the sky and from all the rest of the world. On every side it sat like a lid on the mountains and made of the great valley a closed pot. On the broad, level land floor the gang ploughs bit deep and left the black earth shining like metal where the shares had cut. On the foot-hill ranches across the Salinas River, the yellow stubble fields seemed to be bathed in pale cold sunshine, but there was no sunshine in the valley now in December. The thick willow scrub along the river flamed with sharp and positive yellow leaves.

It was a time of quiet and of waiting. The air was cold and tender. A light wind blew up from the southwest so that the farmers were mildly hopeful of a good rain before long; but fog and rain do not go together.

Across the river, on Henry Allen's foot-hill ranch there was little work to be done, for the hay was cut and stored and the orchards were ploughed up to receive the rain deeply when it should come. The cattle on the higher slopes were becoming shaggy and rough-coated.

Elisa Allen, working in her flower garden, looked down across the yard and saw Henry, her husband, talking to two men in business suits. The three of them stood by the tractor-shed, each man with one foot on the side of the little Fordson. They smoked cigarettes and studied the machine as they talked.

Elisa watched them for a moment and then went back to her work. She was thirty-five. Her face was lean and strong and her eyes were as clear as water. Her figure looked blocked and heavy in her gardening costume, a man's black hat pulled low down over her eyes, clod-hopper shoes, a figured print dress almost completely covered by a big corduroy apron with four big pockets to hold the snips, the trowel and scratcher, the seeds and the knife she worked with. She wore heavy leather gloves to protect her hands while she worked.

She was cutting down the old year's chrysanthemum stalks with a pair of short and powerful scissors. She looked down toward the men by the tractor-shed now and then. Her face was eager and mature and handsome, even her work with the scissors was over-eager, over-powerful. The chrysanthemum stems seemed too small and easy for her energy.

She brushed a cloud of hair out of her eyes with the back of her glove, and left a smudge of earth on her cheek in doing it. Behind her stood the neat white farmhouse with red geraniums close-banked around it as high as the windows. It was a hard-swept-looking little house, with hard-polished windows, and a clean mudmat on the front steps.

Elisa cast another glance toward the tractor-shed. The strangers were getting into their Ford coupé. She took off a glove and put her strong fingers down into the forest of new green chrysanthemum sprouts that were growing around the old roots. She spread the leaves and looked down among the close-growing stems. No aphids were there, no sow bugs or snails or cutworms. Her terrier fingers destroyed such pests before they could get started.

Elisa started at the sound of her husband's voice. He had come near quietly, and he leaned over the wire fence that protected her flower garden from cattle and dogs and chickens.

"At it again," he said. "You've got a strong new crop coming."

Elisa straightened her back and pulled on the gardening glove again. "Yes. They'll be strong this coming year." In her tone and on her face there was a little smugness.

"You've got a gift with things," Henry observed. "Some of those yellow chrysanthemums you had this year were ten inches across. I wish you'd work out in the orchard and raise some apples that big."

Her eyes sharpened. "Maybe I could do it, too. I've a gift with things, all right. My mother had it. She could stick anything in the ground and make it grow. She said it was having planters' hands that knew how to do it."

"Well, it sure works with flowers," he said.

"Henry, who were those men you were talking to?"

"Why, sure, that's what I came to tell you. They were from the Western Meat Company. I sold those thirty head of three-year-old steers. Got nearly my own price, too."

"Good," she said. "Good for you."

"And I thought," he continued, "I thought how it's Saturday afternoon, and we might go into Salinas for dinner at a restaurant, and then to a picture show—to celebrate, you see."

"Good," she repeated. "Oh, yes. That will be good."

Henry put on his joking tone. "There's fights tonight. How'd you like to go to the fights?"

"Oh, no," she said breathlessly. "No, I wouldn't like fights."

"Just fooling, Elisa. We'll go to a movie. Let's see. It's two now. I'm going to take Scotty and bring down those steers from the hill. It'll take us maybe two hours. We'll go in town about five and have dinner at the Cominos Hotel. Like that?"

"Of course I'll like it. It's good to eat away from home."

"All right, then. I'll go get up a couple of horses."

She said: "I'll have plenty of time to transplant some of these sets, I guess."

She heard her husband calling Scotty down by the barn. And a little later she saw the two men ride up the pale yellow hillside in search of the steers.

There was a little square sandy bed kept for rooting the chyrsanthemums. With her trowel she turned the soil over and over, and smoothed it and patted it firm. Then she dug ten parallel trenches to receive the sets. Back at the chrysanthemum bed she pulled out the little crisp shoots, trimmed off the leaves of each one with her scissors and laid it on a small orderly pile.

A squeak of wheels and plod of hoofs came from the road. Elisa looked up. The country road ran along the dense bank of willows and cottonwoods that bordered the river, and up this road came a curious vehicle, curiously drawn. It was an old spring-wagon, with a round canvas top on it like the cover of a prairie schooner. It was drawn by an old bay horse and a little grey-and-white burro. A big stubble-bearded man sat between the cover flaps and drove the crawling team. Underneath the wagon, between the hind wheels, a lean and rangy mongrel dog walked sedately. Words were painted on the canvas, in clumsy, crooked letters. "Pots, pans, knives, sisors, lawn mores, Fixed." Two rows of articles, and the triumphantly definitive "Fixed" below. The black paint had run down in little sharp points beneath each letter.

Elisa, squatting on the ground, watched to see the crazy, loose-jointed wagon pass by. But it didn't pass. It turned into the farm road in front of her house, crooked old wheels skirling and squeaking. The rangy dog darted from between the wheels and ran ahead. Instantly the two ranch shepherds flew out at him. Then all three stopped, and with stiff and quivering tails, with taut straight legs, with ambassadorial dignity, they slowly circled, sniffing daintily. The caravan pulled up to Elisa's wire fence and stopped. Now the newcomer dog, feeling out-numbered, lowered his tail and retired under the wagon with raised hackles and bared teeth.

The man on the wagon seat called out: "That's a bad dog in a fight when he gets started."

Elisa laughed. "I see he is. How soon does he generally get started?"

The man caught up her laughter and echoed it heartily. "Sometimes not for weeks and weeks," he said. He climbed stiffly down, over the wheel. The horse and the donkey drooped like unwatered flowers.

Elisa saw that he was a very big man. Although his hair and beard were greying, he did not look old. His worn black suit was wrinkled and spotted with grease. The laughter had disappeared from his face and eyes the moment his laughing voice ceased. His eyes were dark, and they were full of the brooding that gets in the eyes of teamsters and of sailors. The calloused hands he rested on the wire fence were cracked, and every crack was a black line. He took off his battered hat.

"I'm off my general road, ma'am," he said. "Does this dirt road cut over across the river to the Los Angeles highway?"

Elisa stood up and shoved the thick scissors in her apron pocket. "Well, yes, it does, but it winds around and then fords the river. I don't think your team could pull through the sand."

He replied with some asperity: "It might surprise you what them beasts can pull through."

"When they get started?" she asked.

He smiled for a second, "Yes. When they get started."

"Well," said Elisa, "I think you'll save time if you go back to the Salinas road and pick up the highway there."

He drew a big finger down the chicken wire and made it sing. "I ain't in any hurry, ma'am. I go from Seattle to San Diego and back every year. Takes all my time. About six months each way. I aim to follow nice weather."

Elisa took off her gloves and stuffed them in the apron pocket with the scissors. She touched the under edge of her man's hat, searching for fugitive hairs. "That sounds like a nice kind of way to live," she said.

He leaned confidentially over the fence. "Maybe you noticed the writing on my wagon. I mend pots and sharpen knives and scissors. You got any of them things to do?"

"Oh, no," she said quickly. "Nothing like that." Her eyes hardened with resistance.

"Scissors is the worst thing," he explained. "Most people just ruin scissors trying to sharpen 'em, but I know how. I got a special tool. It's a little bobbit kind of thing, and patented. But it sure does the trick."

"No. My scissors are all sharp."

"All right, then. Take a pot," he continued earnestly, "a bent pot, or a pot with a hole. I can make it like new so you don't have to buy no new ones. That's a saving for you."

"No," she said shortly. "I tell you I have nothing like that for you to do."

His face fell to an exaggerated sadness. His voice took on a whining undertone. "I ain't had a thing to do today. Maybe I won't have no supper tonight. You see I'm off my regular road. I know folks on the highway clear from Seattle to San Diego. They save their things for me to sharpen up because they know I do it so good and save them money."

"I'm sorry," Elisa said irritably. "I haven't anything for you to do."

His eyes left her face and fell to searching the ground. They roamed about until they came to the chrysanthemum bed where she had been working. "What's them plants, ma'am?"

The irritation and resistance melted from Elisa's face. "Oh, those are chrysanthemums, giant whites and yellows. I raise them every year, bigger than anybody around here."

"Kind of a long-stemmed flower? Looks like a quick puff of colored smoke?" he asked.

"That's it. What a nice way to describe them."

"They smell kind of nasty till you get used to them," he said.

"It's a good bitter smell," she retorted, "not nasty at all."

He changed his tone quickly. "I like the smell myself."

"I had ten-inch blooms this year," she said.

The man leaned farther over the fence. "Look. I know a lady down the road a piece, has got the nicest garden you ever seen. Got nearly every kind of flower but no chrysanthemums. Last time I was mending a copper-bottom washtub for her (that's a hard job but I do it good), she said to me: " 'If you ever run acrost some nice chrysanthemums I wish you'd try to get me a few seeds.' That's what she told me."

Elisa's eyes grew alert and eager. "She couldn't have known much about chrysanthemums. You *can* raise them from seed, but it's much easier to root the little sprouts you see there."

"Oh," he said. "I s'pose I can't take none to her, then."

"Why yes you can," Elisa cried. "I can put some in damp sand and you can carry them right along with you. They'll take root in the pot if you keep them damp. And then she can transplant them."

"She'd sure like to have some, ma'am. You say they're nice ones?"

"Beautiful," she said. "Oh, beautiful." Her eyes shone. She tore off the battered hat and shook out her dark pretty hair. "I'll put them in a flowerpot, and you can take them right with you. Come into the yard."

While the man came through the picket gate Elisa ran excitedly along the geranium-bordered path to the back of the house. And she returned carrying a big red flower-pot. The gloves were forgotten now. She kneeled on the ground by the starting bed and dug up the sandy soil with her fingers and scooped it into the bright new flower pot. Then she picked up the little pile of shoots she had prepared. With her strong fingers she pressed them into the sand and tamped around them with her knuckles. The man stood over her. "I'll tell you what to do," she said. "You remember so you can tell the lady."

"Yes, I'll try to remember."

"Well, look. These will take root in about a month. Then she must set them out, about a foot apart in good rich earth like this, see?" She lifted a handful of dark soil for him to look at. "They'll grow fast and tall. Now remember this: In July tell her to cut them down, about eight inches from the ground."

"Before they bloom?" he asked.

"Yes, before they bloom." Her face was

tight with eagerness. "They'll grow right up again. About the last of September the buds will start."

She stopped and seemed perplexed. "It's the budding that takes the most care," she said hesitantly. "I don't know how to tell you." She looked deep into his eyes, searchingly. Her mouth opened a little, and she seemed to be listening. "I'll try to tell you," she said. "Did you ever hear of planting hands?"

"Can't say I have, ma'am."

"Well. I can only tell you what it feels like. It's when you're picking off the buds you don't want. Everything goes right down into your fingertips. You watch your fingers work. They do it themselves. You can feel how it is. They pick and pick the buds. They never make a mistake. They're with the plant. Do you see? Your fingers and the plant. You can feel that, right up your arm. They know. They never make a mistake. You can feel it. When you're like that you can't do anything wrong. Do you see that? Can you understand that?"

She was kneeling on the ground looking up at him. Her breast swelled passionately.

The man's eyes narrowed. He looked away self-consciously. "Maybe I know," he said. "Sometimes in the night in the wagon there—"

Elisa's voice grew husky. She broke in on him: "I've never lived as you do, but I know what you mean. When the night is dark—why, the stars are sharp-pointed, and there's quiet. Why, you rise up and up! Every pointed star gets driven into your body. It's like that. Hot and sharp and—lovely."

Kneeling there, her hand went out toward his legs in the greasy black trousers. Her hesitant fingers almost touched the cloth. Then her hand dropped to the ground. She crouched low like a fawning dog.

He said: "It's nice, just like you say. Only when you don't have no dinner, it ain't."

She stood up then, very straight, and her face was ashamed. She held the flower-pot out to him and placed it gently in his arms. "Here. Put it in your wagon, on the seat, where you can watch it. Maybe I can find something for you to do."

At the back of the house she dug in the can pile and found two old and battered aluminum saucepans. She carried them back and gave them to him. "Here, maybe you can fix these."

His manner changed. He became professional. "Good as new I can fix them." At the back of his wagon he set a little anvil, and out of an oily tool-box dug a small machine hammer. Elisa came through the gate to watch him while he pounded out the dents in the kettles. His mouth grew sure and knowing. At a difficult part of the work he sucked his underlip.

"You sleep right in the wagon?" Elisa asked.

"Right in the wagon, ma'am. Rain or shine I'm dry as a cow in there."

"It must be nice," she said. "It must be very nice. I wish women could do such things."

"It ain't the right kind of a life for a woman."

Her upper lip raised a little, showing her teeth. "How do you know? How can you tell?" she said.

"I don't know, ma'am," he protested. "Of course I don't know. Now here's your kettles, done. You don't have to buy no new ones."

"How much?"

"Oh, fifty cents'll do. I keep my prices down and my work good. That's why I have all them satisfied customers up and down the highway."

Elisa brought him a fifty-cent piece from the house and dropped it in his hand. "You might be surprised to have a rival some time. I can sharpen scissors, too. And I can beat the dents out of little pots. I could show you what a woman might do."

He put his hammer back in the oily box and shoved the little anvil out of sight. "It would be a lonely life for a woman, ma'am, and a scarey life, too, with animals creeping under the wagon all night." He climbed over the single-tree, steadying himself with a hand on the burro's white rump. He settled himself in the seat, picked up the lines. "Thank you kindly ma'am," he said. "I'll do like you told me; I'll go back and catch the Salinas road."

"Mind," she called, "if you're long in getting there, keep the sand damp."

"Sand, ma'am? . . . Sand? Oh, sure. You mean around the chrysanthemums. Sure I will." He clucked his tongue. The beasts leaned luxuriously into their collars. The mongrel dog took his place between the back wheels. The wagon turned and crawled out the entrance road and back the way it had come, along the river.

Elisa stood in front of her wire fence watching the slow progress of the caravan. Her shoulders were straight, her head thrown back, her eyes half-closed, so that the scene came vaguely into them. Her lips moved silently, forming the words "Good-bye—good-bye." Then she whispered: "That's a bright direction. There's a glowing there." The sound of her whisper startled her. She shook herself free and looked about to see whether anyone had been listening. Only the dogs had heard. They lifted their heads toward her from their sleeping in the dust, and then stretched out their chins and settled asleep again. Elisa turned and ran hurriedly into the house.

In the kitchen she reached behind the stove and felt the water tank. It was full of hot water from the noonday cooking. In the bathroom she tore off her soiled clothes and flung them into the corner. And then she scrubbed herself with a little block of pumice, legs and thighs, loins and chest and arms, until her skin was scratched and red. When she had dried herself she stood in front of a mirror in her bedroom and looked at her body. She tightened her stomach and threw out her chest. She turned and looked over her shoulder at her back.

After a while she began to dress, slowly. She put on her newest underclothing and her nicest stockings and the dress which was the symbol of her prettiness. She worked carefully on her hair, pencilled her eyebrows and rouged her lips.

Before she was finished she heard the little thunder of hoofs and the shouts of Henry and his helper as they drove the red steers into the corral. She heard the gate bang shut and set herself for Henry's arrival.

His step sounded on the porch. He entered the house calling: "Elisa, where are you?"

"In my room, dressing. I'm not ready. There's hot water for your bath. Hurry up. It's getting late."

When she heard him splashing in the tub, Elisa laid his dark suit on the bed, and shirt and socks and tie beside it. She stood his polished shoes on the floor beside the bed. Then she went to the porch and sat primly and stiffly down. She looked toward the river road where the willow-line was still yellow with frosted leaves so that under the high grey fog they seemed a thin band of sunshine. This was the only color in the grey afternoon. She sat unmoving for a long time. Her eyes blinked rarely.

Henry came banging out of the door, shoving his tie inside his vest as he came. Elisa stiffened and her face grew tight. Henry stopped short and looked at her. "Why—why, Elisa. You look so nice!"

"Nice? You think I look nice? What do you mean by 'nice'?"

Henry blundered on. "I don't know. I mean you look different, strong and happy."

"I am strong? Yes, strong. What do you mean 'strong'?"

He looked bewildered. "You're playing some kind of a game," he said helplessly. "It's a kind of a play. You look strong enough to break a calf over your knee, happy enough to eat it like a watermelon."

For a second she lost her rigidity. "Henry! Don't talk like that. You didn't know what you said." She grew complete again. "I'm strong," she boasted. "I never knew before how strong."

Henry looked down toward the tractor-shed, and when he brought his eyes back to her, they were his own again. "I'll get out the car. You can put on your coat while I'm starting."

Elisa went into the house. She heard him drive to the gate and idle down his motor, and then she took a long time to put on her hat. She pulled it here and pressed it there. When Henry turned the motor off she slipped into her coat and went out.

The little roadster bounced along on the dirt road by the river, raising the birds and driving the rabbits into the brush. Two cranes flapped heavily over the willow-line and dropped into the riverbed.

Far ahead on the road Elisa saw a dark speck. She knew.

She tried not to look as they passed it, but her eyes would not obey. She whispered to herself sadly: "He might have thrown them off the road. That wouldn't have been much trouble, not very much. But he kept the pot," she explained. "He had to keep the pot. That's why he couldn't get them off the road."

The roadster turned a bend and she saw the caravan ahead. She swung full around toward her husband so she could not see the little covered wagon and the mis-matched team as the car passed them.

In a moment it was over. The thing was done. She did not look back.

She said loudly, to be heard above the motor: "It will be good, tonight, a good dinner."

"Now you've changed again," Henry complained. He took one hand from the wheel and patted her knee. "I ought to take you in to dinner oftener. It would be good for both of us. We get so heavy out on the ranch."

"Henry," she asked, "could we have wine at dinner?"

"Sure we could. Say! That will be fine."

She was silent for a while; then she said: "Henry, at those prizefights, do the men hurt each other very much?"

"Sometimes a little, not often. Why?"

"Well, I've read how they break noses, and blood runs down their chests. I've read how the fighting gloves get heavy and soggy with blood."

He looked around at her. "What's the matter, Elisa? I didn't know you read things like that." He brought the car to a stop, then turned to the right over the Salinas River bridge.

"Do any women ever go to the fights?" she asked.

"Oh, sure, some. What's the matter, Elisa? Do you want to go? I don't think you'd like it, but I'll take you if you really want to go."

She relaxed limply in the seat. "Oh, no. No. I don't want to go. I'm sure I don't." Her face was turned away from him. "It will be enough if we can have wine. It will be plenty." She turned up her coat collar so he could not see that she was crying weakly—like an old woman.

[1937]

For Thought

"The Chrysanthemums" is a story with little action. Instead, Steinbeck concentrates on the elements of symbolism and imagery in narrating his story of a lonely farm wife who has a chance encounter with a traveling tinker down on his luck. The tinker manipulates the emotions of the woman by pretending to have an interest in her prized flowers. When she discovers that he has thrown aside her gift of flower shoots, she upsets her husband with her quietly distraught behavior. Steinbeck suggests that even commonplace, unaware people have depths of emotion they can neither control nor understand.

For Discussion

1. What is the relationship of the Allens to one another and to their farm?
2. What do the chrysanthemums symbolize?

3. Why does Elisa respond in a contradictory manner to the arrival of the tinker? Why is she first hostile and then submissive?
4. How do Elisa's bath and, later, dressing suggest mixed emotions aroused by the tinker?
5. Why does Elisa first show an interest in going to the gory prizefights and then deny her desire to go to one?

Italo Svevo
The Mother

In a valley shut in by wooded hills, and smiling in its spring colours, stood side by side two large, bare houses, all stone and cement. They might have been built by the same hands. The gardens, too, shut in by hedges and facing each other, were of the same size and form. But the lot of the inmates was very different.

In one of the gardens, while the dog was asleep on its chain and the farmer was busy with his fruit trees, some chickens shut off in a corner were exchanging views on their exciting experiences. There were others older in the garden, but the tiny ones, whose bodies had not yet lost the shape of the egg from which they had come, liked to discuss among themselves the life into which they had been plunged, because they were not yet so used to it that they did not see it. They had already suffered and enjoyed, for a life of a few days is longer than it can possibly seem to anyone who has endured it for years, and they knew much, seeing that they had brought a part of their great experience with them from the egg. In fact, they had hardly come into the light before they had learnt that they must look well into things, first with one eye, then with the other, to see whether they were to eat them or be on their guard against them.

And they talked of the world and its vastness, with the trees and the hedges that shut it in, and the house, so enormous and tall. These were all things they could already see, but they saw them better when they talked about them.

One of them, covered with yellow down, gorged full and therefore idle, was not satisfied with talking about the things visible, but drew from the warmth of the sun a memory, which he suddenly expressed: "Undoubtedly we are well off, because there is the sun, but I have heard that in this world you can be still better off, and I am very sorry about it, and I will tell you, so that you may be sorry too. The farmer's daughter said that we are poor specimens because we have not got a mother. She spoke so feelingly that she made me cry."

Another one, whiter and some hours

SOURCE: "The Mother" by Italo Svevo. Reprinted from *The Short Sentimental Journey and Other Stories* by Italo Svevo courtesy of Agenzia Litteraria Internazionale.

younger than the first, so that he still remembered with gratitude the pleasant warmth that he was born from protested: "We have had a mother. It is that little box, which is always warm, no matter how cold it is, and which the chickens come out of full blown."

The yellow one, who had long had the peasant girl's words vividly impressed on his brain, and had therefore had time to magnify them by dwelling on them, dreaming of the mother till he had imagined her as large as the whole garden and as good as bird-food, exclaimed with a contempt that was meant as much for his interlocutor as for the mother of which he was talking: "If it were a question of a dead mother, everyone would have one. But this mother is alive and runs much faster than we can. Perhaps she has wheels like the peasant's cart. So she can come to you without you having to call for her, to warm you when you are likely to be frozen by the cold of this world. It must be nice to have a mother like that near you at night."

A third chicken broke in, brother of the others because he had come out of the same incubator, though it had fashioned him a little differently, with a broader beak and shorter little legs. They called him the bad-mannered chicken, because, when he ate, you could hear his beak clapping together, whereas he was really a duckling who, in his own country, would have passed for a model of manners. In his presence also the girl had talked of a mother. That had happened at the time when a chicken had died of cold and exposure in the grass, with the other chicks round him, not trying to help him, because they do not feel other people's cold. And the duckling, with the air of simplicity which the huge end of his beak gave his tiny face, declared emphatically that, when there is a mother, chickens cannot die.

The desire for a mother soon invaded the whole brood and it was keener, more disturbing, in the minds of the older chicks. Childish illnesses often attack grown-ups and are more dangerous to them. So also do ideas, sometimes. The picture of the mother, as it had taken shape in those little heads heated by the spring, developed in an extraordinary degree, and everything that was good was called mother, fine weather and plenty of food; and when the chickens, ducklings or little turkeys were ill, they became real brothers because they were sighing for the same mother.

One day one of the eldest swore that he would find his mother. He was determined not to live without one any longer. He was the only one of them who had been christened and he was called "Come-Come" because, when the girl with the corn in her apron called, "Come, come," he was always the first to do so. He was already vigorous, a cockerel in whose generous soul the spirit of combat was budding. Tall and lithe as a rapier, he wanted a mother first and foremost to admire him: the mother who was said to be able to give every blessing and therefore also to satisfy ambition and vanity.

One day Come-Come boldly leaped through the thick hedge that surrounded his native garden. In the open he stood suddenly still in amazement. Where could he find his mother in that enormous valley over which was a blue sky even more vast? It was hopeless for one as small as himself to search that immensity. So he did not go too far from his native garden, the world he knew, and thoughtfully made the round of it. Thus he found himself in front of the hedge of the other garden.

"If my mother were in there," he thought, "I should find her in a moment." After escaping from the difficulties of infinite space he had no more hesitation. With a bound he went through that hedge also and found himself in a garden very like the one he had left.

Here also there was a flock of tiny chickens fluttering in the long grass. But here was also an animal not to be found in the other garden. A huge chicken, perhaps ten times the size of Come-Come, was lording it in the midst of little creatures covered only with down, and they, as was clear in a moment, regarded this great, bulky animal as their master and protector. And it looked after them all. It gave warning to those straying too far away with a noise not very unlike that which the girl in the other garden made with her own chickens. But this was not all. Every now and then it bent down over the weakest, covering them with all its body, clearly to give them its own heat.

"This is the mother," thought Come-Come with joy. "I have found her and I shan't leave her. How she will love me! I am stronger and better looking than any of those. And it will be easy for me to be obedient, because I love her already. How beautiful and majestic she is! I will help her to look after all these other stupid creatures too."

Without looking at him the mother called. Come-Come drew nearer, believing that she was calling him. He saw that she was busy scratching the earth with rapid blows of her huge claws, and stood still, watching curiously what she was doing, for it was the first time he had seen the operation. When she stopped, a tiny worm was wriggling on the ground in front of her from which she had scratched the grass. Then she clucked while the chickens round her looked at her ecstatically without understanding.

"Idiots," thought Come-Come. "They don't even understand that she wants them to eat that worm." And fired by his enthusiasm to obey her, he pounced quickly upon his prey and swallowed it.

And then—poor Come-Come—the mother darted furiously upon him. He did not understand at once, because he still suspected that, having only just found him, she had a violent desire to caress him. He would thankfully have welcomed all her caresses, of which he knew nothing, and which he therefore admitted might hurt. But the blows that rained upon him from that hard beak were certainly not kisses. They left no room for doubt. He tried to run away, but the great bird pushed him down, rolled him over and jumped upon him, driving her claws into his stomach.

With a superhuman effort Come-Come got upon his legs and ran to the hedge. In his mad race he knocked over some of the chicks, leaving them there cheeping desperately with their legs in the air. He was thus able to escape, because his enemy stopped for a moment by the fallen. Reaching the hedge, Come-Come, with a leap, and despite all the trunks and branches, managed to hurl his agile little body into safety.

The mother, however, was held up by a thick tangle of foliage. And there she remained, majestically looking out as from a window on to the intruder, who had also stopped, exhausted. She looked at him with her terrible round eyes red with anger. "Who are you that dared to steal the food I dug out of the ground with so much trouble?"

"I am Come-Come," said the chicken humbly. "But who are you and why have you hurt me so?"

She made but one answer to both his questions. "I am mother," and turned her back contemptuously upon him.

Some time later Come-Come, now a splendid cock, was in quite a different farmyard. And one day he heard all his new comrades talking affectionately and regretfully of their mother.

Marvelling at his own cruel fate, he said sadly: "My mother, on the contrary, was a horrible monster, and it would have been better for me if I had never known her."

[1927]

For Thought

In the guise of a pleasant fairy tale set in the form of a fable, "The Mother" entertains the reader with an absurdist view of life and the relationship of humankind to the universe. By reducing the universe to the scope of two adjacent chicken yards, Svevo deliberately trivializes the dangerous heroic quest embarked upon by his protagonist, thereby rendering it laughable. At the same time, however, his disingenuous asides make it clear that his amusing little world of befuddled, motherless chicks is really a microcosm of the world of the human species.

For Discussion

1. What is the tone of the story and how is it achieved? How does the tone contribute to the overall effect of the story?
2. What is the central conflict in the story? How is it resolved?
3. What is the comic basis of the action? (Consider the nature of the quest, the device of mistaken identity, and the conditions surrounding the reversal of fortune.)
4. Accepting the premise of Come-Come as hero, what can one say about his "tragic flaw"?
5. What is the pattern of the story? What element of parody is there in the story?
6. What is the philosophical significance of the "mother's" response to Come-Come's question, "But who are you and why have you hurt me so?"

Dylan Thomas
The Followers

It was six o'clock on a winter's evening. Thin, dingy rain spat and drizzled past the lighted street lamps. The pavements shone long and yellow. In squeaking goloshes, with mackintosh collars up and bowlers and trilbies weeping, youngish men from the offices bundled home against the thistly wind—

"Night, Mr. Macey."

"Going my way, Charlie?"

"Ooh, there's a pig of a night!"

"Goodnight, Mr. Swan"—

and older men, clinging on to the big, black circular birds of their umbrellas, were wafted back, up the gaslit hills, to safe, hot, slippered, weatherproof hearths, and wives called Mother, and old, fond, fleabag dogs, and the wireless babbling.

Young women from the offices, who smelt of scent and powder and wet pixie hoods and hair, scuttled, giggling, arm-in-arm, after the hissing trams, and screeched as they splashed their stockings in the puddles rainbowed with oil between the slippery lines.

In a shopwindow, two girls undressed the dummies:

"Where are you going tonight?"

"Depends on Arthur. Up she comes."

"Mind her cami-knicks, Edna . . ."

The blinds came down over another window.

A newsboy stood in a doorway, calling the news to nobody, very softly:

"Earthquake. Earthquake in Japan."

Water from a chute dripped on to his sacking. He waited in his own pool of rain.

A flat, long girl drifted, snivelling into her hanky, out of a jeweller's shop, and slowly pulled the steel shutters down with a hooked pole. She looked, in the grey rain, as though she were crying from top to toe.

A silent man and woman, dressed in black, carried the wreaths away from the front of their flower shop into the scented deadly darkness behind the window lights. Then the lights went out.

A man with a balloon tied to his cap pushed a shrouded barrow up a dead end.

A baby with an ancient face sat in its

pram outside the wine vaults, quiet, very wet, peering cautiously all round it.

It was the saddest evening I had ever known.

A young man, with his arm round his girl, passed by me, laughing; and she laughed back, right into his handsome, nasty face. That made the evening sadder still.

I met Leslie at the corner of Crimea Street. We were both about the same age: too young and too old. Leslie carried a rolled umbrella, which he never used, though sometimes he pressed doorbells with it. He was trying to grow a moustache. I wore a check ratting cap at a Saturday angle. We greeted each other formally:

"Good evening, old man."

"Evening, Leslie."

"Right on the dot, boy."

"That's right," I said. "Right on the dot."

A plump blonde girl, smelling of wet rabbits, self-conscious even in that dirty night, minced past on high-heeled shoes. The heels clicked, the soles squelched.

Leslie whistled after her, low and admiring.

"Business first," I said.

"Oh, boy!" Leslie said.

"And she's too fat as well."

"I like them corpulent," Leslie said. "Remember Penelope Bogan? a Mrs. too."

"Oh, come *on*. That old bird of Paradise Alley! How's the exchequer, Les?"

"One and a penny. How you fixed?"

"Tanner."

"What'll it be, then? The Compasses?"

"Free cheese at the Marlborough."

We walked towards the Marlborough, dodging umbrella spokes, smacked by our windy macs, stained by steaming lamplight, seeing the sodden, blown scourings and street-wash of the town, papers, rags, dregs, rinds, fag-ends, balls of fur, flap, float, and cringe along the gutters, hearing the sneeze and rattle of the bony trams and a ship hoot like a fog-ditched owl in the bay, and Leslie said:

"What'll we do after?"

"We'll follow someone," I said.

"Remember following that old girl up Kitchener Street? The one who dropped her handbag?"

"You should have given it back."

"There wasn't anything in it, only a piece of bread-and-jam."

"Here we are," I said.

The Marlborough saloon was cold and empty. There were notices on the damp walls: No Singing. No Dancing. No Gambling. No Peddlers.

"You sing," I said to Leslie, "and I'll dance, then we'll have a game of nap and I'll peddle my braces."

The barmaid, with gold hair and two gold teeth in front, like a well-off rabbit's, was blowing on her nails and polishing them without hope.

"You can tell it isn't Saturday night," I said. "Evening, Miss. Two pints."

"And a pound from the till," Leslie said.

"Give us your one-and-a-penny, Les," I whispered, and then said aloud: "Anybody can tell it isn't Saturday night. Nobody sick."

"Nobody here to *be* sick," Leslie said.

The peeling, liver-coloured room might never have been drunk in at all. Here, commercials told jokes and had Scotches and sodas with happy, dyed, port-and-lemon women; dejected regulars grew grand and muzzy in the corners, inventing their pasts, being rich, important, and loved; reprobate grannies in dustbin black cackled and nipped; influential nobodies revised the earth; a party, with earrings, called "Frilly Willy," played the crippled piano, which sounded like a hurdy-gurdy playing under water, until the publican's nosy wife said, No. Strangers came and went, but mostly went. Men from the valleys dropped in for nine or ten; sometimes there were fights; and always there was something doing, some argie-bargie, giggle and bluster, horror or folly, affection, explosion, nonsense, peace, some wild goose flying in the boozy air of that comfortless, humdrum nowhere in the dizzy, ditchwater town at the end of the railway lines. But that evening it was the saddest room I had ever known.

Leslie said, in a low voice; "Think she'll let us have one on tick?"

"Wait a bit, boy," I murmured. "Wait for her to thaw."

But the barmaid heard me, and looked up. She looked clean through me, back through my small history to the bed I was born in, then shook her gold head.

"I don't know what it is," said Leslie as we walked up Crimea Street in the rain, "but I feel kind of depressed tonight."

"It's the saddest night in the world," I said.

We stopped, soaked and alone, to look at the stills outside the cinema we called the Itch-pit. Week after week, for years and years, we had sat on the edges of the springless seats there, in the dank but snug, flickering dark, first with toffees and monkey-nuts that crackled for the dumb guns, and then with cigarettes: a cheap special kind that would make a fire-swallower cough up the cinders of his heart. "Let's go in and see Lon Chaney," I said, "and Richard Talmadge and Milton Sills and . . . and Noah Beery," I said, "and Richard Dix . . . and Slim Summerville and Hoot Gibson."

We both sighed.

"Oh for our vanished youth," I said.

We walked on heavily, with wilful feet, splashing the passers-by.

"Why don't you open your brolly?" I said.

"It won't open. You try."

We both tried, and the umbrella suddenly bellied out, the spokes tore through the soaking cover; the wind danced its tatters; it wrangled above us in the wind like a ruined, mathematical bird. We tried to tug it down; an unseen, new spoke sprang through its ragged ribs. Leslie dragged it behind him, along the pavement, as though he had shot it.

A girl called Dulcie, scurrying to the Itch-pit, sniggered hallo, and we stopped her.

"A rather terrible thing has happened," I said to her. She was so silly that, even when she was fifteen, we had told her to eat soap to make her straw hair crinkle, and Les took a piece from the bathroom, and she did.

"I know," she said, "you broke your gamp."

"No, you're wrong there," Leslie said. "It isn't *our* umbrella at all. It fell off the roof. *You* feel," he said. "You can feel it fell off the roof." She took the umbrella gingerly by its handle.

"There's someone up there throwing umbrellas down," I said. "It may be serious."

She began to titter, and then grew silent and anxious as Leslie said: "You never know. It might be walking-sticks next."

"Or sewing-machines," I said.

"You wait here, Dulcie, and we'll investigate," Leslie said.

We hurried on down the street, turned a blowing corner, and then ran.

Outside Rabiotti's café, Leslie said: "It isn't fair on Dulcie." We never mentioned it again.

A wet girl brushed by. Without a word, we followed her. She cantered, long-legged, down Inkerman Street and through Paradise Passage, and we were at her heels.

"I wonder what's the point in following people," Leslie said, "it's kind of daft. It never gets you anywhere. All you do is follow them home and then try to look through the window and see what they're doing and mostly there's curtains anyway. I bet noboby else does things like that."

"You never know," I said. The girl turned into St. Augustus Crescent, which was a wide lamplit mist. "People are always following people. What shall we call her?"

"Hermione Weatherby," Leslie said. He was never wrong about names. Hermione was fey and stringy, and walked like a long gym-mistress, full of love, through the stinging rain.

"You never know. You never know

what you'll find out. Perhaps she lives in a huge house with all her sisters—"

"How many?"

"Seven. All full of love. And when she gets home they all change into kimonos and lie on divans with music and whisper to each other and all they're doing is waiting for somebody like us to walk in, lost, and then they'll all chatter round us like starlings and put us in kimonos too, and we'll never leave the house until we die. Perhaps it's so beautiful and soft and noisy—like a warm bath full of birds . . ."

"I don't want birds in my bath," said Leslie. "Perhaps she'll slit her throat if they don't draw the blinds. I don't care what happens so long as it's interesting."

She slip-slopped round a corner into an avenue where the neat trees were sighing and the cosy windows shone.

"I don't want old feathers in the tub," Leslie said.

Hermione turned in at number thirteen, Beach-view.

"You can see the beach all right," Leslie said, "if you got a periscope."

We waited on the pavement opposite, under a bubbling lamp, as Hermione opened her door, and then we tip-toed across and down the gravel path and were at the back of the house, outside an uncurtained window.

Hermione's mother, a round, friendly, owlish woman in a pinafore, was shaking a chip-pan on the kitchen stove.

"I'm hungry," I said.

"Ssh!"

We edged to the side of the window as Hermione came into the kitchen. She was old, nearly thirty, with a mouse-brown shingle and big earnest eyes. She wore horn-rimmed spectacles and a sensible tweed costume, and a white shirt with a trim bow-tie. She looked as though she tried to look like a secretary in domestic films, who had only to remove her spectacles and have her hair cherished, and be dressed like a silk dog's dinner, to turn into a dazzler and make her employer, Warner Baxter, gasp, woo, and marry her; but if Hermione took off her glasses, she wouldn't be able to tell if he was Warner Baxter or the man who read the meters.

We stood so near the window, we could hear the chips spitting.

"Have a nice day in the office, dear? There's weather," Hermione's mother said, worrying the chip-pan.

"What's *her* name, Les?"

"Hetty."

Everything there in the warm kitchen, from the tea-caddy and the grandmother clock, to the tabby that purred like a kettle, was good, dull, and sufficient.

"Mr. Truscott was something awful," Hermione said as she put on slippers.

"Where's her kimono?" Leslie said.

"Here's a nice cup of tea," said Hetty.

"Everything's nice in that old hole," said Leslie, grumbling. "Where's the seven sisters like starlings?"

It began to rain much more heavily. It bucketed down on the black backyard, and the little comfy kennel of a house, and us, and the hidden, hushed town, where, even now, in the haven of the Marlborough, the submarine piano would be tinning "Daisy," and the happy henna'd women squealing into their port.

Hetty and Hermione had their supper. Two drowned boys watched them enviously.

"Put a drop of Worcester on the chips," Leslie whispered; and by God she did.

"Doesn't anything happen anywhere?" I said, "in the whole wide world ? I think the *News of the World* is all made up. Nobody murders no one. There isn't any sin any more, or love, or death, or pearls and divorces and mink coats or anything, or putting arsenic in the cocoa . . ."

"Why don't they put on some music for us," Leslie said, "and do a dance? It isn't every night they got two fellows watching them in the rain. Not *every* night, anyway!"

All over the dripping town, small lost people with nowhere to go and nothing to spend were gooseberrying in the rain outside wet windows, but nothing happened.

"I'm getting pneumonia," Leslie said.

The cat and the fire were purring, grandmother time ticktocked our lives away. The supper was cleared, and Hetty and Hermione, who had not spoken for many minutes, they were so confident and close in their little lighted box, looked at one another and slowly smiled.

They stood still in the decent, purring kitchen, facing one another.

"There's something funny going to happen," I whispered very softly.

"It's going to begin," Leslie said.

We did not notice the sour, racing rain any more.

The smiles stayed on the faces of the two still, silent women.

"It's going to begin."

And we heard Hetty say in a small secret voice: "Bring out the album, dear."

Hermione opened a cupboard and brought out a big, stiff-coloured photograph album, and put it in the middle of the table. Then she and Hetty sat down at the table, side by side, and Hermione opened the album.

"That's Uncle Eliot who died in Porthcawl, the one who had the cramp," said Hetty.

They looked with affection at Uncle Eliot, but we could not see him.

"That's Martha-the-woolshop, you wouldn't remember her, dear, it was wool, wool, wool, with her all the time; she wanted to be buried in her jumper, the mauve one, and her husband put his foot down. He'd been in India. That's your Uncle Morgan," Hetty said, "one of the Kidwelly Morgans, remember him in the snow?"

Hermione turned a page. "And that's Myfanwy, she got queer all of a sudden, remember. It was when she was milking. That's your cousin Jim, the Minister, until they found out. And that's our Beryl," Hetty said.

But she spoke all the time like somebody repeating a lesson: a well-loved lesson she knew by heart.

We knew that she and Hermione were only waiting.

Then Hermione turned another page. And we knew, by their secret smiles, that this was what they had been waiting for.

"My sister Katinka," Hetty said.

"Auntie Katinka," Hermione said. They bent over the photograph.

"Remember that day in Aberystwyth, Katinka?" Hetty said softly. "The day we went on the choir outing."

"I wore my new white dress," a new voice said.

Leslie clutched at my hand.

"And a straw hat with birds," said the clear, new voice.

Hermione and Hetty were not moving their lips.

"I was always a one for birds on my hat. Just the plumes of course. It was August the third, and I was twenty-three."

"Twenty-three come October, Katinka," Hetty said.

"That's right, love," the voice said. "Scorpio I was. And we met Douglas Pugh on the Prom and he said, 'You look like a queen today, Katinka,' he said. 'You look like a queen, Katinka,' he said. "Why are those two boys looking in at the window?"

We ran up the gravel drive, and around the corner of the house, and into the avenue and out on to St. Augustus Crescent. The rain roared down to drown the town. There we stopped for breath. We did not speak or look at each other. Then we walked on through the rain. At Victoria corner, we stopped again.

"Good-night, old man," Leslie said.

"Good-night," I said.

And we went our different ways.

[1955]

For Thought

Good-natured high jinks undertaken to dispel the boredom of a rain soaked weekday evening in a small Welsh town form the basis of Dylan Thomas's account of a peeping-tom misadvanture involving two youthful pranksters. Reveling in the richness of free-wheeling metaphorical language, Thomas endows "The Followers" with a special grace of idiom that enhances the comic effect of the harmless caper besides being a delight to the ear in its own right.

For Discussion

1. What is the author's attitude toward the narrator and toward his friend Leslie? How is this attitude conveyed?
2. Analyze significant figures of speech in the story and the way in which they are made comically appropriate.
3. What is the conflict, and what is ironically comic about its crisis and resolution?
4. What ironic contrast is there between the young men's stay at the Marlborough and their brief vigil outside "Hermione's" house?

James Thurber
The Catbird Seat

Mr. Martin bought the pack of Camels on Monday night in the most crowded cigar store on Broadway. It was theatre time and seven or eight men were buying cigarettes. The clerk didn't even glance at Mr. Martin, who put the pack in his overcoat pocket and went out. If any of the staff at F & S had seen him buy the cigarettes, they would have been astonished, for it was generally known that Mr. Martin did not smoke, and never had. No one saw him.

It was just a week to the day since Mr. Martin had decided to rub out Mrs. Ulgine Barrows. The term "rub out" pleased him because it suggested nothing more than the correction of an error—in this case an error of Mr. Fitweiler. Mr. Martin had spent each night of the past week working out his plan and examining it. As he walked home now he went over it again. For the hundredth time he resented the element of imprecision, the margin of guesswork that entered into the business. The project as he had worked it out was casual and bold, the risks were considerable. Something might go wrong anywhere along the line. And therein lay the cunning of his scheme. No one would ever see in it the cautious, painstaking hand of Erwin Martin, head of the filing department at F & S, of whom Mr. Fitweiler had once said, "Man is fallible but Martin isn't." No one would see his hand, that is, unless it were caught in the act.

Sitting in his apartment, drinking a glass of milk, Mr. Martin reviewed his case against Mrs. Ulgine Barrows, as he had every night for seven nights. He began at the beginning. Her quacking voice and braying laugh had first profaned the halls of F & S on March 7, 1941 (Mr. Martin had a head for dates). Old Roberts, the personnel chief, had introduced her as the newly appointed special adviser to the president of the firm, Mr. Fitweiler. The woman had appalled Mr. Martin instantly, but he hadn't shown it. He had given her his dry hand, a look of studious concentration, and a faint smile. "Well," she had said, looking at the papers on his desk, "are you lifting the oxcart out of the ditch?" As Mr. Martin recalled that moment, over his milk, he squirmed slightly. He must keep his mind on her crimes as a special adviser, not on her peccadillos as a personality. This he found difficult to do, in spite of entering an objection and sustaining it. The faults of the woman as a woman kept chattering on in his mind like an unruly witness. She had, for almost two years now, baited him. In the halls, in the elevator, even in his own office, into which she romped now and then like a circus horse, she was constantly shouting these silly questions at him. "Are you lifting the oxcart out of the ditch? Are you tearing up the pea patch? Are you hollering down the rain barrel? Are you scraping around the bottom of the pickle barrel? Are you sitting in the catbird seat?"

It was Joey Hart, one of Mr. Martin's two assistants, who had explained what the gibberish meant. "She must be a Dodger fan," he had said. "Red Barber announces the Dodger games over the radio and he uses those expressions—picked 'em up down South." Joey had gone on to explain one or two. "Tearing up the pea patch" meant going on a rampage; "sitting in the catbird seat" meant sitting pretty, like a batter with three balls and no strikes on him. Mr. Martin dismissed all this with an effort. It had been annoying, it had driven him near to distraction, but he was too solid a man to be moved to murder by anything so childish. It was fortunate, he reflected as he passed on to the important charges against Mrs. Barrows, that he had stood up under it so well. He had maintained always an outward appearance of polite tolerance. "Why, I even believe you like the woman," Miss Paird, his other assistant, had once said to him. He had simply smiled.

A gavel rapped in Mr. Martin's mind and the case proper was resumed. Mrs. Ulgine Barrows stood charged with willful, blatant, and persistent attempts to destroy the efficiency and system of F & S. It was competent, material, and relevant to review her advent and rise to power. Mr. Martin had got the story from Miss Paird, who seemed always able to find things out. According to her, Mrs. Barrows had met Mr. Fitweiler at a party, where she had rescued him from the embraces of a powerfully built drunken man who had mistaken the president of F & S for a famous retired Middle Western football coach. She had led him to a sofa and somehow worked upon him a monstrous magic. The aging gentleman had jumped to the conclusion there and then that this was a woman of singular attainments, equipped to bring out the best in him and in the firm. A week later he had introduced her into F & S as his special adviser. On that day confusion got its foot in the door. After Miss Tyson, Mr. Brundage, and Mr. Bartlett had been fired and Mr. Munson had taken his hat and stalked out, mailing in his resignation later, old Roberts had been emboldened to speak to Mr. Fitweiler. He mentioned that Mr. Munson's department had been "a little disrupted" and hadn't they perhaps better resume the old system there? Mr. Fitweiler had said certainly not. He had the greatest faith in Mrs. Barrows' ideas. "They require a little seasoning, a little seasoning, is all," he had added. Mr. Roberts had given it up. Mr. Martin reviewed in detail all the changes wrought by Mrs. Barrows. She had begun chipping at the cornices of the firm's edifice and now she was swinging at the foundation stones with a pickaxe.

Mr. Martin came now, in his summing up, to the afternoon of Monday, November 2, 1942—just one week ago. On that day, at 3 P.M., Mrs. Barrows had bounced into his office. "Boo!" she had yelled. "Are you scraping around the bottom of the pickle barrel?" Mr. Martin had looked at her from under his green eyeshade, saying nothing. She had begun to wander about the office, taking it in with her great, popping eyes. "Do you really need *all* these filing cabinets?" she had demanded suddenly. Mr. Martin's heart had jumped. "Each of these files," he had said, keeping his voice even, "plays an indispensable part in the system of F & S." She had brayed at him, "Well, don't tear up the pea patch!" and gone to the door. From there she had bawled, "But you sure have got a lot of fine scrap in here!" Mr. Martin could no longer doubt that the finger was on his beloved department. Her pickaxe was on the upswing, poised for the first blow. It had not come yet; he had received no blue memo from the enchanted Mr. Fitweiler bearing nonsensical instructions deriving from the obscene woman. But there was no doubt in Mr. Martin's mind that one would be forthcoming. He must act quickly. Already a precious week had gone by. Mr. Martin stood up in his living room, still holding his milk glass. "Gentlemen of the jury," he said to himself, "I demand the death penalty for this horrible person."

The next day Mr. Martin followed his routine, as usual. He polished his glasses more often and once sharpened an already sharp pencil, but not even Miss Paird noticed. Only once did he catch sight of his victim; she swept past him in the hall with a patronizing "Hi!" At five-thirty he walked home, as usual, and had a glass of milk, as usual. He had never drunk anything stronger in his life—unless you could count ginger ale. The late Sam Schlosser, the S of F & S, had praised Mr. Martin at a staff meeting several years before for his temperate habits. "Our most efficient worker neither drinks nor smokes," he had said. "The results speak for themselves." Mr. Fitweiler had sat by, nodding approval.

Mr. Martin was still thinking about that red-letter day as he walked over to the Schrafft's on Fifth Avenue near Forty-sixth street. He got there, as he always did, at eight o'clock. He finished his dinner and the financial page of the *Sun* at a quarter to nine, as he always did. It was his custom after dinner to take a walk. This time he walked down Fifth Avenue at a casual pace. His gloved hands felt moist and warm, his forehead cold. He transferred the Camels from his overcoat to a jacket pocket. He wondered, as he did so, if they did not represent an unnecessary note of strain. Mrs. Barrows smoked only Luckies. It was his idea to puff a few puffs on a Camel (after the rubbing-out), stub it out in the ashtray holding her lipstick-stained Luckies and thus drag a small red herring across the trail. Perhaps it was not a good idea. It would take time. He might even choke, too loudly.

Mr. Martin had never seen the house on West Twelfth Street where Mrs. Barrows lived, but he had a clear enough picture of it. Fortunately, she had bragged to everybody about her ducky first-floor apartment in the perfectly darling three-story redbrick. There would be no doorman or other attendants; just the tenants of the second and third floors. As he walked along, Mr. Martin realized that he would get there before nine-thirty. He had considered walking north on Fifth Avenue from Schrafft's to a point from which it would take him until ten o'clock to reach the house. At that hour people were less likely to be coming in or going out. But the procedure would have made an awkward loop in the straight thread of his casualness, and he had abandoned it. It was impossible to figure when people would be entering or leaving the house, anyway. There was a great risk at any hour. If he ran into anybody, he would simply have to place the rubbing-out of Ulgine Barrows in the inactive file forever. The same thing would hold true if there were someone in her apartment. In that case he would just say that he had been passing by, recognized her charming house, and thought to drop in.

It was eighteen minutes after nine when Mr. Martin turned into Twelfth Street. A man passed him, and a man and a woman, talking. There was no one within fifty paces when he came to the house, halfway down the block. He was up the steps and in the small vestibule in no time, pressing the bell under the card that said "Mrs. Ulgine Barrows." When the clicking in the lock started, he jumped forward against the door. He got inside fast, closing the door behind him. A bulb in a lantern hung from the hall ceiling on a chain seemed to give a monstrously bright light. There was nobody on the stair, which went up ahead of him along the left wall. A door opened down the hall in the wall on the right. He went toward it swiftly, on tiptoe.

"Well, for God's sake, look who's here!" bawled Mrs. Barrows, and her braying laugh rang out like the report of a shotgun. He rushed past her like a football tackle, bumping her. "Hey, quit shoving!" she cried, closing the door behind them. They were in her living room, which seemed to Mr. Martin to be lighted by a hundred lamps. "What's after you?" she said. "You're as jumpy as a goat." He found he was unable to speak. His heart was wheezing in his throat. "I—yes," he finally brought out. She was jabbering and laughing as she started to help him off with his coat. "No, no," he said. "I'll put it here." He took it off and put it on a chair near the door. "Your hat and gloves, too," she said. "You're in a lady's house." He put his hat on top of the coat. Mrs. Barrows seemed larger than he had thought. He kept his gloves on. "I was passing by," he said. "I recognized—is there anyone here?" She laughed louder than ever. "No," she said, "we're all alone. You're as white as a sheet, you funny man. Whatever *has* come over you? I'll mix you a toddy." She started toward a door across the room. "Scotch-and-soda be all right? But say, you don't drink, do you?" She turned and gave him her amused look. Mr. Martin pulled himself together. "Scotch-and-soda will be all right," he heard himself say. He could hear her laughing in the kitchen.

Mr. Martin looked quickly around the living room for the weapon. He had counted on finding one there. There were andirons and a poker and something in a corner that looked like an Indian club. None of them would do. It couldn't be that way. He began to pace around. He came to a desk. On it lay a metal paper knife with an ornate handle. Would it be sharp enough. He reached for it and knocked over a small brass jar. Stamps spilled out of it and it fell to the floor with a clatter. "Hey," Mrs. Barrows yelled from the kitchen, "are you tearing up the pea patch?" Mr. Martin gave a strange laugh. Picking up the knife, he tried its point against his left wrist. It was blunt. It wouldn't do.

When Mrs. Barrows reappeared, carrying two highballs, Mr. Martin, standing there with his gloves on, became acutely conscious of the fantasy he had wrought. Cigarettes in his pocket, a drink prepared for him—it was all too grossly improbable. It was more than that; it was impossible. Somewhere in the back of his mind a vague idea stirred, sprouted. "For heaven's sake, take off those gloves," said Mrs. Barrows. "I always wear them in the house," said Mr. Martin. The idea began to bloom, strange and wonderful. She put the glasses on a coffee table in front of a sofa and sat on the sofa. "Come over here, you odd little man," she said. Mr. Martin went over and sat beside her. It was difficult getting a cigarette out of the pack of Camels, but he managed it. She held a match for him, laughing. "Well," she said, handing him his drink, "this is perfectly marvellous. You with a drink and a cigarette."

Mr. Martin puffed, not too awkwardly, and took a gulp of the highball. "I drink and smoke all the time," he said. He clinked his glass against hers. "Here's nuts to that old windbag Fitweiler," he said, and gulped again. The stuff tasted awful, but he made no grimace. "Really, Mr. Martin," she said, her voice and posture changing, "you are insulting our employer." Mrs. Barrows was now all special adviser to the president. "I am preparing a bomb," said Mr. Martin, "which will blow the old goat higher than hell." He had only had a little of drink, which was not strong. It couldn't be that. "Do you take dope or something?" Mrs. Barrows asked coldly. "Heroin," said Mr. Martin. "I'll be coked to the gills when I bump that old buzzard off." "Mr. Martin!" she shouted, getting to her feet. "That will be all of that. You must go at once." Mr. Martin took another swallow of his drink. He tapped his cigarette out in the ashtray and put the pack of Camels on the coffee table. Then he got up. She stood glaring at him. He walked over and put on his hat and coat. "Not a word about this," he said, and laid an index finger against his lips. All Mrs. Barrows could bring out was "Really!" Mr. Martin put his hand on the doorknob. "I'm sitting in the catbird seat," he said. He stuck his tongue out at her and left. Nobody saw him go.

Mr. Martin got to his apartment, walking, well before eleven. No one saw him go in. He had two glasses of milk after brushing his teeth, and he felt elated. It wasn't tipsiness, because he hadn't been tipsy. Anyway, the walk had worn off all effects of the whiskey. He got in bed and read a magazine for a while. He was asleep before midnight.

Mr. Martin got to the office at eight-thirty the next morning, as usual. At a quarter to nine, Ulgine Barrows, who had never before arrived at work before ten, swept into his office. "I'm reporting to Mr. Fitweiler now!" she shouted. "If he turns you over to the police, it's no more than you deserve!" Mr. Martin gave her a look of shocked surprise. "I beg your pardon?" he said. Mrs. Barrows snorted and bounced out of the room, leaving Miss Paird and Joey Hart staring after her. "What's the matter with that old devil now?" asked Miss Paird. "I have no idea," said Mr. Martin, resuming his work. The other two looked at him and then at each other. Miss Paird got up and went out. She walked slowly past the closed door of Mr. Fitweiler's office. Mrs. Barrows was yelling inside, but she was not braying. Miss Paird could not hear what the woman was saying. She went back to her desk.

Forty-five minutes later, Mrs. Barrows left the president's office and went into her own, shutting the door. It wasn't until half an hour later that Mr. Fitweiler sent for Mr. Martin. The head of the filing department, neat, quiet, attentive, stood in front of the old man's desk. Mr. Fitweiler was pale and nervous. He took his glasses off and twiddled them. He made a small, bruffing sound in his throat. "Martin," he said, "you have been with us more than twenty years." "Twenty-two, sir," said Mr. Martin. "In that time," pursued the president, "your work and your—uh—manner have been exemplary." "I trust so, sir," said Mr. Martin. "I have understood, Martin," said Mr. Fitweiler, "that you have never taken a drink or smoked." "That is correct, sir," said Mr. Martin. "Ah, yes." Mr. Fitweiler polished his glasses. "You may describe what you did after leaving the office yesterday, Martin," he said. Mr. Martin allowed less than a second for his bewildered pause. "Certainly, sir," he said. "I walked home. Then I went to Schrafft's for dinner. Afterward I walked home again. I went to bed early, sir, and read a magazine for a while. I was asleep before eleven." "Ah, yes," said Mr. Fitweiler again. He was silent for a moment, searching for the proper words to say to the head of the filing department. "Mrs. Barrows," he said finally, "Mrs. Barrows has worked hard, Martin, very hard. It grieves me to report that she has suffered a severe breakdown. It has taken the form of a persecution complex accompanied by distressing hallucinations." "I am very sorry, sir," said Mr. Martin. "Mrs. Barrows is under the delusion," continued Mr. Fitweiler, "that you visited her last evening and behaved yourself in an—uh—unseemly manner." He raised his hand to silence Mr. Martin's little pained outcry. "It is the nature of these psychological diseases," Mr. Fitweiler said, "to fix upon the least likely and most innocent party as the—uh—source of persecution. These matters are not for the lay mind to grasp, Martin. I've just had my psychiatrist, Dr. Fitch, on the phone. He would not, of course, commit himself, but he made enough generalizations to substantiate my suspicions. I suggested to Mrs. Barrows, when she had completed her—uh—story to me this morning that she visit Dr. Fitch, for I suspected a condition at once. She flew, I regret to say, into a rage, and demanded—uh—requested that I call you on the carpet. You may not know, Martin, but Mrs. Barrows had planned a reorganization of your department—subject to my approval, of course, subject to my approval. This brought you, rather than anyone else, to her mind—but again that is a phenomenon for Dr. Fitch and not for us. So, Martin, I am afraid Mrs. Barrows' usefulness here is at an end." "I am dreadfully sorry, sir," said Mr. Martin.

It was at this point that the door to the office blew open with the suddenness of a gas-main explosion and Mrs. Barrows catapulted through it. "Is the little rat denying it?" she screamed. "He can't get away with that!" Mr. Martin got up and moved discreetly to a point beside Mr. Fitweiler's chair. "You drank and smoked at my apartment," she bawled at Mr. Martin, "and you know it! You called Mr. Fitweiler an old windbag and said you were going to blow him up when you got coked to the gills on your heroin!" She stopped yelling to catch her breath and a new glint came into her popping eyes. "If you weren't such a drab, ordinary little man," she said, "I'd think you'd planned it all. Sticking your tongue out, saying you were sitting in the catbird seat, because you thought no one would believe me when I told it! My God, it's really too perfect!" She brayed loudly and hysterically, and the fury was on her again. She glared at Mr. Fitweiler. "Can't you see how he has tricked us, you old fool? Can't you see his little game?" But Mr. Fitweiler had been surreptitiously pressing all the buttons under the top of his desk and employees of F & S began pouring into the room. "Stockton," said Mr. Fitweiler, "you and Fishbein will take Mrs. Barrows to her home. Mrs. Powell, you will go with them." Stockton, who had played a little football in high school, blocked Mrs. Barrows as she made for Mr. Martin. It took him and Fishbein together to force her out of the door into the hall, crowded with stenographers and office boys. She was still screaming imprecations at Mr. Martin, tangled and contradictory imprecations. The hubbub finally died out down the corridor.

"I regret that this has happened," said Mr. Fitweiler. "I shall ask you to dismiss it from your mind, Martin." "Yes, sir," said Mr. Martin, anticipating his chief's "That will be all" by moving to the door. "I will dismiss it." He went out and shut the door, and his step was light and quick in the hall. When he entered his department he had slowed down to his customary gait, and he walked quietly across the room to the W20 file, wearing a look of studious concentration.

[1942]

For Thought

In a story that is actually constructed in three consecutive panels, each involving a crucial confrontation between the two antagonists, Thurber's "The Catbird Seat" reverses the conventional conflict between a brash outsider and a staid organizer. In the author's comic view, it is Mrs. Barrows who is trapped by role stereotypes. Behind Mr. Martin's bland and predictable exterior is a lively imagination. Thurber suggests that people depend on routines for their sense of well-being. Challenge their sense of security, and they will, sometimes, react with courage and intelligence.

For Discussion

1. Traditionally, the crucial confrontation in comic literature involves the tricky, professional, self-effacing ironist who defeats the overconfident, amateurish imposter who has

identified himself with his social function. How closely do Mr. Martin and Mrs. Barrows fit these character types?

2. What other character types (such as clown, fool) also appear in the story?
3. What mannerisms extend Mr. Martin's characterization?
4. What mannerisms characterize Mrs. Barrows?
5. The first part of the story (the first six paragraphs) is expository; the second part (the next nine paragraphs) develops the main action: the third part (the final four paragraphs) resolves the key issue. What events could be classified as development, complication, crisis, reversal, and recognition?
6. How does Thurber use the conventions of the legal trial to increase the story's complexity?
7. How do allusions to animality, enchantment, and insanity support the story's symbolic conflict between reason and delusion?
8. What kinds of literary conventions (hand props, impersonation, messages) are used to forward and complicate the action?
9. What theme or themes emerge from a consideration of the story?

Leo Tolstoy
After the Ball

"So you maintain that a person cannot determine for himself what is good or bad, that it is all a question of environment, that circumstances are the controlling influence. As for me, I believe it's all a question of chance. And this is what I have to say concerning my own life. . . ."

So spoke our esteemed friend Ivan Vasilevitch following a conversation we had just been having about the attainment of individual perfection and the necessity of first changing the circumstances in which people lived. Strictly speaking, no one had said it was impossible for a person to judge for himself what was good or what was bad, but Ivan Vasilevitch would often reply to questions of his own which had arisen out of a conversation and, because of this, tell of some event in his own life. Often he got so carried away by his story that he completely forgot the justification for telling it, especially since he told his stories with such great emotion and candor.

This is exactly what happened on this occasion.

"I can definitely say this for myself. My entire life has been shaped in that fashion and no other—not by environment but by something entirely different."

"By what then?" we all asked.

"Ah, but that's a long story. In order for you to understand what I'm talking about, I'll have to tell you the whole story."

"Go ahead and tell us then."

Ivan Vasilevitch remained thoughtful for a moment and then shook his head.

"Yes," he said, "my entire life was completely altered by the events of one night, or, more exactly, of one morning."

"What happened?"

"What happened was that I was madly in love. I had been in love a number of times before, but this time it was really serious. It was a long time ago. The girl I was in love with already has married daughters of her own. Her name was Varyenka B." Ivan Vasilevitch gave her family name. "Even when she was fifty, she was an extraordinarily beautiful woman, but in her youth—when she was eighteen—she was

SOURCE: "After the Ball" by Leo Tolstoy. Translation by Blaze Bonazza and Emil Roy.

absolutely ravishing—tall, slender, graceful, and stately—really stately. She always carried herself extremely erect as if she were incapable of doing otherwise, with her head held slightly backward. This carriage of hers, along with her beauty and height, gave her a certain royal air that would have frightened people away had it not been for her gentle, happy smile, her charming, sparkling eyes, and her pleasing, youthful manner."

"Ivan Vasilevitch really spreads it on pretty thick!"

"No matter how thickly I spread it on, I couldn't begin to make you understand what she was like. But this doesn't matter. To go on . . . what I am going to tell you about took place in the forties.

"At that time I was a student in a provincial university.

"I don't know whether it was good or bad, but in those days we didn't have study circles with all their theorizing, but instead we were simply young people and we lived like young people—studying and having a good time. I was a happy-go-lucky, lively young fellow, and rich to boot.I kept a spirited team of horses, took young ladies tobogganing in the mountains (skating wasn't popular then), and caroused around with my friends (in those days we drank nothing but champagne; if we had no money, we didn't drink anything at all. We never drank vodka the way we do now). My chief delights were dances and parties. I was a pretty fair dancer and wasn't too bad-looking."

"Come now! Don't be so modest," interrupted one of the young ladies in the group. "We've all seen a picture of you when you were young. Not only weren't you bad-looking, you were actually handsome."

"Well, handsome or not, it doesn't actually matter. What does matter is that at the time of this great love affair of mine I was at a dance at the home of a hospitable, old nobleman during the last days of the carnival season before Lent. He had a wife who was as goodhearted and hospitable as he was, and the two of them greeted their guests at the door. It was a wonderful party. The ballroom was beautiful, and the orchestra was a well-known group of serfs, belonging to a music-loving landlord of those days. There was a sumptuous buffet supper, and the champagne flowed like water. Although I loved champagne, I didn't drink any because I was already drunk with love and didn't need wine. But I danced until I was ready to drop. I danced quadrilles, waltzes, and polkas without stopping, and, of course, as often as possible with Varyenka. She was wearing a white dress with a pink waistband, white kid gloves that didn't quite reach her thin, pointed elbows, and white satin slippers. A rival of mine, an engineer named Anisimov, stole the mazurka away from me. Till this day I haven't forgiven him for it. He asked her for it as soon as she arrived, while I was tied up at the haberdashery shop picking up my gloves. So I didn't get to dance the mazurka with her, but danced it with a German girl that I used to go around with. I'm afraid I didn't pay much attention to her that evening. I didn't talk to her at all or even look at her. I only had eyes for a tall, slender figure in a white dress with a pink waistband, with glowing face, dimpled cheeks, and tender, loving eyes. But I wasn't the only one—everyone was looking at her and admiring her, men and women both. It was impossible not to admire her.

"As I said, strictly speaking I wasn't supposed to be her partner for the mazurka, but actually I danced almost the entire number with her just the same. Without any hesitation, she danced toward me down the entire length of the ballroom. I jumped up without waiting for her invitation and she smiled her thanks for my anticipating her wishes. When I was taken to her and she wasn't able to guess what I represented, she shrugged her thin shoulders and smiled at me with a look of regret and consolation. When the mazurka turned into a waltz, I danced with her for a long time, and she smiled and whispered '*Encore.*' I waltzed on and on with her totally unaware of my own body."

"Totally unaware of your own body! Surely you must have been aware of it when you held her by the waist—not only of your own but of hers too," said one of the guests.

Ivan Vasilevitch suddenly turned red and raised his voice in anger.

"That may be true of you young people today—you don't have anything else on your mind but the body. But that's not the way it was in our day. The more deeply I was in love, the more spiritual the girl seemed to me. Nowadays you people look at nothing but legs and ankles and so forth. You mentally disrobe the woman you are in love with. As for me, the object of my love was always clad in shining armor. Rather than reveal, we tried to conceal nakedness. But you don't understand such things. . . ."

"Don't pay any attention to him, Ivan Vasilevitch. Please continue with your story," said someone else.

"Well, I danced with her so much I didn't notice how the time had passed. The musicians were so tired—you know how it is at the end of a dance—that they just kept playing the mazurka. The mothers and fathers present had already got up from the card tables in the drawing room and were waiting around for supper. House serfs were dashing here and there. It was already past two o'clock. We had to make the most of the last few minutes. I took hold of her once more, and for the hundredth time we danced the length of the ballroom.

"'May I dance the quadrille with you after supper?' I asked her as I escorted her back to her place.

"'Of course, if they don't take me home,' she said with a smile.

"'I don't let them,' I replied.

"'Let me have my fan back,' she said.

"'I regret having to give it up,' I said as I gave her back her little white fan.

"'Here, take this, so you won't be too sad,' she said, plucking a feather out of the fan and giving it to me.

"I took the feather and could only express my gratitude and happiness with a look. I was not only lighthearted and content—I was exhilarated, blissful. I was no longer myself, but some unearthly creature unconscious of evil and capable of nothing but good.

"I hid the feather in my glove and stood there, unable to move from her.

"'Look, they're asking Papa to dance,' she said, pointing at the tall, dignified figure of her father—a colonel with silver epaulets, standing in the doorway with the hostess and some other ladies.

"'Varyenka, come here,' we heard the hostess call out loudly.

"Varyenka went toward the door and I after her.

"'Ask your father to dance with you, my dear. Come now, please do, Pyotr Vladislavovitch,' the hostess begged the colonel.

"Varyenka's father was a very handsome, tall, dignified, and well-preserved old gentleman. He had a very ruddy complexion, a white mustache and side whiskers, his hair was combed forward over his temples, and the same smile that his daughter had played on his lips and in his flashing eyes. He was very well built, with a sturdy soldier's chest decorated modestly with campaign ribbons, broad shoulders, and long, graceful legs. He was clearly an officer of the old school.

"As we got to the doorway, the colonel was refusing to dance, saying that he had forgotten, but at the same time he smiled and dropped his left arm to his side, removed his sword from its belt, and handed it to an obliging young man. He drew a kid glove on his right. 'We must do this right,' he said with a smile, took his daughter's hand, and poised in a quarter-turn, waiting for the beat of the music. As he waited for the music to begin, he briskly tapped one foot, put out the other, and his tall, erect figure glided quietly and smoothly out around the ballroom. The graceful figure of

Varyenka in her white satin slippers floated near him, imperceptibly shortening or lengthening her steps in time with his. Everybody in the ballroom was watching each movement they made. I not only admired them, but looked at them with a feeling close to rapture. I was especially affected by his boots. They were good calfskin boots, but heelless and square-toed instead of being stylishly pointed. Obviously, they had been made by the battalion shoemaker. 'He doesn't buy fashionable boots but wears ordinary ones instead so that he can dress his beloved daughter properly and show her off,' I thought, and those square-toed ordinary boots moved me very much. It was readily apparent that he had once been a very good dancer, but now he was heavy and his legs were no longer responsive enough for all the elaborate, quick steps which he was trying to execute. But nevertheless he danced around the ballroom twice and did very well. When he suddenly spread his feet apart, then brought them together again and dipped to one knee, although somewhat heavily, Varyenka, smiling as she freed her skirt caught by his foot, smoothly circled around him as everyone applauded. Getting up with some effort, he fondly put his hands on his daughter's face and kissed her on the forehead. He then led her over to me, under the impression that I had been dancing with her. I told him that I was not actually her partner.

"'It doesn't matter. Dance with her anyway,' he said, smiling gently and slipping his sword back into its belt.

"Just as the first drop poured out of a wine bottle brings a greater flow after it, so my love for Varyenka set free all the love in my soul. I included the whole world in my love. I loved the hostess with her diamond tiara, her husband, her guests, her servants, and even my rival Anisimov. As for her father, with his square-toed boots and gentle smile just like hers, I felt for him a rapturous, tender sensation.

"When the mazurka was over the hosts invited us to the supper table. Colonel B. declined, begging his host's pardon, saying that he had to get up early in the morning. I was afraid they would take Varyenka home, but she stayed on with her mother.

"After supper I danced the promised quadrille with her, and, although my happiness had seemed boundless before, it still kept growing and growing. We did not speak of love at all. I did not ask her or even myself if she loved me. It was enough that I loved her. The only thing I was afraid of was that something might shatter my happiness.

"When I got home, I undressed and thought about sleeping, but I realized that I couldn't possibly fall asleep. In my hand was the little feather from her fan and one of her gloves, which she had given to me as she was leaving and I escorted her and her mother to their carriage. I looked at these souvenirs and, without closing my eyes, could see her standing there before me, just as she was about to choose between two partners. She guessed my identity in the mazurka and I heard her sweet voice saying, 'Ah, so you are Pride!' Then she joyfully gave me her hand. Or I could see her when she gazed at me with loving eyes over her glass of champagne. But I saw her best of all as she danced with her father, floating gracefully beside him and looking at the admiring onlookers with pride and joy as much for him as for herself. And I involuntarily associated him with her in one deep and tender sensation.

"At this time I was living with my late brother. He never cared much for society and never went to parties. He was in the process of preparing for his examinations and led a very well-regulated life. He was asleep when I got in. As I looked at him with his head buried in his pillow, half-covered by the flannel blanket, I felt sorry for him—sorry because he didn't know and didn't share the happiness I was experiencing. Our serf Petrushka met me with a candle and wanted to help me undress, but I send him away, touched by his sleepy face and disheveled appearance. Trying not to make any noise, I tiptoed to my room and sat down on the bed. But I was so happy I couldn't fall asleep. Besides, it was hot in our overheated rooms and, without taking off my uniform, I stepped out into the hall, put on my overcoat, and went out into the street.

"I had left the ball about five o'clock. The time it took to get home and my sitting there a while took another two hours, so that when I left the house it was already daylight. It was typically late winter weather—misty, with wet snow melting on the roads and water dripping from the roofs. At that time Varyenka's family lived at the edge of town near a large field, on one corner of which was a promenade area, and at the other end, a school for girls. I went down our deserted alley and came out onto the main street, where I encountered passers-by and carters with their sleds loaded with wood, the runners of which cut right through the soft snow down to the pavement. Everything—the horses nodding their heads rhythmically under their shiny yokes, and the carters with pads on their shoulders slushing along in their large boots beside their sleds, the buildings on each side of the street looking so tall through the mist—everything struck me as being dear and important.

"When I reached the field where their house was situated, I noticed something big and black on the corner at the parade area and I could hear the sound of fife and drum. All this time my heart had been singing, and now and then I heard the tune of a mazurka. But this sound was quite different—strident, forbidding.

"'What's going on?' I wondered as I went toward the noise along down the slippery road that cut across the field. After I had gone about a hundred feet, I could make out a group of dark figures through the mist. Evidently they were soldiers. 'Perhaps they're drilling,' I thought, and continued onward behind a blacksmith in a soiled apron, carrying something. Soldiers in black coats were standing in two rows opposite one another, holding their rifles at attention and standing perfectly still. Behind them stood a drummer and a fifer who kept playing that unpleasant, shrill melody over and over again.

"'What are they doing?' I asked the blacksmith, who was standing beside me.

"'They're running a Tartar through the gauntlet for desertion,' said the blacksmith sullenly as he stared angrily toward the far end of the rows.

"I looked there and saw something ghastly coming toward us between the two rows of soldiers. Approaching us was a man stripped to the waist and tied to the rifles of two soldiers who were leading him along. Beside him walked a tall officer in an overcoat and cap, someone whose figure seemed somehow familiar to me. Twisting his whole body and sloshing through the melting snow, the poor wretch being punished, under a storm of blows falling from both sides, came closer to us and then fell backward. As he did, the soldiers leading him by their rifles pulled him forward. When he fell forward, they would pull him back to keep him from falling. Striding at a firm pace and never lagging behind came a tall officer. It was her father with his ruddy complexion, white mustache, and side whiskers.

"With each blow the stretched Tartar turned his pain-contorted face to the side from which the blow came as if surprised and, baring his white teeth, repeated the same words over and over again. Only when he got very near could I make out what he was saying. Rather than speaking he was actually sobbing, 'Brothers, have pity on me; brothers, have pity on me.' But his comrades showed him no pity, and when the procession was directly opposite me, I saw one of the soldiers take a resolute step forward and with a whistling blow strike the Tartar full on the back. The Tartar staggered forward, but the men holding him pulled him up, and then another blow fell on him from the opposite side, and then from this and then from the other side, again and again. The colonel walked alongside them, now looking down at his own square-toed boots, now at the poor wretch, inhaling deeply, puffing out his cheeks, and slowly letting out his breath between pursed lips. When the procession passed me, I caught a glimpse of the Tartar's back between the rows of soldiers. It was absolutely beyond description—reduced to strips of skin, sticky, red, so unnatural I couldn't believe it belonged to a human body.

"'Good God,' muttered the blacksmith standing beside me.

"The procession moved on. Blows continued to fall from both sides on the cringing, stumbling wretch and the drum and the fife continued on in the same fashion. And with firm tread the tall, dignified figure of the colonel moved on between the two rows of soldiers alongside the man being punished. Suddenly the colonel stopped and quickly stepped toward one of the soldiers.

"'Damn you! I'll show you how to do it!' I heard him say in a furious voice. And I saw his strong hand in the kid glove strike the face of a small, frightened soldier because he didn't hit the Tartar's bloody back hard enough with his switch.

"'Get fresh switches!' shouted the colonel, catching sight of me as he turned around. Pretending not to notice me, he scowled fiercely and turned away quickly. I was so thoroughly ashamed that I lowered my gaze, not knowing where to look. I hurried home. All the way there I kept hearing the rolling of the drums and the high-pitched screeching of the fife and then the plea, 'Brothers, have pity on me.' Then I could hear the angry, authoritative voice of the colonel shouting 'Damn you. I'll show you how!' The anguish in my heart was so intense as to make me physically sick, forcing me to stop several times. I felt that I had to expel all the horror which the spectacle had filled me with. I don't recall how I got home and to bed. As soon as I would fall off to sleep, I would see and hear everything all over again. I finally jumped out of bed.

"'The colonel must know something I don't know,' I thought. 'If I knew what he knows, I would understand and what I saw would not torture me so.' But try as I might I couldn't understand what it was the colonel knew, and I couldn't fall asleep until evening and then only after going to a friend's and getting completely drunk.

"Do you think then I concluded that what I had seen was evil? No, not at all. If what was done with such assurance and acceptance by everyone involved as unavoidable, it must be they knew something I didn't know—though I tried and tried to discover what this thing was. But not discovering it, I couldn't enter into military service as I had intended. But not only military service, any service at all. And as you see, I am fit for nothing."

"Now we all know very well how you're not fit for anything," said one of the group. "It would be better to say how many people would be no good for anything if it weren't for you."

"That's nonsense," said Ivan V., sincerely vexed.

"But what about your love?" we asked.

"My love? From that day on my love dwindled away. When she, as she often did, fell into my thoughts with a smile on her lips, I immediately thought of the colonel out on the parade grounds that morning and I would feel so uncomfortable and upset, I began to see her less often. My love for her just faded away.

"Well, that's the way things sometimes happen, and it is things like these that change and direct a person's entire life. And you talk about environment," concluded Ivan Vasilevitch.

[1903]

For Thought

In a story-within-a-story structure, Ivan Vasilevitch, the protagonist in both narratives of "After the Ball", tells the internal story to illustrate his thesis that it is chance, not environment, that rules human destiny. In the events Ivan recounts, however, chance acts to produce the defeat of romantic love and to change the course of his life for a particular reason. Ivan is the kind of sensitive, idealistic young man who is morally shaken by the underlying evil in society.

For Discussion

1. What purpose does the story-within-a-story format serve?
2. What does the elaborate description of Varyenka's beauty prepare for?
3. Of what importance thematically is the time of year at which the ball was held?
4. What do the references to the serfs contribute to the story?
5. How do the colonel's gloves function as a central symbol? How are the square-toed boots used as an ironic or reinforcing symbol?
6. How do the gifts of the glove and the feather from Varyenka's fan serve as ironic peripheral symbols?
7. What is the purpose of the scene in which the colonel dances with Varyenka?
8. What ironic reversal is brought about by Ivan's exhilarated state after the ball?
9. How is music used to create mood and atmosphere in the story? How is the weather used symbolically?
10. What is the central conflict in the story?
11. How does the gauntlet scene complicate the action and alter its outcome?
12. Ivan says that the point of his story is his recognition that chance rules human destiny. What is a fuller statement of the theme, considering the symbols used and the resolution of the conflict?

Ivan Turgenev
Meeting

I was sitting in a birch wood one autumn, about the middle of September. From early morning there had been occasional drizzle, succeeded from time to time by periods of warm sunny radiance; a season of changeable weather. The sky was either covered with crumbling white clouds or suddenly clear for an instant in a few places, and then, from behind the parted clouds, blue sky would appear, lucid and smiling, like a beautiful eye. I sat and looked around me and listened. The leaves scarcely rustled above my head; by their very noise one could know what time of year it was. It was not the happy, laughing *tremolo* of spring, not the soft murmuration and long-winded talkativeness of summer, not the shy and chill babblings of late autumn, but a hardly audible dreamy chattering. A faint wind ever so slightly moved through the treetops. The interior of the wood, damp from the rain, was continually changing, depending on whether the sun was shining or whether it was covered by cloud; the interior was either flooded with light, just as if everything in it had suddenly smiled: the delicate trunks of the not-too-numerous birches would suddenly acquire the soft sheen of white silk, the wafer-thin leaves which lay on the ground would suddenly grow multicoloured and burn with crimson and gold, while the beautiful stems of tall curly bracken, already embellished with their autumn colouring which resembles the colour of overripe grapes, would stand there shot through with light, endlessly entangling and criss-crossing before one's eyes; or suddenly one would again be surrounded by a bluish dusk: the bright colours would instantly be extinguished and the birches would all stand there white, without a gleam on them, white as snow that has only just fallen and has not yet been touched by the chilly sparkling rays of the winter sun; and secretively, slyly, thinly drizzling rain would begin to filter and whisper through the wood.

The foliage on the birches was still almost completely green, although it had noticeably faded; only here and there stood a

Source: "Meeting" by Ivan Turgenev. Translation by Richard Freeborn (Penguin Classics, 1967; pp 168–178).

young tree all decked out in red or gold, and one could not help watching how brightly it flared up when the sun's rays broke, gliding and scintillating, through the myriad network of fine branches only just washed by glittering rain. There was not a single bird to be heard: all had taken cover and fallen silent; only the mocking little voice of the tom-tit tinkled occasionally like a little steel bell.

Before I had stopped in this little birch wood, I had gone with my dog through a grove of tall aspens. I confess that I am not particularly fond of that tree—the aspen—with its pale-mauve trunk and grey-green, metallic foliage which it raises as high as possible and spreads out in the air like a quivering fan; nor do I like the continual flutterings of its round untidy leaves which are so awkwardly attached to their long stalks. It acquires beauty only on certain summer evenings when, rising on high in isolation among low bushy undergrowth, it meets the challenge of the ebbing rays of the sunset and gleams and trembles, suffused from its topmost branches to its roots by a uniform yellow and purple light; or when, on a clear windy day, it is all noisily streaming and babbling against the blue sky, and every leaf, seized by the wind's ardour, appears to want to tear itself free, fly away and hurry off into the distance. But in general I dislike this tree and therefore, without stopping to rest in the aspen grove, I made my way to the little birch wood, settled myself under a tree whose branches began close to the ground and were able, in consequence, to shelter me from the rain, and, having gazed admiringly at the surrounding view, fell into the kind of untroubled and mild sleep familiar only to hunters.

I cannot say how long I was asleep, but when I opened my eyes the entire interior of the wood was filled with sunlight and in all directions through the jubilantly rustling foliage a bright blue sky peered and seemed to sparkle; the clouds had vanished, dispersed by the wind that had sprung up; the weather had cleared, and in the air could be felt that special dry freshness which, imbuing the heart with a feeling of elation, almost always means a peaceful and clear evening after a rainy day.

I was on the point of rising and again trying my luck, when suddenly my eyes lighted on a motionless human form. I looked closely and saw that it was a young peasant girl. She was sitting twenty paces from me, her head lowered in thought and both hands dropped on her knees; in the half-open palm of one of them lay a thick bunch of wild flowers and at each breath she took the bunch slipped quietly down on to her checked skirt. A clean white blouse, buttoned at the neck and at the wrists, gathered in short soft folds about her waist; two rows of large yellow beads fell from her neck on to her bosom. She was very pretty in her own way. Her thick fair hair of a beautiful ash colour was parted into two carefully styled semicircles below a narrow crimson ribbon drawn almost down to her temples, which were white as ivory; the rest of her face was faintly sunburned to that golden hue which is only acquired by a delicate skin. I could not see her eyes because she did not raise them; but I clearly saw her fine, high eyebrows and long eyelashes, which were damp, and on one of her cheeks I saw the dried traces of a tear that had come to rest at the edge of her slightly pale lips and glittered in the sunlight. The whole appearance of her head was very charming; even the slightly thick and rounded nose did nothing to spoil it. I particularly liked the expression on her face for the way in which it was so artless and gentle, so melancholy and full of childish bewilderment at her own grief.

She was evidently waiting for someone. Something crackled faintly in the wood and she at once raised her head and looked round; in the transparent shade her large eyes, bright and frightened, flashed quickly before me like the eyes of a doe. She listened for a few moments without taking her wide-open eyes from the place where the faint sound had been made, then heaved a sigh, turned her head calmly back, bent still farther down and began slowly to finger the flowers. Her eyelids reddened, her lips gave a quiver of bitterness and another tear slipped from beneath her thick lashes, coming to rest on her cheek where it glittered radiantly. Some time passed in this way, and the poor girl did not move save to make a few regretful gestures with her hands and to go on listening and listening. Again something made a noise in the wood and she was instantly alerted. The noise continued, grew louder as it approached, and finally could be heard the noise of rapid, decisive footsteps. She straightened herself and appeared to be overcome with shyness; her attentive features began to quiver and burn with expectation. The figure of a man could be glimpsed through the thicket. She peered in that direction, blushed suddenly, gave a joyful and happy smile, got ready to stand up and once again suddenly lowered her head, growing pale and confused—and she only raised her faltering, almost imploring gaze to the newcomer when he had stopped beside her.

I examined him with curiosity from my hiding-place. I confess that he produced an unpleasant impression on me. To all appearances he was the pampered valet of some rich young master. His clothes displayed pretensions to good taste and dandified casualness: they consisted of a short, bronze-coloured top-coat buttoned up to the neck and inherited, more than likely, from his master, a little rose-tinted neck-tie with mauve tips and a black velvet cap with gold lace edging worn pulled down over the eyebrows. The rounded collar of his white shirt pressed unmercifully up against his ears and bit into his cheek, while his starched cuffs covered his hands right down to the red and crooked fingers which were embellished with gold and silver rings containing turquoise forget-me-nots. His face—ruddy, fresh-complexioned and impudent—belonged to the category of faces which, so far as I have been able to judge, almost invariably annoy men and, unfortunately, are very often pleasing to women. He clearly made an effort to endow his rather coarse features with an expression of superciliousness and boredom; he endlessly screwed up his already tiny milk-grey eyes, frowned, let his mouth droop at the edges, gave forced yawns and with a casual, though not entirely skilled, air of abandon either patted the reddish, artfully coiled har on his temples or twiddled the little yellow hairs that stuck out on his fat upper lip—in a word, he showed off insufferably. He began to show off as soon as he saw the young peasant girl waiting for him; he slowly approached her at a lounging pace, came to a stop, shrugged his shoulders, stuck both hands into the pockets of his top-coat and, with hardly more than a fleeting and indifferent glance at the poor girl, lowered himself to the ground.

'Well,' he began, still looking away to one side, swinging his leg and yawning, 'have you been here long?'

The girl was unable to answer him immediately.

'A long time, sir, Victor Alexandrych,' she said eventually in a scarcely audible voice.

'Ah!' He removed his cap, grandly drew his hand through his thick, tightly coiled hair, which began almost at his eyebrows, and, glancing round with dignity, once more carefully covered his priceless head. 'And I'd almost completely forgotten. After all, look how it rained!' He yawned once more. 'There's a mass of things to be done, what with everything to be got ready and the master swearing as well. Tomorrow we'll be off . . .'

'Tomorrow?' the girl said and directed at him a look of fright.

'That's right—tomorrow. Now, now, now, please,' he added hastily and with annoyance, seeing that she had begun to tremble all over and was quietly lowering her head, 'please, Akulina, no crying. You know I can't stand crying.' And he puckered up his snub nose. 'If you start, I'll leave at once. What silliness—blubbering!'

'No, I won't, I won't,' Akulina uttered hurriedly, making herself swallow her tears. 'So you're leaving tomorrow?' she added after a brief pause. 'When will God bring you back to see me again, Victor Alexandrych?'

'We'll meet again, we'll meet again. If not next year, then later. It seems the master wants to enter government service in St Petersburg,' he continued, speaking the words casually and slightly through the nose, 'and maybe we'll go abroad.'

'You'll forget me, Victor Alexandrych,' Akulina said sadly.

'No, why should I? I won't forget you. Only you've got to be sensible, not start playing up, obey your father . . . I'll not forget you—no-o-o.' And he calmly stretched himself and again yawned.

'You mustn't forget me Victor Alexandrych,' she continued in an imploring voice. 'I've loved you so much, it seems, and it seems I've done everything for you. . . . You tell me to listen to my father, Victor Alexandrych. . . . There's no point in listening to my father . . .'

'Why not?' He uttered these words as it were from his stomach, lying on his back with his arms behind his head.

'There's no point, Victor Alexandrych. You know that yourself . . .'

She said nothing. Victor played with the steel chain of his watch.

'You're not a fool, Akulina,' he started saying at last, 'so don't talk nonsense. I want what's best for you, do you understand me? Of course, you're not stupid, you're not a complete peasant girl, so to speak; and your mother also wasn't always a peasant girl. But you're without any education, so you've got to listen when people tell you things.'

'I'm frightened, Victor Alexandrych.'

'Hey, there, that's a lot of nonsense, my dear. What's there to be frightened of! What's that you've got there,' he added, turning to her, 'flowers?'

'Flowers,' answered Akulina despondently. 'They're some field tansies I've picked,' she continued, brightening slightly, 'and they're good for calves. And these are marigolds, they help against scrofula. Just look what a lovely little flower it is! I've never seen such a lovely little flower before in all my born days. Then there are some forget-me-nots, here are some violets. But these I got for you,' she added, taking out from beneath the yellow tansies a small bunch of blue cornflowers tied together with a fine skein of grass, 'would you like them?'

Victor languidly stretched out his hand, took the bunch, casually sniffed the flowers and began to twiddle them in his fingers, gazing up in the air from time to time with thoughtful self-importance. Akulina looked at him and her sad gaze contained such tender devotion, such worshipful humility and love. Yet she was also afraid of him, and fearful of crying; and taking her own leave of him and doting on him for the last time; but he lay there in the lounging pose of a sultan and endured her worship of him with magnanimous patience and condescension. I confess that his red face vexed me with its pretentiously disdainful indifference through which could be discerned a replete and self-satisfied vanity. Akulina was so fine at that moment, for her whole heart was trustfully and passionately laid open before him, craving him and yearning to be loved, but he . . . he simply let the cornflowers drop on the grass, took a round glass in a bronze frame out of the side pocket of his top-coat and started trying to fix it in place over his eye; but no matter how hard he tried to keep it in place with a puckered brow, a raised cheek and even with his nose, the little eyeglass kept on falling out and dropping into his hand.

'What's that?' Akulina asked finally in astonishment.

'A lorgnette,' he answered self-importantly.

'What's it for?'

'So as to see better.'

'Show it me.'

Victor frowned, but he gave her the eyeglass.

'Don't break it, mind.'

'You needn't worry, I won't.' She raised it timidly to her eye. 'I don't see anything,' she said artlessly.

'It's your eye, you've got to screw up your eye,' he retorted in the voice of a dissatisfied mentor. She screwed up the eye before which she was holding the little glass. 'Not that one, not that one, idiot! The other one!' exclaimed Victor and, giving her no chance to correct her mistake, took the lorgnette from her.

Akulina reddened, gave a nervous laugh and turned away.

'It's obviously not for the likes of me,' she murmured.

'That's for sure!'

The poor girl was silent and let fall a deep sigh.

'Oh, Victor Alexandrych, what'll I do without you?' she suddenly said.

Victor wiped the lorgnette with the edge of his coat and put it back in his pocket.

'Yes, yes,' he said eventually, 'it sure will be hard for you to start with.' He gave her several condescending pats on the shoulder; she ever so quietly lifted his hand from her shoulder and timidly kissed it. 'Well, all right, all right, you're a good kid,' he went on, giving a self-satisfied smile, 'but what can I do about it? Judge for yourself! The master and I can't stay here; it'll be winter soon now and to spend the winter in the country—you know this yourself—is just horrible. But it's another matter in St Petersburg! There are simply such wonderful things there, such as you, stupid, wouldn't be able to imagine even in your wildest dreams! What houses and streets, and the so*ch*iety, the culture—it's simply stupendous!' Akulina listened to him with greedy interest, her lips slightly parted like a child's. 'Anyhow,' he added, turning over, 'why am I telling you all this? You won't be able to understand it.'

'Why say that, Victor Alexandrych? I've understood it, I've understood everything.'

'What a bright one you are!'

Akulina lowered her head.

'You never used to talk to me like that before, Victor Alexandrych,' she said without raising her eyes.

'Didn't I before? Before! You're a one! Before indeed!' he commented, pretending to be indignant.

Both were silent for a while.

'However, it's time for me to be going,' said Victor, and was on the point of raising himself on one elbow.

'Stay a bit longer,' Akulina declared in an imploring voice.

'What's there to wait for? I've already said good-by to you.'

'Stay a bit,' Akulina repeated.

Victor again lay back and started whistling. Akulina never took her eyes off him. I could tell that she was slowly working herself into a state of agitation: her lips were working and her pale cheeks were faintly crimsoning.

'Victor Alexandrych,' she said at last in a breaking voice, 'it's sinful of you . . . sinful of you, Victor Alexandrych, in God's name it is!'

'What's sinful?' he asked, knitting his brows, and he raised himself slightly and turned his head towards her.

'It's sinful, Victor Alexandrych. If you'd only say one kind word to me now you're leaving, just say one word to me, wretched little orphan that I am. . .'

'But what should I say to you?'

'I don't know. You should know that better than me, Victor Alexandrych. Now you're going away, and if only you'd say a word. . . . Why should I deserve this?'

'What a strange girl you are! What can I say?'

'Just say one word . . .'

'Well, you've certainly gone on and on about the same thing,' he said in disgruntlement and stood up.

'Don't be angry, Victor Alexandrych,'

she added quickly, hardly restraining her tears.

'I'm not angry, it's only that you're stupid. . . . What do you want? You know I can't marry you, don't you? Surely you know I can't? So what's it you want? What is it?' He stuck his face forward in expectation of her answer and opened wide his fingers.

'I don't want anything . . . anything,' she answered, stammering and scarcely daring to stretch her trembling hands out towards him, 'only if you'd just say one word in farewell . . .'

And tears streamed from her eyes.

'Well, so there it is, you've started crying,' Victor said callously, tipping his cap forward over his eyes.

'I don't want anything,' she went on, swallowing her tears and covering her face with both hands, 'but what'll it be like for me in the family, what'll there be for me? And what's going to happen to me, what's going to become of me, wretch that I am! They'll give their orphan girl away to someone who doesn't love her . . . O poor me, poor me!'

'Moan away, moan away!' muttered Victor under his breath, shifting from one foot to the other.

'If only he'd say one little word, just one word. . . . Such as, Akulina, I . . . I . . .'

Sudden heart-rending sobs prevented her from finishing what she was saying. She flopped on her face in the grass and burst into bitter, bitter tears. Her whole body shook convulsively, the nape of her neck rising and falling. Her long-restrained grief finally poured forth in torrents. Victor stood for a moment or so above her, shrugged his shoulders, turned and walked away with big strides.

Several moments passed. She grew quiet, raised her head, jumped up, looked about her and wrung her hands; she was on the point of rushing after him, but her legs collapsed under her and she fell on her knees. I could not hold myself back and rushed towards her, but she had hardly had time to look at me before she found the strength from somewhere to raise herself with a faint cry and vanish through the trees, leaving her flowers scattered on the ground.

I stopped there a moment, picked up the bunch of cornflowers and walked out of the wood into a field. The sun was low in the pale clear sky and its rays had, as it were, lost their colour and grown cold; they did not shine so much as flow out in an even, almost watery, light. No more than half an hour remained until evening, but the sunset was only just beginning to crimson the sky. A flurrying wind raced towards me across the dry, yellow stubble; hastily spinning before it, little shrivelled leaves streamed past me across the track and along the edge of the wood; the side which faced on to the field like a wall shuddered all over and glistened with a faint sparkling, distinctly though not brightly; on the red-tinted grass, on separate blades of grass, on pieces of straw, everywhere innumerable strands of autumn cobwebs glittered and rippled. I stopped, and a feeling of melancholy stole over me, for it seemed to me that the sombre terror associated with the approaching winter was breaking through the cheerless, though fresh, smile of nature at this time of withering. High above me, ponderously and sharply sundering the air with its wings, a vigilant raven flew by, turned its head, looked sidewards at me, took wing and disappeared beyond the wood with strident cawings; a large flock of pigeons rose smartly from a place where there had been threshing and after suddenly making a huge wheeling turn in the air settled busily on to the field—a sure sign of autumn! Someone rode by on the other side of a bare hillock, his empty cart clattering noisily . . .

I returned home; but the image of the poor Akulina took a long time to fade from my mind, and her cornflowers, which have long since withered, remain with me to this day.

[1850]

For Thought

Turgenev's unseen narrator, in "Meetings," observes a leave-taking between two unremarkable people. The meeting between the "lovers" deeply affects the narrator emotionally. Although the young and naive woman passionately cares for the valet, he treats her with contempt. In the opinion of the narrator, the woman's love for the young man is misplaced, for he appears to be both conceited and completely insensitive to her feelings. Turgenev implies that love is most valued when given freely and without calculation.

For Discussion

1. What point of view does Turgenev adopt for the story? How is his choice of narrator an effective one? How do the narrator's values affect the reader's sympathy, or lack of sympathy, for the two lovers?
2. How do the season of the year, the weather, and the woodland setting provide the occasion for the story and extend the symbolism of the tale?
3. What contrast does Turgenev create between the peasant girl and the valet? How is this contrast symbolic?
4. What is the theme of the story?
5. What futures can be predicted for the peasant girl and the valet?

John Updike
A & P

In walks these three girls in nothing but bathing suits. I'm in the third checkout slot, with my back to the door, so I don't see them until they're over by the bread. The one that caught my eye first was the one in the plaid green two-piece. She was a chunky kid, with a good tan and a sweet broad soft-looking can with those two crescents of white just under it, where the sun never seems to hit, at the top of the backs of her legs. I stood there with my hand on a box of HiHo crackers trying to remember if I rang it up or not. I ring it up again and the customer starts giving me hell. She's one of these cash-register-watchers, a witch about fifty with rouge on her cheekbones and no eyebrows, and I know it made her day to trip me up. She'd been watching cash registers for fifty years and probably never seen a mistake before.

By the time I got her feathers smoothed and her goodies into a bag—she gives me a little snort in passing, if she'd been born at the right time they would have burned her over in Salem—by the time I get her on her way the girls had circled around the bread and were coming back, without a pushcart, back my way along the counters, in the aisle between the checkouts and the Special bins. They didn't even have shoes on. There was this chunky one, with the two-piece—it was bright green and the seams on the bra were still sharp and her belly was still pretty pale so I guessed she just got it (the suit)—there was this one with one of those chubby berry-faces, the lips all bunched together under her nose, this one, and a tall one, with black hair that hadn't frizzed right, and one of these sunburns right across under the eyes, and a chin that was too long—you know, the kind of girl other girls think is very "striking" and "attractive" but never quite makes it, as they very well know, which is why they like her so much—and then the third one, that wasn't quite so tall. She was the queen. She kind of led them, the other two peeking around and making their shoulders round. She didn't look around, not this queen, she just walked straight on slowly, on these long white prima-donna legs. She came down a little hard on her heels, as if she didn't walk in her bare feet that much, putting down her heels and then letting the weight move along to her toes as if she was testing the floor with every step, putting a little deliberate extra action into it. You never know for sure how girls' minds work (do you really think it's a mind in there or just a little buzz like a bee in a glass jar?) but you got the idea she had talked the other two into coming in here with her, and now she was showing them how to do it, walk and hold yourself straight.

She had on a kind of dirty-pink—beige maybe, I don't know—bathing suit with a little nubble all over it and, what got me, the straps were down. They were off her shoulders looped loose around the cool tops of her arms, and I guess as a result the suit had slipped a little on her, so all around the top of the cloth there was this shining rim. If it hadn't been there you wouldn't have known there could have been anything whiter than those shoulders. With the straps pushed off, there was nothing between the top of the suit and the top of her head except just *her*, this clean bare plane of the top of her chest down from the shoulder bones like a dented sheet of metal tilted in the light. I mean, it was more than pretty.

She had sort of oaky hair that the sun and salt had bleached, done up in a bun that was unravelling, and a kind of prim face. Walking into the A & P with your straps down, I suppose it's the only kind of face you *can* have. She held her head so high her neck, coming up out of those white shoulders, looked kind of stretched, but I didn't mind. The longer her neck was, the more of her there was.

She must have felt in the corner of her eye me and over my shoulder Stokesie in the second slot watching, but she didn't tip. Not this queen. She kept her eyes moving across the racks, and stopped, and turned so slow it made my stomach rub the inside of my apron, and buzzed to the other two, who kind of huddled against her for relief, and then they all three of them went up the cat-and-dog-food-breakfast-cereal-macaroni-rice-raisins-seasonings-spreads-spaghetti-soft-drinks-crackers-and-cookies aisle. From the third slot I look straight up this aisle to the meat counter, and I watched them all the way. The fat one with the tan sort of fumbled with the cookies, but on second thought she put the package back. The sheep pushing their carts down the aisle—the girls were walking against the usual traffic (not that we have one-way signs or anything)—were pretty hilarious. You could see them, when Queenie's white shoulders dawned on them, kind of jerk, or hop, or hiccup, but their eyes snapped back to their own baskets and on they pushed. I bet you could set off dynamite in an A & P and the people would by and large keep reaching and checking oatmeal off their lists and muttering "Let me see, there was a third thing, began with A, asparagus, no, ah, yes, applesauce!" or whatever it is they do mutter. But there was no doubt, this jiggled them. A few houseslaves in pin curlers even looked around after pushing their carts past to make sure what they had seen was correct.

You know, it's one thing to have a girl in a bathing suit down on the beach, where what with the glare nobody can look at each other much anyway, and another thing in the cool of the A & P, under the fluorescent lights, against all those stacked packages, with her feet paddling along naked over our checkerboard green-and-cream rubber-tile floor.

"Oh Daddy," Stokesie said beside me, "I feel so faint."

"Darling," I said, "Hold me tight." Stokesie's married, with two babies chalked up on his fuselage already, but as far as I can tell that's the only difference. He's twenty-two, and I was nineteen this April.

"Is it done?" he asks, the responsible married man finding his voice. I forgot to say he think's he's going to be manager some sunny day, maybe in 1990 when it's called the Great Alexandrov and Petroshki Tea Company or something.

What he meant was, our town is five

miles from a beach, with a big summer colony out on the Point, but we're right in the middle of town, and the women generally put on a shirt or shorts or something before they get out of the car into the street. And anyway these are usually women with six children and varicose veins mapping their legs and nobody, including them, could care less. As I say, we're right in the middle of town, and if you stand at our front doors you can see two banks and the Congregational church and the newspaper store and three real-estate offices and about twenty-seven old freeloaders tearing up Central Street because the sewer broke again. It's not as if we're on the Cape; we're north of Boston and there's people in this town haven't seen the ocean for twenty years.

The girls had reached the meat counter and were asking McMahon something. He pointed, they pointed, and they shuffled out of sight behind a pyramid of Diet Delight peaches. All that was left for us to see was old McMahon patting his mouth and looking after them sizing up their joints. Poor kids, I began to feel sorry for them, they couldn't help it.

Now here comes the sad part of the story, at least my family says it's sad, but I don't think it's so sad myself. The store's pretty empty, it being Thursday afternoon, so there was nothing much to do except lean on the register and wait for the girls to show up again. The whole store was like a pinball machine and I didn't know which tunnel they'd come out of. After a while they come around out of the far aisle, around the light bulbs, records at discount of the Caribbean Six or Tony Martin Sings or some such gunk you wonder they waste the wax on, sixpacks of candy bars, and plastic toys done up in cellophane that fall apart when a kid looks at them anyway. Around they come, Queenie still leading the way, and holding a little gray jar in her hand. Slots Three through Seven are unmanned and I could see her wondering between Stokes and me, but Stokesie with his usual luck draws an old party in baggy pants who stumbles up with four giant cans of pineapple juice (what do these bums *do* with all that pineapple juice? I've often asked myself) so the girls come to me. Queenie puts down the jar and I take it into my fingers icy cold. Kingfish Fancy Herring Snacks in Pure Sour Cream: 49¢. Now her hands are empty, not a ring or a bracelet, bare as God made them, and I wonder where the money's coming from. Still with that prim look she lifts a folded dollar bill out of the hollow at the center of her nubbled pink top. The jar went heavy in my hand. Really, I thought that was so cute.

Then everybody's luck begins to run out. Lengel comes in from haggling with a truck full of cabbages on the lot and is about to scuttle into the door marked MANAGER behind which he hides all day when the girls touch his eye. Lengel's pretty dreary, teaches Sunday school and the rest, but he doesn't miss that much. He comes over and says, "Girls, this isn't the beach."

Queenie blushes, though maybe it's just a brush of sunburn I was noticing for the first time, now that she was so close. "My mother asked me to pick up a jar of herring snacks." Her voice kind of startled me, the way voices do when you see the people first, coming out so flat and dumb yet kind of tony, too, the way it tickled over "pick up" and "snacks." All of a sudden I slid right down her voice into her living room. Her father and the other men were standing around in ice-cream coats and bow ties and the women were in sandals picking up herring snacks on toothpicks off a big glass plate and they were all holding drinks the color of water with olives and sprigs of mint in them. When my parents have somebody over they get lemonade and if it's a real racy affair Schlitz in tall glasses with "They'll Do It Every Time" cartoons stencilled on.

"That's all right," Lengel said. "But this isn't the beach." His repeating this struck me as funny, as if it had just occurred to him, and he had been thinking all these years the A & P was a great big dune and he was the head lifeguard. He didn't like my smiling—as I say he doesn't miss much—but he concentrates on giving the girls that sad Sunday-school-superintendent stare.

Queenie's blush is no sunburn now, and the plump one in plaid, that I liked better from the back—a really sweet can—pipes up, "We weren't doing any shopping. We just came in for the one thing."

"That makes no difference," Lengel tells her, and I could see from the way his eyes went that he hadn't noticed she was wearing a two-piece before. "We want you decently dressed when you come in here."

"We are decent," Queenie says suddenly, her lower lip pushing, getting sore now that she remembers her place, a place from which the crowd that runs the A & P must look pretty crummy. Fancy Herring Snacks flashed in her very blue eyes.

"Girls, I don't want to argue with you. After this come in here with your shoulders covered. It's our policy." He turns his back. That's policy for you. Policy is what the kingpins want. What the others want is juvenile delinquency.

All this while, the customers had been showing up with their carts but, you know, sheep, seeing a scene, they had all bunched up on Stokesie, who shook open a paper bag as gently as peeling a peach, not wanting to miss a word. I could feel in the silence everybody getting nervous, most of all Lengel, who asks me, "Sammy, have you rung up their purchase?"

I thought and said "No" but it wasn't about that I was thinking. I go through the punches, 4,9, GROC, TOT—it's more complicated than you think, and after you do it often enough, it begins to make a little song, that you hear words to, in my case "Hello (*bing*) there, you (*gung*) hap-py *pee*-pul (*splat*)!"—the *splat* being the drawer flying out. I uncrease the bill, tenderly as you may imagine, it just having come from between the two smoothest scoops of vanilla I had ever known were there, and pass a half and a penny into her narrow pink palm, and nestle the herrings in a bag and twist its neck and hand it over, all the time thinking.

The girls, and who'd blame them, are in a hurry to get out, so I say "I quit" to Lengel quick enough for them to hear, hoping they'll stop and watch me, their unsuspected hero. They keep right on going, into the electric eye; the door flies open and they flicker across the lot to their car, Queenie and Plaid and Big Tall Goony-Goony (not that as raw material she was so bad), leaving me with Lengel and a kink in his eyebrow.

"Did you say something, Sammy?"

"I said I quit."

"I thought you did."

"You didn't have to embarrass them."

"It was they who were embarassing us."

I started to say something that came out "Fiddle-de-doo." It's a saying of my grandmother's, and I know she would have been pleased.

"I don't think you know what you're saying," Lengel said.

"I know you don't," I said. "But I do." I pull the bow at the back of my apron and start shrugging it off my shoulders. A couple customers that had been heading for my slot begin to knock against each other, like scared pigs in a chute.

Lengel sighs and begins to look very patient and old and gray. He's been a friend of my parents for years. "Sammy, you don't want to do this to your Mom and Dad," he tells me. It's true, I don't. But it seems to me that once you begin a gesture it's fatal not to go through with it. I fold the apron, "Sammy" stiched in red on the pocket, and put it on the counter, and drop the bow tie on top of it. The bow tie is theirs, if you've ever wondered. "You'll feel this for the rest of your life," Lengel says, and I know that's true, too, but remembering how he made that pretty girl blush makes me so scrunchy inside I punch the No Sale tab and the machine whirs "pee-pul" and the drawer splats out. One advantage to this scene taking place in summer, I can follow this up with a clean exit, there's no fumbling around getting your coat and galoshes. I just saunter into the electric eye in my white shirt that my mother ironed the night before, and the door heaves itself open, and outside the sunshine is skating around on the asphalt.

I look around for my girls, but they're gone, of course. There wasn't anybody but some young married screaming with her children about some candy they didn't get by the door of a powder-blue Falcon station wagon. Looking back in the big windows, over the bags of peat moss and aluminum lawn furniture stacked on the pavement, I could see Lengel in my place in the slot, checking the sheep through. His face was dark gray and his back stiff, as if he'd just had an injection of iron, and my stomach kind of fell as I felt how hard the world was going to be to me hereafter.

[1962]

For Thought

In "A & P" Updike uses a combination of two motifs. One of these involves an important discovery made by the idealistic, adolescent protagonist. The other motif is that of the *beau geste*, or gallant deed, in which the doer of the brave action sacrifices himself for the good of others. Sammy relates the crucial events of a significant day in his life in a manner that gives the reader deeper insight into his prejudices, values, and doubts than he himself may have.

For Discussion

1. What purpose does the first-person point of view serve?
2. How is Sammy characterized?
3. What general conflict is established early in the story?
4. What is Sammy's attitude toward the girls?
5. How is Stokesie used as a foil in the story?
6. What is Sammy's attitude toward his own home and its values?
7. How is Mr. Lengel made unsympathetic?
8. What is the ambiguous significance of Queenie's response, "We are decent"?
9. How and why are Sammy's motives ambiguous rather than purely idealistic?
10. What is the significance of the title?
11. What discovery does Sammy make and how is it important?

Kurt Vonnegut
Who Am I This Time?

The North Crawford Mask and Wig Club, an amateur theatrical society I belong to, voted to do Tennesee Williams' *A Streetcar Named Desire* for the spring play. Doris Sawyer, who always directs, said she couldn't direct this time because her mother was so sick. And she said the club ought to develop some other directors anyway, because she couldn't live forever, even though she'd made it safely to seventy-four.

So I got stuck with the directing job, even though the only thing I'd ever directed before was the installation of combination aluminum storm windows and screens I'd sold. That's what I am, a salesman of storm windows and doors, and here and there a bathtub enclosure. As far as acting goes, the highest rank I ever held on stage was either butler or policeman, whichever's higher.

I made a lot of conditions before I took the directing job, and the biggest one was that Harry Nash, the only real actor the club has, had to take the Marlon Brando part in the play. To give you an idea of how versatile Harry is, inside of one year he was Captain Queeg in *The Caine Mutiny Court Martial*, then Abe Lincoln in *Abe Lincoln in Illinois* and then the young architect in *The Moon is Blue*. The year after that, Harry Nash was Henry the Eighth in *Anne of the Thousand Days* and Doc in *Come Back Little Sheba*, and I was after him for Marlon Brando in *A Streetcar Named Desire*. Harry wasn't at the meeting to say whether he'd take the part or not. He never came to meetings. He was too shy. He didn't stay away from meetings because he had something else to do. He wasn't married, didn't go out with women—didn't have any close men friends either. He stayed away from all kinds of gatherings because he never could think of anything to say or do without a script.

So I had to go down to Miller's Hardware Store, where Harry was a clerk, the next day and ask him if he'd take the part. I stopped off at the telephone company to complain about a bill I'd gotten for a call to Honolulu, I'd never called Honolulu in my life.

And there was this beautiful girl I'd

never seen before behind the counter at the phone company, and she explained that the company had put in an automatic billing machine and that the machine didn't have all the bugs out of it yet. It made mistakes. "Not only did I not call Honolulu," I told her, "I don't think anybody in North Crawford ever has or will."

So she took the charge off the bill, and I asked her if she was from around North Crawford. She said no. She said she just came with the new billing machine to teach local girls how to take care of it. After that, she said, she would go with some other machine to someplace else. "Well," I said, "as long as people have to come along with the machines, I guess we're all right."

"What?" she said.

"When machines start delivering themselves," I said, "I guess that's when the people better start really worrying."

"Oh," she said. She didn't seem very interested in that subject, and I wondered if she was interested in anything. She seemed kind of numb, almost a machine herself, an automatic phone-company politeness machine.

"How long will you be in town here?" I asked her.

"I stay in each town eight weeks, sir," she said. She had pretty blue eyes, but there sure wasn't much hope or curiosity in them. She told me she had been going from town to town like that for two years, always a stranger.

And I got it in my head that she might make a good Stella for the play. Stella was the wife of the Marlon Brando character, the wife of the character I wanted Harry Nash to play. So I told her where and when we were going to hold tryouts, and said the club would be very happy if she'd come.

She looked surprised, and she warmed up a little. "You know," she said, "that's the first time anybody ever asked me to participate in any community thing."

"Well," I said, "there isn't any other way to get to know a lot of nice people faster than to be in a play with 'em."

She said her name was Helene Shaw. She said she might just surprise me—and herself. She said she just might come.

You would think that North Crawford would be fed up with Harry Nash in plays after all the plays he'd been in. But the fact was that North Crawford probably could have gone on enjoying Harry forever, because he was never Harry on stage. When the maroon curtain went up on the stage in the gymnasium of the Consolidated Junior-Senior High School, Harry, body and soul, was exactly what the script and the director told him to be.

Somebody said one time that Harry ought to go to a psychiatrist so he could be something important and colorful in real life, too—so he could get married anyway, and maybe get a better job than just clerking in Miller's Hardware Store for fifty dollars a week. But I don't know what a psychiatrist could have turned up about him that the town didn't already know. The trouble with Harry was he'd been left on the doorstep of the Unitarian Church when he was a baby, and he never did find out who his parents were.

When I told him there in Miller's that I'd been appointed director, that I wanted him in my play, he said what he always said to anybody who asked him to be in a play—and it was kind of sad, if you think about it.

"Who am I this time?" he said.

So I held the tryouts where they're always held—in the meeting room on the second floor of the North Crawford Public Library. Doris Sawyer, the woman who usually directs, came to give me the benefit of all her experience. The two of us sat in state upstairs, while the people who wanted parts waited below. We called them upstairs one by one.

Harry Nash came to the tryouts, even though it was a waste of time. I guess he wanted to get that little bit more acting in.

For Harry's pleasure, and our pleasure, too, we had him read from the scene where he beats up his wife. It was a play in itself, the way Harry did it, and Tennesse Williams hadn't written it all either. Tennessee Williams didn't write the part, for instance, where Harry, who weighs about one hundred forty-five, who's about five feet eight inches tall, added fifty pounds to his weight and four inches to his height by just picking up a playbook. He had a short little double-breasted bellows-back grade-school graduation suit coat on and a dinky little red tie with a horsehead on it. He took off the coat and tie, opened his collar, then turned his back to Doris and me, getting up steam for the part. There was a great big rip in the back of his shirt, and it looked like a fairly new shirt too. He'd ripped it on purpose, so he could be that much more like Marlon Brando, right from the first.

When he faced us again, he was huge and handsome and conceited and cruel. Doris read the part of Stella, the wife, and Harry bullied that old, old lady into believing that she was a sweet, pregnant girl married to a sexy gorilla who was going to beat her brains out. She had me believing it too. And I read the lines of Blanche, her sister in the play, and darned if Harry didn't scare me into feeling like a drunk and faded Southern belle.

And then, while Doris and I were getting over our emotional experiences, like people coming out from under ether, Harry put down the playbook, put on his coat and tie, and turned into the pale hardware-store clerk again.

"Was—was that all right?" he said, and he seemed pretty sure he wouldn't get the part.

"Well," I said, "for a first reading, that wasn't too bad."

"Is there a chance I'll get the part?" he said. I don't know why he always had to pretend there was some doubt about his getting a part, but he did.

"I think we can safely say we're leaning powerfully in your direction," I told him.

He was very pleased. "Thanks! Thanks a lot!" he said, and he shook my hand.

"Is there a pretty new girl downstairs?" I said, meaning Helene Shaw.

"I didn't notice," said Harry.

It turned out that Helene Shaw *had* come for the tryouts, and Doris and I had our hearts broken. We thought the North Crawford Mask and Wig Club was finally going to put a really good-looking, really young girl on stage, instead of one of the beat-up forty-year-old women we generally have to palm off as girls.

But Helene Shaw couldn't act for sour apples. No matter what we gave her to read, she was the same girl with the same smile for anybody who had a complaint about his phone bill.

Doris tried to coach her some, to make her understand that Stella in the play was a very passionate girl who loved a gorilla because she needed a gorilla. But Helene just read the lines the same way again. I don't think a volcano could have stirred her up enough to say, "Oo."

"Dear," said Doris, "I'm going to ask you a personal question."

"All right," said Helene.

"Have you ever been in love?" said Doris. "The reason I ask," she said, "remembering some old love might help you put more warmth in your acting."

Helene frowned and thought hard. "Well," she said, "I travel a lot, you know. And practically all the men in the different companies I visit are married and I never stay anyplace long enough to know many people who aren't."

"What about school?" said Doris. "What about puppy love and all the other kinds of love in school?"

So Helene thought hard about that, and then she said, "Even in school I was always moving around a lot. My father was a construction worker, following jobs around, so I was always saying hello or good-by to someplace, without anything in between."

"Um," said Doris.

"Would movie stars count?" said Helene. "I don't mean in real life. I never knew any. I just mean up on the screen."

Doris looked at me and rolled her eyes. "I guess that's love of a kind," she said.

And then Helene got a little enthusiastic. "I used to sit through movies over and over again," she said, "and pretend I was married to whoever the man movie star was. They were the only people who came with us. No matter where we moved, movie stars were there."

"Uh huh," said Doris.

"Well, thank you, Miss Shaw," I said. "You go downstairs and wait with the rest. We'll let you know."

So we tried to find another Stella. And there just wasn't one, not one woman in the club with the dew still on her. "All we've got are Blanches," I said, meaning all we had were faded women who could play the part of Blanche, Stella's faded sister. "That's life, I guess—twenty Blanches to one Stella."

"And when you find a Stella," said Doris, "it turns out she doesn't know what love is."

Doris and I decided there was one last thing we could try. We could get Harry Nash to play a scene along with Helene. "He just might make her bubble the least little bit," I said.

"That girl hasn't got a bubble in her," said Doris.

So we called down the stairs for Helene to come back on up, and we told somebody to go find Harry. Harry never sat with the rest of the people at tryouts—or at rehearsals either. The minute he didn't have a part to play, he'd disappear into some hiding place where he could hear people call him, but where he couldn't be seen. At tryouts in the library he generally hid in the reference room, passing the time looking at flags of different countries in the front of the dictionary.

Helene came back upstairs, and we were very sorry and surprised to see that she'd been crying.

"Oh, dear," said Doris. "Oh, my—now what on earth's the trouble, dear?"

"I was terrible, wasn't I?" said Helene, hanging her head.

Doris said the only thing anybody can say in an amateur theatrical society when somebody cries. She said, "Why, no dear—you were marvelous."

"No, I wasn't," said Helene. "I'm a walking icebox, and I know it."

"Nobody could look at you and say that," said Doris.

"When they get to know me, they can say it," said Helene. "When people get to know me, that's what they *do* say." Her tears got worse. "I don't want to be the way I am," she said. "I just can't help it, living the way I've lived all my life. The only experiences I've had have been in crazy dreams of movie stars. When I meet somebody nice in real life, I feel as though I were in some kind of big bottle, as though I couldn't touch that person, no matter how hard I tried." And Helene pushed on air as though it were a big bottle all around her.

"You ask me if I've ever been in love," she said to Doris. "No—but I want to be. I know what this play's about. I know what Stella's supposed to feel and why she feels it. I—I—I—" she said, and her tears wouldn't let her go on.

"You what, dear?" said Doris gently.

"I——" said Helene, and she pushed on the imaginary bottle again. "I just don't know how to begin," she said.

There was heavy clumping on the library stairs. It sounded like a deep-sea diver coming upstairs in his lead shoes. It was Harry Nash, turning himself into Marlon Brando. In he came, practically dragging his knuckles on the floor. And he was so much in character that the sight of a weeping woman made him sneer.

"Harry," I said, "I'd like you to meet Helene Shaw. Helene—this is Harry Nash. If you get the part of Stella, he'll be your husband in the play." Harry didn't offer to shake hands. He put his hands in his pockets, and he hunched over, and he looked her up and down, gave her looks that left her naked. Her tears stopped right then and there.

"I wonder if you two would play the fight scene," I said, "and then the reunion scene right after it."

"Sure," said Harry, his eyes still on her. Those eyes burned up clothes faster than she could put them on. "Sure," he said, "if Stell's game."

"What?" said Helene. She'd turned the color of cranberry juice.

"Stell—Stella," said Harry. "That's you. Stell's my wife."

I handed the two of them playbooks. Harry snatched his from me without a work of thanks. Helene's hands weren't working very well, and I had to kind of mold them around the book.

"I'll want something I can throw," said Harry.

"What?" I said.

"There's one place where I throw a radio out a window," said Harry. "What can I throw?"

So I said an iron paperweight was the radio, and I opened the window wide. Helene Shaw looked scared to death.

"Where you want us to start?" said Harry, and he rolled his shoulders like a prizefighter warming up.

"Start a few lines back from where you throw the radio out the window," I said.

"O.K., O.K.," said Harry, warming up, warming up. He scanned the stage directions. "Let's see," he said, "after I throw the radio, she runs off stage, and I chase her, and I sock her one."

"Right," I said.

"O.K., baby," Harry said to Helene, his eyelids drooping. What was about to happen was wilder than the chariot race in *Ben Hur*. "On your mark," said Harry. "Get ready, baby. Go!"

When the scene was over, Helene Shaw was as hot as a hod carrier, as limp as an eel. She sat down with her mouth open and her head hanging to one side. She wasn't in any bottle any more. There wasn't any bottle to hold her up and keep her safe and clean. The bottle was gone.

"Do I get the part or don't I?" Harry snarled at me.

"You'll do," I said.

"You said a mouthful!" he said. "I'll be going now. . . . See you around, Stella," he said to Helene, and he left. He slammed the door behind him.

"Helene?" I said. "Miss Shaw?"

"Me?" she said.

"The part of Stella is yours," I said "You were great!"

"I was?" she said.

"I had no idea you had that much fire in you, dear," Doris said to her.

"Fire?" said Helene. She didn't know if she was afoot or on horseback.

"Skyrockets! Pinwheels! Roman candles!" said Doris.

"Me," said Helene. And that was all she said. She looked as though she were going to sit in the chair with her mouth open forever.

"Stella," I said.

"Huh?" she said.

"You have my permission to go."

So we started having rehearsals four nights a week on the stage of the Consolidated School. And Harry and Helene set such a pace that everybody in the production was half crazy with excitement and exhaustion before we'd rehearsed four times. Usually a director has to beg people to learn their lines, but I had no such trouble. Harry and Helene were working so well together that everybody else in the cast regarded it as a duty and an honor and a pleasure to support them.

I was certainly lucky—or thought I was. Things were going so well, so hot and heavy, so early in the game that I had to say to Harry and Helene after one love scene, "Hold a little something back for the actual performance, would you please? You'll burn yourselves out."

I said that at the fourth or fifth rehearsal, and Lydia Miller, who was playing

Blanche, the faded sister, was sitting next to me in the audience. In real life, she's the wife of Verne Miller. Verne owns Miller's Hardward Store. Verne was Harry's boss.

"Lydia," I said to her, "have we got a play or have we got a play?"

"Yes," she said, "you've got a play all right." She made it sound as though I'd committed some kind of crime, done something just terrible. "You should be very proud of yourself."

"What do you mean by that?" I said.

Before Lydia could answer, Harry yelled at me from the stage, asked if I was through with him, asked if he could go home. I told him he could and, still Marlon Brando, he left, kicking furniture out of his way and slamming doors. Helene was left all alone on the stage, sitting on a couch with the same gaga look she'd had after the tryouts. That girl was drained.

I turned to Lydia again and I said, "Well—until now, I thought I had every reason to be happy and proud. Is there something going on I don't know about?"

"Do you know that girl's in love with Harry?" said Lydia.

"In the play?" I said.

"What play?" said Lydia. "There isn't any play going on now, and look at her up there." She gave a sad cackle. "You aren't directing this play."

"Who is?" I said.

"Mother Nature at her worst," said Lydia. "And think what it's going to do to that girl when she discovers what Harry really is." She corrected herself. "What Harry really isn't," she said.

I didn't do anything about it, because I didn't figure it was any of my business. I heard Lydia try to do something about, but she didn't get very far.

"You know," Lydia said to Helene one night, "I once played Ann Rutledge, and Harry was Abraham Lincoln."

Helene clapped her hands. "That must have been heaven!" she said.

"It was, in a way," said Lydia. "Sometimes I'd get so worked up, I'd love Harry the way I'd love Abraham Lincoln. I'd have to come back to earth and remind myself that he wasn't ever going to free the slaves, that he was just a clerk in my husband's hardware store."

"He's the most marvelous man I ever met," said Helene.

"Of course, one thing you have to get set for, when you're in a play with Harry," said Lydia, "is what happens after the last performance."

"What are you talking about?" said Helene.

"Once the show's over," said Lydia, "whatever you thought Harry was just evaporates into thin air."

"I don't believe it," said Helene.

"I admit it's hard to believe," said Lydia.

Then Helene got a little sore. "Anyway, why tell me about it?" she said. "Even if it is true, what do I care?"

"I—I don't know," said Lydia, backing away. "I—I just thought you might find it interesting."

"Well, I don't," said Helene.

And Lydia slunk away, feeling about as frowzy and unloved as she was supposed to feel in the play. After that nobody said anything more to Helene to warn her about Harry, not even when word got around that she'd told the telephone company that she didn't want to be moved around anymore, that she wanted to stay in North Crawford.

So the time finally came to put on the play. We ran it for three nights—Thursday, Friday, and Saturday—and we murdered those audiences. They believed every word that was said on stage, and when the maroon curtain came down they were ready to go to the nut house along with Blanche, the faded sister.

On Thursday night the other girls at the telephone company sent Helene a dozen red roses. When Helene and Harry were taking a curtain call together, I passed the roses over the footlights to her. She came forward for them, took one rose from the bouquet to give to Harry. But when she turned to give Harry the rose in front of everybody, Harry was gone. The curtain came down on that extra little scene—that girl offering a rose to nothing and nobody.

I went backstage, and I found her still holding that one rose. She'd put the rest of the bouquet aside. There were tears in her eyes. "What did I do wrong?" she said to me. "Did I insult him some way?"

"No," I said. "He always does that after a performance. The minute it's over, he clears out as fast as he can."

"And tomorrow he'll disappear again?"

"Without even taking off his makeup."

"And Saturday?" she said. "He'll stay for the cast party on Saturday, won't he?"

"Harry never goes to parties," I said. "When the curtain comes down on Saturday, that's the last anybody will see of him till he goes to work on Monday."

"How sad," she said.

Helene's performance on Friday night wasn't nearly so good as Thursday's. She seemed to be thinking about other things. She watched Harry take off after curtain call. She didn't say a word.

On Saturday she put on the best performance yet. Ordinarily it was Harry who set the pace. But on Saturday Harry had to work to keep up with Helene.

When the curtain came down on the final curtain call, Harry wanted to get away, but he couldn't. Helene wouldn't let go his hand. The rest of the cast and the stage crew and a lot of well-wishers from the audience were all standing around Harry and Helene, and Harry was trying to get his hand back.

"Well," he said, "I've got to go."

"Where?" she said.

"Oh," he said, "home."

"Won't you please take me to the cast party?" she said.

He got very red. "I'm afraid I'm not much on parties," he said. All the Marlon Brando in him was gone. He was tongue-tied, he was scared, he was shy—he was everything Harry was famous for being between plays.

"All right," she said. "I'll let you go—if you promise me one thing."

"What's that?" he said, and I thought he would jump out a window if she let go of him then.

"I want you to promise to stay here until I get you your present," she said.

"Present?" he said, getting even more panicky.

"Promise?" she said.

He promised. It was the only way he could get his hand back. And he stood there miserably while Helene went down to the ladies' dressing room for the present. While he waited, a lot of people congratulated him on being such a fine actor. But congratulations never made him happy. He just wanted to get away.

Helene came back with the present. It turned out to be a little blue book with a big red ribbon for a place marker. It was a copy of *Romeo and Juliet*. Harry was very embarrassed. It was all he could do to say "Thank you."

"The marker marks my favorite scene," said Helene.

"Um," said Harry.

"Don't you want to see what my favorite scene is?" she said.

So Harry had to open the book to the red ribbon.

Helene got close to him, and read a line of Juliet's. "'How cam'st thou hither, tell me, and wherefore?'" she read. "'The orchard walls are high and hard to climb, and the place death, considering who thou art, if any of my kinsmen find thee here.'" She pointed to the next line. "Now, look what Romeo says," she said.

"Um," said Harry.

"Read what Romeo says," said Helene.

Harry cleared his throat. He didn't want to read the line, but he had to. "'With love's light wings did I o'erperch these walls,'" he read out loud in his everyday voice. But then a change came over him. "'For stony limits cannot hold love out,'" he read, and he straightened up, and eight years dropped away from him, and he was brave and gay. "'And what love can do, that dares love attempt,'" he read, "'therefore thy kinsmen are no let to me.'"

"'If they do see thee they will murther thee,'" said Helene, and she started him walking toward the wings.

"'Alack!'" said Harry, "'there lies more peril in thine eye than twenty of their swords.'" Helene led him toward the backstage exit. "'Look thou but sweet,'" said Harry, "'and I am proof against their enmity.'"

"'I would not for the world they saw thee here,'" said Helene, and that was the last we heard. The two of them were out the door and gone.

They never did show up at the cast party. One week later they were married.

They seem very happy, although they're kind of strange from time to time, depending on which play they're reading to each other at the time.

I dropped into the phone company office the other day, on account of the billing machine was making dumb mistakes again. I asked her what plays she and Harry'd been reading lately.

"In the past week," she said, "I've been married to Othello, been loved by Faust and been kidnaped by Paris. Wouldn't you say I was the luckiest girl in town?"

I said I thought so, and I told her most of the women in town thought so too.

"They had their chance," she said.

"Most of 'em couldn't stand the excitement," I said. And I told her I'd been asked to direct another play. I asked if she and Harry would be available for the cast. She gave me a big smile and said, "Who are we this time?"

[1961]

For Thought

Through the alchemy of sympathetic wit, Vonnegut acquaints the reader with a basically pathetic situation involving two lonely, emotionally stunted young people. He takes this seemingly unpromising situation and turns it into a highly unorthodox but compelling love story. Instead of a sad ending, as one might logically expect from an inauspicious beginning, the author brings about an emotionally satisfying denouement that strikes the reader as being both comically inevitable and just. By slightly altering the question in the title to "Who are we this time?," Vonnegut leaves the reader with the comfortable assurance that Helene and Harry have found the best of all possible worlds in a life together that will be filled with the shared freedom of infinite variety.

For Discussion

1. How does the narrator characterize himself? What purpose is served by this characterization?
2. Trace Helene's characterization through the story and comment on the mixture of passivity and assertiveness in her character.
3. Why is the play that is chosen as the centerpiece of the action, *A Streetcar Named Desire*, so well suited to the structure of the story?
4. What is the narrator's attitude toward his characters? How does it change in the course of the action?
5. What is the critical point in the action? How does it help prepare the reader for the resolution?

Eudora Welty
Death of a Traveling Salesman

R. J. Bowman, who for fourteen years had traveled for a shoe company through Mississippi, drove his Ford along a rutted dirt path. It was a long day! The time did not seem to clear the noon hurdle and settle into soft afternoon. The sun, keeping its strength here even in winter, stayed at the top of the sky, and every time Bowman stuck his head out of the dusty car to stare up the road, it seemed to reach a long arm down and push against the top of his head, right through his hat—like the practical joke of an old drummer, long on the road. It made him feel all the more angry and helpless. He was feverish, and he was not quite sure of the way.

This was his first day back on the road after a long siege of influenza. He had had very high fever, and dreams, and had become weakened and pale, enough to tell the difference in the mirror, and he could not think clearly. . . . All afternoon, in the midst of his anger, and for no reason, he had thought of his dead grandmother. She had been a comfortable soul. Once more Bowman wished he could fall into the big feather bed that had been in her room. . . . Then he forgot her again.

This desolate hill country! And he seemed to be going the wrong way—it was as if he were going back, far back. There was not a house in sight. . . . There was no use wishing he were back in bed, though. By paying the hotel doctor his bill he had proved his recovery. He had not even been sorry when the pretty trained nurse said good-bye. He did not like illness, he distrusted it, as he distrusted the road without signposts. It angered him. He had given the nurse a really expensive bracelet, just because she was packing up her bag and leaving.

But now—what if in fourteen years on the road he had never been ill before and never had an accident? His record was broken, and he had even begun almost to question it. . . . He had gradually put up at better hotels, in the bigger towns, but weren't they all, eternally, stuffy in summer and drafty in winter? Women? He could only remember little rooms within little rooms, like a nest of Chinese paper boxes, and if he thought of one woman he saw the worn loneliness that the furniture of that room seemed built of. And he himself—he was a man who always wore rather wide-brimmed black hats, and in the wavy hotel mirrors had looked something like a bull-fighter, as he paused for that inevitable instant on the landing, walking downstairs to supper. . . . He leaned out of the car again, and once more the sun pushed at his head.

Bowman had wanted to reach Beulah by dark, to go to bed and sleep off his fatigue. As he remembered, Beulah was fifty miles away from the last town, on a graveled road. This was only a cow trail. How had he ever come to such a place? One hand wiped the sweat from his face, and he drove on.

He had made the Beulah trip before. But he had never seen this hill or this petering-out path before—or that cloud, he thought shyly, looking up and then down quickly—any more than he had seen this day before. Why did he not admit he was simply lost and had been for miles? . . . He was not in the habit of asking the way of strangers, and these people never knew where the very roads they lived on went to; but then he had not even been close enough to anyone to call out. People standing in the fields now and then, or on top of the haystacks, had been too far away, looking like leaning sticks or weeds, turning a little at the solitary rattle of his car across their countryside, watching the pale sobered winter dust where it chunked out behind like big squashes down the road. The stares of these distant people had followed him solidly like a wall, impenetrable, behind which they turned back after he had passed.

The cloud floated there to one side like the bolster on his grandmother's bed. It went over a cabin on the edge of a hill, where two bare chinaberry trees clutched at the sky. He drove through a heap of dead oak leaves, his wheels stirring their weightless sides to make a silvery melancholy whistle as the car passed through their bed. No car had been along this way ahead of him. Then he saw that he was on the edge of a ravine that fell away, a red erosion, and that this was indeed the road's end.

He pulled the brake. But it did not hold, though he put all his strength into it. The car, tipped toward the edge, rolled a little. Without doubt, it was going over the bank.

He got out quietly, as though some mischief had been done him and he had his dignity to remember. He lifted his bag and sample case out, set them down, and stood back and watched the car roll over the edge. He heard something—not the crash he was listening for, but a slow, unuproarious crackle. Rather distastefully he went to look over, and he saw that his car had fallen into a tangle of immense grapevines as thick as his arm, which caught it and held it, rocked it like a grotesque child in a dark cradle, and then, as he watched, concerned somehow that he was not still inside it, released it gently to the ground.

He sighed.

Where am I? he wondered with a shock. Why didn't I do something? All his anger seemed to have drifted away from him. There was the house, back on the hill. He took a bag in each hand and with almost childlike willingness went toward it. But his breathing came with difficulty, and he had to stop to rest.

It was a shotgun house, two rooms and an open passage between, perched on the hill. The whole cabin slanted a little under the heavy heaped-up vine that covered the roof, light and green, as though forgotten from summer. A woman stood in the passage.

He stopped still. Then all of a sudden his heart began to behave strangely. Like a rocket set off, it began to leap and expand into uneven patterns of beats which showered into his brain, and he could not think. But in scattering and falling it made no noise. It shot up with great power, almost elation, and fell gently, like acrobats into nets. It began to pound profoundly, then waited irresponsibly, hitting in some sort of inward mockery first at his ribs, then against his eyes, then under his shoulder blades, and against the roof of his mouth when he tried to say, "Good afternoon, madam." But he could not hear his heart—it was as quiet as ashes falling. This was rather comforting; still, it was shocking to Bowman to feel his heart beating at all.

Stock-still in his confusion, he dropped his bags, which seemed to drift in slow bulks gracefully through the air and to cushion themselves on the gray prostrate grass near the doorstep.

As for the woman standing there, he saw at once that she was old. Since she could not possibly hear his heart, he ignored the pounding and now looked at her carefully, and yet in his distraction dreamily, with his mouth open.

She had been cleaning the lamp, and held it, half blackened, half clear, in front of her. He saw her with the dark passage behind her. She was a big woman with a weather-beaten but unwrinkled face; her lips were held tightly together, and her eyes looked with a curious dulled brightness into his. He looked at her shoes, which were like bundles. If it were summer she would be barefoot. . . . Bowman, who automatically judged a woman's age on sight, set her age at fifty. She wore a formless garment of some gray course material, rough-dried from a washing, from which her arms appeared pink and unexpectedly round. When she never said a word, and sustained her quiet pose of holding the lamp, he was convinced of the strength in her body.

"Good afternoon, madam," he said.

She stared on, whether at him or at the air around him he could not tell, but after a moment she lowered her eyes to show that she would listen to whatever he had to say.

"I wonder if you would be interested—" He tried once more. "An accident—my car . . . "

Her voice emerged low and remote, like a sound across a lake. "Sonny he ain't here."

"Sonny?"

"Sonny ain't here now."

Her son—a fellow able to bring my car up, he decided in blurred relief. He pointed down the hill. "My car's in the bottom of the ditch. I'll need help."

"Sonny ain't here, but he'll be here."

She was becoming clearer to him and her voice stronger, and Bowman saw that she was stupid.

He was hardly surprised at the deepening postponement and tedium of his journey. He took a breath, and heard his voice speaking over the silent blows of his heart. "I was sick. I am not strong yet. . . . May I come in?"

He stooped and laid his big black hat over the handle on his bag. It was a humble motion, almost a bow, that instantly struck him as absurd and betraying of all his weakness. He looked up at the woman, the wind blowing his hair. He might have continued for a long time in this unfamiliar attitude; he had never been a patient man, but when he was sick he had learned to sink submissively into the pillows, to wait for his medicine. He waited on the woman.

Then she, looking at him with blue eyes, turned and held open the door, and after a moment Bowman, as if convinced in his action, stood erect and followed her in.

Inside, the darkness of the house touched him like a professional hand, the doctor's. The woman set the half-cleaned lamp on a table in the center of the room and pointed, also like a professional person, a guide, to a chair with a yellow cowhide seat. She herself crouched on the hearth, drawing her knees up under the shapeless dress.

At first he felt hopefully secure. His heart was quieter. The room was enclosed in the gloom of yellow pine boards. He could see the other room, with the foot of an iron bed showing, across the passage. The bed had been made up with a red-and-yellow pieced quilt that looked like a map or a picture, a little like his grandmother's girlhood painting of Rome burning.

He had ached for coolness, but in this room it was cold. He stared at the hearth with dead coals lying on it and iron pots in the corners. The hearth and smoked chimney were of the stone he had seen ribbing the hills, mostly slate. Why is there no fire? he wondered.

And it was so still. The silence of the fields seemed to enter and move familiarly through the house. The wind used the open hall. He felt that he was in a mysterious, quiet, cool danger. It was necessary to do what? . . . To talk.

"I have a nice line of women's low-priced shoes . . . " he said.

But the woman answered, "Sonny'll be here. He's strong. Sonny'll move your car."

"Where is he now?"

"Farms for Mr. Redmond."

Mr. Redmond. Mr. Redmond. That was someone he would never have to encounter, and he was glad. Somehow the name did not appeal to him. . . . In a flare of touchiness and anxiety, Bowman wished to avoid even mention of unknown men and their unknown farms.

"Do you two live here alone?" He was surprised to hear his old voice, chatty, confidential, inflected for selling shoes, asking a question like that—a thing he did not even want to know.

"Yes. We are alone."

He was surprised at the way she answered. She had taken a long time to say that. She had nodded her head in a deep way too. Had she wished to affect him with some sort of premonition? he wondered unhappily. Or was it only that she would not help him, after all, by talking with him? For he was not strong enough to receive the impact of unfamiliar things without a little talk to break their fall. He had lived a month in which nothing had happened except in his head and his body—an almost inaudible life of heartbeats and dreams that came back, a life of fever and privacy, a delicate life which had left him weak to the point of—what? Of begging. The pulse in his palm leapt like a trout in a brook.

He wondered over and over why the woman did not go ahead with cleaning the lamp. What prompted her to stay there across the room, silently bestowing her presence upon him? He saw that with her it was not a time for doing little tasks. Her face was grave; she was feeling how right she was. Perhaps it was only politeness. In docility he held his eyes stiffly wide; they fixed themselves on the woman's clasped hands as though she held the cord they were strung on.

Then, "Sonny's coming," she said.

He himself had not heard anything, but there came a man passing the window and then plunging in at the door, with two hounds beside him. Sonny was a big enough man, with his belt slung low about his hips. He looked at least thirty. He had a hot, red face that was yet full of silence. He wore muddy blue pants and an old military coat stained and patched. World War? Bowman wondered. Great God, it was a Confederate coat. On the back of his light hair he had a wide filthy black hat which seemed to insult Bowman's own. He pushed down the dogs from his chest. He was strong, with dignity and heaviness in his way of moving. . . . There was the resemblance to his mother.

They stood side by side. . . . He must account again for his presence here.

"Sonny, this man, he had his car to run off over the prec'pice an' wants to know if you will git it out for him," the woman said after a few minutes.

Bowman could not even state his case.

Sonny's eyes lay upon him.

He knew he should offer explanations and show money—at least appear either penitent or authoritative. But all he could do was to shrug slightly.

Sonny brushed by him going to the window, followed by the eager dogs, and looked out. There was effort even in the way he was looking, as if he could throw his sight out like a rope. Without turning Bowman felt that his own eyes could have seen nothing: it was too far.

"Got me a mule out there an' got me a block an' tackle," said Sonny meaningfully. "I *could* catch me my mule an' git me my ropes, an' before long I'd git your car out the ravine."

He looked completely around the room, as if in meditation, his eyes roving in their own distance. Then he pressed his lips firmly and yet shyly together, and with the dogs ahead of him this time, he lowered his head and strode out. The hard earth sounded, cupping to his powerful way of walking—almost a stagger.

Mischievously, at the suggestion of those sounds, Bowman's heart leapt again. It seemed to walk about inside him.

"Sonny's goin' to do it," the woman said. She said it again, singing it almost, like a song. She was sitting in her place by the hearth.

Without looking out, he heard some shouts and the dogs barking and the pounding of hoofs in short runs on the hill. In a few minutes Sonny passed under the window with a rope, and there was a brown mule with quivering, shining, purple-looking ears. The mule actually looked in the window. Under its eyelashes it turned targetlike eyes into his. Bowman averted his head and saw the woman looking serenely back at the mule, with only satisfaction in her face.

She sang a little more, under her breath. It occurred to him, and it seemed quite marvelous, that she was not really talking to him, but rather following the thing that came about with words that were unconscious and part of her looking.

So he said nothing, and this time when he did not reply he felt a curious and strong emotion, not fear, rise up in him.

This time, when his heart leapt, something—his soul—seemed to leap too, like a little colt invited out of a pen. He stared at the woman while the frantic nimbleness of his feeling made his head sway. He could not move; there was nothing he could do, unless perhaps he might embrace this woman who sat there growing old and shapeless before him.

But he wanted to leap up, to say to her, I have been sick and I found out then, only then, how lonely I am. Is it too late? My heart puts up a struggle inside me, and you may have heard it, protesting against emptiness. . . . It should be full, he would rush on to tell her, thinking of his heart now as a deep lake, it should be holding love like other hearts. It should be flooded with love. There would be a warm spring day . . . Come and stand in my heart, whoever you are, and a whole river would cover your feet and rise higher and take your knees in whirlpools, and draw you down to itself, your whole body, your heart too.

But he moved a trembling hand across his eyes, and looked at the placid crouching woman across the room. She was still as a statue. He felt ashamed and exhausted by the thought that he might, in one more moment, have tried by simple words and embraces to communicate some strange thing—something which seemed always to have just escaped him . . .

Sunlight touched the furthest pot on the hearth. It was late afternoon. This time tomorrow he would be somewhere on a good graveled road, driving his car past things that happened to people, quicker than their happening. Seeing ahead to the next day, he was glad, and knew that this was no time to embrace an old woman. He could feel in his pounding temples the readying of his blood for motion and for hurrying away.

"Sonny's hitched up your car by now," said the woman. "He'll git it out the ravine right shortly."

"Fine!" he cried with his customary enthusiasm.

Yet it seemed a long time that they waited. It began to get dark. Bowman was cramped in his chair. Any man should know enough to get up and walk around while he waited. There was something like guilt in such stillness and silence.

But instead of getting up, he listened. . . . His breathing restrained, his eyes powerless in the growing dark, he listened uneasily for a warning sound, forgetting in wariness what it would be. Before long he heard something—soft, continuous, insinuating.

"What's that noise?" he asked, his voice jumping into the dark. Then wildly he was afraid it would be his heart beating so plainly in the quiet room, and she would tell him so.

"You might hear the stream," she said grudgingly.

Her voice was closer. She was standing by the table. He wondered why she did not light the lamp. She stood there in the dark and did not light it.

Bowman would never speak to her now, for the time was past. I'll sleep in the dark, he thought, in his bewilderment pitying himself.

Heavily she moved on to the window. Her arm, vaguely white, rose straight from her full side and she pointed out into the darkness.

"That white speck's Sonny," she said, talking to herself.

He turned unwillingly and peered over her shoulder; he hesitated to rise and stand beside her. His eyes searched the dusky air. The white speck floated smoothly toward her finger, like a leaf on a river, growing whiter in the dark. It was as if she had shown him something secret, part of her life, but had offered no explanation. He looked away. He was moved almost to tears, feeling for no reason that she had made a silent declaration equivalent to his own. His hand waited upon his chest.

Then a step shook the house, and Sonny was in the room. Bowman felt how the woman left him there and went to the other man's side.

"I done got your car out, mister," said Sonny's voice in the dark. "She's settin' a-waitin' in the road, turned to go back where she come from."

"Fine!" said Bowman, projecting his own voice to loudness. "I'm surely much obliged—I could never have done it myself—I was sick. . . ."

"I could do it easy," said Sonny.

Bowman could feel them both waiting in the dark, and he could hear the dogs panting out in the yard, waiting to bark when he should go. He felt strangely helpless and resentful. Now that he could go, he longed to stay. From what was he being deprived? His chest was rudely shaken by the violence of his heart. These people cherished something here that he could not see, they withheld some ancient promise of food and warmth and light. Between them they had a conspiracy. He thought of the way she had moved away from him and gone to Sonny, she had flowed toward him. He was shaking with cold, he was tired, and it was not fair. Humbly and yet angrily he stuck his hand into his pocket.

"Of course I'm going to pay you for everything—"

"We don't take money for such," said Sonny's voice belligerently.

"I want to pay. But do something more . . . Let me stay—tonight. . . ." He took another step toward them. If only they could see him, they would know his sincerity, his real need! His voice went on, "I'm not very strong yet, I'm not able to walk far, even back to my car, maybe, I don't know—I don't know exactly where I am—"

He stopped. He felt as if he might burst into tears. What would they think of him!

Sonny came over and put his hands on him. Bowman felt them pass (they were professional too) across his chest, over his hips. He could feel Sonny's eyes upon him in the dark.

"You ain't no revenuer come sneakin' here, mister, ain't got no gun?"

To this end of nowhere! And yet *he* had come. He made a grave answer. "No."

"You can stay."

"Sonny," said the woman, "you'll have to borry some fire."

"I'll go git it from Redmond's," said Sonny.

"What?" Bowman strained to hear their words to each other.

"Our fire, it's out, and Sonny's got to borry some, because its dark an' cold," she said.

"But matches—I have matches—"

"We don't have no need for 'em," she said proudly. "Sonny's goin' after his own fire."

"I'm goin' to Redmond's," said Sonny with an air of importance, and he went out.

After they had waited a while, Bowman looked out the window and saw a light moving over the hill. It spread itself out like a little fan. It zigzagged along the field, darting and swift, not like Sonny at all. . . . Soon enough, Sonny staggered in, holding a burning stick behind him in tongs, fire flowing in his wake, blazing light into the corners of the room.

"We'll make a fire now," the woman said, taking the brand.

When that was done she lit the lamp. It showed its dark and light. The whole room turned golden-yellow like some sort of flower, and the walls smelled of it and seemed to tremble with the quiet rushing of the fire and the waving of the burning lampwick in its funnel of light.

The woman moved among the iron pots. With the tongs she dropped hot coals on top of the iron lids. They made a set of soft vibrations, like the sound of a bell far away.

She looked up and over at Bowman, but he could not answer. He was trembling. . . .

"Have a drink, mister?" Sonny asked. He had brought in a chair from the other room and sat astride it with his folded arms across the back. Now we are all visible to one another, Bowman thought, and cried, "Yes sir, you bet, thanks!"

"Come after me and do just what I do," said Sonny.

It was another excursion into the dark. They went through the hall, out to the back of the house, past a shed and a hooded well. They came to a wilderness of thicket.

"Down on your knees," said Sonny.

"What?" Sweat broke out on his forehead.

He understood when Sonny began to crawl through a sort of tunnel that the bushes made over the ground. He followed, startled in spite of himself when a twig or a thorn touched him gently without making a sound, clinging to him and finally letting him go.

Sonny stopped crawling and, crouched on his knees, began to dig with both his hands into the dirt. Bowman shyly struck matches and made a light. In a few minutes Sonny pulled up a jug. He poured out some of the whisky into a bottle from his coat pocket, and buried the jug again. "You never know who's liable to knock at your door," he said, and laughed. "Start back," he said, almost formally. "Ain't no need for us to drink outdoors, like hogs."

At the table by the fire, sitting opposite each other in their chairs, Sonny and Bowman took drinks out of the bottle, passing it across. The dogs slept; one of them was having a dream.

"This is good," said Bowman. "This is what I needed." It was just as though he were drinking the fire off the hearth.

"He makes it," said the woman with quiet pride.

She was pushing the coals off the pots, and the smells of corn bread and coffee circled the room. She set everything on the table before the men, with a bone-handled knife stuck into one of the potatoes, splitting out its golden fiber. Then she stood for a minute looking at them, tall and full above them where they sat. She leaned a little toward them.

"You all can eat now," she said, and suddenly smiled.

Bowman had just happened to be looking at her. He set his cup back on the table in unbelieving protest. A pain pressed at his eyes. He saw that she was not an old woman. She was young, still young. He could think of no number of years for her. She was the same age as Sonny, and she belonged to him. She stood with the deep dark corner of the room behind her, the shifting yellow light scattering over her head and her gray formless dress, trembling over her tall body when it bent over them in its sudden communication. She was young. Her teeth were shining and her eyes glowed. She turned and walked slowly and heavily out of the room, and he heard her sit down on the cot and then lie down. The pattern on the quilt moved.

"She's goin' to have a baby," said Sonny, popping a bite into his mouth.

Bowman could not speak. He was shocked with knowing what was really in this house. A marriage, a fruitful marriage. That simple thing. Anyone could have had that.

Somehow he felt unable to be indignant or protest, although some sort of joke had certainly been played upon him. There was nothing remote or mysterious here—only something private. The only secret was the ancient communication between two people. But the memory of the woman's waiting silently by the cold hearth, of the man's stubborn journey a mile away to get fire, and how they finally brought out their food and drink and filled the room proudly with all they had to show, was suddenly too clear and too enormous within him for response. . . .

"You ain't as hungry as you look," said Sonny.

The woman came out of the bedroom as soon as the men had finished, and ate her supper while her husband stared peacefully into the fire.

Then they put the dogs out, with the food that was left.

"I think I'd better sleep here by the fire, on the floor," said Bowman.

He felt that he had been cheated, and that he could afford now to be generous. Ill though he was, he was not going to ask them for their bed. He was through with asking favors in this house, now that he understood what was there.

"Sure, mister."

But he had not known yet how slowly he understood. They had not meant to give him their bed. After a little interval they both rose and looking at him gravely went into the other room.

He lay stretched by the fire until it grew low and dying. He watched every tongue of blaze lick out and vanish. "There will be special reduced prices on all footwear during the month of January," he found himself repeating quietly, and then he lay with his lips tight shut.

How many noises the night had! He heard the stream running, the fire dying, and he was sure now that he heard his heart beating, too, the sound it made under his ribs. He heard breathing, round and deep, of the man and his wife in the room across the passage. And that was all. But emotion swelled patiently within him, and he wished that the child were his.

He must get back to where he had been before. He stood weakly before the red coals and put on his overcoat. It felt too heavy on his shoulders. As he started out he looked and saw that the woman had never got through with cleaning the lamp. On some impulse he put all the money from his billfold under its fluted glass base, almost ostentatiously.

Ashamed, shrugging a little, and then shivering, he took his bags and went out. The cold of the air seemed to lift him bodily. The moon was in the sky.

On the slope he began to run, he could not help it. Just as he reached the road, where his car seemed to sit in the moonlight like a boat, his heart began to give off tremendous explosions like a rifle, bang bang bang.

He sank in fright onto the road, his bags falling about him. He felt as if all this had happened before. He covered his heart with both hands to keep anyone from hearing the noise it made.

But nobody heard it.

[1936]

For Thought

In "Death of a Traveling Salesman," Welty employs a technique known as "expressionism," a mode that represents life as a nightmarish experience and the human race's function as a futile quest through a kind of emotional hell. This literary form is characterized by visions and delusions, radical character metamorphoses, and vivid sound and color details and contrasts.

Welty's unlikely hero finds himself journeying into hidden recesses, both of his own mind and of the Southern regional consciousness. His heart has, literally and symbolically, begun to fail him. The proud self-sufficiency of Sonny and his fruitful wife gradually reduce Bowman's surface sophistication to an empty shell. Welty suggests that compassion and charity need deep roots in nature and in nature's rhythms.

For Discussion

1. Summarize the literal narrative at the basis of the impressionistic elements in the story.
2. What foreshadowing of the death of the salesman appears early in the story?
3. How does Welty's point of view paradoxically emphasize both the flatness and the universality of the salesman's character?
4. How are the setting and the atmosphere used to create a mood of frustration, apprehension, and isolation?
5. What elements in the story are comic, or ludicrous? How do they contribute to the story?
6. What is the significance of the name "Beulah"?
7. How does the salesman's palpitating, loud heart take on both literal and symbolic significance?
8. How is money used both at the beginning and at the end of the story as an ironic symbol?
9. What is the critical point in the action; what recognition accompanies it?
10. What does the author accomplish by making Sonny first a son and then a husband and father-to-be?
11. What might be the theme of the story?

Eudora Welty
Lily Daw and the Three Ladies

Mrs. Watts and Mrs. Carson were both in the post office in Victory when the letter came from the Ellisville Institute for the Feeble-Minded of Mississippi. Aimee Slocum, with her hand still full of mail, ran out in front and handed it straight to Mrs. Watts, and they all three read it together. Mrs. Watts held it taut between her pink hands, and Mrs. Carson underscored each line slowly with her thimbled finger. Everybody else in the post office wondered what was up now.

"What will Lily say," beamed Mrs. Carson at last, "when we tell her we're sending her to Ellisville!"

"She'll be tickled to death," said Mrs. Watts, and added in a guttural voice to a deaf lady, "Lily Daw's getting in at Ellisville!"

"Don't you all dare go off and tell Lily without me!" called Aimee Slocum, trotting back to finish putting up the mail.

"Do you suppose they'll look after her down there?" Mrs. Carson began to carry on a conversation with a group of Baptist ladies waiting in the post office. She was the Baptist preacher's wife.

"I've always heard it was lovely down there, but crowded," said one.

"Lily lets people walk over her so," said another.

"Last night at the tent show—" said another, and then popped her hand over her mouth.

"Don't mind me, I know there are such things in the world," said Mrs. Carson, looking down and fingering the tape measure which hung over her bosom.

"Oh, Mrs. Carson. Well, anyway, last night at the tent show, why, the man was just before making Lily buy a ticket to get in."

"A ticket!"

"Till my husband went up and explained she wasn't bright, and so did everybody else."

The ladies all clucked their tongues.

"Oh, it was a very nice show," said the

lady who had gone. "And Lily acted so nice. She was a perfect lady—just set in her seat and stared."

"Oh, she can be a lady—she can be," said Mrs. Carson, shaking her head and turning her eyes up. "That's just what breaks your heart."

"Yes'm, she kept her eyes on—what's that thing makes all the commotion?—the xylophone," said the lady. "Didn't turn her head to the right or to the left the whole time. Set in front of me."

"The point is, what did she do after the show?" asked Mrs. Watts practically. "Lily has gotten so she is very mature for her age."

"Oh, Etta!" protested Mrs. Carson, looking at her wildly for a moment.

"And that's how come we are sending her to Ellisville," finished Mrs. Watts.

"I'm ready, you all," said Aimee Slocum, running out with white powder all over her face. "Mail's up. I don't know how good it's up."

"Well, of course, I do hope it's for the best," said several of the other ladies. They did not go at once to take their mail out of their boxes; they felt a little left out.

The three women stood at the foot of the water tank.

"To find Lily is a different thing," said Aimee Slocum.

"Where in the wide world do you suppose she'd be?" It was Mrs. Watts who was carrying the letter.

"I don't see a sign of her either on this side of the street or on the other side," Mrs. Carson declared as they walked along.

Ed Newton was stringing Redbird school tablets on the wire across the store.

"If you're after Lily, she come in here while ago and tole me she was fixin' to git married," he said.

"Ed Newton!" cried the ladies all together, clutching one another. Mrs. Watts began to fan herself at once with the letter from Ellisville. She wore widow's black, and the least thing made her hot.

"Why she is not. She's going to Ellisville, Ed," said Mrs. Carson gently. "Mrs. Watts and I and Aimee Slocum are paying her way out of our own pockets. Besides, the boys of Victory are on their honor. Lily's not going to get married, that's just an idea she's got in her head."

"More power to you, ladies," said Ed Newton, spanking himself with a tablet.

When they came to the bridge over the railroad tracks, there was Estelle Mabers, sitting on a rail. She was slowly drinking an orange Ne-Hi.

"Have you seen Lily?" they asked her.

"I'm supposed to be out here watching for her now," said the Mabers girl, as though she weren't there yet. "But for Jewel—Jewel says Lily come in the store while ago and picked out a two-ninety-eight hat and wore it off. Jewel wants to swap her something else for it."

"Oh, Estelle, Lily says she's going to get married!" cried Aimee Slocum.

"Well, I declare," said Estelle; she never understood anything.

Loralee Adkins came riding by in her Willys-Knight, tooting the horn to find out what they were talking about.

Aimee threw up her hands and ran out into the street. "Loralee, Loralee, you got to ride us up to Lily Daws'. She's up yonder fixing to get married!"

"Hop in, my land!"

"Well, that just goes to show you right now," said Mrs. Watts, groaning as she was helped into the back seat. "What we've got to do is persuade Lily it will be nicer to go to Ellisville."

"Just to think!"

While they rode around the corner Mrs. Carson was going on in her sad voice, sad as the soft noises in the hen house at twilight. "We buried Lily's poor defenseless mother. We gave Lily all her food and kindling and every stitch she had on. Sent her to Sunday school to learn the Lord's teachings, had her baptized a Baptist. And when her old father commenced beating her and tried to cut her head off with the butcher knife, why, we went and took her away from him and gave her a place to stay."

The paintless frame house with all the weather vanes was three stories high in places and had yellow and violet stained-glass windows in front and gingerbread around the porch. It leaned steeply to one side, toward the railroad, and the front steps were gone. The car full of ladies drew up under the cedar tree.

"Now Lily's almost grown up," Mrs. Carson continued. "In fact, she's grown," she concluded, getting out.

"Talking about getting married," said Mrs. Watts disgustedly. "Thanks, Loralee, you run on home."

They climbed over the dusty zinnias onto the porch and walked through the open door without knocking.

"There certainly is always a funny smell in this house. I say it every time I come," said Aimee Slocum.

Lily was there, in the dark of the hall, kneeling on the floor by a small open trunk.

When she saw them she put a zinnia in her mouth, and held still.

"Hello, Lily," said Mrs. Carson reproachfully.

"Hello," said Lily. In a minute she gave a suck on the zinnia stem that sounded exactly like a jay bird. There she sat, wearing a petticoat for a dress, one of the things Mrs. Carson kept after her about. Her milky-yellow hair streamed freely down from under a new hat. You could see the wavy scar on her throat if you knew it was there.

Mrs. Carson and Mrs. Watts, the two fattest, sat in the double rocker. Aimee Slocum sat on the wire chair donated from the drugstore that burned.

"Well, what are you doing, Lily?" asked Mrs. Watts, who led the rocking.

Lily smiled.

The trunk was old and lined with yellow and brown paper, with an asterisk pattern showing in darker circles and rings. Mutely the ladies indicated to each other that they did not know where in the world it had come from. It was empty except for two bars of soap and a green washcloth, which Lily was now trying to arrange in the bottom.

"Go on and tell us what you're doing, Lily," said Aimee Slocum.

"Packing, silly," said Lily.

"Where are you going?"

"Going to get married, and I bet you wish you was me now," said Lily. But shyness overcame her suddenly, and she popped the zinnia back into her mouth.

"Talk to me, dear," said Mrs. Carson. "Tell old Mrs. Carson why you want to get married."

"No," said Lily, after a moment's hesitation.

"Well, we've thought of something that will be so much nicer," said Mrs. Carson. "Why don't you go to Ellisville!"

"Won't that be lovely?" said Mrs. Watts. "Goodness, yes."

"It's a lovely place," said Aimee Slocum uncertainly.

"You've got bumps on your face," said Lily.

"Aimee, dear, you stay out of this, if you don't mind," said Mrs. Carson anxiously. "I don't know what it is comes over Lily when you come around her."

Lily stared at Aimee Slocum meditatively.

"There! Wouldn't you like to go to Ellisville now?" asked Mrs. Carson.

"No'm," said Lily.

"Why not?" All the ladies leaned down toward her in impressive astonishment.

"'Cause I'm goin' to get married," said Lily.

"Well, and who are you going to marry, dear?" asked Mrs. Watts. She knew how to pin people down and make them deny what they'd already said.

Lily bit her lip and began to smile. She reached into the trunk and held up both cakes of soap and wagged them.

"Tell us," challenged Mrs. Watts. "Who you're going to marry, now."

"A man last night."

There was a gasp from each lady. The possible reality of a lover descended suddenly like a summer hail over their heads. Mrs. Watts stood up and balanced herself.

"One of those show fellows! A musician!" she cried.

Lily looked up in admiration.

"Did he—did he do anything to you?" In the long run, it was still only Mrs. Watts who could take charge.

"Oh, yes'm," said Lily. She patted the cakes of soap fastidiously with the tips of her small fingers and tucked them in with the washcloth.

"What?" demanded Aimee Slocum, rising up and tottering before her scream. "What?" she called out in the hall.

"Don't ask her what," said Mrs. Carson, coming up behind. "Tell me, Lily—just yes or no—are you the same as you were?"

"He had a red coat," said Lily graciously. "He took little sticks and went *ping-pong! ding-dong!*"

"Oh, I think I'm going to faint," said Aimee Slocum, but they said, "No, you're not."

"The xylophone!" cried Mrs. Watts. "The xylophone player! Why, the coward, he ought to be run out of town on a rail!"

"Out of town? He is out of town, by now," cried Aimee. "Can't you read?—the sign in the café—Victory on the ninth, Como on the tenth? He's in Como. Como!"

"All right! We'll bring him back!" cried Mrs. Watts. "He can't get away from me!"

"Hush," said Mrs. Carson. "I don't think it's any use following that line of reasoning at all. It's better in the long run for him to be gone out of our lives for good and all. That kind of a man. He was after Lily's body alone and he wouldn't ever in this world make the poor little thing happy, even if we went out and forced him to marry her like he ought—at the point of a gun."

"Still—" began Aimee, her eyes widening.

"Shut up," said Mrs. Watts. "Mrs. Carson, you're right, I expect."

"This is my hope chest—see?" said Lily politely in the pause that followed. "You haven't even looked at it. I've already got soap and a washrag. And I have my hat—on. What are you all going to give me?"

"Lily," said Mrs. Watts, starting over, "we'll give you lots of gorgeous things if you'll only go to Ellisville instead of getting married."

"What will you give me?" asked Lily.

"I'll give you a pair of hemstitched pillowcases," said Mrs. Carson.

"I'll give you a big caramel cake," said Mrs. Watts.

"I'll give you a souvenir from Jackson—a little toy bank," said Aimee Slocum. "Now will you go?"

"No," said Lily.

"I'll give you a pretty little Bible with your name on it in real gold," said Mrs. Carson.

"What if I was to give you a pink crêpe de Chine brassière with adjustable shoulder straps?" asked Mrs. Watts grimly.

"Oh, Etta."

"Well, she needs it," said Mrs. Watts. "What would they think if she ran all over Ellisville in a petticoat looking like a Fiji?"

"I wish *I* could go to Ellisville," said Aimee Slocum luringly.

"What will they have for me down there?" asked Lily softly.

"Oh! lots of things. You'll have baskets to weave, I expect. . . ." Mrs. Carson looked vaguely at the others.

"Oh, yes indeed, they will let you make all sorts of baskets," said Mrs. Watts; then her voice too trailed off.

"No'm, I'd rather get married," said Lily.

"Lily Daw! Now that's just plain stubbornness!" cried Mrs. Watts. "You almost said you'd go and then you took it back!"

"We've all asked God, Lily," said Mrs.

Carson finally, "and God seemed to tell us—Mr. Carson, too—that the place where you ought to be, so as to be happy, was Ellisville."

Lily looked reverent, but still stubborn.

"We've really just got to get her there—now!" screamed Aimee Slocum all at once. "Suppose—! She can't stay here!"

"Oh, no, no, no," said Mrs. Carson hurriedly. "We mustn't think that."

They sat sunken in despair.

"Could I take my hope chest—to go to Ellisville?" asked Lily shyly, looking at them sidewise.

"Why, yes," said Mrs. Carson blankly.

Silently they rose once more to their feet.

"Oh, if I could just take my hope chest!"

"All the time it was just her hope chest," Aimee whispered.

Mrs. Watts struck her palms together. "It's settled!"

"Praise the fathers," murmured Mrs. Carson.

Lily looked up at them, and her eyes gleamed. She cocked her head and spoke out in a proud imitation of someone—someone utterly unknown.

"O.K.—Toots!"

The ladies had been nodding and smiling and backing away toward the door.

"I think I'd better stay," said Mrs. Carson, stopping in her tracks. "Where—where could she have learned that terrible expression?"

"Pack up," said Mrs. Watts. "Lily Daw is leaving for Ellisville on Number One."

In the station the train was puffing. Nearly everyone in Victory was hanging around waiting for it to leave. The Victory Civic Band had assembled without any orders and was scattered through the crowd. Ed Newton gave false signals to start on his bass horn. A crate full of baby chickens got loose on the platform. Everybody wanted to see Lily all dressed up, but Mrs. Carson and Mrs. Watts had sneaked her into the train from the other side of the tracks.

The two ladies were going to travel as far as Jackson to help Lily change trains and be sure she went in the right direction.

Lily sat between them on the plush seat with her hair combed and pinned up into a knot under a small blue hat which was Jewel's exchange for the pretty one. She wore a traveling dress made out of part of Mrs. Watts's last summer's mourning. Pink straps glowed through. She had a purse and a Bible and a warm cake in a box, all in her lap.

Aimee Slocum had been getting the outgoing mail stamped and bundled. She stood in the aisle of the coach now, tears shaking from her eyes.

"Good-bye, Lily," she said. She was the one who felt things.

"Good-bye, silly," said Lily.

"Oh, dear, I hope they get our telegram to meet her in Ellisville!" Aimee cried sorrowfully, as she thought how far away it was. "And it was so hard to get it all in ten words, too."

"Get off, Aimee, before the train starts and you break your neck," said Mrs. Watts, all settled and waving her dressy fan gaily. "I declare, it's so hot, as soon as we get a few miles out of town I'm going to slip my corset down."

"Oh, Lily, don't cry down there. Just be good, and do what they tell you—it's all because they love you." Aimee drew her mouth down. She was backing away, down the aisle.

Lily laughed. She pointed across Mrs. Carson's bosom out the window toward a man. He had stepped off the train and just stood there, by himself. He was a stranger and wore a cap.

"Look," she said, laughing softly through her fingers.

"Don't—look," said Mrs. Carson very distinctly, as if, out of all she had ever spoken, she would impress these two solemn words upon Lily's soft little brain. She added, "Don't look at anything till you get to Ellisville."

Outside, Aimee Slocum was crying so hard she almost ran into the stranger. He wore a cap and was short and seemed to have on perfume, if such a thing could be.

"Could you tell me, madam," he said, "where a little lady lives in this burg name of Miss Lily Daw?" He lifted his cap—and he had red hair.

"What do you want to know for?" Aimee asked before she knew it.

"Talk louder," said the stranger. He almost whispered, himself.

"She's gone away—she's gone to Ellisville!"

"Gone?"

"Gone to Ellisville!"

"Well, I like that!" The man stuck out his bottom lip and puffed till his hair jumped.

"What business did you have with Lily?" cried Aimee suddenly.

"We was only going to get married, that's all," said the man.

Aimee Slocum started to scream in front of all those people. She almost pointed to the long black box she saw lying on the ground at the man's feet. Then she jumped back in fright.

"The xylophone! The xylophone!" she cried, looking back and forth from the man to the hissing train. Which was more terrible? The bell began to ring hollowly, and the man was talking.

"Did you say Ellisville? That in the state of Mississippi?" Like lightning he had pulled out a red notebook entitled, "Permanent Facts & Data." He wrote down something. "I don't hear well."

Aimee nodded her head up and down, and circled around him.

Under "Ellis-Ville Miss" he was drawing a line; now he was flicking it with two little marks. "Maybe she didn't say she would. Maybe she said she wouldn't." He suddenly laughed very loudly, after the way he had whispered. Aimee jumped back. "Women!—Well, if we play anywheres near Ellisville, Miss., in the future I may look her up and I may not," he said.

The bass horn sounded the true signal for the band to begin. White steam rushed out of the engine. Usually the train stopped for only a minute in Victory, but the engineer knew Lily from waving at her, and he knew this was her big day.

"Wait!" Aimee Slocum did scream. "Wait, mister! I can get her for you. Wait, Mister Engineer! Don't go!"

Then there she was back on the train, screaming in Mrs. Carson's and Mrs. Watts's faces.

"The xylophone player! The xylophone player to marry her! Yonder he is!"

"Nonsense," murmured Mrs. Watts, peering over the others to look where Aimee pointed. "If he's there I don't see him. Where is he? You're looking at One-Eye Beasley."

"The little man with the cap—no, with the red hair! Hurry!"

"Is that really him?" Mrs. Carson asked Mrs. Watts in wonder. "Mercy! He's small, isn't he?"

"Never saw him before in my life!" cried Mrs. Watts. But suddenly she shut up her fan.

"Come on! This is a train we're on!" cried Aimee Slocum. Her nerves were all unstrung.

"All right, don't have a conniption fit, girl," said Mrs. Watts. "Come on," she said thickly to Mrs. Carson.

"Where are we going now?" asked Lily as they struggled down the aisle.

"We're taking you to get married," said Mrs. Watts. "Mrs. Carson, you'd better phone up your husband right there in the station."

"But I don't want to git married," said Lily, beginning to whimper. "I'm going to Ellisville."

"Hush, and we'll all have some ice-cream cones later," whispered Mrs. Carson.

Just as they climbed down the steps at

the back end of the train, the band went into "Independence March."

The xylophone player was still there, patting his foot. He came up and said, "Hello, Toots. What's up—tricks?" and kissed Lily with a smack, after which she hung her head.

"So you're the young man we've heard so much about," said Mrs. Watts. Her smile was brilliant. "Here's your little Lily."

"What say?" asked the xylophone player.

"My husband happens to be the Baptist preacher of Victory," said Mrs. Carson in a loud, clear voice. "Isn't that lucky? I can get him here in five minutes: I know exactly where he is."

They were in a circle around the xylophone player, all going into the white waiting room.

"Oh, I feel just like crying, at a time like this," said Aimee Slocum. She looked back and saw the train moving slowly away, going under the bridge at Main Street. Then it disappeared around the curve.

"Oh, the hope chest!" Aimee cried in a stricken voice.

"And whom have we the pleasure of addressing?" Mrs. Watts was shouting, while Mrs. Carson was ringing up the telephone.

The band went on playing. Some of the people thought Lily was on the train, and some swore she wasn't. Everybody cheered, though, and a straw hat was thrown into the telephone wires.

[1937]

For Thought

In "Lily Daw and the Three Ladies," Welty portrays a brief crisis in the lives of three well-meaning Southern dowagers. The "three ladies" are faced with the sexual maturity of a young, rather simple-minded ward. The primary struggle in the story occurs in the minds of the three women, between their own notions of propriety and their sincere desire for the girl's happiness. A twist in the story brings young Lily both the happiness and the safety so fervently desired by her three guardians.

For Discussion

1. How are the three ladies of the story characterized? Why are they so concerned about Lily Daw?
2. What is Lily Daw's background? From what threats to her life and innocence has she had to be saved?
3. How does Lily combine a simplicity of outlook with honesty and insight?
4. The story's conclusion amounts to a traditional happy ending. How does Welty build suspense? Why would readers accept the ending, unlikely and lacking in credibility as it is?
5. What assumptions about the xylophone player do the three ladies make that are later proven wrong? What strange aspects about the xylophone player ironically make him easier to believe in?
6. How does Welty capture the mood and values of a small Mississippi town?

Eudora Welty
Livvie

Solomon carried Livvie twenty-one miles away from her home when he married her. He carried her away up on the Old Natchez Trace into the deep country to live in his house. She was sixteen—an only girl, then. Once people said he thought nobody would ever come along there. He told her himself that it had been a long time, and a day she did not know about, since that road was a traveled road with *people* coming and going. He was good to her, but he kept her in the house. She had not thought that she could not get back. Where she came from, people said an old man did not want anybody in the world to ever find his wife, for fear they would steal her back from him. Solomon asked her before he took her, "Would she be happy?"—very dignified, for he was a colored man that owned his land and had it written down in the courthouse; and she said, "Yes, sir," since he was an old man and she was young and just listened and answered. He asked her, if she was choosing winter, would she pine for spring, and she said, "No, indeed." Whatever she said, always, was because he was an old man . . . while nine years went by. All the time, he got old, and he got so old he gave out. At last he slept the whole day in bed, and she was young still.

It was a nice house, inside and outside both. In the first place, it had three rooms. The front room was papered in holly paper, with green palmettos from the swamp spaced at careful intervals over the walls. There was fresh newspaper cut with fancy borders on the mantel-shelf, on which were propped photographs of old or very young men printed in faint yellow—Solomon's people. Solomon had a houseful of furniture. There was a double settee, a tall scrolled rocker and an organ in the front room, all around a three-legged table with a pink marble top, on which was set a lamp with three gold feet, besides a jelly glass with pretty hen feathers in it. Behind the front room, the other room had the bright iron bed with the polished knobs like a throne, in which Solomon slept all day. There were snow-white curtains of wiry lace at the window, and a lace bed-spread belonged on the bed. But what old Solomon slept so sound under was a big feather-stitched piece-quilt in the pattern "Trip Around the World," which had twenty-one different colors, four hundred and forty pieces, and a thousand yards of thread, and that was what Solomon's mother made in her life and old age. There was a table holding the Bible, and a trunk with a key. On the wall were two calendars, and a diploma from somewhere in Solomon's family, and under that Livvie's one possession was nailed, a picture of the little white baby of the family she worked for, back in Natchez before she was married. Going through that room and on to the kitchen, there was a big wood stove and a big round table always with a wet top and with the knives and forks in one jelly glass and the spoons in another, and a cut-glass vinegar bottle between, and going out from those, many shallow dishes of pickled peaches, fig preserves, watermelon pickles and blackberry jam always sitting there. The churn sat in the sun, the doors of the safe were always both shut, and there were four baited mouse-traps in the kitchen, one in every corner.

The outside of Solomon's house looked nice. It was not painted, but across the porch was an even balance. On each side there was one easy chair with high springs, looking out, and a fern basket hanging over it from the ceiling, and a dishpan of zinnia seedlings growing at its foot on the floor. By the door was a plow-wheel, just a pretty iron circle, nailed up on one wall and a square mirror on the other, a turquoise-blue comb stuck up in the frame, with the wash stand beneath it. On the door was a wooden knob with a pearl in the end, and Solomon's black hat hung on that, if he was in the house.

Out front was a clean dirt yard with every vestige of grass patiently uprooted and the ground scarred in deep whorls from the strike of Livvie's broom. Rose bushes with tiny blood-red roses blooming every month grew in threes on either side of the steps. On one side was a peach tree, on the other a pomegranate. Then coming around up the path from the deep cut of the Natchez Trace below was a line of bare crape-myrtle trees with every branch of them ending in a colored bottle, green or blue. There was no word that fell from Solomon's lips to say what they were for, but Livvie knew that there could be a spell put in trees, and she was familiar from the time she was born with the way bottle trees kept evil spirits from coming into the house—by luring them inside the colored bottles, where they cannot get out again. Solomon had made the bottle trees with his own hands over the nine years, in labor amounting to about a tree a year, and without a sign that he had any uneasiness in his heart, for he took as much pride in his precautions against spirits coming in the house as he took in the house, and sometimes in the sun the bottle trees looked prettier than the house did.

It was a nice house. It was in a place where the days would go by and surprise anyone that they were over. The lamplight and the firelight would shine out the door after dark, over the still and breathing country, lighting the roses and the bottle trees, and all was quiet there.

But there was nobody, nobody at all, not even a white person. And if there had been anybody, Solomon would not have let Livvie look at them, just as he would not let her look at a field hand, or a field hand look at her. There was no house near, except for the cabins of the tenants that were forbidden to her, and there was no house as far as she had been, stealing away down the still, deep Trace. She felt as if she waded a river when she went, for the dead leaves on the ground reached as high as her knees, and when she was all scratched and bleeding she said it was not like a road that went anywhere. One day, climbing up the high bank, she had found a graveyard without a church, with ribbon-grass growing about the foot of an angel (she had climbed up because she thought she saw angel wings), and in the sun, trees shining like burning flames through the great caterpillar nets which enclosed them. Scarey thistles stood looking like the prophets in the Bible in Solomon's house. Indian paint brushes grew over her head, and the mourning dove made the only sound in the world. Oh for a stirring of the leaves, and a breaking of the nets! But not by a ghost, prayed Livvie, jumping down the bank. After Solomon took to his bed, she never went out, except one more time.

Livvie knew she made a nice girl to wait on anybody. She fixed things to eat on a tray like a surprise. She could keep from singing when she ironed, and to sit by a bed and fan away the flies, she could be so still she could not hear herself breathe. She could clean up the house and never drop a thing, and wash the dishes without a sound, and she would step outside to churn, for churning sounded too sad to her, like sobbing, and if it made her home-sick and not Solomon, she did not think of that.

But Solomon scarcely opened his eyes to see her, and scarcely tasted his food. He was not sick or paralyzed or in any pain that he mentioned, but he was surely wearing out in the body, and no matter what nice hot thing Livvie would bring him to taste, he would only look at it now, as if he were past seeing how he could add anything more to himself. Before she could beg him, he would go fast asleep. She could not surprise him any more, if he would not taste, and she was afraid that he was never in the world going to taste another thing she brought him—and so how could he last?

But one morning it was breakfast time and she cooked his eggs and grits, carried them in on a tray, and called his name. He was sound asleep. He lay in a dignified way with his watch beside him, on his back in the middle of the bed. One hand drew the quilt up high, though it was the first day of spring. Through the white lace curtains a little puffy wind was blowing as if it came from round cheeks. All night the frogs had sung out in the swamp, like a commotion in the room, and he had not stirred, though she lay wide awake and saying "Shh, frogs!" for fear he would mind them.

He looked as if he would like to sleep a little longer, and so she put back the tray and waited a little. When she tiptoed and stayed so quiet, she surrounded herself with a little reverie, and sometimes it seemed to her when she was so stealthy that the quiet she kept was for a sleeping baby, and that she had a baby and was its mother. When she stood at Solomon's bed and looked down at him, she would be thinking. "He sleeps so well," and she would hate to wake him up. And in some other way, too, she was afraid to wake him up because even in his sleep he seemed to be such a strict man.

Of course, nailed to the wall over the bed—only she would forget who it was—there was a picture of him when he was young. Then he had a fan of hair over his forehead like a king's crown. Now his hair lay down on his head, the spring had gone out of it. Solomon had a lightish face, with eyebrows scattered but rugged, the way privet grows, strong eyes, with second sight, a strict mouth, and a little gold smile. This was the way he looked in his clothes, but in bed in the daytime he looked like a different and smaller man, even when he was wide awake, and holding the Bible. He looked like somebody kin to himself. And then sometimes when he lay in sleep and she stood fanning the flies away, and the light came in, his face was like new, so smooth and clear that it was like a glass of jelly held to the window, and she could almost look through his forehead and see what he thought.

She fanned him and at length he opened his eyes and spoke her name, but he would not taste the nice eggs she had kept warm under a pan.

Back in the kitchen she ate heartily, his breakfast and hers, and looked out the open door at what went on. The whole day, and the whole night before, she had felt the stir of spring close to her. It was as present in the house as a young man would be. The moon was in the last quarter and outside they were turning the sod and planting peas and beans. Up and down the red fields, over which smoke from the brush-burning hung showing like a little skirt of sky, a white horse and a white mule pulled the plow. At intervals hoarse shouts came through the air and roused her as if she dozed neglectfully in the shade, and they were telling her, "Jump up!" She could see how over each ribbon of field were moving men and girls, on foot and mounted on mules, with hats set on their heads and bright with tall hoes and forks as if they carried streamers on them and were going to some place on a journey—and how as if at a signal now and then they would all start at once shouting, hollering, cajoling, calling and answering back, running, being leaped on and breaking away, flinging to earth with a shout and lying motionless in the trance of twelve o'clock. The old women came out of the cabins and brought them the food they had ready for them, and then all worked together, spread evenly out. The little children came too, like a bouncing stream overflowing the fields, and set upon the men, the women, the dogs, the rushing birds, and the wave-like rows of earth, their little voices almost too high to be heard. In the middle distance like some white and gold towers were the haystacks, with black cows coming around to eat their edges. High above everything, the wheel of fields, house, and cabins, and the deep road surrounding like a moat to keep them in, was the turning sky, blue with long, far-flung white mare's-tail clouds, serene and still as high flames. And sound asleep while all this went around him that was his, Solomon was like a little still spot in the middle.

Even in the house the earth was sweet to breathe. Solomon had never let Livvie go any farther than the chicken house and the well. But what if she would walk now into the heart of the fields and take a hoe and work until she fell stretched out and drenched with her efforts, like other girls, and laid her cheek against the laid-open earth, and shamed the old man with her humbleness and delight? To shame him! A cruel wish could come in uninvited and so fast while she looked out the back door. She washed the dishes and scrubbed the table. She could hear the cries of the little lambs. Her mother, that she had not seen since her wedding day, had said one time, "I rather a man be anything, than a woman be mean."

So all morning she kept tasting the chicken broth on the stove, and when it was right she poured off a nice cup-ful. She carried it in to Solomon, and there he lay having a dream. Now what did he dream about? For she saw him sigh gently as if not to disturb some whole thing he held round in his mind, like a fresh egg. So even an old man dreamed about something pretty. Did he dream of her, while his eyes were shut and sunken, and his small hand with the wedding ring curled close in sleep around the quilt? He might be dreaming of what time it was, for even through his sleep he kept track of it like a clock, and knew how much of it went by, and waked up knowing where the hands were even before he consulted the silver watch that he never let go. He would sleep with the watch in his palm, and even holding it to his cheek like a child that loves a plaything. Or he might dream of journeys and travels on a steamboat to Natchez. Yet she thought he dreamed of her; but even while she scrutinized him, the rods of the foot of the bed seemed to rise up like a rail fence between them, and she could see that people never could be sure of anything as long as one of them was asleep and the other awake. To look at him dreaming of her when he might be going to die frightened her a little, as if he might carry her with him that way, and she wanted to run out of the room. She took hold of the bed and held on, and Solomon opened his eyes and called her name, but he did not want anything. He would not taste the good broth.

Just a little after that, as she was taking up the ashes in the front room for the last time in the year, she heard a sound. It was somebody coming. She pulled the curtains together and looked through the slit.

Coming up the path under the bottle trees was a white lady. At first she looked young, but then she looked old. Marvelous to see, a little car stood steaming like a kettle out in the field-track—it had come without a road.

Livvie stood listening to the long, repeated knockings at the door, and after a while she opened it just a little. The lady came in through the crack, though she was more than middle-sized and wore a big hat.

"My name is Miss Baby Marie," she said.

Livvie gazed respectfully at the lady and at the little suitcase she was holding close to her by the handle until the proper moment. The lady's eyes were running over the room, from palmetto to palmetto, but she was saying, "I live at home . . . out from Natchez . . . and get out and show these pretty cosmetic things to the white people and the colored people both . . . all around . . . years and years. . . . Both shades of powder and rouge . . . It's the kind of work a girl can do and not go clear 'way from home . . ." And the harder she looked, the more she talked. Suddenly she turned up her nose and said, "It is not Christian or sanitary to put feathers in a vase," and then she took a gold key out of the front of her dress and began unlocking the locks on her suitcase. Her face drew the light, the way it was covered with intense white and red, with a little patty-cake of white between the wrinkles by her upper lip. Little red tassels of hair bobbed under the rusty wires of her picture-hat, as with an air of triumph and secrecy she now drew open her little suitcase and brought out bottle after bottle and jar after jar, which she put down on the table, the mantel-piece, the settee, and the organ.

"Did you ever see so many cosmetics in your life?" cried Miss Baby Marie.

"No'm," Livvie tried to say, but the cat had her tongue.

"Have you ever applied cosmetics?" asked Miss Baby Marie next.

"No'm," Livvie tried to say.

"Then look!" she said, and pulling out the last thing of all, "Try this!" she said. And in her hand was unclenched a golden lipstick which popped open like magic. A fragrance came out of it like incense, and Livvie cried out suddently, "Chinaberry flowers!"

Her hand took the lipstick, and in an instant she was carried away in the air through the spring, and looking down with a half-drowsy smile from a purple cloud she saw from above a chinaberry tree, dark and smooth and neatly leaved, neat as a guinea hen in the dooryard, and there was her home that she had left. On one side of the tree was her mama holding up her heavy apron, and she could see it was loaded with ripe figs, and on the other side was her papa holding a fish-pole over the pond, and she could see it transparently, the little clear fishes swimming up to the brim.

"Oh, no, not chinaberry flowers—secret ingredients," said Miss Baby Marie. "My cosmetics have secret ingredients—not chinaberry flowers."

"It's purple," Livvie breathed, and Miss Baby Marie said, "Use it freely. Rub it on."

Livvie tiptoed out to the wash stand on the front porch and before the mirror put the paint on her mouth. In the wavery surface her face danced before her like a flame. Miss Baby Marie followed her out, took a look at what she had done, and said, "That's it."

Livvie tried to say "Thank you" without moving her parted lips where the paint lay so new.

By now Miss Baby Marie stood behind Livvie and looked in the mirror over her shoulder, twisting up the tassels of her hair. "The lipstick I can let you have for only two dollars," she said, close to her neck.

"Lady, but I don't have no money, never did have," said Livvie.

"Oh, but you don't pay the first time. I make another trip, that's the way I do. I come back again—later."

"Oh" said Livvie, pretending she understood everything so as to please the lady.

"But if you don't take it now, this may be the last time I'll call at your house," said Miss Baby Marie sharply. "It's far away from anywhere, I'll tell you that. You don't live close to anywhere."

"Yes'm. My husband, he keep the *money*," said Livvie, trembling. "He is strict as he can be. He don't know *you* walk in here—Miss Baby Marie!"

"Where is he?"

"Right now, he in yonder sound asleep, an old man. I wouldn't ever ask him for anything."

Miss Baby Marie took back the lipstick and packed it up. She gathered up the jars for both black and white and got them all inside the suitcase, with the same little fuss of triumph with which she had brought them out. She started away.

"Goodbye," she said, making herself look grand from the back, but at the last minute she turned around in the door. Her old hat wobbled as she whispered, "Let me see your husband."

Livvie obediently went on tiptoe and opened the door to the other room. Miss Baby Marie came behind her and rose on her toes and looked in.

"My, what a little tiny old, old man!" she whispered, clasping her hands and shaking her head over them. "What a beautiful quilt! What a tiny old, old man!"

"He can sleep like that all day," whispered Livvie proudly.

They looked at him awhile so fast asleep, and then all at once they looked at each other. Somehow that was as if they had a secret, for he had never stirred. Livvie then politely, but all at once, closed the door.

"Well! I'd certainly like to leave you with a lipstick!" said Miss Baby Marie vivaciously. She smiled in the door.

"Lady, but I told you I don't have no money, and never did have."

"And never will?" In the air and all around, like a bright halo around the white lady's nodding head, it was a true spring day.

"Would you take eggs, lady?" asked Livvie softly.

"No, I have plenty of eggs—plenty," said Miss Baby Marie.

"I still don't have no money," said Livvie, and Miss Baby Marie took her suitcase and went on somewhere else.

Livvie stood watching her go, and all the time she felt her heart beating in her left side. She touched the place with her hand. It seemed as if her heart beat and her whole face flamed from the pulsing color of her lips. She went to sit by Solomon and when he opened his eyes he could not see a change in her. "He's fixin' to die," she said inside. That was the secret. That was when she went out of the house for a little breath of air.

She went down the path and down the Natchez Trace a way, and she did not know how far she had gone, but it was not far, when she saw a sight. It was a man, looking like a vision—she standing on one side of the Old Natchez Trace and he standing on the other.

As soon as this man caught sight of her, he began to look himself over. Starting at the bottom with his pointed shoes, he began to look up, lifting his peg-top pants the higher to see fully his bright socks. His coat long and wide and leafgreen he opened like doors to see his high-up tawny pants and his pants he smoothed downward from the points of his collar, and he wore a luminous baby-pink satin shirt. At the end, he reached gently above his wide platter-shaped round hat, the color of a plum, and one finger touched at the feather, emerald green, blowing in the spring winds.

No matter how she looked, she could never look so fine as he did, and she was not sorry for that, she was pleased.

He took three jumps, one down and two up, and was by her side.

"My name is Cash," he said.

He had a guinea pig in his pocket. They began to walk along. She stared on and on at him, as if he were doing some daring spectacular thing, instead of just walking beside her. It was not simply the city way he was dressed that made her look at him and see hope in its insolence looking back. It was not only the way he moved along kicking the flowers as if he could break through everything in the way and destroy anything in the world, that made her eyes grow bright. It might be, if he had not appeared the way he did appear that day she would never have looked so closely at him, but the time people come makes a difference.

They walked through the still leaves of the Natchez Trace, the light and the shade falling through trees about them, the white irises shining like candles on the banks and the new ferns shining like green stars up in the oak branches. They came out at Solomon's house, bottle trees and all. Livvie stopped and hung her head.

Cash began whistling a little tune. She did not know what it was, but she had heard it before from a distance, and she had a revelation. Cash was a field hand. He was a transformed field hand. Cash belonged to Solomon. But he had stepped out of his overalls into this. There in front of Solomon's house he laughed. He had a round head, a round face, all of him was young, and he flung his head up, rolled it against the mare's-tail sky in his round hat, and he could laugh just to see Solomon's house sitting there. Livvie looked at it, and there was Solomon's black hat hanging on the peg on the front door, the blackest thing in the world.

"I been to Natchez," Cash said, wagging his head around against the sky. "*I* taken a trip, *I* ready for Easter!"

How was it possible to look so fine before the harvest? Cash must have stolen the money, stolen it from Solomon. He stood in the path and lifted his spread hand high and brought it down again and again in his laughter. He kicked up his heels. A little chill went through her. It was as if Cash was bringing that strong hand down to beat a drum or to rain blows upon a man, such an abandon and menace were in his laugh. Frowning, she went closer to him and his swinging arm drew her in at once and the fright was crushed from her body, as a little match-flame might be smothered out by what it lighted. She gathered the folds of his coat behind him and fastened her red lips to his mouth, and she was dazzled by herself then, the way he had been dazzled at himself to begin with.

In that instant she felt something that could not be told—that Solomon's death was at hand, that he was the same to her as if he were dead now. She cried out, and uttering little cries turned and ran for the house.

At once Cash was coming, following after, he was running behind her. He came close, and halfway up the path he laughed and passed her. He even picked up a stone and sailed it into the bottle trees. She put her hands over her head, and sounds clattered through the bottle trees like cries of outrage. Cash stamped and plunged zigzag up the front steps and in at the door.

When she got there, he had stuck his hands in his pockets and was turning slowing about in the front room. The little guinea pig peeped out. Around Cash, the pinned-up palmettos looked as if a lazy green monkey had walked up and down and around the walls leaving green prints of his hands and feet.

She got through the room and his hands were still in his pockets, and she fell upon the closed door to the other room and pushed it open. She ran to Solomon's bed, calling, "Solomon! Solomon!" The little shape of the old man never moved at all, wrapped under the quilt as if it were winter still.

"Solomon!" She pulled the quilt away, but there was another one under that, and she fell on her knees beside him. He made no sound except a sigh, and then she could hear in the silence the light springy steps of Cash walking and walking in the front room, and the ticking of Solomon's silver watch, which came from the bed. Old Solomon was far away in his sleep, his face looked small, relentless, and devout, as if he were walking somewhere where she could imagine the snow falling

Then there was a noise like a hoof pawing the floor, and the door gave a creak, and Cash appeared beside her. When she looked up, Cash's face was so black it was bright, and so bright and bare of pity that it looked sweet to her. She stood up and held up her head. Cash was so powerful that his presence gave her strength even when she did not need any.

Under their eyes Solomon slept. People's faces tell of things and places not known to the one who looks at them while they sleep, and while Solomon slept under the eyes of Livvie and Cash his face told them like a mythical story that all his life he had built, little scrap by little scrap, respect. A beetle could not have been more laborious or more ingenious in the task of its destiny. When Solomon was young, as he was in his picture overhead, it was the infinite thing with him, and he could see no end to the respect he would contrive and keep in a house. He had built a lonely house, the way he would make a cage, but it grew to be the same with him as a great monumental pyramid and sometimes in his absorption of getting it erected he was like the builder-slaves of Egypt who forgot or never knew the origin and meaning of the thing to which they gave all the strength of their bodies and used up all their days. Livvie and Cash could see that as a man might rest from a life-labor he lay in his bed, and they could hear how, wrapped in his quilt, he sighed to himself comfortably in sleep, while in his dreams he might have been an ant, a beetle, a bird, an Egyptian, assembling and carrying on his back and building with his hands, or he might have been an old man of India or a swaddled baby, about to smile and brush all away.

Then without warning old Solomon's eyes flew wide open under the hedge-like brows. He was wide awake.

And instantly Cash raised his quick arm. A radiant sweat stood on his temples. But he did not bring his arm down—it stayed in the air, as if something might have taken hold.

It was not Livvie—she did not move. As if something said "Wait," she stood waiting. Even while her eyes burned under motionless lids, her lips parted in a stiff grimace, and with her arms stiff at her sides she stood above the prone old man and the panting young one, erect and apart.

Movement when it came came in Solomon's face. It was an old and strict face, a frail face, but behind it, like a covered light, came an animation that could play hide and seek, that would dart and escape, had always escaped. The mystery flickered in him, and invited from his eyes. It was that very mystery that Cash with his quick arm would have to strike, and that Livvie could not weep for. But Cash only stood holding his arm in the air, when the gentlest flick of his great strength, almost a puff of his breath, would have been enough, if he had known how to give it, to send the old man over the obstruction that kept him away from death.

If it could not be that the tiny illumination in the fragile and ancient face caused a crisis, a mystery in the room that would not permit a blow to fall, at least it was certain that Cash, throbbing in his Easter clothes, felt a pang of shame that the vigor of a man would come to such an end that he could not be struck without warning. He took down his hand and stepped back behind Livvie, like a round-eyed schoolboy on whose unsuspecting head the dunce cap has been set.

"Young ones can't wait," said Solomon.

Livvie shuddered violently, and then in a gush of tears she stooped for a glass of water and handed it to him, but he did not see her.

"So here come the young man Livvie wait for. Was no prevention. No prevention. Now I lay eyes on young man and it come to be somebody I know all the time, and been knowing since he were born in a cotton patch, and watched grow up year to year, Cash McCord, growed to size, growed up to come in my house in the end—ragged and barefoot."

Solomon gave a cough of distaste. Then he shut his eyes vigorously, and his lips began to move like a chanter's.

"When Livvie married, her husband were already somebody. He had paid great cost for his land. He spread leaves over the ground from wagon to door, day he brought her home, so her foot would not have to touch ground. He carried her through his door. Then he growed old and could not lift her, and she were still young."

Livvie's sobs followed his words like a soft melody repeating each thing as he stated it. His lips moved for a little without sound, or she cried too fervently, and unheard he might have been telling his whole life, and then he said, "God forgive Solomon for sins great and small. God forgive Solomon for carrying away too young girl for wife and keeping her away from her people and from all the young people would clamor for her back."

Then he lifted up his right hand toward Livvie where she stood by the bed and offered her his silver watch. He dangled it before her eyes, and she hushed crying; her tears stopped. For a moment the watch could be heard ticking as it always did, precisely in his proud hand. She lifted it away. Then he took hold of the quilt; then he was dead.

Livvie left Solomon dead and went out of the room. Stealthily, nearly without noise, Cash went beside her. He was like a shadow, but his shiny shoes moved over the floor in spangles, and the green downy feather shone like a light in his hat. As they reached the front room, he seized her deftly as a long black cat and dragged her hanging by the waist round and round him, while he turned in a circle, his face bent down to hers. The first moment, she kept one arm and its hand stiff and still, the one that held Solomon's watch. Then the fingers softly let go, all of her was limp, and the watch fell somewhere on the floor. It ticked away in the still room, and all at once there began outside the full song of a bird.

They moved around and around the room and into the brightness of the open door, then he stopped and shook her once. She rested in silence in his trembling arms, unprotesting as a bird on a nest. Outside the redbirds were flying and crisscrossing, the sun was in all the bottles on the prisoned trees, and the young peach was shining in the middle of them with the bursting light of spring.

[1942]

For Thought

"Livvie" focuses on a conflict that is usually considered comic or bawdy: the contest between an old man and a young man for a young woman. Welty, however, is more interested in Livvie's growing maturity and awareness than in the triangle that develops. At the same time, the story evokes the rich traditions of a South where ties to family, the soil, and past traditions are still strong. The denouement of the story occurs with an acceptance of the natural processes, in which the old prepare the way for the young.

For Discussion

1. How does Welty idealize the situation of an old man marrying a young woman, only to see her leave him for a young man?
2. What contrast does Welty draw between Solomon and Livvie?
3. What precautions does Solomon take to ensure Livvie's faithfulness to him?
4. How is Livvie characterized? Consider the various stages of her developing awareness of her situation.
5. How does Welty describe the setting of the story? How is it idealized?
6. How does the arrival of Miss Baby Marie coincide with and nudge along a change in Livvie?
7. How is Livvie's meeting with Cash McCord an ironic last stage in her growth toward maturity? Consider his symbolic name, his appearance, and Solomon's attempt to isolate Livvie from other people.
8. How is Solomon's reaction to seeing Livvie and Cash together ironic? Consider the watch symbolism.

Edith Wharton
The Other Two

I

Waythorn, on the drawing-room hearth, waited for his wife to come down to dinner.

It was their first night under his own roof, and he was surprised at his thrill of boyish agitation. He was not so old, to be sure—his glass gave him little more than the five-and-thirty years to which his wife confessed—but he had fancied himself already in the temperate zone; yet here he was listening for her step with a tender sense of all it symbolized, with some old trail of verse about the garlanded nuptial doorposts floating through his enjoyment of the pleasant room and the good dinner just beyond it.

They had been hastily recalled from their honeymoon by the illness of Lily Haskett, the child of Mrs. Waythorn's first marriage. The little girl, at Waythorn's desire, had been transferred to his house on the day of her mother's wedding, and the doctor, on their arrival, broke the news that she was ill with typhoid, but declared that all the symptoms were favorable. Lily could show twelve years of unblemished health, and the case promised to be a light one. The nurse spoke as reassuringly, and after a moment of alarm Mrs. Waythorn had adjusted herself to the situation. She was very fond of Lily—her affection for the child had perhaps been her decisive charm in Waythorn's eyes—but she had the perfectly balanced nerves which her little girl had inherited, and no woman ever wasted less tissue in unproductive worry. Waythorn was therefore quite prepared to see her come in presently, a little late because of a last look at Lily, but as serene and well-appointed as if her goodnight kiss had been laid on the brow of health. Her composure was restful to him; it acted as ballast to his somewhat unstable sensibilities. As he pictured her bending over the child's bed he thought how soothing her presence must be in illness: her very step would prognosticate recovery.

His own life had been a gray one, from temperament rather than circumstance, and he had been drawn to her by the unperturbed gaiety which kept her fresh and elastic at an age when most women's activ-

SOURCE: "The Other Two" by Edith Wharton. Originally collected in *The Descent of Man and Other Stories*, Charles Scribner's, 1904.

ities are growing either slack or febrile. He knew what was said about her; for, popular as she was, there had always been a faint undercurrent of detraction. When she had appeared in New York, nine or ten years earlier, as the pretty Mrs. Haskett whom Gus Varick had unearthed somewhere—was it in Pittsburg or Utica?—society, while promptly accepting her, had reserved the right to cast a doubt on its own indiscrimination. Inquiry, however, established her undoubted connection with a socially reigning family, and explained her recent divorce as the natural result of a runaway match at seventeen; and as nothing was known of Mr. Haskett it was easy to believe the worst of him.

Alice Haskett's remarriage with Gus Varick was a passport to the set whose recognition she coveted, and for a few years the Varicks were the most popular couple in town. Unfortunately the alliance was brief and stormy, and this time the husband had his champions. Still, even Varick's stanchest supporters admitted that he was not meant for matrimony, and Mrs. Varick's grievances were of a nature to bear the inspection of the New York courts. A New York divorce is in itself a diploma of virtue, and in the semiwidowhood of this second separation Mrs. Varick took on an air of sanctity, and was allowed to confide her wrongs to some of the most scrupulous ears in town. But when it was known that she was to marry Waythorn there was a momentary reaction. Her best friends would have preferred to see her remain in the role of the injured wife, which was as becoming to her as crepe to a rosy complexion. True, a decent time had elapsed, and it was not even suggested that Waythorn had supplanted his predecessor. People shook their heads over him, however, and one grudging friend, to whom he affirmed that he took the step with his eyes open, replied oracularly: "Yes—and with your ears shut."

Waythorn could afford to smile at these innuendoes. In the Wall Street phrase, he had "discounted" them. He knew that society has not yet adapted itself to the consequences of divorce, and that till the adaptation takes place every woman who uses the freedom the law accords her must be her own social justification. Waythorn had an amused confidence in his wife's ability to justify herself. His expectations were fulfilled, and before the wedding took place Alice Varick's group had rallied openly to her support. She took it all imperturbably: she had a way of surmounting obstacles without seeming to be aware of them, and Waythorn looked back with wonder at the trivialities over which he had worn his nerves thin. He had the sense of having found refuge in a richer, warmer nature than his own, and his satisfaction, at the moment, was humorously summed up in the thought that his wife, when she had done all she could for Lily, would not be ashamed to come down and enjoy a good dinner.

The anticipation of such enjoyment was not, however, the sentiment expressed by Mrs. Waythorn's charming face when she presently joined him. Though she had put on her most engaging tea gown she had neglected to assume the smile that went with it, and Waythorn thought he had never seen her look so nearly worried.

"What is it?" he asked. "Is anything wrong with Lily?"

"No; I've just been in and she's still sleeping." Mrs. Waythorn hesitated. "But something tiresome has happened."

He had taken her two hands, and now perceived that she was crushing a paper between them.

"This letter?"

"Yes—Mr. Haskett has written—I mean his lawyer has written."

Waythorn felt himself flush uncomfortably. He dropped his wife's hands.

"What about?"

"About seeing Lily. You know the courts—"

"Yes, yes," he interrupted nervously.

Nothing was known about Haskett in

New York. He was vaguely supposed to have remained in the outer darkness from which his wife had been rescued, and Waythorn was one of the few who were aware that he had given up his business in Utica and followed her to New York in order to be near his little girl. In the days of his wooing, Waythorn had often met Lily on the doorstep, rosy and smiling, on her way "to see papa."

"I am so sorry," Mrs. Waythorn murmured.

He roused himself. "What does he want?"

"He wants to see her. You know she goes to him once a week."

"Well—he doesn't expect her to go to him now, does he?"

"No—he has heard of her illness; but he expects to come here."

"*Here?*"

Mrs. Waythorn reddened under his gaze. They looked away from each other.

"I'm afraid he has the right. . . . You'll see. . . ." She made a proffer of the letter.

Waythorn moved away with a gesture of refusal. He stood staring about the softly-lighted room, which a moment before had seemed so full of bridal intimacy.

"I'm so sorry," she repeated. "If Lily could have been moved—"

"That's out of the question," he returned impatiently.

"I suppose so."

Her lip was beginning to tremble, and he felt himself a brute.

"He must come, of course," he said. "When is—his day?"

"I'm afraid—tomorrow."

"Very well. Send a note in the morning."

The butler entered to announce dinner.

Waythorn turned to his wife. "Come—you must be tired. It's beastly, but try to forget about it," he said, drawing her hand through his arm.

"You're so good, dear. I'll try," she whispered back.

Her face cleared at once, and as she looked at him across the flowers, between the rosy candleshades, he saw her lips waver back into a smile.

"How pretty everything is!" she sighed luxuriously.

He turned to the butler. "The champagne at once, please. Mrs. Waythorn is tired."

In a moment or two their eyes met above the sparkling glasses. Her own were quite clear and untroubled: he saw that she had obeyed his injunction and forgotten.

II

Waythorn, the next morning, went downtown earlier than usual. Haskett was not likely to come till the afternoon, but the instinct of flight drove him forth. He meant to stay away all day—he had thoughts of dining at his club. As his door closed behind him he reflected that before he opened it again it would have admitted another man who had as much right to enter it as himself, and the thought filled him with a physical repugnance.

He caught the elevated at the employees' hour, and found himself crushed between two layers of pendulous humanity. At Eighth Street the man facing him wriggled out, and another took his place. Waythorn glanced up and saw that it was Gus Varick. The men were so close together that it was impossible to ignore the smile of recognition on Varick's handsome overblown face. And after all—why not? They had always been on good terms, and Varick had been divorced before Waythorn's attentions to his wife began. The two exchanged a word on the perennial grievance of the congested trains, and when a seat at their side was miraculously left empty the instinct of self-preservation made Waythorn slip into it after Varick.

The latter drew the stout man's breath of relief. "Lord—I was beginning to feel like a pressed flower." He leaned back, looking unconcernedly at Waythorn.

"Sorry to hear that Sellers is knocked out again."

"Sellers?" echoed Waythorn, starting at his partner's name.

Varick looked surprised. "You didn't know he was laid up with the gout?"

"No. I've been away—I only got back last night." Waythorn felt himself reddening in anticipation of the other's smile.

"Ah—yes; to be sure. And Sellers' attack came on two days ago. I'm afraid he's pretty bad. Very awkward for me, as it happens, because he was just putting through a rather important thing for me."

"Ah?" Waythorn wondered vaguely since when Varick had been dealing in "important things." Hitherto he had dabbled only in the shallow pools of speculation, with which Waythorn's office did not usually concern itself.

It occurred to him that Varick might be talking at random, to relieve the strain of their propinquity. That strain was becoming momentarily more apparent to Waythorn, and when, at Cortlandt Street, he caught sight of an acquaintance and had a sudden vision of the picture he and Varick must present to an initiated eye, he jumped up with a muttered excuse.

"I hope you'll find Sellers better," said Varick civilly, and he stammered back: "If I can be of any use to you—" and let the departing crowd sweep him to the platform.

At his office he heard that Sellers was in fact ill with the gout, and would probably not be able to leave the house for some weeks.

"I'm sorry it should have happened so, Mr. Waythorn," the senior clerk said with affable significance. "Mr. Sellers was very much upset at the idea of giving you such a lot of extra work just now."

"Oh, that's no matter," said Waythorn hastily. He secretly welcomed the pressure of additional business, and was glad to think that, when the day's work was over, he would have to call at his partner's on the way home.

He was late for luncheon, and turned in at the nearest restaurant instead of going to his club. The place was full, and the waiter hurried him to the back of the room to capture the only vacant table. In the cloud of cigar smoke Waythorn did not at once distinguish his neighbors: but presently, looking about him, he saw Varick seated a few feet off. This time, luckily, they were too far apart for conversation, and Varick, who faced another way, had probably not even seen him; but there was an irony in their renewed nearness.

Varick was said to be fond of good living, and as Waythorn sat dispatching his hurried luncheon he looked across half enviously at the other's leisurely degustation of his meal. When Waythorn first saw him he had been helping himself with critical deliberation to a bit of Camembert at the ideal point of liquefaction, and now, the cheese removed, he was just pouring his *café double* from its little two-storied earthen pot. He poured slowly, his ruddy profile bent over the task, and one beringed white hand steadying the lid of the coffee-pot; then he stretched his other hand to the decanter of cognac at his elbow, filled a liqueur glass, took a tentative sip, and poured the brandy into his coffee cup.

Waythorn watched him in a kind of fascination. What was he thinking of—only of the flavor of the coffee and the liqueur? Had the morning's meeting left no more trace in his thoughts than on his face? Had his wife so completely passed out of his life that even this odd encounter with her present husband, within a week after her remarriage, was no more than an incident in his day? And as Waythorn mused, another idea struck him: had Haskett ever met Varick as Varick and he had just met? The recollection of Haskett perturbed him, and he rose and left the restaurant, taking a circuitous way out to escape the placid irony of Varick's nod.

It was after seven when Waythorn reached home. He thought the footman who opened the door looked at him oddly.

"How is Miss Lily?" he asked in haste.

"Doing very well, sir. A gentleman—"

"Tell Barlow to put off dinner for half an hour," Waythorn cut him off, hurrying upstairs.

He went straight to his room and dressed without seeing his wife. When he reached the drawing room she was there, fresh and radiant. Lily's day had been good; the doctor was not coming back that evening.

At dinner Waythorn told her of Sellers' illness and of the resulting complications. She listened sympathetically, adjuring him not to let himself be overworked, and asking vague feminine questions about the routine of the office. Then she gave him the chronicle of Lily's day; quoted the nurse and doctor, and told him who had called to inquire. He had never seen her more serene and unruffled. It struck him, with a curious pang, that she was very happy in being with him, so happy that she found a childish pleasure in rehearsing the trivial incidents of her day.

After dinner they went to the library, and the servant put the coffee and liqueurs on a low table before her and left the room. She looked singularly soft and girlish in her rosy-pale dress, against the dark leather of one of his bachelor armchairs. A day earlier the contrast would have charmed him.

He turned away now, choosing a cigar with affected deliberation.

"Did Haskett come?" he asked, with his back to her.

"Oh, yes—he came."

"You didn't see him, of course?"

She hesitated a moment. "I let the nurse see him."

That was all. There was nothing more to ask. He swung round toward her, applying a match to his cigar. Well, the thing was over for a week, at any rate. He would try not to think of it. She looked up at him, a trifle rosier than usual, with a smile in her eyes.

"Ready for your coffee, dear?"

He leaned against the mantelpiece, watching her as she lifted the coffeepot. The lamplight struck a gleam from her bracelets and tipped her soft hair with brightness. How light and slender she was, and how each gesture flowed into the next! She seemed a creature all compact of harmonies. As the thought of Haskett receded, Waythorn felt himself yielding again to the joy of possessorship. They were his, those white hands with their flitting motions, his the light haze of hair, the lips and eyes. . . .

She set down the coffeepot, and reaching for the decanter of cognac, measured off a liqueur glass and poured it into his cup.

Waythorn uttered a sudden exclamation.

"What is the matter?" she said, startled.

"Nothing; only—I don't take cognac in my coffee."

"Oh, how stupid of me," she cried.

Their eyes met, and she blushed a sudden agonized red.

III

Ten days later, Mr. Sellers, still housebound, asked Waythorn to call on his way downtown.

The senior partner, with his swaddled foot propped up by the fire, greeted his associate with an air of embarrassment.

"I'm sorry, my dear fellow; I've got to ask you to do an awkward thing for me."

Waythorn waited, and the other went on, after a pause apparently given to the arrangement of his phrases: "The fact is, when I was knocked out I had just gone into a rather complicated piece of business for—Gus Varick."

"Well?" said Waythorn, with an attempt to put him at his ease.

"Well—it's this way: Varick came to me the day before my attack. He had evidently had an inside tip from somebody, and had made about a hundred thousand. He came to me for advice, and I suggested his going in with Vanderlyn."

"Oh, the deuce!" Waythorn exclaimed.

He saw in a flash what had happened. The investment was an alluring one, but required negotiation. He listened quietly while Sellers put the case before him, and, the statement ended, he said: "You think I ought to see Varick?"

"I'm afraid I can't as yet. The doctor is obdurate. And this thing can't wait. I hate to ask you, but no one else in the office knows the ins and outs of it."

Waythorn stood silent. He did not care a farthing for the success of Varick's venture, but the honor of the office was to be considered, and he could hardly refuse to oblige his partner.

"Very well," he said, "I'll do it."

That afternoon, apprised by telephone, Varick called at the office. Waythorn, waiting in his private room, wondered what the others thought of it. The newspapers, at the time of Mrs. Waythorn's marriage, had acquainted their readers with every detail of her previous matrimonial ventures, and Waythorn could fancy the clerks smiling behind Varick's back as he was ushered in.

Varick bore himself admirably. He was easy without being undignified, and Waythorn was conscious of cutting a much less impressive figure. Varick had no experience of business, and the talk prolonged itself for nearly an hour while Waythorn set forth with scrupulous precision the details of the proposed transaction.

"I'm awfully obliged to you," Varick said as he rose. "The fact is I'm not used to having much money to look after, and I don't want to make an ass of myself—" He smiled, and Waythorn could not help noticing that there was something pleasant about his smile. "It feels uncommonly queer to have enough cash to pay one's bills. I'd have sold my soul for it a few years ago!"

Waythorn winced at the allusion. He had heard it rumored that a lack of funds had been one of the determining causes of the Varick separation, but it did not occur to him that Varick's words were intentional. It seemed more likely that the desire to keep clear of embarrassing topics had fatally drawn him into one. Waythorn did not wish to be outdone in civility.

"We'll do the best we can for you," he said. "I think this is a good thing you're in."

"Oh, I'm sure it's immense. It's awfully good of you—" Varick broke off, embarrassed. "I suppose the thing's settled now—but if—"

"If anything happens before Sellers is about, I'll see you again," said Waythorn quietly. He was glad, in the end, to appear the more self-possessed of the two.

The course of Lily's illness ran smooth, and as the days passed Waythorn grew used to the idea of Haskett's weekly visit. The first time the day came round, he stayed out late, and questioned his wife as to the visit on his return. She replied at once that Haskett had merely seen the nurse downstairs, as the doctor did not wish anyone in the child's sickroom till after the crisis.

The following week Waythorn was again conscious of the recurrence of the day, but had forgotten it by the time he came home to dinner. The crisis of the disease came a few days later, with a rapid decline of fever, and the little girl was pronounced out of danger. In the rejoicing which ensued the thought of Haskett passed out of Waythorn's mind, and one afternoon, letting himself into the house with a latchkey, he went straight to his library without noticing a shabby hat and umbrella in the hall.

In the library he found a small effaced-looking man with a thinnish gray beard sitting on the edge of a chair. The stranger might have been a piano tuner, or one of those mysteriously efficient persons who are summoned in emergencies to adjust some detail of the domestic machinery. He blinked at Waythorn through a pair of gold-rimmed spectacles and said mildly: "Mr. Waythorn, I presume? I am Lily's father."

Waythorn flushed. "Oh—" he stammered uncomfortably. He broke off, disliking to appear rude. Inwardly he was trying to adjust the actual Haskett to the image of him projected by his wife's reminiscences. Waythorn had been allowed to infer that Alice's first husband was a brute.

"I am sorry to intrude," said Haskett, with his over-the-counter politeness.

"Don't mention it," returned Waythorn, collecting himself. "I suppose the nurse has been told?"

"I presume so. I can wait," said Haskett. He had a resigned way of speaking, as though life had worn down his natural powers of resistance.

Waythorn stood on the threshold, nervously pulling off his gloves.

"I'm sorry you've been detained. I will send for the nurse," he said; and as he opened the door he added with an effort: "I'm glad we can give you a good report of Lily." He winced as the *we* slipped out, but Haskett seemed not to notice it.

"Thank you, Mr. Waythorn. It's been an anxious time for me."

"Ah, well, that's past. Soon she'll be able to go to you." Waythorn nodded and passed out.

In his own room he flung himself down with a groan. He hated the womanish sensibility which made him suffer so acutely from the grotesque chances of life. He had known when he married that his wife's former husbands were both living, and that amid the multiplied contacts of modern existence there were a thousand chances to one that he would run against one or the other, yet he found himself as much disturbed by his brief encounter with Haskett as though the law had not obligingly removed all difficulties in the way of their meeting.

Waythorn sprang up and began to pace the room nervously. He had not suffered half as much from his two meetings with Varick. It was Haskett's presence in his own house that made the situation so intolerable. He stood still, hearing steps in the passage.

"This way, please," he heard the nurse say. Haskett was being taken upstairs, then: not a corner of the house but was open to him. Waythorn dropped into another chair, staring vaguely ahead of him. On his dressing table stood a photograph of Alice, taken when he had first known her. She was Alice Varick then—how fine and exquisite he had thought her! Those were Varick's pearls about her neck. At Waythorn's instance they had been returned before her marriage. Had Haskett ever given her any trinkets—and what had become of them, Waythorn wondered? He realized suddenly that he knew very little of Haskett's past or present situation; but from the man's appearance and manner of speech he could reconstruct with curious precision the surroundings of Alice's first marriage. And it startled him to think that she had, in the background of her life, a phase of existence so different from anything with which he had connected her. Varick, whatever his faults, was a gentleman, in the conventional, traditional sense of the term: the sense which at that moment seemed, oddly enough, to have most meaning to Waythorn. He and Varick had the same social habits, spoke the same language, understood the same allusions. But this other man . . . it was grotesquely uppermost in Waythorn's mind that Haskett had worn a made-up tie attached with an elastic. Why should that ridiculous detail symbolize the whole man? Waythorn was exasperated by his own paltriness, but the fact of the tie expanded, forced itself on him, became as it were the key to Alice's past. He could see her, as Mrs. Haskett, sitting in a "front parlor" furnished in plush, with a pianola, and copy of *Ben Hur* on the center table. He could see her going to the theater with Haskett—or perhaps even to a "Church Sociable"—she in a "picture hat" and Haskett in a black frock coat, a little creased, with the made-up tie on an elastic. On the way home they would stop and look at the illuminated shop windows, lingering over the photographs of New York actresses. On Sunday afternoons Haskett would take her for a walk, pushing Lily ahead of them in a white enameled perambulator, and Waythorn had a vision of the people they would stop and talk to. He could fancy how pretty Alice must have looked, in a dress adroitly constructed from the hints of a New York fashion paper, and how she must have looked down on the other women, chafing at her life, and secretly feeling that she belonged in a bigger place.

For the moment his foremost thought was one of wonder at the way in which she had shed the phase of existence which her marriage with Haskett implied. It was as if her whole aspect, every gesture, every inflection, every allusion, were a studied negation of that period of her life. If she had denied being married to Haskett she could hardly have stood more convicted of duplicity than in this obliteration of the self which had been his wife.

Waythorn started up, checking himself in the analysis of her motives. What right had he to create a fantastic effigy of her and then pass judgment on it? She had spoken vaguely of her first marriage as unhappy, had hinted, with becoming reticence, that Haskett had wrought havoc among her young illusions. . . . It was a pity for Waythorn's peace of mind that Haskett's very inoffensiveness shed a new light on the nature of those illusions. A man would rather think that his wife has been brutalized by her first husband than that the process has been reversed.

IV

"Mr. Waythorn, I don't like that French governess of Lily's."

Haskett, subdued and apologetic, stood before Waythorn in the library, revolving his shabby hat in his hand.

Waythorn, surprised in his armchair over the evening paper, stared back perplexedly at his visitor.

"You'll excuse my asking to see you," Haskett continued. "But this is my last visit, and I thought if I could have a word with you it would be a better way than writing to Mrs. Waythorn's lawyer."

Waythorn rose uneasily. He did not like the French governess either; but that was irrelevant.

"I am not so sure of that," he returned stiffly; "but since you wish it I will give your message to—my wife." He always hesitated over the possessive pronoun in addressing Haskett.

The latter sighed. "I don't know as that will help much. She didn't like it when I spoke to her."

Waythorn turned red. "When did you see her?" he asked.

"Not since the first day I came to see Lily—right after she was taken sick. I remarked to her then that I didn't like the governess."

Waythorn made no answer. He remembered distinctly that, after that first visit, he had asked his wife if she had seen Haskett. She had lied to him then, but she had respected his wishes since; and the incident cast a curious light on her character. He was sure she would not have seen Haskett that first day if she had divined that Waythorn would object, and the fact that she did not divine it was almost as disagreeable to the latter as the discovery that she had lied to him.

"I don't like the woman," Haskett was repeating with mild persistency. "She ain't straight, Mr. Waythorn—she'll teach the child to be underhand. I've noticed a change in Lily—she's too anxious to please—and she don't always tell the truth. She used to be the straightest child, Mr. Waythorn—" He broke off, his voice a little thick. "Not but what I want her to have a stylish education," he ended.

Waythorn was touched. "I'm sorry, Mr. Haskett; but frankly, I don't quite see what I can do."

Haskett hesitated. Then he laid his hat on the table, and advanced to the hearth-rug, on which Waythorn was standing. There was nothing aggressive in his manner, but he had the solemnity of a timid man resolved on a decisive measure.

"There's just one thing you can do, Mr. Waythorn," he said. "You can remind Mrs. Waythorn that, by the decree of the courts, I am entitled to have a voice in Lily's bringing-up." He paused, and went on more deprecatingly: "I'm not the kind to talk about enforcing my rights, Mr. Waythorn. I don't know as I think a man is entitled to rights he hasn't known how to hold on to; but this business of the child is different. I've never let go there—and I never mean to."

The scene left Waythorn deeply shaken. Shamefacedly, in indirect ways, he had been finding out about Haskett; and all that he had learned was favorable. The little man, in order to be near his daughter, had sold out his share in a profitable business in Utica, and accepted a modest clerkship in a New York manufacturing house. He boarded in a shabby street and had few acquaintances. His passion for Lily filled his life. Waythorn felt that this exploration of Haskett was like groping about with a dark lantern in his wife's past; but he saw now that there were recesses his lantern had not explored. He had never inquired into the exact circumstances of his wife's first matrimonial rupture. On the surface all had been fair. It was she who had obtained the divorce, and the court had given her the child. But Waythorn knew how many ambiguities such a verdict might cover. The mere fact that Haskett retained a right over his daughter implied an unsuspected compromise. Waythorn was an idealist. He always refused to recognize unpleasant contingencies till he found himself confronted with them, and then he saw them followed by a spectral train of consequences. His next days were thus haunted, and he determined to try to lay the ghosts by conjuring them up in his wife's presence.

When he repeated Haskett's request a flame of anger passed over her face; but she subdued it instantly and spoke with a slight quiver of outraged motherhood.

"It is very ungentlemanly of him," she said.

The word grated on Waythorn. "That is neither here nor there. It's a bare question of rights."

She murmured: "It's not as if he could ever be a help to Lily—"

Waythorn flushed. This was even less to his taste. "The question is," he repeated, "what authority has he over her?"

She looked downward, twisting herself a little in her seat. "I am willing to see him—I thought you objected," she faltered.

In a flash he understood that she knew the extent of Haskett's claims. Perhaps it was not the first time she had resisted them.

"My objecting has nothing to do with it," he said coldly; "if Haskett has a right to be consulted you must consult him."

She burst into tears and he saw that she expected him to regard her as a victim.

Haskett did not abuse his right. Waythorn had fet miserably sure that he would not. But the governess was dismissed, and from time to time the little man demanded an interview with Alice. After the first outburst she accepted the situation with her usual adaptability. Haskett had once reminded Waythorn of the piano tuner, and Mrs. Waythorn, after a month or two, appeared to class him with that domestic familiar. Waythorn could not but respect the father's tenacity. At first he had tried to cultivate the suspicion that Haskett might be "up to" something, that he had an object in securing a foothold in the house. But in his heart Waythorn was sure of Haskett's single-mindedness; he even guessed in the latter a mild contempt for such advantages as his relation with the Waythorns might offer. Haskett's sincerity of purpose made him invulnerable, and his successor had to accept him as a lien on the property.

Mr. Sellers was sent to Europe to recover from his gout, and Varick's affairs hung on Waythorn's hands. The negotiations were prolonged and complicated; they necessitated frequent conferences between the two men, and the interests of the firm forbade Waythorn's suggesting that his client should transfer his business to another office.

Varick appeared well in the transaction. In moments of relaxation his coarse streak appeared, and Waythorn dreaded his geniality; but in the office he was concise and clear-headed, with a flattering deference to Waythorn's judgment. Their business relations being so affably established, it would have been absurd for the two men to ignore each other in society. The first time they met in a drawing room, Varick took up their intercourse in the same easy key, and his hostess' grateful glance obliged Waythorn to respond to it. After that they ran across each other frequently, and one evening at a ball Waythorn, wandering through the remoter rooms, came upon Varick seated beside his wife. She colored a little, and faltered in what she was saying; but Varick nodded to Waythorn without rising, and the latter strolled on.

In the carriage, on the way home, he broke out nervously: "I didn't know you spoke to Varick."

Her voice trembled a little. "It's the first time—he happened to be standing near me; I didn't know what to do. It's so awkward, meeting everywhere—and he said you had been very kind about some business."

"That's different," said Waythorn.

She paused a moment. "I'll do just as you wish," she returned pliantly. "I thought it would be less awkward to speak to him when we meet."

Her pliancy was beginning to sicken him. Had she really no will of her own—no theory about her relation to these men? She had accepted Haskett—did she mean to accept Varick? It was "less awkward," as she had said, and her instinct was to evade difficulties or to circumvent them. With sudden vividness Waythorn saw how the instinct had developed. She was "as easy as an old shoe"—a shoe that too many feet had worn. Her elasticity was the result of tension in too many different directions. Alice Haskett—Alice Varick—Alice Waythorn—she had been each in turn, and had left hanging to each name a little of her privacy, a little of her personality, a little of the inmost self where the unknown god abides.

"Yes—it's better to speak to Varick," said Waythorn wearily.

V

The winter wore on, and society took advantage of the Waythorns' acceptance of Varick. Harassed hostesses were grateful to them for bridging over a social difficulty, and Mrs. Waythorn was held up as a miracle of good taste. Some experimental spirits could not resist the diversion of throwing Varick and his former wife together, and there were those who thought he found a zest in the propinquity. But Mrs. Waythorn's conduct remained irreproachable. She neither avoided Varick nor sought him out. Even Waythorn could not but admit that she had discovered the solution of the newest social problem.

He had married her without giving much thought to that problem. He had fancied that a woman can shed her past like a man. But now he saw that Alice was bound to hers both by the circumstances which forced her into continued relation with it, and by the traces it had left on her nature. With grim irony Waythorn compared himself to a member of a syndicate. He held so many shares in his wife's personality and his predecessors were his partners in the business. If there had been any element of passion in the transaction he would have felt less deteriorated by it. The fact that Alice took her change of husbands like a change of weather reduced the situation to mediocrity. He could have forgiven her for blunders, for excesses; for resisting Haskett, for yielding to Varick; for anything but her acquiescence and her tact. She reminded him of a juggler tossing knives; but the knives were blunt and she knew they would never cut her.

And then, gradually, habit formed a protecting surface for his sensibilities. If he paid for each day's comfort with the small change of his illusions, he grew daily to value the comfort more and set less store upon the coin. He had drifted into a dulling propinquity with Haskett and Varick and he took refuge in the cheap revenge of satirizing the situation. He even began to reckon up the advantages which accrued from it, to ask himself if it were not better to own a third of a wife who knew how to make a man happy than a whole one who had lacked opportunity to acquire the art. For it *was* an art, and made up, like all others, of concessions, eliminations and embellishments; of lights judiciously thrown and shadows skillfully softened. His wife knew exactly how to manage the lights, and he knew exactly to what training she owed her skill. He even tried to trace the source of his obligations, to discriminate between the influences which had combined to produce his domestic happiness: he perceived that Haskett's commonness had made Alice worship good breeding, while Varick's liberal construction of the marriage bond had taught her to value the conjugal virtues; so that he was directly indebted to his predecessors for the devotion which made his life easy if not inspiring.

From this phase he passed into that of complete acceptance. He ceased to satirize himself because time dulled the irony of the situation and the joke lost its humor with its sting. Even the sight of Haskett's hat on the hall table had ceased to touch the springs of epigram. The hat was often seen there now, for it had been decided that it was better for Lily's father to visit her than for the little girl to go to his boardinghouse. Waythorn, having acquiesced in this arrangement, had been surprised to find how little difference it made. Haskett was never obtrusive, and the few visitors who met him on the stairs were unaware of his identity. Waythorn did not know how often he saw Alice, but with himself Haskett was seldom in contact.

One afternoon, however, he learned on entering that Lily's father was waiting to see him. In the library he found Haskett occupying a chair in his usual provisional way. Waythorn always felt grateful to him for not leaning back.

"I hope you'll excuse me, Mr. Waythorn," he said rising. "I wanted to see Mrs. Waythorn about Lily, and your man asked me to wait here till she came in."

"Of course," said Waythorn, remembering that a sudden leak had that morning given over the drawing room to the plumbers.

He opened his cigar case and held it out to his visitor, and Haskett's acceptance seemed to mark a fresh stage in their intercourse. The spring evening was chilly, and Waythorn invited his guest to draw up his chair to the fire. He meant to find an excuse to leave Haskett in a moment; but he was tired and cold, and after all the little man no longer jarred on him.

The two were enclosed in the intimacy of their blended cigar smoke when the door opened and Varick walked into the room. Waythorn rose abruptly. It was the first time that Varick had come to the house, and the surprise of seeing him, combined with the singular inopportuneness of his arrival, gave a new edge to Waythorn's blunted sensibilities. He stared at his visitor without speaking.

Varick seemed too preoccupied to notice his host's embarrassment.

"My dear fellow," he exclaimed in his most expansive tone, "I must apologize for tumbling in on you in this way, but I was too late to catch you downtown, and so I thought—"

He stopped short, catching sight of Haskett, and his sanguine color deepened to a flush which spread vividly under his scant blond hair. But in a moment he recovered himself and nodded slightly. Haskett returned the bow in silence, and Waythorn was still groping for speech when the footman came in carrying a tea table.

The intrusion offered a welcome vent to Waythorn's nerves. "What the deuce are you bringing this here for?" he said sharply.

"I beg your pardon, sir, but the plumbers are still in the drawing room, and Mrs. Waythorn said she would have tea in the library." The footman's perfectly respectful tone implied a reflection on Waythorn's reasonableness.

"Oh, very well," said the latter resignedly, and the footman proceeded to open the folding tea table and set out its complicated appointments. While this interminable process continued the three men stood motionless, watching it with a fascinated stare, till Waythorn, to break the silence, said to Varick, "Won't you have a cigar?"

He held out the case he had just tendered to Haskett, and Varick helped himself with a smile. Waythorn looked about for a match, and finding none, proffered a light from his own cigar. Haskett, in the background, held his ground mildly, examining his cigar tip now and then, and stepping forward at the right moment to knock its ashes into the fire.

The footman at last withdrew, and Varick immediately began: "If I could just say half a word to you about this business—"

"Certainly," stammered Waythorn; "in the dining room—"

But as he placed his hand on the door it opened from without, and his wife appeared on the threshold.

She came in fresh and smiling, in her street dress and hat, shedding a fragrance from the boa which she loosened in advancing.

"Shall we have tea in here, dear?" she began; and then she caught sight of Varick. Her smile deepened, veiling a slight tremor of surprise.

"Why, how do you do?" she said with a distinct note of pleasure.

As she shook hands with Varick she saw Haskett standing behind him. Her smile faded for a moment, but she recalled it quickly, with a scarcely perceptible side glance at Waythorn.

"How do you do, Mr. Haskett?" she said, and shook hands with him a shade less cordially.

The three men stood awkwardly before her, till Varick, always the most self-possessed, dashed into an explanatory phrase.

"We—I had to see Waythorn a moment on business," he stammered, brick-red from chin to nape.

Haskett stepped forward with his air of mild obstinacy. "I am sorry to intrude; but you appointed five o'clock—" he directed his resigned glance to the timepiece on the mantel.

She swept aside their embarrassment with a charming gesture of hospitality.

"I'm so sorry—I'm always late; but the afternoon was so lovely." She stood drawing off her gloves, propitiatory and graceful, diffusing about her a sense of ease and familiarity in which the situation lost its grotesqueness. "But before talking business," she added brightly, "I'm sure everyone wants a cup of tea."

She dropped into her low chair by the tea table, and the two visitors, as if drawn by her smile, advanced to receive the cups she held out.

She glanced about for Waythorn, and he took the third cup with a laugh.

[1904]

For Thought

Rather than using a tight plot in "The Other Two" with an inevitable progression of events from inciting incident to complications leading to a crisis, Wharton strings together a series of situations in which ironic reversal of mood is the dominant element. The encounters that alter Waythorn's mood from contentment to perturbation and, finally, back to contentment on a more realistic basis than his initial euphoria are handled by the author with a detached, comically ironic tone. With this tone Wharton renders her main character as slightly foolish, but not satirically so.

For Discussion

1. What is the author's attitude toward her protagonist? What evidence in the text indicates this attitude?

2. How does the language used create the tone of the story?
3. Considering the differences of temperament between Waythorn and Alice, what potential conflict exists?
4. What is th function of Seller's gout in the forward movement of the action?
5. What is the significance of the encounter with Varick at the restaurant?
6. As seen through the eyes of Waythorn, the central intelligence in the story, what is the view of women and their role in life during the period in which the story is set?
7. In what way does the encounter with Varick in Waythorn's office differ from the previous incidents involving Varick? What does this encounter prepare for?
8. What character revelation about Alice is there in the discussion of Haskett's wishes in the matter of Lily's education and the French governess?
9. What is the irony in Alice's "perfection" as a wife?
10. How is the central conflict resolved?

William Carlos Williams
The Use of Force

They were new patients to me, all I had was the name, Olson. Please come down as soon as you can, my daughter is very sick.

When I arrived I was met by the mother, a big startled-looking woman, very clean and apologetic who merely said, Is this the doctor? and let me in. In the back, she added. You must excuse us, doctor, we have her in the kitchen where it is warm. It is very damp here sometimes.

The child was fully dressed and sitting on her father's lap near the kitchen table. He tried to get up, but I motioned for him not to bother, took off my overcoat and started to look things over. I could see that they were all very nervous, eyeing me up and down distrustfully. As often, in such cases, they weren't telling me more than they had to, it was up to me to tell them; that's why they were spending three dollars on me.

The child was fairly eating me up with her cold, steady eyes, and no expression to her face whatever. She did not move and seemed, inwardly, quiet; an unusually attractive little thing, and as strong as a heifer in appearance. But her face was flushed, she was breathing rapidly, and I realized that she had a high fever. She had magnificent blonde hair, in profusion. One of those picture children often reproduced in advertising leaflets and the photogravure sections of the Sunday papers.

She's had a fever for three days, began the father and we don't know what it comes from. My wife has given her things, you know, like people do, but it don't do no good. And there's been a lot of sickness around. So we tho't you'd better look her over and tell us what is the matter.

As doctors often do I took a trial shot at it as a point of departure. Has she had a sore throat?

Both parents answered me together, No . . . No, she says her throat don't hurt her.

Does your throat hurt you? added the mother to the child. But the little girl's expression didn't change nor did she move her eyes from my face.

Have you looked?

I tried to, said the mother, but I couldn't see.

As it happens we had been having a number of cases of diphtheria in the school to which this child went during that month and we were all, quite apparently, thinking of that, though no one had as yet spoken of the thing.

Well, I said, suppose we take a look at the throat first. I smiled in my best professional manner and asking for the child's first name I said, come on, Mathilda, open your mouth and let's take a look at your throat.

Nothing doing.

Aw, come on, I coaxed, just open your mouth wide and let me take a look. Look, I said opening both hands wide, I haven't anything in my hands. Just open up and let me see.

Such a nice man, put in the mother. Look how kind he is to you. Come on, do what he tells you to. He won't hurt you.

At that I ground my teeth in disgust. If only they wouldn't use the word "hurt" I might be able to get somewhere. But I did not allow myself to be hurried or disturbed but speaking quietly and slowly I approached the child again.

As I moved my chair a little nearer suddenly with one cat-like movement both her hands clawed instinctively for my eyes and she almost reached them too. In fact she knocked my glasses flying and they fell, though unbroken, several feet away from me on the kitchen floor.

Both the mother and father almost turned themselves inside out in embarrassment and apology. You bad girl, said the mother, taking her and shaking her by one arm. Look what you've done. The nice man . . .

For heaven's sake, I broke in. Don't call me a nice man to her. I'm here to look at her throat on the chance that she might have diphtheria and possibly die of it. But that's nothing to her. Look here, I said to the child, we're going to look at your throat. You're old enough to understand what I'm saying. Will you open it now by yourself or shall we have to open it for you?

Not a move. Even her expression hadn't changed. Her breaths however were coming faster and faster. Then the battle began. I had to do it. I had to have a throat culture for her own protection. But first I told the parents that it was entirely up to them. I explained the danger but said that I would not insist on a throat examination so long as they would take the responsibility.

If you don't do what the doctor says you'll have to go to the hospital, the mother admonished her severely.

Oh, yeah? I had to smile to myself. After all, I had already fallen in love with the savage brat, the parents were contemptible to me. In the ensuing struggle they grew more and more abject, crushed, exhausted while she surely rose to magnificent heights of insane fury of effort bred of her terror of me.

The father tried his best, and he was a big man but the fact that she was his daughter, his shame at her behavior and his dread of hurting her made him release her just at the critical times when I had almost achieved success, till I wanted to kill him. But his dread also that she might have diphtheria made him tell me to go on, go on though he himself was almost fainting, while the mother moved back and forth behind us raising and lowering her hands in an agony of apprehension.

Put her in front of you on your lap, I ordered, and hold both her wrists.

But as soon as he did the child let out a scream. Don't, you're hurting me. Let go of my hands. Let them go I tell you. Then she shrieked terrifyingly, hysterically. Stop it! Stop it! You're killing me!

Do you think she can stand it, doctor! said the mother.

You get out, said the husband to his wife. Do you want her to die of diphtheria?

Come on now, hold her, I said.

Then I grasped the child's head with my left hand and tried to get the wooden tongue depressor between her teeth. She fought, with clenched teeth, desperately! But now I also had grown furious—at a child. I tried to hold myself down but I couldn't. I know how to expose a throat for inspection. And I did my best. When finally I got the wooden spatula behind the last teeth and just the point of it into the mouth cavity, she opened up for an instant but before I could see anything she came down again and gripping the wooden blade between her molars she reduced it to splinters before I could get it out again.

Aren't you ashamed, the mother yelled at her. Aren't you ashamed to act like that in front of the doctor?

Get me a smooth-handled spoon of some sort, I told the mother. We're going through with this. The child's mouth was already bleeding. Her tongue was cut and she was screaming in wild hysterical shrieks. Perhaps I should have desisted and come back in an hour or more. No doubt it would have been better. But I have seen at least two children lying dead in bed of neglect in such cases, and feeling that I must get a diagnosis now or never I went at it again. But the worst of it was that I too had got beyond reason. I could have torn the child apart in my own fury and enjoyed it. It was a pleasure to attack her. My face was burning with it.

The damned little brat must be protected against her own idiocy, one says to one's self at such times. Others must be protected against her. It is a social necessity. And all these things are true. But a blind fury, a feeling of adult shame, bred of a longing for muscular release are the operatives. One goes on to the end.

In a final unreasoning assault I overpowered the child's neck and jaws. I forced the heavy silver spoon back of her teeth and down her throat till she gagged. And there it was—both tonsils covered with membrane. She had fought valiantly to keep me from knowing her secret. She had been hiding that sore throat for three days at least and lying to her parents in order to escape just such an outcome as this.

Now truly she was furious. She had been on the defensive before but now she attacked. Tried to get off her father's lap and fly at me while tears of defeat blinded her eyes.

[1933]

For Thought

In this disarmingly simple incident involving a throat examination of a child suspected of having diphtheria, "The Use of Force" deals with the disturbing revelation of how easy it is to find release, and even pleasure, in the use of violence when one is faced with the frustration of one's wishes.

For Discussion

1. How many lines of conflict between or within characters emerge in the story?
2. Why has the author chosen to tell the story from the doctor's, rather than from the parents', point of view?
3. How is the doctor characterized?
4. How is the child characterized?
5. To what extent are all of the characters hiding something?
6. How do the doctor and the child react to each other in similar ways?
7. How does the language of the story reveal differing types of discourse, idiom, and degrees of formality?
8. To what extent is the child not only brave and pathetic, but even tragic?
9. What is the theme of the story? How does the title relate to it?
10. How is the conclusion of the story ironic?

Virginia Woolf
The Duchess and the Jeweller

Oliver Bacon lived at the top of a house overlooking the Green Park. He had a flat; chairs jutted out at the right angles—chairs covered in hide. Sofas filled the bays of the windows—sofas covered in tapestry. The windows, the three long windows, had the proper allowance of discreet net and figured satin. The mahogany sideboard bulged discreetly with the right brandies, whiskeys, and liqueurs. And from the middle window he looked down upon the glossy roofs of fashionable cars packed in the narrow straits of Picadilly. A more central position could not be imagined. And at eight in the morning he would have his breakfast brought in on a tray by a man-servant: the man-servant would unfold his crimson dressing-gown; he would rip his letters open with his long pointed nails and would extract thick white cards of invitation upon which the engraving stood up roughly from duchesses, countesses, viscountesses, and Honourable Ladies. Then he would wash; then he would eat his toast; then he would read his paper by the bright burning fire of electric coals.

"Behold Oliver," he would say, addressing himself. "You who began life in a filthy little alley, you who . . ." and he would look down at his legs, so shapely in their perfect trousers; at his boots; at his spats. They were all shapely, shining; cut from the best cloth by the best scissors in Savile Row. But he dismantled himself often and became again a little boy in a dark alley. He had once thought *that* the height of his ambition—selling stolen dogs to fashionable women in Whitechapel. And once he had been done. "Oh, Oliver," his mother had wailed. "Oh, Oliver! When will you have sense, my son?" . . . Then he had gone behind a counter; had sold cheap watches; then he had taken a wallet to Amsterdam. . . . At that memory he would chuckle—the old Oliver remembering the young. Yes, he had done well with the three diamonds; also there was the commission on the emerald. After that he went into the private room behind the shop in Hatton Garden; the room with the scales, the safe, the thick magnifying glasses. And then . . . and then. . . . He chuckled. When he passed through the knots of jewellers in the hot evening who were discussing prices, gold mines, diamonds, reports from South Africa, one of them would lay a finger to the side of his nose and murmur, "Hum-m-m," as he passed. It was no more than a murmur; no more than a nudge on the shoulder, a finger on the nose, a buzz that ran through the cluster of jewellers in Hatton Garden on a hot afternoon—oh, many years ago now! But still Oliver felt it purring down his spine, the nudge, the murmur that meant, "Look at him—young Oliver, the young jeweller—there he goes." Young he was then. And he dressed better and better; and had, first a hansom cab; then a car; and first he went up to the dress circle, then down into the stalls. And he had a villa at Richmond, overlooking the river, with trellises of red roses; and Mademoiselle used to pick one every morning and stick it in his button-hole.

"So," said Oliver Bacon, rising and stretching his legs. "So. . . ."

And he stood beneath the picture of an old lady on the mantelpiece and raised his hands. "I have kept my word," he said, laying his hands together, palm to palm, as if he were doing homage to her. "I have won my bet." That was so; he was the richest jeweller in England; but his nose, which was long and flexible, like an elephant's trunk, seemed to say by its curious quiver at the nostrils (but it seemed as if the whole nose quivered, not only the nostrils) that he was not satisfied yet; still smelt something under the ground a little further off. Imagine a giant hog in a pasture rich with truffles; after unearthing this truffle and that, still it smells a bigger, a blacker truffle under the ground further off. So Oliver snuffed always in the rich earth of Mayfair another truffle, a blacker, a bigger further off.

Now then he straightened the pearl in his tie, cased himself in his smart blue overcoat; took his yellow gloves and his cane; and swayed as he descended the stairs and half snuffed, half sighed through his long sharp nose as he passed out into Piccadilly. For was he not still a sad man, a dissatisfied man, a man who seeks something that is hidden, though he had won his bet?

He swayed slightly as he walked, as the camel at the zoo sways from side to side when it walks along the asphalt paths laden with grocers and their wives eating from paper bags and throwing little bits of silver paper crumpled up on to the path. The camel despises the grocers; the camel is dissatisfied with its lot; the camel sees the blue lake and the fringe of palm trees in front of it. So the great jeweller, the greatest jeweller in the whole world, swung down Piccadilly, perfectly dressed, with his gloves, with his cane; but dissatisfied still, till he reached the dark little shop, that was famous in France, in Germany, in Austria, in Italy, and all over America—the dark little shop in the street off Bond Street.

As usual, he strode through the shop without speaking, though the four men, the two old men, Marshall and Spencer, and the two young men, Hammond and Wicks, stood straight and looked at him, envying him. It was only with one finger of the amber-coloured glove, waggling, that he acknowledged their presence. And he went in and shut the door of his private room behind him.

Then he unlocked the grating that barred the window. The cries of Bond Street came in; the purr of the distant traffic. The light from reflectors at the back of the shop struck upwards. One tree waved six green leaves, for it was June. But Mademoiselle had married Mr. Pedder of the local brewery—no one stuck roses in his buttonhole now.

"So," he half sighed, half snorted, "so—"

Then he touched a spring in the wall and slowly the panelling slid open, and behind it were the steel safes, five, no, six of them, all of burnished steel. He twisted a key; unlocked one; then another. Each was lined with a pad of deep crimson velvet; in each lay jewels—bracelets, necklaces, rings, tiaras, ducal coronets; loose stones in glass shells; rubies, emeralds, pearls, diamonds. All safe, shining, cool, yet burning, eternally, with their own compressed light.

"Tears!" said Oliver, looking at the pearls.

"Heart's blood!" he said, looking at the rubies.

"Gunpowder!" he continued, rattling the diamonds so that they flashed and blazed.

"Gunpowder enough to blow Mayfair—sky high, high, high!" He threw his head back and made a sound like a horse neighing as he said it.

The telephone buzzed obsequiously in a low muted voice on his table. He shut the safe.

"In ten minutes," he said. "Not before." And he sat down at his desk and looked at the heads of the Roman emperors that were graved on his sleeve links. And again he dismantled himself and became once more the little boy playing marbles in the alley where they sell stolen dogs on Sunday. He became that wily astute little boy, with lips like wet cherries. He dabbled his fingers in ropes of tripe; he dipped them in pans of frying fish; he dodged in and out among the crowds. He was slim, lissome, with eyes like licked stones. And now—now—the hands of the clock ticked on, one, two, three, four. . . . The Duchess of Lambourne waited his pleasure; the Duchess of Lambourne, daughter of a hundred Earls. She would wait for ten minutes on a chair at the counter. She would wait his pleasure. She would wait till he was ready to see her. He watched the clock in its shagreen case. The hand moved on. With each tick the clock handed him—so it seemed—pâté de foie gras, a glass of champagne, another of fine brandy, a cigar costing one guinea. The clock laid them on the table beside him as the ten minutes passed. Then he heard soft slow footsteps approaching; a rustle in the corridor. The door opened. Mr. Hammond flattened himself against the wall.

"Her Grace!" he announced.

And he waited there, flattened against the wall.

And Oliver, rising, could hear the rustle of the dress of the Duchess as she came down the passage. Then she loomed up, filling the door, filling the room with the aroma, the prestige, the arrogance, the pomp, the pride of all the Dukes and Duchesses swollen in one wave. And as a wave breaks, she broke, as she sat down, spreading and splashing and falling over Oliver Bacon, the great jeweller, covering him with sparkling bright colours, green, rose, violet; and odours; and iridescences; and rays shooting from fingers, nodding from plumes, flashing from silk; for she was very large, very fat, tightly girt in pink taffeta, and past her prime. As a parasol with many flounces, as a peacock with many feathers, shuts its flounces, folds its feathers, so she subsided and shut herself as she sank down in the leather armchair.

"Good morning, Mr. Bacon," said the Duchess. And she held out her hand which came through the slit of her white glove. And Oliver bent low as he shook it. And as their hands touched the link was forged between them once more. They were friends, yet enemies; he was master, she was mistress; each cheated the other, each needed the other, each feared the other, each felt this and knew this every time they touched hands thus in the little back room with the white light outside, and the tree with its six leaves, and the sound of the street in the distance and behind them the safes.

"And today, Duchess—what can I do for you today?" said Oliver, very softly.

The Duchess opened her heart, her private heart, gaped wide. And with a sign but no word she took from her bag a long wash-leather pouch—it looked like a lean yellow ferret. And from a slit in the ferret's belly she dropped pearls—ten pearls. They rolled from the slit in the ferret's belly—one, two, three, four—like the eggs of some heavenly bird.

"All that's left me, dear Mr. Bacon," she moaned. Five, six, seven—down they rolled, down the slopes of the vast mountain sides that fell between her knees into one narrow valley—the eighth, the ninth, and the tenth. There they lay in the glow of the peach-blossom taffeta. Ten pearls.

"From the Appleby cincture," she mourned. "The last . . . the last of them all."

Oliver stretched out and took one of the pearls between finger and thumb. It was round, it was lustrous. But real was it, or false? Was she lying again? Did she dare?

She laid her plump padded finger across her lips. "If the Duke knew . . ." she whispered. "Dear Mr. Bacon, a bit of bad luck. . . . "

Been gambling again, had she?

"That villain! That sharper!" she hissed.

The man with the chipped cheek bone? A bad 'un. And the Duke was straight as a poker; with side whiskers; would cut her off, shut her up down there if he knew—what I know, thought Oliver, and glanced at the safe.

"Araminta, Daphne, Diana," she moaned. "It's for *them*."

The ladies Araminta, Daphne, Diana—her daughters. He knew them; adored them. But it was Diana he loved.

"You have all my secrets," she leered. Tears slid; tears fell; tears, like diamonds, collecting powder in the rust of her cherry blossom cheeks.

"Old friend," she murmured, "old friend."

"Old friend," he repeated, "old friend," as if he licked the words.

"How much?" he queried.

She covered the pearls with her hand.

"Twenty thousand," she whispered.

But was it real or false, the one he held in his hand? The Appleby cincture—hadn't she sold it already? He would ring for Spencer or Hammond. "Take it and test it," he would say. He stretched to the bell.

"You will come down tomorrow?" she urged, she interrupted. "The Prime Minister—His Royal Highness. . . ." She stopped. "And Diana . . ." she added.

Oliver took his hand off the bell.

He looked past her, at the backs of the houses in Bond Street. But he saw, not the houses in Bond Street, but a dimpling river; and trout rising and salmon; and the Prime Minister; and himself too, in white waistcoat; and then, Diana. He looked down at the pearl in his hand. But how could he test it, in the light of the river, in the light of the eyes of Diana? But the eyes of the Duchess were on him.

"Twenty thousand," she moaned. "My honour!"

The honour of the mother of Diana! He drew his cheque book towards him; he took out his pen.

"Twenty—" he wrote. Then he stopped writing. The eyes of the old woman in the picture were on him—of the old woman his mother.

"Oliver!" she warned him. "Have sense! Don't be a fool!"

"Oliver!" the Duchess entreated—it was "Oliver" now, not "Mr. Bacon." "You'll come for a long week-end?"

Alone in the woods with Diana! Riding alone in the woods with Diana!

"Thousand," he wrote, and signed it.

"Here you are," he said.

And there opened all the flounces of the parasol, all the plumes of the peacock, the radiance of the wave, the swords and spears of Agincourt, as she rose from her chair. And the two old men and the two young men, Spencer and Marshall, Wicks and Hammond, flattened themselves behind the counter envying him as he led her through the shop to the door. And he waggled his yellow glove in their faces, and she held her honour—a cheque for twenty thousand pounds with his signature—quite firmly in her hands.

"Are they false or are they real?" asked Oliver, shutting his private door. There they were, ten pearls on the blotting-paper on the table. He took them to the window. He held them under his lens to the light. . . . This, then, was the truffle he had routed out of the earth! Rotten at the centre—rotten at the core!

"Forgive me, oh, my mother!" he

sighed, raising his hand as if he asked pardon of the old woman in the picture. And again he was a little boy in the alley where they sold dogs on Sunday.

"For," he murmured, laying the palms of his hands together, "it is to be a long week-end."

[1944]

For Thought

Woolf's brief narrative of a day in the life of a wealthy London jeweller is rich in the gestures and textures characteristic of that type of personality, life, and milieu. Oliver Bacon, of "The Duchess and the Jeweller," has risen from the existence of a petty thief in the gutter to a life of luxury and influence. His bargaining session with the Duchess of Lambourne sums up the central issue of the story. He knowingly pays an immense sum for pearls which are worthless in order to buy an entry into the Duchess's society. Woolf implies, however, that both pearls and society may glitter outwardly, concealing the corruption within.

For Discussion

1. How has Woolf carefully cataloged the furnishings and contents of Bacon's shop, the clothing worn by him and the Duchess, and the detailed gestures used by both central characters? How does this detail characterize them and influence the reader's attitudes toward each character?
2. How do Bacon and the Duchess both cooperate and compete? How do their weaknesses and strengths of character balance one another?
3. What ironies emerge from the story?

Glossary

Allegory A didactic narrative in which the characters are an interdependent set of personified abstractions that convey a message, usually moralistic, as in Franz Kafka's "In the Penal Colony."

Atmosphere The feeling of "something in the air" that an author develops through dialogue or description, or other special effects of language. It serves as the conditioning or motivating force in the action, and is exemplified by the queasy feeling the narrator gets from the tarn in Poe's "The Fall of the House of Usher," which sets the stage for the weird events of the story.

Attitude The relation the author assumes toward the subject, the characters, and the action in the story. It may be sympathetic, neutral, or antipathetic. It may be expressed explicitly or ironically. For example, in "The Bride Comes to Yellow Sky," Stephen Crane is indulgently amused by the "little boy" quality of Potter and his antagonist, Scratchy Wilson. He lets the reader know this with his ironic tone.

Character One of the persons in a story. A character may be flat or less developed, like the Young Man in Mary McCarthy's "'Cruel and Barbarous Treatment.'" Or the character may be rounded and complex, like Eudora Welty's traveling salesman. The character may be static and unchanging, like the oldest wife in Lessing's "The Nuisance;" or the character may be developing, undergoing change throughout the story, like Nick in "The Killers."

Characterization The means by which the author creates the sum of traits, thoughts, and actions which, taken together, constitute a character. This is accomplished mainly through dialogue, action, and/or analysis, depending on the point of view in the story. For example, Hemingway uses action and dialogue in "The Killers." Doris Lessing uses action, dialogue, and analysis in "One off the Short List."

Climax The point of greatest tension and decision in the action. It usually coincides with the central character's last chance to make a choice. Once the climax has passed, the choice made by the character leads to the resolution of the story when (in many stories) rewards and punishments are distributed. In "The Catbird Seat" by James Thurber, the climactic moment involves Mr. Martin's decision to outwit rather than to kill Mrs. Barrows.

Complication The development of predictable or unforeseen contingencies in the action, bringing about a change in the direction of the action. In Henry James's "The Real Thing," it involves the painter's discovery that his use of the Monarchs as models is ruining his work and may very likely cost him his commission for the illustrations he is doing.

Conflict The opposition between forces. It may be internal, as with the tensions Laura feels in Katherine Anne Porter's "Flowering Judas." Or it may be external, like the conflict between Potter and Wilson in Crane's "The Bride Comes to Yellow Sky." In most great literature, several lines of conflict usually parallel one another, both on the external and internal levels.

Denouement The unraveling or resolution of the conflict and complications, the final outcome of the sequence of events in a story. Ivan Turgenev's "Meeting," for example, is resolved by the valet's final bored rejection of the peasant girl who is infatuated with him. In James Thurber's "The Catbird Seat," Mr. Fitweiler's decision that Mrs. Barrows has falsely accused Mr. Martin because she has slipped into insanity makes up the resolution, or denouement, of the story.

Dialogue The expression of character through speech. In "The Valiant Woman," Mrs. Stoner's profanity, hackneyed allusions to popular literature, and the use of faulty grammar indicate her shallow, untrained mind.

Exposition The providing of background information. It gives credibility to the main action and sets up a framework within which to proceed. For example, in D. H. Lawrence's "The Rocking Horse Winner," we are told that the young boy's family never has enough money and that Bassett, the gardener, has begun placing bets for him.

Fantasy The use of elements far removed from literal reality. Events may be incredible and characters may shift in a fluid way. The environment may be grotesque or incredibly beautiful. Strong elements of fantasy appear in the stories of Kafka, Poe, Welty, Barthelme, and Coover.

Foreshadowing The use of incidents, characters, tone, imagery, dialogue, and symbolism to suggest what lies ahead. In "Araby," James Joyce prepares us for the boy's eventual disappointment and disillusionment. He does so by using death images at the beginning, revealing the indifference of adults to the boy's aspirations, by delaying the arrival of the uncle, and by using a tone of resigned wisdom throughout the story.

Imagery The use of vivid, sense-stimulating language to create concrete impressions. For example, Moravia uses a crudely carved stone jar in "The Fetish" to reveal aspects of both the husband and wife to Livio.

Insight A recognition by the protagonist of his or her fate or nature, and of the significance of things experienced by that character. At times, it may also refer to the insight the reader gains into the theme of the story and its larger significance. In "Araby," Joyce's hero realizes the difficulty of escaping ugliness through romantic illusions. On the other hand, McCarthy's heroine in "'Cruel and Barbarous Treatment'" gains no insight at all into her pitiable, self-deluded existence.

Irony A reversal of meaning or situation. Poe uses situational irony, a reversal of expectation, in "The Fall of the House of Usher" by having the sounds of Madeline's bursting from the tomb parallel the action of the story his narrator reads to Roderick Usher. Mary McCarthy uses verbal irony, a reversal of meaning, to describe the trivial actions of her heroine in exalted, theatrical terms. Satirical irony may be used by the author to ridicule or poke fun at human folly. The author may also use irony of fate, in which circumstances come about that are the opposite of the outcome expected by the protagonist, but not necessarily by the reader, as in Chekhov's "The Druggist's Wife."

Language The way in which words are put together to create special effects of attitude, tone, atmosphere and mood, setting, dialogue, irony, symbolism, and pace and rhythm. It is used, for example, to further characterization, as when J. F. Powers uses words like "cut" and "spit" to portray Mrs. Stoner in a highly unfavorable light, in "The Valiant Woman."

Metaphor Figurative language, or a nonliteral mode of expression, including the use of symbols like the bazaar in Joyce's "Araby."

Mood The emotional content of a scene or entire story. It is created by the combined effect of atmosphere, setting, exposition, foreshadowing, dialogue, and action. It can range from happiness to sadness, complacency to fear, contentment to deep frustration, and so forth.

Motif The underlying pattern (any recurring idea, phrase, image, or action) that unifies a story by repeatedly recalling its earlier occurrences. A story may have a particular motif in common with other stories. For example, both Welty's "Death of a Traveling Salesman" and Crane's "The Bride Comes to Yellow Sky" use the motif of the perilous journey in different ways.

Motivation All the forces including events, atmosphere, beliefs, and tendencies that cause a character to act as he or she does. In Joyce's "Araby," the boy becomes infatuated with Mangan's sister because of his sensitive, romantic nature. The boy also becomes disillusioned with life because of his impossibly high ideals and overactive imagination.

Narrator The observer-spokesperson of a story. The narrator may possess varying degrees of knowledge about the events and other characters in the story. The townsman narrator in "A Rose for Emily" is at the periphery, and operates from the third-person point of view, even though he employs the pronoun "we."

Pace The tempo and rhythm of a story. Pace and rhythm may be achieved through variations in the length of words and word groups; contrasting or matching syntactical constructions; the sense of pauses or the rapid flow of speech; the deliberate selection of words for ease or difficulty of pronunciation; and the verbatim repetition of words or phrases. In "The Killers," Hemingway uses short, simple sentences that have a flat, reportorial quality, suggesting an objective recording of bare facts and lending an air of tense realism and swift-moving action to the scene.

Plot The arrangement of events in a story into a causal sequence. In Joyce's "Araby," the plot consists of the boy's infatuation, his trip to the bazaar, and his return home.

Point of View The way in which an author has us view the action, and the voice he or she assumes in order to tell the story. The narrator or spokesperson of the story may pretend to know nothing except the externals of character and action, as in Faulkner's "A Rose for Emily;" this point of view is called scenic, or third-person objective. He or she may know all there is to know about one person, as in James' "The Real Thing;" this is known as limited omniscience. A variant of omniscience is central intelligence, in which a single character is aware of all that occurs in the story. The author may use the first-person or third-person form of address and be at the center of action, at the edge of things, or outside the action entirely. He or she may offer editorial comment or be completely objective.

Preparation See foreshadowing.

Probability The logical movement of the action, given the character and situation at the beginning of a story. In Michael Sholokhov's "During the Retreat," it is highly likely that a group of tired, undisciplined soldiers would be taken for deserters by the peasantry and denied food.

Progression The forward movement of the plot when events we thought would happen *do* happen, giving us a sense that things are falling into place. In Sillitoe's "Mr. Raynor the School-Teacher," the unruliness of the boys suggests that Raynor's sexual fantasies will be repeatedly interrupted, and his passivity as a watcher indicates that he will never take action on his fantasies.

Realism A common sense or scientific attempt by the author to present facts that any reasonable observer could verify. Updike's "A & P" shows us the inside of a supermarket that any reader would be familiar with. While realism calls up on our experience and common sense, fantasy calls upon our imagination and suspension of disbelief.

Recognition See insight.

Resolution See denouement.

Reversal A change in fortune experienced by the protagonist from good to bad, bad to worse, or bad to good. In Dorothy Sayers's "The Unprincipled Affair of the Practical Joker," the reversal occurs when Lord Peter appears to discover that the villain has been cheating at cards.

Rhythm See pace.

Setting The location in time and place (temporal and spatial) of the physical background of the action. It may be realistic, even mundane, like the suburban home in "The Country Husband," or surrealistic and fantastic as in "Death of a Traveling Salesman." In either case, its proper function in the story is to help motivate action, working together with tone, atmosphere, imagery, and symbolism.

Structure A metaphorical expression referring to the architecturallike pattern of a story. In a limited sense, the term refers to the pattern of action, or the plot. In its largest sense, structure includes all the elements in a story, the major ones being plot, character and characterization, point of view, language, and theme.

Symbolism The use of objects, characters, situations, or even an entire plot to suggest or stand for something more than the objects or events themselves. In "Silent Snow, Secret Snow," the snow of the title symbolizes the fuzziness with which the boy blots out reality; in "The Lottery," the pile of stones and several of the villagers are used symbolically. In "Gimpel the Fool," the word "fool" takes on a special meaning through the tolerance toward ridicule and shame shown by Gimpel.

Theme The generalization about human life that can be drawn from the resolution or outcome of the conflict and from the supporting evidence provided by attitude, tone, atmosphere, setting, imagery, and symbolism or allegory. In Doris Lessing's "The Nuisance," the theme may be that people prefer to ignore painful moral questions even if a person's rights to dignity and life are violated.

Tone A special effect of language that conveys the stance that the author assumes toward the reader. It may be straightforward or ironic, in earnest or in jest, content or bitter. In Sherwood Anderson's "The Egg," the author is faintly ironic and sympathetic with the father's attempts to interest people in his egg tricks.